OXFORD
Illustrated
ENCYCLOPEDIA

OXFORD
Illustrated
ENCYCLOPEDIA

OXFORD UNIVERSITY PRESS

OXFORD
UNIVERSITY PRESS

Great Clarendon Street, Oxford OX2 6DP

Oxford University Press is a department of the University of Oxford.
It furthers the University's objective of excellence in research, scholarship,
and education by publishing worldwide in

Oxford New York

Auckland Cape Town Dar es Salaam Hong Kong Karachi
Kuala Lumpur Madrid Melbourne Mexico City Nairobi
New Delhi Shanghai Taipei Toronto

With offices in

Oxford is a registered trade mark of Oxford University Press
in the UK and in certain other countries

Argentina Austria Brazil Chile Czech Republic France Greece
Guatemala Hungary Italy Japan Poland Portugal Singapore
South Korea Switzerland Thailand Turkey Ukraine Vietnam

Oxford is a registered trade mark of Oxford University Press
in the UK and in certain other countries

British Library Cataloguing in Publication Data

Data available

ISBN-13: 978-0-19-910444-4

ISBN-10: 0-19-910444-1

1 3 5 7 9 10 8 6 4 2

Printed in China

Contents

Contributors

Editor
Ben Dupré

Coordinating editors
Joanna Harris
Andrew Solway

Assistant editors
Sarah George
Helen Maxey
Louise Spilsbury
Jane Walker

Proofreaders
Susan Mushin
Louise Richmond

Research assistant
Yael Reshef

Indexer
Ann Barrett

Design
Jo Cameron
Oxprint Design Ltd.

Art editor
Hilary Wright

Assistant art editor
Jo Samways

Cover design
Jo Cameron

Photographic research
Charlotte Lippmann

General consultants
Ian Chilvers
Editor of the Oxford Dictionary of Art

Tony Drake
Head of Economics, Oxford School

Joyce Pope
Formerly Senior Lecturer, Natural History Museum, London

Stephen Pople
Formerly Head of Physics, Withywood School, Bristol, and author of Science to 14 *and other books*

Dr Alisdair Rogers
Lecturer, Keble College, Oxford University

Michael Scott
Natural history writer and consultant

Peter Teed
Formerly Headmaster, Goole Grammar School

Consultants
Dr R. E. Allen
Bridget Ardley
Neil Ardley
Norman Barrett
Professor Adrian Brockett
Stuart Corbridge
Frank Eckardt
Dr Honor Gay
Gal Gerson
Gordon Gibson
Narayani Gupta
Professor David Harris
Esmond Harris
Michael Harrison
Peggy Heeks
Rosemary Kelly
Eleanor Kercher
Myrtle Langley
Bryan Loughrey
Bridget Martyn
Dr George McGavin
Vivien McKay
Dr Stuart Milligan
Colin Mills
Dr Jacqueline Mitton
Professor Kenneth O. Morgan
Peggy Morgan
Iain Nicolson
Dr Christopher A. Norris
John O'Connor
Padraig O'Loingsigh
David Parkinson
Professor J. H. Paterson
Chris Powling
David A. Preston
Stewart Ross
Angela Ryalls
Elspeth Scott
Dr Harry Shukman
Professor Charles Taylor
Dr Nicholas Tucker
Eric Tupper
Bob Unwin
Ben Watson
Patrick Wiegand
Elspeth Williamson
Dr Robert Youngson

Authors
Dr R. E. Allen
Bridget Ardley
Neil Ardley
Jill Bailey
Professor Chris Baines
Nicola Barber
Norman Barrett
Dr Michael J. Benton
Professor Adrian Brockett
John R. Brown
Ben Burt
Arthur Swift Butterfield
Kate Castle
Ian Chilvers
Mike Corbishley
Judith Court
Tony Drake
Frank Eckardt
John L. Foster
David Glover
Gib Goodfellow
Susan Goodman
Neil Grant
Dr Alastair McIntosh Gray
Gerald Haigh
Sonya Hinton
Peter Holden
Dr Terry Jennings
Rosemary Kelly
Margaret Killingray
Diyan Leake
Keith Lye
Bridget Martyn
Kenneth and Valerie McLeish
Haydn Middleton
Dr N. J. Middleton
Dr Jacqueline Mitton
Peggy Morgan
Dr Roger Neich
Iain Nicolson
John O'Connor
Dr Stuart Owen-Jones
Chris Oxlade
David Parkinson
Dr David Pimm
Joyce Pope
Stephen Pople
Philip Pullman
Judy Ridgeway
R. J. Ritchie
Dr Alisdair Rogers
Stewart Ross
Theodore Rowland-Entwistle
Michael Scott
Tony Skinner
Nigel Smith
Andrew Solway
Imogen Stewart
Jonathan Stock
John N. Stringer
Professor Charles Taylor
Peter Teed
Teresa Thornhill
Dr Philip Whitfield
Patrick Wiegand
Amanda Williams
Elizabeth Williamson
Jill A. Wright

Introduction

It is 50 years since the first volume of the monumental *Oxford Junior Encyclopaedia* was published. Within a few years the 13th and last volume had appeared, so completing one of the greatest reference works ever published for children. Since then, Oxford encyclopedias have continued to inform and entertain generations of children. Now, for the first time, Oxford is publishing an encyclopedia for children in a single volume.

Balance and depth

The secret of a good encyclopedia is to get the right balance of entries. For this new work we consulted a wide range of subject experts based in many different countries. They helped us to divide up the world of knowledge into separate areas and then advised us on what entries to include in each area. Having carefully laid the foundations, we are confident that this encyclopedia will reliably lead you to the information you are looking for.

Depth is as important as balance: you cannot understand a topic properly unless you get an idea of how it fits into a broader picture. For this reason the articles in this encyclopedia are detailed enough to present facts within a context that makes sense of them. At the same time, it can be frustrating if the information you need is buried in long and complicated articles. So we have aimed for a blend of long and short articles, offering a variety of depth of coverage, and there are a large number of articles in all – nearly 850 – so you will often make a direct 'hit' in looking for a particular topic.

A journey of discovery

You can use this encyclopedia to find your way to a huge amount of information on a wide range of subjects. But the experience of using it should offer much more than that. A carefully planned network of cross-references means that one question will always lead to another, making it not only a book where you can look things up, but also a book to explore, full of unexpected delights and insights.

However cleverly planned and designed, any reference book is only as good as the information it contains. Assisted by our large team of experts, we have aimed to produce articles that combine the best illustrations with text that is lively, accurate and up to date. We hope that the care we have taken in putting this book together will ensure that it becomes for you a trusted companion in an exciting journey of discovery.

Ben Dupré

How to use this book

The *Oxford Illustrated Encyclopedia* has many useful features to help you find the information you need quickly and easily. This guide will help you to get the most out of the book.

The main part of the encyclopedia is a series of entries arranged in alphabetical order, on topics from Aborigines to Zoos. At the end of the book there is a Data file, which contains a Countries fact file, a World history time-line and other useful information.

▼ ► These pages show the main features of the country and continent entries in the encyclopedia. Many major countries, as well as all continents, have entries in the A–Z section. Other countries have a short entry and a list of statistics in the Countries fact file on pages 613–645. There is also a map of the world on pages 646–647, on which all countries are labelled.

Finding what you want

If you are looking for information on a particular topic, the first step is to check whether there is an entry on that topic in the A–Z section. If there is no entry, check the footers at the bottom of the page. These may include the topic you want, and tell you where you can find information on it.

If the topic you are interested in does not have its own entry in the A–Z section, the next step is to look in the *General index* on pages 659–671. This is also arranged alphabetically. Each index entry lists one or more page or pages where there is information on that topic.

Sometimes you may want to know what entries there are on a broad subject area. You may want to know what entries there are on sport, for example, or on animals. The place to look for this information is in the *Subject index* on pages 656–658. Here, all the entries in the A–Z section are listed under subject headings.

Germany

Germany lies in the middle of Europe between the Alps and Scandinavia. Although not as large as France, Spain or Sweden, it has the biggest population of all European countries (excluding Russia).

Much of Germany consists of the Central Uplands, a mixture of ancient block mountains with low hills and plains. Dark forests crown the hills, and castles look down across orchards and vineyards to fertile plains. In the Northern Lowland the sandy soil is not so fertile. Much of this land is covered with heath and pine forest, strewn with rock boulders left by glaciers of the last ice age. In the far south lie the Alps.

Climate

The climate of Germany is temperate (mild) and allows crops such as wheat, maize (corn) and potatoes to grow well. Cattle graze in the damp and mild north-west and in the foothills of the

● In western Germany the Autobahn (motorway) system started by Hitler in the 1930s has been vastly improved and extended. German railways are developing new, high-speed lines which tunnel through hills and climb

d poultry are also
r to the cities.
son for keeping
s are sometimes
the ground for

a single huge city,
es. Many of them,
n, were formerly
such as Bavaria

communist government in power until 1989 neglected older buildings. The state provided housing in the form of monotonous

Key box
- —— country boundary
- ◆ capital city
- ● major cities and towns
- — main roads
- — main railways
- ⊕ main airports

land height in metres
- 2000–5000
- 1000–2000
- 500–1000
- 200–500
- less than 200
- land below sea level

Africa

Africa is the world's second largest continent, covering one-fifth of the Earth's land area. It sits squarely on the Equator, extending almost the same distance to the north and south. Apart from the narrow strip of land at Suez which joins it to Asia, it is completely surrounded by sea.

Almost all of Africa is warm or hot. The countries which lie on the Equator are wet all year round. North and south of the Equator there are two seasons, a wet season and a dry one. The driest parts of Africa are the Sahara, Namib and Kalahari deserts, where it is hot all year and there is hardly any rainfall. The Mediterranean shores and the tip of South Africa have warm, wet winters and hot, dry summers.

● All the independent countries of Africa have entries in the Countries fact file on pages 613–

1 Each continent and many major countries have a map, showing land height and other features.

2 and **3** Locator maps show where a country or continent is in the world. Continental locators (**2**) show the position of a continent on the globe. Country locators (**3**) show the position of a country within a continent.

4 The *scale bar* shows the scale of the map in kilometres and in miles. Each black or white section on the top scale equals 50 kilometres on the ground. Each section on the bottom scale equals 25 miles.

5 The *key box* explains the symbols and colours on the map. Most maps show the land height, and physical features such as mountain ranges, rivers and lakes. Major cities, railways, roads and airports are also shown.

▼▶ These pages from the A–Z section of the encyclopedia show some of the most useful features.

1 The *headwords* are arranged in alphabetical order, to make it easy to find a topic.

2 The *opening paragraph* gives a friendly introduction and an overview of the topic.

3 The *main text* gives a detailed account of the topic.

4 *Captions* usually give extra information about the subject of the picture. This caption tells you about tournaments and jousting.

5 *Feature boxes* look at particular subjects within a topic in more detail.

6 *Margin notes* contain interesting or amazing facts, figures and lists.

7 The *Find out more panel* lists other articles where you can find more information about the topic. The Armour entry, for example has a picture and information about the armour knights wore.

8 Key words are picked out in *italic*.

9 The *footer* lists other alphabetical topics that do not have their own entry in the A–Z section, but which are covered under another headword or in the Data file (pages 612–655). This footer, for example, tells you that there is information on koalas in the entry on Marsupials.

Knights ①

② **Knights were highly trained soldiers on horseback. In the early Middle Ages any talented warrior could become a knight. But gradually the knights formed a group which became a ruling class throughout Europe, with their own rules of behaviour known as the 'code of chivalry'.**

④ ▼ These knights are jousting with long lances at a medieval tournament. The earliest tournaments were practice battles between two picked sides. They were rather like miniature wars, and men were often badly hurt. Jousting was more like a mock duel between individual champions.

③ Early knights formed the finest armies of medieval Europe. They played a vital part in the feudal system of the Middle Ages. In return for estates to live on, they had to serve their lords for about 40 days each year – in warfare, on expeditions or on castle guard. The code of chivalry they followed was meant to help to tame knights who terrorized the people of Europe in peacetime.

Chivalry

Later, Christian knights formed a fixed group of warrior-governors or aristocrats. All knights were expected to serve God and the Church as well as their rulers. True knights should be brave, strong and skilful fighters. The code was used to tame unruly knights. It was an agreement between knights that they should be generous, kind and polite and always protect the weak.

Historians call the years from about 1100 to 1400 the Age of Chivalry, even though not all knights of this time behaved as well as the code suggested they should. By the end of that period most knights had stopped taking the code seriously. Instead of serving God and protecting the weak, they busied themselves with tournaments or with fighting duels of honour.

⑥ • Today in Britain men are still made knights, and given the title 'Sir', as a reward for serving the country in whatever jobs they do. Women who are given a similar reward are referred to as 'Dame' instead of 'Sir'.

find out more ⑦
Armour
Celts
Crusades
Medieval England
Middle Ages

Changing roles

By the 15th century new weapons and new kinds of warfare had come in, making the knights less important to Europe's armies. The weight of their armour greatly limited both their speed and their movement. Many stopped fighting for their rulers, and paid them instead to employ mercenaries, men who just fought for a living. The better-off knights then concentrated on running their estates.

Heraldry ⑤

Medieval knights had patterns on their shields called heraldic devices. Heraldry was the name for the study of these devices. Devices were also worn on helmets, on the drapery of horses and on special outer garments called 'surcoats'. The devices, or 'coats of arms' as they became known, were passed on from one generation to the next and so symbolized whole families, not just individuals.

Devices were often very beautiful, but they were more than just decorations. In tournaments of the Middle Ages devices were the only way of telling one knight from another. And in the heat of real battles these 'coats of arms' helped knights to tell their friends from their enemies.

Charges

Bend

Fess

Saltire

Chevron

Divisions

Quarterly

Paly

▶ The background colour of a shield is its *field* or *ground*. A *charge* is a picture or shape placed on the field. A few simple charges are shown here, but there are hundreds, including animals, birds and weapons. The basic field can be divided up in various ways, called *divisions* or *partitions*, two of which are shown here. ⑧

Armour

Warriors have worn armour to protect themselves in battle for thousands of years. Bullet-proof vests and riot gear are modern forms of armour.

The ancient Greeks wore linen or leather shirts with metal plates sewn on to protect the heart and shoulders. The hoplites (armed foot-soldiers) wore a breastplate of bronze shaped to fit. Roman foot-soldiers and cavalry wore armour of iron hoops protecting the back as well as the front of the body. Romans also used mail, at first made of small metal plates sewn on a leather jerkin, overlapping like tiles on a roof. Later it was made of metal links, known as chain-armour.

In the early Middle Ages, European soldiers wore chain-mail armour. From about 1330 knights wore heavy armour of jointed steel plates. After the development of guns, armour was gradually reduced to a cuirass (breast plate) and helmet. By the 20th century only the helmet remained. From the 1940s a new kind of body armour made of nylon, other plastics and glass fibres came into use.

▼ Some different types of armour.

Greek hoplite (foot-soldier) of the 5th century BC. Helmets were of bronze, and each soldier carried a shield.

Suit of armour, European, late 15th century.

Japanese armour of overlapping metal plates laced together, 19th century.

Modern body armour with overlapping plates of steel alloy or lighter material between layers of fabric.

find out more
Armies
Knights
Weapons

Marsupials

Marsupial records
Largest
Red kangaroo: males may measure 2.5 m in total length, and weigh up to 90 kg.
Smallest
Pilbara ningaui: head-and-body length of adult may be as little as 4.6 cm; weight may be no more than 2 g.

• There are about 280 different kinds of marsupial.

▶ A Tasmanian pademelon with its young feeding in a eucalyptus forest. Pademelons, or scrub wallabies, are hunted for meat and fur.

The group of animals known as marsupials includes kangaroos, koalas and opossums. They are found in Australia, New Guinea, and South and North America. Most female marsupials have a furry pouch on their bellies. This pouch holds and protects the young until they are big enough to fend for themselves.

When baby marsupials are born, they have hardly begun to develop and are very tiny. Some are as small as a grain of rice. But they have strong forelimbs and claws, which they use to crawl through their mother's fur to her pouch. There they find a teat, and fasten themselves to their food supply. Baby marsupials grow fairly slowly.

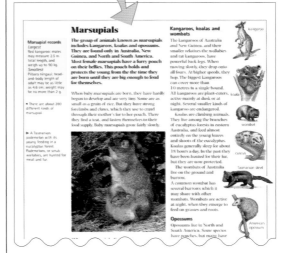

Kangaroos, koalas and wombats

The kangaroos of Australia and New Guinea, and their smaller relatives the wallabies and rat kangaroos, have powerful back legs. When moving slowly, they drop onto all fours. At higher speeds, they hop. The biggest kangaroos can cover more than 10 metres in a single bound. All kangaroos are plant-eaters, active mostly at dusk or at night. Several smaller kinds of kangaroo are endangered.

Koalas are climbing animals. They live among the branches of eucalyptus forests in eastern Australia, and feed almost entirely on the young leaves and shoots of the eucalyptus. Koalas generally sleep for about 18 hours a day. In the past they have been hunted for their fur, but they are now protected.

The wombats of Australia live on the ground and burrow. A common wombat has several burrows which it may share with other wombats. Wombats are active at night, when they emerge to feed on grasses and roots.

Opossums
Opossums live in North and South America. Some species have pouches, but many have

Aborigines

The Aborigines are the original inhabitants of Australia. They have lived there for many thousands of years. Before the arrival of European settlers, they led their lives in close harmony with the land. Their traditional way of life has now mostly disappeared.

The Aborigines probably came to Australia from Asia. They spread over the country in large family groups known as tribes. They moved from place to place, hunting animals and gathering plants for food.

The Aborigines worshipped the land. They believed the spirits of their ancestors had created its features back in a period they called the Dreamtime. They held ceremonies at places sacred to the ancestral spirits.

Europeans began to settle in Australia about 200 years ago. They killed many Aborigines, whose spears and boomerangs were no match for European guns, and used Aboriginal hunting grounds and sacred sites for their settlements and farms. Aborigines also died from diseases, carried to Australia by Europeans, to which they had no resistance.

Today many Aborigines live in big cities or towns. They prefer to be known as Kooris. After years of campaigning, laws which were intended to wipe out their culture have been reversed. Some sacred sites are being returned to their original owners and Aboriginal people now have a voice in running their own affairs.

▲ These Aboriginal rangers in Queensland are sitting underneath ancient cave paintings which were painted by their ancestors many thousands of years ago. Some Aboriginal sites with rock paintings date back between 40 and 60 thousand years.

• The word 'aborigine' comes from the Latin *ab origine* meaning 'from the beginning'.

• Boomerangs are wooden throwing sticks used by Aborigines for hunting. Returning boomerangs have a special curved shape which makes them spin when thrown so that they come back to the thrower.

find out more
Australia
Deserts
Hunter-gatherers

Acid rain

Acid rain is caused by air pollution. When coal, oil and petrol are burned, the smoke given off contains the gases sulphur dioxide and nitrogen dioxide. These gases escape into the atmosphere, where they dissolve in water droplets to form dilute acids. These acids then fall to the ground in rain.

Acid rain is harmful to plants, animals and buildings. Its effects are most severe close to cities and industrial areas. It may be blown by the wind, falling thousands of kilometres from where it was first formed. For example, much of the acid rain in Canada is caused by smoke from factories and power stations in the USA. Although the effects of acid rain are very clear, no one knows for certain how they are produced.

Preventing acid rain

Most of the gases that produce acid rain probably come from power stations and factories, or from the exhaust fumes of motor vehicles. These acid gases can be reduced by using types of coal and oil that contain little sulphur, and by cleaning the waste gases with chemical cleaners before they pass out of factory and power-station chimneys. Cars can be fitted with catalytic converters to reduce the harmful gases in car exhausts. But all these methods are expensive, and some governments and companies prefer not to spend the money. In the long term, only careful use of energy, cleaner factories, and fewer motor cars will reduce acid-rain pollution.

• Acid rain has killed fishes and damaged or killed trees in North America and Europe. It damages crops, and even the water we drink.

find out more
Acids and alkalis
Pollution

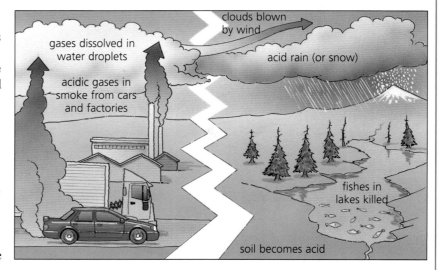

clouds blown by wind

gases dissolved in water droplets

acid rain (or snow)

acidic gases in smoke from cars and factories

fishes in lakes killed

soil becomes acid

Acids and alkalis

Acids and alkalis are chemical opposites. An acid is a sour-tasting substance, such as lemon juice or vinegar. Alkalis are rather soapy substances. Both acids and alkalis are widely used to make products ranging from soap and paper to explosives and fertilizers.

Lemons taste sour because they contain citric acid. The sour taste of vinegar is due to acetic acid, while sour milk contains lactic acid. All these are weak acids. Strong acids are far too dangerous to taste or touch. They are corrosive, which means that they can eat into skin, wood, cloth and other materials.

Alkalis can be strong enough to burn your skin, just like strong acids. If you mix an alkali and an acid together in the right quantities, you will make a neutral substance. This is neither an acid nor an alkali, and it will not burn. Scientists measure the strength of acids and alkalis on a scale of numbers called the pH scale. The scale ranges from 14 (the strongest alkalis) to 0 (the strongest acids).

One of the best-known strong acids is sulphuric acid. It is used to make fertilizers, explosives, plastics, paints, dyes, detergents and many other chemicals. The modern chemical industry, which began 200 years ago, was based on the manufacture of alkalis. Alkali mixtures containing the metals sodium and potassium are widely used in the manufacture of glass, paper, soap and textiles, and in the refining of crude oil.

• Hydrochloric acid is produced in your stomach. It kills most of the germs that you swallow with your food, and helps your stomach to digest the food.

find out more
Chemistry
Soap

▼ The pH scale. Neutral substances, such as pure water, have a pH of 7.

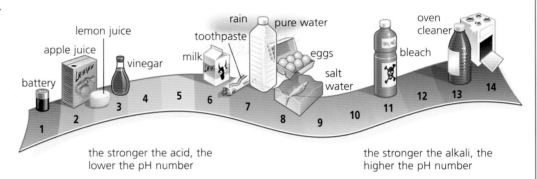

lemon juice
rain   pure water
toothpaste   oven cleaner
apple juice   milk   eggs   bleach
battery   vinegar   salt water
1   2   3   4   5   6   7   8   9   10   11   12   13   14

the stronger the acid, the lower the pH number

the stronger the alkali, the higher the pH number

Advertising

Advertising is a way of bringing information to people. Some adverts inform people about meetings or events. However, most advertising is from companies that make goods or provide services, telling people about the things they have to offer.

People advertise using posters in the street, by putting notices in newspapers, and by short films (commercials) on the television. Much advertising is by direct mail (letters sent to people's homes) and often includes details of competitions and free offers.

Advertising agencies

People who sell goods and services often use advertising agencies to promote their products. Suppose the product is a breakfast cereal. The advertising team decides what sort of people are likely to buy it and what other cereals there are. They then have to think of an idea that will persuade people to buy this particular cereal, such as emphasizing the healthy nature of the ingredients.

Suppose the advertising team decide to make a TV commercial. The agency arranges a script, actors and camera crew are hired, and the film is made. The agency then decides when it is to be shown: in the late afternoon for children to see, or in the evening? Finally, the agency makes sure that the advert is shown and sends their client the bill.

◄ Posters are useful in advertising because they are large and use clear visual images and few words to get their message across. This poster from 1930 advertises the French liner *Liberté*.

• Advertisements have often been criticized for persuading people to buy things they do not want or cannot afford. In an attempt to control this, most advertisers follow a code of practice.

find out more
Designers
Industry

Africa

Africa is the world's second largest continent, covering one-fifth of the Earth's land area. It sits squarely on the Equator, extending almost the same distance to the north and south. Apart from the narrow strip of land at Suez which joins it to Asia, it is completely surrounded by sea.

Almost all of Africa is warm or hot. The countries which lie on the Equator are wet all year round. North and south of the Equator there are two seasons, a wet season and a dry one. The driest parts of Africa are the Sahara, Namib and Kalahari deserts, where it is hot all year and there is hardly any rainfall. The Mediterranean shores and the tip of South Africa have warm, wet winters and hot, dry summers.

• All the independent countries of Africa have entries in the Countries fact file on pages 613–645.

0 | 1000 km
0 | 500 miles

◆ capital city
■ large city
— country boundary
▲ highest peaks (height in metres)

land height in metres
2000–5000
1000–2000
500–1000
200–500
less than 200
sea level
land below sea level

Victoria Falls, one of the largest waterfalls in the world, is on the Zambia–Zimbabwe border. It was given its English name by the explorer David Livingstone. Its African name — *Mosi-oa-Tunya* — means 'the smoke that thunders'.

Landscapes

Africa's chunky shape gives it far less coastline than western Europe and there are few natural harbours. There are a number of African islands; Madagascar, which lies to the south-east, is the largest.

Much of the south and east of Africa is high plateau country. Among the more dramatic highlands are the Ruwenzori range in east Central Africa, and the Drakensberg range along the south-eastern coast. Mount Kilimanjaro in Tanzania is the highest mountain.

The north and west of Africa are in general lower. The area around Lake Chad is an inland basin, and rivers empty themselves into the lake. The Sahara Desert, the largest desert in the world, is also in the north.

The heart of the continent is tropical rainforest. Rainfall here is heavy all year. Away from the forest stretches the savannah – lands of tall grass dotted with trees. They have a wet and a dry season. Most of the large African wildlife live in the savannah, especially in national parks such as the Serengeti.

Africa has four of the world's greatest rivers: the Nile, the Congo, the Niger and the Zambezi. The River Nile is the longest river in the world. Africa also has some of the world's largest freshwater lakes, the largest of which is Lake Victoria. Lakes Tanganyika and Malawi (Nyasa) lie in a great fault (split) in the Earth's surface, called the Rift Valley. A similar valley is filled by the Red Sea.

People and languages

Much of the population of Africa is concentrated in just a few areas. The coast of West Africa, the Nile Valley and the area around Lake Victoria are crowded. But these areas are separated by up to 2000 kilometres of desert or forest, where very few people live.

Over 1000 different languages are spoken in Africa, and very many Africans speak more than one language. In North Africa most people speak Arabic. In West Africa, Hausa, Yoruba, Akan and Malinke are important languages. Most East Africans can speak Kiswahili. South of the Equator people speak one or other of a number of languages known collectively as Bantu.

In the late 19th century, several European nations divided up and ruled most of the continent of Africa. French, Portuguese and English are still spoken in the areas those countries used to rule. ◗

• The first Europeans to reach East Africa were the Portuguese. During the 15th century Portuguese sea captains such as Bartolomeu Dias and Vasco da Gama opened up a sea route to India around the African coast.

▼ In the hot desert lands of North Africa, camels have always played an important role. Camel markets, such as this one in Sudan, do a busy trade.

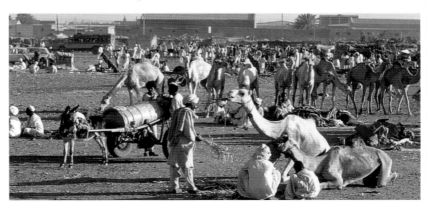

Religion

The Arabic-speaking people of the north are Muslims, as are the majority of the people of Mali, Sudan and northern Nigeria. About half of all Africans are Muslims and the numbers are growing. Christian Churches are strong, too. As well as Roman Catholics and Anglicans, there are many independent African Churches. Traditional African religions have their own rituals and ways of getting advice and guidance from the supreme god. Africans worship with dance and music, and these are important art forms throughout the continent.

African history

Scientists believe that human beings evolved in Africa and spread out to other parts of the world. Very little is known of Africa in prehistoric times, but from about the year 4000 BC powerful empires grew up beside the River Nile, because the soil along its banks was very rich and fertile. The most famous was Egypt in the time of the pharaohs.

From the 5th century AD trading empires arose in West Africa, using camels to cross the Sahara Desert with gold, salt and slaves. Many of their kings adopted the Muslim religion, brought by North African traders and scholars. Other states grew up in the forest areas nearer to the coast. City states on the east coast sent ivory, gold, copper and gum by sea to Arabia, India and China. The gold came from the powerful inland state of Zimbabwe. Its buildings, over 1000 years old, still remain.

The slave trade had long existed in Africa, but in the 16th to 18th centuries it grew enormously. This was because Europeans were taking huge numbers of Africans to be sold into slavery abroad. In the 19th century there were serious wars and disturbances in western Africa as Muslims fought to control states and impose their religion. In southern Africa the Zulu people attacked and conquered neighbouring African groups, and also fought the Dutch (Boers) and British, who were settling on their lands. By the late 19th century much of Africa was conquered and divided up between European nations who imposed new systems of government, language and education, and created countries with artificial frontiers separating people who spoke the same language.

From 1956 onwards, one by one the states of Africa achieved their independence. The new countries kept the artificial boundaries that the Europeans had drawn, and this has been the cause of terrible conflicts in some parts of Africa. Difficult climates, fast-growing populations, lack of resources, and local wars and rebellions have caused widespread famine and unrest in many areas.

◀ Ethiopia has been Christian since the 4th century AD. In the late 12th to 13th centuries, 11 churches were carved out of solid rock in the town of Lalibela. The expertly crafted buildings still attract thousands of pilgrims today.

▲ The South African city of Cape Town is built around one of Africa's few natural harbours. The city began in 1652 as a refreshment station for the trading ships of the Dutch East India company. Today it is a modern city, edged by the shores of Table Bay and the slopes of Table Mountain.

find out more
British empire
Congo, Democratic
  Republic of
Deserts
Egypt
Egyptians, ancient
Grasslands
Mandela, Nelson
Nigeria
Slaves
South Africa
Sudan
Valleys
World music

Aid agencies

There are millions of people in the world today who live in poverty, without a proper place to live or enough food to eat. Aid agencies are organizations that work to improve the lives of people in poor countries all over the world.

find out more
Charities
Refugees
United Nations

Aid agencies provide most help in Africa, Asia, Latin America and, to a lesser extent, in the Middle East and Europe. The United Nations works through its agencies such as the UN International Children's Emergency Fund (UNICEF). Most aid is given by government bodies and goes directly to the countries. More government aid is channelled through the UN and organizations such as the World Bank, which is the largest distributor of aid. A smaller amount is given by voluntary agencies, such as Action Aid or Christian Aid.

◀ Oxfam is an aid agency that raises money for projects worldwide. It also tries to persuade the governments of richer countries to give more money in aid to poorer countries. These children in Cambodia are getting water from a well built with aid from Oxfam.

What aid agencies do

Most aid agencies share two main aims. The first is to try to meet the immediate needs of people affected by natural disasters or war. The second is to help people in longer-term ways with many of the things which those in richer countries take for granted, such as food, shelter, clean water, education and health care.

Aid agencies try to enable people to improve their own lives by providing training, tools and equipment for improving farming methods and water supplies, and education about health and nutrition. They also help people to learn to read and write. Some agencies in Europe and North America try to make people in their own countries aware of the causes of poverty and hardship overseas.

AIDS

AIDS is short for Acquired Immune Deficiency Syndrome. This is a medical condition caused by a virus called HIV (Human Immuno-deficiency Virus).

• AIDS was first recognized in the USA in 1981. It has since been reported in nearly every country in the world and is more common in poor countries with bad health care.

The human body is protected from disease by white blood cells whose job it is to recognize and destroy germs that enter the body. These white blood cells play an important role in the body's *immune system*. HIV kills white blood cells, and weakens the immune system. This means that people with HIV get illnesses, such as pneumonia, more easily than healthy people and that they do not recover so well.

HIV lives in the blood. It is spread by sexual intercourse with an infected person, or by

find out more
Blood
Diseases
Immunity
Viruses

injecting drugs with a needle that an infected person has used. People can also catch HIV from receiving a transfusion of blood already infected with the disease, although today most donated blood is checked for HIV. You cannot catch HIV by breathing the same air as someone with the virus or by touching them.

Scientists have developed treatments such as AZT (an anti-HIV drug) which can help to slow down the spread of the virus. Although there is still no cure for AIDS, it is possible to reduce the spread of HIV through information and education. Scientists are working hard to find a vaccine to protect people against HIV.

▶ A diagram of the Human Immuno-deficiency Virus (HIV) magnified about 200,000 times. The virus enters a white blood cell, reproduces, destroys the cell and goes on to repeat the process in other white blood cells.

protein knob

inner shell

outer skin

genetic material

Air

Although air is all around us, we cannot see, smell or taste it. We can feel it moving when the wind blows. Without air, our planet would be a waterless, empty desert with no living creatures. Air is a mixture of gases, mainly nitrogen and oxygen. We breathe air to obtain the oxygen we need to stay alive.

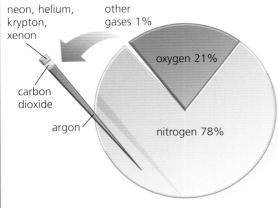

neon, helium, krypton, xenon

other gases 1%

carbon dioxide

argon

oxygen 21%

nitrogen 78%

▲ The different gases found in air.

Air contains tiny amounts of carbon dioxide gas. This is very important as green plants use it, together with water, to make their food. As they do so, they produce oxygen, which is used by humans and other animals. Air also contains many other things: rare gases (such as neon and argon), dust, water vapour, pollen, seeds, tiny microscopic animals, bacteria and pollution from cars and factories.

Atmospheric pressure

A bucketful of air weighs about the same as two pages of this book. The weight of the air above is always pressing down on us. This force pressing on a given area is called atmospheric pressure. At sea level, atmospheric pressure is equivalent to the weight of about 1 kilogram pressing on every square centimetre. This pressure does not squash our bodies because we have air inside us as well as outside.

Atmospheric pressure is measured with a *barometer*. In an aneroid barometer, the most common kind, there is a flat metal box from which most of the air has been removed. The atmospheric pressure tries to squash the box flat but, because the metal is springy, it is not squashed completely. If the atmospheric pressure varies, the lid of the box rises and falls, moving a pointer around a dial to give a reading. A barometer reading is often given in millibars (mb) or in kilopascals (kPa). One kind of barometer, called a barograph, is used in weather forecasting.

Atmospheric pressure is one example of air pressure (the force of air pressing down on a given area of a surface). We can increase the air pressure of a bicycle tyre, for example, by pumping more and more air into the space available.

Vacuums

A vacuum is a completely empty space from which even the air has been removed. Because it is impossible to remove all the air, by 'vacuum' we really mean a partial vacuum from which most of the air has been removed. Space is a vacuum, although it contains some dust and gas particles. Vacuums are used in Thermos flasks and inside some electrical equipment such as televisions and vacuum cleaners. The vacuum inside a Thermos flask is between the inner and outer walls of the container. The flask keeps drinks hot or cold because heat cannot travel very well through the vacuum, so the heat is kept in a hot drink and away from a cold drink.

Air-conditioning

An air-conditioning system keeps the temperature and moisture of the air in a room at comfortable levels (usually between 20 °C and 25 °C and a relative humidity of 35–70 per cent). In an average room, fresh air and air from the room are mixed in an air-conditioning unit about the size of a large box. Some of the air is warmed by passing it over hot pipes, and the rest is cooled over cold water pipes. A mixture of the warm and cold air produces the required temperature.

• In a space as big as a school hall, there is probably over one tonne of air. That is more than the weight of a small car!

• Neon and argon are two of the rare gases found in air. They produce a coloured glow when an electric current is passed through them. The shaped lighting tubes used in colourful advertising signs are filled with neon and argon.

find out more
Atmosphere
Gases, liquids and solids
Greenhouse effect
Oxygen
Plants
Pollution
Weather

▼ Scuba divers carry their own air supply in metal tanks filled with compressed air, which are strapped onto their backs. A special device controls the flow of air into the diver's lungs.

Aircraft

Aircraft is the name we use for flying machines. There are many types of aircraft in use today, for commercial, military, private and recreational purposes. Planes and helicopters are heavier-than-air aircraft which need wings or blades to keep them in the air. Hot-air balloons and airships are also aircraft. They stay in the air because they are filled with a lighter-than-air gas.

Most aircraft have a central body called a fuselage, with wings near the middle and a smaller tailplane and fin at the back. Straight wings work best for carrying heavy loads at low speed, but swept-back wings give a better airflow for fast flying. Some military jets, such as the Panavia Tornado, have 'swing wings' which swing further back for high-speed flight. Some aircraft, such as Concorde, do not have a tailplane. Instead, the wings form a triangular shape, called a delta, which goes all the way to the back. Delta wings are good for high-speed flight but do not perform well at low speed. A few aircraft have their wings at the back and their 'tailplane' at the front. This is called a canard arrangement.

Aircraft normally have a frame made from a light alloy such as duralumin. This frame is covered with a skin of light metal which acts as a shell and makes the fuselage very strong, like a tube. The wings are built in a similar way. Building aircraft with a rigid shell is called monocoque construction. Before it was developed in the 1920s, aircraft had wood or metal frames covered in fabric and braced by wires.

Aircraft power

Powered aircraft come in many shapes and sizes, ranging from simple lightweight microlights to the latest wide-bodied jets that can carry more than 600 passengers over very long distances. Most modern aircraft use jet engines in one form or another. Even where a propeller is fitted, the power may come from a turboprop engine which is based on the jet engine. Some small aircraft have propellers turned by piston engines, which work in a similar way to a motor-car engine. Microlight aircraft are powered by an engine barely bigger than that of a motorcycle. ◆

▲ The giant flying ship *Calcutta* afloat after its launch in 1928. It was the largest passenger aircraft of its kind ever built in Britain, with room for 15 passengers.

• It is now possible to build human-powered aircraft (HPAs) by using new, very strong and light materials such as carbon fibre. These aircraft have an overall weight of just 60 kg. The pilot turns the propeller by pedalling.

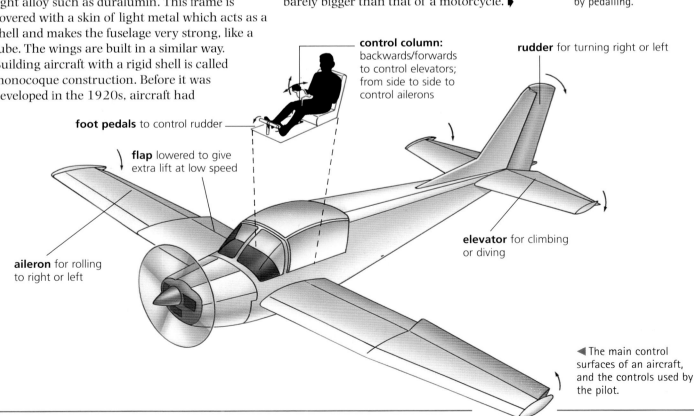

control column: backwards/forwards to control elevators; from side to side to control ailerons

rudder for turning right or left

foot pedals to control rudder

flap lowered to give extra lift at low speed

aileron for rolling to right or left

elevator for climbing or diving

◄ The main control surfaces of an aircraft, and the controls used by the pilot.

▶ A Boeing 777 passenger jet, one of the new generation of air liners.

Aircraft firsts
♦ The Wright brothers' biplane *Flyer* made the first-ever powered flight in 1903.
♦ The Heinkel He-178, which flew in 1939, was the first jet aircraft.
♦ The Boeing 747 'jumbo jet' was the first wide-bodied jet.
♦ Concorde was the first supersonic (faster-than-sound) airliner to enter service. It travels at twice the speed of sound, and can cross the Atlantic in 3 hours.

find out more
Air forces
Airports
Balloons and airships
Engines
Flight
Gliders and kites
Helicopters

▼ This photograph of Wilbur Wright was taken in 1908. During this year he made his record long flight, lasting a total of 2 hours and 20 minutes.

The latest designs
Today's aircraft designers are usually more interested in economy than speed. Many new airliners travel at less than half the speed of the Concorde aircraft designed in the 1960s. Using computers, designers have developed wings that slip more easily through the air, and engines that are quieter and burn their fuel more efficiently. A 'jumbo jet' can carry four times as many passengers as Concorde, using the same amount of fuel.

Computers are an important part of a modern airliner. The autopilot is a computer which can navigate and fly the aircraft for most of its journey. On some aircraft, the pilot does not directly control the plane. Instead, the pilot's controls send instructions to a computer and the computer works out the best way to fly the plane. This system is known as fly-by-wire.

▲ Some aircraft are designed to do special jobs, such as spraying agricultural crops with chemicals.

▶ FLASHBACK ◀
The first aeroplane flight in history was achieved by the Wright brothers in the USA. On 17 December 1903 Orville Wright made a 12-second flight over a distance of 36 metres in *Flyer*. In 1909 Louis Blériot flew across the English Channel. Ten years later, Alcock and Brown made the first non-stop flight across the Atlantic Ocean.

In 1927 Charles Lindbergh completed the first non-stop solo flight across the Atlantic in a specially built plane *Spirit of St Louis*. In 1930 Amy Johnson was the first woman to fly to Australia. Two years later, an American, Amelia Earhart, became the first woman to fly solo across the Atlantic Ocean, in 15 hours and 18 minutes.

Passenger flying developed after World War I. During the 1920s passengers often flew aboard mail planes, sometimes with the mailbags on their laps! By the late 1930s flying was a much more luxurious affair. The first jet aircraft, the Heinkel He-178, flew in 1939. The first jet airliner, the De Havilland Comet, entered service in 1952.

Air forces

find out more
Aircraft
Armies
Helicopters

▼ 'Stealth' aircraft have an outline and surfaces designed to avoid detection by radar and heat sensors.

An air force is a country's military or fighting aircraft and the team of people who organize, fly and maintain them.

In some countries aircraft form a part of army and naval equipment. In others, including the USA, there is a separate air force. Most of the people working in an air force never actually fly. Their job is to put the aircraft in the air.

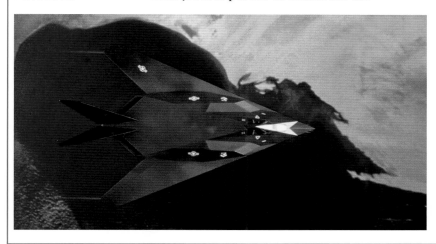

Military aircraft are used in both defence and attack in time of war: to bomb enemy soldiers or warships, to carry troops and supplies into battle, to destroy attacking enemy bombers, and for reconnaissance (looking to see what the enemy is doing). In addition, aircraft can attack a country's industries, roads and railways, and so make it less able to wage war.

Types of aircraft

Air forces use many different kinds of aircraft. *Bombers* are designed to fly long distances and to carry heavy bomb-loads. They may also fire guided missiles from the air, but these have been increasingly replaced by missiles launched from the ground. *Fighters* are small, very fast planes designed to intercept and shoot down enemy bombers, and to fire at targets on the ground or at sea.

Reconnaissance planes carry cameras, radar and other devices to detect enemy defence systems. To counter ground and air reconnaissance, combat aircraft can fly very fast and low to avoid detection by enemy radar and strike at targets deep in enemy territory. *Transport planes* are the largest of all. They are built to ferry troops and supplies.

Airports

Most airports are bustling, noisy places with a huge area for aircraft to take off and land. They are usually located away from city centres to avoid problems of noise and lack of space. Large international airports are open 24 hours a day, providing services for planes and passengers arriving and departing. In the world's busiest airports, over half a million passengers pass through the airport each week.

While waiting for their plane, passengers at most airports can shop, use a bank, or have a meal. There are usually large seating areas. Some airports have giant conveyor belts to carry passengers to other airport buildings, or to a departure gate where they board the aircraft.

Airports handle increasing amounts of goods flown to or from foreign markets as air freight. Warehouses store goods before loading. Bonded warehouses hold arriving goods for inspection by customs officers. Freight is flown either in special holds in passenger aircraft or in containers loaded onto specially designed aircraft.

An international airport employs thousands of workers who clean, refuel and maintain aircraft; load freight and baggage; and prepare food and other items for use by passengers during the flight. Other workers provide the goods and services for passengers on the ground, and there are specialist services such as immigration and passport control, customs and medical staff. All airports have a firefighting service with special equipment in case of accidents. Security staff search people and open or X-ray all baggage looking for bombs, guns and other weapons.

Airport records
Longest runway and highest airport
Bangda Airport, Tibet, 5.5 km, at 4739 m
Busiest airport
Hartsfield International Airport, Atlanta, Georgia, USA, 78 million passengers a year.

◀ An aerial view of Haneda airport in Tokyo, Japan.

• Lack of space led to Hong Kong's international airport being built on land reclaimed from the sea.

find out more
Aircraft
Flight
Radar

Alcohol

Alcohols are clear, colourless liquids that burn easily and evaporate quickly. The best-known alcohol is ethanol, which is the chemical that makes drinks 'alcoholic'. It is so common that it is often just called 'alcohol'.

Alcohols dissolve many things that will not dissolve in water, and are used as a solvent in paints, glues, printing inks, perfumes and aftershaves. Solvents containing alcohols are used to clean electrical goods such as computers. In homes, alcohols are often used for cleaning paintbrushes. Alcohols are also used to make detergents and plastics.

The ethanol in alcoholic drinks is made by a process called *fermentation*. During this process, yeast gradually turns the sugar content of a cereal crop or fruit into ethanol. Beer and lager are made from barley malt fermented with yeast and water. Wine is made by fermenting grape juice with yeast, and cider is made from the juice of apples. Spirits, such as brandy or gin, are made by distilling a liquid such as wine. The liquid is boiled, and most of the alcohol evaporates first. When cooled, it becomes liquid again as almost pure alcohol.

Alcohol is a drug that often changes people's behaviour, and can lead to aggressive or anti-social actions. Most countries have laws to limit the use of alcohol. People who cannot manage without drinking alcohol are called alcoholics. Yet regularly drinking too much alcohol damages the liver and kidneys and can harm the brain.

- A mixture of ethanol with another alcohol called methanol is sold as 'methylated spirits'. Methanol is very poisonous, so a dye and a nasty taste are added to stop people from drinking it.

- Alcoholics feel anxious, ill and unable to face everyday problems without alcohol. They usually need help from doctors and special organizations like Alcoholics Anonymous, which is made up of former alcoholics.

find out more
Biotechnology
Cereals
Drugs
Motor cars

◀ This Brazilian petrol station is selling ordinary petrol as well as fuel made from alcohol. The alcohol, made from plants such as sugar cane, is an alternative fuel to petrol.

Alexander the Great

Alexander the Great was perhaps the most famous and greatest soldier of the ancient world. By the time he died, when he was only 33, his vast empire stretched from Greece in the west to India in the east.

Born 356 BC in Pella, now in Greece
Died 323 BC aged 33

find out more
Egyptians, ancient
Greeks, ancient

Alexander became King Alexander III of Macedonia at the age of 20 after the death of his father, Philip II. He soon set about expanding his empire, and in 332 BC he conquered Egypt. Within the next two years he defeated the Persian army and became king of Persia. He even ordered the magnificent Persian city of Persepolis to be burned and destroyed as a sign of his power. (The ruins of the city are still visible today.) He also invaded northern India, but his exhausted soldiers refused to carry on and he agreed to turn back. He died of a fever shortly after returning to Persia.

Alexander rode into most of his battles on his horse Bucephalus. When the old horse died, Alexander built a city and named it Bucephala after him. He also built many new cities which he named Alexandria, after himself. The most famous is the one in Egypt, which is still an important city today.

When he was a young boy, Alexander had been taught by the philosopher Aristotle to be proud of being Greek. Although he was proud, he also wanted all the people in his new empire to live in peace as friends, not as enemies as before. To help achieve this, he gave important jobs to Persians as well as to Greeks, and even took a Persian princess to be his second wife.

After Alexander's death, no one was able to keep his empire together. After years of war amongst his generals, it was split up into smaller kingdoms, including Macedonia, Egypt and Babylonia.

◀ This Roman mosaic from about 100 BC shows Alexander the Great riding into battle against the Persian ruler Darius III.

Algae

Algae are plants without leaves, stems, roots or flowers. They are found in wet places everywhere, from oceans and rivers to the damp side of a tree. Algae can use sunlight to make food (photosynthesize) like higher plants, but strictly they do not belong to the plant kingdom.

Many kinds of algae are microscopic. When millions grow together in one place, they look like green slime. Such small algae are found in lakes and rivers, and most importantly in the sea.

Floating food

Most of the plant life of the oceans is tiny, single-celled algae. They are known as *phytoplankton* ('plant plankton'). Plankton is the name given to the billions of tiny, floating organisms that live near the surface of the oceans. They form the basic food of many of the animals that live in the ocean. One type of algae among the phytoplankton are the *diatoms*. They do not look like land plants, but have a silica shell that protects the living plant inside. They cannot swim, but many of them have strange, spiky shapes that prevent them from sinking.

When algae grow in huge numbers, they are called *algal blooms*. These cause great harm to sea life, for they are usually poisonous to animals.

Algal sandwiches
Lichens are inconspicuous plants that often form black, orange or greenish-grey patches on rocks, walls and roofs. A lichen is like a sandwich of a fungus and an alga. The alga makes the lichen's food from sunlight and air. On the outside, strands of fungus protect the algal filling.

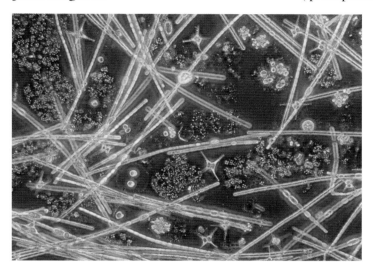

► Some types of phytoplankton, magnified many times. The diatoms can be recognized by their spiky shapes.

find out more
Fungi
Oceans and seas
Plants
Ponds
Seaweeds

Algebra

We use algebra to solve mathematical problems and to examine number patterns. In algebra, unknown numbers are represented by words or letters such as x and y. Scientists use algebra to solve problems and to predict what might happen in an experiment.

Think of a number. Double it. Add 6. Divide that number by 2 and then take away the number you first thought of. You will be left with 3, whichever number you start with. Always! To understand why this happens, mathematicians might write it as an equation, using the letter x (or another letter) to represent 'the number you first thought of':

$$x \times 2 + 6 \div 2 - x = 3.$$

The answer to the equation is always 3, because the number is first doubled, then added, then halved again, and finally taken away. In other words, exactly what is 'put in' is later 'taken out' again. Mathematicians use letters to represent numbers whose values are not known because this allows them to prove whether or not results like this are always true, whatever number you begin with.

Equations

Algebra often involves the use of equations, which are a kind of mathematical sentence showing how one thing relates to another. In most equations, two mathematical expressions are connected by an equals (=) sign. For instance, the equation

$$6x + 4 = 28$$

can be read as '6 times some number plus 4 equals 28'. What number can x stand for here? Often x can stand for several different numbers. For instance, the equation

$$x^2 + y^2 = z^2$$

can be read as 'one number squared (multiplied by itself) plus another number squared is equal to a third number squared'. One trio which works is

$$x = 3, y = 4 \text{ and } z = 5.$$

Can you find any others?

• The word 'algebra' comes from the Arabic word *al-jabr*, meaning setting broken bones. It was used in the title of a book by Muhammad ben Musa about 1200 years ago, meaning 'putting together' the parts of an equation.

find out more
Arithmetic
Mathematics
Numbers

Algeria *see page 613*

Ali, Muhammad

Most experts consider Muhammad Ali to be the greatest boxer of all time. The force of his personality inside and outside the boxing ring won him worldwide fame. He became – and remains – a powerful symbol for black people throughout the world.

After winning the amateur 'Golden Gloves' championship in 1959 and 1960, Cassius Clay (as Ali was then known) became Olympic light-heavyweight champion in 1960. He immediately turned professional and four years later became the heavyweight champion of the world. In that same year, 1964, he became a Muslim and changed his name to Muhammad Ali.

In 1967, because of his religious beliefs, Ali refused to take part in the Vietnam War. He was punished by having his world title taken away from him and was banned from boxing until 1970.

Ali returned to the ring in the 1970s. Although he lost his title twice, he regained it in 1978 and so became the first boxer in history to win the world championship three times. When he finally retired in 1981, he had won 56 of his 61 professional bouts.

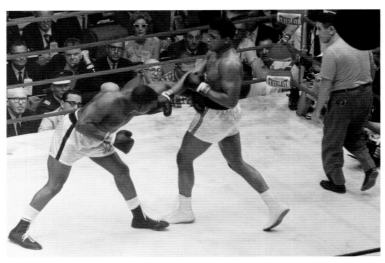

Born 1942 in Kentucky, USA

● 'I am the greatest' became Ali's catchphrase. At the peak of his powers he claimed to be the best-known person on the planet.

◄ Muhammad Ali (right) on his way to defeating Sonny Liston in 1964, to become heavyweight champion of the world for the first time. His success as a boxer was based as much on his clever footwork as on his powerful punches. In his own words, he could 'float like a butterfly, sting like a bee'.

find out more
Boxing and other combat sports

Allergies

You have an allergy if a certain substance makes you sneeze, makes your eyes and nose run, or makes your skin itch. Your body reacts against this substance as if it were a germ and tries to defend you against it.

Many things can cause allergies and these are called *allergens*. Some people are allergic to particular foods. Others react to certain plants, to dust or to animal fur. Sometimes detergents used to wash clothes or bedding cause allergies.

Some allergies can cause quite serious illnesses. *Asthma*, a condition that causes difficulty in breathing, is sometimes caused by an allergy. Asthma is a common illness, especially among children. It is often treated by breathing in a special spray.

Allergies are the most usual cause of a skin complaint called *eczema*, in which the skin becomes dry, cracked and blistered, and very itchy. Young children may suffer from eczema, especially on the inside of their elbows and behind their knees, but it often gets better as they grow up.

Hay fever is an allergy. People with hay fever sneeze and have sore, watery eyes, as though they have a cold. They are allergic to pollen in the air, so hay fever is especially common in late spring and early summer, when flowers and grasses are in bloom and releasing pollen. There are special medicines to help people who suffer from hay fever, making them less sensitive to pollen.

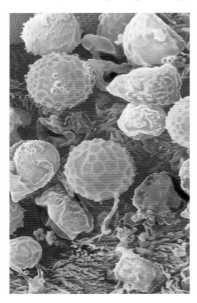

◄ Asthma is sometimes caused by an allergic reaction to pollen and dust in the air. This magnified picture of the inside of a person's trachea (windpipe) has been coloured to show the pollen (pink) and dust (blue) particles that the person has breathed in.

find out more
Complementary medicine
Immunity
Medicine

Amphibians

Frogs, newts and blindworms are amphibians. Amphibians are animals that start their lives in water and change as they grow up, so they are able to live on land as well. All amphibians are vertebrates (animals with backbones) and most have moist, soft skins.

Most amphibians are small animals and, to protect themselves from predators (animals that eat them), many hide during the daytime and are active at night. Many kinds of amphibian have poison glands in their skin which make them taste so nasty that hunting animals avoid them.

Amphibians have very small lungs and breathe partly through their skin. But skin can only breathe if it is kept damp, and so amphibians tend to live near water.

Amphibians are 'cold-blooded' animals. This means that their body temperature and activity depend on the warmth of the air or water around them. When the weather is warm they can be active. When it is cold, they become very sluggish. In cooler parts of the world, such as northern Europe, amphibians hibernate through the winter months.

Metamorphosis

The life of an amphibian begins in water. As it grows up, it changes to adapt to life on land. The process of change is called *metamorphosis*. Most adult amphibians lay large numbers of eggs, or spawn, in ponds or streams. The eggs hatch quickly, but the baby that emerges looks very different from its parents. As it grows, its body changes. It develops lungs and legs, so it can live on dry land. Its diet changes too, and it begins to feed on tiny creatures. Adult amphibians eat flesh, feeding on many sorts of small animals.

Kinds of amphibian

There are three main kinds of amphibian. Blindworms are strange creatures found only in the tropics. They have no legs and a grooved skin, like earthworms, and they burrow

▲ Blindworms are unusual amphibians because only one species lives in water.

through the ground feeding on worms and grubs. Some young blindworms hatch from eggs and some are born live.

Newts and salamanders look like soft-skinned lizards. They are often brightly coloured. Some kinds, such as axolotls, never leave the water. Other kinds crawl up onto land and live in damp woodland areas. One sort hides in logs that people use to make fires, and so it is called the fire salamander.

Frogs and toads have no tails, but they usually have long, powerful hind legs, which they use for jumping and swimming. There are far more kinds of frog and toad than of any other amphibian. They are an important part of the life of tropical forests.

• There are 3500 different kinds of frog and toad, 300 different kinds of newt and salamander and 167 different kinds of blindworm.

• Amphibians were the first vertebrates to live on land. About 400 million years ago there were fishes that had lungs and strong fins. When the pools where they lived dried up, they probably pulled themselves along on their fins. Gradually they became less dependent on water.

• The word 'amphibian' comes from two Greek words and means 'both ways of life'.

find out more
Frogs and toads
Newts and salamanders
Prehistoric life

The life cycle of a frog

Frogs' eggs have no shells. The outside of the egg swells to form a jelly-like protective covering.

A baby frog (*tadpole*) looks rather like a little fish, with a big head and a wriggly tail.

At first the tadpole breathes with gills and feeds on tiny plants that live in the water.

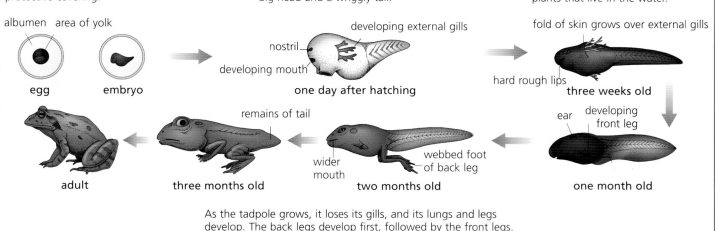

As the tadpole grows, it loses its gills, and its lungs and legs develop. The back legs develop first, followed by the front legs.

Ancient world

By about 5000 BC human beings in Africa, Asia, Europe and America had learned to farm crops and keep animals. This was the first step towards civilization, because it allowed people to live together in communities. Full civilization appeared when villages grew into towns and cities, with government, laws and record-keeping.

The best-known early civilizations are those of the 'ancient world' of Mesopotamia (now Iraq), Egypt, Greece and Rome. But other remarkable cultures flourished elsewhere.

The first civilizations

The first towns were built between about 8000 and 6000 BC. Two of the earliest were Jericho on the River Jordan and Çatal Hüyük in Turkey.

The world's first civilization emerged along the rivers Tigris and Euphrates in an area of Mesopotamia called Sumer. The Sumerians built large cities and pyramid-shaped towers or 'ziggurats'. They dug canals, and traded by sea and land. They also developed the first form of writing.

The second and longest-lived ancient civilization grew up in Egypt beside the River Nile. By 2000 BC other civilizations were spreading across the Middle East and the eastern Mediterranean. The Babylonians took over Mesopotamia. Their king, Hammurabi, was one of the first rulers to write down his laws. Further north, the Hittites, who were fierce warriors, built up an empire in what is now Turkey.

A string of wealthy trading cities emerged in the region called Phoenicia, now Syria and Lebanon, including the great ports of Tyre and Sidon. The Phoenicians were a trading people. They were also great explorers, and settled colonies right across the Mediterranean.

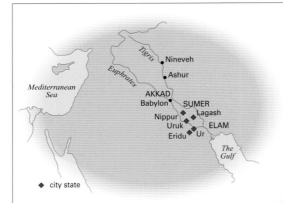

▲ The Sumerian civilization in Mesopotamia.

♦ city state

about 2600	Egyptian pyramids being built
about 2500	Indus civilization begins
about 2000	Beginning of Minoan civilization on Crete
about 1790	Beginning of the reign of King Hammurabi of Babylon
about 1600	Mycenaean civilization flourishing
about 1595	Hittites attack Babylon
about 1500	Shang civilization begins Phoenicians trading in the eastern Mediterranean

area of Olmec influence

▲ The Olmec civilization in Mexico.

776	First Olympic Games in Greece
about 753	Rome founded
605	Nebuchadnezzar becomes king of Babylon
557	Cyrus the Great becomes king of Persia
490	Greeks defeat Persians at Marathon
336–323	Reign of Alexander the Great
146	Romans destroy Carthage
27	Augustus becomes first Roman emperor
AD	
400	Roman empire in decline

Time-line of the ancient world

BC
about 10,000	Farming begins in Asia
about 7500	City of Jericho built
about 3500	City of Ur founded Sumerian writing appears
about 3200	Egyptian hieroglyphic writing begins

area of Shang civilization

▲ The Shang civilization in China.

about 1200	Olmec (Mexico) and Chavin (Peru) civilizations beginning
about 1120	Mycenae destroyed
about 900–650	Assyrian power at its height
814	Phoenicians establish the city of Carthage
about 800	Etruscan civilization beginning

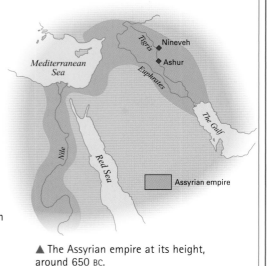

Assyrian empire

▲ The Assyrian empire at its height, around 650 BC.

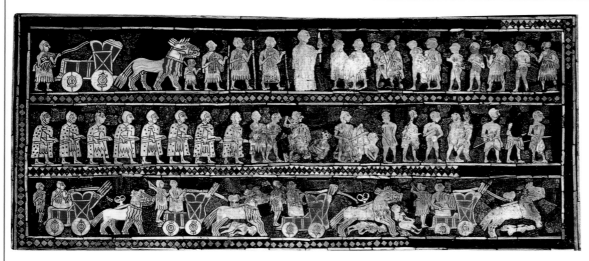

◀ The Standard of Ur is a richly decorated box which was found in one of the 16 magnificent tombs discovered at Ur, one of the greatest of the early cities. Dating from 2500 BC, the two long sides of the box show the Sumerians at war and in victory.

China, India and America

The Chinese were growing rice in about 5000 BC. Their first true civilization, the Shang civilization, flourished some 3000 years later, around the Huang He (Yellow River) and the city of Anyang. The Shang made objects from bronze and invented a very complicated writing system based on pictures. Around 1045 BC the Shang kings were conquered by the Zhou from the west.

Meanwhile, further west, another great river civilization had grown up around the Indus, which lasted for almost 1000 years. At its heart lay the great cities of Harappa, Mohenjo-daro and Lothal. Perhaps 40,000 people lived in Mohenjo-daro. The straight streets were laid out in a grid pattern and larger houses had bathrooms and toilets. The people's wealth came from trade. The Indus culture began to crumble about 1700 BC. After the invasion of Aryans from the north, a new and even richer civilization appeared that gave the world the Hindu and Buddhist religions.

American civilization developed separately. By about 1200 BC two cultures had emerged, the Olmecs of Mexico and the Chavins of Peru. Neither had writing, the wheel or metal tools, but they put up huge buildings and carved stone sculptures of their mysterious, half-human gods.

The glory of the ancient world

The Greek and Roman civilizations (about 900 BC to 400 AD) were the finest of the ancient world. But many other important cultures flourished around the same time.

The warlike Assyrians once controlled an empire that swallowed up Babylonia and reached from Egypt to the Persian Gulf. They too traded widely and built impressive stone palaces. When the Assyrian empire broke up in 612 BC, the Babylonians returned under King Nebuchadnezzar II. He rebuilt the city of Babylon, including a massive, nine-storey ziggurat known as the Tower of Babel.

The Babylonians finally fell to the equally remarkable Persians. Darius I (521–486 BC) ruled the largest empire the world had ever seen, stretching from Egypt and Turkey to the borders of India. It was governed from Persepolis in modern Iran, a city linked to the rest of the empire by a system of royal highways.

The Minoan civilization, on the island of Crete, began in about 3000 BC and survived for over 1500 years. The remains of its stately palaces at Knossos, Mallia and Phaistos survive to this day. Like the Phoenicians, the Minoans grew rich through trade. Their craftspeople were much admired for their pottery and gold working. In about 1450 BC Crete was settled by Mycenaeans from northern Greece, who took over the island's trade and set up markets across the Mediterranean.

The City of Carthage began as a trading post, founded by the Phoenicians in about 814 BC. Until it was destroyed by the Romans in 146 BC, it possessed strong armies and a large fleet of merchant ships. The Etruscans of central Italy were another important civilization overthrown by the Romans. They produced beautiful art and impressive architecture. The Romans copied a great deal from the Etruscans – their capital, Rome, was originally an Etruscan city.

find out more

Alexander the Great
Egyptians, ancient
Greeks, ancient
Romans
Writing systems

▼ A Phoenician ivory furniture panel showing a lion attacking a slave. The Phoenicians were most famous for trading in luxuries like glassware, carved ivory, dyes and jewellery made of precious metals. They were expert at making purple dye, which is how they got their name – 'Phoenicia' comes from the Greek world for purple.

Anglo-Saxons

find out more
Archaeology
Roman Britain
Vikings

The name Anglo-Saxon describes a number of different peoples from Germany and Scandinavia called Angles, Saxons and Jutes who settled in much of Britain from the 5th century AD. The English spoken today comes from the language Anglo-Saxons spoke 1500 years ago.

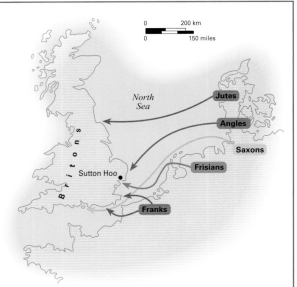

▲ The boundaries between Anglo-Saxon kingdoms were always changing as the kings fought one another for territory. The Britons (Celts) were pushed back to Cornwall and Wales.

In the late 4th and early 5th centuries, Anglo-Saxon soldiers, with their families, were brought over by the Romans as paid fighters to help defend the south and east coasts against pirates and other Saxons. By about 410 the last Roman troops had left Britain. Although some people continued to live in a Roman way, many places began to change and become Anglo-Saxon, as more and more new settlers came from across the English Channel and the North Sea.

▲ This warrior's helmet was found in the remains of an Anglo-Saxon ship at Sutton Hoo, an archaeological site in Suffolk, England. Sutton Hoo is thought to have been the grave of Raedwald, who was not only king of East Anglia but was also High King of Britain. He died in 624 or 625.

Towns and kingdoms

The Anglo-Saxon immigrants to Britain gradually began to take over more land and to build farms, villages and towns. In 200 years, from about 450 to 650, they moved further west and established kingdoms. Some Anglo-Saxon place names survive, such as East Anglia, the kingdom of the East Angles. Other Anglo-Saxon names are still in use today. A *ford* is a crossing, as in Bradford, for example. *Ton* meant farm or village and there are a lot of place names in Britain ending in -*ton*.

Alfred is the most famous of the Anglo-Saxon kings. He ruled in southern England in the 9th century, and during his reign the Anglo-Saxon Chronicles, an important record of events in the kingdom, were begun. Alfred was also responsible for founding a number of new

fortified towns, called *burhs*. These towns were protected by strong banks so that the townspeople and those who lived in the countryside around could take refuge from the new invaders, the Vikings. Canute and his Viking army conquered all England eventually, and in 1016 Canute was accepted as king.

Anglo–Saxon clothes and runes

From the small fragments of cloth found in graves, archaeologists have worked out that women often wore long, flowing gowns fastened at the shoulders with big brooches. On their belts they might have hung a purse. Jewellery such as brooches, necklaces, pins and bracelets has been found too. Men usually wore short tunics over leggings, and cloaks for warmth. Some men were buried with a shield and sword.

The Anglo-Saxons used an alphabet with 33 special letters called *runes*. It was often used to inscribe pots, metal jewellery or special objects made of bone. Christianity introduced Latin to the Anglo-Saxons and some of their handwritten books (called manuscripts) survive today. Some of these manuscripts have drawings too, providing more evidence about the Anglo-Saxon way of life.

● In 597 the Pope sent Augustine, a monk in Rome, to convert the people of Britain to Christianity. There had been some Christian communities in Britain since Roman times, but Augustine converted many more people to the faith. Churches were built – most of wood but some of stone – and a few can still be seen today.

◄ This is a modern reconstruction of an Anglo-Saxon wooden house. Anglo-Saxon villagers kept sheep, cattle and pigs. They hunted deer and ate fish and wild birds.

Animal behaviour

An animal's behaviour includes everything that it does. It may search for food and eat, it may try to escape from its enemies, and it may find a mate and produce and rear young. Even sleep is part of its behaviour.

Most animal behaviour can be broken down into a series of separate actions caused by changes in its circumstances. These changes, which are called triggers, may be internal. For instance, when an animal has digested a meal it feels hungry. This is the trigger for it to search for more food. Its senses pick up external triggers and tell it what is suitable food. For instance, a cheetah in Africa may start to hunt because it is hungry. It will see but ignore large antelopes, but the sight of a Thomson's gazelle will be the trigger to start the chase.

Instinct and learning

The behaviour of many animals looks very clever, but often the cleverness is something that is automatic and cannot be changed. For instance, wasps could no more alter the way they build their beautiful, complex paper nests than they could change their yellow and black colours. Wasps do not have to learn how to make their nests. There are many examples of such unlearned activities, which are often called *innate* (or *instinctive*) *behaviour*.

▼ Like all spiders, this orb-weaver spider from Trinidad in the Caribbean is born knowing how to build the complex web that it uses to catch food.

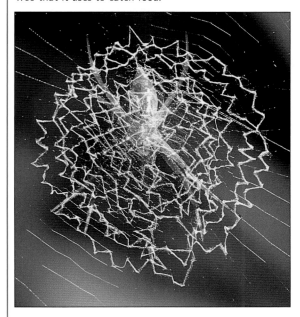

On the other hand, many creatures learn from experience and can change their behaviour. All vertebrates (backboned animals) and a few invertebrates, such as octopuses, behave in ways that are partly learned. An animal's actions are often a complex mix of instinctive and learned behaviour. For instance, all young animals are born with a knowledge of how to eat, but they often do not know what to eat, and have to find out by trial and error. A chick may peck at all sorts of things, such as small stones, but once it has found the right food it does not try to eat inedible things anymore.

Animal language

Many kinds of animal live in groups and need to be able to communicate with each other. Each kind of animal has its own language, although warning noises may be understood by other species. Cats and dogs that share a home do not share a language.

Animals communicate in many ways. Many give and receive information by scent, for instance by using it to mark the boundaries of their territory. Animals also use body language, as when they display specially coloured areas, such as crests or tails, to put across a simple message. When animals are close together, they can communicate using facial expressions. These are important in many mammals. Watch dogs playing and see how they open and narrow their eyes and alter the position of their ears and lips to express meaning. Some animals use sound language. Apes and some kinds of bird are known to have at least 25 sounds with exact meanings.

▲ This chimpanzee is using a stick to dig termites out of a termite mound in Zambia. It has probably learned to do this by copying other chimpanzees, and then trying the behaviour out for itself.

• Many of the things that humans do are innate. We respond to triggers just as other creatures do, but more of our behaviour is learned and our language is hugely complex.

• In the 1950s the Austrian naturalist Konrad Lorenz showed that goslings will follow anything they see during their first 16 hours after hatching. Following is instinctive but what they follow is learned. When introduced to his boots during this 'critical period', young geese followed Lorenz's booted feet everywhere.

find out more
Animals
Hibernation
Migration

Animals

Animals live almost everywhere in the world, from polar regions to hot, dry deserts and steamy forests. The biggest weigh over 100 tonnes, the smallest can only be seen through a microscope.

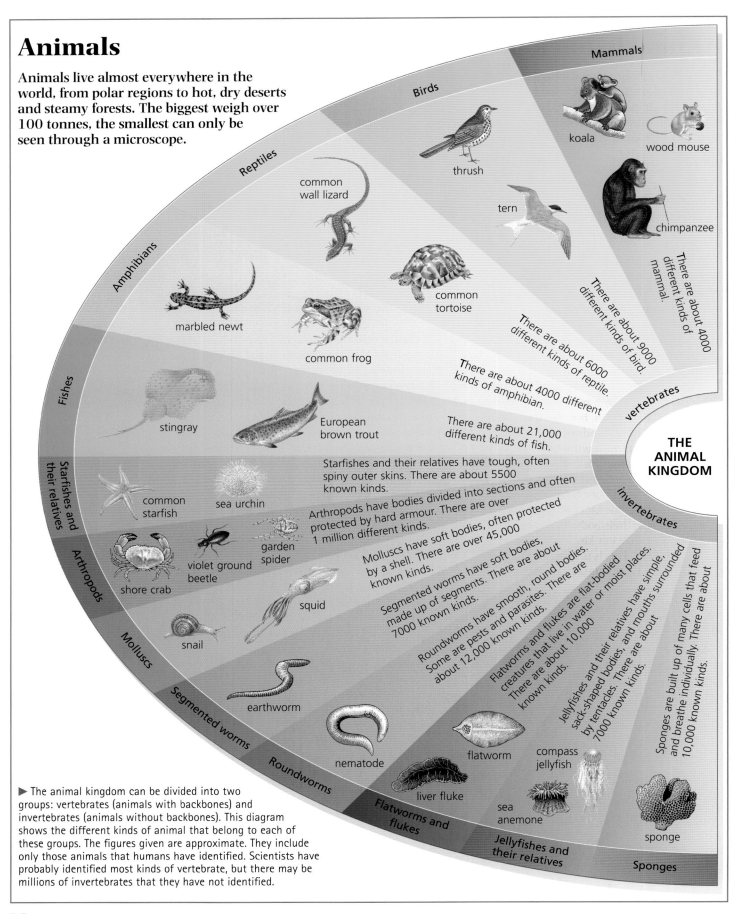

THE ANIMAL KINGDOM

There are about 4000 different kinds of mammal.

There are about 9000 different kinds of bird.

There are about 6000 different kinds of reptile.

There are about 4000 different kinds of amphibian.

There are about 21,000 different kinds of fish.

Starfishes and their relatives have tough, often spiny outer skins. There are about 5500 known kinds.

Arthropods have bodies divided into sections and often protected by hard armour. There are over 1 million different kinds.

Molluscs have soft bodies, often protected by a shell. There are over 45,000 known kinds.

Segmented worms have soft bodies, made up of segments. There are about 7000 known kinds.

Roundworms have smooth, round bodies. Some are pests and parasites. There are about 12,000 known kinds.

Flatworms and flukes are flat-bodied creatures that live in water or moist places. There are about 10,000 known kinds.

Jellyfishes and their relatives have simple, sack-shaped bodies, and mouths surrounded by tentacles. There are about 7000 known kinds.

Sponges are built up of many cells that feed and breathe individually. There are about 10,000 known kinds.

Labels: Mammals, koala, wood mouse, chimpanzee, Birds, thrush, tern, Reptiles, common wall lizard, common tortoise, Amphibians, marbled newt, common frog, Fishes, stingray, European brown trout, vertebrates, invertebrates, Starfishes and their relatives, common starfish, sea urchin, Arthropods, shore crab, violet ground beetle, garden spider, Molluscs, snail, squid, Segmented worms, earthworm, Roundworms, nematode, Flatworms and flukes, liver fluke, flatworm, sea anemone, compass jellyfish, Jellyfishes and their relatives, sponge, Sponges

▶ The animal kingdom can be divided into two groups: vertebrates (animals with backbones) and invertebrates (animals without backbones). This diagram shows the different kinds of animal that belong to each of these groups. The figures given are approximate. They include only those animals that humans have identified. Scientists have probably identified most kinds of vertebrate, but there may be millions of invertebrates that they have not identified.

Animals are one of the five main groups (called kingdoms) into which all living things are divided. It is not always easy to tell animals from plants, but generally animals are able to move about from place to place and must eat food to survive.

All animals eat things that have once been alive. Most, like horses and snails, are *herbivores*, and eat plants. Some, like tigers and sharks, are *carnivores*, and kill and eat other animals. Some, like human beings and worms, are *omnivores*, and eat almost anything. Others, like vultures and dung beetles, are *scavengers*, and feed on dead and rotting plants and animals.

Vertebrates and invertebrates

The word 'vertebrate' comes from the Latin word for a backbone, so vertebrates are animals with backbones. The bodies of vertebrates are supported by the backbone and the other bones in the skeleton. There are five major groups of vertebrates: fishes, amphibians, reptiles, birds and mammals.

Almost all the bigger, more complicated animals are vertebrates, but there are many more different kinds of invertebrates – animals without backbones. These include insects, squids, snails, jellyfishes and worms. Invertebrates do not have bones but may be supported by some kind of hard shell outside or inside their body. There are about 50,000 different kinds of vertebrate that we know of. This is probably less than 1 per cent of all the animals that exist.

Activity

Some animals – birds and mammals – are 'warm-blooded'. This means they are able to keep their body at a constant temperature, however hot or cold their environment. They are always able to be active, but they pay a high price as they have to find a great deal of food to fuel their activity. However, most animals, including reptiles, amphibians, fishes and all invertebrates, are 'cold-blooded'. This means that their body temperature rises and falls with the temperature of their surroundings. In sunshine or hot weather, they can be quite warm and active, but at night or in winter, they are often cold and inactive. The advantage to being so inactive is that they do not need so much food.

Reproduction

Most animals are either male or female, and after mating, the young are born sharing the characteristics of both parents. A small number of animals, such as greenfly and water fleas, are almost all females and, without mating, are able to produce many female young. A few kinds of animal, such as garden snails, are both male and female at the same time, and are able to produce both eggs and sperm. A few others, such as oysters and some fishes, change sex at a certain time in their lives or as a result of changes in their environment. Others still, like some sea anemones, are able to divide their own body, splitting off pieces that grow to make the next generation.

Some animals produce huge numbers of young, but most of these die early, eaten by other creatures. Animals that have long lives and that care for their young tend to have smaller families. Usually the female animal is most important in caring for her family, but in some cases the male helps equally and with some animals he does all the work of looking after the offspring.

- Humankind's use of resources is often wasteful and, in the way that we affect other animals, extremely harmful. Many people now believe that even when we are making use of other animals, as we do in farming, they should be treated with care and kindness.

find out more
Amphibians
Animal behaviour
Birds
Conservation
Ecology
Fishes
Insects
Living things
Mammals
Prehistoric life
Reptiles
Wildlife
Worms
Zoos

Animal records

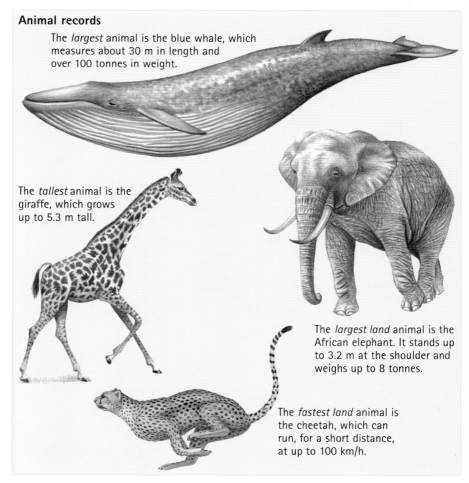

The *largest* animal is the blue whale, which measures about 30 m in length and over 100 tonnes in weight.

The *tallest* animal is the giraffe, which grows up to 5.3 m tall.

The *largest land* animal is the African elephant. It stands up to 3.2 m at the shoulder and weighs up to 8 tonnes.

The *fastest land* animal is the cheetah, which can run, for a short distance, at up to 100 km/h.

Animation

Animation is the technique of making films from a rapid series of still pictures. The pictures may be of drawings (cartoons) or of models, such as puppets.

In many ways animation copies the process used in filming live action, which breaks continuous movements into a series of still pictures, or 'frames', and then projects them in rapid succession onto a screen. The difference is that animators create the impression of movement by making each frame themselves, every one containing a tiny adjustment, barely noticeable on its own.

As with live-action film, it takes 24 frames to make one second of animated-action film. This means that a 10-minute story requires some 14,400 individual pictures.

The cel method

The first animated films, made in the early 1900s, were cartoons. They took a lot of time and effort, as the backgrounds had to be accurately reproduced as well as the moving figures. Cartoon-making was transformed by the invention (in about 1920) of 'cels' – transparent sheets on which the sequence of pictures needed for a particular movement, gesture or expression was drawn. The cels were laid over the background and photographed onto a single frame of film.

Almost all cartoons used the cel method until the recent introduction of computer animation. Disney's *Toy Story* (1995) was the first animated film made entirely of computer images. Computers are also used to create special effects within live-action films, notably for some of the dinosaurs in *Jurassic Park* (1992) and its sequel, *The Lost World* (1997).

► FLASHBACK ◄

Animation is the oldest form of making motion pictures. The first animated films were shown to audiences in the early 1890s by the French artist Emile Reynaud. From 1910 animation began to capture the public's imagination, when cartoon characters like the accident-prone Cartouche and Gertie the Dinosaur became as popular as live performers.

Lasting about five minutes, cartoons were usually shown before the main feature film.

Soon entire studios were devoted to making animated films.

The best-known maker of cartoon films was Walt Disney. Following the success of characters like Mickey Mouse and Donald Duck, he made the bold decision to produce a full-length animated feature film. Most critics thought that audiences would be bored by an 80-minute cartoon, but *Snow White and the Seven Dwarfs* (1937) was a box-office hit and Disney has remained the world's most successful animation studio ever since.

Since the mid-1950s cartoons have been made mostly for television. But animated feature films are as popular as ever, with several film companies hoping to match Disney's success. Don Bluth produced *Thumbelina* (1994) and *Anastasia* (1997), and Steven Spielberg's DreamWorks company made *The Prince of Egypt* (1998).

▲ Model animation was once used to create special effects within live-action films, like the model gorilla built for *King Kong* (1933). Now entire films are made using model animation. Nick Park is shown above adjusting another frame for one of his much-loved Wallace and Gromit films. He has won several Oscars for Best Short Animated Film.

find out more
Cartoons
Disney, Walt
Films
Spielberg, Steven

▼ This sequence of cartoon frames shows a clown taking a bow.

Antarctica

Antarctica is the Earth's fifth largest continent – and the coldest. Nearly all of its huge area is covered with ice over 3 kilometres thick. There is very little wildlife, and for thousands of years there were no people. But since the early 20th century, human activity on Antarctica has steadily grown.

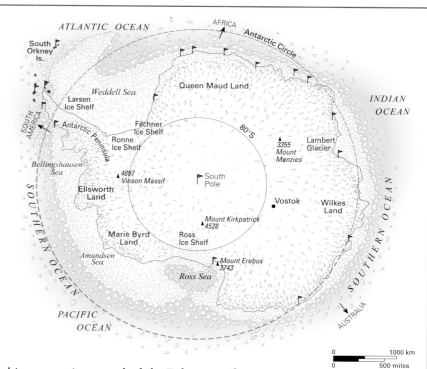

The Antarctic ice-cap has built up over millions of years. The sheet of ice spreads out onto the sea, where huge pieces break off to make icebergs. Geologists who study the rocky areas that are not under ice have discovered coal and the fossils of plants and animals. These finds show that Antarctica once had a warm climate. It began to get cold about 150 million years ago. The climate is made worse by very strong, icy winds. Except in summer, the sea around the continent is full of ice.

Exploration

One of the first explorers to sight Antarctica may have been Captain James Cook, who sailed south in 1774. The first people to set foot on the continent were probably seal hunters in about 1820. But the extreme cold and the ice made exploration difficult. By 1895, people were keen to find out what Antarctica was like. Members of a Belgian party that sailed in 1897 were the first people to spend a winter on the ice.

Between 1901 and 1904 Captain Robert F. Scott led an unsuccessful British expedition to the South Pole. In 1910 Scott began a second attempt, and soon afterwards a Norwegian explorer, Roald Amundsen, also set out for the Pole. Amundsen arrived first, on 14 December 1911, and returned home successfully. Scott and his companions reached the Pole a month later, but died on the return journey.

A continent for research

Since the early 20th century, many countries have sent scientific expeditions to Antarctica, and have set up permanent stations where scientists can live and work. Most scientific research is done in the summer. In recent years, there has also been a small amount of tourism in the summer months.

In 1959 the USA, Russia and 10 other countries signed an Antarctic Treaty, in which they agreed not to make rival claims to territory but to use the Antarctic only for peaceful research. Many more countries have since accepted the treaty, and in 1991 a 50-year mining ban was agreed.

■	land not covered by ice
▲	high peaks (height in metres)
	ice cap (up to 4000 metres thick)
	sea covered by ice all year
	sea covered by ice for part of the year
⚑	scientific stations, permanently occupied

◀ Whole mountain ranges are buried under the Antarctic ice. Just the very tops poke through. The tallest peak is called the Vinson Massif and is 4897 m high.

find out more
Arctic
Continents
Cook, James
Ice
Rain and snow

Antelopes

Most antelopes live in large herds on the grasslands of Africa, where they feed on a wide variety of plants. Antelopes are swift runners, and have long legs, which allows them to avoid predators such as lions. Some antelopes, such as the royal antelope, are tiny, while many, such as the wildebeest, are big, powerful animals.

Often a herd of antelopes consists of females and calves only, although males will join a herd during the mating season. Males fight other males for females and for territory. Their horns are usually spiral or notched so that the rivals' horns lock together when fighting. There follows a trial of strength as they push each other backwards and forwards. Although the fights look fierce, the loser can easily break free and injuries are rare.

A baby antelope can stand within minutes of its birth and is soon an active member of the herd. It becomes independent quickly, as its mother will produce a new calf in the next year.

Antelopes are the prey of many flesh-eating animals, such as lions and other big cats, but humans are their most dangerous enemy. Many species have now become very rare because of over-hunting or the destruction of their habitat. Attempts have been made to domesticate some kinds of antelope, and it is possible that they may become important farm animals in the future.

- There are about 105 different kinds of antelope.

find out more
Cattle
Digestive systems
Grasslands
Mammals
Sheep and goats

◀ This group of animals includes three different kinds of antelope: eland (the large animal to the right), waterbuck (medium-sized and dark brown) and impala (small, reddish-brown). Antelopes graze and browse on a wide variety of plants, which means that many species can live side by side without competing for food.

Ants and termites

Ants and termites are insects which always live in groups, or colonies. Most ant and termite colonies build huge nests. There are many thousands of individuals in a colony, but they all have the same mother: the queen.

Termites eat only plant food, and because of their numbers, they can become pests. Ants feed on many kinds of food, including plants and other animals. Ants can be found worldwide, while termites live only in warm regions, especially Africa, Australia and America.

Most ants and termites do not have wings, but at certain times of the year huge numbers take to the air. After a brief mating flight, the females make new nests and lay eggs. Male ants die after mating, but male termites survive to share the royal chamber with the queen.

The eggs laid by the queen ant hatch into female ants called workers, whose job it is to collect food for themselves, their sisters and the queen. These are the ants that you are most likely to see. When they are out getting food, they make scent trails so that they can find their way back to the nest. Some of the workers become soldier ants, growing large and helping to protect the nest by biting or squirting acid at enemies.

When young termites hatch out, they look like miniature adults, but they do much of the work of the nest.

- There are about 14,000 different kinds of ant and about 2000 different kinds of termite.

- Ants and termites are eaten by a number of large animals such as aardvarks and anteaters. A single insect would not be enough for them, but several thousand provide a feast.

find out more
Animal behaviour
Bees and wasps
Grasslands
Insects

▼ Some kinds of termite build enormous nests, which may rise many metres above the ground. They contain fungus gardens where they grow food, cells for eggs and young, and the royal chamber in which the queen and her mate live.

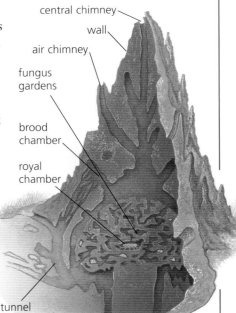

central chimney
wall
air chimney
fungus gardens
brood chamber
royal chamber
tunnel

Apes

Apes are our nearest relatives in the animal kingdom. Like humans, they are intelligent, long-lived mammals, and they generally travel in family parties. There are two main groups of apes. Gorillas, chimpanzees and orang-utans are the great apes, and gibbons and siamangs are the lesser apes.

▼ Chimpanzees live in the forests of central and western Africa. They use gestures and facial expressions to give information to other members of the group, and have a language that includes at least 24 sounds.

• There are 13 kinds of ape: 9 lesser apes and 4 great apes.

• Great apes live about 50 years, while lesser apes live 30 to 40 years.

• Like humans, apes are primates. This means that their hands have a thumb which can be pressed against a finger to pick things up, although they cannot fold it across the palm of the hand. Unlike humans, apes also have long toes and can grasp things with their feet.

The great apes have bodies much like ours. Like us they have no visible tail, and 32 teeth. Vision is their most important sense, and unlike most mammals, they can see colours much as we can. Female apes, like humans, normally have one baby at a time. Young apes develop slowly. A mother does not have another baby until the last one is several years old. A baby chimpanzee continues to feed on its mother's milk until it is about 4 years old. Young chimpanzees learn many things from their mothers, such as how to use a twig as a tool to fish termites out of their nests.

Apes eat mainly leaves and fruit, though some also feed on flesh, such as insects. They wake early and roam through the forest in search of food. During the middle of the day they doze in nests of branches and leaves which they build in the trees. They dislike rain, and sometimes protect themselves by holding a leafy branch over their heads.

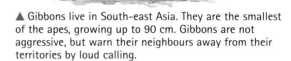

▲ Gibbons live in South-east Asia. They are the smallest of the apes, growing up to 90 cm. Gibbons are not aggressive, but warn their neighbours away from their territories by loud calling.

Apes and humans

There are some obvious differences between apes and humans. The apes all have far more hair covering their bodies than we do. Their arms are much longer and stronger, while their legs tend to be shorter and weaker. Apes can climb very well and often swing about in the branches of trees. They usually walk on all fours. This is known as knuckle-walking, as they put their weight on their knuckles.

In spite of the fact that apes are our close relatives, we have not treated them well. We have killed them, imprisoned them in zoos and experimented on them in laboratories. Worse, much of the forest in which they live has been destroyed. The orang-utan, gorilla and gibbon are all in danger of dying out, and chimpanzees are much less common than they used to be.

▼ Gorillas are the largest of the great apes, growing up to 1.75 m tall. They live in the forests of central Africa. Gorillas are unaggressive creatures, and live in family groups led by a big male, the silverback.

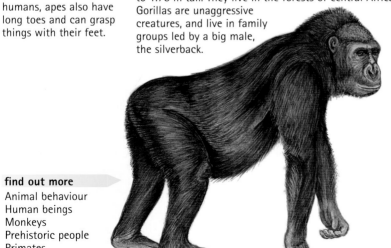

▲ The word 'orang-utan' means 'man of the woods'. Orangs live in forests on the islands of Sumatra and Borneo in South-east Asia. Unlike the other great apes, they mostly live alone.

find out more
Animal behaviour
Human beings
Monkeys
Prehistoric people
Primates

Archaeology

Archaeology is the study of history based on physical evidence. Archaeologists locate, excavate and interpret this evidence to tell us things about the past we might otherwise never know.

Sometimes the remains of the past are so big they can easily be seen, like the great Inca city of Macchu Picchu in Peru. More often, however, archaeologists must seek clues more carefully. To do this they may use hundreds of photographs taken from aeroplanes every year. Archaeological sites may be visible from the air, or crops may grow in different ways if their roots grow over a buried wall or a filled-in ditch.

Excavation

Once a site is discovered, it is carefully measured and detailed records (drawings, photographs and notes) are made. Any surface remains are gathered up, and their position at the site plotted.

Most full-scale excavations today are 'rescue excavations'. These are carried out because the sites are to be disturbed by new roads, buildings or deep ploughing. Excavation of the site means that the archaeologists must destroy most of it in order to understand it.

Interpretation

After an excavation, specialists examine the records and write a report. Many people, including experts in identifying and dating different types of animal bone, fragments of pottery, or

▲ Archaeologists at a burial site in a cave near the Pyramid of the Sun in Teotihuacán, Mexico.

seeds from plants, are needed to put together the 'story' of the site. However, even using the most up-to-date scientific methods it is a difficult job to reconstruct a full picture of the past because not everything will have survived.

find out more
Anglo-Saxons
Aztecs
Celts
Egyptians, ancient
Greeks, ancient
Incas
Maya
Prehistoric life
Prehistoric people
Romans
Vikings

Archimedes

Born about 287 BC in Sicily, Italy
Died 212 BC aged about 75

Archimedes was one of the greatest engineers and mathematicians in ancient Greece. He spent his life studying geometry, and using his ideas to develop new types of machine.

Archimedes was born in the town of Syracuse in Sicily, which at that time was a Greek city-state. He was a wealthy man and a friend of the king of Syracuse.

There is a story that the king wanted to know if his crown was pure gold. He suspected that his goldsmith had mixed some cheaper metal in it. Archimedes could not solve the problem until one day, stepping into his bath, he realized that the water level rose higher the more of his body he immersed.

He ran outside naked shouting 'Eureka! Eureka!' ('I've got it! I've got it!'). Archimedes then put the crown in a bath and worked out its volume by the rise in the water level. Next he immersed a piece of pure gold weighing the same as the crown. As the water level did not rise to the same height, the crown could not have been pure gold and the goldsmith was executed.

Other stories tell of the amazing war machines Archimedes invented to protect Syracuse from the invading Romans. These included large mirrors that focused the Sun's rays and set the Roman ships on fire.

When Syracuse was eventually captured, Archimedes was killed by a Roman soldier.

▼ The engineer, mathematician and philosopher Archimedes at work on one of his inventions.

ARCHIMEDES PHILOSOPHE
Grec. Chap. 23.

• One of the machines that Archimedes is best remembered for is the Archimedean screw, which is used to raise water. In fact, in spite of its name, the screw may have been invented by the Egyptians.

find out more
Geometry
Mathematics

Architecture

Architecture is the business of creating buildings for human use. For centuries European architecture was based on the principles of building developed by the ancient Greeks and Romans. Other cultures have developed their own rules and traditions to determine how buildings should look and be constructed.

Originally master-builders designed buildings and were in charge of construction work. This is still the case in many parts of the world, but in the Western world the jobs of architect and builder have generally become more distinct.

The work of an architect

Architects express their ideas by means of drawing. This may involve drawing by hand or, as computer technology has developed, drawing on screen.

Different types of drawing have different names. The *plan* is a 'footprint' of the building – it shows the shapes of the rooms and the spaces between them. A *cross-section* shows how all the storeys or levels of the building fit together, and *elevations* show the faces of the building and the way the windows and doors are arranged.

The architect also draws *details*. A technical detail might show how a window should open. An ornamental detail might show how a leafy capital (head of a column) should be carved.

Finally, the architect may have a detailed model made or get an artist to produce a *perspective*, a realistic painting or drawing, to show what the finished building will look like.

- The word 'architecture' comes from the Greek word *arkhitekton*, meaning master builder.

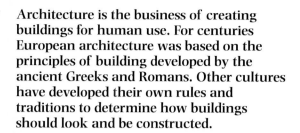

▲ This architectural plan includes the area of the ING Bank shown in the photo (right). The green area is the base of the tower, which is sufficiently well lit for plants to grow.

- The three styles of Greek architecture are known as 'orders'. The Doric order is serious and strong; the Ionic order is light and graceful; and the Corinthian order is rich and lively.

find out more
Bridges
Building
Churches
Houses
Towers
Wren, Christopher

▲ The ING Bank is an example of 'green' architecture. Here, for example, sloping walls and a glass dome with solar panels at the top, make the best use of the Sun's energy.

Architecture through the ages

In the 1st century BC the Roman architect Vitruvius gave a description of the three essential qualities of architecture: usefulness, stability and beauty. A building is useful if it is conveniently planned and pleasant to use. It is stable if it is well and safely built. Finally, it is beautiful if it appeals to the eye, because of its materials, proportions or detailing.

Classical architecture

The term 'classical architecture' describes the kind of buildings seen in ancient Greece and Rome. Greek buildings had a simple form of construction using upright posts (*columns*) and horizontal beams (*architraves*). The columns were of three main styles: Doric, Ionic and Corinthian. The Romans borrowed these types of column and added two more, Tuscan and Composite. These columns formed the basis for a rich system of ornament

▼ This ruined temple, built by the ancient Greeks in Italy, illustrates the Doric order. The columns have no base and a fairly plain capital (the wider section at the top of the column).

▲ The early Gothic cathedral of Bourges, in France. It has very high vaulted ceilings, which are supported on all sides by flying buttresses.

that has been used in buildings inspired by ancient Greek and Roman examples ever since.

Roman buildings were often bigger and more complicated than those of the Greeks. This was partly because they made use of arches. Arches were the basis for two types of roof that the Romans built especially well – domes and vaults. A *dome* is shaped like an upside-down cup and covers a square or circular space, usually in the middle of a large building. A *vault* is usually much longer than it is wide, forming a tunnel-like shape.

Roman architecture formed the basis of much European architecture for many centuries, although it was adapted in different ways in different places. Arches and domes were also an important part of Islamic architecture.

Gothic architecture

In the 12th century a new style of architecture, called Gothic, arose. It used pointed arches, which are stronger than rounded ones and can be put to greater use. Instead of having massively heavy stonework to support the weight of vaults, Gothic buildings have a more skeleton-like system of construction, and therefore look more elegant and airy. Many Gothic churches have huge stained-glass windows. Large Gothic churches often use flying buttresses – external supports that are connected to the wall by an arch.

Renaissance architecture and beyond

By about 1500 the Gothic style was replaced by a revival of Classical features. This was during the Renaissance (meaning 'rebirth') period, when the glories of the ancient world were rediscovered.

Classical architecture was given many variations over the next centuries, but in the 19th century some architects began experimenting with entirely new styles and techniques. Instead of looking to the past for inspiration, they tried to create modern buildings by using industrial materials such as iron and steel.

This revolution in architecture continued after World War I, when many European architects began to experiment with simple forms in what is called the International Style, using new materials, including reinforced concrete and plate glass. The most famous of these architects was Le Corbusier, who worked in France. In the 1930s the German architects Walter Gropius and Mies van der Rohe took these ideas to the USA. There they developed the type of glass-walled, steel-framed office blocks now seen all over the world.

By the 1960s some architects started to mix ideas copied from older buildings in a more decorated 'post-modern' style and to design buildings that expressed the different cultures in the world. Others designed 'green' buildings to help save the Earth's scarce resources.

Some famous architects

William of Sens (died about 1180) helped design one of the first Gothic cathedrals – in Sens, France – and helped rebuild parts of Canterbury Cathedral in England.

The Italian Andrea **Palladio** (1508–1580) reinterpreted classical Roman architecture. The style he developed is known as 'Palladian'.

Antonio **Gaudí** (1852–1926) was a Spanish architect. His buildings include bright colour, unusual materials and daring technical innovations.

The American Frank Lloyd **Wright** (1867–1959) is known for 'organic architecture', which reflects the natural surroundings. His designs make brilliant use of light and space.

The Swiss-born architect known as **Le Corbusier** (1887–1965) was one of the most innovative architects of the 20th century. He thought up many practical solutions to the problems of housing in modern cities.

◀ The remains of Angkor Wat, a magnificent 12th-century temple in Cambodia, South-east Asia. The architecture is strongly influenced by Indian temples of the same period, but the arrangement of the buildings is particular to Cambodia. It is meant to mirror the layout of the Universe according to Hindu beliefs.

Arctic

The Arctic is the area inside the Arctic Circle around the North Pole. It is a huge frozen ocean, surrounded by islands and by the northern coasts of Asia and North America.

The Arctic is cold all year round. In winter the Sun never comes above the horizon, and the sea is frozen over. In summer, temperatures creep above freezing, the edge of the Arctic Ocean melts, and for weeks the Sun never sets. The Arctic Ocean is rich in plankton and fish. These are food for millions of sea birds, which nest in the Arctic in summer, and for seals, whales and other sea creatures.

The land areas around the Arctic Ocean are generally flat and treeless. In winter, the soil is frozen and covered with snow. In summer, plants grow and flower, providing food for animals such as reindeer (caribou) and musk oxen. Meat-eaters like the Arctic wolf and polar bear survive by hunting.

The Arctic region is one of the most sparsely populated areas in the world. The Inuit (Eskimo) have survived here for hundreds of years. More recently, the discovery of oil has brought people from further south to work in the Arctic.

• In 1909 two Americans, Robert Peary and Frederick Cook, both claimed to have been the first to reach the North Pole. There is still dispute about both their claims.

find out more
Antarctica
Ice
Tundra

Argentina

Argentina means 'land of silver', so named because the Spanish explorers who named it vainly hoped to find silver there. It covers most of south-eastern South America and is about five times the size of France.

In the north there is a huge region of subtropical plains and forests, called the Gran Chaco. In the centre lie the vast grassy plains of the pampas with their rich soil. The plains produce about three-quarters of Argentina's wealth. Farmers grow millions of tonnes of wheat and maize there.

People and society

During the first half of the 20th century Argentina became an industrial as well as an agricultural society. But the economy has been through hard times of massive inflation.

In the country districts, most Argentinians are descended from the original Spanish conquerors and Native Americans. In the cities, most are descendants of immigrants, especially Spanish and Italian, who arrived in the 19th century.

► FLASHBACK ◄

In the 1930s Argentina's economy collapsed during the world depression. The first of several military dictatorships followed. In 1946 Juan Perón re-established civilian control and ruled as president until 1955. Military rule sometimes returned, and many people were killed. A return to democratic rule came in 1982 after a 10-week war to capture the Falkland Islands from Britain ended in failure.

◄ There are still a few gauchos, the cowboys of South America, working on the pampas ranches. However, these vast lands are gradually being broken up by fences.

• Argentina was freed from Spanish colonial rule in 1816 by their national hero, José de San Martín.

• Juan Perón was elected president a second time in 1973, but died within a year. His influential and popular first wife, Eva Perón, is the subject of the musical *Evita*.

find out more
Grasslands
South America

Arithmetic

In arithmetic there are four basic operations, which involve combining numbers together: adding, subtracting, multiplying and dividing. We can do simple arithmetic in our head as 'mental arithmetic', but for more complicated calculations we might use an abacus, a calculator or a computer.

At its simplest, adding is nothing more than counting on from one number to another; adding 3 and 3 is the same as starting at 3 and counting on 3 more (3 ... 4, 5, 6). Multiplication is just repeated adding. For example, 7 times 3 is really just the same as

3 + 3 + 3 + 3 + 3 + 3 + 3 (or 7 + 7 + 7).

Subtraction is really just addition in reverse. Finding out the answer to '15 take away 6' is the same as asking, 'What number would I have to add to 6 to get 15?' And in its turn, division is simply multiple subtraction. All complex arithmetic calculations can be done by carrying out a long series of simple additions or subtractions.

Multiplication

The accurate multiplication of large or awkward numbers is needed, for instance, in navigation, astronomy, making machinery or calculating energy needs. Before computers were invented, people had devised lots of ways of multiplying. The simplest of these is a table of multiplications.

1	2	3	4	5	6	7	8	9	10
2	4	6	8	10	12	14	16	18	20
3	6	9	12	15	18	21	24	27	30
4	8	12	16	20	24	28	32	36	40
5	10	15	20	25	30	35	40	45	50
6	12	18	24	30	36	42	48	54	60
7	14	21	28	35	42	49	56	63	70
8	16	24	32	40	48	56	64	72	80
9	18	27	36	45	54	63	72	81	90
10	20	30	40	50	60	70	80	90	100

The table gives the answers to all multiplications between 1 times 1 and 10 times 10. To multiply 4 times 6, find the column with 4 at the top and the row with 6 at the side. The answer, 24, is where the column and row cross.

• Here is a quick method for multiplying a single digit by the number 9. Open both hands in front of you and count from the left the number you want to multiply. Fold down that finger. The number of fingers to the left of the folded one gives you the number of 10s in your answer. Counting the number of fingers to the right of the folded-down finger gives you the number of units in your answer.

find out more
Calculators
Computers
Mathematics
Numbers

Armadillos, anteaters and sloths

Armadillos, anteaters and sloths all belong to a group of mammals known as edentates. This name means 'without teeth', but only the true anteaters are totally toothless.

Armadillos have plates of bone and horn on their backs, heads and tails. They are mainly active at night, when they search for insects, worms and carrion (dead animals). If attacked, some kinds curl up into a ball, while others defend themselves with claws on their front feet. But they are not aggressive, and prefer to escape danger by burrowing underground.

Anteaters eat thousands of ants and other insects a day. Giant anteaters live on the ground; other kinds of anteater live in trees, using their tails to cling onto the branches.

Sloths live in tropical trees, and use their huge, curved claws to hang upside-down from the branches. They rarely come down to the ground, where they are nearly helpless. Sloths have long coarse hair on which tiny plants (algae) live.

• Armadillos, anteaters and sloths are all found in South and Central America; the nine-banded armadillo is also found in parts of North America.

• There are 20 different kinds of armadillo, four kinds of anteater and five kinds of sloth.

• Armadillo means 'little armoured one'.

find out more
Ants and termites
Mammals

▶ Sloths are divided into two groups: one group has three toes, and the other has two toes. This is a three-toed sloth.

◀ As the nine-banded armadillo walks, the only part of its front feet to touch the ground are its large claws.

▲ The giant anteater's tongue is covered with tiny backward-pointed spines. These become sticky with saliva, making it easy to mop up lots of insects.

Armies

The word 'army' is used to describe all of a country's soldiers. Every man or woman who serves in an army has a rank – from private soldier to general – and everyone is assigned to a particular unit.

A modern army has many different units (corps). Infantry units operate on foot, but are often equipped with sophisticated missile weapons, as well as machine-guns and grenades. Signals units gather information and pass on orders. Artillery units support the infantry, providing bombardment with shells. Tank units are the main means of attack in a major war. Engineers build roads, bridges and railways, clear minefields, organize river crossings and mine besieged positions.

There are airborne and parachute units, and in addition medical, catering and intelligence units and military police. Ordnance units provide all the necessary supplies. Transport units move troops using troop carriers and helicopters, amphibious landing craft (which can travel on land and sea) and fleets of lorries.

▶ The purpose of a medal is to mark an important deed. Soldiers can win medals for bravery. This is the Congressional Medal of Honour, the most important military medal awarded in the USA.

▼ A large country such as the USA has several 'armies' made up of a number of corps. These US soldiers are training in the desert in the Gulf.

find out more
Air forces
Armour
Knights
Navies and warships
Weapons

Armour

Warriors have worn armour to protect themselves in battle for thousands of years. Bullet-proof vests and riot gear are modern forms of armour.

The ancient Greeks wore linen or leather shirts with metal plates sewn on to protect the heart and shoulders. The hoplites (armed foot-soldiers) wore a breastplate of bronze shaped to fit. Roman foot-soldiers and cavalry wore armour of iron hoops protecting the back as well as the front of the body. Romans also used mail, at first made of small metal plates sewn on a leather jerkin, overlapping like tiles on a roof. Later it was made of metal links, known as chain-armour.

In the early Middle Ages, European soldiers wore chain-mail armour. From about 1330 knights wore heavy armour of jointed steel plates. After the development of guns, armour was gradually reduced to a cuirass (breast plate) and helmet. By the 20th century only the helmet remained. From the 1940s a new kind of body armour made of nylon, other plastics and glass fibres came into use.

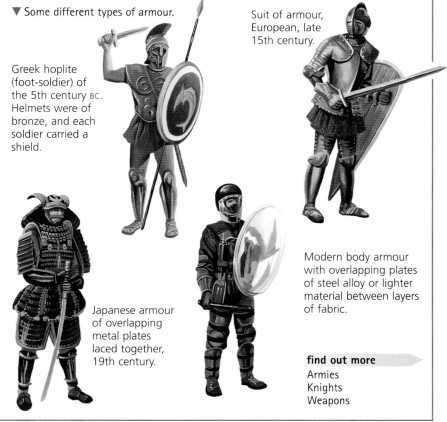

▼ Some different types of armour.

Greek hoplite (foot-soldier) of the 5th century BC. Helmets were of bronze, and each soldier carried a shield.

Suit of armour, European, late 15th century.

Japanese armour of overlapping metal plates laced together, 19th century.

Modern body armour with overlapping plates of steel alloy or lighter material between layers of fabric.

find out more
Armies
Knights
Weapons

Asia

The continent of Asia is the largest in the world, covering one-third of the Earth's land surface. It also has the most people. About two-thirds of the world's population live in Asia. Most of them live in the densely populated southern part of the continent, which is separated from the sparsely populated lands of central and northern Asia by the Himalaya Mountains.

Asia is so large that some parts are more than 2500 kilometres from the sea. This far inland, the climate is very hot in summer, but extremely cold in winter. At this time the land lies under a great cushion of cold heavy air. Cold dry winds blow out from the centre of the continent. In summer the land heats quickly and warms the air, which rises. Wet winds blow in from the sea, bringing heavy monsoon rains to the south. However, the barrier of the Himalayas stops the wet winds from reaching the continent's interior,

• Asia's border with Europe is formed by the Ural Mountains in Russia. The Middle East is usually counted as part of Asia.

◆ capital city
■ large city
●—— Trans-Siberian Railway with major stations
—— country boundary
ᚷᚷᚷ ice cap
▲ highest peaks (height in metres)

land height in metres
more than 5000
2000–5000
1000–2000
500–1000
200–500
less than 200
sea level
land below sea level

0 ——— 1000 km
0 ——— 500 miles

• All the independent countries of Asia have entries in the Countries fact file, pages 613–645.

keeping central Asia, western China and Mongolia dry.

Landscapes

Flat frozen plains of mosses and lichens cover much of the far north. Further south is a band of coniferous forest called the taiga, stretching right across the continent. The steppes of western Asia are grasslands, with rich, black soils that are excellent for agriculture. Much of central Asia, from the Red Sea to Mongolia, is desert. The largest is the bare, rocky Gobi Desert.

The Himalayas separate central Asia from the tropical lands of southern and South-east Asia. They curve in a great arc from Pakistan in the west to Tibet in the east. They form the largest mountain system in the world. The huge peaks reach heights of over 8000 metres, while in some places rivers have cut gorges nearly 5000 metres deep. The rivers that drain the Himalayas, such as the Ganges, the Indus and the Brahmaputra, carry silt and mud to the flood plains to the south, forming rich, fertile soils.

People

The largest number of Asians live in India, Bangladesh and the eastern half of China. Other great centres of population are Japan, Indonesia and Pakistan. The most crowded areas are on the coasts and along the flood plains of rivers in China, India and Bangladesh.

There are also vast areas where few people live. In most of Mongolia, the western half of China and Siberia in Russia the average number of people per square kilometre is less than one.

The majority of Asians live in the country and make their living from some kind of farming.

▼ Rice is the most important crop in large parts of southern and eastern Asia. The seeds are sown in special seed beds, then transferred to a flooded field, or paddy, after 25 to 50 days. This Vietnamese woman is moving some seedlings that are ready for transplanting.

▲ Despite the difficult terrain, there are many kinds of farming and industry in the Himalayas. Rice, sugar cane and other crops are grown; sheep, goats and yaks (above) are reared. About one-third of the Himalayas is forest, used mainly for paper and firewood. The mountains also contain valuable minerals, iron ore and coal.

Rice is the main crop in most of India, China and South-east Asia; wheat is the main crop in Russia and Kazakhstan; and the plains of central Asia are grazed by herds of cattle, goats or yaks. However, in southern and South-east Asia, more and more people are moving to cities. Seoul, Bangkok, Jakarta, Mumbai (Bombay), Kolkata (Calcutta) and several Chinese cities now have more than 5 million inhabitants. Many of these cities have tremendous overcrowding problems.

Asia has some of the world's poorest countries as well as some of its richest. South Asian countries have fewer doctors per person than anywhere else, and many people do not have a balanced diet. The average life expectancy in Laos, for example, is about 50 years, whereas people in Japan usually live to be nearer 80. The death rate for infants is higher in Cambodia than in any other country in the world.

▶ Kolkata, India's second largest and most important city, has problems such as overcrowding caused by poverty and rapid growth. The city is polluted, the streets are mostly narrow and in poor repair, and about a third of the people live in crowded slum housing. Many people have no house at all, and make their home on the pavement.

Aquarius
Jan 21–Feb 19

Pisces
Feb 20–March 20

Aries
March 21–April 20

Taurus
April 21–May 21

Gemini
May 22–June 21

find out more
Constellations

Astrology

Astrologers are people who make predictions from the stars. They believe that the positions of the Sun, Moon and planets among the stars can be used to make forecasts about people's lives and even about world events.

Astrologers may make a plan of where the Moon, Sun and planets are at an important time, such as the date on which someone was born, and then say what they think it means. This plan is called a *horoscope*.

Signs of the zodiac

Astrologers believe that the Sun's position is one of the most important factors. The Sun takes a year to go through a band of sky called the *zodiac*. Thousands of years ago, astrologers divided the zodiac into 12 equal zones called the 'signs' of the zodiac. Your Sun sign depends on where the Sun was in the zodiac on the day you were born.

The signs have the same names as the main constellations through which the Sun passes, but nowadays the signs and constellations do not match up. This is because the path of the Sun among the stars slowly changes and also because the constellations in use today are of different sizes.

Fact or fiction?

Most scientists think that astrology is based on superstition and not on facts. Even so, some people believe that it works. Many popular newspapers and magazines have a horoscope column with a short piece for each sign.

▼ The signs of the zodiac together with their astrological dates.

Cancer
June 22–July 23

Leo
July 24–Aug 23

Virgo
Aug 24–Sept 23

Libra
Sept 24–Oct 23

Scorpio
Oct 24–Nov 22

Sagittarius
Nov 23–Dec 21

Capricorn
Dec 22–Jan 20

Astronomy

Astronomy is the study of the planets, stars and galaxies that make up the Universe. Astronomers try to explain all the things that you can see in the night sky. They also investigate, for example, the age of stars and their distance from the Earth.

Early astronomers watched the movements of the Sun, Moon and stars in order to keep track of time and the seasons. Modern astronomers make observations with the help of telescopes, usually in large observatories. The telescopes gather the light from objects that are too faint to see with the naked eye. As well as sending out light, stars and galaxies give off other kinds of radiation, such as X-rays and radio waves. Astronomers detect these rays with the help of sophisticated telescopes, space satellites and other equipment.

Computers are an important tool in astronomy, helping astronomers to work out what their observations mean. You need to know a lot about science and mathematics to do astronomy as a job, but amateur astronomers can make useful observations as well as have fun with a pair of binoculars or a small telescope.

- Most distances in space are so enormous that it is meaningless to measure them in kilometres. So astronomers use a measurement called a light year (the distance light travels in a year), which is equal to 9.5 million million kilometres.

- The word 'astronomy' comes from the Greek words *astron* meaning 'star' and *nomia* meaning 'arrangement'.

find out more
Copernicus, Nicolas
Galaxies
Galilei, Galileo
Newton, Isaac
Solar System
Stars
Telescopes
Universe

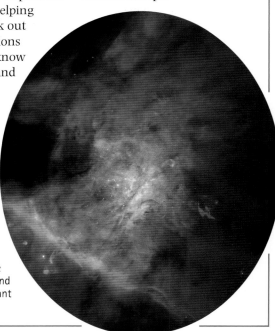

▶ The Orion Nebula, a huge cloud of glowing gas about 1300 light years away from the Earth. The photograph is made up of a series of pictures taken by the Hubble Space Telescope (HST) in orbit round the Earth. Astronomers use powerful telescopes like the HST to help them find out about the very distant parts of the Universe.

Athletics

Athletics are the centrepiece of the greatest of all sporting spectacles, the summer Olympic Games. For athletes, the opportunity to win gold at the Olympics or the world championships is the highlight of their career.

Most athletic events take place within a stadium and are divided into track and field. The track events (running and hurdling) take place on the 400-metre oval track, while the field events (throwing and jumping) are staged in the space within the running track.

Running and hurdling

For both men and women, the running events on the track are divided into the sprints (100, 200 and 400 metres), middle-distance (800 and 1500 metres), and long-distance (5000 and 10,000 metres).

In the *sprint races* the runners use starting blocks to help them get a quick, powerful start, and they must keep in their own lanes throughout. The 100 metres is run straight, while the 200 and 400 metres have a staggered start, so that all the runners cover the same distance.

The 800 metres is run in lanes only to the end of the first bend, and all the longer races (except the 4 × 400 relay) are started on a curved line and not run in lanes. For races of more than one lap, a bell at the finish line is rung to indicate the start of the last lap. These longer races are usually more tactical, with the runners jockeying for position and often waiting until near the end of the race to make a decisive move.

The *relays* are the 4 × 100 metres and 4 × 400 metres. In each of these the four runners run equal legs and must pass the baton to each other in a marked changeover zone. The longer (4 × 400) relay is run in lanes for a lap and a bend.

The *hurdle races* are run over 110 metres (100 metres for women) and 400 metres. In the longer race, the hurdles are staggered right up to the closing straight. Hurdlers are not penalized for knocking over the obstacles, although they may lose time and rhythm in doing so.

In major competitions the *steeplechase* is for men only. It is run over $7\frac{1}{2}$ laps of the track (3000 metres), with four fixed hurdles and a water jump on each lap. All the runners take the same hurdles, usually clearing them, but they put their leading foot on the water-jump barrier, pushing off to land in the shallow end of the water.

The marathon

The marathon is run on a road course over a distance of 42.195 kilometres (26 miles, 385 yards). In major championships it starts and finishes in the stadium. Along the route, refreshment stations provide drinks for the competitors in order to prevent dehydration.

Thousands of people run in 'mass marathons', such as

◀ Michael Johnson of the USA coming home in a time of 19.32 seconds to win the gold medal for the 200 metres at the 1996 Atlanta Olympics. His time shattered the existing world record.

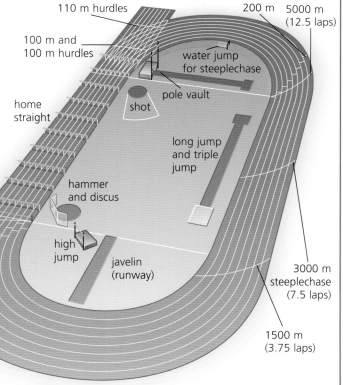

▼ The athletics track, showing the starting positions of the running events, all of which finish in the same place. The positions of some of the field events vary from stadium to stadium.

110 m hurdles

100 m and 100 m hurdles

home straight

finish line

10,000 m (25 laps)

800 m (2 laps)

400 m and 400 m hurdles (1 lap)

hammer and discus

high jump

shot

pole vault

water jump for steeplechase

long jump and triple jump

javelin (runway)

200 m

5000 m (12.5 laps)

3000 m steeplechase (7.5 laps)

1500 m (3.75 laps)

▶ Wang Junxia of China winning the gold medal in the women's 10,000 m at the 1993 world championships. The same year she set the women's world record for the distance, at 29 minutes 31.78 seconds.

find out more
Owens, Jesse

▼ The field events. The triple jump usually uses the same runway and pit as the long jump.

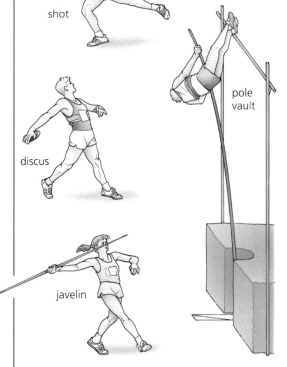

hammer

shot

discus

javelin

those held each year in London and New York. Competitors range from the world's leading runners, who start at the front, to charity runners and elderly joggers, whose aim is just to complete the course.

The marathon is based on the legend of the ancient Greek hero Phidippides. He is supposed to have run the 40 kilometres from the battlefield of Marathon to Athens with the news of the victory of the Greeks over the Persians and then dropped dead on arrival.

Field events

The field events – the four jumps and four throws – take place in special areas inside the track. Men and women compete separately in all the field events.

In the *high jump* and *pole vault*, the bar is raised after each round of jumps or vaults. Competitors are eliminated after failing at three consecutive attempts, until only one is left. This is the winner. In the event of a tie, the number of failed attempts in the course of the competition is taken into account in deciding the placings.

In all the other field events – long jump, triple jump, shot, discus, hammer and javelin – competitors have a set number of jumps or throws, and they are placed according to their best effort.

Multi-events

The multi-events – the decathlon and heptathlon – are tests of an athlete's all-round ability. They are held over two days. Competitors earn points for each event according to their performance time, distance or height, based on a set of standard tables.

pole vault

high jump

long jump

Olympic Games

The Olympic Games are a multi-sport festival, held every four years. There have been separate athletics world championships since 1983, but for most athletes a gold medal at the Olympics is still the ultimate dream. Many other sportspeople, including swimmers, rowers, gymnasts, show-jumpers and weightlifters, also regard competing in the Olympics as the highlight of their careers.

The Winter Olympics, which are held separately in the mid-year between the summer Games, include ice skating, skiing and sled events. Paralympics, for disabled competitors, are held shortly after the summer Games. They include a wide range of sports, including wheelchair racing, tennis, swimming and archery.

The original Olympic Games were held at Olympia, in ancient Greece, from around 776 BC to AD 393. Starting with one foot race, they grew to include throwing and jumping events, boxing, wrestling and chariot-racing. The modern Olympics were founded by Baron Pierre de Coubertin, a French aristocrat. The first modern Games were held in Athens in 1896. Today, the city that hosts the Games is chosen by the International Olympic Committee.

The *decathlon* is for men and consists of 10 events. The five events on the first day are the 100 metres, long jump, shot put, high jump and 400 metres. The second-day events are the 110 metre hurdles, discus, pole vault, javelin and 1500 metres.

The *heptathlon*, for women, is made up of seven events: 100 metre hurdles, high jump, shot put and 200 metres on the first day; long jump, javelin and 800 metres on the second day.

Atmosphere

The atmosphere makes it possible for us to live on the Earth. It consists of layers of air that surround our planet. They are wrapped around the Earth rather like orange peel is wrapped around the fruit inside. The air itself is a mixture of gases, mainly nitrogen and oxygen.

The weight of the atmosphere is quite considerable. Every cubic metre of the air around us contains more than 1 kilogram of air. The weight of all this air above pushing down on us is called atmospheric pressure. It is like having 1 kilogram pressing on every square centimetre of our bodies.

The different layers of the atmosphere merge into one another, so it is difficult to give their exact heights. They vary depending on the time of year, the latitude, and activities of the Sun, such as sunspots and solar flares. We live in the *troposphere*, the lowest layer. It contains 90 per cent of the air in the atmosphere. As you move up through the troposphere, the temperature drops, and on high mountains there is not enough oxygen to breathe easily. The air in the layer above the troposphere, the *stratosphere*, is much thinner, and the temperature rises. The stratosphere contains a gas called ozone, which is a type of oxygen. It absorbs much of the harmful ultraviolet radiation from the Sun.

Above the stratosphere, the temperature drops rapidly. Higher up, in the *ionosphere*, there are layers of particles called ions which carry electrical charges. These layers are very important in bouncing radio signals around our planet. The *exosphere* is where the Earth's atmosphere really becomes part of space. In this layer temperatures can be as high as 1000 °C.

Auroras

High up in the atmosphere, between 80 and 600 kilometres above the ground, huge patches of glowing coloured lights sometimes appear in the night sky. Scientists call this display the aurora. The pattern of lights can look like rays from a searchlight, twisting flames, shooting streamers or shimmering curtains. In the northern hemisphere, the popular name for this display is the 'northern lights'. We are more likely to see an aurora when there are big sunspots on the Sun. Atomic particles from the Sun collide with atoms in our atmosphere, giving off the different coloured lights.

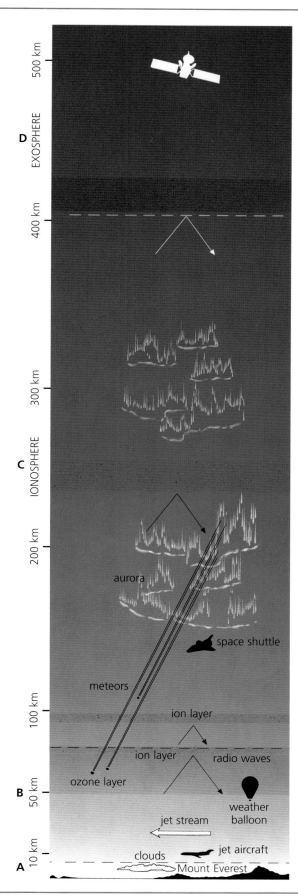

find out more
Air
Greenhouse effect
Oxygen
Radio

D The highest layer, the **exosphere**, contains hardly any gas, only a few molecules of hydrogen and helium.

C Radio signals from Earth bounce off the **ionosphere** before returning to Earth hundreds of kilometres from where they started.

A and **B** Weather balloons carrying instruments are sent up through the **troposphere** (**A**). Clouds form in this layer. In the lower part of the next layer, the **stratosphere** (**B**), long-distance aircraft take advantage of the lack of air resistance, helped by high-speed 'jet-stream' winds.

45

Atoms and molecules

Every material is made from tiny particles called atoms. Often, these are clumped together in groups known as molecules. Atoms are far too small to be seen with a normal microscope.

- Atoms are mostly empty space. If you imagine an atom the size of a concert hall, then its nucleus would be no larger than a grain of salt.

- The molecules in your body are made from four elements – oxygen, carbon, hydrogen and nitrogen.

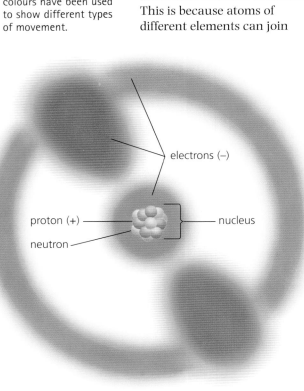

▼ A model of a carbon atom. The nucleus of protons and neutrons is surrounded by clouds of fast-moving electrons. The electrons are all the same, but different colours have been used to show different types of movement.

electrons (–)

proton (+)

neutron

nucleus

Everything is made from about 100 basic substances called *elements*. An atom is the smallest bit of an element you can have. It is so small that more than 4000 million of them would fit across the dot on this letter i! Around 200 years ago, the chemist John Dalton found that the atoms of different elements have different weights. We now know that each element has its own type of atom.

Although there are only about 100 elements, there are millions of different substances. This is because atoms of different elements can join together to make completely new substances called *compounds*. For example, water is a compound of two elements, hydrogen and oxygen.

Compounds and molecules

The smallest bit of water you can have is called a *molecule* of water. It is made up of two hydrogen atoms joined to one oxygen atom. The simplest molecules contain just two or three atoms, sometimes of the same element. But the largest molecules can contain millions of atoms. Many of the molecules in plants and animals are like this.

Inside atoms

Atoms are themselves made of smaller particles, called *electrons*, *protons* and *neutrons*. The protons and neutrons are clumped together in a central *nucleus*. The much lighter electrons speed around this. Each electron carries a negative (–) electric charge and each

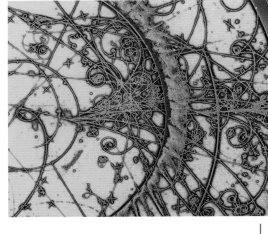

▶ Scientists have found many ways of detecting subatomic particles (electrons, protons, neutrons and quarks). One of the earliest was the bubble chamber. It is filled with a super-heated liquid, which reveals the tracks of electrically charged subatomic particles. In this artificially coloured picture of a bubble chamber you can see the particles' spiralling tracks.

proton an equal positive (+) charge. Neutrons do not have any charge. Each atom has equal numbers of electrons and protons, so overall it is neutral.

J. J. Thomson discovered the electron in 1897, when he found that tiny electrical particles could come from atoms. In 1911 Ernest Rutherford studied how atomic particles were deflected by gold foil and concluded that an atom must be mainly empty space, with a concentrated blob of matter at its centre. He called this the nucleus. Rutherford suggested that electrons might orbit the nucleus rather like planets round the Sun. Nowadays, scientists find it more useful to think of the electrons as clouds of electric charge. To describe their behaviour, they use the mathematics of *quantum mechanics*. They also think that protons and neutrons are themselves made of even smaller particles, called *quarks*.

▼ The molecules of three common substances.

molecule of oxygen gas

molecule of water

molecule of methane gas

 hydrogen atom

 oxygen atom

 carbon atom

Atoms and molecules

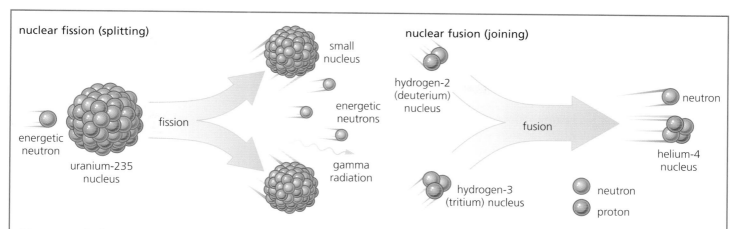

nuclear fission (splitting)

energetic neutron

uranium-235 nucleus

fission

small nucleus

energetic neutrons

gamma radiation

nuclear fusion (joining)

hydrogen-2 (deuterium) nucleus

fusion

hydrogen-3 (tritium) nucleus

neutron

proton

neutron

helium-4 nucleus

Atoms and elements

The atoms of different elements have different numbers of particles in them. Hydrogen, the lightest element, has just one proton in its nucleus. Uranium, one of the heaviest, has 92.

Atoms of any particular element all have the same number of protons (and electrons). But they may have different numbers of neutrons. These different versions of the same element are called *isotopes*. To name isotopes, scientists put a number after the name of the element. Uranium-235, for example, is an isotope of uranium with 235 neutrons and protons.

Fission and fusion

The nuclei of some atoms are unstable. In time, they break up by shooting out tiny particles and, sometimes, high-energy waves. Atoms like this are *radioactive*. The particles and waves carry energy once stored in the nucleus.

Uranium-235 is radioactive. Normally, its nuclei break up slowly. But the process can be speeded up using a *nuclear reactor*. In the reactor, atoms of uranium-235 are bombarded by neutrons. If a neutron strikes a uranium-235 nucleus, the nucleus splits, releasing energy and more neutrons. These may split other nuclei,

and so on, in a chain reaction. The splitting process is called *nuclear fission*. In a nuclear power station, a controlled chain reaction gives a steady supply of heat. In atomic weapons, an uncontrolled chain reaction gives an almost instant release of energy.

Nuclear energy can also be released in another way – by making hydrogen nuclei fuse (join together). This process is called *nuclear fusion*. It is the way the Sun gets its energy and is the power behind the hydrogen bomb. Fusion power stations have yet to be built, but in the 21st century they may become an important source of electricity.

▲ Nuclear fission and nuclear fusion.

find out more
Einstein, Albert
Elements
Gases, liquids and solids
Radiation

▼ A test explosion of a nuclear weapon in 1953. The lines on the left of the picture are smoke trails, used to show the shock waves caused by the explosion. An exploding atom bomb releases as much energy as 16,000 tonnes of high explosive.

Augustus

Born 63 BC in Italy
Died AD 14 aged 76

Augustus was the first emperor of Rome, ruling from 27 BC to AD 14. He was a strong ruler whose reforms left the Roman world more prosperous and stable.

• The Romans honoured Augustus by naming the month of August after him.

• Augustus encouraged builders to make Rome more beautiful. One writer said the emperor could boast that he had found the city built of brick and left it built of marble.

find out more
Caesar, Julius
Cleopatra
Romans

When he was born, Augustus was called Gaius Octavius. When Octavius was only 4 years old, his father died, and he was adopted by Julius Caesar (his mother's uncle) and became his heir. At that time, Caesar was a powerful general, and he would eventually become the dictator of the Roman empire.

Caesar was murdered in 44 BC, and Octavius was determined to avenge his death. He joined forces with Marcus Antonius (Mark Antony) to defeat the murderers Brutus and Cassius. After they had won, Octavius ruled with Antony and another ally, Lepidus, for a while, but soon civil war broke out in the Roman empire. Octavius defeated Antony (together with Cleopatra), and in 29 BC he declared peace throughout the Roman world.

Octavius was now the most powerful man in Rome and took the name Augustus (meaning 'a person to be respected'). He also established a new system of government: that of rule by one man, the emperor. However, he was careful enough to appoint the right people in powerful positions.

▶ This gold coin shows the face of Augustus. It was made in the 1st century AD when he was about 70 years old.

During his long reign Augustus enlarged the Roman empire and created peace for the Roman people for over 30 years. On the deaths of his two grandsons, he adopted Tiberius (his wife's son from her first marriage) as his heir and the next emperor of Rome.

Austen, Jane

Born 1775 in
Hampshire, England
Died 1817 aged 41

Jane Austen is one of the world's most popular novelists. Her dry humour, descriptions of the social manners of the day, and memorable characters have made her novels classics.

◀ This portrait of Jane Austen was drawn by her sister Cassandra.

• All of Jane Austen's novels have been adapted for television or for film. The three most recent popular film successes are *Sense and Sensibility* (released in 1995), and *Emma* and *Persuasion* (both released in 1996). *Pride and Prejudice* was made into a very successful television series in 1995.

find out more
Novels and novelists

Jane Austen was the seventh child of a country clergyman. She was taught by her father and was lucky to receive a better education than many women at that time. Her parents encouraged their children's imaginative play, and converted the rectory barn into a small theatre, where the family could put on plays during the summer holidays. By the age of 12 Austen was writing her own stories, but it was to be nearly another 25 years before her first novel was published.

Austen's novels are as popular today as they have ever been. They are famous for their witty insight into human failings and for their gentle humour. They all have female lead characters and all end, eventually, in a happy marriage. *Sense and Sensibility* (1811) was published first, followed by *Pride and Prejudice* (1813), Mansfield Park (1814), and *Emma* (1816). Both *Northanger Abbey* and *Persuasion* were published in 1818, the year after Austen's death. All of these novels were published anonymously.

Austen herself never married. Instead, she stayed with her family, living in several places, including Bath – the setting for many episodes in her books. The family moved to Winchester in May 1817 to seek medical attention for her ill-health, but Austen died two months later. She is buried in Winchester Cathedral.

Australia

Australia is a large country of great natural beauty. Australian society is varied, combining the culture of its Aboriginal population with the traditions of more recent settlers from all parts of the world.

The Australian landmass has been stable for over 300 million years. There have been no major periods of earthquakes, volcanic activity or mountain-building. This means that wind and water have worn down the land and made it flat.

Landscape

Most of Australia, between the Great Dividing Range in the east and the western coast, is known as the 'outback'. The western half of the country is mostly desert. Few people live there, and plants and animals must adapt to the high temperatures and lack of rain. The central lowlands are also dry and flat, but there is water trapped under the

surface, which can be reached by digging wells.

The Great Dividing Range separate a narrow coastal strip from the dry interior. Because the rainfall here is higher and the soils are more fertile, this is where most Australians live.

Unique plants and animals

Australia was separated from other continental landmasses 65 million years ago. Because of

▲ The Olgas are a group of highly unusual red, dome-shaped rocks near Uluru in central Australia. Australia's natural wonders attract tourists from all over the world.

this long isolation, the country has many plants and animals found nowhere else. Echidnas and duck-billed platypuses are unique mammals that lay eggs. Kangaroos, koalas and wombats belong to a group of mammals called marsupials, which keep

- Australia is the main landmass of the continent of Oceania, which includes New Zealand, Papua New Guinea and the many islands of the central and southern Pacific.

- In the colonial era Australia had its own outlaws similar to the 'Wild West' in the USA. The most famous of these was Ned Kelly, whose murders and robberies made him famous. He became a folk hero to many poor rural dwellers. In a shoot-out with police in 1880 he wore home-made iron armour and a helmet, but was captured and hanged.

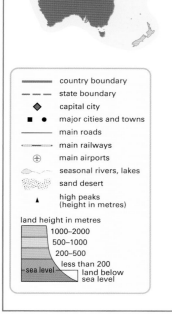

———	country boundary
– – –	state boundary
◆	capital city
■ ●	major cities and towns
———	main roads
⊢⊢⊢	main railways
⊕	main airports
～	seasonal rivers, lakes
⣿	sand desert
▲	high peaks (height in metres)

land height in metres

1000–2000
500–1000
200–500
less than 200
sea level — land below sea level

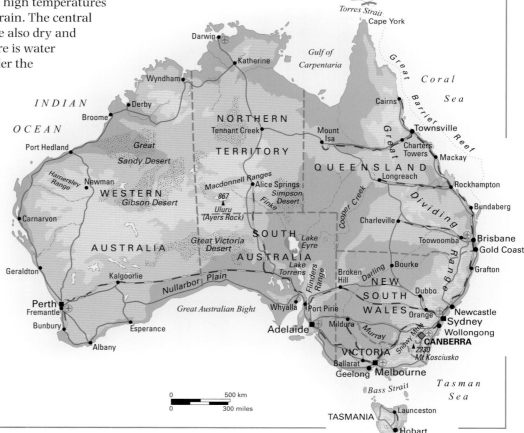

Torres Strait
Cape York
Darwin
Gulf of Carpentaria
Coral Sea
Katherine
Wyndham
INDIAN
Derby
OCEAN
Broome
NORTHERN
Cairns
Tennant Creek
Mount Isa
TERRITORY
Great Barrier Reef
Townsville
Port Hedland
Charters Towers
Mackay
Great Sandy Desert
QUEENSLAND
Hamersley Range
Newman
Macdonnell Ranges
Alice Springs
Simpson Desert
Longreach
Rockhampton
WESTERN
867
Finke
Dividing
Bundaberg
Gibson Desert
Uluru (Ayers Rock)
Charleville
Carnarvon
Cooper Creek
SOUTH
Lake Eyre
Toowoomba
Brisbane
AUSTRALIA
Great Victoria Desert
AUSTRALIA
Range
Gold Coast
Geraldton
Lake Torrens
Broken Hill
Darling
Grafton
Kalgoorlie
Flinders Range
NEW
Dubbo
Perth
Nullarbor Plain
SOUTH
Fremantle
Great Australian Bight
Whyalla
Port Pirie
Mildura
WALES
Orange
Newcastle
Bunbury
Esperance
Adelaide
Murray
Sydney
Wollongong
CANBERRA
Albany
VICTORIA
Snowy River
2230
Mt Kosciusko
Ballarat
Geelong
Melbourne
Tasman Sea
Bass Strait
0   500 km
0   300 miles
TASMANIA
Launceston
Hobart

their young in pouches. Eucalypts, or gum trees, are the most famous Australian trees.

People and cities

Eighty per cent of Australians live in cities and towns along the coasts. The largest city is Sydney, where one in five of the population lives. Outside Australia's south-eastern corner there are a few isolated cities, such as Perth on the south-west coast and Darwin in the tropical north. In the interior there is just one major town – Alice Springs. Other settlements are so remote that they rely on 'flying doctors' for medical care.

Rich resources

European settlers brought many new crops and farm animals to Australia. Where there is enough rainfall, farmers grow wheat, fruit and sugar cane. In drier areas, there are huge sheep and cattle ranches.

Australia is also very rich in minerals and metals. Huge deposits of coal in the east help make the country the world's largest exporter of coal. Ninety per cent of the world's opals come from a single mine, Coober Pedy in South Australia.

Australia's history

The first inhabitants of Australia were the Aborigines. They probably arrived at least 45,000 years ago from Asia, travelling from island to island in dugout canoes. They spread over the country in large family groups known as tribes.

Spanish and Portuguese seafarers first sailed close to Australia's shores in the 17th century. The first European to sail right around Australia was Abel Tasman, a Dutchman. In 1642 he discovered the island that is now named after him, Tasmania. These early voyagers thought that the country was too barren to settle.

In 1770 the British explorer Captain James Cook landed on the more fertile east coast. He named the land New South Wales and claimed it for Britain. The first settlers were convicts and soldiers who were sent by Britain in 1788.

Settlement

During the 19th century more settlers arrived to start farms or make their fortune in the Australian gold fields. They fought with the Aborigines and slowly occupied more and more land. At first they found it hard to make a living. They did not

share the Aborigines' knowledge of the land.

From 1855 Australia gradually obtained greater independence from British rule until, in 1901, it became a self-governing country. Australia has continued to have close links with Britain, but in the last 50 years people from all over the world have come to live there. Australia is now a nation of many cultures and languages. It has also developed more trading links with countries in Asia than with Europe.

▲ Off the coast of Queensland is one of the world's greatest natural wonders, a coral reef called the Great Barrier Reef. It is over 2000 kilometres long and can be seen from space. Thousands of creatures live together on the reef, including parrot fishes, sea cucumbers and tiger sharks.

◄ Sydney harbour, with Sydney Harbour Bridge and the Opera House in the centre. The British troops and convicts who came to Australia in 1788 landed at Botany Bay. But they soon moved north to Sydney's excellent harbour.

find out more

Aborigines
British empire
Continents
Cook, James
Marsupials
Pacific Islands
See also Countries fact file, page 614

Aztecs

find out more
Maya
Mexico
North America
Spain

The Aztecs were a people who created an ancient civilization in the Valley of Mexico in the 14th century.

When the Aztecs came to the Valley of Mexico in about 1345, they built a huge city on an island in Lake Texcoco. They called it Tenochtitlán (now Mexico City) and it became the capital of the Aztec empire. There were canals instead of streets, and raised causeways crossed the lake. Feathers, tools and cacao beans were traded in place of money.

Daily life

Most Aztecs lived in small houses made of mud bricks. Men and boys worked as farmers in the fields. Women and girls looked after the home, ground corn (maize) to make pancakes, and spun and wove cotton cloth.

The emperor had all the power. Below him were high-ranking soldiers, priests and rich merchants. The ordinary people did not have much freedom or say in government. Below them were the slaves.

Conquest and destruction

In 1519 the Spanish conqueror Hernán Cortés arrived at Tenochtitlán. He captured the Aztec emperor, Montezuma II. The Aztecs rebelled, but after fierce fighting they were defeated by the heavily armoured Spaniards. The Spanish then ruled Mexico. They destroyed the temples and the great city of Tenochtitlán.

▲ The Aztecs worshipped many gods. This turquoise mask with eyes and teeth of white shell is thought to represent Quetzalcóatl, the god of learning and priesthood.

capital city
area of Aztec influence
territory paying tribute to Aztecs

0   200 km
0   150 miles

TARASCAN STATE
Tenochtitlán
TLAXCALA
Gulf of Mexico
TEOTITLÁN
XICALANCO
YOPITZINCO
MIXTEC STATES
XOCONOCHCO
PACIFIC OCEAN
MAYAN STATES

▲ At its height, the Aztec empire dominated much of the area that is now Mexico.

Bach, Johann Sebastian

Born 1685 in Eisenach, Germany
Died 1750 aged 65

Johann Sebastian Bach is one of the world's greatest composers. He wrote a wide range of music, all of which is more popular today than it was in his lifetime.

Bach first studied music with his father, and then with his elder brother. Yet it seems he mainly taught himself to compose by copying out the music of the composers he most admired.

When he was 15, Bach found work in the choir in Lüneburg, and two years later he became an organist in Arnstadt. He then worked as a court musician, first for the duke of Weimar and then for Prince Leopold of Cöthen. His last and most important post was as organist and choirmaster at St Thomas's Church in Leipzig, where he settled in 1723.

While working as a court musician, Bach wrote mainly chamber and orchestral works, including the six Brandenburg Concertos. Then, when he worked for the Church, he wrote organ music, cantatas, and great choral works, such as the *St Matthew Passion*. He wrote music as part of the daily routine of his job. The fact that he was a great genius probably never occurred to his employers. His organ music is considered to be the greatest ever written.

Although he was famous in his day (particularly as an organist), Bach's music was virtually forgotten for about 50 years after his death. It was not until the 19th century that people began to realize how great it was and Bach took his place as one of the greatest composers in the history of music.

• Johann Sebastian Bach came from a very musical background. We know of more than 50 members of the Bach family who were musicians of one sort or another. Two of his 20 children, Carl Philipp Emanuel and Johann Christian, became, for a time, even more famous than their father.

find out more
Classical music

▼ This illustration shows Bach playing the harpischord at home with his family.

Bacteria

Bacteria are very simple living things, consisting of a single cell. A row of a hundred would just reach across this full stop. Bacteria are found everywhere: in the ocean depths, in soil, on our skins, even floating freely in the air. They are some of the oldest living things, and fossils have been found of bacteria that lived 3000 million years ago.

Some bacteria can make their own food by using the Sun's energy (photosynthesis), but most live on decaying plants and animals, or as parasites in other living things.

By breaking down dead plants and animals, bacteria return vital nutrients to the soil which are used by plants for growth. But they also cause some of the deadliest diseases of humans, such as tuberculosis, pneumonia, cholera and typhoid.

Unlike single-celled animals and plants, bacteria have no nucleus or distinct parts. They do not have sexes either, but reproduce by dividing in two. They do this so quickly that, given enough food, one bacterium could produce 4000 million million million others in just one day.

▶ FLASHBACK ◀

People once believed that old food went bad because it changed into moulds and microbes (bacteria). In the 19th century the French scientist Louis Pasteur showed that it was microbes in the air that caused the decay rather than a change in the food. He placed freshly cooked food in clean glass containers, sealed one and left the other open to the air. Only food in the open container went bad.

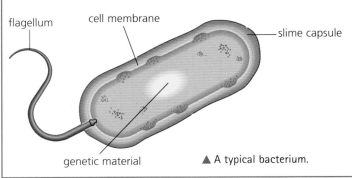

flagellum
cell membrane
slime capsule
genetic material

▲ A typical bacterium.

find out more
Cells
Diseases
Living things
Pests and parasites

Balkans

The south-eastern corner of Europe, known as the Balkans, is one of the great crossroads of the world. In the past many different races, religions and cultures met here, in peace and war.

The complex history of the area explains why Greece, Romania, Bulgaria, Serbia, Croatia, Bosnia and the other modern Balkan states are so different, and why the region has been so troubled.

The Ottoman empire

For hundreds of years the Balkans were part of the Muslim Ottoman empire, ruled from Constantinople (modern Istanbul). From the 1820s, the Balkan peoples began to rebel and set up their own countries.

Greece became independent in 1831, Romania in 1861, Serbia and Bulgaria in 1878, and Albania in 1912.

The Ottoman empire was abolished after World War I. A new kingdom of Yugoslavia was formed, home to Serbs, Bosnians, Croats and other peoples, both Christian and Muslim.

Civil war

After World War II the communist leader President Tito set up a new republic of Yugoslavia. His strict rule held the country together and for a time it prospered. However, after Tito's death in 1980 the old racial and religious squabbles began again.

As the Serbs seemed to be trying to take over the whole

SLOVENIA HUNGARY
Ljubljana Zagreb
CROATIA
BOSNIA-HERZEGOVINA Belgrade ROMANIA
Sarajevo SERBIA & MONTENEGRO
Adriatic Sea BULGARIA Black Sea
Sofia
Tiranë Skopje
MACEDONIA (FYROM) Istanbul
ALBANIA
Aegean Sea TURKEY
GREECE
Athens

◆ capital city

0 — 400 km
0 — 200 miles

• Josip Broz (1892–1980), popularly known as Marshal Tito, made his name during World War II as a guerrilla leader fighting the Nazis. As president of Yugoslavia after the war, he steered a clever middle path between Soviet communism and Western democracy.

country, a bloody civil war broke out in 1991. Slovenia, Croatia, Bosnia and Herzegovina, and Macedonia became independent states. A cease-fire was arranged in 1995 and United Nations troops went in to try to keep the peace.

find out more
Europe
Ottoman empire
United Nations
See also individual Balkan countries in the Countries fact file, pages 613–645

Ballet

Ballet is a form of dance. Ballet dancers are highly skilled, performing movements alone or in patterns with other dancers. The dancing, however difficult or energetic, appears graceful and natural.

◄ Tchaikovsky's ballet *The Nutcracker* (1892) tells a magical Christmas story, in which toys come to life. In this winter scene, from a performance by the English National Ballet in 1989, the ballerinas in the background appear as snowflakes.

Some ballets tell stories, while others are 'abstract', which means there is not a specific story but a mood or feeling that is expressed.

Training and practice

Ballet training begins early. Children of 8 can audition at one of the special ballet training schools. Ballet dancing requires grace, control and flexibility, so the teachers look for children with these qualities.

Ballet dancers have to train hard to develop their strength and skill. The studio in which they train has a rail called the barre that the dancers can hold to keep their balance while they practise. There are mirrors round the walls in which they can see their movements.

Even at the peak of their careers, dancers have to continue to practise hard every day. One of the greatest challenges for ballet dancers, especially ballerinas (female dancers), is to dance gracefully on their toes, or 'on pointe'.

Ballerinas use special shoes with reinforced toes for pointe work.

Ballet dancers also have to know the music they are dancing to extremely well, and remember each step of the ballet, both their own and everyone else's. The person who makes up the sequences of movements for a ballet is called the *choreographer* (meaning 'dance-writer'). The choreographer or the ballet director teaches these sequences to the dancers.

For the last few rehearsals, the dancers practise on stage. The scenery is set up and the dancers wear costumes. Some dancers have to wear wigs and heavy make-up. Finally, the music is played by an orchestra rather than on a piano.

► FLASHBACK ◄

The kind of ballet we know today began about 400 years ago. Watching ballet was a favourite pastime of rich people, and some of them also took part in ballets. The 17th-century French king Louis XIV was a skilful dancer. He took the star part in many court ballets, including one written to celebrate his own wedding.

In the 18th century most ballets were not stage shows on their own but were part of the entertainment in operas. A hundred years later, the first full-length ballets were written to be performed in their own right. Ballets of this kind were especially popular in Russia, where many of the most famous ballets, such as *Swan Lake* and *Sleeping Beauty*, were first produced.

find out more
Dance
Operas and musicals
Stravinsky, Igor

▼ The ballet *Romeo and Juliet* (1936) by the Russian composer Sergei Prokofiev depicts Shakespeare's tragic love story. Here, the famous dance partners Rudolf Nureyev and Margot Fonteyn dance a *pas de deux*, a dance for two people.

▲ The first positions a trainee ballet dancer will learn.

first second third fourth fifth

Famous dancers	Famous ballets and their composers
Gaetano Vestris 1729–1808	*Giselle* Adam (1841)
Anna Pavlova 1881–1931	*Coppélia* Delibes (1870)
Tamara Karsavina 1885–1978	*Swan Lake* Tchaikovsky (1876)
Vaslav Nijinsky 1890–1950	*Sleeping Beauty* Tchaikovsky (1890)
Margot Fonteyn 1919–1991	*Les Sylphides* Chopin (1909)
Rudolf Nureyev 1938–1993	*The Three-Cornered Hat* Falla (1919)
Mikhail Baryshnikov 1948–	

Balloons and airships

In 1783 the first people to fly freely through the air travelled 9 kilometres in a hot-air balloon designed by the Montgolfier brothers in France. A little over 200 years later, people are still using hot-air balloons in record-breaking attempts – this time to fly non-stop around the world.

Nowadays balloon flights are usually for pleasure or sport. Balloons are also used to collect information about the weather, and to carry out scientific experiments and collect data from high up in the atmosphere.

How do balloons fly?

Balloons float in air in the same way as ships float in water. To make a balloon light enough to float, it has to be filled with a gas that is lighter than the surrounding air. So balloons are

▼ Modern hot-air balloons carry gas burners to heat the air inside the balloon. When the burner is turned on, the balloon rises.

filled with hydrogen, helium or hot air.

Until the 1930s, passenger-carrying balloons and airships were filled with hydrogen, the lightest gas. Unfortunately, hydrogen catches fire easily, and was no longer used after a series of bad accidents. In recent years balloons have begun to be used for transport again, but they are filled with helium, an invisible gas with no taste or smell. Helium does not burn, so it is safer than hydrogen.

Parts of a hot–air balloon

The balloon is made of nylon and can be as large as a house when it is inflated. A detachable panel at the top allows the hot air to escape quickly after landing.

A basket hangs from wires or ropes under the balloon. The basket carries the crew and passengers, as well as the gas cylinders and instruments which the crew need to calculate their height, direction and fuel level. The gas burner is fixed to the basket's frame and is used in short bursts to heat the air to make the balloon rise and then keep it at the chosen height. When the air inside cools, the balloon loses height.

Airships

Airships, also called dirigibles (which means 'steerable'), are sausage-shaped balloons powered by engines. Modern airships are quiet, safe and comfortable. They are filled with helium gas. They have an enclosed gondola below, which can carry as many as 20 passengers. The motors which turn the propellers to move the airship forwards are attached to the gondola. The pilot uses a large rudder to steer.

Airships are not much used for commercial passenger flights. Their ability to remain stationary in the air means they are ideal for photographic and television work.

▶ FLASHBACK ◀

In 1793 the first hydrogen-filled balloon flew, just two weeks after the Montgolfier brothers' hot-air balloon had made the first untethered flight with people on board. The first flight of an airship, *La France*, was in 1884. On 6 May 1937 the *Hindenburg* airship burst into flames while landing near New York, killing 35 of the 97 people on board. After this disaster, hydrogen-filled airships were no longer used for commercial transportation.

▲ The hydrogen–filled airship *Graf Zeppelin*. In 1929 it took 10 days to travel all the way around the world.

● Toy balloons are filled with helium, which is lighter than air. This explains why they shoot upwards when you let them go.

find out more
Air
Aircraft
Atmosphere
Flight

Bangladesh

Bangladesh is a flat country in southern Asia formed by the deltas of the Ganges, Brahmaputra and Meghna rivers. About 130 million people live there, making it one of the most crowded countries in the world.

The climate of Bangladesh is hot and wet. Much of the country receives over 2000 millimetres of rain each year, most of it during the monsoon season, between June and September. Monsoon rains can cause devastating floods, as in 1988, when floods killed thousands of people and left over 30 million homeless. From November to May, tropical cyclones (hurricanes) sweeping in from the Bay of Bengal can also cause great destruction.

People

Most Bangladeshis are farmers and live in villages. The low-lying land and abundant water are ideal for rice, which is the country's main crop. Many farmers also grow jute, a plant used to make rope, sacks and carpet backing. The land is criss-crossed by waterways, so boats are the main form of transport.

Bangladeshis are mostly Muslims. Usually the men work the fields, while the women work in and near the home. The typical Bangladeshi household includes several generations of extended family.

▶ FLASHBACK ◀

The modern nation of Bangladesh was founded in 1971. It had been part of British India until 1947. Then the subcontinent was split into India and Pakistan. Pakistan itself was made up of two parts, separated by Indian territory. To the west was West Pakistan (today's Pakistan) and to the east was East Pakistan. In 1971 East Pakistan became Bangladesh after a terrible war in which more than a million people were killed.

◀ Rope-making in Bangladesh. Jute used to be the main fibre used for ropes, but nylon and other synthetic fibres are now often used.

find out more
Asia
India
Pakistan
See also Countries fact file, page 615

Baseball

Baseball is the national summer sport of the USA. It has its origins in the old English game of rounders, which was brought over by colonists in the 1700s.

◀ Babe Ruth, the most famous name in baseball, who became a legend in the 1920s with his big hitting for the New York Yankees. His home run percentage – 714 from 8399 times at bat – has never been beaten.

In baseball, each team of nine players takes it in turn to bat. The pitcher throws the ball and each batter in turn tries to hit it and run. A run is scored when a player moves safely round the three bases and back to home plate. A batter may achieve this at one turn (a *home run*) but is more often advanced from base to base by subsequent batters. The winner is the side with most runs after nine innings at bat.

An inning is over when three players are out. Batters are out when they miss three 'strikes' (pitches that pass over home plate at a hittable height); when a fielder catches the ball; or when they fail to reach first base before a fielder 'tags' (touches) them with the ball.

The highlight of the baseball season is the World Series, which has taken place every year since 1903. It is a best-of-seven decider between the champions of the major leagues in the USA.

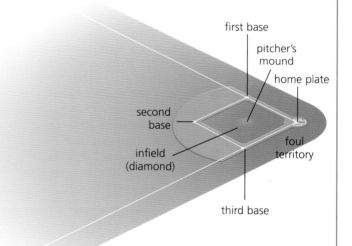

first base
pitcher's mound
home plate
second base
infield (diamond)
foul territory
third base

▲ The baseball field.

• Other countries where baseball is a major sport include Australia, the Netherlands, South Africa, Japan and many in Latin America.

Basketball

Basketball is the most widely played of all indoor sports. The top stars of the US professional league, the National Basketball Association (NBA), are among the world's most highly paid sportsmen.

In basketball, each team may have only five players on court at any one time. All players

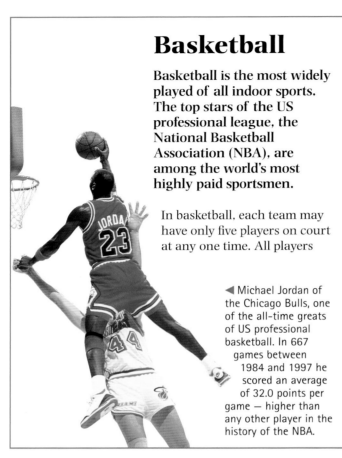

◀ Michael Jordan of the Chicago Bulls, one of the all-time greats of US professional basketball. In 667 games between 1984 and 1997 he scored an average of 32.0 points per game — higher than any other player in the history of the NBA.

play both defence and attack, and players may move freely about the court, but the usual formation is two guards, two forwards and a centre.

The ball may be thrown, passed, tapped, bounced or rolled, but there are strict rules to control how players move with the ball. A player normally has to release the ball within 5 seconds and the team must attempt a shot for goal within 30 seconds of gaining control of the ball. Attackers are not allowed to stay in their opponents' restricted area for more than 3 seconds.

Players may shoot for goal from anywhere on court. They score 3 points for a basket made from outside the three-point line, and 2 points for one made

from inside it. Baskets scored from free throws – awarded when fouls are committed or rules are broken – are worth 1 point each. The team with most points at the end of the game is the winner.

Basketball was invented in the USA in 1891 by a Canadian-born YMCA instructor, Dr James Naismith. He made up the game to keep his students occupied in the severe New England winters.

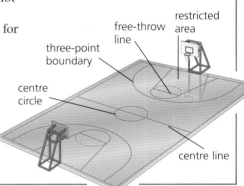

restricted area

free-throw line

three-point boundary

centre circle

centre line

Bats

- There are over 950 kinds of bat, about a quarter of the total number of mammal species.

- There are three kinds of South American vampire bat, which feed only on the fresh blood of mammals and large birds. They do not suck blood, but lap it up. More dangerous to the victim than blood loss is the fact that vampire bats can carry diseases, including rabies.

find out more
Ears
Flight
Hibernation
Mammals
Migration

Bats are the only mammals that have wings and are capable of true flight. During the daytime they are rarely active, resting in dark, hidden places such as caves, lofts and holes in trees. When they emerge, bats are able to find their way in total darkness and silence.

Bats are nocturnal (active at night), and find their way in the dark using *echolocation*. As it flies, a bat makes short, very high-pitched squeaks. When something is nearby, echoes from the squeaks bounce back to the bat's ears, giving it details about the object, such as its distance, size and shape.

Flight requires a lot of energy, so bats eat a large

number of night-flying insects. Some tropical bats feed on larger prey, including other kinds of bat and small creatures such as mice and frogs. Others feed on nectar and fruit.

To conserve energy when they are not active, bats let their body temperature drop. In seasons when food is scarce, bats living in cool regions hibernate (go into a deep sleep), but a few kinds migrate to warmer regions where food is plentiful.

Bats are hunted by some animals, but humans are their main enemy. Some kinds are becoming rare due to pollution and destruction of their homes.

◀ The front part of a bat's wing is supported by the bones of its arm. The wing is also braced by very long finger bones. This fishing bat catches fish with its very large hind feet, which have specially long, strong claws.

Batteries

• The first battery was invented by an Italian physicist, Alessandro Volta. During an experiment he placed card soaked in a salt solution between two piles of coins made of different metals. This produced an electric current, and Volta had made the world's first-ever battery.

Batteries produce electricity when the chemicals inside them react with each other. Small batteries provide the power for torches, radios, watches and pocket calculators. Large batteries can start car engines and can even provide all the power to drive vehicles such as milk-floats.

All materials have positive (+) and negative (−) charges in their atoms. In an electric cell, reactions between chemicals cause the negative charges to concentrate around one terminal, and the positive charges around the other. A battery is really two or more electric cells joined together. However, single cells like the ones used in torches are often called batteries. A car battery consists of six separate cells joined together in the same case.

Different kinds of battery have different chemicals in them. *Zinc chloride* batteries are cheapest, and are often used in torches. *Alkaline* batteries cost more, but last longer because they store more energy. *Lithium* batteries store the most energy, but are much more expensive. In hearing aids, watches and

find out more
Atoms and molecules
Electricity

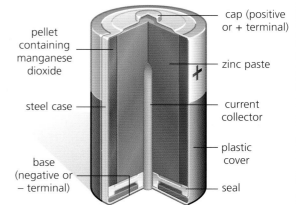

pellet containing manganese dioxide

steel case

base (negative or − terminal)

cap (positive or + terminal)

zinc paste

current collector

plastic cover

seal

▲ A cutaway view of a long-life alkaline battery.

calculators, the batteries need to be thin and small. They are often called *button cells*. Silver oxide, mercury and zinc–air batteries are all button cells.

When batteries are 'flat' and can produce no more electricity, most have to be replaced. Some batteries, such as *nickel–cadmium* ones, are rechargeable. The large *lead–acid* batteries used in car engines are also rechargeable. As the chemicals in rechargeable batteries run out, they can be restored by recharging.

Beans

Beans are the pods and seeds of a group of plants belonging to the pea family. Beans come in all shapes, sizes and colours, from large creamy white butter beans, to tiny green mung beans.

Bean-producing plants grow as bushes or as climbing plants in areas with a temperate (mild) climate such as Europe and parts of North America and China.

Shelled beans, peas and pulses are the only kinds of vegetables that contain much protein. This makes them popular with vegetarians. They are also rich in carbohydrates. Fresh bean pods and seeds contain vitamins A and B and fibre.

Pulses

Pulses are the edible seeds of peas, beans and lentils. The shelled seeds can be easily dried and stored. Before dried beans can be cooked, they must be soaked in water. Dried beans do not regain all their water when they are soaked and cooked, and so contain almost as much energy weight for weight as fresh beans.

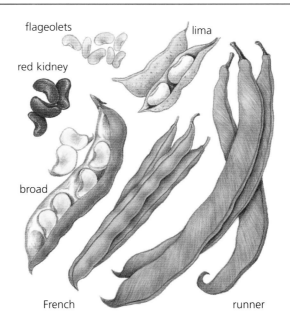

flageolets

lima

red kidney

broad

French

runner

▲ The pods of some beans, such as French and runner beans, are cooked and eaten with the seeds inside. Other beans, including broad and lima beans, are shelled before cooking. Baked beans are made from haricot beans. Some beans can be eaten raw, but others, like kidney beans, are poisonous unless they are boiled in water for at least 15 minutes.

• Coffee is a strong-scented drink made by pouring boiling water over the roasted and ground beans (seeds) of the coffee plant. Like tea, coffee contains caffeine, a substance which stimulates the heart and nervous system. Too much caffeine — more than six cups of tea or coffee a day — can be bad for you.

find out more
Diets
Food
Plants
Vegetables

Bears

find out more
Conservation
Hibernation
Mammals

▶ A female grizzly (or brown) bear with her three cubs. There used to be many brown bears in Europe and North America, but much of the land they lived on is now used for farming. Today they are mostly found in Alaska, Canada and the remoter parts of Asia.

Bears are huge creatures: the biggest bear weighs more than three times as much as a large lion. They are found in a wide range of habitats, from the frozen Arctic to tropical forests. The polar bear feeds mainly on fish and seals, but other bears generally have a varied diet, including fruit, nuts, honey and small animals.

Like human beings, bears can stand upright, but normally they walk on all fours. They have poor eyesight and hearing, but their sense of smell is excellent. They generally live alone. In the autumn, when food is abundant, bears eat a lot before sleeping in a den for much of the winter. However, they do not go into a deep hibernation (winter sleep) and are usually able to wake up quickly.

A female bear produces her cubs in the wintertime, and they stay with her in her den until springtime. The cubs are very small, rarely larger than guinea pigs. They remain with their mother until they are more than a year old. When they leave her, the cubs usually stay together – often for as long as three years.

The giant panda is a relative of the true bears (although the other kind of panda – the red panda – is more closely related to racoons). It is one of the most striking-looking animals in the world, and also one of the rarest: there are perhaps only 500 left in the wild. Pandas live in the high mountains of only three isolated parts of China. Bamboo is their main diet, although they do eat other plants, and occasionally hunt small birds and mammals.

Beatles

George Harrison:
Born 1943
Died 2001 aged 58
John Lennon:
Born 1940
Died 1980 aged 40
Paul McCartney:
Born 1942
Ringo Starr:
Born 1940
All born in Liverpool, England

• In 1996 the three remaining Beatles re-formed to record the single 'Free As A Bird'. They used a recording John Lennon had once made, and added music, vocals and harmonies.

find out more
Pop and rock music

The Beatles are the most famous pop group of all time. During the eight years they were together, they sold millions of records around the world.

The Beatles had their first hit record in 1962 with 'Love Me Do', and this was followed by a run of 20 Top 10 hits. They released 13 albums in the UK (plus several compilations), and also starred in two successful films, *A Hard Day's Night* (1964) and *Help!* (1965).

Their exciting music, written mostly by Lennon and McCartney, together with their rebellious attitudes and humour won them millions of fans. 'Beatlemania' was the term used to describe their amazing popularity. By late 1966, fans at their concerts were so noisy that the Beatles could not hear themselves playing, so they gave up doing live performances.

The following year they released their most famous album, *Sgt. Pepper's Lonely Hearts Club Band*. They introduced many unusual recording techniques in it, as well as new ideas in music and lyrics.

Personal and business pressures made the group split up in 1970. All four went on to record more albums as solo artists, with McCartney and Lennon enjoying particular success. Lennon's songs, particularly 'Imagine' and 'Give Peace a Chance', have become much loved, and were widely played in his memory after he was shot dead outside his New York home in 1980.

▼ The Beatles in 1967: from left to right, George, John, Ringo and Paul. Many of today's bands, particularly Oasis, have been influenced by the Beatles' music and lyrics.

Bees and wasps

Bees and wasps are amongst the most familiar insects. Many live alone, but some, such as honeybees and bumble-bees, live in family groups in a hive or nest.

Each hive or nest is the home of a large number of bees and their mother, the queen bee. Worker bees are females that look after the grubs that hatch from the queen bee's eggs. A small number of the bees in a hive are males, or drones. Their job is to mate with young queen bees, after which they die.

Honeybees make honey from a sugary liquid called nectar, which they suck from flowers. The bees use it to feed their young and as food during the winter, when there are no flowers to provide nectar.

As a bee searches flowers for nectar, she also collects pollen from the flowers into 'pollen baskets' on her hind legs. She takes the pollen back to the hive, where it is used as the main food for the grubs. Some of the pollen also gets stuck on her coat, and it gets brushed onto the next flower she visits, and pollinates (fertilizes) it.

Wasps are closely related to bees. Most people think of wasps as insects with yellow and black stripes that protect themselves with a sting. However, these are social wasps, which are only one of the many different kinds of wasp.

- There are about 25,000 different kinds of bee and over 50,000 kinds of wasp.

- A bee's sting is formed from the egg-laying tube of the female. It is like the needle of a hypodermic syringe and pumps poison from a gland at its base into the enemy. If the sting is used against a human or other mammal, it gets stuck in the skin and the bee dies.

▶ Worker bees at work.

find out more
Animal behaviour
Insects

Workers follow the queen when she lays eggs. She produces a chemical called 'queen substance', which attracts the other bees.

Workers construct the comb from wax made in their bodies. It may be used as a store for honey, or as a nursery for the grubs.

A worker visits a flower to collect nectar and pollen. Bees are the most important pollinators of flowers.

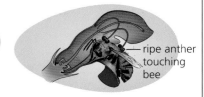

ripe anther touching bee

Beethoven, Ludwig van

Ludwig van Beethoven was one of the most original of all the great composers. His increasing deafness, however, meant that he was never able to hear much of his own music.

Beethoven started playing the violin and piano in public when he was only 8. However, his family life was not always happy, so in 1792 he went to Vienna in Austria to try to make a living as a musician. Although he could be rude and had few social graces, he made influential friends and was soon much in demand as a pianist and teacher.

Then, in 1798, when he was only 28, he began to lose his hearing. At first he could not bear anyone to know of his tragedy. By the end of 1802, though, his hearing loss was serious. At first he was in despair, but he pulled himself together and began to concentrate more than ever on his work. He was completely deaf during the last few years of his life, and he never heard some of his finest music.

Much of the music Beethoven wrote was more powerful and dramatic than anything anyone had written before. It often seemed to tell of a struggle to overcome misfortune and suffering, before ending in peace and calm when all was won. His wide range of music includes the opera *Fidelio*; five piano concertos; 32 piano sonatas; 17 string quartets; the Mass in D; and nine symphonies.

In his last string quartets and piano sonatas, Beethoven struggled to express his musical vision. His audiences found these works difficult to understand, but they are now considered masterpieces.

Born 1770 in Bonn, Germany
Died 1827 aged 56

- Beethoven's music had an enormous influence on later composers such as Brahms, Wagner and Mendelssohn.

find out more
Classical music

▼ Beethoven working on his composing. Until his hearing became too weak, he performed his own piano pieces and conducted his orchestral works.

Beetles

• Ladybirds are small beetles. They are usually brightly coloured, with dark spots on an orange, yellow or red background. Each kind of ladybird has a different pattern and number of spots.

1

• The Goliath beetle is the biggest beetle, as well as the biggest insect. It is about 15 cm long and weighs about 50 g.

find out more
Insects

There are more different kinds of beetle than any other sort of animal. They are easy to recognize because they look as if they are wearing heavy armour. In fact, their front pair of wings are thickened and hinged down to cover the body. Their hind wings are large and papery.

Although there are thousands of different beetles, we do not often see very many. This is because most of them hide away during the daytime, or else keep busy under fallen leaves or among the roots of grasses.

Beetles start life as an egg, and then hatch into a larva (grub). Unlike its parents, it has a soft body, but it has hard biting mouthparts to help it feed and grow. When it has finished growing, the grub finds a safe place to pupate: it goes through a resting stage (pupa), during which the fat body of the larva changes to form the adult beetle. This dramatic change is called metamorphosis.

2

A few beetles are pests because they feed on crops or food stores. However, many more are useful. Some are recyclers, helping to turn decaying matter into nutrients

3

for the soil, which in turn help plants to grow. Others, such as ladybirds, feed off insect pests such as aphids which eat plants, and so are useful to farmers and gardeners.

4

▲ Scientists have discovered over 400,000 different kinds of beetle, and new ones are being found all the time. The ones shown here are a violet ground beetle (1), which cannot fly; a tiger beetle (2), which feeds mainly on other insects; a great diving beetle (3), which lives in water; and an oil beetle (4), which lives in the desert.

Bible

• The Bible was translated from Hebrew and Greek into Latin, the language used in church services all over western Europe for centuries. In the 14th century the religious reformer John Wycliffe organized the first translation of the Bible into English. In the 16th century copies began to be printed in the languages people spoke daily. Today the Bible is printed in over 1100 different languages.

• 'Testament' is a word for an agreement made between people and God.

find out more
Christians
Jews
Printing
Reformation

The Bible is the name given to the Jewish and Christian Scriptures. It is the best-selling and most widely distributed book in the world. The Bible plays an important part in worship and there is a copy in every chapel, church and synagogue.

The Bible has two main parts. The Hebrew Bible, used by both Jews and Christians, is called the Old Testament by Christians. The New Testament was added in the 4th century and is used only by Christians.

The Old Testament

The first Christians were Jews and the Jewish Scriptures were written mainly in Hebrew. Christians rearranged them into 39 books which they called the Old Testament. The books contain myths, legends, history, poetry, hymns and laws for living as God wants people to live. There are stories of prophets such as Amos, Hosea, Isaiah and Ezekiel. Christians believe these prophets prepared the way for the coming of Jesus.

The New Testament

Christians added 27 books called the New Testament. These were written in Greek. They included the life and teaching of Jesus collected in four Gospels. 'Gospel' translates the Greek word 'good news'. The story of the early Church is told in the book called the Acts of the Apostles, and in letters (epistles) written by St Paul and others. These were written in the decades after the death of Jesus.

▼ The monk and Church reformer Martin Luther began a German translation of the Bible in 1521. This version was printed in 1530.

Bicycles

Bicycles are used for sport and leisure, and as an inexpensive means of transport. They also act as delivery vehicles and taxis. Each type of bicycle has special features to make it suitable for a particular job.

Most cycles have a strong but light frame made from hollow metal tubes. The air-filled tyres grip the road and ride smoothly over small bumps. A pull on the brake handles on the handlebars presses rubber brake blocks onto the metal wheel rims and slows down the bicycle.

You change gear by moving levers, which are usually on the handlebars. Low gears are for going uphill or into a strong wind. High gears are for level roads or for going downhill.

▼ In India, bicycles are an important and popular means of transporting produce and other goods.

Bicycle design

Bicycle designers are always improving their designs and trying new materials. Although most bicycle frames are made of steel, many sports bicycles have frames made from lightweight aluminium or titanium, or from strong plastics or carbon-fibre.

A mountain bike has a very strong frame and wheels suited to rough ground, wide chunky tyres for good grip, and lots of low gears for steep hills. A track-racing bike is designed for speed. It has thin tyres, a very lightweight frame, a few high gears, and no brakes. Some have solid wheels for smoother movement through the air. A touring bike is designed for going fast on roads, but can also go along rough tracks.

Racing and other cycle sports

The sport of cycling has several branches, from road and track racing to BMX and mountain biking. In road racing, massed groups of riders battle it out over various distances. A multi-stage road race like the famous Tour de France covers thousands of kilometres and lasts some three weeks.

Track racing takes place on a steeply banked 250-metre oval track. Most track races have elimination heats leading to a final. In *pursuit*, two riders or teams set off at opposite sides of the track and try to catch each other, usually over a distance of 4000 metres (for men) or 3000 metres (for women).

Cyclo-cross and *mountain-bike racing* are cross-country sports. Cyclo-cross riders often have to dismount and carry their bikes over obstacles. In *BMX* (Bicycle Moto-Cross), mainly young riders race small, single-gear bikes over specially built courses. Freestyle BMX riders perform stunts off curved ramps.

▶ FLASHBACK ◀

The first bicycles had a wooden frame and wheels, iron tyres and no brakes or pedals. In 1888 John Boyd Dunlop successfully developed pneumatic tyres for bicycles. By the early 1900s, bicycles looked much like they do today. Lightweight track-racing bicycles, BMX bikes and mountain bikes were introduced in the 1970s.

▲ Mountain bikes are designed so that the rider can carry on cycling even over rugged ground. Downhill racing tests the mountain biker's handling skills.

▲ The hobby horse (velocipede), invented in Germany in 1817.

▲ The Kirkpatrick Macmillan bicycle, with pedals, invented in 1839.

▲ The penny-farthing, invented in the 1860s. (One turn of the pedal made one turn of the wheel.)

find out more
Machines
Materials
Motorcycles

Biology

Biology is the study of living things and the ways in which they interact with the world around them. Biologists study everything about the living world, from the workings of minute bacteria, to the evolution (change) that occurs in animals and plants over millions of years.

Biology is a very broad subject, and it can be studied in many different ways. Some biologists look at large groups of living things. *Population biologists* study whole populations of animals or plants, while *taxonomists* try to classify the different kinds of living things into groups, depending on how closely they are related. *Ecologists* look at how different animals and plants in the same area interact with each other and with their environment.

Other areas of biology look at animals and plants on an individual level. *Anatomists*, for example, study the structure of individual plants or animals, while *physiologists* look at what the different parts do and how they work. Some biologists become experts on particular types of

◀ Some students of biology go on to become veterinarians (vets). In the same way that doctors know all about human biology, vets are expert in animal biology. This vet is applying medicine to the eye of a white rhino, an endangered animal, in Kenya.

living thing. *Zoologists* study animals; *botanists* study plants. *Ornithologists* study only birds, while *entomologists* specialize in insects.

The area of biology that has grown most in the last 100 years is the study of living things at the microscopic level. All living things are made up of tiny cells, and *cell biologists* look at the different kinds of cell and how they work. *Molecular biologists* work on an even smaller scale, studying the chemicals (molecules) that make up cells. These complex molecules, and the chemical reactions that occur between them, are basic to all life on Earth.

find out more
Animals
Cells
Ecology
Evolution
Genetics
Living things
Plants

Biotechnology

Biotechnology is the use of living things to make large amounts of useful products such as drugs, vaccines and medicines. It often involves the use of microbes – tiny single-celled creatures such as bacteria and yeasts.

Microbes have been used in the production of some foods for centuries. Bakers and brewers use microbes called yeasts to make bread and beer. Cheese-making involves the use of bacteria and fungi.

Most modern biotechnology relies on a process known as *genetic engineering*, in which scientists alter the cells of simple animals and plants to give them useful properties. An example of this is the production of human insulin.

• Genetic engineering can also be used to make 'improved' plants. Food plants such as wheat and rice can be given genetic material from other plants to improve their resistance to disease or to help them grow in difficult conditions.

find out more
Bacteria
Fungi
Genetics
Medicine

Insulin is a chemical that controls the levels of sugar in the blood. People with the disease diabetes need insulin as part of their treatment. To make insulin, scientists take a few human cells and extract from them the genetic material (DNA) that has instructions for

making insulin. They copy this material many times, and insert it into microbes, which then produce insulin.

Biotechnology has many other uses in medicine. Microbes can be genetically engineered to produce new drugs and vaccines. They are also used to make human antibodies, substances normally produced in the body which fight disease.

Other products that can be made include enzymes. These are biological substances that speed up chemical reactions in the body. They have many uses in medicine and industry.

◀ Once a microbe has been modified to produce a substance, large numbers have to be grown. Colonies are first grown on flat dishes containing food, as with these fungi. Later, huge numbers are grown in large containers.

Birds

Birds live in all parts of the world: rainforests, deserts, oceans and even the icy wastes of Antarctica. Up in the sky, swans may migrate at a height of 8000 metres. Under the water, penguins may swim to a depth of over 250 metres. There is great variety amongst birds. Some birds eat only plants and some eat only fresh meat. The ostrich grows to be taller than humans, while the bee hummingbird is small enough to fit in the palm of your hand.

Birds are warm-blooded animals. They are the only creatures that have feathers, and all have wings and lay eggs on land. Their bodies are specially designed to enable them to fly efficiently, although a few, such as kiwis and penguins, have lost the power of flight.

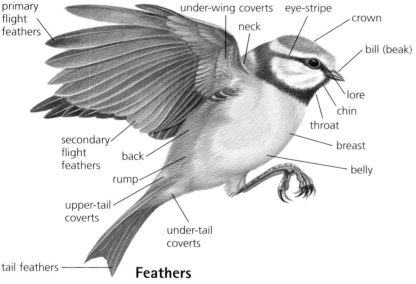

▲ Parts of a bird's body. The upper parts start at the crown and end at the upper-tail coverts. (A covert is a feather covering the base of a bird's tail and flight feathers.) The under parts begin with the chin and finish with the under-tail coverts.

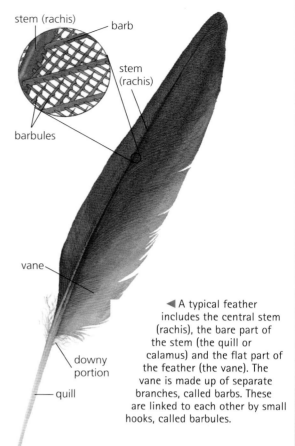

◄ A typical feather includes the central stem (rachis), the bare part of the stem (the quill or calamus) and the flat part of the feather (the vane). The vane is made up of separate branches, called barbs. These are linked to each other by small hooks, called barbules.

Feathers

Feathers cover almost all parts of a bird's body. They are made by the bird's skin, in much the same way that our skin makes hair or fingernails. Usually, only a bird's beak, eyes, legs and feet remain bare.

Feathers have three other important functions. First, they are very good at keeping the bird dry and warm. In cold weather birds fluff up their feathers so that layers of insulating air are trapped between them. Second, the wing feathers enable birds to fly. The flattened curved shapes of the secondary wing feathers help provide the lift that keeps a flying bird in the air. The third important function of feathers is to give birds a streamlined shape, which also aids flight. Feathers can also be used for camouflage or to make a bird obvious. Females are often camouflaged, because they need to stay hidden while sitting on their eggs. Males are often showy and brightly coloured in order to attract a female.

Flight

Birds are specially adapted for flight. Their bones are very light and some are hollow. Their feathers are also light but they serve as a strong covering for the body. In the breeding season females lay eggs at regular intervals and the young develop in a nest so that the mother is not weighed down by carrying them.

Not all birds fly in the same way. Starlings fly in a straight line, moving their wings all the time. Woodpeckers close their wings between flaps and 'bound' along. Larger birds such as gulls often glide, and vultures hardly move their wings as they soar for hours on end.

Some birds, such as kestrels, can hover in the air as they look for prey on the ground, while peregrines, which hunt other birds, can reach speeds of 180 kilometres an hour as they dive to catch their prey. Hummingbirds can also hover in flight while they gather nectar from flowers, their wings beating at an incredible rate of up to 100 times a second. ◗

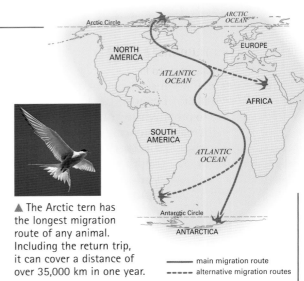

Food

To avoid competing for the same food, different kinds of bird have adapted to different sorts of food. The shapes of their beaks and feet often give us a clue as to what they eat.

Many wading birds have long, strong bills for probing the mud in search of worms or shellfish. Birds of prey have hooked bills for tearing meat. Ducks have flattened bills for filtering water or mud. Sparrows and finches have short, strong bills for cracking seeds.

Some fish-eaters, such as herons, have long legs for wading in water. Others that feed on fish, such as cormorants, have shorter legs and webbed feet to help them swim, dive and chase fish underwater.

▼ Birds' bills are often shaped to help them feed. The curlew (1) uses its long bill to probe mud-flats. Pelicans (2) use their elastic throat pouch as a type of fishing net. The flamingo (3) has a sieve-like bill for filtering food from the water. Eagles (4) tear meat with their hooked bills. The hawfinch (5) has a short, strong bill with which it can crack hard food such as cherry stones.

▼ Japanese cranes performing a complicated courtship dance. The male and female strut around each other with quick, stiff-legged steps and their wings half-spread. The speed of the dance quickens and the birds leap over 4 m into the air and drift down as though in slow motion.

▲ The Arctic tern has the longest migration route of any animal. Including the return trip, it can cover a distance of over 35,000 km in one year.

—— main migration route
----- alternative migration routes

Migration

Many animals, including birds, migrate: they move from one place to another and return again in a different season. While some birds do not travel far from where they hatch, others, especially those breeding in the northern hemisphere, fly hundreds or thousands of kilometres to spend the winter in warmer places where there is plenty of food.

Sometimes only part of a population will migrate. Some mountain birds travel only a few kilometres to lower, warmer levels, while others will move all the way to the coast.

The migrations of small birds can be very long. Wheatears are only a little larger than sparrows, yet each year some fly non-stop from Greenland to North Africa. The tiny ruby-throated hummingbird migrates from North to South America, a journey that includes an 800-kilometre crossing of the Gulf of Mexico.

Sea birds make even longer journeys. Some, such as puffins, go out to sea and spend the winter out of sight of land. Arctic terns fly from their northern breeding grounds to winter in the Southern Ocean, sometimes reaching Antarctica.

Birdsong

Some birds make noises with their bills. A few use their feathers. But most use songs and calls to communicate with other birds.

Calls are usually short and loud, and they may signal danger. They may also be used by courting birds or by young birds begging for food. Some calls help to keep flocks together in thick woodland, or when migrating at night.

It is usually only male birds that sing, to tell other males that they have chosen a place to nest and are prepared to defend the surrounding area (their territory), or to attract a female.

Danger from humans

Young birds must learn to find food and shelter, to survive extreme weather and to avoid enemies. Even so, most will die in their first year. Normally, enough survive to produce the next generation and a balance is created. Unfortunately, humans have the power to upset that balance.

The dodo was a victim of human interference. It was a huge, flightless pigeon relative which lived on the island of Mauritius in the Indian Ocean. Visiting sailors killed many dodos for food, and the cats, pigs, rats and monkeys which the sailors brought with them destroyed the dodos' eggs. By 1681 all the dodos were dead. Since then the great auk, the passenger pigeon and many other birds have also become extinct as a result of human activities.

Birds are also hunted for food and as a sport by some people. Game birds such as pheasants, partridges and grouse are commonly hunted in Europe and North America. However, the activity is managed so that their numbers are not threatened.

Although birds are increasingly being protected by laws throughout the world, damage still occurs. For instance, around the Mediterranean millions of migrating birds are shot or trapped by hunters each year.

The rapid growth of the human population and the huge demand for natural materials have resulted in the destruction of many of the places where birds live. Marshes are drained to make farmland, forests are cleared for timber or for space to build houses or to grow crops, deserts

increase in size because of over-grazing of pasture land by domesticated animals. Even global warming caused by human pollution will affect bird populations.

The origin of birds

Archaeopteryx (from the Greek meaning 'ancient wing') is the earliest known fossil of a bird. It is a 'missing link' between the dinosaurs and the birds as we know them today. The first fossil of *Archaeopteryx* was found in Germany in 1861. It was contained in rocks of the Upper Jurassic period, which are about 145 million years old. The fossil showed an almost complete skeleton, about the size of a pigeon. The creature was similar to small dinosaurs but also had feathers, which showed that it was partly like a bird.

▲ A flock of budgerigars at a waterhole in Australia's North West Territory. Budgerigars are native to Australia but now breed wild in parts of North America too. Like other kinds of parrot, budgerigars are popular as pets. This is partly because they are able to copy human speech.

find out more
Animal behaviour
Conservation
Ducks, geese and swans
Eggs
Flight
Hunting birds
Migration
Sea birds
Songbirds
Wading birds

▶ Domestication involves controlling the living and breeding conditions of birds. Many different birds have been domesticated to provide meat and eggs.

turkey

Chinese goose

rooster

Indian runner

chicken

Black holes

When a massive star collapses it becomes a black hole. Nothing can escape from a black hole because the pull of its gravity is so strong. Only about one star in a thousand is massive enough to have any chance of becoming a black hole. Black holes are difficult to find because they cannot be seen!

find out more
Astronomy
Galaxies
Gravity
Stars
X-rays

A black hole is probably made when a massive star – one which is much 'heavier' than the Sun – runs out of fuel at the end of its life. The inside

◀ Scientists believe that this falsely coloured image made by the Hubble Space Telescope is evidence of a black hole. It shows a spiral disc of hot gas at the centre of the M87 galaxy. The black hole's mass is about 3 billion times greater than the Sun's mass.

of the star falls in on itself and keeps on falling until all its material is crushed down to a tiny volume. While the star is collapsing, the force of gravity at its surface quickly grows stronger. As soon as its gravity becomes strong enough to stop light from escaping, the star becomes a *stellar black hole*. Anything that comes close enough to it will fall in and disappear.

A black hole has to have at least two or three times the mass of the Sun. A less massive star cannot collapse in this way because its gravity is not strong enough. A black hole with 10 times the Sun's mass would have a diameter (width) of 60 kilometres. If the Sun could be made into a black hole, it would have a diameter of 6 kilometres. A black hole with the mass of the Earth would be less than 2 centimetres across!

When material falls in towards a black hole, it becomes very hot and gives off X-rays. Astronomers believe that some of the X-ray 'stars' they have found may be black holes. There are probably 'supermassive' black holes at the centre of certain kinds of galaxy. The very bright centres of these galaxies are lit up by material falling into *galactic black holes* that 'weigh' up to several billion times more than the Sun.

Blindness

Blindness means the loss or lack of sight in both eyes. However, some people are blind in one eye only. 'Partially sighted' means having permanently damaged vision.

• Some scientists believe that it may be possible for blind people to see again by implanting tiny television cameras into their eye sockets.

• Braille is named after its inventor, Louis Braille. He was blinded in an accident in his father's workshop when he was 4 years old, and invented Braille writing when he was only 15.

A few people are born blind, and some become blind because their eyes are damaged by disease or injury.

People who are blind often use their senses of hearing, touch and smell to help them to understand what is happening around them. They also use a range of aids such as trained dogs, books recorded on tape, a kind of raised writing called Braille, and specially adapted computers. Many blind people carry a long white cane. They move this across their path as

they walk to detect obstacles. It also warns other people that they are blind.

About 90 per cent of people who are registered as blind have some sight. Researchers believe that they, and some totally blind people, may be able to see again using various electronic devices. One possibility might be to reactivate the parts of the brain concerned with sight.

Braille

Braille is a special way of printing words so that blind people can read. In Braille, the letters of each word are printed in patterns of up to six small dots. The dots for each letter stick up from the surface of the paper, and the letters can be read by brushing the tips of the fingers lightly across the dots. In Braille writing, the word 'braille' looks like this:

▲ Many blind people do not let their lack of sight stop them from living their lives to the full. This blind man, who is reading Braille, works as a computer software developer.

b r a i l l e

find out more
Disabilities
Eyes
Writing systems

Blood

Blood is the body's transport system. It carries food and oxygen to all parts of the body and removes harmful wastes. It spreads heat evenly around the body, and plays an active part in fighting injury and infection.

Blood is pumped round the body by the heart, a muscular

pump, and travels through tubes called blood vessels. It is made up of a fluid called plasma, with blood cells floating in it. Red blood cells carry oxygen from the lungs to all the other cells of the body. The blood also takes dissolved foods such as glucose (sugar) from the intestines (gut) to other parts of the body and carries away wastes such as carbon dioxide and urea (from the kidneys).

Injury and infection

Blood can protect us from damage and infections in two ways. First, it seals up cuts or

◄ A coloured and greatly magnified photograph of human blood. The red blood cells are coloured red. The white, rough-looking objects are white cells. The small blue objects are platelets, fragments of bone marrow which help the blood to clot.

other damage to the skin by clotting (setting). This stops more blood escaping and prevents dirt and germs from entering. Second, special white blood cells called lymphocytes make antibodies which recognize germs and attach themselves to them. The germs can then be destroyed by other defences, including white blood cells called phagocytes which eat them.

Blood diseases
Anaemia People suffer from anaemia when they do not have enough red cells in their blood.
Haemophilia is an inherited disease. The blood of a haemophiliac does not clot properly.
Leukaemia is a type of blood cancer in which the blood makes too many of a certain type of cell. Choked with the extra cells, the blood cannot function as it should.

• A drop of blood contains about 100 million red blood cells. More than 2 million of them are destroyed and replaced every second.

• The English doctor William Harvey (1578–1657) discovered that blood circulated round the body. Before that doctors had believed that our blood was continually destroyed, and that the food we ate turned into new blood to replace it.

find out more
Diets
Diseases
Hearts
Lungs

Bones

Bones are the hard parts of your body. They form your skeleton, the frame around which your body is built. They give you your shape and enable you to move. Bones contain living cells and can regrow if they break. They are as strong as some kinds of steel, but only one-fifth as heavy.

Bones are made out of a mixture of a tough protein called *collagen*, and very tiny, hard mineral crystals which contain calcium and phosphorus. This mixture gives bones their strength. At the centre of many bones is a soft tissue called *bone marrow*. This contains blood vessels that supply the bone with food and oxygen. The marrow is also the

place where new blood cells continually are made.

As a baby grows in its mother's womb, its bones develop. To begin with they are made of a softer, gristly substance called *cartilage*. During growth most of the cartilage becomes bone, apart from those parts that remain bendy, like the tip of the nose and the ears. In an adult cartilage also forms the smooth surfaces where bones slide against one another at joints. The ends of the ribs are connected to the sternum, or breastbone, by cartilage, which gives the ribcage some flexibility.

Animal bones are made in the same way as human bones,

but some animals have unusual bones. Deer's antlers are bones. They grow from the skull and are shed each year.

shaft

marrow

this end fits into hip bone

compact bone

spongy bone

this end forms part of knee joint

◄ A human thigh bone, cut away to show the internal structure. The thigh bone is the longest bone in the human body.

• A broken bone is said to be fractured. A simple fracture may not need treatment, but if the bone is badly broken, a doctor may put it in plaster until it heals.

find out more
Muscles
Skeletons

Books

Tens of thousands of new book titles are published each year. Thousands of copies of each title are printed. If a book becomes a bestseller, then a million or more copies may be printed and sold around the world. The production of books in large numbers was made possible by the invention of the printing press in the 1400s. Until then, books were created individually by hand.

The idea for a fiction book usually comes from a single author who creates the characters and story. A non-fiction book, such as this encyclopedia, is the work of a large number of editors, authors, designers and illustrators. Authors submit their ideas for new books to a book publisher. Publishers choose, produce and sell books that they think will be popular and will sell well.

The text (words) and pictures for a book can be produced directly on a computer, or changed into computer data. When all the pages have been designed and checked for errors, the text and illustrations are sent to a reproduction house.

• This encyclopedia was produced by a team of people. Editors chose authors to write the articles. Designers planned the layout of each page. Photo researchers found the photographs, and illustrators produced the drawings and diagrams.

• Illuminated manuscripts are hand-made books with beautiful coloured decoration. In medieval times, scribes wrote the text and illuminators decorated the pages with borders, initials and miniature pictures.

find out more
Middle Ages
Novels and novelists
Printing
Stories and story-tellers

Next, the assembled pages are printed onto transparent films that are used to make the metal plates from which the books are printed.

▲ Roald Dahl, the author of such classic children's books as *James and the Giant Peach* and *Matilda*, wrote his stories in a hut at the bottom of his garden. It was often cold, but he wrapped himself in a rug and ate chocolate.

Bowling

Bowling games of various kinds have been played for hundreds of years. Bowls was a very popular sport in the Middle Ages, and most famously Sir Francis Drake is supposed to have been playing bowls when the Spanish Armada was sighted in 1588.

• In bowls the woods have a 'bias' – they are flattened slightly on one side so that they run in a curved line. In *crown-green* bowls, another complication is added by making the green slightly higher in the middle than at the sides.

Apart from bowls, the most popular form of bowling today is tenpin bowling. This started in North America, but is now played in many countries.

Bowls

In the game of bowls heavy wooden or hardened-rubber balls called woods are bowled along a smooth *green*. The game is traditionally played outdoors on close-cut grass, but it is now often played indoors on an artificial surface.

The aim is to bowl the woods as close as possible to a small white ball called the *jack*. A game is played over a number of rounds or *ends*, and in singles each player has four woods.

◄ In this game of bowls, the bowler playing the white woods is 'lying one' – he stands to score one point for the wood at top right.

A point is scored for each wood that lies closer to the jack than the opponent's closest wood, and the winner is the first to reach 21 points. The game can also be played between teams of two or more players.

Tenpin bowling

In tenpin bowling, heavy balls are bowled from one end of a polished wooden lane or *alley* towards 10 skittles, or *pins*, set up in a triangle at the far end. A game is normally played over 10 *frames*, in which each player has two balls to knock down as many pins as possible. Knocking down all 10 pins with the first ball is known as a *strike*.

Tenpin bowling was developed in North America from the game of skittles, or ninepins, which was brought over by Dutch settlers.

Boxing and other combat sports

Combat (fighting) sports are amongst the oldest of all sports. Boxing and wrestling both featured in the ancient Olympic Games.

In China, Japan and other Eastern countries, a number of 'martial arts' have developed. These involve fighting, but they usually have a strong spiritual element as well.

- In 1867 the Marquess of Queensberry helped to establish the rules of modern boxing. The 'Queensberry rules' included making boxers wear gloves and outlawing some of the more dangerous blows.

- Fencing is a sport in which two people fight each other with blunted swords. Three weapons are used. The *foil* is a light sword with a flexible blade. The *épée* is heavier and has a stiffer blade. The *sabre* is a 'cut and thrust' weapon.

find out more
Ali, Muhammad

▼ Rocky Marciano of the USA (left), one of the greatest heavyweights of all time. In 1956 he retired as undefeated world champion, having won all 49 of his professional fights.

Boxing

Boxing is the sport of fist-fighting between two people wearing padded gloves. The boxers are of similar weight, and they fight in a roped-off square called a *ring* for periods of three minutes at a time. Each period is called a *round*. At the end of each round the boxers retire to their corners for a minute's break. Amateur boxers fight for just three rounds, while professionals usually box over 10 or 12 rounds.

The object of boxing is to score points by hitting an opponent while trying to avoid being hit. Boxers can also win by a *knock-out*. This happens when a boxer is knocked to the floor and cannot get up again within 10 seconds, or when the referee stops the fight because one of the boxers is injured or unable to defend himself.

There are many rules and regulations to control modern boxing. In spite of these, many boxers have been badly injured by blows to the head, and a few have even died from their injuries. Because of this, many people feel that boxing should not be allowed.

▲ Women's judo action at the 1996 Atlanta Olympics. Wearing a black belt shows that a person has reached the *dan* (master) grades.

Martial arts

The martial arts are Eastern fighting skills developed over the centuries, often in secret. They are generally linked with religion or self-defence, and many are practised as a way of life.

Judo (meaning 'the gentle way') was developed from ju-jitsu, the Japanese form of self-defence based on using an attacker's own force to defeat him. Competitors wear a loose-fitting white suit with a belt, the colour of which indicates the standard they have reached. The major skills include hip, leg and shoulder throws, but much of the work is also done on the ground.

Karate (meaning 'open hands') has its origins in yoga from India and the self-defence skills of Buddhist monks from medieval China. Competitions involve fights and the performance of moves without an opponent. Physical contact is limited because of the danger involved. Punches and kicks are aimed at particular parts of the body, but they are controlled and pulled back before contact.

Taekwondo ('the way of kick and punch') is a Korean form of unarmed combat. It is similar to karate, with the emphasis on strikes with the hands and feet.

Wrestling

Wrestling is an unarmed combat sport in which two people struggle to throw one another to the ground. In *Greco-Roman wrestling*, the wrestlers are not allowed to hold the body below the waist or use their legs to hold or trip an opponent. *Freestyle wrestling* does not have these restrictions. In both styles a competitor fights an opponent of similar weight. Certain throws and moves earn technical points, but a wrestler may win outright by a *fall*, pinning his opponent's shoulders to the ground for one second.

Brains

find out more
Animal behaviour
Cells
Human body
Nervous systems
Senses

Most animals have a brain, which controls their thoughts and actions. The brain consists of many connected nerve cells (neurons). Some of these pass information from sense organs, such as the ears or eyes, into the brain, while others are connected to nerves that lead from the brain to muscles.

A mammal's brain is the central part of a highly complex nervous system. Encased within the skull, which protects it, the brain is connected to nerves in the spinal cord. The cord runs down from the head inside the backbone. Nerves from the spinal cord are connected to muscles, while other nerves from sense cells in the skin and muscles connect back into the spinal cord.

Processing and control

Most of the brain cells in mammals are connected to other brain cells and process incoming information, carry out thought processes and make complex decisions. Even smaller and less intelligent animals, such as bees, can remember where their hive is and calculate the time of day.

Sense organs rapidly pass information to different parts of the brain as a series of nerve impulses, which act as signals. These may be simple signals, giving information about what part of your body has been touched, or a very complex series of signals using thousands of nerve cells to allow you, for example, to see the shapes of the letters and read the words on this page.

Using information from different parts of the brain, an animal sends signals to its muscles so that they move in a particular way. Some types of movement, such as a single kick, do not require much control, but walking or flying require exact control of the muscles. You would fall over

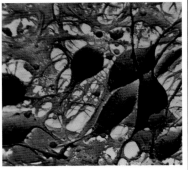

▲ The brain consists of millions of nerve cells like these (shown here magnified many times), carrying millions of messages to and from the brain. All nerve cells have the same basic structure: a large cell body, with a central nerve fibre connecting the cell to thousands of others.

and bump into things if you could not adjust your muscles continually.

Thinking, memory and learning

In humans the cerebral hemispheres, the main sections of the brain, are very large and are involved in consciousness, thought, recognition, memory and personality.

Memory is the ability to recall things and feelings from the past. Part of the action of storing a memory seems to be the making of new links between nerve cells in the brain. It is easier to remember things if you repeat them many times, or if they are very unusual or unpleasant.

Most animals with brains are able to learn. Animals with big, complicated brains are usually able to learn more than those with small brains. Having a large memory, gained through life's experiences, allows an animal to make more complex decisions and generally to respond in a more intelligent manner. Humans, with their large brains and powerful memories, are probably the most intelligent animals.

1

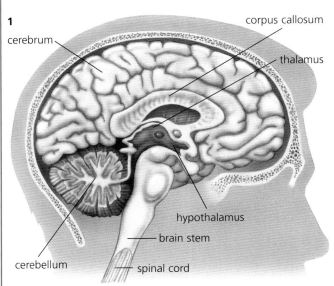

cerebrum
corpus callosum
thalamus
hypothalamus
brain stem
cerebellum
spinal cord

2

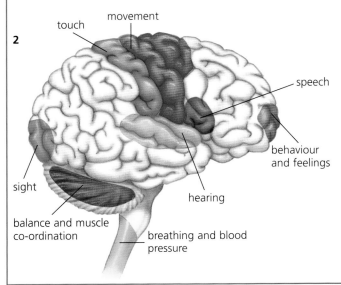

touch
movement
speech
behaviour and feelings
sight
hearing
balance and muscle co-ordination
breathing and blood pressure

◄ A cross-section through the centre of the brain (**1**). The three main parts of the the brain are the brain stem, the cerebellum and the cerebrum. The cerebrum is divided into two halves separated by a deep groove, the left and right cerebral hemispheres. Different parts of the brain carry out different jobs in the body (**2**). The cerebrum controls the senses.

Brazil

Brazil is the biggest country in South America and covers nearly half the continent. It stretches from the foothills of the Andes mountains in the west to the Atlantic Ocean in the east.

The north-eastern corner of Brazil is a vast, harsh, very dry region made up mostly of thorny scrub. In the south the climate is good for crops. Brazil is one of the biggest producers of coffee in the world and also grows sugar cane, tobacco, rice, soya beans, maize (corn) and many fruits.

The rainforest around Brazil's Amazon River is the largest in the world. It has a richer plant life than anywhere else on Earth. However, the forest is being cleared for cattle ranches and farms. As well as adding to global warming, this destruction is robbing many Native Americans of their forest homes.

Brazil is one of the 10 biggest industrial nations in the world. There are deposits of iron ore and other minerals. Much of the ore is used for steel-making,

and the steel is used to make motor cars, locomotives, ships and other goods.

▶ FLASHBACK ◀

The Portuguese were the first Europeans to colonize Brazil in 1500. That is why Brazilians are the only South Americans whose language is Portuguese. In 1825 Brazil became independent under Emperor Pedro I. Brazil became a republic in 1889. As well as the original native peoples, Portuguese colonists, and African slaves, many other nationalities have emigrated to Brazil from Europe, the Middle East and the Far East.

◀ In Brazil the few very wealthy people live in luxury, while the millions who are poor live in shanty towns like this one in São Paulo.

find out more
Forests
Rivers and streams
South America
See also Countries fact file, page 616

Bread

Bread comes in many shapes and sizes. As well as tin-shaped and cottage loaves, there are flat pitta breads from the Middle East, puffed-up puris from India, corn bread from America, millet cakes from Africa, and many other varieties.

Whatever the shape or size, the basic ingredients of bread are flour and water. The bread you eat is probably made from wheat flour, but flour can also be made from rye, oats, corn and other

cereals. Sometimes cheese, nuts or herbs are added to give bread extra flavour or texture.

Flat bread and risen bread

Bread which stays completely flat when cooked is made by mixing flour with water and salt into a soft dough. Flat-bread flour is made from maize (corn), millet, barley or buckwheat. The dough is rolled out and cooked straightaway on a metal plate over a fire or on a stove. Indian chapatis and Mexican tortillas are made like this. The bread does not rise and is called unleavened bread.

Leavened bread uses yeast as well as flour and water, and the mixture is left to stand for a while before cooking. The yeast reacts with the sugars in the flour and causes the dough to ferment. This produces carbon dioxide gas which helps the dough to rise and swell. The bread is then baked in a hot oven. You can see the tiny holes of air in the bread.

◀ Bread has been called the 'Staff of Life'. It is such an important part of what most people eat that it is known as a staple food. As well as protein, bread contains plenty of starch (a carbohydrate), and is a good source of dietary fibre, calcium and some of the B vitamins.

• Wholemeal bread is made from flour which is milled from the whole grain. Brown flour has 15% of the outer coating and germ of the wheat sieved out, while white bread has 30% removed. This process removes some nutrients that are good for you, so in several countries the millers have to replace them by law.

find out more
Cereals
Diets
Food

Breathing

• People usually think that respiration means breathing. However, breathing is just the means of getting oxygen so that respiration can take place.

• Some animals do not use lungs and air for respiration. For example, fishes use their gills to get oxygen from the water.

• Plants make their own oxygen for respiration through the process of photosynthesis. They use energy from the Sun to turn carbon dioxide in the air and water into glucose and oxygen.

▶ Breathing in and breathing out.

Breathing is the forcing of air in and out of the lungs. The body gets the energy it needs by a process called respiration. This process is fuelled by the gas oxygen, which is extracted from air in our lungs.

When you breathe in (inhale), your chest gets bigger as air is sucked into the lungs. This happens because muscles pull the ribs upwards and outwards, and a sheet of muscle below the lungs, called the diaphragm, is pulled downwards. When you breathe out (exhale), your ribs get lower and are drawn in and the diaphragm rises.

The brain controls the speed of our breathing. This is to provide enough oxygen at all times for the body's needs. When you are still, your energy needs are low; you require little oxygen and your breathing is slow and shallow. You will probably breathe in and out about 12 times every minute. However, if you start exercising hard, you need much more energy. Without thinking about it, you automatically find yourself breathing faster and more deeply.

Respiration

Respiration is the process by which the oxygen we breathe in reacts with food to release energy. The oxygen passes into the red blood cells through tiny blood vessels in the lungs. The blood then carries the oxygen to every cell in the body where respiration occurs. In these cells oxygen is combined with sugars and fats in food to release energy plus some water and the waste gas carbon dioxide. The blood then carries the carbon dioxide back to the lungs, from where it is breathed out every time we exhale.

Some creatures can get their energy without oxygen. This is called anaerobic respiration. They include microbes living in thick mud, and parasites living inside an animal's gut. When you run very quickly, your muscles respire anaerobically because they cannot get enough energy from normal respiration. This produces lactic acid as a waste product instead of carbon dioxide, and it is this acid that causes your muscles to ache.

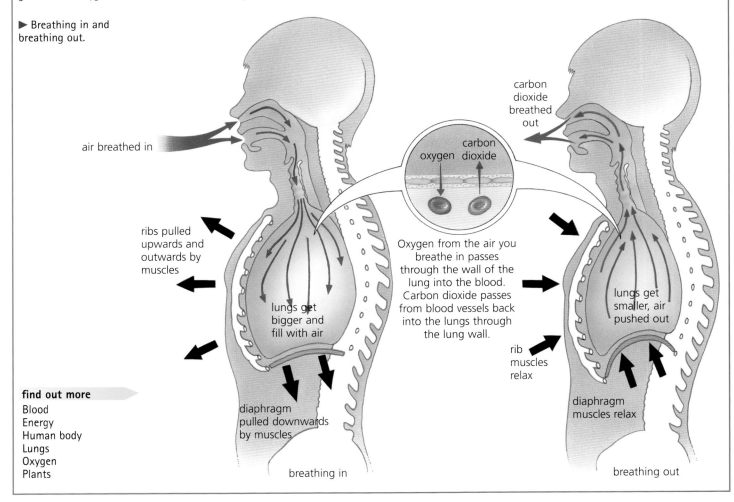

air breathed in

carbon dioxide breathed out

oxygen carbon dioxide

ribs pulled upwards and outwards by muscles

lungs get bigger and fill with air

Oxygen from the air you breathe in passes through the wall of the lung into the blood. Carbon dioxide passes from blood vessels back into the lungs through the lung wall.

lungs get smaller, air pushed out

rib muscles relax

diaphragm pulled downwards by muscles

diaphragm muscles relax

breathing in

breathing out

find out more
Blood
Energy
Human body
Lungs
Oxygen
Plants

Bricks *see* Building

Bridges

Bridges carry roads, railways or footways over water, valleys and ravines or above other roads. Most are fixed, but some can be raised or swung round.

- The longest suspension bridge in the world is the bridge over the Akashi Strait in Japan, completed in 1997.

▲ This magnificent bridge spans the River Seine in Normandy, France. With a span of 856 m, it is the longest cable-stayed bridge in the world.

find out more
Architecture
Railways
Rivers and streams
Roads

With all bridges, the problem for engineers is to design and build structures which will not sag or crack under the weight they have to carry. There are several ways of doing this.

Beam bridges have rigid beams which are supported at each end. The earliest bridges used this idea. They were just tree trunks or slabs of stone resting between the banks of a stream. Modern beam bridges are often long, hollow boxes made of steel or concrete.

A *clapper bridge* is a beam bridge in which two or more stones or pieces of wood act as beams and are supported by piers of stone or wood. A *truss-girder bridge* is a type of beam bridge which uses a rigid steel framework as a beam.

Cantilever bridges have long, rigid sections like beam bridges. However, these sections are supported in the middle rather than at their ends. Each section extends out equally on either side of its supporting pier so that it balances.

Arch bridges take the strain of the main span with an arch that pushes on the ground at each end. Modern arch bridges often have a light, open structure.

Suspension bridges are best for very large spans. The road or rail deck is suspended from steel cables which hang between towers. The ends of these cables are anchored on either side of the span. Older suspension bridges have chains or even ropes rather than cables.

Cable-stayed bridges have cables attached to masts. The cables support the deck and transmit its load to the masts, putting them under large compression (squashing) forces.

▶ **FLASHBACK** ◀

The Romans built many of their bridges using concrete made by mixing volcanic soil, lime and water. At the end of the 18th century, when methods of making large cast-iron girders developed, iron bridges were built. The first was at Coalbrookdale, England, in 1779. The Menai Suspension Bridge, built in the 1820s by the Scottish engineer Thomas Telford, lasted for over 100 years before the iron chains needed to be replaced. By the 1880s bridges were being built of steel, which is stronger and less brittle than cast iron.

▼ Various types of bridge.

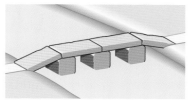

clapper bridge

arch bridge

truss-girder bridge

cantilever bridge

cable-stayed bridge

suspension bridge

▼ A poor family in a
slum house before World
War I. Millions of homes
had no bathrooms and
only an outside toilet.

Britain since 1900

During the 20th century Britain lost its position as the world's most powerful country. But society became fairer, and despite two world wars and the Great Depression, the average family's standard of living rose sharply.

These changes were well under way in the period before World War I. Suffragettes campaigned for votes for women and trade unions called strikes for better pay and conditions. The Liberal government introduced old-age pensions. By 1914 British industry had been overtaken by the USA and Germany.

Between the wars

World War I (1914–1918) cost almost a million British lives and left Britain with huge debts. It also speeded up the rate of change. In 1918 women over 30 got the vote in national elections. In 1921 Ireland was divided between the Catholic Irish Free State and Protestant

▶ In the 1960s, 'Swinging Britain' was the cultural centre of the world. This trend was led by fashion designers like Mary Quant and bands like the Beatles, which gave British 'pop' a huge international following.

Ulster, which remained in the United Kingdom.

Times were tough for the traditional industries – coalmining, iron and steel, and shipbuilding – and unemployment remained high. Hard-pressed workers resorted to strikes. The biggest of these was the nine-day General Strike of 1926. The Great Depression (from 1929 onwards) deepened the misery, and by 1932 unemployment stood at 2.7 million.

Nevertheless, the middle class grew, suburbs spread, and people were buying more things. Politics changed, too. The Liberals lost popularity to the Labour Party, although in 1931 a coalition (all-party) National Government was formed to deal with the problems of the Great Depression.

War and welfare

In 1939 Britain was at war again. Enemy German planes regularly bombed London and other cities. Air-raid shelters were built and children were evacuated to the countryside. Winston Churchill's coalition government rationed food and other necessities. With most men aged between 18 and 50 in the forces or doing war work, women kept the country going.

After World War II ended in 1945, a Labour government introduced the 'Welfare State' to help poorer families. Its reforms included better unemployment pay and pensions, child allowances and setting up the National Health Service. All children under 16 had free education. The government also took over ('nationalized') several large industries, including coalmining and railways.

The 50s and 60s

The British empire was broken up between 1947 and 1970 as former colonies became independent. Thousands of immigrants came to Britain, creating a multicultural society, and racism was officially made illegal.

The country prospered. Slums were cleared, and most homes now had bathrooms, fridges and televisions. Millions of new cars began to clog up the roads. Harold Macmillan's Conservatives won the 1959 election with the slogan 'You've never had it so good'.

Towards the millennium

The 1970s were plagued by inflation, unemployment and strikes. Rising oil prices made matters worse, and by 1982 unemployment was over 3 million. The discovery of oil fields beneath the North Sea and joining the European Economic Community (now the European Union) in 1973 brought some relief. Margaret Thatcher's Conservative government (1979–1990) curbed the power of trade unions, cut government

▶ The Channel Tunnel was more than just a great feat of engineering. It was a symbol of Britain's willingness to work more closely with Europe.

spending and sold off many nationalized industries. Unemployment remained high, and the gap between rich and poor grew.

Terrorism caused over 3000 deaths in Northern Ireland between 1968 and 1994. Violent crime increased, divorce rates rose, and there was a decline in organized religion.

Britain seemed unsure about where it stood in the world. It fought wars in the Falklands (1982) and the Gulf (1991), and found the European Union difficult to work with. In 1997 Tony Blair led a Labour government to power. The Scots and Welsh voted for their own assemblies, and in Northern Ireland there were important steps towards peace. The economy did well, and unemployment came down. In 2003 Blair joined the USA in a war against Iraq, despite much opposition at home and in much of the rest of the European Union.

find out more
Beatles
British empire
Churchill, Winston
European Union
Ireland, Republic of
Scotland
Twentieth-century
  history
Wales
World War I
World War II

British empire

At its height, in about 1900, the British empire included one-quarter of the world's population and land area.

In about 1600 English ships sailed as far as North America and India. Here they found a wealth of useful goods and fertile lands from which Britain could obviously benefit. The colonists either drove the native people from their lands, as in North America and Australia, or took control of the people, as in India, imposing their culture and systems of administration over them.

Effects of the empire

Britain imported food and raw materials for its factories from all over the empire, while selling back manufactured goods. Luxuries from abroad, such as spices and silks, were sold at home. British missionaries went out to bring Christianity to native peoples. The empire also gave many Britons work.

In some ways the colonies benefited from the railways, roads, schools and hospitals that the British built and the legal and administrative systems they set up. However, British rulers often had little respect for local traditions, customs and beliefs, and native peoples were sometimes used as virtual slaves.

By 1980 almost all Britain's old colonies had gained their independence, many after violent protests. Some joined the Commonwealth of Nations.

• Members of the Commonwealth of Nations accept the English monarch as Head of the Commonwealth.

find out more
Australia
Canada
Caribbean
India
North America
Slaves
South Africa

◀ This map shows the great extent of the British empire at its peak, in 1914.

British kings and queens *see page 653* • **British prime ministers** *see page 654* • **Brunei** *see page 617*
   75

Buddhists

The Buddhist religion began between the 6th and 5th centuries BC. An Indian prince called Siddhartha Gautama found a way of life that he believed could make all beings peaceful and happy. He became known as Buddha, the 'enlightened one', and today he has followers all over the world.

The turning point in Siddhartha's life came at the age of 29, when he travelled beyond the palace grounds and was confronted with old age, sickness and death. He realized that these things were a part of life, and that they should be accepted. He left his home to study different religions in the hope of finding the cause of such suffering and the meaning of life. Disappointed, he focused all his energies on meditation (deep thought) instead. In this way he finally understood the truth about the way things are. Buddhists call this being enlightened.

Teachings
Buddha spent the rest of his life teaching others what he had discovered. He taught that true happiness and contentment come when we accept the fact that everything changes, when we respect the life of every living thing, and when we are generous, kind and compassionate. Problems arise when we think of ourselves as

• Buddhists believe in *karma*, the idea that good or evil deeds get a just reward either in this life or, through rebirth, in other lives.

• Buddha himself began the spread of Buddhism by sending monks out to teach people in their own languages. First, Buddhism spread over India, then along the Silk Road to China and through Korea to Japan. Although it later almost died out in India, it established itself in Sri Lanka, Tibet and South-east Asia. In the 20th century Buddhism has started to grow in Western countries.

▶ Buddhists show respect for Buddha by putting flowers, incense and candles before his statue. They keep statues of Buddha in their homes to inspire them to try to follow his teachings and become enlightened. This bronze statue of Buddha was made in Thailand in the 14th century.

▲ Prayer wheels like this one are a speciality of Tibetan Buddhism. As they are turned, scrolls inside the cylinders are believed to release several million prayers up to the heavens. Tibetans still look upon the Buddhist monk Dalai Lama as the rightful ruler of their country, even though he lives in exile in India because Tibet is currently under Chinese control.

somehow separate, making us unable to live in harmony and peace. He taught through his own example as well as through stories and parables.

The Buddha taught four truths, which Buddhists call 'noble truths':
1 Life is full of suffering and therefore unsatisfactory.
2 Suffering has a cause and that cause is attachment to greed or desire.
3 Suffering can end when we stop clinging to impermanent things.
4 There is a path or way of life that can lead to enlightenment, a state of inner peace called *nirvana*.

It is called the eightfold noble path:
● *Right understanding* seeing the world as it really is
● *Right intentions* those of kindness and compassion
● *Right speech* not lying or gossiping
● *Right action* not harming living things, not stealing, not having wrong sexual relationships and avoiding alcohol and drugs
● *Right livelihood* earning a living in a fair and honest way without hurting others
● *Right effort* knowing what you can do and using just the right amount of effort
● *Right mindfulness* being alert to what is going on in and around you
● *Right concentration* applying the mind to meditation and to everything that you do.

Way of life

Buddhists say that they depend on three precious things – the Buddha, his teachings (*dharma*), and the community (*sangha*). Buddhists call them the three jewels or 'triple gem'.

▲ Most Thais are Buddhists, and a majority of the men spend some part of their lives as monks learning about their religion in one of the country's 27,000 *wat* (temples).

The Buddhist community is made up of monks and nuns, and of householders and their families. Monks and nuns live a very simple way of life. They own little except their robes and alms bowl (for offerings of money or food), and spend their time in meditation and study.

Householders give monks and nuns their food, clothing and somewhere to live. The monks and nuns give the householders what is called 'the greater gift', the gift of the dharma (teachings). They may also give advice if people ask for it. Families visit temples and monasteries to worship and meditate, for festivals, and to talk to the monks and nuns.

The branches of Buddhism

There are two main branches of the Buddhist religion – Theravada and Mahayana. Theravada means doctrine (*vada*) of the elders (*thera*). This is the kind of Buddhism practised in Sri Lanka, Myanmar (Burma) and Thailand. Theravada Buddhists believe that theirs is the original form of Buddhism. Their rituals are few and simple, and focus on the memory and teachings of Buddha. It is sometimes called 'the little way'.

Mahayana means 'the great way'. It is called great because it claims to provide many ways to enlightenment for a variety of people. There are Mahayana Buddhists in Tibet, Nepal, China, Korea, Japan and elsewhere. They rely for help on bodhissatvas, those beings who, on the threshold of nirvana, hold back and are prepared to be reborn into the world in order to help others to reach enlightenment. Mahayana Buddhists have elaborate rituals and focus on many buddhas and bodhisattvas.

• Nirvana means the blowing out (extinction) of desire and attachment.

• Meditation is an act of contemplation, a way of relaxing the mind and body in order to focus on religious thoughts. Mediation is central to the Buddhist religion.

find out more
Festivals and holidays
India
Monks and nuns
Religions

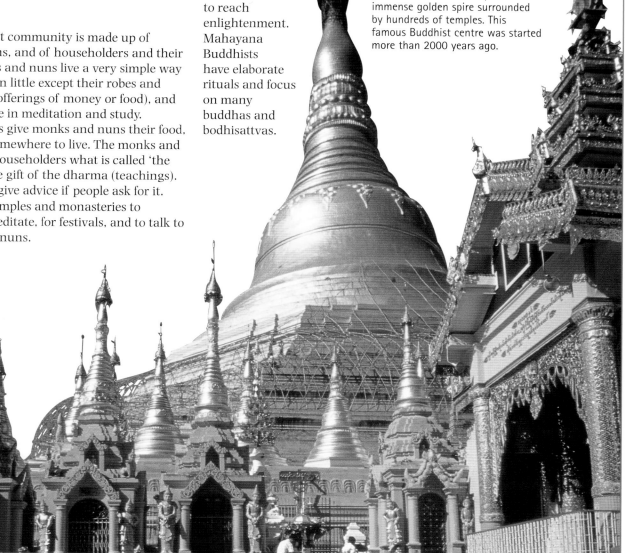

▼ The Shwe Dagon Pagoda in Rangoon, Myanmar's capital, is an immense golden spire surrounded by hundreds of temples. This famous Buddhist centre was started more than 2000 years ago.

Building

Building work uses a wide range of materials. These range from simple ones such as clay and wood, to the steel, glass and concrete used to create the giant multi-storey structures found in modern cities.

There are two main methods of building. One involves constructing walls of a solid material like earth, brick or stone. These are called *load-bearing walls*, and they support the floors and the roof of the building. The other method involves constructing a framework of timber, steel or concrete. The frame bears the load of the floors and often the roof. The framework of timber buildings usually includes the roof structure. The frame can be covered or filled in with material (cladding or infilling), which can be lightweight as it does not carry loads.

• One of the most famous iron buildings of the 19th century was the Crystal Palace in London, which looked like a giant greenhouse. Glass was used to fill the spaces in the framework.

Building a brick house

Before work can begin on building a brick house, a surveyor examines the soil and underlying rocks on the site to decide what foundations will be needed. The surveyor makes a plan of the plot of land to show its size and shape, and the nearest roads and water, gas and electricity supplies. Next, an architect draws a detailed plan showing every wall, door and window with exact measurements and information about the materials to be used. The builders use this to estimate the costs.

During building, an inspector from the local council checks regularly that building regulations are being observed. These regulations make sure the building is well built and safe.

Next, bulldozers level the ground ready for building work. The builders dig trenches where the house walls are to be built and pour concrete into them. The concrete sets hard to make a firm

▼ How a typical single-storey brick house is built.

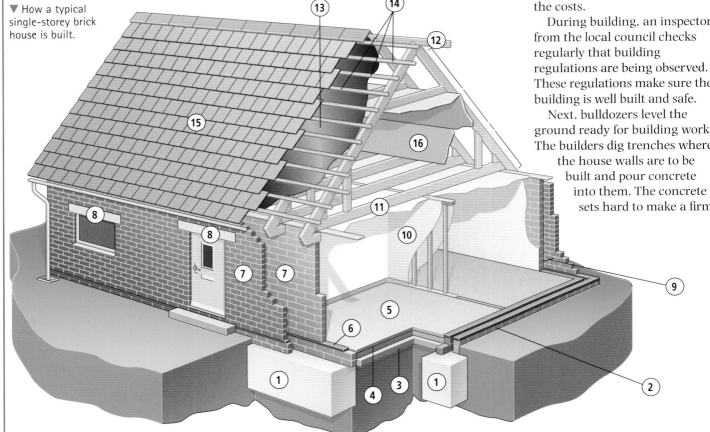

Strong, firm **foundations** (**1**) are needed for a house, to prevent it it sinking into the ground or tilting over. **Footing walls** (**2**) finish level with the ground floor. They support the concrete slab of the ground floor and the structure above. To make the ground floor, **hardcore** (**3**) (broken bits of building material) is spread around the footing walls, and concrete is poured on. A **waterproof membrane** (**4**) (plastic sheet) goes on next, followed by a layer of **concrete flooring** (**5**).

The **damp-proof course** (**6**) prevents moisture from being sucked up the **walls** (**7**) from the earth (rising damp). Steel 'ties' in the mortar hold the inner and outer walls together. Concrete **lintels** (**8**) span the openings of doorways and windows. The **wall cavity** (**9**) keeps out rain and helps to keep the house warm in winter and cool in summer. Inner dividing walls are often made of **plasterboard** (**10**).

The main pieces of the roof framework are triangular **trusses** (**11**). A **ridge piece** (**12**) joins the trusses together at the top. **Waterproof felt** (**13**) covers the timber framework. **Battens** (**14**) (thin strips of timber) are laid on top of the felt, and **tiles** or **slates** (**15**) are nailed to the battens. **Insulating material** (**16**) is laid inside the roof space, to stop heat escaping through the roof.

Building materials

Bricks are moulded from clay and baked in a kiln. *Mortar*, a mixture of sand and cement, is used to stick the bricks together. It sets hard when it dries. The simplest framed buildings are made with a framework of timber (wood). Some Malaysian, Japanese, Chinese and medieval European timber-framed houses are decorated with ornate patterns and carving. Nowadays timber-framing is usually covered with bricks, wooden boards (weatherboarding) or panels. Iron and later steel have been used since the 18th century to make framed buildings. On modern steel-framed buildings, glass can be used as cladding as well as for windows. The concrete used for frames is reinforced with steel to make it stronger.

▲ In many hot countries, bricks are still made from clay in the traditional way. They have to be baked hard in the sun before they can be used for building work.

▲ The timber-framed guildhall at Thaxted in Essex, England, dates from the 15th century.

wide base as foundations for the walls. Once the 'footing' walls have been built on the concrete foundations, the concrete floor is laid, together with a layer of waterproof material, called the damp-proof course (DPC). It separates the foundations from the walls above. As the bricklayers build the walls upwards from the footings, they lay the bricks in horizontal patterns (bonds), overlapping them to prevent weak vertical joins up the face of the wall.

Most houses in wetter climates have a pitched (sloping) roof, so that rainwater runs off easily. As soon as the roof is in position, the carpenters fit the doors and windows and, if the house has more than one storey, the staircase. Plumbers fit the water system and electricians lay wiring for lights and electrical sockets. Plasterers finish the inside walls with a layer of plaster, which is decorated when dry. The new house is finally ready.

Multi-storey buildings

A building with more than five storeys is called a multi-storey

building. Unless there is solid rock just below it, a tall building needs deep foundations to stop it sinking, slipping sideways or being blown over in a gale. Most tall buildings are supported by *piles*. These are often huge steel or reinforced-concrete girders that are hammered deep into the ground.

The core walls of the building are built first. They are made by pouring concrete into wooden casings (shutterings). The core contains the main water and

electrical installations, such as lifts and lavatories. On top of it, at roof level, is the plant room which houses the lift and air-conditioning machinery.

A steel or concrete framework, which supports the concrete floor, is built around the core. Next the cladding panels are bolted on. These can be made of brick, metal (usually steel or aluminium), glass or concrete. Cladding that is bolted onto the outside of the frame is called *curtain walling*.

• Cement is made by burning a mixture of clay and limestone at such high temperatures that it melts. When cool, it forms small lumps, called clinkers, which are ground to a fine grey powder. Cement is mixed with water and crushed stone or sand to make concrete. The wet cement binds all the materials together to make a strong, hard-wearing material.

◄ The framework of huge modern buildings is often made from concrete reinforced with steel rods or bars. You can clearly see the steel rods in this building under construction in Thailand.

find out more
Architecture
Houses
Materials

Bushmen

Bushmen, who are also called San, are a group of people in southern Africa. Most of them live in or near the Kalahari Desert in Botswana and Namibia.

Some San people work on farms, while others are nomads (wanderers). There are probably about 80,000 Bushmen altogether. The nomads live in bands of 25 to 30 people. Each band has its own area. These nomadic groups are hunter-gatherers. They have learned how to survive in harsh desert conditions and can find food and water where there appears to be nothing but sand or scrub.

Bushmen use bows and poison-tipped arrows to kill wild animals. Boys are taught to hunt, and they are not allowed to marry until they have killed one large animal. Other members of the band gather roots, berries, nuts and seeds.

Moving from place to place

The band often needs to move to find food and water. They carry their babies on their backs in leather pouches and carry water in ostrich shells. Their few possessions are light and easy to carry. Sometimes they build semicircular shelters with branches and grass and live in them for several weeks. At night, they often listen to stories told by the older people.

• The Bushmen were probably the first people in southern Africa. They have probably lived there for more than 20,000 years. Rock paintings by ancestors of the Bushmen have been found which are thousands of years old.

find out more
Deserts
Hunter-gatherers
Prehistoric people
South Africa

▼ This Bushwoman has bound a python, caught by members of her tribe, into a tight circle before cooking it in a fire in the sand.

Butterflies and moths

Butterflies and moths are familiar insects which are found almost everywhere in the world. Most butterflies are brightly coloured, day-flying insects, while most moths are active at night and are drab in colour.

Most butterflies and moths live for less than a year. They cannot chew their food. Instead, they use their long, tube-like tongues to suck up liquids, such as the sugary nectar from flowers.

The surface of a butterfly's wings is covered in thousands of tiny scales and is brightly coloured. The underside is often grey and brown. When its wings are folded, it is usually hidden from creatures that might eat it. Moths too are difficult to see when at rest.

Because of their beauty, butterflies have been collected on a vast scale. Some of the big tropical butterflies, such as the morphos from Brazil, have been used as jewellery. Even some of the small European butterflies are in danger of dying out, largely because of the destruction of their habitats and the plants on which their caterpillars feed.

Mating, eggs and caterpillars

Butterflies find and court their mates with a show of colour. Moths use their excellent sense of smell to find a mate. After mating, female butterflies and moths lay batches of eggs on suitable food plants, and then die.

These eggs hatch into caterpillars, which are similar to the maggots or grubs of other insects. Caterpillars spend most of the time feeding. When they have grown big enough, they pupate (enter a resting stage). In the pupa (chrysalis) the butterfly develops and then emerges as an adult.

• There are about 20,000 different kinds of butterfly and about 120,000 different kinds of moth.

• Many butterflies travel long distances on migration. Comma butterflies have flown from the Sahara to northern Europe, a distance of 3000 km, in 14 days.

◄ This monarch butterfly has just emerged from its pupa, and is spreading its wings for the first time.

find out more
Insects
Migration
Silk

Byzantine empire

For over 1000 years, the city of Byzantium was the centre of the eastern Roman empire, the Byzantine empire, and it became one of the largest and richest cities in the world.

Byzantium (now the city of Istanbul in Turkey) was an ancient Greek town which was easy to defend because there was sea on three sides. Constantine the Great, the first Christian emperor of Rome, made it the capital of the whole empire instead of Rome, and in AD 330 he changed its name to Constantinople.

Gains and losses

While the western Roman empire was crumbling, the eastern empire stayed strong. In the 6th century the Byzantine emperor Justinian won back parts of Italy, Spain and North Africa. But from the 7th century the empire was continually being attacked. After attempts by Slavonic tribes and Muslim Arabs failed, Turks from the east succeeded in occupying Palestine in 1071. The emperor appealed to the Christians of western Europe for military help in 1099. The result was the Crusades. The Byzantine empire lasted another 250 years. Finally the Turks captured Constantinople in 1453 and made it the capital of the Ottoman empire.

• In the 6th century, Byzantine emperor Justinian's most lasting achievement was a Code of Roman Law. He had all the laws that had been made over 1000 years put into a single legal system. This is still the basis of the legal system in France, Italy, Scotland and many other countries.

find out more
Christians
Churches
Crusades
Holy Roman Empire
Ottoman empire
Romans

▼ The greatest of all the Byzantine churches was the cathedral of Saint Sophia in Istanbul. The walls are covered in glowing mosaic pictures of stories from the Bible and of famous Byzantine figures. This beautiful mosaic shows Empress Zoe, the most powerful woman in the Byzantine empire.

Caesar, Julius

Julius Caesar was a powerful Roman general with great ambitions. He used his vast army to win a civil war against his political rivals and make himself the sole ruler of the mighty Roman empire.

Born 100 BC in Italy
Murdered 44 BC
aged 55

find out more
Augustus
Cleopatra
Romans

Julius Caesar was born into an important Roman family and soon became a successful politician. He served his time in the army and then held various public offices. In 60 BC he was elected to serve for one year as consul, the highest position in Rome. He was now in charge of the state's administration and the armed forces, although he held power jointly with another consul. He then governed provinces in northern Italy and Gaul (part of modern France).

◄ This painting by Lionel Noel Royer from 1899 uses accounts from Caesar's time to reconstruct a scene in which Vercingetorix, who led a doomed rebellion against Roman rule, surrenders to Caesar.

From there he conquered a vast new area in Gaul and Germany and invaded Britain twice, in 55 and 54 BC.

Caesar was now a very powerful leader with a huge army under his control. He decided not to disband his troops, as he should have done by law, and marched into Italy in 49 BC. Caesar had declared war on the Roman state, and this meant civil war. Pompey the Great fought against Caesar. The war lasted until Caesar's victory in 45 BC, and the next year he was appointed 'dictator for life', making him the sole ruler. However, not everyone wanted to be ruled by one man, and on the day called the Ides of March (15 March) in 44 BC, Caesar was stabbed to death outside the building where the senate (parliament) of Rome met.

Calculators

A calculator is a machine which does arithmetic. We use simple calculators to help us with mathematics at school, or checking bills at home. Scientists, engineers and accountants use more advanced calculators which can do very complicated sums. Today's calculators are electronic ones containing a tiny silicon chip to work out the calculations.

- A shop till is a type of calculator. It adds together prices and prints out a list of them with a total. Most supermarket tills read prices automatically from the barcode printed on each item.

A simple calculator can add and subtract, multiply and divide, and work out percentages. Inside its electronic 'brain', numbers are represented by tiny electric circuits being switched on or off. The 'brain' works using the binary system of numbers, which has only the digits 0 (off) and 1 (on), instead of the digits 0 to 9 in the decimal system. Any number that you enter into the calculator is changed into binary, and calculations in binary are changed back to decimal so that you can see the results in the display.

- A calculator's 'brain' can only add and subtract. It does multiplication and division by doing additions or subtractions over and over again.

▲ This Japanese office worker is using an abacus. It has seven beads on each wire, with a bar that separates off two beads in each row. Sums are done by sliding the beads along the wires.

Types of calculator

Basic pocket calculators can do simple calculations, and have just a few keys. Most have a simple eight-digit display, and a memory for storing numbers. They are powered either by small batteries or by a solar panel. Desktop calculators are larger than pocket calculators. Some are mains-powered and print numbers on a paper roll as well as showing them on the display. Scientific calculators are more complicated calculators which work out mathematical functions or process statistics.

▶ FLASHBACK ◀

The abacus was probably the first calculating device. It was invented over 5000 years ago, and is still used in some countries. Sums are done by sliding wooden beads along wires held in a wooden frame. Beads represent different units, for example 1s, 10s, 100s, and so on.

The first mechanical calculating machines were built in the 17th century. They used levers and gears to carry out calculations, and were not reliable until the 19th century. In the 1830s the Englishman Charles Babbage designed a machine called the Analytical Engine, which was a programmable mechanical calculator. Unfortunately, it was too complicated to be built at the time. In the 1930s and 1940s, scientists in the United States developed large electronic calculating machines. The first desktop electronic calculator became available in 1963, and by the end of the 1970s cheap pocket calculators were commonplace.

- The components inside some pocket calculators are so tiny that they will fit into a credit card-sized case or a wrist-watch.

How a calculator works
When you enter a calculation on the keypad, the two numbers and the operation (add, subtract, multiply, divide) are stored as binary numbers in the calculator's memory registers. The arithmetic unit does the calculation and stores the result in one of the memory registers. The result (the answer) is sent to the display memory, and you read it in decimal form in the display.

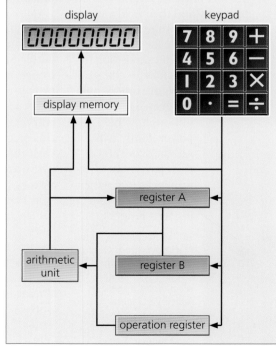

display | keypad

find out more
Arithmetic
Computers
Electronics
Information technology
Numbers

Calendars

A calendar is a way of grouping days so as to help people organize their lives. It is needed for planning farming, business, religion, and domestic life. Western countries use the Gregorian calendar, which was proposed in 1582 by Pope Gregory XIII.

The solar year (the time it takes the Earth to complete its orbit around the Sun) is actually 365 days, 5 hours, 48 minutes and 46 seconds long. The Gregorian calendar is based on the solar year. An extra day, 29 February, is put in the calendar every four years (called *leap years*). This helps to keep the calendar in step with the seasons, but there is still a small difference that adds up over many years.

The word 'month' comes from the name Moon. The Gregorian calendar is divided into 12 months with 30 or 31 days (28 or 29 in February). The Moon actually takes about $29\frac{1}{2}$ days to go through its phases as it orbits the Earth, so the months do not quite keep in step with the Moon's phases.

Other societies and communities use different calendars, often based on the Moon. The Jewish calendar has 12 months of 29 or 30 days. An extra month is put in seven times in a 19-year period. The Islamic calendar has 12 lunar months of 30 or 29 days and does not keep in step with the seasons.

Days of the week

People have organized days into blocks of seven, called weeks, for a very long time. The Romans named the days of the week after the Sun, the Moon and the planets, which were themselves named after the Roman gods. The Anglo-Saxons used their own versions of the names of the Norse gods.

• In the Chinese calendar, each year is named after one of 12 animals: rat, ox, tiger, hare, dragon, snake, horse, sheep, monkey, rooster, dog and pig.

◀ This French lunar calendar dates from 1680. By turning the two wheels and using the table of dates, the Moon's appearance on any given date could be worked out.

• A millennium is a period of 1000 years. 1 January of the year 2000 is the beginning of the third millennium in the Gregorian calendar.

find out more
Festivals and holidays
Seasons
Time

Camels

Camels are the largest animals of the desert. They are well suited to the harsh, waterless environment. For centuries they have been domesticated and used to carry heavy loads long distances across hostile landscapes.

Camels' bodies are adapted to save water in the dry desert.

They do not sweat, and they lose very little moisture in other ways. But most importantly, a camel can go without drinking for long periods, losing up to 40 per cent of its body weight. A camel will replace the liquid it has lost as soon as it reaches water and may drink over 50 litres in one go. A camel's two-toed, broad-padded feet are ideal for walking on loose sand or gravel, and it can close its nostrils against sandstorms.

There are two kinds of camel, and both have been domesticated. The one-humped Arabian camel, from the Middle East, is no longer found in the wild. However, some domesticated ones have been released in parts of the world (such as Africa and Australia) and have become semi-wild. The two-humped Bactrian camel, from the rocky deserts of central Asia, is now rare in the wild.

The llama and its close relative the alpaca are grazing animals from South America. They are related to camels, although they have no hump. They are valued for their long, fine wool. Llamas are also used to carry heavy loads in high mountain areas.

◀ The Bactrian camel has quite long, shaggy fur which helps keep it warm in the extreme conditions in which it lives in the wild.

• There are six members of the camel family: the Arabian camel, the Bactrian camel, the llama, the alpaca, the guanaco, and the vicuña.

• Camels' humps do not contain water but fat, which is used up in times of hardship.

◀ The Arabian camel has longer legs and is not as heavily built as the Bactrian camel.

find out more
Deserts
Mammals

Calvin, John *see* Reformation • **Cambodia** *see page 617*

Cameras

We use cameras to take photographs or record moving pictures. Cameras which make photographs range from disposable ones that fit inside your pocket, to the single-lens reflex cameras used by keen amateur and professional photographers. Other cameras, such as cine-cameras and camcorders, are used to re-create a moving scene.

- Infrared cameras make pictures in the dark using the heat radiation given off by, for example, the bodies of animals.

- Digital cameras have no film. The picture is recorded by a special microchip and can then be viewed on a computer screen.

To take a good photograph, the camera must let just the right amount of light hit the film. This is called the correct *exposure*. Most cameras have an *aperture* (opening) which changes in size to let more or less light through the lens.

Types of camera

All-plastic disposable cameras are the simplest and cheapest type of camera. The more sophisticated compact cameras have automatic focusing (autofocus), automatic exposure, motorized film wind-on, and an automatic flash unit. A zoom lens allows you to pick out a smaller or wider section of a scene.

Whatever you see in the *viewfinder* when taking a photograph appears in the final picture. Compact cameras have a viewfinder close to the lens, but in a single-lens reflex (SLR) camera you look through the lens itself.

Cine-cameras, TV and video cameras

A cine-camera takes 24 pictures (called frames) every second on a long strip of film. When the developed film is projected, the frames appear quickly one after the other.

TV cameras change the picture into electrical signals. With video cameras and camcorders the pictures are stored or handled electronically.

▶ FLASHBACK ◀

The first proper camera was built by Frenchman Joseph Niepce in 1826. It was a wooden box with a lens on the front. Another Frenchman, Louis Daguerre, invented the first practical camera in the 1830s. Inside the camera, the image fell on a plate coated with a chemical. In sunlight, the light part of the picture became dark and the darker parts were left lighter, making a negative picture. A few years later an Englishman, William Fox Talbot, discovered how to make multiple positive prints on paper from a negative (we use this same idea today).

In 1888, American George Eastman introduced the first Kodak camera, which used a roll of flexible film. Small cameras with interchangeable lenses were introduced in the 1920s, and cameras with electronic autofocus and automatic exposure in the 1970s.

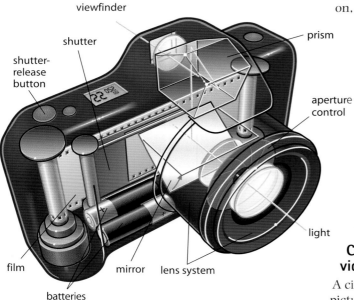

▲ The main parts of a single-lens reflex (SLR) camera.

viewfinder · shutter · shutter-release button · prism · aperture control · light · film · mirror · lens system · batteries

A camera's sturdy lightproof body protects the delicate parts inside, and stops light getting to the film. When you take a photograph, a *shutter* opens for a split second to let light hit the film. The *lens* collects light and focuses it on the film inside to make a small picture, or image. In most cameras the lens can be adjusted to make a sharp and clear image on the film. This is called *focusing*. Light-sensitive chemicals in the film record the image. Later, the film is processed to produce the finished photograph.

find out more
Photography
X-rays

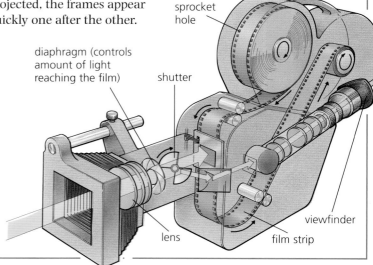

▼ The main parts of a cine-camera (movie camera).

sprocket hole · diaphragm (controls amount of light reaching the film) · shutter · lens · viewfinder · film strip

Camouflage

Most kinds of wild animal are hard to see because they are camouflaged – coloured or shaped to match the places in which they live. Their camouflage is a source of protection because they cannot easily be seen by animals that hunt them.

Hunters in turn need camouflage, both for protection against animals that hunt them and so that they remain unseen as they close in on their prey.

Countershading, where an animal's back is darker than its underside, is a form of camouflage that almost every animal has. Stronger light falling on the animal's back makes its rounded body appear to be all one colour and flat. It is then harder to see.

Some animals have *disruptive coloration* – their skin or fur is broken up by spots or stripes. This helps them merge into the dappled light around them. They may also have a *disruptive shape* – the outline of their body is broken up with spines or flaps of skin, making them difficult to see. These bits may be shaped and coloured to look like leaves or thorns on a plant.

Some camouflage copies the patterns and colours of animals that taste unpleasant or have a sting. For instance, harmless hoverflies look like wasps, which scares away hunters such as dragonflies.

Although camouflage is vitally important, it is not enough. Stillness and silence are part of the trick of not being seen.

find out more
Animal behaviour
Food chains and webs
Lizards

◀ Some of the most effective camouflage is found in tropical rainforests. This leaf-imitating insect in the Costa Rican rainforest is very hard to tell apart from the real thing.

Camping

Camping involves living and sleeping in a tent or caravan, rather than in a house or other permanent building.

For some people, living in tents is a way of life. Tents are used as homes by Mongolian nomads (wandering people) and by the Bedouin in the Middle East and North Africa. They were also used by ancient civilizations such as the Assyrians.

Recreational camping

Camping for pleasure is called recreational camping. This includes family camping holidays and camps organized for young people by school and youth organizations, such as the Guides and Scouts.

Most family camping holidays are based on organized campsites, which hire land for camping and provide shopping, washing and toilet facilities. Some families may own or hire a large *frame tent*, which can be packed and moved by car or trailer. Many people prefer to use *caravans*, especially in Europe and North America. These have many of the features of home, including a toilet, carefully fitted into the small space available.

Camping in which people tour on foot, carrying their accommodation and food with them, is called *backpacking*. This usually involves moving every day to a new location. Light, compact equipment is needed, including a small tent and a sleeping bag. When backpacking in remote regions, it is important to carry enough food and water, a torch, a good map and a compass.

• As well as for recreational camping, tents are used for a wide variety of other purposes: by the armed forces, for example, and by explorers. Large tents used for weddings and exhibitions are called *marquees*.

◀ A campsite at night, showing a frame tent (left) and two ridge tents.

find out more
Gypsies
Houses
Youth organizations

Canada

Canada is the world's second largest country. It stretches 5000 kilometres from the Pacific Ocean to the Atlantic Ocean and almost the same distance from near the North Pole to half-way to the Equator.

Even though Canada is so vast, most people live in the south-east, near the border with the USA. Much of the rest of Canada is unpopulated. The north is covered in snow and ice, the high Rocky Mountains, though tree-covered, are mostly home to wildlife, and the interior plains where wheat is grown are sparsely inhabited by ranchers.

Settlement

Three out of every four Canadians live in cities. Along the Atlantic and Pacific coasts, cities with safe harbours flourish. The largest of these on the

▲ Snowploughs and trucks clear the roads in snow-bound Ottawa, Canada.

Atlantic, Halifax, began as a British naval base. Vancouver on the Pacific grew as the port at the western end of Canada's first continental railroad.

Between the coasts, cities are strung along railroads, highways and the Great Lakes–St Lawrence Seaway in the south. Half of Canada's population and most of its large cities are found along this water system.

• Snow covers much of Canada from November until April. Sometimes a midwinter warm spell melts the snow, but then more replaces it. In the country people ski and skate and travel over frozen lakes on snowmobiles, a Canadian invention similar to a motorcycle. Summers are generally warm.

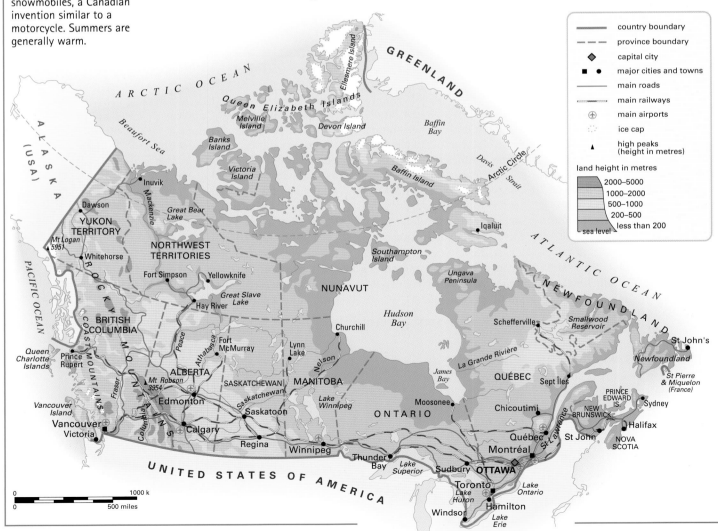

Map legend:
- country boundary
- province boundary
- ◆ capital city
- ■ ● major cities and towns
- main roads
- main railways
- ⊕ main airports
- ice cap
- ▲ high peaks (height in metres)

land height in metres
- 2000–5000
- 1000–2000
- 500–1000
- 200–500
- sea level — less than 200

0 — 1000 k
0 — 500 miles

Resources

Canada is very rich in farmland, forest and minerals, and has one of the world's largest developments of hydroelectricity. It exports wheat and other grains, timber and paper, and zinc, gold, nickel and platinum. There are huge deposits of oil, natural gas and coal.

Canada's forest-product industries employ many thousands of workers; and it manufactures aluminium products for the North American aircraft industry.

People and culture

Most Canadians speak one of Canada's two official languages, French or English. Most of Canada's 500,000 native people speak one of 11 native languages and English or French, which they learn in school. Canadians who are half French and half Native American are known as métis, and have separate lands and a separate culture. Both English and French are widely used, French especially in Québec Province. However, there are tensions between the two cultures. Many French Canadians want Québec to leave Canada and become an independent country. The new Inuit territory of Nunavut was founded April 1 1999 and now occupies part of what used to be the Northwest Territory.

Canada's history

The original Canadians emigrated from Asia during the Ice Age at least 25,000 years ago. Many bands of people crossed what is now the Bering Sea, when sea levels were lower. The Inuit of Canada, whom Europeans once called Eskimos, arrived 4000 years ago along the Arctic coast. The Native Americans here have many distinct language and cultural groups. The Haida of the west coast are known for their totem poles; the Ojibway perfected the birch-bark canoe; and the Cree invented the toboggan.

European settlement

In 1497 John Cabot, an Italian navigator who had settled in England, landed in Nova Scotia. He explored the St Lawrence estuary and claimed the area for the king of England. British colonists settled in the warmer lands to the south. In the 17th century the French sent 10,000 settlers to the St Lawrence River to farm and trade for fur. The Native Americans helped the French fur traders and became their partners.

In the 18th century the French and English fought over these valuable lands. The British gained control after the capture of the city of

Québec in 1759, although the French were given rights of language and education. When the USA became independent, thousands of Britain's supporters fled to Canada, including some slaves. Canada outlawed slavery in 1834 and runaway slaves continued to escape to Canada from the USA for almost 30 years.

New Canadians

Canadians were afraid that the USA might try to take them over. As a result, several of the biggest colonies formed the Dominion of Canada in 1867. Each colony became a province. The new country purchased land and planned a cross-continental railroad. As the number of settlers increased and moved westwards, new provinces were founded.

At first most immigrants to Canada came from Britain, but settlers from eastern and northern Europe followed. To begin with they found low-paying jobs on the wheat farms of the prairies and in the timber industries. Gradually they sought better jobs in the cities. In the 1960s many arrived to do construction work, but started their own businesses. Today most immigrants are from Asia and the Caribbean.

▲ Peyto Lake in Banff National Park, Alberta, Canada. Established in 1885 as Canada's first national park, Banff is situated on the eastern slopes of the Rocky Mountains.

find out more
British empire
France
Inuit
North America
United States of America
See also Countries fact file, page 618

▼ Upper Fort Garry, Hudson Bay, on the east coast of Canada, in 1845. Hudson Bay was discovered by the English explorer Henry Hudson in 1610. It became the site of the company that dominated the early economy of Canada.

Canals

Most canals have been built for use by boats moving heavy loads. Other canals are built for irrigation or drainage. In the past 100 years, ship canals have been built to join seas and oceans. Today, canals are still used to transport enormous loads, as well as for boating holidays.

- Thomas Telford (1757–1834) was famous for his canal-building, which included England's Ellesmere Canal, the Caledonian Canal in the Scottish Highlands, and the Göta Canal in Sweden.

▲ Barges carrying goods along a stretch of China's Grand Canal. Work on the canal began in the 6th century BC and continued over hundreds of years. Today, the canal is 1794 km long.

- The horses that pulled narrow boats along canals could not pass through small tunnels, which were usually built without towpaths. Members of the crew had to lie on their backs on the top of the boat and 'leg' their way through by pushing with their feet on the tunnel roof.

find out more
Georgian Britain
Industrial Revolution
Ships and boats

Canals are usually built in places where there is no river, or where rivers flow too fast or are too narrow and winding for boats. The long thin boats that were used to carry large loads on the canals are called *narrow boats*. The early ones were pulled by horses led along the canal towpath, but narrow boats were later motorized. On wider waterways, large barges are used, some of them pushed or pulled by tugs. Some tow boats can pull up to 50 barges at a time carrying very heavy

▶ The Miraflores Locks, one of three sets of enormous locks along the Panama Canal. Completed in 1914, the canal allows ships to go from the Atlantic and Caribbean to the Pacific without travelling around the continent of South America.

loads. This is such an economical form of transport that canals and waterways are likely to be used extensively in the 21st century.

Different types of canal

Huge ship canals that join seas and oceans have dramatically reduced the time taken by ships to travel around the world. The Suez Canal links the Mediterranean and the Red Sea, allowing ships to travel from Europe to India and the East without having to sail around Africa.

Other canals link rivers and lakes. In North America, the St Lawrence Seaway allows large ships to reach Lake Ontario from Lake Erie and so opens up 3830 kilometres of waterway, from the west of Lake Superior to the Atlantic. In Europe, an extensive network of canals connects the Rhine and the Rhône and other main rivers. This means that large

loads can be transported long distances and across national borders throughout the continent.

Locks

Canals cannot go up or down slopes. So, where a canal passes through hilly country, a series of locks is needed. A lock is a section of canal with watertight gates at each end. The water outside the two gates is at different levels. By altering the water level inside the lock, boats and ships can move from one water level to another. In this type of lock, which is called a *pound lock*, a boat can be raised or lowered by up to 9 metres.

▶ FLASHBACK ◀

Irrigation canals have been built since at least 3000 BC. The Romans built canal systems for military transport throughout northern Europe. In the 13th and 14th centuries drainage canals were adapted to carry boat traffic in the Netherlands. In the 17th century several important canals were constructed in France. In the UK, canal building started in about 1750 with Brindley's Bridgewater Canal in Lancashire.

Cancer

find out more
Diseases
Smoking

• Lung cancer is usually caused by tobacco smoke. It is most likely to develop in a person who smokes, but it can also develop in a person who regularly breathes in other people's smoke ('passive' smoking).

▶ Medical treatment for cancer can have unpleasant 'side-effects', such as hair loss and nausea (a feeling of sickness). This cancer patient is being given a special drug that reduces the nausea, enabling him to lead a fairly normal life while he undergoes chemotherapy.

Cancer is the name given to a number of serious diseases. They happen when cells in the body increase rapidly and form a swelling called a tumour. Sometimes cells break off the tumour, spreading the cancer to a different place in the body.

There are many types of cancer and many different causes. Some kinds are caused by chemicals, viruses or radiation (invisible rays of energy). For example, leukaemia – cancer of the

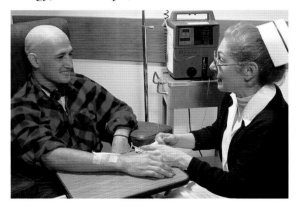

bone marrow – can be caused by exposure to radiation. Cancer of the skin, called melanoma, may develop if a person spends too much time in the sun, without protection. Cancer can be inherited. It may also be related to psychological stress. In richer countries of the world cancer is one of the main causes of death. Some cases of cancer could be prevented if people stopped smoking, exercised more and ate healthier food.

Many cancers can be cured, especially if they are found early enough. Often a tumour can be removed by a surgeon. Chemotherapy (drug treatment) may be successful. Radiotherapy, where special rays (gamma rays) are directed at the tumour, can also cure it. Anti-cancer drugs may cause hair loss, but the hair grows again when the treatment stops.

There are examinations for people who have a higher risk than average of developing certain cancers. Women can be checked for early signs of breast cancer or cancer of the cervix (neck of the womb). Men can be tested for cancer of the prostate gland (part of the reproductive system). Anyone who has been cured of cancer has regular check-ups to make sure that cancer is not developing again.

Carbon

Carbon is an element found in countless different things. It is the black material you see on burnt wood or toast. Plants and animals are mainly made from materials containing carbon. Other things with carbon in them include vinegar, alcohol, plastics and disinfectants.

Pure carbon can exist in three very different forms: graphite, the black material used as the 'lead' in pencils; diamond, which is the hardest substance known; and a newly discovered group of materials called the fullerenes. Although all of these forms are made up only of carbon, the carbon atoms are arranged differently, so they look different and have different properties.

When foods and fuels are burnt, the carbon in them combines with oxygen to form a gas called *carbon dioxide*. When carbon combines with hydrogen, it forms a family of materials called *hydrocarbons*. These include natural gas, petrol, paraffin and diesel oil. Carbon also combines with hydrogen and oxygen to form foods like sugar and starch. These are called *carbohydrates*.

▼ Carbon is used again and again in a process called the *carbon cycle*. Plants take in carbon dioxide from the air through their leaves. Carbon is then transferred to animals, which release it back into the air as they breathe. When plants and animals die their bodies decompose (rot). Over millions of years they form fossil fuels, which we can burn as a source of energy.

find out more
Coal
Diamonds
Elements
Greenhouse effect
Oil
Plants

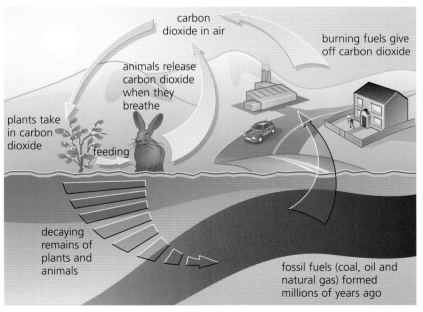

carbon dioxide in air

burning fuels give off carbon dioxide

animals release carbon dioxide when they breathe

plants take in carbon dioxide

feeding

decaying remains of plants and animals

fossil fuels (coal, oil and natural gas) formed millions of years ago

Caribbean

The Caribbean Sea stretches over 3000 kilometres from the coast of Central America to Trinidad and Barbados. The Caribbean also includes all the islands around the sea, the Caribbean coastlands of Central and South America, and the countries of Guyana, Suriname and French Guiana. These do not touch the Caribbean Sea but have links with the island chain.

• Because of the history of colonization, when many of the Caribbean islands were settled by Europeans, a variety of languages is spoken. They include Spanish, French, Creole, Dutch, English and a language called Papiamento.

▼ The islands of the Caribbean are sometimes called the West Indies.

Some of the islands are very large. Cuba, the largest, is over 1100 kilometres long, and has a population of over 10 million. There are more than 20 independent or self-governing countries in the region, and hundreds of smaller islands, many of which are so small that no one lives on them. Some islands are built up from coral reefs, and are so flat that they hardly rise above the sea. Others have steep-sided mountains, 2000–3000 metres high, covered with thick rainforest. Many of these mountains are volcanoes, some of which are still active.

Climate

The Caribbean has a warm, tropical climate, but the islands and coasts are cooled by breezes

▲ The land on Antigua, one of the Leeward Islands, is not so good for farming, but there are beautiful sandy beaches. More than 100,000 tourists visit the island every year.

from the sea. In the mountains it is quite cool. Rainfall is heavy, but comes in short, violent showers, so there is plenty of sunshine too. Most rain falls from June to November. From February to April, it can be very dry. There is much more rainfall in the mountains than on the coast. Occasionally, during the rainy season, there is a violent storm known as a hurricane. Hurricanes can cause very serious damage.

Life and work

Many tropical crops thrive in the Caribbean climate. Sugar cane, bananas, coffee, spices and cocoa are all grown for export. There are few minerals or energy resources, except for some bauxite and a little oil and natural gas. (Bauxite, from which aluminium is made, is mined in some islands.) Many factories have been set up and farming has been modernized. Tourism and banking are important in many places.

There is now a strong North American influence on the Caribbean way of life. Many people have relatives in the USA and Canada, travel

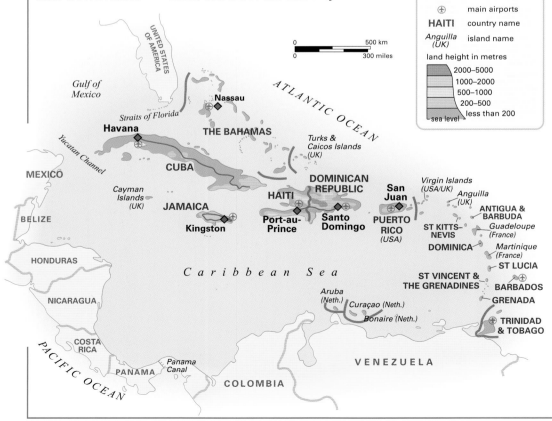

——	country boundary
◆	capital city
——	main roads
⊕	main airports
HAITI	country name
Anguilla (UK)	island name

land height in metres

	2000–5000
	1000–2000
	500–1000
	200–500
	less than 200
	sea level

0 500 km
0 300 miles

UNITED STATES OF AMERICA

Gulf of Mexico

ATLANTIC OCEAN

Nassau

Straits of Florida

Havana

THE BAHAMAS

Turks & Caicos Islands (UK)

Yucatan Channel

CUBA

MEXICO

Cayman Islands (UK)

DOMINICAN REPUBLIC

San Juan

Virgin Islands (USA/UK)

Anguilla (UK)

JAMAICA

HAITI

ANTIGUA & BARBUDA

BELIZE

Kingston

Port-au-Prince

Santo Domingo

PUERTO RICO (USA)

ST KITTS–NEVIS

Guadeloupe (France)

DOMINICA

Martinique (France)

ST LUCIA

HONDURAS

Caribbean Sea

ST VINCENT & THE GRENADINES

BARBADOS

NICARAGUA

Aruba (Neth.)

Curaçao (Neth.)

GRENADA

Bonaire (Neth.)

TRINIDAD & TOBAGO

COSTA RICA

PACIFIC OCEAN

Panama Canal

PANAMA

COLOMBIA

VENEZUELA

there to study or on holiday, and watch American TV programmes. However, many people in the Caribbean are also now placing much more emphasis on their own culture and identity.

Caribbean history

Five hundred years ago the Caribbean islands were home for two groups of Native Americans, the Arawaks and the Caribs. Up to 50 Arawak or Carib families lived with their chief in a village. Every few years they moved their thatched huts and their sleeping hammocks to a new place for farming. The Arawaks lived mostly in the western islands. The Caribs lived on the South American mainland and in the eastern Caribbean.

European empires

In 1492 Christopher Columbus sailed into the Caribbean from Spain. He hoped he had sailed around the world to the East Indian islands. Other explorers recognized that these were different islands, which they named the West Indies. The

◀ Toussaint l'Ouverture was the most famous leader of the black armies who fought against the French in St Dominique. In 1804, renamed Haiti, the island became the first independent black country in the Caribbean.

Spanish built up an empire in the Caribbean and the Americas. Many Arawaks died in fighting or from European diseases.

French, Dutch and English sailors began to raid the Spanish empire and captured many islands, especially in the Caribbean. There were many wars between the settlers and the Caribs. Today, only a few people on the smaller islands have Carib ancestors.

Slave life

Over a period of about 200 years, about 5 million men, women and children were brought from West Africa and sold as slaves to sugar and tobacco plantations.

As time went on, the African traditions they brought with them combined with the ways of the Europeans. Many Caribbean people today speak Creole languages with French or English words and mainly African grammar. Music and dance forms combine African and Caribbean traditions.

Slavery did not completely end in British colonies until 1838. Slavery lasted in the French islands (Martinique and Guadeloupe) until 1848, and in the Spanish islands (Cuba and Puerto Rico) until 1886. After slavery was abolished the British and Dutch hired workers from India to work on plantations in Trinidad, Guyana and Suriname, where their descendants are known as 'East Indians'.

Independence

Although most ex-slaves left the plantations to find work or set up businesses on their own, Europeans kept the best land and did little to see that black people had jobs, schools or health care. Some people had to emigrate to find work. Many West Indians went to the USA, Canada or Europe.

In the 1920s and 1930s, most people in the Caribbean were still desperately poor. Trade unions and political parties were formed to press for better conditions and, later, for independence. Jamaica, and Trinidad and Tobago, achieved independence in 1962. Suriname became independent in 1975. Most of the former British colonies are now independent countries, but the French islands are governed as if they were districts of France. Puerto Rico, once a Spanish colony, is linked to the USA.

▲ Grenada, St Vincent, St Lucia and Dominica are known as the Windward Islands. Bananas have been an important export crop on these islands for a long time. The workers at this banana plantation are washing and sorting banana bunches.

• Marcus Garvey, a black rights campaigner from Jamaica, tried to bring together the people who had left the Caribbean. He wanted to unite them as members of a single nation with its roots in Africa. In 1914 he started his Universal Negro Improvement Association and he inspired many black people to work towards independence.

• The independent states of the Caribbean have individual entries in the Countries fact file, pages 613–645.

find out more
Africa
British empire
Columbus, Christopher
Slaves
South America

Carroll, Lewis

Born 1832 in Cheshire, England
Died 1898 aged 65

Famous characters in Lewis Carroll's books
The Mad Hatter
The Queen of Hearts
The Duchess
The Cheshire Cat
Tweedledum and
  Tweedledee
The Walrus and the
  Carpenter
The Jabberwock

find out more
Stories and story-tellers

Lewis Carroll was the author of two classic children's stories – *Alice's Adventures in Wonderland* and *Through the Looking-Glass*.

Lewis Carroll's real name was Charles Dodgson. He was the third child in a family of 11, and he and his brothers and sisters spent a lot of time playing literary games and making up puzzles and word-games.

Carroll worked as a mathematics teacher at Oxford University and made friends with the Dean of Christ Church College. He used to entertain the Dean's eldest daughters – Alice, Lorina and Edith – by making up amazing stories. One day in 1862, while on a river trip with the three girls, Carroll made up the story of a girl called Alice who had fantastic adventures when she went underground. The girls loved it and Alice asked him to write it down. Other people read it and urged him to get it published. *Alice's Adventures in Wonderland* first appeared in 1865, and the sequel, *Through the Looking-Glass*, was published in 1872.

Carroll's amazing adventure stories are unique. Strange, often nonsensical, things happen in them, often for no particular reason, but they somehow seem to make sense. Nothing like them had been published for children before and they became huge successes.

▼ This illustration from *Alice's Adventures in Wonderland* shows the Duchess advising Alice on how to play croquet using a flamingo as a croquet mallet.

Cartoons

• The original meaning of the word 'cartoon' is a drawing used as a pattern for a painting, tapestry or stained-glass window.

find out more
Animation
Disney, Walt
Drawing

▶ 'Peanuts' by Charles Schulz first appeared in the USA in 1950. It is the most popular cartoon in the world, and has appeared in more than 2000 newspapers in 68 countries, in 26 different languages.

Cartoons are drawn to amuse people. Some cartoons make a joke in a single frame (one drawing). A strip cartoon uses several frames to tell a funny story. Most cartoons also have words to accompany them.

Single-frame cartoons have been used since the 18th century to poke fun at politicians or to highlight social problems.

Single-frame cartoons that are simply meant to be funny became very popular in the 20th century. This popularity spread from the magazine *The New Yorker* in the USA to other magazines and newspapers all over the world. Today most national newspapers include this sort of amusing cartoon as well as political or social cartoons. The first strip cartoon, 'The Yellow Kid', appeared in a newspaper in the USA in 1896. It was enjoyed by many, and others like it soon followed.

Comics use many frames to tell a story. What the people say is written in speech bubbles next to the speaker's mouth. Sometimes the action is described at the bottom of each frame. A lot of comics have a superhero as the main character. One of the most popular is Superman, who was created in 1938. Other favourite comics include *Spider-Man* and, in Britain, the *Beano*.

Castles

Castles are strong buildings, or groups of buildings, that were designed to protect the people who lived in them from attack. They were usually the homes of chieftains, kings or knights.

• The word 'castle' comes from the Latin *castellum*, which means 'a little fort'. The word 'fort' comes from the French word for 'strong'. Forts are usually built as soldiers' headquarters. The Romans built forts for their armies and strong walls to protect their towns.

find out more
Crusades
Knights
Middle Ages
Normans
Weapons

Most castles date from the Middle Ages and were built in Europe. Asian countries such as China, India and Thailand have their own strongholds, but these are usually known as *forts*. They are often not strong in themselves but are protected by strong walls.

The first true castles were built in 10th-century France. Many started as a simple wooden tower (*keep*), built on a high mound (*motte*) and encircled by a wall made of earth or wood. There was sometimes a surrounding ditch filled with water, called a *moat*. Builders often put up fences round the foot of the mound. The area between the fence and the wall formed a yard known as a ward or bailey. Such castles are called *motte-and-bailey* castles.

Motte-and-bailey castles were very popular with the Normans, and during the 11th century they became common all over western Europe. In many places builders remade the keeps and outer walls in stone. This was to stop attackers from setting fire to them. Baileys became bigger too, so that more buildings could be added.

Builders constantly thought of ways to make their castles safer from attack. After 1100 European builders got many ideas from the crusaders, who had seen the mighty fortresses of their Arab enemies. They made the outer walls much thicker, usually with a second wall inside. Along the top was a walkway for the soldiers to patrol. A wall called a *battlement* ran along the walkway. It protected the patrols, but it also had openings in it so that attackers could be fired upon. Towers guarded each section of the wall. The *drawbridge* at the main gateway was the first thing to be raised in case of attack. Stables, gardens, kitchens and a chapel were often built inside the bailey.

Enemy attempts to capture castles were called *sieges*. It was possible to fire arrows at the attackers through narrow slits in the walls or through the gaps in the battlements. If they came closer, the defenders could drop heavy objects on them or pour hot oil through holes beneath the battlements.

The arrival of gunpowder in Europe in the 15th century meant that castles could be attacked and conquered much more easily. They were still built, but not to stand up to sieges. Many look powerful, but some are just light-hearted reminders of the medieval past.

▶ A cut-away illustration of a medieval European castle. Inside the keep were rooms for eating and sleeping, and storerooms for keeping supplies. The great walls around the castle protected the people inside from attack. Inside the walls was the yard or bailey, which often had gardens for growing food and stables for keeping animals.

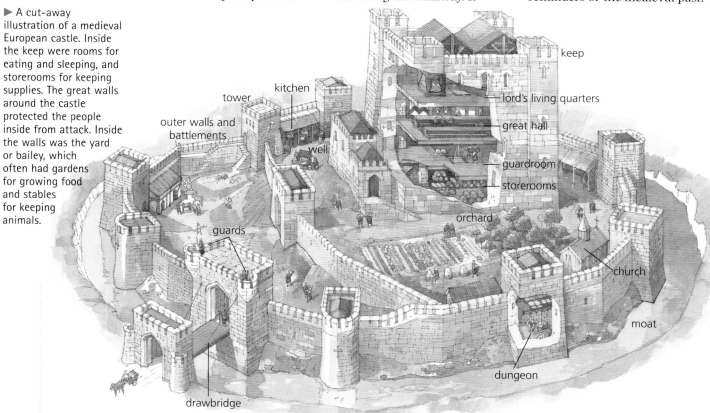

tower · kitchen · keep · lord's living quarters · outer walls and battlements · well · great hall · guardroom · storerooms · orchard · church · guards · moat · dungeon · drawbridge

Cats

The cat family includes wild cats such as lions, tigers, leopards and cheetahs, and domestic cats that people keep in their homes as pets.

serval

Cats are supreme hunters. Their diet consists mainly of meat, so wild cats must kill to survive. Most cats are very fast over a short distance, but they give up if their prey runs too far. They have lithe bodies and strong legs with padded feet that enable them to move silently. Their eyesight is also good, and many of them hunt at night or when the light is dim. Their eyes are large and look forward, rather than seeing all round.

Cats have an excellent sense of hearing, and the long whiskers growing around their face also help them to sense their surroundings. If their whiskers are touched, even very lightly, cats are aware of it. This not only enables them to avoid bumping into things at night, but they may be able to feel the disturbance of the air if their prey makes a dash for safety.

Most cats use their strong and sharp claws to catch their prey. All cats except cheetahs can retract (pull in) their claws, so they do not become worn and blunt when they walk.

- There are 37 kinds of wild cat. The lion, tiger, jaguar, leopard and snow leopard are known as 'big cats'. Smaller wild cats include the lynx from Europe, Asia and North America, the ocelot from Central and South America, and the serval from Africa.

▼ Tigers are protected animals but they are often killed illegally, even in nature reserves. Unless this killing is stopped, it is likely that there will be no tigers left in the wild by the early 21st century.

▲ A lion eating a zebra that it has killed. An adult male lion may eat 40 kilograms of meat in a single meal, but then he will probably not feed again for several days.

Lions

Lions live in grassland or scrub country. A few hundred remain in one reserve in India; the rest live in Africa. Unlike most members of the cat family, lions live in groups, called prides. A pride usually consists of about a dozen animals. At least two of them are adult males, the rest females and their cubs. The females in a pride are usually sisters, and remain together all their lives. The males rarely stay with the same pride for more than three years.

The lionesses do most of the hunting. Sometimes two or more work together to stalk an antelope or zebra, which are their main food. However, although the females may make the kill, the males usually feed first.

Tigers

Tigers are big cats that live in forested areas. At one time they were found throughout much of eastern and southern Asia, but now they survive mainly in India, Sumatra and Siberia.

Male tigers live alone in large territories, although these may overlap the living areas of several females. They are chiefly active at twilight or at night, using their sight and sense of hearing to stalk their prey. They may travel up to 20 kilometres in a night and can leap as far as 10 metres in a single bound. They are good swimmers and can climb quite well. Their main food is large mammals such as wild pigs, buffalo and deer.

Leopards and cheetahs

Leopards live in much of Africa and Asia, in forests, grasslands and even deserts. They usually live alone and defend their territories from others. They climb trees very well and often rest up in the branches. They also hide the remains of their meals in trees, out of reach of most scavengers. They mainly hunt medium-sized grazing animals such as small antelopes and pigs, but will resort to smaller prey, even insects.

▼ The cheetah is now a protected animal. The main threat to its existence is the destruction of its natural home and the prey it finds there.

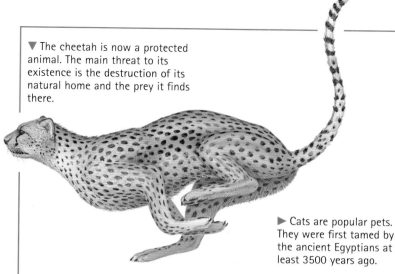

▶ Cats are popular pets. They were first tamed by the ancient Egyptians at least 3500 years ago.

Cheetahs usually live in small groups on grassy plains in eastern and southern Africa. They are able to hunt in the daytime because they can run faster than any other animal, reaching up to 100 kilometres per hour. But they cannot keep this speed up for long, and an average chase lasts for less than half a minute. They usually hunt small antelopes or the young of some larger animals. A cheetah's claws are blunt, so it kills its prey by knocking it off balance and then throttling it.

Jaguars and pumas

The jaguar's beautiful blotched coat camouflages it in the South American forests, where it is usually found. Jaguars live alone in large territories. They are active mainly at night, when they hunt large ground prey such as peccaries, capybaras and tapirs. They are good swimmers and sometimes feed on fish. They occasionally even catch crocodiles.

Pumas (also known as cougars or mountain lions) live in remote parts of North and South America. They live alone and do not have fixed dens; instead they travel through their territory, usually over 30 square kilometres. They have very good eyesight and hearing, but their sense of smell is poor. They have powerful hind legs, and it is said that they can leap upwards more than 5 metres. Their main prey is deer, usually sick or old ones. They make about one kill a week, and drag the carcass to a safe place to be eaten over several days.

Cats in danger

Many of the world's wild cats are now close to dying out. This is partly because of the destruction of their habitat. Also, some cats are hunted because they have attacked domestic animals or even humans, and others are killed by hunters. Many are killed, however, for their beautiful, thick, soft fur, which is often patterned with spots or stripes. The fur is highly prized for making coats or even rugs. Today many cats are protected by law in most parts of the world.

• There are over 500 million domestic cats around the world.

find out more
Ecology
Grasslands
Mammals
Pets

▼ Pumas rarely attack domestic animals. Even so many are shot by farmers and cattle-herders.

▲ The number of jaguars in the world today is very low because of hunting and forest clearance by humans.

Record-breaking cats
Largest
Lions, shoulder height up to 1.2 m
Largest domestic breed
Ragdoll, males weigh up to 9 kg
Smallest domestic breed
Singapura, males weigh up to 2.7 kg, females up to 1.8 kg
Fastest
Cheetah, up to 100 km per hour

Cattle

Cattle include a number of large plant-eating animals such as cows, buffaloes and bison. A few kinds of cattle are still found in the wild, but most live as farm animals and are a vital source of milk, meat and leather.

There are several different kinds of wild cattle, including yaks, bison and buffaloes. Many live in forested areas where they can find plenty of food and safe, shady places to rest. However, some, such as yaks, live in high mountain areas of the Himalayas. Others, such as American bison, live on vast plains where they graze on the plentiful grass.

Cattle are social animals and live in groups led by a bull. Both the males and females have horns. They are straight or curved and last all through the animal's life. The horns of water buffalo are bigger than those of any other animal.

Cattle are now very rare in the wild, largely as a result of human hunting, but they are common as farm animals. Most farm cattle are descended from the aurochs, which once roamed Europe but became extinct about 350 years ago. Today there are about 200 different domestic breeds. They are mostly bred for their milk, meat and leather. However, some are also used for pulling ploughs and heavy loads. Cattle droppings can be used as fertilizer, and sometimes they are dried out and used as fuel on fires. Some cultures also use cattle as a measure of wealth: the more cattle a person has, the richer they are.

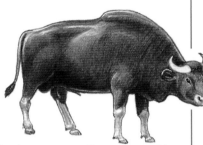

▲ Domestic cattle, such as the Friesian (left), look quite different from wild cattle, such as the gaur of South-east Asia (right).

- Cattle digest their food using a complex, four-chambered stomach. They are known as ruminants, as are antelopes, sheep, deer and giraffes. All these animals re-chew food that has been swallowed and then brought back into the mouth. This process is known as 'chewing the cud'.

- There are 12 different kinds (species) of cattle.

find out more
Digestive systems
Farming
Mammals
Milk

Caves

The most spectacular caves in the world are found in areas with lots of limestone, such as the Carlsbad Caverns in New Mexico, USA. Impressive stalactites and stalagmites form in many of these limestone caves. Caves also occur in seashore cliffs and in volcanic areas.

Limestone rock is made up mainly of calcium carbonate, which dissolves in rainwater. Water seeps through cracks and joints in limestone rock, which is permeable (lets water through easily). Gradually the water widens the cracks and joints. Sometimes it makes a deep tunnel down through the permeable rock, called a swallow hole. Underground rivers also wear the limestone away, leaving large caves and sometimes lakes.

Caves can occur in rocks such as basalt (cooled lava from volcanoes). When the surface of the liquid lava cools and hardens, a cave may be left when the lava below stops flowing. Sea caves are formed by waves hurling stones and rocks at the cliffs, and by the force of the waves themselves.

Stalactites and stalagmites

Stalactites hang down from the ceiling of a cave as thin stone columns. Stalagmites rise from the floor as pillars of stone. Sometimes they join together to form a whole column of rock. Every time a drip of water forms on the cave roof, some of the water evaporates leaving a tiny deposit of calcium carbonate. These deposits grow very, very slowly to form stalactites, while deposits pile up on the cave floor to form stalagmites.

▼ A cross-section of an underground cave system.

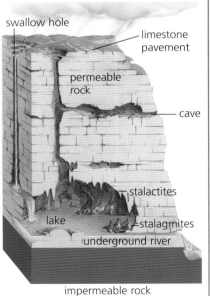

Cave records
Deepest cave
Réseau du Foillis, French Alps: 1455 m deep
Biggest cave system
Mammoth Cave system, Kentucky, USA: over 530 km of caves and passages
Longest (unsupported) stalactite
Gruta do Janelão, Brazil: about 10 m long
Tallest stalagmite
In Krásnohorská cave, Slovakia: about 32 m tall

find out more
Erosion
Rocks and minerals

Cavalry *see* Armies

Cells

Cells are the building blocks of life. Some very simple plants and animals have only one cell, but most living things are made of huge numbers of cells. A newborn baby has about 5 million million cells in its body, and an adult has over 10 times that number. Most cells are so tiny that they can be seen only by using a powerful microscope.

Cells can look different, but most have the same basic parts. They are each surrounded by a cell membrane which holds them together and controls which substances can enter or leave. Inside this membrane, the cell is divided into two parts: the nucleus and the cytoplasm.

The *nucleus* contains the body's genes. Genes control what features a plant or animal will have. They contain a chemical, DNA, which forms a kind of code or blueprint setting out how the cell will develop. Genes are arranged in groups on structures called *chromosomes*. When a cell divides, each chromosome makes an exact copy of itself so that the new cell has a complete blueprint.

The *cytoplasm* surrounds the nucleus and contains food and many other substances. It is a kind of chemical factory where the materials needed for living, growing and changing are produced. The nucleus controls what goes on in the cytoplasm by sending chemical messages to it. The cytoplasm contains a number of structures called *organelles*, each surrounded by its own membrane.

Different organelles have different tasks. The *endoplasmic reticulum* makes various chemicals that the body needs and breaks down waste materials. The *mitochondria* are the powerhouses of the cell. Here, the cell uses oxygen to break down glucose from food to provide energy. In plant cells, organelles called *chloroplasts* contain the green pigment chlorophyll, which traps the energy of sunlight. This is used to build up sugars for food from carbon dioxide and water.

Not all cells contain a nucleus. In very simple cells, such as those of bacteria, the DNA is free in the cytoplasm. Instead of chromosomes, there is a single circular strand of DNA. These cells do not have organelles either.

Tissues and organs

Tissues are groups of similar cells that work together to perform a particular function. For example, muscle tissue is made up of cells called muscle fibres. These contain protein fibres which can shorten (contract) in response to nerve signals. Nerve tissue consists of cells with long, thin nerve fibres and a cell membrane that can transmit electrical nerve impulses.

Organs are groups of different kinds of tissue, containing different types of cell, which work together to carry out a particular function. For example, the heart contains muscle tissue for pumping, nerve tissue for controlling the pumping, and blood vessels for supplying the other cells with food and oxygen.

• The oldest forms of life are microscopic, single-celled organisms, such as bacteria and certain algae. Over time, groups of single-celled organisms began to cluster together in colonies. Some simple animals, such as sponges, are in some ways like masses of colonial cells living in a single co-operative structure.

find out more
Animals
Bacteria
Genetics
Living things
Plants
Viruses

▲ A typical animal cell. Animal cells have a faint outline when seen under a microscope, because they are enclosed only in a thin cell membrane.

Labels: mitochondria, microtubules, cell membrane, nucleus, centrioles, vesicle, endoplasmic reticulum, ribosomes, pore

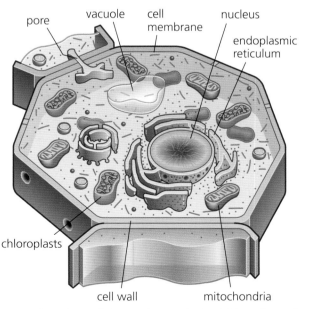

▲ A typical plant cell. Plant cells are clearly visible under a microscope because they have a thick cellulose cell wall outside the cell membrane.

Labels: pore, vacuole, cell membrane, nucleus, endoplasmic reticulum, chloroplasts, cell wall, mitochondria

Celts

The Celts are an ancient European people. They are known as a fierce and warlike people, but this may be because they left no written records and the Greeks and Romans who wrote about them were, for most of the time, their enemies.

Many Europeans are descended from the Celts, and Celtic place names (such as London and Paris) and river names (such as Rhine, Danube and Thames) are still used today

Conquest and defeat in Europe

The Celts' first homeland was probably in what is now southern Germany and the Czech Republic. They were warriors, farmers and traders, who used iron weapons to conquer more lands, and iron tools to farm them. By 400 BC Celtic tribes were settled in the British Isles, Spain, France and Italy. Fellow Celts were soon advancing into the Balkans, and in about 276 BC a Celtic people even moved into Asia Minor (now Turkey). Their opponents found the Celtic warriors terrifying. To scare their enemies in battle, Celtic warriors combed their hair to make it stand on end, often tattooed or decorated their bodies, and rushed shouting into battle.

It must have seemed for a while that the Celts would make all Europe their own. But they showed little interest in creating an empire, or in making a union of all their territories. From about 200 BC, the Celts rapidly lost ground: to the Germans in the north, the Dacians in the east and the Romans in the south.

Celtic Britain

Celtic-speaking people first came to Britain in about 700 BC and tribes of invaders kept on coming until the 1st century BC. Each tribe had its own rulers and quite possibly its own gods. For this reason the tribes often fought each other, and did not join forces against the successful Roman invaders who came after AD 43.

After the Roman occupation, the new Anglo-Saxon settlers edged the Celts out too. Celtic culture did linger on in Cornwall and in the highlands of Wales

► High crosses were usually gifts from powerful chiefs and kings. Many were built in the 9th and 10th centuries at important Christian centres. The coils and spirals in this design are typical of the work of the Celtic craftspeople; no one knows whether they had any special meaning.

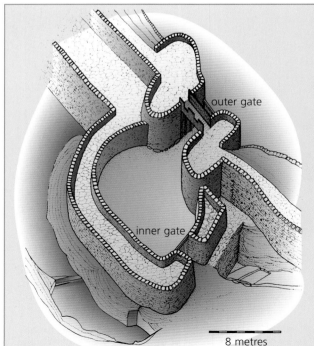

Hillforts
Celtic people built hillforts as a strong defence against enemy tribes and wild animals. They chose hills which had their own defences, such as cliff edges. Then they built huge banks of earth all around by digging out deep ditches. Some hillforts have steep stone walls in front of these banks of earth. The entrances made enemies twist and turn between high walls, leaving them open to attack from swords, spears or slings. But even the sling-throwers able to kill an enemy at 60 metres away were no match for the giant catapults of the Roman artillery and the Celts were forced out of their hilltop towns.

8 metres

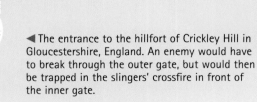

◄ The entrance to the hillfort of Crickley Hill in Gloucestershire, England. An enemy would have to break through the outer gate, but would then be trapped in the slingers' crossfire in front of the inner gate.

• Celtic myths and legends were passed on by word of mouth. Many people in Cornwall, Ireland, Scotland and Wales today continue to tell them. The stories are about giants like Ysbadaden, who propped his eyelids open with pitchforks; wizards like Merlin, who helped King Arthur; and warriors like Geraint of Cornwall or Gawain of Wales.

and Scotland. Ireland was never invaded by the Romans or Saxons. It remained a Celtic country until the Vikings came in the 9th century AD. So the Irish people went on speaking their Celtic or 'Goidelic' language.

Celtic society and beliefs

The Celts had a carefully organized society with laws made by nobles who were leaders – princes or chiefs – of their own tribes or clans. They lived not only in hillforts, but also on farms and in small 'villages' made up of five or six families. As well as vegetables, they grew wheat and barley to make bread; the barley was also used to make beer. They reared cows, goats, horses, pigs and sheep, and used dogs for hunting wild boar. They liked to wear multi-coloured and embroidered clothes finished off with patterned bronze or gold jewellery.

Celtic people worshipped dozens of gods and spirits, and the Sun and Moon. They made offerings to please their gods and their Druids made both animal and human sacrifices.

Druids were the priests of the Celtic peoples who lived in Gaul (now mainly France) and Britain in the 1st century BC. Druids could be male or female and they acted as chiefs and judges as well as priests. 'Druid' comes from the Greek word for oak, *drus*. Druids believed that the oak tree was sacred and they held important religious ceremonies in oak groves.

• The Celtic warrior-chief King Arthur is the hero of many Celtic myths and legends. The stories say he ruled all Britain and conquered most of western Europe. His 12 most trusted warriors were called the Knights of the Round Table.

◀ This Celtic silver cauldron was found in Denmark, but was probably made in south-eastern Europe. The detailed scenes on it show gods and goddesses, bulls and bullfights, processions of warriors and sacrifices.

find out more
Anglo-Saxons
Ireland, Republic of
Roman Britain
Scotland
Wales

• There are over 2000 kinds of centipede and about 8000 kinds of millipede.

find out more
Animals
Skeletons

▼ The centipede's flattened body enables it to squeeze through narrow spaces in soil or rotten wood. Its eyesight is poor, but its long antennae help it to track its prey.

Centipedes and millipedes

Centipedes and millipedes are best known for the extraordinary number of legs they have. As a group, they are called myriapods, which means 'many-footed animals'.

The legs of these animals are attached to a series of segments that make up the body. Centipedes have one pair of legs on each segment, but millipedes

▶ Millipedes have a row of stink glands along their sides from which they produce unpleasant chemicals when disturbed. Some millipedes protect themselves by rolling up into a tight ball.

have two. Like insects and spiders, they have external skeletons.

The name centipede means 'hundred feet'. A few kinds of centipede have far more than this, but most have fewer. At first, young centipedes do not have many feet, but they grow more legs as they grow larger and longer. Centipedes move fast, for they are hunters, tracking insects, grubs and worms. They use poison fangs to overcome their prey. Some tropical centipedes can give an unpleasant bite if they are handled, but most are entirely harmless to humans.

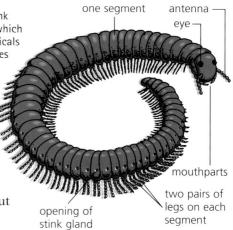

one segment   antenna
eye
mouthparts
opening of stink gland
two pairs of legs on each segment

The name millipede means 'thousand feet', but none of them has more than 400 feet. They cannot move fast, but their legs provide enough power to burrow through leaf litter and loose soil to search for soft or decaying plants to eat. Those in forests are good recyclers, returning chemicals to the soil for plants to use again.

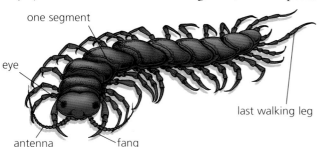

one segment
eye
antenna   fang
last walking leg

Cereals

One of the most important kinds of food we eat is made from the seed of a type of grass. Since prehistoric times people have grown plants of the grass family, called cereals.

The seeds of the cereal plants are called grains. They are quite large and full of carbohydrates, which are filling and provide the body with a quick source of energy. The grains also contain some protein, vitamins and minerals, and have plenty of fibre. Most of the fibre is found in bran, the grain's outer layer.

The most common cereals are wheat, maize, oats, rye, barley, millet and rice. Cereal grains can be eaten whole or processed. Ready-to-eat breakfast cereals are made mainly from maize, rice and wheat. Some breakfast cereals use the whole grain and they are more nutritious than those which do not. Cereal grains can also be ground into flour to make bread, pasta, porridge and puddings.

find out more
Bread
Diets
Farming
Food
Grasses
Prehistoric people

▲ **Rice** is one of the most important cereal crops. Over half the world's population eats rice as a staple food. Rice is grown standing in water. The seedlings are planted out in flooded paddy fields in warmer parts of the world. This field is in Madagascar.

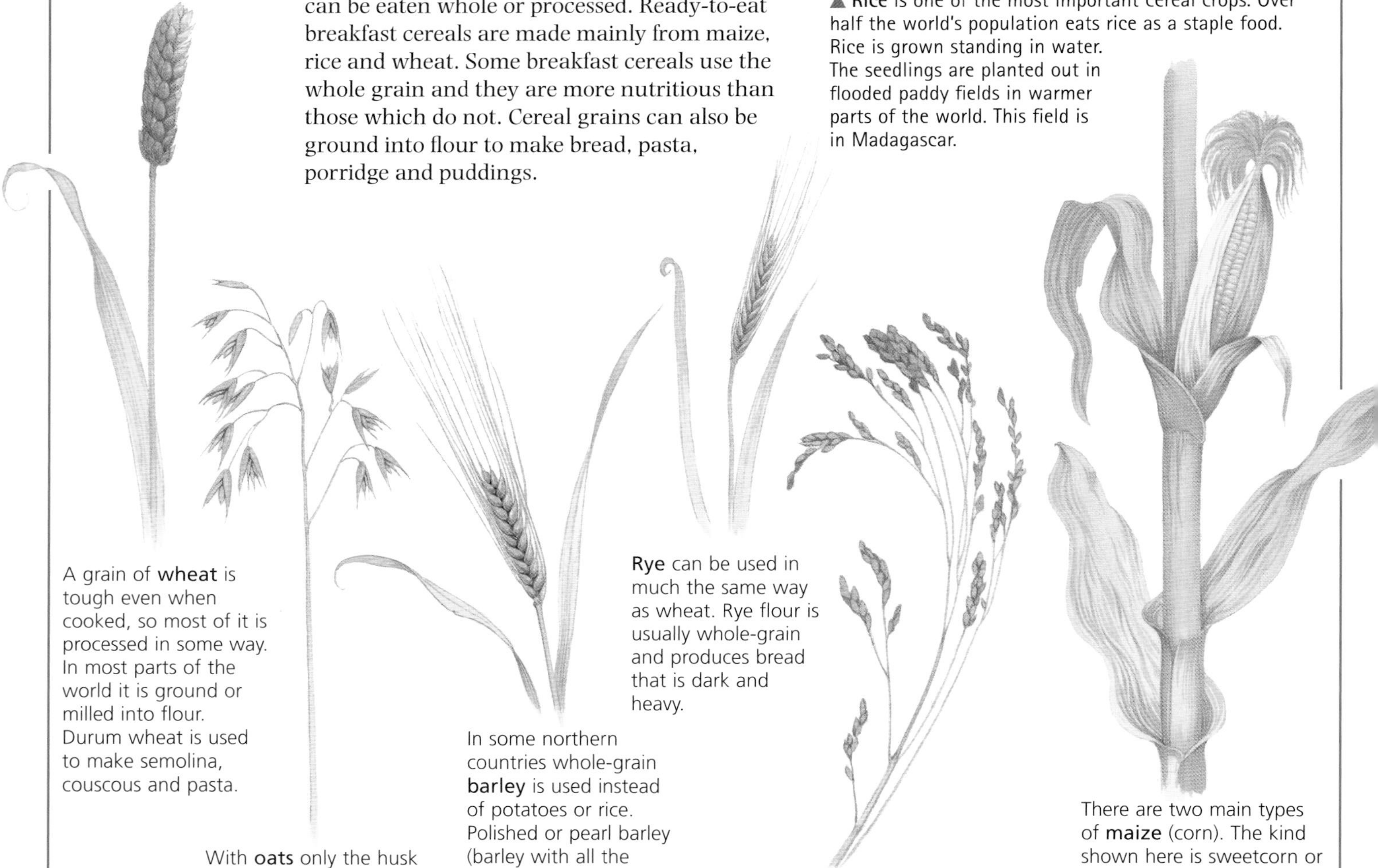

A grain of **wheat** is tough even when cooked, so most of it is processed in some way. In most parts of the world it is ground or milled into flour. Durum wheat is used to make semolina, couscous and pasta.

With **oats** only the husk is removed in the milling, so oatmeal retains most of the fibre and all the nutrients of the grain. In northern Europe, ground or flaked oats are used to make porridge and oatcakes.

In some northern countries whole-grain **barley** is used instead of potatoes or rice. Polished or pearl barley (barley with all the husks removed) is used in soups. Most barley, however, is either malted for making beer or whisky, or fed to cattle.

Rye can be used in much the same way as wheat. Rye flour is usually whole-grain and produces bread that is dark and heavy.

Millet can be used instead of rice, or be ground into flour and made into porridge or unleavened bread.

There are two main types of **maize** (corn). The kind shown here is sweetcorn or corn-on-the-cob. It is eaten fresh as a vegetable. The other kind produces smaller, more starchy grains which can be ground and cooked in various ways. Maize contains fat as well as starch, and this is often extracted to make corn oil.

Chad *see page 618* • **Chamber music** *see* Classical music • **Chameleons** *see* Lizards

Chaplin, Charlie

Charlie Chaplin was the best-known comedian of the silent-film era. His films are still popular today, especially those in which he plays a sad tramp.

Charles Chaplin first appeared on stage at the age of 5. In 1910, after some success as a teenage actor, he went to the USA. Four years later he got his first film roles, and soon became a favourite with cinema audiences. He later took over the writing and directing of his films. In 1919 he joined other stars and directors to found their own film company, called United Artists.

In his most famous films, such as *The Kid* (1920) and *The Gold Rush* (1925), Chaplin played a little tramp who had a small moustache, wore baggy trousers and a bowler hat, and carried a cane which he twirled around. The tramp was often bullied by powerful people, but he usually managed to bounce back and was always on the side of weaker or poorer people. These films made Chaplin the best-loved comedian of the era. He made many silent films, and after the arrival of 'sound' at the end of the 1920s he also made successful talking pictures. These included *The Great Dictator* (1940).

In later years, Chaplin was excluded from the USA because he was suspected of supporting communism, and he refused to let his films be shown there. However, in 1972 he returned in triumph to be awarded a special Oscar for his unique contribution to the film world. Two years before he died, he was honoured by the country of his birth when he was knighted to become Sir Charles Chaplin.

Born 1889 in London, England
Died 1977 aged 88

◄ Charlie Chaplin was born into poverty but became one of the highest-paid film stars in the world. He is shown here at the height of his fame in *The Gold Rush* (1925).

find out more
Films

Charities

Most charities are organizations that raise money to help people in need, such as children or the blind. But other charities work to protect animals, and still others to save the Earth's resources.

Charities raise funds for their activities by collecting money from the public and from businesses. Charities raise funds in many ways. They often have door-to-door or street collections, and some hold sponsored events. Many countries have state lotteries, which help to raise funds. Television stations sometimes run marathon fund-raising evenings called 'telethons'.

In most countries there are laws which control the ways in which a charity can operate. In such countries, organizations wishing to become charities register with the appropriate government department. The government then ensures that they follow laws about how they spend their money and keep their accounts.

One of the most famous charities in the world is the International Red Cross (known as the Red Crescent in Muslim countries). It acts as a go-between for countries involved in war and sends medical aid where it is most needed. Most countries have agreed never to fire on people, hospitals and ambulances displaying the Red Cross or Crescent.

◄ Sponsored walks and runs are a popular way of raising money, and many marathon runners are sponsored to raise money for charity. In 1980 a runner called Terry Fox, who had an artificial leg, ran 5373 km across Canada to raise more than 24 million Canadian dollars for charity.

Some famous charities
Campaign
Friends of the Earth
Greenpeace
Medecins sans frontiers
Red Cross
Salvation Army
Save the Children Fund
World Wide Fund for Nature

find out more
Aid agencies

Charlemagne

Charlemagne was a soldier and conqueror who became the greatest ruler of the early Middle Ages. He is regarded as one of the main founders of Western civilization.

Born about 742 probably in Aachen, now in Germany
Died 814 aged 72

• Charlemagne built magnificent palaces in Aix-la-Chapelle (Aachen) and in other parts of his kingdom, such as Zürich, Paris and Frankfurt. His court became a centre of art and learning as he encouraged artists, musicians, writers and scholars.

find out more
Byzantine empire
Holy Roman Empire
Middle Ages

Charles (later called Charlemagne) was the eldest son of Pepin, king of the Franks. The Franks had invaded part of the Roman empire and settled in what is now France and Germany. When King Pepin died in 768, he divided his kingdom between his two sons, Charles and Carloman. Three years later Carloman died, and Charles became the sole ruler.

Charles's aim as king was to enlarge the kingdom he had inherited and at the same time to spread Christianity among the people he conquered. During his long reign of over 40 years he organized about 60 military campaigns. His empire extended to include what is now France, most of Germany, and parts of Hungary, the Czech Republic, Slovakia, Italy, Spain and the Balkan countries.

His conquests earned him the name Charlemagne ('Charles the Great'). Pope Leo III asked him to take over part of Italy, and in 800 he was crowned emperor of what was later to become known as the Holy Roman Empire. After Charlemagne's death, his mighty empire fell apart.

◀ Charlemagne was both the ruler of much of Europe and the head of the Church within his empire. This engraving by Hieronymus Wierix shows him in both of these roles: he is standing astride the lands of his empire while wearing a bishop's hat.

Chaucer, Geoffrey

Geoffrey Chaucer was the most important English writer before Shakespeare. His collection of short stories – *The Canterbury Tales* – is regarded as one of the greatest works of its time.

Born about 1340 in London, England
Died 1400 aged about 60

• Chaucer was the first court poet to write in English. (Previous poets had written in French or Latin.) The language he wrote in is called Middle English. Here Chaucer describes a *werte* (wart):
*... thereon stood a toft of herys,
Reed as the brustles of a sowes erys;*
(... on it grew a tuft of hairs,
Red as the bristles on a sow's ears;)

find out more
English language
Stories and story-tellers

Geoffrey Chaucer worked as a page in the royal household before becoming a court poet. His duties included entertaining the court with music, songs and stories. He also went on diplomatic missions, travelling to France and Italy. While he was in Italy, he read books by Italian writers and later used some of their stories in his own writing.

In 1374 Chaucer was made Controller of Customs in the Port of London, but he left after 12 years and began writing *The Canterbury Tales*. This, his most famous work, is a group of tales told by pilgrims who go on a pilgrimage together to Canterbury. The pilgrims come from all walks of life and include a knight, a miller, a nun and a doctor. Through the tales, both sad and funny, we learn a lot about each character, as well as about life in the Middle Ages.

Chaucer also wrote other long poems. These are mainly about love and include Chaucer's first truly great piece of work, *Troilus and Criseyde*.

▼ Chaucer's *Canterbury Tales* is made up of 24 stories, although he had planned to write more. Some are written in prose and some in verse. This illustration shows part of *The Nun's Tale* and is taken from a very early edition of the tales.

Cheese

Most cheese is made from cow's milk, but the milk of other animals such as sheep, goat, buffalo, yak and camel is also used.

Simple fresh cheeses are made by heating milk with lemon juice or vinegar. These acid liquids cause the particles of fat and protein in the milk to stick together and form curds (solids) which separate from the liquid or whey. Hard cheeses such as Cheddar and mature soft cheeses such as Brie are made by adding rennet to milk. The rennet acts in the same way as the acid liquids and causes curds to form in the milk. The curds are cut, heated, drained and spooned into moulds. They may also be pressed. The cheeses are left to ripen and mature for a few days, months or even a year.

Types of cheese

There are hundreds of different cheeses. Each has its own exact recipe which gives it its character. Hard cheeses have a natural dry rind, which is formed by the curds at the edge of the cheese drying out. They may be brushed, oiled or bandaged to make them rough or smooth. Soft cheeses like Camembert are washed with moulds, which grow on the outside of the cheese to form a fluffy white rind. Other cheeses are washed with bacteria to give them a reddish-coloured rind with a strong smell. Blue cheeses, such as Stilton, are injected with penicillin moulds which grow in the curd to form the blue veins that can be seen in the mature cheese. Fresh soft cheese does not have time to form a rind, as it is eaten shortly after it is made.

▶ A dairy worker checking cheese on an automated production line.

- Most cheese has a high fat content of around 40–50%. Cheese is also a good source of protein and calcium as well as the vitamin B complex and vitamins A, D and E. A 100-g piece of cheese contains the same amount of calcium as a similar quantity of bread and nearly as much as the same amount of milk.

find out more
Diets
Farming
Food
Milk

Chemistry

Chemistry is the science that looks at substances. Chemists study how substances differ from one another – for example, one substance may burn easily, while another does not. They also study how different substances react together.

The most basic kinds of substance are called *elements*. These are substances made of only one kind of atom. But atoms can also join together, through chemical bonds, to form new substances called *compounds*. Water is a compound: it is made up of two atoms of hydrogen joined to one atom of oxygen.

When two or more substances react together, the chemical bonds between them change. When coal burns, for example, carbon atoms in the coal join up with oxygen from the air to make carbon dioxide. All chemical reactions involve making or breaking chemical bonds.

There are chemical changes going on around us all the time. Burning gas in a fire or a cooker is a chemical process. Boiling an egg until it goes hard is a chemical change. And a battery produces electricity by chemical changes.

The chemical industry develops processes by which quite simple chemicals can be made into useful products such as plastics and synthetic fibres, medicines, batteries and fertilizers.

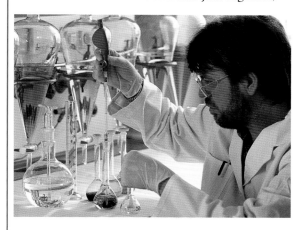

◀ A chemist carrying out a titration. This is a method for finding out how much of one substance there is in a solution by adding a measured amount of another substance. If the chemist knows how the two substances react, and how much of the second substance he has added to the mixture, he can work out how much of the first substance is in solution.

- Chemists use letters for different atoms: carbon, for example, is C, oxygen is O, and hydrogen is H. Compounds can be written using these letters: water is H_2O.

- *Organic chemistry* is the study of compounds of carbon, many of which are found in living things. *Inorganic chemistry* is the study of chemicals that do not contain carbon.

find out more
Atoms and molecules
Elements
Gases, liquids and solids

Children

Childhood is the time of life when babyhood is over and you are not yet an adult. The end of childhood is marked by the beginning of puberty or adolescence.

How long you are thought to be a child depends on the society in which you live. In some societies the end of childhood is set legally as the age at which you can vote in elections. The UN Commission on Human Rights defines children as those under the age of 18.

Skills and ideas

Childhood is a time of rapid growth and change. Skills and ideas develop through learning, as your body and brain grow and change. You are able to control all kinds of movements more accurately. Language also develops rapidly from the first words at about 1 year old to about 2600 words at 6 years. You learn how to think about the future and to plan and predict what may happen. Ideas about right and wrong develop through the example and teaching of adults.

Playing is one of the main ways of learning about the world. You can practise for real-life situations by pretend play. Young children tend to play alongside other children. As they get older, they learn to play together. They learn to follow rules so that games can run smoothly, and friends become very important.

- Thomas Barnardo was the founder of a charity to care for children in need. He became aware of the plight of homeless children while working as a doctor in London's East End. By the time of his death in 1905, nearly 60,000 needy children had been sheltered and trained in Dr Barnardo's Homes, and the charity continues his good work today.

- Today the majority of the countries in the United Nations accept the Convention on the Rights of the Child set up in 1990 to protect the world's children. However, millions of children all over the world still lack the basic rights of food, education and freedom from abuse.

find out more
Families
Growth and
   development
Schools and universities
Toys
United Nations

▼ In rich countries children go to school. They have time to play and learn. In many poor parts of the world children may go to school very little. They have to work to help their families when they are very young. These Indian children are carrying heavy stones for dam-building.

Independence

Small children are dependent upon their parents, or other adults they know well, to make them feel safe and happy. By the time they reach their teens, children become more independent. They have gained the confidence and experience to take some responsibility for themselves. They go shopping, use public transport and arrange their own social life. Many stay away from home on school trips or with friends. It is still helpful to have caring adults to support and advise.

At 4 months babies can sit propped up against something. They smile, hold toys and try to reach things.

At about a year children can stand, maybe even take a few steps and say simple words.

At 3 years old children can dress themselves, catch a ball, join in family conversations, and ride a bike (with stabilizers).

At around 6 children learn to read and write in their first years at school.

At 12 children have developed analytical skills and can carry out investigations and experiments for themselves.

◀ Childhood is a time of rapid growth. Fastest growth takes place during the first 2 years of life and again between 10 and 15 years for girls, and between 12 and 17 years for boys.

China

Chinese inventions
1st century AD
Magnetic compass
Ship's stern rudder
Canal locks
Seismograph
2nd century
Paper
3rd century
Wheelbarrow
5th century
Horse-collar harness
6th century
Suspension bridge
9th century
Gunpowder
11th century
Movable-type printing
Mechanical clock

China has the world's largest population: over 1.2 billion people live there. It is also the third largest country in the world by area.

China has over 4000 years of written history. For most of this time it has been ruled by a series of emperors, but since 1949 it has been led by the Chinese Communist Party.

Landscape

The most isolated and barren part of China is the Tibetan plateau in the west. Two rivers, the Huang He and the Chang Jiang (Yangtze), flow from the plateau towards the sea in the east. The Huang He carries large amounts of fine yellow silt called loess. When the river floods, the loess is left behind, producing very rich soils.

Bamboo forests across much of central China are home to the giant panda and other rare animals. The south is tropical, hot and humid. It often has typhoons (hurricanes), but the climate is good enough to grow three crops of rice a year. ◗

▲ A Tibetan woman milking a yak. Yaks are natural inhabitants of the Tibetan plateau that have been domesticated. Tibetans make use of their milk, hair and meat.

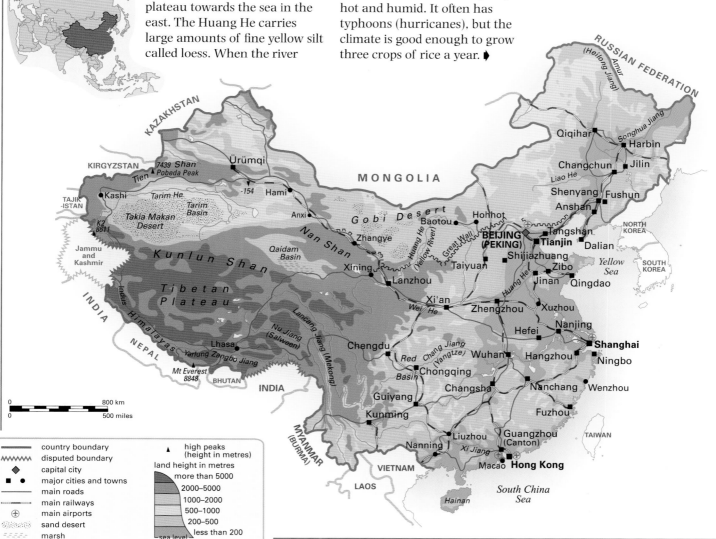

country boundary
disputed boundary
capital city
major cities and towns
main roads
main railways
main airports
sand desert
marsh

high peaks
(height in metres)
land height in metres
more than 5000
2000–5000
1000–2000
500–1000
200–500
less than 200
sea level

0 800 km
0 500 miles

▲ The Huang He used to be called the Yellow River because of the yellow colour given to it by the loess (silt).

• After 200 years of Chinese rule, Tibet became independent in 1912. The Chinese re-took Tibet in 1951, drove out the Dalai Lama (the traditional ruler) and tried to force Chinese communist ways on the Buddhist people.

Dynasties	Starting date
Xia	about 2000 BC
Shang	about 1500 BC
Zhou	about 1030 BC
Qin	221 BC
Han	206 BC
Time of the three kingdoms	AD 220
Sui	581
Tang	618
Five dynasties	907
Song	960
Yuan	1279
Ming	1368
Qing (Manzhou)	1644
Nationalist Republic	1912
People's Republic	1949

People

Ninety per cent of China's population belong to a people called the Han, but they speak many different dialects of Chinese. There are also over 50 non-Han minority groups with their own languages and traditions. The largest group is the Zhuang, who live in the centre of the country.

Most Chinese live in the countryside and work the land. In the north they grow mostly wheat and potatoes. Rice is more common in the south, where it is warmer and wetter. There is not enough suitable land for animals such as cattle, so farmers keep pigs, ducks and chickens. Many fruits come from China, such as peaches, apricots, tangerines and lychees.

Villages and cities

Village life is very traditional, but in recent years there have been changes. Couples have been encouraged to have fewer children, to help control population growth. Small factories and workshops have been set up to provide

▶ A road junction in the Chinese city of Kunming. Bicycles are a much more important form of transport in China than cars, buses or lorries.

alternatives to farming and to stop country people moving to the cities.

For most of the 20th century China was a poor country, but in the past 20 years its economy has boomed. Chinese factories now make half the world's toys. They also produce steel, textiles, shoes, ships and cars. These new industries have changed the cities. Shanghai is building a huge new office district and new shopping malls. People in cities can now afford colour television sets, although the countryside remains quite poor.

Much of the investment in cities and factories has come from Hong Kong. Hong Kong was a British colony from 1842 until 1997, when it once more became part of China. Its key position and its natural harbour have made it a thriving trading centre.

China's history

Chinese civilization is one of the oldest in the world. From at least 2000 BC until the 20th century, China was ruled by a series of 'dynasties', each named after the family of the ruling emperor. The first four dynasties that we know much about were the Shang, Zhou, Qin and Han (around 1500 BC–AD 220). They united China as a single country, introduced irrigated rice-growing, and built the Great Wall to keep out 'barbarians' from the north. Buddhism came to China during this period, the arts and literature flourished, and philosophers such as Confucius were much respected.

During the Tang and Song dynasties (618–1279), China governed much of central and South-east Asia. The country was then conquered by the Mongols, who swept over the Great Wall and set up the Yuan dynasty (1279–1368). The Italian merchant Marco Polo visited China at this time.

Revolution

In 1368 the Yuan were defeated by the Chinese Ming dynasty, who governed the country until 1644. Beijing was laid out by the Ming emperors. At the centre was a sacred palace, the Forbidden City, where China's emperors continued to live until 1911.

When Portuguese explorers reached China by boat in 1517, they found a powerful, well-organized, sophisticated society, but one that was rigid and unwilling to change. By the 19th century, China's power had waned. Europeans trading with China found excuses to

China

◀ The 2700-km Great Wall of China was built between 221 and 210 BC. It was extended 400 years later, then rebuilt in the 15th and 16th centuries. It is the only man-made object that can be seen from space.

• In 1989 many democracy campaigners were killed during a demonstration in Tiananmen Square in Beijing. There was an international outcry over this massacre.

• To control floods and generate electricity, China is building a huge dam on the Chang Jiang river, in an area called the Three Gorges. It will create a lake nearly 1000 km long, and over a million people will lose their homes.

seize Chinese ports. This was how the British took control of Hong Kong in 1842.

By 1900 a number of Western-educated Chinese were worried that their country might be divided up between the Europeans and made into colonies. In 1911, led by Sun Yixian (Sun Yat-sen), they organized a revolution that overthrew the Qing (Manzhou) emperor, Pu Yi, and made China a republic.

Mao and after
Sun Yixian's democratic government quickly collapsed. After a period of unrest and a long civil war, General Jiang Jieshi (Chiang Kai-shek), came to power. His most serious rivals were the communists, led by Mao Zedong.

In 1937 Japan attacked China, and until 1945 the Chinese were united against the Japanese invaders. But after Japan's defeat, civil war broke out. Mao emerged victorious in 1949, and set up the communist People's Republic of China. Jiang Jieshi fled to Taiwan, where he headed a pro-Western government.

For 30 years Mao was the most powerful figure in China.

Under communism education, health and the rights of women improved a lot. But private businesses were not permitted, and agriculture and industry made unsteady progress. After Mao's death in 1976, the new leaders began to allow some private enterprise, and with help from abroad the economy boomed. But opposition to the government was still not allowed, and and some countries refused to trade with China because of this. However, relations with other countries have gradually improved, industries have done well and the economy has grown.

find out more
Asia
Buddhists
Confucians
Dragons
Mao Zedong
Mongol empire
Polo, Marco
Taoists
Writing systems
See also Countries fact file, page 619

◀ In 1900 the ordinary Chinese tried to drive out the European 'foreign devils' from their country. The Boxer rebellion, as it was known, was crushed by huge numbers of European soldiers.

Chocolate

The slab of chocolate you may buy from a shop comes from cocoa (cacao) beans. So does the powder used to make drinking chocolate or cocoa, and good-quality chocolate used in cooking.

First, whole cocoa pods containing the beans are stored in boxes or under leaves until the flesh begins to ferment. The beans are then dried in the sun and roasted until the shells fall away. The remains are called 'nibs'. These nibs are ground until the fat (cocoa butter) in them liquefies. The resulting dark liquid (cocoa mass) is heat-treated and then cooled in moulds or rolled into bars. If the cocoa butter is taken out, cocoa powder is left.

The main ingredients of plain chocolate are cocoa mass, cocoa butter and sugar. Milk chocolate has powdered milk added to it.

• The cacao tree grows wild in the tropical rainforests of Brazil. It is now also cultivated in West Africa and Indonesia.

find out more
Beans
Food

How chocolate is made

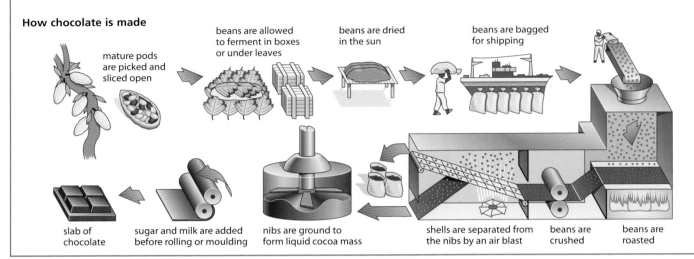

mature pods are picked and sliced open

beans are allowed to ferment in boxes or under leaves

beans are dried in the sun

beans are bagged for shipping

slab of chocolate

sugar and milk are added before rolling or moulding

nibs are ground to form liquid cocoa mass

shells are separated from the nibs by an air blast

beans are crushed

beans are roasted

Choirs

A choir is a group of singers who either sing all together or who sing different parts of the same piece of music. Men and women sing in choirs at religious ceremonies, to entertain people, and above all to enjoy themselves.

Choirs can have over 1000 singers or as few as 4 or 5, but most have between 20 and 100 members. Each person sings at the most suitable pitch for their voice. The highest voices are the sopranos (women) or trebles (boys), then come altos (men) and contraltos (women), and lastly tenors and basses, who are men.

Singing has long been part of the religious ceremonies in Christian churches. Some of the most beautiful and complex choral music has been written for highly trained church choirs.

Small choirs called chamber choirs often sing madrigals. In these, each person's voice interweaves with the others in intricate rhythms and melodies. The words are usually on the subjects of love and war.

In many parts of the world, including most of Asia and Africa, modern choirs often still sing traditional music in the same way as their ancestors. One common example is for one voice to lead and a larger group to sing an answering phrase, in a kind of musical conversation. In the USA in particular, gospel choirs give this kind of performance of Christian hymns and spirituals, often bringing in jazz and soul rhythms as well.

• Some choirs are made up only of men. Many of these male-voice choirs developed when groups of men got together to drink and sing. Many 19th-century composers also gathered groups of their male friends together and wrote songs for them to perform.

◄ Choirs sometimes travel around the world to perform at international events. This Chinese children's choir is singing at Expo 86, a world trade fair held in Vancouver, Canada, in 1986.

find out more
Music
Operas and musicals
Singing and songs

Christians

The Christian religion began with the life and teachings of Jesus, a Jew who lived in Palestine from about the year 4 BC to AD 29. Within a hundred years of his death, missionaries had taken Christian teachings to many countries around the Mediterranean Sea. There are now Christians all over the world.

Jesus taught Christians that God rules as a loving father, who asks his children to believe in him in order to find happiness on Earth and, after death, in heaven. The most important thing for all Christians is to love God and to care for the people around them, particularly those less fortunate than themselves.

Who was Jesus?

There are four written accounts of the life of Jesus in the New Testament of the Bible, called the Gospels of Matthew, Mark, Luke and John. According to these stories, Mary was visited by the angel Gabriel who told her that she would give birth to Jesus, who was the son of God, not of her husband Joseph.

At about the age of 30, Jesus was baptized by his cousin John the Baptist. John was a prophet (someone who feels an inner call to preach to people about God). Jesus then began to preach and to heal the sick and disabled himself. He taught his followers to love both God and their neighbours. They came to believe that he was the Messiah or Christ (a king whom the Jewish people believed was coming to save them). The ruling Roman government felt threatened and had him arrested and sentenced to death by crucifixion (being nailed to a cross). On the third day after his death, Jesus rose from the dead. Easter Sunday is the day for celebrating his resurrection. The followers of Jesus soon became known as Christians.

▲ Orthodox churches are full of icons like this one of Jesus from Saint Sophia, Istanbul, Turkey. Icons are special pictures of Jesus, his mother Mary, or of a saint, which people believe have the power to do good and channel God's grace into the world. They are honoured by Orthodox Christians with candles and a kiss.

▼ Christmas is a Christian festival which celebrates the birth of Jesus. Most Christians hold the celebration on 25 December. Children in Germany dress up as kings on 6 January to mark the end of the Christmas festival.

The teaching of Jesus

Jesus' life was a good example of his own teaching on self-sacrifice and love for other people. Even as he was dying on the cross, he prayed to God to forgive the soldiers who had nailed him there. He encouraged his followers not to worry about food, clothes and homes, but to depend on God and care for one another. In his parables, Jesus talked about the kingdom, or rule, of God. It is described as having had small beginnings, like a mustard seed which grows into a great tree. It is described as being precious, like a pearl, and as involving celebration, so that being invited into the kingdom is like being given an invitation to a party. Being part of the kingdom of God also involves using what talents you have as well as you can.

▲ This 15th-century illustration shows St Paul being converted to Christianity. St Paul had a great influence on Christian teaching.

The spread of Christianity

Jesus chose 12 men from among his followers to carry on his teaching. They were called apostles, meaning 'those who are sent out'. In the Bible, the Acts of the Apostles tells the story of the spread of Christianity from Palestine, through parts of Greece and other Mediterranean lands to Rome. One of the first Christian missionaries to reach Rome was St Paul, who was put to death for his beliefs. Gradually Christianity spread throughout the Roman empire. But many early Christians were still harassed and

▲ Many Christians go on pilgrimages — trips to places which are sacred or holy to them. These pilgrims are at Lourdes in south-west France where the Christian shrine of St Bernadette has a reputation for miraculous cures.

• Heretics were Christians who disagreed with Church leaders over matters of religion, choosing for themselves what to believe. Something a heretic believes which does not agree with the Church's teaching is called a 'heresy'.

• At the time Jesus was born, the Romans dated years from the legendary foundation of Rome. About 500 years after Jesus lived, Christian scholars worked out a new system counting from what they thought was the year of his birth. Their calculations were wrong. Later historians realized that Jesus was born four years earlier. BC means 'before Christ' and AD means after Christ was born. (AD is short for *anno domini*, which means 'in the year of our Lord'.)

persecuted for their beliefs. Some were even killed for the amusement of the Roman crowds. The first emperor to accept the teachings of Christ publicly was Constantine. In AD 313 he allowed Christianity to be recognized, and persecution ended.

In the 11th century the Western and Eastern Churches split. Rome continued to be the headquarters of the Christian church in the West, and Constantinople (Byzantium, now Istanbul) became the centre for the Eastern Orthodox Churches. It was Greek monks who took Christianity to Russia, where it became the official religion in 988.

There were Christian churches on the north coast of Africa, which was part of the Roman world, from at least the 2nd century. Hundreds of years later, from the 15th century, European traders and missionaries took Christianity into the vast African continent, where there are now many independent Churches.

In South America, Spanish and Portuguese soldiers and missionaries established Roman Catholic Christianity from the 16th century onwards. The Pilgrim Fathers took Protestant Christianity to North America in the 17th century.

The Christian way of life

Some Christians try to study the Bible and learn to listen to God as well as talk to him through prayer, every day. On Sundays they usually go to church or chapel with other Christians, because Sunday is the day Jesus rose from the dead. Other Christians may never go to church, or pray much, but they still believe in God and try to live a Christian way of life.

In their church services Christians remember the last supper which Jesus had with his friends, the 12 disciples, before he died. This service of remembering and sharing in these events is called the Mass, Holy Communion, the Eucharist or the Lord's Supper. The main part of this worship is sharing bread and wine that has been blessed. This is one of the two gospel *sacraments* – outward actions which show an inner relationship with God.

The other sacrament is baptism (often called christening), a service in which people are given their Christian names and become members of the Christian Church. If baptized as a baby, a Roman Catholic or Anglican child later confirms the decision to be a Christian, which was first made on its behalf by its parents, in a service called confirmation. ◗

▼ John the Baptist immersed people in the River Jordan to show that they repented and their sins were washed away. Today Christians are usually baptized in blessed water in the font of a church or in a river or sea like these Christians in the Caribbean.

▲ St Basil's Cathedral, an Orthodox church in Moscow, Russia.

Christian groups

There are three main groups of Christians today. **Eastern Orthodox Christians** live mainly in Greece, Romania, Russia, Serbia and Bulgaria. Their history goes back in an unbroken line to the beginnings of Christianity. Eastern and Western forms of Christianity drifted apart for some centuries before there was a break in 1054 over the authority of the Pope and the exact words used in the creed (an explanation of Christian beliefs). A striking feature of the Orthodox Churches is their colourful and majestic form of worship (the liturgy).

The Catholic Church continued the unbroken line of Christianity in the West until the time of the Reformation. For most of the

◄ This is Pope John Paul II celebrating a Mass in Rome. He was Pope from 1978 to 2005. Pope is a Christian title from the Latin word *papa*, which is an affectionate way of saying father. It was originally part of the title of all Christian bishops, but is now used particularly for the bishop of Rome, who is the head on Earth of the Roman Catholic Church.

Other Christian groups

Some Christian groups have split off from the mainstream Churches to form their own denominations. Two such groups are the Quakers and the Methodists.

The Quakers are members of the Society of Friends, founded by George Fox and other Puritans in England in the 1660s. They believe that all Christians have the 'inner light' of God within them, and do not need priests or ministers to help them understand God's teachings. Instead they worship together as equal 'friends'.

John Wesley

The Methodist Church was founded by John Wesley, a priest who formed a group of young men to lead 'methodical' lives, praying and reading the Bible together, and going to church regularly. He originally wanted to remain loyal to the Church of England, but a split came in 1784 when he broke their rules by ordaining a group of Methodist preachers, and the movement grew into a separate Church.

George Fox

time its centre of authority has been the Vatican in Rome, where the Pope lives. For hundreds of years Catholics sang the Mass and said prayers in Latin because this was the language of educated people in Western Europe. Today there are more members of the Roman Catholic Church than of any other Christian denomination. It has members all over the world and they use their everyday language for worship.

Protestants believe that at the time of the Reformation in the 16th century they returned to beliefs and a way of life closer to that of the Bible. They did this in protest at some practices of the Roman Catholic Church. There are now very many different kinds of Protestant Church because of their emphasis on individual interpretation of Scripture and personal commitment rather than an acceptance of a traditional form of Christianity. Some Protestant groups are named after their ideas. For example, those served by presbyters (ministers) are Presbyterians; those organized as separate congregations are Congregationalists. Baptists believe they should wait until they are adults to be baptized.

• In the New Testament of the Bible, Matthew alleges that Herod the Great, king of Judea from 40 BC, ordered the 'Massacre of the Innocents'. He had all children under 2 killed in an attempt to ensure the death of Jesus, whom he foresaw as a rival. Jesus and his family escaped to Egypt.

find out more
Bible
Churches
Festivals and holidays
Reformation
Religions

Christmas *see* Festivals and holidays

Churches

Churches are buildings in which Christians meet for worship. The word church comes from the Greek word for 'the Lord's house'.

One of the first churches to be built was old St Peter's in Rome. Begun in AD 326, after Christianity became legally tolerated in the Roman empire, it became so famous that it was copied all over western Europe.

These first western churches, including St Peter's, were copied from the halls (basilicas) where the Romans conducted public business. The names of parts of a basilica are also used for parts of a church, including the nave and the aisle.

Churches in western Europe have been built in many different styles, though most of them are cross-shaped. In the Middle Ages the Gothic style with pointed arches was used. Churches built after the Renaissance in the 15th and 16th centuries used ideas from Greek and Roman buildings. In the 19th century, however, Christians imitated the style and workmanship of medieval masons because they thought that these craftsmen had been inspired by God.

Eastern (Orthodox) churches look very different from western churches because they were built with many arches and domes. They are called 'Byzantine' after Byzantium (now Istanbul), the capital of the Eastern Roman Empire.

Today churches around the world are built in many exciting new styles and shapes. Many are cross-shaped, but others are circular, fan-shaped or square, with the seats and altar arranged to help worshippers join in the service.

Inside a church

From the earliest times, Christians decorated their churches with pictures and carvings that told stories from the Bible and the lives of the saints. Early Christian and Byzantine churches were lined with mosaics. Medieval European churches had wall-paintings, stained glass, statues and carvings. In Orthodox churches wooden panels painted with pictures of saints (icons) stand in front of the altar. For Protestants the spoken word of God is more important than pictures, so their churches are often quite plain.

Cathedrals

A cathedral is the main church of a diocese – a district under the control of a bishop. The first cathedrals were built in the 4th century, but the great age of cathedral building was from 1000 to 1500. Most cathedrals were gradually built and rebuilt over many centuries. They often contain many different styles of architecture.

Medieval cathedrals were places of craftsmanship and learning. The buildings were the work of the most skilful masons, carvers and glaziers.

Stained-glass windows
Stained-glass artists work with glass, lead and light. The artist plans the window carefully, drawing a full-scale design, called a cartoon, which shows the positions of the lead lines and the colours of the glass pieces.

Once the glass has been cut out, the artist starts to lay out the network of leads. Following the outline of the cartoon, the leads are bent and the glass pieces slid into place. Then the leads are soldered together and any gaps filled with cement.

find out more
Architecture
Christians

◀ Cut-away drawing of an English medieval church. Many western European churches are arranged like this. The congregation faces east towards the altar. Medieval Christians believed that Christ's Second Coming would happen in the east.

1 tower
2 font
3 nave
4 pews
5 porch
6 aisle
7 lectern
8 pulpit
9 transept
10 lady chapel
11 chancel
12 choir stalls
13 altar
14 vestry

Churchill, Winston

Winston Churchill was the prime minister of Britain during most of World War II. His strong leadership helped steer the country to victory in 1945.

Born 1874 at Blenheim Palace, Oxfordshire, England
Died 1965 aged 90

• 'Never in the field of human conflict was so much owed by so many to so few.'
Winston Churchill on the skill and courage of British airmen during the Battle of Britain, 1940

find out more
Britain since 1900
World War II

Winston Churchill was the grandson of the seventh Duke of Marlborough. His political career started in 1900 when he was elected to Parliament as a Conservative. However, in 1904 he fell out with his party and joined the Liberals, and he held several posts while they were in government. Before and during World War I he served as head of the Admiralty, but he resigned from government to command troops in France for a time. After serving again as a Liberal minister after the war, he returned to the Conservative Party, and was Chancellor of the Exchequer from 1924 to 1929.

Churchill did not hold a government post during the 1930s. He warned that there was a danger of another world war, but many people ignored him. However, when World War II did break out, he was put in charge of the Admiralty once again. Then, when German armies were overrunning Europe in May 1940, King George VI asked him to be prime minister and lead a coalition government of all parties. His courage and speeches inspired people to withstand air raids and military defeats, and carry on to victory.

Churchill remained prime minister until the 1945 general election brought Labour to power, just before the end of the war. He was prime minister again from 1951 to 1955, before giving up politics in 1964.

▼ Churchill on his way to the House of Commons in London on 8 May 1945. This was VE Day, the day on which the Allies celebrated their victory against Hitler's forces in Europe.

Circuses

At a circus, the audience sit around a circular space called the circus ring, and watch people, and sometimes animals, perform tricks and feats of skill.

• Animal acts have become less popular since the 1980s because many people feel that they are cruel to animals.

• From 1883 Buffalo Bill, former US Cavalry man, began his Wild West Shows. These were rather like circus shows with horse tricks, shooting displays, mock battles, and lots of 'cowboys and Indians'. The show featured stars like Annie Oakley, who was such a good shot she could split a playing card held edge-on from 30 paces away.

At a circus show there may be jugglers, clowns, acrobats, trapeze artists, plate-spinners, tightrope-walkers, magicians, knife-throwers, fire-eaters, sword-swallowers, and many others. Sometimes animals, such as horses, perform as well.

Many circuses in Europe are travelling shows with the circus ring and the audience all housed in an enormous tent called the Big Top. There are few large travelling circuses left in western Europe, but in Russia and eastern Europe circuses flourish and are housed in permanent buildings.

◄ Clowns provide comic entertainment between the other acts.

► FLASHBACK ◄

Circuses began in ancient Rome. Some Roman circuses included feats of skill, like chariot racing. In others the audience went to see wild animals or gladiators fighting. The modern circus developed from the late 18th century when horse-riding displays were given in London. There were soon similar shows all over Europe. The really big circuses developed in America with the famous Barnum and Bailey's Circus, formed in 1880.

Some performers have become famous too. In 1859 tightrope-walker Charles Blondin became the first person ever to cross the Niagara Falls on a high wire. In the early years of the 20th century, the magician Harry Houdini became renowned for his amazing escape tricks.

Classical music

When we talk about classical music, we usually mean the kind of music that is performed in concerts, religious services, opera and ballet. The term 'Classical' can also be used to describe music from the Classical period of Western music, which lasted from about 1750 to 1800.

▲ Music for string quartet (two violins, a viola and cello) has been the dominant form of chamber music since the 1750s, when it was first developed by Joseph Haydn. Haydn and many of the composers who followed him found this combination of strings a particularly effective way of expressing inner thoughts and feelings.

• Music written for a small room or 'chamber', and so for a small number of instrumental players, is known as *chamber music*. It is most often written for three players (trio), four players (quartet) or five players (quintet).

Western classical music is only one of the many different classical music traditions around the world. In India, for example, classical music makes use of note-patterns and rhythms that have been used for centuries, but which are not written down. In Japan, the tradition of classical court music, called *gagaku*, dates back to the AD 700s.

The Western tradition

In the West, the earliest music that we know much about (*plainsong*) was sung in the Christian Church from around the 9th century. Very little is known about music before this date because it was not written down and so preserved. Plainsong reached its height around the 13th century.

During the Renaissance period (from about 1400 until 1600), music for the Church became more elaborate. Composers such as the 16th-century Italian Giovanni Perluigi Palestrina wrote complicated settings of the words of the Mass. Music also developed outside the Church, as first Italian, then English, composers set poetry to music in short vocal pieces called *madrigals*.

The Baroque period (from about 1600 until 1750) saw the birth of opera as well as the continued development of both religious (sacred) and non-religious (secular) music.

Probably the greatest of all Baroque composers was Johann Sebastian Bach. He wrote a vast amount of sacred music and also developed secular forms of music such as the concerto. At the same time, George Frideric Handel was writing dramatic oratorios. Ever since its first performance in 1742, Handel's oratorio *Messiah* has been extremely popular.

Classical and Romantic

The second half of the 18th century is known as the Classical period in Western music. At this time most composers and musicans were employed either by the Church or by wealthy patrons. It was quite usual for a prince or nobleman to keep an orchestra at court for his entertainment, as well as a composer to write music for it.

The Austrian composer Franz Joseph Haydn worked for much of his life at the court of Prince Esterházy in Vienna. He wrote over 100 symphonies, as well as developing new kinds of chamber music such as the string quartet. Haydn's music set a style which was

Some musical forms

Concerto: a piece written for an instrumental soloist, or soloists, accompanied by orchestra. The composer makes the most of the contrast between the solo and the orchestral sounds.

Madrigal: a poem set to music and written for a small group of unaccompanied voices. This form was popular in the Renaissance.

Oratorio: a story told through solo singers, chorus and orchestra. The story is usually religious, and there is no acting, scenery or costumes. A *Passion* is an oratorio telling the Easter story of the Passion (suffering) of Christ.

Sonata: a piece of music for a solo instrument or two instruments (duo), without orchestral accompaniment.

Suite: A series of related pieces, often including slow 'dances' such as an allemande, courante, sarabande or gigue. This form was very popular in the Baroque period.

Symphony: a large-scale work for orchestra. Symphonies are usually divided into contrasting sections, called movements.

the inspiration for many other composers of the Classical period.

The genius of Wolfgang Amadeus Mozart was recognized during his own lifetime, but he never had a long-standing patron. Without this security his life was one of struggle and hardship. He composed in a greater variety of forms than Haydn, and his love of the theatre led him to write operas, such as *The Marriage of Figaro* and *The Magic Flute*.

The major figure of the end of the Classical period is Ludwig van Beethoven. Beethoven used musical forms such as the symphony and the concerto, and expanded them to suit his own purposes. Other composers in the 19th century took their lead from Beethoven, developing new forms to express feelings through their music.

This time became known as the Romantic period in music, art and literature.

The Romantic period (the 19th century) was a time of revolution, during which the power of the monarchy and nobles declined and a new class of wealthy people emerged. In many of Europe's cities public concert halls were built. Composers and performers no longer had to please a patron – they had to please the public.

The Hungarian pianist Franz Liszt and the Italian violinist Niccolò Paganini wrote and performed works designed to dazzle audiences with their difficulty. In contrast, the Austrian composer Franz Schubert composed hundreds of expressive songs to be performed to small groups of friends and admirers. In the world of opera, the Italian Guiseppe Verdi wrote operas based on stories from literature and history, while Richard Wagner, a German, turned to myths and legends as inspiration for his epic works.

The modern period

In the late 19th and early 20th centuries, some composers began to react against the emotional style of Romantic music. They looked for new

▲ Opera originated in Italy at the end of the 16th century. It is a form of drama in which the actors sing, rather than speak, with the accompaniment of an orchestra. Opera flourished in the 19th century, and one of its leading composers was Gioacchino Rossini. This is a scene from his opera *La Cenerentola*, a version of the Cinderella story.

ways to say new things in music. Claude Debussy, a Frenchman, was one of the first composers to explore new harmonies and sounds. He found inspiration in nature, and tried to re-create the impression of, for example, moonlight or the sea in his music.

The Austrian composer Arnold Schoenberg invented the 'tone row' – a row of 12 notes upon which he based whole pieces. His ideas influenced many 20th-century composers, particularly Anton Webern and Alban Berg. The

Russian-born composer Igor Stravinsky experimented with rhythm in the ballet music *The Rite of Spring*. He also developed the 'neoclassical' style, in which compositions are based on works written in the Baroque period but have a distinct, 20th-century flavour.

Later 20th-century composition included the experiments of John Cage and the electronic music of Karlheinz Stockhausen. Some composers, such as John Tavener, turned back to the Church for their inspiration. Others, including Steve Reich, John Adams and Arvo Pärt, tried to take music to a pure, uncomplicated level. Today, most composers are open to a very wide range of influences from all over the world.

 Training in Western classical music takes place in many non-Western countries. Japan, for example, has produced lots of world-famous classical musicians. This is partly because Japanese children are encouraged to play instruments at an early age, but mainly because the training methods are effective.

• The composer John Cage wanted to make people aware of the many different sounds going on around them, sounds that they normally would not notice. So in 1952 he wrote a piece of music called '4 Minutes 33 Seconds', in which a pianist sat and played nothing at all. The 'music' came from the natural sounds in the concert hall.

find out more

Cleopatra

Born about 69 BC in Egypt
Died 30 BC aged about 39

▶ Cleopatra (centre) pictured in a relief on the walls of the Birth House of the Temple of Mathor, Dendera, Egypt. On the right is Ra, the god of the Sun. Cleopatra regarded herself as the daughter of the Sun god.

find out more
Augustus
Caesar, Julius
Egyptians, ancient
Romans

Cleopatra is ancient Egypt's most famous queen. She succeeded in holding onto power for many years before (as legend has it) she died by letting herself be bitten by a poisonous snake.

On her father's death in 51 BC, Cleopatra ruled Egypt with her younger brother Ptolemy XIII. (It was the custom for brother and sister to be married and to rule jointly.) However, at this time Egypt was no longer independent of the expanding Roman empire. Cleopatra was forced out by the Romans in 48 BC, but was soon restored to power by Julius Caesar, who allowed her to rule with another of her brothers. Caesar had fallen in love with Cleopatra and they lived together openly in Rome. She had a son called Caesarion, and stayed with Caesar until he was assassinated in 44 BC. She then returned to Egypt and ruled jointly with her son.

A civil war soon followed in the Roman world, and by 41 BC Cleopatra had become an ally and then the mistress of the victor, Mark Antony. Antony made his base in the capital of Egypt, Alexandria. He permitted Cleopatra and Caesarion to be joint rulers of Egypt and Cyprus. Cleopatra had three children by Antony, each of whom was proclaimed ruler of a part of the Roman empire, with Antony as 'king' in the east.

However, civil war broke out again in the Roman empire in 31 BC. Antony and Cleopatra were defeated at the battle of Actium by Octavius (later the Emperor Augustus). They both committed suicide rather than be taken prisoner.

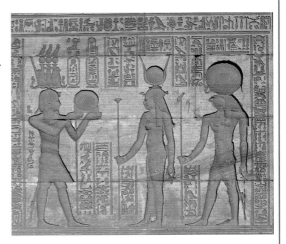

Cliffs

• One 5-kilometre stretch of cliff in Greenland is estimated to hold 1.6 million breeding guillemots.

• The highest cliffs in the world are sea-cliffs on the Hawaiian Islands, which reach up to 1005 m. However, these are not sheer vertical cliffs.

▶ The cliffs of Moher in County Clare, on the west coast of Ireland, rise to a height of 230 m.

find out more
Coasts
Erosion
Oceans and seas
Rivers and streams
Sea birds
Seashore

Cliffs are steep, rocky slopes that are found both inland and along coastlines. They formed when the sea, fast-moving rivers or ancient ice glaciers cut into the base of the rock. The rock above then fell away too, leaving a sheer wall of rock.

When the rock is soft, a cliff constantly crumbles away, and nothing can live on it. But if the rock is hard and stable, plants can begin to grow, anchored by their roots in rock cracks. Only special kinds of plant can cope with the amount of salt spray to which they are exposed on sea-cliffs. Common cliff plants include thrift (sea pink), sea campion and rock samphire. Different plants grow on inland cliffs, depending on whether the cliff face is damp and shady or exposed to hot sunshine.

Bird life

On sea-cliffs, the layering of the rock and the effects of the weather sometimes produce flat ledges where sea birds come ashore to nest. A cliff provides a safe place for them to lay their eggs, away from egg-eating hunters like rats and foxes. Flying hunters, such as gulls or skuas, may wait near sea-cliffs to catch unwary birds or to steal their eggs.

The number of birds nesting on sea-cliffs can be enormous. Razorbills, kittiwakes and gannets nest on the sheer cliff face. Crammed together on ledges, guillemots rest their eggs on their feet instead of building a nest. Puffins nest in burrows on the grassy cliff-top. To lie safely on a cliff-top and watch the activity of all the sea birds below can be a very exciting experience.

Climate

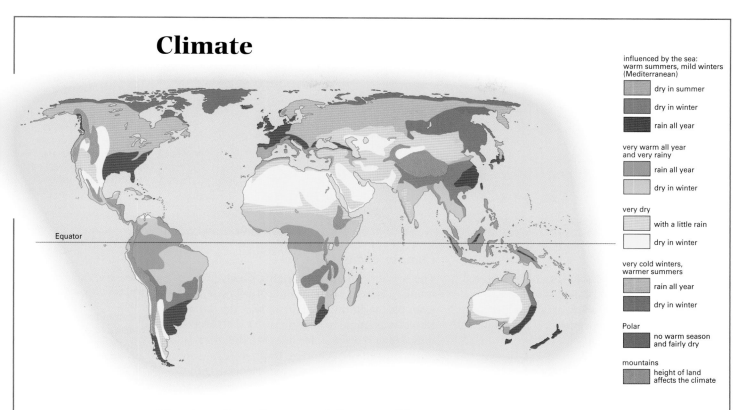

influenced by the sea:
warm summers, mild winters
(Mediterranean)

- dry in summer
- dry in winter
- rain all year

very warm all year
and very rainy

- rain all year
- dry in winter

very dry

- with a little rain
- dry in winter

very cold winters,
warmer summers

- rain all year
- dry in winter

Polar

- no warm season
  and fairly dry

mountains

- height of land
  affects the climate

Climate and weather are not the same thing. The weather may change from day to day – it may be warm and dry one day, and cool and rainy the next. The climate of a place is the pattern of its weather over a long period of time. Climate is often described in terms of temperature and rainfall.

▲ This map of the world shows the different types of climate, and where they occur on Earth.

Every place on Earth has its own climate, which may be similar to the climate of other places faraway. For example, the Mediterranean region has a similar climate to California, in the USA, and to south-eastern Australia. The main factors that affect climate are: latitude (distance from the Equator), altitude (height above sea level), distance from the sea, and type of wind.

Latitude

The latitude of a place affects how much heat it receives from the Sun's rays. At the North and South Poles, which are at high latitudes, the Sun's rays fall at a very low angle. Much of their heat is absorbed as they pass through a thick layer of the Earth's atmosphere. As a result, the *polar* climate is cold, with short summers and long dark winters.

The areas around the Equator are the tropical areas, or tropics, where the Sun is almost overhead at noon for much of the year, and the hours of daylight are the same month after month. The tropics receive more sunlight than

anywhere else in the world. The *tropical* climate is warm all year round, usually with marked dry seasons and wet seasons.

In the mid-latitudes (between the polar regions and the tropics) are the *temperate* regions, which have distinct seasons. Here the Sun is low in the sky in winter, and high in summer, resulting in long summer days and short winter ones.

Altitude and distance from sea

The height of a place above sea level affects its temperature – the higher you go, the cooler it becomes. Mountainous regions are generally cooler than lowland areas. Some mountains, for example Mount Kilimanjaro in tropical Africa, may have snow all year round. This type of climate is a *montane* (mountain) climate.

In general, water warms up and cools down much more slowly than land. As a result, in winter the sea is often warmer than the land, and in summer it is often cooler. Coastal areas and islands in temperate regions such as northern Europe tend to have less extreme variations in temperature when compared with areas such as the central USA and eastern Europe, which are further away from the sea. So places near the sea have a *maritime* climate, which is milder than the *continental* climate of places further inland.

• Mountain ranges may produce an effect called a *rain shadow*. As moist air passes over a mountain, it rises and water vapour condenses to form rain clouds. Rain falls on the mountainside facing the wind, but the other side is drier because no moisture is left in the air. The vast Tibetan plateau lies in the rain shadow of the Himalayas.

find out more
Atmosphere
Clouds
Deserts
Greenhouse effect
Maps
Rain and snow
Seasons
Weather
Wind

◄ Wild animals move along a dried-up river-bed in Kenya, in East Africa, in search of water and fresh grazing land. The climate of much of the country is dry, with some places receiving less than 25 cm of rain in a year. Many rivers, like this one, are without water for large parts of the year.

Winds

Winds carry moisture in clouds and as water vapour. They may also be dry, as well as hot or cold. Winds tend to blow in particular directions in different parts of the world.

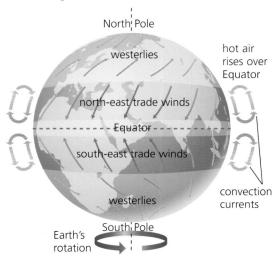

▲ Winds are the result of the uneven heating of air masses around the Earth, and they are also influenced by the rotation of the Earth. They move around the world in a series of wind belts.

In the tropics, the land surface is hot and so heats the air above. The hot air rises, cools and sheds its water content, producing the heavy rainfall that is typical of a tropical climate. Cooler air from places to the north and south of the Equator replaces the rising hot air. These are called *trade winds*. As the air rising from the Equator moves from the tropics towards the Poles, it becomes cooler and more dense, so it descends towards the Earth. It has already shed its water content as rain, so the regions beyond the trade winds contain many deserts, for example the Sahara Desert and the central Australian desert.

Climate change

The world's climate is changing slowly over many hundreds or thousands of years. For example, we know from fossils that the Sahara Desert was home to flowing rivers with crocodiles only 5000 years ago. Ice ages are the most important climate changes that temperate areas like northern Europe have experienced. Only 18,000 years ago northern Europe and North America were covered by an ice-sheet.

Scientists believe that there are many natural reasons for climate change. These include long-term changes in the Earth's orbit around the Sun, and variations in the amount of the Sun's heat that reaches the Earth's surface. Recently it has been suggested that our climate is also affected by human activity. By burning large amounts of fossil fuels such as coal and oil, we are releasing increased amounts of carbon dioxide and other gases into the atmosphere. Higher levels of these so-called greenhouse gases may be responsible for increasing the greenhouse effect. This increase may result in *global warming* – a rise in the world's temperatures.

• Major volcanic eruptions are a possible cause of climate change. They add large amounts of ash and gases into the upper atmosphere. The ash reduces the amount of heat from the Sun that reaches the Earth.

• Scientists predict that the Earth's average temperature will increase by between 1 °C and 3.5 °C in the 21st century.

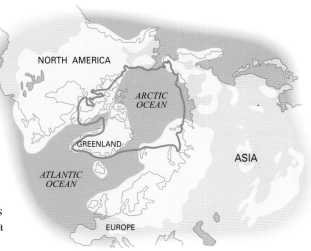

◄ The last ice age began about 1.8 million years ago and ended around 11,000 years ago. The climate was much colder than today, and much of the northern hemisphere was covered in ice. During this ice age there were at least 17 periods called 'glacials' when ice-sheets were expanding. These were interrupted by warmer periods when the ice melted.

⬭ present-day limit of permanent ice

☐ approximate extent of glaciers

Clocks and watches

People have kept time for many thousands of years. Shadow sticks were used as long ago as 3500 BC, and the ancient Egyptians measured time with water clocks. Mechanical clocks with an hour hand and a minute hand were not made until the 17th century. Modern clocks and watches use a quartz crystal to keep the time extremely accurately.

Shadow sticks and sundials tell you the time from the changing length and direction of a shadow cast by the Sun as it moves across the sky. Water clocks were used in Egypt from about 1400 BC. Time was measured by how long it took water to flow out of holes in a container. The Greeks and Romans made more complicated water clocks, in the form of a cylinder into which water dripped from a reservoir. The time was read from a float.

Mechanical clocks

Mechanical clocks get their power from a weight that falls slowly or from a spring that has to be wound up. The first mechanical clocks were made in the 14th century. They did not have hands or a dial, but made a bell ring every hour. People began to put striking clocks in public places in large cities in Europe.

The first pendulum clock was built by the Dutchman Christiaan Huygens in the 17th century. It was much more accurate than any other clock at that time. A clock pendulum

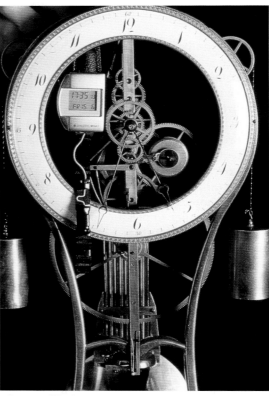

▶ This pendulum clock dates from the 18th century. The wrist-watch on top of it is controlled by radio signals from an atomic clock kept in Frankfurt, Germany. The atomic clock uses a metal called caesium to keep time, and is the most accurate clock of its kind in the world.

consists of a stiff rod with a weight on the end, that is free to swing to and fro. A pendulum of a given length always swings at the same rate. It was this regular swing that helped the pendulum clock keep such accurate time.

In 1675 Thomas Tompion made the first accurate watch. It used a small balance spring to keep time instead of a pendulum. John Harrison took up the challenge of making a chronometer, a particularly precise clock, that would keep accurate time on long sea journeys. In 1772 he was awarded a £20,000 prize as the first successful maker of a chronometer.

Modern timepieces

In the 19th century clocks driven by electric power were first made, and by 1918 they could use the signal from mains electricity to keep time. Mechanical wrist-watches were first popular around 1900, when they were made mainly in France and Switzerland. Today, many clocks and watches use the natural vibrations (100,000 per second) in a quartz crystal to keep time, and their power comes from batteries. Even a small watch can be like a tiny computer, with a built-in alarm and stopwatch and the time shown by a digital electronic display.

Atomic clocks are so accurate that they gain or lose less than a millionth of a second every year. They work by measuring the frequency with which certain atoms vibrate. International atomic time is kept by atomic clocks in laboratories around the world.

- Sand-glasses, which have been in use since the Middle Ages, are still often used as kitchen egg-timers. The sand takes a certain length of time to flow from one half of a glass container to the other.

- Pocket watches became possible after the invention, in about 1500, of the mainspring (a tightly wound coil) to give the power.

- The first electric clock was invented in 1843 by Alexander Bain.

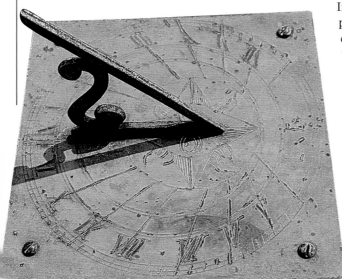

▲ Sundials are a kind of shadow clock. As the Sun moves across the sky, the shadow changes position. You read the time by seeing where the shadow falls on the dial.

find out more
Calendars
Time

Clothes

People usually choose a clothing style that suits a particular use: they may want a garment that is comfortable, hard-wearing, practical or perhaps simply fashionable. Most people in the world today buy ready-to-wear clothes which are mass-produced in factories or workshops. Such clothing is much cheaper to produce than traditional clothes made by hand.

In the countries of the developed world in particular, styles of clothing are often similar. This is partly because both the textiles and the designs are exchanged when different countries trade with each other. Also, many large clothing manufacturers have factories in several parts of the world, producing garments such as sportswear and denim jeans. Although these factories are in different locations, they produce the same styles of clothing.

Design

Designers decide what clothes will look like, and also plan how they will be manufactured. The choice of shape and the type of material depend on whether the clothes are intended to be fashionable, casual, for sport or for work. The sort of weather they are designed for controls what weight the material should be, and whether the garment should cover the whole body or part of it.

The designer's main task is to produce a prototype – a master pattern from which hundreds or thousands of identical garments can be made. The designer drapes the fabric over a dummy and cuts and pins it into shape. The pieces of material are then taken off the dummy, flattened out, and the shapes are traced to make a pattern. The pattern has to be fitted together very tightly onto the flat material to make sure that as little as possible is wasted. Each section is cut out, several layers of material at a time, with electric cutters or lasers. Today, computers can help to work out pattern shapes and how they can be fitted together on the material.

Manufacture

The separate pieces of the garment are then sewn together, often by a number of workers. One may sew up the main body of the garment; another puts in the sleeves; a third joins together the collar and cuffs, and so on. In factories where hundreds of the same garment are made daily, one machine may put together

◀ This woman in Gujurat, northern India, is employed to sew clothes by hand in her own home. In many developing countries the clothing industry relies on thousands of individual workers like her, instead of bringing the whole process together in a factory.

particular parts, such as pockets. Machines are used for pattern-cutting and for many small-scale sewing operations. Computerized machinery can often be reprogrammed to deal with fast-changing fashions, but many operations are still done by hand.

When all the pieces of material have been sewn together, the garment must be pressed to remove creases or to add in pleats that mould it into shape. Finally, the finished garments are carefully checked before they are sold.

▶ FLASHBACK ◀

Until the 1600s outer garments were made by men tailors, and women only made shirts and underwear. After women started to make women's clothes, men still made corsets and riding habits.

• The 'rag trade' is a term used to describe the cheaper end of the clothing industry.

• When the sewing machine became available in the 1850s, dressmakers could work more quickly and produce many more pieces of clothing in a day.

find out more
Dress and costume
Sewing and knitting
Shoes
Textiles

▼ The different stages in the manufacture of a piece of clothing.

The designer creates an original design using a computer.

The prototype garment is fitted onto a dummy.

A laser beam is used to cut through many layers of fabric at a time.

Skilled sewers use automatic sewing machines to sew together the different pieces of the garment.

The quality of the garments is checked before they are packed and distributed to shops and traders.

Clouds

Clouds form in different shapes and appearances at varying heights in the sky. Thin wispy cirrus clouds may form up to 15 kilometres above the ground, while low-lying stratus clouds can suddenly appear on high ground, creating problems for hikers and climbers.

The Earth's atmosphere contains lots of water vapour. But since the temperature in the air is not always the same everywhere, the water vapour sometimes changes back to a liquid by condensation. Clouds are formed when water vapour condenses to become small droplets in the air. These droplets are so small they are not heavy enough to fall to the ground as rain. They stay in the air and come together to form clouds.

Thunderstorms

Thunderstorms come from cumulonimbus clouds, the biggest in the sky. They bring heavy rain, thunder and lightning. Thunderstorm clouds have electrical charges. At the top the charge is positive, while at the bottom the charge is negative. The ground below a thunderstorm is also positive. When all these charges build up, there is a lightning flash which very briefly lights up the sky. Thunder is the noise we hear when the air in front of a stroke of lightning expands rapidly because of the great heat. Thunderclouds have bigger droplets than other clouds. Very big drops are too heavy to stay in the cloud and fall as rain. When the air in the cloud is very cold, the raindrops freeze and fall as hailstones.

▲ Low-lying nimbostratus clouds give us most of our heavy rain. They are dark grey and threatening.

find out more
Atmosphere
Climate
Rain and snow
Weather

height
−9 km ①
−8 km
−7 km ②
−6 km
−5 km
−4 km ③
−3 km ④
−2 km ⑤
−1 km ⑥ ⑦

1 **Cirrus** clouds consist of ice because they occur at heights where the temperature is always below freezing-point.
2 **Cirrocumulus** is often seen when fair weather approaches after a depression. A 'mackerel sky' (a form of cirrocumulus) means that rain is on the way.
3 In summer, layers of **altocumulus** clouds can be seen in late evening or early morning.
4 A veil of even, grey **altostratus** cloud is an almost certain sign of rain.
5 **Cumulonimbus** is the thundercloud of hot, still summer weather.
6 **Stratus** cloud often appears suddenly over high ground. It may thicken and turn to fog, drizzle or rain.
7 Heavy, cauliflower-shaped **cumulus** clouds are formed by currents of warm rising air.

Coal

The coal we are most familiar with – bituminous coal – is hard, black and shiny. It is the most common kind of coal and burns easily. Another kind of coal, called lignite, is soft and brown. All coal is the fossilized remains of plants. These plants grew with the help of the Sun's energy millions of years ago.

Some coal is simply burned as fuel, not only in household fires but also in power stations, to produce electricity. Much coal is also turned into coke, by baking it rather than burning it. Coke is a valuable smokeless fuel, and is also used in making iron from iron ore. When coke is made, coal tar and ammonia are also formed.

• In places such as Ireland and Scotland, peat is dug up, dried and burned as fuel. It is rather smoky.

• Highly compressed peat produces anthracite, a hard black coal which burns slowly with very little smoke.

find out more
Fossils
Geology
Mining
Power stations
Rocks and minerals

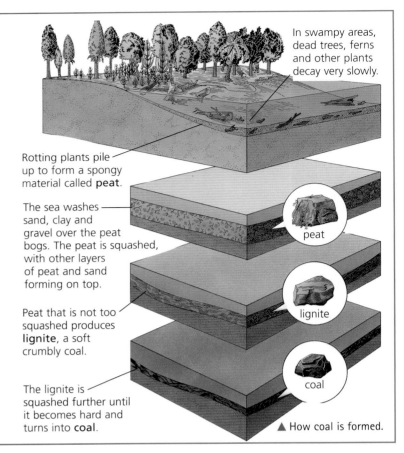

In swampy areas, dead trees, ferns and other plants decay very slowly.

Rotting plants pile up to form a spongy material called **peat**.

The sea washes sand, clay and gravel over the peat bogs. The peat is squashed, with other layers of peat and sand forming on top.

Peat that is not too squashed produces **lignite**, a soft crumbly coal.

The lignite is squashed further until it becomes hard and turns into **coal**.

peat

lignite

coal

▲ How coal is formed.

Coasts

A coast is the boundary where land meets sea. The world has about 312,000 kilometres of coastline. Many of the world's major cities, such as New York, Sydney, Shanghai and Rio de Janeiro, lie on the coast. Fertile plains along low-lying coasts, such as those in Bangladesh, are home to millions of people.

The pattern of coastlines is constantly changing as some coasts are worn away by the sea and others are built up by mud and sand. Waves are amazingly powerful forces that can wear away cliffs and carve out caves. They pound the worn-away rock into smaller and smaller pieces that are swept along the coast,

helping to wear away more rocks. In the process these pebbles are worn down to sand and deposited as beaches. Each year, billions of tonnes of sand and silt are carried to the oceans by rivers. This material is then washed in by breaking waves to build up the beach.

Some stretches of coastline are fast disappearing under the waves, for example along the east coast of England. In many

parts of the world there are natural sea defences such as salt marshes, sand dunes and mangrove swamps, which absorb the impact of the waves. However, many of these natural barriers are gradually being destroyed by human activities.

• Where a river drops a lot of sand or mud as it enters the sea, it may build out the coast to form a huge fan-shaped delta, such as the Mississippi or Nile delta.

find out more
Cliffs
Climate
Erosion
Greenhouse effect
Oceans and seas
Rivers and streams
Seashore

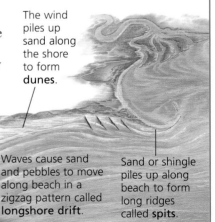

The wind piles up sand along the shore to form **dunes**.

The sea wears away cliffs to produce rocks and sand.

Waves cause sand and pebbles to move along beach in a zigzag pattern called **longshore drift**.

Sand or shingle piles up along beach to form long ridges called **spits**.

Breaking waves carry sand and shingle up the beach.

Colour

We live in a world full of colour. A rainbow arching its colours across the sky is a beautiful sight. The pictures we see on our television screens are filled with colour. Even the light from the Sun or an electric light bulb contains a mixture of colours – all the colours of the rainbow. How do we see all this colour?

All light travels like the ripples across a pond when you drop a stone in. The distance between the top of one ripple and the top of the next is called the *wavelength*. Light of different colours has different wavelengths. Red light has the longest wavelength and violet the shortest. The wavelength of the light makes us see different colours, although our brain also has an important part to play. Nobody knows exactly how we see all the shades of all the different colours.

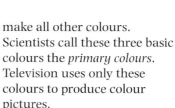

▲ When mixing light beams, only three basic colours – red, green and blue – are needed to make all the other colours. When the three colours are mixed together they produce white, because they contain all the colours in the spectrum.

White and coloured light

Although the light from the Sun seems colourless, it is made up of all the colours of the rainbow. We call this spread of colours a *spectrum*. Whenever our eyes receive this mixture of colours, we see it as white light.

To make beams of light of different colours, you can put sheets of transparent coloured plastic (filters) in front of a torch beam of white light. A red filter gives you a red light beam. A green filter gives you a green light beam. If you shine the red beam and the green beam onto a sheet of white paper, you will see yellow where they overlap! When light is added together in this way, only three basic colours – red, green and blue, each in different proportions – are needed to

make all other colours. Scientists call these three basic colours the *primary colours*. Television uses only these colours to produce colour pictures.

Paints and inks

Mixing paints or inks gives different colours from mixing beams of light. When you mix paints, colours are taken away. The paint on the walls of a room absorb most of the colours in white light. So when you see blue walls, for example, you are seeing only the colours in the blue part of the spectrum. All the colours in the red part of the spectrum are absorbed by the paint.

Printers can make most colours by mixing inks of three basic colours: magenta (a bluish red), yellow and cyan (a greenish blue).

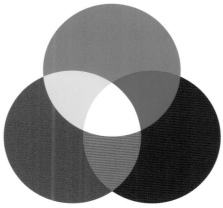

▲ When mixing paints, dyes or inks, the three primary colours – red, blue and yellow – are used. When these colours are mixed together they produce black.

find out more

Eyes
Light
Paints and dyes
Printing
Television

▼ Raindrops can act like tiny prisms, splitting sunlight into different colours. Only one colour from each raindrop reaches our eyes, but because there are thousands of drops we can see the whole rainbow. When a beam of sunlight goes into a raindrop, it is refracted (bent) and split up. It is then reflected from the back of the drop and is split up even further as it comes out.

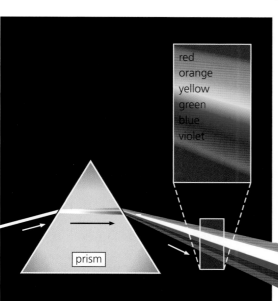

red
orange
yellow
green
blue
violet

▲ A glass prism splits white light into the colours of the spectrum. We can see the invisible light rays because they are bouncing off specks in the glass or smoke particles in the air.

Columbus,
Christopher

Born 1451 in Genoa,
Italy
Died 1506 aged 54

find out more
Caribbean
Explorers
South America

▼ This statue of
Columbus is from
Cartagena in Italy.

Christopher Columbus is one of the most famous explorers and navigators of all time. He came across the Americas while trying to find a westward route from Europe to the Far East.

→ first voyage, 1492–1493
→ fourth voyage, 1502–1504

SPAIN
Azores
Palos
Cadiz
Madeira
Bahamas
Cuba
Canary Islands
ATLANTIC OCEAN
Hispaniola
Jamaica
HONDURAS
Caribbean Sea
Martinique
AFRICA
Cape Verde Islands
Trinidad
SOUTH AMERICA

0   1200 km
0   900 miles

▲ This map shows two of Columbus's voyages across the Atlantic Ocean.

On 3 August 1492 Columbus, funded by the king and queen of Spain, set sail with three small ships, *Santa Maria*, *Niña* and *Pinta*, and about 90 men. After 9 weeks they sighted land. It was, in fact, one of the Bahamian islands, but Columbus was convinced it was the Indies and that he was very near Japan. He thought the local people were 'Indians', which is why Native Americans are sometimes so called.

Columbus returned to Spain a hero, and was given the titles of Admiral of the Ocean Sea and Viceroy of the Indies. This meant that he could set up and govern colonies in the new land. He went on a second voyage in 1493, when he visited Jamaica, and a third trip in 1498, when he set foot on mainland South America.

Although he was a good explorer, Columbus was not a good governor. Complaints were made about his harsh rule and he was arrested and sent back to Spain. However, he was soon pardoned, and in 1502 he was allowed to make one more voyage. He died in 1506, still believing he had reached the Far East. He never realized that he had, in fact, found a land that no European at the time knew existed.

Comets

Comets are icy objects which travel through the Solar System. A bright comet in the night sky looks like a hazy patch with a long wispy tail. The most famous comet, Halley's Comet, can be seen from the Earth every 76 years.

▶ The comet Hale–Bopp as photographed from California, USA, in March 1997. Its gas and dust tails are clearly visible. The comet was first discovered on 23 June 1995.

find out more
Gravity
Solar System
Sun

Comets travel in orbits through the Solar System. They evaporate gas and dust and grow long tails when they are near enough to the Sun's heat and light. The tails are caused by the light and streams of atomic particles from the Sun.

Comets that are bright enough to be seen easily by the unaided eye are quite rare, but astronomers using telescopes find 20 or 30 comets every year. When a comet comes near Earth, it gets brighter over a few weeks. A check from night to night shows that it moves slowly among the stars. Then it gradually fades and disappears.

Most comets are seen only once. They are pulled towards the Sun by the force of its gravity, then they vanish into distant space. Others get trapped by the gravity of the Sun and planets and keep moving around the Sun in long oval orbits.

Halley's Comet

Halley's Comet is named after the astronomer Edmond Halley. He observed a bright comet in 1682, and realized that it had appeared at least twice before. Halley predicted that it would reappear in 1758, although he did not live to see it.

Communication

Communication is the passing of signals from one living thing to another. For humans, communication ranges from a simple smile or a wave, to a message on the Internet.

Most communication in the animal kingdom is to do with finding a mate, warning others of danger or keeping in touch with young. The signs and symbols that animals use to communicate with each other include smells, sounds, gestures and displays. Humans seem to be the only animals that can produce a highly complex language.

Writing and printing

About 5000 years ago people used writing for the first time. In the beginning they made symbols on clay or parchment scrolls. They communicated over long distances with written messages carried by runners or messengers travelling on horseback.

Until the 15th century, written documents were made and copied by hand. Then, in 1450, the first great communications revolution began. Johann Gutenberg developed the first practical printing system, producing pamphlets and books in large numbers. This meant that ideas and education could be shared by many more people.

Wires and waves

In the 19th century a series of discoveries and inventions produced a second revolution in

• In 1794 the Frenchman Claude Chappe invented a signalling system called *semaphore*. Two movable arms on top of a tall tower were set at angles to spell out words according to a code. Using a telescope, the signals could be read from another tower up to 16 km away.

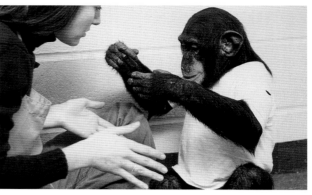

▲ Chimpanzees are believed to be the most intelligent animals after human beings. Researchers have successfully taught them to use sign language and languages which involve picture symbols. In this photograph a researcher is teaching a chimp the sign language for 'box'.

communications. The invention of railways greatly increased the speed at which letters could be delivered. Then, in 1837, the telegraph was invented. This sent messages, coded as a series of long and short bleeps, along electric wires.

In 1876 a Scottish-born inventor, Alexander Graham Bell, developed the telephone, enabling people in distant locations to speak directly to each other for the first time. Later, in 1895, the Italian Guglielmo Marconi made the first long-distance radio transmission using radio waves. Wireless technology developed rapidly throughout the 20th century. It is used in mobile communications between vehicles, and as a means of mass communication through radio and television broadcasts.

Global communications

Since the late 20th century people have been able to talk to each other from opposite sides of the world using a phone they can carry around in their pocket. The world's telephone network has also been combined with computer technology. This has enabled people to send and receive electronic mail and to obtain information from databases all over the world.

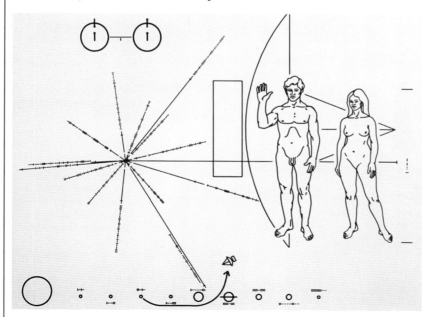

◀ The plaque attached to the *Pioneer 10* and *11* spacecraft. It shows where the spacecraft come from in case they are ever examined by another intelligent species. The 'dumb-bell' symbol at top left represents a molecule of hydrogen, the most common element in the Universe. Below this, the lines radiating from a central point show the positions of 14 pulsars (cosmic sources of radio energy) relative to our Sun. Below the human figures is a plan of the Solar System showing the early stages of the spacecraft's journey from Earth.

Communists

'Workers of all countries, unite!' So wrote Karl Marx and Friedrich Engels, who together were the founders of modern communism. Communism is a political theory. It calls for a society in which all property and businesses are owned by the people, and in which each person is paid according to their needs, whatever their abilities are.

Marx, a German political writer living in London, England, developed the ideas on which communism is based in his influential book *Capital* (1867–1894). In it, he claimed that one day workers would rise in revolution, destroy the rich and set up communism across the world.

▶ Fidel Castro, communist leader of Cuba since 1959, speaking in front of a poster of Che Guevara, who fought with Castro to overthrow the Cuban dictator Batista.

However, communist revolutions did not come about in rich, industrial states, but in underdeveloped countries, such as Russia and China. Under communism people were better educated, and unemployment and extreme poverty were eliminated. But, as Marx had wanted, communist states were dictatorships. In Stalin's Russia and Mao Zedong's China everything was controlled by the Communist Party. This led to much corruption and cruelty. By the 1990s most communist governments, including those in Poland and the former Soviet Union, had collapsed.

Some of the communists' ideals live on in *socialism*, a moderate version of communism. This rejects revolution and dictatorship, but accepts the need for justice and equal opportunities for all.

find out more
China
Dictators
Mao Zedong
Russia
Stalin, Joseph

Compact discs

Compact discs (CDs for short) have many different uses. You can listen to recorded music on audio CDs. You can look up an encyclopedia entry or play a game on a CD-ROM, which stores computer programs and other data. Almost any sort of information can be recorded on a CD.

Compact discs are made of plastic, about 1 millimetre thick, and normally measure 12 centimetres across. On a CD, information is coded as binary numbers (just the digits 0 and 1). Groups of 0s and 1s represent larger numbers, which in turn represent sounds, pictures, letters and so on. The first CDs were developed in the early 1980s.

Recording on a CD

A laser beam makes a recording by burning pits into the surface of a compact disc. A master disc is made from this. The master disc stamps the pits into transparent plastic discs. The pitted side is coated with aluminium and a layer of lacquer, and then the label is put on. On the underside of the disc, the reverse of the pits comes out as a pattern of 'steps' and 'flats' (no step). A flat represents a 1 in binary, and a step represents a 0.

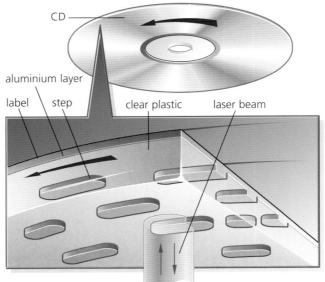

CD
aluminium layer
label
step
clear plastic
laser beam

find out more
Computers
Electronics
Information technology
Lasers
Recording

● DVDs (digital video discs or digital versatile discs) use the same technology as compact discs, but can hold about 15 times as much information as a CD-ROM.

◀ Inside a CD player, a laser beam reads the pattern of steps and flats on the underside of the CD. Electronic circuits turn this pattern into electrical signals, which are used to form the sounds you hear or the words and pictures you see on the screen.

Complementary medicine

Complementary medicine includes various forms of medical treatment that do not involve the use of artificial drugs or surgery, which are features of traditional Western medicine. Some treatments are based on ancient remedies or on Eastern methods of healing, but others are fairly new ideas.

Most of the therapies (systems of healing) used in complementary medicine are run according to the standards of a governing organization, and the practitioners are usually trained and qualified. The therapies may be used alongside treatment given by qualified medical doctors and are said to 'complement' standard medical care.

Many of the treatments seem to be of real benefit to patients, although it is possible that when a person 'believes' in the treatment they make it work.

Varieties of treatment

There are many kinds of complementary medicine. Some have a 'holistic' approach. This means that, in the treatment, attention is paid to the overall well-being of the patient, not just to a specific physical problem.

Traditional *Chinese medicine* is based on very complicated ideas called 'yin and yang' and the 'five phases', which relate to inner harmony and balance. This harmony and balance also depends on the smooth flow of *qi* (pronounced 'chee'), a sort of life-energy which is thought to be responsible for the proper working of all parts of the body. There are many different forms of ancient Chinese treatment, including

▲ A traditional Chinese acupuncture study figure of an adult female. It shows the meridians (energy pathways) and points where needles are inserted.

find out more
Diseases
Health and fitness
Medicine

Other types of complementary medicine
Alexander technique is a method of correcting bad habits of posture, breathing and muscular tension. It was developed by an Australian therapist in the 1930s.
Aromatherapy uses 'essential' oils that give plants their aroma (smell) to bring about a positive effect on the mind and body. The oils are usually massaged into the patient's skin.
Herbalism is the use of plants and plant products as 'natural medicine' instead of artificially-produced drugs, which can be harmful.
Reflexology is a treatment in which certain parts of the feet (reflex points) are pressed to relieve problems in various parts of the body.
Shiatsu is a Japanese treatment, similar in theory to acupuncture. Instead of using needles, however, the practitioner uses finger or palm pressure on various points on the body.

---

acupuncture, osteopathy and moxibustion, in which dried herbs are burnt next to the skin. Chinese medicines are made from herbs and animal parts.

The ancient Chinese practice of *acupuncture* is one of the best-known and most successful forms of complementary medicine in the West. It is used for relieving pain, curing disease and improving general health. The practice involves inserting long, fine metal needles into the body at specific points along the 12 'meridians', the *qi* pathways in the body. Although the needles may be far from the part of the body that the acupuncturist is treating, they are connected to it by the meridians.

Backache and other pains in the joints and muscles are very common complaints in the modern world. Osteopathy and chiropractic are popular methods of treating them. *Osteopathy* involves pushing, pulling, twisting and pressing various bones in the body to get them back into their proper positions. *Chiropractic* involves similar treatment but it focuses specifically on the spine.

Homeopathy is based on the belief that if a sick person shows symptoms of a disease, it means that their body is battling against it. If a patient is given a minute quantity of a substance that produces the same type of symptoms as the illness, the body's own natural healing process will be encouraged to fight the illness.

◀ In India and Sri Lanka, many hospitals practise Ayurvedic medicine. This is an ancient system of Indian medicine that is based on principles found in the Hindu scriptures. The doctor in this Sri Lankan hospital is applying a herbal paste to the patient's knee to treat her inflamed knee-joint.

Computers

Computers are electronic machines that can be programmed to do a huge number of different tasks. In homes, schools and offices, they are used to produce documents, create designs, make calculations, store lists and search for information. In factories, computers operate tools and robot arms. There are even computers inside washing machines and microwave ovens.

Computers work by processing *data*. Data is information. It can be numbers, words, pictures, sounds – in fact, almost any sort of information. As the computer operates, it follows instructions stored in its electronic memory. These instructions are called a *program*. The reason a computer can do so many different jobs is that the program can be changed easily. This means that the same computer can be a word processor, an encyclopedia, or a powerful mathematical calculator.

Hardware and software

A computer system is made up of two parts, the hardware and the software. The hardware is the actual computer itself – the electronic parts, the screen and the keyboard. Software is the programs and data that the computer uses. *Systems software* is software that the computer needs to do basic jobs, such as sending words and pictures to the screen. *Applications software* is software that allows the computer to do different jobs – word-processing, storing information, doing calculations or playing games.

Inside a computer

At the heart of every computer is a tiny microchip, a small slice of silicon imprinted with an extremely complicated electronic circuit. This is the *microprocessor*. It is the part of the computer that does all the calculations and carries out the instructions it gets from programs. The computer also has a set of memory chips for storing programs and data. There are two types of memory – RAM (Random Access Memory) and ROM (Read-Only Memory). RAM is the computer's short-term memory, where it stores data it needs quickly. Everything stored in the RAM is lost when the computer is turned off. ROM is where the computer stores data it will need again and again. It takes longer to read or to store data in the ROM, but the data is not lost when the computer is turned off.

The microprocessor carries out programs stored in the memory. As the microprocessor follows the program instructions, it gets pieces of data from the memory, does something with them, such as adding them together or multiplying them, and then stores the results. A microprocessor understands only a few dozen simple instructions. But when these instructions are combined in a program, it can do very complicated calculations and tasks.

▲ A computer's power is measured by how many instructions it can carry out each second. Today's personal computers (PCs) operate at around 300 MIPS (millions of instructions per second), but supercomputers like this CM-5, which is as tall as a wardrobe, can operate at over 10,000 MIPS. Instead of using a single microprocessor, like a PC, it can use up to 1024 processors.

● Computer circuits recognize only two numbers, 0 and 1. These are called *binary numbers*. Binary numbers are based on two. This means that the number one is written as 1, but two is 10 (one 2 and no 1s), three is 11, and so on. Computers store and process data using binary numbers.

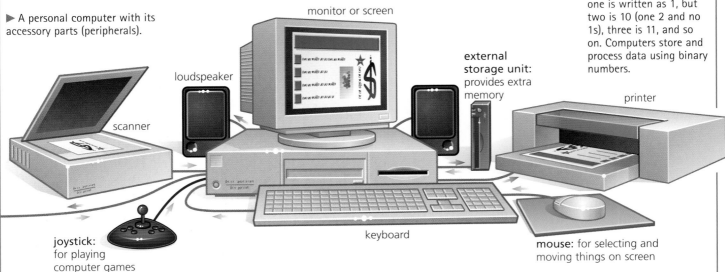

▶ A personal computer with its accessory parts (peripherals).

monitor or screen

loudspeaker

external storage unit: provides extra memory

printer

scanner

joystick: for playing computer games

keyboard

mouse: for selecting and moving things on screen

 Concentration camps *see* Holocaust

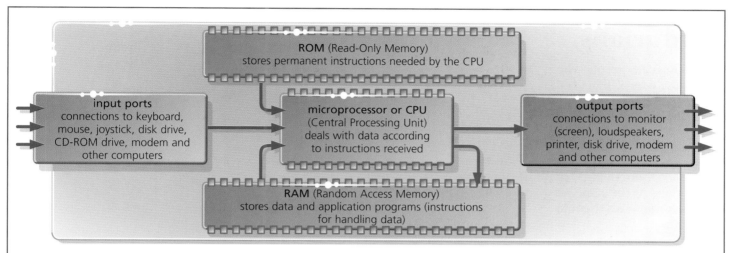

ROM (Read-Only Memory)
stores permanent instructions needed by the CPU

input ports
connections to keyboard, mouse, joystick, disk drive, CD-ROM drive, modem and other computers

microprocessor or CPU
(Central Processing Unit) deals with data according to instructions received

output ports
connections to monitor (screen), loudspeakers, printer, disk drive, modem and other computers

RAM (Random Access Memory)
stores data and application programs (instructions for handling data)

Peripherals

Peripherals are devices attached to a computer, which send it data and receive data from it. *Input devices* are used to get data into the computer. The most common input device is the keyboard. Others include a mouse, CD-ROMs, scanners (which copy pictures into the computer), microphones and digital cameras. *Output devices* are used to get information out of the computer. The most common output devices are monitors, which display words and pictures, and printers, which print out data. Loudspeakers and earphones are also output devices.

Some peripherals are both input and output devices. Disk drives are the most common of these. Disk drives store data on magnetic disks (floppy disks), CDs or DVDs (digital versatile discs). They can write data from the microprocessor onto a disk, or they can read data from the disk and send it back to the microprocessor. A modem can send information from one computer to another through the telephone network.

▶ FLASHBACK ◀

In the mid-1830s, before scientists understood electricity, a British mathematician called Charles Babbage designed a mechanical computer called an analytical engine. Unfortunately it was far too complicated to build in his lifetime.

▶ Technicians changing the wiring of ENIAC (the Electronic Numerical Integrator And Calculator). ENIAC was completed in 1946 and was one of the first electronic computers. Changing the wiring created different circuits between ENIAC's 18,000 valves, and so changed its 'program'.

The first electronic computers were developed in the 1940s. Instead of microchips, they used thousands of electronic valves, which looked rather like light bulbs and were about the same size. These huge computers were not as powerful as today's small portable computers. In the 1950s electronic valves were replaced by transistors, which were much smaller – about the size of a pea – and computers became smaller and more powerful.

In 1972 the first microchips were made. In the late 1970s and early 1980s the first personal computers (PCs) were produced. Since then, microprocessors have become more and more powerful and computers have become cheaper. Today, computer scientists are experimenting with computer systems called *neural nets*, which can solve problems by learning for themselves.

▲ Flow diagram showing how data is processed in a computer.

• The amount of information a computer or a disk drive can store is measured in *bits* and *bytes*. One bit of memory stores either a 0 or a 1. One byte is eight bits: enough to store one letter of the alphabet.

find out more
Calculators
Compact discs
Electronics
Information technology
Internet

Confucians

Confucians are people who follow the way of life suggested by the Chinese teacher Confucius, who lived in the 6th and 5th centuries BC. They believe, as Confucius did, that the most important thing in life is to treat others in the same way as you would wish them to treat you.

Confucius was the son of a poor nobleman. He worked for a time as a government official, but after his mother's death he gave up his job and went home to mourn for three years, as was the custom of the time. While there, he began to study ancient Chinese history and literature. He spent most of his remaining years as a travelling teacher of young noblemen and officials.

Teachings

Some years after Confucius's death, his teachings were collected into a book called the *Analects*. They teach that the best kind of life is one full of peace and harmony. A person creates harmony by avoiding any extreme action or bad thoughts. Confucius believed that peace in the world depends on the proper organization of each country; that a peaceful country depends on a peaceful family; and that peaceful family life depends on the harmony inside each individual.

The teachings of Confucius were developed and handed on by Mengzi (Mencius) in the 4th century BC. Much later, in AD 1190, his most important teachings were printed and published so that they could be read all over China.

◀ A portrait of Confucius.

• Confucius is the Western spelling of the Chinese name Kongzi, which means 'Kong the master'.

• Confucius devoted much of his life to relieving suffering among the poor by working for government reforms. For almost 2000 years, up until 1912, all students who were training to be Chinese officials had to study his ideas.

find out more
Buddhists
China
Religions
Taoists

Congo, Democratic Republic of

The Democratic Republic of Congo (formerly Zaire) is in central Africa. It is Africa's third largest country by area, after Sudan and Algeria.

One of the world's longest rivers, the Congo, runs through the country. The river forms a great basin covering three-fifths of the country, which is mostly rainforest. Around the basin the land rises to high grassy plains. Mountains rise in the south and east. The climate is hot and rainy.

The Congo has about 200 groups of people, each with its own language. Most people are farmers, growing crops such as cassava, maize (corn) and rice for food, and coffee to sell. The chief export is copper.

Congo was once ruled by powerful African kings, but the kingdoms lost their power in the 16th century. European traders sold many people from the area as slaves. In 1885 King Léopold II of Belgium declared the country to be his personal property. Belgium ruled the country, which they called the Belgian Congo, from 1908 until it became independent in 1960.

In 1961 the new prime minister was assassinated and the country was torn apart by civil war. General Mobutu Sese Seko seized power. He made the country very poor. In May 1997 Mobuto was overthrown. Since then there has again been civil war.

• Zaire was renamed Democratic Republic of Congo in 1997.

◀ Fishermen haul up their fish traps at Boyoma Falls on the Lualaba River. Beyond the falls, the river becomes the Congo.

find out more
Africa
Refugees
See also Countries fact file, page 619

    Congo, Republic of *see page 619* • **Conifers** *see* Trees and shrubs

Conservation

With more and more people wanting space for houses, factories and farms, there is less and less space for other living things. Conservation is action to stop rare animals and plants from dying out and to stop common animals and plants from becoming rare. It also aims to protect the wild places where all these animals and plants live.

In the past, some animals became extinct (died out) because they could not cope with natural changes around them. The dinosaurs may all have died out when a meteor from space crashed into the Earth. This sent clouds of dust into the air, that blotted out the Sun and made the weather too cold for them. However, humans have greatly speeded up the rate at which plants and animals are becoming extinct.

For example, the dodo that lived on the island of Mauritius was a slow-moving bird that could not fly. When the first humans discovered Mauritius, they found that the dodo was easy to kill and good to eat. In less than a century, they had killed every dodo. Many other animals have also been made extinct by humans killing them and destroying their homes.

Animals in danger

Many other living things are in danger of becoming extinct. At least 1000 different kinds of birds and mammals are now extremely rare, and nobody can even begin to guess how many kinds

▲ No more than 400 mountain gorillas survive in the mountain forests of central Africa, yet some are still shot by poachers. A recent war in the countries where they live has reduced numbers still further.

of insects and plants are in danger. The giant panda from China is a famous example. Less than 1000 pandas survive in the wild, because so much of the wild bamboo forest in which they live has been chopped down by people to make

▼ For many centuries, animals have been made extinct by human hunting. In the last 350 years, 95 different birds and 40 different kinds of mammal have become extinct, including the penguin-like great auk from the islands of the North Atlantic, the passenger pigeon of North America, and the quagga (a kind of zebra) from Africa.

• The rarest animal in the world is probably the Spix's macaw. A single male bird was found in a wood in Brazil in 1990. About 30 other Spix's macaws live in zoos, and a few females have now been released back into the wild, in the hope that they will breed with the male to save the species.

Carolina parakeet
extinct 1918

quagga
extinct 1883

aurochs
extinct 1627

passenger pigeon
extinct 1914

giant moa
extinct about 1500

dodo
extinct 1681

flightless ibis
extinct about 1000

giant lemur
extinct about AD 500

way for fields. Several kinds of rhinoceros are in danger because of hunting for their horns, and tigers are threatened by hunting for their skins.

Rare birds that need conservation include the bald eagle – the national bird of the United States – and the Mauritius kestrel from the island where the dodo once lived. Thanks to the work of conservationists, these animals are now commoner than they were, but they still need help if they are to survive.

None of these plants and animals can survive unless we protect their habitats – the wild places in which they live. Many of the rarest animals live in the tropical rainforest, but the rainforest itself is in danger. Every minute, an area of rainforest the size of 20 football pitches is cut or burnt down, either for the valuable timber from its trees or to make way for farming. All the animals that live there then lose their homes.

In the sea, coral reefs are almost as full of life as rainforests, but only about a tenth of them are still in good condition. The rest have been damaged by waste chemicals, by mud washed down rivers, by too many human visitors and even by coral mining.

Positive action

Since about 1970, people have realized how seriously these plants, animals and wild places are threatened, and have begun to do something. Conservation charities like the World Wide Fund for Nature (WWF) have spent huge sums of money trying to protect rare animals and plants and their habitats. Governments have passed laws to stop animals being killed, and they have set up nature reserves and national parks to keep their best pieces of countryside safe.

Perhaps the most important change is that people have begun to recognize the value of wild plants and animals. As well as the pleasure we

find out more
Ecology
Green movement
Pollution
Zoos

▼ People who protect wildlife and wild places are called conservationists. These young conservationists are cleaning up a river to make it a better home for plants and animals.

▲ Every year, an area of rainforest twice the size of Austria is destroyed by humans. In this satellite photograph, taken over western Brazil, the natural forest (shown in pink) is being cut down to make way for farmers' fields (shown in blue and green).

get from seeing a beautiful animal in its habitat (even if it is only on television), many living things have other values for humans. For example, a medicine from a rare plant called the rosy periwinkle from the rainforest of Madagascar is now used to cure a disease called leukaemia. The rainforest and the oceans also have an important role in locking up the gases, produced by factories and power stations, that are causing global warming. However, this can only happen if these wild places are kept in good condition.

The variety of life

In 1985 an American scientist invented a new word: *biodiversity*. It combines the words 'biological' (referring to living things) and 'diversity' (meaning lots of different kinds), so it means the total variety of all living things on Earth. Biodiversity is part of the natural 'wealth' of our planet. We all become a little poorer for each bit of biodiversity that is lost. The sheer variety of living things also helps to keep the environment in good working order. Biodiversity is therefore an important measure of the health of the planet.

In 1992, at an international meeting called the Earth Summit in Rio de Janeiro, Brazil, world leaders signed a document promising they would protect the biodiversity of their countries, and help poorer countries do the same. That means that everyone around the world has a part to play in saving living things and their habitats.

　Constantine the Great *see* Byzantine empire

Constellations

If you look at the night sky, you can pick out patterns made by the brighter stars. For thousands of years, people have been giving names to the groups of stars that make these patterns. These named groups are the constellations. Some of them were named by the Greeks 2000 years ago, and Arab and Chinese astronomers had their own constellations too.

There are 88 constellations and they cover the whole sky. They were probably invented as a way of referring to particular stars. Although the stars in a constellation appear to us to be in a group, they are really vast distances away from each other. Astronomers have agreed where the imaginary boundary lines between the constellations are, and the official names they use are in Latin. Many of the old names of constellations are of animals, like Leo (the Lion) and Cygnus (the Swan), and of people from Greek myths, such as Perseus and Andromeda. Among the recently named constellations you will find Octans (the Octant) and Horologium (the Clock).

The constellations you can see at any one time vary according to the season, the time of night and where you are on the Earth. If you live in the northern hemisphere, some of the easiest constellations to find are in the sky on winter evenings. Orion (the Hunter) has three very bright stars in a row making his belt. Near him you can find Taurus (the Bull) and Gemini (the Twins). On summer evenings, three of the brightest stars are in Aquila (the Eagle), Cygnus and Lyra (the Lyre). They stand out as a giant triangle and can help you find some of the other constellations. From the southern hemisphere people see different constellations, such as Crux Australis (the Southern Cross) and Centaurus (the Centaur).

The zodiac

We cannot see the stars during the day because the Sun is too bright, but if we could we would notice the Sun slowly moving through the star patterns. It makes a trip right round the sky once a year, travelling through a band of constellations called the zodiac. The ancient Greeks divided the zodiac into 12 equal zones, called the 'signs' of the zodiac. Each sign corresponds roughly to one of the zodiac constellations, though the official constellations that astronomers use are not all equal in size. People called astrologers make predictions about people's lives, based on the signs of the zodiac.

▲ This colourful 18th-century print brings the constellations of the zodiac to life.

find out more
Astrology
Astronomy
Seasons
Stars

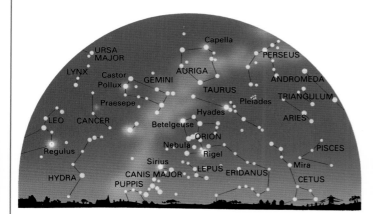

▲ This star chart shows some of the constellations visible from the northern hemisphere in winter. You would need to stand facing south around midnight in December in Europe to see the sky looking like this.

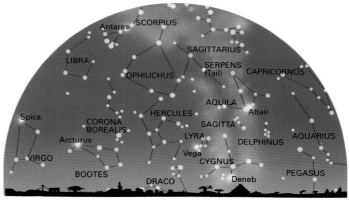

▲ This star chart shows some of the constellations visible in winter in the southern hemisphere. You would need to stand facing north around midnight in June in Australia to see the sky looking like this.

Continents

The large masses of land on the Earth's surface are called continents. They cover 29 per cent of the total surface area. Millions of years ago, all the continents were joined together in one giant landmass, called Pangaea. Gradually this supercontinent broke up into smaller pieces to form the seven continents we know today.

plate boundaries
— moving apart
- - - - moving together
— passive

▲ This map shows the present-day position of the world's continents, as well as the names and the boundaries of the rocky plates that make up the Earth's crust.

• Liquid rock is pushing up through a deep crack in the middle of the floor of the Atlantic Ocean. As the two halves of the ocean floor are forced apart, the continent of Africa is moving gradually to the east and South America to the west.

Europe is the smallest continent. Some people insist that it is really part of Asia because there is no clear division between the two. (The Ural Mountains and the Ural river are usually taken to be the boundary.) Oceania is counted as a continent although it is made up of Australia, New Zealand and other Pacific islands.

The heart of each continent is a flat slab or 'shield' of ancient rock. Around this lie regions on which are piled great thicknesses of sedimentary rocks. At the edges are mountains. Continents are generally 30–40 kilometres thick. Continental rocks are much older than the rocks which lie under the oceans.

Moving plates

• The Earth's plates are all moving in different directions. North America will eventually reach Russia to the west. Africa may move northwards, closing off the Mediterranean Sea.

The rocky surface of the Earth is divided up into several large plates. These great rafts of rock 'float' on top of the liquid rocks of the mantle, the Earth's main inner layer. The plates move slowly over the Earth's surface. Over millions of years this movement, although only a few centimetres each year, has caused continents to split apart and collide.

The explanation of these plate movements is called *plate tectonics*. On some parts of the ocean floor, plates pull apart. New crust forms when hot, liquid rocks (magma) from undersea volcanoes rise to plug the gap. The magma rises

through weak areas of the Earth's crust to form underwater mountains (mid-oceanic ridges), rift valleys, and volcanic mountains or islands. Deep-sea trenches form where one part of the ocean floor is pushed under another.

At other plate boundaries, when one plate edge is forced under another, earthquakes can occur. Great mountain ranges such as the Himalayas and the Andes form where one plate pushes against another.

Continental drift

We can find evidence of how the continents gradually drifted to their present-day positions when we see how well the coastlines of different continents match up. For example, Africa and South America fit neatly together. Identical fossils of ferns and reptiles have been found in South America, Africa, India, Antarctica and Australia. These plants and animals could not have crossed the oceans, so they must have lived on the same landmass at some time in the past.

▼ About 200 million years ago, Pangaea began to split into the supercontinents of Laurasia and Gondwanaland. These landmasses broke up further to become the continents we know today.

250 million years ago

175 million years ago

present day

Cook, James

James Cook was a sailor and navigator who explored and mapped the Pacific Ocean and its islands. He claimed Australia and New Zealand for the British empire.

James Cook was 18 before he first worked on sailing ships. Nearly 10 years later, with England on the brink of war with France, Cook joined the Royal Navy as a seaman. He soon won promotion and was entrusted with the navigation of a ship.

In 1768 he was given command of the ship *Endeavour*. His main task was to take some astronomers to the Pacific island of Tahiti, but he was also given secret orders to search for the Great Southern Continent which people believed existed.

On that voyage around the world from 1768 to 1771, Cook explored and charted the coast of New Zealand and the eastern coast of Australia. The following year he sailed south of the Antarctic Circle, before cruising the Pacific Ocean to visit and chart many of the islands.

Cook was promoted to captain before going on a trip to find a possible sea route running north of Canada from the Pacific. He was the first European to visit the Sandwich Islands (Hawaii), and he passed through the Bering Strait between Alaska and Siberia into the Arctic Ocean. He was then forced to stop and turn round by a thick pack of ice. He returned to Hawaii to pick up food and water, but was killed by islanders in a scuffle on shore.

Born 1728 in Yorkshire, England
Died 1779 aged 50

find out more
Australia
Georgian Britain
New Zealand
Pacific Islands

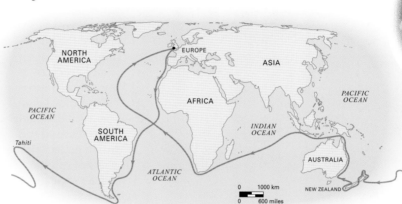

◄ James Cook sailed around the world on his first voyage. He sailed his small ships over a wider area of unknown seas than any other explorer.

Cooking

Cooking can make food look and taste much more interesting. Different ideas about which foods to cook together have contributed to the very different dishes found all over the world.

Almost all food can be eaten without any cooking at all. Most people eat raw fruit, and raw vegetables in salads, and some like raw fish. However, many foods are much easier to chew and digest if they have been cooked. Cooking also helps to destroy harmful bacteria.

Cooking up changes

Cooking causes chemical changes to take place in all food. These changes are irreversible. You cannot unboil an egg. Cell walls soften and the cells tend to separate. This can be seen if you look at mashed potato through a strong lens. Some of the contents of the cells may escape. Water, for example, evaporates during dry roasting, and a roasted joint of meat shrinks as it cooks. Colour and nutrients may be lost into the water when food is boiled.

Starch granules in food swell on cooking and become quite jelly-like. This is why flour is used for thickening. The protein in egg sets, and so eggs are used to set dishes like soufflés and sponge cakes.

find out more
Diets
Food
Heat
Household equipment
Spices

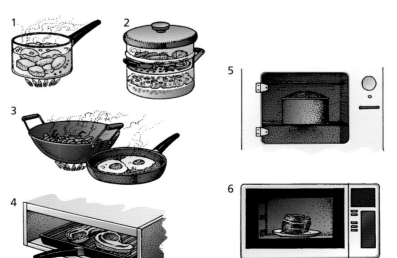

◄ Some different cooking methods. When you **boil** food (1) you cook it in water boiling at 100 °C. In **steaming** (2), the food is heated by steam from water boiling beneath it. **Frying** (3) involves heating the food in hot fat. When you **grill** food (4), it is heated by radiant heat. **Baking** (5) heats food in an oven using hot air. A **microwave** oven (6) uses very short-wavelength radio waves to penetrate and heat the food.

Copernicus, Nicolas

Born 1473 in Poland
Died 1543 aged 70

Nicolas Copernicus was the first person to work out that the Sun is at the centre of our Solar System, and all the planets orbit around it.

▶ This map of the Solar System was published by Copernicus in about 1530. In it he demonstrates how the Earth orbits the Sun, and how its position in relation to the Sun at different times of the year affects its climate and creates the seasons. He also shows the orbits of Saturn, Jupiter and Mars.

find out more
Astronomy
Galilei, Galileo
Solar System

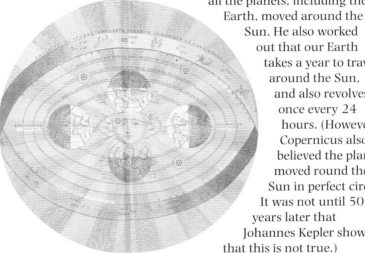

When Nicolas Copernicus started studying astronomy, everyone believed that the Earth was at the centre of the Universe, and that the Earth did not move. Copernicus, however, realized that this picture did not agree with astronomical observations. He believed that all the planets, including the Earth, moved around the Sun. He also worked out that our Earth takes a year to travel around the Sun, and also revolves once every 24 hours. (However, Copernicus also believed the planets moved round the Sun in perfect circles. It was not until 50 years later that Johannes Kepler showed that this is not true.)

Copernicus set out his Sun-centred theory in a famous book, *De revolutionibus*. This was printed in 1543, just a few weeks before he died. His ideas were considered very controversial. They challenged views about the Solar System which had been held since the times of the ancient Greeks. They also challenged the Church's belief that God created the Earth at the centre of the Universe.

Copernicus's book was regarded as a source of evil ideas, and in 1616 it was put on the 'Index', a list of books that Roman Catholics were not allowed to read. Copernicus's theory was the subject of a famous trial in 1633, when the great astronomer Galileo was forced against his will to declare that the Earth did not move at all.

Cotton

Fibres from the cotton plant are used to make clothing fabric which is cool and comfortable to wear. Cotton fabric absorbs moisture and lets it out, so your skin can breathe. Cotton fibres are also made into towelling, cheesecloth, curtaining, furniture fabric and heavy-duty industrial fabrics.

Cotton grows in tropical and subtropical areas. Each plant produces seed pods (bolls) which contain about 30 seeds. The ripened bolls burst open to reveal a fluffy mass of fibres. When the fluffy mass is separated from the seeds, it is known as cotton lint, which is what is used to make fabrics. The cotton seeds are not thrown away. The fat is extracted to produce an edible oil, and the seeds are then processed into cattle cake and fertilizer.

Machinery is used on the largest cotton plantations for almost all jobs, from sowing to picking. On the smaller plantations in poorer countries, the cotton worker uses teams of oxen or buffalo and picks the cotton by hand. Although harvesting by machine is quicker, hand-picking is often better because the cotton pickers pick only the really ripe bolls.

Cotton fibres vary in length between about 2 and 4 centimetres. Short and medium-length fibres account for about 90 per cent of world production of cotton fabric. The finest fabrics are made from long fibres. Cotton fabric is easily dyed and printed. It can be treated so that it is waterproof. Also, it is not affected by static electricity in the atmosphere and therefore stays clean much longer than other materials. It is now frequently reinforced with other fibres, such as polyester and Acrilan.

◀ Cotton-harvesting by machine in California, USA.

• Cotton is grown on a commercial basis in more than 75 countries. The largest producers are the USA, China and Uzbekistan, followed by India and Pakistan.

• A cotton worker can pick 110 kg of seed cotton by hand a day. A machine can pick the same amount in just one hour.

find out more
Clothes
Materials
Sewing and knitting
Textiles

Countries

A country is a territory (land) with its own people. Some countries are self-governing. We call them *sovereign countries*. The government of a sovereign country has the right to make laws for its own people. It can also print currencies, sign treaties with other sovereign countries, and even declare war. Most sovereign countries are members of the United Nations, which at present brings together over 190 countries.

Territories that are not fully self-governing but are ruled by another country are called *colonies* or *dependent territories*. There are around 60 such territories in the world. For example, Anguilla, in the Caribbean, is a dependency (dependent territory) of the United Kingdom.

If a country has a head of state who is born to the position, like a king or queen, it is a *monarchy*; if it does not, it is a *republic*. The Netherlands is a monarchy, but France and the USA are republics. Most countries are democracies, which means that they have elected governments. A few, such as Bhutan, are ruled directly by monarchs, while others, such as North Korea, are run by unelected dictators.

Developed and developing countries

Countries are often divided into two main groups: developed and developing, or less developed, countries. Development is the process

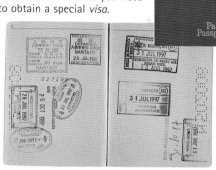

▼▶ To enter another country or to re-enter your own country you usually need a *passport*. Sometimes your passport is stamped (below) when you enter and leave a country. To enter some countries you need to obtain a special *visa*.

by which the inhabitants of a country or a region generally become richer, healthier and more educated. As a country becomes developed, it builds more and improved roads and communications, more industries, and more banks, schools and hospitals.

Developed countries are concentrated in the northern hemisphere, while much of the southern hemisphere consists of developing countries. For this reason they are sometimes referred to as 'the North' and 'the South'. The term 'First World' is also often used for the developed countries. The former Soviet Union (the USSR) and countries of Eastern Europe used to be known as the 'Second World'. The 'Third World' refers to developing countries.

Country records
Largest country
– by area
Russia
17,075,400 sq km
– by population
China 1,277,760,056
Smallest country by area and by population
Vatican City
0.44 sq km,
population 1000

• Malaysia, Singapore, Mexico and Chile are examples of 'Newly Industrializing Countries' (NICs). These are developing countries that are rapidly approaching the living standards of developed countries.

find out more
Democracy
Government
United Nations
See also Countries fact file and map of the world, pages 612–647

▼ This world map uses a scale that compares the wealth rather than the physical size of different countries. It measures 'gross domestic product' (GDP) (the value of all the goods and services produced within a country in a year).

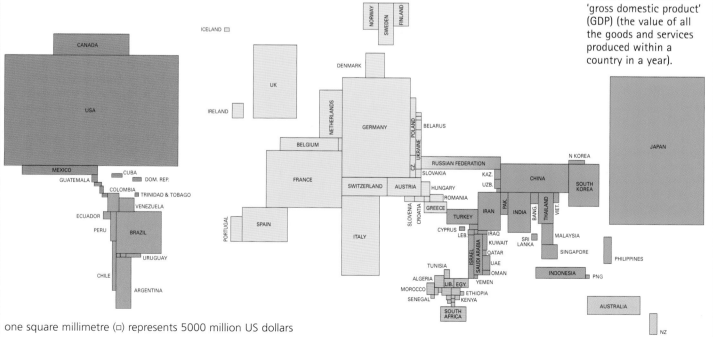

one square millimetre (□) represents 5000 million US dollars

Crabs and other crustaceans

Crustaceans are a large and successful group of animals including crabs, lobsters, barnacles and woodlice. The name crustacea means 'crusty one', a suitable name for animals that are covered in hard armour.

- There are about 150,000 different kinds of crustacean. Of these, over 6000 are lobsters and about 4500 are crabs.

Like their relatives the insects, crustaceans have jointed legs; unlike insects, their head and thorax (the middle part, which is separate in an insect) are usually joined into one segment, and they have two pairs of antennae (feelers), not one. Most crustaceans spend their lives in the sea or in fresh water.

▼ Members of the main crustacean groups. With the exception of the shore crab, all these animals are shown five times larger than they are in real life.

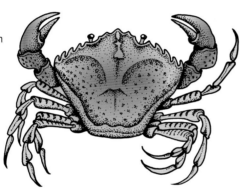

Crabs, like this shore crab (shown actual size), are heavily armoured and most live in the sea. Many are fast-moving scavengers.

Daphnia, or water fleas, seem to jump through the water as they swim. *Daphnia* females produce young without mating.

Acorn barnacles are protected by plates of shell. Their hairy feet comb the water for fragments of food and for oxygen.

Cyclops swim jerkily, like *Daphnia*. Most live in still, fresh water. The females carry two egg sacs.

Fish lice are parasites that feed on the blood of their host. They often live in the gills of fish.

Ostracods are sometimes called seed shrimps. Their hinged shell makes them look like small seeds in the water.

▲ Lobsters, such as the common lobster shown here, belong to the 'walking' group of crustaceans. Large lobsters have very big 'claws' or pincers on their first pair of legs. One of the claws is much larger than the other and is specially designed for stabbing or crushing prey.

Some of the most ancient fossils known are crustaceans, dating back over 500 million years. Most of these early types had a large number of legs which, as they swept through the water, gathered fragments of food from it.

Today, many small, swimming crustaceans are filter-feeders – the legs have fine hair-like projections which sweep food in the water towards the animal's mouth. Other crustaceans live on the sea-bed and have legs suitable for walking and grasping food.

Crustacean variety

The appearance and size of crustaceans are extremely varied. Lobsters are the giants among crustaceans, the biggest weighing over 20 kilograms. The smallest are tiny copepods, just a fraction of a millimetre long, which live between grains of sand on beaches or float in the sea.

Many crustaceans, such as shrimps, prawns and lobsters, have long bodies with a fan-like tail at the end. Some, like ostracods, have a hinged shell that makes them look like small seeds.

Life cycles

Crustaceans tend to be long-lived animals. Although some kinds may migrate short distances to suitable breeding places, in general, once they are adult, they live in a small area and do not move from it. Only in the earliest phases of their life after hatching do they travel freely.

Most marine (sea-dwelling) crustaceans produce large numbers of tiny larvae – young forms that are very unlike their parents. At this stage, they are part of a mass of plankton (minute plants and animals), swept along by the currents of the oceans. Many of them are eaten by fishes or other animals.

As they grow, crustaceans cast off and regrow their shell many times. During the course of its life a large crab or lobster may shed its shell 20 times. Each time, it emerges with a new, soft covering and must remain in hiding until this has hardened into a strong armour. The larger the animal grows, the longer this takes.

Crabs

Crabs are amongst the most familiar crustaceans. They are mainly scavengers, feeding on dead and rotting remains, and small-scale hunters. In turn they are preyed on by many creatures, including humans, who prize the flesh of these large crustaceans.

Some crabs camouflage themselves with sponges or pieces of seaweed that they attach to their shells. Hermit crabs have long, soft bodies which they hide inside the shells of sea snails. Some kinds then place sea anemones on their shell. They probably do this to frighten off any hunting animals, as the sea anemone has a painful sting.

Krill and shrimps

Shrimps and various shrimp-like crustaceans are extremely abundant in the oceans. Many creatures that look like shrimps live in the open sea, though they may not be closely related to the inshore kinds. Krill are probably the most important of these. Huge numbers live in the cold waters of the Arctic and Antarctic seas, where they feed on microscopic plants and animal. In turn, krill are the basic food for many birds, seals and baleen whales. Like many other

▲ The animal plankton shown here are the larvae (young) of various different kinds of crustacean, including krill. In the Atlantic Ocean, between January and April, there are as many as 20 kg of krill in every cubic metre of water.

marine crustaceans, they have a row of light-producing organs down each side.

Living in tropical seas is a shrimp that uses sound as a weapon. Pistol shrimps have a large claw that can make a sharp, cracking noise. At close range small prey can be stunned or even killed by the noise.

Other shrimps often seen in warm waters are 'cleaners', or barber shrimps. They help fishes by pulling off and eating tiny parasitic animals living on their skin and in their gills. In return the shrimps are not harmed by the fishes, which in other circumstances might eat them.

Copepods and barnacles

There are many different kinds of copepod, which are also amongst the most abundant animals in the oceans. They and their relatives have a very important position at the base of ocean food chains. They feed on the smallest sea-living plants, and they themselves are eaten by other invertebrates and fishes. These are in turn eaten by bigger hunters.

Goose barnacles are among the animals that feed on copepods. Unlike the acorn barnacles of the seashore, goose barnacles have fragile shells. But they feed in the same way as shore barnacles, kicking long, feathery legs into the water to comb tiny sea creatures such as copepods into their mouths.

▲ The delicate and dainty arrow crab lives in the Atlantic around the coasts of North and South America. To feed, it perches on underwater rocks and gathers detritus (bits that are floating around). Later, it picks out edible particles from the detritus.

• The commonest land crustaceans are woodlice. They breathe with gills, which must be kept moist, so they cannot survive in really dry places. They mainly feed on rotting vegetation.

• Shrimps and prawns are important as human food. They are caught in huge numbers from inshore waters around the world. In recent years many prawn farms have been set up, often causing the destruction of valuable mangrove swamps.

find out more
Animals
Food chains and webs
Oceans and seas
Seashore
Whales and dolphins

Cranes

Cranes are used to lift and move heavy objects. They are found in docks and harbours, on building sites, and on ships. Breakdown trucks carry mobile cranes. Travelling cranes move loads in factories. In scrapyards, special cranes fitted with electromagnets move loads such as old cars.

Cranes usually make use of wires, ropes or cables running through grooved wheels called sheaves. A simple pulley (a rope over a wheel) enables you to lift a heavy weight by pulling downwards. More wheels make lifting even easier.

The arm of a crane (the jib or boom) is a long structure that supports the cable system. The hook is gradually wound in by cables running round a drum. To balance the weight of the load, a block of iron or concrete is attached to the other end of the jib. The jib and tower usually consist of an open metal framework made of triangles.

• The Gottwald MK 1000 crane, nicknamed 'Birdie One', made the heaviest lift by a single mobile crane when it placed a 742-tonne reactor inside a New Zealand refinery.

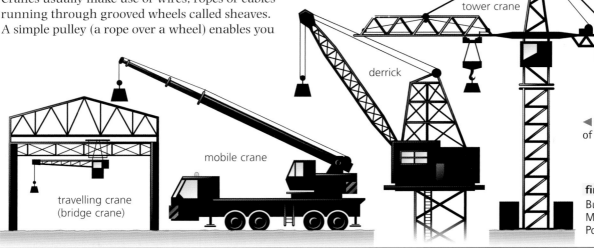

tower crane

derrick

mobile crane

travelling crane (bridge crane)

◄ Some different types of crane.

find out more
Building
Machines
Ports and docks

Cricket

Cricket is an 11-a-side game played with bat and ball. It began in Britain and is particularly popular in various Commonwealth countries, which used to form part of the British empire. In recent years, the strongest international teams have come from Australia and the West Indies.

In a game of cricket the players on the batting team try to hit the ball to score runs. One run is scored each time the two batsmen run from one wicket to the other. If they hit the ball across the boundary of the field, they score four runs, or six if it crosses the boundary without bouncing.

The fielding side tries to get the batsmen out. This can happen in a number of ways. The most common are when a batsman is *bowled out*, if a bowler hits the wicket with the ball; *leg before wicket* (LBW), if any part of the batsman's body (except the hand) stops the ball hitting the wicket; and *caught out*, if the ball hits the bat and is caught by a fielder before it bounces.

Bowlers take it in turns to bowl a sequence of six deliveries (an *over*) at each wicket. The batting team's innings ends when 10 batsmen are out or when they declare their innings closed. Then it is the other team's turn to bat. Each team may have one or two innings. The side that scores more runs overall is the winner.

Most matches of two innings per side are scheduled to last three or four days, but international (Test) matches are played over five days. Tests are played between the main cricketing countries, which are currently England, Australia, South Africa, West Indies, New Zealand, India, Pakistan, Sri Lanka and Zimbabwe.

In limited-overs (one-day) cricket, each team has one innings and bats for a specified maximum number of overs, usually 50. The cricket World Cup is a limited-overs tournament, with as many as 12 nations taking part over a period of a month.

sight screen

boundary

outfield

wickets

pitch

▲ A cricket ground.

• Cricket as we know it today began in the 18th century. The first great club was Hambledon, a village in Hampshire, England, who were good enough to take on and beat 'All England'.

find out more
Grace, W. G.

Crime

All countries have laws which govern how people should behave to each other, to each other's property, and towards the state itself. A crime is an action which breaks the criminal law of a country.

• Smugglers are criminals who avoid paying taxes when moving goods from one country to another. They may also deal in illegal goods such as narcotics (drugs) or arms (weapons). Selling narcotics is a crime because they may damage drug users' lives.

• Highway robbers (criminals who steal from road travellers) are uncommon today. They thrived when travel was slow and lonely. In the Middle Ages attacks by robbers were so common that it was dangerous to travel alone. The great age of highwaymen in Britain was in the 17th and 18th centuries when coach travel was more common but routes often passed through deserted places.

Many crimes have been regarded as crimes for centuries and in countries all over the world. Murder and other forms of unlawful killing are crimes. So are assault and other forms of violence towards a person, including rape and other sexual offences. Theft, robbery, burglary, criminal damage to property, fraud and forgery are all considered to be crimes.

In some cases omitting to do something may be a crime. Wilful neglect of a child so as to cause suffering is a crime. Failure to pay for a television licence is a crime in the United Kingdom.

Organized crime

Organized crime is the term used to describe illegal operations which are run like a big business. Crimes like this are carried out by criminals who work in gangs. There are gangs in every major country of the world. Many of the biggest gangs are in the USA. Some modern gangsters, like the Mafia, are involved in the illegal drugs trade. Japanese gangsters, called *yakuza* (meaning 'good for nothing'), are also highly organized and very powerful.

Probably the most famous time for gangsters was the Prohibition period in the USA. Between 1920 and 1933 alcoholic drinks were banned

find out more
Law and order
Police
Taxes

▲ During the days of the American Wild West, many outlaws such as Jesse James and Billy the Kid ran gangs. Jesse James and his elder brother Frank ran a particularly vicious gang that held up stagecoaches and trains and robbed banks.

and gangs grew rich running illegal drinking dens. The best known prohibition gangster was Al Capone, who dominated organized crime in Chicago from 1925 to 1931.

The Mafia

The Mafia is a secret society which began in Sicily long ago. In the 20th century it spread to mainland Italy and to the USA, where many Italian immigrants had settled. The Mafia is involved in many criminal activities including obtaining money from people using threats or force, selling illegal drugs, running illegal gambling operations, kidnapping and various acts of terrorism.

The Mafia is organized into a network of 'families'. The Italian and US governments have put many suspected Mafia members on trial, but it is difficult to obtain evidence against them because Mafia members are sworn to secrecy.

◄ Mafia suspects wait behind bars while on trial in Italy. In recent years a number of senior Mafia members have agreed to give evidence against their former colleagues, resulting in several highly publicized trials.

Crocodiles and alligators

Crocodiles and alligators are hunting animals that live in rivers, lakes and the edge of the sea in warm parts of the world. They belong to an ancient group of reptiles which has changed little since the days of the dinosaurs.

Crocodiles and alligators are ferocious hunters when in water, using the power of their flattened, oar-like tails to drive them towards their prey. Their jaws are set with sharp pointed teeth, which are ideal for holding fish, their main source of food. Big, old crocodiles can tackle larger creatures and can sometimes be a danger to humans and livestock.

A female usually makes a nest of mud and plant debris near the water's edge, although some kinds dig a hole in the sand. She lays her eggs and stays on guard until they are ready to hatch. When they hatch, she gathers them into her huge mouth and carries them to the water. She continues to guard them as they may be eaten by other animals.

Large crocodiles and alligators have few natural enemies, as they are protected by a thick, leathery skin armoured with small plates of bone. However, the skin of young ones makes valuable leather, and many have been killed for this. Some are farmed for their leather and meat, but many kinds of crocodile in particular are endangered and need careful conservation.

▼ Alligators have shorter, blunter snouts than crocodiles. No lower teeth can be seen when an alligator shuts its mouth. However, when a crocodile's mouth is closed, the large tooth fourth from the centre on the lower jaw still shows near the front of the mouth.

• Crocodiles may grow up to 6.5 m long; alligators up to 5.8 m.

• There are 13 different kinds of crocodile, 2 alligators, and 5 caymans.

find out more
Reptiles

Chinese alligator

African crocodile

fourth lower tooth visible when jaws closed

Cromwell, Oliver

Oliver Cromwell was the Puritan leader fighting on the side of Parliament against the king during the English Civil War. Cromwell and his men never lost a battle, and his victories made him the most powerful man in England.

Cromwell was 41 when he first joined the English Parliament in 1640, and he was a strong supporter of Parliament's powers. When the English Civil War began, he trained his own cavalry, nicknamed 'Ironsides' because they were such good fighters. They joined Parliament's victorious 'New Model Army', which Cromwell later commanded.

After winning the war, Cromwell and other army leaders tried to make a deal with Charles I, but the king broke his promises. Charles was put on trial for bringing war to his people and publicly beheaded. It is said that Cromwell came on his own to look at the dead king, and muttered sadly: 'Cruel necessity'.

Cromwell was determined to defend the new 'Commonwealth' (republic) of England. He distrusted the Irish, and carried out a ruthless conquest of Ireland. When the Scots tried to help the young Charles II, he defeated them too.

Cromwell became 'Lord Protector' in 1653. He tried to rule with Parliament, although he also used his army to enforce what he thought right. He allowed more religious freedom than usual (except in Catholic Ireland), and won a high reputation abroad. When Parliament offered him the crown, he refused it. But when he died, his funeral was as grand as any king's.

Born 1599 in Huntingdon, England
Died 1658 aged 59

▼ Oliver Cromwell with his soldiers following his victory in the battle of Marston Moor in 1644.

find out more
Stuart Britain

Crusades

Crusades were wars waged by the knights of Europe against non-Christian peoples in the Middle Ages. The best-known crusades were against the Muslims of the Middle East between 1096 and 1291.

The crusaders wanted to help the Christian emperor of Constantinople in his wars with the Muslim Turks. They also wanted to seize the holy city of Jerusalem, and to protect Christian pilgrims who went there. But perhaps they were keenest of all to win lands, fame and fortune.

The four crusades

Pope Urban II called for the first crusade in 1095. From then until 1291 thousands of ordinary men and women fought alongside knights in a series of wars which were part of four different crusades.

By 1100 the crusaders had won and there was a Christian king in Jerusalem. However, in 1187 Saladin, the Muslim sultan of Egypt, recaptured the city. Attempts to reclaim it, made by England's Richard I ('the Lionheart') and the French king Philip II, failed.

In 1204 the fourth and final crusade took Constantinople rather than Jerusalem. Crusaders looted the city which they held until 1261. By 1291 all other remaining Christian strongholds had fallen to the Muslims.

▼ This medieval French illustration shows crusaders loading their ship with supplies before setting out on the journey to Jerusalem.

• 'Crusade' comes from the Latin word *crux*, which means 'cross'. The first crusaders had the Christian cross sewn onto their clothes.

find out more
Byzantine empire
Knights
Middle Ages

Crystals

We may think of a crystal as a clear, sparkling object like a diamond. But to a scientist, the word has a very different meaning. Any solid in which the atoms are arranged in a regular pattern is a crystal.

If you look at salt grains through a magnifying glass, you will see that each grain is a tiny crystal. The salt crystals are always the same basic shape – a cube. Like all substances, salt is made from millions of tiny atoms. In salt, there are two types of atom, sodium and chlorine, arranged in a regular formation. The cubic shape of the salt crystals is a result of this regular arrangement.

Pure crystals of a particular substance always have the same basic shape, because the atoms of that substance always arrange themselves in the same way. However, crystals of different substances can be different shapes and sizes. Some substances form large crystals. Quartz, for example, can form crystals as big as a person. Other substances, such as metals, are made up of very tiny crystals, too small to see.

Forming crystals

Large crystals only form under certain conditions. For example, if a substance is dissolved in water, crystals will form if the water evaporates. They can also form if a liquid cools down and solidifies. You can see crystals formed in this way on a cold morning, when water on the outside of a window cools down and forms patterns of ice crystals on the panes.

▲ This photograph of the surface of the metal palladium has been magnified many times to show the tiny crystals that make up the metal.

◄ The cubic shape of salt crystals can be seen in this photograph.

Growing salt crystals
To grow your own salt crystals, add some salt to a little warm water and stir until it dissolves. Pour the liquid (called salt solution) into a saucer and leave on a windowsill for a day or so. As the water slowly evaporates, salt crystals will appear.

find out more
Atoms and molecules
Diamonds
Gases, liquids and solids
Gems and jewellery
Ice
Rocks and minerals
Salt

Curie, Marie

Born 1867 in Warsaw, Poland
Died 1934 aged 66

Marie Curie was a physicist who spent her life studying radioactive materials. She invented an instrument to measure radioactivity. With her husband Pierre, she discovered the element radium.

Marie Curie grew up in Warsaw, the capital of Poland. Her name was then Marya Sklodowska. Women could not go to university in Poland at this time, so Marya went to study in Paris, France, where she changed her name to Marie. In 1894 she married a chemist called Pierre Curie, who, realizing that his wife was a great scientist, began to work as her assistant.

Marie Curie devoted her life to the study of radioactive substances. She discovered that a substance called pitchblende – the ore from which uranium is extracted – was a thousand times more radioactive than the uranium itself.

To find out what was making the pitchblende so radioactive, the Curies tried to separate out the tiny quantity of unknown radioactive material from several tonnes of pitchblende. Some years later they ended up with a pinch of a highly radioactive element which they called radium. They also discovered a second radioactive element, called polonium. In 1903 the Curies received the Nobel prize for physics.

The dangers of radioactivity were not properly understood at that time, and as a result of her work, Marie died from leukaemia – a type of cancer that can be caused by radiation.

• When she was a student in Paris, Marie Curie was so poor that she sometimes fainted with hunger during her classes. However, she still managed to come top of the class in the exams.

find out more
Atoms and molecules
Nobel prizes
Radiation

▼ Marie and Pierre Curie at work in their laboratory in Paris. Pierre was killed in an accident in 1906, but Marie carried on with her work and received a second Nobel prize in 1911, this time for chemistry.

Dams

A dam is a barrier built across a stream, river or estuary. It is used to prevent flooding, to generate electricity by hydroelectric power, or to hold water for drinking or irrigating land. The dam blocks the water flow and the water collects behind it to form a reservoir.

Modern dams are mainly of two types, embankment dams and masonry dams.

Embankment dams are wide banks of earth or rock. The base is much wider than the top, because the pressure of the water is always greatest at the bottom of a dam. A layer of stones protects the dam wall from the water. A waterproof barrier, called a grout curtain, stretches down into the ground.

Embankment dams are usually used across broad rivers because the materials of which they are made are cheap and easy to obtain. They can withstand movements of their foundations because they are made of loose material. However, water can gradually seep through and weaken them. To combat this, engineers either line the dam with a layer of waterproof clay, or provide outlets to allow some of the water to drain away.

Masonry dams are usually built of concrete. They are used across deep, narrow valleys because only reinforced concrete can withstand the high pressures at the dam's base. The simplest type of masonry dam is a gravity dam, in which the dam wall is very thick at the base.

Record-breaking dams
Highest: the Nurek Dam on the River Vakhsh, Tajikistan, is 300 m high. On its completion, the Rogunskaya Dam, also across the River Vakhsh, will be 335 m.
Biggest volume: when completed, the Syncrude Tailings Dam in Alberta, Canada, will contain 540 cubic kilometres of earth and rock.
Biggest reservoir: the Kakhova Dam, on the River Dnieper in the Ukraine, holds back 182,000 cubic kilometres of water.

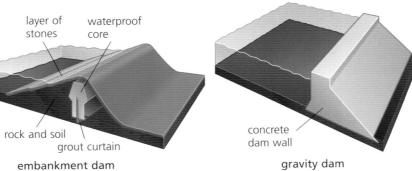

layer of stones
waterproof core
rock and soil
grout curtain
embankment dam

concrete dam wall
gravity dam

find out more
Hydroelectric power
Rivers and streams

Dance

Dancing has been a popular activity throughout history and throughout the world. People dance for many reasons – for ceremonies, for celebrations, for entertainment, and just for fun. Many dances have cultural or traditional importance.

▲ A women's dance in Angola, Africa. In traditional African dance, it is rare for men and women to dance in the same style, even if they are dancing together. Men's movements tend to be fast and forceful, while the women's movements are graceful and fluid.

▼ This sequence shows a dance exercise devised by Merce Cunningham. The exercise is performed smoothly to develop a strong, supple spine.

All types of dance have special steps and movements that must be learnt, and these skills are called technique. Some kinds of dance are made for performing to an audience. They often tell a story, or communicate ideas or feelings. Other kinds of dance are social: they are designed for everyone to join in.

Choreography

Choreography comes from two Greek words, *choreia* meaning 'dance' and *graphia* meaning 'writing'. Choreography means making new dances. The idea for a dance can come from a story, a painting or a piece of music.

Choreographers work with the dancers, teaching them steps and movements that will express their ideas. They make patterns from the movements, perhaps choosing a group of steps, called a motif, to use regularly through the dance. This helps the audience to make sense of the patterns and shapes that they see. The choreographer works closely with the designer and the composer to make sure their ideas are in harmony.

Dances can be written down. This is called *choreology* or *dance notation*. Dance companies often write down their dances and video them so that they have a complete record of the piece.

Modern dance

Modern theatre dance has existed for less than a hundred years. The pioneers were dancers like Martha Graham and Doris Humphrey in the USA, and Mary Wigman in Germany, who were interested in creating movement to express emotions or states of mind. In the 1950s the choreographer Merce Cunningham and others began to create dances in which the movement was chosen for its own sake, not as a means of expressing an emotion or idea. During the 1960s and 1970s post-modern dancers, working initially in the USA, rejected formal dance techniques and tried to develop more relaxed, fluid ways of moving. Their work often involved very simple movements like walking, running, standing and rolling.

▲ Odissi is a flowing, graceful style of dance that originated in Orissa, in eastern India. It was originally a type of temple dancing. Devadasis, female temple dancers, used dance to worship and praise the gods, and to tell stories and songs about them.

African dance

In Africa dances were developed to celebrate weddings, successful hunts, harvests – in fact, any kind of event. Along with the dancing is music such as drumming, singing, clapping and chants. African dancers usually move with the legs bent and the weight low: the feet often stamp out rhythms on the ground. The back bends and stretches in snaky, rippling movements, while the hips circle and sway. African dancers also often sing and clap as they dance.

When Africans were taken to the Americas as slaves during the 17th, 18th and 19th

centuries, they took their dances with them. Many new styles developed from the combination of African dancing with existing American styles. Tap dancing is a mixture of clog dancing, Irish step dancing and African dance, while the jazz dancing seen in musicals has many movements that come from African dance. Caribbean dancing and Latin American dancing also show the influence of African dance.

Indian dance

Dance in India is a very ancient art. Dancers were performing in Hindu temples nearly 2000 years ago. Today, there are many different styles of performance.

In Indian dancing, the legs are bent and there are few jumps. Dancers often wear bells on their ankles and stamp out complex rhythms. The dancer's body, arms, hands and face are very mobile. Many of the movements are gestures: there are, for example, 67 different gestures, or *mudras*, for the hands in one kind of Indian dance, and 36 different glances.

Indian dance performances can last several hours, often continuing all night. Dance styles throughout the Far East, particularly in Java and Japan have been strongly influenced by Indian dance.

Folk dancing

A folk dance is special to the part of the world it comes from. Each area has folk dances of its own. In Britain, morris dancing is probably the best-known type of folk dance. Clog-dancing, in various forms, is found in Britain, Ireland and the USA.

Nowadays most folk dances are for entertainment, but centuries ago the dancers had more serious purposes. Some folk dances were performed to bring good luck and ensure good crops. Many became part of religious ceremonies. In the Far East, people dressed as dragons or lions danced to frighten away evil spirits. The Maori of New Zealand performed war-dances to delight the gods of war and terrify the enemy. People in dry areas, for example the Aborigines in Australia and the Native Americans of the North American plains, performed rain-dances to please the sky-gods and to bring rain.

▲ This sequence shows a jazz walk. This combines fast sideways stepping with hip swings.

Social dancing

Social dancing is dance where people get together to dance and enjoy themselves. Sometimes people dance together in large groups, perhaps in a circle, in a procession, in long lines, or in squares. Other social dances are for couples: these include ballroom dances such as the waltz and the quick-step, Latin dances such as the tango and the salsa, and rock-and-roll dances such as the jive. More recently, people have begun to dance by themselves on social occasions. At a club or disco, dancers choose for themselves what they will do: there are no set steps or rules.

◄ Social dancing in a club. There are no formal rules to modern social dancing of this kind, but definite styles do develop.

▲ This dance piece by the choreographer Mark Morris is a rich mixture of ancient and modern. The movement and costumes are modern, but they are set to an opera written in the 18th century by Jean-Philippe Rameau.

• In eastern European countries, people still dance at weddings, baptisms and other family occasions. In Britain and the USA children play games such as 'Ring a Ring o' Roses' or 'Oranges and Lemons'. Although we seldom think of such games as folk dances, that is what they are.

find out more
Ballet
Operas and musicals
World music

Darwin, Charles

Born 1809 in
Shrewsbury, England
Died 1882 aged 73

• Darwin became ill a year or so after his return from the *Beagle* voyage, and his health gradually declined. For the last 40 or so years of his life he was an almost permanent invalid, but he continued his scientific work until his death.

find out more
Evolution
Prehistoric life
Prehistoric people

Charles Darwin was a scientist who came up with the revolutionary idea that plants and animals evolve (change) over time by a process called natural selection.

Darwin did not pursue his interest in plants and animals seriously until he became friends with the cleric and botanist John Stevens Henslow at Cambridge University. On Henslow's recommendation, he was invited to join the naval survey ship, HMS *Beagle*, as naturalist and gentleman companion for the captain. He set sail on 27 December 1831.

For Darwin, the most important part of the five-year voyage was visiting the Galapagos Islands, west of Ecuador. He noticed that the finches on the different islands were closely related, yet the finches from any one island were different from all the others. Also, they all looked similar to a type of finch that lived on the South American mainland. Darwin decided that some of the finches must have first reached the islands accidentally and then evolved separately on each island.

Darwin concluded that, over many generations, living things evolve and adapt to their environment through a process of natural selection. This means that only the best-adapted survive and produce offspring. In 1859 Darwin published his theories in his book *The Origin of Species*. It was very unpopular because it went against the belief that all kinds of plants and animals were created by God and had not changed since. Today few people doubt the logic of Darwin's arguments.

▶ Darwin is shown here studying plants in a conservatory.

Deafness

• American Sign Language (ASL) is used by more than half a million deaf people, and is the fourth most common language in the USA.

Deafness is being unable to hear sounds. Some people are totally deaf and cannot hear anything at all. Others, who are partly deaf, can hear some sounds.

We hear sounds when sound waves travel down the ear passage to the eardrum, then through the middle ear to the cochlea in the inner ear. The cochlea changes vibrations caused by the sound waves into nerve impulses which go along a nerve to the brain.

Some people are deaf because sound is blocked on its way to the cochlea. This may be due to wax in the ear passage, a heavy cold with catarrh, or damage to the eardrum. Ear wax can be removed by washing it out of the ear canal, but other causes may need surgery.

Deafness also occurs when the cochlea, or the nerve from the cochlea to the brain, is damaged. A defect causing deafness can also be inherited.

Sign language

People who are deaf still need to communicate. They can do this by learning a special sign language which uses the hands, the face, and the upper body. The meaning of the signs depends as much upon the person's movements and facial expression as their hands. Sign language can be communicated as quickly as spoken language. There are many different sign languages. American Sign Language is used by more than half a million deaf people.

▶ This person is using sign language to say 'Hello! I am pleased to meet you.'

find out more
Disabilities
Ears
Sound

Hello!   I   (am)   pleased   to meet   you

Deer

• There are 45 different kinds of deer.

Deer are graceful animals, with slim bodies and long, slender legs. Most live in herds in cool woodlands. Deer are alert, swift-footed animals, and they use their speed to escape the many hunting animals that try to catch them.

Most deer produce only one baby at a time. The mother leaves it hidden in the undergrowth, where it is well camouflaged by its spotted coat. She returns to feed it twice a day. After a few weeks it is strong enough to join the herd.

Males of most kinds of deer have antlers. The size of the antlers shows a male's age and position in the herd. They are often used in fighting for females. Fighting males lock antlers and push, until the weaker deer breaks away. Unlike all other kinds of deer, reindeer (caribou) females have antlers, but they are smaller than those of the males.

In parts of northern Europe and Asia reindeer have been domesticated, and in a few places they are still ridden or used to pull sledges. A few kinds of deer, such as red deer, are now being farmed for their meat.

• Antlers, which are made of bone, are shed and regrown each year. When they are growing, they are covered with live furry skin ('velvet') which is later rubbed off. This leaves an antler of bare bone that lasts for just one breeding season before falling off.

find out more
Forests
Mammals

▶ The Chinese water deer is a tiny, shy creature that lives in the marshes of China and Korea.

▶ The adult male red deer is one of the largest mammals in Europe. Its antlers can grow to be more than 1 m long.

▶ The moose is the largest of the deer family. Called a moose in North America, in Europe it is known as an elk.

Democracy

find out more
Elections
Government
Greeks, ancient
Parliaments

Democracy means 'rule by the people'. The earliest democracy was in the Greek city of Athens, about 2500 years ago. It involved a meeting of the free men of the city, who voted on what the city should do in matters of peace and war.

Today countries are too big for such meetings to be held. Instead, the people elect representatives to a parliament or a congress. The representatives then make decisions on the people's behalf. In this way the people have their say, by choosing representatives who are likely to vote the way they want them to. If they do not like what their representatives say or do, they are free to vote against them in the next election. This is known as *representative democracy*.

In such a democracy everybody over a certain age is allowed to vote in elections, whatever their race, religion or sex. Decisions are taken, and laws are passed, by a majority vote. In some countries, certain decisions must be taken by a minimum proportion of those voting, perhaps two-thirds. In other cases a majority of just one vote is enough.

Voting usually takes place at *general elections*. In democratic political systems, people get the chance to vote in private (secret ballot) with no one to see how they have filled in their ballot paper.

◀ In ancient Greek cities, the Agora or market place was also the political and legal centre. This is the west side of the Agora in Athens, where the main government buildings stood.

Deserts

A desert is a large, extremely dry area of land. Geographers say that a 'true' desert receives less than 250 millimetres of rain in an average year. Yet rainfall in the desert can vary a great deal from year to year, and is difficult to predict. A desert may have heavy rains in one year, followed by several years with no rain at all. To survive in the desert, the people and wildlife living there have to adapt to the changing conditions.

• In coastal deserts, such as the Namib Desert in south-western Africa, fog may be the most reliable source of water for many smaller animals and plants.

▼ Cracked mud lies on the surface of the Atacama Desert in Chile. The longest period of drought ever recorded occurred in the Atacama. It lasted for 400 years, ending in 1971 when rain finally fell.

The map below shows that most deserts are near the tropics of Cancer and Capricorn. These are the *hot deserts*, where the Sun shines constantly from cloudless skies. During the night, the clear skies allow heat to escape, and it can become surprisingly cold. In coastal areas, fog may roll into the desert at night and dew sometimes forms at dawn.

The deserts of central Asia are not near the tropics. They are far inland, where the winds are dry. Deserts such as the Gobi are hot in summer and bitterly cold in winter. The polar regions, including Antarctica and Greenland, also receive very little rain, sometimes only up to 130 millimetres a year. These areas are known as the *cold* or *polar deserts*.

Desert landscapes

Sand covers only a small area of most hot deserts. Only about one-tenth of the Sahara Desert, for example, is sandy, and most other

▲ A gemsbok (oryx) stands before sand dunes in Africa's Namib Desert. During a long period of drought, large animals such as this often move to other areas where there is more rain.

hot deserts have even less sand. The remaining desert areas consist mainly of vast flat expanses of gravel and boulders, and some mountainous regions. In places, wind has carried the sand over long distances and piled it up to form *dunes*. These sand dunes are constantly moving as sand is blown up one side of the dune and then rolls down the steep face on the other side.

The landscape in some older desert areas has been eroded (worn away) by wind and water for thousands of years. Wind-blown sand acts like sandpaper, wearing away the softer layers of rock. Mountains have been eroded, often by the wind, to form strange shapes, such as the flat-topped mesas (tablelands) of Arizona, USA. Water is also important in shaping the desert. When storms occur, they sweep down the wadis (dry valleys) and flood over the land. The water wears away the rocky surfaces to produce steep-sided gorges and great spreads of rock and gravel.

Spreading deserts

In some parts of the world, particularly around the Sahara, the desert areas are expanding, and destroying the fertile lands that

▼ The world's principal deserts.

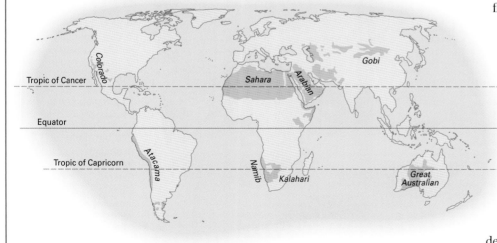

Colorado
Tropic of Cancer
Sahara
Arabian
Gobi
Equator
Atacama
Tropic of Capricorn
Namib
Kalahari
Great Australian

surround them. We call this process *desertification*. Its main causes are overgrazing by livestock, the cutting-down of trees, mainly for firewood, and changes in the climate, which have resulted in longer periods of drought. Once the grass has been eaten and the trees have been removed, the desert soils become dry and dusty, leading to increased erosion of the land.

To reclaim some of the newly created desert areas, trees are planted to reduce the damaging effects of the wind. New methods of farming are also being introduced, and farmers are being encouraged to reduce the size of livestock herds.

Desert peoples

At one time, the only permanent settlements in hot desert areas were in oases and in the valleys of rivers like the Nile, which flows through the desert. Today, there are probably more people than ever living in the deserts. New settlements have grown up where deposits of oil and valuable minerals such as uranium are found. Water for these settlements can be extracted from deep wells or brought in by pipelines or lorries.

Many traditional desert inhabitants are *nomads*, who move around in search of fresh grazing land for their animals. Nomads live in tents or build new shelters each time they stop. In the deserts of Arabia and in the Sahara, the Bedouin peoples graze their herds of camels, sheep and goats, which they sell. The nomadic Bushmen of the Kalahari and the Aborigines in Australia have special skills for finding water, and can survive by eating desert plants and animals.

▲ A Turkana woman waters her livestock in a dried-up river-bed in the desert region of northern Kenya.

Desert wildlife

Desert plants and animals face similar challenges in order to survive in the harsh hot desert conditions. Many animals avoid the heat by sleeping during the day and coming out to find food at night. Insects and other small animals shelter in the sand, while larger animals keep cool by seeking shade under a tree or a rockface.

Desert wildlife also has to survive with little or no water for long periods of time. Camels can live for several weeks without a drink. They store fat in their humps, and their bodies produce water by breaking down this stored fat. Many desert plants store water in their stems, leaves or roots. Some have a thick waxy coating that reduces the amount of water lost through their leaves.

Desert records

Largest hot desert
Sahara Desert,
8.4 million sq km

Highest temperature
58 °C, recorded in
Libya in 1922

Longest drought
400 years, in the
Atacama Desert, Chile

Highest sand dunes
430 m high, in eastern
Algeria

• Places in the desert where water lies at or close to the surface are called *oases*. The soil here may be quite fertile, and trees, shrubs and crops can all flourish because their roots can reach water.

• Cacti, which store moisture in their fleshy stems, have tiny spines instead of leaves so that they do not lose water in the dry desert air.

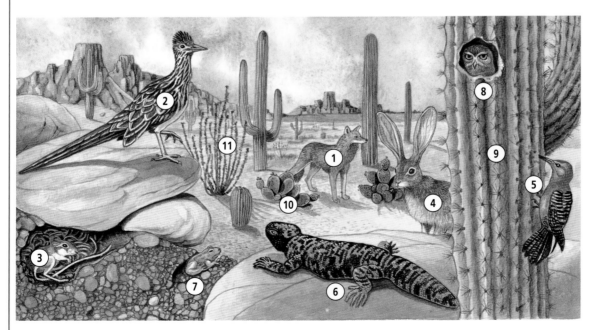

◄ Wildlife in the Sonoran Desert in Arizona, USA.
1 coyote
2 roadrunner
3 kangaroo rat
4 jackrabbit
5 Gila woodpecker
6 Gila monster
7 spadefoot toad
8 elf owl
9 saguaro cactus
10 jumping cholla
11 ocotillo

find out more
Aborigines
Bushmen
Camels
Climate
Erosion
Plants
Tundra
Wells and springs

Designers

Designers are creative problem-solvers who produce plans, in an illustrated (drawn) form, that meet the needs they or others have identified. They have to make the best use they can of all the available resources, including materials, space and time. A well-designed solution will look good as well as work well.

Designers work in a wide range of fields. Industrial designers may design cars, or household objects, such as kettles. Fashion designers design new clothes; graphic designers produce posters, advertisements and page layouts for books. On a larger scale, interior designers try to improve the appearance and environment inside a building. Landscape designers tackle gardens, parks and even new towns.

► Most big companies and organizations have a 'logo' or trademark. Logos are examples of graphic design. If the design is a good one, people will remember it, and when they see it again they will know which company it stands for.

The need for a design may be identified by the designer, or the designer may work to a brief (instructions provided by someone else). Good designers approach their work creatively, looking at the 'problem' from many different angles. They may use design models, discarding them if they do not work properly or do not look as they want them to.

The final stage of turning the finished design into reality is called *realization*. If the design is for a product that people will use, the product will be tested to make sure it works well enough before it is mass-produced.

◄ The original Coca-Cola bottle was designed in 1916 by Alex Samuelson. Most Coke is now sold in cans or plastic bottles, but the company still uses the original bottle in advertisements because it is so popular and creates a particular image.

find out more
Advertising
Architecture
Books
Building
Dress and costume
Furniture
Models
Parks and gardens

Diamonds

Diamond is the hardest known natural substance. Natural or 'rough' diamonds look like small pebbles of cloudy glass. The finest stones are either colourless or blue-white. Diamonds sparkle brilliantly only after they have been cut and polished.

Diamonds are crystals of pure carbon, and they are found in all shapes and sizes. They were formed under great heat and pressure, often deep inside the cores of ancient volcanoes. Natural diamonds are found in rocks and gravels in areas as far apart as South Africa, Australia, Brazil, India and Siberia. South Africa and Russia are the world's largest producers of natural diamonds.

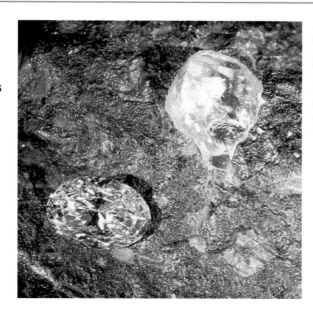

◄ A rough diamond and a polished diamond lie on top of a piece of kimberlite, a rock from which diamonds are extracted.

• The largest diamond ever discovered is the Cullinan, which was found in 1905 in South Africa. Its uncut weight was 621 g, or 3105 carats (1 carat – the unit in which the weight of diamonds is measured – equals 0.2 grams).

• Graphite is the substance found in pencil 'lead'. It is squeezed in giant presses at a very high temperature. However, the diamonds produced from graphite are minute.

Synthetic diamonds are made out of graphite, another form of pure carbon. These (as well as small natural diamonds) are used to make dentists' drills, glass-cutting equipment and the teeth of diamond saws used for cutting rocks. Because diamond is such a hard material, one diamond can be cut only by another. Diamonds are often used to make items of fine jewellery, such as rings, brooches and necklaces.

find out more
Carbon
Crystals
Gems and jewellery
Rocks and minerals

Born 1812 in
Portsmouth, England
Died 1870 aged 58

find out more
Novels and novelists
Victorian Britain

► An illustration
from *David Copperfield*
showing David walking
with Mr Micawber. This
book was Charles
Dickens's most popular
novel and his own
personal favourite.

Dickens,
Charles

**Charles Dickens was one
of the greatest novelists of
Victorian England. His
books – with their many
memorable characters – are
as much loved today as they
were 150 years ago.**

Because his family was very
poor, Charles Dickens spent
some of his childhood working
in a factory. This proved a very
bitter experience, although he
was eventually able to take up
his studies again for a few years.

When he was 15 he became
a lawyer's clerk, before getting
work as a newspaper reporter
covering debates in the House of
Commons. His genius for
describing comic characters
and his anger about social
injustice soon became apparent.
In 1836 he began his first
novel, *The Pickwick Papers*. As
with all his other novels, it was
published in instalments in a
magazine before being
published as a book. It was so
popular that by the age of 24
Dickens was famous in Britain
and in the USA.

Dickens wrote stories of such
power that Parliament was

sometimes forced to take action
against the abuses he described
so vividly. For example, after his
book *Nicholas Nickleby* was
published, some of the cruel
boarding-schools he described
were made to close down
following such bad publicity.
And in his book *Oliver Twist* he
made people more aware of
how badly many orphans were
being treated.

Dickens also had a wonderful
gift for creating larger-than-life
characters in his novels. Some
of the best known are the
villainous Fagin in *Oliver Twist*,
the bitter Miss Havisham in
Great Expectations, and the
over-optimistic, unreliable Mr
Micawber in *David Copperfield*.
These characters were brought
to life still further when Dickens
started a series of public
readings of some of his most
popular novels.

Dictators

**Dictators are rulers who have complete
power over the countries they govern. Many
dictators seize power by force.**

• Many countries,
especially in Africa and
Latin America, were
ruled by dictators during
the 20th century.

Most dictators have the title of president, but they
are not democratic heads of state elected by their
people. Most dictators favour one-party states
and ban all parties apart from their own. They
may also censor (control) the content of
newspapers, books, films and television in order
to suppress views different to their own.

Fascist and communist dictators
The most notorious dictators of modern times
were fascists and communists. Fascism began
in Italy after World War I. Benito Mussolini
abandoned elections and democratic discussion
and brutally put down criticism and opposition,
using a strong army and secret police. Similar
methods were used by Adolf Hitler, the Nazi
dictator of Germany from 1933 to 1945, and
Joseph Stalin, the communist ruler of the USSR
from 1924 to 1953. Fascist dictator Francisco
Franco ruled Spain for 36 years, until 1975.

find out more
Caesar, Julius
Democracy
Germany
Hitler, Adolf
Italy
Russia
Spain
Stalin, Joseph

▼ Benito Mussolini set up the Italian fascist party in 1919
and 3 years later took power as leader of the government.
He ruled as dictator until 1943.

Diets

The range of foods that you eat most of the time is called your diet. Your diet should provide all the things that your body needs for growth, repair and health. Sometimes people change their diet for health reasons. This may be to lose weight, to control a disease, to prepare for sporting events, because they are allergic to some foods or because they are pregnant.

A healthy diet is one that provides the right nutrients (nourishing food substances) in the right amounts. A diet that includes plenty of cereals, fruit and vegetables provides a good balance of nutrients. A diet that is mostly made up of chips, sweets and salty snacks is much less healthy, because it is unbalanced. It contains too much fat, sugar and salt, and not enough protein and vitamins.

Nutrition

Nutrition is the process in which nutrients are taken into the body. All food contains nutrients, which provide us with energy and the raw materials for living. They include proteins, fats, carbohydrates, minerals and vitamins. Each nutrient has its own particular function in the human body. Proteins are the main body-builders; carbohydrates and fats are important for energy; vitamin C helps to protect us against infection; vitamin D and calcium help good

• Starvation occurs when a person suffers from a severe lack of food. At least one-tenth of the world's population suffers from hunger. Most of them live in developing countries and many of them are children and young people. Every year about 15 million children die of starvation and related causes. They are so underfed that they cannot resist disease.

▼ This graph shows the differences in average diet between a number of developed and developing countries.

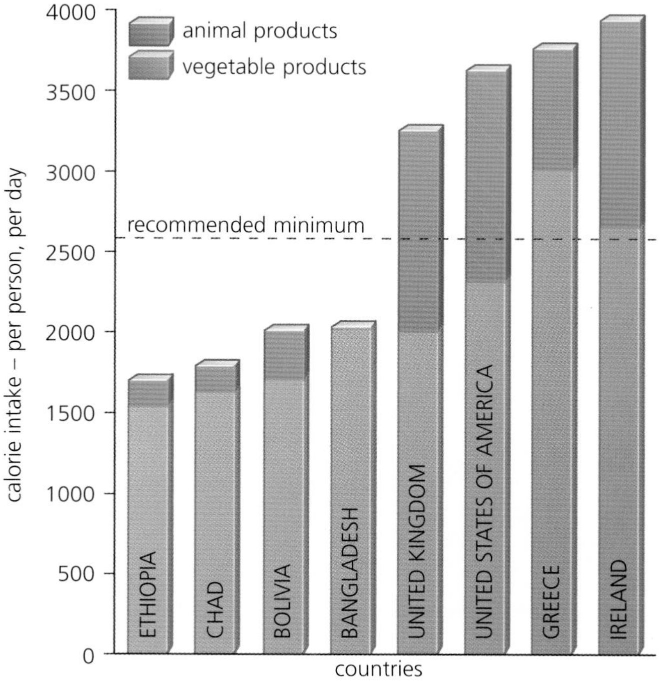

▲ A child suffering malnutrition during a famine in Sudan, Africa. She and thousands like her have stomachs swollen not from overeating, but from a lack of food, which also causes repeated infections, such as diarrhoea.

strong bones and teeth to grow. Altogether, there are 13 major vitamins: A, C, D, E, K and eight different B vitamins. By eating a range of healthy foods you will be giving your body the vitamins it needs to perform many important chemical processes.

We should eat a variety of different foods to make sure we get all the nutrients in roughly the right combination. *Malnutrition* means bad feeding and it can result from being under- or over-nourished. More than half the world's population suffers under-nutrition because, especially in some poor countries, they do not have enough to eat. In Western nations people usually suffer malnutrition because they eat too much of the wrong types of food.

Diet around the world

People's diets vary from country to country. The people who live around the Mediterranean Sea eat a lot of starchy food in the form of pasta, plenty of fruit and vegetables, olive oil and a little fish. This Mediterranean diet is very balanced. The people of Japan and China are also often

The graph:

y-axis: calorie intake – per person, per day (0 to 4000)

Legend:
- animal products
- vegetable products

recommended minimum (dashed line at approximately 2600)

x-axis (countries): ETHIOPIA, CHAD, BOLIVIA, BANGLADESH, UNITED KINGDOM, UNITED STATES OF AMERICA, GREECE, IRELAND

healthier than those in many Western countries. They eat a lot of vegetables and cereals, especially rice, but little sugar and hardly any milk or cream.

Many people in Europe, North America and Australia eat a large amount of meat, eggs, cream, cakes, sweets, sugar and biscuits. This kind of diet is unbalanced and people who eat it are more likely to be overweight. Obesity (being very overweight) can lead to heart disease, high blood pressure, diabetes and certain cancers.

Diet and weight

The only sensible way to get, and stay, slim, is to eat less fattening food (fats, oils and sugars), and take more exercise. This will help remove excess fat and make you feel healthier. Clever advertisements and magazine articles are full of diets that are supposed to make you slim. In fact no food has any special slimming properties.

Dieting in order to reach a desired shape can cause eating disorders if the diet is not properly controlled. There are three main kinds of eating disorder: anorexia nervosa, bulimia nervosa and compulsive eating. Sufferers of anorexia nervosa try to eat as little as possible, or even nothing at all. People with bulimia eat very large amounts of food (binge) and then make themselves sick to get rid of the food. Compulsive eaters cannot help eating, even if they are not hungry. All of these conditions are very serious and sufferers may die as a result. They need careful treatment from friends, family and doctors to help them to learn to eat sensibly again.

Vegetarians

Vegetarians are people who do not eat meat, poultry or fish. Some people, such as Buddhists and Jains, choose to be vegetarians for religious reasons. Others believe that killing animals is morally wrong. Many object to the way animals bred for slaughter are treated. Others believe that producing meat is an inefficient way of feeding a population and that land should be used to grow things like soya beans, which can feed many more people than if the same area were used to feed livestock. Some people choose a vegetarian diet simply because they think it is healthier to avoid eating meat.

Vegetarians obtain the protein they need from nuts, seeds, pulses, cereals, soya products (such as tofu) and quorn, and from egg and milk products. All of the other nutrients they need should be present in their normal diet. Vegans, who do not eat dairy products, may take a supplement of vitamin B12, but many foods already contain this vitamin (such as yeast extracts, some soya milks and some cereals).

Special diets

Pregnant women have an increased need for certain vitamins and minerals such as vitamin B6, iron and zinc to help their baby develop. To get these extra nutrients they should eat more oily fish such as tuna and sardines, and more raw fruit and vegetables. Athletes need increased quantities of starchy foods such as bread or pasta. These foods give them increased energy.

Some people cannot eat certain foods as they cause allergies such as skin rashes. Others must avoid foods they cannot digest. People with coeliac disease, for instance, cannot digest gluten in wheat and so avoid all things made from wheat flour.

find out more
Allergies
Cereals
Fats
Food
Proteins

Fats and oils give you a lot of energy, but if you eat more than you need, they make you fat and cause heart disease.

Sweet foods give you energy but nothing else. They rot your teeth and make you fat.

Processed foods have some goodness removed, and salt, sugar, colouring, preservatives and other chemicals added.

Fruit gives you energy, vitamins and minerals to keep you healthy.

Vegetables and cereals give you energy, vitamins, minerals and fibre. They do not make you fat.

Low-fat proteins build you up without making you fat.

Digestive systems

Your digestive system breaks down the food you eat into small particles that can be absorbed into the blood. Digestion takes place in the gut, which is really a long tube that stretches from your mouth to your anus. If you laid this tube out in a straight line, it would be about 7 metres long.

You chew your food to break it into small pieces which are easy to swallow. The front teeth bite off a chunk, then the tongue pushes it to the back teeth, which grind it up and mix it with saliva. *Saliva* is produced by the salivary glands. It softens the food and begins to digest it. When the food is well chewed, you swallow it.

The chewed food passes down your gullet (*oesophagus*) into your stomach. Muscles in the

• The appendix is a small, worm-shaped organ in the lower gut. Most mammals have a similar organ. In plant-eaters it is used to digest grass. In humans it no longer has any function, but it may become infected and cause severe pain in your right side. This is called *appendicitis,* and often has to be treated by an operation.

▶ The human digestive system.

▼ A carpet of villi 0.5—1.0 mm high lines the small intestine. These villi give the intestine a huge surface area for absorbing digested food. Your small intestine has an inside surface area of 10 square metres.

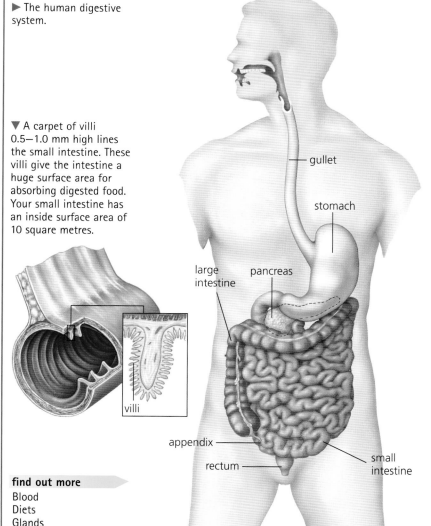

villi

Rumination

Bison, like all cattle and some other large, plant-eating animals, are *ruminants*. Ruminants have complicated stomachs, usually made up of four parts. When food is first swallowed, it goes to the *rumen*, where it is broken down before being returned to the mouth as *cud* for a thorough chewing, called *rumination*. When it is swallowed a second time, it goes to the *reticulum*. From there it passes to the remaining areas of the stomach until the digestive process is complete. Sheep, deer, antelopes and giraffes are all ruminants.

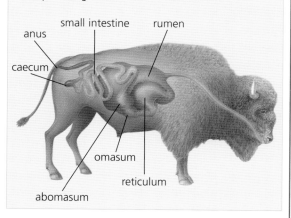

gullet push it forward by squeezing together behind it and relaxing in front of it in a movement called *peristalsis*. The *stomach* is a strong muscular bag which expands as more food passes into it. In the stomach the food is mixed with acid and digestive juices called *enzymes* which kill any bacteria and help to break the food down. Muscles in the stomach wall churn it up until it becomes a runny mush.

Partly digested food passes from the stomach into the small intestine. Enzymes in the wall of the intestine, and from a gland called the *pancreas*, continue digestion. They break the food down into small molecules – sugars, fats and amino acids (from proteins). These can pass easily through the wall of the small intestine into the blood. First these molecules are carried to the *liver*. The liver stores excess foods and changes some poisons, such as alcohol, into harmless substances. From the liver the digested food is carried in the blood to all parts of the body, where it provides energy and materials for growth and repair.

The parts of food which cannot be digested, such as fibre from vegetables and fruit, pass into the large intestine, which is made up of the colon, rectum and anus. The undigested food remains in the colon for between 12 and 36 hours. Water and salt are removed from it during this time. It then passes into the rectum and out of the anus as faeces.

Dinosaurs

Dinosaur records
*Longest dinosaur
Diplodocus* 27 m
*Tallest dinosaur
Brachiosaurus* 12 m
*Smallest dinosaur
Compsognathus*
75–91 cm; 3 kg
*Heaviest dinosaur
Ultrasaurus* 120
tonnes

• At the time of the first dinosaurs, the dry land of the Earth formed one supercontinent, called Pangaea. Animals were able to reach all parts of Pangaea, and so, when it split to form separate continents, dinosaurs lived on all of them.

• The word 'dinosaur' means 'terrible lizard'. More than 1000 different kinds of dinosaur are known, and more are found every year.

Dinosaurs were prehistoric reptiles. Many of them were very big, larger than any other animal that has ever lived on dry land, but some were as small as chickens. Dinosaurs inhabited the Earth for about 160 million years, and the last ones became extinct 64 million years ago – more than 60 million years before the first human-like creatures appeared.

For most of the time that dinosaurs lived the climate worldwide was fairly warm and there were few high mountains. Most dinosaurs lived on broad plains by slow-flowing rivers.

The first dinosaurs appeared over 220 million years ago. They were quite small and ran on their hind legs. The main difference between them and their ancestors was that their legs were 'under' their bodies (like human legs), instead of sticking out to the sides. This gave them greater control over their movement and meant that they could reach food and escape from enemies more easily. They fed on insects and other small prey. They survived and thrived and many different kinds developed, some of which were very large.

Main dinosaur groups

Scientists have divided dinosaurs into two main groups based on the shape of their hip bones. One group is called the Saurischia, which means 'reptile-hipped', because reptiles such as crocodiles have their hip bones arranged in this way. The other group is called Ornithischia, which means 'bird-hipped', because the hip bones of birds are arranged like this. There are differences between the two groups. The reptile-hipped dinosaurs had their teeth in the front of their mouth. Though they could bite and nip and tear, they could not really chew their food. All the flesh-eaters were saurischians. The bird-hipped dinosaurs had their teeth at the back of their mouth, and often had a horny beak at the front. They

◄ Fossilized dinosaur footprints like this one are one of the clues that help scientists find out how big dinosaurs were and how fast they moved.

could grind up tough plant food. All the bird-hipped dinosaurs fed on plants (although none ate grass, which did not appear until after the dinosaurs had died out). Many of them had armoured plates of spikes or bone on their bodies.

Warm-blooded or cold-blooded?

Scientists do not know whether dinosaurs were warm-blooded or cold-blooded. A cold-blooded animal like a lizard needs heat from the Sun to keep warm and to become active. Warm-blooded animals, such as birds and human beings, can be active all the time. Because the Earth's climate as a whole was warmer, it would have been easier for cold-blooded dinosaurs to remain active for much of the time. The big dinosaurs could stay warm through the night because it would take a long time for their massive bodies

► Dinosaurs such as *Tyrannosaurus* (opposite) and the slimmer, more ostrich-like *Stenonychosaurus*, walked on their hind legs, rather like chickens.

▼ Other dinosaurs walked on all fours. Some of these, like *Triceratops* (top), had a bony neck shield. Others had horns or plates of bone on their bodies, like *Euoplocephalus* (bottom).

to lose heat. This may be one reason many of the dinosaurs were so large. Smaller dinosaurs may have kept themselves warm by being active, or they may have been truly warm-blooded.

The end of the dinosaurs

No one knows why the dinosaurs disappeared. For 160 million years, new kinds of dinosaur had evolved as others became extinct (died out). But at the end of the Cretaceous period, 64 million years ago, the dinosaurs disappeared quite suddenly.

Scientists do not know exactly how long this disappearance took. It could have happened in a short time or it might have taken as much as a million years. Many other kinds of animals became extinct at about the same time. Most of them were large, although many smaller species disappeared as well, including the mosasaurs, the last of the great sea reptiles.

So what happened? One suggestion is that this was a time of great changes in climates and habitats. The dinosaurs could not adapt to the new conditions and just died out. Another theory, popular today, is that the Earth was hit by a giant meteorite. The impact sent up a huge cloud of dust which blacked out the Sun. This lowered the temperature, and plants and animals died off everywhere. Only those that could withstand the cold were able to survive and spread out across the Earth.

Discovering dinosaurs

Everything that we know about dinosaurs has been learned from fossils. If scientists discover a new kind of dinosaur, they study its bones to work out the shape of its body and how it walked and ran, and what other kinds of dinosaur it is related to. The position in which some dinosaur fossils have been found tells us that certain kinds of dinosaur lived in herds.

There may also be other fossils such as leaves, insects or shells that tell us about the climate and the plants that lived at the time. Dinosaur teeth often survive, and can tell us whether the animal ate flesh or plant food. A few dinosaur eggs have been found, and these suggest that some kinds of dinosaur, like most reptiles alive today, did not look after their young.

All these things help us to understand the dinosaurs, but there are many things that we do not yet know about them. What colour were they? How noisy were they? How long did they live? Scientists are still searching for the answers to these questions.

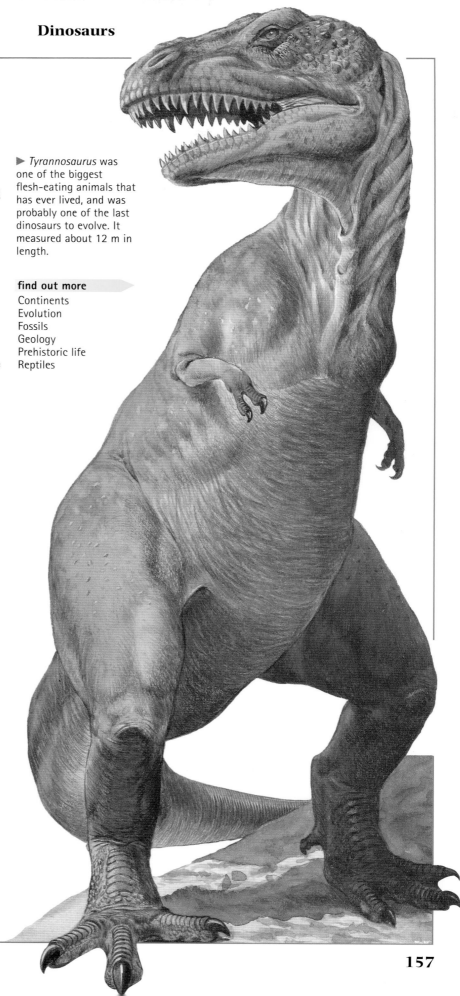

▶ *Tyrannosaurus* was one of the biggest flesh-eating animals that has ever lived, and was probably one of the last dinosaurs to evolve. It measured about 12 m in length.

find out more
Continents
Evolution
Fossils
Geology
Prehistoric life
Reptiles

Disabilities

A disability means that part of your body does not work properly. People may suffer from a mental or physical disability. They usually need help to live their lives more easily.

This 4-year-old girl has Down's Syndrome, a mental disability. About one in 650 babies is born with the syndrome. Many of them grow up to lead near-normal lives.

A person is disabled when part of their body is missing or damaged. Sometimes a body part does not work well because the brain is damaged and cannot send proper messages to that part of the body.

Some kinds of disability stop you hearing or seeing properly. These are called *sensory disabilities* because they affect your senses. There are also people who have *learning disabilities*. They may have trouble thinking, reasoning, understanding and remembering. They cannot learn as easily as other people.

Causes of disability

We do not always know why people are disabled. Sometimes people inherit a disability from their parents. If a pregnant woman takes drugs, drinks a lot of alcohol or smokes, this may damage the baby before it is born. Occasionally there are medical problems during the birth of a baby, which may cause it brain damage.

Other disabilities may be caused by disease or by an accident. People may also develop physically disabling conditions such as arthritis as they grow old.

Cerebral palsy and Down's syndrome

Cerebral palsy (also called spastic paralysis) is a serious illness in which a person's muscles do not work properly, causing disablement. It happens because the part of the brain that controls movement does not work properly for some reason. It can begin before, during or very soon after birth.

People with cerebral palsy can often be helped by special exercises called *physiotherapy*. They learn to control their movements with the help of the undamaged parts of their brain.

Down's syndrome is a disability that some babies are born with. It is usually caused by a defect in the egg (ovum) of the mother. It affects facial features, giving a broader, flatter face than normal, a short neck and upward-slanting eyes. People with Down's take longer than normal to learn how to do things, but many lead a fulfilling life.

Living with disability

How much help a disabled person gets depends very much on where they live in the world. In Britain there are special schools for disabled children, but, where possible, they go to the same schools as other children. Sometimes there is a special person in a school to help disabled pupils.

New buildings are now often built in such a way that people in wheelchairs can easily use them. Cars and buses can also be altered for disabled users.

Many disabled people take an active part in sport. There is a special Olympic Games for the disabled. There are also workshops for disabled people that teach skills they can use to support themselves.

find out more
Blindness
Deafness

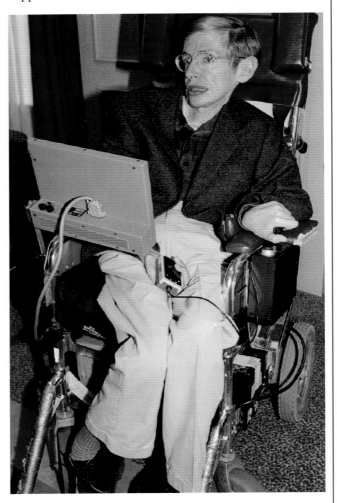

▼ Stephen Hawking is a leading physicist and has written a best-selling book called *A Brief History of Time* (1988). Because of a muscle-wasting disease he is confined to a wheelchair and uses a computerized voice synthesizer to communicate. Even such severe physical disability need not prevent people fulfilling their potential.

Diseases

When a person has a disease, their body is affected in some way, often unpleasantly. A person may be born with a disease or they may get one as a result of an injury, from an infection, or from some other cause.

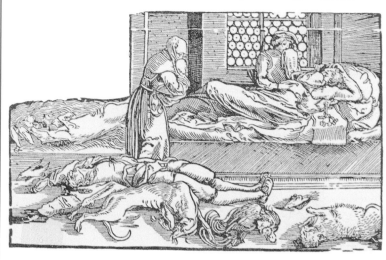

▲ In the past diseases were called plagues. In the 14th century one such plague, known as the Black Death, killed 25 million people. It was spread to humans by bacteria carried by flea-infested rats. This illustration shows victims of the disease.

Diseases range from those that are very serious, even fatal, such as AIDS, to minor ones, such as the common cold. Some diseases, such as diabetes, are potentially serious, but if treatment is available they can be kept under control.

Infectious diseases

Many diseases are infectious. This means that the germs that cause them pass from one person to another, either carried in the air or through some sort of physical contact. These germs include bacteria, viruses, prions and fungi.

The diseases caused by *bacteria* include food poisoning, whooping cough and tuberculosis (TB). Bacteria also cause tetanus (a type of blood poisoning) in humans and animals, and canker in fruit trees. Bacteria can be killed by antiseptics or antibiotics. People can also be protected against certain types of bacteria before they have a chance to harm them by receiving vaccines.

This protection is called immunization.

Viruses cause several diseases in humans, including AIDS, rabies, measles, chicken pox, influenza (flu) and the common cold. Viruses also cause diseases in other animals and plants. New viruses sometimes appear, such as the HIV virus that causes AIDS. Antibiotics will not cure viral infections, but there are some anti-viral drugs.

Prions are much smaller than bacteria and viruses and consist only of protein. Scientists think that prions cause BSE ('mad cow disease'), which is believed to be passed to humans from infected beef.

Fungi cause athlete's foot, ringworm and other infections in humans. They also cause foot rot in cattle and many plant diseases. Fungal infections can be treated with special powders and creams that kill the fungus.

Epidemics

Occasionally a large number of people get the same disease at the same time in the same place. This is called an epidemic. Epidemics of diseases such as cholera and typhoid are often caused by people eating and drinking food and water that contain germs. Epidemics of diseases such as measles and flu are caused by germs that are spread by coughing and sneezing or by touching someone with the disease.

Educating people about the need for cleanliness when handling food and about the proper disposal of waste can help prevent the outbreak of an epidemic. Epidemics can also be prevented by giving people vaccines to protect them against certain diseases.

Quarantine is another way of trying to stop the spread of a disease. Because some diseases

• New diseases are appearing all the time. One recent disease is SARS (Severe Acute Respiratory Syndrome), a type of pneumonia that is often fatal. It first appeared in China in autumn 2002, and within a few months had spread across eastern Asia.

▼ Louis Pasteur was a great French scientist who discovered that bacteria cause diseases. He developed vaccines for several diseases in animals including rabies and anthrax, which kills cattle and sheep.

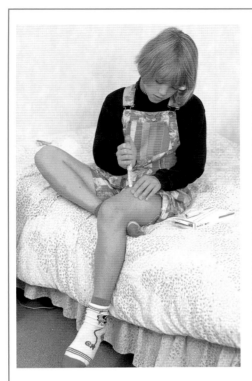

◄ Diabetes is a fairly common disease, affecting 4% of the world's population. Like most diabetes sufferers, this girl has to inject herself daily with the chemical insulin because her body does not produce it naturally. The body needs insulin to break down sugar in the blood.

Sometimes a baby is born with part of its body not working properly. For example, its heart may have a hole in it, causing the blood to flow incorrectly. Such conditions, called developmental diseases, can often be cured by surgery.

disease. Food containing vitamins and minerals is essential to good health. Vitamin C, found in fresh fruit and vegetables, is important for your blood. The mineral calcium, in cheese and milk, helps to strengthen your bones and teeth. Iron also helps to make healthy blood and is found in some vegetables. Food containing too much fat can cause heart disease. Too much sugar can decay the teeth and too much salt can cause high blood pressure.

▼ This picture shows microscopic prion fibres (coloured orange) in the brain of a cow infected with BSE ('mad cow disease'). Prions are virus-like germ that attack nerve cells in the brains of various animals, including humans.

take a long time to develop, it may be some time before an infected person starts to feel ill. However, during this time, called the *incubation period*, they could pass the disease to someone else. If they are kept in quarantine (separate from other people), this may stop the disease from spreading. Plants and animals that may be diseased are also held in quarantine. In Britain, animals from abroad are held in quarantine for six months to make sure that they do not have rabies. Rabies can be spread to humans if they are bitten by an infected animal. It is a very serious disease that causes death if it is left to develop.

Inherited and developmental diseases

Inherited diseases are passed by parents to their children. Haemophilia, a disease in which the blood is slow to clot, is one example. Special treatment can help people with inherited diseases, though they can rarely be completely cured.

Mental illness

Mental diseases, also called mental illness, are problems of the mind. Serious forms of mental illness are called psychoses and less severe ones are called neuroses. They often cause people to behave in an unusual manner, and some sufferers may see and hear things that are not there. They also may hurt themselves or other people.

Some people become very unhappy and are said to be suffering from depression. This may be caused by overwork, stress or the death of someone close to them.

Sometimes people with mental disease need close attention and have to stay in hospital until the illness is under control. They are treated by doctors called psychiatrists.

Good health

Preventing disease by being healthy is better than trying to cure a disease once it has taken hold. Proper diet is one way of helping your body to fight

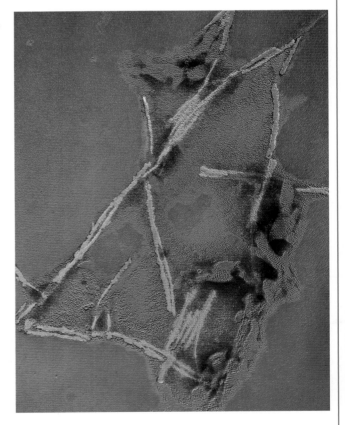

Keeping clean, taking regular exercise, controlling your weight, not smoking or taking drugs, not drinking too much alcohol – these are all ways in which you can help to keep yourself healthy. Scientific research into ways of preventing and curing disease is being carried out all the time in many countries of the world.

find out more
AIDS
Biotechnology
Cancer
Complementary
 medicine
Diets
Disabilities
Drugs
Health and fitness
Immunity
Medicine
Psychologists

Disney, Walt

Born 1901 in Chicago, USA
Died 1966 aged 65

Walt Disney was brilliant at creating cartoon characters and bringing them to life. He founded the famous film company that bears his name.

Walter Disney grew up on a Missouri farm, and enjoyed sketching the animals around him. He later worked for an advertising agency before starting on cartoon films for the Laugh-O-gram company in Missouri. He formed his own film company in 1923 and created Mickey Mouse in 1928. The success of such characters as Mickey, Donald Duck, Pluto and Goofy eventually led to full-length animated films. The first of these were *Snow White and the Seven Dwarfs* (1937) and *Pinocchio* (1940) .

Walt Disney Productions made more cartoons than any other company. It also made family films with real actors, such as *20,000 Leagues Under the Sea* (1954), and films such as *Mary Poppins* (1964), which combined cartoon characters and real actors. Disney is still one of the most successful film companies in the world, making films for all ages.

In 1955 Walt Disney opened Disneyland, the huge amusement park in California. The even bigger Walt Disney World in Florida opened five years after his death. Tokyo Disneyland opened in Japan in 1983, and Disneyland Paris opened in France in 1992.

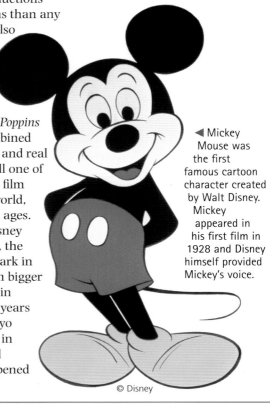

◀ Mickey Mouse was the first famous cartoon character created by Walt Disney. Mickey appeared in his first film in 1928 and Disney himself provided Mickey's voice.

© Disney

find out more
Animation
Films

Doctors

Doctors are people who have been trained to prevent and cure illnesses.

• People can have the title Doctor even if they have not studied medicine. These people are called Doctors of Philosophy. This means that after studying for a degree at university they have gone on to do several years of original research and have written a long essay (a 'thesis') on their subject.

A doctor's training varies from country to country, but normally students study medical sciences for two or three years, then practise dealing with patients for another two or three years. After this they spend many years learning more about the special area of medicine that they want to concentrate on.

There are two main types of medical doctor: the family doctor or general practitioner (GP), and the specialist. People who are ill usually go first to a GP, who diagnoses (identifies) any problem, and decides whether to treat them or to send them to a specialist for treatment.

Specialist doctors usually work in hospitals. They can specialize in many areas, including surgery, looking after children or old people, or treating particular diseases.

▶ FLASHBACK ◀

People have been practising medicine for thousands of years. The ancient Greek doctor Hippocrates of Cos, who lived about 2400 years ago, has had a great influence on Western medicine.

It is only quite recently that women have had the legal right to become doctors.

▼ This graph compares the number of people per doctor in countries around the world. In Niger, for example, there is one doctor for every 53,000 people, whereas Italy has one doctor for every 200 people.

find out more
Complementary
  medicine
Diseases
Health and fitness
Hospitals
Medicine
Nurses

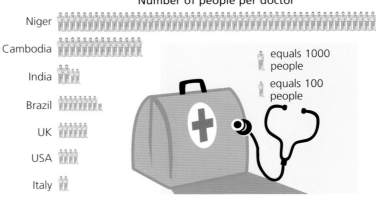

Number of people per doctor

Niger
Cambodia
India
Brazil
UK
USA
Italy

equals 1000 people
equals 100 people

Dogs

There are more than 100 different breeds of domestic dog that live and work with people all over the world. All these breeds are descended from just one ancestor, the wolf. But there are many other kinds of wild dog as well, including wolves, foxes, jackals and coyotes.

All dogs are hunters, and most can run fast. They possess very good senses of sight, hearing and smell. All these senses help them to hunt, but for most wild dogs sight is the most important. They use their excellent sense of smell to communicate with each other. Like all hunters, dogs are intelligent animals.

Wild dogs

Wolves live in family groups called packs. The pack centres around a breeding pair who mate for life and can contain up to 20 members. Wolf cubs are fed and cared for by all members of the pack. Because wolves hunt together, they can kill animals that are much larger than themselves. They feed mainly on deer, usually preying on the weaker ones.

After a kill, a wolf can eat about 9 kilograms of meat in one go.

Jackals live in the warm, dry climates of Africa, Asia and south-eastern Europe. They usually feed on rodents, lizards, birds and insects, although they can hunt larger animals, such as small antelope. They also scavenge, eating the leftovers from lions' kills and sometimes human rubbish. Jackals are hunted as a pest, and because of this and the destruction of their habitat, Simien jackals are now an endangered species.

Unlike wolves and jackals, most foxes live alone, although cubs remain with both parents for the first few months of life. Foxes live in most regions north of the tropics, and in Australia, where they were brought by European settlers. They eat a wide variety of foods, such as small rodents, insects, and even woodland fruits. Some foxes kill game birds, but most do not, and they are often useful in destroying pests.

Domestic dogs

Dogs were the first animals to be domesticated and they are now found wherever there are human beings. All dogs have the same biological make-up and behaviour patterns, and they are capable of inter-breeding, producing cross-breeds (mongrels). Dogs look so different from each other because they have been bred by people for different purposes.

The domestication of dogs began towards the end of the Palaeolithic period (Old Stone Age), about 10,000 BC. It may have come about because wolves were attracted to scavenge for food at the rubbish tips left by the humans of that time. Perhaps wolf cubs were sometimes found and kept, and

▲ Jackals usually live in pairs. Once mated, they will stay together for life. This family of golden jackals from Ngorongoro, Tanzania, has just caught a flamingo. Cubs stay with their parents for at least six months.

• There are 2 different kinds of wolf, 21 different kinds of fox and 4 different kinds of jackal. Other wild dogs include the African hunting dog, the bush dog, the dhole and the racoon dog.

◄ Red foxes survive well in many different conditions. They are found over more of the world than any other carnivore (flesh-eater). They have recently taken to living in towns and cities, although they are still wary of humans.

Record-breaking dogs

Tallest
Irish wolfhound, shoulder height about 110 cm
Heaviest
St Bernard, weight about 100 kg
Smallest
Chihuahua, weight under 1 kg
Fastest
Over long distances, saluki; over short distances, greyhound

• The coyotes of North and Central America have, like foxes, adapted well to living beside their human neighbours and now inhabit regions which were formerly the territory of wolves.

• Dingos were probably introduced into Australia by the Aborigines 5000 to 8000 years ago. They can sometimes be tamed, and become affectionate pets.

find out more
Animal behaviour
Mammals

▼ Humans have bred dogs for all sorts of jobs, so the variety among breeds of dog is enormous.

people discovered, as they grew up, that they could be useful. It took several thousand years to transform wild wolves into tame dogs, but by about 5000 years ago dogs were playing an important part in people's lives.

Wolves defend their territories, so dogs could easily be trained to guard the human living places that they shared. Wolves also defend their pack. In ancient times large breeds of dog were used for fighting in battles, defending their human pack. They have also been trained to hunt, to herd animals and to fight each other for sport. In the days before central heating, people sometimes kept themselves warm by cuddling small dogs, called 'lap dogs'.

A useful companion

Today our understanding of dog behaviour has made it possible for us to train dogs to do new and more difficult jobs. Some are guide dogs for the blind and hearing dogs for the deaf. Others are trained as sniffer dogs to help track down terrorists and drug dealers, and others as disaster dogs, to find people buried in avalanches or the rubble of earthquakes. They are also used for experiments in laboratories. Large dogs, such as bouviers, were often used to pull small carts, and in the Arctic sledge dogs are vital to human survival.

▲ All breeds of domestic dog are descended from the wolf. Wolves were once widespread but have now been reduced to small populations in Europe, Asia and northern regions of North America.

Because dogs are hunters, they like chasing games and must have plenty of exercise. Pet dogs that are not given enough to do can sometimes become bored and destructive. Like wolves, dogs are pack animals, attached to and obedient to their group. One reason why they have taken so well to domestication and human companionship is that people have become their 'pack'.

chihuahua · Afghan hound · cocker spaniel · Airedale · cairn terrier · bulldog · chow chow · bouvier

Dragons

Dragons are mythical creatures: a mixture of bird and snake, and of good and evil. People have been telling stories about dragons for a very long time.

• One of the most famous dragons is the Nidhögg, the 'Dread Biter', found in Norse legends. The Nidhögg threatens to destroy the Universe. He gnaws the roots of the giant tree, Yggdrasil, the Mighty Ash. People of the time thought that the tree was the Universe.

find out more
Myths and legends

For Christians, the dragon stood for evil – Satan or the Devil. The Archangel Michael defeated the dragon, proving that good overcomes evil. The ancient Egyptians had a similar myth. Their dragon, Apophis, spread chaos and darkness over the Earth each night, and was overcome by the Sun-god, Ra, each morning.

The dragon that Saint George, the patron saint of England, is supposed to have killed was white, with bat-like wings, and it terrorized the people of Lydia in the Middle East. The daughter of the King of Lydia was offered to the dragon as a sacrifice, but Saint George killed the dragon and rescued the princess.

Some good dragons

In the Far East the dragon is seen as a force for good. The Chinese dragon, *Long*, is king-like: he lives in rivers, lakes and oceans, and roams the skies. For over 2000 years the Chinese people have performed special dances to *Long*, asking him to send them rain to feed the Earth. In ancient Chinese stories a dragon guards the house of the gods. Another dragon became the emblem of the emperors.

▼ This dragon mask is being worn as part of a dance in Bali, Indonesia.

Drake, Francis

Born about 1543 in Devon, England
Died 1596 aged about 53

Francis Drake was a sea captain during the reign of Elizabeth I. He was the first Englishman to sail around the world, and he played an important role in the defeat of the Spanish Armada.

• Drake was playing bowls near Plymouth harbour when the Spanish Armada was first sighted.

• Drake died of a fever at sea during yet another raid on Spanish colonies in the Americas.

find out more
Elizabeth I
Tudor England

Francis Drake learned to sail when he was 13. Ten years later he joined a fleet that took him on two trips taking slaves from Africa to America. A surprise attack by Spaniards made Drake a lifelong enemy of Spain.

At the time of Elizabeth I, England and Spain were enemies. Elizabeth allowed Drake to plunder and steal from Spanish ships as long as he was doing it 'unofficially'. He went on several successful voyages, seizing treasure from Spanish colonies in South America and the West Indies. Drake was behaving little better than a pirate, but he was popular in England for his daring deeds.

In 1577 Drake set sail on a three-year journey of exploration and looting. His ship, the *Golden Hind*, was the only one of the fleet to finish the trip, making him the first Englishman to sail around the world. When he arrived back home, he was knighted by Elizabeth I on board the *Golden Hind*.

In 1587 Drake raided the Spanish harbour of Cádiz and burned a fleet that was being prepared to invade England. The Spaniards equipped a new invasion fleet, which they called the Invincible Armada. When it sailed in 1588, Drake was one of the English leaders who helped to defeat it. This great victory made him an even more popular hero.

▼ A portrait of Francis Drake painted at the height of his fame as an explorer and admiral.

Drama

A drama is a story that is performed. The people who play the parts of different characters in the drama are called actors. All over the world, and throughout history, people have enjoyed watching and acting in drama.

▼ Gillian Anderson (FBI Agent Dana Scully) in a scene from *The X-Files*, the hit American science-fiction series. Television dramas like *The X-Files* can make international stars of their actors.

• Mime is a type of drama in which the actors do not speak or make any noise at all. They show their feelings through facial expression and bodily movement. They can make the audience believe in things that are not physically there, such as walls, balls and tables. Elaborate forms of mime are used in an Indian classical dance form called 'Kathakali'.

Many people go to the theatre to see plays being performed live. People also go to the cinema to watch films, which are a form of drama. And millions of people watch soap operas, situation comedies and various other types of drama on television. They may also listen to plays on the radio.

A play can make us laugh or cry, become excited or frightened. By clever use of words and acting, the playwright (the person who writes the play) and the actors involve us, the audience, in some way. But as well as just entertaining us, many plays

▶ This woodcut from 1745 shows people in Coventry, England, watching a performance of a mystery play. Mystery plays were a popular kind of drama in medieval Europe. They usually told stories from the Bible, and were acted by working people who were members of the 'mysteries' or craft guilds.

help us to understand more about the world in which we live and the problems and feelings that we share.

To become a professional actor you have to spend time studying exactly how other people do things. It is important to make the audience feel that you really are the person you are pretending to be. Otherwise no one will believe the story. You do this by using exactly the right movement, facial expression and speech.

The beginnings of drama

It is possible that early drama dealt with the origins of the Universe, food, life, death and religion. Perhaps, if hunters acted a successful catch before setting out, they could make it come true. Prehistoric people may have acted out all sorts of rituals, but because they were never written down, very little is known of them.

As civilizations developed, plays were written down and learned. This meant that they could be performed over and over again by different groups of actors.

The Greeks

About 2500 years ago, the Greeks began to develop a powerful kind of drama. Their plays told of the sufferings endured by famous characters as they struggled to please their rather strict gods. These plays nearly all had unhappy endings and were called *tragedies*. The three greatest writers of Greek tragedies were Aeschylus, Sophocles and Euripides.

The Greeks also wrote *comedies*. A comedy is a play that not only makes the audience laugh, but also has a happy ending. The plays by Aristophanes poked fun at politicians and their ideas. Other more light-hearted

Australian Aborigines used drama as part of their religious ritual. They acted out stories from myth. Here the Tjapukai Theatre performs the myth of the fire-makers. The actors' bodies are painted with ritual patterns.

comedies were about everyday things such as couples falling in love and all the obstacles they had to overcome.

Greek drama was very different from the plays written today. All the actors were men and they all wore masks. A large group of them, called the 'chorus', told much of the story. This chorus spoke and moved together, and sometimes sang and danced.

Elizabethan theatre

In Europe in the Middle Ages, the main subject for drama was Bible stories. But during the reign of Queen Elizabeth I of England in the 16th century, people began to use drama to tell other kinds of stories. In London, special theatres were built and people paid to see professional actors perform newly written plays. The greatest playwright of this period was William Shakespeare. Many of his later plays were especially written for the famous circular Globe Theatre in London.

Melodrama

In the 19th century melodramas became very popular. These were vivid, exciting stories with a lot of music and fighting, and the

audience cheered the hero and booed the villain. Almost every melodrama ended with good overcoming bad. The scripts of these plays were printed, together with drawings of the characters and scenes, to be cut out and used in toy theatres by Victorian children. They show us how actors of the time stood and gestured.

Oriental theatre

In the 20th century Western drama was influenced by theatre in China, Japan and other Eastern countries. *Kabuki* is a popular form of Japanese theatre that mixes music, dance and mime. The plays are based on ancient legends and are performed by men, who wear elaborate make-up and splendid costumes. Japanese *No* drama also uses music, dancing and elaborate costumes. The actors wear masks. It is based on Buddhist and Shinto religious ritual. Both No and Kabuki are based on set movements, though Kabuki is more light-hearted.

Beijing opera is a Chinese theatre form that features acrobatics, operatic singing, dancing and dialogue. The stories are based on myth, history and fiction.

Changing ideas

These days, as well as comedies, tragedies and melodramas, there are many other kinds of drama: plays without words, or plays where the actors themselves have made up the script; plays on television; pantomimes and musicals with enormously expensive and complicated sets; and plays with no scenery at all.

▲ This mask from Japanese No theatre represents a demon. It was made in about 1280.

Famous playwrights

Sophocles (about 495–406 BC) was a great Greek writer of tragedy. His seven surviving plays include *Antigone* and *Electra*.

Kalidasa (5th century BC) was probably the greatest Indian writer ever. His most famous play was *Sakuntala*.

William Shakespeare (1564–1616) is considered the greatest English playwright. His most famous plays are probably four of his tragedies: *Hamlet*, *Macbeth*, *Othello* and *King Lear*.

The comedies of the French dramatist **Molière** (1622–1673) often attack human weaknesses such as hypocrisy and meanness. *Le Malade imaginaire* ('the imaginary invalid') is about someone who thinks he is more ill than he really is.

The plays of the Russian dramatist **Anton Chekhov** (1860–1904) mix seriousness with humour. *The Cherry Orchard* is one of the greatest dramas ever written.

The German playwright **Bertolt Brecht** (1898–1956) was a major influence on 20th-century drama. *Mother Courage and her Children* was one of his most famous plays.

Tennessee Williams (1911–1983) was an important American playwright. *A Streetcar Named Desire* and *Cat on a Hot Tin Roof* are famous for their brilliant dialogue and emotional tension.

Drawing

▲ *Two Women Resting*, a drawing by Henry Moore (1898–1986). Moore made pen-and-ink sketches similar to the one above as a basis for his sculptures.

• There is a close relationship between drawing and writing. In some ancient languages, like Chinese, the written words were originally simple drawings of the things the words represented.

Drawing is the creation of pictures or designs using the same kind of tools and materials that we use for writing. Pens, pencils, crayons and charcoal are all common drawing implements.

Artists use drawings in many different ways. Some drawings are intended as finished works of art; these are often highly detailed and delicate in treatment. Often, however, artists use drawing as a way of trying out new ideas or as part of the planning of a larger work, such as a painting or sculpture. These kinds of drawing range from rapid sketches, done to jot down a sudden idea before it is forgotten, to elaborate designs in which every detail is worked out precisely.

We usually think of drawing as being an artistic activity, but this is not always so. Many drawings are made to provide information or to help people construct things. Architects' plans and engineers' drawings are two examples of these 'working drawings'. Although these drawings are meant to be functional rather than decorative, they are often attractive to look at.

The development of drawing

Humans have made drawings since prehistoric times. The first drawings were made by scratching marks on earth, rock or tree bark with pointed sticks or stones. Charcoal (charred wood) is another very old drawing tool, popular with the Romans. It was not until the invention of paper, however, that drawing became a highly developed art form. Paper was invented in the Far East and came to Europe in about the 12th century AD. By the 14th century there was a flourishing paper industry, and it was soon after this that drawing became a central part of the work of most artists.

The first famous artist to produce a large number of drawings was the Italian Leonardo da Vinci, who used them in his scientific studies as well as in his work as a painter. Leonardo used several different sorts of drawing technique, including chalk, ink and silverpoint. In silverpoint the artist draws on special paper with a metal rod tipped with silver. The silver reacts with chemicals coated on the paper and produces a wonderfully delicate line. Many other drawing techniques produce their own typical effects. Charcoal, for example, is not suitable for capturing precise detail, but it is ideal for bold, broad impressions.

Today the most popular drawing tool is the pencil, because it can be used in so many ways and is easily available. The 'lead' pencil with varying degrees of hardness or softness was invented in the 1790s by a Frenchman, Nicolas-Jacques Conté, who like Leonardo was both an artist and a scientist. Pencil leads are in fact made of graphite and clay rather than lead.

The latest drawing tools are special computer programs that can reproduce electronically many of the qualities of traditional drawings.

find out more
Animation
Building
Cartoons
Designers
Leonardo da Vinci
Painting
Writing systems

◀ This drawing of an elephant is by the 17th-century Dutch artist Rembrandt. He is most famous for his portraits, but he also liked to paint and draw animals.

Dress and costume

People choose to wear certain clothing – to have a particular style of dress – for many different reasons, practical, cultural and personal. In many parts of the world, people wear clothing that protects them from the climate. Some people like to wear bright, distinctive clothes for decoration or to identify with a particular group.

◀ This woman from Rajasthan in India wears the traditional dress of her region: a brightly coloured long skirt and blouse.

Climate has the most basic influence on the choice of clothing. When it is hot, light-coloured clothes and hats are usually preferred as they deflect the Sun's rays. This type of clothing is worn all year round in hotter regions of the world. In colder regions, clothing is usually woollen and multi-layered for warmth.

Dress for work and play

The work that people do can dictate what they wear during work hours. People in the police force, nursing and sales, for example, have to wear uniforms so that members of the public will recognize them. Some schools also require students to wear uniforms so that it is clear what school they go to. Wearing a uniform may also help them to feel that they are a part of the school.

In other jobs, workers need to wear special clothes for their own protection. Certain types of work bring people into contact with dangerous substances. In these situations, workers wear outfits specially designed to shield them from harm, sometimes covering every part of their bodies. Protective clothing is also worn by members of the armed services.

Sports players wear special clothing for their sport. Athletes, for example, wear leotards or shorts and vests to allow complete freedom of movement. By contrast, American footballers wear elaborate helmets and special padding on their bodies to guard against injury.

Traditional dress

In some countries many people wear the same style of dress as each other. This style is handed down from generation to generation. One country may have several different styles of traditional dress. In India, for instance, Rajasthani women wear brightly coloured long skirts and blouses. Further

▲ Firemen wear special clothing that protects them from getting burnt. Their overalls and hood are made of a fire-resistant material, and a helmet protects their head from falling debris. The fluorescent (glowing) stripes on their clothes make them visible to each other through dense smoke.

north in the Punjab they wear *shalwar* (loose trousers) and *kamiz* (a long shirt). In the south and east the sari is the normal dress for women, though it can be tied in different ways. All over India traditional clothes are worn for everyday work as well as for special occasions.

In European countries hardly anyone now wears traditional styles of dress for everyday use. But in some regions people wear national dress (sometimes called folk costume) for festivals, weddings and other celebrations.

▶ Through the centuries in Europe, one style of costume has slowly changed into another.

early 15th century

late 16th century

mid-18th century

early 19th century

early 20th century

Dress and costume

India

20th-century China

Japan

69% Artwork

Bedouin, Negev Desert, Israel

Berber, Atlas Mountains, Morocco

Cameroon

Bella, Mali

Masai, Kenya

Native American, Andes, South America

Inuit, Canada

▼ Some people choose fashions that make a statement. This teenage punk rocker is wearing clothes, make-up and a hairstyle that are designed to attract attention and look shocking.

Fashion

Fashion is a way of dressing that is particular to a time or place. In the Western world the style of dress has changed a lot since ancient times. Until the 19th century, new and daring styles were worn only by wealthy people. Clothes made of especially expensive fabric were fashionable, especially clothes like full skirts that required vast amounts of costly material. In the 16th century there was even a fashion for cutting holes in top clothes to show off another layer of extravagant fabric beneath.

In the 19th century many people would copy new styles from the illustrations in pocket books, which were like magazines. Poor people wore secondhand clothes and altered them to make them more fashionable. Then the upper classes would quickly bring about another change in fashion; they tried to assert their higher social position by wearing distinctive clothing.

Fashion has now become big business, and many people want to wear the latest styles. Those who can afford it will wear the most fashionable clothes, designed by top fashion houses in Paris, Milan, New York or London. Designers show their ideas at fashion shows, where they are photographed and videoed immediately. Designs will then be adapted and mass-produced by chain stores for sale in the mass market. Fashions are sometimes set by ordinary people, too, especially groups of young people.

Changes to fashion affect not only clothing such as trousers or skirts, but all of the accessories that go to make a complete fashionable outfit, for example, gloves, bags, scarves, belts, hats and shoes. Make-up, too, is influenced by fashion.

▼ An exhibition of clothes by the Japanese fashion designer Issey Miyake, modelled at a fashion show in Paris. Like many leading designers, the clothes he exhibits are his most experimental designs, serving more as works of art than as clothes that will be bought and worn by the public.

▲ Across the world, clothing has been influenced by such factors as climate and cultural values. The Inuit man, for example, wears animal skins to keep warm. The Bedouin woman wears a dress that covers her entire body, because in her society women are not supposed to show bare skin.

find out more
Clothes
Shoes
Textiles

Drought *see* Rain and snow

Drugs

People take drugs because they have a particular effect on their mind or body. Most drugs are taken to help cure illnesses and to relieve pain. But sometimes people take drugs because they like the way they make them feel. Most of these drugs are illegal and have serious side effects.

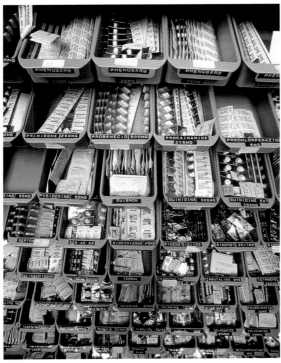

▲ A selection of the pills used for a range of medical purposes, including gout, malaria and tuberculosis.

All drugs used to be made from plants and animals. We now know that many of these were useless, but some are still used today. Opium, from poppies, was used to dull pain for many centuries. In the early 1800s, scientists learned how to isolate (separate) the painkiller morphine from the opium poppy. Soon many other drugs were isolated, making it easier to study them. It then became possible to make some drugs from chemicals (synthetic drugs), which is how most drugs are made today.

The main types of drug used in medicine include antibiotics to kill bacteria; vaccines to fight diseases; analgesics to relieve pain; anaesthetics to stop pain during operations; tranquillizers to calm people down; and sedatives to help people sleep. Some drugs are so strong that they can only be prescribed (ordered) by a doctor.

Antibiotics

Diseases such as sore throats, food poisoning and pneumonia are caused by bacteria. Antibiotics damage or kill bacteria in different ways, and it is the doctor's job to choose the correct antibiotic to fight the bacteria that is causing the disease.

Penicillin was the first antibiotic to be discovered. In 1928 the Scottish scientist Alexander Fleming noticed that colonies of bacteria he had grown had been stunted by a mould, Penicillium notatum. He realized that the mould was producing a substance that killed the bacteria, which he called penicillin. Today, penicillin is used to treat many serious infections.

Drug addiction and abuse

People can come to believe that they cannot manage without taking drugs, even though the drugs may be harming them. This is called drug addiction. The alcohol in alcoholic drinks and the nicotine in tobacco are both drugs that can cause addiction. It is possible to become addicted to drugs prescribed by a doctor. Even drinking too much coffee can become addictive.

Drugs such as heroin and cocaine create a physical dependence, where the body will not function properly if the drug is withdrawn. Other substances, like tobacco, are addictive only because the user cannot break the habit of using them. It is possible to change a habit but it takes a lot of determination. Many people need professional help to overcome an addiction.

• Prehistoric people probably learned that eating certain plants could relieve pain. The ancient Chinese, Egyptians and Greeks all used remedies obtained from plants.

• As well as curing people, drugs can have other effects which are unpleasant or even dangerous. Before drugs are made available to the public, they are tested for safety, first on animals then on human volunteers (clinical trials).

• Drugs such as cannabis, Ecstasy, LSD, cocaine and heroin are illegal, and anyone found with them will face severe punishment. Supplying these drugs is a huge international criminal trade.

◀ These drugs officers have just uncovered a large quantity of cocaine being smuggled illegally through the Panama Canal.

find out more
Alcohol
Bacteria
Diseases
Medicine
Smoking

Ducks, geese and swans

Wildfowl is the name we often give to the large group of birds which includes ducks, geese and swans. They are usually found near water and have webbed feet, short legs and oily feathers.

There are three main groups of ducks. Dabbling ducks, such as mallards and shovelers, filter the surface water to find food. Diving ducks, such as pochards and sawbills, search below the surface for vegetable matter. Perching ducks, including muscovies and the colourful mandarins, nest and perch in trees.

True geese are found only in the northern hemisphere. They graze on grass and other vegetation. They spend much of the year in large flocks and many make long migrations. Grey geese include the greylag goose, which is the ancestor of many farmyard geese. Among the black geese is the Canada goose of North America, which has also been introduced into Britain.

Swans feed on grass and water plants. They have long, flexible necks which allow them to reach plants up to a metre below the surface of the water. Several kinds of swan are long-distance migrants. Bewick's swans fly from the Russian tundra to north-west Europe for the winter. The closely related whistling swan breeds in Arctic Canada and winters in the southern USA.

- Swans and geese keep the same mate all their lives, but ducks usually find a new mate each season. For this reason, male ducks usually produce richly coloured feathers each breeding season, in order to attract females. Female ducks, and geese and swans of both sexes, are more plainly coloured throughout the year.

- There are 147 different kinds of ducks, geese and swans.

find out more
Birds

▼ The mute swan (right) with a cygnet (young swan), the greylag goose (centre) and the shoveler duck (left). Geese are smaller than swans but bigger than ducks, and spend less time in water than either of them.

Ears

We use our ears to detect sound. Other mammals have ears similar to ours, and birds, reptiles, amphibians and fishes are able to hear sounds, although their ears do not work in quite the same way. Some insects have ears on their legs or body.

The part of the ear that you can see is called the outer ear. Its funnel shape enables it to collect sound waves and focus them on a thin membrane called the *eardrum*. The eardrum then vibrates, which causes the group of tiny bones (*ossicles*) that are attached to it to vibrate too. This vibration in turn moves the liquid in a snail-shaped chamber inside the inner ear called the *cochlea*. Inside the cochlea, sensitive hair cells, attached to nerves, send messages to the brain. These nerve messages enable us to hear and understand sounds, including speech and music.

The ear and brain working together can separate sounds depending on how loud or soft, and how high or low pitched they are. Having two ears helps us to tell where a sound is coming from, as it will be louder in one ear than the other unless it is straight ahead or immediately behind. The lowest sounds humans can hear are at 20 vibrations a second (a low hum) and the highest are 20,000 vibrations a second (a high-pitched hiss).

Your sense of balance is controlled in the inner ear. Any change in the position of your head causes fluid in three *semicircular canals* to move. This information is then passed by nerve cells to the brain. Without this information you would be unable to move without falling.

find out more
Bats
Deafness
Senses
Sound

▼ Sounds make the eardrum vibrate. This makes the ossicles vibrate, which makes sensory hairs in the cochlea vibrate. These send nerve impulses to the brain where we hear the sound.

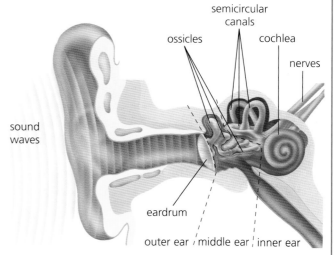

semicircular canals

ossicles

cochlea

nerves

sound waves

eardrum

outer ear / middle ear / inner ear

Dyes *see* Paints and dyes

Earth

The Earth is one of the nine planets in the Solar System. It is a huge rocky ball whose surface is two-thirds water and one-third land. The layers of air that surround the Earth make up its atmosphere. The atmosphere contains oxygen, which is essential to living things. The Earth is tiny compared with some of the other planets, or with the Sun. Jupiter and Saturn are hundreds of times bigger than Earth, and the Sun is over a million times bigger.

The Earth is constantly moving. It spins round in space like a top, and at the same time it travels around the Sun in an orbit (path) that takes one year to complete. Satellite photographs taken from space

▲ An eruption of Krafla, a large, active volcano in Iceland. Since the year 1500, about one-third of the Earth's total lava flow has come from Iceland's volcanoes.

show the Earth as a blue ball covered with masses of swirling cloud. Closer views can show its surface features, such as the shapes of the continents, the oceans, the great snow-covered mountain ranges, and even large rivers and cities.

Inside the Earth

We live on the outer part of the Earth, which is called the *crust*. It is made up of hard rocks and is covered with water in places. The crust is about 5 kilometres thick under the oceans and up to 30 kilometres thick under the land.

Beneath the crust lies a ball of hot rock and metals. The inside of the Earth is extremely hot, and below about 70 kilometres the rocks are molten (melted). This molten rock comes to the surface when a volcano erupts. The deeper below the surface, the hotter and denser (thicker) the rock becomes. The main inner layer of molten rock, immediately below the crust, is called the *mantle*. It surrounds the hot

metallic centre, which is called the core. The core is partly solid and partly liquid metal.

How the Earth developed

The Sun, like other stars, developed from huge spinning clouds of gas, called nebulas. The Sun is thought to have formed about 5000 million years ago. When it first formed, a broad disc of dust and gas swirled around the Sun. Some of the dust and gas collected together to form larger lumps of material, which became the planets of the Solar System. One of these planets was Earth.

When it was first formed, about 4600 million years ago, the Earth is thought to have been a ball of molten rock. The surface was probably as hot as 4000 °C. It took many millions of years for the surface to cool down enough for a solid crust to form.

▼ A cross-section of the Earth shows the different layers beneath the outer layer, or crust. Scientists find out about the inside of the Earth by measuring the speed at which the waves from earthquakes travel through the layers.

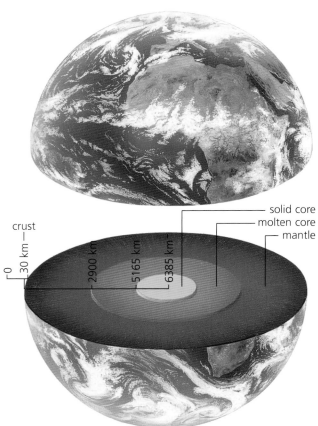

crust
0
30 km
2900 km
5165 km
6385 km
solid core
molten core
mantle

Earth statistics

Average distance from Sun
149,600,000 kilometres
Surface area
510 million square kilometres
Distance from surface to centre (average)
6368 kilometres
Distance around Equator
40,075 kilometres
Area of land
149 million square kilometres (29%)
Area of oceans and seas
361 million square kilometres (71%)
Volume
1,083,230 million cubic kilometres
Weight
76 million million million tonnes
Greatest height
8848 m Mount Everest
Greatest depth
11,035 m Marianas Trench
Age
4600 million years (cooled to 1000 °C and first rains, 4300 million years ago)
First living things
about 3500 million years ago
Temperature at core
5000 °C

At first, the Earth had no atmosphere, just like most of the other planets today. However, volcanic eruptions all over the surface produced enough gases to create a primitive atmosphere. This early atmosphere had no oxygen, and the first forms of life on Earth survived without oxygen. They are believed to date from 3500 million years ago. Oxygen, which is mainly produced by plants, came later, when plants started to develop and spread across the Earth.

No rocks on Earth are as old as the Earth itself. The oldest rocks are a little less than 4,000 million years old. But by time these rocks were formed, the earliest rocks had already been worn down to sediments and used to form new rocks. The earliest evidence of life is found in rocks from about 3500 million years ago. These contain fossils of tiny creatures called blue-green algae. Fossils of a few other primitive animals appear in rocks about 1000 million years old, then there is a sudden explosion of life in rocks from about 550 million years ago. The first mammals developed 200 million years ago, and the dinosaurs are thought to have become extinct 65 million years ago. The first human beings probably arrived only about 2 million years ago.

Remote sensing

Satellite photography of the Earth is called remote sensing because scientists can observe or 'sense' major features of the Earth from a distance. Remote sensing allows weather forecasters to see the large-scale patterns of clouds, which can be used to predict the weather.

It provides information about climate and agriculture, for example crop yields, and helps geologists to find valuable minerals. Remote sensing also enables scientists to assess the effects of human activities on forests, deserts and waterways. Today, the quality of the photographs is so good that houses and even cars can sometimes be identified.

▲ Below the surface of the world's oceans are long mountain chains called oceanic ridges. Here, hot lava from below the surface pushes up to form a new ocean crust. The 'black smokers' in the picture are hydrothermal vents, where water heated to over 300 °C escapes from the hot rocks.

▶ This photograph of the Earth taken from space shows Egypt and the Sinai peninsula. The Red Sea is in the bottom-left corner of the photo; the dark band across the centre is the River Nile, which opens out into the Nile Delta, where it meets the Mediterranean. The Suez Canal runs between the Mediterranean and the top-left fork of the Red Sea.

find out more
Atmosphere
Continents
Earthquakes
Evolution
Geology
Mountains
Oceans and seas
Seasons
Solar System
Time
Universe

Earthquakes

Earthquakes happen when the surface of the Earth moves. A small earthquake feels like a distant rumble, but the most serious ones can destroy whole buildings, rip apart roads and bridges, and destroy electricity and gas services. Often fires break out and great floods occur. Many people may be killed as buildings collapse on top of them.

The Earth's crust is divided into great plates which are moving extremely slowly all the time. The edges of these plates mark lines of weakness in the crust. When two plates can no longer move easily against each other, pressure builds up under the surface until suddenly it becomes too great. Then the plates jerk against each other and an earthquake happens. The city of San Francisco, USA, has experienced numerous earthquakes. It lies on the San Andreas Fault, which marks the boundary between two plates.

The earthquake's *focus* (the place where the violent movement begins) is usually no more than 100 kilometres below the surface. The point on the Earth's surface directly above this is the *epicentre*, although the destructive power of the earthquake may not be greatest at this point. During the 1985 earthquake in Mexico City, the epicentre was some distance from the city. Earthquakes also happen out at sea, often deep down in ocean trenches. They cause huge waves called *tsunamis* to form, often travelling towards the shore at up to 800 kilometres an hour.

▼ This section of highway collapsed as a result of the powerful earthquake that devastated the Japanese city of Kobe in 1995.

- The size of every earthquake is measured on a scale from 1 (tiny) to 10 (total devastation). The scale, known as the Richter scale, measures the forces involved and the effects of the earthquake.

- *Seismologists* (people who study earthquakes) map where faults are and monitor slight movements in the surface, but they are unable to forecast accurately when and where an earthquake will happen, or how powerful it will be.

find out more
Continents
Earth
Volcanoes

Eclipses

We see an eclipse when the Earth, the Moon and the Sun line up in space. If the Moon moves between the Earth and the Sun, there is an eclipse of the Sun. If the Earth is between the Sun and the Moon, we see an eclipse of the Moon.

The Moon goes round the Earth once a month, but it only goes directly in front of the Sun a few times each year. Although the Sun is very much bigger than the Moon, it is also a lot further away. By chance, the Moon and the Sun look about the same size as seen from Earth, so the Moon sometimes just covers the Sun to make a total eclipse. When this happens, the sky goes dark and the Sun's corona, a faint halo of glowing gas, can be seen around the black disc of the Moon. Even then, a total eclipse can be seen only from places along a narrow strip of the Earth's surface, just a few kilometres wide. In any one place, total eclipses of the Sun are rare. Partial eclipses, when the Moon covers just part of the Sun, are seen much more frequently.

Eclipses of the Moon are easier to see because they are visible from all the places where the Moon has risen. During an eclipse, the Moon looks a lot darker and reddish, but it does not disappear completely.

Total eclipses of the
Moon
9 November 2003
4 May 2004
28 October 2004
3 March 2007
28 August 2007
Total eclipses of the
Sun
23 November 2003
29 March 2006
1 August 2008
11 July 2009

find out more
Moon
Sun

▼ Eclipses of the Moon last for several hours while the Moon passes through the Earth's shadow.

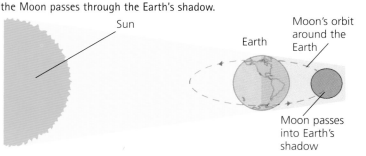

Sun

Earth

Moon's orbit around the Earth

Moon passes into Earth's shadow

▼ Total eclipses of the Sun last for a few minutes while the Moon covers the Sun.

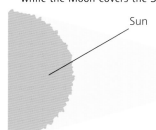

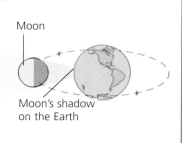

Sun

Moon

Moon's shadow on the Earth

Ecology

Ecology is the science that studies how plants and animals live together, and how they affect, and are affected by, the world around them. Scientists who study ecology are called ecologists.

▲ The leafy treetops (the *canopy*) of the Amazon rainforest are the richest habitat in the world. Ecologists use many techniques to study the canopy at close quarters. This biologist is using climbing equipment to reach an artificial nest hole high above the rainforest floor. He is holding an egg that was laid in the hole.

There are many complicated links between plants, animals and their environment. For example, thrushes eat the berries of trees like the mountain ash. The seeds inside the berries pass through the gut and come out in the thrush's droppings. The seeds then grow into new trees, which produce more berries. In bad summers, the trees produce few berries and the thrushes cannot feed so many young, so the number of thrushes falls. The trees therefore depend on the thrushes, and the thrushes depend on the trees, and both are affected by the weather.

To take another example: voles and lemmings are small mammals that live in northern countries. In years when the weather is kind, they have lots of young. This means there is also plenty of food for the owls that hunt them. The owls are therefore able to raise lots of young, and so the next year there are many more owls. They kill large numbers of their prey (the voles or lemmings), so the numbers of the voles and lemmings drop. The numbers of the owls, voles and lemmings therefore rise and fall in a way that is closely linked together. The job of an ecologist is to try to understand how these kinds of natural processes work.

Careful study

Ecologists often need to make careful measurements as part of their study. So, in the example above, they might count the number of owls and lemmings, measure how much grass is available for the lemmings to eat, and record careful details of the weather. Putting all these measurements together, they can begin to understand the processes that control the numbers of the different animals.

Animals are also linked together in what ecologists call food chains. In the sea, for example, tiny plants float near the surface, using the Sun's energy to make their own food. These are eaten by tiny, floating animals. These tiny animals are eaten by small fishes, which are eaten by bigger fishes. Then the bigger fishes might be eaten by a penguin, and the penguin might be killed and eaten by a seal. The animals involved therefore depend on other animals lower down the food chain, and all their food comes originally from the energy of the Sun captured by the tiny plants.

Living spaces

Ecology also shows how plants and animals depend on all the features that make up their surroundings, called their *environment*. So cacti and rattlesnakes, for example, are adapted (designed by nature) to live in the desert environment, and this is described as their *habitat*. To survive there, they must have ways of

thrush

seeds in droppings

new tree

mountain ash

▲ The thrush and the mountain ash depend on each other. The thrush needs the tree's berries for food, while the mountain ash needs the thrush to spread its seeds.

• Deserts, rainforests and coral reefs are examples of ecosystems. Even a small pond can be an ecosystem in itself.

• The complex way in which the lives of plants and animals are linked together is called the 'balance of nature'. A change in one part of an ecosystem often causes changes elsewhere that bring the system back into balance. However, the ecosystem is very finely balanced. If the changes are too great, it may break down altogether.

175

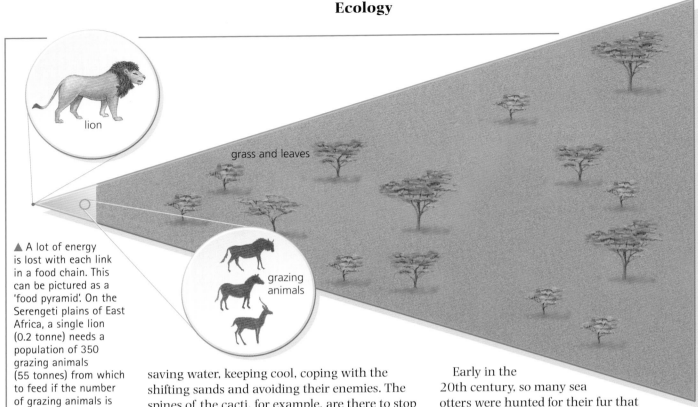

lion

grass and leaves

grazing animals

▲ A lot of energy is lost with each link in a food chain. This can be pictured as a 'food pyramid'. On the Serengeti plains of East Africa, a single lion (0.2 tonne) needs a population of 350 grazing animals (55 tonnes) from which to feed if the number of grazing animals is going to stay stable. The grazing animals, in turn, need 6500 tonnes of grass and leaves from which to feed.

saving water, keeping cool, coping with the shifting sands and avoiding their enemies. The spines of the cacti, for example, are there to stop them being eaten by animals, while rattlesnakes have a special way of moving over the hot ground. The lives of all the plants and animals in any habitat depend on each other and on their surroundings. The living system that ties them all together is called an *ecosystem*.

Lessons for life

One of the lessons of ecology for humans is that, if we disturb the balance of nature in any ecosystem, the result is difficult to predict but often damaging to us and to many other kinds of living things. The story of what happened to the Californian sea otter illustrates this.

Early in the 20th century, so many sea otters were hunted for their fur that they almost died out. Sea otters feed on smaller animals, including sea urchins. With the sea otters gone, huge numbers of sea urchins built up in California, USA. They soon used up all the large seaweeds, called giant kelps, on which they fed. Underwater 'forests' of kelp were replaced by bare, rocky areas called 'sea urchin barrens'. But the kelp forests were the breeding place for many fishes off the Californian coast. When the kelp disappeared, the fishes died out. The fishing industry had to close down, and so did the canning factories. Hundreds of people lost their jobs – and all because the killing of sea otters had disturbed the balance of nature.

▶ The disappearance of the Californian sea otter, as a result of hunting, had unexpected effects that led to many fishermen and factory workers losing their jobs.

find out more
Conservation
Food chains and webs
Forests
Grasslands
Green movement
Oceans and seas
Rivers and streams
Wetlands

Economics

We are all consumers, buying the goods and services we need. Most people are also producers, working to make goods or provide services. Economics is all about how we produce the things people need and want and about how those goods and services are shared out.

There are many economic problems in the world. People's wants are endless, but resources – things we need for production – are limited. In poor countries people have very little, whilst in better-off countries people often have more than they need. Many countries also suffer from inflation, when prices keep going up and up, and unemployment, when people cannot find jobs.

Capitalism and communism

In communist countries, the government decides what things people need and arranges for them to be produced. In capitalist countries people are free to set up businesses producing what they think consumers might want to buy.

Countries that use elements of both systems are called *mixed economies*. In a mixed economy, most businesses belong to private individuals and shareholders, but the government provides some services, such as law and order, and defence.

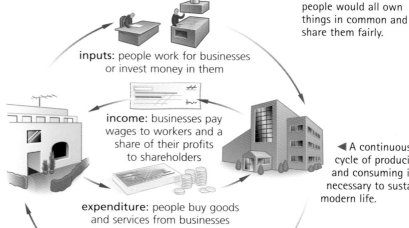

inputs: people work for businesses or invest money in them

income: businesses pay wages to workers and a share of their profits to shareholders

expenditure: people buy goods and services from businesses

output: businesses produce goods and services for sale to people

◀ A continuous cycle of producing and consuming is necessary to sustain modern life.

• German philosopher and economist Karl Marx developed the communist idea of economics in the 19th century. He said that people would all own things in common and share them fairly.

find out more
Communists
Democracy
Employment
Industry
Money
Trade

Edison, Thomas

Born 1847 in Ohio, USA
Died 1931 aged 84

• In 1869 Edison was offered a large sum of money for his design of a telegraph device. With this money he set up a research laboratory, which he called his 'invention factory'. He used to boast that this laboratory made a small invention every 10 days and a big one every six months.

find out more
Electronics
Inventors
Light
Recording

Thomas Edison was one of the greatest inventors of all time. He patented (registered with the government) over 1000 inventions, including the electric light bulb.

From the age of 7, Thomas Edison was taught at home by his mother, who encouraged his interest in science. By the time he was 10, he had made his own laboratory and was starting to do his own experiments.

One of Edison's most important inventions was the world's first machine for recording sounds, the phonograph. The whole of our modern recording industry, which includes music, film, television and video, developed from this invention.

Edison also helped to invent the electric lamp. The one he designed consisted of a wire, or filament, inside a glass bulb from which all the air had been taken out to create a vacuum. His breakthrough came when he eventually found the right material from which to make the filament.

While he was experimenting, Edison found that a current could also flow across the vacuum to a plate inside the bulb. He did not understand why, but we know today that it is due to electrons escaping from the filament: it is known

▶ This photograph of Thomas Edison was taken in 1888 after he had worked continuously for five days and five nights to improve his latest invention, the phonograph (shown beside him).

now as the Edison effect. This discovery led to the invention of the electronic valve (used before transistors and microchips were invented), and was really the beginning of the whole of our modern electronics industry.

Ecosystems *see* Ecology • **Ecuador** *see page 621* • **Education** *see* Schools and universities

Eggs

An egg is the cell made by a female animal which, when joined with a sperm from a male, can grow into a new animal. Almost all animals produce eggs.

Most animals lay their eggs. The eggs are normally covered with a protective layer of jelly or a tough shell. Fish eggs are laid in the sea or in lakes and rivers; turtle and crocodile eggs are laid in sand; frogs' eggs (frogspawn) are laid in ponds; and birds' eggs are laid in nests.

The eggs of many insects have shells that are very nutritious. The young insects eat these shells as soon as they hatch. Insects also often lay their eggs on a plant that will be the food of the young when they hatch.

Birds' eggs

A bird's egg has several layers. On the outside is a hard shell for protection. Inside are membranes (thin walls) and the *albumen* (white). This is a watery substance that cushions and protects the growing chick. Right in the centre of the egg is the *yolk*, which is made of fat and proteins to feed the growing chick.

When an egg is laid, if it has not been fertilized, a chick will not develop. If it has been

◄ Many kinds of cuckoo lay their eggs in other birds' nests and leave the 'foster mother' to rear the young birds. This cuckoo egg has been laid in a dunnock's nest. When the cuckoo hatches, it will push the other eggs out of the nest so that it can eat all the food brought by the foster mother.

fertilized, a chick grows. It must then be *incubated* (kept warm), and the parents do this by taking turns to sit on the eggs. At the end of the incubation period the young bird hatches by breaking out of the egg.

find out more
Birds
Cells
Mammals
Pregnancy and birth
Sex and reproduction

▼ A cross-section of a chicken's egg. The chick sits on a ball of food called the yolk. This floats in a jelly called the albumen which gives it moisture. The shell gives protection and also lets oxygen pass through to the growing chick.

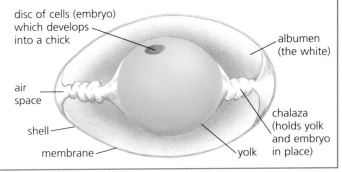

disc of cells (embryo) which develops into a chick

air space

shell

membrane

albumen (the white)

chalaza (holds yolk and embryo in place)

yolk

Egypt

Egypt is a large country in North Africa. Most of Egypt is desert, but at the heart of the country is the narrow, fertile strip of the Nile valley, where over 90 per cent of all Egyptians live.

Most parts of Egypt have hot, dry summers and mild winters. The Nile runs along a narrow valley for most of its length, but fans out into a fertile delta almost 250 kilometres wide.

Egypt is a Muslim country, and Arabic is the main language. Over half the population live in the Nile delta, many of them in Cairo, Africa's largest and fastest-growing city. Overcrowding is a major problem in Cairo.

Many Egyptians are farmers, or *fellahin*. They grow wheat,

rice, cotton, dates, and other fruit. Because of the dry climate, the fields have to be irrigated from the Nile.

► FLASHBACK ◄

By AD 200 many Egyptians had become Christians. During the 7th century the country was invaded by Arabic people, and it

has remained an Arabic-speaking state. Since 1922 it has been an independent country. In 1967 and 1973 Egypt was at war with Israel. Then in 1979 Egypt recognized the state of Israel. Since then the country has played a more moderate part in the continuing tensions between Arabs and Israelis.

► The felucca is a traditional boat on the Nile. This felucca is being used as a ferry.

find out more
Africa
Deserts
Egyptians, ancient
Middle East
See also Countries fact file, page 621

Egyptians, ancient

Egypt became a single kingdom in about 3100 BC. This makes it one of the oldest states in the world. The ancient Egyptians conquered other countries and established a vast empire. They became famous for their great buildings, their statues and their ability to farm a land which was largely desert.

- The Egyptian empire came to an end in 30 BC when the Romans invaded and Egypt became part of the Roman empire.

- The Egyptians were good at engineering. They built special 'Nilometers' to measure the height of the flood waters in July, to work out how much water they could use when ploughing began in October.

▼ Tutankhamun (about 1370–1352 BC) is one of the best known of all the Egyptian kings. His fame is based mainly on the amazing treasures found inside his tomb when it was discovered in 1922. These include a solid gold coffin, a throne, jewellery, weapons, chariots and this beautiful gold funeral mask, which shows what the young king actually looked like.

▲ This painting comes from a tomb in Thebes. It shows the nobleman Nebamun as a hunter throwing a stick at birds. Notice the great variety of birds in the air and fishes in the River Nile below his boat of reeds.

Egypt could never have become a prosperous and powerful country without the River Nile. Each year the Nile floods the land, bringing water to a country which has very little rainfall. The river also washes fertile mud onto the soil. The Egyptians were able to grow corn for bread, and lettuces, onions, peas, cucumbers and other vegetables. Once the crops were growing, the Egyptians were able to water the soil by digging irrigation channels from the Nile. The Egyptians regarded the River Nile as a god, called Hapy, who was generous to them. He was not always reliable though, and there were years of drought and sometimes floods.

The king and the government

The rulers of Egypt were called *pharaohs*. The pharaoh was a king but was also thought to be a god after death. He was the High Priest of the Egyptians, the chief judge and also the commander-in-chief of the army. The king usually married his own sister and their son would become the next pharaoh.

A large number of officials, appointed by the king, ran the government. Some would have been relatives of the king. These officials looked after government departments such as the treasury, the civil service, the foreign office and the public records.

Ordinary Egyptians

A lot of ordinary Egyptians worked on the land as farmers. People not only planted crops but kept animals such as cows, sheep, goats and pigs. They also hunted animals such as deer, and trapped birds and fished, sometimes just for sport.

There were also a large number of special jobs to be done. Some Egyptians were fishermen, or boat-owners moving goods up and down the Nile. Builders were needed for the towns, palaces and the tombs. Craftspeople were trained to be tomb-painters or statue sculptors, or to make objects such as furniture

and jewellery. Some Egyptians were good engineers.

Pyramids and other buildings

Very important buildings, such as pyramids and temples to the gods, were built of stone cut from quarries. All the other buildings (people's houses, palaces and government buildings) were made of mud bricks. Earth was mixed with straw and water and put into wooden moulds. Once it had dried hard in the sun it could be used as a

▼ This map of ancient Egypt shows how all the major settlements were along the banks of the life-giving Nile.

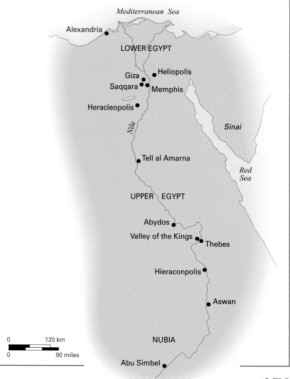

Mediterranean Sea

Alexandria

LOWER EGYPT

Giza • Heliopolis
Saqqara • Memphis

Heracleopolis

Nile

Sinai

Red Sea

Tell al Amarna

UPPER EGYPT

Abydos
Valley of the Kings • Thebes

Hieraconpolis

Aswan

NUBIA

0   120 km
0   90 miles

Abu Simbel

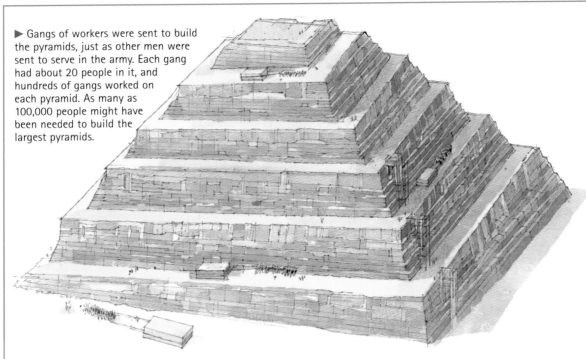

► Gangs of workers were sent to build the pyramids, just as other men were sent to serve in the army. Each gang had about 20 people in it, and hundreds of gangs worked on each pyramid. As many as 100,000 people might have been needed to build the largest pyramids.

• The ancient Egyptians are famous for using a kind of reed called papyrus to make writing materials. They used papyrus to write on and for painting pictures. They used pictures (called hieroglyphs) for their writing, which we can translate today.

▼ Animal mummies, like this cat mummy from Abydos, were found in tombs. To mummify a human or animal body, specialist workers removed the liver, lungs and other organs, then dried out the rest of the body using a type of salt. After about 70 days, when the body was completely dry, it was wrapped in linen bandages and sealed inside a coffin.

Egyptian gods and goddesses

The Egyptians worshipped over 750 gods. The gods ruled the upper world where humans lived, and the underworld where souls went after death.

Four Egyptian gods

Ra Egyptians believed that the world was brought to life by Ra (right), the Sun-god. Every day Ra sailed through the sky, bringing light to the world. Every evening he began a night-long voyage through the caves and tunnels of the underworld.

Osiris and Isis Osiris (second from right) and Isis (second from left) were the king and queen of all humans. Their brother, Set, the storm-god, murdered Osiris, cut his body into 14 pieces and floated them down the Nile. Osiris went to the underworld, where he became ruler of the dead. On each anniversary of his death, Isis wept for him and her tears caused the yearly Nile floods.

Anubis Ancient Egyptians believed that when a body died, the ka, or spirit-self, lived on. Jackal-headed Anubis (left), god of tombs, weighed each ka's heart against the Feather of Truth on a pair of scales. Wicked kas were handed over to the Eater of Corpses. Good kas were led to Osiris, who gave them eternal happiness.

building brick. Bricks lasted for a long time because the climate in Egypt is dry and hot.

The pharaohs and other important people of ancient Egypt were buried in fine tombs from the earliest times. In about 2686 BC a new type of tomb was built for the Pharaoh Zoser at Saqqara. It is called a step pyramid because it was built as series of steps or platforms. Later, engineers worked out how to build smooth-sided pyramids of enormous height. Later still, tombs cut into rock were used as burial places. The most famous is that of Tutankhamun, in the Valley of the Kings at Thebes.

In pyramids the actual burial place was reached by a long passage carefully blocked and hidden from tomb-robbers. Pyramids were built close to the Nile so that stone blocks could be brought to the site by boat and moved on sledges. The body of the pharaoh also arrived by boat.

The afterlife

The Egyptians were very religious and believed that gods played a great part in their lives. They also believed that there was life after death. They thought that the dead person made a journey to the next world and continued to live the same sort of life there. The king would still be a king; a farm labourer would still be a farm labourer. To help in this journey, the rich were given a painted tomb with a variety of their possessions. The Egyptians also tried to preserve the body of a dead person in a life-like way using a special technique called mummification.

find out more
Ancient world
Cleopatra
Egypt
Seven Wonders of the World
Writing systems

Einstein, Albert

Born 1879 in Württemberg, Germany
Died 1955 aged 76

Albert Einstein was a scientist who revolutionized physics in the 20th century. Without his radical ideas, lasers, television, computers, space travel and many other things that are familiar today might never have been developed.

▶ This portrait of Albert Einstein was made in 1921. This was the year in which he was awarded the Nobel prize for physics.

• Although Einstein's scientific ideas were used to develop nuclear weapons, he himself was a prominent campaigner for world peace.

find out more
Atoms and molecules
Physics

Albert Einstein was unhappy at school and his teachers thought he was not very clever. However, despite this poor start, it was not long before he became really interested in mathematics and started studying seriously. After spending some time in Italy, he went to Switzerland, and there his skills as a mathematician and scientist were recognized. In one year, when he was only 26, Einstein published several scientific papers that completely changed the way scientists think.

In 1914 he moved back to Germany. His scientific work made him world-famous and he was awarded the Nobel prize for physics in 1921. However, the rise of the Nazi Party meant he suffered abuse because he was Jewish. Eventually he had had enough, and in 1933 he went to the USA, where he lived for the rest of his life.

Einstein's scientific ideas were so unusual that at first people found them difficult to understand. He developed theories about time and space (relativity) and about how very tiny particles such as electrons and protons behave (quantum theory). Now his theories are essential to the way scientists think about atoms and the Universe.

Elections

Elections are the way in which people can choose a person or group to represent or lead them.

Members of groups and clubs often hold elections to choose an organizing committee. Elections may also be held to choose a trade union official, a local councillor, or a member of a parliament or congress. In a democratic election, the voters have a choice of candidates, and voting takes place in secret so that no one can be forced to vote for someone they do not want. In elections to parliaments and local councils, candidates are often organized into political parties.

In *general elections* voters decide who shall govern a country. In some countries, such as France, the USA and Russia, voters get the chance to elect the president in addition to members of parliament. In other countries, such as Britain, the majority party in the parliament forms the government, and the leader of that party becomes leader of the government.

In a general election all the voters in a country go to special places called *polling stations* to cast their votes. Voters usually get a ballot paper which shows the names and details of all the candidates in the election. They then put a mark (usually an X) against the name of the person they wish to vote for and place the ballot paper in a ballot box. Later, when voting is completed, the boxes are emptied and the votes are counted.

• In the 'first past the post' system of election, everyone has a single vote, and the candidate who receives the most votes wins. Under proportional representation (PR) the total numbers of votes are added up and the political parties have as many members elected as their share of the votes.

◀ A 75-year-old invalid from a squatter camp outside Cape Town is helped to cast his vote in South Africa's first all-race elections, held on 26 April 1994.

find out more
Democracy
Government
Parliaments

Electricity

Electricity makes cling-film stick to your hands, and sparks jump through the air. It is also one of the most useful forms of energy we have. It can power torches, TVs, tumble-driers and trains. It can come from batteries, or from massive generators hundreds of kilometres away.

Electricity is lots of tiny particles called *electrons*. These come from inside atoms. Everything is made of atoms, so there is electricity in everything. But you do not notice its effects until something makes the electrons move from their atoms.

Rubbing can make electrons move. When cling-film rubs on your hand, it pulls electrons away from atoms in your skin. The atoms try to pull the electrons back again, so the cling-film sticks to your hand. Scientists say that the cling-film has electric charge, or *static electricity*, on it.

Batteries and generators can push electrons through wires. The electrons flow between the atoms of metal that form the wire. The flow is called an electric *current*.

• At very low temperatures (–200 °C or less) some materials become *superconductors*. These are perfect conductors which do not need a battery to keep a current flowing through them.

▼ Special symbols are used for drawing circuits. These are the ones that would be used in a diagram of the circuit below.

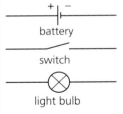

battery

switch

light bulb

Conductors and insulators

Materials that let current flow through are called *conductors*. Metals, such as copper and aluminium, are good conductors. So is carbon.

Materials that do not let current flow through are called *insulators*. They include rubber, and plastics such as PVC.

In most electric cables, the wires are made of copper, with PVC insulation around them to stop the current passing from one wire to another – or into anyone who touches the cable.

Some wires, especially thin ones, warm up when a current flows through them. In an electric cooker, the current makes the metal element red-hot. In a light bulb, a filament (thin wire coil) gets so hot that it glows white.

Using circuits

To make a small bulb light up, it can be connected to a battery. This has two terminals, one positive (+) and one negative (–). If these are linked by a conductor, such as a bulb and connecting wires, electrons flow from the negative terminal round to the positive. The complete loop through the wires, bulb and battery is called a circuit. With a switch in the circuit, you can turn the current on and off. Switching off pulls two contacts apart and breaks the circuit.

A circuit like this could also be used to run an *electromagnet* – a magnet that can be

▲ Air is normally an insulator. But with 10,000 volts or more, it can be made to conduct ... in a flash.

switched on and off. This is an iron bar with a coil of wire wound round it. When a current flows through the coil, it produces a magnetic field which is made stronger by the iron. The magnetic effect of a current is also used in electric motors and loudspeakers.

Many circuits run on mains electricity rather than on batteries. Mains electricity comes from huge generators in power stations. When you plug in a kettle, for example, you are connecting it to the big mains circuit.

Generating electricity

Generators, or *dynamos*, produce electricity when turned. The dynamo on a bicycle is turned by a small wheel which presses against the tyre. Inside the dynamo, a magnet is rotated close to a coil of wire. As the magnetic field moves through the coil, a current is generated. It flows backwards and

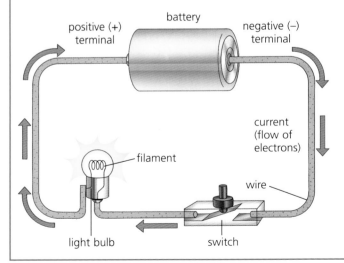

positive (+) terminal

battery

negative (–) terminal

current (flow of electrons)

filament

wire

light bulb

switch

◄ In an electric circuit the battery pushes the electrons from the negative (–) terminal through the wire to the positive (+) terminal. The bulb lights up as the electrons flow through its filament (thin wire coil). The switch turns the current on and off by pulling the contacts apart and so breaking the circuit.

Amps, volts and watts

Scientists measure current in amperes ('amps'). The higher the current, the more electrons are flowing every second.

The *voltage* of a battery or generator tells you how hard it pushes out electrons. A 1.5-volt battery is safe to touch. But a 230-volt mains socket pushes electrons so hard that the flow through your body might kill you if you touched a wire inside.

Electrons carry energy from a battery or generator. When the electrons pass through a bulb, the energy is spent as heat and light. The *power* of the bulb is measured in watts. The higher the power, the more energy is spent every second, and the more heat and light are produced every second.

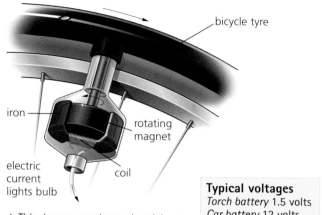

forwards, as first one end of the magnet and then the other sweeps past. Current like this is called *alternating current* (AC). The generators that produce it are known as *alternators*. (The 'one-way' current from a battery is called *direct current*, or DC.)

The huge generators in power stations are alternators. The moving magnet is a powerful electromagnet, and the generator is turned by turbines driven round by the force of high-pressure steam, gas or water.

Mains electricity

At a power station, current from the generator is passed through a *transformer*. This steps up the voltage before the power is carried across country by overhead transmission lines. Increasing the voltage reduces the current. The electrons are pushed harder, so fewer are needed to carry the energy, and thinner lines can be used.

▲ This dynamo produces electricity to run the lights on a bicycle. It is turned by the bicycle tyre. Inside the dynamo, a rotating magnet generates current in a fixed coil.

▼ Large power stations can generate 2000 megawatts of electricity (1 megawatt equals 1 million watts). At substations more transformers reduce the voltage, and cables carry power to homes, schools, shops, offices and factories.

Typical voltages
Torch battery 1.5 volts
Car battery 12 volts
Mains supply 230 volts (UK), 110 or 220 volts (Canada and USA)
Underground train 600 volts
Lightning flash 100 million volts

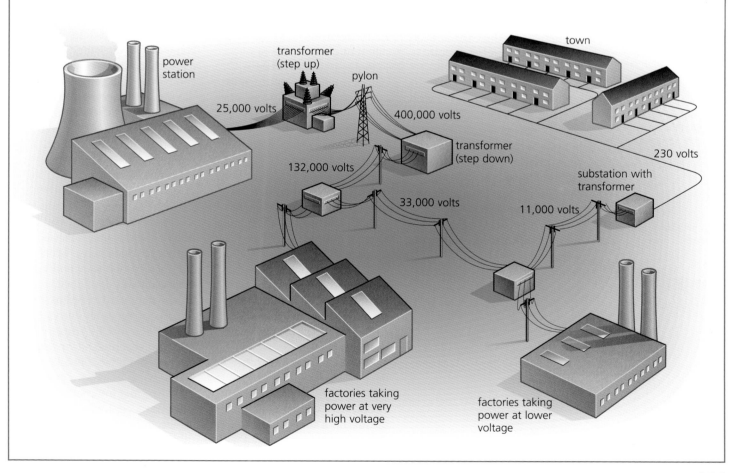

power station

transformer (step up)

pylon

town

25,000 volts

400,000 volts

132,000 volts

transformer (step down)

230 volts

33,000 volts

substation with transformer

11,000 volts

factories taking power at very high voltage

factories taking power at lower voltage

Electronics

Electronics help us in many ways in our daily lives. TVs, telephones, computers, CD players, watches – all these devices use electronics.

find out more
Computers
Electricity
Information technology
Recording

Electronic circuits work by using changing electric currents called *signals*. These signals can carry information, such as sound, pictures, numbers or instructions. They can produce sounds from loudspeakers or pictures on a TV, send messages across the world, or control the flight of an airliner.

Analogue and digital
There are two main types of electronic circuit – analogue and digital. In an *analogue circuit*, the electric current changes smoothly. For example, when you speak into a microphone, it produces an electric signal that changes smoothly in the same pattern as the sound waves. In a *digital circuit* the current is either on or off. Digital circuits send signals as long strings of 'ons' and 'offs'. These represent strings of numbers, each one measuring the strength of the signal at one particular moment.

Electronic components
Electronic circuits are built from a few basic parts, called components. *Transistors* are the most important components. They can be used to amplify (boost) the strength of a signal, or to switch other circuits on or off. *Resistors* reduce the flow of electricity through a circuit. They make sure that all the other components get the right amount of current. *Diodes* work as electronic valves. They let the current flow in one direction but not in the other. *Capacitors* can store electricity, to smooth out the flow of current. They can also be used to pass on one signal but not others. Tuning a radio to a particular radio station is done using capacitors.

▼ A microchip resting on a person's finger.

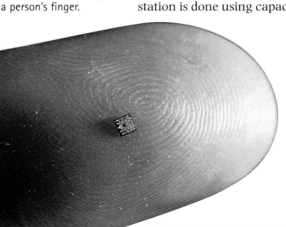

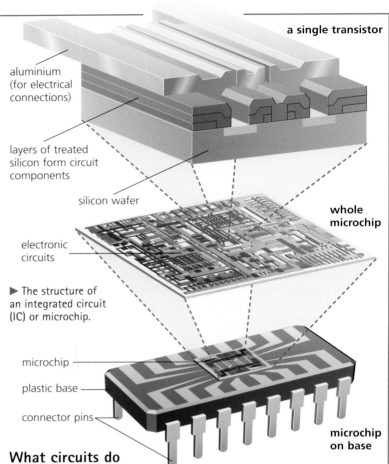

a single transistor

aluminium (for electrical connections)

layers of treated silicon form circuit components

silicon wafer

electronic circuits

whole microchip

▶ The structure of an integrated circuit (IC) or microchip.

microchip

plastic base

connector pins

microchip on base

What circuits do
In an electronic circuit, different components are joined together to perform different jobs. One of the most common circuits is an *amplifier*. Electronic signals are often weak. In an amplifier, transistors use the small, changing current of the original signal to regulate a much stronger current from another power source. The powerful current thus becomes a much stronger 'copy' of the original weak signal.

Another common circuit, used particularly in computers, is the *adder*. This can take two digital signals, corresponding to two numbers, and add them together.

Most of today's electronic devices use *integrated circuits* (ICs), or *microchips*. An IC is a circuit with thousands of parts, formed on a single chip of silicon. The chip is treated with chemicals so that different parts behave like transistors, resistors, capacitors, diodes or connecting wire. An IC may be the timer in a watch, the amplifier in a radio, or the 'brain' of a computer.

▶ FLASHBACK ◀
Ambrose Fleming invented the diode valve in 1904. It did the same job as a modern diode, but looked rather like a light bulb, and was about the same size. In 1906 the triode valve, which did the same job as a modern transistor, was developed. Valves were used in radios and other equipment for over 40 years. Then in 1947 three scientists invented a transistor made out of a piece of silicon. It was about the size of a pea. In 1958 the first integrated circuit was produced. It could fit hundreds of transistors onto a single silicon chip.

Elements

The elements are the basic materials that everything on the Earth and in the whole Universe is made of – including us. About 90 different elements are found in nature. Scientists have given each one a name and a chemical symbol. Oxygen and silicon are the most common elements on Earth.

Each element contains only one kind of atom, so it cannot be split up into different materials. The atoms of an element all behave in the same way. However, most familiar materials are not pure elements but *compounds* (combinations). To make a compound, the atoms of two or more elements join together to make a completely different material. Water is a compound. It is made from hydrogen and oxygen.

Hydrogen and oxygen are both gases, and water is nothing like either. Sugar is another compound. It is made from hydrogen, oxygen and carbon.

New elements

Scientists have made new elements by shooting tiny atomic particles at some heavy elements. So far they have made at least 11 new elements, though tiny amounts of two of these were later found in nature.

The periodic table

At the end of the 19th century, a Russian chemist, Dimitri Mendeléev, arranged all the chemical elements into a pattern called the periodic table. In it, all the elements are arranged in a continuous pattern of horizontal rows in order, starting with the lightest atoms and ending with the heaviest. Each vertical column makes up a group of elements with similar properties.

◄ Drops of the element mercury. It is a metal, but unlike other metals mercury is liquid at room temperature. It is extremely poisonous to humans and other animals.

• About 99% of the Earth is made of just eight elements.

• At ordinary temperatures most elements are solids. Only 2 elements (bromine and mercury) are liquids and 11 are gases.

find out more
Atoms and molecules
Chemistry
Gases, liquids and solids
Metals
Oxygen

▼ The periodic table.

the most reactive groups of metals

| H hydrogen 1 | — the symbol used for the element |
| — the element's name |
| — the *atomic number* tells you how many protons (particles with a positive charge) are in one atom of the element |

the most reactive non-metals (the *halogens*)

the *inert* (least reactive) gases

																He helium 2
Li lithium 3	Be beryllium 4											B boron 5	C carbon 6	N nitrogen 7	O oxygen 8	F fluorine 9	Ne neon 10
Na sodium 11	Mg magnesium 12											Al aluminium 13	Si silicon 14	P phosphorus 15	S sulphur 16	Cl chlorine 17	Ar argon 18
K potassium 19	Ca calcium 20	Sc scandium 21	Ti titanium 22	V vanadium 23	Cr chromium 24	Mn manganese 25	Fe iron 26	Co cobalt 27	Ni nickel 28	Cu copper 29	Zn zinc 30	Ga gallium 31	Ge germanium 32	As arsenic 33	Se selenium 34	Br bromine 35	Kr krypton 36
Rb rubidium 37	Sr strontium 38	Y yttrium 39	Zr zirconium 40	Nb niobium 41	Mo molybdenum 42	Tc technetium 43	Ru ruthenium 44	Rh rhodium 45	Pd palladium 46	Ag silver 47	Cd cadmium 48	In indium 49	Sn tin 50	Sb antimony 51	Te tellurium 52	I iodine 53	Xe xenon 54
Cs caesium 55	Ba barium 56	La lanthanum 57	Hf hafnium 72	Ta tantalum 73	W tungsten 74	Re rhenium 75	Os osmium 76	Ir iridium 77	Pt platinum 78	Au gold 79	Hg mercury 80	Tl thalium 81	Pb lead 82	Bi bismuth 83	Po polonium 84	At astatine 85	Rn radon 86
Fr francium 87	Ra radium 88	Ac actinium 89															

metals

non-metals

Ce cerium 58	Pr praseodymium 59	Nd neodymium 60	Pm promethium 61	Sm samarium 62	Eu europium 63	Gd gadolinium 64	Tb terbium 65	Dy dysprosium 66	Ho holmium 67	Er erbium 68	Tm thulium 69	Yb ytterbium 70	Lu lutetium 71
Th thorium 90	Pa protactinium 91	U uranium 92	Np neptunium 93	Pu plutonium 94	Am americium 95	Cm curium 96	Bk berkelium 97	Cf californium 98	Es einsteinium 99	Fm fermium 100	Md mendelevium 101	No nobelium 102	Lr lawrencium 103

• In the past there were many species of elephant living over most of the world apart from Australia. Some were much bigger than the elephants of today. They have now all died out.

find out more
Conservation
Mammals
Prehistoric life

Elephants

Elephants are the biggest living land animals. There are two kinds of elephant: one lives in Africa, south of the Sahara Desert, the other in South-east Asia. African elephants are rarely tamed, but Asiatic ones are often used to move heavy objects such as logs, and for ceremonial processions.

Both kinds of elephant live in herds. Each herd is led by an old female, who is followed by her young offspring and her adult daughters and their families. The elephants in a herd remain together for many years.

Young males leave the herd when they become sexually mature, at the age of about 12 years. Males may form herds, but these may change from one day to the next.

▼ A young African elephant uses its trunk to pull up grass as it grazes.

Trunks, tusks and teeth

An elephant's trunk is formed from its upper lip and nose. It is boneless but muscular, and has one or two finger-like points at the tip. The elephant uses it to smell, breathe and drink. The trunk is also used as a hand. It is strong enough to break down a branch and delicate enough to pick a single fruit the size of a raspberry.

An elephant's tusks are really just big teeth. Most of a tusk is made of dentine (ivory). Elephants use their tusks for defence and in feeding. They continue to grow throughout the elephant's whole life, so one with very large tusks is likely to be an old animal.

To support its large bulk, an elephant needs huge amounts of food. An adult elephant eats about 150 kilograms of grass, leaves, twigs and fruit each day. Such tough food needs to be thoroughly chewed, and elephants have grinding teeth in the back of their mouths. When these teeth get worn out, they are replaced by another set which pushes in from behind. When the last of these wears out, the animal becomes weakened by lack of food and dies of starvation or disease.

▲ Elaborately decorated tame Asiatic elephants take part in a festival at Trichipooram in southern India.

Elephants in danger

Present-day elephants are endangered because humans are increasingly taking over the land where they live and also killing them for their valuable ivory tusks. Ivory has always been much prized for carving and making luxury items. Poaching for ivory has severely reduced the populations of African elephants, and many African countries now ban its export.

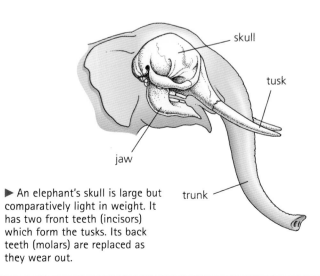

skull

tusk

jaw

trunk

▶ An elephant's skull is large but comparatively light in weight. It has two front teeth (incisors) which form the tusks. Its back teeth (molars) are replaced as they wear out.

Elizabeth I

Elizabeth I was the queen of England from 1558 to 1603. During her reign England became more powerful and prosperous, and literature and the other arts flourished.

Elizabeth's early life was not easy. Her father, Henry VIII, did not want a daughter, and when she was 2 years old, her mother, Anne Boleyn, was executed. She was in great danger during her Catholic sister Mary's reign because she was a Protestant: when she was 21, she was imprisoned in the Tower of London for allegedly plotting against Mary. Not surprisingly, the 25-year-old woman who became queen in 1558 had learnt to hide her feelings. She was also cautious, clever and quick-witted.

Elizabeth was a strong-willed woman. In 1559 she changed the country's religion from Catholicism to Protestantism, even though this created many problems for herself and her people, particularly the Catholics. She often put off difficult decisions. Although Mary Queen of Scots was a great threat because Catholics thought she should be queen, Elizabeth took 19 years to agree to her execution.

Elizabeth hated spending money. She avoided an expensive war with Philip II of Spain for as long as possible, although she secretly encouraged the attack and plunder of Spanish ships. When the Spanish Armada set out to invade England, Elizabeth was an inspiring war leader and yet, after the victory, she did not pay the English sailors who had done the fighting.

Elizabeth was a woman in a world of powerful men. Everyone expected her to marry, and she once promised Parliament she would marry 'as soon as I can conveniently' – but it never proved to be convenient.

Born 1533 in London, England
Died 1603 aged 69

find out more
Drake, Francis
Henry VIII
Reformation
Tudor England

◄ When she was older, Elizabeth I wore thick white make-up and a red wig (she may have lost her hair when she had smallpox). She took great care to ensure that she looked like an impressive queen in all her portraits. This one was painted to celebrate the English victory over the Spanish Armada in 1588.

Employment

People who work for a living are said to be employed. Organizations which produce goods and services need to hire workers; they are *employers*. The workers they hire are *employees*.

Some people's work involves taking natural resources from the land and sea, such as coalminers extracting coal from the ground. These jobs are in the *primary* sector of employment. The primary sector provides raw materials for workers to make goods or buildings. This is the *secondary* sector of employment. People in the *tertiary* sector work in service industries, providing services for businesses or consumers, for example in banks or hotels.

Trade unions
Groups of workers who band together to ask for better wages or conditions are called trade unions, or labor unions in the USA. Employers and unions sometimes reach agreements that are acceptable to both sides. However, if talks break down, they are in dispute and trade unions may take action to make employers agree to their demands. They may even strike (stop work) to get what they want. Trade unions also support their members in other situations, for instance where the safety of workers is at risk, or where an employee has been unfairly dismissed.

• Some unions represent workers who have the same skill or work in a particular industry. General unions represent workers in many different industries. It is often useful for unions to act together so they have also formed national and international associations.

◄ Unemployed workers in Germany queuing at an employment office. Job centres and employment agencies help people find work. In countries with a welfare state, unemployed workers may be given payments to help them and their families to live.

find out more
Economics
Industrial Revolution
Industry

El Salvador *see page 621* • **Embroidery** *see* Sewing and knitting

Energy

Our bodies depend on energy, as do our homes, vehicles and factories. On Earth, the Sun is the source of nearly all of our energy. Without energy, nothing would live, move or change.

It is hard work pedalling uphill or moving heavy objects about. To scientists, *work* is done whenever a force makes something move. The greater the force and the further it moves, the more work is done.

If something has energy, it means that it is capable of doing work. An engine uses the energy in its fuel to move a car along. A battery can store the energy needed to turn an electric motor. And some winds carry enough energy to blow trees over. Hot things also have energy. In any material, the tiny particles (atoms) of which it is made are always on the move. Heating the material makes its atoms move faster.

Scientists measure energy in joules (J). A litre of petrol stores about 35 million joules. But this energy is not a 'thing'. It is just a measure of how much work can be done. The energy can be used to produce motion that you can see (such as a car speeding up) or tiny movements that you cannot see (like the atoms moving more quickly when something gets hot).

Changing forms

Energy can exist in many different forms. Things that are moving, such as cars and winds, have *kinetic* energy. Springs or other stretched or compressed materials have *potential* energy. So does anything in a position where it can fall. When hot materials cool down, they give off heat, or

The energy that radiates from the Sun's surface as heat and light is the source of almost all the energy we use.

Weather systems are driven by heat radiated from the Sun. Hot air rising above the Equator causes belts of wind around the Earth. Heat and wind lift water vapour from the oceans and so bring rain and snow.

Green plants use the energy in sunlight falling on their leaves to produce their own food from water and carbon dioxide.

Solar panels use the energy from the Sun to heat water. Solar cells use sunlight to produce small amounts of electricity.

Coal, oil and natural gas are formed from the remains of plants and animals that lived millions of years ago. We extract them from the ground and burn them to get energy. This energy is used to power engines, to make electricity and for heating.

We get energy from the food we eat. The food may be from plants or from animals that feed on plants.

For centuries people have been using the power of the wind to move ships, pump water and grind corn. Today, huge wind turbines are used to turn electrical generators.

thermal energy. Foods, fuels and batteries store *chemical* energy – their energy is released by chemical reactions. Light and sound are types of *radiant* energy. Electric currents carry *electrical* energy. And energy that comes from the nucleus (centre) of an atom is called *nuclear* energy.

Energy can change from one form to another. When you kick a ball, your muscles change chemical energy from your food

into kinetic energy. As the ball moves through the air and across the ground, friction slows it down and its kinetic energy is changed into thermal energy (heat).

Scientists have discovered that, although energy can change into different forms, it cannot be made or destroyed. People may talk about 'using energy', but in fact it never gets used up. It just gets passed on in another form. Eventually, most

▲ How the Sun provides the Earth's energy.

● Lifting this book 5 cm takes about 1 joule (J) of energy.

● An average 11-year-old needs about 10,000 kilojoules (kJ) of food energy a day. (1 kJ equals 1000 joules.)

of it ends up as heat, but it is so spread out that it cannot be detected or used.

Energy from fuels

Industrial societies need huge amounts of energy to run their homes, vehicles and factories. More than 80 per cent of this energy comes from burning coal, oil and natural gas. These are called *fossil fuels*, because they formed from the remains of plants and tiny sea creatures that lived on Earth many millions of years ago. They include fuels made from oil, such as petrol, diesel and fuel for jet planes.

Most large power stations burn fossil fuels. The heat is used to boil water and make steam. The force of the steam turns turbines which drive generators.

There are two main problems with burning fossil fuels. First, their waste gases pollute the atmosphere. These gases include carbon dioxide, which traps the Sun's heat and may be causing global warming. Second, fossil fuels cannot be replaced. Supplies will eventually run out, so we must find alternatives.

Nuclear fuel, used in nuclear power stations, does not burn. Instead, its energy is released as heat by nuclear reactions. Nuclear power stations produce no waste gases, but they are expensive to build, and produce dangerous radioactive waste which must be stored safely for centuries. Nuclear accidents are rare, but when they do occur, radioactive gas and dust may be released. These cause cancer. They may contaminate the local area and be carried thousands of kilometres by the wind.

In developing countries, wood is the main fuel for 2 billion people. Unlike fossil

fuels and nuclear fuel, wood is a *renewable* energy source, because new trees can be grown. At present, however, not enough trees are being planted to replace those cut down for timber, papermaking and fuel.

Alternative energy

To reduce our use of fossil and nuclear fuels, alternative energy sources are needed. There are many possibilities. *Hydroelectric* schemes generate electricity using the flow of water from a lake behind a dam. *Solar panels* use the Sun's radiant energy to heat water, while *solar cells* use it to generate electricity. In *wind farms*, generators are turned by giant wind turbines (windmills). *Biofuels* are made from plant or animal matter. In Brazil, for example, many cars run on alcohol made from sugar cane. Gases from sewage, dung and rotting waste can be used as fuels, and some power stations burn rubbish as their fuel.

All of these alternative energy sources are renewable, but none can be used without affecting the environment in some way. For example, creating a lake for a hydroelectric scheme changes the landscape and destroys habitats for wildlife. Also, none

▲ Hydroelectric power uses fast-flowing water to turn generators which produce electricity. This energy source is renewable because the water is constantly resupplied through rain.

of these sources can yet provide enough energy to meet our present demands.

For these reasons, many people think that we should find ways of being less wasteful with our energy. These could include greater use of public transport and bicycles instead of cars, better insulation in our homes, manufacturing goods that last longer before they are thrown away, and recycling more of our waste materials.

▼ This solar-powered car, called *Sunraycer*, has been developed by the giant US car manufacturer General Motors. Rows of solar cells on the back and sides of the car use sunlight to charge the batteries that run its electric motor.

- Power, measured in watts, tells you the rate at which energy is being spent. A power of 1 watt (W) means that 1 joule of energy is being spent every second.

- The Sun runs on nuclear energy. It has enough stored to keep it shining for another 5000 million years.

- Seven million tonnes of household rubbish contains the same amount of energy as 2 million tonnes of coal.

Typical powers
Light bulb 60 watts (60 joules per second)
TV set 120 watts
Hotplate 1500 watts
Small car engine 45 kilowatts (45,000 joules per second)

find out more
Coal
Electricity
Greenhouse effect
Hydroelectric power
Oil
Pollution
Power stations
Sun
Waste disposal
Wind

Engines

Engines produce the power to drive vehicles and machines. Engines are themselves machines that burn fuel and turn the resulting heat into motion.

Steam engines, which mostly use coal as fuel, were the first successful engines. Until the beginning of the 20th century steam engines powered trains, ships and many machines. Over the last 100 years they have largely been replaced by internal-combustion engines, fuelled by petrol or diesel oil. Most airliners and military aircraft are powered by jet engines, which burn kerosene.

Many machines and some vehicles, especially trains, are powered by electric motors. Electric motors are not usually regarded as 'true' engines, since they do not produce motion directly from heat.

Steam engines

The first really practical engine was a steam engine built in 1705 by Thomas Newcomen. It pumped water from deep mine shafts. Newcomen's engine was very inefficient, but in 1765 the design was improved by James Watt. The first steam-powered railway locomotive was built in 1803 by Richard Trevithick.

In a steam engine, heat from a burning fuel (usually coal) heats water to make steam. The steam pushes on a piston to produce movement. The piston can be used to turn a wheel, which may then drive a locomotive or power a pump.

Many power stations and some ships are powered by modern steam engines called *steam turbines*. A turbine is a kind of fan or propeller, with many blades. When high-pressure steam pushes against

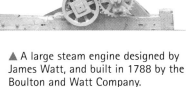

▲ A large steam engine designed by James Watt, and built in 1788 by the Boulton and Watt Company.

the turbine blades, they spin round very fast.

Petrol and diesel engines

Cars, motorcycles, trucks and buses are all powered by *internal-combustion engines*. Most of these use petrol or diesel oil as their fuel. In this type of engine, fuel is exploded inside a closed cylinder. The force of the explosion pushes out a piston inside the cylinder. The movement of the piston pushes round a crankshaft, which is fixed to a heavy

• The biggest jet engines produce as much power as 500 large car engines. The steam turbines in large power stations produce as much power as 5000 large car engines. But most powerful of all are the rocket engines that lift spacecraft into orbit. They produce as much power as 500,000 large car engines, but only for a few minutes at a time.

▶ A single cylinder of a petrol engine, showing how it works. The engine is called a four-stroke engine because the piston goes through a series of four movements, or strokes. The heavy flywheel helps to keep the crankshaft and piston moving after the power stroke. Most petrol engines have four or more cylinders, so that each cylinder is on its power stroke at a different time.

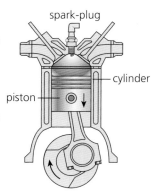
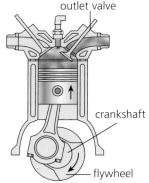

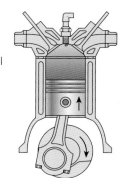

Power stroke
A mixture of petrol and air is exploded in the cylinder by a spark from a spark plug. The expanding hot gases push the piston out.

Exhaust stroke
The outlet valve opens as the piston moves in again. The piston pushes the burnt gases out of the cylinder.

Induction stroke
The inlet valve opens as the piston moves out once more. A mixture of petrol and air is sucked into the cylinder.

Compression stroke
Both valves close as the piston moves in, compressing the petrol/air mixture. The cylinder is ready for the next power stroke.

▶ Technicians making final adjustments to two Formula 1 racing engines. Each engine has 10 cylinders, arranged in two rows of five. Extra-light materials and special fuels help to make these engines much more powerful than normal engines of a similar size.

• On a flight from London to Hong Kong a Boeing 747 jumbo jet with four jet engines uses enough fuel to fill a car's petrol tank 3500 times. This much fuel would take a car over 2 million km.

flywheel (the flywheel helps to keep the crankshaft turning smoothly). The turning of the crankshaft drives the wheels of the vehicle.

Most trucks and buses, and some cars, use four-stroke diesel engines. In a diesel engine, air drawn into the engine is compressed so much that it becomes very hot. Diesel oil is squirted straight into the cylinders. It starts to burn as soon as it meets the hot air, so the engine does not need spark-plugs. Diesel engines are less powerful and more expensive than petrol engines of the same size, but they use less fuel and last longer.

Jet engines

Jet engines are very powerful engines, used mainly to drive aircraft. They have fewer moving parts than internal-combustion engines, and they need less looking after. The first jet engine was designed by Frank Whittle in 1937.

In a basic jet engine (*turbojet*), air is sucked in at the front, then compressed and forced into a combustion chamber. Fuel is added and burnt in the chamber. This produces very hot gases, which

shoot out of the back of the engine. As the gases escape, they drive the aircraft forward. They also push round a turbine, which turns the compressor that draws in air at the front of the engine.

Turbofan engines are quieter than turbojets and use less fuel. Most large airliners use turbofan engines. In a *turboprop* engine, the hot gases are used to drive a propeller. Turboprops are often used in helicopters.

Rocket engines

All the engines described so far burn a mixture of fuel and air. The oxygen in the air is vital to combustion; without it, the fuel will not burn. Rocket engines do not need air, because they carry their own oxygen supply with them. This means that they work in space.

A simple firework rocket is a tube open at one end and filled with gunpowder. One of the chemicals in gunpowder contains oxygen, so it does not need air to burn. As the gunpowder burns, hot gases rush out of the tube and shoot the rocket into the sky.

Some spacecraft engines use a solid fuel rather like the gunpowder in a firework. Other rockets have two liquid fuels – liquid hydrogen and liquid oxygen. The hydrogen and oxygen are fed to the engine's combustion chambers, where they mix and burn.

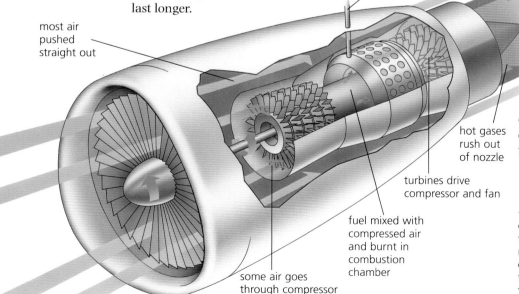

fuel pumped in from tanks

most air pushed straight out

hot gases rush out of nozzle

turbines drive compressor and fan

fuel mixed with compressed air and burnt in combustion chamber

some air goes through compressor

◀ Inside a turbofan engine. These engines have huge fans at the front to collect air. Some of this air is mixed with fuel in the combustion chamber, but most is pushed around the chamber and out of the nozzle at the back.

England

England forms the largest part of the United Kingdom, a country in north-west Europe.

• The other parts of the United Kingdom are Scotland, Wales and Nothern Ireland.

England is a cool, moist region. The surrounding sea stops the land from becoming too hot or cold. The weather is very variable, and it is mostly affected by depressions (areas of low pressure) which move eastwards across the Atlantic Ocean, bringing cloud and rain.

Landscape

The landscape varies across the country. The Lake District has mountains made from the oldest rocks in Britain. Much high moorland is found in the south-west peninsula of Cornwall and Devon. To the east and south of England the coastline is smooth, with long sandy beaches. The North Sea coast is more rugged, and the beaches are mostly shingle.

Much of lowland England has long ridges of low hills, including the Cotswolds, Chilterns and North and South Downs. Many southern hills are made of chalk, and their soil is very thin. East Anglia is low and flat. The rocks here are soft clay and peat. Parts of the East Anglian Fens are as much as a metre below sea level.

▶ A view from Buckden Pike in the Yorkshire Dales, North Yorkshire. North Yorkshire is the largest county in England, and the most rural.

Cities

England contains some of the most crowded regions in the world. A great chain of cities stretches from London to Liverpool. The industrial cities of the north grew rapidly in the 19th century. Nearby coal provided the energy for their factories.

Today there are still contrasts between the north and the south. In the north there is higher unemployment because the older industries have declined. In the south, particularly in and around London, houses are more expensive because more and more people want to live there. London is one of the world's oldest and greatest capital cities and is a focal point for modern manufacturing industry and tourism. It is an important financial centre and part of the economic centre of Europe.

find out more
Anglo-Saxons
Britain since 1900
British empire
Celts
English language
Europe
Georgian Britain
Medieval England
Middle Ages
Northern Ireland
Prehistoric people
Roman Britain
Scotland
Stuart Britain
Tudor England
United Kingdom
Victorian Britain
Vikings
Wales

——	country boundary
◆	capital city
■ ●	major cities and towns
——	main roads
┅┅	main railways
⊕	main airports
▲	high peaks (height in metres)

land height in metres
500–1000
200–500
100–200
less than 100
sea level — land below sea level

192

English language

More than 300 million people today use English as their main language, and many more learn it as a second language. Its use originally spread around the world during the 17th century, a time of far-reaching exploration, trade and colonization.

- English is spoken as the main language in Britain, North America, the Caribbean, Australia, New Zealand, India and parts of Africa. These are all regions that used to be British colonies.

There are many different forms or varieties of English around the world. Even within Britain there are dialects and regional variations. *Dialects* have many local words and phrases that are understood only in the area in which they are spoken. There are also different local ways of pronouncing words, called *accents*.

American English

British	American
autumn	fall
nappy	diaper
petrol	gasoline
sweets	candy
tap	faucet
trousers	pants
pavement	sidewalk

find out more

Languages

▶ FLASHBACK ◀

The oldest form of English – Old English – was spoken by the Anglo-Saxons about 1500 years ago. It would not be easy to recognize much of it today. English has been changed over the years by the various peoples who have come to conquer or live in Britain, especially the Vikings from Scandinavia, and the Normans from Normandy, now part of France.

The Normans spoke a form of French with many words that came from Latin, the language of the ancient Romans. The form of English which then developed is called Middle English. Unlike Old English, it is possible to understand a good deal of it today.

The modern English that we use nowadays is a rich mixture of words from many places, which is one of the reasons why some words are rather difficult to spell.

▼ As well as local languages, English is spoken throughout Britain's former colonies. This road sign in Sri Lanka is written in English, Sinhalese and Tamil.

Erosion

All around us, the rocky surface of the Earth is being slowly worn away by the action of water, wind and sun. Tiny pieces of rock are then carried away by water and wind and deposited in other places, especially in the sea. This process is called erosion.

- 'Erosion' comes from the Latin word meaning 'to gnaw'.

- Soft rocks are eroded more quickly than hard ones. Hard rocks may lead to the formation of a waterfall along a river or headlands at the seaside.

Erosion is the work of moving water, ice or wind. It is usually a slow process. But during storms, water and wind are much more powerful. They carry bigger fragments of rock and erode the land more quickly. Rivers are deepening and widening their valleys all the time, but a river in flood can erode more land in a few hours than it would normally do over many years.

The breaking-down of rocks by snow and frost, sun and rain is called *weathering*. When rocks are exposed to the atmosphere, they are affected by the weather. Constant heating and cooling can split some rocks. When water in these split rocks freezes and then expands, it cracks them. Rainwater is a weak acid and can dissolve or change the chemicals in rocks. Weathering can be speeded up by plant roots and burrowing animals.

The rock pieces that have been broken up by weathering are moved away by water, ice and wind. Although weathering and erosion are different, they both work together to reshape the landscape.

find out more

Glaciers
Ice
Rivers and streams
Rocks and minerals
Soil
Valleys

▲ The pounding action of sea waves has worn away the cliff to form a cave.

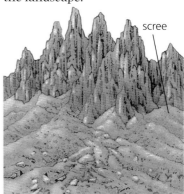

scree

▲ Scree (piles of rock fragments) forms around the base of mountains as a result of ice erosion.

Europe

Europe is the smallest continent, yet it is the most crowded, with about one-eighth of all the world's people. Over the past 500 years Europeans have settled in every other continent, and today European languages can be heard all over the world.

- There is no clear boundary between eastern Europe and western Asia. The Ural Mountains in Russia make a convenient line on the map, so Russia is partly in Europe but mainly in Asia. The countries between the Black and Caspian seas are usually counted as part of Europe. But many people consider Azerbaijan and Armenia to be Asian. Turkey is usually counted as part of western Asia.

▼ This time-line shows some of the major events in the history of Europe from the time of the ancient Greeks, about 2500 years ago, to the present day.

Europe is a continent of peninsulas and islands. In fact, it is really a westward extension of Asia. There are two main sea inlets: the Baltic Sea to the north and the Mediterranean Sea to the south. The main mountains are the Alps, a line of jagged, snow-capped peaks stretching between France and Austria. The Pyrenees, between Spain and France, and the mountains of Scandinavia, Greece and the Balkans are not so high. The North European plain, from Brittany in France to Russia, is low and mainly flat.

Climate

Most winds in Europe come from the west. They are wet because they have crossed the Atlantic Ocean. Depressions move over Europe all the time, bringing quick changes in the weather. In winter, warm Atlantic ocean currents keep the coasts free from ice. Far from the sea, though, winters can be calm, clear and very cold. The Mediterranean region has warm, wet winters and hot, dry summers. There are long periods of sunshine and clear, blue skies in summer.

Countries and languages

The borders of European states changed many times in the 20th century. Norway, Finland and Albania were made countries before World War I. Poland, Czechoslovakia, Hungary, Yugoslavia, Iceland and Ireland won independence shortly afterwards. The Baltic states of Estonia, Latvia and Lithuania became independent states in 1920, but in 1940 they were forced to join the USSR. In 1991 they became independent again. Malta and Cyprus date from the 1960s.

Some new states have changed again. Czechoslovakia divided into the Czech Republic and Slovakia in 1993. Between 1991 and 2003 Yugoslavia broke up into Croatia, Slovenia, Macedonia, Bosnia and Herzegovina, and Serbia and Montenegro.

The languages spoken in Europe can tell us something of the early history of the continent. German, Dutch, Danish, Swedish and English are all Germanic languages. Polish, Bulgarian, Czech, Slovak and Serbo-Croat are Slavonic languages related to Russian. Italian, Spanish, Romanian and French developed out of the Latin language which was spoken all over the Roman empire.

Because Europeans have settled all over the world, European languages can be heard all over the world: English in North America and Australia; French in Canada and South-east Asia; Spanish and Portuguese in Central and South America; English, French, Portuguese and Dutch in Africa.

500	400	300	200	100 BC		AD 1	100	200	300
			R O M A N S						
G R E E K S									
		Rome expands in Italy	Roman expansion continues	Rome dominant in Mediterranean			Peak of Roman expansion	Romans attacked by tribes from beyond Rhine and Danube	Christianity spreads
		Plato and Aristotle active	Rivalry between Rome and Carthage	146 Rome defeats Carthage and Greece	58–50 Julius Caesar conquers Gaul	AD 29 Jesus Christ crucified	122 Construction on Hadrian's wall begins		313 Emperor Constantine makes Christianity official religion
Greek city states emerge	480 Greeks defeat Persians at battle of Salamis	338 Macedonian takeover of Greece			55 BC Caesar invades Britain				
Celtic tribes move west	479–404 Athens builds empire in north and north-east Mediterranean				31–30 Roman civil war	AD 43 Claudius invades Britain and makes it a Roman province			330 Capital of Roman empire moves to Constantinople (Byzantium)
	431–404 War between Athens and Sparta	336–323 Empire of Alexander the Great			27 BC Augustus proclaims Roman empire	Christians persecuted			395 Division of Roman empire into eastern and western parts
					4 BC Jesus Christ born				

Europe

400	**500**	**600**	**700**	**800**	**900**	**1000**	**1100**	**1200**
E A R L Y M I D D L E A G E S I N W E S T				M I D D L E A G E S				
		B Y Z A N T I N E E M P I R E I N E A S T						
Anglo-Saxons settle in Britain 410 Rome captured by Visigoths	Christian missionaries convert people in France, England and Germany 523 Benedict founds order of monks	Kingdom of Franks strong Pope's authority grows	Muslim Moors conquer Spain; invade France 723 Charles Martel defeats Moors at Poitiers	Establishment of Holy Roman Empire under Charlemagne Beginning of feudal system Vikings raid Ireland, England, France and Italy 845 Vikings sack Paris 878 Alfred defeats Vikings in England	Russians converted by Greek Christians 911 Vikings rule Duchy of Normandy 962 Otto the Great crowned Holy Roman Emperor 966 Kingdom of Poland established	Christendom divides: Roman Catholics in West; Eastern Orthodox in East 1066 Normans conquer England 1095 First crusade	French kings extend power Crusades continue 1171 Normans conquer Ireland 1187 Muslims reconquer Jerusalem	Gothic architecture 1240 Mongol 'Golden Horde' conquers Russia 1271–1295 Marco Polo in China

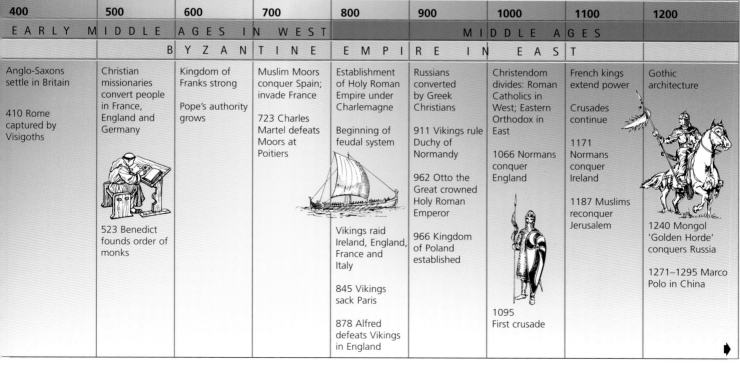

Modern Europe

It is generally reckoned that modern European history began with the French Revolution of 1789 and the wars that followed it. Victorious French armies spread the ideas of liberty and equality. The remains of the old feudal system were swept away and democracy spread across the continent. After the defeat of the French emperor Napoleon in 1815, other attempts to turn back the clock did not last long.

The population of Europe was growing fast. Towns and cities sprawled. By the middle of the 19th century railways, mines and steam-powered factories were changing the face of the continent. Europe's manufactured goods flooded markets all around the globe. The countries of Europe had never been so rich or so powerful.

Europeans used their technology and wealth to seize territories overseas. The British empire was the largest and most successful.

War and unity

By 1900 Europe was already being overtaken by the United States. The Great Depression, fascist dictatorships and two world wars completed the process. They left Europe bankrupt, exhausted and divided. Russia had become communist in 1917. Now leader of the Union of Soviet Socialist Republics (USSR), it controlled the eastern half of the continent. The democratic states of western Europe relied on the US for military protection and economic aid.

Remarkably, the countries of western Europe recovered. Learning from past mistakes, they put aside past differences in favour of economic and political co-operation. The Treaty of Rome in 1957 set up the European Economic Community, which in 1991 became the European Union (EU) with a European Parliament. By 1995 the 15 member countries, working as a single market and planning a single currency, had become a major world economic power.

Many of the countries of eastern Europe may become part of the European Union in the future. Closer ties are being established. Europe is in economic competition with other parts of the world and its prosperity is under threat.

The changing face of Europe

Meanwhile, during 1989 and 1990 communism collapsed in eastern Europe. Democracy spread to Russia and the countries it had controlled since the 1940s – notably Poland, Czechoslovakia, East Germany, Hungary, Bulgaria and Romania. Their peoples enjoyed rights and freedoms they had previously only dreamed of.

The collapse of communism had other effects. The reunited Germany began to dominate the continent. The USSR, Czechoslovakia and Yugoslavia broke up into independent countries. Sometimes, as in Yugoslavia, this was accompanied by bloody civil war. Several of the smaller new countries found it hard to compete with the richer, more efficient nations of the West.

find out more
Ancient world
Byzantine empire
Charlemagne
Christians
European Union
France
Germany
Greeks, ancient
Industrial Revolution
Italy
Middle Ages
Napoleon Bonaparte
Normans
Ottoman empire
Renaissance
Romans
Russia
Spain
Twentieth-century
 history
Vikings
World War I
World War II

1300	1400	1500	1600	1700	1800	1900
RENAISSANCE AND REFORMATION			M O D E R N N A T I O N S			
Venice, Florence, Genoa powerful city states	Italian renaissance	Reformation of Church in northern Europe	European colonies in America	Age of Enlightenment	Russian empire expands	Electronic and nuclear technology
1326 Ivan I Grand Prince of Moscow	Gutenberg invents print		30 Years War between Catholics and Protestants (1618–1648)	Industrial and agricultural revolutions	European empires in Africa and Asia	End of European empires
1337 Hundred Years War begins	Russians expel Mongol Golden Horde		1648 Peace of Westphalia establishes nation-state system	1776 American independence from Britain		Independent states in Asia and Africa
1347 Black Death	Navigators to India and Caribbean	Spanish conquer Aztecs and Incas	1642–1649 English Civil War		Abolition of slavery and serfdom in British, French and Russian empires	1914–1918 World War I
	1423 Turks capture Constantinople	English–Spanish naval struggle			1815 Napoleonic wars end at battle of Waterloo	1917–1991 Soviet Union
		1526 Turks besiege Vienna			1861 Unification of Italy	1939–1945 World War II
	1492 Columbus sails to Caribbean	1588 English defeat Spanish Armada		1789 French Revolution	1870 Unification of Germany	1957 European Union formed

European Union

find out more
Europe

European Union member

member from May 2004

member from 2007

0   1000 km

0   600 miles

The European Union consists of a number of countries in Europe which have agreed to work more closely with each other. They hope that by working together they can maintain a peaceful and prosperous Europe.

In 1957 six countries – Belgium, France, West Germany, Italy, Luxembourg and the Netherlands – signed the Treaty of Rome to form the European Economic Community. By 1998 the Community had grown into a European Union (EU) of 15 countries.

In 1993 a single market was created within the countries of the Union, allowing money, goods, services and people to move freely without customs

◀ Member countries of the European Union in 1998.

and other controls at frontiers. A single currency, the euro, was introduced in 1999 in 12 of the member states, to make it easier for businesses to trade with each other. Euro notes and coins came into use in January 2002.

Institutions of the Union

The European Union is run by the Council of Ministers and the Commission. The Council of Ministers, made up of ministers from each country's government, has the final say on Union policies. The Commissioners take routine decisions and propose new laws. The members of the European Parliament are elected by voters in each member state. Euro MPs comment on the Commissioners' proposals. The Court of Justice has the power to enforce European Union law on member states.

Evolution

find out more
Archaeology
Darwin, Charles
Dinosaurs
Fossils
Genetics
Prehistoric life

▶ Darwin's theory of evolution can explain the development of the pterosaur, an ancient flying reptile that lived over 150 million years ago. It began as a four-footed lizard (1). Over millions of years, small folds of skin developed between its feet, which enabled it to glide from tree to tree (2). Over many more generations the folds, and the bones and muscles supporting them, grew to form wings (3).

Evolution is the way new kinds of plants, animals and other living things come into being as a result of many small changes over a long period of time.

Evidence from fossils in ancient rocks shows that over millions of years new kinds of creature have appeared. At the same time some of the old forms, such as the dinosaurs, have become extinct (died out).

In the 19th century the biologists Charles Darwin and Alfred Russel Wallace proposed a theory to explain how

evolution takes place. The theory of *natural selection* (sometimes called the 'survival of the fittest') argues that the offspring of an animal or plant that are most likely to survive are those best suited to the present conditions and best able to compete for the things they need, such as food, water, light and space. These 'fit' individuals are also more likely to produce offspring, which in turn will inherit the special characteristics that made their

parents fit. In a few generations that kind, or species, of plant or animal will contain more fit creatures and will gradually change. This may eventually lead to the development of a new species.

3

2

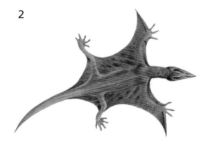

1

Explorers

Today, people know something about even the remotest countries of the world. But 500 years ago people had scarcely any knowledge of countries other than their own and even thought the world was flat! Our knowledge of other lands was opened up by the great explorers of the world.

During the thousand years before Christ, Greek and Phoenician traders explored the Mediterranean Sea. The Chinese sailed to South-east Asia to trade. The Polynesians sailed huge areas of the Pacific Ocean.

Great advances

By the 15th century, stronger ships made exploration easier. Many early explorers went on map-making expeditions. Later, most set out to discover gold, spices and other riches, although some Europeans went to the Americas to introduce Christianity.

From the 18th century many went to study the geography, plants and animals of the world. Many places are named after their explorers.

Explorers in the 20th century have found new challenges. The North and South Poles were reached; the highest mountains were climbed; undersea vessels explored the depths of the oceans; and spacecraft ventured to the Moon and beyond.

find out more
Antarctica
Columbus, Christopher
Cook, James
Drake, Francis
Magellan, Ferdinand
Polo, Marco
Space exploration

▼ North African explorer Ibn Batuta wrote vivid descriptions of North and West Africa, India and China in the 14th century. He travelled more than 120,000 km in his life – further than Marco Polo, who lived at about the same time.

Explosives

Explosives are used in bombs, missiles and other weapons. They are also found inside fireworks and the flares set off by people lost at sea or in mountains. Explosives are more widely used for peaceful jobs like demolishing buildings and breaking up rocks in quarries and mines.

The high-pressure gas given off by an explosive expands violently to produce a noisy explosion. All explosives have a fuel, which burns rapidly, and a chemical that provides oxygen for burning.

Gunpowder and the explosives used in shells, guns and some rockets are *low explosives*. They can be set off by heat or even an electric spark. They are tightly packed inside a container so that the gas pressure can build up rapidly. Inside a firework container an explosive mixture, which includes gunpowder, burns, and pressure builds up. This forces out showers of sparks or sends a rocket up into the air.

High explosives such as dynamite and gelignite explode so fast that they shatter everything around them. They are used in bombs and for rock-blasting. They are set off by a small explosion from a detonator. *Plastic explosive*, a high explosive that can be moulded into shape, is used by terrorists because it is easy to hide and difficult to detect.

▶ FLASHBACK ◀

As early as the 9th century AD the Chinese made fireworks using gunpowder, the first explosive to be discovered. It was first used for firing guns in 14th-century Europe. Dynamite was invented in 1866 by the Swedish chemist Alfred Nobel, who later developed other high explosives, including gelignite.

• Always be careful with fireworks; their heat and explosive power can burn, blind and even kill.

find out more
Fire
Nobel prizes
Rockets
Weapons

▶ Fireworks behind Sydney Harbour Bridge in Australia. The beautiful colours of fireworks are produced by chemicals (compounds) containing certain metals. Calcium or strontium compounds produce red, sodium produces yellow, copper or barium makes green, and potassium makes violet.

Eyes

Eyes are like living cameras. They focus light from surrounding objects to form a picture which your brain can understand. Your eyes give you a clear, moving, three-dimensional, coloured picture of the outside world. They allow you to recognize things by their colour, shape and brightness.

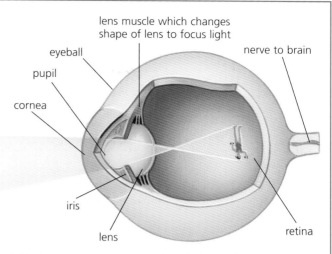

▲ The human eye, cut away to show its internal structure. The image at the back of the eye is upside-down. The brain interprets it the right way up.

At the front of the eye is a clear, round window called the *cornea*. Tears from tear glands keep it moist and clean and, together with your eyelids and eyelashes, help protect it from damage.

Behind the cornea, the lens focuses light onto a layer of light-sensitive cells at the back of the eye called the *retina*. The images focused on the retina are detected by these cells, which send messages along nerves to the brain. The brain interprets them and converts them into what you see. On the retina directly opposite the lens is a patch called the yellow spot.

This is the part which is most sensitive to colour.

Just behind the lens is a sheet of muscle called the *iris*. This is the coloured part of the eye. It has a round hole at its centre called the pupil. In bright light the iris muscles contract and make the *pupil* smaller, to stop too much light entering the eye. In dim light the muscles relax and the pupil opens and lets in more light.

We need two eyes, because with only one eye we would find it difficult to judge distance and depth.

Why do people wear glasses?
Many people need to wear glasses or contact lenses to correct their vision. Some people are *short-sighted* and can see objects clearly only when they are close to their eyes. Others are *long-sighted*, and can see things clearly only when they are far away. It is the job of an *optician* to test your eyes and decide whether you need to wear glasses or contact lenses, and what kind you should have.

We do not know when glasses were invented, but they were being worn in Europe and China in the 13th century. They became more popular in the 15th century with the development of printing.

• Some people have difficulty telling colours apart. They are *colour-blind*. Other people cannot tell red from green. About one boy in 10 is born with red–green colour-blindness, although hardly any girls are affected.

find out more
Blindness
Brains
Cameras
Colour
Nervous systems
Senses

▼ This tarsier from the Philippines has large eyes which help it to hunt for food in the night. In the dark its pupils expand to collect as much light as possible. In daytime or bright light its pupils become very small.

▼ The eyes of insects, like this dragonfly, are made up of hundreds of narrow, light-sensitive tubes. Each tube cannot make a proper picture but all the tubes together can. Eyes like this are called *compound eyes*. Crustaceans, such as crabs, also have compound eyes.

Fairies

find out more
Myths and legends

Fairies are very small, make-believe beings in human form, who have magical powers.

Fairies have wings, and include pixies (also called 'fair folk'), goblins (or 'hobgoblins'), elves and leprechauns. They can be beautiful and kind, but many look strange and are mischievous (naughty), and even dangerous. Pixies, for example, lead travellers astray and frighten people. Some children believe in the 'tooth fairy', a friendly fairy who takes teeth that have fallen out,

◀ Fairies are often associated with flowers. In this painting, *The Fairy's Funeral* by John Anster (1832–1906), some of the fairies are shown wearing flowers and even being part plant themselves.

and replaces them with a silver coin. But even friendly fairies should not always be trusted. For example, people taken to fairyland cannot leave if they eat or drink there.

A 'goblin' is another name for an imp – a small, ugly, mischievous devil. Elves are similar to goblins. There are good elves in fairy tales, but only the bad ones bother with humans. Goblins and elves like to play tricks on humans, whom they hate. They turn milk sour, and make wailing noises to scare people at night.

Leprechauns are Irish shoemaker-elves. They are said to bury gold in holes and mark the place with a rainbow. There is a fairy myth that anyone who manages to catch a leprechaun and keep a close watch on it can make it lead the way to the buried treasure.

Fairs

• Today there are permanent fun-fairs in some holiday resorts, such as Blackpool in England, Coney Island in New York City, USA, and the Tivoli Gardens in Copenhagen, Denmark.

• Modern trade fairs and exhibitions, such as the Frankfurt Book Fair in Germany, are usually annual events. They attract customers and businesses from all over the world.

find out more
Trade

Many modern fairs, with roundabouts and sideshows, are the continuation of local markets. These were held once or twice a year for people to meet to buy and sell their goods or services. Modern trade fairs are often devoted to one line of business, such as computer software or antique fairs.

During the Middle Ages most of the trade of Europe was carried out at fairs. The fairs of Champagne, Aix-la-Chapelle and Brie in France attracted merchants from all over Europe. One of the most important fairs began as a local fair in Leipzig, Germany, in the 12th century. It grew into a market for fur, leather, glassware and textiles. In London St Bartholomew's

fair was held in Smithfield. Cloth, animals and other goods were on sale there, and plays were performed. The fair was held annually until the middle of the 19th century.

In Africa and Asia too there are fairs which have continued for centuries. In Timbuktu (now in Mali) during the Middle Ages merchants from southern Africa exchanged their gold and ivory for salt from North Africa.

▼ The famous camel fair at the city of Pushkar in Rajasthan, India. There are camel races and thousands of people from India and overseas camp out in tents during the fair.

Families

A family is a group of people who are related to each other by birth, marriage or adoption.

In most societies, people live in family groups which provide care for children and for the old. Although living arrangements are very different from one country to another, most people throughout the world still choose to live together as families.

find out more
Children
Marriage

Types of family

The marriage of two people is usually the basis of a family. In Western countries most families consist of one or two parents and some children. This is called a *nuclear family*. The children will in their turn leave home and start new nuclear families when they grow up.

An *extended family* may include grandparents, aunts, uncles and cousins. In many societies extended families live together under one roof or in nearby houses and are able to support and help one another. This way of living is very common in Asia and Africa.

But we all belong to an extended family of children, parents, grandparents, aunts and uncles even if we do not see them very often.

One-parent families consist of one parent and one or more children. This can happen because the parents separate or get divorced, or because one parent dies. If the parents divorce, they are no longer part of each other's family, although they are both part of their children's family.

Step-families arise when parents who are divorced or widowed marry again. The new partner then becomes a step-parent, and children may have stepbrothers and stepsisters. In the past, when men and women often died younger, it was very common for widows and widowers to marry again. So children in earlier centuries often lived with their stepmothers or stepfathers. Today many children live with step-parents, but more commonly as a result of divorce and remarriage.

Adoption

There are two ways in which children become part of a family. They can be born into a family, or adopted. Babies or children who lose their natural parents may be adopted by other couples, or in some cases by a single person. Their new, adoptive parents bring them up as if they were their natural children. Being adopted is like being in an ordinary family. You take that family's name and are part of it forever.

Foster children

Foster children are the children in a family whose own parents are unable to look after them for some reason. Children may be fostered because one parent is ill, or in some cases because their parents have neglected or ill-treated them.

Great care is taken to find children a family that is right for them, and the children have the right to choose for themselves. Even so, moving into a new family can be difficult. A social worker visits regularly to check everyone is happy with the arrangement. Sometimes foster children stay only a short while with their new family, but sometimes they remain there until they have grown up.

▼ These pictures show three generations of the same family: grandmother, mother and daughter. The special features that they share and which make them look alike are called 'family resemblances'.

grandmother

mother

daughter

- In 1845 the Great Famine began in Ireland, after the failure of the potato crop, the country's staple food. By 1849 1 million people had either died from starvation or disease, or emigrated to North America.

- In 1974 Bangladesh suffered famine after disastrous floods destroyed the rice harvests. About 300,000 people died of starvation, either through food shortages or because they could not afford to buy the food that was available.

find out more
Aid agencies
Diets
Farming
Food
Refugees

Famine

When a large number of people are starving because they do not have enough to eat, we say there is a famine. Famines have been common throughout human history, from the Bible's account of seven years of famine in ancient Egypt to the African famines of the 20th century.

Famines may be caused by climatic disasters such as drought or flooding, as well as by pests and diseases. A drought can destroy crops that need rainwater to grow properly, and floodwaters can drown crops and sweep them away. Both droughts and floods helped to cause famines in African countries such as Sudan, Ethiopia and Mozambique during the 1980s.

Human action can cause famine or make it worse. There were a number of famines in parts of Europe during World War II. Many famines, in African countries in particular, have occurred during civil wars. The wars disrupt farmers' work and make the distribution of food difficult.

Other causes have been suggested for famine. Sometimes traditional farming methods cannot produce enough food while a population is growing fast. Another basic cause of famine is poverty. People may not have enough money to buy food even when it is available in their markets. In 17th-century Britain, in years of poor harvests, famine occurred because the inhabitants of the fast-growing towns were fed while peasants in the countryside starved.

▲ A young boy at a famine relief centre near Mogadishu in Somalia (1992). During famines, food is distributed from such centres, which are usually run by international aid agencies.

Faraday, Michael

Born 1791 in London, England
Died 1867 aged 75

Michael Faraday was one of the greatest scientists of all time. His most important achievements were the invention of the transformer, a vital part of most modern electrical equipment, and of the electric generator.

Faraday's researches covered many subjects in both chemistry and physics. He was especially interested in the effect of electric currents on chemicals, and the way electric currents are produced from chemicals in cells (batteries). He also studied how gases turn to liquids at low temperatures, and how to make new kinds of glass for the lenses of microscopes.

Faraday knew that the French physicist André-Marie Ampère had shown that when electricity flowed in a coil, the coil behaved like a magnet. Faraday thought that if electricity could produce a magnet, then a magnet could produce electricity.

His experiments proved that this idea was right: when a piece of iron inside a coil becomes magnetic, an electric current flows in the coil. Faraday had, in fact, discovered the transformer. By moving a magnet in and out of a hollow coil, a current flowed in the coil and Faraday had discovered the principle of the generator.

▼ Michael Faraday giving one of his famous Royal Institution Christmas Lectures for young people, which he started in 1826. They have been held every year since, except for three years during World War I, and are now watched by millions of people on television.

find out more
Electricity
Magnets

Farming

Most types of farming produce food for people to eat. Farmers make the best use they can of the natural resources available to them (such as soil and climate) to produce crops and rear animals.

▲ In the developed world at harvest time, most farm work is done by machine. Machines like this carrot picker are complicated and very expensive, but they save the farmer a lot of time and hard work.

• Market gardens are small farms where vegetables are grown to be taken straight to the market where they are sold. Tomatoes, lettuces and spring onions are just a few of the crops that need to be sold soon after they are picked. They are best grown close enough to the market to get them there before they go rotten.

Different types of plants and animals need different conditions to grow, so there is a variety of types of farming around the world.

Types of farming

Dairy farming produces milk, butter and cheese from cows that graze in grassy fields. Dairy farms are usually quite close to large cities so that fresh milk can quickly reach people's kitchens.

Arable farming involves ploughing the land and planting seed or small plants to grow crops. The most important arable crops are rice, wheat, maize (corn) and potatoes.

Mixed farming involves both crops and livestock. The main area is the corn belt of the midwest USA. Here farmers grow maize to feed to hogs (pigs) and cattle. Oats and hay are also grown as feed, as well as other crops such as soy beans and wheat. Mixed farming is found in Europe, too, in a region that stretches from northern Portugal and Spain across Britain, France, Germany and Poland and into the Ukraine.

Mediterranean farming is found in areas with a Mediterranean climate, where winters are mild and wet, summers long and dry, and rainfall is quite low. There are areas like this around the Mediterranean Sea, and there are others in California, Chile, South Africa and Australia. Winter crops include wheat, barley and broccoli. Summer crops include peaches, citrus fruits, tomatoes, grapes and olives.

Shifting cultivation is a common type of farming in many tropical countries. It is different from settled farming because shifting cultivators raise crops in a place only for as long as the soil allows the crops to grow well. After a year or so in one place the farmer moves on, chops away the natural vegetation from another area, and leaves the first plot to return to its natural state. After about a decade the old site may be reused. Shifting cultivation is practised in the tropical forests of Central and South America, Africa and South-east Asia. Farmers grow maize, rice, manioc, yams, millet and other food crops.

Farm animals

Sheep, cattle, pigs, chickens and goats are all farm animals. Sheep are kept both for their meat and wool, and are generally left to graze on grasslands. The grasslands usually cannot be used for other types of farming because they are too steep or too dry. Dogs often help to round up the sheep and to protect them and their lambs from wild animals such as wolves and eagles.

Lamb and mutton (from older sheep) are popular meats in many regions of the Middle East. Pigs are not kept on farms in the Middle

▼ Kamba people ploughing with oxen near Emali, Kenya. Soil is ploughed to bury weeds. The earth is then broken up and raked over to make it ready for planting.

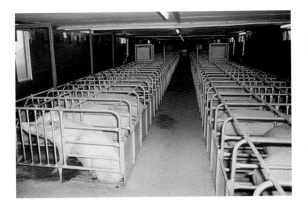

▶ Pregnant sows being kept in stalls. This form of intensive farming was banned in the countries of the European Union in 1998.

East, however, because most people there are Muslims and do not eat pork. Chickens are found on farms in many regions of the world. In western Europe and North America large numbers of chickens are kept indoors in row upon row of small cages, often never seeing the light of day. Farmers feed these 'battery hens' each day and collect their eggs.

Keeping battery hens is an example of *intensive farming*, in which farmers organize their animals and crops to get the maximum food from them. Intensive farming uses lots of machinery to make it more efficient. Tractors are used to plough fields and plant seed, and chemical fertilizers make plants grow stronger, while pesticides kill pests and herbicides kill weeds.

Pastures and cattle ranges

Much of the beef in hamburgers eaten in North America comes from cattle that graze in Central and South America. To expand cattle-ranching, tropical forests have been cut down to provide grasslands for 'hamburger cattle'. Cattle also graze on natural grasslands such as the pampas of Argentina.

In countries where intensive farming is practised, some cattle are not only fattened on pastures, they are also injected with drugs that make their bodies produce more meat. Where this is not done, the farming is 'extensive' rather than intensive, as quite large areas of grassland are needed to fatten one cow. In parts of East Africa, where grasslands are not good enough to feed cattle all the year round, farmers have to move their herds with the seasons to find new grazing land.

Grain farming

Grain (cereals) is the most important food source for most people in the world. The main types of grain are wheat, maize and rice. Grain can be made into many different kinds of food. Wheat is mainly eaten as pasta in Italy and as bread in North America and elsewhere. The USA, Argentina, Australia and Ukraine are the world's main areas of wheat production. Farming in these countries is mostly intensive. The use of machines, fertilizers, pesticides and herbicides means that the amount of grain produced from a hectare of field (its 'yield') in North America is over four times that produced from a hectare of field in Africa. The USA is the world's biggest exporter of grain. Nearly every African country has to import grain.

Organic farming

There are problems with some modern farming methods. Fertilizers and pesticides cause pollution of soil and water, and they may kill plants and animals that the farmer does not want to kill. Very small traces of the chemicals may also be left in crops, which can make them dangerous to eat.

▶ In North America there are large areas of intensive farming where the wheat or, in this case, ripe barley is harvested with combine harvesters.

▲ Trucks irrigating (watering) crops in the USA. Without such irrigation much of this land would be too dry for crops to grow properly.

▲ A traditional boom-type irrigation system on the River Nile, Egypt. The beam swings like a see-saw to dip the bucket in the water. Irrigation, using simple systems like this or motorized pumps in wealthier countries, is very important to farmers in the drier parts of the world.

Farmers who choose to farm organically do not use artificial chemicals on their land. They use compost and manure from farm animals to fertilize the land, and other plants to control insects. Animals kept on organic farms are allowed to roam in the open air and are not confined for long periods. The number of organic farms in the USA and Europe has grown in recent years. Many people believe that food grown organically tastes better and is safer than food produced by intensive methods.

Farms of the future

Some of the problems of arable farming, including the effects of poor weather or pests, can be solved by breeding new crops. This sort of breeding, using 'plant genetics', has gone on for centuries, but it is likely to become more and more common in farming in the future. In laboratories, scientists take samples of the crops they want to improve and cross them with wild varieties that have a certain quality that is beneficial to the new plant. It is a long and difficult business, and can take many years. This battle will always continue, because although a new plant can be made to resist a disease, it is usually attacked by a different disease just a few years after it is introduced to the fields.

Feeding the world

When people cannot get enough to eat, it seems obvious that farming is not producing enough food. Sometimes this is true, such as when climatic disasters, like droughts or floods, ruin harvests, but it is not always the case.

The world produces enough food to feed everyone on the planet, but problems arise when food is not in the right place at the right time. In the 1980s in Europe, for example, farmers were encouraged by their governments to produce so much food that excess 'food mountains' were created that cost a lot of money to store. Some of the food could have been sold or given to people who needed it; but this did not always happen.

Agricultural revolutions

The first agricultural revolution of modern times began in Britain in the 18th century. Between 1750 and 1870 there was a huge increase in farm output. Farmers learned how to drain their fields and enclose them in hedges. They found that by alternating crops they could use a field continuously, without having to leave it empty (fallow) for a time. Also, stock breeders developed larger and fatter animals.

In the late 18th and early 19th centuries farm machinery rapidly developed, mostly in the USA. First reapers, then threshers, and then combine harvesters appeared. Steam engines were used to power the traction engines used for ploughing and threshing. This mechanical revolution meant that more food could be grown by fewer people.

The latest agricultural revolution began in the 1960s and is still going on. It is called the 'Green Revolution'. Plant breeders have created new varieties of grains such as rice, wheat and maize that give higher yields. This has helped countries such as India, the Philippines and Mexico that have fast-growing populations.

• Most farmers have different jobs to do at different times of the year. Springtime is when lambs are born, while in winter sheep may have to be protected from harsh weather. Autumn is harvest time for crops such as wheat, and time to sow the seed for next year's crop. In areas like the steppes (grasslands) of central Asia the harvest must be brought in before the cold winter sets in.

Fats

Fats are substances found in food and they form an important part of your diet. They contain essential vitamins and your body uses them as a source of energy. It also stores energy as fat. But if you eat too many fatty foods, you will put on weight.

Fats do not dissolve in water, and they feel oily or greasy to the touch. Some fats, such as butter, lard and margarine, are solid at normal room temperature. Other fats, such as sunflower oil, corn oil and olive oil, are liquid.

Fats are made up of different kinds of fatty acid. Some of these must be present in the diet, but others can be made by the body from other foods, such as sugar and starch. So it is possible to put on weight by eating non-fatty foods.

Eating too much fat is also thought to be a cause of diseases such as cancer and heart disease. In general, plant oils such as olive oil and sunflower oil, which are made up of *unsaturated* fatty acids, are healthier than animal fats, like butter and lard, which are made up of *saturated* fatty acids. Saturated fatty acids are thought to increase the risk of disease, whereas unsaturated fatty acids are thought to reduce it.

▶ The chemical structure of saturated and unsaturated fat molecules. Fat molecules are made up of carbon atoms arranged in chains, with hydrogen atoms attached to them. Saturated fat is fully laden with hydrogen atoms. Unsaturated fat has double bonds between some of the carbon atoms, and fewer hydrogen atoms.

Hidden fat

Peanuts contain 50% of their weight as fat. *Double cream* contains 50% of its weight as fat. *Chocolate* contains 40% of its weight as fat. *Eggs* contain 12% of their weight as fat.

• The only foods that have no fats at all are raw fruits, vegetables and sugar.

find out more
Diets
Diseases
Food
Health and fitness

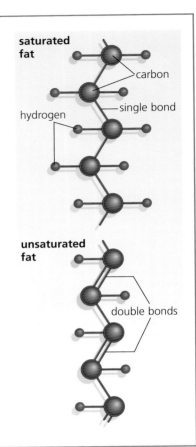

saturated fat — carbon — single bond — hydrogen

unsaturated fat — double bonds

Fax machines

A fax machine sends a copy of pages of text and pictures to another fax machine. It also prints copies of text and pictures sent by other fax machines. The word 'fax' is short for facsimile, which means 'exact copy'.

Office fax machines first became popular in the early 1980s. Some have a telephone handset for talking to the person operating the other machine.

Sending and receiving a fax

Once the sending machine has dialled the receiving machine and the receiving machine has answered, it begins to scan the document. It changes the pattern of light and dark in the pages of text and pictures (the document) into electrical signals, then sends these signals over the telephone network to the receiving machine.

The receiving fax machine takes the signals from the sending machine one line at a time. It sends them to a line of tiny heating elements. Where the original document was dark, the heating element is turned on, and where it was light, the element is turned off. Heat-sensitive paper moves past the heating elements, and where the elements are on, the paper turns black. Gradually, the pattern of light and dark on the original document is drawn line by line.

▶ How a fax machine works.

• With some personal computers, you can send documents directly to a fax machine. You can also receive faxed documents on the computer. They appear on the screen and can be stored or printed out.

• The idea of fax originated in Germany in 1902. For many years newspaper offices used fax to receive pictures quickly from around the world.

find out more
Information technology
Photocopiers
Telephones

0s and 1s sent as digital signals, one line at a time, through the telephone network.

Heating elements turn the line of 0s and 1s into a series of hots and colds.

0 0 1 1 0 0 0 1 1 0 0 0 1 1 0 0

light sensors

Light sensors change blacks and whites of image into electrical 0s and 1s.

sending fax

heating elements

receiving fax

Heat-sensitive paper turns black where it is heated.

Festivals and holidays

• These are just a few of the many thousands of festivals and holidays celebrated all over the world. Different regions and countries use their own calendars, and dates change in many cases from year to year, so these pages can only show roughly when they happen. Festivals and holidays listed without a coloured dot are secular (non-religious) or national holidays.

⬤ Christian
⬤ Jewish
⬤ Buddhist
⬤ Hindu
⬤ Sikh

Autumn

⬤ *Harvest festival*
Churches are decorated with produce in thanksgiving.

⬤ *Rosh Hashanah*
New Year's Day commemorates the creation of the world.

⬤ *Yom Kippur*
Day of Atonement to fast, pray and ask forgiveness.

⬤ *Navaratri*
Nine-nights festival held in honour of the goddess Durga.

⬤ *Simchat Torah*
Rejoicing in the Law by parading and even dancing with the scrolls in the synagogues.

⬤ *Kathina Day*
The end of the rainy season retreat when new robes are offered to monks.

⬤ *All Saints' Day* 1 November
Celebration of the lives and work of all the saints.

⬤ *All Souls' Day* 2 November
Commemoration of all the faithful Christians who have died.

⬤⬤ *Divali*
Hindus and Sikhs light lamps indoors and outdoors, give presents and send cards.

▲ A Fastnacht parade in Basel, Switzerland. Fastnacht is a carnival celebrated in German-speaking countries to mark the eve of the Christian period of fasting, Lent. It has been celebrated since medieval times.

Remembrance Day
The Sunday nearest to Armistice Day on 11 November, which was the end of World War I, to remember those who died in both World Wars.

Thanksgiving
The fourth Thursday in November in the USA; the second Monday of October in Canada.
A celebration of the harvest of the first settlers.

⬤ *Guru Nanak's Birthday*
Sikhs celebrate the birthday of their founder in the gurdwaras, singing hymns and hearing teachings.

Winter

⬤ *Christmas Day*
25 December
Catholic and Protestant Christians celebrate the birth of Jesus.

⬤ *Christmas* 6–7 January
Eastern Orthodox Christians celebrate Jesus' birth.

Yuan Dan
Chinese New Year's Day, celebrated with fireworks, the Lion Dance, and the giving of flowers and sweets.

Deng Jie
The Chinese Lantern Festival marks the lengthening of days.

⬤ *Shrove Tuesday*
Pancake Day, when leftovers are eaten before Lent. In many Catholic countries, Carnival is celebrated. ▶

▶ Families watch stilt dancers in a New Year procession in northern China.

► A ticker-tape parade in New York City. The people of New York welcome celebrities, such as Nelson Mandela, by showering them with ticker-tape (paper strings from computers and tape machines) in their progress through the streets.

find out more
Religions
Saints

Spring

● *Holi*
A spring festival in India with processions, bonfires and people throwing coloured water over each other.

● *Mothering Sunday*
Traditionally Christians visited their mother church and took gifts to their mothers.

● *Palm Sunday*
Commemorates the arrival of Jesus in Jerusalem at the beginning of Holy Week. Palm branches were laid on the ground and waved to welcome him.

● *Good Friday*
The day on which Jesus was crucified.

● *Passover* or *Pesach*
Jews remember the Exodus (going out) of their ancestors from slavery in Egypt and also celebrate the barley harvest with a special meal at home.

● *Easter Sunday*
Christians celebrate the resurrection of Jesus after his death on the cross the Friday before (Good Friday).

● *Baisakhi* or *Vaisakhi*
Sikhs remember the day Guru Gobind Singh gave their community the 5 'Ks', symbols of Sikh identity.

● *Pentecost (Whit Sunday)*
Christians remember how the Holy Spirit came to give Jesus' followers courage six weeks after Easter.

● *Wesak* or *Vesak*
Theravada Buddhists celebrate the birth, enlightenment and death of Gautama Buddha.

Summer

● *Raksha Bandhan*
Sisters tie threads of red and gold round their brothers' wrists as a protection from harm. The brothers give them presents in return.

● *Janmashtami*
Hindus celebrate the birthday of Krishna with images of the baby Krishna, singing, dancing and sweets.

Muslim festivals

Muslim festivals do not take place during the same season each year. Muslims use a lunar calendar (based on the Moon) and their year is shorter than those adjusted to the movements of the Sun. Each festival is earlier than it was the year before.

▲ Id-ul-Fitr street festivities in Bombay, India. Id-ul-Fitr is the Muslim festival to mark the end of Ramadan, the month of fasting.

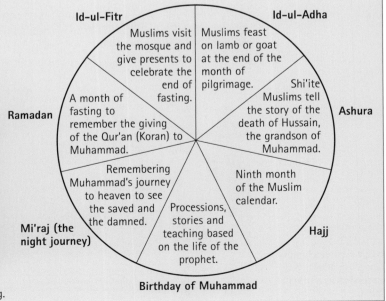

Id-ul-Fitr — Muslims visit the mosque and give presents to celebrate the end of fasting.

Id-ul-Adha — Muslims feast on lamb or goat at the end of the month of pilgrimage.

Ashura — Shi'ite Muslims tell the story of the death of Hussain, the grandson of Muhammad.

Hajj — Ninth month of the Muslim calendar.

Birthday of Muhammad — Processions, stories and teaching based on the life of the prophet.

Mi'raj (the night journey) — Remembering Muhammad's journey to heaven to see the saved and the damned.

Ramadan — A month of fasting to remember the giving of the Qur'an (Koran) to Muhammad.

Films

In Paris in 1895 the Lumière brothers projected the very first films onto a screen in front of a paying audience. Films have been a popular source of entertainment and an important art form ever since. Some film actors and actresses have become 'stars', their names and faces known all over the world.

The first films to be made were very short, but soon longer 'feature' films were being produced as entertainment. Cinemas opened in major towns around the world and many countries had their own film industries. The most important film-making centre was Hollywood, California, in the USA. Early films had no sound, although piano players or orchestras often provided a musical accompaniment. One advantage of silent films was that everybody could understand them, whatever language they spoke. Many of the clever techniques and exciting special effects still used in film-making today were developed in the early days.

The coming of sound

The first major sound film, nicknamed a 'talkie', was *The Jazz Singer* in 1927. This started a 'golden age' of Hollywood films, which lasted until television became popular in the 1950s. With the coming of sound, many countries began to make films in their own languages, but movies made in Hollywood continued to be very popular around the world.

- Films can be very expensive to make. Today a major blockbuster can cost £50 million or more. This money is raised by the producer.

- India has the world's biggest film industry, making about 900 films each year, compared with around 250 in the USA. It is based in Bombay (now Mumbai) and is known as 'Bollywood'.

▶ Making a film.

1 The **director** controls the actors' performances and the look of each shot, and so creates the film's pace and atmosphere.

2 Film **actors** play their parts shot by shot, often having to wait while the camera angle or lighting is changed.

3 The **camera crew** is made up of a camera operator, an assistant, a **clapper loader** who operates the clapperboard, a **focus puller,** who adjusts the focus, and **grips**. The grips' job is to move the camera smoothly during shots.

4 The **cinematographer** controls the lighting, the camera movement and the framing of each shot.

5 The **sound team** records the sound through a microphone suspended on a long boom. They listen for sound quality through headphones, and record background sound.

6 The **lighting team** controls the many powerful lights needed in filming to create the right atmosphere. The chief lighting engineer is called the **gaffer**.

7 The **continuity assistant** checks that every detail of each shot is correct.

8 Actors are carefully dressed and made-up each day for filming.

9 The **editor's** job is to join (splice) together the shots and sounds that go into the final film. Today editing is made easier because the information can be fed into a computer.

10 The **sound mixer's** job is to take the three soundtracks – the dialogue, the special effects and the music – and mix them onto a single track.

▲ *The Wizard of Oz* (1939), starring Judy Garland, was one of the earliest films to be made in colour. The opening scenes were shot in black and white to make the Technicolor land of Oz even more fantastic.

By the 1930s, millions of people were going to the cinema, often several times a week. Huge film studios in Hollywood and elsewhere turned out more and more new films. They usually stuck to the kinds of film which they knew audiences liked. Popular film 'genres' (type of film) developed, such as comedies, romances and westerns. Many films had similar plots. People often went to see films because their favourite stars were playing the leading roles.

As well as the main feature, audiences would see a cartoon or a documentary. In the days before television, there were also weekly newsreels. Films and weekly film serials made specially for children were often shown in the afternoons.

Films in the age of television

Since the arrival of television, film-makers have had to invent new ways of attracting audiences. The epic *Ben Hur* (1959) was filmed on a wide screen with stereo sound. It was a great box-office success and won 11 Oscars. In the 1970s directors such as Steven Spielberg introduced spectacular special effects into their films, which made action adventures and science fiction even more thrilling. A younger generation of filmgoers went to see these films in new 'multiplex' cinemas, many of which had 10 screens or more.

Modern film technology is changing at a rapid pace. Today, most people watch films on TV, video or DVD (digital video disc), rather than in the cinema. It may soon be possible to interact with the action, or even take part in it yourself!

Film 'genres'

Action and adventure movies are fast, fun and often spectacular. Famous stars of this genre are the swashbuckling Errol Flynn and Harrison Ford, who starred in the Indiana Jones trilogy.

Comedies are the oldest kind of movie. Some popular comic stars are the Marx brothers, who appeared in such comedy classics as *Duck Soup* (1933) and, more recently, Robin Williams.

Costume and melodrama films tell stories of people's lives, sometimes set in the past and sometimes those of real historical people. Bette Davis and Emma Thompson are two successful actresses of this genre.

Crime movies tell sinister and compelling stories of gangsters, thieves and private eyes. Humphrey Bogart is the classic Hollywood detective.

Horror movies play on our worst nightmares, sometimes with the help of gruesome special effects. Boris Karloff as Frankenstein's monster and Christopher Lee in such films as *The Mummy* have created unforgettable figures of horror.

Romances are love stories. Famous screen lovers are Clark Gable and Greta Garbo.

Musicals, with their lively song-and-dance routines, are pure entertainment. Fred Astaire and Ginger Rogers were a hugely successful dance partnership, who starred in many musicals. Amitabh Bachan was a major star of Indian popular musicals in the 1970s and 1980s.

Westerns, tales of 'cowboys and Indians', gunfights and tough lawmen, are a speciality of American cinema. John Wayne and Clint Eastwood are two of the greatest film gunslingers.

Science-fiction films are among the most popular and successful films of all time. The *Star Wars* and *Alien* trilogies are classics of this genre.

▼ *Gone With The Wind* (1939), starring Vivien Leigh and Clark Gable, won 10 Oscars and topped the box-office charts for 25 years.

find out more
Animation
Cameras
Chaplin, Charlie
Disney, Walt
Photography
Spielberg, Steven

▼ A scene from *Star Wars* (Special Edition 1997). The original *Star Wars* trilogy used miniatures and models to create its special effects. For the films' re-release in 1997 the special effects were improved by computer simulation, and animated characters such as Jabba the Hut, seen here with Harrison Ford, were superimposed over live actors. The first *Star Wars* trilogy is the most successful film series ever made.

Fire

find out more
Electricity
Gases, liquids and solids
Heat
Oxygen

All fires require three things to burn: fuel, heat and oxygen. The fuel must be turned into a gas before it can burn. The burning gases combine with oxygen in the air to produce lots of heat. As the burning gases and tiny particles of soot stream upwards, they glow as red-hot or even white-hot flames.

Once a fire is burning, the burning gases from the fuel, such as coal, make enough heat to keep the coal hot, so it produces more gas, and so on. Unless oxygen is present, the gases cannot burn. (A fire blanket or foam from an extinguisher will smother a fire by preventing the oxygen in the air from reaching it.)

Fire brigades or departments are responsible for fighting and

◄ These fire-fighters are tackling a blaze from three different levels. Water is being pumped to their hoses from a nearby water mains.

preventing fires. In the USA, for example, there are more than 20,000 fire departments, many of them staffed by volunteers instead of full-time fire-fighters. Fire-fighters are trained to enter blazing buildings, and often need to wear breathing apparatus in the smoke-filled surroundings. Every fire brigade has several different kinds of fire tender, equipped to tackle blazes. The main fire-fighting weapon is a powerful jet of water pumped from a hose. Many tenders carry a tank full of water. Foam, rather than water, is used to smother the flames of fires involving petrol.

Fire safety
Prevention
- Keep all doors shut, especially at night.
- Unplug the TV set at night and when leaving the house.
- Do not drape clothes over lights or heaters.
- Do not play or experiment with fire.
- Install smoke alarms in your home.

In the event of fire
- Shut the door to the fire, unless this traps someone.
- Tell an adult immediately.
- Get everyone out of the building.
- Never go back into a building that is on fire.
- Call the fire brigade and give the address clearly.

First aid

People who are trained in first aid know what action to take in medical emergencies. They try to prevent a victim's condition from getting worse and to make them as comfortable as possible until expert medical help arrives.

There are certain emergency situations that are fairly common. These include unconsciousness, shock, choking and bleeding. It is useful for everyone to know some first aid in these situations.

Unconscious people can die by inhaling their own saliva or vomit. To try and avoid this they should be placed in the 'recovery position' (see right). But if there are signs of injury to the person's backbone, they should not be moved at all.

A person in shock looks very pale and has cold and clammy skin, a rapid pulse and rapid, shallow breathing. They should be placed in the recovery position. You should not try to warm them up or give them a drink without a doctor's permission.

If a person is choking, you should take any obvious blockage from their mouth, bend them over, face-down, and slap them sharply between the shoulders up to four times.

Bleeding can be controlled by pressing on the wound with your hand or with a clean cloth. If an arm or leg is bleeding, it helps to raise it. You should call a doctor if the bleeding does not stop, if something is stuck in the wound, or if it was caused by an animal.

If a person has a burn, you should run cold water over it – until the pain stops for a small burn; longer for a large one. You should cover it with a dry, non-fluffy sterile dressing.

find out more
Bones
Breathing
Health and fitness
Hospitals
Medicine

◄ The recovery position. Turn the body so that the head is to one side, and pull both the arm and the leg on that side up so they are at right angles to the body. Loosen clothing around the neck and pull the chin forwards so the tongue does not block the throat. Clear the mouth of any blockage.

Fireworks *see* Explosives

Fishes

Fishes are cold-blooded animals with backbones, gills and fins. They all live in water, and can be found in ponds, lakes and rivers, and in the sea. Most sea-dwelling fishes live in the shallows close to land and in the surface waters of the great oceans.

pectoral fin
nostrils
spiny dorsal (back) fin
soft dorsal fin
tail fin
scales
gill cover
gill opening
vent
anal fin
lateral line
pelvic fin

▲ Most fishes have a skeleton of bone and are covered with a protective armour of scales, made of very thin plates of bone. Sharks and their relatives have skeletons of gristly cartilage. There are about 21,000 different kinds of fish, of which more than 20,000 are bony fishes.

Fish records
Largest
Whale shark, up to 18 m long, over 40 tonnes
Largest freshwater fish
Arapaima, up to 3 m long and 200 kg
Smallest fish
Pygmy goby, up to 11 mm long, 4–5 mg
Fastest
Sailfish, about 109 km/h
Largest number of eggs
An ocean sunfish contained an estimated 300 million eggs

▼ A lionfish hunts among a school of cardinal fish off the coast of Borneo in Indonesia. Cardinal fishes, like many kinds of fish, live in groups called schools with others of the same age and species. Fishes in a school behave as a single unit. When threatened by danger, they swim close together, twisting and turning like a single fish.

Water is about 800 times as dense as air, so fishes have to work hard to swim through it. The fastest fishes, such as mackerel and tuna, have long, tapering, streamlined bodies and crescent-shaped tails. Slower-moving fishes, such as tench and carp, have rounder bodies and squarer tails. Some kinds of fish, such as rays and turbot, live on the sea-bed. They have flattened, camouflaged bodies and are slow-moving, and so they are hard to see.

When they swim, most fishes use powerful zigzag muscles which move their bodies and tails from side to side. Only very few kinds paddle along with their fins, which are mainly used for balancing, stabilizing and braking.

Fishes do not sink in the water even when they are totally still. Most kinds of fish have an internal *swim bladder*, a gas-filled bag which holds them up. When they swim, all their energy goes into pushing forwards through the water. Other animals have to use some of their energy to stay up when swimming.

The life of a fish

Most fishes are born from eggs, although a few kinds are born live. Usually fishes have a definite breeding season. Some, like eels and salmon, migrate long distances to reach the best place to spawn (produce eggs).

In most fishes the females lay huge numbers of eggs. These are almost always fertilized by the male outside the female's body. It is unusual for fishes to take any care of their young, although some produce smaller families and do look after them. Among these it is often the male, rather than the female, that cares for the young.

Fishes that live in fresh water or near the seashore usually lay eggs that sink to the bottom, where they may be hidden among plants. Fishes that live in the open sea generally lay very tiny eggs that float. When these hatch, they become part of the sea plankton. Very few of these tiny fishes survive, as they provide food for many other animals.

The senses of a fish

Fishes have the same basic senses as we do: sight, hearing, touch, smell and taste.

Most fishes have eyes on the sides of their heads, which gives them all-round vision. Many fishes have good colour vision. This is important in the

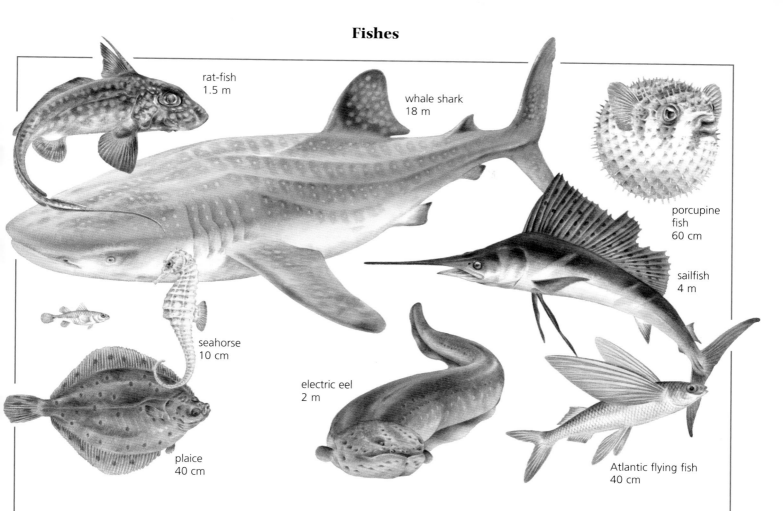

rat-fish
1.5 m

whale shark
18 m

porcupine
fish
60 cm

sailfish
4 m

seahorse
10 cm

electric eel
2 m

plaice
40 cm

Atlantic flying fish
40 cm

courtship of some species, and in others that can change their colour to match their surroundings.

Fishes' ears are inside their skulls. They work as organs of balance as well as of hearing. Sounds travel very well under water, and many fishes make noises to communicate with each other.

Many fishes live where there is little light, so their sense of touch is important. A fish's main organ of touch is its *lateral lines*. These are a series of very sensitive nerve endings that lie just below the skin along the fish's sides. Any movement in the water is detected by the lateral lines, and the fish can tell that there is an enemy or a possible meal nearby. Some fishes have 'whiskers', called *barbels*, round their mouth which they use to explore the sea- or river-bed.

Most fishes have a very good sense of smell and can recognize the scents of other fishes. Many use smell to find their prey. Some, if they are injured, release a special substance from their skin into the water. When other fishes of the same species smell this, they swim quickly to safety. Salmon probably use their sense of smell when they migrate back to the stream where they were born to lay their eggs.

The sense of taste is related to the sense of smell. Some fishes have large numbers of taste buds in and around the mouth.

Fish food

Freshwater fishes eat all sorts of food, including water plants, snails, worms, insects and their larvae, and other fishes. Some fishes, like grey mullet, suck up mud from the river-bed and

digest the tiny creatures that live there. They are called detritus feeders.

In the open sea, where there are no rooted plants, most fishes are carnivores (flesh-eaters), feeding on a wide range of animals including shrimps, squid and other fishes. Others – including some very large fishes, such as basking sharks – are filter-feeders. The fish takes a mouthful of water, closes its mouth and pushes the water out over its gills. The plankton is filtered out by special combs called gill rakers, which are attached to the gills, and the fish then swallows it.

Some of the strangest of all fishes are those that live deep in the ocean. Most have huge mouths and teeth and some can swallow creatures bigger than themselves, as they have few chances to feed and may not eat again for months.

▲ Almost half the 43,000 species of animals with backbones (vertebrates) are fishes. Some of the species that have evolved are very strange indeed.

find out more
Animals
Fishing
Oceans and seas
Ponds
Rivers and streams
Sharks and rays
Swimming and diving

Fishing

There are three kinds of fishing: fishing for sport, for food to live by or for profit.

• In fish 'farms' lakes, rivers and parts of the coast are stocked with fish which are kept in cages or released to be caught and eaten.

Sports fishing, or angling, is the most popular pastime in many countries across the world. While these individuals fish for pleasure, many poorer people must fish to feed themselves and their families. The fishing industry is one of the biggest industries in the world. It employs many people to catch, process and sell fish for profit.

▲ In game fishing, or fly-fishing, the artificial flies attract fish by looking like food. The rod is lifted sharply above the fisher's head and then the line is propelled forward to land gently on the water.

Sports fishing

There are three main types of sports fishing: coarse fishing, game fishing and sea fishing.

Coarse fishing, or bait fishing, is the cheapest, easiest and most popular form of fishing. The word 'coarse' refers to the type of fish caught, many of which are not edible. This kind of fishing uses a simple rod, a reel and line, hooks, weights, floats and bait (food to lure the fish).

Game fishing, or fly-fishing, involves catching game fish, such as salmon or trout. Fly-fishing is often said to be the most entertaining form of fishing because of the fish and methods involved. The hooks are dressed (disguised) as artificial flies to attract the fish and you use a rod to 'cast' a fly. Tinsel, wool, fur and feathers are used, and dressing flies is an art in itself.

Sea angling is a recent form of the sport. It started with fishing off piers, using tackle and methods similar to coarse fishing. You can also

cast from the beach or rocks, and many more anglers fish from anchored or moving boats.

The fishing industry

There are two main types of industrial fishing: inshore fishing and deep-sea fishing. Inshore fishing boats stay near the coast and catch fish using rods and lines or small nets. They sail and return the same day.

Most of the world's fish catch comes from the deep oceans, too far from land for ships to catch and return the same day. Deep-sea fishing ships are much bigger than those that fish inshore. They can stay at sea for months. Many trawlers feed their catches into a 'factory ship', where the fish are cleaned, gutted and frozen while at sea.

Fishing ports in Europe and elsewhere are suffering unemployment because so many fish have been caught from some oceans that the wild fish stocks are running out. The European Union is trying to limit the number of fish caught so that stocks can be conserved for the future.

▼ These are the three main types of net used to catch most of the world's fish. Drift and purse-seine nets are used to catch fish near the surface; trawls catch fish near the ocean floor. The nets of some modern ships are too heavy to be dragged on board, so some have great pipes which suck up the catch from the net while it is still in the water.

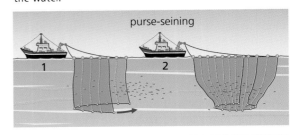

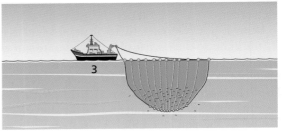

find out more
Conservation
Fishes
Oceans and seas
Ports and docks

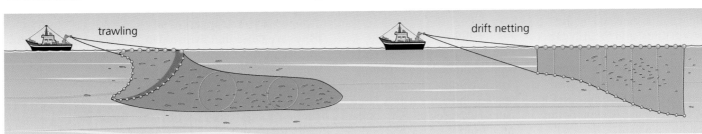

Fleas and lice

Fleas and lice are wingless insects that live as parasites on other animals. A parasite is an animal that lives by feeding on another animal (its host), usually causing it harm in the process.

Fleas live on mammals and birds. They have backward-pointing hairs and sharp claws, so they are difficult to dislodge if the host tries to scratch them away. They can walk slowly, but if they need to move quickly they jump using their powerful back legs.

Fleas feed on blood: the bite itches because the host's body reacts against chemicals in the flea's saliva. Fleas lay their eggs in the nests or beds of their hosts. The young that hatch out look like tiny worms. Some fleas breed at the same time of year as their hosts, so that when the host's young are born there is a crop of fleas ready to live on them.

Two kinds of insect are called lice. One group is the bird lice, or biting lice. As their name suggests, they are found mainly on birds, where they nibble at feathers and skin. The other group is called the sucking lice. These feed on mammals' blood.

They cling closely to their hosts with gripping claws. Unlike fleas, lice attach their eggs, called nits, to the host's hair.

The human louse may live in hair, or in clothes which are close to the skin. Head lice can easily be spread where people are living close together, and perhaps sharing combs. It is important to control lice, as they can carry diseases.

▲ A flea (left) and a louse (right) magnified many times. They often carry diseases which they can pass on to their host when they bite it to suck its blood.

- Fleas have been known to jump more than 30 cm, about 200 times their body length.

- There are about 1750 different kinds of flea, about 2600 kinds of biting louse and about 250 kinds of sucking louse.

find out more
Insects
Pests and parasites

Flies and mosquitoes

Flies are among the insects we see most often. Many people think they are dirty and spread disease, but this is not true in most cases.

Flies can be very useful. Some live on decaying plants and animals and can change these dead things into chemicals which help the soil. Other flies are pollinators, helping plants to spread by carrying pollen from flower to flower.

Flies vary a lot in shape. One big group, which includes mosquitoes and midges, have slender, soft bodies. A second group, which includes horseflies, have short, hard bodies. The third and largest group includes houseflies and hoverflies. All of these have short, well-armoured bodies.

Flies spend the first part of their lives as larvae, which are called grubs or maggots. Some larvae live in the flesh of dead mammals or birds; some hunt tiny soil-dwelling animals; and other kinds live in water. A few types of larva burrow into the skin of cattle and other animals.

Mosquitoes are small flies, many of which carry diseases. A person can catch the disease if they are bitten by the female mosquito (the male feeds only on plants). Malaria is one of the

▲ A male mosquito's feathery antennae are sensitive to sound vibrations: they are its 'ears'. This mosquito is about six times its actual size.

most serious diseases spread by mosquitoes: it probably kills a million people, mostly children, each year – more than any other infectious disease. Taking anti-malarial tablets reduces the chances of infection if you happen to be bitten.

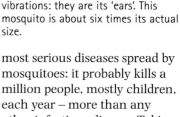

◀ The male horsefly sucks nectar from plants but the female sucks blood from horses, cattle and humans. This horsefly is about three times its actual size.

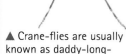

▲ Crane-flies are usually known as daddy-long-legs.

- There are at least 90,000 different kinds of flies and mosquitoes.

- All flies have two pairs of wings. The front pair are used for flying, while the tiny hind pair are probably used to help with balance.

find out more
Diseases
Insects

Flight

Insects were flying nearly 350 million years before the first person dreamed of taking to the air. About 200 million years later, the first birds developed the ability to fly. It was not until 1903 that the very first powered plane flight took place. To be able to fly, any animal or machine has to get up into the air, stay up there, and control its movements.

When a bird takes off, it jumps into the wind and flaps its wings. The feather-covered wings are well adapted to flying. As the wing moves down, it pushes against the air and this produces an upward force. The air is also pushed backwards by the wing so that the bird moves forwards. As the wing comes up, it is twisted and air passes between the feathers to cut down resistance. A bird tucks its legs up in flight so its body shape is smooth and streamlined. It uses its tail feathers to change direction.

How an aircraft flies

Most aircraft have wings with an arched cross-section like those of birds. The shape is called an *aerofoil*. Air moving over this aerofoil creates lift, but unlike bird's wings, aircraft wings cannot be flapped. Therefore air must be kept flowing over them.

The aircraft in the picture is moved forwards using a propeller that turns very quickly. Its engine is similar to the one in a car, although more powerful. As the aircraft builds up speed, the air rushing over the wings creates the lift needed to raise it into the sky. Aircraft designers have to ensure that the shape of the plane is streamlined. This reduces drag, which is caused by the resistance of the air as a plane moves through it.

• Early attempts by humans to fly with artificial wings failed because no one had the strength to flap them quickly enough. Bats are the only mammals to have perfected the art of flying.

find out more
Aircraft
Balloons and airships
Bats
Birds
Engines
Gliders and kites
Helicopters
Insects

◄ The forces on an aircraft in flight.

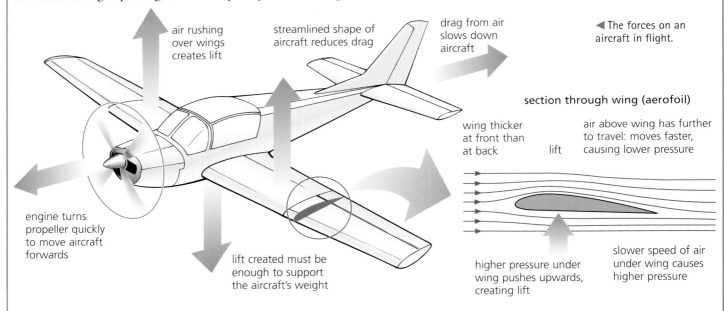

air rushing over wings creates lift

streamlined shape of aircraft reduces drag

drag from air slows down aircraft

engine turns propeller quickly to move aircraft forwards

lift created must be enough to support the aircraft's weight

section through wing (aerofoil)

wing thicker at front than at back

lift

air above wing has further to travel: moves faster, causing lower pressure

higher pressure under wing pushes upwards, creating lift

slower speed of air under wing causes higher pressure

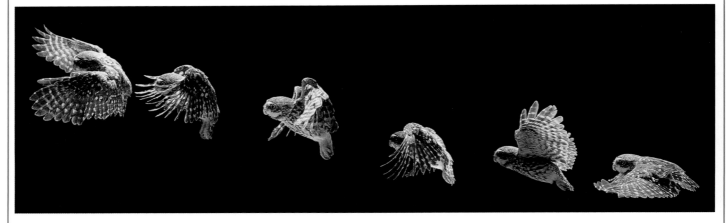

▼ A little owl in flight. To flap their wings, birds have powerful muscles attached to a strong breastbone.

Flowering plants

Flowering plants are the most successful group in the plant kingdom. There are nearly 250,000 species, found in every part of the world. The smallest is the least duckweed, a tiny water plant scarcely 1 millimetre across. The largest flowering plants are trees, which can grow to 95 metres or more in height.

Flowering plants are so called because they reproduce using flowers. The brightly coloured and scented flowers that we see in the countryside and in gardens are only one type of flower. Flowers of plants like grasses are small and inconspicuous, while other flowers, like the catkins of some trees, do not look like typical flowers at all.

Parts of a flower

There are many different types of flower, but they all have the same basic structure. Each part of the flower is designed to do a particular job.

The outermost parts of a flower are the leaf-like *sepals*. They protect the flower when it is in bud. *Petals* are the most visible part of the flower. They are often coloured and scented to attract insects.

Stamens contain the plant's male sex cells. The male sex cells are tiny *pollen grains*, which are spread from plant to plant. *Carpels* contain a flower's female sex cells, the *ovules*. These are like the plant's eggs. An ovule cannot grow into a new plant until it has linked up with a pollen grain.

In most flowering plants, each flower has both stamens and carpels. However some plants, such as oak and willow trees, produce separate male and female flowers. ▶

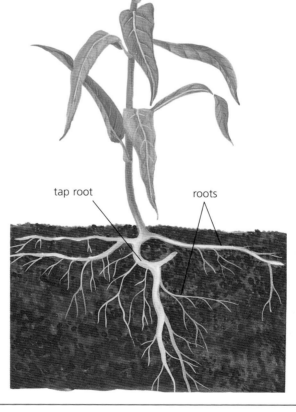

anther (sac containing pollen)

petal

sepal

stamen

carpel

stigma (sticky or feathery structure for catching pollen)

ovary with ovule inside

bud

flower

fruit

seeds

leaf

stem

tap root

roots

◀ Parts of a flowering plant.
Leaves make food for the plant, using energy from sunlight, carbon dioxide from the air, and water. This process is called photosynthesis.
Stems are the main support of the plant. They also contain the tubes that carry water up from the soil to the leaves, and food from the leaves to other parts of the plant.
Roots anchor a plant and draw in water from the soil, along with the minerals needed for growth. The main (tap) roots may reach far down into the soil, while a mass of fibrous roots spreads out through the soil surface.

• All flowering plants belong to a group of plants known as *angiosperms*. There are two subgroups. One includes grasses, lilies and orchids. The other includes most common flowers and all broadleaved trees.

Orchids
Orchids are the largest flowering plant family, with at least 18,000 known species. Most grow in tropical countries, partly because insects to pollinate them are more common there. Some tropical orchids grow high above the ground, with dangling roots which absorb water and minerals from the rain.

Pollination and fertilization

A flower's pollen has to combine with an ovule on the same or another flower before the ovule can become a seed. But first, the pollen has to get to the ovule. This process is called *pollination*.

Most flowers have developed ways to ensure that pollen from one flower is carried to another flower of the same species. There are two main ways that this transfer takes place: by animals and by wind.

find out more
Fruit
Grasses
Plants
Trees and shrubs
Wood

▲ Hazel trees have both male and female flowers. These catkins are the male flowers. They are shedding a dust of pollen into the air, to be carried away on the wind.

▲ A honeybee on a swamp rose (the smaller insect is a hoverfly). The bee is searching for nectar, which it uses to make honey. Bees also collect pollen, in special 'pollen baskets' on their back legs. The yellow dust on this bee's legs is pollen.

Insects are the most common animal pollinators, especially bees and butterflies. Insects are attracted to a flower by its colour and smell. They come in search of *nectar*, a sweet, sugary liquid found in a tiny cup at the base of each petal. While the insect is searching for nectar, pollen grains stick to its body. Some of this pollen is then left behind on the next flower the insect visits.

Wind-pollinated flowers need to be in a position to catch the breeze. Their pollen grains are small and light so that they can float on the slightest breeze. Pollen is produced in huge quantities, because each grain only has a very small chance of reaching another flower. Spreading, feathery structures (*stigmas*) on each flower act like nets to catch pollen drifting past in the breeze.

Once a pollen grain has reached another flower of the same kind, it grows a tiny tube down into the carpel, to join up with an ovule inside. Once it reaches the ovule, the two cells combine. This is *fertilization*. Once the ovule has been fertilized, it can start developing into a seed. At the same time, the part of the carpel around the seed (the *ovary*) swells to form a fruit, such as a fleshy berry, a nut or a dry capsule.

Life cycles of flowering plants

Each growing season, a flowering plant increases in size until it is ready to flower and set seed. *Annuals* are plants which flower once and die within a year, leaving their seeds to survive the winter or dry season. *Biennials* also flower only once, but take two years to do so. In the first year they produce stems and leaves, and store food, usually in their roots. The shoot then dies but the root survives underground. In the second year, the plant uses the stored food to grow a new shoot. It then flowers, releases its seeds, and dies. *Perennial* plants flower year after year, each year storing food in their roots for the next year's growth.

▼ The talipot palm has one of the largest flower clusters in the world. It only flowers once, then dies, exhausted by the effort of producing so many flowers.

Food

Food is vital for life. It supplies you with energy, and with the materials your body needs for growing, repairing wounds, and staying healthy.

Everything the body does needs energy. Your muscles use energy when you move and your brain uses energy when you think. You use energy even when you are asleep. Energy keeps your body warm, your heart beating and your lungs working.

Food for energy

The smallest amount of energy that you need to stay alive is called your basal metabolic rate (BMR). The average adult BMR is between 6000 and 7000 kilojoules a day (a kilojoule is a unit for measuring energy). The amount of energy you need on top of your BMR, when you wake up and start moving, depends on your age, your sex and how energetic a job or activity you are doing – a young athlete uses far more energy than an elderly retired person.

• Water is as important to the body as any food. You can live without food for a week or more, but water is necessary every day. Most people need about 2 litres of water a day.

• There are many different kinds of protein in food from plants and animals. Many people get protein from both animal and plant food. Vegetarians do not eat meat, but they can stay healthy with proteins from plants.

▼ Different foods supply different amounts of energy as this food chart shows.

▲ These village children in Zambia are preparing flour to make bread – a good source of carbohydrate energy.

Nutrients

The substances the body uses for energy and growth are called nutrients. There are five types of nutrient: carbohydrates, fats, proteins, vitamins and minerals.

Carbohydrates are our main source of energy. They are found in sugary foods such as sweets, honey, jam and treacle, and in starchy foods such as bread, potatoes and rice.

Fats are also energy-rich nutrients. Fatty foods include butter and cream, which come from animals, and oils from plants, such as olive oil and maize-seed oil. Fats can supply twice as much energy as the same weight of carbohydrates. But instead of using them straightaway, fats can be stored under the skin.

Proteins are needed to help your body replace damaged and worn-out parts. Everyone needs plenty of protein because bodies are rebuilding themselves all the time. Vegetables such as lettuce and cabbage have very little protein, while meat (especially liver and kidney), cheese, eggs, fish, milk, beans (including tinned baked beans) and peas are high-protein foods.

Vitamins and *minerals* are nutrients which are essential for good health. Vitamins take part in many important chemical changes in the body. Most vitamins come from food, but the body can make vitamin D from sunlight. You need minerals such as iron for healthy red blood cells, and calcium and phosphorus for healthy bones and teeth. Calcium also helps your muscles and nerves work properly. ◗

Types of food	Kilojoules per 100 g	
Meat and fish: mostly protein with some fat and oil. Many vitamins, especially in fish oil.	600 to 1200 kJ	
Eggs and dairy produce: mostly fat, especially butter and cheese. Eggs have a lot of protein and many vitamins.	300 to 3000	
Cereals: mostly starchy carbohydrate with a little protein. Some vitamins.	1000 to 1600	
Vegetables: contain a lot of water, some carbohydrate and protein. Very little fat. Very rich in vitamins and minerals.	40 to 350	
Fruit: contain a lot of water with some carbohydrate and a little protein. Rich in vitamin C.	100 to 300	
Sweets and cakes: mostly carbohydrate, especially sugar, with some fat and a little protein. No vitamins.	1000 to 2300	

Food processing

Food may just be washed, trimmed and packed before being sold, or it may be processed to turn it into ready-made dishes such as cakes and casseroles. Food grown in one part of the world may be transported for use far away in another, so it may need processing for longer storage. If food is not processed, it may be spoiled by bacteria and moulds present in the air.

There are a number of preserving methods. The easiest way is to remove water. Water can be removed by drying in warm air, or by adding sugar, salt, vinegar or certain chemicals. These substances, known as *preservatives*, take the place of water in the food. *Canning* and *bottling* use heat treatment to kill bacteria. The food is then packed without any air and can be kept for years. Food can also be chilled in a fridge; *freezing* keeps it fresh for even longer. *Radiation* can also kill bacteria and preserve food.

Additives

Additives are natural or artificial substances that are added to food in small amounts to perform certain tasks. In Europe most are identified by a special E number (the 'E' stands for European, meaning they have been approved by the European Commission). They are listed with the ingredients on the product label. E numbers do not cover flavourings.

Some additives are used to maintain freshness and lengthen shelf life; others are needed to make products in the form in which they are known and enjoyed. Raising agents, for example, are used in cakes. Others are used to improve the flavour of the food, its appearance or its nutritional value.

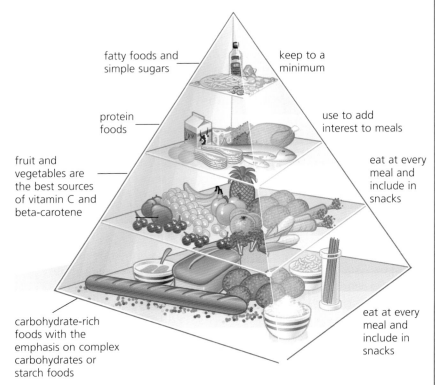

fatty foods and simple sugars — keep to a minimum

protein foods — use to add interest to meals

fruit and vegetables are the best sources of vitamin C and beta-carotene — eat at every meal and include in snacks

carbohydrate-rich foods with the emphasis on complex carbohydrates or starch foods — eat at every meal and include in snacks

▲ This food pyramid gives advice on how and when to eat food of different types.

Food around the world

In most parts of the world people eat a lot of the foods that grow particularly well in the area where they live. These are known as staple foods. They are often cheaper than imported foods, and they can be a good source of energy and body-building materials. Rice is a staple food in parts of India, southern China and South-east Asia. In north-east China noodles and steamed buns made of wheat are more common. Maize (corn) is a staple food in Central and South America. Wheat and potatoes are staple foods in North America and Europe.

Different crops need different climatic conditions and soils. Tropical fruits and vegetables only grow where it is warm or very hot throughout the year. They include groundnuts (peanuts), bananas and plantains, pineapples, mangoes, yams and okra.

North and south of the tropics are the temperate zones. Here quite different fruits and vegetables grow, including olives, grapes, oranges, aubergines and figs. Apples, pears, strawberries, blackberries, potatoes, carrots and wheat grow further north or south of the tropics. In countries bordering the sea, fish form a major part of the diet. In central Europe meat is often preserved and eaten as sausages.

● Fruit and vegetables, wholemeal bread and pasta, brown rice, peas and beans all contain lots of fibre. Fibre is not a nutrient but it is important because it helps the body to get rid of waste products.

◀ Inside a tuna-fish canning plant in Thailand.

find out more
Beans
Bread
Cereals
Cheese
Cooking
Diets
Farming
Milk
Spices
Sugar
Vegetables

Food chains and webs

All living things need food to stay alive. Green plants make their own food, using sunlight, water and carbon dioxide from the air. Animals cannot do this. They have to get their food either by eating plants or by eating other animals. So the plants and animals which live in an area are all connected to each other by the way that they get their food.

When green plants use sunlight to make their food, they are storing some of the Sun's energy. Plant-eating animals (*herbivores*) get this energy directly from the plants, by eating them. The herbivores are eaten in turn by flesh-eating animals (*carnivores*), which may themselves be eaten by other carnivores. But even for these animals, the energy in their food comes originally from plants.

The simplest food chains

The plants and animals which live in an area are all linked together by energy and food, forming a food chain. In a garden, caterpillars may eat a cabbage plant. Some of the energy stored in the cabbage is passed to the caterpillars. If a thrush then eats a caterpillar, some of the energy is passed to the thrush. Cabbage, caterpillar and thrush are all links in the food chain.

There may be only two links in a food chain, as when a horse eats grass. If large carnivores feed

▲ In a few food chains, a plant is the carnivore rather than an animal. The Venus fly-trap grows in soils that are short of certain minerals that the plant needs for growth. It gets the extra minerals by catching and digesting insects in its specially adapted 'fly-trap' leaves.

on smaller carnivores, there may be three or more links in the food chain. If we use our original example, a fox may kill and eat the thrush. Then the food chain has four links.

Food webs

In real life, food chains are rarely quite so simple. Many different food chains may interconnect to form a food web. All living things are linked together in food webs. A change in the numbers of animals or plants in one part of a food web (for example, as a result of pollution) can affect all the other parts of the web. Human activities often disrupt natural food webs, putting the whole living system (the *ecosystem*) out of balance.

• Scavengers and decomposers are an important part of most food chains. *Scavengers* are animals such as vultures, hyenas and some kinds of beetle. They feed on dead plants or animals. *Decomposers* are certain types of bacteria and fungi, which break down the remains of dead animals. This puts minerals back into the soil and helps new plants to grow.

◄ A food web. In many meadows, field voles eat grass. Kestrels often hunt and kill the voles. The grass, voles and kestrels make a simple food chain (red arrows). Other kinds of animals also feed on grass – cattle, sheep, deer, rabbits, snails and grasshoppers. In turn, there are many carnivores which feed on these herbivores.

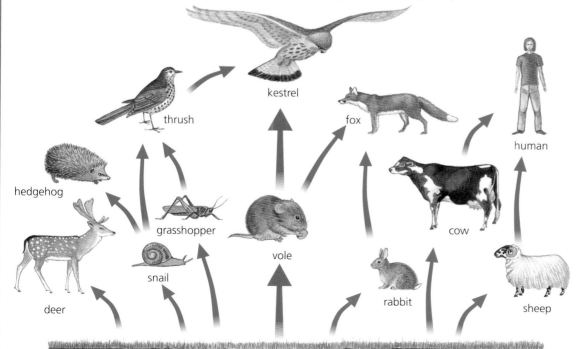

thrush
kestrel
fox
human
hedgehog
grasshopper
cow
vole
snail
deer
rabbit
sheep

find out more
Ecology
Energy
Food
Plants

Football

There are several different games called football played with round or oval-shaped balls. In spite of the name, in all but one of these sports – Association Football, or 'soccer'– players are allowed to handle the ball.

• There are references to a game similar to soccer throughout the Middle Ages in Europe. The modern game as we know it began in the public schools of southern England in the 19th century.

▼ Football (soccer) pitch.

goal line

halfway line

goal area

centre circle

touch line

penalty spot

penalty area

▼Bulgaria score their first goal in their 2-1 victory over Germany in the 1994 soccer World Cup. The eventual winner of the tournament was Brazil, who won again in 2002 to become world champions for a record fifth time.

Sports such as rugby football and American football have major followings in many countries, but soccer is the most widely played by far. In most places it is simply known as 'football', and it is the most popular game in the world.

Soccer

A professional football match is played between two teams of 11 players and lasts for 90 minutes, with a 15-minute break between halves. Players may use any part of their body, except hands and arms, to play the ball. Only the goalkeepers are allowed to handle the ball, and then only when they are in their own penalty area.

The object of the game is to score goals by kicking or heading the ball into the opponents' goal. Players move up the field by passing or running with the ball (dribbling). The game is controlled by a referee. The referee may caution, or 'book', a player for certain offences (displaying a yellow card), and send players off for the rest of the game (red card) for more serious offences or for a second bookable offence.

Soccer competitions

The World Cup is the most important international competition in football. It takes place every four years. Over 170 countries enter the regional qualifying rounds, with 32 going on to the finals in a particular host country. The competition has been dominated by European and South American countries, but African and Asian teams have made great progress in recent tournaments. The first Women's World Cup was held in China in 1991 and was won by the USA.

The club champions of each country are decided on the basis of a *league competition*. The top clubs are arranged in a number of divisions, and each team usually plays the others in the same division twice in a season, once at home and once away. The team in the top division with the most points at the end of the season becomes the national champions.

Some national competitions are organized on a *knockout* basis, in which clubs progress through a number of rounds to a final. The oldest and most famous of these is the English FA (Football Association) Cup, which started in the late 19th century. Over 500 clubs enter this competition, and the final is televised to countries all over the world.

Australian rules and Gaelic football

In Australian rules football two teams of 18 players compete with an oval ball on a large oval pitch. Players may hit the ball with the palm of the hand or punch it, but they are not allowed to throw it. They can also run with the ball, as long as they bounce or touch it on the ground every 10 metres. Features of the game are the long kicks from the hand, and the high, spectacular catches called 'marks'.

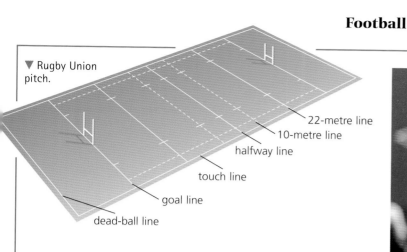

▼ Rugby Union pitch.

22-metre line
10-metre line
halfway line
touch line
goal line
dead-ball line

Gaelic football is a 15-a-side game played mainly in Ireland. It is played with a round ball, and the goal combines rugby posts and a soccer net. In many ways the game resembles Australian rules football. The game features long kicks, high jumps to catch the ball, and plenty of physical contact. Running with the ball is allowed, provided the player 'hops' (bounces) the ball from foot to hand every four steps.

Rugby

The two forms of rugby are running, passing and kicking games, with plenty of hard physical contact. Rugby Union, played 15-a-side, is the more widely played game. It is strongest in the British Isles, France, South Africa, New Zealand and Australia. Rugby League, a 13-a-side game, is played chiefly in Australia and in the north of England, where it began. Both games are played 40 minutes each way.

In both Union and League the main object is to score a try by touching the ball down behind the opponents' goal line. Goals (converted tries), penalty goals and drop goals (dropping the ball and kicking it on the bounce) are scored by kicking the ball over the crossbar. The ball can be kicked forward and thrown from player to player by hand, but it must not be passed in a forward direction.

In Rugby Union the forwards of the two teams battle for the ball, which they then feed back to the scrum-half and then to the fly-half, who together control the pattern of the game. The halves decide whether to gain ground by kicking the ball upfield, or by setting up running and passing moves with the three-quarter backs. In Rugby League, a team is allowed five plays (tackles), after each of which the tackled player taps the ball back to a team-mate with his foot. After the sixth tackle the ball is handed over to the other team.

American football

American football is the national sport of the USA. It is a game of explosive action and much physical contact, so players wear helmets with face guards and padded clothing.

Professional teams have squads of 45 players, but only 11 are allowed on the field at any one time. A game is divided into four 15-minute quarters, but the clock is stopped for a variety of reasons and games usually last 3 hours or more.

A touchdown worth 6 points is scored by taking the ball across the goal line or by catching a pass while in the end zone. The attacking side advances the ball in a series of plays called *downs*. Teams have four downs in which to move the ball at least 10 yards forwards. If they fail to do so, the ball is handed over to their opponents.

The ball is moved by running with it or by passing – one forward pass, usually made by the quarterback, is allowed on each down. Only the ball-carrier may be tackled, but players may obstruct opponents by blocking.

▲ Terrell Davis, star running back of the Denver Broncos, makes another major gain in his team's victory over Green Bay in the 1998 Super Bowl. The Super Bowl is the climax of the American football season, when the two top teams of the National Football League meet to decide the overall champions.

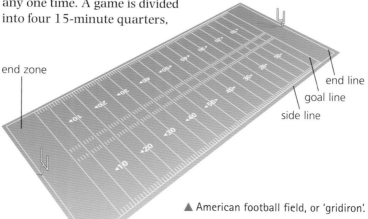

end zone
end line
goal line
side line

▲ American football field, or 'gridiron'.

find out more
Pelé

Forces and pressure

'Force' is the word we use for a push or a pull. A force will make a still object move. It will make a moving object travel faster, more slowly, or in a different direction. Together, two or more forces can make something stretch, squash, bend, twist or turn.

Gravity is a force of attraction – it tries to pull things together. There is a gravitational attraction between all objects. The more mass things have, and the closer they are, the stronger is the gravitational pull between them. The force of gravity between you and the Earth is strong enough to keep you on the ground.

Friction is the force which tries to stop one material sliding over another. If you throw a ball, the ball has to 'slide' through the air. This causes a type of friction called *air resistance*. For cars and other vehicles, air resistance is a nuisance. However, parachutists use air resistance to slow their descent.

If you stretch a rubber band, you feel a force called *tension*. Tension forces support climbers on ropes and goods in shopping bags. They are very useful. They even hold up your clothes! *Compression* (squashing) forces are the opposite of tension forces. They are produced when you lie on a bed, sit on a chair, or just stand on the ground. Without compression forces nothing could ever support your weight.

Scientists measure force in newtons (N). It takes a force of about 5 newtons to switch on a light, and 20 newtons to open a canned drink.

Different kinds of force

Scientists think that there are five kinds of force in the Universe: gravitational, magnetic, electric and two types of nuclear force. You feel a

Pressure

Pressure tells you how concentrated a force is. If the same amount of force is spread across two areas, one large and one small, the pressure acting on the smaller area will be greater than that on the larger area. Pressure is measured in newtons per square metre (N/m^2), also called pascals (Pa).

Pressure from gases like air pushes out in all directions. In liquids like water (and in gases), the pressure gets greater as you go deeper down in the liquid. If divers go too deep under the sea, the water pressure will crush them.

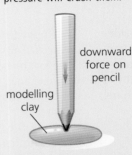
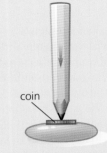

downward force on pencil

modelling clay

coin

▲ When force is applied to a pencil, the point will sink easily into a lump of modelling clay.

▲ The force applied to the pencil here is spread by the coin. The pressure on the modelling clay is less and so it is squashed only a little.

magnetic force if you hold a magnet close to a piece of iron or steel. You can see the effects of an electric force if you pull a comb through your hair and then hold it close to some tiny pieces of paper. Electric and magnetic forces are generally known by a single name – electromagnetic forces.

▼ This sequence of events shows just some of the forces involved when playing on a tree. (**1**) The boy is using the *tension* in the rope to help him climb the tree. (**2**) The boy is exerting a *compression* force by standing on the branch. (**3**) The boy uses *friction* to help him hold onto the branch as he swings. (**4**) The boy's hands slip, and *gravity* pulls him down to the ground.

Forests

A forest is a large area of land covered mainly with trees and undergrowth. Some forests, such as the great Amazon rainforest, have existed for thousands of years. Vast areas of forest have been destroyed by human activity, but others have been planted, and a fifth of the world's land is still covered by forest.

Forests create their own special environment. At ground level they are generally shady and cool, because the crowns of the trees shade the forest floor. The air is still, because the trees shield the forest interior from the full force of the wind. The days are cooler and the nights warmer, making the forest a sheltered place for wildlife.

Types of forest

Forests can grow wherever the temperature rises above 10 °C in summer and the annual rainfall exceeds 200 millimetres. Different climates and soils support different kinds of forest.

Rainforests thrive in the humid tropics. The weather is the same all year round – hot and very rainy. The rainforest has such a dense tangle of vegetation that it is often difficult to distinguish the various layers. Plants, including some orchids, even grow perched on the trunks and branches of trees and fallen logs. There are many different kinds of tree: a small patch of forest may contain over 100 different tree species.

Deciduous forests are found in temperate climates, where it is cool in the winter and warm in the summer. There are many fewer different types of tree than in the rainforest. The main trees are deciduous, which means that they shed their leaves in winter (or in the dry season in some regions). The trees also produce flowers, fruits and nuts at particular times of the year. When the trees are leafless in springtime, the forest floor receives plenty of light, so smaller plants may grow and flower.

Coniferous forest is found further north and higher up mountain slopes than any other kind of forest. The main trees are conifers (cone-bearing trees) such as pines. Most are evergreen (they keep their leaves all year), with needle-like leaves coated in wax to reduce water loss. Conifers can survive drought and the freezing of soil water in winter. Their branches slope downwards, so that snow easily slides off. Some conifer forests have arisen naturally, but others

have been planted by people, in order to grow wood for timber, paper and other uses.

The importance of forests

Forests have important functions. Like all green plants, trees absorb carbon dioxide from the air, and release oxygen. So forests are major suppliers of the oxygen humans and all animals need, and they help stop the levels of carbon dioxide in the air from rising too high. This is important because high levels of carbon dioxide in the air cause global warming. ◗

▼ **The structure of a forest**
In the rainforest shown here, the larger trees form an almost continuous *canopy* over the roof of the forest. A few very tall trees, called *emergents*, grow through the canopy into the sunlight above. Below the canopy smaller trees and young saplings form the *understorey*. Below them are shrubs and briars, and on the *forest floor* a layer of smaller shrubs and plants. Each layer of the forest has its own animal communities.

1	harpy eagle	**6**	sloth
2	macaw	**7**	ocelot
3	spider monkey	**8**	poison frog
4	cock of the rock	**9**	capybara
5	tree boa	**10**	coral snake

Forests

varnishes, dyes, corks, rubber, kapok, insecticides and medicines such as antibiotics.

Vanishing forests

Every year the world consumes 3 billion cubic metres of wood. In Britain and much of north-west Europe, human beings have cut down most of the trees. In tropical regions, an area of rainforest the size of a football pitch is cut down every second.

Many rainforests grow on very poor soils. Most of the goodness of the land is locked up in the plants. When rainforest is cut down and burned, the remaining soil is often too poor to support crops for long. The soil is easily washed away in the tropical rains, and silts up lakes and reservoirs. The area may even turn to desert.

Forests, especially tropical rainforests, contain a huge variety of plants and animals. If forests are cut down at the present rate, around half the world's remaining rainforests will have vanished by the year 2020, with the loss of around one-tenth of all the species on Earth. Scientists and others are campaigning to stop this destruction of the Earth's resources.

find out more
Conservation
Greenhouse effect
Trees and shrubs
Wood

▼ Rot and decay
When trees die or parts of the tree fall, they quickly rot. Woodpeckers drill holes in soft rotting trunks, and bark beetles excavate tunnels under the bark, allowing fungi to enter. Fungi break down the tree's tissues and absorb the nutrients. When the fungi die, they in turn are broken down by bacteria. The dead plant material gradually crumbles into the soil, and the nutrients it contained escape into the soil, to be taken up by new plants.

▲ Autumn in a deciduous forest in Utah, USA. As the leaves die, the chemical that makes leaves green is broken down, and they turn many different colours. By shedding their leaves for the winter or during the dry season, the trees are able to save energy and greatly reduce the amount of water they need.

A forest acts like a giant sponge, absorbing rainfall and only gradually releasing it into rivers. By holding the water back, the forest prevents disastrous flooding further downstream. Forest cover also prevents the soil being eroded (worn away) and silting up rivers and lakes.

Forests provide shelter and food for many animals. Leaves, flowers, fruits, seeds and nuts are food for insects, birds and small mammals, such as squirrels and mice, which in turn are food for larger birds and mammals. The moist forest soil has its own community of worms, centipedes, beetles, ants, and the eggs and larvae of many insects.

Forests provide people with an enormous range of important products. For large areas of the world, firewood is the main source of energy, the only source that people can afford. Wood is used for house frames, shipbuilding, papermaking, packaging, fencing and many other purposes. The fruits and nuts of forest trees provide food and spices. Forest trees also provide oils for cooking and industry, syrups, resins,

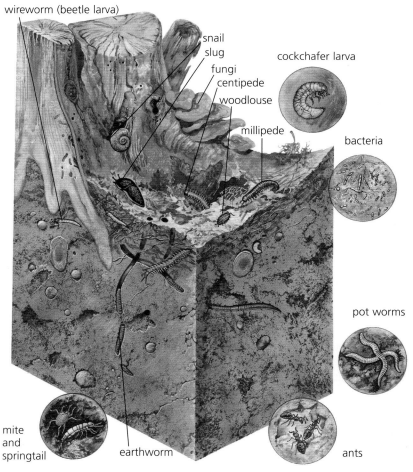

wireworm (beetle larva)
snail
slug
fungi
centipede
woodlouse
cockchafer larva
millipede
bacteria
pot worms
mite and springtail
earthworm
ants

Fossils

Fossils are the remains of animals and plants that died long ago. By studying fossils, we can discover what kinds of animals and plants lived on the Earth many millions of years ago.

Most fossils show us only the hard parts of the ancient animal or plant. These include the materials making up the shells and bones, which do not rot away. The commonest fossils are ancient sea shells. This is because most of the rocks that contain fossils were formed in the sea, and shellfish have always been common. Other sea creatures can also be found quite often.

Types of fossil

The Ordovician and Silurian mudstones (510–412 million years old) contain fossil graptolites, animals which floated near the sea surface. In limestones of that age you can find corals and brachiopods, a group of shellfish that look at first sight like clams, though they were really very different.

In some rocks of Devonian age (412–355 million years ago) fishes are the commonest fossils. In coal-rich areas you are most likely to find plants of the Carboniferous age (355–290 million years ago), such as ferns, from which the coal is formed.

Permian and Triassic rocks (290–205 million years old) were generally formed on land, and fossils are therefore rare. Rocks formed in the Jurassic and Cretaceous seas (205–66 million years ago) are often full of shellfish, such as oysters. They may also contain the bones of sea reptiles. Dinosaur fossils are mainly Jurassic and Cretaceous in age, but they are not often found because dinosaurs lived on land.

Unusual fossils

The rarest and most exciting fossils show us the soft parts of long-dead animals. These include insects trapped in amber, a resin that oozes from certain trees and then dries hard. Every detail of these animals can be seen because their bodies have not decayed at all. Very occasionally, whole mammoths, deep-frozen for thousands of years in the soil of Siberia, are discovered. Their flesh is often preserved very well. We can tell from preserved mammoth hair that these animals were reddish in colour.

Fossilized animal droppings, footprints and burrows are called *trace fossils*. Among the most exciting trace fossils to have been found are dinosaur footprints. Commoner trace fossils include burrows and crawling marks made by ancient sea creatures. These are often the only evidence we have that certain soft-bodied animals existed.

◀ A selection of fossilized ammonites. Ammonites were coiled shellfish related to present-day squids. They lived from the Devonian to the Cretaceous period (400 to 64 million years ago).

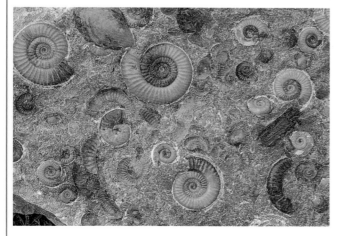

- The word 'fossil' comes from a Latin word meaning 'dug up'.

- Anyone can look for fossils. The best place to look is on a beach, where the waves keep washing away the rock and uncovering new fossils. Other good places include cuttings at the sides of roads or old quarries. But all of these places can be dangerous, so you should always go with an adult.

find out more
Coal
Dinosaurs
Evolution
Geology
Prehistoric life
Rocks and minerals

How fossils are formed

1 When a dead animal sinks to the sea-bed, scavenging animals and bacteria soon remove its flesh.

2 Sediments pile on top and dissolved minerals seep into the remains. Minerals from the water replace the chemicals in the bones.

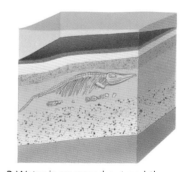

3 Water is squeezed out and the rock becomes hard and compact.

4 Millions of years later the rocks are lifted up and become dry land. Rain, wind or the sea wear them away until the fossil is exposed.

France

France is the largest country in western Europe. It has many different landscapes and ways of life.

Most of Europe's climate types are found within France. Brittany benefits from the warm North Atlantic Drift, and its mild, damp weather contrasts with the varied temperatures of the interior plains such as Alsace. The Mediterranean south has hot, dry summers, and the spiny, deep-rooted plants growing there can resist drought.

Landscape

France's longest river, the Loire, rises in the high plateaux (level ground) of the centre. Here there are extinct volcanoes that form the cone-shaped peaks of the Auvergne. There are also deep gorges where the River Tarn cuts through dry limestone uplands known as the Causses. Smaller uplands include the forested Vosges in the east and the moorlands of Brittany in the north-west. Elsewhere there are wide plains, most extensive in the Paris Basin and in Aquitaine around the city of Bordeaux. High mountains provide the borders with Italy and Spain.

Food and farming

France's large size and variety of physical conditions make it the world's second largest exporter of agricultural goods. A lot of wheat is grown, especially on the large farms of the northern plains, providing flour for the crusty bread the French buy daily. Maize (corn) is grown mainly to feed livestock, and in summer many of the fields are yellow with sunflowers, which provide both food for animals and oil for cooking.

France has some famous breeds of cattle, including the pale-coated Charolais and the rich-brown Limousin, which are exported to many other countries. Dairy cows, most of which feed on the lush pastures of the north-west, produce milk for the cities and for cheeses such as Brie and Camembert, for which France is famous. Roquefort is a cheese made from the milk of sheep.

Vines flourish in many parts of France. The most extensive vineyards are in the south, but some of the best-known wines come from grapes grown on the sunny slopes of Burgundy and (to the north on the River Marne) Champagne. Great skill goes into the blending and maturing of these wines, which are sold throughout the world.

The south also produces many other fruits and vegetables, but irrigation water is needed in the dry summer.

Industry

France possesses only limited resources of coal and other fuels. Huge quantities of electricity (70 per cent of France's needs) are generated by nuclear power stations and from hydroelectric dams in the mountains and on rivers such as the Rhône.

Loss of jobs in steel-making and textiles has created employment problems in the older industrial regions of the north-east. New science-based industries flourish in Toulouse, Grenoble and other cities of the south. Concorde, Airbus, the Ariane space rocket and high-speed trains (TGV) are typical

Map legend

- country boundary
- ◆ capital city
- ■ ● major cities and towns
- main roads
- main railways
- ⊕ main airports
- ▲ high peaks (height in metres)

land height in metres

- 2000–5000
- 1000–2000
- 500–1000
- 200–500
- less than 200
- sea level

• The Tour de France is one of the world's most famous cycle races. The route includes sections in all the mountainous areas of France, where the competitors face long, steep hill climbs.

products of French technical skills. Tourism is also important in the economy.

France's history

Before Roman times the land we now call France was divided into many small kingdoms and tribes. The Romans, who knew the region as Gaul, conquered it in the 1st century BC and held it for 500 years.

The Franks

The name 'France' comes from the tribe of Franks who invaded Gaul in the 5th century AD. The Frankish king Clovis (465–511) defeated the last Roman governor of Gaul, accepted Christianity and established Paris as his capital.

The mightiest early French king was Charlemagne ('Charles the Great') (747–814). His huge empire included all modern France (except Brittany), much of central Europe, and northern Italy. In 800 the Pope crowned him Roman emperor. Although the empire broke up after his death, France was now an important European kingdom.

War and peace

Over the following centuries the French kings spent much of their time fighting rivals, notably the dukes of Normandy and Burgundy and the kings of England. The Hundred Years War fought between the English and French lasted from 1337 to 1453. Inspired by Joan of Arc, the French won.

By 1483 the Burgundians had also been defeated and France's borders were much as they are today. The huge country was one of the richest in Europe. It boasted wonderful cathedrals, such as Chartres, Reims and Notre Dame in Paris, thriving cities and wealthy merchants. Most of the peasants, however, remained desperately poor.

Master of Europe

During the 16th century, France was torn by civil wars between Protestants (Huguenots) and Catholics. The conflict was ended by Henry IV, and during the 17th century France thrived. By the mid-1680s, Louis XIV, who was known as the 'Sun King', was master of Europe. Louis' palace at Versailles was the political and cultural capital of the continent. ◗

▼ Almost one-fifth of the population of France live in the city and suburbs of the capital, Paris. This glass pyramid, loved and hated in equal measure, stands in front of the Louvre, the city's most famous museum.

▲ Beaujolais vineyards in the Rhône valley. The wine industry is an important part of France's economy and each year millions of bottles are exported around the world.

France's strength worried its neighbours, particularly England. Four long wars, between 1702 and 1783, left France tired, bankrupt and without many of its overseas territories. The French people were fed up with the corrupt and unfair way they were governed.

Revolution and war

In 1789 France exploded into revolution. In the name of 'liberty, equality and fraternity', the people swept away the old government and set up a parliament (the National Assembly). In 1793 they executed Louis XVI and his wife, Marie Antoinette. During a bloodthirsty Reign of Terror, 17,000 nobles and other 'enemies of the people' were executed.

In an effort to stop the Revolution spreading, other European states invaded France. The French drove them back and under Emperor Napoleon I (Napoleon Bonaparte) conquered most of western Europe. The success of the French people spread the ideas of fair government and human rights across the continent.

Industry and empire

In the 19th century France underwent political turmoil, especially in Paris. But in the regions industrial towns

▶ A painting depicting the storming of the Bastille on 14 July 1789, the huge prison in Paris. The act of capturing it symbolized the destruction of the once-powerful monarchy. France's national day is celebrated on 14 July each year.

expanded, linked by a network of railways, and business people grew richer.

French adventurers conquered a huge overseas empire. By 1900 the French flag flew over much of Indo-China, north and west Africa, and many Pacific islands. Colonial trade added to France's wealth. However, France's position at home was threatened by the creation of the enormous German empire. In 1870–1871 France was invaded by German armies. Again, in 1914, the two countries went to war.

The 20th century

The early 20th century was a nightmare for France. World War I devastated large areas of the country and left the people exhausted and dispirited. The Great Depression hit France heavily. Poverty and unemployment rose and

governments struggled to keep control. In 1945, after four years of German occupation during World War II, the French seemed a broken people.

However, with US economic help, France's new leaders brought about an 'economic miracle'. Workers' incomes doubled in 20 years and the country grew strong and rich again. It set aside the past by giving independence to its colonies and working closely with Germany to found the European Union.

Not everyone was happy with France's conservative society and government. Students led riots in 1968 and the French Communist Party was prominent in opposition. After 1968 France became a more liberal society and by the 1990s it was once again a wealthy, powerful and respected nation.

• General Charles de Gaulle (1890–1970) fought in World War I, and from his base in England led the Free French during World War II. In 1958 he was seen as the only man capable of uniting the nation and was elected president. Until 1969 he played a major part in the creation of modern France.

find out more

Canada
Celts
Charlemagne
Curie, Marie
Europe
European Union
Holy Roman Empire
Joan of Arc
Louis XIV
Middle Ages
Napoleon Bonaparte
Normans
Romans
Twentieth-century
  history
World War I
World War II
*See also Countries fact
  file, page 623*

◀ Students demonstrate against the government in 1968. Many French felt that President de Gaulle had lost touch with the young and underprivileged.

Frank, Anne

Born 1929 in
Frankfurt, Germany
Died 1945 aged 15

Anne Frank was a brave Jewish girl who wrote a diary while in hiding from the Nazis during World War II. Anne died in a Nazi concentration camp, but her diary survived and her story has moved many millions of readers.

After the rise of Hitler in Germany, Anne Frank's father, Otto, moved his young Jewish family to Amsterdam in the Netherlands. They lived happily there until the Nazis invaded in 1942. When the family heard of the Nazi plans to send all Jewish people to concentration camps, they went into hiding in some sealed-off rooms at the top of Otto Frank's former warehouse, with another Jewish family. Dutch friends smuggled them tiny rations of food.

In her diary, Anne Frank wrote about daily events and the cramped conditions in which they lived. She also wrote of her longing to be outside in the fresh air again. In spite of everything, she always seemed to remain hopeful, writing 'I still believe that people are really good at heart'.

On 4 August 1944, after two years in hiding, the secret rooms were broken into and the Franks were taken to concentration camps. Anne's mother died in one camp. Anne and her sister both died of typhus in another camp, shortly before the war ended. Their father survived and published Anne's diary, which had been found by friends, in 1947.

• Anne Frank's diary has been translated into over 30 languages and the Franks' hiding place in Amsterdam has been turned into a museum.

find out more
Hitler, Adolf
Holocaust
Jews
World War II

▲ Anne Frank, sitting in front of the diary that was to touch the hearts of millions of people across the world.

Frogs and toads

• There are about 2600 different kinds of frogs and toads. They live in moist habitats throughout the tropical and temperate areas.

Frogs and toads are amphibians, like newts and salamanders, and like them, they spend the early part of their lives in water. The main differences between frogs and toads and other amphibians is that they do not have tails and that they have powerful hind legs for swimming and jumping on land.

▶ This fire-bellied toad shows its bright underside to an enemy to signal 'red for danger'. The poison in its skin tastes so unpleasant that other animals soon learn not to touch it.

Frogs and toads are all good swimmers and on land most move about by leaping in a zigzag pattern. Many are active mainly at night. All adult frogs and toads feed on other small animals. Some catch their prey with long, sticky tongues, others leap and grab insects in their mouths. Some have sucker pads on their toes which make them very good climbers. There is no very clear distinction between animals called frogs and animals called toads. True toads usually have drier, wartier skins than frogs.

Frogs and toads have small lungs, but they also breathe partly through their moist, soft skins. If their skin were to dry out, they would suffocate.

In the breeding season males call to attract their mates. Each kind of frog or toad has its own croaking or trilling song and many males have throat pouches which they can blow out to increase the volume of sound.

Frogs and toads are preyed on by many other animals for food. Some protect themselves by camouflage – their colouring matches their background so they cannot be seen easily. They also have powerful poison glands in their skin, and some of these are brightly coloured to warn enemies to steer clear. The poison-dart frogs of South America have such powerful poison in their skin that the native people used to tip their arrows with it.

• You will find a feature box on the life cycle of a frog under Amphibians.

find out more
Amphibians
Camouflage
Newts and salamanders

Freud, Sigmund *see* Psychologists • **Friction** *see* Forces and pressure

Fruit

We most commonly use the word 'fruit' for types of fruit that we can eat, such as apples, oranges and pears. However, scientists also use the word to describe the part of a flowering plant where the seeds develop. The fruit encloses and protects the seeds as they develop, then helps to spread them when they are ripe. Different kinds of fruit spread their seeds in different ways.

Fruits we eat, like apples, oranges and bananas, are called 'soft fruits'. Other fruits form dry or papery containers round the seeds. These are 'dry fruits'.

Animals spread the seeds of some fruits. They eat the sweet flesh of soft fruits, and drop the seeds inside, or else the seeds pass through the animal's gut without being digested and fall to the ground in the droppings. Fruits that are sticky or have tiny hooks ('burs') hitch rides by sticking to an animal's fur or feathers.

Many plants use the wind to spread their fruits and seeds. Sycamore, maple and ash all have winged fruits, while dandelions and thistles have parachutes of hairs. Poppies and orchids produce tiny seeds, light enough to float on the breeze when they are shaken from the fruit.

Plants growing near a river or the sea, like the coconut palm, may use water currents to carry their fruits. Other fruits split or burst open to

▲ Stages in the growth of a tomato from a fertilized flower. After fertilization, the flower petals wither and drop off, and the ovary (the part containing the seeds) swells into a round green fruit. When the seeds are ready, the tomato ripens from green to red and develops a sweet flavour.

flower

fruit

release ripe seeds. On a hot day you may hear the popping broom pods as they suddenly twist open and fling out their seeds.

Growing fruit

Different kinds of fruit grow in different climates. Fruit like apples, pears, plums and raspberries are grown in temperate regions, where summers are warm but the winter is chilly. Oranges, lemons and other citrus fruits grow best where there are warm summers and mild, wet winters. Fruits that grow best in the hot, wet tropics include mangoes, avocados, pineapples, bananas and papayas. It is sometimes possible to grow tropical fruits in other climates, but only in a greenhouse.

• Nuts are not soft fruits, but they contain rich food and many animals eat them or bury them to eat later.

• 'Vegetables' like tomatoes, cucumbers and peppers are really fruits, and contain seeds inside.

find out more
Flowering plants
Plants
Vegetables

▲ Oranges are a kind of soft fruit. The juicy flesh and the outer skin develop from the ovary of the flower. The 'pips' in the centre are the seeds.

▲ Some fruits are winged, like this field maple. Such fruits are called 'keys' and they spin through the air like helicopters.

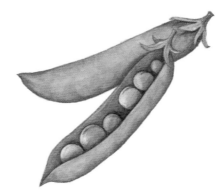

▲ Pea pods are a type of dry fruit. They dry out as they ripen, then split to release the seeds.

▲ Strawberries are 'false fruits', because the fleshy part that we eat is not strictly the fruit, but a swollen stem.

Funerals

Saying goodbye to a person who has died is very important. A funeral is the last ceremony (rite) of respect by families and friends, and everyone tries to be there.

Religions teach that death is not the end of life and that it is wrong to be completely miserable when a person dies. So funerals are often a mixture of sadness and hope, loss and celebration.

Funeral traditions

There are different traditions about what should be done with the body of a dead person. Hindus, Buddhists and Sikhs prefer cremation (burning). Hindus like to scatter the ashes of the person on the River Ganges if this is possible. They believe that all life is one and that returning the remains of a person to a sacred river is a good end for them.

Jews and Muslims prefer to bury their dead. Jews teach that everyone should have the simplest coffin available because all men and women are equal before God. For the same reason Muslims are buried in simple white robes. Jews are buried facing Jerusalem and Muslims face towards Mecca.

Christians nowadays can choose burial or cremation. Funeral services are held in a church or in a chapel of remembrance attached to a cemetery or a crematorium. For those of no religion, a secular funeral may celebrate the life of the deceased person. Various humanist and other associations will help organize this. The traditional Irish wake, a social gathering of relatives and friends, comes from the custom of a 'wake', or watch, over the body of the dead person.

find out more
Religions

▼ Tombs are special places for the burial of the dead. They can be underground vaults, a chamber cut into rock or a monument to house a great leader. These terracotta soldiers were made to guard the tomb of Zheng, the first Qin emperor. The tomb, at Mount Li in China, was huge — big enough for 8000 of these life-size soldiers.

Fungi

Fungi are an important group of living things. They get their food by breaking down the tissues of living or dead plants or animals. Many fungi can only be seen with a microscope. A few, such as mushrooms and toadstools, grow much larger.

Most fungi grow as networks of tiny threads called *hyphae*. These spread through the material on which the fungus is growing, and absorb food. Fungi reproduce by way of microscopic *spores*, which act like tiny seeds. They are produced in a part of the fungus called the *fruiting body*.

Mushrooms and toadstools

Mushrooms and toadstools are the fruiting bodies of some kinds of fungus. They are usually umbrella-shaped, with a thick stalk and a broad cap. Beneath the cap there are hanging curtains called gills or pores, where the spores develop. Many kinds of mushroom are edible, but only two are grown widely for food. There is no easy way to tell a poisonous mushroom from an edible one, so it is safest to eat only ones from the shops.

Fungi in the soil

One vital role of fungi is to decompose (rot) dead plants, animals and their wastes. Fungi break the dead matter down into chemicals that are recycled back into the soil. Other fungi are essential partners in the growth of trees and other plants. They live in or around their roots in a mass called a *mycorrhiza*. The roots protect the fungi, which in turn provide food for the plants.

Helpful fungi
Yeasts are a type of fungus used in making bread, beer and wine. Other fungi produce penicillin and other antibiotics, which attack bacteria harmful to humans.

• There are about 70,000 known species of fungus. Although they are plant-like, fungi are usually put in their own kingdom, the Mycota.

• Some fungi grow so fast that a single spore can produce more than 1 km of hyphae in 24 hours.

◀ Four of the many kinds of fungus.
1 Field mushroom 2 Shaggy ink cap
3 Leaf rust 4 Bracket fungus.

find out more
Algae
Plants

Fur *see* Hair

Furniture

Furniture is designed to be useful and attractive. Most pieces of furniture serve a single purpose – for instance, a bench is for sitting on and a cupboard is for storing things. However, some furniture performs more than one function – a sofa bed, for example. Other furniture is designed to meet a particular need, such as a cabinet for a television.

- Antique furniture is furniture that is many years old and has artistic value. Most collectors expect it to be at least 100 years old.

find out more
Designers
Household equipment
Materials
Wood

▼ Furniture designers today choose clean, simple shapes, often using new materials. The furniture chosen for this bathroom, in a penthouse flat in London, England, is an extreme example of modern, almost futuristic, furniture design.

We use furniture every day, so it needs to be comfortable. The designers of school furniture design chairs and work surfaces to fit children of different sizes: sitting on a chair that is too big or too small can be tiring. But furniture can also be too comfortable; if it does not support the body properly, for example, it can cause back pain in later life.

Furniture makers use wood, cane, glass, metal, plastic and a variety of other materials. Strong, lightweight furniture can be made from such materials as hollow metal tubing, laminated woods and fibreglass. Foam rubber and new spring devices are used in upholstery.

Styles around the world

Furniture has developed differently throughout the world, depending on the needs of the people in a particular region. In traditional Chinese furniture, for instance, the wooden joints fit together tightly without glue, screws or pegs, allowing the wood to expand and contract as temperature changes. The Japanese traditionally use few pieces of furniture. Rooms often include movable partitions for creating different arrangements of space, so furniture has to be small and portable. In the past, people sat on the floor and slept on mats, so beds and chairs were unnecessary.

▶ FLASHBACK ◀

The first pieces of furniture were made in prehistoric times from slabs of stone and chunks of wood. By 2000 BC, Egyptians were making finely carved furniture that was beautiful as well as useful. Egyptian styles influenced later civilizations of the ancient world, including the Greeks and Romans, who used marble, bronze, terracotta, ivory and bone in their furniture. For thousands of years all fine furniture was designed to suit the tastes of the nobility and other wealthy people.

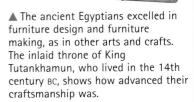

▲ The ancient Egyptians excelled in furniture design and furniture making, as in other arts and crafts. The inlaid throne of King Tutankhamun, who lived in the 14th century BC, shows how advanced their craftsmanship was.

In Western Europe during the later Middle Ages (1100–1500) most people worked outdoors, and only had basic furniture; chairs and beds were for the privileged rich. Since that time, many different furniture styles have been introduced. As tastes changed and furniture makers learnt new methods, furniture became lighter and more elegant. Designers sometimes revived and adapted earlier styles to suit the times. By the end of the 18th century, some of the best designers had become famous, and their designs were widely copied.

As ordinary people's standard of living improved from about 1800 onwards, the demand for furniture grew. Eventually this demand was met by mass-producing furniture in factories. Most 20th-century furniture is machine-made.

Galaxies

Our Sun and all the stars you can see in the night sky belong to a giant family of stars that we call our Galaxy. It contains around 100,000 million stars. The view we have of the Galaxy from inside it is known as the Milky Way. Beyond our own Galaxy, there are countless other galaxies scattered all through the Universe.

If you could go far out in space to look at our Galaxy, you would see a flat, circular shape with a bulge in the middle and a pattern of spiral arms. Between the stars there are giant clouds of gas and dust, some of them shining brightly and some dark.

The Milky Way

On a dark night, the Milky Way looks like a hazy band of light stretching across the sky. You can look at it through binoculars or a small telescope on a clear night, and see that it is the light from vast numbers of faint stars.

The Milky Way circles the whole sky. You can see parts of it wherever you are on the Earth. In the north, the constellations (groups of stars) it goes through include Auriga (the Charioteer), Cassiopeia, and Cygnus (the Swan). Dark patches in the Milky Way are really clouds of dust cutting out the light from the stars. The most famous one, 'the Coalsack', is in the Southern Cross.

Kinds of galaxy

Our Galaxy is a *spiral galaxy*, which measures about 100,000 light years across. (One light year is equivalent to 9.5 million million kilometres, the distance that light travels in a year.) Many large galaxies have beautiful spiral shapes. *Elliptical galaxies* are just flattened balls of stars. Another kind of galaxy is irregular, and has no particular shape.

Many of these galaxies send out strong radio waves that can be picked up by radio telescopes. Galaxies tend to cluster together in space. Our own Galaxy belongs to a cluster called the Local Group.

Other galaxies

The nearest galaxies to Earth are the two Magellanic Clouds. They look like little clouds of stars and can be seen only from the southern hemisphere. They are about 180,000 light years away. The biggest galaxy in our Local Group is called the Andromeda Galaxy. It can just be seen by eye as a misty patch. It is a spiral galaxy, 130,000 light years across and just over 2 million light years away.

• A quasar (quasi-stellar radio source) is something that sends out radio waves and looks like (but is not) a star. Quasars are embedded in galaxies. The most distant ones are more than 10 billion light years away. They shine so brightly that they swamp the fainter light of their parent galaxy.

▼ An image of the Whirlpool Galaxy, which is formed from a separate spiral galaxy (NGC 5194) and its companion. The two are linked by a faint bridge of gas. The Whirlpool Galaxy is around 13 million light years away from Earth.

▼ An image of the elliptical galaxy M87, which is 50 million light years away from Earth. M87 is believed to have a black hole at its centre. The jet to the side, which leads into the centre of the galaxy, is probably caused by gas and stars falling into the black hole.

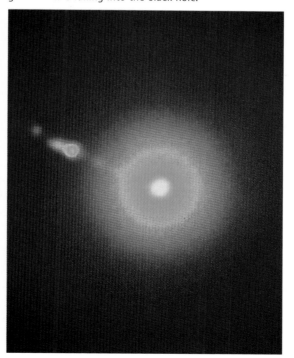

find out more
Astronomy
Black holes
Constellations
Stars
Telescopes
Universe

Galilei, Galileo

Born 1564 in Pisa, Italy
Died 1642 aged 77

Galileo Galilei (or simply Galileo, as he is usually known) was one of the leading figures of the Renaissance. This was a period of exciting change in Europe, when many discoveries in science and the arts were made.

Galileo was supposed to study medicine at university, but he was much more interested in mathematics and physics. He abandoned medicine and, at the age of 25, became professor of mathematics.

In 1609 Galileo heard news of the invention of the telescope in the Netherlands, and he set about building a small one for himself. When he used it to study the sky, he soon made some very important discoveries. He saw four moons circling the planet Jupiter, craters on the surface of the Moon, spots on the Sun, and rings around Saturn.

From his studies of Venus, he became convinced that all the planets, including Earth, moved around the Sun. This went against the thinking at the time, which was that all the planets

and the Sun travelled around the Earth. The Christian Church believed God had created the Earth at the centre of the Universe, and punished anyone who said otherwise. When the astronomer Copernicus had published his ideas about the Sun-centred Universe 20 years before Galileo was born, his book was officially banned by the Church.

Galileo's views on the subject and the books he wrote landed him in serious trouble with the Church. He was forced to say he did not agree with Copernicus in order to avoid torture or even execution. But, even though he said this in public, he never changed his real belief.

◀ It was not until 1992 that the Church finally acknowledged that it had been wrong to condemn Galileo for his theories about the Solar System.

find out more
Astronomy
Copernicus, Nicolas
Renaissance
Solar System
Telescopes

Gandhi, Mahatma

Born 1869 in Porbandar, India
Died 1948 aged 78

Mahatma Gandhi led the Indian people in their struggle for independence from British rule. Many Indians think of him as the father of modern India.

• Although his real name was Mohandas Gandhi, he was known as Mahatma Gandhi. 'Mahatma' means 'great soul'.

• Gandhi believed that peoples and nations should be self-sufficient. He set an example by devoting part of each day to spinning home-made cloth.

Mohandas Karamchand Gandhi was 24 years old and working as a lawyer when he went to South Africa to work on a court case. He ended up staying for 18 years as he tried to help his fellow countrymen in South Africa in their struggle against the racial discrimination they suffered.

Gandhi returned to India in 1914 and before long he emerged as the leader of the Indian National Congress Party. The party's aim was to make India independent from Britain. Even though all the protests Gandhi led were peaceful, he was still imprisoned many times by the British.

During the long campaign for independence, Gandhi struggled in vain to overcome the growing gap between the Hindu and Muslim populations of India. Eventually these differences led to the creation of the separate Muslim state of Pakistan in 1947. India and Pakistan both became independent from Britain in that year but there continued to be explosions of violence between Hindus and the Muslims who were left in India. Gandhi appealed for peace, hoping that the two sides could work out a way of living together. His dream was cut short when he was killed by a Hindu extremist in January 1948.

▼ In 1930 Gandhi walked 400 kilometres to the seashore, where he picked up some natural salt of his own as a protest against the British ruling that Indian people had to pay tax on the salt they used.

find out more
British empire
India
Pakistan

Gases, liquids and solids

Everything around us is a gas, a liquid or a solid. These are the three states of matter. The three states seem very different, but substances can change from one to another when heated or cooled.

Every material is made from tiny particles, called atoms and molecules. The way in which these particles stick together and move determines whether something is a solid, a liquid or a gas. Each state has its own special features.

The states of matter

At the temperatures and pressures normally encountered on Earth, most substances are found in one particular state. Iron, for example, is a solid, while oxygen is a gas. However, iron can be heated in a furnace until it becomes a liquid, and oxygen can be made liquid at low temperatures and high pressures.

A *solid* has shape and strength. You can pick it up and turn it around. If you stretch, squash or twist a solid, it resists the forces that are trying to change its shape. It behaves like this because its particles (atoms or molecules) are held together by strong forces of attraction. The particles move, but only by vibrating. The hotter the solid, the faster its particles vibrate.

A *liquid* does not have shape or strength like a solid. It flows and takes up the shape of its container. It offers little resistance to stretching and twisting, but it does resist squeezing. For example, you cannot force a cork into a bottle

▼ The particles in any substance move around in all directions. In a solid they stay fairly close together. In a liquid the particles move around more freely, and in a gas they move around even more than in a liquid.

▶ At room temperature carbon dioxide is a gas, but if compressed it can be turned into a liquid. If the liquid is then allowed to expand, it freezes to a snow-like powder called *dry ice*. At room temperature the dry ice sublimes (turns directly from a solid to a vapour). The vapour is heavier than air, so it pours, like water.

that is filled to the brim. A liquid behaves like this because its particles, although close together and vibrating, are free to tumble over each other, like grains of rice in a sack.

A *gas*, such as air, does not have shape, strength or a fixed volume. It completely fills whatever container it is in. It behaves like this because its particles have enough speed to escape from the forces trying to hold them together. They whizz around, constantly knocking into each other and the container walls. These collisions put pressure on the container. If you heat a gas, its pressure increases. The particles move faster, so their collisions have a stronger effect.

Ice, water and steam

Water is the only substance that is commonly found as a solid, a liquid and a gas. Below 0 °C, it takes the form of solid ice, with its molecules held together in a rigid pattern. When heated, the molecules begin to break free from each other, and the ice melts to become liquid water. Once liquid, the water starts to *evaporate* – faster molecules escape from its surface to form a gas called water vapour. When water is heated to 100 °C, under normal atmospheric conditions, it evaporates so rapidly that big vapour bubbles form in it – the water boils.

Floating
Different substances have different *densities* – a certain volume of one substance has a different weight from the same volume of another. A litre of oil, for example, weighs less than a litre of water. One substance can float on another if it is less dense. This is why oil and wood float on water.

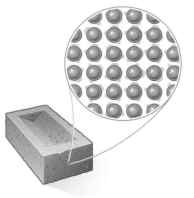

solid

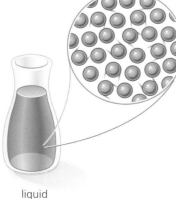

liquid

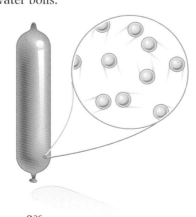

gas

find out more
Air
Atoms and molecules
Forces and pressure
Heat
Hydrogen
Ice
Metals
Nitrogen
Oxygen
Water

Gems and jewellery

Gemstones (or 'gems' for short) are beautiful, rare and hard-wearing materials. Most gemstones, for example diamonds and rubies, are single crystals of a mineral. Others, such as pearls and amber, come from plants or animals and are known as organic gemstones. Because most gems have a sparkling and transparent appearance, people have used them throughout history to make beautiful items of jewellery.

◄ An insect has been trapped in this piece of amber, an organic gemstone made from the sticky resin of pine or fir trees. Long ago, the oozing resin flowed over the insect and hardened around it.

It is possible to manufacture some gems by imitating the conditions under which they were formed in the Earth's crust. Large synthetic rubies are used in lasers. Graphite, another form of carbon, can be heated to very high temperatures and pressures to produce diamonds for use in industrial tools.

- The largest pearl in the world was found inside a giant clam in the Philippines in 1934. The Pearl of Laozi weighs 6.37 kg and is valued at over $33 million.

- Jewellery is sometimes worn to protect the wearer against danger or bad luck. A Christian person might wear a disc with a picture of St Christopher, the saint who is believed to protect travellers.

find out more
Crystals
Diamonds
Rocks and minerals

▼ These village children in the state of Gujarat, northern India, are dressed in traditional costume. They are adorned with many different items of jewellery, particularly earrings and bracelets. In India, jewellery is usually worn to indicate a person's wealth and status.

Most gems are unusual forms of quite common minerals. Quartz is a common mineral that forms part of many rocks. A perfect quartz crystal may contain minute traces of iron, making it into the purple gemstone amethyst or a yellow variety known as citrine. Traces of impurities can transform corundum, another common mineral, into coloured gems like blue sapphires and red rubies. Emeralds and aquamarines are simply different-coloured forms of the mineral beryl. What makes these gemstones precious is that they are perfect single crystals. The chemical composition and the arrangement of atoms of each crystal are so perfectly ordered that the gemstone is transparent.

Organic gemstones

Pearls are organic gemstones that are sometimes formed inside the shells of certain kinds of shellfish, such as oysters and freshwater mussels. The shellfish line their shells with mother-of-pearl, which is a special type of chalk. If a piece of grit or other foreign object becomes trapped inside the shell, the shellfish coats it with layers of mother-of-pearl to form a pearl. Tiny beads of mother-of-pearl can be deliberately inserted into the shells of shellfish to produce cultured pearls. These are mainly produced in Japan and Australia. Amber, another organic gemstone, is the fossilized remains of resin, produced long ago by a pine or fir tree.

Jewellery
People have worn jewellery since prehistoric times, when objects from nature, such as shells, bones or feathers, were used as personal decoration. Most jewellery is worn on the body – earrings, finger and toe rings, nose studs, bracelets and necklaces. Other types, such as brooches and buckles, are fastened to clothing. Jewellery can be made from a wide variety of materials, ranging from inexpensive ones such as seeds, wood and plastic, to precious gems such as sapphires and emeralds.

One use of jewellery is as simple decoration; costume jewellery, for example, is worn to complement clothes and to look fashionable. Jewellery may also be worn to send a message about the wearer – as a symbol of their status. In Canada, engineers may wear an iron ring to show that they have qualified. In many cultures, married people choose to wear a ring on a particular finger. A monarch may have splendid jewellery to indicate the importance of his or her position. Jewellery made from precious gems may be worn to show people how wealthy the wearer is. Such precious jewellery may also be worn in order to keep it safe.

Genes *see* Genetics

Genetics

The young of all living things are similar to their parents. A mother rabbit always has baby rabbits; apple seeds always grow into apple trees. Children inherit characteristics from their parents. Genetics is the study of how these characteristics pass from one generation to the next.

▼ Identical twins (below) look very alike because they have the same genetic material. They both grow from a single egg that splits after it has been fertilized. Non-identical twins look less alike: they grow from different eggs and do not have the same genetic material.

Different kinds of animal or plant are obviously different from one another. But there are also smaller differences between animals or plants of the same kind. Pansy flowers, for example, can be many different colours, while female spiders are bigger than males. Some of these differences are due to *heredity*. Heredity is the inheritance of characteristics from our parents.

Environmental influence

Not all of an individual's characteristics are inherited. Some things about us are purely the result of our environment and upbringing. Reading and writing, for example, are things that we learn. We also have characteristics that result from a combination of both inheritance and environment. Our body shape is partly due to heredity, but how much we eat can have a major influence on it.

Chromosomes and genes

Characteristics are passed on from parents to their offspring through structures called *chromosomes*. These are found inside the cells that make up the body. Each cell carries inside it a complete blueprint of the whole plant or animal.

There are a number of chromosomes in a cell, and they are arranged in pairs, one from each parent. Different animals and plants have different numbers of chromosomes – humans, for example, have 46 chromosomes arranged in 23 pairs.

Arranged along the length of each chromosome, like beads on a necklace, are units called *genes*. Each gene carries information about a particular characteristic of the plant or animal. A human gene, for example, might carry information about eye or hair colour. More complicated features such as body shape are the result of many genes working together.

Every chromosome in a cell is different. But the chromosomes of a pair carry genes for the same characteristics. So for each characteristic we have two genes.

Genes produce the different characteristics of an animal or plant by controlling the making of proteins. There are thousands of different proteins, each with an important job in the body. Each gene controls the making of one or a small number of these proteins. Which genes your cells have influences which proteins are produced.

Passing on genes

A new animal or plant is made by the joining together of two special cells, called *sex cells*, one

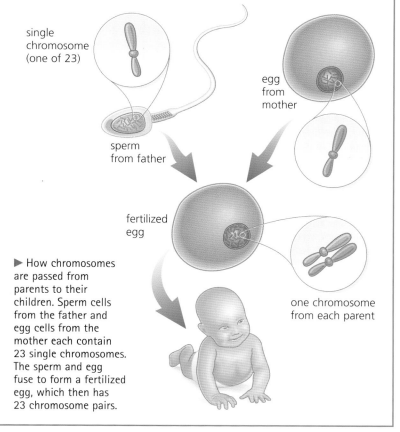

single chromosome (one of 23)

sperm from father

egg from mother

fertilized egg

one chromosome from each parent

▶ How chromosomes are passed from parents to their children. Sperm cells from the father and egg cells from the mother each contain 23 single chromosomes. The sperm and egg fuse to form a fertilized egg, which then has 23 chromosome pairs.

◀ Genes are made from a chemical called *DNA*. Each gene is one section of an enormously long DNA molecule. DNA is like a long ladder, twisted into a spiral. The 'rungs' of the ladder carry coded information that body cells can use to make proteins.

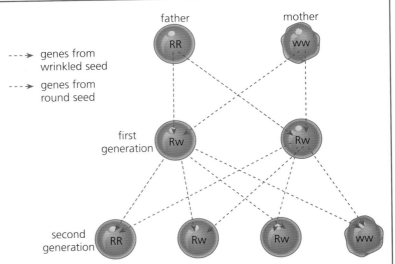

- - - ▸ genes from wrinkled seed
- - - ▸ genes from round seed

▲ Breeding wrinkled-seed pea plants with round-seed pea plants. The offspring from these plants produce only round seeds. But if two of the offspring plants are bred together, they produce a mixture of round and wrinkled seeds, with about three times as many round seeds as wrinkled seeds. The symbols inside the peas show the gene pairs in the plants in each generation. The round-seed gene, R, is dominant over the wrinkled-seed gene, w.

from each parent. Sex cells are different from all other cells in the body, in that they do not have a complete set of chromosomes. Each sex cell contains only half the normal number of chromosomes, one from each chromosome pair. When two sex cells join, the resulting cell (which becomes the new animal or plant) has the normal number of chromosomes – half from the mother and half from the father.

find out more
Biotechnology
Cells
Proteins
Sex and reproduction

Dominant genes

The characteristics we inherit are passed on through pairs of genes. But if we have two genes for each characteristic, which one does the body use? Or does it use both?

Of the two genes we inherit for any characteristic, one of them is usually *dominant* over the other. For example, in pea plants, there is a gene that controls whether the pea seeds are smooth or wrinkled. A plant with a smooth-seed gene from each parent will have smooth seeds, and a plant with a wrinkled-seed gene from each parent will produce wrinkled seeds. But the smooth-seed gene is dominant over the wrinkled seed gene. So if a plant inherits a smooth-seed gene from one parent and a wrinkled-seed gene from the other, it will produce only smooth seeds.

This dominance of one gene in a pair over another means that animals and plants carry within their chromosomes many 'hidden' genes. These do not show as characteristics because they are masked by a dominant gene.

Genetic engineering

Scientists' improved understanding of genetics has made it possible to 'engineer' living cells to give them useful properties. For example, microbes (tiny, single-celled creatures such as bacteria and yeasts) can be modified (changed) to produce medically useful vaccines, hormones and other chemicals that are normally made only in the human body.

Genetic engineering has many important uses, but many people are worried by it. They do not like the idea that one day babies may be 'designed' to have specially chosen characteristics.

▶ Dolly the sheep, born in 1997, was the first large animal to be cloned from an adult. A cell from a Dorset sheep (Dolly's mother) was injected into an unfertilized sheep's egg that had had its nucleus removed. The two cells were fused using a spark of electricity. The new cell was placed in the womb of a third sheep, where it grew into Dolly, who had exactly the same genetic material as her mother. Dolly herself developed a number of health problems, and had to be put down in 2003.

Geology

The Earth is nearly 5 billion years old. The science of geology tries to explain the history of planet Earth – how it was first formed and how it has changed over time.

Geologists (scientists who study the Earth) realized a long time ago that the Earth was very ancient. For example, they could see the great changes that had taken place through time by studying fossils. The Earth is still changing all the time as new rocks are being formed, for example when volcanoes erupt and when rivers deposit layers of particles (sediment).

Dating rocks

Rocks that are deposited in layers, for example sedimentary rocks, can be dated using a method called *relative dating*. The layers are often made up of different minerals and may contain fossils. Assuming that the oldest layers of rock are at the bottom and that the youngest are at the top, geologists work out the age of the rocks from the slight differences in their contents.

However, rocks that are folded or crumbled, or that do not have layers in the first place, cannot be dated in this way. They require *absolute dating* techniques. Many of these techniques measure the radioactive material in the rocks. Granite, for example, contains radioactive material that decays at a constant rate. By measuring the radioactive material left in the rock, it is possible to say when the rock was formed. This method can even find out the exact age of Moon rocks and meteorites.

Geological time

The Earth's geological history involves such enormous amounts of time that they cannot be measured in years. Instead, geological time is divided into individual eras, many millions of years long. A jump from one era to the next is marked by a major change in the type of living things found on Earth. Each era is divided into geological *periods*, which are marked by smaller changes in the animal and plant life.

Geologists

Many geologists specialize in particular subject areas. *Stratigraphers* study the Earth's history by looking at different rock layers. *Palaeontologists* use fossils to help them study ancient plant and animal life. *Geophysicists* study earthquakes, volcanoes and the Earth's magnetic field.

▼ The chart illustrates the Earth's geological history, and the types of fossil found in rocks from different periods

Era	Period	Epoch	Evolution and events
CAINOZOIC 'time of recent life'	QUATERNARY	Holocene Pleistocene	The Great Ice Age Early humans appear
	TERTIARY	Pliocene Miocene Oligocene Eocene Palaeocene	Many mammals appear Alpine earth movements create Alps, Himalayas and Rockies
MESOZOIC 'time of middle life'	CRETACEOUS		Dinosaurs die out Chalk deposited
	JURASSIC		Many dinosaurs
	TRIASSIC		First dinosaurs and mammals
PALAEOZOIC 'time of ancient life'	PERMIAN		Continents move together to form the giant landmass Pangaea
	CARBONIFEROUS		Great coal swamp forests
	DEVONIAN		Caledonian earth movements Ferns and fishes
	SILURIAN		First land plants
	ORDOVICIAN		Animals without backbones
	CAMBRIAN		Trilobites First shellfishes
PROTEROZOIC 'time of first life'	PRECAMBRIAN		First jellyfishes and worms Algae

Millions of years ago: 2, 66, 135, 205, 250, 290, 355, 412, 435, 510, 550

find out more
Earth
Fossils
Mountains
Prehistoric life
Rocks and minerals

Geometry

One way of deciding whether a square is a square, for example, is to look for features (properties) that all squares have. This way of looking at shapes and figures, such as squares, is called geometry. It is a branch of mathematics.

Geometry looks at the properties of two-dimensional figures such as squares and triangles, and three-dimensional ones such as pyramids and cubes. One property of all squares, for example, is that the diagonals of a square (lines drawn from corner to opposite corner) always cut each other exactly in two, and the two diagonals are exactly the same length.

Other properties of figures, such as their areas and the relationships between their angles, are also important in geometry.

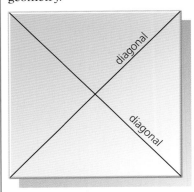

Symmetry

A common property of figures is symmetry, where a figure can be divided by lines to produce two or more exactly similar parts. The diagonal line across a

square described earlier is called the *line of symmetry*. It divides the square into two triangles of exactly the same shape and size. When the two parts of a divided figure have the same shape, size and position, this is known as *bilateral* ('two-sided') *symmetry*. A square also has *rotational symmetry* because it looks the same if you rotate it by half a turn.

◀ Some three-dimensional figures.

cube

sphere

cone

◀ Some two-dimensional shapes.

triangle (3 sides)

pentagon (5 sides)

decagon (10 sides)

circle (infinite number of sides)

◀ These triangles are named according to the size of their angles.

right-angled triangle

obtuse-angled triangle

acute-angled triangle

Shapes and angles

It is usual to name two-dimensional shapes by the number of sides they have. Triangles have three sides, quadrilaterals have four; then come pentagons, hexagons, heptagons, octagons, nonagons, decagons, and so on. A circle has an infinite number of sides.

In two dimensions, there are regular polygons (shapes with all the sides and all the angles equal) for any number of sides. In three dimensions there are only five different regular solids: the tetrahedron (four-faced), cube (six-faced), octahedron (eight-faced), dodecahedron (twelve-faced) and icosahedron (twenty-faced). Geometers (people who study geometry)

◀ Two lines of symmetry of a square. The two sides on either side of the diagonal line are symmetrical, and the top half is symmetrical with the bottom.

have worked out ways to calculate the areas and volumes of these regular shapes.

Angles are measured in degrees (°). Lines at the corner of a square are at right angles (90°) to each other. Triangles can be classified by the size of their angles. A triangle can have one angle greater than 90° (an *obtuse-angled* triangle), or it can have one angle of exactly 90° (a *right-angled* triangle), or all three angles can be less than 90° (an *acute-angled* triangle).

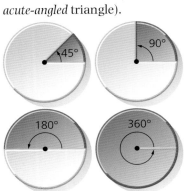

• The word 'geometry' comes from two Greek words: *ge* meaning 'Earth' and *metria* meaning 'measurement'.

• Trigonometry deals with the links between lengths and angles in triangles and other figures. When some measurements are known, others can be calculated. Trigonometry is of great practical importance in navigation and surveying.

◀ One complete turn of a circle is 360°. A quarter turn results in an angle of 90° (a right angle) and a half-turn produces an angle of 180°.

find out more
Mathematics

Georgian Britain

For over a hundred years, from 1714 to 1830, Britain was ruled by four kings called George. This time is often known as the Georgian period.

For much of this period, Britain was at war with its long-standing enemy France, until the struggle ended in 1815 with the Duke of Wellington's victory over Napoleon at the battle of Waterloo. They also clashed in the rich trading areas of India and North America, where both wanted to build an empire. Britain won control of much of India and Canada, but lost the rest of North America when the 13 American colonies won their independence in 1783. However, the first settlement at Botany Bay in

▲ A portrait of George III. During his reign Britain lost one part of its empire, the 13 American colonies.

▲ The wealth of a country squire came from his huge estates, and his favourite sports were usually hunting and shooting.

Australia in 1788 enlarged what was by then the 'British empire'.

The four Georges

George I was the Elector (ruler) of Hanover, a German state; he was a great-grandson of the English King James I. George I became king because he was the nearest Protestant heir to the throne and the Protestant ruling classes in Parliament did not want the Catholic Stuarts back in power. He was a cold, stiff man, who went back to Hanover whenever he could. This left small groups of ministers, led by Robert Walpole, to make government decisions.

George II was a fiery character who, like his father, preferred Hanover, leaving Walpole in control of the country until 1742. William Pitt (the Elder) became chief minister from 1756 even though George II detested him.

The hard-working, well-meaning George III took his position as king very seriously. In 1766 he made William Pitt (the Elder) prime minister, and after Pitt died, he gave the job to Pitt's son, William Pitt (the Younger). But George III developed a disease which sent

him mad, and his son, later George IV, ruled for him for nine years as Prince Regent. George IV won little respect because of his extravagance and his wild social life. His brother William IV ruled from 1830 until 1837, when Victoria became queen.

Country life

Most of the people of Britain still lived in the countryside. Most landowners sat in Parliament as MPs, or in the House of Lords. At home, they ran local affairs. In the local lawcourts punishments were harsh. People caught sheep-stealing or poaching were hanged, or transported in terrible conditions to the colonies.

From about 1750 many landowners created more 'enclosures', by fencing off part of their own and common land, to take advantage of new farming methods. In many places villagers could no longer make a living once they had lost their strips of land to farm and the use of the common land to rear a few animals. They were

1714 **George I**
1715 Jacobite rebellion
1721 Robert Walpole in power
1727 **George II**
1745 Jacobite rebellion
1746 Battle of Culloden; Bonnie Prince Charlie defeated
1759 Wolfe captured Québec, Canada
1760 **George III**
1776 American colonies declared independence
1777 Watt built steam engine
1789 French Revolution
1793 War against France
1800 Ireland lost its own parliament
1801 Act of Union with Ireland
1805 Battle of Trafalgar
1807 Slave trade abolished
1810 Prince George regent
1815 Battle of Waterloo
1820 **George IV**
1830 **William IV**

Two Jacobite rebellions

Jacobites were people who wanted the descendants of the Stuart James II (James VII of Scotland) to win back the throne. The name comes from Jacobus, which is Latin for James.

In 1715 James, son of James II, landed briefly in Scotland. Because he claimed the throne, he was called the Old Pretender ('pretend' in those days meant 'claim').

In 1745 Charles Edward, James's son, called Bonnie Prince Charlie, occupied Edinburgh for a time, and invaded England. He was defeated at Culloden in 1746.

▲ William Hogarth's engraving *The Enraged Musician* (1741) shows some aspects of the lives of the poor in Georgian Britain.

forced to work as labourers on very low wages, or they drifted to the growing towns in search of work. People were also driven off the land in the Highlands of Scotland as landowners introduced huge and profitable herds of sheep.

Trade, industry and transport

British ships, protected by the powerful navy, brought trading wealth to merchants and bankers. Sugar, cotton and tobacco poured in from the Caribbean. The trade in African slaves brought wealth to Bristol and Liverpool. Tea, luxury textiles and expensive dyes came from India and China. Britain exported corn, herrings, lead, tools, weapons and, in increasing amounts, woollen and cotton textiles.

At the end of the 18th century the 'Industrial Revolution' brought rapid changes in the economy, in the way people worked and lived,

and in transport too. By the 1780s industrial towns like Birmingham, Manchester and Glasgow were growing fast. From the 1780s canals were built so that barges could transport heavy goods, and in 1825 the first railway opened.

Elegance and poverty

Rich and fashionable people spent the winter 'season' in London and Edinburgh, attending balls, parties and concerts. It was also fashionable to 'take the waters' at spa towns such as Bath and Harrogate,

because it was believed that their mineral waters could cure diseases.

The number of schools for rich girls increased, but most taught little more than drawing, dancing and good manners. A good marriage was still the only way for most women to get on in society. Rich boys were usually sent to boarding school and there were grammar schools for wealthier middle-class children.

The great gap between rich and poor remained, though craftspeople and tradespeople could live well. In the country, villagers often lived in leaking, ramshackle cottages, existing on a diet of bread, cheese, peas and turnips. Many of the children in a poor family might die before the age of 5. Some villages had schools, but for the very poor, a child's wages were needed to keep the family going.

In the growing industrial towns, families were crowded into dark, stinking courtyards with one water pump which up to 50 people might share. Only a few employers, such as the social reformer Robert Owen, provided decent conditions for their workers and schools for the workers' children.

▼ Charing Cross, London, in 1794. The 18th century was a boom time for builders and architects who designed spacious squares and elegant housing for Georgian cities.

Germany

Germany lies in the middle of Europe between the Alps and Scandinavia. Although not as large as France, Spain or Sweden, it has the biggest population of all European countries (excluding Russia).

Much of Germany consists of the Central Uplands, a mixture of ancient block mountains with low hills and plains. Dark forests crown the hills, and castles look down across orchards and vineyards to fertile plains. In the Northern Lowland the sandy soil is not so fertile. Much of this land is covered with heath and pine forest, strewn with rock boulders left by glaciers of the last ice age. In the far south lie the Alps.

Climate

The climate of Germany is temperate (mild) and allows crops such as wheat, maize (corn) and potatoes to grow well. Cattle graze in the damp and mild north-west and in the foothills of the mountains, but pigs, cattle and poultry are also kept in large battery units near to the cities, especially in the east. One reason for keeping animals indoors is that winters are sometimes very cold, with snow covering the ground for many weeks.

Cities and states

Germany is not dominated by a single huge city, but has a network of large cities. Many of them, including Munich and Dresden, were formerly capitals of independent states such as Bavaria and Saxony that were united into the German empire in the 19th century. These cities inherited splendid palaces and art museums. In western Germany the cities have been well maintained and are prosperous, but in the east the

- In western Germany the Autobahn (motorway) system started by Hitler in the 1930s has been vastly improved and extended. German railways are developing new, high-speed lines which tunnel through hills and climb over valleys to keep an almost dead-level track, even in the mountains.

▼ The Rhine in western Germany, Europe's busiest waterway. It can carry large barges laden with coal and other heavy goods from Basel to the North Sea. The hills above the Rhine are used for farming and the area is famous for its white wine.

——	country boundary
◆	capital city
■ ●	major cities and towns
——	main roads
⇥	main railways
⊕	main airports

land height in metres
- 2000–5000
- 1000–2000
- 500–1000
- 200–500
- less than 200
- sea level — land below sea level

communist government in power until 1989 neglected older buildings. The state provided housing in the form of monotonous prefabricated blocks of apartments on the fringes of the cities.

Bavaria and Saxony are now two of the 16 Länder (federal states) around which the country's federal system of government is built. These states vary greatly in size and population. But they are all important because each has its own constitution, elected parliament and government headed by a minister-president. These governments have responsibility for education, police and local government. They also have local taxation powers.

People

The majority of Germans speak German as their first language, but there is a big minority of people who were born outside Germany. The former West Germany had a large number of people who originally came to the country as 'guest workers' to take jobs in factories when

Germany

▲ Berlin today. Older buildings in the eastern part of Germany had been neglected, but today they are being renovated along with the rest of the city.

● Before reunification East Germany relied for most of its electricity output on low-grade brown coal, which caused a high level of air pollution. Its salt, potash, uranium and chemical industries endangered lives of people living nearby, and also poured pollutants into the Weser and Elbe river systems. Since 1990 many of the most polluting plants have been closed down.

Germany was short of labour in the 1960s. The majority of these are from Turkey; the rest are from Bosnia, Croatia, Yugoslavia, Italy, Spain, Greece and Portugal.

German law guarantees admission to anyone claiming German family connections. After the relaxation of frontier controls in the former USSR and eastern Europe from 1989, hundreds of thousands of people arrived from Polish Silesia, Hungary, Romania and the Soviet Union. Germany's liberal immigration laws have also brought an influx of political refugees from countries such as Iran, Lebanon, Sri Lanka and Romania, the latter mainly gypsies.

Economy

Germany is the leading economic power in Europe, and one of the world leaders. The former West Germany was famous for high-quality industrial products, such as machine tools, motor vehicles, and its electric and electronic equipment, and chemicals. East Germany had a good reputation as a supplier of machinery, electrical equipment, chemicals and ships to the former USSR and other communist countries. But after the collapse of communist rule in eastern Europe in 1989 and the reunification of Germany in 1990, very few products from what had been East Germany could compete in a free market. Factories closed and for a while people faced unemployment.

▶ When Otto von Bismark was Prussian prime minister, his armies captured neighbouring lands. These victories persuaded other German states to join a German *Reich* (empire) with Prussia.

Agriculture is not a very profitable industry in western Germany because of the large number of small family farms. The farms of communist East Germany had been combined into huge co-operative (collective) units. After reunification in 1990 their sales suffered from poor marketing.

Germany's history

Already in Roman times there were German tribes in the area north of the River Rhine occupied by modern Germany. When the Roman empire collapsed, some of these tribes, the Franks, invaded Gaul. Charlemagne, their greatest king, was crowned in AD 800. After he died, his empire was divided into West Francia (modern France) and East Francia, or Franconia.

First German empire

King Otto I of Franconia (reigned 936–973) spread his power over all the German-speaking people of Europe, down the River Rhone and into Italy. He was crowned by the Pope in AD 962, and the Holy Roman Empire was born. Some of his descendants were strong emperors, especially Frederick II ('the Great'), who, during his reign (1212–1250), joined southern Italy and Sicily to the empire. Others were weak and lost power to the dukes and princes of Germany.

Between 1452 and 1806 this empire was ruled by the Habsburgs from Vienna. Their greatest emperor was Charles V (reigned 1519–1556), but after his death the emperors gradually lost power. In the end, the empire covered only what are now Austria, parts of Hungary, the Czech Republic, Slovakia, Croatia, Slovenia and Bosnia. The rest of Germany was ruled by 400 princes, dukes and bishops.

Second German empire

By the 19th century many German-speaking people wanted to be united again in one country. In 1871 the German princes invited the king of Prussia (a German state) to become emperor of Germany. The first chancellor (prime minister) was Otto von Bismarck. He tried to make life better for people by starting old-age pensions and payments for sickness and accident. People worked hard, building railways, new factories and a navy to make Germany strong.

Germany

◄ Hitler and his Nazi party set out to destroy all opposition. Young people were enrolled into the 'Hitler Youth' where they were taught that National Socialism was the only right form of government. Nazis burned any books that praised democracy, denounced war or were written by Jews (left) in their attempts to impose total control over people.

find out more
Bach, Johann Sebastian
Beethoven, Ludwig van
Charlemagne
Dictators
Einstein, Albert
Europe
European Union
Hitler, Adolf
Holocaust
Holy Roman Empire
World War I
World War II

World War I and the Weimar Republic

Rivalry between Germany and other nations led to World War I (1914–1918). Six million German people were killed or wounded and by the end of the war many were starving. Some Germans blamed the emperor (Kaiser) for this, and he was overthrown. A republic was proclaimed in the city of Weimar. This republican government soon ran into trouble. By 1923 money had lost its value and people's savings had become worthless. Unemployment was rising and by 1932 there were 6 million people without work.

Third German empire: the Third Reich

In 1933 Adolf Hitler, leader of the Nazis, became chancellor. He promised to unite all the German-speaking people into a new German empire (the Third Reich). Germans who opposed Hitler were silenced and many died in concentration camps. Jews were persecuted, and those who could migrated abroad. Hitler's armies took over Austria in 1938 and Czechoslovakia in the spring of 1939. When they invaded Poland later in 1939, World War II began.

Defeat, division and reunification

When Allied troops defeated Germany in 1945, they discovered that 6 million Jews had been exterminated in what became known as the 'Holocaust'. Most German cities had been reduced to ruins. Money was valueless.

At the end of the war, Austria became a separate country again. Czechoslovakia and Poland were restored (with changed boundaries) and expelled at least 12 million Germans. Germany was divided into four zones of occupation, and Berlin into four sectors. In 1949 the Russian zone became the German Democratic Republic (East Germany), with the Soviet sector of Berlin as its capital. It was closely controlled by a dictatorial government.

The zones of the USA, Britain and France were combined to form the Federal Republic of Germany (West Germany), a democracy with a capitalist economy. Bonn was its capital. The three western sectors of Berlin formed an 'island' within East German territory.

By 1961 the East German economy had been greatly weakened by the loss of approximately 2.5 million people migrating to West Germany. In response to this, the communist government erected the Berlin Wall, a system of fortifications along the western boundary encircling West Berlin to prevent escape. The wall came down in October 1989, when massive demonstrations led to the fall of the communist government of East Germany. Free elections were held in March 1990, and Germany was reunited on 3 October that year with Berlin as the country's capital.

▼ The Berlin Wall was a powerful symbol of the East–West divide in Germany. When the communist government fell in 1989, the Berlin Wall was brought down by thousands of jubilant demonstrators.

Ghosts

A ghost is the form of a person or some other creature that is no longer alive. Some people believe that the ghosts of their ancestors continue to share in their lives.

In many parts of the world, such as South America, Africa and the Caribbean, people believe that *shamans*, or medicine men, receive their healing powers through the ghosts of dead healers. People also believe that a ghost may enter into a living person and 'possess' him or her. To get rid of an unwanted ghost, a priest says prayers that will release it from this world and let it rest.

Some people, particularly in Europe, have always been very frightened of ghosts. They say that ghosts haunt places where they were unhappy in their lifetime, or where they were killed. Many stories are told about such ghosts.

Sometimes people claim to have seen ghosts when they themselves are very tired. Soldiers who have been fighting for long hours and days report that they have suddenly seen the figures of their dead comrades – fellow soldiers killed earlier in the battle – fighting beside them.

Spirits called *poltergeists* are invisible but very noisy and mischievous. They move objects around, laugh, scream or make the sound of footsteps, and break things. Kinder ghosts, such as the Russian *domovoy*, appear at night when everyone is asleep, and clean the kitchen, do the ironing, and put the children's toys away.

• The Christian festival of Hallowe'en (short for All Hallows' Eve) takes place on 31 October, the night before All Saints' Day on 1 November. This is the night when ghosts and other spirits are supposed to roam the Earth. In pre-Christian times these dates were the end of the old year and the beginning of the new.

◀ The photographer who took this picture of the Tulip Staircase in the Queen's House, Greenwich, England, claims that it was taken during normal opening hours and that he did not see the figures at the bottom of the staircase. It was taken on 19 June 1966.

find out more
Myths and legends
Religions

Glaciers

A glacier is a moving mass of ice. Glaciers usually form when enough snow builds up an ice layer on the land. They can be seen today in the European Alps and other high mountain ranges, in Alaska and northern Canada, New Zealand, Greenland and Antarctica.

A glacier usually begins high in the mountain. The layers of ice at the bottom where it rests on the ground become soft and slippery, and the glacier begins to move downhill in fits and starts. The ice may move smoothly for a while, until it meets an obstruction such as a bend or a mound of broken rocks.

Glaciers move at different speeds, usually between 1 centimetre and 1 metre per day. The middle part moves faster, and the edges, which rub against the sides of the valleys, may move more slowly. Glaciers can pass right into the sea, where large pieces of ice break away and float off as icebergs. They may retreat if the climate or weather becomes warmer.

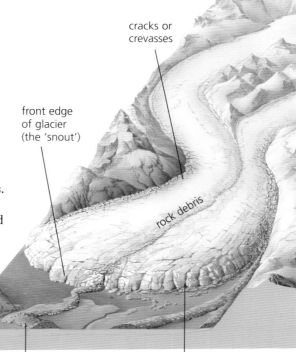

cracks or crevasses

front edge of glacier (the 'snout')

rock debris

rocks and soil are dumped in heaps called moraines

ice cuts away rocks and boulders

◀ A glacier as it flows through a valley, making it wider and deeper. The valley is changed from a V shape to a U shape.

Glacier records
World's largest
Lambert Glacier, Antarctica, 514 km long
World's fastest
Quarayac Glacier, Greenland, 20 m per day

find out more
Antarctica
Arctic
Climate
Ice
Valleys

Glands

Glands are special organs which make chemicals that the body needs, such as sweat and saliva. Some produce chemicals called hormones that control important life processes.

The chemicals produced by glands are called *secretions*. Sweat glands in your skin produce sweat, and salivary glands in your mouth produce saliva. Glands in the stomach and the wall of the gut make digestive enzymes which break down food.

Hormones

Hormones are made and stored in glands, and released into the blood to be carried around the body. Humans have many different hormones.

If hormones do not carry out their job properly, it can lead to disease. In the disease called diabetes, the pancreas does not produce enough insulin, so the blood is too sugary. People who are diabetic feel very tired unless their condition is treated.

Hormones also control important processes in other animals. For instance, in insects and crabs hormones control moulting (shedding of the external skeleton). In plants hormones control growth and flowering.

▶ Some of the main glands of the body.

When boys reach puberty, their **testes** start to produce a hormone called testosterone which causes their voice to get deeper, their beard to grow and their sex organs to enlarge.

The **pituitary gland** produces hormones which control growth, reproduction and milk production, and hormones that control other glands.

The **thyroid gland** produces thyroxine, which increases the activity of certain body processes.

The **pancreas** produces the hormone insulin, which makes the liver absorb sugar from the blood.

Women's **ovaries** produce sex hormones that control the menstrual period and egg production.

find out more
Digestive systems
Growth and
  development
Sex and reproduction

Glass

Window panes, tumblers, ornaments, cooking vessels and windscreens are just a few of our everyday uses of glass. Special glass is used for lenses, telescope mirrors and furnaces. There is even bulletproof glass to resist machine-gun fire.

Much of the glass used today is produced by heating a mixture of sand, soda ash and limestone in a large furnace at a temperature of 1500 °C. Before the ingredients are added, some broken glass is put in to speed up the process.

As the mixture melts, any impurities rise to the surface and are skimmed off. The molten glass is allowed to cool until it looks like thin, sticky toffee. It is then moulded or rolled into sheets.

The cheapest kind of glass, used for windows, is *sheet glass*. The molten glass is lifted from the furnace and passed through rollers to form a flat sheet. *Plate glass* is made by flattening molten glass into sheets. The sides are then ground and polished by machine. In 1952 Alastair Pilkington invented a method to make *float glass*, which has a smooth, polished finish. Car windscreens are made by combining layers of float glass and plastic material to make *laminated glass*.

• Some high-quality glass products are still blown by hand today. The glass-blower blows down a hollow iron tube which has been dipped into molten glass.

find out more
Lenses
Recycling

◀ In the float-glass method, a thin layer of molten glass is floated on the perfectly flat surface of a tank filled with molten tin. The glass formed has a clear, smooth surface.

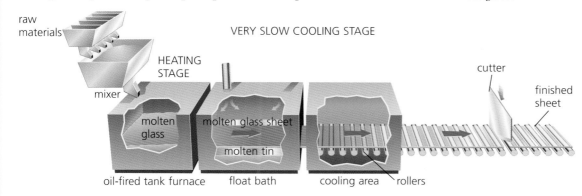

raw materials
mixer
HEATING STAGE
molten glass
VERY SLOW COOLING STAGE
molten glass sheet
molten tin
cutter
finished sheet
oil-fired tank furnace
float bath
cooling area
rollers

Gliders and kites

Gliders and kites use the force of the wind to stay up in the air. Gliders are flown for pleasure and in competitions, often involving long-distance flights or acrobatics. Hang-gliders are really fold-up gliders with portable wings.

▲ A view along the wing of a banking glider. When seen in the air, it is easy to distinguish a glider from a powered aircraft. Gliders have long flexible wings, a thin streamlined body and a distinctive tail.

A glider does not have an engine to keep it moving. Its fuselage (body) is lightweight and streamlined to cut down air resistance. The wings are long to create as much lift as possible at the glider's low cruising speed. Most gliders have one seat, although those used for training have two.

Gliders are either towed up into the air behind a powered aircraft or launched from the ground by a car or powered winch. Once in the air, the pilot releases the towline and is free to soar like a bird.

A glider can gain height if the pilot finds a *thermal*, a current of warm air that rises from the ground on a sunny day. If the glider circles in the thermal, it will gain height. Pilots can also use the air flow over a hill to gain height.

Hang-gliding

Most hang-gliders carry one person, the pilot, who hangs underneath in a special harness. Some are strong enough for a pilot and a passenger. The pilot gets airborne by running into the wind off a hill or cliff. For safety reasons, the pilot wears a crash helmet and always carries a parachute. Hang-gliding is not only a popular outdoor activity but also a competitive sport.

Kites

Kites are flown at festivals, in competitions, for enjoyment, and for practical jobs too. In some parts of Asia, people fish by hanging hooks from kites. Samoans have used kites to pull canoes, and kites that could lift a soldier were used by the British army in 1906.

Kites were invented in China about 3000 years ago. The first kites were probably made of silk on a bamboo frame and flown from a single line. Modern

stunter kites have a plastic covering over an aluminium frame and are attached to two lines. By pulling on one line more than the other, you can turn the kite so that it swoops and soars.

▶ **FLASHBACK** ◀

In 1853, after a lifetime of testing model gliders, George Cayley built the first glider to carry a person into the air. Later a German, Otto Lilienthal, learnt to control his gliders using body movements like today's hang-glider pilots. The first gliders for sport were built in Germany in the 1920s. During World War II, airborne assaults were made by troops carried in large gliders. After a period when it was largely forgotten, hang-gliding was revived in the 1960s.

▲ Kite-flying is a popular sport in Japan. This man is preparing to fly his kite at a kite festival in Hamamatsu, Japan.

• In 1847, an 11-year-old American boy landed his kite on the far side of the Niagara River gorge so that work could start on a suspension bridge. The kite line was used to pull the first cables across the gorge.

◀ Once airborne, the pilot controls the hang-glider by moving a control bar, which is part of the glider's triangular frame.

find out more
Aircraft
Flight

Gold

Pure gold is a soft yellowish metal. It has been a valuable material since ancient times – gold coins were first made by King Croesus of Lydia in about 600 BC. Because gold does not react with other chemicals in its surroundings, it does not corrode (wear away).

Gold is generally hardened by alloying (mixing) it with copper or silver. The gold content of alloys is measured in *carats*. Pure gold is said to be 24 carats; an alloy of equal parts of gold and, say, silver is said to be 12-carat gold; 18-carat gold is 18/24 pure gold (75% gold).

Gold is widely used to make jewellery, ornaments and other precious objects. Dentists use gold for filling and capping teeth, while gold or alloys of it are used to make electrical contacts for the electronics industry.

Mining gold

Most gold is obtained from mines. Rock containing veins of gold is blasted out with the help of explosives and then crushed by heavy machinery. The powdered rock is treated with chemicals to extract the gold. Around 100 tonnes of gold-bearing rock have to be mined to produce 1 kilogram of gold.

Shallow metal pans are used to collect grains of gold found in sand or gravel on some river-beds. The sand is washed over the pan edge while the gold sinks to the bottom.

• The great Californian gold rush started after James Marshall found gold at Sutter's Hill in January 1848. The prospectors who followed him in 1849 became known as 'the Forty-Niners'.

• South Africa produces three-quarters of the world's gold, after which come the USA and Australia. South Africa still makes gold coins, called krugerrands, but they are for investment purposes.

◀ Inside a gold refinery, hot molten gold is carefully poured into a mould.

find out more
Gems and jewellery
Metals
Mining

Golf

Golf is one of the few truly international sports. Huge TV audiences follow the major tournaments, while millions of keen amateurs of all ages practise and play throughout the year.

A golfer uses a set of clubs to hit a ball towards a hole cut in the ground. Players may use a maximum of 14 clubs, from which they choose the one most suitable for the type of shot required. Playing individually or in pairs over a set number of holes, the winner is the player or team that takes fewest strokes to get the ball into the hole (*stroke play*) or wins the most holes (*match play*).

Each hole begins on an area of raised ground called the *tee*, where the first stroke is played. A strip of shortish grass, the *fairway*, stretches from the

◀ Jack Nicklaus of the USA chips out of a bunker at the 1991 US Masters. No other player in history has come close to his record of 18 wins in the majors.

tee to the smooth *green*, where the hole is cut and marked with a flag. Alongside the fairway is longer grass, the *rough*. Trees, bushes and hazards, such as streams and bunkers of sand, all help to make the course more difficult to play.

On a full-sized golf course, golfers play a round of 18 holes. Each hole has a *par* score, between 3 and 5, which is the number of strokes that a leading (scratch) player is expected to take. The par score for an 18-hole course is usually between 70 and 72.

Most big tournaments last four days, with one round played each day. These include the four 'majors' – the US and British Opens, the US Masters and the US PGA. There are regular 'tours', in which the top players take part in a tournament a week during the season.

• Golf has been played in Scotland since the 15th century. The Royal and Ancient Golf Club, the guardian of the rules of golf, was founded at St Andrews in 1754.

• The oldest and most important match-play event is the Ryder Cup. This is played every two years between the leading players of Europe and the USA.

• A score of 1 below par is known as a *birdie*, and 2 below par as an *eagle*. One shot over par is called a *bogey*, 2 over par a *double bogey*, and so on.

Government

The government of a country is the organization that is responsible for running that country. Its decisions affect everyone. The school you attend, the roads you travel on, your family's income – all these may depend on the government.

▲ Four US presidents (from left to right): George Bush (senior), Bill Clinton, Gerald Ford and Jimmy Carter. Presidents of the USA are elected for four years and no president may serve for more than two four-year terms. The US president is head of state, prime minister and commander-in-chief of the armed forces.

Governments make and change the laws. They also make sure that these laws are obeyed. The government has to defend the country and is in charge of the armed forces.

Democracy and dictatorship

There are two main types of government. Many, such as those in Europe and North America, are *democracies*. People vote in elections for candidates put forward by political parties. These parties are groups of people with similar ideas on how to govern the country. The party that wins the most votes or the most seats in the country's parliament becomes the government until the next election.

Another kind of government is a *dictatorship*. In a dictatorship one person or one political party controls the country. There is no freedom to disagree with the government and there are no free elections. Sometimes the armed forces seize power in a country. This is known as a military government or dictatorship.

The parts of government

In any system of government the most important person is the head of the government. They usually have the title 'prime minister' or 'president'. They are in charge of the

executive branch of the government. It is the job of the executive branch to see that laws and decisions by the government are carried out. In some countries the head of the government is the leader of the biggest political party in the parliament. In other countries, such as the USA, the head of the government is elected directly by the people.

The head of the government appoints ministers. Each minister is in charge of a part of the government's work. So there may be a minister of education, of transport, of defence, and so on. The finance minister is in charge of the country's economic policies. In Britain the finance minister is called the Chancellor of the Exchequer, and in the USA, Secretary to the Treasury.

• The extent of a president's power varies. In some countries, such as India, the president is a ceremonial head of state and the prime minister has the real power. In others, such as Zimbabwe, the president runs the government.

• In many countries important ministers belong to the Cabinet. The Cabinet is a committee that discusses long-term government policy. The word 'cabinet' means a small room, which is where the first Cabinet meetings took place in London in the late 17th century.

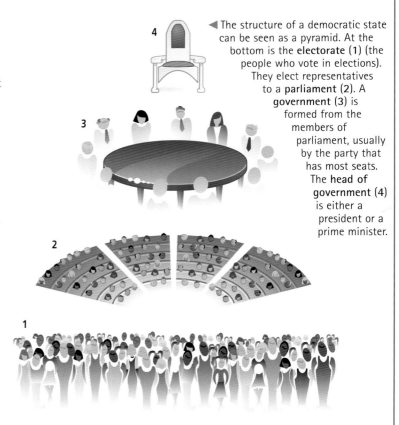

◀ The structure of a democratic state can be seen as a pyramid. At the bottom is the **electorate** (1) (the people who vote in elections). They elect representatives to a **parliament** (2). A **government** (3) is formed from the members of parliament, usually by the party that has most seats. The **head of government** (4) is either a president or a prime minister.

◄ Some countries, such as France, Italy and Japan, have many political parties, none of which is usually strong enough to win an election on its own. Two or more parties may form a *coalition* (alliance) to become the government. This is the Italian coalition government in 1997.

Quite a few countries, called *monarchies*, such as Britain, Denmark and Jordan, have a royal family, with a monarch (king or queen) as their head of state. The governments of such countries rule on the monarch's behalf, even if the monarch has no practical involvement in governing. Countries without this kind of hereditary system are called *republics*. In a republic a president is the head of state.

Making laws is the job of the *legislature*. In Britain this is Parliament and in the USA it is Congress. Many countries, including France, call their parliament the National Assembly. An important job of members of the parliament is to keep watch over what the government does. They question and criticize the government, and have the power to vote against it. If the government loses the support of parliament, it may have to resign and call an election.

Looking after people

During the 20th century many governments took responsibility for people's well-being. *Welfare states* are countries where the government provides a great deal of help to people through unemployment pay, old-age pensions and health care. One of the first welfare states was set up in Sweden in the 1930s.

A very important task for modern government is managing the economy. This means trying to provide jobs for as many people as possible. Governments try to make sure that prices do not rise too much and that the standard of living rises steadily for its citizens.

All governments have to raise a great deal of money to pay for all the things that they do. They do this by making people pay *taxes*. Everyone who has an income pays taxes such as income tax and also sales tax (for example VAT). The government also makes businesses pay taxes.

No one likes paying taxes, and if the government raises taxes too high it will become unpopular. At the same time many people want the government to spend more money on the welfare state and on improving vital services such as health care and education. It is difficult for a government to strike the right balance between raising taxes and improving services. But if they get it wrong, a democratic government may lose power at the next election.

Governments employ large numbers of permanent staff known as *civil servants*. They do all the detailed work and make sure that government decisions are carried out. All capital cities, such as Washington, Paris, London and Moscow, have huge office buildings, called ministries, where civil servants work.

Local government

Some government work is given to local governments (councils). Councils are in charge of areas such as counties, towns and villages. Councillors are elected to serve on these councils. Their responsibilities vary from one country to another. Generally, they run local services including schools, rubbish collection and repairing minor roads. Some councils decide where new homes or factories should be built. Residents have to pay a tax to their local council, which is used to pay for local services. Local councils usually have to follow the decisions of the central government.

• The world's first woman prime minister was Mrs Sirimavo Bandaranaike, who became premier of Sri Lanka in 1960. Other female prime ministers include Britain's Margaret Thatcher, Pakistan's Benazir Bhutto and Turkey's Tansu Ciller.

• As part of the welfare state the government employs social workers to help people who are having difficulty coping with everyday problems. These services are very expensive to provide.

▼ This teacher in Stockholm, Sweden, is working in a pre-school day-care centre. Centres such as this are one of the services provided by the Swedish government for its people.

Grace, W. G.

W. G. Grace is the most famous figure in the history of cricket. His astonishing performances and larger-than-life appearance on and off the field made him a national celebrity in Victorian England. More than any other person, he was responsible for making cricket a national institution and an international sport.

William Gilbert Grace was taught to play cricket, along with his two brothers, by his mother. Mrs Grace must have been a very good coach, because all three Grace brothers ended up playing first-class cricket for their home county, Gloucestershire.

Grace was qualified as a doctor, but cricket was his life's work. 'W. G.', as he was known, played his first major match at the age of 16 and carried on playing cricket until the age of 60. During this time he set new standards in every aspect of the game. Although best remembered as a batsman, he was also an outstanding bowler and fielder.

During the course of his career, Grace scored 54,896 runs (including 126 centuries), took 2876 wickets and held 877 catches. He simply towered over the game: in the 1871 season his batting average of 78.25 was more than twice as high as the next best player, and in 1876 he scored 344, 177 and 318 not out in three consecutive first-class innings. He also captained Gloucestershire, leading them to win the county championship, and was captain of England against Australia on 13 occasions, both at home and abroad.

Born 1848 in Gloucestershire, England
Died 1915 aged 67

◀ W. G. Grace drew huge crowds wherever he played. He was such an attraction that the admission fee to the ground was sometimes doubled if he was playing.

● Grace did not let personal matters get in the way of his cricket. On the 1873 tour to Australia, he took his wife with him on their honeymoon!

find out more
Cricket

Graphs

A graph is a way of showing information in picture form. Instead of listing a mass of numbers, a graph presents them in a way that shows up any patterns in the numbers. It also lets you compare different numbers.

There are many different types of graph. Three of the most useful are line graphs, bar charts and pie charts.

Line graphs are a simple way of comparing numbers. They are used to present many different kinds of information, such as population figures, the temperature of a sick person, the amount of money a country earns or the amount of goods it sells. The lines with the numbers on are called axes.

Bar charts are useful for comparing different things, such as how many vehicles of different types drive past your house each day.

A pie chart looks like a pie with different slices. It is used to show the relationship between a whole and the different parts into which it can be divided, for example the percentage of the world's population found in each of the major continents. Pie charts are good for getting a quick impression of amounts but not for reading off detailed information.

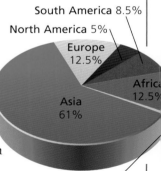

South America 8.5%
North America 5%
Europe 12.5%
Africa 12.5%
Asia 61%
Oceania 0.5%

▲ This pie chart shows how the world's population is distributed between the major continents.

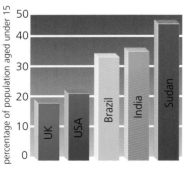

▲ This bar chart compares the percentage of children in the population of five countries. Children make up less than 20% of the UK's population, but almost half of Sudan's.

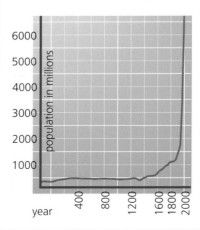

◀ This line graph shows the population of the world from around 200 BC to the present day. At a glance you can see how the population increase has been sharp since the 18th century, and very sharp during the 20th century.

find out more
Mathematics
Numbers
Statistics

◀ Flowering cocksfoot grass, and a diagram of one floret. Grass flowers use the wind to spread their pollen (male sex cells). The flowers consist of two or three florets. Each floret contains three anthers on long stalks, and two feathery stigmas. The anthers contain pollen, which they release into the wind. The stigmas catch pollen from other flowers. (In a real floret, stigmas and anthers do not appear at the same time.)

find out more
Cereals
Flowering plants
Food
Grasslands

Grasses

Grasses are the most successful flowering plants, with about 900 different kinds. Extensive grasslands cover more than a fifth of the world's land surface.

The grass stem is divided into sections by nodes (joints), with a leaf attached at each node. Part of the leaf wraps round the stem to form a sheath: the rest forms a long, thin blade. Most grasses are *herbaceous*. This means that they do not have woody stems and die right down to the ground after flowering. An exception is bamboo, which has woody stems up to 40 metres high. Many grasses are annual: they live for a season, produce a large quantity of seeds, and then die.

Grasses for food

In the prairies of North America and the savannah of Africa, grasses are food for huge herds of grazing animals. For people too, grasses are a very important food. Wheat, maize, rice, sugar cane and bamboo are all types of grass. About half the energy that humans around the world take in from food comes from wheat, maize and rice alone.

Why grasses are successful

Grasses survive because they grow quickly and soon produce seed. Their tall, thin shape means that they fit easily between other plants. If flattened, the stem will grow to bring the flower stalk upright again. Many grasses have short shoots, which lie close to the ground, so they can go on growing even if heavily grazed.

Grasshoppers and crickets

Grasshoppers and crickets are insects that have existed since before the dinosaurs. Most are plant-eaters, though some feed on other small creatures. Almost all have huge hind legs, and can leap long distances.

• There are about 13,000 different kinds of grasshoppers and crickets.

• In the Old Testament of the Bible a plague of locusts is one of the plagues with which God punished the Egyptians to make them free the Israelites.

The animals that we usually call grasshoppers have short, rather thick antennae, so they are often known as the short-horned grasshoppers. Most are active during the daytime. Crickets have long, hair-like antennae which are much longer than their bodies. Many crickets are active at night.

Both grasshoppers and crickets 'sing'. Grasshoppers do this by rubbing a row of little pegs on their hind legs against a vein on the side of their forewings. Crickets rub their wings together. Only the males sing, courting females with a song that also warns off other males. Though it is easy to hear grasshoppers and crickets, they are usually so well camouflaged that they are very difficult to see.

Several kinds of large grasshopper are known as locusts. Most of the time they are harmless, but sometimes huge swarms of them gather together and destroy all the plants in an area as they feed. In the Middle East and Africa, locusts have been the most feared of all pests since farming began.

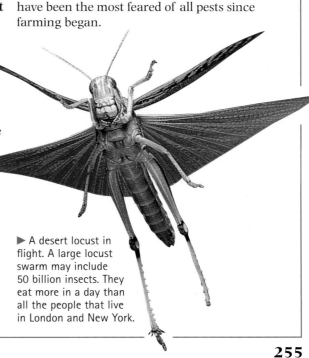

▶ A desert locust in flight. A large locust swarm may include 50 billion insects. They eat more in a day than all the people that live in London and New York.

find out more
Insects
Pests and parasites

Grasslands

Grasslands cover more than a fifth of the Earth's land surface. Grass is an important food for many animals, and humans grow and eat grasses like wheat and rice. Grasslands are of many different types, from the desolate steppe lands of Central Asia to the rich farmlands of North America.

• Some parts of the steppes of Russia, Kazakhstan and Mongolia are still roamed by camels and horses. Some of the animals are wild, others are used by nomads, who move about with their animals and live in large round tents made of felt (*yurts* or *gers*).

Grasslands have different names in different parts of the world. There are hot savannahs in East Africa, and veld in southern Africa. In North America there are the fertile prairies, in South America the dry pampas and chacos. The huge areas of grassland in Central Europe and Asia are called steppes, while in western Europe there are meadows and downlands.

Animals

All sorts of animals live on the world's grasslands. Australia's grasslands are home to many of the country's best-known animals, such as kangaroos, emus, kookaburras, and flocks of brightly coloured budgerigars, parrots and cockatoos. Some of the world's largest animals live on the savannahs of East Africa. They include giraffes, elephants and black rhinos.

The North American prairies are home to prairie dogs, small rodents that feed on the grasses. They eat the grass roots as well as the leaves, but they also collect and bury grass seeds, so helping to 'plant' new grasses. The rattlesnake is common in the grasslands of North America. The 'rattle' is in the tip of its tail: the snake rattles when it is disturbed or when coiled ready to strike.

▲ This rolling farmland in Washington State, USA, was once grassland. Much of what used to be prairie is now used to grow cereals such as wheat and maize (corn), which are themselves types of grass.

Most grasslands have a host of tiny animals, which are not usually seen. Earthworms, ants and beetles live in the soil, roots and leaves. Termites build large 'skyscraper' homes of soil in the grasslands, up to 7 metres high.

People and grasslands

Humans have changed grasslands in many parts of the world. Three hundred years ago, there were probably 60 million bison ('buffaloes') roaming the prairies of North America. Settlers from Europe shot bison for their meat and hides, and by the beginning of the 20th century fewer than a thousand were left. During the 20th century the prairies have been changed even more dramatically. The grasslands have been ploughed up and turned into rich farmland. Grasslands have been ploughed for crops in other regions too, such as the steppes of the Ukraine and Russia. In other areas, such as the pampas of Argentina, grasslands are used to graze beef cattle.

find out more
Cereals
Farming
Grasses

◄ Herds of giraffes, wildebeest, zebra and eland graze together on the East African savannah. Grazing in mixed herds enables the animals to help warn each other of danger from predators. Each animal eats different plants or parts of plants. Giraffes, for example, can reach leaves high on the acacia trees, and their tough mouths are not damaged by the trees' huge thorns.

Gravity

Gravity is the pulling force that holds us all down onto the Earth's surface. In fact, everything has a gravitational pull towards everything else; even two people attract each other. The more massive the object, the larger the pull, so the pull of the Earth drowns out the tiny pulls that we have on each other.

The force of gravity pulling us towards our planet gives us our weight; it makes us feel heavy. Our weight depends on where we are because the pull of gravity gets less if we move further away from the centre of the Earth. A man standing at the North Pole would weigh very slightly less if he moved to the Equator, and less again if he then climbed a high mountain.

Other planets, smaller than the Earth, have a weaker gravitational pull, so we would weigh less on them. On a more massive planet we would weigh more, even though the mass of our bodies stays exactly the same as on Earth. Your weight on Earth is about six times more than it would be on the Moon, while on the planet Jupiter you would weigh about three times as much as you do on Earth.

Gravity and the Universe

The pull of the Earth's gravity holds the Moon in its orbit circling round us, and the Sun's gravity keeps the Earth and the other planets in their orbits. Gravity also holds the Sun and 100,000 million other stars in a gigantic group called the Galaxy. In fact, the Sun and the planets would

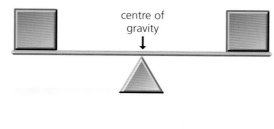

centre of gravity

A see-saw resting on a central pivot. There are two boxes of the same size, one on each end of the see-saw. The see-saw is perfectly balanced.

The same see-saw resting on the same pivot. This time there is a larger box on one end of the see-saw, with the same-size box as before on the other end. The see-saw is tipped, with the end with the larger box on the ground and the other end in the air.

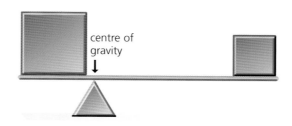

centre of gravity

The same see-saw, with the same large and small boxes on it as in the previous diagram. But this time the central pivot has been moved towards the larger box. The see-saw is now perfectly balanced again.

not exist at all if gravity had not pulled together particles of gas and dust to make them.

Centre of gravity

You can balance on a narrow beam because gravity pulls you down equally on either side of the beam, so you do not fall off. A pencil will also balance across another pencil when half its weight is one side of the balancing point and half the other side. The point where the pencils cross is the *centre of gravity* of the balancing pencil. All its weight seems to be concentrated at that point. If you add a small piece of modelling clay to one end, it will balance at a different point because the extra weight has moved the centre of gravity.

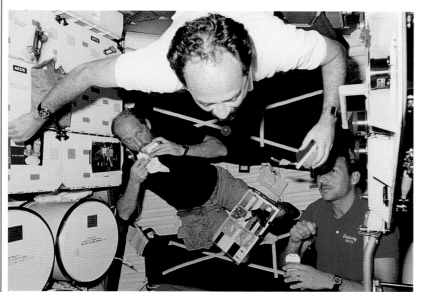

◄ Everything in space floats around because the effects of gravity are tiny. Things become weightless. This floating astronaut on board the Space Shuttle *Discovery* is weightless, as is the bubble of strawberry drink he is trying to catch.

• People often use the word 'weight' when they really mean 'mass'. Mass is the amount of matter in something. Weight is the force of gravity pulling us towards our planet. The more matter there is in something, the more strongly gravity acts on it and the heavier it is.

find out more
Forces and pressure
Newton, Isaac
Universe

Greeks, ancient

The ancient Greeks have had an enormous influence on the modern world. Their art and architecture are copied, their literature is widely read, their plays are still performed. A system of government first used by the Greeks – democracy – is now used in most countries of the world.

Greek civilization began about 1600 BC in a number of small but rich kingdoms on mainland Greece and on the island of Crete. Around 1200–1000 BC they were destroyed by invaders, fire and earthquakes. Some of the best-known remains are the city of Mycenae (south of Athens) and the buildings of the Minoans at Knossos on Crete.

▼ The Acropolis ('high city') of Athens as it may have looked in the 5th century BC.
1 Sanctuary of Zeus
2 Parthenon (the temple of Athens's goddess Athene)
3 Theatre of Dionysus
4 Erechtheum, the temple of Athene and Poseidon
5 Statue of Athene
6 Sanctuary of Artemis
7 The gateway or Propylaea

▲ The myth of the Cretan Minotaur – the bull-headed, flesh-eating monster that lived in a maze – comes from the early period of Greek civilization. On this Athenian pot from the 6th century BC the beast is shown being killed by the young Greek hero Theseus.

City states

By the 9th century BC, after long years of war and turmoil, Greece was settling down again. The region was divided into hundreds of city states, each consisting of a city or village and its surrounding land. The city states governed themselves and made their own laws. Hard labour was done by slaves, and women had little say in what went on.

Because Greece was both rich and divided, neighbouring powers were tempted to invade. The most dangerous threat came from the Persian emperor Darius I. The wars between the Greeks and the Persians lasted from 499 to 479 BC. Although Darius's successor Xerxes burned Athens in 480 BC, in the end the Greeks drove off the invaders.

The 'golden age'

After the defeat of the Persians, Greece enjoyed a brief 'golden age' during the 5th century BC. Athens, the most successful city state, built up a trading empire in the eastern Mediterranean under the leadership of Pericles. Athens was also a centre of art, literature and philosophy (the 'love of wisdom'). Athenian craft workers produced beautiful pottery, decorated with scenes from daily life and the adventures of gods and heroes. The ruins of its grand buildings, such as those on the Acropolis, survive to this day. Open-air theatres, holding as many as 10,000 spectators, put on plays by remarkable

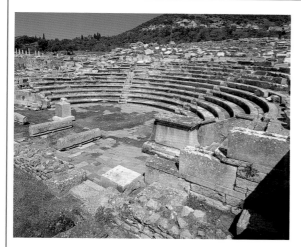

◄ The theatre at Epidaurus. The Greeks built their open-air theatres on hillsides so the audience had a good view and could hear every word spoken. Many modern theatres follow this basic design.

dramatists, including Euripides, Sophocles and Aristophanes.

Exercise was an important part of Greek life. Athletes from all over the Greek world met to compete in athletics games. The most famous was the Olympic Games, held at Olympia in honour of the god Zeus.

Rise and fall

Athens's great rival was the military state of Sparta, which controlled much of the southern part of the Greek mainland (the Peloponnese). Athens was wealthier and had a more powerful navy. It was also democratic ('ruled by the people'): all of its male citizens had a say in the government of the state. Spartans valued military skills above art and philosophy, and all Spartan men had to be in the army.

The two city states first went to war in 459 BC, when Sparta won. A second war broke out in 431 BC and lasted for over 25 years. Athens again lost and the city was captured. After this,

Greek power declined until the time of Alexander the Great, the Macedonian king from 336 to 323 BC, who conquered a huge empire and spread Greek ideas across Asia to northern India. His empire broke up after his death, and by the 2nd century BC Greece was under Roman rule.

Greek beliefs

The Greeks believed in gods and goddesses with semi-human personalities. These were worshipped with statues, temples, feasts, processions, sacrifices, games and plays. Because a god or goddess controlled almost every activity, from hunting to lighting a fire, the Greeks dared not forget them for an instant. Before starting something important, Greeks consulted oracles, holy places where a priest or priestess could foretell the future. The most popular oracle was at the temple of Apollo at Delphi.

Greek gods and goddesses

The chief god was Zeus, ruler of all lesser gods and mortals. He lived on top of Mount Olympus with his wife Hera, the goddess of marriage. Zeus had two brothers: Poseidon and Hades. Poseidon, married to Amphrite, ruled the kingdom of water – rivers, lakes and the sea. He dug new waterways with an enormous three-pronged spear, or trident. Hades ruled the Underworld with his wife Persephone, whom he stole from the corn goddess Demeter. Persephone was allowed back to the world for six months each year to allow crops to grow. The Underworld, where the spirits of the dead went, was a horrible maze of dark tunnels inhabited by ghosts and monsters.

Other important gods and goddesses included Aphrodite, the goddess of love and beauty; Apollo, the god of prophesy, music and medicine; Ares, the god of war; Artemis, the goddess of the Moon and hunting; Dionysus, the god of wine and the theatre; and Hermes, the messenger god.

Poseidon, ruler of the water kingdom, with his trident.

- Historians and archaeologists have long been fascinated by two 'missing' Greek cities, Atlantis and Troy. Atlantis, which was supposed to have disappeared beneath the sea, has never been found. But in 1871 the site of Troy was found in Turkey. The real city was not as grand as that of the legendary Trojan War. This is based on a real siege of about 1210 BC, when Greek armies are supposed to have captured the city by hiding men inside a wooden horse.

- Sport was so important to the ancient Greeks that during the time of the Olympic Games (held every four years between 776 BC and 394 AD) war was banned.

Ancient Greece

BC

about 2000	Minoan civilization begins in Crete
about 1600	Mycenaean civilization begins
about 1450	Mycenaeans invade Crete
about 1210	Greeks capture Troy
1100–800	'Dark Age' of Greek civilization
about 900	City of Sparta founded
about 750	Greeks setting up colonies overseas
776	First recorded Olympic Games
about 590	Tyrants driven out of Athens
508	Democratic reforms in Athens
490	Greeks defeat Persians at battle of Marathon
461	Pericles becomes leader of Athens
about 447	Parthenon built at Athens
431–404	Athens and Sparta at war
336–323	Reign of Alexander the Great
146	Greece under Roman rule

find out more
Alexander the Great
Ancient world
Archimedes
Armour
Democracy
Drama
Myths and legends
Philosophers
Romans
Slaves
Theatres

Greenhouse effect

Some of the gases in the Earth's atmosphere act naturally like the glass in a greenhouse. They trap heat from the Sun to help keep the surface of the Earth warm. However, human activities have increased the amounts of these greenhouse gases in the atmosphere and they are now trapping too much heat. Scientists believe that this greenhouse effect is causing the world to become warmer.

The atmosphere is a mixture of gases, but our modern lifestyle is upsetting the natural balance of these gases. Exhaust gases from vehicles and power stations add about 6 billion tonnes of carbon dioxide (the main greenhouse gas) to the atmosphere each year. The destruction of huge areas of forest leaves fewer plants to absorb the gas. Methane, another greenhouse gas, is released by animal waste, swamps, paddy-fields, and oil and gas rigs. Nitrous oxide comes from car exhausts and fertilizers. Chlorofluorocarbons (CFCs) are used in refrigerators, aerosols and foam packaging. They are present only in small quantities in the atmosphere, but they are 10,000 times more effective than carbon dioxide at trapping heat.

Scientists believe that we can slow the greenhouse effect if we produce less greenhouse gases. We could burn fewer fossil fuels, like petrol, oil, natural gas and coal, if we develop more efficient heating systems and engines, design buildings which waste less heat, and create transport systems with fewer vehicles.

find out more
Atmosphere
Climate
Energy
Pollution
Power stations

▼ How greenhouse gases trap energy from the Sun.

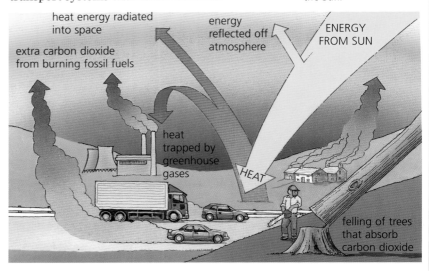

heat energy radiated into space

energy reflected off atmosphere

ENERGY FROM SUN

extra carbon dioxide from burning fossil fuels

heat trapped by greenhouse gases

HEAT

felling of trees that absorb carbon dioxide

Green movement

People who are worried about what humans are doing to the Earth have formed a number of groups to campaign for measures to protect the environment. Together, these groups are known as the green movement.

In many countries, people concerned about green issues have formed political parties. By the end of the 1980s, there was a party known as the Greens or a similar name in almost every country in western and northern Europe. In the 1990s Green parties began to emerge in eastern Europe. In the USA, environmental groups have put forward candidates in elections since the 1980s. Green parties have also developed in such countries as Australia, Canada and New Zealand.

Environmental groups

Many other groups involved in green issues are not political parties. Organizations such as Greenpeace, Friends of the Earth and the Worldwide Fund for Nature raise funds for projects such as the creation of reserves where endangered animals and their habitats can be protected. They also campaign to stop the cutting down of irreplaceable forests, to reduce levels of pollution, to stop dumping of dangerous wastes in the oceans, and on many other environmental issues.

find out more
Acid rain
Conservation
Greenhouse effect
Pollution

▼ Members of Greenpeace trying to stop a beam trawler from putting out its nets. The nets of beam trawlers can cause damage to the sea-bed.

Growth and development

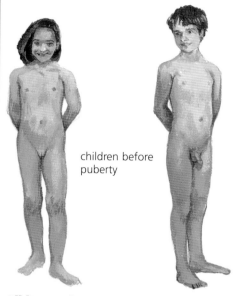

children before puberty

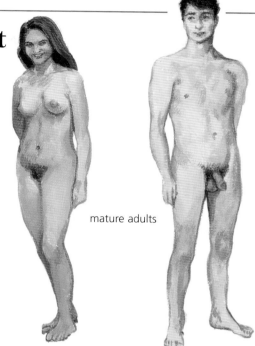

mature adults

◄ During puberty a child's body develops into that of an adult.

• The stage in human social development between childhood and adulthood is known as *adolescence*.

find out more
Animals
Cells
Children
Glands
Living things
Plants
Sex and reproduction

All living things are able to grow. Food is essential for growth, but the kind of food needed is different for plants and animals. Plants need only carbon dioxide gas from the air, water and mineral salts from the soil, and sunlight for growth. Animals need water too. But they also need many complicated foodstuffs like starches, proteins, fats and vitamins. They can only get these by feeding on the bodies of other animals or plants.

Although the foods used are different, the ways in which animals and plants grow are similar. To get bigger, living things make more cells. They change the food they take in into the material for new cells. These are formed when the cells that are already present divide into two. The faster this cell division goes on, the faster a plant or animal will grow.

In plants the cell division is concentrated at special growing points – often at the tips of twigs or roots. In a bud, tiny new leaves and sections of stem are produced out of new cells. They are then expanded to full size when the cells 'blow up', like minute balloons, with extra water.

Human development

Animals grow at different speeds at different times of their life. A human grows fastest as a baby, with different parts of his or her body growing at different rates. After infancy, the overall rate slows down, except for a growth spurt during puberty.

Puberty is a time, usually beginning in your early teens, of physical and emotional changes, when your body develops so that you are capable of producing a baby. During puberty, first girls then, a year or two later, boys go through a period of rapid growth. At the end of puberty, usually between the ages of 16 and 20, they will have grown to their full height.

With the increase in height go other physical changes that turn young teenagers into young adults. These are controlled by hormones, chemical messengers of the body. In girls, the breasts develop, pubic hair grows, the body becomes more curved and the voice less childlike. *Periods* (menstruation) also begin. In boys, the voice 'breaks' (deepens), hair grows on the face, above the penis and elsewhere on the body, and muscular power increases. The penis and testicles also get larger.

Ageing and death

Ageing occurs at different rates for different people. However, everyone experiences a loss of muscle tissue throughout their adult life and loses strength. Women lose their ability to reproduce after they reach the menopause, when they are 45 to 50 years old. This is when their ovaries stop producing eggs and periods stop. The rate at which the body converts food into energy also slows down and the skeleton weakens.

Death is simply the end of life. The heart stops beating, breathing stops, and soon afterwards all activity in the brain stops.

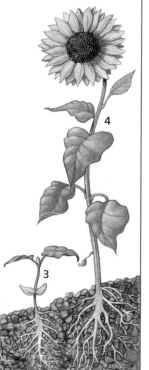

▼ A sunflower plant begins as a seed. Roots grow (1), then a shoot pushes its way through the surface (2). The first leaves are special ones called cotyledons. Then the first full-sized leaves appear (3). At the top of the stem, a flower bud forms becoming a sunflower (4).

Gymnastics

Gymnastics was one of the nine original sports of the first modern Olympic Games in 1896. Its beginnings go back to the times of the ancient Greeks and Romans, whose young men used gymnastic exercises to become fit soldiers.

The best-known gymnastics competitions are the world championships, held every two years, and the Olympic Games, staged every four years.

Both events start with team competitions in compulsory and voluntary exercises. The 36 best gymnasts then go forward to the individual all-round finals, which are followed by individual finals on each piece of apparatus.

Gymnastic exercises

Men perform on six pieces of apparatus, women on four.

Both men and women perform *floor* exercises, which demand strength as well as tumbling skills such as somersaults and back flips. The women's optional exercise is done to music.

The *vault* is used longways for men, sideways for women. Gymnasts launch themselves from the springboard, then somersault off the horse, thrusting with their hands.

The *beam*, for women only, requires balance, as the gymnast must work on a narrow strip only 10 centimetres wide. Expert beam performers can execute many floor skills such as back flips and somersaults.

On the *parallel bars* men gymnasts perform handstands, turns, releases and re-grasps. They make frequent changes of direction as well as swinging and circling movements.

The *asymmetric bars*, for women only, require routines made up mostly of swinging movements from bar to bar. The exercise must flow without pausing or stopping.

On the *horizontal bar* men gymnasts perform continuous swinging movements without stopping. The movements must include circles, twists and changes of grasp.

The *rings* are the greatest test of strength for men gymnasts, particularly arm and shoulder strength. The gymnast must also keep the rings from swinging when he performs handstands or swinging movements.

On the *pommel horse* men gymnasts support their weight with one or both hands on the pommels (handles), or any other part of the horse, while carrying out circular movements with their legs.

Other gymnastic sports

Other gymnastic sports include *rhythmic gymnastics*, for women only, and *sports acrobatics*, in which men or women perform in combinations such as pairs, trios and fours. Rhythmic gymnasts use hand apparatus such as hoops, ribbons, balls, ropes and clubs, while sports acrobatics involves tumbling and circus-style balances.

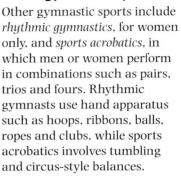

horizontal bar

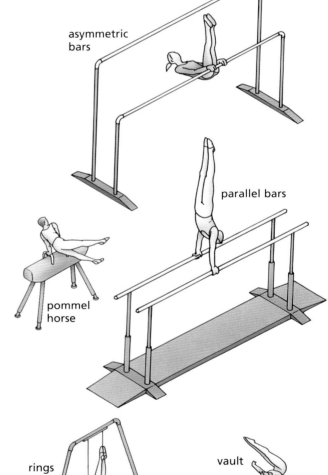

asymmetric bars

parallel bars

pommel horse

rings

vault

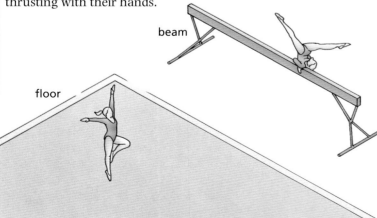

beam

floor

springboard

Gypsies

Gypsies, also known as Romanies, are an independent group of people. They live mostly in Europe and North Africa, but also in North and South America.

Some Gypsies live in houses, but many are travellers who move

from one place to another. They often have problems finding places where they are allowed to camp for a while. Some areas, however, have special campsites for Gypsies and schools for their children.

Most Gypsies are self-employed, doing work such as dealing in scrap metal or offering a service on a short-term basis, such as fruit-picking

at harvest-time. Some may make goods to sell, including baskets and lace, while others sometimes work as musicians, dancers or circus performers.

Because Gypsies live quite differently from most other people, some non-Gypsies regard them with suspicion and try to make them change to fit in more with the rest of society. Gypsies have been treated badly for centuries, but they have so far managed to maintain their distinctive way of life.

Many Gypsies speak a special language called Romany. It is probably derived from a northern Indian language, but it has words from several other languages including Greek and Turkish.

◀ These Gypsies in Romania are living a typical traveller's life. They live in this wagon, and move from place to place to find work.

• In Britain, Romany people are called Gypsies. In France they are called Bohemians or Marouches. In Spain they are Gitanos, and in Sweden they are Tartars.

• Gypsies as well as Jews were put to death in the concentration camps run by Nazi Germany.

Hair

Humans and other mammals are the only animals that have hair on their skin. The hair may be thin and patchy, as it is on humans, but most mammals have lots of it, tightly packed together.

A thick coat of hair, such as you find on a dog, is usually called fur. True fur is made of two sorts of hair: an inner layer of very fine hair that traps a layer of still air close to the animal's body, and an outer layer of thicker guard hairs.

Hair helps to control body temperature. It usually forms a waterproof, insulating coat that keeps down heat loss. Hair also gives an animal its characteristic markings. These are made out of hairs of

different colours and lengths. An animal's markings are often used for camouflage and can be important in attracting a mate.

Animal hairs have other functions, too. For example, whiskers are specialized hairs that act as sensory organs for certain animals that are nocturnal (active at night). Porcupines and hedgehogs have sharp hairs called quills which are used for defence.

The structure of hair

Hairs grow out of a little pit in the skin called a *hair follicle*. The hair itself is dead and is made out of dead skin cells filled with a tough protein called keratin. Hairs do not last for ever. They grow for a while and then fall out and are replaced by new ones. The average life of a long hair on your head is between three and five years.

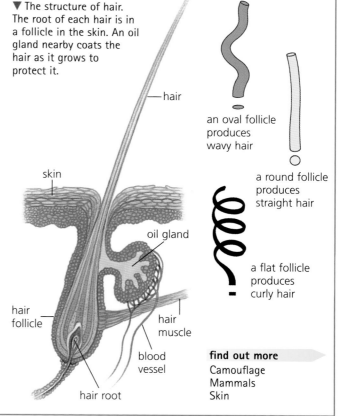

▼ The structure of hair. The root of each hair is in a follicle in the skin. An oil gland nearby coats the hair as it grows to protect it.

hair

skin

oil gland

hair follicle

hair muscle

blood vessel

hair root

an oval follicle produces wavy hair

a round follicle produces straight hair

a flat follicle produces curly hair

find out more
Camouflage
Mammals
Skin

Health and fitness

Good health is hard to define. The World Health Organization calls it 'a state of complete physical, mental and social well-being'.

- Hygiene includes the basic rules for keeping clean and healthy. For example, we need to have regular baths, wear clean clothes, and wash our hands after using the toilet in order to avoid spreading bacteria that cause disease.

Good health depends on many different things. We need to live in a healthy environment, look after our own bodies and have good medical care when we are ill.

Many diseases are caused by the environment in which we live. Food that is not fresh or is poorly prepared can make us ill. Dirty water can lead to cholera, and dirty air to bronchitis. Bad housing conditions cause accidents, and the health of people at work can be damaged by fumes, noise, machinery or stress.

Smoking tobacco and drinking too much alcohol are also damaging to the health. Eating the right kinds of food is an important way of keeping healthy.

Fitness

Keeping as fit as possible helps people live full and healthy lives. Any exercises people do should give them stamina, strength and suppleness. Exercises such

▲ There are many forms of exercise that people do to keep themselves fit and healthy. One of the most popular is running. These runners are competing in the New York Marathon.

as jogging, skipping or cycling will build up stamina by strengthening the lungs, heart and blood system. Whatever exercise they do, people should always build up their level of fitness over a period of time: they should start gently and build up gradually to avoid injuring themselves.

find out more
Complementary medicine
Diets
Doctors
First aid
Medicine

Hearts

A heart is a muscular organ that pumps blood around the body. All vertebrates (animals with backbones) have hearts, as do many larger invertebrates, including earthworms, crabs, insects, snails and squids.

find out more
Blood
Human body

► How the human heart works.

In humans, the heart is in the middle of the chest. It is made up of four muscular chambers: two atria and two ventricles. Their strong contractions as they pump the blood are our heartbeats. The *pulse* is a wave of blood being pushed by a heartbeat along a blood vessel (tube) running from the heart. These blood vessels are close to the surface at the wrist and neck, which are the best places to feel your

pulse. Measuring your pulse rate tells you how fast your heart is beating. A normal rate is about 65–85 beats per minute for an adult.

How blood circulates

The left side of the heart takes in oxygen-carrying blood from the lungs. It then pushes it out along thick-walled blood vessels called *arteries* into very thin blood vessels called *capillaries*. The capillaries carry the blood to and from all parts of the body before joining up with thin-walled blood vessels called veins. The veins carry the blood, which now contains the waste gas carbon dioxide, back to the right side of the heart and the circulation begins again. The heart pushes the blood with the waste carbon dioxide out to the lungs and the gas is breathed out when you exhale.

pulmonary arteries carry blood from heart to lungs

head

right atrium

vena cava (vein) carries blood from body to heart

lung

lung

aorta (artery) carries blood from heart to body

left atrium

pulmonary veins carry blood from lungs to heart

valves

right ventricle

left ventricle

valves

body

Heat

When hot things cool down, their temperature drops and they give off energy. Scientists call this thermal energy, or heat. Heat can travel through solids, liquids, gases, and even through empty space.

find out more
Atoms and molecules
Electricity
Energy
Fire
Gases, liquids and solids
Measurement
Radiation

• As something becomes colder, its atoms or molecules move more slowly. Eventually, they reach a point at which they can lose no more speed. This happens at −273 °C, or *absolute zero*. It is the lowest possible temperature. The Kelvin scale measures temperatures using absolute zero as its starting point. On this scale water freezes at 273 K.

All materials are made up of tiny particles, called atoms and molecules. These are constantly on the move. For example, in a solid object such as an iron bar, the atoms are not still. Each one is vibrating. If the bar is heated up, its atoms get more energy and vibrate faster. With enough heat, they may vibrate so much that they start to break free. At this point the solid melts.

Conduction

If you put one end of a metal spoon in a hot drink, the heat eventually reaches the other end. Heat flows through the metal by conduction, which means that fast-moving atoms at the hot end gradually pass on their energy to slower-moving ones at the colder end. Metals are good *conductors* of heat. Poor conductors of heat are called *insulators*. Air is one example. Wool, feathers and plastic foam all insulate well because they trap air.

Convection

Air is a poor conductor, but it can carry heat in another way – by convection. If air is heated, it rises, and cooler air flows in to take its place. When the hot air cools down again, it sinks. As a result, a circulating current – called a *convection current* – is set up in the air. This is how the air in a room is warmed up by a fire or a radiator. Convection can also take place in liquids.

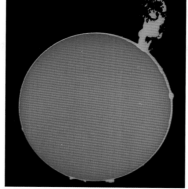

▲ Radiation from the Sun travels millions of kilometres through empty space to heat the Earth.

Radiation

Between the Sun and the Earth, there is empty space. Yet heat from the Sun still reaches us. This is because the heat energy is carried by the Sun's radiation. It travels through space as invisible waves. All hot things lose heat by radiation. The hotter they are, the more they radiate.

Temperature

Temperature tells you how hot something is. It is measured using a thermometer, which has a scale marked on it to show the degree of hotness. Most countries use the Celsius scale (sometimes called the centigrade scale). On this scale water freezes at 0 °C and boils at 100 °C. Temperatures below 0 °C are given minus numbers.

Temperature is not the same as heat. The amount of heat needed to make an iron wire red-hot, for example, would hardly raise the temperature of an iron frying pan at all. Also, different substances need different amounts of heat to change their temperature. For example, it takes more heat to raise the temperature of a kilogram of iron by 1 °C than it does to raise the temperature of a kilogram of aluminium by the same amount.

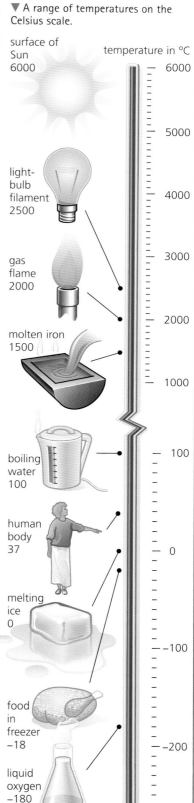

▼ A range of temperatures on the Celsius scale.

temperature in °C

surface of Sun 6000 — 6000

— 5000

light-bulb filament 2500 — 4000

gas flame 2000 — 3000

molten iron 1500 — 2000

— 1000

boiling water 100 — 100

human body 37 — 0

melting ice 0

— −100

food in freezer −18 — −200

liquid oxygen −180

absolute zero = −273

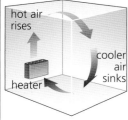

hot air rises

cooler air sinks

heater

▲ Convection currents quickly carry heat around a room.

Hedgehogs, moles and shrews

Although they look very different, hedgehogs, moles and shrews are in fact closely related.

Hedgehogs are covered with hundreds of spines. If a hedgehog feels threatened, it can roll up into a prickly ball and most enemies will leave it alone. Hedgehogs rest during the daytime, but in the evening they set out to look for food. They use their sense of smell to find insects, snails, slugs, grubs and frogs. They hibernate (sleep) through the winter.

Moles are active, burrowing creatures that spend most of their lives in long tunnels underground. They feed mainly on insects, worms and grubs in the soil. Moles are built for digging, with stumpy, powerful bodies and short legs. They have very poor eyesight but an acute sense of smell. They are also very sensitive to movement when they are underground.

Shrews are among the most active of all mammals, hunting small prey day and night. Their tiny bodies burn energy so quickly that some can starve to death if they go more than 4 hours without a meal. Shrews have stink glands on their sides which ensure that hunters such as weasels and cats leave them alone. Birds, however, have a poor sense of smell, and owls and birds of prey often hunt for shrews to eat.

- There are 14 different kinds of hedgehog, 26 different kinds of mole, and 289 different kinds of shrew.

- A mole's fur is short and velvety, so that it can move either forwards or backwards in its tunnels and not rub its fur up the wrong way.

- Hedgehogs have about 3000 spines. They are actually thick hairs, and each one is hollow so all together they weigh very little.

◀ A hedgehog (left), a shrew (centre) and a mole. They all belong to a group of mammals known as insectivores. As the name suggests, insects form an important part of their diet. Hedgehogs grow up to 30 cm long, moles are 7–18 cm long, and shrews about 7 cm.

find out more
Mammals

Helicopters

Helicopters can take off and land vertically from any flat area, even a roof. They are used to carry people and equipment on short-distance journeys to and from inaccessible places such as offshore oil rigs, and between airports and across towns. They carry soldiers quickly around the battlefield, and can fly from ships. Helicopters are also ideal for rescue work on mountains or at sea because they can hover.

Instead of wings, helicopters have long thin blades (the rotor) on top. The engine makes the blades turn. As they spin round, they push air downwards and this lifts the helicopter upwards. By tilting the blades the pilot can make the helicopter take off, hover or land. Helicopters usually have a smaller tail rotor to stop the helicopter spinning round in the opposite direction from the main rotor. Helicopters are noisier and smaller than most other aircraft.

▶ The pilot changes the angle, or pitch, of the spinning blades to control whether the helicopter moves up, down or forwards.

- Helicopters cannot fly as fast as other aircraft. Their top speed is about 400 km per hour.

find out more
Aircraft
Flight

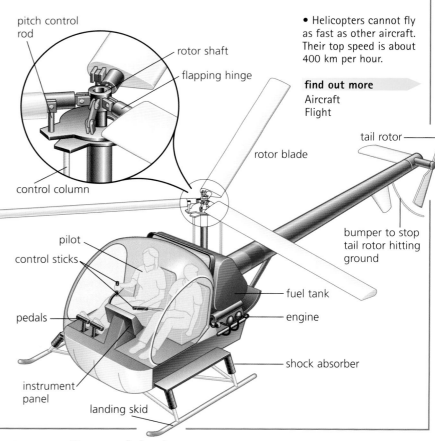

pitch control rod
rotor shaft
flapping hinge
control column
rotor blade
tail rotor
bumper to stop tail rotor hitting ground
pilot
control sticks
pedals
instrument panel
landing skid
fuel tank
engine
shock absorber

Henry VIII

Born 1491 in London,
England
Died 1547 aged 55

Henry VIII is one of England's most famous kings. He was a powerful figure who dealt ruthlessly with anyone who opposed him and few people close to him escaped some trouble.

• As an old man, Henry was a terrifying figure. He could often be unpredictable and impatient and suffered from fits of depression. He had a painful ulcer on his leg, and was so overweight that a machine had to haul him upstairs.

find out more
Elizabeth I
Monks and nuns
Reformation
Tudor England

After Henry VIII came to the throne in 1509, he seemed to have everything. He was handsome, religious, well educated and musical. He had a new wife, Catherine of Aragon, and a loyal minister, Thomas Wolsey, who was his Lord Chancellor.

However, Henry wanted a son to succeed him as king. Catherine had given birth to a daughter, Mary, and he wanted to marry Anne Boleyn, a lady of the court, instead. Wolsey failed to persuade the Pope to give Henry a divorce, and he was dismissed. To get his own way, Henry broke with the Pope and the Catholic Church. He married Anne Boleyn in 1533 (and divorced Catherine afterwards), became Supreme Head of the English Church, and destroyed the monasteries because he wanted their wealth.

Anne Boleyn produced a daughter (who became Elizabeth I), and in 1536 she was beheaded for alleged treason. Henry's next wife, Jane Seymour, died in 1537 giving birth to Henry's long-awaited son, Edward (who became Edward VI). Henry also married and later divorced Anne of Cleves, and Catherine Howard, who was beheaded in 1542 for being unfaithful. He finally found some peace with his sixth wife Katherine Parr.

▲ Henry VIII, king of England and Wales from 1509 to 1547, painted by Hans Holbein the Younger.

Hibernation

Hibernation is a kind of deep sleep in which some animals spend the winter. Most hibernating animals are small creatures that feed on insects, or other food that becomes scarce when the weather is cold.

• Some animals that live in hot, dry places go into a kind of summer hibernation, called *aestivation*, if their food supplies disappear. Insects, snails, mammals and even some fishes aestivate.

• Many animals without backbones (invertebrates) hibernate. Snails and ladybirds cluster together in a safe place. Many butterflies come into buildings.

find out more
Animal behaviour
Animals
Migration

Many cold-blooded animals, such as amphibians and reptiles, hibernate. These animals get their warmth from their surroundings. When the weather gets cold, their body temperature falls, they breathe slowly, and their heartbeat slows down. They become so sluggish that they can scarcely move. Because they are using hardly any energy, they can remain in this state for many months. They hibernate in safe places that are unlikely to freeze.

Warm-blooded hibernators

Almost all warm-blooded hibernators are mammals, including bats, hedgehogs and dormice. When they hibernate, they effectively cease to be warm-blooded: their temperature drops, and their breathing and heartbeat slow down.

Hibernating mammals feed a great deal in the summer, so that by the autumn they are carrying a lot of extra fat. This fat enables them to survive without feeding for months on end. Some hibernators, such as hamsters, make stores and wake up every now and then for a snack.

Many other mammals sleep for much of the winter. Badgers may not come out of their dens for days or even weeks, and bears snooze away the cold months. These animals do not really hibernate, because their bodies are functioning at a normal rate.

▼ This Daubenton's bat is hibernating for the winter in a cave. The outer parts of its body are so cool that water vapour in the air of the cave has condensed to form dew on its fur.

Hindus

Hinduism is a religion that began over 4000 years ago in the Indian subcontinent. Hindus themselves call it the *Sanatana Dharma*, 'eternal truth' or 'teaching'. Many Hindus do not like to use the word religion, but say instead that they follow a total Hindu way of life which affects what they eat and who they marry as well as how they worship.

- Over 80% of the population of India are Hindus. Other Hindus live in North America, Africa, Indonesia, Nepal, Sri Lanka, the Caribbean and Britain.

- Hindus believe that the god Vishnu had 10 avatars or incarnations (new forms) whom he could send down to Earth to help people. These include Krishna, Buddha and Rama, the hero of the epic poem, the *Ramayana*.

▼ Some Hindu temples are enormous, with towers built to look like the Himalaya mountains, the home of the gods. Others, like this street temple in Mumbai (Bombay), India, are small shrines where people can bring their offerings and say their prayers.

Hindus have many different beliefs and practices. They think that everyone has his or her own way of finding a path to God. This means that Hindus are very tolerant of differences within their religion and between different religions. You can still be a Hindu if you do not believe in God, or if you think that God is not a person but a force called Brahman. You can worship God as male (Shiva or Vishnu), as female (Durga, Lakshmi or Saraswati), with a partly animal form (Ganesh or Hanuman), or through an abstract symbol such as fire. In some way or other, these are all pointing to one true God.

Hindus can worship God just as easily in their homes as in temples. You can get to God through loving devotion (*bhakti*), knowledge through study and meditation (*jnana*), and good deeds (*karma*).

Basic ideas

Hindus think that it is very important to teach others *dharma*, the truth about the way things are. Dharma is also the word used for our duty, according to our age and place in society.

All living things have eternal souls (*atman*). These are reborn many times in both animal and human forms. What we will come back as in the next life is determined by our actions (*karma*) in this life, which can result in an improved or worsened fate. The word for the constant round of rebirth is *samsara*.

◀ Ganesh is part-animal, an elephant-headed form of God who can be seen at the entrance of Hindu temples or houses. His title is 'remover of obstacles', and Hindus give offerings to him when they are beginning something, such as starting school or a new business, or going on a long journey.

The soul in each of us is part of the eternal soul, God. It is as if God poured himself into the world at creation. This means that we are all part of God and each other. So when we hurt other living things – trees, animals or humans – we hurt ourselves. Many Hindus respect animal life to the extent of becoming vegetarians. They also think of the cow, which gives people milk to drink, and the oxen, which work for them and provide dung for fuel and fertilizer, as mothers, and never eat beef.

All beings wish to be free from the round of rebirth and return to God. Hindus call this liberation (*moksha*). This may be a state of loving devotion in a community of souls, or it may be returning to the source of being, like a river to the ocean.

Way of life

Some Hindus renounce the world. They do not marry and, wearing distinctive orange robes, live either in religious communities or completely on their own, relying on other people for food. In India people feel that it is an honour to give to a holy person.

Those Hindus who marry often live in an extended family. Many arrange marriages for their children to partners from a similar kind of family. This, and the job they do, might reflect the old 'caste' system,

◀ A Hindu temple in Colombo, Sri Lanka. The elaborate carvings on the tower include images of the gods.

find out more
Festivals and holidays
Gandhi, Mahatma
India

Sacred books

There are two types of Hindu sacred writings: things heard (*sruti*) and things remembered (*smrti*). The sruti are the most sacred and contain the four Vedas and the Upanishads. The books are written in Sanskrit and contain many great sayings about God and the world.

The smrti contain the Laws of Manu and the two great epic poems, the *Mahabharata* and the *Ramayana*. These stories are constantly re-told, acted, danced and painted. The famous *Bhagavad Gita* (Song of the Lord) is part of the *Mahabharata*. Lord Krishna, an incarnation of the god Vishnu, teaches how to worship God by doing your duty in the world. Rama, the hero of the *Ramayana*, is also an incarnation of Vishnu, who comes to Earth to help good overcome evil. The story is one of those remembered at the festival of Divali.

▼ There are many places of pilgrimage for Hindus in India. These holy places are often temples or rivers, and some are mountains. The Ganges is considered a sacred river and thousands of Hindu pilgrims travel to the holy cities along its banks every year. Those who visit Varanasi bathe in the river to make themselves pure, and take home Ganges water as a blessing.

▼ Sadhus are holy men who wander alone all over India, coming together occasionally for religious gatherings. They live on offerings given by ordinary Hindus.

when you were born into an occupation and set place in society. Now education, city life, new laws against such discrimination, and the fact that many Hindus live abroad, have lessened caste divisions.

Families enjoy meeting for worship at home or in a temple. Hindus are very hospitable. Their weddings, other celebrations and many colourful festivals are opportunities for generosity and warm celebrations. One Hindu festival is Divali. 'Divali' means garland of lights. Lakshmi, the goddess of wealth, is believed to visit clean, brightly lit homes at this time.

Hitler, Adolf

Adolf Hitler was the dictator of Nazi Germany. His determination to rule over much of Europe resulted in the outbreak of World War II.

In 1921 Hitler became the leader of the National Socialist German Workers' Party, or Nazis for short. In 1923 the Nazis tried to overthrow the government, but the attempt failed and Hitler went to prison for nine months.

While in prison he wrote *Mein Kampf* ('my struggle'), stating that all Germany's problems were caused by Jews and communists, and that Germany needed a strong Führer (leader) in order to be great again. He believed that he should be that leader. His first taste of power came in 1933 when he was made chancellor (chief minister) by President Hindenburg.

When Hindenburg died in 1934, Hitler became president, chancellor and supreme commander of the armed forces. All opposition to his rule was crushed. Millions were sent to concentration camps, and Jews gradually lost all their rights.

In 1938 Hitler's forces invaded Austria and in 1939 they occupied Czechoslovakia. They invaded Poland the same year, and this triggered the beginning of World War II. Many more Jews and others died in extermination camps, and millions of soldiers and civilians were also killed. When, in 1945, it became clear that the Nazis had been beaten, Hitler shot himself in his underground shelter in Berlin.

Born 1889 in Braunau-am-Inn, Austria **Died** 1945 aged 56

find out more
Dictators
Germany
Holocaust
World War I
World War II

◀ Adolf Hitler, centre, and other Nazi leaders at a rally. The swastika (cross with L-shaped bars) which they are all wearing was adopted by Hitler as the emblem of the Nazi Party. It was even made part of the German national flag in the years 1935–1945.

Hockey

Modern ice hockey began in Canada in the 1870s, as a winter version of field hockey that could be played on frozen ponds and lakes.

In spite of their common origins, the two forms of hockey have developed quite separately and each has its own set of rules.

Hockey

Hockey (or field hockey) is played indoors or outdoors by two teams of 11 players (men or women). The object is to score by hitting the ball with a stick into the opposing side's goal. Outfield players are only allowed to use the flat side of the hooked stick. The goalkeeper can handle the ball, and wears special clothing to give protection against high-speed shots.

Ice hockey

Ice hockey is a six-a-side game played on skates on an ice rink.

◀ Canadian Wayne Gretsky, probably the greatest ice-hockey player of all time, seen here playing for the Los Angeles Kings in 1988.

Instead of a ball, a small flat rubber disc called the puck is used. The aim is to strike the puck with the stick into the opposing goal. Either side of the stick can be used to move the puck.

The rink is surrounded by waist-high barrier boards. The puck can bounce off these and still be in play, so the game flows quickly with few stoppages. There are frequent collisions both between players and against the barrier boards, so all players wear helmets and padded clothing.

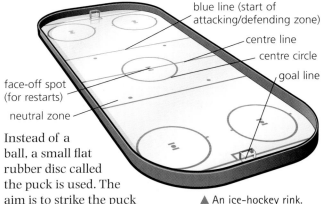

blue line (start of attacking/defending zone)
centre line
centre circle
goal line
face-off spot (for restarts)
neutral zone

▲ An ice-hockey rink.

• India, Pakistan, Germany and Britain are among the strongest nations in (field) hockey. The strongest teams in ice hockey come from North America, Russia, and northern and eastern Europe.

Holocaust

The word 'holocaust' originally meant 'a burnt sacrifice', but it has come to mean the horrific killing of millions of Jews by Nazis before and during World War II.

The Nazi Party rose to power in Germany between the world wars. It gained supporters by promising strong leadership at a time when there was weak government, poverty and unemployment. As soon as the Nazis were in power and Adolf Hitler became Führer (leader), Nazis were taught to believe that 'true' Germans, or 'Aryans', were superior to all other races. When Hitler declared that many of Germany's problems were caused by the Jews, a terrible persecution of all Jews began. Many were forced to live in ghettos (restricted areas), where they died of starvation and disease. Over 1 million were shot.

Concentration camps

The Nazis rounded up Jews in Germany and in the countries that they occupied during the war, and sent them to concentration camps. These were prison camps where Jews had to work hard with little food, and very many of them died. Some of the camps became 'death camps' with gas chambers in which Jews were deliberately killed. In Auschwitz, in occupied Poland, gas chambers killed and burned 12,000 people a day. Four million Jewish men, women and children died in these terrible camps.

• As well as Jews, gypsies, mentally handicapped people, homosexuals and communists were also sent to the camps, and many died.

◄ Children standing behind a barbed wire fence at the Nazi concentration camp at Auschwitz, southern Poland, in 1945. Films and photographs of what Allied soldiers found in these camps after the war were shown all over the world, and they still cause horror when they are seen today.

find out more
Dictators
Germany
Hitler, Adolf
Jews
World War II

Holy Roman Empire

In AD 800 the pope crowned Charlemagne 'Charles Augustus, Emperor of the Romans'. Charlemagne's empire was a pale shadow of the old Roman Empire and it soon broke up. But Charlemagne's title was not forgotten.

Some 150 years later, King Otto I of Germany conquered northern Italy. In 962, as a reward for helping Pope John XII defeat his enemies, he was crowned Roman emperor. Over the next 850 years the title was given to a German prince.

From the 12th century onwards the emperors called themselves Holy Roman Emperors because they claimed to have some control over the Church. The popes, of course, did not agree and there were bitter squabbles. In 1084 Emperor Henry IV drove the pope into exile and a century later Emperor Frederick Barbarossa set up an 'anti-pope'!

▶ King Otto I ('Otto the Great').

▶ The Holy Roman Empire occupied much of central Europe from the 11th century to the 17th century.

The Habsburgs

Until the 17th century the empire stretched from northern Germany to Siena in Italy. But the emperor had only a vague control over this area and his power depended on his family possessions. In 1438 the three bishops and four princes who elected the emperor chose Duke Albert of Habsburg. Thereafter the emperor was always a Habsburg.

The most powerful emperor was Charles V, who was also king of Spain. After he resigned in 1556 the Holy Roman Empire became increasingly meaningless, so that the French philosopher Voltaire remarked that it was 'neither holy, nor Roman, nor an empire.' It was finally abolished in 1806.

1 HAMBURG
2 BILLUNG
3 NORDMARK
4 MEISSEN

KINGDOM OF DENMARK
FRIESLAND
SAXONY
LUSATIA
THURINGIA
LOTHARINGIA
FRANCONIA
BOHEMIA
MORAVIA
SWABIA
BAVARIA
AUSTRIA
CARINTHIA
KINGDOM OF BURGUNDY
KINGDOM OF ITALY
CORSICA
PATRIMONY OF ST PETER
DUCHY OF APULIA
SARDINIA

0   200 km
0   150 miles

find out more
Charlemagne
Germany
Romans

Horses

For thousands of years, and in almost all parts of the world, people have used horses for riding, to pull heavy loads and for sport and leisure. Herds of wild horses still survive in some parts of the world – though all but the zebras of Africa are very rare.

Wild horses live in herds in open grassland, in Africa, the Middle East and Asia. They have sharp senses of sight, hearing and smell, and can detect hunting animals from a distance. They are strong runners, and use their speed over long distances to escape from danger. Herds of feral horses (domestic horses gone wild) survive in many places, especially in the Americas and Australia.

Domestication of horses

Horses were first domesticated by prehistoric people in central Asia over 6000 years ago. At first, they were used to pull lightweight chariots, but when larger breeds were developed, people began to ride. At first they rode without saddles or stirrups. The Roman cavalry were the first to use saddles regularly, and stirrups were only introduced into Europe from Asia in the 9th

▲ Zebras live in family groups. As a family moves, it keeps a strict order. A mare (adult female) leads. She is the dominant female and is followed by her young, and then by up to six more mares and their foals. Right at the back comes the stallion, the father of all of the foals, who fights off predators, such as lions.

century AD. With the arrival of the horse collar at about the same time, people began to use horses to pull heavy weights.

During the Middle Ages, the armour worn by knights was so heavy that only very big horses could carry their weight. Huge animals, called the great horses, were bred. More lightweight, speedier horses were bred in the countries surrounding the Mediterranean Sea. These were the ancestors of the fast, slender-limbed horses such as the Arab breeds. Today there are over 150 breeds of domestic horse, and they are used more for pleasure than for work.

Horse sports

Horse-racing is an ancient sport: the Greeks and the Romans matched their fastest horses against each other. Today the fastest horses run in flat races and are usually thoroughbreds – horses whose ancestry dates back to three stallions that lived in the early 18th century. Some races are over jumps. Hurdles are small jumps, usually about 1 metre in height. Steeplechases include much bigger and more dangerous jumps. Cross-country events involve jumping natural obstacles.

In *show-jumping* events riders take their horses round a constructed course of obstacles. The courses are short, but the obstacles can be very large, and the horses often have to carry out complicated movements. Riders sometimes spend years training horses. Young riders can get their first taste of show-jumping at *gymkhanas*, where they jump their ponies over simple, low obstacles.

Horse records
Largest
One Percheron stood 21 hands (over 2 m), and weighed nearly 2 tonnes
Smallest
The Falabella: adults about 70 cm (7 hands)
Fastest
69.2 km/h averaged over 400 m

• There are seven different kinds of horse, of which two (donkeys and horses) have been domesticated.

• A pony is a small horse, standing less than 142 cm (14 hands) at the withers (the high-point between its shoulder-blades).

find out more
Grasslands
Mammals

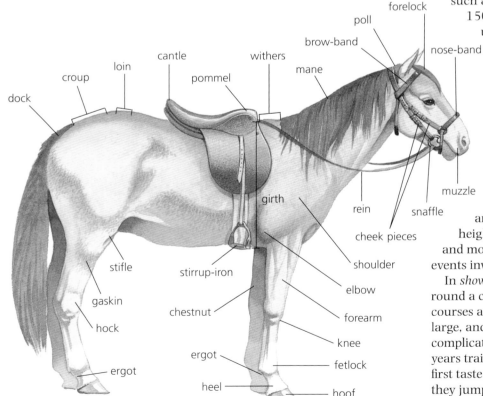

forelock
poll
brow-band
nose-band
cantle
withers
mane
loin
pommel
croup
dock
muzzle
girth
rein
snaffle
cheek pieces
shoulder
stifle
stirrup-iron
elbow
gaskin
chestnut
forearm
hock
knee
ergot
ergot
fetlock
heel
hoof

Horsetails *see* **Plants**

Hospitals

Hospitals provide medical care for people when they are ill or injured and cannot be cared for by a doctor at home. They may also be centres for research, or teaching hospitals, providing training for doctors and nurses.

In many countries hospitals are part of a public health service and treatment is free. There are also some privately run hospitals where patients may have to pay. Large district or general hospitals may have from 300 to over 1000 beds. They provide a wide range of treatments, including emergency care after accidents, surgery, drug treatment and tests.

Types of hospital

General hospitals deal with two sorts of patient: out-patients and in-patients. Out-patients visit the hospital to be seen by a doctor. If the doctor decides that they need to stay in the hospital for a while, they are given a bed and become in-patients.

If a person is injured, they will probably arrive at the accident and emergency (casualty) department in an ambulance. If they need an operation, they will be taken to an operating theatre.

Some hospitals specialize in a particular kind of treatment and care. These include maternity hospitals (caring for women giving birth),

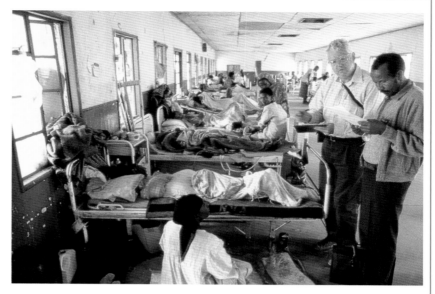

▲ A ward in the Hargeisa hospital, Somalia. The hospital has 245 beds, filled with patients suffering from gastro-enteritis, tuberculosis and injuries from the Somalian civil war.

psychiatric or mental hospitals for people who are mentally ill, paediatric hospitals for children, and geriatric hospitals for old people.

Clinics are medical centres which people attend for treatment and advice. Clinics often concentrate on preventing disease. For instance, pregnant women may attend clinics to learn about keeping healthy. In Western countries clinics often specialize in a particular area, such as diabetes or asthma. In developing countries, where there are fewer hospitals, clinics often serve as general medical centres. Sometimes mobile clinics are used to take medical services to rural areas.

● The word 'hospital' comes from a Latin word meaning 'guest house'.

▶ FLASHBACK ◀

Hospitals existed in ancient Greece and Rome, and even earlier in the East. They were often part of a temple and provided care for the poor. In the Middle Ages in Europe, hospitals were mainly run by nuns and monks. As well as caring for the sick and disabled, they provided shelter and food for travellers and the poor.

From the 13th century, many fine hospitals were established in Italy and France. The first hospital in the Americas was built by the Spanish in Mexico in 1524. In England in the 16th century Henry VIII founded hospitals in London, including St Thomas's and St Bartholomew's. In the rest of Europe, hospitals continued to be provided by the Church. During the 18th century some new English hospitals were founded, but in many areas there were no hospitals. People who could afford it were treated at home. Infection made operations dangerous and in hospitals people died as often as they were cured.

● Paramedics are highly trained health-care workers, such as nurses and emergency medical technicians, who share responsibility for patient care with doctors. Paramedics perform routine medical procedures, usually in a particular area of health care.

▼ A nurse attends a patient in the intensive care unit (ICU) of a hospital in the USA. The ventilator monitor to which the patient is connected monitors the oxygen and carbon dioxide levels of the air he breathes out, and is equipped with an automatic alarm system.

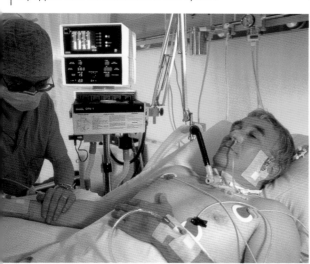

find out more
Doctors
Health and fitness
Medicine
Nightingale, Florence
Nurses
Operations

Household equipment

Home life in Europe and North America was much harder work 200 years ago than it is today. People fetched water from a well, cooked food over an open fire, and did the washing and cleaning by hand. Today, most homes have a constant supply of water and electricity. Equipment such as microwave ovens, refrigerators and washing machines makes our daily life much easier, enabling us to spend less time on household chores.

Most modern houses are connected to mains electricity, drains, water, and possibly a gas supply as well. These are called *services*. Basic equipment is built into the house, including taps, sinks, a bath or shower, a toilet, and a central-heating system. Large, heavy items of household equipment, such as cookers, washing machines, tumble driers and refrigerators, are usually kept in one place. Mains electricity provides an instant power supply for most of these machines, and electronics can make them even more useful and efficient. Controlled by a microchip, a dishwasher can wash, rinse and dry dirty crockery and cutlery at the press of a button.

Equipment such as vacuum cleaners, food mixers, irons and electric kettles needs to be movable. Most of these items are powered by mains electricity but the trailing electrical cables can get in the way. Cordless irons and kettles use mains power but lift free from their base and cable.

Cookers

Until the 18th century most cooking was done over an open fire of wood, coal or peat. Then ovens and hobs were placed beside the grates that enclosed the open fire. Later, the ovens and hobs were linked by hot plates placed over the fires. In the early 19th century the closed range was introduced for cooking and for heating water. Modern cookers use gas, electricity or solid fuel such as coal or wood. Microwave ovens produce heat when the microwaves enter the food inside the oven. They cook food more quickly than conventional ovens and so save energy.

On some electric cookers, the hobs use heat from tungsten halogen lamps instead of coiled elements which are heated by the flow of electricity. Another type of hob, called an induction hob, will heat up the base of a metal saucepan which, in turn, heats up the food. The rest of the hob, apart from the area in contact with the pan, stays cool.

● In a microwave oven, microwaves cause the food molecules to jump about. The resulting friction between the molecules brings about a rise in temperature, cooking the food from the inside.

find out more
Electronics
Refrigerators
Waste disposal
Water

▼ Vacuum cleaners are used to clean carpets and other flooring. A fan makes a partial vacuum inside the cleaner. The air rushes in, bringing dust and dirt with it.

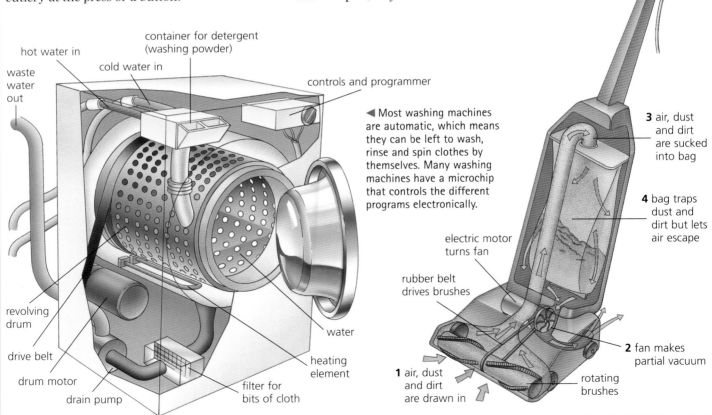

hot water in

container for detergent (washing powder)

cold water in

waste water out

controls and programmer

◄ Most washing machines are automatic, which means they can be left to wash, rinse and spin clothes by themselves. Many washing machines have a microchip that controls the different programs electronically.

3 air, dust and dirt are sucked into bag

4 bag traps dust and dirt but lets air escape

electric motor turns fan

rubber belt drives brushes

revolving drum

drive belt

drum motor

drain pump

filter for bits of cloth

water

heating element

1 air, dust and dirt are drawn in

rotating brushes

2 fan makes partial vacuum

Houses

Houses are made from different materials and come in many shapes and sizes, to suit various climates and ways of life. A bungalow in an Australian suburb is a house, but so is a flat in a high-rise block in Hong Kong.

▲ The nomadic (wandering) people of Mongolia live in tents called gers (yurts). The ger is covered with skin or cloth. Inside it is draped with brightly coloured rugs.

Despite 20th-century improvements in central heating, air-conditioning and insulation, houses last longer and are more pleasant to live in if they are designed to suit the climate. Sloped roofs are best in rainy areas; thick walls and small windows keep rooms cool in hot countries; and verandas or porches are often used as outdoor rooms in countries that have warm summers.

Materials

Houses can now be built from materials brought from distant places by modern transport, but in many countries builders still use local materials. Traditional materials include stone, timber, clay (often made into bricks), straw, reeds or turf.

The Inuit, who live in Arctic regions, use snow blocks for their homes (igloos). Near the Congo River, in Africa, houses are made of woven

▶ A mud-brick house in Yemen, in the Arabian Desert. This style of building is found throughout the Middle East and North Africa.

▶ In some coastal areas of Benin, in Africa, huts are built on stilts to raise them well above the water level. The huts are made of bamboo from the nearby bamboo forests.

bamboo mats. In Saudi Arabia the earth of the desert is pressed together into mud-brick houses. Wood is still used for building in countries that have large forests, such as Canada and the Scandinavian countries.

Wood is used for some of the world's most modern houses. This one, on the USA's east coast, blends well into the surrounding woodland.

▼ Blocks of flats (tenements) that were built up to 400 years ago still stand in Edinburgh's city centre, Scotland.

Style

European-style houses are typically built in rows (terraces), in pairs (semi-detached), or on top of each other in blocks of flats (apartment blocks). This saves land, which is expensive in towns and cities. It also makes the houses cheaper to build and to buy.

The idea of building flats is a very old one. In the ancient Roman town of Ostia, the remains of three-, four-, and five-storey blocks of flats can still be seen. By today's standards these flats were quite large – the largest of them had 12 rooms.

With modern building methods, apartment blocks can be built more than 50 storeys high, as in Hong Kong, Kuala Lumpur and other crowded cities of South-east Asia.

find out more
Architecture
Building
Castles

Human beings

Today there are over 5.5 billion human beings on Earth. All humans belong to the same animal species – *Homo sapiens sapiens*. Like cats, horses and dolphins, humans are mammals, and of all the mammals they are the most successful.

▶ Skin colour is the result of how much melanin (dark colouring) your skin contains, and that depends on which part of the world your ancestors came from. Melanin protects the skin from the Sun's burning rays, so people with dark skin originally came from hot, sunny countries. Pale-skinned people came from colder countries where the sunshine is weaker.

• Most democracies have included some idea of 'human rights' in their constitution. These include the right to free speech, to vote, to follow your own religion and to have a fair trial in a court of law. Amnesty International, an organization founded in 1961, campaigns against abuses of basic human rights.

The key to the success of humankind is our intelligence. It has enabled us to use fire, make tools, construct shelters, grow food and clothe our bodies. We have increasingly adapted the environment to our needs. As a result, human beings have spread throughout the world, from forests and deserts to remote islands and the Arctic ice.

Social animals

Human beings are social animals. This means that we grow up in families and choose to live our lives in groups. Since prehistoric times human beings have banded together in tribes and clans to share important tasks such as food-gathering and child-rearing, and to provide security for each other. Our skill with language enables us to share knowledge and ideas, helping to keep the group together.

About 10,000 years ago small human groups discovered how to grow crops and settled down to farm the land. Since then, human settlements have grown from simple villages to vast cities, where millions of people live and work, and from which money, food and goods are traded across the world.

Rich variety

Tall and short, fat and thin, black and white: although human bodies are all built to the same plan, they are all different. Some of this variety is explained by the fact that human beings have adapted to their environment as they have spread. The Inuit people of the Arctic, for example, have relatively short stocky bodies. This shape helps them to keep warm by reducing the surface area through which heat can escape. In contrast, people who live in hot dry climates, such as the Watusi in central Africa, have tall slender bodies, which are less likely to overheat.

As well as physical variety, there is a huge variety in human culture from place to place. The food we eat, the music we listen to and the religion we follow are just some of the things that make up our culture. Today, as people are more mobile, cultures are mixing more and more.

However, when people move from one culture to another they may keep links with their original culture, or 'roots'. *Ethnic groups* are communities of people who feel they have a common cultural identity. They may share a language, a religion and traditional customs. The USA, for example, is often called a multi-ethnic society because many people there would describe themselves as being members of an ethnic group (for instance Jewish, Hispanic or Chinese) at the same time as being American.

▼ At various times in history groups of human beings have shown great cruelty towards other groups simply because they have different ethnic backgrounds. In the 1990s in the former Yugoslavia, Bosnian Serbs attempted to 'cleanse' the land of non-Serbian peoples. These Bosnian Muslims are being kept prisoner by Serbs, who forcibly removed them from their houses and land.

Human body

Like the bodies of all animals, the human body is made up of billions of tiny cells. Particular kinds of cells are grouped together to form tissues, and these in turn are organized together into organs such as the heart and the lungs.

Some groups of organs and tissues work together in *systems* to perform particular jobs. There are eight main systems in the human body.

The *skeleton* is a system of bones and joints that supports the soft parts of the body and provides a framework for muscles to attach to. *Muscles* make the limbs and organs of the body move.

In the *digestive system* food is broken down into a liquid form from which nutrients that the body needs can be absorbed into the blood. The *excretory system* is the body's waste disposal unit. It is made up of the kidneys and the bladder.

The windpipe (trachea) and the lungs are the *respiratory system*. This system enables us to take in oxygen, which our bodies use to produce energy from our food. The *circulatory system* is made up of the heart, the blood vessels and the blood. The blood carries nutrients and oxygen to all the body tissues, and takes away waste materials.

The *nervous system* is made up of the brain, the spinal cord and a network of nerves. It is the body's communication and control system. The *reproductive* *systems* of males and females work together to produce new human beings.

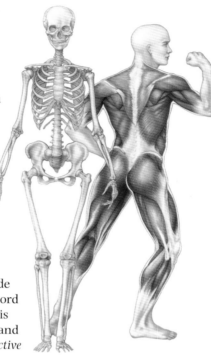

◀ The skeleton and the muscular system.

find out more
Blood
Bones
Brains
Breathing
Cells
Digestive systems
Ears
Eyes
Glands
Growth and development
Hair
Hearts
Kidneys
Lungs
Muscles
Nervous systems
Noses
Pregnancy and birth
Senses
Sex and reproduction
Skeletons
Skin
Sleep
Teeth

Hunter-gatherers

Hunter-gatherers are people who live by hunting animals, fishing, and gathering wild foods such as fruits, nuts, vegetables and honey.

Hunter-gatherers live in some of the harshest places in the world. The Inuit live in the Arctic, the Bushmen in the Kalahari Desert, the Australian Aborigines in the outback, and the Pygmies in the rainforests of central Africa. Hunter-gatherers live healthy lives where others could not survive at all. This is because of their deep knowledge of their environment, the animals and plants, the weather and the seasons. Our human ancestors hunted wild animals over 2 million years ago, and hunting and gathering was the way of life of all humankind until about 11,000 years ago. It was only when people discovered how to grow crops that they stopped living in this way.

◀ These hunter-gatherers, who belong to the Masai people of East Africa, are using a homemade ladder to gather honey from a baobab tree in the Tarangire area of Tanzania.

How hunter–gatherers live
It is mostly the men who hunt and the women who gather, but this is not always the case. Hunter-gatherers are skilled hunters, hunting alone or in groups. They make weapons, nets, traps and tools out of natural materials such as wood, bone, ivory and stone.

Most hunter-gatherers move from place to place so that they can always get food and water. Many live in small groups known as bands. These bands may be just a single family and are rarely bigger than 100 people. They follow the migrations of the wild animals that they hunt, and plan their movements very carefully.

• Today only about 0.001% of the population of the world are hunter-gatherers.

find out more
Aborigines
Bushmen
Inuit
Prehistoric people
Pygmies

Human rights *see* Human beings • **Hummingbirds** *see* Birds • **Hungary** *see page 625*

Hunting birds

Hunting birds, or 'birds of prey', such as eagles, falcons and hawks, are superbly equipped to hunt and kill other animals for food. They have hooked bills, and powerful feet with talons. Their sight is better than ours and they have good hearing.

▶ This red kite soars in the sky hunting for prey. Most birds of prey have such good eyesight that they can spot a meal from a great height.

Vultures are powerful birds related to these hunters, but they usually feed by scavenging on the remains of dead animals (carrion). Owls are sometimes called the nocturnal (night-time) birds of prey, but they are not closely related to falcons or vultures.

Out to kill

Hunting methods and types of prey vary enormously. Harriers fly low over the ground searching for small mammals and birds. Sparrowhawks have long legs for grasping prey. They also have short, broad wings and long tails for manoeuvring in the woods where they live. Peregrines use their speed to kill other birds in flight. Lammergeyers drop bones onto rocks from a height to get at the marrow. Honey buzzards that eat bees have blunt talons for digging out bees' nests. Vultures soar, searching for signs of carrion, and rarely hunt live prey.

Most owls hunt at night. Their large, forward-facing eyes allow them to see in poor light and to judge distance accurately. Owls have very good hearing, so they can hunt even in total darkness. Great grey owls can hear their prey moving under the snow. An owl's soft feathers allow it to fly silently, so its prey does not hear it approaching. Some owls eat small animals, others catch insects, and a few catch fish.

Falconry

Falconry is an ancient sport that uses trained birds of prey to hunt wild birds and other animals. It may have originated in China 4000 years ago. It was common in Europe in the Middle Ages and has recently been revived. Hawks, falcons, eagles and buzzards are the most commonly kept species. Once all birds were taken from the wild. Now most are bred in captivity.

Hunters hunted

For years humans have shot, trapped and poisoned hunting birds to protect game birds from being preyed on by them. Many have been taken into captivity for falconry. Certain chemical pesticides used in farming are also harmful to hunting birds, because their prey becomes poisoned. The most harmful of these have been banned in many countries. Many populations, such as peregrine falcons, have declined rapidly as a result of chemical poisoning.

Hunting-bird records
Largest
Andean condor: length 116 cm
Largest owl
Eagle owl: length 70 cm
Smallest
Black-legged falconet: length 14 cm; elf owl: 13–15 cm

• Owls swallow their prey whole and then bring the inedible parts back up as pellets or castings. If you pull these pellets apart, you can see what the owl has eaten by the bones and other food remains in them.

◀ Ospreys catch their prey by diving into the water feet first and grabbing the fish with their talons. Their feathers are waterproof, and their nostrils close as they dive.

find out more
Birds
Eyes
Food chains and webs

Hydroelectric power

The downhill flow of water in fast-moving rivers or from waterfalls and dams is a source of energy. In the past, this energy was used to turn wheels for milling grain or to provide power for factories. Modern hydroelectric power (HEP) schemes harness this energy to produce electricity.

An HEP scheme usually has a large dam, made of earth, concrete or stone, to hold back the water in a reservoir. Large pipes carry the water from the reservoir to turbines (special water wheels), which drive the generators that produce electricity.

In a *pumped-storage system*, water runs between two reservoirs at different levels and generates electricity. At night, when demand for energy is low, this electricity is used to pump the water back to the upper reservoir. This water is used to generate electricity in the day, when demand is greater.

- The world's first electric power station, in Godalming, UK, was driven by water from a local river.

- The Itaipú hydroelectric project in Brazil and Paraguay is designed to provide over 12 million kilowatts of power.

- In countries with large rivers and waterfalls, much electricity is generated by water power, an energy source that will never run out.

find out more
Dams
Electricity
Energy
Power stations
Tides
Water

▼ In a hydroelectric power scheme, water flowing from a dam turns turbines that drive the generators to produce electricity.

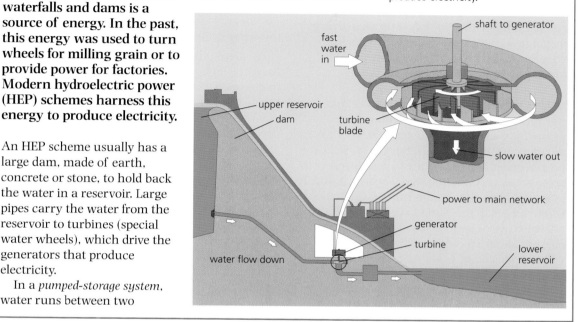

fast water in
upper reservoir
dam
turbine blade
shaft to generator
slow water out
power to main network
generator
turbine
lower reservoir
water flow down

Hydrogen

Hydrogen is a very light, invisible gas that burns easily. It is also the commonest element in the Universe. However, nearly all of the Earth's hydrogen is locked away in other substances.

Hydrogen atoms are the lightest of all atoms. They stick together in pairs to form molecules of hydrogen gas. When hydrogen gas burns, it combines with oxygen in the air to form water. Each water molecule is made up of two hydrogen atoms joined to one oxygen atom. (The chemical formula for water is H_2O.)

Nearly all of the Earth's hydrogen is combined with other elements in substances such as water, oil and natural gas. Industry gets most of its hydrogen from natural gas. Hydrogen can also be extracted from sea water. Passing an electric current through the water splits it into hydrogen and oxygen atoms.

find out more
Atoms and molecules
Balloons and airships
Elements
Gases, liquids and solids
Rockets

◀ The fuel tank in this experimental car is being filled with liquid hydrogen, which produces no pollution. However, liquid hydrogen is expensive to produce and must be stored at extremely low temperatures.

Uses of hydrogen

The chemical industry uses hydrogen in the manufacture of ammonia, soap and plastics. The food industry uses it to turn oils into margarine.

Being so light, hydrogen floats in air. At one time, airships and balloons were filled with hydrogen. But in the 1930s there were terrible accidents when airships caught fire. Today, airships are filled with helium gas.

Hydrogen is used as rocket fuel. One day it may be widely used as a fuel in cars and trucks. Hydrogen-powered engines are non-polluting and produce only water vapour (extracting hydrogen in the first place causes some pollution).

Our Sun is mainly hydrogen. It gets its heat and light by releasing the nuclear energy in hydrogen atoms.

Ice

Ice is water that is frozen solid. Ice cubes, hail, snow, icicles, frozen puddles and ponds, and glaciers are all composed of the same basic substance – ice. Individual crystals of ice stick together to form larger blocks of ice. Millions of tiny ice crystals measuring only a few millimetres across are packed together tightly to form huge lumps of floating ice called icebergs.

Under a magnifying lens you would see that snowflakes are composed of numbers of six-pointed, star-like crystals. Bigger blocks of ice are also made up of ice crystals, but the crystals are too numerous and too tightly packed together to be seen. Most crystals measure between 1 and 20 millimetres, but the crystals that make up the oldest glaciers in the world have been repeatedly re-formed over a long period, and some now measure about 50 centimetres across.

The expansion of water as it freezes into ice can produce a very powerful force. Freezing water in winter can burst pipes and damage car engines unless they have antifreeze in them. On mountainsides, rainwater seeps into cracks in the rocks. If the water freezes, it expands with such force that it will split the rocks and make pieces fall off.

▼ Icebergs floating in Jokulsarlon Lake, Iceland. The ice has 'calved' from the nearby Vatnajokull glacier, one of the largest in Europe.

If you press ice very hard, it will begin to melt. The best snowballs are made when the snow melts a little if you press it together. If it is much colder than 0 °C (the freezing point of pure water), then the ice and snow will stay frozen and the snow will be too cold to melt when you squeeze it.

Ice-sheets and icebergs

Large areas of ice and snow which permanently cover the land are called ice-sheets. They are all that remain of the great sheets of ice that once covered large parts of the world. The world's main ice-sheets are found in Antarctica and Greenland.

Icebergs are huge lumps of ice that break away from ice-sheets (and glaciers) and float in the sea. Only about a ninth of an iceberg shows above the surface. The part that is hidden under the water may be wider than the part that shows. This is a great danger to shipping. The largest icebergs break away from the edge of Antarctica, such as from the Ross Ice Shelf. This area of floating ice is as large as France. Icebergs in the Arctic are smaller than the Antarctic ones, but they are often taller. Glaciers reach the sea around Greenland, and as the ice begins to float, huge lumps 'calve' or break off.

Icebergs begin to melt as they drift away from the polar regions. Cold currents carry icebergs great distances. The cold Labrador Current can carry Arctic icebergs into the busy North Atlantic shipping routes. The International Ice Patrol warns ships about drifting icebergs.

▲ These flower-shaped patterns of frost are really crystals of ice. Frost forms during very cold nights when the air temperature falls below the freezing point of water (0 °C). Moisture in the air freezes into tiny ice crystals where the air is in contact with surfaces such as blades of grass and windows.

Iceberg records
Largest iceberg
Over 31,000 sq km (335 km long and 97 km wide), seen in the South Pacific Ocean in November 1956
Tallest iceberg
167 m high, seen off west Greenland in 1958

find out more
Antarctica
Arctic
Crystals
Gases, liquids and solids
Glaciers
Greenhouse effect
Rain and snow
Water

Immunity

Immunity is the body's ability to defend itself against infection and fight disease. Different parts of your body make up the immune system.

When 'foreign bodies', such as viruses and bacteria, invade your body they can cause disease. The immune system recognizes that chemical groups (molecules) called *antigens* on the surface of these 'invaders' are not part of your body and that the germs that carry them are not wanted. It immediately starts to make *antibodies*, which react with the antigens, making the germs harmless. Once the antibodies against a particular disease have been formed, your body can produce them again when faced with the same 'invaders'. This is called *active immunity* and may be long-lasting. When antibodies from someone who is already immune are injected into you, you have *passive immunity*. This only lasts a number of weeks.

Various parts of the body are involved in the immune system. The thymus helps in the development of the immune system. White blood cells fight 'invaders', and make antibodies. Bone marrow helps make white blood cells. The lymph nodes help get rid of bacteria, and make antibodies and white blood cells. The spleen helps keep the blood clean, and makes antibodies. The tonsils also help to protect you from infection.

tonsils
thymus
lymph nodes
bone marrow
lymph vessels
spleen

◄ The human immune system.

• Vaccinations or immunizations are injections of harmless germs. You do not get ill, but your body's immune system responds by producing antibodies as if you had been invaded by a disease-causing germ.

find out more
AIDS
Bacteria
Blood
Diseases
Viruses

Incas

The Incas were native South Americans who developed an empire in and around the Andes mountain range in the 15th and early 16th centuries. At its greatest, their territory extended for about 4000 kilometres and they ruled about 12 million people.

The Incas probably began as mountain people who moved to the valley of the Cuzco (now Peru) in about AD 1000. They gradually conquered neighbouring nations until they ruled the whole region.

Life, work and government
Almost every Inca man was a farmer, making food and clothing for himself and his family. The Incas grew maize (corn), potatoes, tomatoes, peanuts and cotton, and raised guinea pigs, ducks, llamas, alpacas and dogs.

Inca palaces, temples, irrigation systems and fortifications can still be seen throughout the Andes. The Incas also built a network of highways and minor roads over and through the mountains. They used impressive engineering techniques to construct short rock tunnels and vine-supported suspension bridges.

The ruler of the empire was thought to be a god and descended from the Sun. He was known as the Inca and he had absolute power over a highly organized system of government. Below him were the rulers, nobles, common people, and a special group of craftspeople and servants.

In 1532 Spanish invaders, led by Francisco Pizarro, arrived in Peru and captured the ruling emperor Atahualpa. The Incas resisted, but by the 1570s they had been utterly crushed by the Spaniards and their empire was at an end.

0   1000 km
0   600 miles

▲ The territory under the influence of the Inca empire at the height of its power.

◄ This young girl was buried on a volcano 500 years ago as a gift to the mountain gods, an Inca human sacrifice.

find out more
South America

India

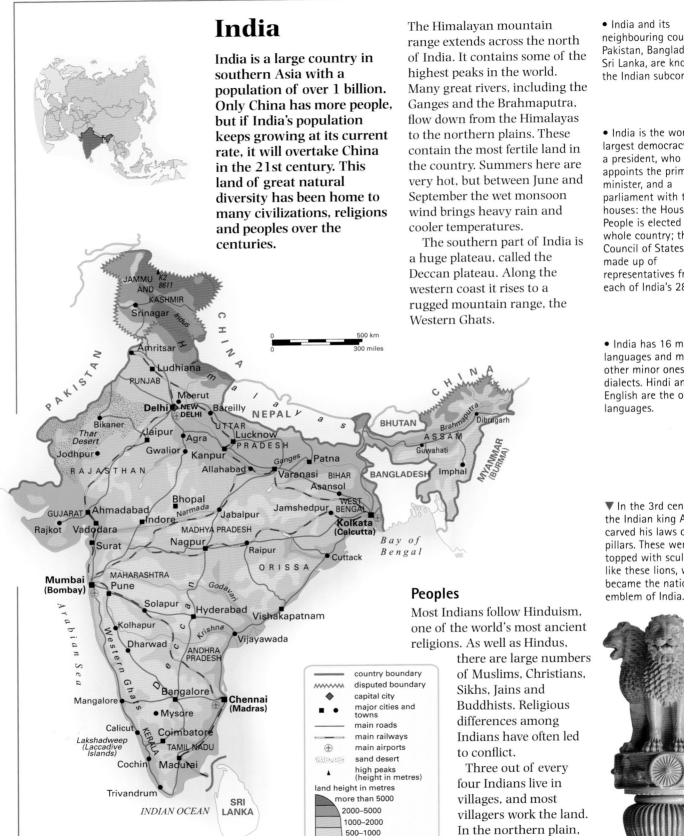

India is a large country in southern Asia with a population of over 1 billion. Only China has more people, but if India's population keeps growing at its current rate, it will overtake China in the 21st century. This land of great natural diversity has been home to many civilizations, religions and peoples over the centuries.

The Himalayan mountain range extends across the north of India. It contains some of the highest peaks in the world. Many great rivers, including the Ganges and the Brahmaputra, flow down from the Himalayas to the northern plains. These contain the most fertile land in the country. Summers here are very hot, but between June and September the wet monsoon wind brings heavy rain and cooler temperatures.

The southern part of India is a huge plateau, called the Deccan plateau. Along the western coast it rises to a rugged mountain range, the Western Ghats.

- India and its neighbouring countries, Pakistan, Bangladesh and Sri Lanka, are known as the Indian subcontinent.

- India is the world's largest democracy. It has a president, who appoints the prime minister, and a parliament with two houses: the House of the People is elected by the whole country; the Council of States is made up of representatives from each of India's 28 states.

- India has 16 major languages and many other minor ones and dialects. Hindi and English are the official languages.

▼ In the 3rd century BC the Indian king Asoka carved his laws on pillars. These were topped with sculptures, like these lions, which became the national emblem of India.

Peoples

Most Indians follow Hinduism, one of the world's most ancient religions. As well as Hindus, there are large numbers of Muslims, Christians, Sikhs, Jains and Buddhists. Religious differences among Indians have often led to conflict.

Three out of every four Indians live in villages, and most villagers work the land. In the northern plain, wheat is the main crop. In the south and east,

Map legend
- country boundary
- disputed boundary
- ◆ capital city
- ■ • major cities and towns
- main roads
- main railways
- ⊕ main airports
- sand desert
- ▲ high peaks (height in metres)
- land height in metres
  - more than 5000
  - 2000–5000
  - 1000–2000
  - 500–1000
  - 200–500
  - less than 200
  - sea level

where it is wetter, rice is the most important crop. Farmers also grow maize (corn), millet, bananas, groundnuts, lentils, sugar cane, pepper, tea, coffee, tobacco and cotton.

In order to feed its rapidly growing population, new types of rice and wheat were introduced in the 1960s to produce bigger crops. This was called the Green Revolution. However, regular droughts and floods still destroy crops.

▲ Cooking on the street in Mysore, southern India. Indian food is famous for its richness and variety, but most Indians have a very simple diet. In the south, this may be rice and dal, a dish made from puréed lentils or split peas.

Mines and factories

India is rich in minerals. It has large deposits of coal, iron ore, bauxite (from which aluminium is made), manganese and zinc. Factories build everything from bicycles and sewing machines to ships and aircraft. In rural areas, small workshops turn out pottery, cloth and other craft goods.

India has its own space industry, and has launched satellites. In such a large country, these are vital for communications. Bangalore, in the south, has an important computer industry. Its workers write software programs that are used throughout the world.

Cities

India has two of the world's largest cities, Mumbai (Bombay) and Kolkata (Calcutta), both with over 10 million inhabitants. Many people travel to the cities from rural areas, because there is not enough work for them to do on the land. In the cities many of them find work, but it is much harder for them to find somewhere to live. To help solve this problem, the government has improved roads and railways, so that villagers can travel to the city each day.

India's history

The earliest civilization in this area grew up around the city of Harappa in the Indus valley, in what is now Pakistan, and extended east into present-day India. Around 2500 BC the people of this region built huge irrigation (watering) systems, heated baths and temples, and invented their own writing.

The next stage in India's development followed the arrival of the Aryan people from central Asia in about 1500 BC. The Aryans developed the Sanskrit language and two great religious faiths, Hinduism and Buddhism.

In the third century BC, under the wise leadership of the Mauryan kings Chandragupta and Asoka, a single Indian nation began to emerge. It was based on the state of Magadha around the River Ganges, and extended west to Afghanistan and south almost to Sri Lanka.

Between AD 320 and 467 India enjoyed a golden age under the great kings of the Gupta dynasty. The many fine

temples built during this period included one at Sarnath, where Buddha had first taught. Indian dance, music and poetry flourished.

Muslims and Christians

In the 8th century a third great religion was introduced into India. This was Islam, carried by Arab conquerors sweeping through the mountain passes of the north-west. Southern India was not seriously affected, and in the 9th century the Hindu Chola people set up a vast and wealthy trading empire that stretched from Sri Lanka to the Ganges.

▲ Children harvesting wheat in Rajasthan, northern India. The monsoon rains do not reach the north-west of India, and a large part of Rajasthan is desert.

▼ Huge film posters dominate the streets of Mumbai (Bombay). Mumbai has the largest film industry in the world, producing about 900 films each year.

◀ The Taj Mahal at Agra is probably India's most famous landmark and one of the most beautiful buildings in the world. It was built between 1632 and 1649 by the Mughal emperor Shah Jahan in memory of his wife, Arjumand Banu Begam.

From the 13th century onwards northern India was hit by wave after wave of Mongol invaders from central Asia. In one attack, in 1398, Tamerlane ('Timur the lame') sacked Delhi and killed most of its inhabitants. A little over a century later the Muslim warlord Babur invaded India and founded the Mughal (Persian for Mongol) empire, which lasted until 1858.

The most successful Mughal emperor was Akbar (1556–1605). He conquered fresh lands and kept people happy by tolerating the Hindu religion. By this time, however, yet another group of people had arrived – Christians from Europe. They came as traders but soon seized bases of their own. Then, taking advantage of squabbles between Indian princes, they gradually took over more and more of the country.

The British were the most successful of the new arrivals. In the 18th century they drove out their French rivals. By the 19th century they controlled most of the country. In 1876 the British queen Victoria became Empress of India.

An independent nation
The British ruled India less harshly than most conquerors. Efforts were made to improve agriculture and relieve famine. A fine railway system was built and Western-style education was introduced. In 1885 the Indian National Congress was set up by educated Indians to ask for more of a voice in their own government. When the British turned down their demands, a movement for full independence was born.

From 1919 the most important leader of the independence campaign was Mohandas (Mahatma) Gandhi. His successful non-violent tactics involved refusing to co-operate with the British. The British gradually gave way, and after World War II they agreed to full independence for India.

Unfortunately, the Hindu and Muslim politicians could not agree what form Indian independence should take. The British solved the problem in 1947 by dividing the country into the largely Hindu nation of India and the Muslim state of Pakistan.

Under prime minister Jawaharlal Nehru (1947–1964), India began to build up its industry, and by the 1980s the economy began to boom. However, from time to time religous differences have led to ugly violence. There have also been three wars with Pakistan (1947, 1965, 1971), and tensions between the two countries remain high.

• The Amritsar massacre (1919) shocked people all over India. A crowd had gathered in a small park to listen to nationalist leaders. As large meetings were forbidden, the British General Dyer told the people to leave. He then ordered his troops to open fire. 379 people were killed and about 1200 wounded in the gunfire.

• In 1984 there was a leak of dangerous gas from a US chemicals factory in Bhopal, in Madhya Pradesh. Over 3000 people died and as many as 250,000 were injured in the world's worst ever industrial disaster.

find out more
Asia
Bangladesh
British empire
Buddhists
Dance
Gandhi, Mahatma
Hindus
Jains
Mongol empire
Muslims
Pakistan
Sikhs
See also Countries fact file, page 625

◀ Hinduism has many gods, and each part of the country has its own festivals, temples and sacred places. The Rathayatra (car festival) takes place at the temple of Jagannatha in Puri, eastern India, every June. Thousands of people gather to haul heavy wooden images of the god Jagannatha and his brother and sister from the temple at Puri to another temple, in the country.

Indonesia

Indonesia, in South-east Asia, is the world's largest island chain. It is made up of over 13,000 islands, scattered over 8 million square kilometres of ocean. Only 3000 of these islands are inhabited, and 60 per cent of people live on just one island – Java.

The Equator runs through the middle of Indonesia. The climate is hot, and the annual rainfall is over 2000 millimetres in most parts. This hot, wet climate means that farmers can grow rice, which is the country's basic food.

In many of the outer islands, such as Borneo and Sumatra, there are dense rainforests. Unfortunately, much of Indonesia's forest is being cleared for mining, oil exploration, farming and timber. In recent years the economy has boomed thanks to the discovery of oil and natural gas, and the building of factories that make shoes, textiles and electronics.

Many different peoples live in Indonesia. In the rainforests some tribes still live traditional lives, either hunting or clearing small plots to grow food, then moving on and letting the forest return. Other people have settled in Indonesia, including Hindus, Buddhists and Muslim traders.

Indonesia was a Dutch colony until 1949. From independence until 1998 Indonesia had only two leaders, Presidents Sukarno and Suharto. President Suharto was forced to stand down in 1998, when economic problems led to mass demonstrations.

▼ Children playing in Ambon City, Indonesia. Even in quite large cities, Indonesians live in small communities called kampongs, each of which is like a village.

• Following 23 years of brutal occupation by Indonesia, the people of East Timor finally voted in 1999 to become independent. UN troops were sent to the island to restore order, and East Timor became a fully independent country on 20 May 2002.

find out more
Asia
See also Countries fact file, page 626

Indoor games and sports

For thousands of years people have invented games and sports to amuse themselves when confined within a house or other building. Often these are played in social or family situations, or when darkness or bad weather prevent people from moving outside.

Such amusements have been developed throughout the world. Some, especially those for young children, are largely a matter of luck. Others require a great deal of skill on the part of the players.

Card games

Most card games are played with a pack of 52 playing cards, which are divided equally into four suits: spades, clubs, hearts and diamonds. Each suit has the numbers 1 (ace) to 10 followed by the picture cards – jack, queen and king.

Amongst the most popular card games are 'trump-and-trick' games, which include *whist* and *bridge*. In games of this kind the ace usually ranks highest, followed by the picture cards and number cards in descending order. One suit is made *trumps*, which means that cards of that suit beat any card of another suit. One player leads (plays the first card) and the others must follow suit (play a card of the same suit) if they can. Each round or *trick* is won by the highest card of the suit led, but if a player cannot follow suit, they may play a trump and the highest trump wins. The winner is the player or team that wins the most tricks.◗

▲ A hand of cards from a standard pack, showing the four suits (from left): spades, hearts, clubs and diamonds.

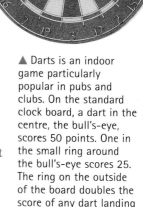

▲ Darts is an indoor game particularly popular in pubs and clubs. On the standard clock board, a dart in the centre, the bull's-eye, scores 50 points. One in the small ring around the bull's-eye scores 25. The ring on the outside of the board doubles the score of any dart landing within it. The smaller inner ring trebles a dart's score.

Playing cards came to Europe from the Muslim world, probably in the 14th century. At that time the suit signs were swords, batons, coins and cups, which are still used in some countries. India, China and Korea also have traditional packs of playing cards. The Indian cards are usually round, and have 8, 10 or 12 suits of 12 cards each. Chinese playing cards are very small and narrower than European cards.

Board games

Many different kinds of board game are played throughout the world, and many of them have been popular for hundreds of years. A few board games are decided by chance or luck alone, but most require some amount of skill on the part of the players.

▲ The chess pieces set up at the beginning of play. From left to right, the black pieces are: rook, knight, bishop, king, queen, bishop, knight, rook. In front of these stand a row of eight pawns.

Games of pure chance are usually 'race' games, such as the children's game *snakes and ladders*. The winner – the player who reaches a certain square first – is decided by throwing numbered dice, over which the players have no control.

Games such as Monopoly and backgammon are a mixture of chance and skill. Even though luck (usually the throw of dice) plays a part, choices made by the players in the course of the game also help to decide the winner. *Backgammon* is one of the oldest board games that people still play. Its name comes from the Saxon (it means 'back game' because sometimes pieces have to go back to the beginning), but the Romans played this game too.

Luck plays little or no part in games of skill – the outcome is decided by the players' ability to make the most advantageous moves available. Such games are often 'war' games, which involve capturing an opponent's pieces. The most popular of all such games today is chess.

Chess is a game of great skill that calls for the ability to plan moves and recognize threats several steps ahead. Each player has an 'army' of 16 pieces with which to fight a battle. There are six different kinds of piece – king, queen, bishop, knight, rook and pawn – and each has its own special way of moving about the board. If a player moves onto a square occupied by an opposing piece, that piece is captured and removed from the board. The object of the game is to trap (*checkmate*) the enemy king by putting it in a position where it cannot escape capture.

Table-top games

Various indoor games, including billiards, snooker and pool, are played on a large, flat, cloth-covered table with six pockets. In these games, each of the two players tries to *pot* the balls (knock them into the pockets) by striking them with a *cue-ball*, which is hit with the tip of a stick called a *cue*.

In *billiards*, there are just three balls: a white cue-ball for each player and one red ball. Points are scored by potting the balls, by sending the cue-ball into a pocket 'in off' one of the other balls, or by getting the cue-ball to hit both the other balls (a *cannon*). The winner is the player who reaches an agreed score first, or who has the highest score after a certain time.

In *snooker* there are 22 balls: 1 cue-ball, 15 reds and 6 colours. A player must first pot one of the red balls (scoring 1 point) and then one of the colours, which are worth between 2 points (yellow) and 7 (black). The colour ball is put back on the table, and the player tries to pot another red. The turn or *break* continues until the player fails to score or plays a foul shot. When all the reds have gone, the colours are potted in sequence from yellow to black, which marks the end of the game or *frame*. The winner of the frame is the player with the most points. Most professional matches are decided over a fixed number of frames.

▲ Table tennis is a popular indoor sport for two or four players. The ball has to clear the net and bounce on the table beyond it. Volleying is not allowed, and the ball must bounce just once. The service must bounce on both sides of the net.

▼ Snooker table and balls set up at the start of play. The 15 red balls, arranged in a triangle, are worth 1 point each. The yellow ball is worth 2, green 3, brown 4, blue 5, pink 6 and black 7.

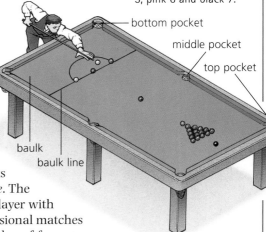

bottom pocket

middle pocket

top pocket

baulk

baulk line

Industrial Revolution

From the beginning of the 18th century, machines were increasingly used to do work formerly done by hand. Later, canals and railways were built to carry raw materials and finished goods. Such developments represented a revolution in the way people lived and worked, and together make up what we now call the Industrial Revolution.

Steam engines were at the heart of the Industrial Revolution. The first was invented in 1698 by Dr Thomas Savery to pump water out of Cornish tin mines. Improvements made later by Thomas Newcomen and James Watt meant that steam engines could be used for all kinds of manufacturing work and thereby made cheap mass production in factories possible.

Textiles

Until the Industrial Revolution, linen and wool had been spun and woven in people's homes. The introduction of machines, such as John Kay's flying shuttle, invented in 1733, speeded up the weaving process. James Hargreaves's spinning jenny (1764) enabled one person to spin as much thread as 16 had done before. By the beginning of the 19th century people no longer worked at home but in new mills and factories, which were built to house great new machines that had to be powered by water wheel or steam engine.

Iron

In 1713 Abraham Darby began using coke instead of charcoal to smelt (make) iron. This meant ironworks were not so reliant on woodland and made cast iron cheaper. By 1784 Henry Cort had developed a method of removing some of the impurities of cast iron to make wrought iron. Ironmaking became one of Britain's most important industries and iron was used to build the tools, bridges, machines and later railways of the Industrial Revolution.

Coal and canals

Steam engines as well as the iron industry required coal for fuel, and the growing population needed coal for heat and cooking. Canals were constructed to take coal where it was needed. Between 1759 and 1840 about 6840 kilometres of canals were dug in Britain. This formed the most important transport network before the railways were built.

The continuing revolution

Later stages of industrialization included the development of steel and shipbuilding, and the chemical, electrical and motor industries. These industrial methods spread first to Europe, then to the USA, Canada, Japan and Russia, and then to all the major countries of the world. Industrialization continues to develop and spread, particularly in electronics.

◀ The spinning frame, a machine for spinning cotton, which Richard Arkwright invented in 1768. Thanks to machines like this, cotton became more popular than wool and played a vital part in Britain's economy right up until the 20th century.

▲ Thomas Savery's first steam engine proved unsafe, and it was Thomas Newcomen who developed a much safer engine in 1712. His steam-powered water pump was rather slow, but it solved the problem of flooding in the coalmines. There is a steam-powered water pump in use in the centre of this 19th-century English painting of the pit-head of a coalmine.

find out more
Canals
Engines
Georgian Britain
Industry
Iron and steel
Railways
Roads
Victorian Britain
Watt, James

Industry

Industry is any sort of activity that is done to produce the goods and services that people need. There are many types of industry, including manufacturing, farming, mining, banking and tourism.

- When people make things at home or in a small workshop and sell them through a local market stall or shop, this is called a *cottage industry*. Potters who sell their pottery and knitters who sell their woollen garments through local outlets belong to cottage industries.

- *Industrialized countries* are those that have a lot of manufacturing, or secondary, industry. Now that some countries have a majority of their workforce in tertiary occupations, some people talk of '*post-industrialization*', meaning that these countries are developing service industries to take the place of factories.

An industry is a group of firms or businesses that are all making the same, or similar, products. For example, the world's car-making industry contains a number of individual firms, such as Ford, Volvo, Volkswagen, Renault and Honda. Each of these firms makes cars for sale to the public and aims to make a profit from the sales. Before the cars are manufactured, the firms need to buy raw materials (such as steel and glass), component parts (such as lights and batteries) and energy (such as electricity and gas) from other industries. For any product you buy, you can trace a 'chain of production', which will take you through a number of industries before the product reaches you, the consumer.

Primary industry

The different kinds of industry are divided into three types: primary, secondary and tertiary. Primary industry is the name given to all those industries that take natural resources from the Earth and sea. The mining and quarrying industries extract minerals (such as coal, oil and copper) and stone from the ground. These materials are then taken to be used in factories and power stations and on building projects.

▲ Advances in computer technology have made it possible for more people to work from home. Workers can use personal computers and modems to send data down the telephone lines to their head office. *Teleworking*, as this is known, saves workers time because they have to do less travelling, and it saves companies money because they do not have to provide offices and other facilities for the workers.

Fishing, farming and forestry are also primary industries. Most of the fish, food and timber produced by these industries is then processed by other industries.

◄ Workers in a rock quarry in Karnataka, India. In India almost three-quarters of the population work in primary industries. Countries such as India are trying to build up their manufacturing industry. As workers can usually earn higher wages in the new factories than on the land, people are moving to the cities in search of jobs.

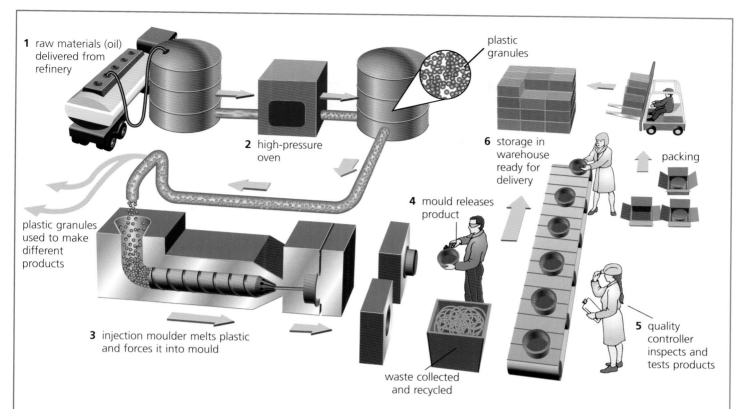

1 raw materials (oil) delivered from refinery

plastic granules

2 high-pressure oven

plastic granules used to make different products

6 storage in warehouse ready for delivery

packing

4 mould releases product

3 injection moulder melts plastic and forces it into mould

waste collected and recycled

5 quality controller inspects and tests products

Primary industry is not as important now as it once was in the most advanced economies of the world. In Japan and the USA, for instance, primary industries produce only 2 to 3 per cent of the country's Gross Domestic Product (or GDP, the total value of goods and services provided in a country in one year).

In developing countries, however, primary industry may still account for a large proportion of a country's goods and services. For example, more than half of Kenya's exports are agricultural products such as tea and coffee.

Secondary industry

Firms that take raw materials and turn them into products for the public belong to the manufacturing or 'secondary' industries. These businesses make all sorts of products, from matches to space rockets. The construction or building industry is a secondary industry.

Manufacturers talk about the 'market' for their products. This means the number of people who might buy the products. The bigger the market, the more chance there is of making a profit and the more businesses there are likely to be in that particular industry.

Before deciding where to build a factory, the owners will have to ask a number of important questions. The first may be whether the site is in an area targeted for development by government,

and therefore eligible for government subsidies (financial help). The people who work in the factory (the labour force) are also important. Are there enough of them, with the necessary skills, within easy reach of the factory? If the raw materials used in production are heavy and expensive to move, will it be a good idea to locate the factory close to the source of raw materials? Transport links are also vital for getting raw materials to the factory and the finished goods to the market. Are there good roads, railways, airports or sea ports close to the factory site? Only when all these questions have been answered can a decision be made about where the factory should be built.

Tertiary industry

Tertiary industry offers people a service. Transporting and selling goods to the public are service activities. So are health care, education, banking, insurance and tourism. They do not make anything, but the services they provide help to improve people's standard of living.

The leisure industry includes skating rinks, hotels, restaurants, swimming pools, cinemas, theatres and wildlife parks. This type of industry has been growing rapidly in recent decades in most of the economies of Europe and North America, and may account for more than half the industrial output of such countries.

▲ The production process in a factory making plastic washing-up bowls. Mass production of goods in factories means that more goods can be made using fewer people. Goods are cheaper because the cost of buying the machines to make them is spread over more items.

• The materials, workforce, energy and money needed to run a factory are called 'inputs' by people in industry. The product made is called the 'output'.

Information technology

When you write a story on a word processor, take money out of the bank, buy food at a supermarket, or program a microwave oven to cook a meal, you are using information technology (IT for short). IT includes all the uses of computers, from controlling industrial robots to playing games.

Businesses, schools, banks and individuals all use computers to store huge amounts of data (information), such as names and addresses, wages, exam results, or details of bank accounts. This data can be called up on a screen instantly, changed, printed on paper, or sent to another computer. Today, with an ordinary personal computer, you can use the Internet to link up with computers all around the world.

You can see IT at work when you visit a supermarket or shop. At the till, the assistant uses a laser scanner to read the barcode on each item. The barcode tells the shop's computer what the item is, and the computer tells the till the name and price of the item. If a shopper pays with a plastic card, the till operator 'swipes' the card through the till. The till reads the data stored on the card's magnetic strip, for example the shopper's bank account number. It then sends the data, and the price of the goods, along a telephone line to the bank's computer.

Creative computers

Scientists and engineers use computers to work out very complicated calculations that would have been impossible to do before they had computers. For example, they can create

computer models of buildings to check if they will stand up to hurricanes or earthquakes. Designers use CAD (computer-aided design) to look at a design, for example of a new car, from all angles on the computer screen. Using high-speed supercomputers, graphic artists can produce a full-length animated film from just a few drawings.

Keeping control

One of the most common uses of computers is to control everyday machines, such as washing machines and video recorders. The computers send out signals to turn motors, pumps or switches on and off, and receive signals from electronic sensors telling them what the machine is doing. In factories, computers control larger machines, for example machine tools such as lathes and drills, and robots programmed to do everything from packing boxes to painting and welding. They make sure that parts are made accurately every time, and that the whole product is put together correctly and efficiently.

◀ Schoolchildren in the UK using computers to access the Internet. Today children are beginning to use the Internet as a part of their learning. They can connect to sites all around the world to find up-to-date information about a huge range of subjects. They can also communicate with children in other schools by e-mail.

IT terms

ATM *(automatic teller machine):* a machine that reads the information from the magnetic strip on a credit card when the card is 'swiped'.

On-line shopping: with a computer linked to the telephone network or the Internet, you can order and pay for goods. The goods are delivered later.

Smart card: a credit card-sized plastic card with a microchip embedded in it. The chip can hold far more information than the magnetic strip on a normal card.

find out more
Calculators
Communication
Compact discs
Computers
Electronics
Fax machines
Internet
Robots
Telephones
Virtual reality
Word processors

Insects

Together with birds and bats, insects are the only animals that can fly. There are more insects than any other kind of animal. About a million different species have so far been identified, and new ones are being discovered all the time.

An insect's body is divided into three main sections. Its mouth, eyes and antennae (feelers), with which it smells as well as feels, are on its *head*. The *thorax* is concerned with movement: most insects have three pairs of legs and two pairs of wings attached to the thorax. The main part of the gut and digestive system is in the *abdomen*, and so are the sex organs.

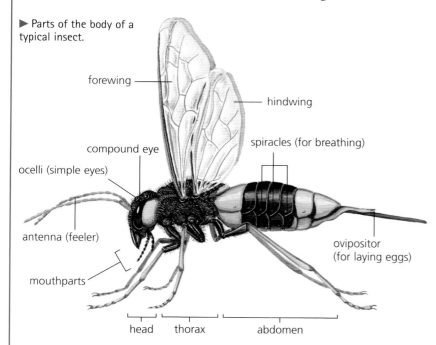

▶ Parts of the body of a typical insect.

- forewing
- hindwing
- compound eye
- spiracles (for breathing)
- ocelli (simple eyes)
- antenna (feeler)
- ovipositor (for laying eggs)
- mouthparts

head　thorax　abdomen

• Dragonflies are the fastest-flying of all insects. Some reach speeds of over 50 km an hour. They are very agile in flight and are able to fly backwards.

find out more

Ants and termites
Bees and wasps
Beetles
Butterflies and moths
Fleas and lice
Flies and mosquitoes
Grasshoppers and crickets

A skeleton on the outside

Like crabs and spiders, to which they are related, insects have bodies that are supported and protected by a hard outer armour, the *exoskeleton*. This is waterproof and prevents them from drying up in the air. It enables insects to live almost everywhere in the world, even in deserts and on mountains.

The great disadvantage of the exoskeleton is that it cannot stretch, so all insects have to shed their skin (*moult*) in order to grow. As a result, they grow in a series of jumps. After feeding and growing for a time, the hard exoskeleton splits and the insect, which has grown a new flexible skin beneath the old one, wriggles out. At first this new cover is soft and can expand to allow for growth. But it hardens quite quickly to protect and limit the insect once more.

Insects in the environment

Scientists think that there are probably at least 7 million kinds of insect that we do not yet know about. One reason for the great numbers of different sorts of insect is that they are all small and very many of them can share the same environment. Even a single tree may be home to many insects. Some may be among the roots, some on or under the bark and some on the leaves. Some may be active during the daytime, while others are active at night. Different kinds of insect are active at different times of the year.

Most insects feed on only one type of food, but between them they can eat almost anything. Because of this, some of them are pests of human crops and stores. Most, however, do no damage and are a vital part of the world that we share with them. Bees and butterflies, which pollinate flowers and crops, are useful to us. So are many other insects, such as ladybirds and some hoverflies, which feed on pests such as

▼ These ladybirds are feeding on aphids (greenfly), which are considered pests because they attack crops and spread disease. Aphids reproduce very quickly. During the summer all aphids are female. They do not lay eggs, or even mate, but give birth to live female young, which in turn are able to reproduce in 10 days' time.

Incomplete metamorphosis

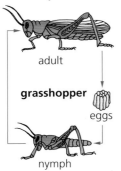

grasshopper

adult

eggs

nymph

Complete metamorphosis

butterfly

adult

pupa

eggs

larva

aphids (greenfly). But we rarely think of the most important insects. These are the recyclers, such as beetles and cockroaches, which feed on the remains of dead plants and animals. As these remains pass through the insects, they are broken down into chemicals which fertilize the soil when returned to it. Plants can then make use of these chemicals when they grow.

The main groups of insects

It is likely that the first insects, which evolved more than 300 million years ago, had no wings, although their bodies were divided into three sections, like the insects of today. A few kinds of *wingless insects* still survive. They are scavengers, and are common wherever there are dead leaves and plants. The young, when they hatch from the egg, look like tiny versions of the adults.

Most insects have wings and can fly. Some, like grasshoppers and bugs, produce young which look like their parents, but at first have no wings. At each moult their wings get bigger. At last, when they are fully grown, they are able to fly. As adults, they feed on the same food as they did before. Insects that develop in this way are said to undergo *incomplete metamorphosis*.

The third group of insects have young that hatch from their eggs as larvae (grubs). They

▲ A shield bug sucks sap from a flower. Bugs are a large and varied group of insects that have one thing in common: they cannot eat solid food. All bugs have long, thin, sharp-tipped mouthparts to pierce the stems, leaves or fruit of plants to suck up the sap, or the skin of animals to drink blood.

look very different from their parents and they feed on different food. When they are fully grown, they turn into pupae, a kind of resting stage during which they change to the adult form. Many of the adults feed chiefly on nectar, and are important as pollinators of flowers. Most of the more familiar insects go through this form of development, known as *complete metamorphosis*.

Wingless insects

silverfish

bristletail

Insects with incomplete metamorphosis

termite

book louse

earwig

dragonfly

shield bug

Insects with complete metamorphosis

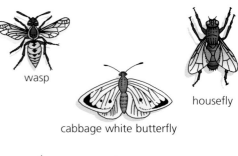

wasp

cabbage white butterfly

housefly

soldier beetle

lacewing

Insurance

People take out insurance to make sure that if their property is lost or stolen, or they are injured in some way, there will be a sum of money available to replace goods, to make up for loss of earnings or to cover the cost of medical treatment.

The basic idea of insurance is that each year a large number of people put a sum of money (called a *premium*) into a pool of money. That fund then provides the money to pay compensation to the few unfortunate people who suffer a loss or accident of some kind.

The details of each insurance arrangement are set out in a document issued by the insurance company called a *policy*. You can insure yourself against almost anything, from house or vehicle damage to losing your job. Many major sports stars insure themselves against serious injury that may shorten their careers.

Pensions

A pension is a sort of insurance people take out to ensure they are paid a regular income when they retire. Some pension schemes are rewards for past services. More often, they are contributory. This means that a person pays a certain amount every week while earning, and draws a pension based on those contributions.

• When the payout from an insurance policy is a fixed sum, it is known as assurance. Insurance is when the payout is proportionate to the loss.

▶ A fire-insurance policy drawn up in 1682 between Nicholas Barton and Sam Brookes to insure a house in London, England, against fire. People in England first started to insure their property against loss due to fire after the Fire of London in 1666.

find out more
Economics

Internet

The Internet ('the Net' for short) is a huge computer network that connects millions of computers. It is a fast and efficient way of sending information around the world. Any two computers connected to the Internet, wherever they are, can exchange information.

To join the Internet, you need a personal computer, a modem and a telephone line. You can use the Internet to send electronic messages to other users (this is called *e-mail*), hold electronic conversations, transfer computer files, or find information on thousands of different subjects. The number of people connected to the Internet, and the amount of information passing through it, are increasing rapidly. Some experts think that the Net will change how we work and live.

The fastest growing area of the Internet is a system called the *Worldwide Web* ('the Web' for short), which allows you to look at information stored on the Internet. To look at this information (text, pictures, sounds and video clips), you need a program called a *Web browser*. It finds the information on a *Web site*, and displays it on your screen.

The Internet works by linking together many small computer networks belonging to organizations such as businesses, universities and government departments.

▶ Most computers belonging to individuals, schools and small organizations that are linked to the Internet are connected through an Internet service provider (ISP).

Internet jargon
Surfing the Net Browsing through information on the Internet.
Netiquet The unwritten rules of good behaviour for Net users.
Snailmail Net users' word for normal mail.

find out more
Computers
Information technology

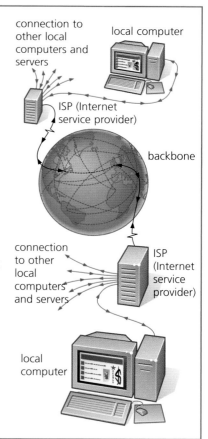

connection to other local computers and servers

local computer

ISP (Internet service provider)

backbone

connection to other local computers and servers

ISP (Internet service provider)

local computer

Inuit

The Inuit live in the Arctic lands of Greenland, Canada and Alaska. Although some people call them 'Eskimos', they prefer 'Inuit', as it is their own name for themselves. It simply means 'people'.

In Arctic regions for much of the year the ground is covered with snow and ice, and the sea is frozen over. But there are many wild creatures, such as seals, walruses and polar bears, that the Inuit can hunt, and they can fish in the lakes and the sea.

Inuit hunting trips often involve travelling long distances over many days. The meat they bring back feeds their families. Nowadays they are able to buy what they cannot get or make for themselves at trading stores. This includes guns, metal tools and clothes made in factories far away. But for Arctic life, the clothes that Inuit women make from animal skins are often more suitable.

Most of the Inuit live in villages or small towns on the sea coasts. In the past they would move from one place to another throughout the year, living in tents or igloos (houses made from blocks of snow). They walked, rode on sledges pulled by dogs, or paddled boats. Nowadays, they often have motorized vehicles.

Although some Inuit still make their living from their land and its animals, the development of towns has led to an increase in the number of people doing modern jobs.

▶ This Inuit man uses a skidoo (motorized sledge) to get about. The Inuit's traditional way of life is gradually changing with the introduction of new technology.

• The language of the Inuit is Inuktitot. Many of them live in the Nunavut province in Canada.

find out more
Arctic
Canada
North America

Inventors

An inventor is someone who makes something new or who finds new ways of using old ideas. What they make is called an invention.

◀ Alexander Graham Bell invented the telephone in 1876. In this photograph, taken in 1892, he is making the first phone call from New York to Chicago.

We usually think of inventions as objects such as cars, washing machines and rockets, but they can also be processes like making paper or canning food. Everything made by people has an inventor. Hundreds of inventors are remembered by name because of the impact that their invention has had on our lives. Examples of such inventors include Marconi (radio), Baird (television), Edison (electric light) and Bell (telephone). Sometimes the invention takes the name of the inventor: Biro pens, Hoovers, Diesel engines. Most modern machines are so complex that they are invented by teams of people, rather than by a single person.

Famous inventors	see article on
Archimedes	Archimedes
Babbage, Charles	Computers
Baird, John Logie	Television
Bell, Alexander Graham	Telephones
Brunel, Isambard Kingdom	Ships and boats
Daguerre, Louis	Cameras
Diesel, Rudolf	Engines
Edison, Thomas	Edison, Thomas
Faraday, Michael	Faraday, Michael
Ford, Henry	Motor cars
Gutenberg, Johann	Printing
Leonardo da Vinci	Leonardo da Vinci
Marconi, Guglielmo	Radio
Montgolfier brothers	Balloons and airships
Stephenson, George	Railways
Talbot, William Henry Fox	Cameras
Trevithick, Richard	Railways
Volta, Alessandro	Batteries
Watson-Watt, Robert	Radar
Watt, James	Watt, James
Whittle, Frank	Engines
Zworykin, Vladimir	Television

Iran

Iran is the biggest non-Arab country in the Middle East. It has a variety of landscapes, from the snowy mountains in the north to the hot dry deserts near the Gulf in the south. Tehran, the capital, is a crowded and bustling city with a backdrop of mountains.

Iran is a Muslim country, and its people mainly belong to the Shi'ah sect. It has a very rich heritage of literature, music, painting and architecture. Rice forms the basis of food in Iran, which tends to be more varied and delicately cooked than elsewhere in the region. A speciality is caviar (fish eggs) from the Caspian Sea. The most important industry is oil. Most of Iran's earnings come from oil wells in the south.

Iran used to be called Persia and was the centre of an ancient civilization. In the 7th century AD the Arabs conquered Persia. The country was ruled by a series of dynasties (families). The last royal ruler was Muhammad Reza Shah, who tried to modernize and westernize the country. But in 1979 there was a revolution led by the religious leaders, or ayatollahs. Iran became an Islamic republic, led by Ayatollah Khomeini.

In 1980 war broke out between Iran and neighbouring Iraq. The struggle lasted eight years, and hundreds of thousands of people were killed. In 1989, soon after the end of the war, Ayatollah Khomeini died. Iran's relations with western countries improved and Iranian society became more relaxed.

◄ Iranian carpets are superbly designed and among the finest in the world. These men are washing carpets in the river.

find out more
Iraq
Middle East
Muslims
See also Countries fact file, page 626

Iraq

Iraq is one of the biggest and most powerful Arab states of the Middle East. It is a Muslim country, and more than half the population belong to the Shi'ah sect.

Iraq is mostly a desert country. However, two great rivers, the Tigris and the Euphrates, run through the country, and the land close to them is green and fertile. Mountains are found in the north and east of the country. The two major cities of Iraq are Baghdad, the capital, and Basra, Iraq's only port.

Since the 1930s Iraq has grown rich from sales of oil. The skylines of Iraq's cities are dominated by modern high-rise buildings. But many Iraqis still live in small villages and work on the land. Rice and beans form the basis of the national diet. But in Baghdad the speciality is grilled fish.

► FLASHBACK ◄

Mesopotamia, the area where some of the world's most ancient civilizations began, was part of what is now Iraq. This area has been settled for over 12,000 years. Mesopotamia was conquered by Muslim Arabs in the 7th century AD and Iraq became a major centre for Islamic study.

In 1980 Iraq launched an eight-year war against Iran that cost hundreds of thousands of lives. Then in 1990 Iraq's dictator Saddam Hussein invaded the oil-rich state of Kuwait. A powerful army from many countries, backed by the United Nations, expelled Iraq after six months, but Saddam himself remained in power. In 2003 the USA and UK, claiming Saddam illegally held weapons of mass destruction, went to war against Iraq and overthrew Saddam. Many people around the world thought this war was unjustified.

find out more
Ancient world
Iran
Kurds
Middle East
Muslims
See also Countries fact file, page 626

◄ The spiral minaret at Samarra. The minaret, and the Great Friday Mosque next to it (now in ruins), were built in the 9th century, when Samarra was the capital of Iraq. It is an important centre for Shi'ah Muslim pilgrims.

Ireland, Republic of

The Republic of Ireland is a country in north-west Europe. It covers most of the island of Ireland, which is often called the 'Emerald Isle' because its mild and moist climate helps to cover the countryside with lush grass.

Much of the Irish coast faces the Atlantic Ocean. It is a rugged coastline, broken up by numerous bays, inlets, peninsulas and sandy beaches. Most of the country's mountains and moorlands are near the coast, in places such as Wicklow and Waterford in the south-east, Cork and Kerry in the south-west, Clare, Galway and Mayo in the west, and Sligo and Donegal in the north-west. About 15 per cent of the land is covered by peat bogs, and the turf from these is used for heating and as an energy source.

Agriculture and industry

About three-quarters of the country's land is suitable for agriculture. Beef and dairy cattle are raised in large numbers on the lush pastures, and cereals, potatoes and sugar beet are important crops. Much of the country's industry is based on this agriculture, and its dairy and beef products are major exports. Other world-famous Irish products are linen, crystal glass, whiskey and beer. Many new industries have recently been set up, and the production of computer components is particularly important. Tourism is another important industry. Fishing and fish-farming are carried on in small ports around the coast, and the mining industry is growing because of recent discoveries of mineral deposits.

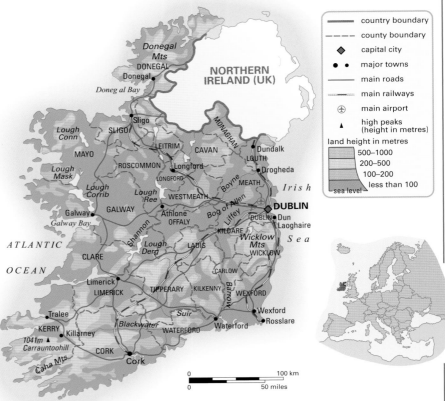

Ireland's history

Around 300 BC Celtic people came, after which there were no new settlers for 1000 years. In that time the Celtic language developed into Gaelic. The island, which was now called Ériu, was divided into about 100 kingdoms.

Early Ireland was a centre of Christianity. From the 5th century bishops, such as St Patrick, came to organize the Church. Monasteries became centres of art, law and literature.

In the 9th century Viking (Norse) raiders founded Dublin and other ports, and traded with lands as far away as Russia. In 1171 the English king, Henry II, invaded Ireland. From that time all English kings claimed lordship over parts of Ireland and wanted the Irish to accept English laws and ways of government.

◄ The lush landscape of the Ring of Kerry in Killarney, Ireland.

• Irish lawyer Daniel O'Connell (1775–1847) was a famous campaigner for Catholic Irish people's rights. O'Connell and his supporters made the British parliament pass the Catholic Emancipation Act of 1829. This allowed Catholic men to serve in the British parliament and to hold other public offices. He is most remembered for his efforts to unite all classes of Irish people, without ever using violence.

• The parliament of the Irish Republic is based in Dublin and consists of two houses, the Seanad (Senate) and the Dáil. The head of the government is the Taoiseach (prime minister). The country's president is elected every seven years.

◀ Dublin, capital of the Republic of Ireland, sits at the mouth of the River Liffey. Dublin was the centre of English rule from 1171 until 1921.

English conquest and rebellion

King Henry VIII was declared king of Ireland, but he and his Tudor successors had to fight before all Ireland was conquered. Whole Irish communities were killed before, in 1601, an English army defeated the last Irish forces. James I gave land in Ulster, in the north, to Protestant English and Scottish landowners and companies.

In 1641 the Irish revolted against English rule and many Protestants were killed. In 1649 Oliver Cromwell's army crushed the rebels and gave over more Ulster land to Protestants. Catholics briefly regained their position when Catholic James II became king, but he was defeated in 1690. For the next 100 years the parliament in Dublin was run by Protestant landowners.

Revolution and the Act of Union

Catholics resented this, and so did some Protestants. In 1798 a group of Protestants led a revolution in which many Catholics also took part. The British decided that Ireland could only be governed if it was united with England.

This happened with the Act of Union of 1801, which Catholics saw as a betrayal. The Dublin parliament was closed and only Protestants could be elected to Parliament in London. In 1829 Catholics were granted freedom from the laws which barred them from parliament, public office and some professions, but this was followed by a failed attempt to cancel the Act of Union.

The fight for independence

In the first half of the 19th century a potato blight (disease) caused terrible famine and thousands died or left the country. Many Irish blamed Britain for the famine. Many politicians began to fight for Home Rule and an Irish government run by the country's own citizens. However, this was opposed by Unionists, mainly Protestants, who feared Catholic rule.

Just before World War I, Britain promised Home Rule, and large numbers of Irish served with Britain's army. After the war, the nationalist party, Sinn Féin, won the elections. Instead of going to London, they set up a parliament in Dublin. At the same time, the Irish Republican Army (IRA) began a war with Britain which lasted until 1921.

In 1921, a treaty was agreed in which six of Ulster's nine counties remained part of the United Kingdom, while the other 26 counties became the Irish Free State, as part of the British Commonwealth. In 1932 Eamon de Valera became prime minister and set about winning full independence. In 1937 the Free State became Éire (modern Irish for Ériu) and in 1949 the Republic of Ireland was established.

Peace in our time?

The peace settlement of 1921 was designed to ensure continued Protestant control in Northern Ireland. This was bitterly resented by Republicans and a position of stalemate lasted until 1968, when Northern Irish Catholics began campaigning for equal civil rights. This began a period of 'troubles' – riots, shootings and bombings carried out by armed groups on both sides. In 1998, after four years of negotiation and fragile cease-fires, a peace plan was finally agreed. This plan gave the Republic a voice in Northern Irish affairs, in return for which it agreed to drop its claim to the province.

● Ireland was linked to Britain and Europe until the end of the last ice age, when the sea level rose and so formed the Irish Sea. The first human settlers were probably Middle Stone Age hunters who crossed from Britain around 6000 BC, followed by Neolithic (New Stone Age) people in about 4000 BC.

find out more
Celts
Cromwell, Oliver
Europe
Northern Ireland
Prehistoric people
Tudor England
Vikings
See also Countries fact file, page 626

▼ At Easter 1916 some nationalists tried to win full independence from Britain by force. After the Easter Rising street fighting continued for about a week, until the leaders, except Eamon de Valera, were executed.

Iron and steel

Iron and steel are used for making buildings, cars, ships, trains and many other things. There are many different kinds of iron and steel. Most of the iron produced is used to make steel. Steel is a mixture of iron and other products.

Iron comes from the ground, sometimes in its pure form but mostly combined with rocky materials in the form of ores. The commonest iron ore is called haematite. These ores are heated in a blast furnace to make iron.

Making iron

Iron is made in a *blast furnace* – a tall oven made of steel and lined with fireproof bricks. A mixture of crushed iron ore, coke and limestone is fed into the furnace and heated by a continuous blast of hot air.

The three substances react together inside the furnace to form iron and a waste material called *slag*. These are drained separately through tap holes at the bottom of the furnace while they are still molten. When the slag solidifies, it is sold for road-building. Some of the iron solidifies in moulds to form a rather brittle kind of iron, called *cast* or *pig iron*. Most of the molten iron is turned into steel.

Steel-making

To make steel, excess carbon and unwanted impurities in the iron are removed in an oxygen furnace. Molten iron is poured into the furnace. Scrap steel may be put in as well. Then some quicklime is added and a jet of oxygen is turned on. The impurities burn away, leaving a small amount of carbon in the iron so that it is hard but not brittle. Other metallic elements may then be added to the molten steel to make an alloy (metal mixture) which has special properties. Stainless steel, for example, is an alloy of steel and chromium which, unlike ordinary steel, does not rust.

Steel can also be made in electric-arc furnaces. A large electric current is carried into the furnace to produce the heat needed to melt the scrap and solid iron inside. This process produces both steel and slag (waste material).

◄ Inside the hot-rolling mill at a steel foundry. Red-hot slabs of steel travel backwards and forwards under huge rollers. They are taken out when they have been rolled into steel sheets of the right thickness.

find out more
Industrial Revolution
Metals
Prehistoric people

► FLASHBACK ◄

Iron was first made by heating a mixture of iron ore and charcoal over a fire. While it was still hot, the iron was beaten into shape with a stone to make knives and axes.

The introduction of the blast furnace to England at the beginning of the 16th century allowed pig iron to be made continuously. The first cheap method of making steel used the Bessemer process, invented in England in 1856 by Henry Bessemer.

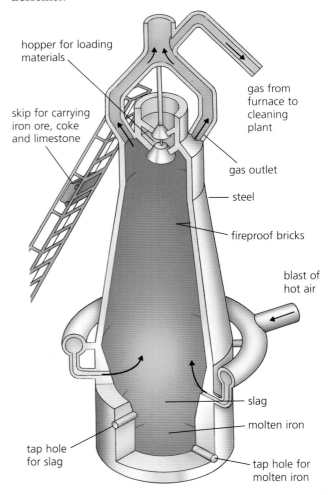

▼ Making iron in a blast furnace.

hopper for loading materials

skip for carrying iron ore, coke and limestone

gas from furnace to cleaning plant

gas outlet

steel

fireproof bricks

blast of hot air

tap hole for slag

slag

molten iron

tap hole for molten iron

Islands

▲ Kayangel Atoll is part of the Caroline Islands in the Pacific Ocean. This aerial photograph shows a ring of coral reefs just below the water's surface surrounding a deeper lagoon.

• Some countries, for example Indonesia, are made up of a large group of islands, which is called an *archipelago*.

• The white sand found on many beaches in tropical areas is made of broken-up coral.

find out more
Caribbean
Continents
Darwin, Charles
Jellyfishes and corals
Pacific Islands
Volcanoes
Wildlife

▼ How different kinds of island are formed.

An island is an area of land that is entirely surrounded by water. Islands are found in lakes or rivers, and also in oceans and seas. They come in many different forms and sizes. The world's largest island is Greenland.

Some islands are small landmasses that have become separated from the mainland. Others are formed when the sea level rises after large ice-sheets have melted, for example the British Isles. Lowland areas are flooded, leaving the areas of land in between as islands.

Some mountainous islands are the tops of volcanoes that have erupted on the ocean floor. Hawaii, some of the Caribbean islands and the Aleutian Islands are examples of volcanic islands. Many low-lying islands in warm seas are made of coral. An example is the Maldives in the Indian Ocean. The skeletons of the tiny coral animals form a solid mass, called a *reef*. Sometimes the coral forms a circular ring called an *atoll*, which encloses an area of water known as a *lagoon*. Atolls tend to form around the submerged rim of a volcano. When a thin layer of soil collects on the atoll and plants begin to grow there, it becomes a coral island.

Island life

The first plant to grow on many tropical islands is the coconut palm, whose nut is carried long distances by the sea. Other plants may arrive as seeds carried by birds that have been blown off course.

Many islands, such as Madagascar, are home to kinds of plant and animal that are found nowhere else on Earth. On some islands there are no mammals, but there may be reptiles, some of which are very large because they face less competition for food and other resources than they would on the mainland. Giant tortoises were at one time found on many islands.

When sea levels fall, land bridges may form, allowing humans and other animals to cross to new islands. Long ago, Australia was linked to Asia when the Torres Strait between the two continents was exposed.

continental island
rising sea level covers low-lying land

volcanic island
lava is deposited on the ocean floor — the lava builds up above sea level to form an island

coral atoll
a volcanic island, surrounded by a coral reef, is sinking — a lagoon forms between the sinking island and the coral reef — the island sinks below sea level and the reef becomes an atoll

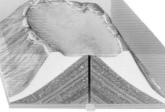

Israel

Israel is the country created in the Middle East for Jewish people. Any Jew is entitled to settle in Israel. The country was founded within the Arab world in what was Palestine, against the wishes of the Arabs.

Most Israelis live on the coastal plain, where fruit and vegetables are grown. Most industry is located here, too. The largest cities on the coast

▶ The Dome of the Rock shrine (background right) is sacred to both Muslims and Jews. It is one of many holy sites in Israel's capital Jerusalem.

find out more
Egypt
Jews
Middle East
See also Countries fact file, page 626

are Tel Aviv and Haifa. Israel's capital, Jerusalem, is further inland. Many Israelis live in rural settlements called *kibbutzim*, growing food or making other products. In the past, members of a *kibbutz* shared everything from childcare to money, but today they are becoming more like ordinary villages.

▶ FLASHBACK ◀

At the end of the 19th century a group called the Zionists put forward the idea of creating a Jewish state in Palestine. Over the next 50 years, thousands of Jews emigrated to the area, and fought to set up a Jewish state. Israel was created in 1948, under the leadership of David Ben-Gurion. From its creation, it was involved in a series of wars with its Arab neighbours. In these wars Israel took land from Egypt, Jordan and Syria. Many Palestinian Arabs had to leave Israel and move to Jordan or Lebanon. Since 1979, however, Israel has made peace agreements with Egypt and Jordan, and an initial agreement to allow Palestinian Arabs to govern themselves in some areas. But despite these agreements, tension and violence between Arabs and Israelis has continued.

Italy

Italy consists of a long peninsula leading south from the Alps and two large islands, Sicily and Sardinia.

The richest farmland is in the north, in the wide flat valley of the River Po. Rows of apple and pear trees grow between strips of wheat and maize (corn). There are acres of sugar beet, and rice grows on the wettest lowland. Vines are grown everywhere, making Italy one of the world's biggest producers of wine. In Sicily there are huge orchards of almond trees and lemons.

Industry

During the 20th century, Italy developed rapidly. It is now the world's fifth largest economy. But this economic growth is uneven. The northern cities are the industrial centres. Turin (Fiat cars), Milan (fashion accessories) and Florence (shoes and fine textiles) are world leaders

● Foreigners are often puzzled by Italy's politics. There are over 20 parties, many of them based in only one region, so governments are usually formed by coalitions (alliances) of politicians.

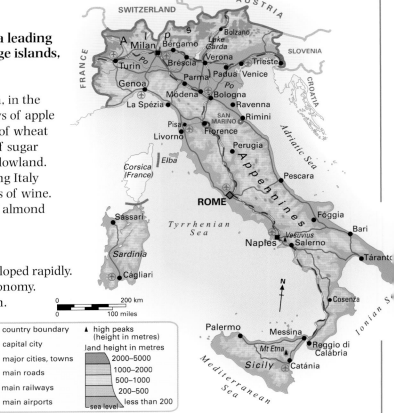

in design and engineering. But the south and the islands are still farming areas, and quite poor. During the 19th century, thousands of southerners migrated to the USA. Now they travel to the northern cities. The government has invested heavily in roads, dams and irrigation projects to overcome the south's geographical isolation and improve its agriculture.

Italy's history

Two thousand years ago, the Roman empire was expanding its power around the shores of the Mediterranean, and the people of Italy must have felt they were at the centre of the world. Four hundred years later barbarian tribes crashed through Italy and captured Rome in 410. In the following four centuries, the buildings left by the Romans fell into disrepair. But as more people became Christians, the skills of engineers and artists were rekindled in order to build and decorate new churches.

The Middle Ages

Throughout the Middle Ages, there were separate Italian cities. The Pope was the ruler of Rome and the lands around. Venice was one of the most powerful states. It grew very rich from its merchants who traded all around the Mediterranean. They used their wealth to build palaces and churches, and to pay artists to decorate them.

By the 15th century people were becoming more interested in the art of the ancient Romans and there was a great rebirth, or *renaissance*, of ideas from the Greeks and Romans. Once again Italy was the inspiration for European thinkers and artists.

Unification

Life in medieval Italy was not peaceful. There was often war between cities and conflicts within cities. Italy remained a jigsaw of small countries for another 300 years. Then, in 1860, a soldier, Giuseppe Garibaldi, and a politician, Camillo Cavour, managed to liberate Italy from Austrian rule, and forge it into a single country.

In 1861 Victor Emmanuel II of Sardinia and Piedmont was accepted as king of a united Italy. Venice joined in 1866 and Rome in 1870. The Pope refused to accept what had happened, and the Vatican remained independent.

Italian Republic

Italy sided with the Allies (French, British and Americans) in World War I, but afterwards fell under the control of the fascist dictator Benito Mussolini. Mussolini lost power in 1943 and was killed in 1945. After World War II Italians voted to become a republic. To stop the country falling into the hands of a dictator again, the new system of elections made it impossible for one party to gain power.

During the 1990s Italy's government was shaken by a series of scandals, and there were investigations into links between the Mafia (an international criminal organization based in Sicily) and politicians.

◀ Garibaldi (right) meets Victor Emmanuel II in 1860, the year before the latter became king of a united Italy.

▲ Venice was once a great trading centre built on islands in a lagoon. It is now in danger because it is sinking into the lagoon.

● Vatican City is the world's smallest independent country. It occupies 0.44 sq km in the Italian capital, Rome, and it is the headquarters of the Roman Catholic Church, and the home of the Pope. Independent since 1929, it is all that is left of the Papal States, the area of central Italy ruled by the popes until 1870.

find out more
Columbus, Christopher
Dictators
Europe
Galilei, Galileo
Leonardo da Vinci
Michelangelo
Middle Ages
Polo, Marco
Renaissance
Romans
World War I
World War II
See also Countries fact file, page 626

Jains

Jains are members of an ancient Indian religion. They are known for their compassion and sympathy for all forms of life.

◀ Jains inside Mount Abu temple in Rajasthan, India.

Although the Jain religion began in India, where most Jains still live, there are also small communities of Jains in North America, East Africa and Britain.

The name Jain is taken from the title *jina*, which means 'one who conquers or overcomes'. Jains believe that we have immortal souls and that after death we are born again as another human being or animal. 'Overcoming' refers to the business of escaping from this cycle of reincarnation.

The most famous jina and the founder of the Jains lived in the 5th and 6th century BC. He is known as Mahavira, a title which means 'the great hero'. Jains respect 24 jinas, whom they also call *tirthankaras*, which means 'ford-makers', those who help others across the rivers of life.

Many Jains gain liberation by giving up family life. Their basic needs are provided by other Jains who lead normal lives but who have great respect for anyone who fasts and renounces the world. Jains teach tolerance for other people's beliefs as well as the importance of speaking the truth.

All Jains try to avoid harming any form of life. The word for this non-harming is *ahimsa*, and for Jains it includes being strict vegetarians. Jains have their own festivals and places of pilgrimage, such as Mount Abu in Rajasthan, India, where there is a group of superb temples built of white marble.

• There are about 6 million Jains throughout the world, but most of them live in India. Although their numbers are relatively small, their influence has been great, for example on the non-violent movements led by Mahatma Gandhi in India.

find out more
Gandhi, Mahatma
India
Religions

Japan

Japan is a country of many islands in the north-west Pacific Ocean. It is a wealthy, bustling country, and its industries make goods which sell all over the world. The main island, Honshu, is where most people live.

Thickly wooded hills and mountains occupy two-thirds of Japan. Many short, fast rivers flow from the mountains to the sea. The country has more than 60 active volcanoes and is often shaken by earthquakes. The highest mountain, Mount Fuji, is an old volcano, but it has not erupted since 1707.

Japan's climate varies from north to south. In the north winters are cold and snowy, and summers are short. In the south the climate is hot and humid.

People

Because so much of Japan is mountainous, three-quarters of the people live in or near the towns and cities in a narrow coastal plain. Many people live in suburbs and commute to work. Long tunnels and bridges link the main islands.

Imagine having to learn 1850 different characters instead of the 26 letters of our alphabet! That is what Japanese children have to do. All children must go to school until they are at least 15. Most go on to high school, and many go to college or university.

The traditional arts of Japan are very simple, elegant and formal. The Japanese pioneered bonsai (growing miniature trees). They also perfected origami, or paper folding. The favourite kind of poetry is the haiku, which is just 17 syllables

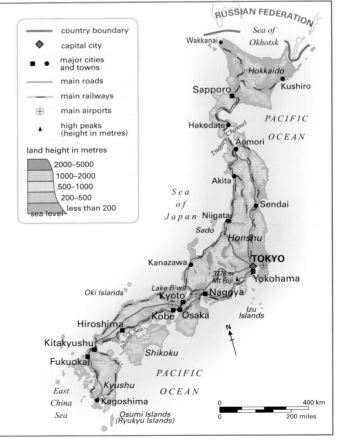

country boundary
capital city
major cities and towns
main roads
main railways
main airports
high peaks (height in metres)

land height in metres
2000–5000
1000–2000
500–1000
200–500
less than 200
sea level

◀ The flowering of the cherry blossom in spring is a traditional time for celebration in Japan. Groups of people picnic under the cherry trees. Karaoke (singing along to a song on tape) is also popular.

long. Japan is also the home of many martial arts, such as judo, karate and sumo wrestling.

Industry and farming

Japan has become a rich and powerful manufacturing country. It is a leading producer of cars, ships and television sets, and sells a great deal of electronic equipment. But it has to import nearly all its raw materials and its coal and oil.

Each of Japan's islands has large areas of farmland. Farms are often run by families. Rice is the main crop. Most meals are based on rice, and Japanese eat more fish than meat. Although farmers now use machines to plant the young seedlings, a great deal of the work has to be done by hand.

Japan's history

Stone Age people first settled in Japan more than 10,000 years ago. According to legend, the first emperor of Japan was Jimmu, who reigned in 660 BC, but little is known about the early Japanese empire. Emperors were regarded as divine gods, but from about AD 800 the real rulers were the noble Fujiwara family.

In 1160 power passed to a succession of warriors, who took the title of shogun (general). European traders arrived in the 16th century, but in 1637 the shoguns banned almost all foreign trade. Japan remained cut off from the rest of the world until 1854, when a US fleet under Commodore Matthew Perry forced the Japanese to open their ports once more.

The shoguns became very bad rulers, so in 1867 the emperor Mutsuhito (Meiji) took away their powers and ruled the country himself. Japan quickly built up its industry and armed forces. In a succession of wars between 1894 and 1937, Japan gained control of Korea, Taiwan and large areas of China.

In 1939 World War II broke out in Europe. Japan began to attack European colonies in Asia, and within five months it had conquered most of Southeast Asia. The Japanese also bombed the US naval base at Pearl Harbor in Hawaii, which brought the USA into the war. Japan eventually surrendered after the USA dropped atomic bombs on two Japanese cities, Hiroshima and Nagasaki.

American and Allied forces occupied Japan until 1952. Since then Japan has adopted a democratic government and become one of the world's most important industrial nations. However, it still has an agreement not to develop its army and navy.

find out more
Asia
Boxing and other
  combat sports
Shintoists
World War II
*See also Countries fact
  file, page 627*

▼ One of a series of coloured prints entitled *Thirty-six Views of Mount Fuji*, by the Japanese artist Hokusai. He was perhaps the greatest artist of the *ukiyo-e* (pictures of the floating world) school.

Jazz

▲ Count Basie and Joe Williams led one of the most popular jazz bands of the 1930s and 1940s. They played a type of jazz known as swing. With its fast and driving rhythm it was good for dancing to.

Some great jazz musicians
Trumpet
Louis Armstrong, Miles Davis, Dizzy Gillespie
Saxophone
Ornette Coleman, John Coltrane, Jan Garbarek, Stan Getz, Charlie Parker, Sonny Rollins
Piano
Earl Hines, Keith Jarrett, Thelonious Monk, Oscar Peterson, Art Tatum
Double-bass
Jimmy Garrison, Charles Mingus
Drums
Art Blakey, Elvin Jones, Max Roach
Composers
Duke Ellington, Gil Evans, Michael Gibbs, Charles Mingus
Singers
Ella Fitzgerald, Billie Holiday, Sarah Vaughan

find out more
Musical instruments
Orchestras and bands
World music

Jazz has developed in less than 100 years into a kind of music that is popular, highly creative and full of energy. It was created mainly by black American musicians, and has progressed rapidly through several styles.

Jazz has two important features that make it different from other kinds of music: improvisation and 'swing'. Improvisation means that the players make up the music as they go along. They often use particular melodies or harmonies, but the music they play is never quite the same twice. Swing is the rhythm that drives the music along. As they play, the musicians emphasize the beat of the music, so giving it tremendous energy.

Jazz musicians play solos on brass and wind instruments, such as trumpets and saxophones. They are accompanied by a piano or guitar, a bass and drums – the rhythm section. There are also jazz singers.

Jazz styles

Jazz originated in the city of New Orleans in the southern USA in the early years of the 20th century. People began to mix the strong rhythms brought from Africa by slaves with the simple melodies and harmonies brought from Europe by settlers. A style called *New Orleans jazz*, later known as *traditional jazz*, emerged. Three or four players – often a trumpet, trombone and clarinet – played with a rhythm section. In the 1920s jazz bands began to feature solos. The greatest of the early solo players was the trumpeter Louis Armstrong.

Jazz groups soon grew, and developed into 'big bands'. Composers now wrote down the music, and players took solos at set points. This style of jazz was known as *swing*. It became very popular in the USA in the 1930s. Pioneers of swing include Duke Ellington and Count Basie. Glenn Miller achieved huge fame as a big-band leader in the 1940s.

A reaction to swing took place in the 1940s with a style called *bebop*. It featured fast, complicated melodies and rhythms, and was mainly played by small groups. The pioneers of bebop were Charlie Parker and Dizzy Gillespie.

► Billie Holiday was the greatest jazz singer of the 1930s, and her recordings are still popular today. She had a very individual voice and interpreted songs with great emotion.

In the 1950s a style of jazz known as *cool jazz* developed, with simpler melodies and a more restrained approach. Musicians experimented with instruments such as the flute and French horn. Miles Davis and Dave Brubeck were leaders of this jazz style.

By 1960 some jazz musicians began to demand more freedom. Led by Miles Davis and John Coltrane, they began to improvise on a scale of notes in a style known as *modal jazz*. Then other musicians developed *free jazz*, in which musicians could play anything at all.

The 1970s saw the development of many new styles. One of these was known as *jazz-rock* or *fusion*. Miles Davis was again the pioneer. He mixed jazz with rock music, taking over the strong beat of rock and the electric instruments.

Today, there are players of all jazz styles, from early traditional or swing to recent fusion, who play to jazz audiences all over the world. Jazz music has also had an important influence on pop music.

Jefferson, Thomas

Born 1743 in Virginia, USA
Died 1826 aged 83

find out more
United States of America

▶ Thomas Jefferson (wearing the red waistcoat) signing the Declaration of Independence. In this important document he wrote the now famous words: 'all men are created equal and independent', and therefore they have rights which no one can take away. These rights include 'the preservation of life and liberty, and the pursuit of happiness'.

Thomas Jefferson was president of the USA from 1801 to 1809, but he is most famous for his part in writing the American Declaration of Independence. This historic document formed the basis of the US constitution and renounced all connections with Britain.

When Thomas Jefferson was born, Virginia was still a colony ruled by Britain. His father died

when he was 14 and he inherited an enormous plantation, together with some slaves. After going to college, he became a lawyer, and in 1769 he was elected to the House of Burgesses, a local parliament. Many Virginians felt that Britain should allow the colonists to rule themselves. Jefferson agreed. He wrote that London had no right to make laws for people who had left England. Many people read and discussed his ideas and he was chosen to draft what became the Declaration of Independence. This formed the basis of the US constitution, the theory of government on which the USA was founded. This declaration led to the American Revolution (1775–1783) which secured US independence from England.

Jefferson did not fight in the war, choosing instead to return to Virginia. He was elected governor of Virginia (1779–1781) and then rose up the political ladder, as well as serving on diplomatic missions to Europe. In 1801 he became the third president of the USA. During his presidency, the size of the USA doubled. Jefferson dedicated the last years of his life to what was one of his proudest achievements, the University of Virginia.

Jellyfishes and corals

Jellyfishes, corals and sea anemones belong to the same group of animals. They all have a simple tube-shaped or cup-shaped body.

• There are 6500 different kinds of coral and sea anemone, and 200 different kinds of jellyfish.

• Several related but different sorts of creature are often referred to as jellyfishes. These include the Portuguese man-of-war, the sting of which is dangerous to humans.

find out more
Islands
Oceans and seas
Seashore

Much of a jellyfish's bell-shaped body is made up of a stiff, jelly-like material. From the edge of the bell, long tentacles trail into the sea. These tentacles are covered with stinging cells which are powerful enough to paralyse prey such as fishes, shrimps and other sea animals.

Sea anemones and their relatives the corals look like plants but are in fact creatures called polyps. A polyp has a simple, cup-shaped body with a ring of tentacles around the mouth. The tentacles are studded with stinging cells that paralyse and kill any tiny creature that touches them.

Sea anemones are entirely soft-bodied. They live in shallow or deep water, attaching themselves to a hard surface such as a rock, a coral or a shell. If they are taken out of water, they are just like blobs of jelly, but when covered with water they look like flowers, with their frill of short tentacles.

▲ Sea anemones and corals can often be found together. Here a sea anemone lives on a sea-fan coral.

A coral polyp is able to take minerals from the sea water and build them into a hard cup-like skeleton that supports and protects it. Some corals live alone in cold or deep water, but many others are colonial animals and share a huge skeleton. These are the builders of coral reefs. Such reefs are home to many kinds of fishes and other creatures.

Jesus *see* Christians • **Jet engines** *see* Engines • **Jewellery** *see* Gems and jewellery

Jews

Jews are the followers of Judaism, the Jewish religion of the ancient Hebrews. Some Jews may feel part of the Jewish people and their culture but not the religion.

- Three major festivals, Passover, the Festival of Weeks (Pentecost) and the Feast of Tabernacles, celebrate the escape from Egypt, the giving of the Ten Commandments and sheltering in the wilderness.

- Jacob is the traditional ancestor of the people of Israel. In a dream, Jacob saw a ladder stretching between Earth and heaven. God told Jacob that he would always be with him and that his descendants would have a special land and history. God later gave Jacob the name of Israel ('one who struggles with God').

Religious Jews believe that God has a relationship or covenant (contract) with everyone who leads a good life. The covenant of the Jewish people with God began with Abraham and continued with Moses.

Abraham and Moses

Abraham was a wealthy trader who lived in Mesopotamia (modern Iraq) in about 1800 BC. At the age of about 75 he followed God's call to leave his country and go to a new land, Canaan. He settled there and proved his faith in God by agreeing to sacrifice his beloved son, Isaac. God let Isaac live, and blessed them both as the founders of a great nation. Abraham is important to Jews because God led him to the

The Jewish synagogue

A synagogue is the place where Jews come together for study and prayer. The focus of the synagogue is the Torah, which is written by hand on a scroll and placed in a cupboard or alcove called the Holy Ark (below). A light burns in front of the Ark as a symbol of the presence of God. The first ark was a portable chest for the Ten Commandments given to Moses.

Another important part of a synagogue is the *bimah* (reading desk) which is usually in the centre. From this desk a member of the congregation reads the portion of Scripture for the week. The main services are led by a rabbi or any learned person appointed by the community.

promised land of Israel, which they have called their own ever since.

Later, so it is claimed in the Scriptures, when the Israelites were slaves in Egypt, God used Moses to lead them out of Egypt (the Exodus). The Hebrews wandered in the wilderness for 40 years until, on Mount Sinai, they made a covenant with God and God gave them the gift of the Torah (law or teaching), which includes the Ten Commandments. The Torah describes how people should treat their families, strangers, animals and the land, as well as how to worship.

Scriptures

The story of God and the Israelites is told in the Hebrew Bible. Jews are encouraged to learn the Hebrew language and to study and discuss the meaning of the text. It comprises three sections: the Law (*Torah*), the Prophets (*Neviim*), and the Writings (*Ketuvim*). The Law is the core

◀ This family in Jerusalem, Israel, is celebrating Passover, called *Pesach* in Hebrew. Passover is an eight-day festival which recalls the 'passing over' of the Angel of Death over Jewish houses, so that only the first-born sons of the Egyptians were killed by plague. The deaths were a warning from God to the Egyptians, who finally let the Jews leave after 3000 years of slavery.

▲ The Western or Wailing Wall is the only part of the Temple which survived in Jerusalem after the Romans destroyed it in AD 70. These Jewish pilgrims have come to the Wall to pray. Everyone who comes to the Wall must be suitably dressed. Men wear head coverings and women must cover their shoulders.

of the Jewish Scriptures. The English names of these five books of Moses are Genesis, Exodus, Leviticus, Numbers and Deuteronomy.

Famous prophets (*Neviim*) included Isaiah, Jeremiah, Ezekiel, Amos and Hosea. They constantly reminded people to keep their covenant with God. The third section of the Hebrew Bible (*Ketuvim*) contains the stories of Job, Ruth, Esther and Daniel. There are also psalms, and poetry such as the Song of Songs.

The Talmud is the record of debates of the rabbis (religious teachers) up to about AD 500. Talmud means 'study', and the rabbis help people to apply the law to their everyday lives.

A special and suffering people

Jews have one of the oldest religions in the world. For nearly 4000 years they have struggled to follow it and keep it from being destroyed. Palestine was ruled by various empires including the Babylonian, Persian, Greek, Roman, Ottoman and British; the people were exiled and their temple in Jerusalem destroyed.

▶ When a Jewish boy is 13 and a girl 12, they 'come of age'. A boy becomes Bar Mitzvah, a son of the commandments, and a girl Bat Mitzvah, a daughter of the commandments. This boy is ready to celebrate his Bar Mitzvah. He is wearing the *tephillin*, leather boxes containing verses from the Jewish Scriptures, on his forehead and also bound to his arm; a prayer shawl (*tallit*); and a cap (*kippah*) as a sign of respect.

These exiles began the diaspora (dispersal) of Jews to many parts of the world. In AD 135 the Romans exiled all Jews from Jerusalem, and for the next 18 centuries most Jews lived all over the world. Wherever they went, they tried to maintain a distinctive way of life and worship. Persecutions (called 'pogroms') began because Christians saw them as outsiders. This prejudice against Jews is called anti-Semitism. The last terrible persecution was the Holocaust (*Shoah*) in Nazi Germany in the 1930s and 1940s when over 6 million Jews were killed. After this it was agreed by the United Nations in 1947 that there should be a Jewish state in Palestine. This was to be called Israel.

A way of life

Getting married and having a family is an important part of being Jewish. Rabbis are expected to marry like everyone else. Jewish boys and girls learn about their religion and way of life first of all at home with their mothers.

The focus of each week is the Sabbath. This is a day of rest, recreation and prayer lasting from dusk on Friday to dusk on Saturday. It begins in the home when the mother welcomes the Sabbath by lighting two candles and the father says a special blessing over wine and bread before the evening meal. On Saturday morning the family will probably go to the synagogue for prayers and to meet friends. On other days children go to classes at the synagogue to learn Hebrew, the language of the Jewish Bible, and prepare for their Bar Mitzvah celebration, when at the age of 12 or 13, they become full members of the Jewish community.

● The word 'Hebrews' is used in the Bible as another name for Jews. 'Hebrew' may have originally meant a kind of slave, and it may have been used to refer to the Israelites because they had once been slaves.

● David and Solomon, who lived in the 10th century BC, were two of Israel's most famous kings. David united the tribes of Judah and Israel into one nation and brought the Ark with the Ten Commandments to Jerusalem. His son Solomon's most important work was the building of the Temple, which made Jerusalem a holy city.

find out more
Bible
Festivals and holidays
Holocaust
Israel
Religions

Joan of Arc

Born 1412 in Domrémy, France
Burnt at the stake 1431 aged 18

Joan of Arc was a young peasant girl who, inspired by God, led French troops in a battle against the English during the Hundred Years' War. She was later captured by the English, who claimed she was a witch and burnt her at the stake.

• Twenty-five years after her death, the French king proclaimed Joan of Arc innocent, and nearly 500 years after her death the Pope declared her a saint.

When Joan was 13 years old, she heard some voices which she believed had come from God. They spoke about the sufferings of France at the hands of the English, who had invaded under Henry V. The true heir to the French throne, Charles the Dauphin, was a refugee. The voices told Joan to lead the fight against the English.

Joan persuaded Charles of her mission. He sent her with troops to Orléans, the last city in northern France still resisting the English. Within a week of her arrival in May 1429, the siege of Orléans was over. Within two months, the English had been defeated in battle and Charles had been crowned King of France.

However, after a year she was captured by the English and King Charles made no attempt to rescue her. Joan was put on trial as a witch and a heretic (a person who disagrees with the teaching of the Church). Her accusers insisted that it was the Devil who had inspired her to wear men's clothes and to claim such power for herself. Joan was found guilty and was burnt at the stake in Rouen in May 1431.

find out more
France

▼ This painting of Joan of Arc in battledress at the coronation of Charles VII was made by Jean-Auguste Dominique Ingres in 1854.

Kennedy, J. F.

John Fitzgerald Kennedy was one of America's most popular and inspiring presidents. Tragically, he was in office for only two years before being shot and killed by an assassin.

John Kennedy ('Jack' to his family) was one of nine children. He did well at college, but he hurt his back while playing football and never fully recovered from the injury. During World War II, he commanded a small ship. It was sunk by the Japanese, but Kennedy, although badly injured, managed to lead his men to safety. For this he was awarded a medal for heroism.

Kennedy's father was a strong-minded man who was determined that one of his sons would become a politician. The whole family helped Jack by contributing campaign funds and canvassing voters. He became a Democrat member of the House of Representatives in 1946, and a senator in 1952.

In 1960 he was elected president of the USA. Although he was energetic and intelligent, Kennedy soon faced problems. He gave American help to Cuban refugees trying to invade communist Cuba. They failed, making the USA look foolish. Nevertheless, Kennedy did stop the USSR from building nuclear missile bases on Cuba in 1962. He also sent military advisers and troops to Vietnam, which led, after his death, to American involvement in the Vietnam War. At home, he proposed laws to give black Americans equal rights, but Congress did not pass these laws until after he was killed in 1963.

Born 1917 in Brookline, Massachusetts, USA
Assassinated 1963 aged 46

find out more
United States of America
Vietnam War

▼ In November 1963 Kennedy travelled to Dallas, Texas, to gather support in the American South. He was shot and killed by a gunman while travelling in this open car.

Kidneys

As the blood travels round your body, it collects unwanted waste and poisons. Your kidneys' job is to clean your blood and get rid of this waste matter. They do this by filtering the blood and passing the waste out of the body in urine.

• All fishes, amphibians, reptiles, birds and mammals have kidneys that are basically similar to those of a human.

▶ A kidney cut in half. Kidneys are part of the body's waste-disposal system. They filter blood to stop your body being poisoned by its own wastes.

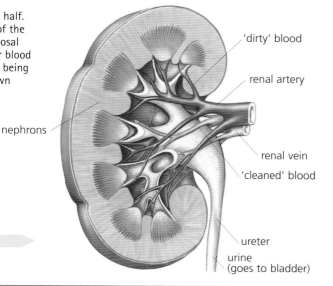

nephrons

'dirty' blood

renal artery

renal vein

'cleaned' blood

ureter

urine (goes to bladder)

find out more
Blood
Human body

You have two bean-shaped kidneys towards the back of your body, just above the waist. Each one is joined to the bladder by a tube called a ureter. Urine passes down the ureters to the bladder, and from there you pass it out of your body when you urinate.

How the kidneys work

Blood enters the kidneys at high pressure and then passes into millions of tiny tubes called nephrons, where waste products are filtered out as urine. The main waste in urine is a chemical called urea. This contains nitrogen, which is formed when proteins are broken down in the body. The cleaned blood leaves the kidneys by the renal veins. Your kidneys filter your blood about 50 times a day.

If the kidneys stop working, a dialysis machine can carry out their job. Three times a week the blood is passed into the machine for several hours and the waste products are removed. Healthy kidneys may also be transplanted into someone else whose kidneys are not working properly. If one kidney stops working, the other will get larger and do the work of two.

King, Martin Luther

Martin Luther King was the leader of the black civil rights movement in the USA in the 1950s and 1960s. He was an inspiring and committed leader, who finally gave his life in the struggle to win equal rights for black people.

Born 1929 in Atlanta, Georgia, USA
Assassinated 1968 aged 39

find out more
Slaves
United States of America

▶ Martin Luther King at the Washington demonstration of 1963. His speech inspired millions of people to campaign for civil rights: 'I have a dream, that my four little children will one day live in a nation where they will not be judged by the colour of their skin but by the content of their character.'

Martin Luther King believed that the best way for black people to win equal rights was by non-violent protest against unfair laws. In 1955, he became a minister in Montgomery, Alabama. The buses there had separate seats for blacks and whites; King led a campaign to get rid of this separate seating.

King and his supporters were attacked and imprisoned for their non-violent protests, but their following continued to grow. Over 200,000 people marched to Washington in 1963, in support of equal rights for black people.

In 1964, King was awarded the Nobel Peace Prize. That same year, a new law made it an offence to discriminate against black people in public places, and the following year the US government gave all black adults the vote.

By 1966 other black leaders began to oppose his non-violent methods. He also became unpopular with some people, especially the government, because he opposed the Vietnam War. In April 1968 King went to Memphis, Tennessee, to support a strike by black refuse collectors. He was shot and killed by a sniper, while standing on the balcony of his motel room. Today, the anniversary of his assassination is a national holiday in the USA.

Kings and queens

A king or queen is a ruler over a kingdom, which may be a tribe or country. A queen may be the monarch of a country in her own right, or she may be the wife of a king. Sometimes a king or queen is chosen by the people, but most often the crown is passed on from parent to child.

Most prehistoric tribes had kings, usually their finest warrior. There are many stories of kings in ancient Greece, such as Theseus, king of Athens. The Jewish kings described in the Bible, such as David and Solomon, were thought to receive their power from God himself.

There were also famous queens in ancient times. The Queen of Sheba came from Arabia to visit the court of King Solomon in Israel. Boudicca, widow of a Celtic British king, led an army of resistance against the Romans.

Royal families

In some countries the same royal families have ruled for many years. These are called dynasties, and those of ancient Egypt and of China often lasted for hundreds of years. In Europe two of the greatest royal families were the Habsburgs of Austria and the Bourbons of France.

Japan has the oldest royal family in the world. Seventy generations of the same family have ruled since 660 BC. Morocco has been ruled by the same family since the 17th century.

Kings and queens today

There are few countries with powerful kings or queens any more. They have either been deposed (removed from the throne), and sometimes killed, or else they have handed their powers over to an elected parliament, as in the United Kingdom. There are more powerful kings in Thailand, Nepal, Morocco and Lesotho.

▲ Elizabeth II has been Queen of the United Kingdom since the death of her father, King George VI, in 1952. In her role as head of state she undertakes around 400 public engagements a year, both at home and abroad. Here she can be seen attending an official banquet in Malaysia.

The main job of a king or queen today is as ceremonial head of state, doing what in other countries is done by an elected president. They appoint a prime minister, sign bills from parliament, welcome important guests, take part in various ceremonies and visit other countries.

- Why have there been fewer queens than kings? One reason is that in many countries, when a monarch dies, the crown is always inherited by the eldest son. A girl will only become monarch if there is no elder son. In some other countries no female monarchs are allowed, and in the absence of a son the crown will pass instead to a male relation.

Royal families today
Africa
Lesotho
Morocco
Swaziland
Asia
Bhutan
Japan (emperor)
Nepal
Thailand
Middle East
Bahrain
Jordan
Kuwait
Oman
Saudi Arabia
Oceania
Tonga
Europe
Belgium
Denmark
Liechtenstein
Luxembourg
Monaco
Netherlands
Norway
Spain
Sweden
United Kingdom

▶ Henry VI became King of England when he was only 1 year old. However, it was not until 1442, when he was 21 years old, that he was given full royal power.

find out more
Charlemagne
Cleopatra
Elizabeth I
Henry VIII
Victoria

Knights

Knights were highly trained soldiers on horseback. In the early Middle Ages any talented warrior could become a knight. But gradually the knights formed a group which became a ruling class throughout Europe, with their own rules of behaviour known as the 'code of chivalry'.

Early knights formed the finest armies of medieval Europe. They played a vital part in the feudal system of the Middle Ages. In return for estates to live on, they had to serve their lords for about 40 days each year – in warfare, on expeditions or on castle guard. The code of chivalry they followed was meant to help to tame knights who terrorized the people of Europe in peacetime.

▼ These knights are jousting with long lances at a medieval tournament. The earliest tournaments were practice battles between two picked sides. They were rather like miniature wars, and men were often badly hurt. Jousting was more like a mock duel between individual champions.

Chivalry

Later, Christian knights formed a fixed group of warrior-governors or aristocrats. All knights were expected to serve God and the Church as well as their rulers. True knights should be brave, strong and skilful fighters. The code was used to tame unruly knights. It was an agreement between knights that they should be generous, kind and polite and always protect the weak.

Historians call the years from about 1100 to 1400 the Age of Chivalry, even though not all knights of this time behaved as well as the code suggested they should. By the end of that period most knights had stopped taking the code seriously. Instead of serving God and protecting the weak, they busied themselves with tournaments or with fighting duels of honour.

• Today in Britain men are still made knights, and given the title 'Sir', as a reward for serving the country in whatever jobs they do. Women who are given a similar reward are referred to as 'Dame' instead of 'Sir'.

find out more
Armour
Celts
Crusades
Medieval England
Middle Ages

Changing roles

By the 15th century new weapons and new kinds of warfare had come in, making the knights less important to Europe's armies. The weight of their armour greatly limited both their speed and their movement. Many stopped fighting for their rulers, and paid them instead to employ mercenaries, men who just fought for a living. The better-off knights then concentrated on running their estates.

Heraldry
Medieval knights had patterns on their shields called heraldic devices. Heraldry was the name for the study of these devices. Devices were also worn on helmets, on the drapery of horses and on special outer garments called 'surcoats'. The devices, or 'coats of arms' as they became known, were passed on from one generation to the next and so symbolized whole families, not just individuals.

Devices were often very beautiful, but they were more than just decorations. In tournaments of the Middle Ages devices were the only way of telling one knight from another. And in the heat of real battles these 'coats of arms' helped knights to tell their friends from their enemies.

Charges

Bend

Fess

Saltire

Chevron

Divisions

Quarterly

Paly

▶ The background colour of a shield is its *field* or *ground*. A *charge* is a picture or shape placed on the field. A few simple charges are shown here, but there are hundreds, including animals, birds and weapons. The basic field can be divided up in various ways, called *divisions* or *partitions*, two of which are shown here.

Korea

Korea is a peninsula in north-east Asia. Since 1948 it has been divided into two countries, North and South Korea.

Korea was first united in the 7th century AD, under the rule of the kingdom of Silla. Except for short periods, it remained independent until 1910, when the Japanese took control. After World War II, Soviet troops occupied North Korea, and US troops occupied South Korea. Since then, the country has remained divided.

South Korea

South Korea is a republic, governed by a president and a state council. Much of South Korea is mountainous, but most people live in the lowland areas (only about a third of the country). Rice is the main farm crop. The country has few natural resources, but it has achieved remarkable economic growth. By the late 1990s it was the world's 11th largest economy, but there were worries about the country's huge debts to foreign banks.

North Korea

North Korea is a communist country. It is mountainous and heavily forested, but it has huge deposits of coal, iron ore and other minerals. These are used in industries such as metal-making and chemicals. The state owns all farms and factories, and provides free health, housing and education. In world politics, North Korea is isolated. Visitors are discouraged and foreign companies are restricted to special areas.

- In 1950 the North Koreans invaded South Korea and there was war, which lasted until 1953.

- North Korea was ruled by Kim Il Sung from 1948 until his death in 1994, and then by his son, Kim Jong Il.

find out more
Asia
China
Japan

———	country boundary
◆	capital city
■ ●	major cities and towns
———	main roads
⊢⊣⊢⊣	main railways
⊕	main airports

Kurds

The Kurds are a Muslim people of the Middle East. They have a population of between 24 and 27 million, but have never had their own independent country.

Several thousand years ago the Kurdish people came from central Asia to the Zagros Mountains, a region that today falls in a number of countries. Kurds call this region Kurdistan.

Traditionally, Kurdish men are skilled fighters. This reputation meant that they were in great demand as paid soldiers in foreign armies. They used to wear tunics, baggy trousers and turbans, while Kurdish women wore brightly coloured dresses over bloomers. Today most Kurds living in towns and cities wear Western clothes.

From 1514 until 1918, Kurdistan belonged to the Ottoman and Persian empires. However, the Kurds, who lived as tribal nomads (wandering people), were left to rule themselves.

Since the 1920s most Kurds have lived as ethnic (non-native) minorities in the various states that make up Kurdistan. They have struggled for their cultural and national rights. In Turkey, since 1984, the PKK (Kurdish Workers' Party) has fought with the Turkish army for a separate Kurdish state. In the 1980s and 1990s the Kurds in Iraq suffered greatly at the hands of the dictator Saddam Hussein. He used chemical weapons against them, killing tens of thousands and making over 1 million homeless.

find out more
Iran
Iraq
Middle East
Turkey

▼ The hilly region of Kurdistan is divided by many national borders. In Turkey many Kurdish villages have been destroyed by the army and families have had to move to the cities to make new lives. This family (right) is on the move in eastern Turkey.

most people Kurds

Lacrosse

Lacrosse is a team game played with a hard rubber ball and a special netted stick called a crosse. The ball is moved rapidly around the field and from end to end – in a good game, the ball scarcely touches the ground – so it makes an excellent spectator sport.

Lacrosse is played separately by teams of men and women (10 a side for men, 12 a side for women). Body contact is allowed in the men's game, so players wear protective padding, helmets and faceguards. Body contact is forbidden in the women's game.

A lacrosse pitch is about the size of a football field, with a goal 1.83 metres square at each end. The object is to score goals, which players can do only if they are outside a circle surrounding each goal. The ball can be caught and carried in the crosse and also slung from it. Players learn the skill of running with the crosse almost upright, rapidly twirling it to and fro to keep the ball cradled in the net.

Lacrosse has its origins in a game called baggataway ('ball game') played by the native peoples of North America several hundred years ago. The stick used to catch and throw the ball reminded European settlers of a bishop's crozier (*la crosse*), which is how the game got its name.

The game was later introduced from Canada to a number of other countries. Today it is played in many parts of the world, including the USA, Britain, Australia, New Zealand and South Africa.

◀ A player 'cradles' the ball, keeping the ball in the crosse by making a series of rapid half-turns of the stick while running.

• In the game of baggataway, each side would sometimes number several hundred and the game could continue for up to three days. It was very rough, and participants could be quite seriously injured.

Lakes

Lakes are areas of water surrounded by land. They occur where water can collect in hollows in the Earth's surface, or behind barriers which may be natural or artificial. The world's largest lake is the Caspian Sea, which receives water from the Volga and Ural rivers.

Crater lakes lie in the natural hollows of old volcanoes. The Eifel district of north-west Germany has hundreds of lakes lying in extinct craters. Lake Bosumtwi in Ghana lies in a crater that was probably made by a meteorite.

Glacial lakes form where ice-sheets and glaciers have left the ground very uneven. They have scraped and hollowed out hard rock or dumped sand, gravel and clay in uneven layers. Such lake districts are found in Finland and in northern Canada. Lakes may fill holes in the glaciated valley floor, as in the Lake District in north-west England.

Rift-valley lakes are long thin lakes such as Lake Malawi, Lake Tanganyika and Lake Turkana in East Africa, and the Dead Sea between Israel and Jordan. When the Earth's crust slipped down between long lines of faults, the water filled part of the floor of the valley.

Artificial lakes are created by humans. People have built earth, stone and huge concrete dams to hold back rivers for water supply, irrigation or hydroelectric power.

• The world's largest lake is the Caspian Sea in central Asia, with an area of 371,000 sq km. The deepest lake is Lake Baykal in Siberia, Russia, which is 1741 m deep.

find out more
Dams
Glaciers
Mountains
Ponds

▼ Some different kinds of lake.

crater lake   rift-valley lake   glacial lake

Languages

Languages are for communicating facts and ideas, for asking questions, for telling people what to do, for creating stories and poems, and for explaining things.

No one is sure exactly how many languages there are in the world, but there are certainly well over 4000. In Africa alone there are about 1300 languages. In Europe over 30 main languages are spoken. But these European languages are generally not completely different.

Language families

English, German, Gaelic and Sanskrit, an ancient Indian language, all belong to a great Indo-European family of languages. About 5000–6000 years ago, people in southern Russia and the Danube area of Europe probably spoke a sort of original Indo-European language. Over the years different forms of the language developed as people spread over larger areas. These languages include the Celtic group of languages, Greek and Latin, the Germanic and Slavonic languages, and Hindi.

There are other families of languages. One includes Finnish, Hungarian and perhaps Turkish. Others include the Chinese languages and the languages of Japan and Korea.

There are four families of African languages, one of which includes Arabic. Some languages do not seem to belong to any family. The Basque language spoken in northern Spain is unlike any other.

Languages in use

Some people are bilingual – they speak more than one language equally well. They may have been brought up by parents who speak different languages or have lived in two countries. In some countries it is normal to use a mother tongue at home and an official language at work and on formal occasions. In parts of India and Africa children learn two or three languages at school.

Some languages, including English and French, are used as *international languages*. People from different countries may use one of these languages to speak to each other.

Sometimes languages are adapted into special forms. *Pidgins* are simplified languages used by groups of people with no language in common. English and Chinese merchants and diplomats used Chinese pidgin English for over 300 years. If a pidgin becomes a native language of a people, it is called a *creole*. In some Caribbean countries, people speak creoles based on English mixed with words borrowed from French and Dutch.

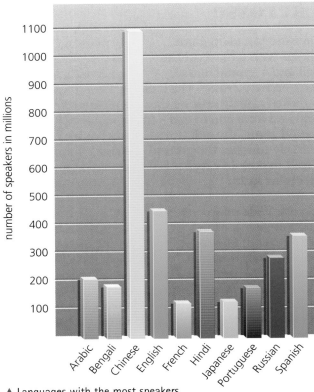

▲ Languages with the most speakers.

Grammar

Grammar is the way we construct language in order to say something. If you want people to understand what you mean, you have to use the right kinds of words and put them in the right order. Words can be grouped into sorts called *parts of speech* (see below). Most important of these are nouns (which name things), verbs (which tell you what is happening) and adjectives (which describe things). Nearly all sentences have a verb and at least one noun.

• The Italian, Spanish, Portuguese, Catalan, French and Romanian languages all developed from Latin. These are known as the Romance languages.

find out more
Communication
English language
Symbols
Writing systems

▼ Examples of the parts of speech and the two articles in English.

interjections are words that you call out (oh, gosh, hey)

definite article (the)

nouns tell you what is being talked about (cake, brother, love)

pronouns stand for people or things already mentioned (she, me, it)

indefinite article (a)

'Ouch!' cried the hairy gorilla as he fell clumsily in a heap.

verbs tell you what is happening or what someone is doing (sit, push, be)

adjectives describe things (red, big, fast)

conjunctions join phrases and sentences (and, because, if)

adverbs tell you the way in which things happen or are done (suddenly, easily, fast)

prepositions tell you about position or direction (in, on, to, off)

Lasers

Lasers produce a narrow beam of bright light. Ordinary light is a mixture of colours, but laser light is just one pure colour. Lasers are used in a wide range of everyday situations – to read bar codes at supermarket tills, to play compact discs, to carry telephone signals over long distances and to make 3D pictures called holograms.

A laser beam is much narrower than that of an ordinary lamp. Laser light is different in other ways as well. First, it has a single wavelength, which explains why it is a single pure colour. Second, the light waves move exactly in time with each other. Waves of ordinary light are sent out in disorganized bursts.

How lasers work

Some lasers have a crystal in them. Others have a tube containing gas or liquid. An electrical discharge or flash of bright light gives extra energy to the atoms in the laser material. A few atoms lose this energy by giving out light. These trigger other atoms into losing energy and sending out light waves, and so on.

Mirrors at each end of a laser send the light to and fro so that more and more atoms are triggered into sending out light. One of the mirrors is only partly reflecting. Light escapes through it, either as a steady beam or as a sudden pulse, depending on the type of laser.

Using lasers

Some supermarket tills use lasers to 'read' the bar codes on the things you buy. The laser beam is reflected from the bars

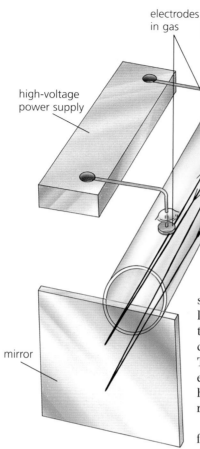

electrodes in gas

high-voltage power supply

laser beam

mirror letting out some light

mixture of helium and neon gas in tube

mirror

◀ Inside a helium–neon gas laser.

in pulses which are changed into electrical signals. Doctors use lasers to burn away birthmarks and some cancer cells. Military lasers guide missiles to their targets, and factories use powerful lasers to cut through metal, glass and cloth for clothing.

Holograms

The special single-colour light from a laser is used to make a hologram. Unlike an ordinary flat picture of an object, the picture stored in the hologram has depth, so you can see round the sides of the object as though it were solid and really there.

▶ Doctors use lasers to perform delicate eye surgery. If the retina (the part of the eye that contains light-sensitive cells) becomes loose, a laser can be used to stick it back in place. The laser beam is sent to the patient's eye in a series of pulses.

To see the picture stored in some holograms a beam of laser light is shone on them, but the holograms used on credit cards work with reflected light. They give a 3D image which is easy to see if you place the hologram upright under a reading lamp.

Holograms are used in factories to show up small differences in machines and parts which should be exactly the same. Holography has been used on the Space Shuttle to show which of its protective tiles have become loosened during flight.

• LASER stands for Light Amplification by Stimulated Emission of Radiation.

• DANGER! Never look directly down a laser beam. It could damage your eyes and even make you blind.

find out more
Atoms and molecules
Compact discs
Eyes
Information technology
Light
Radiation
Recording
Telephones

Law and order

The rules of a country are known as its laws. The government of a country has to make sure that people obey the law. If they do not, then they are punished. The police, courts and prison services carry out the law. Together they make up a system of 'law and order'.

▲ This scene from a US courtroom shows a case being heard in front of a judge and jury. The woman at the centre is a lawyer. She is speaking directly to the jury, whose job it is to decide whether the defendant (the person on trial) is innocent or guilty.

• The Code of Justinian is a collection of Roman laws. Ten wise men compiled it on the orders of the emperor Justinian, who reigned over the Byzantine empire from 527 to 565.

Laws are different from country to country. Today's law in many European countries, such as France, Germany and Italy, is based on laws from the ancient Roman empire. English law is the basis of law in the USA and many other English-speaking countries. Some countries base their law on religious ideas. Many Arab countries use Islamic law based on the Muslim holy book, the Qur'an (Koran).

Criminal law

Criminal law deals with people accused of committing a crime such as murder, robbery or assault. The police investigate crimes and arrest suspects. Criminal courts decide whether a person charged with a crime (a defendant) is innocent or guilty. Judges and magistrates listen to the evidence and the legal arguments of a case. The law sets a maximum punishment for every crime.

In many countries, including France, Britain and the USA, serious crimes, such as murder, are dealt with in front of a judge and jury. Judges make sure the trial is carried out properly and decide on questions of law and punishments. The job of the jury, in countries which use a jury system, is to listen to the evidence and decide whether or not the accused person is guilty. Jury systems vary across the world, but in general jury members are chosen randomly and usually consider a case in complete secrecy before announcing their verdict.

Two important people in court are the prosecuting and defending lawyers. Prosecutors present the evidence against the accused. Defending lawyers do all they can to prove their client's innocence. Everyone who gives evidence in court takes an oath promising to tell the truth.

Civil law

Civil law deals with matters such as divorce, family disputes and disputes over property. If a person suffers loss, damage or harm because of a breach of civil law, they can take the offender to court. Lawyers advise people in such cases. Often people go to court to get compensation for an injury or damage.

▼ One of the oldest systems of law we know of was put together nearly 4000 years ago by Hammurabi, king of Babylon. He had 282 laws carved on this large block of black stone, called a stele. Hammurabi based his code on many older laws. They set out the principle of 'an eye for an eye', which was later challenged by Christian teaching.

International law

Every country has slightly different laws, so attempts have been made to agree on a set of basic human rights that everyone in the world should have. In 1948 the United Nations adopted a Universal Declaration of Human Rights. It states that everyone has the right to life, security, freedom and protection by the law. However, countries are not legally bound to follow this declaration. European countries also have an agreement on certain human rights. Anyone who feels they have been wrongly treated can complain to the European Commission of Human Rights.

▼ The European Court of Human Rights in Strasbourg is the court to which an individual can appeal if they believe that their human rights have been violated by one of the member states of the European Union.

▲ Many prisons today are becoming more and more overcrowded. One solution is the use of prison ships. This prison ship, *The Resolution*, is heading for its mooring off Britain's coast. Prison ships like this can hold up to 500 prisoners.

▼ Elizabeth Fry, seen here reading the Bible to women prisoners and their children, was a Quaker who worked to reform prisons in England in the early 19th century. Prisons at that time were often violent places and full of disease. She worked to ensure that women prisoners were always looked after by women staff. She also managed to get prisons to start educating or training some of their prisoners, so that it was sometimes possible for them to get jobs when they were released.

find out more
Crime
Government
Police

Punishment

Most people found guilty of fairly minor crimes are punished by having to pay a fine. Some may be made to do community service – to spend a certain number of hours working on something that helps the community. Others may be put on *probation*. For a certain period a probation officer gives them advice and keeps an eye on their behaviour.

For more serious crimes people may be sent to *prison*. The purpose of prison is to punish the offender and protect the public. It is also to rehabilitate offenders. This means providing prisoners with skills that will help them to find work when they are released, and also to avoid a return to crime.

In the past most countries executed people for serious crimes such as murder. In more than 80 countries the death penalty is now banned. However, executions still take place in many other countries, including the USA.

Lenin

Born 1870 in
Simbirsk, Russia
Died 1924 aged 53

Lenin was the leader of the communist revolution in Russia in 1917. Under his leadership, the old Russian empire was transformed into the Union of Soviet Socialist Republics (the USSR).

• On the 100th anniversary of Lenin's birth, a third of the people of the world were living in countries run by communist governments. By 1991, however, the USSR had broken up and several other countries soon abandoned communism.

find out more
Communists
Russia
Stalin, Joseph

As a young man, Vladimir Ilich Ulyanov (as Lenin was then called) became increasingly aware of what he saw to be the problems of his country: a weak tsar (ruler), a corrupt Church and nobility, and millions of poor and angry peasants and factory workers. Like many people, he saw revolution and the communist ideas of Karl Marx as the solution.

As a student, Ulyanov was often in trouble because of his political beliefs. Eventually he was sent to prison and then into exile in Siberia. While he was in Siberia he took the name 'Lenin', from the River Lena.

In 1898 the Russian Social-Democratic Workers' Party was formed. In an effort to gain power, Lenin helped to split the party in 1903, leading the Bolsheviks ('Majority') against the Mensheviks ('Minority'). The Bolsheviks later became the Russian Communist Party.

Lenin lived in exile for 12 years, but returned to Russia in 1917 when the tsar was overthrown and a new government came to power. That same year, he led the Bolsheviks to victory in a revolution against this government and thus became the ruler of Russia. The Bolshevik (or Soviet) government became a virtual dictatorship and defeated their opponents in the Russian Civil War (1918–1921). Lenin led his country – now the Union of Soviet Socialist Republics (USSR) – until his death from a stroke in 1924.

▼ After the 1917 revolution, posters and statues of Lenin were put up all over Russia.

Lenses

The lenses in spectacles are specially shaped pieces of glass or plastic that bend a beam of light as it goes through them. Lenses range from tiny ones found in microscopes to huge ones, over one metre wide, used in astronomical telescopes. The lenses we use most often are the ones in our eyes.

There are two types of lens. A *convex* lens is thicker in the middle. A magnifying glass is a convex lens. A *concave* lens is thinner in the middle. Spectacles worn by short-sighted people have concave lenses.

Looking through lenses

If you hold a lens above a newspaper, you will see that a convex lens makes the words look bigger and a concave lens makes them look smaller. If you hold a convex lens in front of a sheet of card facing a window, the lens makes a small, upside-down picture of the window on the card. We call this picture an *image*. The lenses in our eyes help make an image of what we are looking at, inside our eyes. In the same way, a camera lens makes an image on the film inside the camera.

We use magnifying glasses to make things look larger and clearer. Stronger magnifying glasses have fatter lenses which magnify more. However, a thick lens will only make a clear picture near the middle of the lens. Near the edges, where the lens is thinner, the picture will be blurred.

We look through the lenses of microscopes, binoculars and telescopes to see things that are too small or too far away to be seen with our eyes alone. These lenses vary in size, from under 2 millimetres in a microscope to over 1 metre in the biggest astronomical telescopes. In all these instruments each 'lens' is really several lenses joined together. These make clearer pictures than single lenses, which produce pictures with blurred or coloured edges.

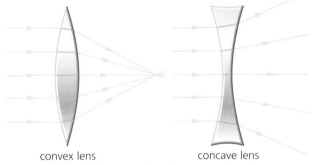

convex lens   concave lens

▲ When a beam of light goes through a convex lens, it narrows down to a point as the lens focuses the light. A concave lens spreads out a beam of light.

find out more
Cameras
Eyes
Microscopes
Telescopes

Leonardo da Vinci

Leonardo da Vinci was a multi-talented genius and one of the leading figures of the Renaissance period. He was an artist, designer, inventor and engineer.

As a teenager, Leonardo was apprenticed to a leading Italian artist who taught him painting, sculpture, metal-casting, jewellery-making and costume design. By the age of 20 he was good enough to be a master painter, but he had so many interests that he produced relatively few paintings and left several of them unfinished. The pictures that he did complete, however, show that he was one of the greatest and most original artists of his time.

Leonardo had enormous curiosity. He was one of the first people to dissect (cut apart) human bodies to find out how muscles and bones really work. He was fascinated by nature and wanted to understand the laws that govern it. He planned buildings and worked out how to divert rivers and to construct canals. He invented weapons and even acted as military adviser to the duke of Milan. Amazingly, he also designed flying machines nearly 400 years before the first powered aircraft flew.

Leonardo was greatly admired in his lifetime. However, his scientific work was often far ahead of that of his contemporaries, and most of his ideas remained in his notebooks and were not developed.

> **Born** 1452 in or near Vinci, Tuscany, Italy
> **Died** 1519 aged 67

◀ Leonardo da Vinci's painting *Mona Lisa* (1503–1506), which is now in the Louvre museum in Paris, France, is probably the most famous painting in the world.

find out more
Drawing
Painting
Renaissance

Letters and diaries

find out more
Frank, Anne
Information technology
Postal services

• One of the earliest diaries still in existence is the *Kagero nikki* (*The Gossamer Years*), written by a Japanese noble woman in the 10th century AD. It describes her unhappy marriage.

Letters and diaries are both personal forms of writing that are used by many people, and in everyday situations. People usually write letters to communicate with someone else, whereas they keep diaries mainly as a private record.

More letters are written today than ever before, but most are business letters. Now, instead of writing letters, people tend to keep in touch with their friends and families by telephone, and sometimes even by e-mail.

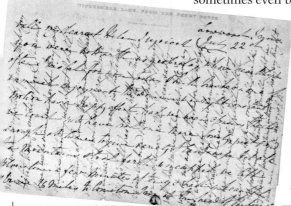

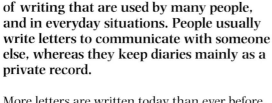

◀ This letter was written in 1839 in Cumbria, England. The writer ('E. B.') has 'crossed' her letter — that is, she has written down the page and then turned the paper round and written across the page as well. Letters were frequently crossed in the 19th century, when paper was more expensive and less easily available than it is today.

'Keyhole into history'

The letters and diaries of some famous people – people who led very dramatic lives, or who wrote particularly well – have been published. These documents can tell us a lot about the past. They are also often enjoyable to read because they are funny or moving.

The apostle St Paul wrote some famous letters to Christian communities in the 1st century AD, to help them understand their new religion and follow its teachings. These letters, or 'epistles', form part of the Bible.

The Paston family from Norfolk, England, who lived during the 15th century, kept hundreds of letters. These letters were published in six volumes in the early 20th century. They provide fascinating insights into the way people lived at that time and the kind of English they spoke.

The most famous diary in the English language was written by Samuel Pepys in the 17th century. It is full of entertaining pictures of everyday life. It also records the plague of 1665 and the Great Fire of London the following year. Pepys wrote his diary in code, so that other people could not read the sometimes extremely rude things he said about them.

Light

Light is a type of radiation. It comes from the Sun, a lamp, or anything that glows. Light can pass through glass or water, but it bounces off materials that look solid. We need light to see, but we can also use it to communicate with each other.

• Light from a hot or glowing material comes from its atoms. The atoms give out the light in tiny bursts of wave energy called *photons*.

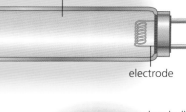

glass tube   phosphor coating   mercury vapour

electrode   electrode

▲ In a fluorescent light, an electric current flows between the electrodes at either end of the tube. The current causes the mercury vapour inside the tube to give off invisible ultraviolet light. This ultraviolet radiation makes the phosphor coating on the inside of the glass tube glow white.

▶ In a filament light bulb, an electric current heats a coil of thin wire, the filament, making it glow white-hot. The hot filament would burn up in air, so the bulb is filled with argon gas to stop this from happening.

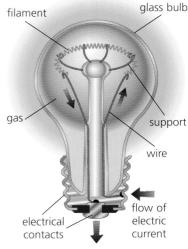

filament   glass bulb

gas   support

wire

electrical contacts   flow of electric current

The Sun, lamps, TVs and fires give off their own light. But most things do not. We only see them because they reflect light into our eyes. White surfaces reflect most light and look bright. Black surfaces reflect hardly any light. Mirrors reflect in a regular way. The light bounces off in the same pattern as it arrives. As a result, your eyes see an image in the mirror.

Light normally travels in straight lines. If it is blocked, a shadow forms where the light cannot get through. When light passes into glass, water or other clear material at any angle other than 90°, it bends. This effect is called *refraction*. It occurs because the light travels slower in the clear material than in air. Refraction makes a straw leaning in a glass of water look bent.

Colours and waves

White light is a mixture of all the colours of the rainbow.

▼ A dentist using ultraviolet light to cement braces onto a young girl's teeth. The UV light causes a chemical reaction in the cement, which hardens it. Although UV light itself is invisible to the eye, the light source gives out some visible light.

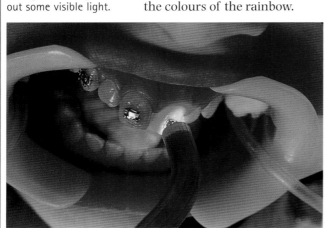

When white light passes through a prism (a triangular piece of glass), the colours are bent by different amounts and a range of colours called a *spectrum* is formed.

Light is lots of tiny waves, which travel through space rather like ripples travelling across the surface of a pond. The waves are extremely small – more than 2000 of them would fit across a pinhead. The distance from one 'peak' of a wave to the next is called the *wavelength*. Different colours have different wavelengths. Red light waves are the longest, and violet waves the shortest.

The light that we can see is just one member of a whole family of *electromagnetic waves*. Others include infrared, ultraviolet, radio waves and X-rays. All these waves travel through space at the same speed: about 300,000 kilometres per second. Nothing can travel faster than this. If you could travel at the speed of light, you could go round the Earth more than seven times in one second!

Lamps and lighting

If a material is heated to more than about 700 °C, it starts to glow. The Sun, candles and many lamps give off light because they are hot. In most light bulbs there is a tiny filament (thin wire) made of tungsten metal. This glows white-hot when an electric current is passed through it.

Electricity can be used to produce light in other ways too. Many street lamps are filled with sodium vapour. Passing a current through the vapour makes it glow yellow. Similarly, a tube filled with neon gas glows red. In a fluorescent light, the current makes mercury vapour give off invisible ultraviolet radiation. The inside of the tube is coated with a special powder that glows when it absorbs the ultraviolet light. Fluorescent paints use the same effect. They give off extra light when they absorb the ultraviolet radiation that is naturally present in sunlight.

Light signals

Flashing lamps have long been used to send signals across land or between ships at sea. Now, telephone calls, TV pictures and computer data can be carried thousands of kilometres by sending flashes of laser light along *optical fibres*. These fibres are hair-thin strands of glass. A beam of laser light put in at one end cannot escape from the sides and comes out of the other end. High-speed electronic circuits flash the laser on and off millions of times a second. The flashes are digital signals, which means that they stand for numbers. At the far end, more circuits can turn these signals back into sounds or pictures.

▶ FLASHBACK ◀

Lamps that burn animal or vegetable oils have been used since prehistoric times. The first candles were made in Egypt about 2000 years ago. Gas lamps became available in the early 1800s, but they flickered badly and were not very bright. These problems were solved by covering the flame with a mantle – a cloth bag coated with chemicals that glow with a brilliant-white light when hot.

The first electric filament bulbs were made by Joseph Swann and Thomas Edison in the late 1870s. The filament bulbs that we use today were developed from these. They are cheap, but produce more heat than light. Low-energy bulbs use small fluorescent tubes. They give as much light as a filament bulb but use only one-fifth of the amount of electricity.

◀ A lamplighter lighting a gas lamp in a city street in the early 1900s. Around this time, electric street lights were starting to replace gas lamps in many cities.

• Thomas Young (1773–1829) was a British physicist who made important discoveries about light. He was the first person to show that light is a kind of wave. He also found out that our eyes can only detect three colours — red, green and blue — and that all the other colours can be made up of mixtures of these three.

Lincoln, Abraham

Abraham Lincoln was president of the USA from 1861 to 1865. His presidency was dominated by the American Civil War.

Abraham Lincoln's family was very poor and he had less than a year of proper schooling. When he was 22, Lincoln went to Illinois, where he qualified as a lawyer. It was there that he became involved in politics, eventually serving a term in the US Congress.

He first became famous as one of the leaders of the anti-slavery movement. His popularity in the northern states resulted in him being elected president of the USA in 1861. However, on his election many southern states (which wanted to keep slavery) reorganized themselves as an independent nation, called the Southern Confederacy. This division in the country was the beginning of the American Civil War, which lasted until 1865, when the northern armies defeated the southern armies.

In 1863 Lincoln made a speech at a soldiers' cemetery after the terrible battle of Gettysburg, which the armies of the northern states had won. Few people realized it at the time, but the speech summed up the spirit of democracy. He said the soldiers had died so 'that government of the people, by the people, for the people, shall not perish from the Earth'.

After the war, Lincoln had plans for healing the division in his country, but he was killed before he could carry them out.

He was shot dead while at the theatre by John Wilkes Booth, a fanatical supporter of the southern states.

Born 1809 in Kentucky, USA
Died 1865 aged 56

▶ Abraham Lincoln in 1864, the year after he announced his Emancipation Proclamation. He decreed that all slaves in America should be set free. People living in the Southern Confederacy refused to do this. However, after they lost the war, they were forced to comply.

find out more
Slaves
United States of America

Living things

Human beings are living things, as are whales and mosquitoes, oak trees and mosses, even bacteria. Despite their differences in size and appearance, living things have several things in common: they are able to grow for part or all of their lives; they are able to reproduce (to make a new generation of young); and they are able to react to changes in their surroundings.

This reaction to change can take many different forms. A plant may react to a change in the weather by losing its leaves or opening its flowers. An amoeba (a single-celled animal) might move towards a smell that may mean food. Larger, more complex animals behave in still more complicated ways.

THE FIVE KINGDOMS

Bacteria and blue-green algae (kingdom **Monera**): about 4000 species

Protozoa and algae (kingdom **Protoctista**): about 80,000 species

Fungi (mushrooms, moulds): about 72,000 species

Plants: about 270,000 species

Animals: about 1,320,000 species

heliozoan
amoeba
fly agaric mushroom
moss
tulip
Scot's pine
lugworm
rat
swallow
spider
sea anemone
frog
shark

spore-producing
flowering
cone-bearing
invertebrates
vertebrates

▲ Living things can be divided into five kingdoms.

An example of classification

Kingdom Animalia	All animals belong to the kingdom Animalia.
Phylum Chordata	All animals that have a stiffening rod in their backs in the early stages of their lives belong to the phylum Chordata (chordates).
Subphylum Vertebrata	All animals that have backbones belong to the subphylum Vertebrata (vertebrates).
Class Mammalia	All animals that breathe air, are hairy and feed their young on milk belong to the class Mammalia (mammals).
Order Perissodactyla	All animals that are hoofed and have an odd number of toes – including horses and their relatives – belong to the order Perissodactyla.
Family Equidae	All horse-like animals, from about 60 million years ago to the present day, belong to the family Equidae.
Genus Equus	All single-toed horses, from about 5 million years ago – including horses, donkeys and zebras – belong to the genus Equus.
Species Equus caballus	The domestic horse belongs to the caballus species. The scientific name for any animal species combines its genus and species name, so the domestic horse is properly known as Equus caballus.

Classifying life

Ever since ancient times, human beings have tried to improve their understanding of the natural world by classifying (grouping together) similar living things. Today, plants, animals and other living things that are similar in structure are classified under a system developed over 200 years ago by a Swede, Carolus Linnaeus.

The basic unit of the Linnaean system is the individual. Although no two individuals are exactly the same, some are clearly very alike. They belong to the same *species*, a group that is able to breed successfully in the wild. Similar species belong to the same *genus* (plural: genera). They cannot breed together. Genera are grouped into *families*, which consist of clearly related animals or plants. For instance, all cats belong to one family; all dogs to another.

Families are put together into *orders*. Cats and dogs both belong to the same order, along with bears and weasels among other flesh-eaters. Orders are grouped into *classes*. All mammals belong to one class. A number of classes together make up a *phylum* (plural: phyla). A phylum includes animals with basic similarities, though these are often masked by adaptations to a particular way of life. Finally, the phyla are grouped into five *kingdoms* – animals, plants, fungi, Protoctista and Monera.

● More than 1.75 million different species of living thing have been identified, and more are being discovered all the time. The total number could be in the region of 13 million! The numbers of identified species belonging to the Monera and Protoctista kingdoms are probably only a tiny proportion of the total numbers that exist.

find out more
Animals
Bacteria
Fungi
Plants
Viruses

Lizards

Lizards are small, agile reptiles. Most live in warmer, drier parts of the world, and can often be seen sunning themselves or scuttling away from danger.

- There are about 3000 different kinds of lizard, more than any other kind of reptile. The largest lizard is the Komodo dragon, which grows to over 3 m long and weighs over 100 kg.

All lizards have sharp eyesight and a good sense of hearing. They generally feed on insects and other small animals. Some are burrowers, hunting their prey underground. Lizards' skin is silky smooth and their legs are small. Some, like slow-worms, have no legs at all.

Lizards have many enemies. They protect themselves by moving quickly and by camouflage – they match their environment and so are difficult to

find out more
Reptiles

see. Some types of lizard shed their tails if caught by a predator, and so escape. The tail will grow again.

Chameleons are small lizards that have a very special kind of camouflage. They change colour, sometimes in as little as two minutes. In bright sunshine they are a rich green, while at night they become whiter. A frightened chameleon may turn pale, while an angry one goes blackish green.

Generally, lizards avoid people, but geckos like to live in buildings. They have suction pads on their feet which help them to climb walls or walk upside-down on ceilings. They are welcome in many houses, because they feed on flies and other household pests.

Most lizards lay eggs, but some kinds give birth to live young, and a few even feed developing young through a placenta like mammals.

common wall lizard

blue-tailed day gecko

chameleon

Lorries and buses

Lorries and buses are large vehicles used for transport by road. Lorries (or trucks) carry heavy goods, and specially designed ones can tip heavy loads, carry liquids in a tank, or keep food refrigerated. Buses carry passengers on short local journeys as well as over longer distances.

- Very large lorries are sometimes called 'juggernauts'. Juggernaut is the name of a Hindu temple and god, whose image is traditionally carried in a huge, unstoppable chariot.

find out more
Engines
Motor cars
Roads

▼ This colourful bus is carrying passengers through a mountain pass in northern Pakistan.

The heaviest lorries can weigh 40 tonnes or more. Most lorries are powered by diesel engines and can have as many as 16 gears. They are often built with the same basic cab and chassis (frame), but different bodies are bolted on depending on the load to be carried. Some lorries are in two parts. The front part, with the engine and cab, is called the tractor unit. This pulls the rear part, a trailer which carries the load. Lorries like this are known as *articulated lorries*, because the whole unit bends where the two parts join.

▶ FLASHBACK ◀

Lorries, powered by steam or electricity, first appeared in the 1890s. Lorries with petrol engines were introduced in the early 1900s and were widely used for carrying supplies during World War I (1914–1918). During the 1920s, reliable and longer-lasting diesel engines became available and have been used ever since.

▼ A long-distance articulated freight lorry speeds along an empty highway in Nevada, USA.

Llamas *see* Camels • **Locusts** *see* Grasshoppers and crickets

Louis XIV

Born 1638 at Saint-Germain-en-Laye, France
Died 1715 aged 76

• Louis XIV's palace at Versailles was enormous. About 5000 courtiers and attendants lived inside.

find out more
France

Louis XIV was the king of France from 1643 to 1715. During his long reign, literature and the other arts flourished, but he had much less success in his attempts to gain new territories in Europe.

Louis became the king of France at the age of 4 on the death of his father, Louis XIII. His mother, Anne of Austria, at first ruled for him, helped by her powerful chief adviser, Cardinal Mazarin. After Mazarin died in 1661, however, Louis was determined to be the only ruler. As he said himself, 'L'état, c'est moi' ('I am the state').

Louis had many good ideas for improving the towns and countryside of France. Art, music and literature also flourished as he encouraged brilliant writers, artists and musicians to come to his court. However, there was a darker side to his reign as well. He fought expensive wars in the Netherlands and against Spain to gain new territories, but he was defeated when other countries joined together against him. At home, he was cruel to the Huguenots (Protestants) who, after a century of freedom, were told in 1685 that they had to become Roman Catholics. Two hundred thousand of them refused and left the country.

A magnificent palace at Versailles, just outside Paris, was built on Louis's orders and he moved his court there in 1682. However, the life of luxury he lived angered his subjects, many of whom were struggling to survive. When he died, he was a lonely figure, and his body was buried to the jeers of the watching crowd.

▼ Louis XIV portrayed in his coronation robes. He became known as the Sun King because he chose the Sun as his royal badge.

Lungs

• All mammals, birds, reptiles and air-breathing amphibians have lungs. Most fishes do not have lungs. However, one group that does is called the lungfishes. Their lungs are filled with air when they put their noses through the water surface. They also have gills which they use underwater.

• The disease bronchitis is an inflammation (swelling) of the air passages of the lungs.

find out more
Breathing
Human body

Humans and many other animals have organs called lungs which are used for respiration, the process by which the body gets the energy it needs to function. The lungs absorb oxygen from the air breathed in, and extract the waste gas carbon dioxide from the blood after respiration.

Air gets to and from the lungs via the windpipe (trachea) which leads from the throat. The trachea divides into two main air tubes called *bronchi*, one going to each of the two lungs. The bronchi continue to branch and divide into thousands of very tiny air tubes called *bronchioles*. At the end of each bronchiole is a group of tiny air-filled sacs called *alveoli*.

The oxygen from the air breathed in passes from these alveoli into tiny blood vessels (capillaries) nearby. It then travels around the body to special cells where respiration takes place. Respiration uses oxygen to release energy from food, and it produces water and carbon dioxide as by-products. Carbon dioxide is not needed by the body, so it is carried in blood vessels back to the lungs. It passes through the alveoli into the bronchioles and is breathed out when you exhale.

▶ Air flows in through the nose and mouth, down the windpipe and into the lungs via the two bronchi. The lungs are like a soft pink sponge because they are made up of millions of tiny air tubes (bronchioles) which end in air sacs (alveoli) covered with blood vessels.

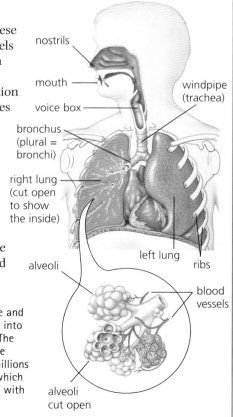

nostrils
mouth
voice box
windpipe (trachea)
bronchus (plural = bronchi)
right lung (cut open to show the inside)
left lung
ribs
alveoli
blood vessels
alveoli cut open

Machines

Machines are devices that make work easier. A machine can be as simple as a door handle, or as complex as a computer. Most machines, even big and complicated ones like railway engines or printing presses, are made up of five simpler machines: the wedge or ramp, the lever, the wheel and axle, the screw and the pulley. These simple machines can be joined together to do a complex job.

A *wedge* or *ramp* is used to raise a heavy weight (the load) a small amount. By moving the load up a slope, less effort is needed but the load has to move further. The powerful sideways force of a wedge (an axe) is used to split wood. A *wheel and axle* is another way of moving a heavy load easily. The wheel's turning action can become a strong turning force at the axle, as when a spanner turns a bolt. All motor vehicles and many other machines have wheels and axles.

Power is transmitted from one part of a machine to another in different ways. Gears, belts and chains are three common devices for transmitting power and for making parts of a machine run faster, slower or in different directions. Fast and complex machines are often controlled by electronic devices. Electrical sensors can tell when it is time to switch on other parts of the machine and check that everything is running smoothly and safely.

- A screw moves with great force. It turns round many times to move only a short distance. A screw-jack produces enough force to lift a car.

find out more
Engines
Forces and pressure
Robots

Gears and belts

Gears are used inside machines to transmit power in different directions or at different speeds. Most gears are made up of an axle and a wheel with teeth around the outer edge. A small gearwheel will turn a larger one more slowly, but with more force and in an opposite direction. The teeth of the two wheels are meshed (locked together) to make this possible. *Belts* and *bands* drive household machines like washing machines, food processors and video recorders. When you connect two wheels with a belt (a *pulley*), both wheels turn in the same direction. Different sizes of pulley turn the machines faster or slower.

Chains

If a belt has to transmit too much power, it will slip. A *chain* overcomes this problem because it fits over teeth, called sprockets, on the gearwheels. The pedals on a bicycle turn a big gearwheel, called a chain wheel. The bicycle chain turns a little gearwheel, called a sprocket wheel, which is connected to the back wheel. Some bikes have several chain wheels and sprocket wheels. When you change gear, you move the chain so that it fits over the gearwheels which are best for the job. You use the smallest chain wheel and the biggest sprocket wheel for steep hills, and the biggest chain wheel and the smallest sprocket wheel for speed on the flat and for downhill.

The lever

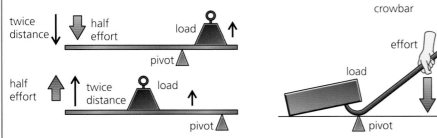

crowbar   wheelbarrow

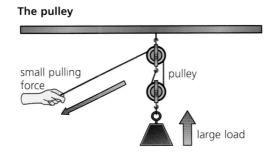

◀ A *lever* moves a heavy load easily. The pivot of the lever can be in different places. The pivot on a crowbar is closer to the load than to you, so a small effort lifts a large load. In a wheelbarrow, the load is between you and the pivot.

▶ A *pulley* lifts heavy loads by making it possible to pull downwards, which is easier than pulling upwards. Pulleys magnify the pulling force. Big pulley systems have many sets of wheels. With a pulley system called a chain hoist, one person can lift a motor car engine.

The pulley

chain hoist

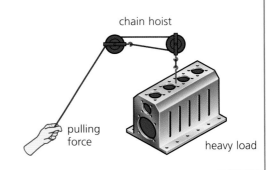

Magellan, Ferdinand

Born about 1480 in Sabrosa, Portugal
Died 1521 aged about 41

Ferdinand Magellan was a famous navigator. He was the first man to find a route from the Atlantic Ocean to the Pacific Ocean.

Ferdinand Magellan was convinced that the Far East could be reached by sailing west from Europe. Other explorers had believed this was possible, but none had yet managed to find a way of sailing round or through the Americas.

In 1519 Magellan set sail from Spain with five small ships and 268 men. One ship was wrecked in a storm off South America, and another turned back. But with the others, Magellan battled against bad weather and eventually found a passage between Tierra del Fuego and the mainland of South America. (This passage is now called the Strait of Magellan.) He emerged into calm sea, which he named the Pacific (peaceful) Ocean.

The ships sailed across the Pacific Ocean to the island of Guam, and then on to the Philippines. They had succeeded in reaching the Far East by sailing westwards. Shortly afterwards, however, Magellan was killed there in a skirmish.

Only one out of the original five ships made the complete voyage around the world, returning to Spain in 1522.

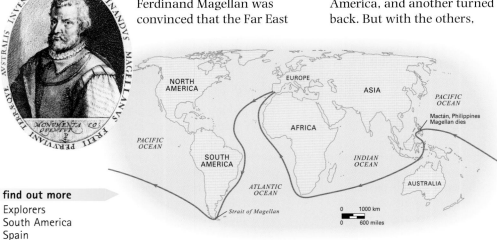

◄ Ferdinand Magellan commanded the first expedition to sail around the world. Although he did not live to see the voyage completed, it provided the first proof that the Earth is round.

find out more
Explorers
South America
Spain

Magnets

find out more
Faraday, Michael
Metals
Navigation

● The space around a magnet, where it attracts or repels, is called the *magnetic field*.

▼ The forces from a magnet seem to come from two points near its ends: called poles. One is a north pole, the other is a south pole. Iron filings show the lines of force in a magnet.

Magnets are all around you in your home. Some hold refrigerator and wardrobe doors shut. Others are hidden, for example in the doorbell and the telephone.

Magnets attract iron, nickel, cobalt and most types of steel. But there are many metals they do not attract, including copper, aluminium, brass, tin, silver and lead.

If you put a steel needle next to a magnet, it too becomes a magnet and stays magnetized when you take the magnet away. An iron nail also becomes magnetized near a magnet, but it loses its magnetism when the magnet is removed. Magnets that keep their magnetism are called permanent magnets. Most are made of steel or alloys (metal mixtures).

How magnets work

Scientists think that, in materials like iron and steel, each atom is a tiny magnet. Normally the atoms point in all directions and their magnetic effects cancel. But when a material is magnetized, its atoms line up, and it becomes one big magnet.

▼ The disc-like object hanging from this scrapyard crane is an *electromagnet*, a type of magnet that can be switched on and off. The magnet has an iron core which only becomes magnetized when an electric current passes through it. The electromagnet is used to separate and lift heavy objects from among the waste.

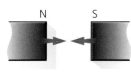

like poles repel each other

opposite poles attract each other

Mammals

Mammals are the creatures that most of us think of when we use the word 'animals'. We know them best among all living things, because many of our domestic animals and pets are mammals and so are we. In general, mammals are far more intelligent than other animals.

Mammals are found almost everywhere in the world, from the cold lands and seas of the Arctic to hot deserts and steamy forests. There are about 4000 different kinds of mammal. Some are plant-eating, some flesh-eating, and some are omnivores – they eat both plants and flesh. They live in many different environments. Bats can fly; whales live only in water; moles are burrowers; antelopes and horses are runners; monkeys are climbers.

What is it about these animals, different in size, appearance and way of life, that makes us group them all together as mammals?

They have five things in common:
- All mammals have bones, including a backbone.
- All mammals have lungs and breathe air.
- All mammals are warm-blooded.
- All mammals have some fur or hair on their bodies at some stage in their life.
- All female mammals feed their babies on milk.

The first mammals were small and evolved at about the same time as the dinosaurs, 220 million years ago. When dinosaurs died out 65 million years ago, the numbers of mammals increased dramatically, and they quickly developed into shapes and sizes that suited them for life in almost every habitat. Mammals became the dominant land animals, and the biggest

▲ A young orang-utan suckles at its mother's breast. The name mammal comes from the Latin word for breast, *mamma*, as all female mammals produce milk to feed their young.

animals on land and in the sea. Almost all large mammals, such as rhinoceroses, tigers and gorillas, are now under threat of extinction, mainly because of the activities of human beings.

Mammal groups

Mammals are divided into three groups depending on how their young develop.

The monotremes
Monotremes are the only mammals that hatch from eggs. There are only three kinds of monotreme, and they all live in Australia or New Guinea: two kinds of echidna, or spiny anteater, and the duck-billed platypus. When the young platypuses hatch from their eggs, they

Mammal records
Largest
Blue whale, up to 33 m in length and about 120 tonnes in weight
Smallest
Several kinds of shrew have a head-and-body length of less than 4.5 cm and weigh about 2 g. The hog-nosed bat of Thailand is about the same weight.
Tallest
Giraffe, up to 5.3 m

▼ A grey seal cub suckling. Seals are mammals that spend most of their lives in water, although they have to come ashore to produce their young.

lap up milk from tiny glands on their mother's belly.

platypus

bat

porpoise

koala

The placentals
Most mammals, including whales, bats, giraffes, hippopotamuses and human beings, are placentals. Young placentals grow inside their mother's body for a long while before they are born. They are nourished through a special organ called the placenta which develops within the mother's body. Food and oxygen pass from her through the placenta to the young, and waste products are returned the same way.

giraffe

find out more
Animals
Marsupials
Pregnancy and birth
Prehistoric life

hippopotamus

The marsupials
Baby marsupials are minute when they are born – some are no larger than a grain of rice – but all depend on their mother's milk to complete their growth. Most crawl up their mother's belly to a pouch, although a few are lodged in a fold of skin like a wallet. There they feed on milk and grow in safety. Marsupials, such as koalas, are found mainly in Australia and New Guinea, but some also live in South and North America.

Mandela, Nelson

In 1964 Nelson Mandela was imprisoned for life for protesting against apartheid, South Africa's system of racial discrimination. During the 26 years he was detained he became an important symbol for the anti-apartheid movement, which campaigned for his release all over the world.

• In 1993, together with F. W. de Klerk, the white president who released Mandela and legalized the ANC party, Mandela was awarded the Nobel Peace Prize for helping to abolish apartheid.

Although Nelson Mandela is related to the Xhosa royal family, he spent much of his early childhood herding cattle. After university, he qualified as a lawyer.

Mandela helped form the Youth League of the African National Congress (ANC) in 1943. The Youth League stressed the need for the ANC to identify with the hardships and struggles of ordinary black people against racial discrimination.

The ANC led peaceful mass protests against apartheid ('separate development'), the policy introduced by the National Party in 1948 to justify and strengthen white domination. Many protesters were imprisoned or killed. In 1960 the ANC was outlawed. In reply, Mandela and others established 'Umkhonto we Sizwe' (Spear of the Nation), a guerrilla army, in 1961.

In 1964, after months in hiding, Mandela was arrested and imprisoned for life. As a result of years of internal and international pressure, Mandela was eventually released in 1990 by President F. W. de Klerk. Mandela led the ANC in negotiations, resulting in the first democratic elections to be held in South Africa. The ANC won easily, and Mandela became president. In his new role, Mandela promoted reconciliation amongst all South Africans.

find out more
Nobel prizes
South Africa

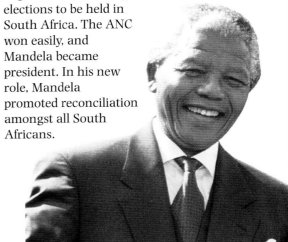

▶ Nelson Mandela celebrates his historic inauguration as president of South Africa in Pretoria, 10 May 1994.

Maori

find out more
New Zealand
Pacific Islands

▼ A Maori carver at work.

The Maori are the people who first settled in the South Pacific islands of New Zealand. They arrived about 1000 years ago from the tropical islands of eastern Polynesia.

The Maori brought many useful tropical plants with them to New Zealand, or Aotearoa as they know it. In the colder climate many of their plants died, but the taro and sweet potato flourished, and the forests and coastal waters of the new land provided other food.

Soon Maori spread over both main islands. They used wood from the dense forests to build houses and canoes, and became very skilled at woodworking.

Classic Maori culture

About 500 years ago, improved growing techniques led to an increase in population. Competition for land became intense. Tribes banded together, building large fortified villages. High-born chiefs ruled over commoners, and slaves were taken in warfare. Both men and women decorated their bodies with deep-blue tattoos. By the time Captain Cook reached New Zealand in 1769, Maori culture had become very complex.

European times

The Europeans brought with them guns, Christianity and diseases. In the Land Wars of the 1860s, many tribes lost their best lands.

After a long period of decline, the Maori population is now growing fast. During the 1950s and 1960s Maori people moved into the cities. The Maori language is being revived and Maori culture is growing stronger. Gradually, some of the injustices of the past are being put right.

Mao Zedong

Born 1893 in Hunan, China
Died 1976 aged 82

• In 1937, when the Japanese invaded China, the nationalists retreated to the mountains, but Mao sent in the 'people's liberation army' to help people in occupied villages. This is one of the reasons why, when the Japanese were defeated at the end of World War II, the people supported Mao.

find out more
China

Mao Zedong was one of the founders of the People's Republic of China in 1949. As Chairman Mao he led China with his own brand of communism, as set out in the little red books given to all his people.

As a boy, Mao loved the stories of rebel leaders who stood up for the peasants, and he was one of the first to join the new Chinese Communist Party in 1921. At first the communists worked with the Guomindang (Nationalist Party) led by Jiang Jieshi (Chiang Kai-shek) until Jiang had many of them killed in 1927. Mao's communists and Jiang's nationalists continued to fight each other until after the end of World War II when the people supported Mao in a civil war against the nationalists.

In 1949 Mao's forces captured the capital, Beijing, and set up the People's Republic of China. Mao encouraged the peasants to overthrow the landlords and work together on collective farms. In 1957 he ordered the peasants to join their farms into large 'communes', and to build new dams or open factories. These were part of Mao's plan for a 'Great Leap Forward' in industry. However, many of the schemes failed, and in 1959 Mao retired. Then, in 1966, he re-emerged to start the 'Cultural Revolution'. This movement was intended to keep Chinese communism free from outside influence and at the forefront of life in China. This, and many of his other plans and ideas, were lost when Mao died in 1976.

▼ The children surrounding Mao's painting are all dressed in traditional 'Mao' jackets, wearing red badges and holding copies of Mao's little red book.

Maps

A map is a plan of an area, viewed from above. We use many different kinds of map. Street maps, for example, show you where you are, and how to reach the place you want to go to. By contrast, physical maps tell you about the natural features of an area, whether of a country or of a continent.

- Before a map can be made, the positions of all the main features, such as hills, roads and churches, must be found. This is called *surveying*. Map surveys are now carried out using a satellite navigation system called the Global Positioning System (GPS).

- There is a map of the world on pages 646–647.

find out more
Continents
Navigation
Weather
See also articles on individual countries and continents

▼ These two world maps are drawn on different *projections*. This means that they have been flattened out in different ways. Map A is an equal area map, which means that the relative areas of the continents are correct. However, the shapes of the continents have been distorted slightly. On map B the shapes of the land areas are more accurate, but their relative sizes are incorrect.

Road maps, street maps and railway maps are made simply to show routes. *Theme maps* show special information about places. Geological maps, for example, show which rocks make up the landscape. Economic maps show a wide range of economic information, such as the average income for each inhabitant of a country, how much money countries earn from their exports, and so on. Historical maps show a country or a region at a particular period in the past. *Physical maps* show the natural features of an area of land, such as hills and rivers. *Topographic maps* also show these features, together with human features such as towns, roads and country boundaries. Land height is shown by colours. The colour green, for instance, is often used to show low land. *Political maps* include countries and their boundaries, capital cities and sometimes other towns or administrative areas, but do not tell you much about what the land looks like. Colours on these maps are used to mark out the different areas, rather than to give information about land height or the kind of vegetation.

World maps

The most accurate way to look at the size and shape of the Earth's landmasses is to use a globe. However, globes are awkward to carry about and you cannot see the entire Earth's surface at a glance.

A world map is convenient to use but it has to be read with care. It is impossible to flatten the curved surface of the Earth without stretching or cutting part of it. There is always some distortion in the shape or size of the landmasses and oceans on a world map.

Latitude and longitude

Latitude and longitude are imaginary lines that tell you exactly where a place is on the Earth's surface. They help you to find and describe the position of any place on a map. Latitude tells you how far the place is to the north or south of the *Equator*, an imaginary line around the centre of the world dividing it into the northern and southern hemispheres.

Longitude tells you how far a place is to the east or west of a special line called the Prime Meridian, which passes through Greenwich in London, England.

Both latitude and longitude are measured in degrees (°). There are 360° in a complete circle, so longitude runs east and west from 0° to 180°. All the longitude lines meet at the Poles. The latitude of the Equator is 0° and the Poles are 90° north and 90° south. The latitude lines are parallel to the Equator. Each degree of latitude is about 111 kilometres.

The *tropics* are imaginary lines marking the places furthest away from the Equator where the Sun is overhead for part of the year. The Tropic of Cancer is at $23\frac{1}{2}$° north of the Equator, and the Tropic of Capricorn is at $23\frac{1}{2}$° south of the Equator. The area between these lines is called the tropics.

Scale

The amount of detail included on a map depends on its scale. Atlas maps are small-scale maps that show large areas with little detail. The maps used by walkers and climbers, however, are large-scale maps that show small areas in a lot of detail. If you are out walking, it is very important to understand scale. What looks like a short distance on the map could turn out to be a very long way.

A

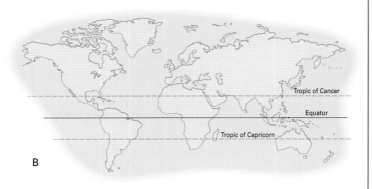

B

The scale of a map can be shown by a scale line or bar. This is divided up to show what distances on the map mean on the ground. Scale can also be shown in numbers. A scale of 1:50,000 means that one of any unit on the map represents 50,000 of the same unit on the ground. One centimetre along a road on the map would mean 50,000 centimetres along the real road – that is 500 metres or half a kilometre.

Reading maps

Maps do not show everything. You would need an aerial photograph if you wanted to see what a place actually looked like. Maps only show the things that the map maker has decided to include. Supermarkets, for example, are not usually shown, but on many maps churches are included because church spires and towers are good for helping you to find your way around. The landscape features that are shown are marked by simple symbols. Some symbols are like pictures, and others are initial letters (for example, T for telephone). It is always important to refer to the key or legend of the map to find out what the symbols mean.

On some maps the height of the land is shown by lines joining places of the same height above sea level. These imaginary lines, which do not cross each other, are called *contours*. If they seem to join up or stop, they represent a cliff or vertical slope. With practice you can learn to read the pattern of the contours so that you can picture the landscape.

Before using a map outdoors, it is helpful to turn it so that it faces north. This is called setting or orientating the map. You can use a compass to help you.

▲▼ Compare the topographic map of the continent of Europe (above) with the satellite image (below) of the same landmass. The colours in the map show different land heights. The white patches in the bottom picture are snow, which can be seen in parts of northern Europe as well as on mountain ranges in the south.

Marriage

When a man and a woman make a legal agreement to live together as husband and wife, sharing their property and probably having children, it is called marriage.

find out more
Religions

• Many homosexual couples – gay men and lesbian women – also want to make a legal, public commitment to each other. In 1989 Denmark became the first country to legalize a union between members of the same sex.

▼ This Roman Catholic bride is accompanied down the aisle of the church by her father. She is wearing white, which, traditionally, is worn as a symbol of the bride's virginity.

To get married you can promise in front of a registrar of marriages and two witnesses to live with the other person for life. The registrar then gives you a certificate to say that you are legally married.

Religious ceremonies

Many religions have a special ceremony for marriage in their places of worship. This often includes the necessary legal part of marriage. If it does not, the couple can have both a legal and a religious wedding.

Jewish marriage is a contract between two people which is blessed by God. A Muslim marriage is a civil contract between two families, which is usually exchanged at home. Muslim men can marry up to four wives in Muslim countries, but rarely do so.

In some societies, such as in certain Hindu, Sikh and Muslim countries, arranged marriages take place, in which parents help to arrange whom their children marry through family contacts. In some arranged marriages, the young couple may have never previously met.

Wedding customs

A wedding is the ceremony that takes place when a man (the groom) and woman (the bride) get married. The couple often wear traditional costumes, for example Sikh and Hindu brides may wear red.

People of different religions have different wedding customs. Eastern Orthodox Christians crown the bride and groom, who are treated like a king and queen on their wedding day.

▲ This Hindu couple in Kashmir are walking round a sacred fire during their wedding as a symbol of their unity.

Protestant and Catholic Christian couples exchange wedding rings and make marriage vows in front of a minister or priest. The Sikh groom leads his bride around the Sikh holy book, which will play a central part in their lives together. The Jewish bridegroom crushes a glass under his foot to show that love is finely made and easily destroyed.

Divorce

Divorce is the ending of a marriage according to the law. Some religions do not allow divorce, but see marriage as lasting for ever. For Christians, although ideally marriage is for life, divorce is allowed by some Churches, and a second wedding or blessing may take place in church. Divorce is allowed by Jews, Muslims and Sikhs, but with great sadness.

Marsupials

The group of animals known as marsupials includes kangaroos, koalas and opossums. They are found only in Australia, New Guinea, and North and South America. Most female marsupials have a furry pouch on their bellies. This pouch holds and protects the young from the the time they are born until they are big enough to fend for themselves.

When baby marsupials are born, they have hardly begun to develop and are very tiny. Some are as small as a grain of rice. But they have strong forelimbs and claws, which they use to crawl through their mother's fur to her pouch. There they find a teat, and fasten themselves to their food supply. Baby marsupials grow fairly slowly.

Where marsupials live

Marsupials are found mainly in Australia, New Guinea and South America. This is because for much of the last 100 million years Australia and South America have been island continents. When they became separated from the other continents, almost the only mammals living in Australia were marsupials, and in South America some mammals were marsupial. In both continents marsupials evolved into many different sorts of animal. When South America became joined to North America about 10 million years ago, most of the South American marsupials were killed off by more successful mammals which invaded from the north.

Kangaroos, koalas and wombats

kangaroo

The kangaroos of Australia and New Guinea, and their smaller relatives the wallabies and rat kangaroos, have powerful back legs. When moving slowly, they drop onto all fours. At higher speeds, they hop. The biggest kangaroos can cover more than 10 metres in a single bound. All kangaroos are plant-eaters, active mainly at dusk or at night. Several smaller kinds of kangaroo are endangered.

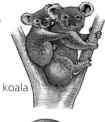
koala

Koalas are climbing animals. They live among the branches of eucalyptus forests in eastern Australia, and feed almost entirely on the young leaves and shoots of the eucalyptus. Koalas generally sleep for about 18 hours a day. In the past they have been hunted for their fur, but they are now protected.

wombat

The wombats of Australia live on the ground and burrow. A common wombat has several burrows which it may share with other wombats. Wombats are active at night, when they emerge to feed on grasses and roots.

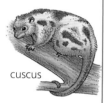
cuscus

Opossums

Opossums live in North and South America. Some species have pouches, but many have two folds of skin on their bellies, or no pouch at all. Most opossums live in forests and have hairless tails that they use to cling to branches. They feed mainly on small animals, including insects.

Tasmanian devil

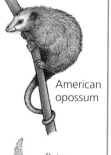
American opossum

flying opossum

▶ Marsupials vary greatly in appearance and in how they live. There are grazing, climbing, burrowing, and flesh-eating marsupials. The Tasmanian wolf has not been seen since 1936, so it is almost certainly extinct.

Tasmanian wolf

Marsupial records
Largest
Red kangaroo: males may measure 2.5 m total length, and weigh up to 90 kg.
Smallest
Pilbara ningaui: head-and-body length of adult may be as little as 4.6 cm; weight may be no more than 2 g.

• There are about 280 different kinds of marsupial.

▶ A Tasmanian pademelon with its young feeding in a eucalyptus forest. Pademelons, or scrub wallabies, are hunted for meat and fur.

• The Virginia opossum pretends to be dead if it is caught, or badly frightened. This is known as 'playing possum'. Often its enemy loses interest and the opossum makes its escape.

find out more
Australia
Mammals

Materials

Materials are the substances that things are made of – from the concrete and steel used for buildings and bridges, to the paper and ink used to make this book. All materials come originally from substances such as rocks, oil, plants or animals.

Many of the materials around us have been used for hundreds of years. They include wood and paper from trees; cotton from cotton plants; leather from cattle, wool from sheep; and materials such as pottery, stone, concrete, slate, glass and many metals, which are made from substances that have been dug out of the ground. These traditional materials still have many uses. But countless new materials have been developed that can be lighter, stronger and cheaper than traditional ones.

Modern materials

Plastics are probably the most important modern materials. They can be hard or soft, rigid or flexible, transparent or coloured. They can be moulded easily, and they are hard-wearing and long-lasting. However, plastics are not strong enough to be used for building, and they melt or burn at quite low temperatures.

Many new types of metal have been created by making *alloys*. An alloy is a combination of two metals, or a metal with a small amount of another substance. Alloys can be made with many different properties. For example, new steel alloys can be used at much higher temperatures than ordinary steels, and alloys that combine aluminium and titanium are extremely light and strong.

At very high temperatures, even the best metal alloys become too soft to be useful, and *ceramic materials* must be used. Ceramics are materials that are made by baking at high temperatures, like pottery. They do not lose strength at these temperatures and they insulate (keep heat in) well. However, they break easily under stress, rather than bend.

Composites are mixtures in which fibres, pieces or sheets of a strong material are surrounded by another, less rigid material. The fibres make the material strong, while the surrounding material stops the fibres from breaking. Composites such as carbon-reinforced plastics are used to make aircraft wings, helicopter rotor blades and sports equipment such as tennis rackets. Composites can also be made in which the fibres are embedded in a metal or a ceramic material, rather than plastic. These materials are very expensive, but they can be used at high temperatures.

Many other materials have been developed for particular

▲ Top racing bicycles are made of very sophisticated materials. This cycle frame is made of a light, strong carbon-fibre composite. It is made in several pieces, with the fibres in each piece arranged in a way that best meets the stresses on that part of the frame. The pieces are bonded together with a very strong glue.

purposes. These include metals developed for storing radioactive waste, which will remain stable for hundreds of years, and materials that can be used inside the body for making heart valves and artificial hip joints.

▼ The underside of the Space Shuttle gets extremely hot as it drops through the atmosphere on landing. Ceramic tiles are used to protect the metal skin of the craft from the heat.

● Liquid crystals are unusual materials that change colour when heated, or when an electric current is passed through them. They are used to make displays for calculators and portable computers. They can also be used to make fabrics that change colour as they get warmer and colder.

find out more
Cotton
Glass
Industry
Iron and steel
Metals
Oil
Paper
Plastics
Textiles
Wool

Mathematics

Mathematics has all sorts of uses. We use it to check our supermarket bills, to estimate how much wallpaper is needed for a room, or to work out the best shape for a bridge.

Among other things, mathematics has to do with finding out about numbers and shapes. The main branches of pure mathematics are arithmetic, geometry and algebra. Pure mathematicians are interested in ideas, such as the relations between different numbers and shapes. Others are interested in mathematical ideas that can be used in different areas, such as science and engineering.

Mathematics is growing and changing as mathematicians find new problems to interest them. They argue about which problems are the most important ones to pursue, and about who has the right answer. One special thing about modern mathematics is that, to a mathematician, finding the answer is not enough. There must be a careful explanation of exactly why each answer must be the right one.

▶ FLASHBACK ◀

People have been doing mathematics for at least as long as we have written records. A leading mathematician in ancient Greece was Pythagoras. He is best remembered for his theorem, a simple rule in geometry that links the lengths of the sides of right-angled triangles.

Many famous mathematicians first showed their brilliance at a very young age. In the 17th century, Blaise Pascal in France had published a geometry book by the age of 16, and had invented an adding and subtracting machine by the time he was 19. He also helped to devise the theory of probability.

◀ The Greek mathematician Pythagoras believed that mathematics held all the secrets of the Universe, and that some numbers were magical.

find out more
Algebra
Arithmetic
Geometry
Numbers
Probability
Statistics

Maya

The ancient Mayan people of Mexico and Central America developed the highest civilization in the New World before the arrival of the Europeans.

▼ Ancient Maya occupied an area of some 495,000 sq km, including parts of what are now southern Mexico, Guatemala, Belize, Honduras and western El Salvador.

Between about 1200 BC and AD 300, the Maya were simply one of several cultures developing around the Gulf of Mexico. The Maya were a farming people, growing maize (corn), cotton, beans, chilli and cacao (source of chocolate).

Rise and fall

Mayan civilization reached its peak between AD 300 and 900.

The chief gods of the Maya were the Sun, the Moon, the Earth and four rain gods. Mayans also studied astronomy because the stars and planets were thought to influence all life on Earth.

This Mayan civilization used stone tools and jade for decoration. They made fine woodwork, basketwork and pottery, and colourful cottons. Farmers traded in cacao beans, jaguar pelts, bird feathers and salt.

The early Mayan cities were already in decline when they were conquered by the Spanish in the 16th century. Modern Mayans live in southern Mexico, Guatemala, Belize and west Honduras. They speak Spanish and some 20 dialects of the Mayan language.

find out more
Ancient world
Mexico
North America

▼ This beautifully carved stone pillar from Honduras was made by a Mayan sculptor in the 8th century AD.

area of Mayan influence

0   400 km
0   300 miles

Gulf of Mexico

PACIFIC OCEAN

Measurement

How tall are you? How much do you weigh? How long does it take you to walk to school? The answers to all these questions are measurements.

Measurements are numbers that give us information about the world around us. We use them to buy and sell things, to build roads, to design machines, to cook meals, to do experiments and to plan our lives.

Making measurements

All measurements, whether simple or complicated, are written with a number and a unit of measurement. For example, you might be 1.5 metres tall and weigh 45 kilograms. To make measurements like these, you need measuring instruments.

Lengths can be measured with rulers and tapes. Surveyors use accurate tapes which give measurements on a digital read-out. For longer distances instruments that use pulses of infrared radiation or laser beams can be used. Using a micrometer gauge, lengths as small as one millionth of a metre (less than one hundredth the thickness of a hair) can be measured accurately.

Masses and *weights* are measured with scales and balances. Weight can be measured using a spring balance. The amount the spring stretches indicates the object's weight. A set of balancing scales compares an unknown mass with a known one.

Time can be measured with watches and clocks. It is now possible to buy a clock that has a radio link to an atomic clock, and is accurate to within 1 second in 1.7 million years.

◄ This surveyor is using a *theodolite* to measure the angle between the point where he is standing and the rule in the foreground. Accurate measurements of angles, combined with a single accurate length measurement (the baseline), can be used to calculate distances that could not easily be measured directly.

Temperatures are measured with thermometers. A digital thermometer has an electrical sensor and displays the temperature on a digital display.

Measuring systems

Scientists and others who make measurements must agree standard values for basic units of measurement. Everyone has to agree, for example, how long a metre is, otherwise measurements made in different places cannot be accurately compared. The set of standards for different kinds of unit together make up a *measurement system.*

Early standard units for length were based on parts of the body. For instance, an inch was the width of a man's thumb, and a yard was the distance around his waist. But people's thumbs and waists vary in size, and more reliable standards were needed.

Today, the *metric system* or *SI (Système Internationale)* is used in many parts of the world. In this system the basic measure of length is the metre, while mass is measured in kilograms. All other measures of length and mass are found by multiplying or dividing these basic measures. A millimetre, for example, is a thousandth of a metre.

The standard metre in the metric system was first defined as one ten-millionth of the distance between the North Pole and the Equator. But as scientific measurements became more accurate, a better standard was needed. So since 1983 the metre has been defined as a certain fraction of the distance that light travels in a vacuum in one second.

Usage des Nouvelles Mesures.

▲ The metric system was first introduced in France in around 1800. This illustration shows some of the units of measurement they used at that time. They are the litre (volume), the gram (weight), the metre (length), the are (a unit of area, equal to 100 square metres), the franc (currency) and the stère (a unit for solid measures, equal to one cubic metre).

• Once the basic units of a measuring system have been agreed, then units for all the different quantities we wish to measure can be made up from them. For example, area can be measured in square metres, volume in cubic metres, and speed in metres per second.

• For many years the imperial system of measurement was used in the USA, the UK and some other countries. Its measures of mass and length were based on the pound and the yard. A pound is just under half a kilogram; a yard is slightly less than a metre.

Medicine

Medicine is the practice of preventing and treating disease. Through the study and practice of medicine, our lives have been improved in countless ways.

The history of medicine can be traced back to the first person who we could describe as a doctor – an Egyptian called Imhotep, who died about 5000 years ago. People even visited his tomb believing that they would be cured.

Early developments

The ancient Greeks helped to start the system of modern medicine. Hippocrates of Cos, who lived in the 5th century BC, argued that diseases were not caused by magic, as many people believed, and that they could be explained if patients were examined carefully. He also taught people about the importance of diet and hygiene (keeping clean) in order to be healthy. His ideas spread through Greece and the Roman empire.

During the early Middle Ages in Europe, medical knowledge progressed very little. But in other parts of the world such as Persia (Iran), China and India, medicine was developing.

From the 9th century onwards, medical schools were founded in various parts of Europe. They taught a more scientific approach to medicine and big advances were made. Medicine developed rapidly during the following centuries, with scientists making many important discoveries about disease and its treatment.

▼ Knowlege of human anatomy (the structure of the body) leapt forward during the 16th century. This was because doctors began to cut up real corpses for the first time, to find out how the human body was put together.

▲ Modern medicine is so advanced that we can discover whether an unborn child (fetus) is developing normally. This laboratory technician is checking sample cells from the fluid that surrounds the fetus to discover whether the fetus has a genetic disorder.

Harvey and Lister

In the 17th century, the English physician William Harvey began to question the theories of the ancient Greek physician Galen about the working of the heart. In his book *On the Motions of the Heart and Blood* (1628) Harvey accurately described the circulation of the blood. This was of enormous importance in the understanding of how the body works.

Later, in the 19th century, after the French chemist Louis Pasteur proved the existence of germs, the English surgeon Joseph Lister introduced the idea of antiseptic (germ-free) surgery. After this, surgery was much safer.

Modern medicine

Developments in modern medicine have improved our lives in many ways. It is now possible to discover some serious diseases before a person actually starts to feel ill. This is called *screening* and it means that doctors can start to treat patients very early in the development of a disease. Many tests are carried out in laboratories. Blood tests, for example, tell a doctor a great deal about a person's health.

Machines are also of great use in medicine. Scanners, for example, show doctors images of the inside of the body. Other machines pick up signals from the heart or the brain, or check that an unborn baby is developing properly.

Thousands of drugs are now available to help in the treatment of illnesses, and scientists are developing new ones all the time. There is also a growing interest in non-Western medicine that does not involve drugs.

• Because the medieval period is so long, this article covers only the years after about 1100. The time before that is dealt with in Anglo-Saxons and Normans. The period after 1485 is dealt with under Tudor England.

NORMANS
1100 Henry I
1135 Stephen and Matilda

PLANTAGANETS
1154 Henry II
1170 Murder of Archbishop Thomas Becket
1189 Richard I
1199 John
1215 Magna Carta
1216 Henry III
1272 Edward I
1295 English Model Parliament set up
1307 Edward II
1327 Edward III
1337–1453 Hundred Years War
1348 First outbreak of Black Death
1377 Richard II
1381 Peasants' Revolt

LANCASTER
1399 Henry IV
1413 Henry V
1415 Henry V defeats the French at Agincourt
1422 Henry VI
1455–1485 Wars of the Roses

YORK
1461 Edward IV
1476 William Caxton sets up his printing press
1483 Edward V
1483 Richard III

▶ John, king of England from 1199 to 1216, used every means he could to raise the money to pay for wars to win back French land. When he began to act illegally, his subjects made him sign a great list of their rights called Magna Carta ('great charter').

Medieval England

We call the years between about AD 410 and 1485 in England the 'Middle Ages' or 'medieval times'. It is not a very exact period. The Middle Ages did not suddenly begin when the last Roman armies sailed away in 410, or end when Henry VII came to the throne.

For much of the Middle Ages English kings had possessions in France as well as England. Henry I ruled Normandy, Brittany and Maine, while Henry II governed an empire that stretched from the Scottish border to the Pyrenees.

The medieval kingdom

After King John had lost some of these possessions to France, successive kings fought the Hundred Years War (really a series of small wars) to try to win them back. Edward III and Henry V had spectacular short-term successes, but eventually the French were too powerful.

Meanwhile, English kings attempted to win control of the whole of the British Isles. Henry II conquered parts of Ireland, but his successors were unable to retain his conquests. Wales fell to the armies of Edward I, who made his son Prince of Wales. The Scots successfully resisted English conquest.

King, law and parliament

Although medieval kings wielded immense power, an

▲ After destroying the French army at Agincourt in 1415 (above), Henry V, king of England from 1413 to 1422, continued his assault on France until the French king let Henry marry his daughter, and so become his heir. In the nine years he ruled, Henry became the most powerful man in Europe.

unpopular monarch rarely lasted long. The hated Edward II was murdered by his enemies and Queen Matilda's reign was ravaged by civil war. Furthermore, ambitious barons were always ready to fight for the crown. The best known of these contests was the Wars of the Roses, fought between the families of York and Lancaster, both heirs of Edward III.

Despite war and rebellion, England was one of the best-governed states in Europe. Successful kings kept in touch with their barons and, later, with representatives from the counties. The assemblies of barons became the House of Lords and the assemblies of non-noble representatives became the House of Commons. The two Houses made up a Parliament.

◀ When Archbishop Thomas Becket refused to change the system allowing churchmen to be tried in their own courts, he was murdered in Canterbury Cathedral. This stained-glass window of Becket, later declared a saint, shows him tending a sick person.

God's will

The Christian Church in England was a branch of the hugely rich and powerful Roman Catholic Church, headed by the Pope. It was the largest landowner and it controlled the schools and universities. The Church even had its own system of law, allowing churchmen to be tried in their own courts. This led to bitter squabbles between the king and the Church.

'Field full of folk'

In the early Middle Ages most people were agricultural peasants. They lived in small villages, where their freedom was restricted by the *feudal system*. In the feudal system society was structured rather like a pyramid. Great numbers of ordinary people formed its broad base, and their hard work on the land provided for everyone above them – the knights, lords, barons and king.

Outbreaks of the Black Death (the plague) killed more than a third of the population, causing a labour shortage. This and the peasants' own complaints made the feudal system increasingly unworkable.

Changing times

The Middle Ages were full of changes. Royal power was limited by Parliament. Towns expanded and a prosperous merchant class grew up. The broad open fields of the early Middle Ages, in which peasants farmed their own strips of land, started to be replaced by enclosed fields. By the 15th century the Church, with its wealth and services in Latin, was increasingly out of touch with people's needs.

The invention of printing meant that books were more widely available, and the Renaissance introduced exciting new art and ideas from southern Europe.

• Angered by bad government and feudal restrictions, in 1381 the south and east of the country rose in revolt. The peasants marched on London, killing, burning and looting. The Peasants' Revolt was mercilessly crushed.

find out more
Anglo-Saxons
Chaucer, Geoffrey
Crusades
Joan of Arc
Knights
Middle Ages
Normans

Mediterranean

The Mediterranean Sea stretches over 3000 kilometres from west to east. When we talk about the Mediterranean, we often mean both the sea and the shores surrounding it, where more than 100 million people live.

The Mediterranean region has mild, wet winters and hot, dry summers. The eastern Mediterranean is drier than the west. The coast of North Africa, especially Libya, is desert. It can be very hot here, as it is also in the far south of Italy.

The mountains are wetter and cooler than the coastal plains. In summer, a dry dusty wind often blows from the Sahara. This is the sirocco. In winter comes the mistral, an icy wind from northern Europe, bringing with it a sudden chill.

Shipping and ports

The Mediterranean has been an important sea route since before the civilizations of Greece and Rome. Today, ocean-going tankers bring oil through the Suez Canal and luxury liners take tourists cruising through the islands. Marseille is the largest Mediterranean trading port.

• Over 30 million tourists visit the Mediterranean each year. The Spanish coasts of the Costa del Sol, Costa Brava and Costa Blanca are especially crowded. So too are the Riviera coasts of France and Italy, the Greek islands and Tunisia in North Africa.

find out more
Africa
Europe
Middle East
Oceans and seas

▲ A bronze mirror from Egypt. Bronze, a mixture of copper and tin, was probably the first alloy to be made.

Metals

The Earth is made of about 90 different basic substances, called elements. Of these, about three-quarters are metals. For thousands of years, people have been making use of metals. Today they are used for everything from needles to bridges.

Although there are many different metals, they all have certain properties in common. Except for mercury, which is a liquid, metals are all solids at room temperature, and pure metals are shiny when polished. Metals are good conductors of electricity and heat. Most are fairly strong, and can withstand crushing or stretching without breaking. However, they are also *malleable*, which means that they can easily be shaped by hammering or rolling. Many metals are also *ductile* – they can be drawn out into wires.

From ore to metal

Only metals such as copper, silver and gold, which do not easily combine with other materials, are found in a pure state in nature. Most metals are found in the ground as *ores* – rocks that are particularly rich in one type of metal. Some ores are much more common than others. Gold, silver and platinum are very rare. Aluminium, by contrast, is the most abundant metal on Earth. It is found mostly as *bauxite*, a mixture of aluminium oxide with materials such as sand and iron oxide.

Once an ore has been dug out of the ground, it is usually crushed to a powder, which allows many of the larger impurities to be either floated or washed away. Next, the pure metal has to be extracted. Some ores (for example iron and tin)

▼ The properties and uses of some metals.

Metal	Properties	Uses
Aluminium	Light and strong, especially in alloys. Good conductor of electricity and heat.	Principal building material for aircraft. Used for parts of cars, trains and ships, and in all kinds of machines. Soft-drink cans, doors and window-frames, saucepans, electric cables.
Copper	Reddish-yellow, quite soft, easily shaped. Very good conductor of heat and electricity.	Electrical wires and cables; also for water pipes and sometimes roofing. Important alloys include bronze and brass.
Gold	Yellow, shiny metal. Excellent conductor of electricity.	Main use as a precious metal in jewellery and coinage. Also used for electrical connections in electronics.
Iron	Pure iron greyish, malleable, easily magnetized. Alloys have wide range of properties.	Most widely used metal, mostly as its alloy, steel. Used for making huge range of products, from bridges, cars and machinery of all kinds, to needles and paper clips.
Lead	Soft, easily shaped. Does not rust. Very heavy.	Used for small, heavy weights, for example in yacht keels, and for waterproof joins on roofs. Also for plates in car batteries, and shielding around radioactive materials.
Magnesium	Light, silver-white metal. Burns with brilliant white flame.	Makes strong, light alloys with aluminium that are used in aircraft and cars. Pure metal used in fireworks.
Mercury	Silvery-white; liquid at room temperature. Good conductor of electricity. Poisonous.	Used in some electrical switches and long-life batteries. Used to be widely used in thermometers and barometers.
Nickel	Silvery-white, hard metal. Magnetic.	Thin layer of nickel on steel can prevent rust. Used in iron and steel alloys, for example stainless steel. Also used in coins.
Silver	White, shiny metal; easily shaped. Best conductor of heat and electricity.	Used as a precious metal in jewellery, ornaments and coins. Chemicals made from silver form the light-sensitive coating on photographic film.
Tin	Soft, silvery-white, does not rust or corrode.	Mainly used in tin-plating. Tin alloys include solder, pewter and bronze.
Tungsten	One of heaviest, hardest, stiffest metals. Highest melting-point of all metals.	Main use is for the filaments of light bulbs. Added to special hard steels used for the cutting edges of drills and saws.
Uranium	Heavy, yellowish metal; radioactive.	Used as a fuel in nuclear reactors.
Zinc	Bluish-white, brittle metal; does not rust.	Used to galvanize steel: thin coating of zinc on steel prevents rusting. Used for diecast metal parts such as car door handles. Important alloys include brass and solder.

▲ A coppersmith in Marrakesh, Morocco, finishing a large bowl. Copper is soft and easy to work, even when cold.

are purified by *smelting*, which involves heating them fiercely in a furnace with coke or coal. Other metals, such as aluminium, are purified by passing an electric current through the melted or dissolved ore. This process is known as *electrolysis*.

Shaping and alloying

Purified metals can be shaped in various ways. Hot metal may be rolled into thin sheets, or worked into shape by hammering while hot. Molten metal may be poured into a mould (cast), or it may be squeezed like toothpaste through a shaped hole to make bars, girders or wire.

Pure metals have relatively few uses. Much more useful are mixtures of metals, or metals mixed with small amounts of non-metals. Such mixtures are called *alloys*.

Alloys can have very different properties from the metals they are made from. Pure iron, for example, is fairly soft and

stretches easily, but adding a small amount of carbon to it produces a form of steel called mild steel. This is hard and strong, and is used for buildings, bridges, car bodies and many other purposes. Brass is an alloy of copper and zinc, and bronze is made from copper and tin. Both are much harder and stronger than the metals from which they are made. More recently, alloys of aluminium have become important materials because of their hardness, lightness and strength.

Corrosion

Metals can be chemically attacked by air, water or other substances in their surroundings. This kind of damage is called corrosion. Rust, which forms on iron and steel, is the most common type of corrosion, but other metals also corrode. Copper and bronze get a green covering called verdigris, and a black tarnish forms on silver.

Various methods are used to prevent iron and steel from rusting. Usually these involve coating the metal with something to keep out air and water. Bridges and steel girders are painted with special anti-rust paint, while food cans are coated with a thin layer of tin, which does not rust and is not poisonous. Machine parts and tools are greased to stop rusting. Many alloys that do not corrode have also been developed.

► FLASHBACK ◄

The first metals to be used were gold, silver and copper, because they sometimes occur in the pure state. Copper was first used

before 6000 BC in western Asia. About 4000 BC, in Egypt, people first learned to make copper from copper ore. The first alloy to be developed was bronze. Iron is thought to have been widely used in the Middle East from about 1200 BC.

During the Middle Ages, our knowledge of metals was advanced by alchemists, who were trying to turn other metals into gold. In the 16th century various writers brought together most of the existing knowledge about making metals and alloys. By the 18th century the development of the blast furnace for smelting iron, and the use of coke instead of charcoal in the smelting process, meant that iron could be made in much larger quantities then previously. A series of advances in the 19th century made it possible to produce large quantities of steel cheaply. In the late 19th century the modern process of electrolysis was developed, and aluminium became available in large quantities for the first time.

find out more
Atoms and molecules
Gold
Iron and steel
Materials

▼ Rusty cars in a scrapyard. The orange powdery rust is iron oxide, a chemical formed when iron reacts with oxygen in the air.

find out more
Atmosphere
Earth
Moon
Solar System

▼ This crater in Arizona, USA, was made by a meteorite about 25,000 years ago. The crater measures 1.2 km across and is 200 m deep.

Meteors and meteorites

On a dark, clear night you might see a meteor as a sudden streak of light flashing across the sky. Meteors are the hot glowing gases which are created when pieces of rock and dust from space plunge into the Earth's atmosphere. When the pieces of rock are big enough to fall right to the ground, we call them meteorites.

The common name for meteors is 'shooting stars', but they are not really stars. As the particles of dust and pieces of rock enter the Earth's atmosphere, most of them burn up completely. When they do this, we just see the red-hot flash that we call a meteor. As the Earth travels round the Sun, it sometimes passes through swarms of meteors. On these days we can see showers of meteors which all seem to come from a small area of the sky.

Meteorites

Meteorites are pieces of rock from space which are big enough to fall to the ground. About 500 largish ones strike the Earth each year. There are three main kinds of meteorite: some are stony, some are nearly all iron, and some are a mixture. They are different from the rocks the Earth is made of, so scientists like to find and study them.

A really large meteorite would make a big round crater in the ground. Meteorites made the craters on the Moon and planets. Long ago, when the Solar System first formed, there were many more large pieces of rock drifting in space but, fortunately, we think that nearly all of them have fallen onto the planets by now.

Mexico

Mexico is the most northerly country of the Spanish-speaking Americas. Its landscape changes from dry deserts in the north, through ranges of high mountains and volcanoes, to low tropical jungle in the south-east.

• Central and southern Mexico has been the home of a number of ancient civilizations, such as the Maya and the Olmecs.

find out more
Aztecs
Maya
North America
*See also Countries fact
file, page 631*

The capital, Mexico City, is 2200 metres above sea level, and although it is usually warm during the day it can be cold at night. Down at sea level in the south-east of Mexico it is warm all the year round. The peninsula known as the Yucatán is very flat and hot and has some fine beaches of white coral sand.

Large oil deposits have been discovered off Mexico's east coast. But Mexico has not become as rich as some oil-producing countries because oil prices fell and foreign debts took most of the money. Today many Mexicans are still very poor. Millions of Mexicans have journeyed to the USA in the 20th century to find better-paid jobs.

▶ FLASHBACK ◀

Modern Mexico dates from the 16th century, when the Spaniards conquered the Aztecs. The Mexicans gained their independence in 1821, after 11 years of war. For a century after that, dictators ruled the country. The present republic emerged after a series of revolutions and upheavals from 1910 to 1929.

▼ More than 18 million people live in Mexico City, one of the largest cities on Earth. Beyond Mexico City you can see two of Mexico's highest volcanoes, which are both over 5000 metres high. Their names come from old Aztec words: Iztaccíhuatl and Popocatépetl.

Mice, squirrels and other rodents

Mice, rats, gerbils, hamsters, guinea pigs, squirrels, beavers and porcupines all belong to the group of animals known as rodents. About half of all of the known kinds of mammals are rodents, and they are found in almost all parts of the world, from hot tropical forests to deserts and cold tundra. Many other mammals and birds feed on rodents, so most kinds of rodent produce enormous numbers of young so that some will survive.

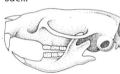

▼ A skull of a rat, showing the razor-sharp incisor teeth at the front of the jaw and the grinding teeth at the back.

The name 'rodent' comes from the Latin word meaning 'to gnaw'. At the front of their mouths rodents have only two razor-sharp incisor teeth in the upper jaw and two in the lower jaw. At the back of their mouths are grinding teeth, because rodents feed mainly on plants, though many eat insects and other small creatures as well.

Mice and dormice

Different kinds of mice are found throughout most of the world. They live in almost all habitats, from the harshest deserts to lush tropical rainforest. Most mice have little contact with human beings. Only one, the house mouse, has become a common pest, mostly because of the damage it causes.

Dormice are small, plump, furry-tailed rodents with long whiskers and large eyes. They are good climbers and usually live in woodlands or rocky places. The word 'dormouse' means 'sleep mouse', and most dormice hibernate (go into a deep sleep) for more than six months in winter.

wood mouse

Rats

The most common rats are the black rat and the brown rat. Both have become major pests to humans. They eat almost anything, and both can carry diseases, some of which may be passed to human beings or domestic animals. The Black Death, which is said to have killed a third of the population of Europe in the Middle Ages, was caused by germs carried by the fleas of black rats.

Black rats need warmth and so they live mostly in countries with hot climates. Brown rats are more hardy and can be found in almost all parts of the world, partly because humans have brought them on board ship by mistake.

• Brown rats have been tamed and make excellent pets, despite the bad reputation of their wild relatives. They are very clean and much friendlier than the more commonly kept rodents, such as hamsters and gerbils.

Voles and lemmings

Voles are sometimes mistaken for mice, but they have shorter tails and legs, and blunt faces with small eyes and ears. They are most often found in fields and meadows, though some live in woodland or desert areas. They rarely live for more than a year, but females can produce several litters of young in this time. Many of the young are eaten by foxes, owls or other predators.

Some voles are known as lemmings. Lemmings are found in burrows or rock crevices in northern tundra regions of America, Europe and Asia. About once every four years the number of lemmings increases dramatically. Many move away from where they were born to find new sources of food. In their hurry, some may rush into rivers or even the sea, where they drown. This has caused people to believe, mistakenly, that lemmings commit suicide.

lemming

Gerbils, hamsters and guinea pigs

In the wild, almost all true gerbils live on the edge of deserts in Africa and the Middle East. They escape from the daytime heat in deep burrows and come out at night to feed. There are many kinds of gerbil and many kinds of jird and sand-rat, their close relatives. Often people keep jirds as pets, but call them gerbils by mistake. Jirds have shorter hind legs than gerbils and are a bit rounder and fatter.

Hamsters are plump-bodied rodents. Most have short faces, and short legs and tails. They live in burrows in the fields of Europe and western Asia. All hamsters have huge pouches at the side of their mouths. These are used like built-in shopping baskets to carry food. Golden hamsters are popular as pets.

Guinea pigs are small tail-less rodents. They got their name because when they were first brought to Europe from South America in the 16th century, people thought they looked like tiny pigs. ▶

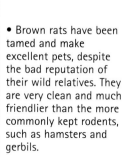

eastern chipmunk

Squirrels

Squirrels are found in almost all parts of the world. Unlike most small mammals, they are active during the day. Like many rodents, though, squirrels store extra food, usually by burying it.

Tree squirrels, such as the grey and red squirrels, are well adapted for tree-climbing. Their sharp claws help them to cling onto branches, while their long fluffy tail helps them to keep their balance. *Flying squirrels* have membranes (thin layers of skin) between their legs that enable them to glide (rather than fly) from tree to tree. Other types of squirrels are known as *ground squirrels*, and include prairie dogs, chipmunks and marmots.

Porcupines and beavers

Porcupines are large rodents with sharp spines or quills over most of their bodies, which they use for defence. There are two main groups of porcupines. New World (American) porcupines live mainly in trees. They have flexible tails, which help them to climb and keep their balance, and they generally have short quills. Old World porcupines live in warm areas, from southern Europe to Borneo and Malaya. Most kinds live on the ground and have long black-and-white quills.

Beavers are water-living rodents found in northern parts of Europe, Asia and North America. More than any other animal, except humans, they are able to change their environment. They build dams across streams by dragging stones, mud and logs from trees they have cut down with their sharp teeth. Usually the dam contains a lodge – a space in which they live and store food. Because beaver fur is valuable, the number of beavers in the world is low and they are specially protected.

grey squirrel

Old World porcupine

◄ A beaver's lodge, made of branches and compacted mud, can be as tall as a human, although most of it is underwater. The central chamber is lined with twigs and in spring two to eight young are born here. Part of the roof is made only of sticks, so that some air can get in.

find out more
Animals
Ecology
Mammals
Pets

Michelangelo

Born 1475 in Caprese, Italy
Died 1564 aged 88

• For the last 30 years of his life, Michelangelo worked mostly as an architect. He was mainly responsible for the magnificent dome of the church of St Peter in Rome.

Michelangelo was a sculptor, painter and architect. He was the most famous artist of his time, and many people consider him to be the greatest artist that ever lived.

Michelangelo Buonarroti lived during the Renaissance, a period of great change in Europe, when many dramatic developments were made in science and the arts. At the age of 13, Michelangelo became apprenticed to a painter. He studied the great art and artists of the past, and learned how to paint frescos (paintings on walls and ceilings which are done when the plaster is still wet). He also took up sculpture, which was to become his greatest love.

Almost all of Michelangelo's work as a painter and sculptor was concerned with the human figure. He was extremely good at drawing, and no artist before or since has matched his mastery in depicting nude figures in complex poses.

For all his great gifts, Michelangelo was a difficult personality. He quarrelled easily, and was often bitter and depressed. He was furious when Pope Julius II asked him to paint the ceiling of the Sistene Chapel in Rome. Michelangelo thought it was a plot by his enemies to keep him away from sculpting. However, the painting turned out to be one of the most astonishing creations in the history of art. It took four years of agonizing effort. When he was in his 60s, he also painted a magnificent fresco of The Last Judgement on the wall behind the altar in the Sistine Chapel.

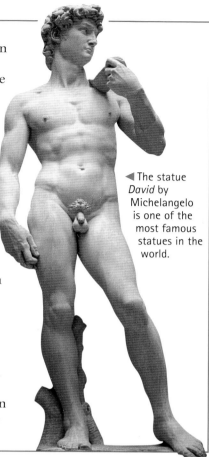

◀ The statue *David* by Michelangelo is one of the most famous statues in the world.

find out more
Renaissance
Sculpture

Microscopes

• There are two main types of electron microscope: the transmission electron microscope (TEM), which looks at thin slices of specimens, and the scanning electron microscope (SEM), which looks at the surface of specimens. The most powerful type – the scanning tunnelling microscope – can see individual atoms in a specimen.

A microscope makes tiny things look much larger, and it lets us see things which are too small to see normally. We use microscopes in schools and in science laboratories. The most powerful microscopes, called electron microscopes, can magnify things several million times.

The most common type of microscope is the *optical microscope*. It has two lenses: the objective lens, which creates a magnified image of the specimen (the object you are looking at), and the eyepiece lens, which acts like a magnifying glass to magnify that image. The specimen is lit from underneath with sunlight or light from a lamp. It must be cut into a very thin slice and mounted on glass to support it and keep it flat. A simple optical microscope can magnify a specimen by about 100 times. So a hair, which is about one-tenth of a millimetre thick, would look 10 millimetres thick. The best optical microscopes can magnify up to about 2000 times.

The *electron microscope*, a more powerful type of microscope, does not magnify with light. Instead, it fires a stream of tiny particles called electrons at the specimen, and detects how they pass through it or bounce off it.

▶ FLASHBACK ◀

The first microscope was probably made in Holland in about 1590. In the 17th century a Dutchman called Anton van Leeuwenhoek made many important discoveries about animal life with a simple, single-lens microscope. The first electron microscope was built in Germany in 1931.

◀ These hairs on the underside of a stinging nettle leaf are shown about 25 times bigger than their real size. The picture was taken by a scanning electron microscope, and the colours have been added by a computer.

find out more
Lenses
Telescopes

Middle Ages

The Middle Ages (or the 'medieval period') covers the years between about AD 410 and 1500, the first three centuries of which are sometimes called the 'Dark Ages'. We call the period before the Middle Ages 'ancient times' (the time of the Egyptians, Greeks and Romans). After the Middle Ages come 'modern times'.

Medieval Europe was divided into dozens of small states. Countries such as Scotland and Portugal were roughly the same as they are today. Other areas, like Germany and Italy, consisted of many smaller states. Some states consisted of just a single city. At this time people's religious beliefs were more important to them than the countries they happened to live in.

One Church for all

The people of Europe described themselves as living in 'Christendom', the area where Christians lived, roughly the same as Europe. There were two branches of the Christian Church. Western Europe was Roman Catholic, under the leadership of the Pope. The people of eastern Europe belonged to the Orthodox Church, which had its headquarters in Constantinople (now Istanbul). Other forms of Christianity were not allowed. Catholic services were much the same all over western Europe, and the services were even given in the same language – Latin.

For people living in the Middle Ages death was never very far away; doctors had far less knowledge and skill and diseases like the Black Death killed many. Medieval people believed hell was real and full of torments and that going to church was the main way of pleasing God and reserving a place in heaven.

The first estate

There were three groups, or 'estates', of people in Christendom. Church men and women belonged to the first and most important estate. There were thousands of Church officials. Some were rich and mighty, like the Pope, archbishops, bishops and abbots, who ran large

▲ This map shows the main countries in Europe in about the year 1200.

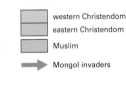

0 ——— 500 km	
0 ——— 300 miles	

	western Christendom
	eastern Christendom
	Muslim
➤	Mongol invaders

monasteries. Most, however, were poor and humble, like the parish priests, monks and nuns.

The Church's main tasks were to pray, to teach, and to help ordinary people live religious lives. Later, some said the Church was too rich, too powerful and too concerned with worldly matters. Even so, in 1500 the Church was still a mighty organization. It owned almost a quarter of all the land in Christendom and great wealth in buildings, jewels and precious metals.

• Throughout the Middle Ages in Europe there were many revolts by peasants against their poor conditions. In 1358, for example, there was a massive peasants' revolt in northern France. All such revolts were crushed without mercy.

◄ The Gothic cathedral in Milan, built in the 14th and 15th centuries, still looms over the city today. In medieval Europe religion was an important part of everyone's life. On Sundays and other 'holy days', everyone had to attend religious services. Huge and splendid cathedrals like this were built by the wealthy and powerful Church all over Europe during the Middle Ages.

► The English king, Edward III (right, dressed in red) receives an ambassador from Robert Bruce (king of Scotland) in 1327. The 15-year-old English king is surrounded by the nobles of his court. While the Church looked after people's souls, the rulers and soldiers of the second estate were supposed to look after their bodies. Ordinary people had no say in government.

The village of Montaillou

In the 1970s some fascinating documents telling us about 14th-century village life in Montaillou, France, were discovered. Each year there were 90 religious festivals or 'holy days'. The main food was bread made from wheat or millet. A popular soup included bacon, bread, cabbages and turnips. Sweet foods were rare.

Only four or five of the villagers could read or write. Hardly any of the children went to school, and at 12 boys were expected to do grown-up jobs. People did not shave or wash very often and women spent hours picking fleas off their relatives and friends. Families normally decided who their children would marry and most villagers married someone else from Montaillou.

The second estate

Kings, queens and nobles made up the second estate of medieval Europe. In many parts of Europe, lay people (those not in the Church) were part of a feudal system. This placed everyone in a sort of pyramid of importance. The king was at the top and the common people at the bottom. Nobles were chief soldiers, under whom served the knights, who all swore to serve their superiors. In return, they were given lands to live on. In wartime the knights served by fighting. In peacetime, based in their castles, they served by helping their lords to rule.

The third estate

We know very little about the lives of the ordinary folk (peasants), the third and by far the largest of the three estates. Hundreds of books about the first and second estates survive, but very little was written about the peasants.

Apart from religion, the most important thing for these people was work. The nobles and the Church relied on them for food, clothing and taxes. The peasants also had to fight for their lords. Some ordinary people lived on lonely hill farms. Others lived in the growing towns and cities. But by 1500, eight or nine people out of

ten still lived in villages and worked the fields. For them, things had not changed much for hundreds of years. Virtually no ordinary medieval homes are standing today: most were rough cottages of mud, sticks and straw, which burned down or fell to ruin centuries ago.

The end of the Middle Ages

Most medieval people knew little of the outside world. They could not read about it in books and travel was difficult, dangerous and expensive. By 1500 all this was beginning to change. European explorers had sailed to India and across the Atlantic to the 'New World', later known as the Americas. Cheap printed books were helping many more people to read and write. Artists and thinkers were saying that life was more than just a preparation for heaven, and criticism of the Church and the Pope was growing. People were starting to think of themselves not chiefly as part of Christendom, but as members of a nation, such as France, Castile (central Spain), or Sweden. The Middle Ages were coming to an end.

► This painting was made in the 15th century, near the end of the Middle Ages. It shows medieval country workers on an estate. Workers are shown sheep-shearing, wood-chopping, hay-cutting, apple-picking and ploughing. The lady of the house is seen carrying freshly picked flowers.

Middle East

Three continents – Europe, Asia and Africa – join in the Middle East. Three religions – Judaism, Christianity and Islam – had their beginnings there. For thousands of years, the Middle East has been a crossroads for travellers and traders. It has also been an area of great conflict.

The Middle East includes the whole of the Arabian Peninsula, Egypt, Israel, Iran, Iraq, Jordan, Lebanon, Syria and Turkey. It was named the Middle East because for the British and other Europeans it was half-way to the 'Far East'. Asians call the same area West Asia.

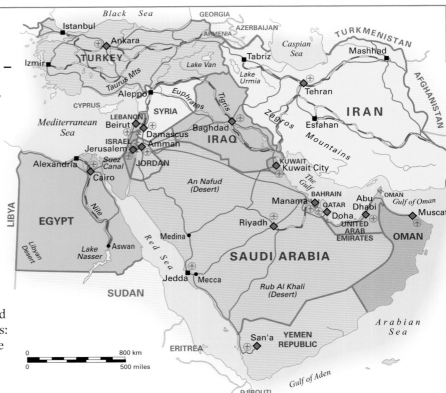

Landscape and climate

The region is full of variety. There are large sand deserts, but also three of the world's great rivers: the Nile, the Tigris and the Euphrates. There are spectacular mountain ranges, some snow-capped, but also vast flat stretches of lowland. The climate is hot and dry, although snow can fall on high ground near the Mediterranean, and desert nights can be cold. In Arabia temperatures soar to 50 °C and people wear lots of loose clothes to protect themselves from the fierce sun. In some areas rain does not fall for years, but when it does, rivers suddenly appear and rush down the dry valleys.

People and resources

Most people in the Middle East are Arabs, and Arabic is the common language. There are also Iranians, Turks, Kurds and other smaller groups of people. Most live in towns or villages. Some peoples are nomadic. This means that they move from place to place with their herds of sheep, goats and other animals.

The major natural resource of the Middle East is the vast deposits of oil and natural gas. The sale of oil and gas overseas has brought great wealth to some countries and some of the people. Agriculture is also important. Cotton, tobacco, and fruits such as dates, oranges, grapes and olives are grown. Egypt makes a lot of money by taxing ships passing through the Suez Canal.

The Middle East's history

The Middle East has played an enormously important part in history. It was the birthplace of farming and towns. Writing was developed there, as well as the three great religions of Judaism, Christianity and Islam.

◀ The Prophet's Mosque at Medina, Saudi Arabia, is one of the two most sacred sites in the world for Muslims. The prophet Mohammed is buried there.

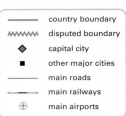

——	country boundary
⋀⋀⋀⋀	disputed boundary
◆	capital city
■	other major cities
——	main roads
⊨⊨⊨	main railways
⊕	main airports

find out more
Christians
Egypt
Iran
Iraq
Israel
Jews
Muslims
Ottoman empire
Turkey
*See also individual
  Middle Eastern
  countries in Countries
  fact file, pages
  613–645*

◀ An oil refinery in Saudi Arabia. In 1973–1974 the Arabs caused worldwide chaos by raising the price of their oil and refusing to supply countries that supported Israel in the Arab–Israeli conflict.

The earliest civilization began about 5000 BC in Sumer, part of Mesopotamia (modern-day Iraq) around the Tigris and Euphrates rivers. The Sumerians built cities and canals and invented a type of writing called cuneiform. By 3000 BC, along the banks of the Nile, the remarkable Egyptian civilization was also flowering.

The Jewish (or Hebrew) people, who lived at the eastern end of the Mediterranean, believed in one almighty God. About 2000 years ago a Jew named Jesus claimed to be the son of God. His followers, the Christians, spread his teachings far and wide. Later an Arab named Muhammad began another new religion – Islam. By AD 750 Muslims (followers of Islam) had conquered a huge empire and spread Arab civilization from India to Spain.

The Ottoman empire

Much of the Arab empire was taken over by the Ottoman Turks, another powerful Muslim people. The Ottoman empire was at its height during the 16th and 17th centuries, but in the 19th century it began to break up. Some areas where Arabs lived, such as Arabia, became independent countries. Others, including Syria, Lebanon, Palestine, Jordan and Iraq, were governed by Europeans until after World War II.

In Roman times the Jews had been driven from their native land and scattered all over Europe and the Middle East. In the 20th century, encouraged by the promises of European politicians, many Jews began to return to the region where their ancestors had lived. Some fled there to escape persecution in Nazi Germany.

Israel and oil

In 1948 the United Nations allowed the Jews to set up a country of their own – Israel. But Arabs were already living there in a land they called Palestine. Fighting broke out and other Arab

countries, particularly Egypt, Syria and Jordan, joined in on the Palestinian side. Helped by American money and arms, the Israelis defeated the Arabs three times (1948–9, 1967 and 1973) and conquered more Arab land.

By now the Europeans had left the Middle East, which was divided into the countries we see today. But the Palestinian Arabs had no country. They lived as refugees, often in poverty and hardship. From bases in Lebanon and Syria, their young men fought the Israelis with terrorism. Only in the 1990s did the Palestinians, led by Yasser Arafat, get some say in the government of the areas where they live.

The discovery of oil made some Arab states extremely rich and powerful. Saudi Arabia, guardian of the Muslim holy cities of Makkah (Mecca) and Medina, is one of the wealthiest countries in the world. The Iraqi dictator Saddam Hussein used his oil money to buy weapons to wage war against Iran (1980–1988) and Kuwait (1990–91). In 2003 the USA and UK accused Saddam of possessing illegal weapons of mass destruction, and overthrew him in another war.

• Palestine is an area of the Middle East made up of parts of Israel and Jordan. In 1948, the state of Israel was created and Palestine was divided between Jews and Arabs. Some of the land allocated to the Palestinian Arabs was later occupied by Israel. The PLO (Palestine Liberation Organization) represents the Arab people who lived in Palestine before the creation of the state of Israel.

▼ Palestinian policemen trying to maintain order on the border between the Gaza Strip and Israel. The Gaza Strip has been for many years an area of conflict between Israel and the Palestinian people. In 1993 an agreement with the Israelis gave the Palestinians some degree of self-rule.

Migration

Migration is the regular movement of animals to and from a particular area. The most common type of migration is seasonal, when animals travel from one area to another at different times of the year.

The journeys made by migrants are often very long. The Arctic tern, for example, travels from the pack ice of the Antarctic to the most northerly parts of Europe, Asia and North America to breed. By contrast, some kinds of hummingbird move only a few hundred metres up and down a mountain slope as the seasons change.

Migration may also take place on a longer time scale. Salmon spend the first part of their lives in rivers, migrate to the ocean as adults, and then return to the rivers to breed. Eels do the opposite – they hatch in the sea and migrate to fresh water to grow. A few kinds of animals are on the move almost constantly. Wildebeest in Africa and, in the oceans, some kinds of whales make a circular tour in the course of a year.

In winter some birds and other animals move away from their breeding areas to places where the weather is warmer. Migrants in northern Europe include starlings, some kinds of bat, and reindeer (caribou).

Human migration

People also migrate. They are *emigrants* from the country they leave, and *immigrants* in the country where they settle. Unlike most animal migrants, once human migrants settle somewhere new, they are unlikely to return to their old home.

find out more
Animal behaviour
Animals
Birds
Refugees
Tundra
Turtles and tortoises

▼ Some green turtles migrate over 2000 km, from their feeding grounds on the coast of Brazil to Ascension Island in the Atlantic Ocean, to breed. This strange migration probably evolved over millions of years.

ATLANTIC OCEAN
BRAZIL
Ascension Island

Milk

Humans and all other mammals produce milk to feed their young. It is nourishing and helps to protect the young from disease.

Fresh milk contains many of the essential nutrients needed for health. These include protein, fat, calcium and vitamins A, D and E. Milk may be taken from cows, goats, buffalo, camels, sheep, reindeer and other mammals.

Using milk

Milk is used in hot and cold drinks and in cooked dishes such as sauces, soups and puddings. Some mothers need or prefer to use milk powder to make a substitute for breast milk for their babies.

Milk fresh from the cow can be a dangerous source of bacteria. So milk is pasteurized (heat-treated) to kill off any germs that might be present. It may also be heated for longer, to preserve, condense or dry it. Some milk has its fat content reduced by separating off most of the cream to give skimmed or semi-skimmed milk.

Milk products

Milk is also used to make butter, yoghurt, cream and cheese. Butter is made from cream separated off from the milk. Yoghurt is made from milk that has been thickened and slightly soured by the action of certain bacteria. Cream is a concentration of the fatty part of the milk.

find out more
Cattle
Cheese
Diets
Farming
Food
Mammals

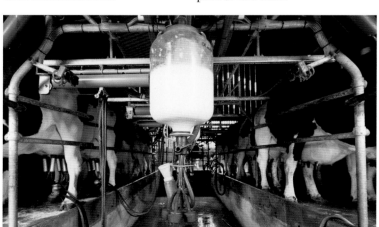

◄ These Friesian cows are being milked by machine in a milking parlour in the UK.

Mining

Mining is the process of digging rocks and minerals out of the ground. (A mineral is any substance that can be mined from the ground.) Diamonds, coal and ores (minerals from which we extract metals) are just some of the materials that we mine. Many people think that mining always takes place far underground. In fact, although some mines are very deep, others are near or at the surface of the ground.

When materials such as coal, iron ore and aluminium ore lie near the surface of the ground, they are dug up by *opencast mining*. In this kind of mining, giant excavators strip off the surface soil. Power shovels and excavators then dig out the materials and load them into lorries or railway trucks.

Most gold is obtained by *underground mining*. Shafts are dug down to the level of the ore-bearing rock. Tunnels are then dug out from the shaft to that layer. The roofs of the tunnels are often held up with metal props. The ore is removed from the rock with explosives. It is then loaded onto railway wagons, taken to the shaft and lifted to the surface.

Underground coal is mined by tunnelling. Coal is quite soft, so it is often cut by machines. In mines that are not so highly mechanized, a gap is cut beneath the coal, and then the coal is brought down with explosives or by pneumatic drills. In all coalmines, hydraulic props are used to support the roofs of the tunnels while the coal is being cut away.

Other forms of mining

Underwater mining is used to obtain tin ore. This kind of mining is called *placer mining*. Because tin ore is heavy, it tends to settle in the beds of streams or rivers. The ore is extracted by large floating dredges (a kind of scoop). Diamonds and gold, which are also heavy, are sometimes extracted by placer mining.

Stone or rock is dug out of a *quarry* (a pit or hole in the ground). In one type of quarry, large blocks of stone are cut and trimmed by special machines. The rocks quarried in this way include granite, marble, limestone, sandstone and slate. They are used for buildings and ornamental uses such as statues. Another type of quarry produces aggregate (broken stone) for road-making.

Mining dangers

Mining has always been one of the most dangerous jobs. Dusty mine air can damage miners' lungs, and explosives sometimes cause accidents. There is always the risk of poisonous gases, flooding, fire, or the roof of the mine collapsing, trapping the miners deep underground.

• The gold-mines of South Africa are the world's deepest mines, going down over 3 km.

▶ Different methods of mining.

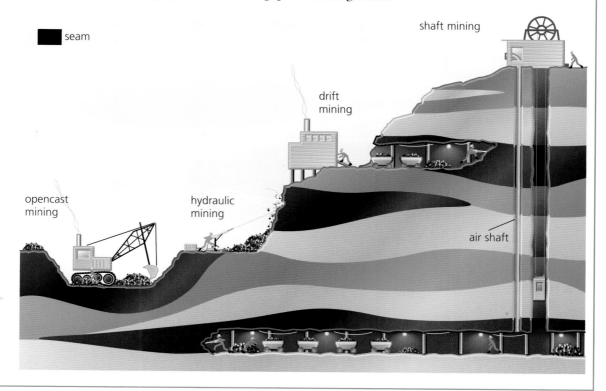

seam

opencast mining

hydraulic mining

drift mining

shaft mining

air shaft

find out more
Coal
Gold
Oil
Rocks and minerals
Salt

Mirrors

Any polished surface which reflects light is a mirror. Most mirrors are made of smooth glass backed with a very thin layer of metal, often aluminium. As well as the mirrors we use in our homes and our motor vehicles, mirrors are found inside scientific instruments such as microscopes. Huge mirrors are used inside astronomical observatories and in solar power stations.

If you put an object (say, a mug) in front of a flat mirror, you see its image in the mirror. Light from the mug bounces off the mirror so that it seems to come from behind it. This is where the image appears to be. The image is reversed, but it is the same size as the mug, and as far behind the mirror as the mug is in front.

Not all mirrors are flat. *Convex* mirrors bulge outwards. They make things look smaller but give you a wider view. They are often used as driving mirrors in cars and security mirrors in shops. *Concave* mirrors curve inwards. They are sometimes used as make-up or shaving mirrors, because they magnify things which are close.

▶ These mirrors at a funfair have a curved surface. They produce a distorted image.

With distant things, they produce a tiny, upside-down image. In large telescopes they are used instead of a lens to collect and focus the light.

Kaleidoscopes

Kaleidoscopes use mirrors to make colourful five- or six-sided patterns. The mirrors are fixed at an angle to each other inside the barrel of the kaleidoscope. Tiny bits of coloured material move around as the barrel turns. They are reflected several times in the mirrors, creating a series of changing patterns.

find out more
Lasers
Lenses
Light
Telescopes

Models

A model is a copy of an object, such as a car or an aeroplane. Models of things such as spacecraft, futuristic buildings or dinosaurs are often used when making films and TV programmes. Architects, planners and designers use models, often on a computer screen, to show what new buildings and machines will look like.

A model is made to look just like the real-life object. Although most models are on a much smaller scale, they are usually in proportion to the real object. For example, a quarter-scale model of a car will be a quarter of the length, width and height of the full-size car, and all the details will be quarter-size as well. Accurately scaled models like this are normally found only in museum displays and exhibitions. Most models (like toy cars) have some details left out.

Making models of trains, boats, cars and planes has been a popular hobby ever since these forms of transport were invented. Model boats have been found which were made over 3000 years ago. Model railways are always built to scale so that all the different parts (such as tracks, stations and engines) fit together properly.

Computer models

With the help of a computer model, a vehicle designer can alter an image, see it from different angles, and try out the effects of wind or other forces. Scientists use computer models widely, for example to investigate the structure of chemicals or to study weather patterns for forecasting.

◀ New car designs are developed and tested using computer-modelling. Before a new car goes into production, a full-size model is usually built out of wood and clay to check out the designer's ideas.

• The word 'model' also describes a person who displays clothes at fashion shows. Models also appear in advertisements for clothing, cosmetics and many other products.

• Most model aircraft are built from lightweight balsa wood. They are powered either by a coiled-up length of rubber or by a tiny engine. Some are radio-controlled from a handset.

find out more
Computers
Designers
Information technology
Toys

Money

Money is what we use to pay for things we want to buy. Money can be in the form of coins, notes or money held in a bank account. Cheques, debit cards and credit cards can also be used to pay for things.

Each country has its own particular type of money, called its *currency*. The main units of currency have names such as dollar, pound, franc, mark and yen. Banks, post offices and travel agents will all change currency for visitors going abroad. With computers and satellite communications, vast sums of money are moved around the world every day, by banks exchanging one currency for another.

From cows to coins

In the earliest times, when people wanted to trade they would have exchanged (bartered) their goods or services. Then gradually many different things came to be used as money in various parts of the world – sharks' teeth, shells, cocoa beans, cows and precious stones. In time, people saw that gold and silver were particularly suitable to be used as money. These precious metals keep their value because they are scarce, they look beautiful and they do not rust. Coins that we would recognize as such today were first made in Lydia (modern Turkey) in the 7th century BC. Gold coins were in use as currency in China in the 4th century BC, by which time coins were being used all around the Mediterranean.

Gold is very heavy to carry. By the 18th century people started to leave their gold in banks which gave them paper notes in exchange.

▲ These shells from Lau Lagoon in the Solomon Islands, Oceania, form part of the traditional *kula* exchange system of this region. In this system, red shell necklaces and white shell bracelets are passed in opposite directions around a circle of islands to seal trading agreements and social relationships.

These notes were only for large amounts. Then, as now, most European countries had coins for smaller amounts.

Banks and cheques

Keeping a lot of cash is not very safe, so most people and businesses keep their money in a bank or building society. To open an account you just need some money to pay into it. Instead of paying with banknotes, an account holder can write a cheque which instructs their bank to pay the money into the account of the *payee*. Cheques are also useful if you have to send a payment by post. Another safe way of sending money by post is to buy a postal order from a post office. For regular bills standing orders can be used to move money from one bank account to another.

Banks and some building societies also offer savings or deposit accounts. The bank is able to pay you interest on your savings because it lends your money to other people who need it. The borrowers then pay interest to the bank.

Credit cards

When people are given credit, it means that they can have something and pay for it later, usually with interest added. A credit card is a small plastic card which has the owner's details printed on a magnetic strip. A credit card holder pays by signing a slip of paper showing how much is owed. The shop sends the slip to the credit card company, which pays for the item and then sends a monthly bill to the credit card holder.

▲ We call the place where coins are made a 'mint'. The coins being made at this mint in Philadelphia, USA, have writing as well as pictures on them. The writing is often in a kind of code, to save space.

• In 1999 all the members of the European Union (except the UK, Denmark and Sweden) began to use a new common currency, the euro. At first only governments and businesses used euros for financial exchanges. But in January 2002 euro notes and coins came into use, and the old currencies, such as the French franc and the German mark, disappeared.

find out more
Economics
Gold
Trade

Mongol empire

The Mongol empire became the largest in the history of the world. It was created by the brutal leader Genghis Khan and his followers.

▼ Genghis Khan was one of the most terrifying soldiers in history. Here, he is entering battle behind his general, Gebe.

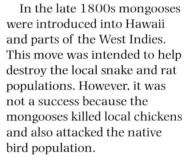

Genghis Khan, the son of a Mongol chief, was named Temujin when he was born. He was only 9 when his father died. When he grew up he begged 20,000 soldiers from a friendly chief, and set about making himself leader of all the Mongol tribes.

By 1206 Temujin had united eastern and western Mongolia. He won his empire through brutal leadership and unimaginable cruelty. He took the title 'Genghis Khan', which means 'universal ruler'. He and his sons and grandsons, including Kublai Khan, went on to conquer an area that stretched from Russia in eastern Europe across to China.

In the late 14th century the empire was in decline. Tamerlane, great-grandson of a minister of Genghis Khan, planned to rebuild it. By 1404 he had conquered regions from the Black Sea to the Indus. A hundred years after Tamerlane's death in 1405, the empire had completely disintegrated.

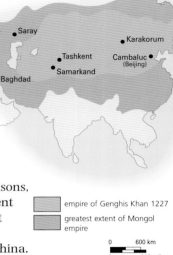

empire of Genghis Khan 1227

greatest extent of Mongol empire

| 0 | 600 km |
| 0 | 900 miles |

find out more
Asia
China
Polo, Marco

Mongooses

Mongooses are small, short-legged mammals with pointed faces and long bushy tails. They are found in the warmer parts of Europe, Asia and Africa.

Mongooses are fast-moving, agile hunters. They are a very widespread and successful group of animals. None of the 31 different kinds is in danger of extinction.

Mongooses feed mainly on small animals, from insects to birds and small mammals. They also eat birds' eggs and even fruits. They are daring hunters and are best known for their ability to kill snakes, including poisonous ones. They are not immune to the poison, but are so quick that they can avoid the snake's strike.

Most mongooses are solitary creatures, living either alone or in pairs. Some live in family groups, and a few, like the dwarf mongoose and the slender-tailed meerkat, live in larger groups, sometimes numbering up to 40 animals. Females have between two and four young at a time.

In the late 1800s mongooses were introduced into Hawaii and parts of the West Indies. This move was intended to help destroy the local snake and rat populations. However, it was not a success because the mongooses killed local chickens and also attacked the native bird population.

• The largest mongoose, the white-tailed mongoose, grows to a length of up to 58 cm, not including the tail. This is more than double the length of the tiny dwarf mongoose, the smallest of all the mongoose family.

◀ A mongoose will grab a snake by its neck. Once this happens, the fight is over and the snake is eaten by the mongoose.

find out more
Mammals
Snakes

Monkeys

Monkeys are primates, as are human beings, but it is not true to say that we are descended from them. However, monkeys are like us in many ways, particularly the way in which they use their hands for holding things.

▼ The golden marmoset has a reddish-gold coat. Unlike most other monkeys, marmosets have claws rather than nails on their hands and feet.

• The New World monkeys from South America have flat noses with nostrils set wide apart and opening to the side. The nostrils of the Old World monkeys from Africa and Asia are much closer together.

find out more
Apes
Human beings
Mammals
Primates

Monkeys have very good eyesight, which is important as many of them spend a lot of their time leaping between branches. Like humans, most monkeys have five fingers and toes on their hands and feet, and nails rather than claws.

Monkeys are sociable animals, living within groups of their own kind. Within the group each monkey knows its place, and the leader is rarely challenged. There may be noisy arguments and occasional fights, but group members are unlikely to seriously hurt each other.

Female monkeys usually give birth to one baby every few years. These are mostly carried by their mother, at first clinging to her underside and later riding on her back. Young monkeys develop slowly, and they do not usually become adults for several years.

New and Old World monkeys

There are two main groups of monkeys. Those that live in South America – the New World monkeys – all live in trees. They are wonderful climbers, and many have prehensile (gripping) tails which they use like an extra hand. New World monkeys include spider monkeys, howler monkeys, marmosets and tamarins.

The other kind of monkeys – the Old World monkeys – are found in forested areas of Africa and the warm parts of Asia. None of these has a prehensile tail, although most have some kind of tail. Some, like baboons, live mainly on the ground. Others, such as the colobus monkeys, are expert climbers and rarely leave the tree-tops.

When they are resting, all of the Old World monkeys sit upright. They have areas of hardened skin on their

buttocks, which act as built-in cushions. None of the New World monkeys have this patch.

Monkeys at risk

Some monkeys have become pests, raiding crops from farms and taking food left out in open places. In India, monkeys are sacred animals and are protected, but in many parts of the world they are now becoming very rare. This is partly because they are hunted for food, for their skins, and sometimes for use in laboratories, but mostly because the forests in which they live are being destroyed.

► The spider monkey has a strong, prehensile (gripping) tail that has a sensitive tip. It can be used like an extra hand to feel for food.

◄ The mandrill is a kind of baboon. The coat of the male is dark but he has a bright red nose and bright blue cheeks. He also has a blue-red patch on his buttocks. Males have these markings to help them attract females.

▼ Colobus monkeys are either black and white – like this one – or red. Many thousands used to be killed because their coats were much in demand for making clothes.

Monks and nuns

Monks and nuns are men and women who give over their lives completely to god. They usually live in monasteries and convents with others in the same religious order.

▲ Nuns eating a meal at a French convent. Many convents and monasteries have a rule of silence so that members do not lose a feeling of connection with God.

● A monastery is a religious community of monks. Christians also call them abbeys or priories, and the senior monk an abbot or prior. The places where nuns live are called nunneries, abbeys or convents. The senior nun is an abbess or is sometimes called the 'mother superior'.

▶ Buddhist monks accepting offerings. Young boys often take the vows and follow the rules for just a few months. Others decide to remain monks for the whole of their lives. But if they wish to leave the monastery and live an ordinary family life, they may do so.

Monks and nuns spend their time in formal prayer and meditation, but also work in caring and religious ways. Some are teachers, others nurse the sick, or spend their time travelling to wherever they are needed. Since they do not have partners and children to think about, they can give their time to anyone who wants help.

Hindu and Buddhist monks

In India there have always been people who have left family life for a life of meditation. They become dependent on the generosity of others for

food and clothing. Hindus who renounce the world and live alone in this way are called *sanyasins* and wear saffron-coloured robes. Ordinary people feel it is an honour to help them to live lives of meditation that point to a world beyond this one. There are also Hindu religious communities or monasteries. Here there are simple rooms where the monks live, a large room for them to meditate together or teach, a shrine room for worship, and somewhere for guests.

Buddhist monasteries (*viharas*) are similar. Right from the beginning of their history, Buddhist monks and nuns have had places to live during the three months' rainy season. The land for the monasteries and the material for building them are a gift from ordinary Buddhists and are never owned by the monks and nuns themselves, who also travel a great deal.

The first Christian monks

For Christians the monastic idea began soon after the death of Jesus. The early Christians shared their possessions and lived a life of prayer and dependence on God. Then in the 3rd century an Egyptian Christian, Antony, heard some words of Jesus read out in church: 'Go, sell all that you have and give to the poor.' He, and others at that time, did leave everything and went to live in the deserts of Egypt and Syria. These early Christians felt closer to Jesus by living as he had done, with no possessions, relying only on prayer to God.

The first monks lived alone. Later they chose to live in groups of caves, or built simple huts together. Their life of prayer was balanced with work, such as making reed baskets. People from the towns came to visit them to ask their advice, as they had a reputation for being wise.

Benedictine monks

One of the most important people in the history of Christian monks is St Benedict. He lived in Italy in the 6th century, but the rules he set out for his community of monks became a pattern all over the Christian world for many centuries. Those who follow his rules are called Benedictines.

Benedictine monks have to make certain vows (promises), and these are similar to the kinds of promise made by other Christian monks and nuns. Two examples are: to give up personal possessions, which is the vow of poverty, and not to marry, which is the vow of chastity.

The Middle Ages

All over Europe men and women continued to 'imitate Christ' by living in religious houses and following the rules of St Benedict. Many monasteries also served as farms, as hospitals and as places of learning. Some men who wanted to live as monks decided that this was too much like living in the everyday world. So they joined new monastic orders, such as the Carthusians or Cistercians, and followed a harder, stricter rule.

The first friars were penniless wandering preachers. They followed the teachings and ideas of Francis of Assisi (Franciscans) or of St Dominic (Dominicans).

Old and new

In England the monasteries were closed down in the reign of Henry VIII at the time of the Reformation (in the 16th century). But on the continent of Europe the old monasteries continued and new religious orders were founded, including the Roman Catholic order,

the Society of Jesus. Jesuits, as they were called, became famous as teachers, preachers and missionaries. Today there are more monks and nuns in southern Europe than there are in the north.

▼ Before the development of printing in the 15th century, Bibles, prayer books and collections of psalms were copied and often decorated by hand. In the early Middle Ages these manuscripts were made by monks.

• The Carthusians are named after their first monastery in the Grande Chartreuse, a group of mountains in the French Alps. The Cistercians are likewise named after their monastery at Cîteaux in eastern France. Both orders have strict rules about prayer, work, fasting and silence. Trappists is a later name for Cistercians.

find out more
Buddhists
Christians
Hindus
Middle Ages
Reformation
Saints

Moon

The Moon is the Earth's natural satellite. It travels round the Earth while the Earth travels round the Sun. The Moon is made of rock and looks like a small planet. It is just over a quarter of the Earth's size.

It takes the Moon about one month to orbit the Earth. In that time its shape as seen from

Earth changes from a thin crescent to a Full Moon and back again.

The Moon does not give out any light of its own. It reflects some of the sunlight that falls on it. Half of it is lit by the Sun, and the other half is in darkness. At New Moon, the Moon cannot be seen because the dark side is facing the Earth. As the Moon moves on round the Earth, we see more and more of its sunlit part.

▲ A Full Moon viewed from a spacecraft. Dark plains, called *maria*, are visible on the left. Large numbers of craters can be seen on the right.

Nearly everywhere on the Moon there are craters. Most of them were made by huge lumps of rock (meteorites) that crashed into the Moon.

Until recently the Moon was thought to have no air or water. But in 1998 the space probe *Lunar Prospector* found ice at the poles. Lunar ice could provide water and rocket fuel for future space missions.

Moon facts
Distance from Earth
384,000 km
Diameter
3476 km
Mass
0.0123 of the Earth's
Surface gravity
0.165 of the Earth's
Surface temperature
120 °C maximum to
−163 °C at night
Time to orbit Earth
29.53 days

▶ In this diagram, the inner circle of Moons shows how the Sun always lights up half of the Moon. The outer circle shows how each phase looks from the Earth.

find out more
Eclipses
Meteors and meteorites
Satellites
Solar System
Space exploration

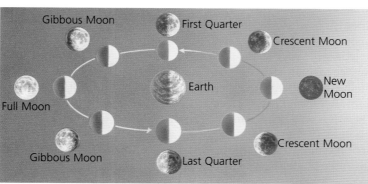

Gibbous Moon
First Quarter
Crescent Moon
Earth
New Moon
Full Moon
Gibbous Moon
Last Quarter
Crescent Moon

Moors and heaths

Moors and heaths are open treeless areas. Some are found where it is too wet or windy, or the soil is too poor and peaty, for trees to grow. Others were formed when people cleared the trees for hunting or to graze sheep or cattle.

Heaths are covered in low-growing heather-like shrubs, while moors are made up of coarse grasses and sedges. If grazing is very heavy, heaths turn into grassy moors. Heaths can become very dry in summer, and fires are common, caused either by lightning or by humans. Without fires or grazing, heaths would soon return to woodland.

Heaths

Heaths are harsh, windswept places. The heathers and their relatives which form the main vegetation are woody shrubs growing close to the ground, with small, bell-shaped flowers. The tiny leaves have a waxy coating to prevent the plant from losing too much water. Heathers provide shelter to many animals. Some related plants, such as cranberry and blueberry, have fleshy berries that provide food for many birds and small mammals. The juicy berries are also popular with people, for making jams and fruit pies.

Heaths are often used for grazing sheep. The tender young heather shoots make good fodder, and farmers often deliberately set fire to the heath from time to time to encourage new growth. Grouse shooting is also a profitable use for moors and heaths.

◀ Moors and heaths are generally bare of trees, but occasional rowan trees (also called mountain ash) are found on this moorland in Lancashire, UK.

Heaths are found on acid soil. When the land was covered by forest, the fallen leaves added nutrients to the soil and made it less acid. Without the trees, the nutrients were soon washed away, leaving very acid soil, poor in nutrients. Because of its acidity, very few bacteria can live in this soil, so plant material does not rot away. Dead bog mosses in the heath pile up and form a spongy material known as *peat*. In some areas, peat is dried and used as fuel.

Moors

Grassy moors are found mainly where the rainfall is very high or where the rock below the surface (usually slate or the similar, but softer, shale) stops rainwater from draining away. The soil is waterlogged most of the time. Waterlogged soils do not have many bacteria to rot down the plant material, so moors also build up peat. The coarse grasses that grow here often form large tussocks (clumps). Water collects in the dips between the tussocks, forming small boggy patches. Insects thrive in boggy moorland pools, and are themselves food for other animals.

find out more
Coal
Grasslands
Wetlands

▼ Heaths and moors are full of bird life. Overhead, birds of prey such as buzzards (shown below), kestrels and peregrines hunt for birds and small mammals.

Motor cars

There are more than 500 million cars in the world today, and over 50 million new cars are produced each year. Cars come in a variety of shapes and sizes. Most have four wheels, though some have only three, and at least one has 26!

Saloon cars have a closed-in compartment for passengers, with a separate boot for luggage. *Hatchbacks* are like saloons, but they have a luggage space behind the back seat instead of a separate boot. They have a door at the back and the rear seats fold down to give more luggage space. *Estate cars* are similar to hatchbacks, but have a larger luggage space behind the seats. *MPVs* (multi-purpose vehicles), also known as *RVs* (recreational vehicles) or people carriers, are roomy vehicles with an extra row of seats. *Limousines* are large luxury cars, used by wealthy people and at special occasions such as weddings. *City cars* are small cars designed to be economical, as well as easy to drive on busy streets.

In most cars, only two of the wheels (front or back) are driven by the engine. However, in four-wheel drive (4 × 4) cars, the engine drives all four wheels. Four-wheel drive cars are designed for driving across rough terrain.

Designed for safety

Modern cars are designed with safety in mind. The passenger compartment is built so that it does not collapse in an accident, while the front and rear parts of the car's body are designed to crumple in an accident. This kind of design makes the impact of an accident less violent for the people inside the vehicle. Seat belts stop the driver and passengers from being thrown through the windscreen, and special locks stop the doors from bursting open. Car windows are made from safety glass, which has no sharp edges. Bars inside the doors protect passengers from sideways-on collisions. Anti-lock braking systems (ABS) help to prevent cars from skidding. Many cars are now fitted with airbags. In an accident, these inflate like balloons and cushion the car's occupants as they are thrown forwards. ◗

• The world's longest car was specially built for its owner in the USA. It is over 30 m long, has 26 wheels, and a swimming pool in the back.

▼ The different parts of a car.

The **engine** is the heart of the car. It runs on petrol or diesel fuel and provides the power to drive the wheels.

The **transmission system** takes the power from the engine via the gearbox to the wheels.

The **gears** allow the car to be driven at different speeds with the engine working efficiently.

The **cooling system** uses water (or sometimes air) to keep the engine cool.

The **exhaust system** carries waste gases from the engine to the air. The catalytic converter makes these gases less polluting.

The **steering-wheel** is used to control the car by turning the front wheels.

The **brakes** are used to slow the car down. They are attached to the wheels.

The **electrical system** uses a battery to power the starter motor and spark plugs when starting up. Once started the engine powers an alternator (a type of generator) which supplies electricity and recharges the battery.

The **suspension** joins each wheel to the body of the car. It uses springs to give the passengers a smooth ride.

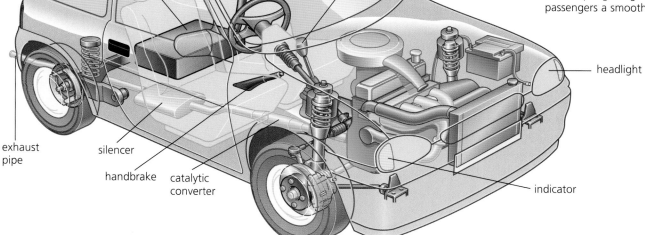

fuel tank

tail lights

gear lever

headlight

exhaust pipe

silencer

handbrake

catalytic converter

indicator

▲ To reduce pollution levels, some cities are encouraging people to use electric cars. Although these do not go as quickly as other cars, they do not produce polluting gases. Most electric cars use mains electricity to recharge their batteries, which is usually generated in power stations that burn coal or oil. However, the power stations are less polluting than car engines. The batteries of this electric car can be recharged from solar cells on the roof of the owner's home. The car can travel 150 km before its batteries run out, and it has a top speed of 100 km an hour.

Vehicle pollution

Motor cars give out exhaust gases, and some of these gases pollute the air around us. One of the main polluting gases produced by cars is carbon dioxide. Although it is not poisonous, carbon dioxide is one of the gases that traps heat from the Sun in the so-called greenhouse effect. Increased amounts of carbon dioxide in the atmosphere may be trapping too much heat, and so contributing to global warming.

Car engines that burn petrol also produce small amounts of unburned fuel, highly poisonous carbon monoxide gas, and chemicals called nitrogen oxides, which can cause smog in city areas. Petrol engines can now be fitted with devices called catalytic converters, which turn the harmful gases into carbon dioxide and water.

Cars with diesel engines do not need catalytic converters, but their exhaust gases contain tiny particles that may cause damage to human lungs. In general, those cars that burn the least fuel produce the smallest amounts of polluting gases. To use fuel economically, a car needs to be lightweight and as streamlined as possible. Also, it should not be driven at high speeds. One of the best ways to reduce pollution is for people to leave their car at home and to travel on foot or by bicycle, bus or train.

► FLASHBACK ◄

The first vehicle powered by a petrol engine was a wooden motorcycle. It was built in 1885 in Germany by Gottlieb Daimler. In 1886 Karl Benz built a three-wheeler which many people consider to be the first true motor car. Daimler and Benz went on to manufacture four-wheeled motor cars.

In the early days of motoring, passengers sat in open cars that had no roof. Early motoring was expensive. But in 1907 Henry Ford in Detroit, USA, started to manufacture a cheap reliable car, called the Model T. He was able to sell his cars more cheaply by making them on a production line. Each car was put together, piece by piece, as it moved through the factory. This was a much cheaper and quicker method than building one whole car at a time. By the 1920s, a wide choice of cheap cars was available, and closed-in saloon cars became popular.

From the 1960s onwards, more and more electronic equipment was used in cars. Today, a car with an engine that is run by an electronic system can travel almost twice as far on one litre of fuel as a similar car from 50 years ago. Car safety also became a priority around this time. All cars are now fitted with seat belts, and it is compulsory to wear them in many countries. The first air bags were fitted to cars in the 1980s. During the 1990s, many major car manufacturers began to sell electrically powered cars. In the future, as the number of car users increases, it will be even more important to make all cars safer, more fuel-efficient, and less polluting.

• The most popular car ever made is the Volkswagen Beetle. More than 20 million have been built around the world.

find out more
Designers
Engines
Greenhouse effect
Motorcycles
Motor sports
Pollution
Roads

▼ This is a copy of the three-wheeled vehicle built by Karl Benz in 1886 in Germany. The car had a top speed of 12.8 km an hour.

Motorcycles

A motorcycle is much stronger and heavier than a pedal bicycle. It is powered by a petrol engine. Motorcycles can transport one or two people. They are also used for sport and for leisure activities. Many people, such as police officers and delivery and messenger workers, ride motorcycles while doing their job. It is much easier to move through busy traffic on a motorcycle than in a car.

Motorcycles have a frame rather like that of a bicycle. The engine, gearbox, fuel tank, saddle and other parts are all bolted to this frame. The front and rear wheels have hydraulic dampers (shock absorbers) to stop the bike bouncing up and down too much. The engine is connected to a gearbox and turns the rear wheel, usually by means of a chain. Engines range in capacity from less than 50 cc (cubic centimetres) to over 1200 cc. Motorcycles with an engine capacity of 50 cc or less are called mopeds. Small motorcycles

▶ This motorcycle has an engine capacity of 650 cc. Its petrol engine is cooled by air.

generally have air-cooled, two-stroke petrol engines. Larger and more expensive machines usually have four-stroke engines and may also have water cooling.

The front brake, throttle, clutch, and lighting controls are mounted on the handlebars. The rear brake is applied by a foot pedal. Gear changes may also be made by foot. However, many motorcycles have automatic gearboxes.

• The first motorcycle with a petrol engine was made by Gottlieb Daimler in Germany in 1885.

find out more
Engines
Motor sports

twist-grip throttle
front brake
fuel tank
front fork with dampers and springs
engine
rear brake
gearbox
chain drive to rear wheel
disc brake

Motors

A motor is any machine that is capable of moving something, but when people talk about a motor, they usually mean an electric motor. Electric motors are used in lots of the equipment we use every day, such as vacuum cleaners, food mixers, washing machines, video recorders and lawnmowers.

A simple electric motor has a coil which can spin between the poles of a magnet. When an electric current is passed through the coil, it becomes magnetized. This magnetic effect creates poles that are repelled by like poles on the magnet. The coil's north pole is repelled by the magnet's north pole, and the coil's south pole is repelled by the magnet's south pole. As a result the coil turns until its own north and south poles are next to the opposite poles of the magnet.

At this point, a device called a commutator reverses the direction of the current that is flowing through the coil. This reverses the poles of the coil, so it is pushed round another half-turn. This cycle is continually repeated to keep the motor moving.

To run smoothly, real motors have several coils and the commutator has many sections to reverse the current for each coil. For a stronger turning effect, a powerful electromagnet is used instead of an ordinary permanent magnet.

Many motors use alternating current (AC) instead of the 'one-way' direct current from a battery.

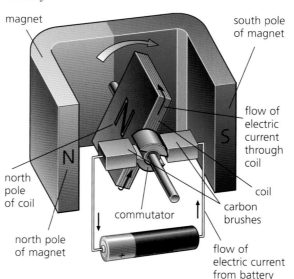

magnet
south pole of magnet
north pole of coil
flow of electric current through coil
coil
carbon brushes
north pole of magnet
commutator
flow of electric current from battery

◀ In a simple electric motor, the electric current magnetizes the coil. The magnetized coil turns between the poles of the magnet until its own poles are next to the opposite poles of the magnet. At this point the commutator reverses the direction of the current flowing through the coil, forcing the coil to make another half-turn.

find out more
Electricity
Engines
Magnets

Motor sports

Motor sports include a variety of competitions between motor cars of all shapes and sizes. Some motor sports are extremely popular, attracting huge live audiences and millions of television viewers.

In most motor sports, the cars are specially built or modified for racing. They have to meet particular regulations (a 'formula') that govern engine design and other details.

Formula 1

The most important motor-car races are the Grand Prix events for Formula 1 cars. There are 19 races in the season. Thirty or more of the world's top racing drivers take part, competing for a dozen or so teams. Drivers are awarded points for finishing in the first eight. The driver with the most points at the end of the season is the world champion.

Grand Prix circuits vary from about 3 kilometres to nearly 7 kilometres. The total distance for most races is just over 300 kilometres. All Grand Prix circuits have sharp twists and turns, which test a car's manoeuvrability and a driver's skill, and long straights, where engine power is important.

Other motor sports

Motor rallies, which take place on ordinary roads, are long-distance events that often last several days. Rally cars must be based on regular models, but they are adapted to cope with the rough conditions. The drivers start each stage at intervals and are penalized for arriving late at check points or for changing car parts. The winning car is the one that finishes with the fewest penalty points.

The most important US motor sport is *Indycar racing*, a series of races held each year. The cars are designed to handle steeply banked oval tracks as well as twisting road circuits. The highlight of the Indycar calendar – the Indianapolis 500 – attracts crowds of up to 300,000 spectators.

The *Le Mans 24-hour race* dates back to 1923, and is held on a 13.6-kilometre circuit near Paris, France. The cars are two-seater sports cars with closed cockpits. Two or three drivers take turns at the wheel and cover as much distance as they can in 24 hours.

▲ Juha Kankkunen of Finland on his way to winning the British RAC Rally in 1993. That year Kankkunen won his fourth world championship, a record equalled by fellow Finn Tommi Makinen in 1999.

• In *drag-racing*, two vehicles race over a straight 400-metre track from a standing start. 'Dragsters' are specially built cars which race in several classes. 'Top-fuellers' reach speeds of 350 kilometres per hour and races may last less than 6 seconds.

Motorcycle racing
Motorcycle world championships are held every year on specially built circuits. The champion is decided on the results of 12 or more Grand Prix races.
Speedway, on bikes with no brakes or gears, is held on oval dirt tracks about 400 metres long. There are championships for teams and individuals.
Motocross, or *scrambling*, takes place on very rough cross-country courses, where riders have to cope with hills and mud.

◄ French driver Alain Prost in his McLaren car at the 1989 Monaco Grand Prix, one of the highlights of the Formula 1 season.

find out more
Motor cars
Motorcycles

Mountains

High up in the mountains, you can find some of the most dramatic scenery in the world – jagged snow-capped peaks, deep gorges, large valley glaciers and fast-flowing rivers and streams. Mountains continually challenge the human spirit of adventure, with each generation of climbers seeking new ways to conquer the highest peaks.

As mountains rise above the surrounding land, they are soon attacked by water, wind, rain and ice. The softer rocks are eroded (worn away) to form valleys, and jagged peaks form as the valleys are cut back into the hills. Young and rapidly rising mountains have high, steep-sided peaks and deep valleys and gorges. In time, the mountain peaks and the valley sides are worn away, the hills become lower and more rounded, and the valleys become wider, with slower-flowing, less powerful rivers. In old age, a mountain range may become little more than a gently rolling plain. ◗

▼ Mountains are formed in different ways. *Fold mountains* are created when the ocean floor between two moving plates is squeezed upwards. *Block mountains* form when huge blocks of rock are tilted or lifted up along lines of weakness, called faults. When molten lava cannot break through strong rocks above, it forces the rocks to bulge upwards forming a *dome mountain*.

• In the Rocky Mountains, or Rockies, of North America there are mountains with gentle slopes and rounded tops, but others are tall with jagged rocky peaks. Many reach over 4000 metres above sea level.
Highest peak: Mount Elbert, 4402 m

• The Alps in Europe consist of several separate mountain ranges of steep slopes and jagged snow-capped peaks. In places there are huge limestone cliffs and canyons, as well as permanent snowfields and glaciers.
Highest mountain: Mont Blanc, 4808 m

• The Andes is a series of mountain ranges with many peaks over 6700 metres, including some active volcanoes. High plateaux separate some ranges, and in the south, glaciers push down to the Pacific Ocean.
Highest peak: Aconcagua, 6960 m

Mountain records
Highest mountain above sea level
Mount Everest, Himalayas, 8850 m
Largest single mountain mass
Mauna Loa, Hawaii (the total height of the mountain is 9350 m, although only 4170 m are above sea level)
Biggest mountain range on land
Himalaya–Karakoram–Hindu Kush range, 3800 km long, with 14 mountains over 4000 m
Longest underwater mountain range
Indian/East Pacific Ocean Cordillera, 19,000 km long

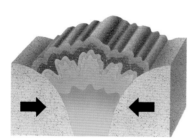

fold mountains: Alps, Europe; Himalayas, Asia; Rocky Mountains, North America; Andes, South America

block mountains: Sierra Nevada Mountains, USA; Black Forest Mountains, Europe; Ruwenzori Mountains, East Africa

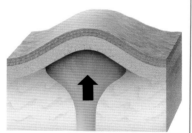

dome mountains: Black Hills, South Dakota, USA

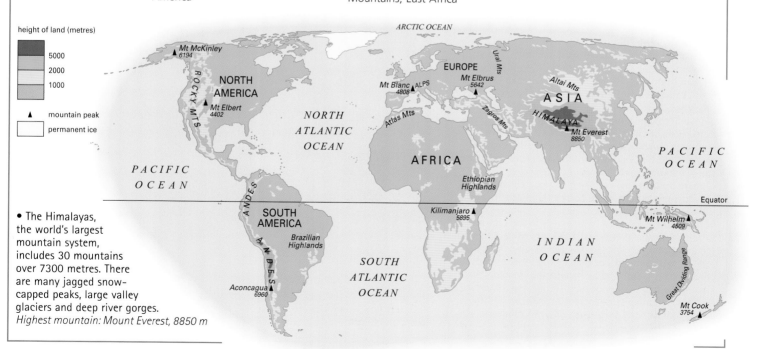

height of land (metres)

5000
2000
1000

▲ mountain peak
☐ permanent ice

ARCTIC OCEAN

▲ Mt McKinley 6194

ROCKY MTS

NORTH AMERICA

▲ Mt Elbert 4402

NORTH ATLANTIC OCEAN

PACIFIC OCEAN

EUROPE

Ural Mts

Mt Blanc 4808 ALPS
Atlas Mts

Mt Elbrus 5642

Altai Mts

ASIA

Zagros Mts

HIMALAYA

▲ Mt Everest 8850

AFRICA

Ethiopian Highlands

Kilimanjaro ▲ 5895

PACIFIC OCEAN

ANDES

SOUTH AMERICA

Brazilian Highlands

SOUTH ATLANTIC OCEAN

Aconcagua 6960

Equator

INDIAN OCEAN

Mt Wilhelm ▲ 4509

Great Dividing Range

Mt Cook 3754 ▲

• The Himalayas, the world's largest mountain system, includes 30 mountains over 7300 metres. There are many jagged snow-capped peaks, large valley glaciers and deep river gorges.
Highest mountain: Mount Everest, 8850 m

Mountain climate

As you climb up a mountain, the temperature falls by 1°C for every 150 metres. There is snow on the top of high mountains even at the Equator. Also, there is less oxygen in the atmosphere the higher up you go. Winds are often extremely strong, and the weather can change very quickly.

Mountains have a dramatic effect on the climate of surrounding areas. As the clouds rise over the mountains, they shed their rain, so the side of a mountain range where the wind blows is often very wet, but the sheltered side (the 'rain shadow') gets very little rain. Parts of the southern Himalayas are very wet because monsoon winds drop rain and snow over the mountains. To the north, the winds become dry and desert conditions exist.

Mountain life

Conditions in mountain areas are harsh and difficult for the people and wildlife trying to survive at such altitudes. People tend to settle in sheltered valleys, by water sources on the mountain slopes, or near deposits of minerals such as zinc, silver, coal and iron ore. Roads and railways follow the valleys. Fast-flowing mountain rivers are often dammed to produce hydroelectric power.

Many mountain people make a living from farming. In the Alps, in Europe, farmers move their dairy cattle to high pastures in spring, and bring them down to the valleys in autumn. Crops may be grown on raised terraces on the slopes. The terrace walls trap rainwater and prevent soil from being washed away. Other activities in mountain areas include mining, forestry and tourism. Tourists are attracted to mountains by the dramatic scenery. They also come to enjoy walking, climbing, skiing, fishing and hunting.

Mountain plants and animals have to cope with extremes of temperature, hot days and cold nights, and very high winds. Mountain soils are often thin, as soil is washed down the slopes. Above a certain altitude, called the tree-line, trees cannot grow as conditions are too harsh. Lower slopes are often covered with forests. Sheep, goats and other long-haired animals are well suited to harsh climates. In the Himalayas, yaks (mountain cattle with long shaggy hair) are reared for their meat and milk and as a means of transporting people and heavy loads. Many animals, such as mountain hares, grow extra thick coats in winter.

Avalanche danger

An avalanche is a mass of snow which comes loose from a steep mountain slope and hurtles down to the valley below. In any mountainous area with bare slopes and heavy snow, avalanches are a danger, particularly when the snows begin to melt. On some mountains, new forests are planted to reduce the danger, and walls and snow fences help to break up any avalanches. Trained patrols issue forecasts and warnings, especially in popular skiing areas.

Mountain climbing

The sport of climbing and exploring mountains became popular after the successful ascent of Mont Blanc, in the European Alps, in 1786. In 1953 Edmund Hillary, a New Zealander, and Tenzing Norgay, a Sherpa tribesman, were the first people to climb Mount Everest, the world's highest mountain. Since then, numerous expeditions of climbers have ascended Everest. Mountain climbing continues to provide an exciting challenge to many people, with many peaks and routes still waiting to be conquered.

There are two kinds of climbing: rock climbing and ice climbing. In both kinds, two or three people are usually roped together for safety. Rock climbers insert nuts (small steel wedges) into cracks in the rock and attach karabiners (snaplinks) and ropes to hold them in the event of a fall. Ice climbers wear crampons (spiked steel frames) on their boots and carry ice axes with curved picks. They climb by hammering the picks and kicking the front spikes of their crampons into the ice. On very high mountains there is so little oxygen that climbers must carry their own supply in cylinders.

◄ An avalanche on Mount McKinley, Alaska, USA. Avalanches are a particular danger after a warm spell. When the snow starts to thaw, one snow layer can slide over another and crash down the mountain slopes.

find out more
Continents
Hydroelectric power
Lakes
Rivers and streams
Rocks and minerals
Volcanoes

Mozart, Wolfgang Amadeus

Born 1756 in Salzburg, Austria
Died 1791 aged 35

Wolfgang Amadeus Mozart is considered by many to be the greatest composer of all time.

Mozart was the son of a composer, and by the time he was 5 years old, he was able to compose quite decent pieces of music himself. He was also able to play the harpsichord and violin better than much older musicians.

In 1762 Mozart and his sister Anna were taken by their father, Leopold, on a performing tour around Europe. The young Mozart caused a sensation everywhere he went. After the tour, he joined his father as a court musician in Salzburg. However, he hated it there, and in 1781 he left to try to earn his living in Vienna.

Mozart tried to live on money from the public performances of his operas and by teaching and giving concerts, but he did not manage his money well and constantly struggled against poverty. All the same, he composed with extraordinary fluency and speed. Amongst his many works, Mozart composed at least 41 symphonies, 30 piano concertos, 23 string quartets, 35 violin sonatas and 17 piano sonatas. Finest of all, perhaps, are his operas, which include *The Marriage of Figaro* and *The Magic Flute*.

• Because of Mozart's financial difficulties, there was no money to pay for his funeral after his death from an unknown illness. He was buried in Vienna in a multiple grave, a common resting place for people with little or no money.

find out more
Classical music
Operas and musicals

▼ Mozart, his sister Anna and his father performing in Paris as part of their hugely successful European tour.

Muscles

Muscles are parts of an animal's body that make the other parts move. They are needed for all kinds of movement, including walking, running, lifting things, blinking, pumping blood and swallowing food.

• The largest human muscle is the gluteus maximus, which is around the buttocks and the top of the legs. The smallest human muscle is inside the ear.

• All muscles need energy to work. Blood carries oxygen and glucose (a sugar made from digested food) to the muscles. Through the process of respiration, the muscles get the energy they need to work properly.

find out more
Bones
Hearts
Human body
Skeletons

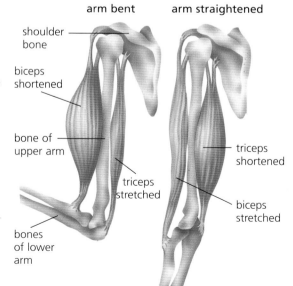

arm bent   arm straightened

shoulder bone
biceps shortened
bone of upper arm
triceps stretched
bones of lower arm
triceps shortened
biceps stretched

Muscles are made up of muscle cells, and are controlled by nerve signals from the brain. They work by contracting (getting shorter). Muscles cannot lengthen themselves, but they can be stretched when other muscles pull at them.

There are about 650 muscles in the human body, and there are three types. The first type is attached to the bones and is used to move the body. It only works when you want it to, so it is called a *voluntary muscle*. When you want to move, it pulls against the skeleton, bending it at joints such as the elbow and the knee.

The second type of muscle can contract without you thinking about it, so it is called an *involuntary muscle*. An example of an involuntary muscle is the muscle around the gut which pushes food along it.

The third type of muscle is found in the heart. This is the *cardiac muscle* which pumps blood around the body. It can work continuously for years without getting tired.

◄ There are at least two muscles at each joint. In the upper arm the biceps and triceps muscles work together to bend and straighten the arm.

Music

Music is sound that is organized into pleasing or interesting patterns. These patterns may communicate a particular mood or idea. They may stimulate the hearer to move around, or they may relax and soothe. Music is a vital part of everyday life in all parts of the world. It is used as an important part of religious ritual; it can be used to calm and ease the mind; and it is also used to delight and entertain.

Music is as old as human beings. The first humans made simple musical sounds by clapping their hands, or striking two sticks together. They noticed the twang made by their hunting bows, and the sound produced when they beat hollow sticks on the ground. About 12,000 years ago, people were making simple flutes from hollow bones. Other instruments such as bells and rattles are known to have been important in the rituals of the ancient Egyptians, and the Chinese.

Melody, harmony and rhythm

The simplest form of music is a collection of notes, sung or played one after the other, which form a melody, or tune. In Western music, each note has a definite *pitch* (the height of the note), which is given a letter name from A to G.

When two or more notes with different pitches are sounded together, this is called harmony. Certain groups of notes that sound pleasant to our ears form the basis of most Western music. A group of two or more notes is called a chord. Harmony is often used to support the melody.

As well as varying the pitch of a note, you can also vary the length that you sound the note. Some notes can be short, and some can be long. The combination of long and short sounds in music adds rhythm to the pattern of sounds. Rhythm is a vital element in all music, and it forms the basis for some traditions, for example Indonesian gamelan music.

Writing music down

In most parts of the world, music has never been written down. It has been learned and passed on from parent to child, or teacher to pupil. The ancient Greeks had a system for writing down music, but it has been lost.

In the West, people started to write down music some time around the 9th century AD. Over the centuries, a standard system for writing down all Western-style music has developed. Music is written down on a *stave* (see the picture on the following page). The higher the note on the stave, the higher is its pitch. The type of symbol used for a note tells you how long the note should be.

A *scale* is a series of notes arranged in order of pitch. There are many different kinds of scale. For example a raga is a kind of scale used in Indian music, and a pentatonic scale has five notes and is used widely in Far Eastern music. The scales most widely used in Western music have eight scale notes. They are based on patterns of pitches called tones and semitones. These patterns make up two kinds of scale, known as major and minor. Music in a major scale tends to sound happy, while music in a minor scale has a sadder sound.

▶ Written music from around 1430. The beautiful initial 'I' was painted by the artist Fra Angelico. The earliest musical notation had no stave at all. Later a grid of lines was introduced, which by the 13th century had become a four-line stave. The actual notes are indicated by thick horizontal or diagonal pen strokes, with thin vertical lines on the longest notes.

Composing
Someone who writes music is called a composer. Composers arrange sounds to make music. The complete *score* of a piece of music usually has several parts, each for a different instrument or voice. Composers work in many different ways. Some compose at the piano; some hear the sounds they want to write down in their heads. Songwriters often start with the words of a song (the *lyrics*), and compose a melody around the lyrics. And some composers experiment with electronic sounds and work in studios with computers.

Music notation

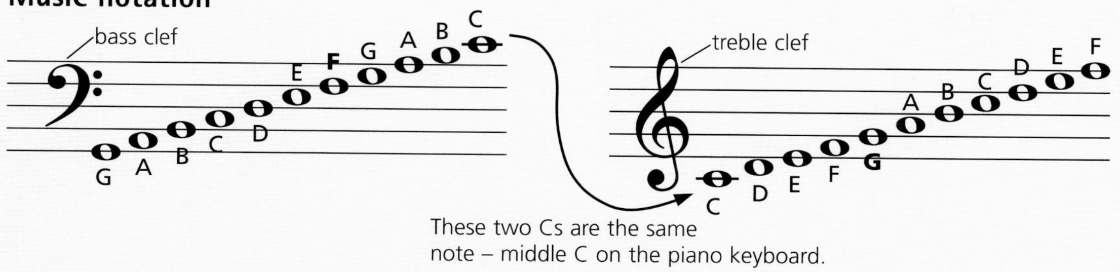
bass clef
G A B C D E F G A B C
treble clef
C D E F G A B C D E F
These two Cs are the same note – middle C on the piano keyboard.

◀ The notes of the *treble clef* and the *bass clef*. The centre loop of the treble clef curls around the second line up on the stave. It tells you that this note is G. The loop of the bass clef starts on the second line down on the stave, and indicates that this note is F.

semibreve (4 beats)
minim (2 beats)
crotchet (1 beat)
quaver (half-beat)
semiquaver (quarter-beat)

◀ The length of a note is shown by its symbol. Some notes have different symbols depending on whether they are alone or in groups.

1 2 Alla marcia—3
4
5
f
9
6
mf
f
10
8
7

◀ This is an arrangement for piano of the Toreador Song from Georges Bizet's opera *Carmen*.

• Music words help the performer interpret the music – for example presto (very fast), vivace (full of life), allegro (fast and lively), andante (walking pace) and adagio (leisurely). Other words indicate how loud or soft to play: *pianissimo* (*pp*), very soft; *piano* (*p*), soft; *forte* (*f*), loud; *fortissimo* (*ff*), very loud.

1 Key signature. The flat sign (♭) is the key signature. It tells you which major or minor scale the piece is based on. This piece is in F major. Every time you see the note B, you must play B flat.

2 Time signature. The numbers $^2/_4$ are the time signature. The top number tells you the number of beats in the bar (2). The bottom number tells you what kind of beat it is (4 stands for a crotchet).

3 'Alla marcia' means 'like a march'. It gives an idea of the tempo (speed) and the style of the piece.

4 Bar lines divide up the bars. Every bar in this piece has two beats.

5 Dotted notes. A dot after a note makes the note worth half as much again. So a dotted quaver is $^3/_4$ beat.

6 Accidentals. Flats, sharps and naturals within the music are called accidentals. A flat sign (♭) tells you that the note you play must be lowered by a semitone. A sharp sign (♯) tells you the note must be raised by a semitone. A natural sign (♮) cancels a sharp or flat.

7 Rests. In music, silence is shown by rests. In this bar there is a quaver rest (𝄾, half a beat) and a, crotchet rest (𝄽, a whole beat).

8 Grouping notes. Phrase marks show which groups of notes belong together. A long phrase mark indicates one 'sentence' within the piece; a short mark (a slur) shows that the two notes should be played as a pair.

9 Ties. A tie joins two notes of the same pitch across a bar line. It tells you to continue the note across the bar line.

10 Dynamics tell the player how loud or soft a composer would like the music to be played. The 'hairpin' (>) means get softer from *f* (*forte*), which is loud, to *mf* (*mezzo forte*), which is quite loud.

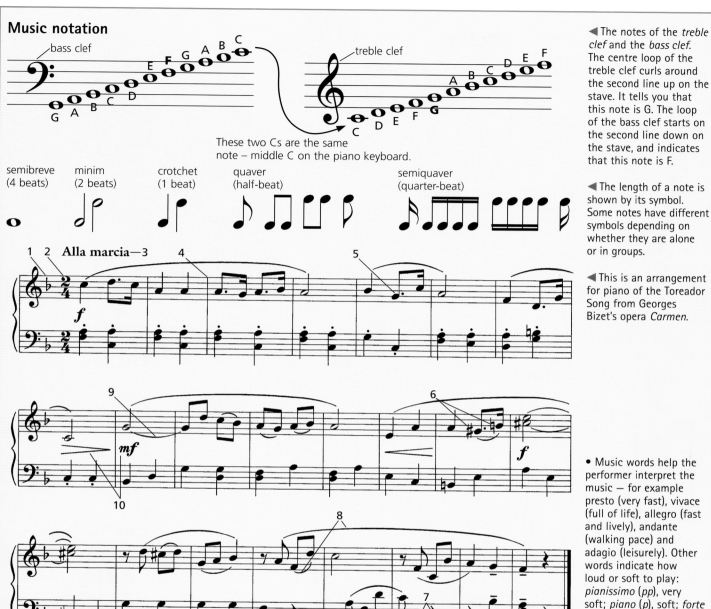

Musical instruments

find out more
Classical music
Jazz
Music
Orchestras and bands
Pop and rock music
World music

Human beings have made musical instruments since prehistoric times. Instruments vary in different regions of the world to suit the different styles of music that have developed there. Even so, there are similarities in the way they produce sounds.

Musical instruments can be grouped into four main sorts: stringed instruments, wind instruments, keyboard instruments and percussion instruments.

Stringed instruments

Stringed instruments produce sound when the player makes one or more strings vibrate. The strings can either be plucked or bowed.

Plucked instruments are played either with the fingers or with a plectrum (a 'plucker'). With instruments like the guitar or banjo, one hand plucks while the other hand 'fingers' the strings, pressing on them in different places to produce different notes. Some instruments have frets (ridges) on the fingerboard to fix the pitch and improve the quality of the sound. On harps and lyres both hands are used for plucking.

Bowed instruments use a bow drawn across the strings to produce the sound. One hand uses the

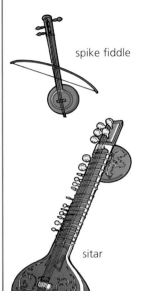

spike fiddle

sitar

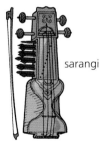

sarangi

isen

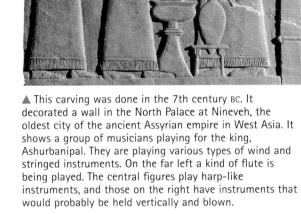

▲ This carving was done in the 7th century BC. It decorated a wall in the North Palace at Nineveh, the oldest city of the ancient Assyrian empire in West Asia. It shows a group of musicians playing for the king, Ashurbanipal. They are playing various types of wind and stringed instruments. On the far left a kind of flute is being played. The central figures play harp-like instruments, and those on the right have instruments that would probably be held vertically and blown.

bow while the other 'fingers' the notes as for a guitar or banjo. Violins and violas are played tucked under the chin, but for larger instruments such as cellos, you stand the instrument on the ground or rest it on your lap. Most bowed stringed instruments can also be plucked: this is called playing 'pizzicato'.

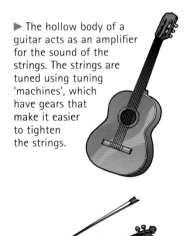

▶ The hollow body of a guitar acts as an amplifier for the sound of the strings. The strings are tuned using tuning 'machines', which have gears that make it easier to tighten the strings.

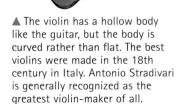

◀ Cello is short for 'violoncello'. It is midway in size between the viola and the double-bass, and it has a very mellow sound. Like the violin, it is a much-loved instrument and many composers have written works for it. It is held upright on the floor between the legs of the seated player.

harp

▶ The modern harp has up to 47 strings and seven pedals. Although the modern harp is a complex instrument, much simpler versions have existed since ancient Egyptian times.

▲ Stringed instruments have developed in various forms all over the world. They include the Turkish spike fiddle, the Indian sitar and sarangi, and the Japanese samisen.

▲ The violin has a hollow body like the guitar, but the body is curved rather than flat. The best violins were made in the 18th century in Italy. Antonio Stradivari is generally recognized as the greatest violin-maker of all.

Wind instruments

To play a wind instrument you have to blow it in some way. There are two kinds of wind instrument: woodwind and brass.

Although the term 'woodwind' implies that these instruments are made of wood, this is only true of some of them. In the Western world *woodwind instruments* were once all made of wood, but many are now made of metal and plastic. They can be made of anything, from wood to bone or pottery.

Woodwind instruments have a hole or holes that are blown down or across. Some, such as the clarinet and oboe, have reeds that vibrate when you blow through them. The reeds may be doubled, as in the oboe and bassoon, so that they vibrate against each other. Different notes on the instrument are usually made by 'stopping' (covering) other holes in the instrument: the more of the holes you cover, the lower the note. On many modern woodwind instruments there are connected metal keys. These enable the player to cover several holes at once without having to move their fingers very much.

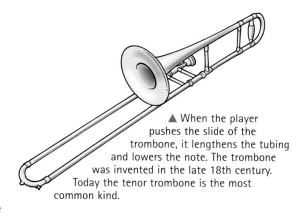

▲ When the player pushes the slide of the trombone, it lengthens the tubing and lowers the note. The trombone was invented in the late 18th century. Today the tenor trombone is the most common kind.

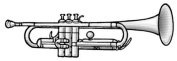

▲ The trumpet is popular for all kinds of music: classical, jazz, brass-band and rock. The sound it makes can be changed by using mutes – muffling devices that fit into the bell (wide end). There are mutes for all brass instruments except the French horn.

Brass instruments are long, funnel-shaped tubes that are often coiled to make them easier to hold. The longer and wider the funnel, the deeper the notes the instrument can produce.

The mouthpiece on a brass instrument is made of metal and can be detached. To play a note you have to make your lips vibrate in the mouthpiece, in a similar way to 'blowing a raspberry'. With instruments like the bugle, which have a fairly simple design, you play different notes by changing the shape of your lips. Instruments such as the trumpet and the trombone, however, have valves or slides that open up extra lengths of tubing, so that you can play more notes.

Keyboard instruments

A keyboard is a row of keys, some of which are normally black and some white. You press these keys to make the sound.

When you press a piano key, it sets off a mechanism that makes a small wooden hammer hit one, two or three strings, all tuned to the same pitch, to produce a note. When you take your finger off the key, a damper touches the strings to stop them vibrating. In a harpsichord the keys activate a mechanism to pluck the strings rather than hit them.

Another popular keyboard instrument is the organ. Organs can work either by pumping air through different-sized pipes, or by electronics. Pipe organs are much older, and usually much bigger. Organ pipes range from the size of a

◄ The flute produces sound as air is passed across the mouth-hole. It is one of the great instruments of the orchestral woodwind section and is also an extremely popular solo instrument. Music for the flute ranges from J. S. Bach to modern jazz.

► The clarinet, a woodwind instrument, has a single reed and a system of both holes and keys for the fingers to work. There is a whole family of clarinets, from the large contrabass clarinet to a very small clarinet for the highest notes.

► The saxophone was invented by Adolphe Sax in the 1840s. Although made of brass, the saxophone has a reed (like the clarinet) and belongs to the woodwind family. There are seven different kinds of saxophone, from the small sopranino to the baritone, which plays the lowest notes. The instrument has had its greatest success in jazz music.

▼ The panpipes are classed as a woodwind instrument. They are made up of a row of tubes of different lengths, joined together, and are played by blowing across the tops, with each tube giving one note. The panpipes are one of the most ancient instruments, and are found in various forms all over the world.

▲ Harpsichords were popular keyboard instruments in Europe from the 15th to 18th centuries. Like the grand piano, which was developed in the 18th century, the strings run horizontally, but unlike the piano, they are plucked by a quill rather than hit by a hammer when the keys are pressed. Many – like the one pictured here – were made both to look and to sound beautiful.

peashooter for the highest notes, to huge giants as tall as a house for the lowest notes. Besides keyboards for the hands, large pipe organs have a pedal board for the feet. They also have several complete sets of different-sounding pipes, activated by stops (knobs).

Percussion instruments

Percussion instruments include anything that can be banged, clicked, shaken, rasped or scraped to make a sound. Instruments such as xylophones and tubular bells have many different notes and can be used to play tunes.

▶ Cymbals and maracas are examples of percussion instruments. The cymbals have been played since ancient times and are found in many different regions of the world. They are often played in pairs and banged together. The maracas are from South America. They were originally made from a gourd (a dried-out fruit), with its dried seeds making the rattling sound. Now they are usually made of wood or plastic.

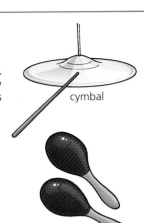

cymbal

maracas

However, most percussion instruments, such as tambourines and maracas, do not play specific notes. They are used to play rhythms.

The percussion instruments in orchestras originally came from many different countries. Tambourines and kettledrums came from the Middle East, xylophones and marimbas from Africa, glockenspiels and wood blocks from the Far East, while bongos and maracas are from South America.

▼ ▶ A drum is a percussion instrument which is essentially a skin stretched over a hollow bowl or tube. The sound is made by the vibrations of the skin when it is struck by hands or beaters. Some, such as the tom-tom and bass drum, are strictly rhythm instruments – they have no particular pitch (highness or lowness to their tone). Others, such as the orchestral kettledrums (known as timpani) are tuned to precise pitches.

orchestral
kettledrum

bass drum

tom-tom
barrel drum

Electronic instruments

There are two kinds of electronic instrument. Some *amplify* (make louder) the sound of an instrument. For example, the sound of an electric guitar is produced by plucking the strings, but this sound is picked up, often modified and then amplified through a loudspeaker. Electric violins, pianos and flutes all work in a similar way.

The second group of electronic instruments actually *produces* a sound electronically. This group includes synthesizers, which produce a huge variety of original sounds, and drum machines, which imitate the sound of percussion instruments. It also includes some of the earliest electronic instruments to be invented: the theremin and the ondes martenot. The theremin was invented in 1920. It produces an eerie, whining sound. The ondes martenot was invented in the late 1920s. It makes strange swooping sounds.

▲ Bands such as the Chemical Brothers, pictured here, use synthesizers and other instruments that produce sound electronically.

▼ The xylophone is made up of tuned wooden bars. The bars, or 'keys', lie in two rows like piano keys and have metal or plastic resonators hanging vertically beneath them. They are played using beaters with wooden, rubber or plastic tips.

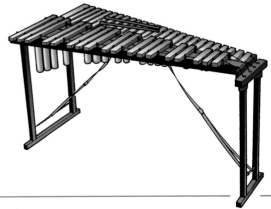

Muslims

Muslims are the followers of the religion of Islam. Islam means submitting to the will of God. Muslims believe that obeying God, Allah, and living in the way God expects brings peace with other people.

Muslims respect all the prophets who taught people to worship one God and to do good deeds. These include Abraham, Moses and Jesus. For Muslims, Muhammad, who died in AD 632, is the last and greatest of these prophets.

The prophet Muhammad

While a trader, Muhammad used to pray alone in a cave on Mount Hira outside Makkah (Mecca), and there he received his first messages from God. Muhammad began to preach to the people of Makkah that there is only one God, Allah, and that they were wrong to worship idols (images). He was attacked for his beliefs, so he and his followers, known as Muslims, moved to Medina for safety. This move is called the *hijra* (migration). From Medina he preached and organized armed resistance to Muslim enemies. When he re-entered Makkah he did so peacefully and all Meccans became Muslims.

For all Muslims, Muhammad is the example of a person whose life is rightly guided by God. The messages Muhammad received from God were later written down in the Qur'an (Koran). For Muslims this is the record of how God wants them to live.

▲ The Qur'an is the Holy Book of Muslims. This mother is teaching her children how to read the Qur'an in Arabic.

Way of life: the five pillars

Muslims sometimes talk about the 'House of Islam', the community in which they live their religious life. Islam is very much a way of life and its house is built on the foundation of the Qur'an and supported by five 'pillars'. These pillars are:

1 The statement of faith called the *shahadah*. 'There is no God except Allah, Muhammad is the messenger of Allah.'

2 Prayer (*salah*), five times a day. This may be performed anywhere that is clean, normally at home or in a mosque. The times of prayer are dawn, noon, mid-afternoon, just after sunset, and before going to sleep. These are flexible if people are travelling or ill. ◗

• The first Muslim community began in Medina in AD 622, and later Islam became the main religion of the Arabian peninsula. Later there were other powerful Islamic empires: the Ottoman empire based in Turkey, the Safavid empire in Persia and the Mughal empire in northern India. The influence of Islam spread and today there are Muslims all over the world.

▼ The Ka'bah inside the Great Mosque at Makkah is the most important Muslim pilgrimage shrine. It contains a sacred black stone which, according to legend, dates back to the time of Abraham. Pilgrims walk around it seven times. Men wear special pilgrimage dress called *ihram*. Women must have their heads covered, but not their faces.

3 Alms (*zahah*) should be given to the poor or anyone in need at least once a year.

4 Fasting (*sawm*) between dawn and dusk, especially during the month of Ramadan. This helps self-discipline, brings you closer to God, and gives you more time for religious things and sympathy for the poor. Children, pregnant women and the sick need not fast.

5 Pilgrimage (*hajj*) once in a lifetime if one can afford to travel to Makkah.

Growing up in Islam

Young Muslims are taught a variety of things at home, usually by their mother. These include the foods that are allowed (*halal*) and what is forbidden (*haram*), and how to pray.

Once boys and girls become adolescent, parents prefer them to be educated separately. Many think that their roles are very different in life. Some parents arrange marriages for their children to try to make sure that they have a partner and the support of an extended family.

Interpreting the tradition

Muslims believe that everything they need to know to live as good people is there in the Qur'an. However, there were no nuclear weapons or organ transplants in the 7th century. The *ulama* are religious scholars who help to interpret the tradition of Islam for the present day.

▲ The Dome of the Rock in Jerusalem is an important Muslim shrine. It was built in about AD 690 to cover the sacred spot from where Muslims believe the prophet Muhammad ascended to heaven.

▲ To prepare for prayer, a Muslim must wash the hands, mouth, nostrils, face and forearms, then wipe the head, ears and neck, and finally wash the feet. Then Muslims stand, kneel and bow in a certain order as they say their prayers. In a mosque the leader of the prayer faces in the direction of the holy city, Makkah.

If the Qur'an does not deal directly with a problem, Muslims look at the *Hadith*, the traditions about the life and sayings of the prophet Muhammad. The Qur'an and Hadith together are the foundation of the *Shari' ah* (law) which guides Muslim life.

Sunni and Shi'ah Muslims

The majority of Muslims belong to a broad group called the Sunni Muslims. The word *sunnah* means a custom and refers to the traditional Muslim code of behaviour. Sunni Muslims do things in the most traditional Muslim way, based on the example of Muhammad in the collection of stories about his life.

Shi'ah Muslims live mainly in Iran and Iraq, and there are smaller groups in many other countries. Shi'ah is short for *shi' at Ali*, the party of supporters of Ali. Ali was the cousin and son-in-law of Muhammad. In 656 he became the fourth leader (*khalifah*) after the prophet's death, but he was assassinated. His sons, Hasan and Husayn, were also killed. Muslims see the death of Husayn, who was massacred with a small army of followers, as a martyrdom. The idea of innocent suffering and the dignity of being a martyr for Islam is a strong model for Shi'ah Muslims when they are fighting against what they believe to be oppression and injustice.

Muslims emphasize that Sunni and Shi'ah Muslims share more than they disagree about. They all believe that the Qur'an is the word of God and that Muhammad is the messenger of Allah. They all observe the five pillars and can pray together in the same mosques, with small variations in the way they pray.

● In 1979 Muslim fundamentalists, who observe strict traditional Muslim laws, came to power in Iran under the leadership of Ayatollah Khomeini. Fundamentalism has also increased in power and influence in Algeria, Egypt, Pakistan, Indonesia and other Muslim countries.

find out more
Festivals and holidays
Marriage
Middle East
Ottoman empire
Religions

Mussels and oysters

Mussels and oysters belong to a large group of animals called bivalve molluscs. These animals have two shells, joined by a hinge of elastic tissue. Some bivalves live in rivers and lakes, but most are found in the sea.

Most bivalves, such as cockles and razorshells, bury themselves in soft mud or sand, using a muscular 'foot' to burrow their way down.

▲ A common mussel. A large mussel filters about 1.5 litres of water an hour to gets its food.

• There are over 20,000 kinds of bivalve mollusc. The other important groups of molluscs are gastropods (slugs, snails, limpets) and cephalods (squids and octopuses).

find out more
Animals
Oceans and seas
Seashore
Slugs and snails
Squids and octopuses

▶ There are about 1000 kinds of freshwater mussel known. They live in streams, lakes and ponds in most parts of the world.

To feed, they push a long tube up to the surface and suck in water containing plankton (tiny floating plants and animals). The water also holds oxygen, so bivalves breathe and feed at the same time.

Mussels and oysters are unusual in that they live attached to rocks. Mussels are attached with strong threads that hold them safe from the crashing waves. They are sometimes left above sea level as the tide falls, but they do not usually spend very long out of water. Most oysters cement themselves to rocks, usually below low-tide level.

Like other bivalves, mussels and oysters feed on plankton, which they suck into their

▶ One side of a true oyster shell is flat and the other side, in which the body lies, is rounded. Oysters anchor the rounded side of the shell to the seabed and use the flat side as a lid. If danger threatens, they snap the lid firmly shut.

shells with water. Sometimes, by accident, a grain of sand gets inside the shell in a place where it cannot be swept away by a current of water. When this happens, the creature covers the grit with layers of scaly material (mother-of-pearl) to get rid of the irritation. If a perfectly round pearl is formed, it may be very valuable, as humans turn such pearls into expensive jewellery.

Myanmar

Myanmar is a country in South-east Asia. Until 1989 it was called Burma. Much of the country is covered by mountains and thick tropical rainforest. Most people live along the Irrawaddy River, which runs from north to south.

Myanmar's climate is tropical, and May to September is the season of the monsoon rains. About half the country is covered by trees, including teak trees. In recent years large areas of forest have been cut down, and this has led to landslides and flooding. The country is rich in oil and natural gas as well as timber.

For over 900 years Myanmar has been the land of the Burman people. Some Buddhist

temples date from the 11th century. British troops invaded Burma in the 19th century. For over 60 years Burma was a British colony. It became independent in 1948. A key figure in the independence struggle, Aung San, was killed shortly before independence.

Since independence, Burma has been governed for periods by military leaders. Since 1989 there has been a military government, which changed the name of the country to Myanmar. In 1990 elections were held, but the military did not let the winning party, National League for Democracy (NLD), take power. One of the NLD's leaders was Aung San Suu Kyi, daughter of Aung San. She was held under house arrest until 1995. Since then she has continued to speak out for democracy.

• Parts of the fabulous golden Shwe Dagon Pagoda, in Myanmar's capital, Yangon (Rangoon), are over 2000 years old.

• Burmans are the biggest of the ethnic groups in Myanmar. There are also 50 other ethnic groups. Most of these live in the mountainous regions.

find out more
Asia
See also Countries fact file, page 632

▲ The temple on Mount Popa, in the Pegu mountains, is a centre of Burmese folk religion. Believers worship a group of spirits called *nats*. Mount Popa is considered to be the home of the most important *nats*.

Myths and legends

All around the world people have made up stories, or myths, to explain things they do not understand, such as 'How was the Earth formed?' or 'Why does spring follow winter?'. The questions are the same everywhere, but the stories are different, because they come from groups of people with different cultures and beliefs, and who live in different parts of the world.

• Mermaids and mermen are creatures of myth and folklore who are part-human and part-fish. They live under the sea in coral palaces, but sometimes come ashore and even fall in love with human beings. But they have to return to the sea after a while, or they die.

▶ In this 19th-century silk painting, Isanagi stirs the waters of the sea of mud to create the island of Onokoro in Japan, while Isanami looks on.

Many myths tell of gods and goddesses, or of strange creatures – monsters, giants and dragons – with magical and sometimes terrible powers. Legends are often like myths, but they are stories based on real people or places that have become exaggerated as people have told and retold them. They usually describe the adventures of especially skilled, brave or clever people.

Creation myths

People everywhere have told stories about how the world was formed and how the human race began. These stories are called creation myths.

Monsters and giants

Lots of stories have been told about monsters and giants, especially about humans or gods who have fought them and won, or outwitted them with their clever tricks.

Coatlicue was a monster in Aztec myth who had crocodile jaws. One day she swallowed every other creature in the world, and dived to the bottom of the sea. Two gods, Wind and Shadow, teased her, dragged her to the surface and forced her to disgorge them all. They then threw her crocodile fangs into the sea, where they turned into jagged rocks. Coatlicue occasionally grumbles and shakes herself in her underground prison, and this is what causes earthquakes.

Many stories say that giants were the first kind of creature that ever lived on Earth, and that they fought a battle with the gods, which the gods won. In Greek myth, all the gods joined together to destroy the giants, but could only finally defeat them with the help of a human being – the hero, Heracles (Roman Hercules).

One of the most famous of all giants is Goliath, a soldier in the Philistine army, who fought against David, a shepherd boy in ancient Israel. David won the fight by killing Goliath with a stone from his sling. David and Goliath are historical characters, so the story of David and Goliath is a legend, and not a myth.

According to a Japanese myth, the twin gods Isanami and Isanagi created the world from a sea of lifeless mud. They took a long spear, with a tip made of stars, and stirred the mud until it thickened and stuck to the spear-point. Bits of mud splashed back into the sea. Small lumps of mud made islands, and bigger lumps made continents. Grass grew, and trees and flowers covered the new land.

Greek myth tells of a time when only gods and giants, called titans, lived in the Universe. One day one of the titans, Prometheus, sat idly making tiny models of gods out of clay. The goddess Athene came along and breathed life into these mud dolls, and the human race was born.

Seasons and weather

Many myths have been created to explain why it is cold in winter and warm in summer. Others tell of why the Sun shines, or why lightning strikes.

Native Americans have a story of Old Man Winter, who lives in the frozen north, and Summer Queen, whose home is the warm south. Once a year, Old Man Winter walks south, bringing the snow and ice. Then, when six months have passed, Summer Queen forces him back to his snow-kingdom, and brings the spring.

The Norse people, who lived about 1500 years ago in the lands that are now Norway, Sweden, Denmark and Iceland, told many stories about their gods and goddesses. One of their best-known

▶ Thor, the Norse storm-god, raises his hammer above his head to strike his enemies with thunder and lightning.

gods was Thor, the storm-god. Thor was the bearer of lightning, which he carried inside a huge hammer. This hammer was the gods' best weapon against their enemies, the giants. Thor could kill a giant with a single thunderbolt.

Legends

Many legends are in fact well-known folk tales that have become attached to one person. For example, there is a story about a marksman who is forced to shoot an apple from his son's head. This is a folk tale, but people now think of it as being about the Swiss hero William Tell.

The legend of Robin Hood was probably based on the adventures of several outlaws who lived in the forests of England in the 12th and 13th centuries. According to the legend, Robin Hood 'stole from the rich and gave to the poor'. Among the 'merry men' who followed him were Little John, Friar Tuck and Will Scarlet. They lived in the open air, and ambushed wealthy travellers.

The legend of the Pied Piper of Hamelin tells of a time when the town of Hamelin in Germany was overrun by rats. One day a young man came to the town and offered to get rid of the rats – for a price. The poor people accepted his offer, and the young man started to play on his pipe. As he played, the rats began to follow him. They followed him out of the town and down to the sea, where they all plunged in, never to return.

The piper went back to the town to claim his fee, but now the people felt that his price was too high. So the young man began to play on his pipe

again. This time the children of the town followed him. They followed him up into the mountains, where there was an opening in the rock. They followed him into the rock, never to return – except for one, the slowest child, who went back to the town to tell the tale.

◀ This painting by Arthur Rackham shows the children of Hamelin following the Pied Piper out of the town.

find out more
Celts
Dragons
Egyptians, ancient
Greeks, ancient
Religions
Romans
Seasons
Vikings

Names

Ever since people have used language, they have given names to people, things or places they know or have heard about. Names are a vital way of identifying the people and things around us.

Many people have family names, or surnames, and a first name (or forename). Others follow a different custom and do not have a surname. It is quite common for a Muslim brother and sister to have no family name at all. However, there is a great variety of first names. Hindu people might be called Arun or Anwadha; Muslims might be Akram or Asmat; Christian names include Anne and Andrew. Jewish names such as Rachel and David come from the Bible.

- In England surnames began as a way of identifying a particular person. A man called John might become John Fisher (if he was a fisherman), or John Brown (if he had dark hair), or John Wood (if he lived in a wood).

- Some places are named after a person. Athens takes its name from the ancient Greek goddess Athene. In the USA the capital city is named after the first president, George Washington.

find out more
Anglo-Saxons
Romans

Place names

Sometimes people in two countries have different names for the same place. The water that the British call the Channel is known to the French as La Manche ('the sleeve'). Some countries change their name when they become independent because they do not want to be called by their colonial name.

The African country which was known as the Gold Coast renamed itself Ghana.

In North America the early Spanish explorers named many settlements after saints, such as San Francisco (St Francis). A number of US states, such as Dakota and Kansas, were named after the Native American peoples that lived there.

Byzantium to Istanbul: name changes through history

Some cities have been renamed several times throughout their history, perhaps because they have been conquered, or even because a new person has come to power. Istanbul, in Turkey, situated in two continents (Europe and Asia), is one major city whose name has changed. Towards the end of the 8th century BC a new colony was founded by the Greeks. They called it **Byzantium**. In AD 330 Constantine I made the city the seat of the Roman empire, and renamed it **Constantinople**. In 1453 the city was conquered by the Turks and made the capital of the Ottoman empire. It was renamed **Istanbul**, but it was not until the 20th century that this became its official name.

Napoleon Bonaparte

Napoleon Bonaparte was a great military leader who became ruler of France. He was the emperor from 1804 to 1814 and again in 1815.

Born 1769 in Ajaccio, Corsica
Died 1821 aged 51

- Although Napoleon is perhaps best known for his military campaigns, he also made many notable reforms as a statesman. He reorganized the French legal system in what became known as the Code Napoléon. It was adopted throughout the Napoleonic empire and influenced legal systems around the world. It remains the basis of French law today.

find out more
France
Nelson, Horatio

Napoleon Bonaparte was a brilliant general who, by 1799, had led his troops to several victories in Europe. France at this time was going through a difficult phase. With his help, the old government was overthrown and Napoleon became France's new leader.

Over the next 5 years, he made many changes to improve the lives of ordinary people. His armies were successful abroad, although his navy was defeated by Nelson at the battle of Trafalgar in 1805. In 1804 he became emperor, and by 1807 he ruled a vast empire.

However, things began to go wrong and the French people became weary of Napoleon's rule. In 1814 he was banished to Elba, in the Mediterranean, but he escaped and regained power. This time, however, Britain, Prussia, Russia and Austria combined to defeat him at the battle of Waterloo in 1815. He died in exile in St Helena in the south Atlantic.

◄ Troops sent to stop Napoleon on his return from exile on the island of Elba in 1815 welcome him instead as their emperor. His victory was short-lived.

Navies and warships

Every country with a sea coast maintains some form of navy, if only to patrol the coastline against smugglers. Naval ships are used in times of war to hunt and destroy enemy ships, submarines and aircraft, and for launching missiles against land targets.

Modern sea warfare relies heavily on submarines equipped with guided missiles and torpedoes, and on air power. Instead of huge battleships, small, mobile ships such as destroyers and frigates carrying guided missiles are built. Aircraft carriers are the largest naval vessels of all; the biggest can carry over 90 aircraft. They carry high-speed assault planes, which are launched into the air using steam catapults or, in smaller ships, special ramps. Helicopters are used for anti-submarine patrols and for supporting commando-type landings.

For combined landing operations, modern navies are equipped with troop- and tank-carrying assault craft and 'logistic landing ships', which are designed to carry bulky stores and equipment. Mine-laying is still a part of sea warfare, and was used in the Persian Gulf during the Gulf War between Iran and Iraq in the 1980s. To combat this, navies keep a number of vessels specially designed to detect mines and dispose of them. These usually have hulls built of glass and reinforced plastics, which do not attract magnetic mines. Most naval vessels are packed with radar and other electronic equipment which can detect and track missiles.

▶ FLASHBACK ◀

Fleets of warships have existed since the days of ancient Greece. The earliest English navy was the Saxon fleet organized by Alfred the Great in the 890s to fight off a Viking invasion.

The great days of the British navy began with the defeat of the Spanish Armada in 1588. During the 18th and 19th centuries the British navy ruled the seas of the world, winning the decisive battle of Trafalgar over the French in 1805. The British Royal Navy reached its greatest size in 1914, when it had 542 major warships. Since then, numbers have been gradually reduced.

After the end of World War I the navies of the USA and Japan expanded the fastest. In the first half of the 20th century Japan had a very powerful navy.

• Many countries maintain very strong navies. In 1997 the largest were those of the USA, with about 354 warships and 623,000 men, and the Russian Federation, with fewer men (about 490,000), but about the same number of warships.

find out more
Helicopters
Ships and boats
Submarines
Weapons

▼ An aircraft carrier (top) and a missile cruiser (bottom), two of the most important kinds of naval warship.

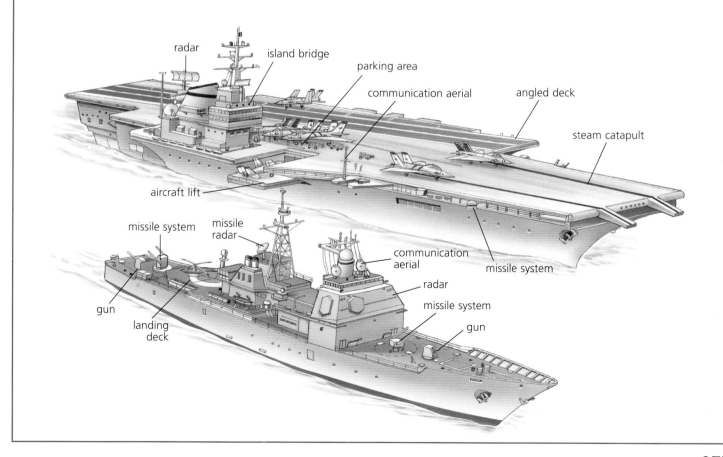

radar
island bridge
parking area
communication aerial
angled deck
steam catapult
aircraft lift
missile system
missile radar
communication aerial
missile system
radar
missile system
gun
landing deck
gun

Navigation

Navigation is knowing your position – at sea, on land or in the air – and where you will be a little while later. To do this, you need to work out your present position and you need to know your speed and the direction in which you are moving. The simplest way of navigating is with a magnetic compass. Today, more and more navigation is done by satellite.

A *magnetic compass* has a small magnetized needle that can turn freely. The Earth's magnetism pulls the needle so that it always points to the magnetic north pole, and from that you can work out your direction.

However, magnetic north is not in quite the same direction as true north, so ships and aircraft use a more accurate *gyrocompass*. It consists of a gyroscope (a heavy wheel that spins on its axis). Once it is spinning at very high speed, the gyroscope keeps pointing in the same direction. Other sensors detect any changes in motion so that a computer can work out how the position of the ship or aircraft is changing.

Lighthouses

The brilliant sweeping beam from a lighthouse helps passing ships to work out exactly where

▶ A walker checks his location with a satellite navigation receiver. Each GPS satellite sends out a signal with its identity and position and the exact time from an atomic clock. In the receiver, a tiny computer compares the arrival times of the signals from different satellites and uses the information to calculate its position to within 100 metres.

they are. Each lighthouse has a distinctive code of flashing beams. In foggy conditions, some lighthouses also send out deep horn notes. Lighthouses usually mark locations that are dangerous to shipping, such as islands, rocks or reefs.

Most modern lighthouses are operated by computers from the mainland. Previously, up to three lighthouse keepers at a time used to keep the lighthouse working.

Navigation by satellite

Many walkers, climbers, sailors, pilots and motorists now navigate with the help of a network of satellites called the Global Positioning System (GPS). The GPS has a ring of satellites around the Earth in geostationary orbit – their motion matches the Earth's rotation so that they stay in fixed positions above the ground. The satellites transmit synchronized radio signals that can be picked up by a small receiver below.

▶ FLASHBACK ◀

Simple compasses using lodestone, a magnetic rock, may have been used in China in the 5th century BC. By the 12th century AD European sailors navigated with compasses made from lodestone.

The Pharos at Alexandria, in Egypt, was the first great lighthouse. Built in about 280 BC, it was one of the Seven Wonders of the ancient world. Torches in its windows guided ships into harbour. The same method was used for 1400 years, until oil lamps, and later electric lights, were used.

find out more
Earth
Geometry
Magnets
Maps
Radar
Satellites
Seven Wonders of the World

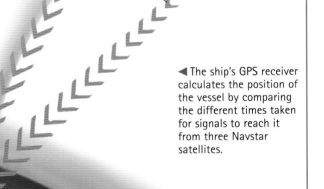

Navstar 2

Navstar 1

time signal

Navstar 3

◀ The ship's GPS receiver calculates the position of the vessel by comparing the different times taken for signals to reach it from three Navstar satellites.

ship with GPS receiver

Nelson, Horatio

Born 1758 in Norfolk, England
Died 1805 aged 47

find out more
Georgian Britain
Napoleon Bonaparte

Horatio Nelson was Britain's greatest admiral. He defeated Napoleon's navy at the battle of Trafalgar in 1805, and this ensured that Britain was saved from being invaded by the French.

Horatio Nelson joined the navy when he was 15, and just six years later was given command of his own ship. Despite frequent illnesses, he soon made a name for himself as a skilled commander who was also popular with his men.

His first opportunity to really prove himself came when Britain declared war on the French in 1793. He was blinded in his right eye during a battle in 1794, and more

◄ In this painting, Nelson is shown dying on the deck of his ship, the *Victory*. Having been assured of his fleet's success, his last words were said to be, 'Thank God I have done my duty.'

injuries followed – eventually his right arm had to be cut off at the elbow. However, this did not hold him back. He destroyed the French navy in the battle of the Nile in 1798, and in 1801 he defeated the Danes at the battle of Copenhagen. He was rewarded with the rank of vice-admiral that same year.

Nelson's greatest success was to be his last. In 1805 his fleet of 27 ships encountered 33 French and Spanish vessels at Cape Trafalgar, off the coast of Spain. Nelson signalled to his own fleet: 'England expects that every man will do his duty.' His forces won a famous victory, but during the fighting he was shot and he died on the deck of his ship, the *Victory*. England was now safe from invasion from Napoleon's forces but had lost one of its greatest heroes.

Nervous systems

• Reflexes are built into your nervous system. They are actions which you do without having to think, such as pulling your hand away if you touch something hot.

• Pain is an unpleasant feeling that warns us of damage to our bodies. Nerve endings in the skin and other parts of the body carry the pain message to the spinal cord and into the brain.

find out more
Brains
Cells
Glands
Human body

The nervous system of humans and other vertebrates (animals with backbones) is made up of the brain, the spinal cord and a network of nerves. It is the body's communication and control system.

The nervous system ensures that all the parts of an animal's body are co-ordinated and that the animal responds to any changes in its surroundings.

The brain and the spinal cord make up the *central nervous system*. This is protected by bone: the brain by the skull and the spinal cord by the backbone. The *peripheral nervous system* is made up of the nerves that connect all the parts of the

body with the brain and the spinal cord.

The nerves carry electrical messages (nerve impulses). Nerve impulses only travel in one direction, which is why we need two different sets of nerves: sensory and motor nerves. *Sensory nerves* carry

information from the sense organs, such as the eyes, ears, nose, taste buds and touch sensors in the skin, to the brain. The brain sends out nerve impulses through the *motor nerves* to the part of the body where action is needed, such as a muscle or a gland.

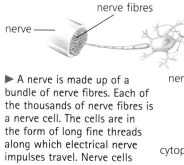

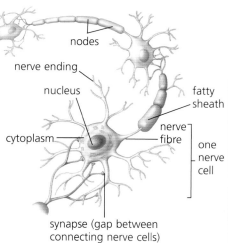

▶ A nerve is made up of a bundle of nerve fibres. Each of the thousands of nerve fibres is a nerve cell. The cells are in the form of long fine threads along which electrical nerve impulses travel. Nerve cells communicate with each other across gaps called synapses. Nerve fibres carry messages in the form of electrical impulses. These impulses travel very quickly, reaching speeds of up to 160 metres per second.

nerve fibres
nerve
nodes
nerve ending
nucleus
fatty sheath
cytoplasm
nerve fibre
one nerve cell
synapse (gap between connecting nerve cells)

Newspapers and magazines

Millions of newspapers and magazines are sold every day. They are the cheapest and most popular source of written information and entertainment in the world. There are many different kinds of newspapers and magazines to cater for all interests and ages.

- No matter how unusual your interest may be, somewhere there will be a magazine to suit it. Today's publishing industry provides magazines on almost every subject, from sailing to computer news and from Hollywood gossip to business investment.

Newspapers and magazines usually cost the reader money, but this alone is never enough to pay for the whole cost of producing them. Successful magazines make huge sums of money from advertising because colour printing and glossy paper can make products look very attractive. Newspaper advertisements are very expensive because newspapers are read by millions of people.

Newspapers

There are many different sorts of newspaper: daily and weekly, national and local, and in many areas now there are free newspapers which contain mainly advertisements. All newspapers employ reporters to collect and write about the news. No paper can afford to have reporters everywhere in the country or the world. News agencies, such as the Exchange Telegraph and Reuters, employ people to gather news from all over the world, and then they sell it to any newspaper that will pay for it.

▶ Most newspapers in the West are owned by private individuals who can express their opinions on the editorial pages. Not all countries allow free speech in newspapers. Some have *censorship*, which means that stories have to be checked first to see that the government does not object to what is being said.

Putting the newspaper together

In newspapers, advertisements are laid out first; then the news. The news editor decides which stories to include and which to put on the front page. At this stage, a rough outline of the pages will be designed. But before the paper is 'put to bed' (ready for printing) stories will be rewritten, cut, extended or scrapped. Headlines and subheadings will be added and photographs will be chosen.

When it is time to produce the newspaper itself, electronic typesetting machines create the printing plates automatically (see above). These are then put on the presses for printing, and huge machines fold the pages, gather them together and cut them ready for sending to newsagents.

Magazines

New magazines are being created all the time. When a new interest catches on, magazines quickly appear in the shops to feed the new demand. Some survive for years, but others quickly vanish when the subject becomes unfashionable. Women's magazines are a very important part of the industry. Most are edited by women and reflect women's interests – in news and public affairs, careers, travel, health and many other subjects. Comics are a type of magazine containing stories in cartoon form. They are usually aimed at younger readers and are hugely popular.

More than half of all magazines are sent direct to their readers, rather than being sold in shops. This is called *direct-mail selling*. Scientific and technical journals are sold in this way. When scientists make a new discovery, they write an account of their findings for a scientific journal.

Newton, Isaac

Born 1642 in Lincolnshire, England
Died 1727 aged 84

• Despite being a brilliant scientist, Newton was renowned for being absent-minded. He could also be sensitive to criticism, and was very modest about his amazing achievements. He was knighted in 1702 for his great contribution to scientific understanding.

find out more
Colour
Forces and pressure
Gravity
Light

Isaac Newton was one of the greatest physicists and mathematicians that has ever lived. Today he is best remembered for discovering the law of gravity, and working out the three standard laws of motion.

Many people have heard the story of Newton sitting in an orchard and seeing an apple fall. He was only 23, but his studies at Cambridge University had started to make him think in a new way about the movement of the Earth, the Moon and the planets. He realized that, just as the force of gravity pulled the apple to Earth, so gravity also kept the Moon in its orbit. Without gravity, the Moon would fly off into space. Newton developed this idea into his theories of motion and gravitation.

Newton also made an important discovery while making a telescope. He noted

◀ Because he was master of the Royal Mint for nearly 30 years, Newton's portrait was chosen to be on the back of the last English one-pound note. This is the illustration on which the portrait was based.

that the bright images he saw through it had coloured edges. His determination to find out why this happened resulted in him being the first person to realize that white light is a mixture of all the different colours of the rainbow. He showed that a prism or raindrops in the air make a spectrum (rainbow) of colours by splitting up the white light.

Newton's greatest book, written in Latin and usually called *Principia* (1686–1687), included his three laws of motion. It has had an enormous effect on the way scientists have thought ever since. After the publication of *Principia*, Newton became active in public life. He was appointed master of the Royal Mint, and from 1703 until his death he was also president of the Royal Society.

Newts and salamanders

Newts and salamanders are amphibians, like frogs and toads. They have long narrow bodies, long tails and short legs with webbed feet for swimming.

They use their powerful tails to propel themselves through the water. Like frogs, newts and salamanders have moist skins and live in damp places. They feed on worms and insects, and some use their tongues to catch their prey. Most newts and salamanders spend their adult lives on land, but some live mainly in water.

Some newts and salamanders lay their eggs in water. These eggs hatch into tadpoles, which feed on small water animals. Others lay their eggs on land, in damp hollows under old logs or stones. The tadpole stage takes place inside the eggs, and the tiny young eventually hatch out from the eggs. A few kinds give birth to live young. A few salamander tadpoles never really grow up. An adult

axolotl is like a giant tadpole, still with feathery gills on the outside of its head.

Most newts and salamanders produce poisonous slime from glands in their skin. They may be brightly coloured to warn enemies of their poison.

▼ The fire salamander has bright yellow markings on its black body, tail and head, to warn enemies of its poisonous skin. It spends most of its time on land, living in damp places.

▶ Like most newts, the marbled newt lives mainly on land but returns to water to breed.

find out more
Amphibians

New Zealand

New Zealand is a country made up of two main islands in the Pacific Ocean. The islands were named in 1642 by the Dutch explorer Abel Tasman. But the Maori people, who had discovered and settled the land 600 years earlier, call New Zealand 'Aotearoa' ('land of the long white cloud').

New Zealand is in a major earthquake zone. There are many active volcanoes in the North Island, and around the town of Rotorua there are bubbling mud pools, geysers, hot springs and mineral pools to bathe in. The South Island has a spectacular mountain range, with several peaks over 3000 metres high.

Climate and people

New Zealand's mild climate and good soil encourage growth of fruit and vegetables. There is good grazing for animals all year, so livestock farming, particularly of sheep, is an important part of the economy. Outdoor pursuits are popular, especially rugby, sailing, fishing and hiking. New Zealanders value their unpolluted, nuclear-free country, and have campaigned against nuclear tests in the Pacific.

Wildlife

When the Maori first arrived in New Zealand, they found an uninhabited land covered in forest, full of unusual ferns and huge, ancient kauri trees. There were no mammals except for bats, and the most distinctive creatures were flightless birds. Today much of the forest has gone, and some of the birds have been hunted to extinction. Mammals such as rats, introduced from abroad, now compete with the natural wildlife for food and space.

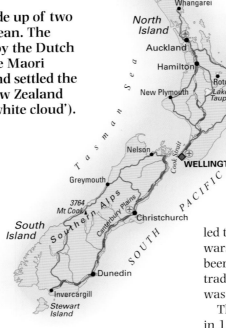

▶ FLASHBACK ◀

Captain James Cook visited New Zealand in 1769, and soon afterwards traders, missionaries and settlers from Britain began to arrive. There were disputes over land between the new arrivals and the Maori, which led to a series of fierce land wars. By 1870 the Maori had been defeated. As a result, the traditional Maori way of life was almost destroyed.

The invention of refrigeration in 1869 encouraged sheep and dairy farming, as lamb and butter could now be sold abroad. Until the UK joined the European Union in 1973, much New Zealand produce was sold there. Today, however, New Zealand has stronger trading links with Australia and South-east Asia.

find out more
Cook, James
Maori
Pacific Islands
Wool
See also Countries fact file, page 633

▼ Milford Sound, in the south-west of the South Island, New Zealand, is a fjord (a steep-sided valley flooded by the sea). It marks the end of the Milford walking track, which is thought to be one of the most beautiful walks in the world.

Nigeria

Nigeria has more people than any other African country, although by area it is only Africa's 14th largest country. It is named after the Niger, Africa's third largest river.

High plains cover most of northern and central Nigeria, with high mountains in the east, on the border with Cameroon. Along the coast in the south are sandy beaches, mangrove forests, and the swampy Niger delta. Inland are grassy plains with some woodland.

About 400 groups of people live in Nigeria, each with its own language. The largest groups are the Muslim Hausa and Fulani peoples in the north, the Yoruba in the south-west, and the Ibo in the south-east.

Two-thirds of Nigerians live in farming villages. In southern Nigeria, women run the markets, work in factories and play a major role in society. By contrast, most women in the north do not work outside their homes.

Nigeria's main export is oil. Money from oil sales has enabled Nigeria to set up many new industries, although much poverty remains.

From 1861 Britain gradually took control of Nigeria, occupying the kingdom of Benin in 1894 and uniting the various regions into a single colony in 1914. Nigeria was granted independence in 1960. From time to time since 1966, its rulers have been army officers. A civil war in the south-east between 1967 and 1970 began in part because of the discovery of oil off Port Harcourt. In the 1990s a period of violent military government was followed by a return to democracy in 1999.

◄ Western clothes are common in the cities, but many Nigerians wear long white or brightly coloured robes, especially on market days, when they meet their relatives and friends.

find out more
Africa
Oil
Sculpture
See also Countries fact file, page 634

Nightingale, Florence

Florence Nightingale was a nurse who organized the care of soldiers injured in the Crimean War. She was one of the founders of modern nursing and became an English national heroine.

Florence Nightingale always wanted to be a nurse, but her family did not think it was a respectable job. It was not until 1851 that she got her own way and started work in a small London hospital. She was so successful that she was asked to go to the Crimean War to take charge of the nursing of wounded British soldiers.

Nightingale set sail in 1854 with 38 nurses. Within a month they had 5000 men to look after. She worked 20 hours a day. When her story was published in English newspapers, she became a national heroine. Grateful people donated £45,000 – a huge sum in those days – and she built the Nightingale training school for nurses at St Thomas's Hospital, London.

However, the strain of her work in the Crimea caused her health to get worse, and from 1857 she was an invalid. Despite the fact that she spent the last 52 years of her life in bed or on her couch, she carried on helping to train nurses.

Nightingale's sight gradually got worse and by 1901 she was blind, although she still carried on working. In 1907 she became the first woman ever to be awarded the Order of Merit.

Born 1820 in Florence, Italy
Died 1910 aged 90

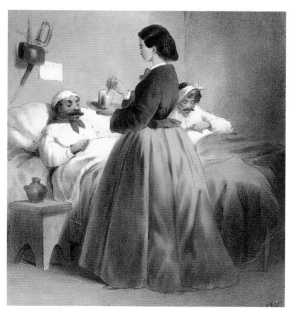

◄ Florence Nightingale became known as 'the lady with the lamp' while nursing in the Crimea. Every night she visited the wards, checking on the welfare of the soldiers by the light of her lamp.

find out more
Hospitals
Medicine
Nurses

Nile *see* Africa *and* Egypt

Nitrogen

The gas nitrogen makes up 78 per cent of the air we breathe, and it is found (combined with other elements) in all living things. Because nitrogen does not readily react with or attack other substances, it is often added to food packages, such as crisp packets. This method keeps the food fresh and stops it from spoiling.

Nitrogen is a chemical element, as are carbon and oxygen. When nitrogen combines with these and other elements, nitrogen compounds are formed. Some of these, especially amino acids and proteins, are essential to life.

Nitrogen can be separated out from air by cooling the air until the gases in it become liquid. Nitrogen becomes a liquid at a temperature of −196 °C. This very cold liquid is used to produce low temperatures, for example in rapidly freezing food to preserve it.

The nitrogen cycle

Although people and other animals breathe in nitrogen all the time, the nitrogen that they need enters their bodies in another way, as part of a constant movement of nitrogen called the nitrogen cycle. In this cycle, nitrogen moves from the air into plants and animals and back again, helping to sustain life as it does so.

The food that animals eat contains the essential nitrogen compounds. These compounds are present in plants, and people and animals get them either by eating plants or by eating animals that have fed on plants. Plants absorb nitrogen compounds from the soil through their roots. These compounds come mainly from the decaying remains of dead plants and animals.

▼ Scientists use liquid nitrogen to store materials at very low temperatures. For example, cells from human beings, such as sperm and egg cells, are frozen and then thawed when needed.

- Farmers often help crops to grow by spreading fertilizers containing nitrogen compounds (nitrates). However, using such fertilizers can cause large amounts of nitrates to build up in the soil. Rainwater may then wash them into water supplies, rivers and seas. High levels of nitrates in drinking water may cause illness.

find out more
Air
Atmosphere
Gases, liquids and solids
Proteins

Nobel prizes

Nobel prizes are named after Alfred Nobel, the inventor of dynamite. In his will he left a huge fund for prizes to be given to people who helped humankind.

find out more
Explosives
Weapons

The Nobel Foundation was set up at the start of the 20th century to carry out Alfred Nobel's wishes. The 9 million dollars he left were used to give prizes in five fields: literature, physics, chemistry, physiology and medicine, and peace. The first prizes were awarded in 1901. From 1969 onwards a sixth prize was awarded for economics. Nobel prizes are awarded on 10 December each year, the anniversary of Alfred Nobel's death. Each award consists of a gold medal, a sum of money and a certificate.

Perhaps the most famous Nobel prize is that awarded for peace. One famous winner of the Nobel Peace Prize is Nelson Mandela, who was awarded the prize together with F. W. de Klerk in 1993 for helping to abolish apartheid. The Dalai Lama, exiled leader of Tibet, won the award in 1989, and in 1991 it was given to Aung San Suu Kyi for her non-violent struggle for democracy and human rights in Myanmar (Burma).

Alfred Nobel

Alfred Bernhard Nobel was born in Sweden in 1833. His father was an inventor and maker of mines and explosives. Nobel himself became obsessed with explosives. He invented a much safer explosive, which he called 'dynamite'. This was mainly used for blasting through rock. He also invented an explosive for firing bullets or shells out of guns.

Nobel became very wealthy, but died a very sad man. He had hoped that terrible weapons would prevent war because no one would dare use them. Unfortunately, he was wrong.

▶ Alfred Nobel, Swedish inventor and manufacturer.

Normans

The first Normans were 'Northmen' – tall, fair-haired Vikings from Scandinavia. They came to the fertile lands of northern France to steal goods and land. In 911 the king of the Franks made a deal with Rolf, the Viking leader. The king granted him land. In return, Rolf became a Christian, and probably promised to be loyal to the king. That was the beginning of Normandy.

The dukes of Normandy, from Rolf onwards, were strong rulers and powerful fighters. They controlled their tough followers by giving them land, and they expected loyalty and obedience in return. Most of Normandy was very fertile. The coast had good harbours. The Seine joined Normandy to Paris and the heart of France, so the Normans could trade and travel easily. They became rich and independent.

The Normans learned to speak French. They had come to a Christian land and soon became Christian themselves. The Church in Normandy grew strong and well organized, run by good and well-educated bishops.

Warriors

The Normans were effective fighters, especially when fighting on horseback. They bred special warhorses, and saddles and stirrups gave them firm control of their mounts. Norman knights learned to use long, heavy lances, so when they charged, their enemies faced an array of deadly spikes bearing down on them. Norman armies

▲ Norman knights gave money and land to found monasteries. They built impressive round-arched churches and cathedrals. Durham Cathedral in England (above), completed in 1133, still retains its Norman character.

had foot-soldiers and archers too. It is not surprising the Normans conquered other lands beyond Normandy.

Travels and conquests

Southern Italy had no strong ruler, and was on the route which pilgrims took to the Holy Land. To the south lay Sicily, controlled by Saracens (Muslims). Norman adventurers turned up there from AD 1000 to make their fortunes. One such adventurer was Robert Guiscard. He and his brother, Roger, managed to win most of southern Italy and Sicily. Normans ruled there as kings of Sicily until 1194.

In 1066 Duke William of Normandy claimed the English throne when the old king, his cousin Edward the Confessor, died. But he had to defeat the English Harold of Wessex, who had already taken the crown. So 'William the Conqueror' invaded England. The battle of Hastings was long and hard, but finally Harold was killed, and the English fled. After that, the Normans ruled England.

Soon after, in 1095, two groups of Normans (from Normandy and southern Italy) joined the first crusade to win back Jerusalem from the Muslims. They helped to capture Jerusalem, and set up a Norman kingdom round Antioch, in modern Turkey. ◗

▼ Map showing Norman lands in about 1090.

Norman states
× battle
→ Robert and Roger Guiscard, Norman adventurers to the Mediterranean 1042

Scandinavia
NORWAY
SCOTLAND
North Sea
SWEDEN
Estonians
IRELAND
Durham
DENMARK
Lithuanians
WALES
ENGLAND
Prussians
Hastings
Canterbury
Atlantic Ocean
BRITTANY
NORMANDY
Rouen
Paris
Seine
POLAND
Kiev
KIEV RUS
THE GERMAN EMPIRE
FRANCE
HUNGARY
LEON & CASTILE
Portugal
Black Sea
CALIPHATE OF CORDOVA
Rome
BYZANTINE
Constantinople
Seljuks of Rum
Naples
EMPIRE
Mediterranean Sea
SICILY
Palermo
Antioch (Norman)
Levant
ALMORAVID EMPIRE
Holy Land
Jerusalem

0 500 km
0 300 miles

English rebellions

On Christmas Day, 1066, Duke William of Normandy was crowned William, King of England (William I). He faced risings against the Normans every year until 1070. In the marshy fens of East Anglia, the rebel Hereward the Wake held out until he was betrayed. Later, Vikings from Norway attacked in Yorkshire and stirred up trouble amongst those who hated the Normans. William stormed north. His soldiers killed rebels and burned villages and crops.

Normans and English

Before 1066 England had been in close touch with Normandy because Edward the Confessor was half Norman. After 1066 English customs and laws did not disappear; William's taxes were collected by the local sheriff, just as they had been in Anglo-Saxon times.

All the same, there were great changes for ordinary English people. Almost everywhere their local lord was no longer English but a Norman baron. Many churls (free men) in the village lost their land. Serfs (slaves) almost disappeared. Most of the poorest villagers became villeins, who had to work for their lord at set times. He controlled their lives in all kinds of ways, so they were really no better off.

Ordinary people still spoke English, but if you were educated and wanted to get on, you had to speak Norman French and Latin. It was about 300 years before poetry and stories were written down in English again, as they had been in Saxon times. Norman place names made from Latin or French words appeared: Pontefract, meaning 'broken bridge' in Latin; or Beaulieu, French for 'beautiful place'. Many French words have become part of modern English, including government, parliament, music and poem.

The Christian Church was already strong during Anglo-Saxon times. The Normans built churches all over England. Some were great cathedrals, as at Durham, and many were ordinary village churches.

Norman England was now closely linked to Normandy, and to the rest of western Europe. Because the Norman Conquest brought great changes, it is often called the beginning of the Middle Ages in England.

• In 1085 William decided he needed to know who owned English land, how much it was worth, who lived there, and what taxes he could expect. He divided the country into seven districts, and by the end of 1086 barons in each district had collected the information. This huge survey, called the Domesday Book, still exists today.

find out more
Anglo-Saxons
Castles
Crusades
English language
France
Medieval England
Vikings

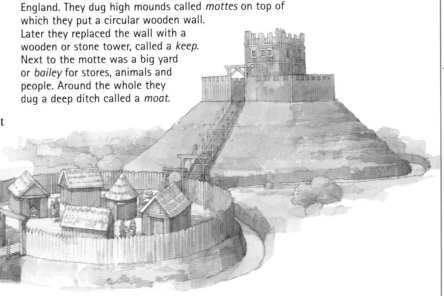

▼ The Norman invaders built castles very quickly in England. They dug high mounds called *mottes* on top of which they put a circular wooden wall. Later they replaced the wall with a wooden or stone tower, called a *keep*. Next to the motte was a big yard or *bailey* for stores, animals and people. Around the whole they dug a deep ditch called a *moat*.

North America

North America is the third largest continent in the world. It is made up of Canada, the United States of America, Greenland, Mexico, and the countries of Central America and the Caribbean. The ancestors of the Native Americans came there over 25,000 years ago from Asia. Five hundred years ago Europeans began to settle there, followed by immigrants from the rest of the world.

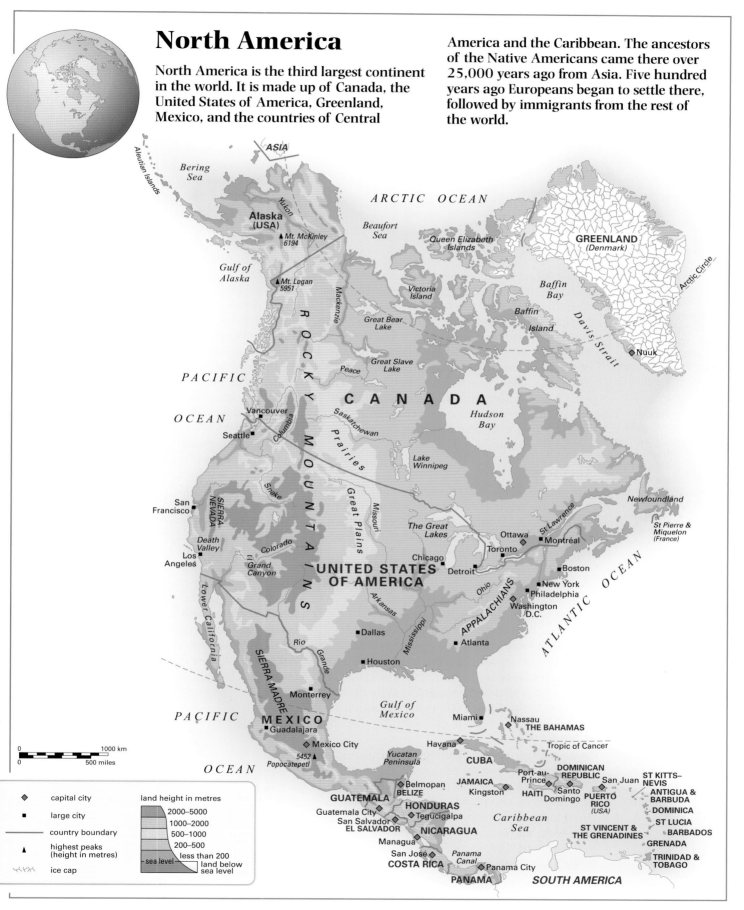

ASIA

Aleutian Islands

Bering Sea

ARCTIC OCEAN

Alaska (USA)

▲ *Mt. McKinley 6194*

Beaufort Sea

Queen Elizabeth Islands

GREENLAND *(Denmark)*

Arctic Circle

Yukon

Gulf of Alaska

▲ *Mt. Logan 5951*

Mackenzie

Victoria Island

Baffin Bay

Baffin Island

Davis Strait

Great Bear Lake

PACIFIC

Great Slave Lake

Peace

Nuuk

R O C K Y

Vancouver

Saskatchewan

C A N A D A

Hudson Bay

OCEAN

Seattle

Columbia

Prairies

Lake Winnipeg

Snake

Great Plains

Missouri

Newfoundland

San Francisco

SIERRA NEVADA

M O U N T A I N S

The Great Lakes

St Lawrence

Ottawa ◆

Montréal

St Pierre & Miquelon (France)

Death Valley

Colorado

Toronto

Chicago

Detroit

Boston

ATLANTIC

Los Angeles

Grand Canyon

UNITED STATES OF AMERICA

Ohio

New York
Philadelphia

Washington D.C. ◆

APPALACHIANS

OCEAN

Lower California

Arkansas

Mississippi

Dallas

Atlanta

Rio

Grande

Houston

Monterrey ◆

SIERRA MADRE

PACIFIC

MEXICO

Gulf of Mexico

Miami

Nassau
THE BAHAMAS

Guadalajara

Mexico City ◆

Havana

Tropic of Cancer

5452 ▲

Popocatepetl

Yucatan Peninsula

CUBA

OCEAN

Port-au-Prince

DOMINICAN REPUBLIC

San Juan

ST KITTS– NEVIS

◆ **Belmopan**
BELIZE

JAMAICA

Kingston

HAITI

◆ *Santo Domingo*

PUERTO RICO *(USA)*

ANTIGUA & BARBUDA

GUATEMALA

Guatemala City ◆

HONDURAS

◆ *Tegucigalpa*

Caribbean Sea

DOMINICA

San Salvador
EL SALVADOR

NICARAGUA

ST VINCENT & THE GRENADINES

ST LUCIA

BARBADOS

Managua ◆

Panama Canal

GRENADA

San José ◆

◆ *Panama City*

TRINIDAD & TOBAGO

COSTA RICA

PANAMA

SOUTH AMERICA

0 ___ 1000 km
0 ___ 500 miles

◆ capital city

■ large city

— country boundary

▲ highest peaks (height in metres)

ᴎᴎᴎ ice cap

land height in metres

2000–5000
1000–2000
500–1000
200–500
sea level
less than 200
land below sea level

▲ Alaska is the largest state of the USA, but it is also the most sparsely populated. This picture shows the icy landscape in the northernmost part of Alaska, which lies within the Arctic Circle.

● Greenland is the world's largest island. Although situated near North America, it is actually a self-governing part of Denmark. It is a mountainous and rocky island with a polar climate, so it is only sparsely populated. The people are a mixture of Danish and Inuit (Eskimo) origin.

● Central America is a narrow stretch of land, only 82 km wide at the Panama Canal. Spain once ruled the territories now occupied by Guatemala, El Salvador, Honduras, Nicaragua, Costa Rica and Panama. Belize was a British colony.

North America is rich in natural resources, including timber, oil, gas, gold and many metals. These have enabled the continent's societies to become wealthy and successful. Although Native Americans had farms and cities, it was the Europeans who developed the land and resources of North America. They cleared forests and drained land to create farms on fertile soils. The search for timber and minerals, especially gold, helped to open up the continent rapidly in the 19th century as immigrants from Europe crossed the ocean.

Landscape

The west is dominated by several mountain ranges, including the Sierra Nevada of California and the Rocky Mountains or 'Rockies'. This is a series of mountain ranges running like a giant backbone down the west-centre of North America to Mexico. To the east of the Sierra Nevada the Colorado River has cut through this high land to form the Grand Canyon. On the eastern side of the continent lie the Appalachians, low mountains of ridges and valleys. Between this range and the Rockies are huge plains, across which the Mississippi and Missouri rivers run. To the north, the waters of Hudson Bay lead to the bleak Arctic. To the south are the Gulf of Mexico and the Caribbean Sea.

Climate

Almost all parts of the continent have warm or hot summers. Only the edge of the Arctic and the high mountains are cool in summer. In winter the northern and central parts of the continent are bitterly cold. There are no mountains to stop icy Arctic air blowing south. The Sierra Nevada do, however, block wet air from the Pacific Ocean. Deserts on the eastern side of these mountains get little rain. Death Valley in California is the

hottest and lowest place on the continent. The coastline on the Gulf of Mexico and the Caribbean Sea often suffer from hurricanes.

People

In the USA and Canada descendants of Native American peoples such as the Cree, the Apache and the Navajo became small minorities after Europeans arrived. Some now live on reservations, while others have migrated to the cities. The governments are negotiating with Native Americans over land rights which would enable them to live their own ways of life. In Mexico, Europeans and Native Americans married each other. Their descendants are called *mestizos*. A third of the population belongs to Native American groups, speaking traditional languages.

The people of North America present a mixture of languages and cultures. The largest numbers of early immigrants came from Spain, France and the British Isles. English and Spanish are the most widely spoken languages, and French is spoken in parts of Canada. Black North Americans trace their ancestors back to Africans transported as slaves before 1808. There are also large numbers of Italians, Greeks, Irish, Germans, Chinese and Russians. Recently immigrants have come from Cambodia and other countries in South-east Asia.

North American history

The first Americans came in distinct waves from Asia beginning over 25,000 years ago. They adapted their ways of life to the continent's many landscapes. In the cold north they became hunters and gatherers. Along the coasts they lived by fishing. Where soils were good they grew maize (corn), squash and beans. In Mexico, people such as the Mayans and Aztecs founded great cities and civilizations.

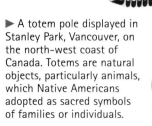

▶ A totem pole displayed in Stanley Park, Vancouver, on the north-west coast of Canada. Totems are natural objects, particularly animals, which Native Americans adopted as sacred symbols of families or individuals.

Native Americans

Native Americans were called Indians by the first European explorers, who thought they had arrived in the East Indies (eastern Asia). The Italian explorer John Cabot discovered mainland North America in 1497. He thought he had arrived in China. The Spanish conquerors, called conquistadores, overthrew the Aztec empire. They used Native American people to work their new farms and mines. In the lands to the north, both Native Americans and Europeans benefited from contact. The Native Americans led the Europeans on explorations and provided them with food in return for iron pots and knives. But over time Native Americans were forced off their land. Many pushed westwards into other lands.

Colonies

During the 16th century Spaniards had settled in Mexico and southern parts of what is now the United States, and the French were settling in Canada and along the Mississippi.

The first permanent English settlement was at Jamestown, Virginia, in 1607. These settlers grew tobacco for sale to Britain. The second colony, Plymouth Colony (later part of Massachusetts) was formed by a group of Puritans. They were called the Pilgrim Fathers because they were seeking a place where they could follow their religion without persecution. By 1733 Britain ruled 13 colonies, which ran along the Atlantic coast of North America.

Settlers' lives

Life for the first settlers in the Atlantic colonies was hard. They built simple houses of wood. They had to make most of their own furniture and clothing. Although not all the land was good, there was plenty of it. Most people farmed,

although some turned to fishing and trade. Many were Quakers, Puritans and other Protestants who led sober, hard-working lives.

A rich land

By 1760 the British colonies were growing prosperous. Immigrants had flocked in, lured by the prospect of owning land and making a new life. Most were from the British Isles, but others came from Germany, the Netherlands and France. Towns and cities grew up, with postal services, newspapers, and schools and colleges. The northern Atlantic colonies, called New England, had their own governors and law-makers. Each town and colony valued its independence. In the southern colonies slaves worked on huge plantations.

Wars of independence

In 1759 the British armies defeated French forces and the whole of Canada came under British rule. In the Atlantic colonies people had grown tired of paying high taxes to Britain. They fought for their independence during the American Revolution (1775–1783) and finally gained their freedom as the United States of America on 15 April 1783. In 1821, the Mexicans successfully rebelled against their Spanish rulers. Canada became an independent country in 1867.

▲ Relations between Native Americans and colonists were often hostile, but a few individuals were moved to help the 'enemy'. According to legend, Pocahontas, the daughter of a Native American leader, flung herself down and successfully saved the life of a captured English captain after she begged her father to spare him.

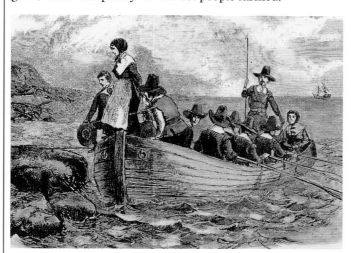

◄ The Pilgrim Fathers coming ashore in North America in 1620. Their colony flourished when Native American farmers taught them how to grow corn (maize).

find out more
Aztecs
Canada
Caribbean
Continents
Festivals and holidays
  (Thanksgiving)
Grasslands
Maya
Mexico
Mountains
Religions
Slaves
South America
United States of
  America
Washington, George
*See also individual
  North American
  countries in the
  Countries fact file,
  pages 613–645*

Northern Ireland

Northern Ireland occupies the north-east corner of Ireland. It is the smallest of the four areas that form the United Kingdom of Great Britain and Northern Ireland.

▶ In Belfast many walls are covered with political murals (paintings), like this one in support of the Irish nationalist party Sinn Féin.

find out more
Britain since 1900
Ireland, Republic of
United Kingdom

Northern Ireland is a beautiful land of fertile plains and small mountains. Farming is an important industry. Irish linens and tweeds are world-famous and its factories also produce clothing and materials from synthetic fibres. There are also newer industries making aircraft, chemicals, tobacco products and alcohol.

▶ **FLASHBACK** ◀

Northern Ireland was formed in 1921 from six of the nine counties of Ulster. Two-thirds of the Northern Irish population were Protestants and one-third was Catholic. The Protestant Unionists wanted to keep Northern Ireland in the UK. Many Catholics were nationalists and wanted it to join the Republic of Ireland.

The period from 1969 was known as the 'troubles', when both nationalist and Unionist groups used shootings and bombings to further their causes. In 1998 a peace plan was agreed that involved establishing closer ties between Northern Ireland and the Republic. At the same time, the plan recognized that Northern Ireland would remain part of the UK so long as a majority of its people wished it to do so.

Noses

find out more
Elephants
Human body
Senses
Whales and dolphins

Most fishes, amphibians, reptiles, birds and mammals have two nostrils. These are tubes running from the front of the head into the mouth. In most mammals these tubes end in a special bulge on the face called a nose.

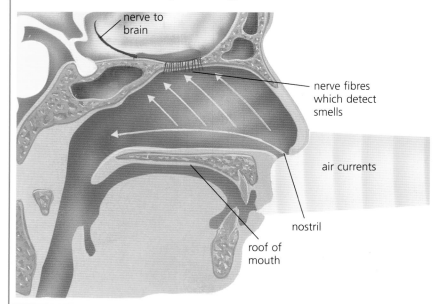

nerve to brain

nerve fibres which detect smells

air currents

nostril

roof of mouth

The nose and its tubes have two important functions. First, they are a route for air to enter the lungs when the mouth is shut or filled with food. Second, the walls of the nostrils are lined with special nerve cells that respond to odours in the air. These send messages to the brain, and this produces the sense of smell. Humans and other animals also use their nose when they eat, as many food 'tastes' are actually detected by the nose.

Human beings can distinguish between 10,000 and 40,000 different odours. However, many animals have a much better sense of smell. A bloodhound, for example, has a sense of smell that is around one million times better than that of a human, which is why they are used by the police to find hidden drugs or to search for clues that will help solve a crime.

Noses come in all shapes and sizes. An elephant's nose, together with its upper lip, forms the trunk. A whale's nose is the blow-hole on top of its head.

◀ Chemicals in the air you breathe dissolve in moisture-covered nerve ends in your nose. These chemicals make the nerves send messages to your brain, so producing your sense of smell.

Novels and novelists

A novel is a long story written in everyday language (prose) rather than in poetry. Most novels are based around a set of characters, and have a plot – a series of connected events that link the characters together and move the story along.

The novel is a form of writing that developed in Europe about 400 years ago. Today novels are written, published and read all over the world. A number of different 'genres' (types) have developed, such as romance, detective, science fiction, horror and children's.

The earliest novels

The first novel of all was probably *Don Quixote*, written by the Spanish writer Cervantes and published in two parts in 1605 and 1615. It tells the story of Don Quixote, who dreams of being a chivalrous knight, and roams the country on his old horse in search of adventures, accompanied by his more practical squire, Sancho Panza. In the 18th century, writers such as Daniel Defoe, Henry Fielding, Samuel Richardson and, later, Fanny Burney helped to make the novel popular in England. *Robinson Crusoe* (1719), by Defoe, describes how the hero survives after being shipwrecked on a desert island.

The 19th century

The novel became extremely popular during the 19th century. At the beginning of the century Walter Scott's historical novels, such as *Waverley* (1814) and *Ivanhoe* (1819), were hugely successful. Jane Austen wrote six witty and realistic novels which gently mocked the manners and behaviour of her day. Her best-known novel is *Pride and Prejudice* (1813), which tells the story of the romance between Elizabeth Bennet and the proud Mr Darcy.

In mid-19th century Britain, many more people learned to read, there were more libraries, and books became cheaper to produce. Many novels came out in instalments in the numerous literary journals that flourished. Writers could reach a much wider audience.

In 1847 the Brontë sisters, Charlotte, Emily and Anne, each published a novel: Charlotte *Jane Eyre*, Emily *Wuthering Heights*, and Anne *Agnes Grey*. At first they published under the made-up

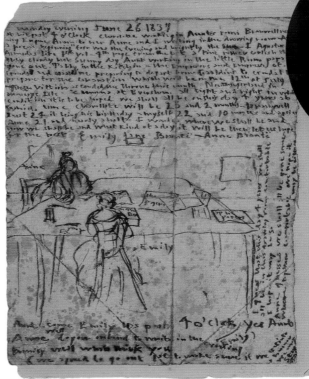

◀ ▲ The Brontë sisters, Charlotte (above) and Emily and Anne (left – pictured writing in this diary sketch by Emily) spent most of their lives in Haworth, a small town in Yorkshire, England, where their father was the clergyman. No other family of novelists has ever achieved as much as these shy, unwordly sisters.

names Currer, Ellis and Acton Bell. Many women wrote novels, but some thought that they would be taken more seriously if they presented themselves as men, rather than as women. *Jane Eyre* and *Wuthering Heights* were both very successful, and the identities of the sisters soon became known. *Jane Eyre* is the story of an orphan girl's search for happiness and independence. *Wuthering Heights*, set on the Yorkshire moors, portrays the passionate love between Cathy and Heathcliff that survives death.

Charles Dickens was the most popular and successful of the Victorian novelists. His books, such as *David Copperfield* (1850) and *Great Expectations* (1861), are full of larger-than-life characters, caught up in fast-moving plots. They also contain fierce criticisms of the evils of Victorian society, such as greed, and child labour and poverty. ◗

Novels for young people

Many novels written for young readers have come to be regarded as 'classics'. Some of them feature animals, such as Kenneth Grahame's *The Wind in the Willows* (1908), the story of Rat, Mole, Badger and Toad, and their life on the river. Others have children as their central characters, such as Enid Blyton's books on the Famous Five and Secret Seven. In *The Hobbit* (1937) and *The Lord of the Rings* (1954–55), J. R. R. Tolkien created the world of Middle Earth, inhabited by elves, dwarves and wizards.

• The first English detective novel was *The Moonstone* (1868), by Wilkie Collins. A few years later Arthur Conan Doyle created the most famous of all detectives, the subtle and sharp-eyed Sherlock Holmes. American detectives have tended to inhabit a more realistic, urban world. The tough detective Philip Marlow, who features in the novels of Raymond Chandler, is the classic world-weary private eye.

▲ The Russian novelist Leo Tolstoy at work in his study.

The popularity of the novel spread, particularly in France, Russia and the USA. French writers such as Gustave Flaubert, Emile Zola and Honoré de Balzac produced closely observed and dramatic portraits of life in 19th-century French society. Zola's novel *Germinal* (1885) is a powerful story of family life in a poor mining community.

Two Russian novelists of the same period who have achieved lasting fame are Leo Tolstoy and Fyodor Dostoevsky. Many people consider Tolstoy's *War and Peace* (1863–1869) to be the greatest novel ever written. It charts the fortunes of three families and paints a broad picture of Russian life at the time of the Napoleonic wars.

In the USA writers such as Nathaniel Hawthorne, Hermann Melville and Mark Twain were writing novels about life in the 'new world'. In *The Adventures of Tom Sawyer* (1876) and *The Adventures of Huckleberry Finn* (1884), Mark Twain wrote about the exciting lives led by the people who lived on and around the Mississippi River in the mid-19th century.

The 20th century

At the beginning of the 20th century, people began to be much more interested in psychology – the way the human mind works. This influenced the kinds of novel that were written.

In books such as *Women in Love* (1921), D. H. Lawrence closely examined his characters' secret feelings. A year later, James Joyce broke new ground in his famous novel *Ulysses* (1922) by representing the free flow of his characters' thoughts in the style of his writing. He records their jumbled-together impressions, emotions, memories and fantasies – often without separating them by using commas or full stops.

Many novelists have been interested in political subjects. In novels such as *Things Fall Apart* (1958), the Nigerian writer Chinua Achebe wrote about the changes in African society as people moved away from a traditional way of life. The Russian writer Alexander Solzhenitsyn caused a sensation when he published *One Day in the Life of Ivan Denisovitch* (1962), based on his own experiences in a Soviet labour camp. The black American writer Alice Walker, author of *The Color Purple* (1982), said: 'I write all the things I should have been able to read'. She said this because, when she was growing up, there were almost no novels that described what it was like to be black in America.

find out more
Austen, Jane
Carroll, Lewis
Dickens, Charles
Drama
Poetry
Stevenson, Robert Louis
Stories and story-tellers

Horror and science fiction

The horror novel is about the dark side of the human imagination. It began in the 18th century when there was a fashion for 'gothic' novels, full of ruined castles and sinister villains, such as *The Mysteries of Udolpho* (1794), by Ann Radcliffe. A later classic of this genre is *Dracula* (1897), by Bram Stoker.

In *Frankenstein* (1818), by Mary Shelley, a scientist, Dr Frankenstein, uses his skill to create a monster. *Frankenstein* was one of the first science-fiction novels. The genre of science fiction was developed further by Jules Verne in *Journey to the Centre of the Earth* (1864), and H. G. Wells in *The War of the Worlds* (1898). Developments in science and technology in the 20th century inspired many science-fiction novels. Aldous Huxley's *Brave New World* (1932) and George Orwell's *1984* (1949) drew gloomy pictures of a future in which people's actions and thoughts were controlled.

▶ This early illustration from *Frankenstein* shows Dr Frankenstein running away in horror as the monster he has created stirs into life.

Numbers

We use numbers in almost everything that we do – when deciding which bus or train to catch, when finding out how much something costs or how old someone is, or when looking for a house number in a street. It would be very difficult to manage without numbers. Since early times, people have developed many ways of writing down numbers. We use special symbols, called *numerals*, to write them down.

There are many words for naming numbers. In English, we count using words like six, sixteen and sixty, and then join them together to make new names like sixty-six. As we count higher, more names are needed, for example hundred (ten tens), thousand (ten hundreds), million (a thousand thousands) and billion (a thousand millions).

The Hindu-Arabic system of writing numbers uses 10 numerals from 0 to 9. Roman numerals consist of letters such as I (1) and V (5). Some of the symbols used for writing down numbers give you an idea of what the number is. For example, the Chinese symbols for one, two and three have one, two and three lines in them in turn. However, with the Hindu-Arabic symbols, the link with the number is not obvious. A visitor from Mars could not tell that the symbol 2 meant two just by looking at it!

Decimal and binary systems

The Hindu-Arabic numeral system, with its 10 symbols, is called a decimal system (from the Latin word *decem* meaning ten). Although there are only 10 symbols to choose from, we can still write down any number. This is because we use the idea of *place value*. When two or more symbols are put next to each other, the value of each depends on its position. For example:

thousands	hundreds	tens	ones
2	2	2	2

means two thousands + two hundreds + two tens + two ones. In our place-value system, each place is worth 10 times the one on its right.

The binary system uses just two symbols, 0 and 1. Mathematicians say that the *base* of binary is two (just as the base of the decimal system is ten). Each place is worth two times the one on its right. For example:

eights	fours	twos	ones
1	1	0	1

in binary means one eight + one four + no twos + one one (making 13). Binary is very useful in computers because numbers can be stored by switching tiny circuits *off* for 0 and *on* for 1.

Prime numbers

Prime numbers are the essential 'building blocks' from which all other numbers are made. They are numbers which cannot be made by multiplying two smaller whole numbers together. Two, three, five, seven and eleven are all prime numbers. Can you think of any more primes?

Numbers that can be made by multiplying two smaller whole numbers together are called

▲ This clock face, which decorates the tower of St Nicholas's Church, Prague, in the Czech Republic, combines a number of different systems of measuring time.

Percentages

	Fraction	Proportion
1%	$\frac{1}{100}$	1 in every 100
10%	$\frac{1}{10}$ $\left(\frac{10}{100}\right)$	1 in every 10
20%	$\frac{1}{5}$ $\left(\frac{20}{100}\right)$	1 in every 5
50%	$\frac{1}{2}$ $\left(\frac{50}{100}\right)$	1 in every 2
75%	$\frac{3}{4}$ $\left(\frac{75}{100}\right)$	3 in every 4
80%	$\frac{4}{5}$ $\left(\frac{80}{100}\right)$	4 in every 5
100%	1 $\left(\frac{100}{100}\right)$	all

• Some numbers are difficult to write as decimals. The square root of 2 is the number which we multiply by itself to get 2. A calculator gives an approximate value of 1.414213562, but however many places of decimals we use, it will still not be enough to give the value exactly.

• If you add or multiply two even numbers, the answer is always even. If you add two odd numbers, the answer is always even. But if you multiply two odd numbers, the answer is always odd.

number word		symbols (numerals)				
English	Welsh	Arabic	Chinese	Urdu	Hindu	Roman
one	un	١	一	١	٩	I
two	dau	٢	二	٢	٢	II
three	tri	٣	三	٣	٣	III
four	pedwar	٤	四	٤	४	IV
five	pump	٥	五	٥	५	V
six	chwech	٦	六	٦	६	VI
seven	saith	٧	七	٧	७	VII
eight	wyth	٨	八	٨	८	VIII
nine	naw	٩	九	٩	९	IX
ten	deg	١٠	十	١٠	٩٠	X
fifteen	pymtheg	١٥	十五	١٥	٩४	XV
fifty	deg a deugain	٥٠	五十	٥٠	४٠	L
hundred	cant	١٠٠	百	١٠٠	٩٠٠	C
five hundred	pum cant	٥٠٠	五百	٥٠٠	४٠٠	D
thousand	mil	١٠٠٠	一千	١٠٠٠	٩٠٠٠	M

Nursery rhymes *see* Poetry

composite numbers. Six is a composite number, because it can be made like this: 6 = 2 × 3. In this example, the 2 and the 3 are called *factors.* All composite numbers can be made by multiplying primes together.

Fractions and percentages

Fractions allow you to write numbers which are not whole numbers. They allow you to divide up the gap between whole numbers so that a more accurate measurement can be given. There are two standard ways of writing fractions: $\frac{3}{4}$, which is called a *vulgar fraction,* and 0.75 which is a *decimal fraction.* The vulgar fraction $\frac{3}{4}$ is a way of writing 'three-quarters' in number form. The top number is called the *numerator* and the bottom number is the *denominator.*

A decimal fraction such as 16.25 is read as 'sixteen point two five' and not as 'sixteen point twenty-five'. Decimals use the idea of place value in just the same way as whole numbers do. Each place is 10 times smaller than the one to its immediate left. The 2 in 16.25 stands for two-tenths, and the 5 stands for five-hundredths.

A percentage is a special kind of fraction. 25 per cent (25%) is another way of writing $\frac{25}{100}$,

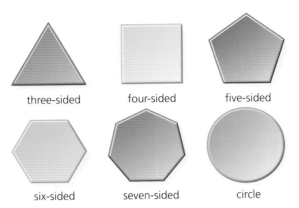

three-sided   four-sided   five-sided

six-sided   seven-sided   circle

◀ A circle has an infinite (never-ending) number of sides. The more sides a shape has the more like a circle it becomes.

which is a quarter. 50% is another way of writing $\frac{50}{100}$, which is a half. So the percentage symbol % is a way of telling you that you have a fraction with 100 on the bottom.

Percentages are useful for giving information about proportions. For example, if you get 80 questions right out of 100 in a test, you can say that your score is 80%. Percentages are often used to give information about wage increases or price rises. If the price of coffee rises by 10%, the increase on a jar of coffee costing 80p will be $\frac{1}{10}$ × 80p, which is 8p. So the new price will be 88p (80p plus the extra 8p).

• When goods are sold with a tax on them, the tax is given as a percentage. A tax of 15% means that you have to pay an extra 15 for every 100 pounds, dollars, pence or cents of the basic price. If something costs £100, the price will be £115 after adding tax.

find out more
Arithmetic
Mathematics
Probability

Nurses

A nurse is someone who looks after people who are sick. Professional nurses are highly trained and work together with doctors to ensure the best care for their patients.

Trainee nurses normally study at a nursing school for three years before they qualify. Nursing assistants or aides can begin work after 11 to 18 months of training. Once they have qualified, many nurses specialize in a particular area of patient care and will continue to study and take exams. They might choose to care for babies or old people, or people suffering from a particular disease such as cancer.

In most countries the majority of nurses work in

hospitals. The other main type of nurse is the community nurse, who visits people in their own homes. Some nurses also work in industry, in homes for elderly people, or as private nurses for a single patient.

▶ FLASHBACK ◀

Modern nursing began in the middle of the 19th century. Medicine was becoming a much

more scientific subject, and doctors were observing their patients more carefully to see what was wrong and what could be done to help them. They needed reliable helpers who were trained to assist them and the patients, and so nurse training schools were set up. One of the first of these was founded at Kaiserwerth in Germany in 1833.

• Mary Seacole was a Jamaican nurse. She was not allowed to go with Florence Nightingale and her nurses to the Crimean War in 1854 because she was black, so she decided to go at her own expense. She helped the soldiers to get food and medicines, and showed great bravery in very dangerous situations.

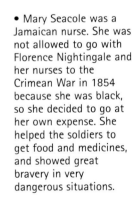

◀ Nurses have a particularly vital role to play in countries where there are few doctors. This community nurse in Ghana, West Africa, is weighing a baby to check that it is getting enough food to eat.

find out more
Doctors
Hospitals
Medicine
Nightingale, Florence

Oceans and seas

Oceans and seas cover 71 per cent (over 360 million square kilometres) of the Earth's surface. They contain about 1370 million cubic kilometres of water. The five major oceans – the Pacific, Atlantic, Indian, Arctic and Southern – are connected to each other by open water.

• Parts of the Arctic and Southern Oceans form permanently frozen ice shelves stretching out from the coast. In slightly warmer areas, the sea freezes only in winter, forming pack ice up to 2 m thick.

• Some sea creatures use the wind to drift across the sea. The Portuguese man-of-war has a gas-filled float to catch the wind. The bubble-raft snail produces a froth of bubbles as a float.

▼ A cross-section of the ocean floor.

The average depth of water in the oceans is 4000 metres, but in some ocean trenches it may be as much as 11,000 metres deep. This water is constantly moving, driven by winds, waves, tides and currents. Waves, whipped up by the wind, stir the surface, but do not move the mass of the water. This is done by tides, which shift the water in time with the phases of the Moon. Water circulates between the oceans in currents. The surface currents swirl slowly in a clockwise direction in the northern hemisphere and anticlockwise in the south.

ARCTIC OCEAN

Arctic Circle

NORTH AMERICA

EUROPE

ASIA

NORTH ATLANTIC OCEAN

AFRICA

PACIFIC OCEAN

Equator

SOUTH AMERICA

SOUTH ATLANTIC OCEAN

INDIAN OCEAN

OCEANIA

PACIFIC OCEAN

Antarctic Circle

SOUTHERN OCEAN

▲ The world's oceans. They contain almost 97% of all the water found on Earth.

The ocean floor

Much of the ocean floor is a flat plain, but in places mountains rise thousands of metres up from the sea-bed. Sometimes they push through the sea's surface as islands. Many of these are active or extinct volcanoes. Running down the centre of the ocean floor in several of the oceans is a ridge of mountains, which is continually being built up by outpourings of lava. As the rock is forced outwards from the ridge by the new lava, the ocean floor spreads.

Much of the ocean floor is covered in sand or mud brought in by rivers. In places, hot springs bubble up, depositing sulphur and other minerals. The remains of microscopic plants and animals from the surface sink down to the bottom to form a layer of tiny particles (sediment). Here, pressure from the water above and from other sediment layers slowly turns the sediment into rock.

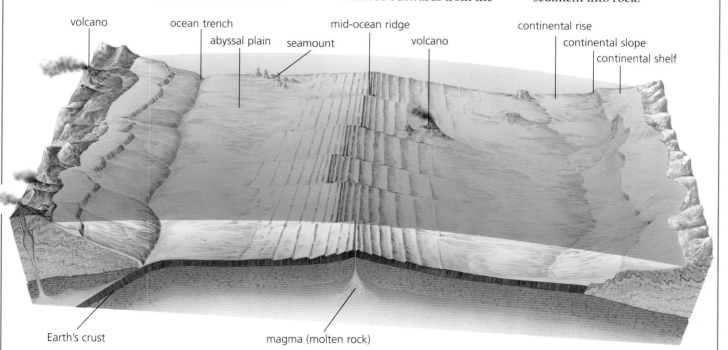

volcano

ocean trench

abyssal plain   seamount

mid-ocean ridge

volcano

continental rise

continental slope

continental shelf

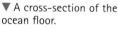
Earth's crust

magma (molten rock)

Ocean zones

The oceans can be divided into three zones. The sunny surface waters at the top – the *photosynthetic zone* – contain most of the ocean fishes as well as a floating community of billions of microscopic creatures called plankton. Below this zone lie the more dimly lit *twilight zone* and, reaching down to deep cold waters, the *dark zone*. Fewer life forms, mainly flesh-eating fishes, live in the lower zones.

Most of the ocean is at around the same temperature – about 4 °C. As you go down deeper, the pressure of the water above increases steadily, making it difficult to move quickly. The temperature also falls to around 2 °C in deep water. The amount of light decreases, until at 1000 metres there is no light at all.

Life at the top

The plant and animal plankton in the photosynthetic zone provides food for tiny animals, such as shrimps, prawns, and the young of starfishes, crabs and other sea animals. Away

▼ Many bottom-dwelling fishes rely on smell and taste. The tripod fish uses three fins to prop itself above the sea-bed while smelling for prey.

▶ The oceans can be divided into three zones. The photosynthetic zone at the top receives enough sunlight to photosynthesize and produce food. It contains most of the ocean's fishes as well as plant and animal plankton. The twilight and dark zones beneath are home to fewer life forms, mainly carnivorous fishes. This diagram is not to scale.

from the sheltered coastal waters there are fewer different kinds of animal, but many fishes and a few large mammals like whales, dolphins and porpoises live here. Some, such as baleen whales and basking sharks, feed by filtering the water for plankton. Others, such as white sharks and barracuda, hunt other fishes.

Deep-sea life

In the cold, dark waters of the deep ocean, hunters can spot the silhouettes of their prey against the faint light above. Here, many fishes have silvery scales along their sides to reflect any light and disguise their shapes. Others are flat-sided, giving them very narrow silhouettes.

Many fishes have huge mouths and can eat prey larger than themselves. Gulper eels and hatchet fishes swim with their large mouths open to catch whatever they can.

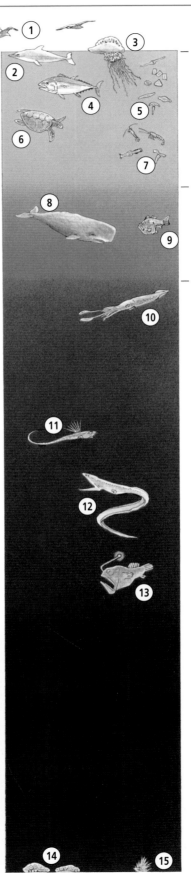

This diagram is not to scale.

photosynthetic zone (up to 200 m deep)

twilight zone (up to 1000 m deep)

dark zone (the average sea depth is 4000 m, but it reaches 11,000 m at its deepest point)

1 gulls
2 dolphin
3 jellyfish
4 tuna
5 plant plankton
6 turtle
7 animal plankton
8 sperm whale
9 hatchet fish
10 squid
11 rat-tail
12 gulper eel
13 angler fish
14 sea cucumbers
15 actinarian

find out more
Continents
Earth
Fishes
Food chains and webs
Mountains
Seashore
Tides
Waves

Oil

Oil is one of the most important substances we use today, and it supplies more of the world's energy than any other fuel. Oil spills from tankers and rigs can cause widespread harm to the oceans and their wildlife. Also, the gases produced when we burn oil are damaging the Earth's atmosphere.

Oil is a fossil fuel, like coal and natural gas. It is the remains of tiny plants and animals which lived in the sea millions of years ago. When they died, they sank to the bottom and were covered by layers of mud and sand. Over the years, the mud and sand slowly turned to rock. Eventually, the weight of rock, combined with heat and the activity of bacteria, changed the animal and plant remains into oil (and natural gas). Deep down under layers of solid rock, the oil became trapped in the holes of porous rock, rather like water in a sponge. The geological name for this oil is *petroleum*.

The search for oil

Oil companies search for petroleum under the sea-bed or under land once covered by sea. After identifying areas where the rocks are most likely to contain oil, test drillings are made. At the drilling site, a framework tower called a *derrick* is erected. Under the derrick, a huge drill is turned by a diesel engine. As the drill hole deepens, the drill is lengthened by adding drill pipes from above. The cutting end of the drill is called the *bit*. It has hardened steel teeth, and there may also be diamonds on it for cutting very hard rock. To keep the bit

cool, watery mud is pumped down the drill pipes and out through holes in the bit. If oil is found, it flows up through the drill hole. The hole then becomes an oil well.

Where oil is found under the sea-bed, the derrick and drilling equipment are built on an *oil rig*. Some rigs float, while others rest on legs on the sea-bed. Semi-submersible rigs are held down on the sea-bed by flooding their legs with water. The choice of rig depends on the sea-bed, the depth of water and the likely weather conditions. The rigs used for natural gas are similar to those used for oil.

Oil flowing from an oil well is called *crude oil*. After fitting valves to control the flow of crude oil, oil is pumped from the well and carried away by pipeline, tanker ship, rail or road to a refinery. Natural gas is produced from wells both on land and offshore. It is carried from the gas-producing areas by long-distance pipelines or as a liquid by tanker ships.

At the refinery

At the refinery, crude oil is separated into several substances, starting with a process called *fractional distillation*. This takes place inside a tall distillation tower. The crude oil is heated until most of its liquids boil and turn into vapours. These vapours rise up, cool, and become liquids again at different temperatures, so they flow out of the tower at different levels. The thicker heavier liquids are broken down further in a process called cracking, making more petrol and light oils.

▶ At an oil refinery, crude oil is separated into different substances, called fractions, inside a distillation tower.

▲ Workers on an oil rig are known as 'roughnecks'. They may have living quarters on the rig itself, although for safety reasons they often live on a separate platform.

find out more
Energy
Greenhouse effect
Plastics
Pollution
Rocks and minerals

• It is estimated that the world's supply of oil will only last for another 30 to 60 years.

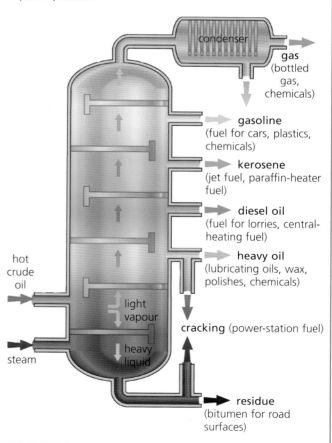

Operas and musicals

Operas and musicals are like plays set to music. They tell stories through words and songs and sometimes through dance.

Operas have little or no spoken dialogue and are usually set to classical music, whereas musicals generally have quite a lot of spoken dialogue and use more modern music.

Operas

Opera was invented in Italy towards the end of the 16th century. Musicians took stories from Greek and Roman myths and fitted them with songs and a musical accompaniment.

For many years opera was chiefly an entertainment for the very rich. Many aristocrats had private opera houses and companies of singers, while others regularly visited theatres that specialized in opera.

In the mid-18th century, towns and cities throughout Europe began to build public opera houses, and operatic fashions changed. The stories of many 19th and 20th century operas are political, about kings, queens and revolutionaries of the past. Operas are also based on stories of love, jealousy and murder.

The main parts in operas are performed by solo singers. Sometimes their music is like a conversation. This type of singing is known as *recitative*. But at high points in the story the singers may express their feelings in big solo songs called *arias*. At other times the singers join together in duets (two voices), trios (three voices), and so on. Many operas also have *choruses*. These are choirs of people who play crowds of soldiers, villagers, or whatever other kind of people the story needs.

Musicals

Musicals have their origins in 19th-century operettas ('little operas'). In operettas, songs and spoken dialogue were used to tell stories that were often comic and fantastical, with complicated stage sets and exotic costumes. Proper musicals began in the USA in the late 1920s and 1930s in the heyday of dancers such as Fred Astaire. Dancing was more important in musicals than in operettas, and the stories were usually about ordinary people.

The first film musical was *The Jazz Singer* (1927). Film-makers realized they could do many things on film that were not possible on stage, and film musicals became all-singing, all-dancing extravaganzas with little regard given to plot or storyline.

Fashions changed again in the 1940s, however, and a new kind of musical developed that has remained popular to this day. These musicals have a proper storyline which is highlighted by songs and dances: all three aspects are equally important. These musicals were originally performed on stage, but many, including *West Side Story* (1957), *The Sound of Music* (1959) and *Grease* (1972), were also made into hugely popular films.

▼ *Starlight Express* is one of London's longest-running musicals. It is unusual in that the performers wear rollerskates, and at times they skate amongst the audience on specially designed tracks.

Some famous operas
Orfeo, Monteverdi (1607)
The Marriage of Figaro, Mozart (1786)
The Barber of Seville, Rossini (1816)
La Traviata, Verdi (1853)
Carmen, Bizet (1875)
Madama Butterfly, Puccini (1904)
Salome, Richard Strauss (1905)

Some famous musicals
Showboat, Kern (1927)
Oklahoma!, Rodgers and Hammerstein (1943)
The Sound of Music, Rodgers and Hammerstein (1959)
West Side Story, Bernstein (1957)
Evita, Lloyd Webber and Rice (1978)
Les Misérables, Boubil and Schonberg (1985)

find out more
Classical music
Dance
Films
Singing and songs

◀ In the 17th century many operas were put on by rich noblemen at their own expense. These operas often involved fantastic scenery and a huge cast dressed in elaborate costumes. This opera, based on a story from Roman mythology, was staged at the court of the French king Louis XIV at Versailles.

Operations

A medical operation is the treatment of a disease or injury by going into the body and removing or repairing the damaged part. Operations are usually performed in hospital in rooms called operating theatres. The doctors who carry out operations are called *surgeons.*

An operation involves a team of people and several machines. First the *anaesthetist* gives the patient an anaesthetic, a drug that stops them feeling pain. This may be a local anaesthetic, under which the patient stays awake while the operation is being carried out. A general anaesthetic makes the patient totally unconscious and unaware of anything.

The chief surgeon performs the operation using special surgical instruments, and is helped by assistant surgeons. An operation is also attended by nurses specially trained to work in an operating theatre. Other people operate special machines, such as X-ray equipment or a heart–lung machine. When the surgeon has completed the operation, he or she may leave an assistant to stitch up the incision (cut). Then the patient will be returned to a ward to recover from the operation.

Types of surgery

In *transplant surgery* surgeons replace or repair parts of the body with parts from other people. *Microsurgery* is used for operations such as those on the eye, the inner ear, the brain and the spinal cord. The part of the body being treated is greatly magnified by a special microscope and the surgeon uses very tiny instruments to carry out the work.

Keyhole surgery is the popular name for a method of operating called 'minimally invasive

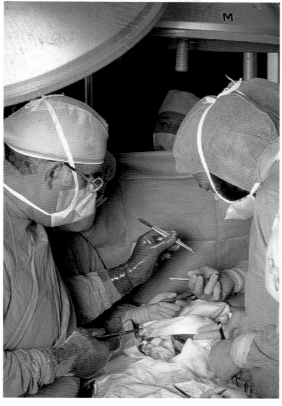

◀ Surgeons performing a kidney transplant operation in Minneapolis, USA.

surgery'. The surgeon passes a flexible telescope or camera through three or four small incisions (cuts) in the skin, and examines the patient. Certain operations can be performed using keyhole surgery, without the need for a large incision. In *cryosurgery*, extreme cold is used to remove unwanted tissue, such as cataracts or cancerous growths.

▶ FLASHBACK ◀

Operations have been performed for thousands of years, especially to repair broken bones and to treat wounds. Skulls more than 10,000 years old have been found with holes drilled in them. This operation, called trepanning, was probably done in the belief that it would release evil spirits from the patient's head. During the Middle Ages, surgery was dirty, painful and dangerous. Simple operations, such as pulling teeth and blood-letting, were often carried out by barbers, who had little or no training.

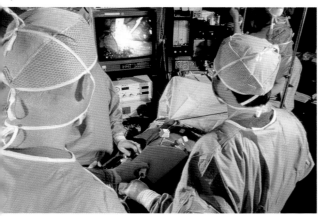

◀ These surgeons in a hospital in Hong Kong are removing a gall bladder by keyhole surgery. They are using an instrument called a laparoscope, which contains a tiny camera. This camera provides a view of the gall bladder on the screen, which the other surgeons use to guide their instruments and remove the gall bladder without the need for large incisions.

● In the past, three main problems made operations particularly dangerous for the patient: pain, risk of infection and shock caused by bleeding or infection. In modern surgery, these problems have largely been solved.

● The most operations carried out in one day were 833 cataract operations performed by Dr M. C. Modi in India.

find out more

Diseases
Doctors
Hospitals
Lasers
Medicine
Scanners

Orchestras and bands

Orchestras and bands are groups of people who play musical instruments together. There are many different kinds of orchestra and band across the world, including Japanese gagaku ensembles, Russian balalaika orchestras and Jamaican steel bands. Pop groups are also often known as bands.

• In Japan, gagaku is the name for the court orchestra. Gagaku music is probably the oldest type of orchestral music in the world. The gagaku orchestra can range in size from a chamber orchestra of about 20 people to large 'symphony' orchestras with over 100 players.

In Western countries, an orchestra always includes stringed instruments, often with the addition of woodwind, brass and percussion instruments. In contrast, a band is usually made up of woodwind, brass and percussion instruments.

Development of the orchestra

In ancient Greek theatres the orchestra was the name given to the semicircular area in front of the stage, where the chorus sang and danced. In the 16th and 17th centuries, when the first orchestras were formed to accompany operas, they too played in front of the stage. The term 'orchestra' was gradually transferred from the area to the players themselves.

Soon composers began to write for the orchestra on its own. The most famous orchestra of the late 17th and 18th centuries belonged to the glittering court of King Louis XIV of France. It was called 'The King's Twenty-four Violins', and the king employed composers to write stately, graceful music for it. His most influential composer and conductor was Italian-born Jean-Baptiste Lully.

There was no standard structure for the orchestra until the 18th century, when

▲ Part of the string section of a youth orchestra. The development of the orchestra has had a lot to do with the success of the string section. During the reign of Louis XIV, the king's highly successful group of string players started to play with groups of oboe- and bassoon-players. Since then, the orchestra has grown and the strings have remained at its centre.

orchestras became more organized, with instruments divided into string, woodwind and brass sections. Composers such as Haydn and Mozart wrote concertos and symphonies for these skilful orchestras. During this time, the average orchestra contained between 30 and 40 players. But

► The arrangement of a modern symphony orchestra.

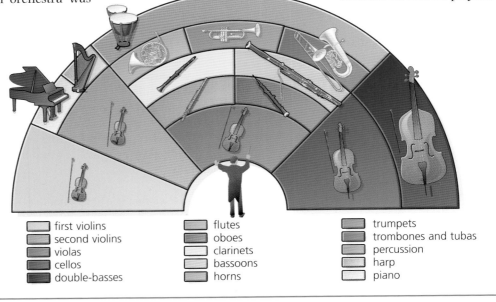

first violins	flutes	trumpets
second violins	oboes	trombones and tubas
violas	clarinets	percussion
cellos	bassoons	harp
double-basses	horns	piano

over the next century, the orchestra grew rapidly to over 100 players for works by Romantic composers such as Berlioz and Mahler.

In the 19th century, public concert halls were built in many towns and cities. Today, the world's best-known orchestras are linked to specific cities, such as the New York Philharmonic and the Royal Concertgebouw Orchestra of Amsterdam.

The modern orchestra

Most modern orchestras in the Western tradition play a wide variety of music, from classical symphonies by Mozart or Haydn to 20th-century works by Aaron Copland or Michael Tippett. Orchestras accompany solo instrumentalists and singers as well as choruses. They may play for operas or ballets, record background music for films or television commercials, or play backing tracks for pop and rock bands.

Orchestras come in many sizes, from the large symphony orchestra to much smaller groups called chamber orchestras. Professional orchestras are made up of highly skilled musicians, who are paid for playing their instruments. But there are also many amateur orchestras in

schools, colleges and towns, in which people play for fun.

Most of these orchestras have a conductor. The conductor, usually holding a white stick called a baton, directs the orchestra, indicating the beat and interpreting the music.

The leader, or concert-master, of an orchestra is the senior violinist, who sits at the front of the first-violin section and helps the conductor with musical direction. In most countries, the leader takes a solo bow at the start of each concert, just before the conductor walks on stage.

Bands

A band is usually made up of woodwind, brass and percussion instruments.

Some bands are named after the type of instruments they include. All the instruments in a *brass band* are of the 'brass' family, except for some

percussion. The most common ones are cornets, flugelhorns, saxhorns, trombones and tubas. Brass bands tend to play for outdoor occasions.

A *wind band* combines woodwind instruments including the flute, oboe, clarinet and bassoon with military instruments such as trumpets and trombones. Wind bands play a wide variety of music, from classical to pop.

Other types of band are named after the kind of music that the band plays. In the past *military bands* played an active role in a fighting force, helping soldiers march in step and encouraging them in battle. Today, military bands are mostly for show, playing at state occasions and for parades.

Marching bands are really simplified military bands that play less complicated music. They often appear at special events such as sports competitions.

Jazz band describes almost any group of musicians who play jazz together. However, when there are 10 players or more playing from written-out music, it is known as 'big band'.

◀ The gamelan is the traditional orchestra of Indonesia. It is made up of instruments such as tuned gongs, xylophones, metallophones (with bars of metal), cymbals, drums, flutes and fiddles. Its sound inspired many 20th-century Western composers, including Claude Debussy, Benjamin Britten and John Cage.

• Brass bands started in Britain in the 19th century. Mill- and mine-owners bought brass instruments and encouraged their workers to learn to play. Today, many schools, factories and towns still have their own brass bands.

◀ Steel bands were first formed in the Caribbean island of Trinidad in the 1940s. The players play tuned oil drums, called 'pans'. The traditional music of steel bands is called calypso, but today they also play arrangements of other types of music.

find out more
Classical music
Jazz
Music
Musical instruments
Operas and musicals
Pop and rock music
Theatres
World music

Ottoman empire

A Turkish leader, Uthman, founded the Ottoman kingdom in north-east Turkey in the 14th century. The Ottoman empire was at the height of its power in the 16th and 17th centuries. Altogether the Ottoman family ruled for more than 600 years.

The Ottoman Turks and their empire took their name from Uthman (1258–1326). The capital of their empire, Constantinople, was captured from the Byzantine emperor in 1453. To win the city, Mehmed II, the Turkish sultan, had his ships dragged overland to the harbour to bypass Constantinople's sea defences.

The sultan was the religious head over all Muslims within the empire. All his ministers and servants were originally military slaves, and so were his personal troops, the Janissaries. They were taken as boys from the Balkan lands, spent all their lives in barracks and were not allowed to marry.

In 1683 the Ottoman army threatened to capture Vienna but Austrian and Polish troops turned them back. From about 1800 the empire began to break up. The Greeks fought and won their independence in 1829.

In World War I, the Turks fought on the side of Germany and Austria and were defeated in 1918. The lands of the old empire became independent countries and the new Republic of Turkey was created in Asia Minor.

▶ The greatest of the sultans was Suleiman the Magnificent, who ruled from 1520 to 1566. He filled his court with painters, poets and craftsmen, and employed architects to build aqueducts, bridges, public baths and mosques.

● Constantinople actually became Istanbul after the Turks took over in the 15th century, but the name was not officially changed until the Turkish Post Office changed it in 1926.

find out more
Balkans
Byzantine empire
Holy Roman Empire
Middle East
Turkey

Owens, Jesse

Jesse Owens was an outstanding black athlete who set world records in sprints, hurdles and the long jump. Today, he is best known for his role in the 1936 Berlin Olympics, where his feats on the track helped to expose the stupidity of Hitler's racist ideas.

In May 1935 Jesse Owens, a 22-year-old student at Ohio State University, took part in a college track meeting. Within 45 minutes he had equalled the world record for the 100-yard sprint, and broken the records for the 220-yard sprint, the 220-yard hurdles and the long jump.

In the following year, 1936, the Olympic Games were held in Berlin, Germany. Adolf Hitler,

the leader of Nazi Germany, hoped that the Games would help to prove his theory that the 'Aryan race' of white Europeans was superior to all other people. He felt sure that such white athletes, particularly the specially chosen German ones, would win most of the gold medals.

Jesse Owens – a black athlete – proved Hitler very wrong, finishing the Olympics with four gold medals. Even the Germans themselves recognized that this black athlete had proved himself the outstanding sportsman of the Games. There was nothing Hitler could do to destroy the symbolic value of Owens's triumphs.

After retiring from athletics, Owens took on a role in public life. He was heavily involved in community work, especially with youngsters.

Born 1913 in Alabama, USA
Died 1980 aged 67

● Jesse Owens's first name was really a nickname. It came from the initials of his real names, James Cleveland – J. C., hence 'Jesse'.

◀ Owens winning gold in Berlin. In winning four gold medals, he equalled the Olympic record for the 100 m, broke the Olympic records for the 200 m and the long jump, and ran the final leg in the world-record-breaking US 4 × 100-m relay team.

find out more
Athletics
Hitler, Adolf

Oxygen

Oxygen is a gas which makes up one-fifth of the air we breathe. There is more oxygen on Earth than anything else, although most of the atoms of oxygen are combined with those of other substances. Oxygen atoms combine with atoms of hydrogen to make water.

When fuels such as oil and natural gas burn, they combine with oxygen and give out heat

energy and carbon dioxide. This process is called *combustion*. When materials combine with the oxygen in air, they 'oxidize' (this happens when iron rusts).

Living things need oxygen to release energy from their food. This process, which is called *respiration*, takes place in the cells of their bodies. As animals respire, they take oxygen from the air. Plants, on the other hand, give out oxygen into the air.

► FLASHBACK ◄

Joseph Priestley, an English chemist, discovered oxygen (although he gave it a different name) in the late 1700s. Around the same time in

◄ Welders burn a mixture of oxygen and other gases in their torches. The mixture produces a very high flame temperature that can melt steel.

France, Antoine-Laurent Lavoisier realized that air contains two gases: 'oxygen' and 'azote' (which we now call nitrogen).

▼ This patient is receiving oxygen treatment inside a pressure chamber. Pure oxygen helps to speed the healing process in people suffering from gas poisoning, ulcers and burns.

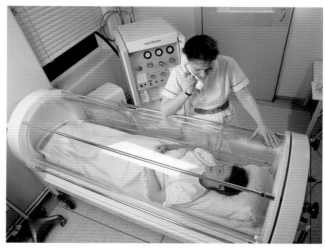

find out more
Air
Breathing
Elements
Gases, liquids and solids
Plants
Pollution
Water

Pacific Islands

There are about 10,000 islands in the Pacific Ocean, spread over a very large area. The islands can be divided into three regions: Micronesia, Melanesia and Polynesia.

Each island region has a distinct group of people with its own way of life. Melanesians are dark-skinned and live in the south-west Pacific. Polynesians are lighter skinned, and live in the eastern Pacific. Micronesians live in the western Pacific.

Most of the islands are coral reefs and volcanic peaks. Coconut palms provide copra (dried coconut flesh) and coconut oil, both important exports. Bananas, pineapples and other tropical fruits are also grown.

► FLASHBACK ◄

Europeans first came to the islands in the 18th century. They brought new diseases that killed many people, and gradually took more land

from the native peoples. During World War II the islands saw battles between the USA and Japan. Several islands have been used to test atomic bombs.

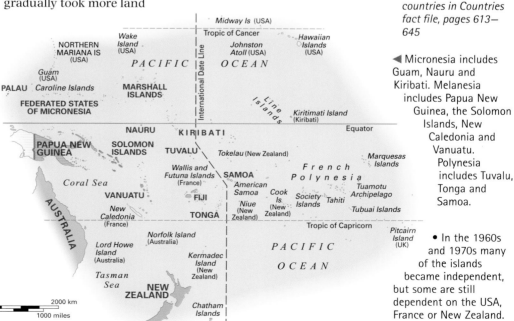

find out more
Australia
Cook, James
Islands
New Zealand
See also individual countries in Countries fact file, pages 613–645

◄ Micronesia includes Guam, Nauru and Kiribati. Melanesia includes Papua New Guinea, the Solomon Islands, New Caledonia and Vanuatu. Polynesia includes Tuvalu, Tonga and Samoa.

• In the 1960s and 1970s many of the islands became independent, but some are still dependent on the USA, France or New Zealand.

Oysters *see* Mussels and oysters • **Ozone** *see* Pollution • **Paint** *see* Paints and dyes

Painting

People paint pictures for many different reasons. Today lots of people paint as a hobby, purely for pleasure, but in the past almost all paintings were done for a specific purpose and often for a particular place.

There are many different kinds of painting. Paintings vary in many ways – in style, subject, technique and size. Some paintings are so small that they can easily be held in the palm of the hand, while others are so large that they cover entire walls or the ceilings of grand churches or palaces.

Tools of the trade

Artists have used a great variety of materials and tools to create paintings. Most of the paintings that you see in art galleries are done in oil colours on canvas. These materials have been very popular from the 15th century to the present day because they are so adaptable. *Canvas*, a rough cloth made of linen or cotton, can be cut easily to any size or shape and weighs much less than wooden panels, which

had previously been the most popular surface for movable paintings. In *oil colours* the pigment (colour) is mixed with linseed oil or some other vegetable oil. This kind of paint can be used to create all manner of different effects.

Before oil paint was developed, the most popular kind of paint was *tempera*. In this the base, or 'medium', is egg rather than oil. Tempera paint can produce beautiful, detailed results, but it is harder to use than oil paint because it is difficult to blend. The artist has to use lots of tiny strokes of the brush, building up effects gradually.

Two other painting techniques have been of particular importance in the history of art. *Fresco*, which is used for large-scale paintings on walls or ceilings, is a difficult technique that involves painting quickly on wet plaster. *Watercolour* is generally used for fairly small pictures on paper. The medium is usually gum arabic and the paints are diluted with water.

The pigments used in paint have been made from many different substances, including clays, rocks, metal ores and minerals. In the 20th century many bright new colours have been made from dyes, and in the 1940s artists began using a new type of paint called *acrylic*. This has some of the qualities of oil paint, but it is soluble in water and dries much more quickly than oils. Many professional artists now prefer it to oil paint.

Apart from canvas, wood, paper and walls, artists have used many other surfaces as a 'support' for painting. These include metal, glass, slate, ivory (used particularly for miniature portraits), and silk, which is very popular in Chinese painting.

▲ Jan van Eyck's *The Arnolfini Marriage* (1434) is a fine example of his skill in handling oil paint. Van Eyck was a master of exquisite detail. He has painted a reflection of the main scene in the mirror at the back of the room. If you look closely you can see a figure in blue between the other two. This is the artist.

▶ The ceiling of the Sistine Chapel, Rome. From 1508 to 1512 Michelangelo worked on top of a 20-m-high scaffolding to paint a massive series of ceiling frescos. The painting turned out to be one of the most astonishing creations in the history of art. This part tells the story of Adam and Eve's expulsion from Paradise.

Religious painting

The earliest paintings that we know of were done on the walls and ceilings of caves about 30,000 years ago. Many experts think that these paintings had some kind of religious or magical purpose. They may have been part of rituals to help the people who painted them to have success in hunting the animals shown.

Religion has certainly played a major part in the painting of most cultures of the world. In Europe, it was virtually the only subject for a period of about 1000 years, from the fall of the Roman empire in the 5th century to the Renaissance in the 15th century. During this time religion dominated the lives of most people, and they took great pride in decorating their local church. At a time when most people could not read, paintings on the church walls helped them to understand the teachings of the Bible.

Broadening horizons

During the 15th century other subjects became popular in painting, particularly portraits and mythological scenes. Mythology had been one of the main subjects in Greek and Roman painting, but Sandro

Botticelli was the first artist since ancient times to paint really large and imposing mythological scenes.

It was not until the 17th century that landscape and still life – two of the most popular subjects today – became fully established in Europe. They flourished mainly in the Netherlands, and it was there that paintings began to have the same kind of mass appeal that they have today.

Painting as self-expression

In order to make a living, artists had to paint pictures that they thought would appeal to other people, but some artists began to regard painting as a way of expressing their feelings. The personalities of great painters had always come through in their work, but the desire for intense self-expression did not become common until the early 19th century.

Since then, the subject of painting has gradually come to be regarded as less important than an artist's personal treatment of it. Eventually the subject matter disappeared altogether in the form of abstract art. The first purely

▲ This 14th-century painting showing grooms feeding horses is by the Chinese artist Jen Jen-Far. Chinese paintings were usually done in ink and watercolour. Some pictures were never displayed, but taken out of a box to contemplate, rather like opening a book to read a poem.

• Brushes are the painter's chief tools. They are usually made from animal hairs. Badger, donkey, cat, ermine, mink and camel are some that have been used. Bristle brushes are made from tough, hard-wearing hair from pigs. They are used for oil painting. Sable brushes are fine and soft, made from hairs from the tail-tip of a mink or similar animal. These brushes are best for watercolour painting. Many modern brushes are made of nylon.

◄ This watercolour of a Swiss Alpine landscape is by the English painter J. M. W. Turner (1775–1851). He was particularly interested in light and colour. Watercolour can be used very quickly, so it is ideal for sketching out of doors. The paper usually shows through the paint to some extent, and this can produce delicate and subtle effects.

◄ *Rouen Cathedral* by Claude Monet (1840–1926). Monet was one of the greatest French Impressionist painters. These painters used dabs of bright colour, which merged together, creating hazy, dappled images of flickering light and shade.

In addition to this type of personal style, there are other kinds of style, national or regional style. For example, a typical Chinese painting looks completely different to a typical European painting. It is done in a different technique, like a sort of ink drawing, and shows a different outlook on life, often one that is more mystical. In the same way there may be various clues that help to indicate the period in which a picture was painted, because artists working at the same time often share similarities of outlook.

Like-minded artists sometimes deliberately group together to explore ways of painting in a particular style. One of the most famous of these groups (or 'schools') were the Impressionists in late 19th-century France. These painters wanted to break away from traditional subjects and to paint life in a fresh way. Instead of showing things in great detail, they tried to give an impression of what the eye sees at any moment. At first many people found Impressionist paintings shocking. Now they are among the most popular of all paintings.

◄ This watercolour, *Swinging*, is by Vassily Kandinsky (1866–1944), one of the first artists to paint totally abstract pictures. In this kind of art, lines, colours, shapes, patterns and textures exist for their own sake rather than to represent something.

abstract pictures were painted in about 1910, and abstraction has been one of the most important approaches to art ever since.

Styles of painting

Style is a distinctive way of doing something. Sometimes an artist has such an individual style that we can tell at a glance that he or she has painted a particular picture. Botticelli's style, for example, is exquisitely graceful, whereas van Gogh's style is marked by a highly personal use of energetic, thickly textured brushstrokes, and strong, sometimes dazzling colour.

Some famous painters

The Italian **Giotto** (about 1267–1337) was a very influential medieval painter. He painted frescos of religious subjects.

The Flemish painter Peter Paul **Rubens** (1577–1640) painted biblical and mythological scenes that were bold and full of colour.

The Dutch painter Jan **Vermeer** (1632–1675) specialized in everyday scenes of Dutch people. His use of light and colour gave calm to his paintings.

Vincent **van Gogh** (1853–1890) painted ordinary things: a chair, his bedroom, a bunch of sunflowers. His excited, bold brushstrokes show deep emotion and a sort of frenzy.

The Mexican Diego **Rivera** (1886–1957) painted huge murals (wall paintings) with scenes from the life and history of ordinary Mexican people.

The Spanish painter Salvador **Dalí** (1904–1989) is one of the most famous artists of the 20th century. His paintings portray very weird scenes, like images from a dream.

find out more

Cartoons
Drawing
Leonardo da Vinci
Michelangelo
Picasso, Pablo
Prehistoric people
Renaissance

Paints and dyes

Paints are coloured coatings put on houses, vehicles and other firm surfaces to make them look better, and to protect them from the weather and air pollution. Dyes are chemicals that change the colour of materials.

• Around 3000 years ago, the Phoenicians made a magnificent purple dye, called Tyrian purple, from the juices of crushed sea-snails. In Roman times, only the emperor was allowed to wear cloth dyed with Tyrian purple.

• The vehicle used to make the first paints was animal fat. Later, gum arabic, gelatine, egg-white and beeswax were used to make paint.

▲ A scene inside a paint factory. The vats contain a yellow fluid that is to be used as a liquid pigment in the manufacture of paint. The yellow colour of the pigment comes from iron oxide.

▶ This man in Gujrat, north India, is using a method called 'tie and dye' to add coloured patterns to a piece of cloth. The cloth is knotted, sewn, bunched or twisted, or small objects are sewn into it. When the cloth is dipped in dye, the tied areas are not coloured by dye.

find out more
Colour
Painting
Textiles

The first paints and dyes were made from natural materials such as clays, rock ores and plants. Most modern paints and dyes are made from chemicals.

Paints

Paint consists mainly of two types of substance – pigments and vehicles. The *pigments*, the coloured parts of paint, are usually in the form of fine powders. The *vehicles* get their name because they carry the pigment of the paint. They are liquids that dry to a tough film, binding the pigment to the surface being painted.

The pigments and vehicles in modern paints are mostly made artificially. In a paint factory, the pigment particles and vehicle are mixed together in a machine called a mill. Some-times special machines whirl sand through the paint at high speed to mix it thoroughly.

Paints are made in thousands of different colours and for all purposes. Paints for outdoor use need to be hard-wearing. They contain plenty of special oils, which make them slow to dry but give a hard, glossy finish. Some indoor paints, such as those used on walls and ceilings, consist mainly of water and contain no oil. Special paints are made to cover metal surfaces, to resist heat or to prevent mould.

Dyes

At one time, dyes were made from plants and animals. For example, saffron, a yellow dye, comes from the crocus plant. A red dye that has been used to colour army uniforms (and can be used as a food colouring) comes from the cochineal insect of South America. Today, the chemical industry makes thousands of different-coloured dyes, called synthetic dyes. When cloth is dyed, special chemicals called mordants are used to help the dye penetrate the fabric and stay fixed. If you have done any dyeing at home, you may have used salt as a mordant. When dyes cannot be washed out and do not fade, we say that they are fast.

▶ FLASHBACK ◀

People painted pictures in caves in France and Spain as early as 30,000 BC. The earliest pigments were obtained from clays and other rocks and metal ores. Five thousand years ago, the ancient Egyptians crushed minerals such as malachite and cinnabar to make pigments. They dyed wool, silk and cotton with beautiful colours obtained from berries and plants. The Greeks made a blue-green colour called verdigris from copper suspended over vinegar.

In the Middle Ages people obtained new pigments from plants and by burning minerals. In 1828 a synthetic blue was manufactured from soda, china clay, coal and sulphur. The first synthetic dye was made in 1856 using chemicals obtained from coal tar.

Pakistan

Pakistan is a country in south-west Asia, with the mighty River Indus at its centre. The Indus flows 2900 kilometres from the plateau of Tibet, passing around the Himalayas, through the Karakoram Mountains and south to the Arabian Sea.

The plains of the Indus make up about one-third of Pakistan. Here, the months of May to August are unpleasantly hot, while in mid-July the monsoon brings 400 to 500 millimetres of rain. Away from the Indus valley, much of the country is either mountainous or very dry. In the northern mountains it is often bitterly cold. The Karakorams have some large glaciers and very little grows there. In south-west Pakistan, Baluchistan is a hot, dry desert. In this region there are large gas fields from which gas is piped to the cities.

People

The Indus valley is where most Pakistanis live. The river's water is used to irrigate the land for food crops such as wheat, and especially cotton, which is Pakistan's main export. The largest city in Pakistan is Karachi, where over 5 million people live and work.

Pakistan is an Islamic nation. Almost all Pakistanis are Muslims, and Pakistan's laws are based on Islamic law. But though they share the same religion, there are many different ethnic groups within Pakistan, each with its own customs and culture. Punjabis, for example, cook their meat in a clay oven, called a tandoor, while

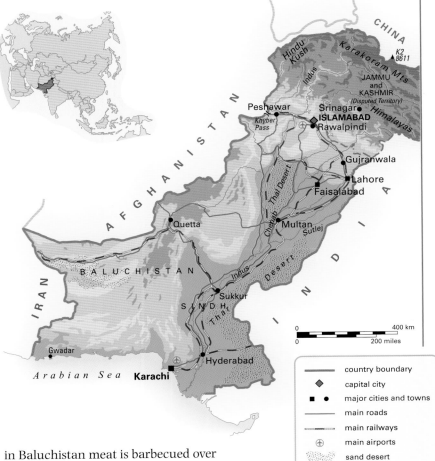

in Baluchistan meat is barbecued over an open fire and eaten as kebabs.

▶ FLASHBACK ◀

The Indus valley was the site of the great civilization of Harappa and Mohenjo-daro (about 2500–1600 BC). The invasion of Alexander the Great in the 4th century BC was the first of a series of invasions into the rich lands of the Indus valley and the Punjab (the land of the five rivers). Muslim rulers controlled the region from the 13th century until the 1750s, when the British East India Company began to take control.

From 1858, for almost a hundred years, Pakistan was part of British India. But when in 1947 India gained independence, it was divided into two nations: Pakistan and India. The new state of Pakistan was in two parts, West and East, separated by Indian territory. However, in 1971 East Pakistan became an independent nation, Bangladesh. Since Pakistan's independence, democratic government has alternated with times when the president has been an army officer.

▼ Cotton is Pakistan's most important crop. These women from the Punjab are drawing out and twisting thick cotton 'rope' into long, thin fibres.

Map labels: CHINA, Hindu Kush, Karakoram Mts, K2 8611, Indus, JAMMU and KASHMIR (Disputed Territory), Himalayas, AFGHANISTAN, Peshawar, Khyber Pass, Srinagar, ISLAMABAD, Rawalpindi, Gujranwala, Lahore, Faisalabad, Thal Desert, Chenab, Multan, Sutlej, Quetta, BALUCHISTAN, Indus, INDIA, Thar Desert, IRAN, Sukkur, SINDH, Gwadar, Hyderabad, Arabian Sea, Karachi

0 400 km
0 200 miles

Key:
— country boundary
◆ capital city
■ • major cities and towns
— main roads
main railways
⊕ main airports
sand desert
▲ high peaks (height in metres)
land height in metres
more than 5000
2000–5000
1000–2000
500–1000
200–500
less than 200
sea level

• The highest mountain in Pakistan is in the Karakorams. It is called K2 and is 8611 m high, making it the second highest mountain in the world.

find out more
Bangladesh
India
Ancient world
See also Countries fact file, page 634

Paper

Most of the paper that we use today has been made from wood pulp. The pulp comes mainly from coniferous trees such as pines and firs. We cut down millions of these trees each year to make paper, but most of them are specially grown for this purpose. We can also make perfectly good paper from waste paper, and many newspapers are now made from recycled paper.

The first stage in papermaking is to change the wood from the logs into wood pulp. They may be ground between heavy rollers or 'cooked' with chemicals to break the wood into fibres. These fibres are made into a thin slush, by adding water, and cleaned. 'Beaters' fray the fibres so that they will easily mat together. After this stage, chemicals and dyes may be mixed in.

At the 'wet end' of the papermaking machine, the liquid pulp goes onto a fast-moving belt of fine wire mesh. The water drains away or is sucked off. The remaining pulp, which still consists of about 80 per cent water, passes onto the rollers. They squeeze out even more water and press the fibres firmly together to form a 'web' of paper. It is dried by heated rollers before it finally emerges in a huge continuous roll.

▼ At the paper mill, wood pulp is obtained from logs. The pulp is cleaned, beaten, drained, pressed and dried before it finally emerges as a huge continuous roll of paper.

• Origami is the Japanese art of paper folding. Paper models are made by folding squares of coloured paper, without cutting or pasting. In Japan, origami is used to decorate gifts and religious shrines.

• Some paper is moistened and passed through heated rollers to give it a glossy surface. Other papers are given coatings of china clay to make high-quality paper for art and for printing.

find out more
Books
Materials
Recycling
Wood

Recycling paper

Paper can also be made from waste paper. When the waste paper is soaked in water, it breaks down into its original fibres. These can be used over and over again. At present only 25 per cent of the world's paper is recycled, but this amount could easily be increased to 75 per cent. For every tonne of waste paper collected and reused, at least two trees are saved. Waste paper is easy to collect, and many towns and cities have special paper banks where people can deposit their old newspapers and other waste paper. Many newspapers are printed on recycled paper which has been de-inked and cleaned.

► FLASHBACK ◄

In ancient Egypt, a form of writing material called papyrus was made from the stems of the papyrus reed. (The name 'paper' comes from papyrus.) Strips of reed were soaked in water to make them stick together. The sheet was hammered and dried, and then polished with ivory or a smooth shell.

True paper was first made in China about 1900 years ago. The Arabs learned the method from the Chinese in the 8th century, and Muslims took the industry to Spain. Paper was made in Europe during the Middle Ages, but it was rare and expensive. For centuries paper was made from plant fibres obtained from pulped cotton and linen rags. During the 19th century wood pulp replaced these plant fibres.

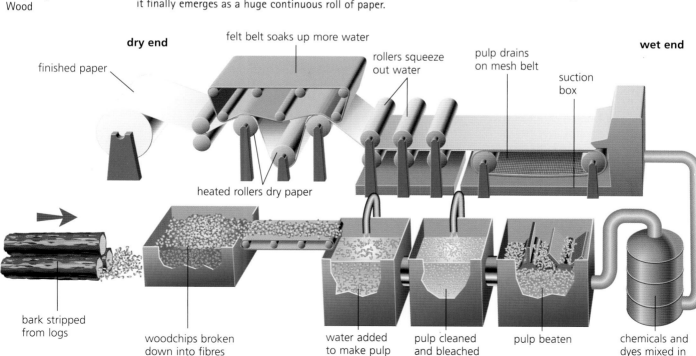

dry end — felt belt soaks up more water — rollers squeeze out water — pulp drains on mesh belt — suction box — **wet end**

finished paper

heated rollers dry paper

bark stripped from logs

woodchips broken down into fibres

water added to make pulp

pulp cleaned and bleached

pulp beaten

chemicals and dyes mixed in

Parachutes

A parachute slows the fall of a person or object through the air, or slows a landing aeroplane. Parachutes are used for military operations, for dropping supplies into areas far from roads or rivers, and for sport. The Space Shuttle uses huge parachutes to slow it down on landing.

A parachute, or 'canopy', is an umbrella-shaped bag, usually made of nylon. It resists the movement of the air past it, and acts as a brake. This helps to make the parachutist's landing a soft one. Sport parachutes may be small and arched, and are controlled by pulling on cords. They can glide and turn rather like hang-gliders. Surprisingly, they sometimes have holes in them to make them stable, and to stop them swinging. Military parachutes have a small parachute, called a drogue, to pull out the main one.

Skydiving

Skydiving is the popular name for parachuting sports. Skydivers make their jumps from specially prepared aircraft. They perform manoeuvres in the air, either before or after they open their parachutes. Sometimes they aim to land on a ground target.

The part of a jump before the parachute opens is called *freefall*. Skydivers can vary the speed of their fall and perform aerial manoeuvres by changing their body position. When teams of skydivers link up in special formations during freefall, it is called 'relative work'.

▼ More than 30 skydivers have linked up in the air to form a parachute pyramid. When teams of skydivers link up in special formations with their parachutes opened, it is called 'canopy relative work' (CRW).

• The first successful parachute was made of cloth over a bamboo frame. Its designer, André Garnerin, made a hazardous landing outside Paris in 1797.

• Any object falling to Earth reaches a certain speed limit called its 'terminal velocity'. It exists because of the air resistance on the falling object. For the average person this speed limit is nearly 200 kilometres per hour, and is reached in about 10 seconds.

find out more
Flight
Gliders and kites

Parks and gardens

Ever since people first settled in one place, they have wanted green space around them. The first gardens were places to grow food, herbs or medicines, but gradually flowers became more important. Public parks were first created in Victorian England, but the idea soon spread to Europe and America.

Victorian city parks had a range of exotic plants, often in large conservatories. Other attractions included aquariums, a bandstand, a playground, bowling greens and boating lakes. Today, many city parks are becoming more natural than in Victorian times, with wild-flower meadows and city woodlands instead of lawns and flower beds. On the edges of towns there are large country parks, where people can picnic and enjoy the fresh air.

Gardens for all occasions

In the medieval garden the main plants were herbs, grown either to flavour food or for use as medicines. Most of the big houses, mansions and stately homes of the past had very extensive gardens, but today European gardens tend to be smaller and easier to care for. Lawns are a common feature, because they are easy to maintain with a lawnmower. By contrast, traditional Japanese gardens are designed to strict rules. They use such things as raked sand, rugged rocks, and clipped shrubs to create a kind of miniature landscape. In the hot countries around the Mediterranean, fountains and pools are important features of gardens.

Famous parks
◆ Central Park, New York
◆ Bois de Boulogne, Paris
◆ Hyde Park, London
◆ Tiergarten, Berlin
◆ Disneyworld, Florida
◆ Legoland, Billund, Denmark

◄ A fairground ride at Alton Towers theme park, Derbyshire, UK. Theme parks are very different from other types of park. They are permanent fun-fairs, with rides, shooting galleries, restaurants, and other things to see and do.

Parliaments

Parliaments are law-making assemblies. They are an important part of the government of a country, known as the legislature. In democratic countries they are usually elected by voters.

- The US Congress has a Senate and a House of Representatives. The British parliament consists of the House of Lords and the House of Commons (which contains Members of Parliament, or MPs, elected by voters).

▶ The Althing of Iceland is the oldest parliament in the world. It has been meeting since AD 930.

Many countries, including Britain, Australia, Canada and New Zealand, call their law-making bodies assemblies or parliaments. In the United States of America the law-making body is called Congress; in Norway it is called Storting; and in Israel it is the Knesset.

Apart from making laws, parliaments may also have the power to keep a watch on government. The US president can only spend money if his budget is approved by Congress. Many parliaments have committees, which may meet before the press and TV cameras, to make sure that government ministers act properly.

Most members of parliament belong to a political party, which is a group of politicians who share similar ideas. Some parliaments are dominated by two or three main parties. In parliaments with a large number of parties, parties often form alliances (called coalitions) to gain more power. When one party (or a coalition of parties) has more than half the members of parliament, it is effectively in control of the parliament because it should be able to win any vote. It can form a government and choose policies. The other party (or parties) becomes the opposition, offering alternative views on political issues.

find out more
Democracy
Elections
European Union
Government

Peace movement

There are more than 1400 peace groups in the world, with a membership of millions. The peace movement is a worldwide opposition to war.

- There are a number of environmental groups such as Friends of the Earth and Greenpeace (both founded in 1969), which have many of the same aims as the peace movement itself.

Peace campaigns often focus on nuclear weapons, but the numerous peace organizations do differ in their aims, some wanting an end to all weapons manufacture, others simply opposed to any increase in arms. The peace movement began almost as soon as the first atomic bomb was dropped on Hiroshima, Japan, in 1945. The development of the more lethal hydrogen bomb led to the first mass rallies in the 1950s.

In the 1960s the peace movement switched its attention from nuclear weapons to war. In the USA and in Europe huge demonstrations forced the US government to withdraw from the Vietnam War. Later, many Europeans protested against the US nuclear missile bases in Europe. With the end of the 'cold war', when the communist countries and the USA and its allies ceased to be political enemies, the movement felt one of its main aims had been achieved.

find out more
Vietnam War
Weapons

▼ Crowds of anti-nuclear protesters at a rally in Germany.

Pelé

Born 1940 in Três Corações, Brazil

Pelé is generally considered to be the greatest football player of all time. He starred in Brazil's World Cup-winning teams of 1958 and 1970.

• In his long footballing career Pelé scored a record 1217 goals in 1254 first-class matches, including 76 in his 92 full internationals.

Edson Arantes do Nascimento was given the nickname 'Pelé' when he played football as a boy. He showed so much promise for his junior team that he was signed by the top Brazilian club Santos. The following year, when he was only 16, he was picked to play for Brazil. A year later, in 1958, he scored two goals to help Brazil beat Sweden 5–2 in the World Cup final, having scored three against France in the semi-finals.

Brazil won the World Cup again in 1962, but Pelé missed the final after being injured in their second match. He was hurt again in the 1966 World Cup, in England, when he was repeatedly and brutally fouled as Brazil were knocked out in the first stage. However, Pelé made up for this failure in 1970 in Mexico, when he again inspired Brazil to World Cup victory.

Pelé retired in 1974, but the following year he signed a deal to play in the newly established North American League for the New York Cosmos, and he led them to the title in 1977.

Throughout his long career, Pelé showed that he was the complete footballer. He had all the gifts of control, dribbling, passing and shooting, as well as great vision and inventiveness. In addition, he was a wonderful ambassador for the game.

▶ Pelé heads the ball past an Italian defender in the 1970 World Cup final in Mexico City. Brazil went on to beat Italy 4–1 and so to win the championship for the third time.

find out more
Football

Pests and parasites

find out more
Diseases
Fleas and lice
Flies and mosquitoes
Slugs and snails
Weeds
Worms

Any living thing that harms humans or human activities can be called a pest. A parasite is a living thing that steals food and shelter from another animal or plant, but gives nothing in return.

▼ These fish lice are parasites of fishes.

In some cases, parasites can also be pests. The varroa mite, which is a parasite on honey bees, is also a serious pest as it weakens the entire bee colony. Infections of varroa have affected honey production in many countries.

Pests

Most pests affect our food in some way, either by eating food crops or by causing disease. Some bacteria and fungi cause diseases in food plants. Insect pests include mosquitoes, which spread disease among animals by drinking their blood, and aphids, which weaken crops by feeding on their sap. Snails and slugs are pests in the garden, and rats and mice can be pests in the house.

Plant pests are often controlled by the use of chemicals called pesticides, which kill the pest but not the plant. Pesticides can cause damage to the environment, so farmers may also use other types of pest control. They may grow crops that are resistant to some pests, or release animals that feed on the pests.

Parasites

The animal or plant that a parasite lives on is called its *host*. Animal parasites like fleas and lice live on the skin of their hosts. They are called *external parasites*. Other parasites, such as tapeworms and hookworms, are *internal parasites*, that live inside their hosts.

A parasite of a large or long-lived host does not generally kill it, but can weaken it and may cause disease. Parasites of small creatures such as insects are often of a similar size to the host, which they usually kill.

Pets

Pets are animals that we keep for company, comfort and affection. We share our lives – and often our homes – with them and we care for them as if they were part of the family.

It is important to be sure that you really want a pet and can care for it for all of its life. Many people get a pet, particularly a young one such as a kitten or a puppy, and then decide a few months or years later that they do not want it any more. Each year, animal rescue organizations take in hundreds of thousands of unwanted pets.

Before you decide to get a pet, you need to ask yourself several questions. Have you got the time to look after a pet? All pets need regular attention throughout their lives. They must not be ignored because you are ill, on holiday, or can think of something better to do. Do you have enough space for a pet? For animals such as cats, dogs, rabbits and guinea pigs you really need a garden. Can you afford a pet? Small pets are usually the cheapest to look after, but you will need to buy bedding each week as well as food. If your pet becomes ill, will you be able to afford to take it to the vet?

▶ FLASHBACK ◀

We do not know exactly when people first began to keep pets, but in Israel there is a tomb where a human and a dog were buried together about 12,000 years ago. The dead person's hand rests on the dog's shoulder.

The pharaohs of ancient Egypt kept cats and dogs as pets.

▼ This boy from Malaysia has a pet loris, a small primate that normally lives in forests. Such animals do not make the best pets because they are used to living in the wild.

• Pets need a lot of care and attention. Dogs need to be taken for walks at least twice a day, and cats like to have easy access to outside areas. Pets that live in cages are easier to look after. These include hamsters, gerbils and guinea pigs. Perhaps the easiest pets to care for are fishes, although they need regular feeding and their aquariums need to be kept clean.

find out more
Cats
Dogs
Mice, squirrels and
  other rodents
Primates

Philippines

The Philippines is a country made up of 7107 islands scattered over a wide area of the Pacific Ocean. Together, they have a land area about the size of Italy. The capital, Manila, is on the largest island, Luzon.

The islands have three seasons: rainy from June to October, cool from November to February, and hot from March to May. Earthquakes are common, and there are several active volcanoes. This part of the Pacific Ocean also suffers from violent typhoons (hurricanes) between June and December.

Many of the islands were once covered by tropical rainforests. However, large areas of forest have been cut down and sold abroad. Rice is the main food crop, but there are also large farms producing crops for export, such as pineapples. The Philippines is rich in mineral resources. The most important of these is copper, but there are also deposits of gold, silver and iron ore.

The islands of the Philippines were ruled by Spain for over 300 years. The country was named after King Philip II of Spain. The USA took control for the first half of the 20th century, and the country became independent in 1946 after three years of Japanese occupation. Ferdinand Marcos became the country's president in 1965, but he was a harsh ruler. Opposition to him grew over many years, until in 1986 he was overthrown by a popular uprising. The leader of the opposition to Marcos, Corazon Aquino, was president until 1992, and since then there have been free elections to the presidency.

◀ Many rice fields in the Philippines are on steep hillsides. They are terraced in a series of steps, with a low wall to retain water.

find out more
Asia
Cereals
Pacific Islands
*See also Countries fact
file, page 635*

Philosophers

Early philosophers tried to work out answers to mighty problems, such as the meaning of life and the basis of right and wrong.

◀ A detail from Raphael's painting *The School of Athens*, showing Plato (left) walking with Aristotle. At Plato's Academy Aristotle became a teacher himself, and also wrote books about politics and ethics — the study of whether behaviour is right or wrong.

Today most philosophers are far less ambitious and talk and write about the way we use ideas to understand our world. Take a word like 'fair', for example. Does it mean that everyone should be treated in exactly the same way? If you are sharing out a cake, is it fair to give everyone the same-size slice? Or does it mean that people should be treated in a way that is right for them – to give bigger slices to older children and smaller slices to younger children, who have smaller appetites? These are the sort of word problems that philosophers study.

Greek philosophers

There were three hugely influential philosophers in ancient Greece. Socrates (469–399 BC) was the first to use a set of rules, or logic, to discuss important matters. He also questioned the way people thought and acted.

We only know about Socrates's ideas because his follower Plato (429–347 BC) published them. Plato believed, like Socrates, that the right way to teach was to ask questions and let the pupils discover the answers for themselves.

The ideas of Aristotle (384–322 BC), who attended Plato's Academy, remained a key part of university education in Europe from the 13th to the 17th century. He was regarded as the supreme authority in science and philosophy for a long time.

• The word 'philosophy' comes from the Greek *philosophia*, which means 'love of wisdom'.

find out more
Greeks, ancient
Religions

Photocopiers

A photocopier is a machine that makes a copy of a document, for example a page of text, a drawing or a picture. The copy, which may be a black-and-white or a colour one, is called a photocopy.

Most photocopiers work by a process called *xerography* (pronounced 'zerography'), which uses light and static electricity. The drum inside a photocopier is charged with negative static electricity. When you press the copying button, a light shines onto the document to be copied. The white parts of the document reflect light onto the drum, knocking the negative charges off its surface. Dark parts of the document reflect no light onto the drum, leaving the negative charges in place on these areas of the drum.

The ink particles in the photocopier toner are positively charged so that they are attracted to the negatively charged parts of the drum. The toner then sticks to a clean sheet of paper that is pressed against the drum. The paper is then heated to melt the toner, and the copy is complete.

• Sophisticated photocopiers can make several copies of documents with hundreds of pages, and organize the pages in the right order. Some machines can make the original document bigger or smaller on the copy.

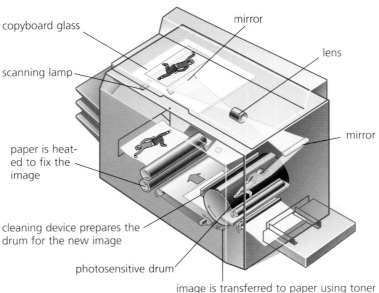

copyboard glass

mirror

scanning lamp

lens

paper is heated to fix the image

mirror

cleaning device prepares the drum for the new image

photosensitive drum

image is transferred to paper using toner

◀ A photocopier uses the process of xerography. The pattern of light and dark on the document being copied becomes a pattern of charge or no charge on the drum's surface.

find out more
Electricity
Fax machines
Paper
Printing

Photography

Photography is the art of taking pictures with a camera. It includes everything from deciding on a subject to developing and printing the photograph.

Many people take photographs for pleasure, often to create a record of holidays and family occasions. But photography has many other uses, for example in journalism, advertising, science and medicine.

This photograph of riders on a carousel at Hampstead Fair was taken in August 1923. The angle from which the picture has been taken makes the most of the way the people are being carried through the air.

Taking a picture

To take a good photograph, you need to think about how to *compose* it. The composition of a photograph includes how the subject is arranged, how it fills the frame, what shapes, colours and tones are present, and how light is used. Posed photographs are carefully arranged to achieve their effect. Unposed shots depend on capturing things as they happen.

Outdoor photography uses natural light. Skilled photographers can make good use of sunlight and shadows. In indoor photography the subject can be lit using a flash or lamps.

Developing and printing

After you have taken a photograph, the film has to be developed to make the image appear. Washing the film in chemical solutions changes it where it has been exposed to light. Usually the developed film is a *negative*. This means that areas that were light in the original image are dark on the film, while dark areas appear light. To make a positive image, light is shone through the negative onto a piece of light-sensitive paper. This is then developed to produce a *print*.

Many special effects can be used in developing and printing. A photograph can be cropped so that parts of it are not shown. Paint can be blown on with an airbrush. Images from separate photographs can be printed together to form a single picture.

Photographers

Newspaper photographers are present at all kinds of event – from sports competitions to political meetings and even wars. They try to take dramatic photographs for publication. Photojournalists are journalists who present the events they are reporting through photographs.

Studio photographers often take portraits of people or work with models. They take care arranging and lighting their subjects. Their photographs may appear in magazines and advertisements.

Scientific and medical photographers use special techniques to photograph specimens and experiments. In *photomicrography* a camera is attached to a microscope to photograph the structures of materials or cells. In *astronomical photography* images from Space are recorded on film exposed to light or other types of images collected by large telescopes.

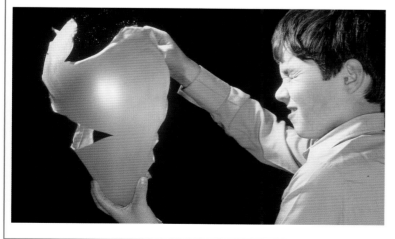

This photograph of a balloon bursting has been taken using high-speed photography. In this kind of photography the film may be exposed for as little as one-millionth of a second. It can be used to photograph rapid events such as explosions, or the flight of birds and insects.

Some famous photographers

Julia Margaret Cameron (1815–1879) created powerful, close-up portraits.

Dorothea Lange (1895–1965) was a photojournalist who took pictures of migrant workers in the USA in the 1930s.

Cecil Beaton (1904–1980) was a fashion and society photographer, who created highly decorative and beautiful images.

Henri Cartier-Bresson (1908–2004) was skilled at creating fully composed and expressive pictures out of the passing moment.

Robert Capa (1913–1954) was a war photographer famous for his grim photographs of death. He was killed by a land mine in Vietnam.

• Some cameras do not use film, but record digital images on magnetic discs or memory chips. These digital pictures can be transferred directly to computers to be altered before being printed.

find out more
Cameras
Films
Newspapers and magazines
Scanners
X-rays

Physics

Physics is the part of science concerned with discovering the basic forces and laws of the Universe. Physics tries to explain how matter and energy behave. Physicists try to understand everything, from the tiniest particles inside atoms to the creation of the whole Universe.

Physicists are interested in what happens to matter when it is cooled to almost absolute zero, or heated to the temperature at the centre of a star. They study how electrons move inside the materials used to make computer chips, how liquids flow, and how energy is transformed from one form to another.

The first scientist we would now call a 'physicist' was Galileo Galilei. His ideas and experiments helped Isaac Newton to develop his laws of motion and his theory of gravity. During the 18th century physicists gained a better understanding of heat and light, and also began to experiment with the mysterious forces of electricity and magnetism. The basic laws of electricity and magnetism were discovered in the 19th century by Michael Faraday, James Clerk Maxwell and others. In the late 1800s radioactivity and subatomic particles were observed for the first time.

The early 20th century saw some remarkable new ideas, including Einstein's theories of relativity. These gave a new understanding of time and space. The theory of quantum mechanics, developed by Max Planck and others, explains how matter behaves at the scale of the atom. Quantum theory made possible the incredible progress in electronics which led to the computer age.

find out more
Atoms and molecules
Einstein, Albert
Electricity
Electronics
Energy
Faraday, Michael
Galilei, Galileo
Gravity
Magnets
Newton, Isaac
Radiation

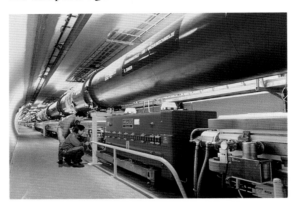

◄ Physicists at work inside the European particle physics laboratory near Geneva, Switzerland. Part of the laboratory's complex equipment is housed in this tunnel, which is built in a ring shape 27 km long.

Picasso, Pablo

| Born 1881 in Málaga, Spain |
| Died 1973 aged 91 |

Many people consider Pablo Picasso to be the greatest artist of the 20th century. He was very adventurous as a painter and sculptor, changing his style many times during his lifetime. He has also had a great influence on other artists.

• Picasso was successful with a wide range of artistic forms. He was famous for his drawings, paintings, collages, prints, theatre sets, sculptures and pottery.

find out more
Painting
Sculpture

Picasso hated school and never learned to write well, but from an early age he showed a truly exceptional talent for art. People soon realized that Picasso was a genius, but he wanted to do things in his own way, even if he disappointed those who expected him to become a traditional painter. When he was 23 Picasso left Spain and moved to Paris, France. He remained in France for the rest of his life.

As his extraordinary talents developed, Picasso constantly broke the rules of artistic tradition, often shocking the public with his strange and powerful paintings. He did not usually try to 'copy' real life; instead, he developed new forms to give fresh ways of looking at the world around us.

Picasso's stunning originality revealed itself in a succession of bold and highly individual styles throughout his life, and his work is often divided into a series of different 'periods'. Perhaps his most famous style was *cubism*, in which objects and people are broken up into geometrical units, or small cubes.

► *Child Holding a Dove* was painted during Picasso's 'blue period' (1901–1904). During this period he used many cold and moody tones in his paintings.

Pigs

Pigs are mammals that have short legs, heavy bodies, short tails (which are often curly), and a snout for a nose. Most of them have a coarse, bristly coat, although many farm pigs have a smooth skin.

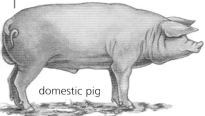
domestic pig

Pigs are common as domestic animals that are kept on farms and then killed for their skin and meat. These pigs have been domesticated over the centuries from wild pigs.

Wild pigs are strong and self-protective. They live in many parts of the world, mostly in forested areas, and include the warthog from Africa, and the wild boar from parts of Europe, Asia and Africa. (The European wild boar is the ancestor of the domestic pig.) Wild pigs have a coat of coarse hair, which is generally brown or grey in colour.

Most wild pigs make a short burrow, roughly lined with twigs or grass, in which they hide or rest. Sows (female pigs) produce their litter of five or six young in their burrow. The piglets are helpless at birth and

wild boar

warthog

remain in the burrow for the first few days of their life.

Wild pigs are generally peaceable animals, but if they are attacked they defend themselves with their large, sharp canine teeth (tusks). These curve up out of the mouth to make effective weapons.

Pigs feed on grasses and small plants, and often use their long snouts, which are strengthened with a special bone, to dig up roots. However, pigs are not vegetarians, and farm pigs are often fed on scraps which can include fish or meat, as well as corns and grains.

- In spite of their reputation, pigs are not exceptionally dirty. However, they may sometimes wallow in mud, probably to keep their skins cool.

- The peccaries of Central and South America look and behave rather like pigs, but they are not closely related. They move about in large groups which may turn as one on an intruder.

find out more
Farming
Mammals

Pirates

Pirates are robbers who steal from ships at sea. They appeared as soon as people had learned how to make sea-going ships, at least 7000 years ago.

By the time of the ancient Greeks and Romans, piracy was a constant danger to Mediterranean sea travellers. The 16th and 17th centuries saw the 'golden age' of piracy. After this, with powerful navies patrolling the world's oceans, piracy declined. However, pirates still roam the islands and channels of the Caribbean and South-east Asia.

Pirates around the world
Spanish ships passing through the Caribbean with treasure plundered from the Americas were easy targets for pirates famous for their cruelty. Edward Teach, known as Blackbeard, scared his victims by hanging lighted fuses about his head and seized their rings by cutting off their fingers.

For centuries the pirates most feared by Europeans were the Muslim corsairs of North Africa, who sailed massive galleys with up to 300 oarsmen. The great Corsairs Dragut Reis and the Barbarossa (Red Beard) brothers captured slaves for sale or ransom.

European pirates arrived in the 17th century, using Madagascar as a base. The most successful pirate of this era was Henry Avery, an ex-naval

▶ Pirates would get rid of prisoners or enemies by making them 'walk the plank'. Victims would be forced to walk off the board to certain death.

captain who disappeared with a shipload of diamonds.

Piracy in the Far East was on a grand scale. The 17th-century Chinese pirate Ching Chihlung commanded over 1000 boats.

- The term piracy is also used to describe the breaking of copyright laws. Copyright laws prevent the reproduction of books, music or other artistic works, such as films or photographs, without permission. 'Video pirates' are people who illegally copy and sell video tapes.

- Anne Bonny and Mary Read wore men's clothing and made a living by piracy until captured in 1720. Their accomplices were hanged, but Anne and Mary were spared execution because they were pregnant.

find out more
Drake, Francis

Plants

• The study of plants is called botany, and people who study them are called botanists.

Plants range in size from giant trees to tiny mosses. They include the largest and the oldest living things. But unlike animals, plants do not usually move around. Instead, they grow rooted in the soil or attached to the ground or to rocks.

Plants do not feed like animals, although they have to take in chemicals from the soil or from their surroundings to grow. Instead of eating, most make their own food in special 'chemical factories' in their leaves.

Green factories

The most important difference between plants and animals is how they get their food, and this also helps to explain the shape and form of a typical plant. Most plants are green in colour and have leaves. These leaves are spread out in a way that catches most sunshine.

Plants, like animals, are made up of microscopic 'building blocks' called cells. The plants are green because their cells contain a green chemical called *chlorophyll*, and the chlorophyll is bundled into packages called *chloroplasts*. The chloroplasts are the chemical factories that make the plant's food. To do this, the plant also needs two 'raw materials' from its surroundings. These are the gas carbon dioxide, which is common in the air, and water. The carbon dioxide passes into the plant's leaves through special pores in their surface, while the water is taken up by the plant's roots. The chlorophyll in the plant's leaves absorbs energy from sunlight, and this energy is used to turn carbon dioxide and water into various kinds of energy-rich sugars. These sugars are the plant's food. The whole process of making food using sunlight is called *photosynthesis*.

A waste product of photosynthesis is the gas oxygen. This is fortunate for humans and other animals, because we need oxygen to breathe. In the process, we breathe out carbon dioxide, which would eventually poison us, if plants did not turn it into oxygen. Plants therefore have an important role in recycling the air that we breathe.

Food stores

The sugars produced by plants in photosynthesis can be joined together and stored as more complex chemicals called starches. These are often stored in parts of the plant's roots or underground stems, which swell up into bulging growths called tubers. Sometimes we eat these starch stores as food. Carrots, for example, are swollen roots, and potatoes are swollen underground stems.

The plant can break down the starch and the sugars whenever it needs energy, for example at night when there is no sunlight to provide energy, or when it needs extra energy to grow or to produce seeds. Plants also need other chemicals (called *minerals*) to build all the parts that make up their cells. These chemicals are taken in by the plant's roots, dissolved in water.

▼ (1) Roots reach down into the soil to gather the water and minerals the plant needs for growth. (2) The roots of some plants swell up and are used to store the plant's food, as in a carrot.

1

2

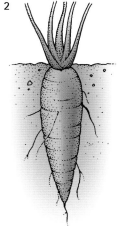

Plant variety

We can think of a tree as a 'typical' plant. Its roots anchor it in the ground and absorb water and minerals. The main job of its stem or trunk is to hold up the leaves, so they can collect sunshine and carbon dioxide for photosynthesis. Tube-like cells inside the stem carry water from the roots to the leaves, and other tubes transport sugars to wherever the plant needs them for energy. Twigs and branches spread out the leaves so they can best collect sunshine. Plants such as mosses and liverworts are much simpler in design, but they still photosynthesize and they still fit the basic pattern of a plant.

Some plants are not green: they contain no chlorophyll and cannot photosynthesize. These plants get their food in different ways. Plants such as mistletoe live as parasites, which means they 'steal' from other plants. Their roots grow into the roots or stem of another plant and draw off the sugars, minerals and water they need to live and grow. Other plants such as toothwort get all the goodness they need from dead plant material in the soil. Their roots release chemicals which break up fragments of dead leaf or twig in the soil to release sugars and minerals, which the plant then absorbs through its roots.

There are some groups of living things which are very plant-like, but which scientists do not regard as true plants. Many algae, for example, are made up of a single cell which contains chlorophyll and can photosynthesize. But some algae move about like animals, and so algae are

▲ Mosses have a simpler structure than flowering plants. They have no proper roots, and collect all the water and minerals they need from the rain that falls on them.

generally regarded as a separate group (or kingdom) of living things (even though seaweeds are giant algae which look very much like plants). Mushrooms and toadstools also look like plants, but they are actually the fruiting body of a fungus, which is mostly made up of a tangle of tiny threads in the soil. The fungi are therefore put in another kingdom. The plant kingdom therefore includes just mosses, liverworts, ferns, conifers and true flowering plants.

Spreading the kind

Because plants do not move about like animals, they cannot find their way to new places where it might be better to live, and they cannot meet and mate with others of their kind, as animals do. Plants therefore need outside help both to breed and to spread themselves. Flowering plants produce male and female sex cells in different parts of their flowers. They rely either on the wind or on animals to carry the male sex cells (called pollen) to the female sex cells of another flower. There, the sex cells can join, in a process called fertilization, to produce seeds.

Seeds allow new plants to grow, and help to spread their kind. They are usually enclosed in a fruit. The fruit is designed to carry the seed away from the parent plant. This helps the plant invade new areas, and ensures that the young plant

▼ Flowers like the ones on these cacti are designed to attract insects, which then help the plant by carrying pollen to another flower so that fertilization can occur. The shape and colour of different flowers attract particular insects. This helps to ensure the pollen is carried only to the right kind of plant.

Herbs

We normally think of herbs as plants, like mint and parsley, whose leaves are used as flavourings for food. But in botany, a herbaceous plant is one that does not have a woody stem, and dies right down to the ground after flowering. Not all the plants that we use as herbs are actually herbaceous. For example, bay leaves are herbs that grow on a small tree.

does not compete with its parent for space and sunlight.

Different life cycles

Other plant groups spread and multiply their kind in slightly different ways. Conifers, for example, also have tiny flowers that spread pollen for fertilization. But their seeds are usually produced on a woody cone that does not completely enclose the seed. Some conifers, such as yew trees, have juicy berries instead of cones, but the seed is still not completely enclosed. The seeds from cones are spread by the wind, while the berries are spread by animals.

Ferns, mosses and liverworts have more complicated lifecycles. Instead of seeds they spread by *spores* – dust-like particles that are spread in the wind. The spores grow into young plants that are quite unlike the adults; they are tiny green flaps than can only survive in damp places.

▶ Mistletoe grows attached to branches, high in a tree. Its roots penetrate the branches and collect minerals and water from the tree, but its green leaves still make their own food by photosynthesis. Its sticky white berries are spread to other trees by birds.

These produce sex cells in tiny pockets on their underside. The male sex cells swim through a film of moisture on the surface of the flap to the pockets containing the female sex cells, which they then fertilize. An adult fern, moss or liverwort then develops from the fertilized cells.

find out more
Algae
Flowering plants
Forests
Seaweeds
Trees and shrubs

▼ Plants are divided into different groups, according to how they reproduce.

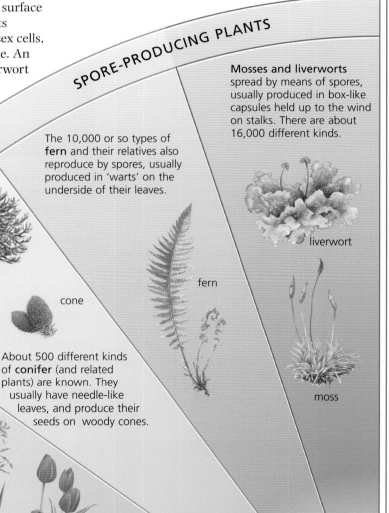

SPORE-PRODUCING PLANTS

Mosses and liverworts spread by means of spores, usually produced in box-like capsules held up to the wind on stalks. There are about 16,000 different kinds.

liverwort

The 10,000 or so types of **fern** and their relatives also reproduce by spores, usually produced in 'warts' on the underside of their leaves.

fern

moss

CONE-BEARERS

monkey-puzzle tree

cone

About 500 different kinds of **conifer** (and related plants) are known. They usually have needle-like leaves, and produce their seeds on woody cones.

MONOCOTYLEDONS

The 240,000 known types of **flowering plant** are divided into two groups, depending on the number of leaves that spring directly from their seeds. Monocotyledons produce a single leaf inside each seed.

grass

tulip

FLOWERING PLANTS

dicotyledons

Dicotyledons are flowering plants with two leaves ready-formed inside their seeds.

oak tree

sunflower

Plastics

You can find things made of plastics all around you: telephones, television sets, computers, tapes and disks, toothbrushes, clothes, and countless other things. Plastics are chemically made materials which can easily be moulded into any shape. They can be very hard and strong or they can be soft and stretchy. With such a wide range of properties, plastics have become some of the most useful modern materials.

In some ways, plastics are better than natural materials, such as wood, metal, glass and cotton. They do not rot like wood, or rust like iron and steel. Plastic bottles and cups do not break if you drop them. Electrical appliances are made of plastics because they do not conduct electricity. Plastics can be made with a wide range of different characteristics and shapes. They may be transparent, like glass, or made in any colour; they can be formed into ultra-light solid foams for packaging or into flexible synthetic fibres that are woven into cloth.

Making plastics

Plastics are made from gases and liquids, most of which are extracted from crude oil. The chemicals used to make plastics have small molecules (particles). When heated, often under

pressure, the small molecules join up in chains to form long molecules. Substances with long-chain molecules, such as plastics, are called *polymers*. When the long-chain molecules of a plastic bend, this makes the plastic flexible. When the molecules interlink so that they cannot bend, the plastic is a rigid and tough one.

▲ Helmets and other protective sportswear are made from a very tough plastic called polycarbonate.

▼ Two methods of making plastic objects.

Some common plastics

Name	Properties	Uses
polythene	strong, flexible, not easily damaged by gases or liquids	bags, sacks, pipes, bottles
nylon	strong, hard-wearing	clothes, carpets, other textiles
PVC (polyvinyl chloride)	flexible, water-resistant, insulates electricity	hoses, boots, rainwear, covering for electrical wires
Kevlar	very strong, bullet-proof	bullet-proof vests, cables, aircraft parts
fibreglass	very strong, water- and weather-resistant	boat hulls, storage tanks
acrylic	clear, rigid, weather-resistant	car lights, motorcycle windscreens
polystyrene	lightweight, good insulator against heat and cold	food packaging, disposable cups

Blow moulding

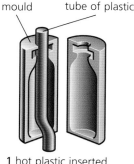

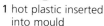

mould   tube of plastic   compressed air   finished bottle

1 hot plastic inserted into mould

2 mould closed

3 compressed air forced in, shaping plastic to mould

Extrusion

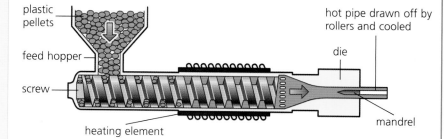

plastic pellets

feed hopper

screw

heating element

hot pipe drawn off by rollers and cooled

die

mandrel

Plastic pellets are fed through a hopper into a barrel. They are heated to turn them into a liquid, which is pushed by a screw through a die and mandrel. The die and mandrel shape the plastic into a pipe.

find out more
Atoms and molecules
Materials
Oil

Poetry

▲ In Homer's epic poem, *The Odyssey*, the hero Odysseus describes how the Greeks defeated the Trojans after 10 years of war by building a wooden horse and leaving it outside the walls of Troy. The Trojans took the horse inside their city, and immediately the Greek warriors hidden inside the horse burst out and ransacked the city. Stories and characters from *The Odyssey* and *The Iliad* have been used again and again in Western poetry and painting.

Poetry puts words into patterns. The *haiku*, a type of poem that comes from Japan, has a strict pattern of lines and syllables: 17 syllables, arranged in three lines of 5, 7 and 5. A haiku should present one 'picture'. This example is by the 17th-century Japanese poet Matsuo Basho:

On a withered branch
a silent crow has settled:
an autumn nightfall.

Poetry is difficult to define. 'If you want a definition' wrote Dylan Thomas, 'poetry is what makes me laugh or cry or yawn, what makes my toenails twinkle. All that matters about poetry is the enjoyment of it.' Samuel Taylor Coleridge described poetry as 'the best words in the best order'.

Poetry involves using language in unusual and exciting ways, often to express something about our experience as human beings. Poets frequently create meanings through the sounds of words or by organizing lines into particular patterns. In describing things, they often use 'images': unexpected comparisons which help us to understand what something is like.

The earliest poetry

Some of the oldest poems are long stories written in verse. They are known as 'epic' poems and usually have a cast of gods and heroes. The *Mahabharata*, which dates from the period 400 BC to AD 200, is a great epic poem about the ancient peoples of India. It has nearly 100,000 verses and tells of a civil war between two branches of the same family.

The Greek poet Homer is believed to be the author of two epics, composed around the 8th century BC, about the gods and heroes of ancient Greece. *The Iliad* describes the siege of Troy, while *The Odyssey* recounts the wanderings of the hero Odysseus, and includes his famous encounter with the giant Cyclops. Troy is also the starting point of *The Aeneid*, an epic poem by the Roman poet Virgil, who lived in the 1st century BC. He retells the famous episode of the wooden horse, but is mainly interested in the Trojan hero Aeneas, whom the Romans saw as their ancestor.

One of the earliest English poems to have survived is the epic *Beowulf*. Written down around the 8th century AD in Anglo-Saxon, it tells of the adventures of a powerful hero, Beowulf, who kills the monster Grendel but is himself finally killed by an enraged dragon. The most famous English epic is *Paradise Lost*, which was written by John Milton in the 17th century. It retells the Bible story of how Satan tempted Adam and Eve into disobeying God. Milton, who was blind, composed the 12 books of his epic in his head and dictated them to his daughter.

Poetry and stories

Epics are not the only poems that tell stories. Chaucer's *Canterbury Tales*, written in the 14th century, is based around a group of pilgrims on their way to Canterbury who decide to pass the time with a story-telling competition.

Ballads are another kind of story-telling (or 'narrative') poem. They are usually written in a regular rhythm with a fixed rhyme-scheme, and have four lines in each stanza. Many ballads tell of the adventures of folk heroes such as the Australian outlaw Ned Kelly. One of the most famous ballads is the haunting 'Rime of the Ancient Mariner' by Samuel Taylor Coleridge, in which the ancient mariner of the title stops a 'wedding guest' and compels him to listen to his tale of a terrifying sea voyage:

'God save thee, ancient Mariner!
 From the fiends that plague thee
 thus!
 Why lookst thou so?' With my
 cross-bow
 I shot the Albatross.

▼ The Italian poet Dante Alighieri (1265–1321) wrote an epic poem called *The Divine Comedy*, which describes his journey through Hell, Purgatory and Paradise. It is regarded as one of the most beautiful poems ever written.

Poetry and nature

Poets have always taken a special interest in the natural world. William Wordsworth, the most famous English poet of nature, caused a great deal of argument in the 19th century through his belief that truth can be found in nature rather than in human society. In a poem called 'Lines Composed above Tintern Abbey', he called nature:

The anchor of my purest
  thoughts, the nurse,
The guide, the guardian of my
  heart, and soul
Of all my moral being.

The Irish poet Seamus Heaney writes poetry that is rooted in the farmland of his youth. The English poet Ted Hughes describes the beauty and also the cruelty of life in the wild. In his series of poems *Crow*, the bird is portrayed as both savage and brave.

Imagination and the individual

Wordsworth and Coleridge belong to a group of English poets we call the 'Romantics'. Other famous Romantic poets are Percy Bysshe Shelley, Lord Byron and John Keats. These poets believed strongly in the value of a person's individual experience and in the power of the imagination. Keats is famous for the rich, sensual images he uses in such poems as 'Ode to Autumn', which opens with the lines:

Season of mists and mellow
  fruitfulness,
Close bosom-friend of the
  maturing sun;
Conspiring with him how to load
  and bless
With fruit the vines that round
  the thatches run.

Many 20th-century poets have chosen to write about things that disturb them. Sylvia Plath often considered illness, suffering and death in her poetry, while in her poem 'Not Waving But Drowning' Stevie Smith reflected the painful lives that some people lead privately. Maya Angelou writes about her life as a black American woman; here she describes Africa, the continent of her ancestors, as if it was a woman:

Thus she has lain
  sugar cane sweet
  deserts her hair
  golden her feet
  mountains her breasts
  two Niles her tears
Thus she has lain
Black through the years.

Love and humour

Poetry is especially suited to the expression of powerful emotions such as love. Many love poems are written in a form called the sonnet, a type of poem which has 14 lines and a regular rhyme scheme. Possibly the most famous of all love poems is the sonnet by William Shakespeare which begins:

Shall I compare thee to a
  summer's day?
Thou art more lovely and more
  temperate.

It is a mistake to think that poetry is always serious. When, in 1846, Edward Lear published *The Book of Nonsense*, it was an immediate success – with its selection of limericks such as this one:

There was an old man with a
  beard,
Who said 'It is just as I feared!
Two Owls and a Hen,
Four Larks and a Wren
Have all built their nests in my
  beard!'

▶ The 18th-century English poet and artist William Blake made etchings of his poems, and then printed and coloured them. His poem 'The Tyger', illustrated here, is a good example of his powerful and visionary poetic style.

Poetry and change

Poets are often misunderstood and attacked in their lifetime because they attempt to do something special with the language they are using and the subjects they choose.

In 1922 T. S. Eliot published an extraordinary poem called *The Waste Land*, which combined everyday speech with some extremely unusual images in its description of what the poet saw as the empty, worthless aspects of life in his own century. Traditional critics hated his modern approach to writing, but younger ones saw it as an important and exciting break with the past.

• Today many poets perform their poems. Benjamin Zephaniah delights audiences listening to favourites such as 'I love me mudder'.

find out more
Carroll, Lewis
Chaucer, Geoffrey
Drama
Shakespeare, William
Stories and story-tellers

Poland

Poland is a large country in north-eastern Europe. Much of the land is wide and flat, with mountains to the south.

The Vistula is Poland's longest river. It flows north from the Tatra Mountains in the south, through the Carpathians, to the woods of central Poland, before reaching the lakes of the north and finally the pine forests of the coast. Poland still has large areas of unspoilt land, where elk, wild boar, wolves and even brown bears still roam.

Work and industry

About a third of the population works on the land, growing potatoes, sugar beet and cereal crops. Poland exports tinned ham, bacon, pickled vegetables, jams and fruits. Heavy industry is centred around the rich coalfields and mineral reserves of Silesia in the south, and shipbuilding in the north.

find out more
Copernicus, Nicolas
Curie, Marie
Europe
World War II
See also Countries fact file, page 635

▶ The organization Solidarnosc (Solidarity) was set up in the early 1980s as a trade-union movement. It began in the shipyards of Gdansk under the leadership of Lech Walesa (right), who was later elected president.

▶ FLASHBACK ◀

For hundreds of years Poland was a kingdom, until at the end of the 18th century Russia, Austria and Prussia conquered it and divided its land among themselves.

In 1918 Poland became independent once more, as a republic not a kingdom. The Poles suffered severely in World War II under German occupation, and at the end of the war the USSR took over a fifth of Polish territory. Poland was ruled by the Communist Party until 1989, when the first free elections were won by Solidarnosc (Solidarity).

Police

The main job of policemen and policewomen is to investigate and solve crimes, but they carry out many other tasks as well.

Police officers carry out regular patrols ('beats'), on foot or in vehicles, to prevent crime and help the public. They keep radio contact with the main control room. They may also be on traffic patrol, when they have to direct traffic, deal with accidents and enforce traffic laws.

The officers who investigate more serious crimes are usually detectives, who wear plain clothes rather than a uniform. They are supported by experts (police officers and civilians) who help to find evidence. 'Scenes of crime officers' search for fingerprints and other clues.

Other police officers specialize in juvenile crime or in meeting children in schools. Others keep records of crimes, storing any information that might help solve future crimes.

• Police forces around the world often work together. The International Criminal Police Organization (Interpol) links the police of over 180 different countries from its headquarters in Paris, France, so that they can work together to track down criminals.

• In the USA there are more than 40,000 police forces, organized at state, county, city and village level. The Federal Bureau of Investigation (FBI) investigates crimes across the whole of the USA.

find out more
Crime
Law and order

▼ Everyone's fingerprints are different. After a crime, police dust aluminium powder over any fingerprints to make them show up. They then try to match those prints with those of known criminals or suspects.

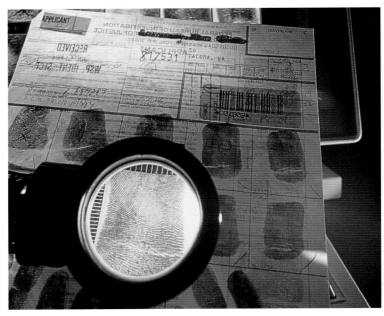

Pollution

We cause pollution when we do damage to our surroundings. Leaving litter is one form of pollution. But chemicals and waste from factories, farms, motor cars and even houses cause much more serious pollution, which can affect the air, water and the land.

Pollution is not something new. Six hundred years ago, the air over London was thick with smoke from coal fires. Over the years, laws have been passed to stop some kinds of pollution. Many countries now have government departments whose job is to limit the damage pollution does.

Air pollution

Factories, power stations and motor vehicles make waste gases, soot and dust, which are all released into the air. The polluted air damages people's lungs. Some kinds of air pollution can even cause brain damage. Waste gases in the air can also cause acid rain, which damages trees, lake and river life, and buildings.

Ozone is a gas produced naturally from oxygen in the upper atmosphere. A thin layer of ozone surrounds the world, and protects us from the harmful ultraviolet rays in sunlight. Ozone is destroyed by pollution from burning fuels and by chemicals called CFCs released from some refrigerators and aerosols. If the ozone layer is badly damaged, more people will get skin cancer.

Water pollution

Acid rain can pollute lakes and rivers. But there are many other kinds of water pollution. Some towns and villages pump untreated sewage into rivers or the sea, while factories sometimes release poisonous chemicals and wastes. These pollutants can kill fishes and other water animals and plants. Farmers use fertilizers and chemical pesticides that can also be washed into rivers and streams after heavy rainfall. The sea can also be polluted by spillages of oil from oil tankers and oil rigs.

Pollution on land

People cause pollution when they thoughtlessly dump their rubbish or litter. Some kinds of rubbish rot away quite quickly, but many plastic materials will never decay.

Radioactive waste from nuclear power stations could cause very serious pollution. Nearly all nuclear waste is safely contained for now, but small amounts do sometimes escape into the air or water. Many scientists are worried about the long-term effects of this type of pollution, because nuclear waste can stay radioactive for thousands of years.

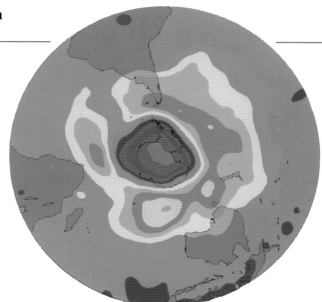

▲ Pollution is causing thinning of the ozone layer, especially over the Poles. This satellite picture taken above the Antarctic shows ozone levels in the upper atmosphere. In the blue, purple and grey area at the centre there is virtually no ozone at all.

▲ In some large cities, the air is so polluted that people wear face masks to filter out dust and soot from the air.

◀ Water pollution in New Zealand. The wastes from a factory pour out from a pipe directly into the sea, close to a beach.

find out more
Acid rain
Climate
Conservation
Ecology
Greenhouse effect
Recycling

Polo, Marco

Born about 1254 in
Venice, Italy
Died 1324 aged
about 70

Marco Polo was one of the few Europeans in the Middle Ages to venture into the heart of the unknown Chinese empire. On his return he wrote a fascinating account of the countries he visited and the splendours of Emperor Kublai Khan's court.

• Marco Polo's book is a description of the Mongol empire. He began by describing Kublai Khan and the magnificent state in which he lived. He then wrote about the Summer Palace, and the hunting parties in the country south-east of Beijing. There are fascinating details too about his travels inside China.

find out more
Explorers
Mongol empire

Marco Polo was an 18-year-old merchant when he set out for China in 1271 with his father and uncle, Niccolò and Maffeo Polo. They travelled by ship to Turkey and then overland on the Silk Road, along which merchants from China regularly brought silk to Europe. The whole journey took almost four years.

The emperor of China, Kublai Khan, welcomed them warmly to his court at Khanbalik (now Beijing). Marco Polo's father and uncle settled down as traders. Marco, who had a gift for languages, became a civil servant and travelling diplomat, reporting back to Kublai all that he saw. He was sent on many missions, visiting India, Burma (now Myanmar) and Ceylon (now Sri Lanka).

In 1292 the Polos set out for home. They went by sea, via what is now Singapore, Sri Lanka and the Persian Gulf. They arrived in Venice in 1295 with a fortune in jewels, having been away for 24 years.

Marco Polo spent the last 30 years of his life as a Venetian merchant. At one time he was captured in a sea fight by the Genoese, and became a prisoner in Genoa. It was during this time that he dictated the now-famous story of his travels.

▼ Marco Polo with elephants and camels arriving from India at Hormuz in the Persian Gulf.

Ponds

A pond is a small, shallow body of water. Some are created by farmers and gardeners. Others form naturally in wet hollows and ditches, fed by rain or melting snow. Ponds attract animals to drink, and birds coming to look for food.

Ponds are usually shallow, so the water contains plenty of oxygen for the pond animals to breathe. Tiny oxygen bubbles are also produced by pondweeds as they photosynthesize (make food using sunlight). The surface of the pond heats up by day and cools down quickly at night. In shady, deeper water the temperature changes less.

Most ponds change with the seasons. In winter, the floating plants sink to the bottom, or are

torn up by the wind. In cold countries, a winter cover of ice protects the deeper water below from cold air, allowing frogs, toads and fishes to survive at the bottom of the pond.

Disappearing ponds

If left alone, many ponds eventually silt up and disappear. In hot climates the

pond may shrink or even disappear during the dry season, as the water evaporates.

In recent years, many village ponds have been drained so that the land can be built on or farmed. Others have been filled in as rubbish dumps or become polluted by fertilizers or pesticides.

find out more
Rivers and streams

yellow iris

damselfly

pond skater

whirligig beetle

coot

water boatman

mallard

young pike

duckweed

pond snail

common newt

great diving beetle

tadpoles

dragonfly nymph

caddis larva

stickleback

Ponies *see* Horses

Pop and rock music

Pop and rock music is a powerful part of popular culture today. It can take many forms, from a catchy tune on the radio to a piece of rhythmic soul music or an exciting rock concert.

Today pop and rock music is produced all over the world. Although it is often influenced by local musical styles, all music that has a pop and rock sound is a development of music that originated in the USA in the 1950s.

▲ The Rolling Stones in 1964. Like their contemporaries the Beatles, they wrote most of their own songs and dressed in the fashions of the period, but their music was more influenced by American music – soul music, in particular. They achieved great success on both sides of the Atlantic for several decades.

Rock 'n' roll roots

American rock 'n' roll singers such as Elvis Presley, Chuck Berry, Little Richard and Jerry Lee Lewis first became popular in the late 1950s. Their music was inspired by the blues-singing tradition of the American southern states, and had influences from country-and-western and jazz music. Although all of these stars played rock 'n' roll, each of them had a distinctive sound and image. Also they all gave exciting and memorable stage performances. The growth of television at that time also strengthened their popularity.

Songwriting and politics

Folk music was one of the first forms of popular music to include political ideas in its lyrics (song words). During the 1930s and 1940s the American singer songwriter Woody Guthrie sang about poverty and injustice in his country. His music inspired the most famous folk musicians of the 1960s – Joan Baez and Bob Dylan. The anti-war songs of Baez and Dylan expressed the feelings of many young people as America's involvement in the Vietnam War dragged on. The same mood was expressed by many of the groups that played at Woodstock, an enormous rock-music festival held in New York State in 1969.

Since then numerous pop records have contained a political message or have tried to promote a social cause. In the 1970s reggae artists such as Bob Marley and Peter Tosh wrote song lyrics about social and moral issues – particularly issues relating to the situation of black people. In 1985 Live Aid, a huge pop-music event featuring many top groups, raised over 40 million pounds to ease famine in Africa. From the late 1980s, many performers used rap and ragga to express their personal views in a strident manner.

Dance music

Although pop music can have a serious political or social

▼ Chuck Berry was one of the first great rock 'n' roll stars of the 1950s. His electric-guitar playing set the style for a generation of guitarists. Many of his songs, such as 'Maybellene' (1955) and 'Johnny B. Goode' (1958), are classics of rock 'n' roll music.

▼ Johnny Rotten's band the Sex Pistols were one of the first British punk-rock bands. Punk rock emerged in the mid-1970s as an expression of rebellion against authority and socially 'polite' behaviour. Punk-rock musicians were largely self-taught and their success encouraged many young people to have a go at playing rock music.

message, often its purpose is simply to entertain people and encourage them to dance. This was especially true of the rhythm-based soul and disco music that developed during the 1970s. Techno, hip-hop and jungle-beat music, which became highly popular in dance clubs during the 1990s, took this even further. The dance rhythm was the most important element, with any melody or vocal line coming second.

Dance music can be listened to at home and on the radio, but it is ideally suited to the social atmosphere of a club or disco. However, multi-million-selling pop acts of the 1980s and 1990s, such as Madonna and the Spice Girls, managed to combine a danceable rhythm with a catchy tune and lyrics. Their success had a lot to do with the way their image was carefully designed to appeal to teenagers. Full use was also made of television and other media so people could not help but notice them.

▼ The British group Queen were part of a theatrical style of music known as glam-rock. Their song 'Bohemian Rhapsody' (1975) featured elements of classical music and opera. The video of the song is considered to be the first successful pop video.

Images of pop

If pop artists are to become successful they have to find the 'right' look and stage manner. They are often responsible for creating fashions in clothes and hairstyles as they search for a new look that will get them noticed by the public.

The development of music videos to promote recordings made image and presentation all the more important. In the late 1970s bands like Queen, who had a very theatrical approach, really took advantage of this new medium. Their dramatic videos brought greater attention to their records. The launch of the music-video channel MTV in 1981 meant that no new record release was complete without a promotional video.

Links between pop music and TV and film have also grown. Many TV personalities, such as Jason Donovan and Kylie Minogue from the Australian soap opera *Neighbours*, have gone on to have chart success, and film soundtracks often include pop songs. Several pop stars, including Madonna, Sting and David Bowie, have starred in top movies.

Pop music and technology

Traditionally pop and rock musicians would write some lyrics and then compose a melody and chord structure for the song, using a guitar or piano. This would be recorded in a studio by the band, who would then perform concerts to promote the new recording.

Today pop music is often written using computer software and studio editing techniques. The result is that much pop music is no longer either recorded or performed live. Also, with the growth of TV and video, there is little need for many acts to promote their new recordings by going on tour. However, in the 1990s, guitar-based rock bands such as Oasis put new life into the tradition of live performance.

The music industry

Pop and rock music has become an important industry in many countries, involving the employment of hundreds of thousands of people. Top acts sell millions of records worldwide and can make a big contribution to a country's exports and wealth. Today the music industry is 'big business'. Most stars are bound by a legal contract to one of a few large multi-national companies, and in many ways they are promoted just like any other consumer product.

▶ In the 1990s Oasis went against the trend of most other bands, who were relying on modern technology for their sound. Oasis reminded people that with a few guitars, a drum-kit and the ability to write and sing good songs, you can create great rock music, in the tradition of the Beatles and the Rolling Stones.

▲ Some pop groups today make huge amounts of money out of selling products which display their image. Pictures of the British group the Spice Girls appeared on a vast range of products. The Spice Girls were a phenomenally successful group, and each of their first three singles sold over a million copies.

find out more
Beatles
Jazz
Music
Musical instruments
Presley, Elvis
World music

Popes see Christians

Population

Today, there are more than 6 billion people in the world. The population of the world has grown steadily since about 1750. Since the early 20th century, and particularly from about 1950 onwards, this growth has been very rapid.

The population is the number of people found in a particular place. We talk about the population of the world, a continent, a country, a city or a village. Governments count the population of their countries using a *census*. The earliest census counts are those of China, which go back over 3000 years. Censuses have been carried out since 1790 in the USA and since 1801 in the United Kingdom. Today, most countries carry out population censuses, many of them on a 10-yearly basis. The population between census counts can be estimated or worked out from records of births and deaths and the numbers of people who have moved.

Population patterns

Scientists who study population figures and patterns are called *demographers*. They try to predict what the world's population will be in future decades by studying the present population figures and rates of growth.

The world population first started to increase rapidly during the 18th century, at the beginning of the Industrial Revolution. Most of this increase was in Europe, and in the Americas and Oceania where Europeans settled. Today, a fast growth in population is typical of many countries in Africa, Asia, and Central and South America. These countries are sometimes referred to as 'the South' since many are in southern parts of the world. In Europe and North America, on the other hand, population is now growing slowly or even declining. These countries are sometimes called 'the North'.

The population structure (the number of people in each age group) of these two sets of countries is also different. In the South there are many young people. Half the population may be under 25 or 30 years old. In the North fewer babies are born, but not so many children and young people die, so the numbers in each age group are more equal. In proportion to the total population, there are more elderly people.

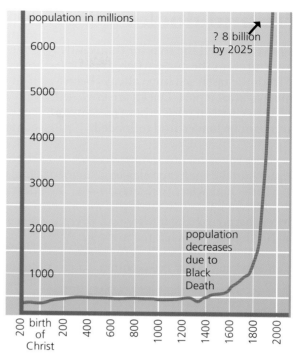

? 8 billion by 2025

population decreases due to Black Death

▲ This graph gives an idea of how the population of the world has grown over the past 2000 years.

• The population of China is bigger than that of any other country: nearly 1.3 billion (1300 million) people. During the 1980s Chinese families were told to have just one child.

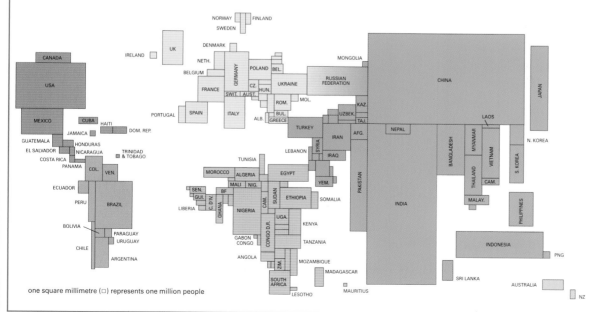

one square millimetre (□) represents one million people

◄ This map of the world shows where people live on the Earth. The size of each country has been drawn to indicate how many people live there, not how much land the country covers.

World population in the 20th century

1900	1550 million
1930	2070 million
1960	3003 million
1990	5300 million
1999	6000 million

find out more
Countries
Ecology
Industrial Revolution

Ports and docks

People have travelled the seas for thousands of years. Places on the coast where there is shelter from the open sea have always been good spots to start a port. Docks are enclosed areas of water within ports where passengers and cargo can be loaded and unloaded.

In some places where there is not much of a natural harbour, the landscape may be changed to make a better and bigger port. In the 13th century Rotterdam, in the Netherlands, was a small fishing harbour 25 kilometres up a river from the North Sea. Today, it is the world's busiest port. Ships dock all the way to the sea along a channel dug in the 19th century.

▲ Some trading ports handle only fish. There are small fishing ports along coasts around the world. These colourful blue and red fishing boats are in a small fishing port in Vietnam.

Trading and passenger ports

Many countries buy and sell goods from other countries. To deal with the very large ships that carry goods across the oceans ports may need to hold water up to 30 metres deep. Special cranes and loading equipment on the dockside load the containers from trains and lorries on and off the container ships.

Some ports are mainly for people travelling on ships and ferries. Cross-channel ferries between England and France carry cars, lorries and pedestrians. The ferries are very popular, but they have lost business to the Channel Tunnel since it opened in 1994.

Docks

In some docks ships enter and leave through a lock. This means that the water in the dock can be kept at a constant level, even though the sea level outside is changing with the tides. In dry docks – docks without water – ships can be inspected and repaired. There are various dock structures. The oldest is the *quay wall*, which is simply a long wall along the shore. The quay wall protects the shore and the resting ships and provides a platform for loading and unloading. A *wharf* is a rectangular platform which runs alongside the shore, and has a runway connecting it to the shore. A *pier* is simply a platform supported by beams and girders which stretches over the water. The platform is usually built of reinforced concrete, though wood or metal may be used. *Pontoon docks* rise and fall with the changing water level. To get ashore, a trestle, hinged at the shore end, rests freely on the pontoon at the other end.

1
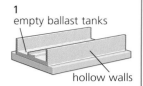
empty ballast tanks
hollow walls

2

3

supports to hold the ship level

4

▲ A dry dock. When its ballast tanks are empty, the dry dock floats in the water (1). When the ballast tanks are filled, the dock sinks below the water. A ship can float into the dock (2). Once the ship is in the dock, the ballast tanks are pumped out again (3). The dock rises until the floor is out of the water. The ship can now be repaired (4).

◄ Aerial view of the harbour of Salerno Campania in south-west Italy. Many industries, such as shipbuilding, engineering, refineries and food-processing plants, grow up around ports like this because it is cheaper and more convenient to be close for unloading and loading.

find out more
Fishing
Ships and boats

Postal services

Sending a letter from France to Australia

The letter is collected from the postbox and taken to a sorting office.

The mail is sorted into bundles according to destination, and these are put onto vans or trains.

As the mail is going overseas, it has to be taken there on a boat or a plane.

The bundles of mail are dealt with at the local sorting office.

The local postal service delivers the letter.

Every country in the world has an official postal service. This vital form of communication is a way of collecting, transporting and delivering letters and parcels. As long as an item is properly addressed and paid for, it can be taken anywhere in the world.

The basic system is the same in all countries. The country from which the item is sent keeps the money paid, and handles mail from other countries free of extra charge. In some countries letters are delivered direct to people's homes. In others, people collect them from the nearest post office.

Stamps

Postage stamps are used to show that the price of sending a parcel or letter has been paid. Individual countries have their own national stamps. The design on postage stamps can be used for a variety of purposes; for example, to honour the country's leader or national heroes, to recall or celebrate a special event, or to show aspects of the history or geography of a country.

When mail goes through the postal system, stamps are marked with an inking stamp so they cannot be reused. Companies which send a lot of mail may use a franking machine instead of stamps.

They pay a sum of money to the post office and the machine will frank envelopes or labels until that amount of money is used up.

Moving with the times

Official postal services in many countries today are in competition with private courier services, which promise special benefits such as extra security or more rapid delivery.

Modern technology is also providing other ways of sending letters and documents. Electronic mail (e-mail) systems send information from one computer to another either by cable or by telephone link. Fax (facsimile) machines code information so that it can be sent along telephone lines and decoded at the receiving fax. Individuals and companies may have this equipment for their own use. In some countries, post offices and courier companies offer e-mail and fax services to help the public send messages more quickly.

• In 1874 the General Postal Union established international co-operation between mail services of different countries.

• Philately is the study of stamps. Many philatelists collect stamps according to a chosen theme, perhaps old stamps, stamps of a certain country, or stamps that depict a particular thing, such as trains or birds. The value of stamps varies a great deal depending on their condition and rarity.

find out more
Fax machines
Information technology
Letters and diaries

◄ In 1837 Rowland Hill, one of the key reformers of Britain's postal system, suggested that the sender pay postal charges, not the receiver. He also suggested a simplified scale of charges based on the weight of the item, not the distance it has to be sent (within the country). Following Hill's reforms the first Penny Black and Twopence Blue were introduced in 1840.

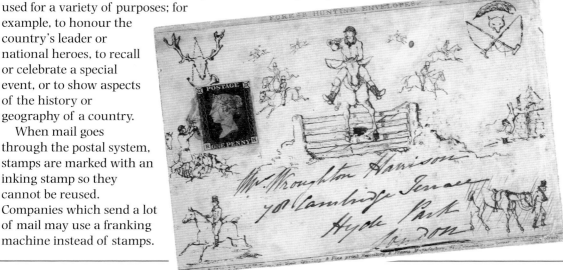

Pottery

Containers and other objects made from baked clay are known as pottery. Pottery is also the name given to the art of making such objects. It is the oldest known technology involving the use of fire.

▼ Pots are made all over the world. This potter is working on a wheel-made pot in a village in Indonesia. The pots are made of local clay and decorative patterns are cut into them by hand.

• Mugs made in a factory are cast in a mould. The mould is made up of two halves. Clay is diluted with water and poured into the mould. The plaster of the mould absorbs some of the water, but a coating of clay forms inside the mould. When the clay left is firm, the two halves of the mould are opened and the mug is taken out. The handle is then added, and the mug is fired in a kiln.

Clay looks and feels like mud, but it has special qualities. When it is wet, it can be shaped. When it is baked until it becomes red-hot, it changes into a permanent solid material.

Many different kinds of clay can be used to make pottery. Those that are fired at the lowest temperatures (below 1100 °C) are used for making *earthenware* (for example, flowerpots). When dug out of the ground, these clays may be grey, brown, cream or blue-black. They are often found near rivers and lakes, where they have been deposited by water. Unglazed earthenware is not waterproof.

Stoneware is fired at a higher temperature than earthenware (above 1200 °C). It is strong and waterproof because the clay particles fuse together during firing to form a kind of glassy stone. Stoneware clays contain some impurities, so they are rarely white.

China clay (kaolin) is white and can be fired at a very high temperature of up to 1400 °C. It is one of the ingredients used to make *porcelain* and *bone china*. This kind of pottery is very fragile and translucent, which means that light can be seen through it.

The potter's wheel

Before the potter's wheel came into use, all pots were made using hand-building techniques such as pinching, coiling or slabbing. Although a skilled craftsperson can make beautiful pieces of pottery using these methods, the invention of the potter's wheel meant that more elaborate pieces could be made more quickly.

To make a pot on a wheel, the potter 'throws' a ball of clay onto the middle of the wheel. The wheel is made to spin, using hand or foot power, or electricity. The potter works the clay into a wet mound, hollows it out with the fingers into a cup shape, and then draws up the sides of the pot.

Firing and glazing

For centuries potters fired their pots in bonfires. These pots were fragile and often discoloured by the ashes. Potters gradually learned to fire their pots in a *kiln*. This is a kind of oven that can reach very high temperatures, so producing much stronger pots.

A glaze is a thin layer of melted glass which covers the clay pot. This makes it smooth, waterproof and often very colourful. Lead, common salt, wood ash or other ingredients are added to the glaze to make it melt on the pot when it is fired. Coloured glazes are made by adding colouring agents. Cobalt makes a beautiful blue. Copper makes blue, green or red. Iron makes yellow, pale blue, green, brown or black.

▼ A lot of pottery is beautifully decorated, such as this Chinese porcelain vase made towards the end of the Ming dynasty (1388–1644).

Power stations

• Waste materials such as paper or the gas from rubbish tips are burned by some power stations as a useful additional source of power. One power station in the USA even burns drugs captured by the police.

▼ How power stations work.

When you plug a kettle, a television or another electrical appliance into the mains, the electricity comes from a power station that may be hundreds of kilometres away. The most common kind of power station burns coal or oil. Other important kinds burn natural gas or are powered by nuclear fuels.

In a power station, the electricity comes from huge generators. To deliver power, the generators must be turned. Usually, they are driven by huge wheels with fanlike blades or vanes on them.

These wheels are called *turbines*. When a stream of moving liquid or gas strikes them, they spin round. Most turbines are turned by jets of steam from a boiler. However, they can also be turned by running water, wind or gas. The power output of a large power station is 2000 megawatts (2 billion watts) – enough to supply electricity to over a million homes.

Different types of power station

Power stations which use fuels are of three main types: coal- or oil-fired, nuclear-powered, or CCGT (combined-cycle gas turbine). In a *coal- or oil-fired power station*, oil or powdered coal is burned to turn water in the boiler into steam, which drives the turbines. After use, the steam is cooled, condensed (changed back into a liquid) and reused in the boiler. To cool the steam, cooling water passes through huge cooling towers where the heat is removed by an upward draught of air. The cooled water can then be used again in the cooling tower, or it is pumped into a nearby river or lake.

Instead of a furnace for burning fuel to raise steam, a *nuclear power station* has a nuclear reactor to do the same job. The core of the reactor contains a nuclear fuel, such as the radioactive metal uranium-235. In the reactor, heat is released by the fission (splitting) of the atoms of uranium-235. This process releases an enormous amount of heat which is used to boil water. In a pressurized-water reactor (PWR), heat is carried away from the core by water. In an advanced gas-cooled reactor (AGR), carbon dioxide gas is used instead. Control rods are lowered into the reactor's core to slow the rate of fission. Of the 400 or more nuclear power stations in the world, more than half use PWRs.

Combined-cycle gas turbine power stations have a jet engine which uses gas as its fuel. The shaft of the engine turns one generator. The heat from the jet exhaust makes steam to drive another generator. CCGT stations produce less power than other kinds of power station, but they can start up rapidly when demand for power rises. Also, they are more efficient so they can extract more energy from each litre of fuel burned.

Waste heat

Fuel-burning and nuclear power stations use heat energy to drive their generators. Unfortunately, they deliver less than a half of their energy as electricity. The rest is wasted as heat, although this loss is not due to poor design. Once heat has been removed by the cooling

Oil- or coal-burning power station

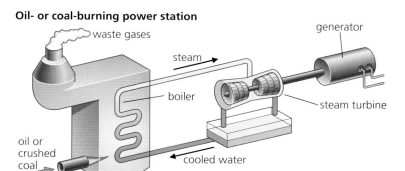

Nuclear power station

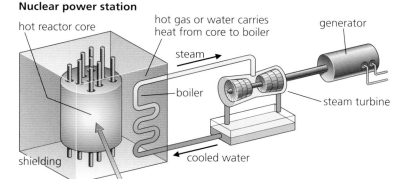

Combined-cycle gas turbine (CCGT) power station

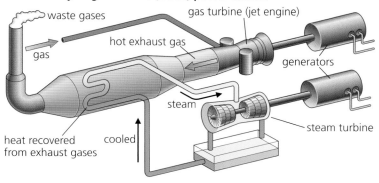

◀ Electricity from this coal-fired power station is carried by wires to nearby cities and towns, and to other areas where it is needed.

• In 1986, a major accident at the Chernobyl nuclear power station in the Ukraine released a huge cloud of radioactive material into the atmosphere. Thirty-one people were killed in the accident itself, and thousands are still suffering from its after-effects.

• A typical nuclear power station produces about 60 tonnes of waste every year, of which about 1 tonne is highly radioactive.

water, it becomes so spread out that it is no longer useful for the generating process. To make steam, concentrated heat is needed at a high temperature. Some power stations use their cooling systems to supply hot water to the houses in their area. This cuts down on energy wastage by using the fuel more efficiently.

Polluting gases

Fuel-burning power stations pollute the atmosphere with unwanted exhaust gases from their chimneys. All give out carbon dioxide, which adds to global warming. Coal-fired stations also give out sulphur dioxide, which causes acid rain. The amount of damage can be reduced either by burning only low-sulphur coal, or by fitting special equipment in the chimneys to control the amount of polluting gases released. However, such equipment is expensive and does not get rid of all the harmful gases.

Nuclear power stations do not burn their fuel, so they do not produce large amounts of polluting gases. However, they produce highly radioactive waste which needs safe storage for thousands of years. Also, very high safety standards are needed to make sure that nuclear power stations do not leak radioactive materials into the atmosphere.

Alternative power schemes

The world's supplies of oil, natural gas and coal are limited, so, where possible, it makes sense to use power stations that do not need these fuels and that produce no polluting gases. Although it may be difficult to provide all the electricity we want without nuclear power, some people say that the risks are too great. We need to find safer and less polluting ways of generating power.

Hydroelectric power uses the flow of water from a lake behind a dam to drive its turbines. Tidal power schemes use the power of the rising tide. Wind farms are collections of aerogenerators: generators turned by giant windmills.

Geothermal power stations use the heat from underground rocks to make steam for their turbines. Cold water is pumped down to the rocks through one borehole and comes up a second borehole as hot steam. In areas where hot water occurs naturally deep in the ground, steam comes out of cracks in the ground.

▶ FLASHBACK ◀

The world's first power station, with a water-driven generator, was built in Surrey, England, in 1881. It supplied power for a new electric street-lighting system. The first power station in the USA opened in 1882. Its generator was driven by a steam engine. Power stations with steam turbines appeared in about 1900. The first power station to use a nuclear reactor was opened at Obninsk, in Russia, in 1954. The first nuclear power station to provide electricity for public use began working in 1956 in the UK.

• When the nuclei of hydrogen atoms fuse (join) together, large amounts of energy are released in a process called nuclear fusion. (Fusion is the source of the Sun's heat.) In the 21st century, fusion power stations may become an important source of electricity. Unlike today's nuclear power stations, they will produce almost no radioactive waste.

find out more
Acid rain
Electricity
Energy
Greenhouse effect
Hydroelectric power
Pollution
Radiation
Sun
Tides
Wind

◀ The core of a nuclear reactor. This reactor is being used for research and not to generate power. The nuclear fuel rods at the centre are being heated to very high temperatures. The blue glow is caused by highly charged particles travelling through water faster than light does.

Pregnancy and birth

A woman is pregnant when she is carrying a growing baby inside her. Pregnancy comes to an end when the baby is born. Pregnancy occurs in all animals that give birth to their young live rather than as eggs. This includes almost all mammals.

In humans (as in other mammals) pregnancy begins when a sperm from the father fertilizes an egg inside the mother and the fertilized egg begins to grow. This is called *conception*.

The growing fertilized egg is called an *embryo*. It soon becomes attached to the wall of the mother's uterus (womb) through a spongy structure called the *placenta*. The placenta contains many blood vessels, through which food and oxygen are passed from the mother's blood, via the umbilical cord, to the growing embryo.

After eight weeks of development the embryo is called a *fetus*. By 12 weeks the fetus, although only 8 centimetres long, looks like a tiny human being. It has hands, feet, eyes, nose, mouth and ears, and is moving. It will be another 12 weeks or so before it has grown enough to have any chance of surviving if born early. Normally birth takes place about 40 weeks after conception.

During those 40 weeks the womb has to grow enormously to provide room for the growing baby. It is this that gives a pregnant mother a 'tummy bulge'. The mother's breasts also become bigger. At the end of pregnancy they start to produce milk to feed the newborn baby.

Birth

There are three stages to birth (labour). In the first, the neck of the womb, the cervix, gradually opens. It stretches to about 10 centimetres so that the baby's head can be pushed through.

In the second stage, the womb muscles contract to push the baby down the birth canal. Once the head is born, the rest of the body slides out quite easily. The baby still has the umbilical cord that supplied it with nourishment from the placenta. This is removed, and the cord end forms the baby's navel (tummy button).

In the third stage, soon after the baby is born, the placenta becomes detached from the wall of the womb and is pushed out of the mother's body by more muscle contractions. The womb slowly shrinks back to its normal size.

Midwives

Midwives help women give birth. They are the experts in normal birth and are qualified to give total care through pregnancy and birth and for at least two weeks afterwards. Midwives are different from nurses, though many have trained as nurses.

The word 'midwife' means 'with woman'. In medieval times the midwife was usually one of a group of female friends who helped the woman in childbirth. Today some midwives are men.

▶ A newborn baby. The stump of the umbilical cord usually drops off 7–10 days after birth.

- Pregnancy may last from 12 days in some small marsupials to over a year in large whales.

- Sometimes a developing baby dies during pregnancy and the womb expels the fetus. This is called a *miscarriage*. Sometimes, if the baby is not developing normally, or if the mother is ill or there are other problems, a woman may go into hospital to have the fetus removed. This is an *abortion* and is usually done in the early stages of pregnancy.

- Occasionally, if a baby cannot be born naturally, the doctor may give the mother an anaesthetic and remove the baby by making a cut in the mother's abdomen and the wall of the womb. This is called a *caesarian birth*.

find out more
Children
Doctors
Hospitals
Nurses
Sex and reproduction

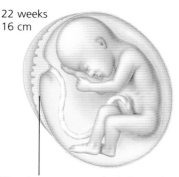

The **umbilical cord** carries blood containing food and oxygen to the baby from the mother, and carries away waste.

6 weeks
0.5 cm

9 weeks
1.7 cm

The **amniotic sac** is a bag of fluid in which the baby floats inside the womb.

22 weeks
16 cm

The **placenta** roots the baby to the wall of the womb, and passes blood to the umbilical cord.

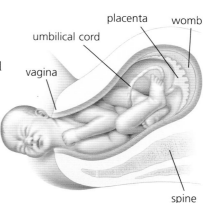

placenta   womb

umbilical cord

vagina

spine

▲ During labour, muscles around the womb push the baby out, usually head first, through the vagina. Labour may take several hours.

Prehistoric life

The term 'prehistoric life' means all the living things that existed before humans began to write about their history. We know about some plants and animals only from their fossils as they lived before human beings. Cave paintings and physical remains tell us about other animals that were well known to our ancestors. Many of these animals are now extinct.

When the Earth was first formed, about 4600 million years ago, there was no life at all, for its surface was too hot for any living things to exist. Scientists think that life first started in the muddy surfaces heated by volcanoes. The oldest fossils known date back about 3500 million years. They are much like bacteria of the present day.

Life in the sea

Hundreds of millions of years passed and some of the living things began to use the Sun's energy to make food. In this process, called photosynthesis, they used carbon dioxide in the atmosphere and gave off oxygen as a waste product. Plants still use this method of making food today. There is evidence that very small and simple plants existed about 3000 million years ago. As a result of plant activity, oxygen gas became part of the Earth's atmosphere, gradually building up to levels similar to those found today.

The first animals were probably like some single-celled creatures of today, such as Euglena, which makes a green scum on ponds. As time

▲ These living stromatolites in Australia are made up of layers of blue-green algae and rock. The oldest known fossils are of stromatolites 3500 million years old.

went on, the single cells combined to make larger life forms. The first chains of plant cells date back about 1000 million years, and geologists have found the remains of some of the first complex animals in rocks that date back over 600 million years: first sponges, then jellyfishes and worm-like creatures.

About 570 million years ago many kinds of animal developed hard shells, which became fossilized much more easily than the soft bodies of earlier creatures. Fossils of this age include corals, brachiopods, starfishes, snail-like animals,

- Ninety-nine per cent of all the different kinds of animal that have ever lived are now extinct.

- An extinction is the total disappearance of a particular species (kind) of plant or animal. Although there have been several great extinctions, very few phyla (major groups) of animals have disappeared completely.

▼ Evolution of life began more than 3500 million years ago. This time-line shows only the last 550 million years. Scientists can never be sure of the exact time an animal or plant evolved, so the time-line shows only when something was living rather than when it first appeared. Some of the kinds of animals that lived 500 million years ago, such as the starfishes, are still living today, but most are now extinct. (These drawings are not to scale.)

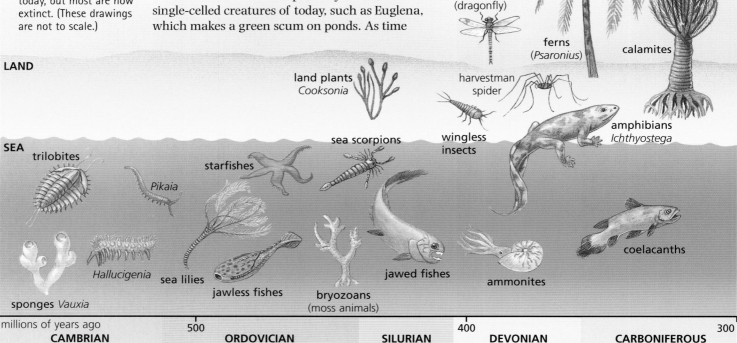

winged insects (dragonfly)

ferns (*Psaronius*)

calamites

harvestman spider

LAND

land plants *Cooksonia*

sea scorpions

wingless insects

amphibians *Ichthyostega*

SEA

trilobites

Pikaia

starfishes

Hallucigenia

sea lilies

jawless fishes

bryozoans (moss animals)

jawed fishes

ammonites

coelacanths

sponges *Vauxia*

millions of years ago	500		400		300
CAMBRIAN	ORDOVICIAN	SILURIAN	DEVONIAN	CARBONIFEROUS	

and most important, trilobites, which were armoured creatures related to crabs and insects.

The first fishes, whose remains are found in slightly later rocks, were armoured with heavy bone to protect them against hunting invertebrates (animals without backbones). Eventually many kinds of fish, including sharks and the ancestors of bony fishes, lived in the seas and fresh waters.

Life on land

From the fresh waters, plants and animals began to invade the land. This began about 400 million years ago, when a few small plants, fungi, mites

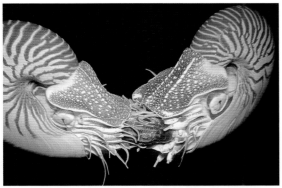

▲ Nautiluses, like the two in this picture, are sometimes called 'living fossils'. Their ancestors, known as nautiloids, include ammonites and were common 450 million years ago, during the Ordovician period.

and insect-like creatures lived on the muddy shores of estuaries and lakes. Some of the animals fed on the plants. In time plants grew larger and covered much of the land, making suitable habitats for many kinds of animal.

Unlike most modern fishes, many fishes at this time could breathe dry air, for they had lungs as well as gills. Some had pairs of large fins, supported by leg-like bones. It is thought that these fishes lived on the bed of pools or rivers, using their fins like legs to walk over the mud. They were all flesh-eaters, and it is likely that they sometimes scrambled right out of the water to grab prey such as an insect or snail from the bank.

In time, amphibians developed from such 'walking fishes'. Amphibians (which include today's frogs and salamanders) are able to survive out of water for at least part of their lives, although they have to return to water to breed. The first amphibians dragged themselves over the ground. But a few developed stronger legs, and were able to lift themselves clear of the rough surface. The descendants of these developed into reptiles. ▶

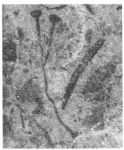

▲ *Cooksonia*, one of the first land plants. The photograph shows a fossil of the plant. The illustration shows how scientists think it looked. It had a waxy outer layer (cuticle) to prevent it drying out, and tubes in the stems to transport water and food.

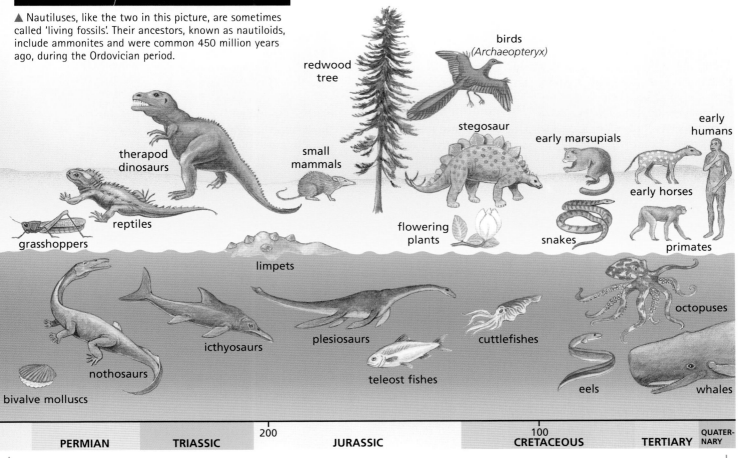

redwood tree

birds (*Archaeopteryx*)

therapod dinosaurs

small mammals

stegosaur

early marsupials

early humans

reptiles

flowering plants

early horses

grasshoppers

snakes

primates

limpets

octopuses

nothosaurs

icthyosaurs

plesiosaurs

cuttlefishes

teleost fishes

eels

whales

bivalve molluscs

200			100		
PERMIAN	**TRIASSIC**	**JURASSIC**	**CRETACEOUS**	**TERTIARY**	**QUATER-NARY**

◀ After insects, pterosaurs were the first animals to fly. They were reptiles that had gradually developed wings over millions of years, taking to the skies over 200 million years ago. It became extinct 70 million years ago. Birds were the next animals to fly, and finally bats, which are the only flying mammals.

The first reptiles

The first reptiles lived about 280 million years ago. Their skin was probably hard, dry and waterproof, and their eggs probably had a shell like those of modern reptiles.

Slowly the early reptiles spread across the continents, adapting to many different ways of life. Some returned to the water. Plesiosaurs and pliosaurs swam like the seals of today, while ichthyosaurs were the equivalent of dolphins. Great lizards called mosasaurs also lived in the seas. Flying reptiles soared above. Dinosaurs were among the numerous reptiles on land. Some of these were larger than any other land animals, before or since.

The first mammals and birds

Most reptiles were heavy-bodied and slow-moving, but a few developed in such a way that they were able to move faster and so escape from predators (hunting animals). Changes in their skull and their ribs suggest that they breathed regularly, like mammals. The first true mammals had developed from these mammal-like reptiles by the time of the earliest dinosaurs.

Birds evolved later. The earliest bird that we know of lived about 147 million years ago. It was clearly related to small flesh-eating dinosaurs.

When the dinosaurs finally died out about 65 million years ago, mammals, birds and modern types of fishes and flowering plants survived. In a relatively short period of time huge numbers of mammals and birds occupied much of the land and the seas. In time the mammals were left as the largest living creatures.

The coming of humans

One of the most recent mammals to evolve was humans. Our ancestors in prehistoric times shared their world with many animals that are now extinct. We know about these animals from cave paintings, engravings, fossils and other remains.

At the end of the last ice age in Europe, hunters in France and Spain painted pictures of animals on the walls of caves. Most were of wild horses, deer and bison, which were their main food. Other animals well known to our ancestors but now extinct are the mammoth, the woolly rhinoceros, the cave lion and the cave bear.

Most of what we know about prehistoric animals is from their fossilized remains, but a few creatures have been completely preserved, and we can see their muscles and skin. In parts of Siberia and North America woolly mammoths fell into crevasses in the frozen ground and were unable to get out. These animals were in a natural deep-freeze, in which they were preserved for over 10,000 years.

In North America the remains of a kind of extinct elephant called a mastodon tell us that these creatures were sometimes hunted successfully by humans. One fossil skeleton has been found with a small stone implement stuck into one of the bones.

• All domestic animals, including our pets, cows, horses and pigs, are descended from wild species. People in prehistoric times caught and tamed animals that could be useful to them. Tamed wolves helped in hunting; cattle, horses, sheep, goats and camels were kept for meat, milk, fur and hide and were often used to transport loads.

find out more
Animals
Cells
Dinosaurs
Evolution
Fossils
Geology
Plants
Prehistoric people

▼ These sabre-toothed cats ranged over North and South America about 2 million years ago, and probably fed on large mammals. It is thought that they attacked the soft underbellies of their prey, using their teeth to remove its innards.

Prehistoric people

Prehistory is the name archaeologists give to the enormous period of the past before written records began. It includes the evolution of modern humans from the ancestors that we share with today's great apes. Archaeologists have to work out how people developed and lived in that time from what little physical evidence survives.

• When 19th-century European archaeologists began to find prehistoric stone and metal tools they divided prehistory into three periods: the Stone Age, the Bronze Age and the Iron Age.

▲ Evidence of how prehistoric peoples lived is also found in the cave paintings they made. The most famous are in the woods of Lascaux in the Dordogne area of France. The cave walls are covered in a range of animals, dating from between 15,000 and 14,000 BC.

Homo sapiens made carvings, delicate stone tools, clay models and wonderful cave paintings.

modern humans

Neanderthal people wore clothes and used flint knives. They also buried their dead.

Homo erectus ('upright man') had a bigger brain than *Homo habilis*, was able to make better tools, and to make fires.

Homo habilis ('handy man') was less ape-like than *Australopithecus*, stood about 1.6 m tall, had a larger brain and probably used tools.

other australopithecines (types of 'southern ape')

One of the best examples of *Australopithecus afarensis* is known as Lucy. She was 1.5 m tall and had a small brain. She could walk upright, although she would have spent time climbing trees.

Australopithecus ramidus (*Australopithecus* means 'southern ape')

▲ How modern humans evolved over the last 5 million years. Many human-like species, such as *Homo habilis* and Neanderthals, are not the direct ancestors of modern humans. Some of these species overlapped with each other in time.

Our ancestors separated from the ancestors of modern gorillas nearly 7 million years ago, and from the ancestors of modern chimpanzees over 5 million years ago.

Millions of years ago

0

0.5

1

2

3

4

The further back you go in time, the more chance there is that things people used will have rotted away. It is usually only bones, and the stone tools or metal parts of things that survive.

The evolution of people

The animals that eventually evolved into humans separated from the ancestors of the great apes over 5 million years ago. Some human-like species which evolved later are not direct ancestors of modern humans.

The earliest kinds of fossil that are believed to be from ancestors of humans have been found in Africa and are over 4 million years old. Scientists think that the modern kind of human beings evolved from *Homo erectus* ('upright man'), although the fossil record does not tell us where and when *Homo sapiens* ('thinking man'), which is what we are, first arose.

Neanderthals were *Homo sapiens* and their fossils have been found in Europe and western Asia. Genetic evidence suggests that a newer type of human, *Homo sapiens sapiens*, developed in Africa about 100,000 years ago and spread to other continents, gradually replacing the Neanderthals. The fossil record is not good enough to make us sure of all the details, but by 10,000 years ago modern people lived almost everywhere.

Hunters and gatherers

Through most of prehistory, people everywhere obtained their food from wild plants and animals. They hunted, fished and gathered fruits, roots and other plant foods. They moved seasonally ▶

Prehistoric people

▶ This timeline shows the development of prehistoric peoples around the world, from the time when the first human-like 'hominids' evolved, about 5 million years ago, until 700 BC. Scientists have recently found skeletons of a species of human which is no taller than a modern three-year-old child. They are thought to be 18,000 years old and have been nicknamed the 'hobbit' after the Lord of the Rings characters.

5,000,000–2,000,000 BC	2,000,000–250,000 BC	250,000–120,000 BC	80,000–30,000 BC	50,000–25,000 BC	25,000–10,000 BC	10,000–8000 BC
Early tree-dwelling 'hominids' evolve in Africa.	Upright humans *Homo erectus* evolve, spreading to Asia and Europe.	Modern humans *Homo sapiens* evolve in Africa and spread north.	*Neanderthals*, a now extinct type of *Homo sapiens*, live in Europe and western Asia.	Modern humans, like those of today (*Homo sapiens sapiens*), spread through Europe and Asia into Australia and the Americas. A wide variety of tools (knifes, axes, adzes, scrapers, awls, harpoons, needles) made in a variety of materials (wood, bone, stone, antler, reed, leather, flint).	Early round houses, cave-painting and carving in Europe and western Asia.	Climate changes as ice age ends.

▼ This drawing shows what archaeologists think a hunters' camp looked like in a place called Pincevent, on the banks of the River Seine in France, about 12,000 to 10,000 years ago. The people hunted reindeer for food and skins, gathered plant foods and cooked their meals in the open.

from camp to camp and became expert observers of plant and animal life in the landscapes they occupied. They were the world's first 'ecologists'. They made tools, mostly of stone and wood, and lived in small family groups, occasionally joining other groups at tribal gatherings. They did not need to spend all their time getting and processing food, and had leisure to express themselves artistically in rock and cave paintings and by carving models of animals and people.

Farmers

From about 10,000 years ago, at the end of the last ice age, some hunter-gatherers began to cultivate plants and keep animals in small herds. This change took place earliest in the Middle East, where some people were already living all year in small settlements. Their populations grew and they became more dependent on the

cultivation of cereals, such as barley and wheat, and other grain crops, such as peas and lentils, the seeds of which were nutritious, easily stored, and could be sown for future harvesting.

They raised goats, sheep, and later pigs and cattle, which provided regular supplies of meat and other useful products. As agriculture developed, settlements became larger and people began to specialize in different crafts such as pottery, weaving and metal-working.

In a few other parts of the world people also began to cultivate plants they had previously gathered, such as rice in China, maize in Mexico and sorghum in tropical Africa. Agriculture gradually spread from these early centres and, as it did so, more plants and animals were 'domesticated': for example, asses, horses and camels in western Asia, and llamas and alpacas in South America. By 3000 BC farming had largely replaced gathering and hunting as the dominant way of life in Europe. And in the Middle East the first civilizations had become established.

8000–7000 BC	7000–6000 BC	5000–4000 BC	4000–3000 BC	3000–2000 BC	2000–1000 BC	1000–700 BC
Beginning of farming in western Asia. Wild cereals (wheat and barley) and legumes (peas, lentils) cultivated. Village settlements in the eastern Mediterranean, Syria and Jordan.	Goats, sheep, pigs and cattle domesticated in western Asia. Linen, textiles and pottery first made. Copper used in Anatolia, Turkey. Rice cultivated in China.	Copper and lead used in Anatolia. Domestication of asses, horses and camels in western Asia.	Sumerian civilization. First writing. Metalwork in copper, tin, bronze, lead, silver, gold. Irrigation. Sails. Maize cultivated in Mexico. Cotton grown in Peru. Llama domesticated in Peru. Agriculture established across Europe. Stone temples and tombs in Europe.	First pharaohs in Egypt; hieroglyphic writing system. Chariot invented in Mesopotamia. Indus civilization with cotton textiles. 'Beaker culture' spreads copper and textile technology through western Europe.	Bronze technology throughout Europe. Stonehenge completed.	Olmec culture in Mexico. Celts spread into central Europe and Britain. Iron technology in Europe by 700 BC.

▲ Stone circles were built in Europe from about 3000 BC to about 1200 BC as ceremonial or religious monuments. Archaeologists think that Stonehenge (pictured) in England was also used to observe the Sun and Moon.

Prehistoric technology

In many parts of the world prehistoric people used flint and other types of stone, such as obsidian, to make their tools and weapons. As they became more skillful, they developed specialized tools, such as stone axes for butchering large animals, flint blades for skinning them, and differently shaped stone and bone barbs for spears and arrows with which to kill birds, fish, reptiles and small mammals. They also made baskets for collecting plant foods, but these are seldom found by archaeologists because they decay easily. The first farmers needed additional tools, especially stone axes for felling trees to make room for fields, and grindstones for processing grains. Most prehistoric peoples also learned how to make pottery and to spin and weave wool, hair and other fibres.

Discovering metals

The discovery of how to use metal was made at different times and in different parts of the world.

Copper was the first metal to be used, before 6000 BC in western Asia. Later it was found that mixing copper and tin produced a harder and more useful metal, bronze. Later still, people discovered that they could make iron by 'smelting': melting iron ore and charcoal together. While hot, the iron was beaten into shapes with stones to make knives and other tools and weapons.

The first people to use iron lived in Anatolia (part of Turkey today) in about 2000 BC. In Britain people began using iron in about 700 BC. Some of it was made into bars and used for currency. In China iron was being smelted by the 6th century BC, and in West Africa iron was being worked before 500 BC.

Prehistory to history

The period of prehistory varies from place to place depending on the time when writing began in an area. In China prehistory ends with the invention of writing in the Shang period (from about 1600 BC). In most of America prehistory lasted until the Europeans arrived in the 16th century. In Britain the prehistoric period ended with the Roman invasion in AD 43, as it did for other countries too, as they were conquered by the Romans, who kept written records.

find out more
Africa
Ancient world
Archaeology
Aztecs
Celts
China
Evolution
Human beings
Hunter-gatherers
Incas
Maya
Prehistoric life

▼ On 19 September 1991 two hikers in the Alps found the remains of a man whose body had been preserved in the ice for 5300 years. He still had clothes and boots, a quiver and two arrows, a copper axe, a stone-pointed 'fire striker', a small flint dagger, a simple haversack, a sewing kit and lots of trapping equipment. He had apparently died while hunting in the mountains.

Presley, Elvis

Born 1935 in
Mississippi, USA
Died 1977 aged 42

Elvis Presley was the world's most popular rock and roll singer in the 1950s and 1960s. He was hugely influential, and he is still much imitated today.

• Elvis Presley sold 500 million records in his lifetime.

• Elvis Presley's house, Graceland, is a place of pilgrimage for his fans. Thousands visit every year to see some of his personal belongings and to visit his grave, which is in the grounds.

Elvis Aron Presley was born into a poor family in East Tupelo, Mississippi. As a teenager, he spent much of his time with black musicians, learning a lot about blues and gospel music. In 1953 he paid to make a record at Sun Records in Memphis, Tennessee. The owner liked his unusual mixture of country, blues and gospel styles, and offered him professional recording work.

Soon after Presley's first local hit he created a sensation on television by swivelling his hips while singing. Adults were outraged, but teenagers loved it. By 1956 he was a national star, with hits such as 'Hound Dog', 'Blue Suede Shoes' and 'Heartbreak Hotel'. Known as the 'King of Rock 'n' Roll', he eventually recorded 94 gold singles and over 40 gold albums. He also starred in 33 films.

By the mid-1960s, he was being challenged by other stars, but he continued touring and recording. In the 1970s he spent more and more time in Graceland, his huge mansion in Memphis. He died there in 1977.

find out more
Beatles
Pop and rock music

▶ Elvis Presley pictured at the height of his popularity. His life was cut short by heart failure at the age of 42. Many people believe his unhealthy lifestyle was to blame: he ate huge amounts of fast food and took lots of different types of drugs.

Primates

'Primates' is the name given to the group of mammals to which human beings belong. It also includes apes, monkeys and various 'lesser primates', including the lemurs of Madagascar, the pottos of Africa and the lorises of Asia.

Except for humans, most primates live in tropical forests. When they climb trees, they hold on to the branches with their fingers and toes. Many of them have a thumb that folds across the palm of the hand and a large toe that folds across the base of the foot. This enables most primates to grip things very strongly with both their hands and their feet.

Eyesight is a primate's most important sense. Its eyes are at the front of its face, so it looks at things using both eyes together. This is called binocular vision, and it enables primates to judge distances accurately. This is very important when they leap among the branches. Most primates do not have a good sense of smell, though, as a large nose would get in the way of their vision.

Most primates are social creatures that live in family groups. They have large brains, and are more intelligent than most other animals. In general, primate mothers have only one baby at a time. It is usually cared for by its mother and learns both from her and by playing with other members of the group.

Many primates have a long tail. In most cases it is used only for balancing, though some South American monkeys

▲ A slender loris from southern India, so called because it has long, slender arms and legs. It is a nocturnal animal (active at night), spending its nights using its huge eyes to look for insects and other small animals. It spends the days curled up asleep in the trees.

have a prehensile (gripping) tail that they can use like an extra hand. Humans, like their closest relatives the apes, have no tail.

• Lemurs, lorises and pottos are known as prosimians, or lesser primates. Prosimians have several features that distinguish them from other primates, including a wet nose with slit-like nostrils.

find out more
Apes
Human beings
Mammals
Monkeys
Pets

Printing

Printing is a way of making many identical copies from one original. For every page in a magazine, for every stamp, poster, book or cereal packet, there is one original. A printing plate is made from this original, and then hundreds, thousands or even millions of copies are printed.

Nearly all the printed material we see is made up of type (words or numbers), photographs and artists' illustrations. This article has all three. A novel may have only type, while a stamp usually has type and a photograph or illustration.

Type is mostly set on a computer very similar to a word processor, and all the typefaces (different kinds of type) and sizes are stored electronically in its memory. Sometimes artists'

Type is any letter, number or other character used in printing.
Typography is the design and layout of the type.
Typefaces: *serif* type has a slight projection finishing off the stroke of a letter; *sans serif* type has no serifs; *script* type imitates handwriting.

serif   sans serif   script

typo gra *phy*

Styles:
Roman   *Italic*
Bold   ***Bold Italic***

Type sizes: type is measured in points (72 points = 25.4 mm = 1 inch). The top part of a letter is called the ascender, the bottom part the descender.

---

illustrations and photographs are also stored in this way. Designers can also use the computer to arrange the type and illustrations on the page.

A finished page can be stored electronically and used to produce film from which the printers can make printing plates. Alternatively, the computer can print out just the type on special paper, and use it together with the illustrations and photographs to make the finished original, which is called camera-ready artwork.

Printing plates

Before any printing can be done, the words and pictures on the camera-ready artwork have to be transferred to the *plate* (printing surface), which is usually metal. The plate is coated with a light-sensitive material, which hardens when exposed to light. The image of the original is transferred by placing a negative film of the original over a printing plate and exposing it to bright light. After exposure, the plate is washed. Those parts of the plate that were masked from the light

wash away, but the image of the original remains in those areas where the light shone through the negative.

Type is solid black, but black-and-white photographs and illustrations need a range of different tones from black to very light greys. The tones are produced by breaking the picture up into a pattern of very small dots called a *halftone*. Each dot prints solid black, but little dots with big white spaces between them appear light grey. Big black dots with very little white spaces between them appear almost black.

Printing processes

We use two main printing processes: *lithography* and *gravure*. A third process, *letterpress*, using a printing surface with a raised image, was for many years the main printing technique, but it is now little used.

Lithography ('litho') is the most widely used printing

▲ The main photo shows a print worker checking the quality of a sheet of colour printing (part of the printing press can be seen on the right). The enlarged section above shows how printed colour photos are made up from tiny dots of just four colours: magenta (a bluish red), yellow, cyan (a greenish blue) and black. All other colours can be made by combining these four.

• An offset litho printing press can print on a giant reel of paper (a web) at speeds of more than 500 metres per minute.

Lithography

The letter image is greasy and so attracts printing ink.

One roller spreads water over all the plate except for the greasy parts.

A second roller spreads ink which sticks to the greasy letters. It is repelled by the wet parts of the plate.

The inked letter is transferred to the paper.

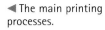

◀ The main printing processes.

find out more

Books
Drawing
Newspapers and
 magazines
Photocopiers
Word processors

Gravure

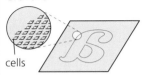

cells

The letter consists of hundreds of tiny cells sunk into the plate.

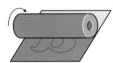

A roller spreads ink over the whole plate.

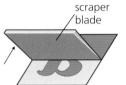

scraper blade

A metal blade scrapes ink off the plate surface, leaving it only in the cells.

The inked letter is transferred to the paper

process today. The image on the printing plate is the whole 'picture' of type, illustrations and photographs. Litho plates are usually made of aluminium, which can be easily wrapped around a cylinder. On the printing press, the inked image is offset (transferred) from the plate onto a rubber cylinder and from there onto the paper.

In gravure the printing plate has cells (like tiny wells) sunk into its surface. Making gravure plates is very expensive, so this process is usually used for very large print runs such as for magazines or packaging.

▶ FLASHBACK ◀

The first printed books were made in China by hand-carving characters and designs back-to-front onto a flat block of wood,

then inking the block and pressing paper or cloth against it. The earliest surviving book, a collection of Buddhist sermons, was printed in China in AD 868. Movable type, which consists of a different piece of type for each character, was invented in China by Pi Sheng between 1041 and 1048.

All printing in Europe was done from wooden blocks until about 1450, when Johann Gutenberg of Germany developed movable metal type which could be used again and again. He also developed a special press that could make many copies of a page quickly. This is the letterpress form of printing, used by all printing presses for the next 350 years. Around 1800 the process of lithography was introduced.

Printmaking

In the early 1400s artists began to experiment with ways of printing pictures using the same basic principle as the printing press. They cut a design into a smooth, flat block of wood, applied ink to it, and then pressed it very hard against a sheet of paper. A picture made in this way is called a print or engraving.

In the mid-1400s, a method of printmaking called line engraving was invented. The design was cut in a metal plate (usually copper) so that finer lines and more detail could be included in the print. Colour prints are made by using several blocks or plates, one for each colour. A more recent technique is silkscreen printing, in which the artist cuts a design in a stencil and places it on top of a screen made of fine silk mesh. The artist squeezes colour through the parts of the screen that are not covered by the stencil onto the paper below.

• In a printmaking technique called *etching*, the artist uses a needle to draw onto a copper plate covered with a thin layer of wax. The plate is then placed in acid, which eats away the metal where the wax has been scratched off. The design is transferred onto the plate, which is printed in the normal way. The Dutch artist Rembrandt (1606–1669) was a great etcher.

• The German artist Albrecht Dürer (1471–1528) was one of the greatest ever masters of engraving and wood-block prints.

▼ To print this colour picture, four printing plates are needed. Each plate makes its impression separately. Black is always printed last.

yellow plate

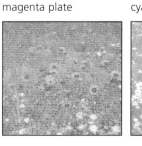

magenta plate

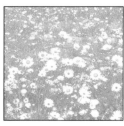

cyan plate

black plate

Probability

Some probabilities
*Throwing a double
with two dice:*
1/6 (people sometimes
call this 1 in 6)
*Throwing a double six
with two dice:*
1/36
*Being dealt all four
aces in a hand of 13
playing cards:*
1/379
*Being dealt a complete
suit (all hearts, clubs,
diamonds or spades) in
a hand of 13 cards:*
1/158,753,389,900

A probability is a number somewhere between 0 and 1. It gives a more precise estimate of how likely you think something is to happen. The nearer a probability is to 1, the more likely it is to happen. The probability of a tossed coin landing as 'heads' (or 'tails') is $\frac{1}{2}$, because there are only two ways it can come down.

The probability of throwing a head with a single coin (a one in two chance) can be expressed as a percentage (50 per cent), as a decimal (0.5), or as a fraction ($\frac{1}{2}$). If you throw a dice, there are six ways it can land, so the probability of throwing the number you want is 1/6. Probability also tells us the likelihood of several things happening one after the other. For example, the probability of getting two heads when you toss two coins is $\frac{1}{4}$, because the coins can land in four different ways: HH, HT, TH, TT. Find out the probability of getting two heads with three coins. Do you think that this would be a good bet?

Gamblers bet on the results of horse races or football matches. They also try to win money on games of chance, such as roulette, poker and backgammon. Lotteries are another way of trying to win money through chance. Prizes are awarded to those people whose chosen numbers match the numbers drawn at random from a drum. The probability of winning the top prize in a national lottery may be as low as 1/10 million.

▼ Bookmakers, like these ones at a racecourse in Ireland, accept bets on the results of horse races. When they bet, gamblers are trying to win money by predicting the future.

find out more
Numbers
Statistics

Proteins

Proteins are among the most important substances that make up living things. They can carry out almost any task that a living cell requires.

1 The body's genes carry the information for making many proteins on a long molecule called DNA.

DNA

mRNA

2 One gene, with the instructions for making an individual protein, is copied to another molecule, called mRNA (messenger RNA).

3 Tiny particles called ribosomes use the instructions from mRNA to join a string of amino acids together in a specific order.

ribosome

4 Once a protein chain has been formed, it folds itself into a particular shape.

protein chain of an enzyme

5 Some more complex proteins are made up of several protein chains.

chain A   chain B

chain B   chain A

◀ How proteins are made.

Proteins are large complicated molecules. They are built of smaller units called amino acids, strung together in chains. An average protein is about 500 amino acids long. All the proteins found in living things are made from only 20 different amino acids.

There are two main types of protein. *Structural proteins* make up the bulk of such body tissues as muscles and ligaments. *Enzymes* are proteins that help chemical reactions in the body to occur quickly and efficiently. In digestion, for example, enzymes help break down food into smaller parts so that it can be absorbed into the body.

The different functions of structural proteins and enzymes depend on their shapes. The amino-acid chains of structural proteins make long, straight shapes that can join together in threads, bundles or sheets. But in enzymes, the chains fold up into complex shapes, each one designed to help a particular chemical reaction.

find out more
Cells
Diets
Food
Genetics
Glands

Psychologists

Psychologists are people who study the workings of the human mind, often with the aim of helping others to understand themselves better. Some psychologists carry out research; others work in a wide variety of settings within the community, to help people with different needs.

- The word 'psychology' comes from two Greek words meaning 'study of the mind'. 'Psychiatry', also from Greek, means 'curing the mind'.

▶ The Austrian doctor Sigmund Freud (1865–1939) was one of the pioneers of modern psychology. He introduced the idea that the unconscious mind influences people's thoughts and behaviour, and developed a method of treating people with problems known as psychoanalysis.

find out more
Brains
Diseases
Medicine

Within the community, educational psychologists help children in school who are having trouble with their work or their behaviour. Occupational psychologists help people find the right job for their type of personality. Clinical psychologists help people with personal problems, such as shyness or lack of confidence, and those with serious mental problems.

Clinical psychologists use various forms of therapy (treatment) to help people with their problems. These therapies usually involve prompting people to talk about their problems so that they learn to understand themselves better. They may then recognize where they sometimes go wrong and how best to put this right in the future.

The field of *psychiatry* is similar to clinical psychology in that it also concerns itself with mental illness. However, psychiatrists are trained medical doctors and may treat their patients with drugs.

No one really knows what causes mental illness. Some kinds seem to be caused by disturbances in the chemistry of the brain. It upsets the way people think, feel and behave. Sometimes people who are mentally ill need to stay in hospital until their illness is under control.

Puppets

Puppets are a bit like dolls, but they are made to move by the use of the fingers or by pulling strings or pushing rods that are attached to them. Puppets may resemble people, animals or imaginary creatures, and are often used in drama, where they mime the actions of the story.

- Punch and Judy is the best-known puppet play in Britain. The story is told by a single puppeteer, who uses hand (glove) puppets and stands hidden in a booth.

Puppets range in size from tiny finger puppets to huge figures, larger than people. There are many different types, but the four most common are glove puppets, rod puppets, shadow puppets and marionettes. Glove puppets fit on the hand and are worked by the fingers. Rod puppets are moved by rods attached to the puppet's arms and legs. Shadow puppets are also often worked by rods, but they are flat, and a light behind them casts their shadows onto a screen. Marionettes, or string puppets, are operated from above by strings fastened to different parts of the puppet.

For centuries puppets have been used to act out folk stories and scenes from religious books. In medieval Europe puppets enacted stories from the Bible and famous battles and scenes from history. There are puppet theatres in many parts of the world today, which use elaborate costumes, staging and music, especially in India, Japan and Java. In Japan the puppet theatre is one of the three main types of theatre, along with No and Kabuki.

find out more
Drama

▶ In this Thai puppet show, the puppeteer uses finely carved shadow puppets, which create interesting shadows. Music is played in the background on Thai instruments.

Pygmies

Pygmies live in the hot forests of central Africa. They are small people, usually less than 1.5 metres in height. They were probably the earliest inhabitants of the region.

Pygmies live in groups of up to 100 people. They get their food by hunting animals with bows and arrows, spears and nets, and gathering food plants, such as berries and nuts. They regard honey as a delicacy. When they find some, they often celebrate.

Pygmies live in camps, which they occupy for only a few weeks before moving to a new site. Their homes are made of frames of branches covered by leaves. In the camps, adults make arrows, baskets and cloth from tree bark, boys learn hunting skills, and girls work with their mothers. Many pygmies are skilled potters. Pygmies enjoy singing, dancing and telling stories that show their love for the forest, which they call 'mother and father'. The forest supplies nearly all their needs and they try not to harm it.

Long ago, pygmies probably lived throughout central Africa, but farmers have taken most of their land. Their way of life is changing. Some pygmies have left the forests and some children are now attending school. The Twa pygmies, who live in Burundi, Rwanda and the Democratic Republic of Congo (formerly Zaire), have adopted much of the language and culture of neighbouring tribes.

However, the Mbuti pygmies of the Ituri forest, also in the Democratic Republic of Congo, have remained relatively unchanged.

▼ A pygmy hunter from Cameroon.

find out more
Africa
Hunter-gatherers

Rabbits and hares

• There are 21 different kinds of rabbit and 22 kinds of hare.

find out more
Mammals
Pets

Rabbits and hares are small furry mammals with long ears. In general, hares have bigger ears and larger bodies than rabbits, who are their close relatives.

Rabbits and hares are so similar that in some parts of the world creatures that should be called hares are known as rabbits. For example, some kinds of North American hare are often called rabbits or jackrabbits.

Rabbits

Rabbits are gnawing animals, feeding on plants. They usually live in groups and shelter in burrows. When they feed, they stay close to home for safety. They rely on their good eyesight and senses of hearing and smell to warn them of enemies. They are hunted by many predators, including human beings.

Baby rabbits are blind and furless at birth. Although their mothers feed them only twice a day, they grow quickly. They are ready to face the outside world by the age of 3 weeks. Most kinds of rabbit produce a large number of young in a year.

Hares

Unlike rabbits, hares live alone, usually in grassy places. They do not dig burrows, but make a shallow trench, called a form, to shelter in. A hare lies quite still when a dog or a fox approaches. It leaps away only when the enemy is very near. It can run very fast, zigzagging and jumping high, so that it can still watch its enemy.

Baby hares are called leverets. They are open-eyed, furry and active within minutes of being born. Their mother hides them near to her form and feeds them every evening, but they are soon able to look after themselves.

◄ During the mating season male hares leap, chase and 'box' each other to attract the attention of females.

Racoons

Racoons are among the most familiar animals in the Americas. Many racoons have discovered that humans produce lots of edible waste. They often make their dens in lofts and outhouses to be near to dustbins and rubbish tips.

- The name 'racoon' comes from 'aroughcoune', a Native American name for the animal. It means 'he scratches with his hands'.

- Racoons are best known for their striped tails, which were worn by hunters of the American West, such as Davy Crockett.

- There are seven members of the racoon family.

find out more
Mammals

Most racoons live in forests, near water, and they climb and swim well. They are more active in the evening than in the day. They eat almost anything: wild fruit, birds' eggs and insects in the forests, worms, fish, frogs, young muskrats, crayfish and clams in the water. They have front paws like little hands, with long, mobile fingers that can

break open shells and even undo catches and locks.

Normally racoons live alone, and a male may travel a long distance to find a mate. Most females have a family of four or five young, born in April or May. The young develop slowly. Born blind and helpless, they do not leave the den until they are about 8 weeks old, and are not weaned until the end of the summer.

The red panda is the only member of the racoon family to live outside the Americas. It lives in mountain forests in China and the Himalayas. Red pandas are good climbers. They sleep by day in tree dens and are active at night, searching for fruits, acorns and plant shoots, and sometimes catching insects and other small animals.

◄ A racoon raiding a henhouse for eggs.

Radar

Radar is short for RAdio Detection And Ranging. It can tell us the position of a moving or stationary object, even when it is far away or in dark or foggy conditions. Radar tells air-traffic controllers the height and position of aircraft around busy airports. It has many other important uses, including catching speeding motorists.

Most large aircraft have on-board radar to warn them of nearby planes as well as bad weather ahead. A ship's radar equipment detects other ships or hazards in the area. Weather forecasters use radar to detect approaching storms or hurricanes. Radar helps scientists to study the atmosphere and other planets, and to track spacecraft before they reach their orbits. It can also warn of attacking missiles, aircraft or ships.

Radar was invented by a British scientist, Robert Watson-Watt. In 1935 the British government asked him to find out whether beams of radio waves could destroy enemy aircraft. During his research he realized that radio waves would bounce off a plane. He devised a way of

using reflected waves from an aircraft to find out its position and the direction it was moving. Watson-Watt had invented the first radar system for detecting enemy planes.

find out more
Airports
Radiation
Radio
Waves
Weather

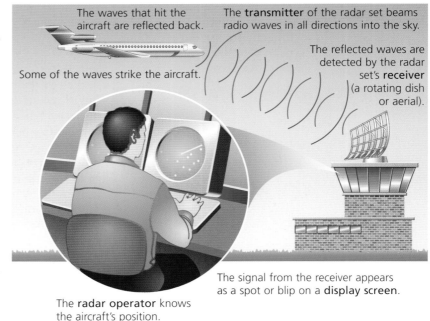

The waves that hit the aircraft are reflected back.

Some of the waves strike the aircraft.

The **transmitter** of the radar set beams radio waves in all directions into the sky.

The reflected waves are detected by the radar set's **receiver** (a rotating dish or aerial).

The **radar operator** knows the aircraft's position.

The signal from the receiver appears as a spot or blip on a **display screen**.

Radiation

Radiation is energy on the move. Some kinds of radiation energy, such as radio signals and light, travel as invisible waves. Other kinds of radiation are tiny particles that shoot out from atoms at enormous speeds. The cosmic rays speeding around out in space are made up of tiny particles.

The materials inside the reactors of nuclear power plants are examples of *radioactive materials*. Radioactive materials can produce a mixture of radiations, some of which are particles and some of which are waves.

Radioactivity

The atoms inside radioactive materials can change into different kinds of atom by throwing out tiny atomic particles. There are two kinds of particle, called alpha and beta. Alpha particles travel more slowly than beta particles, but they are much heavier and generally have more energy. Alpha particles lose their energy easily and can be stopped by a thick sheet of paper. Beta particles lose their energy less easily and can pass through a sheet of aluminium.

Radioactive materials also throw out gamma rays. These travel as waves, and can pass through several centimetres of lead.

Radiation dangers

Small amounts of nuclear radiation come from radioactive materials inside the Earth all the time. This is called *background radiation*, and it

▶ This computer picture shows the spread of radioactivity across the northern hemisphere following an accident at the Chernobyl nuclear power plant, in the former Soviet Union, in April 1986. Many people died or became ill with radiation sickness.

normally does us no harm. However, too much radiation can be dangerous. For example, a natural radioactive gas called radon leaks up through the ground in some places and can collect in people's homes. Special pumps can get rid of the gas.

The radioactive materials in nuclear power plants are surrounded by thick concrete walls to stop the radiation escaping. A serious accident at a nuclear power plant can release radioactive dust and gas into the environment, contaminating water supplies and food. The radiation released in this way may cause cancer, perhaps many years later.

▶ FLASHBACK ◀

In 1873 James Clerk Maxwell predicted the existence of invisible kinds of radiation similar to light. Heinrich Hertz discovered radio waves in 1887, and so confirmed Maxwell's predictions. Then, in 1895, William Röntgen discovered X-rays. In 1896 Henri Becquerel found that uranium gives off an invisible radiation that affects photographic plates. He called this effect radioactivity.

▼ Most types of wave radiation belong to the same family. They are called *electromagnetic waves*. You can see the different types in the chart below.

• Doctors sometimes use nuclear radiation to destroy cancer tumours. Although the doses given are quite small, there are often unpleasant side-effects for the patients.

find out more
Atoms and molecules
Curie, Marie
Energy
Heat
Light
Power stations
Radio
Scanners
Sound
Stars
Waves
X-rays

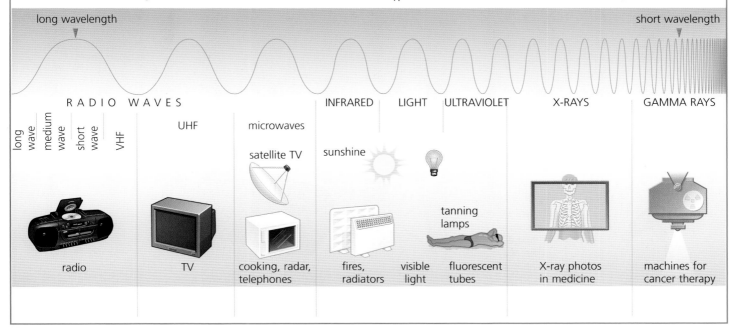

long wavelength   short wavelength

RADIO WAVES   INFRARED   LIGHT   ULTRAVIOLET   X-RAYS   GAMMA RAYS

long wave | medium wave | short wave | VHF | UHF | microwaves | sunshine | tanning lamps

satellite TV

radio | TV | cooking, radar, telephones | fires, radiators | visible light | fluorescent tubes | X-ray photos in medicine | machines for cancer therapy

Radio

Radio lets you listen to someone speaking into a microphone thousands of kilometres away. The sounds themselves do not travel that far. Instead, they are changed into radio waves which travel through the air. When they reach your radio, they are changed back into a copy of the original sounds.

Radio waves are a kind of electromagnetic radiation. Like other kinds of radiation, such as light and X-rays, they can travel long distances at incredible speed – 300,000 km per second (the speed of light).

Sending sounds by radio

When someone speaks, their voice sends sound vibrations through the air. A *microphone* turns the vibrations into tiny changing currents called electrical signals. A *transmitter* is a device for making powerful radio waves, which are sent out in a continuous stream called a *carrier wave*. In simple transmitters, the electrical signals from the microphone control the strength of the radio waves being sent out, making them pulsate to match the sound vibrations. The pulsating waves are sent out from the transmitter through an *aerial* (a metal rod or wire). If the transmitter is powerful enough, the radio waves can travel thousands of kilometres.

The radio waves (called radio signals) are picked up by an aerial in a *receiver* (such as your radio at home). The receiver turns the pulsations into electrical signals, which are then turned back into a copy of the original sound in a *loudspeaker*.

Uses of radio

We use radio waves for many types of communication, apart from sound broadcasting. Police, fire, taxi and ambulance crews use two-way radios. Mobile phones are linked to the main telephone network by radio. Ships and aircraft use radio for communication and for navigation. Television uses radio waves for transmitting pictures and sound.

◀ This little boy is listening to a portable radio in a street in Beijing, China. Portable radios are powered by batteries and can be used almost anywhere.

• DAB (Digital Audio Broadcasting) is the latest way of receiving a radio station. As the signal is digital, it allows a clearer signal to be broadcast.

▶ FLASHBACK ◀

Radio signals were first transmitted over a distance of more than 1.5 kilometres by the Italian inventor Guglielmo Marconi in 1895. In 1901 he sent a radio message across the Atlantic Ocean from Cornwall, England to Newfoundland, Canada. It was later found that the radio waves bounced off an upper layer of the atmosphere, which explained how they could travel so far.

An American station, KDKA, started the first regular public broadcasting in 1920. In the 1950s the first small, portable radios began to appear.

find out more
Atmosphere
Electronics
Radiation
Recording
Satellites
Television
Waves

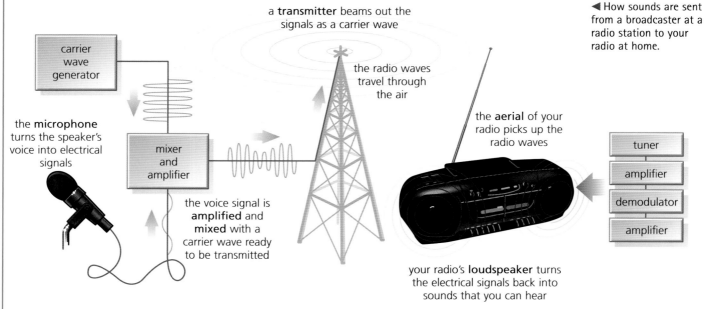

◀ How sounds are sent from a broadcaster at a radio station to your radio at home.

the **microphone** turns the speaker's voice into electrical signals

carrier wave generator

mixer and amplifier

the voice signal is **amplified** and **mixed** with a carrier wave ready to be transmitted

a **transmitter** beams out the signals as a carrier wave

the radio waves travel through the air

the **aerial** of your radio picks up the radio waves

tuner

amplifier

demodulator

amplifier

your radio's **loudspeaker** turns the electrical signals back into sounds that you can hear

Railways

Railways run on smooth metal tracks that allow heavy loads to be moved more efficiently than on roads. Locomotives (railway engines) are used to pull trains carrying either passengers or freight. A single locomotive may pull a load weighing thousands of tonnes.

Commuter trains carry large numbers of people to and from their work. High-speed passenger trains are widely used in Europe and Japan, the fastest ones travelling at speeds of over 300 kilometres per hour. Freight trains carry cargo. They are often manufactured specially to carry materials or goods such as oil, chemicals and cars. Some freight trains are over 500 metres long, and several locomotives may be needed to pull very heavy loads.

Types of locomotive

Most railway locomotives are powered either by electricity or by diesel engines similar to those in trucks and buses. In big diesel locomotives, the engine turns a generator which supplies electricity to motors between the wheels. Locomotives that use this system are known as diesel-electric locomotives. Electric locomotives can be small but powerful. Electric motors turn the wheels, supplied with electricity either from overhead wires or from an extra rail alongside.

Recent developments in locomotive design have involved lifting trains above the track, either with a cushion of air (the hover-train) or by the use of magnetic levitation (the maglev). Powerful magnets fitted onto the vehicle and onto a guide rail below are used to make the maglev trains 'float' above the track, clear of the rails. These trains can travel at high speeds because there is no contact with the track and so no friction to slow them down. In Germany and Japan maglev test vehicles have reached speeds of about 500 kilometres per hour. Not all maglev trains travel at high speeds. The low-speed, driverless trains used to transport people around some large airports are also maglev vehicles.

Constructing railways

The route for a railway needs to be as level as possible. Any slope or gradient has to be very gradual to stop the locomotive wheels from slipping. Curves have to be gentle because a train cannot turn sharply at high speed. Viaducts are built to carry the railway across valleys, and

Trams

Trams are passenger-carrying vehicles that run on rails laid in the street. The top of each rail is level with the surface of the road so that other vehicles can cross the rails without any difficulty. Modern trams are electric-driven, and are quiet, comfortable and fast.

Horse-drawn trams were first used in the USA in about 1830 and in Britain in 1858. In some places, the horses were replaced by steam tram locomotives. The old trams were noisy and slow and got in the way of other vehicles.

tunnels carry it through hills. In the early days of railway building, much of the work was done by hand, with teams of thousands of people moving earth and laying tracks.

The railway track is made of steel rails laid on concrete or wooden sleepers. These help to take the weight of the passing train and keep the rails level. Short gaps are often left between the lengths of railway track to allow the rails to expand in warm weather. Without the gaps, the rails would bend out of shape. The two rails are laid a fixed distance apart, known as the *gauge*. The most common gauge is 1.44 metres. Russia, Finland and Spain use a wider gauge.

▲ The high-speed Eurostar train carries passengers between Britain and mainland Europe via the Channel Tunnel.

Railway signals

To avoid collisions, a railway line is divided into sections with a signal at the beginning of each section. A train can pass a signal only if it shows the right colour or the right position. The signals are operated from a signal box. In modern signal boxes, a computer ensures that only one train is travelling on each section of line. The signal box

• Local services often use trains known as diesel multiple units (DMUs). In these, small diesel engines are mounted under the floor of each coach.

• On very steep slopes a special toothed 'rack rail' is used between the outer rails. A powered gearwheel on the locomotive, called a pinion, engages the teeth so the train can pull itself uphill without slipping.

- One of the finest achievements of railway engineering was the construction of a railway between Bristol and London, under the guidance of Isambard Kingdom Brunel. The Great Western Railway, as it was called, took eight years to build and was completed in 1841.

- In 1863 two North American companies, the Union Pacific and the Central Pacific, started to build a railway across the continent. One company worked eastwards from the Pacific coast and the other westwards from the Missouri River. Six years later the two lines met in Utah.

- The largest working steam engine in the world is the Union Pacific 'Challenger', which was built during World War II and restored in the 1980s.

- The London Underground has over 400 km of track, more than any other underground railway. New York has the most stations (466), and Moscow carries the most passengers (over 6 million a day).

find out more
Engines
Magnets
Tunnels
Victorian Britain

▲ On many railways, traffic is controlled from signal centres fitted out with sophisticated computer equipment.

also controls the route of each train. The train is steered by special moving rails, called *points*, which make it change direction wherever the tracks divide.

Underground railways

The first underground railways, or *subways*, were shallow tracks built for steam engines, not far below street level. The first part of the London Metropolitan Line was opened in 1863. Engineers later developed techniques of tube-tunnelling at 25 to 28 metres below ground. A deep-level line running under the River Thames opened in 1890. In the USA, the first stretches of the New York subway opened in 1904.

▶ FLASHBACK ◀

The first steam railway locomotive was built by Richard Trevithick in 1804 and ran in an iron-works in Wales. Another Englishman, George Stephenson, designed many early railway locomotives as well as the first passenger railway, which opened in 1825 between Stockton and Darlington in England. He also supervised the building of the Liverpool to Manchester railway, which opened five years later and marked the beginning of the 'railway age'. The famous steam locomotive 'The Rocket' was designed by Stephenson and built by his son Robert. It was completed in 1829.

Railways continued to expand throughout the 19th century. Public railways opened in Belgium and Germany in 1835, and in the next 20 years construction started in many parts of the world. Railways brought great changes to the way people lived, enabling them for the first time in history to travel long distances every day to work. Steam locomotives were widely used until the 1960s and are still in use in some countries.

▼ A United States mail train crossing the Sierra Nevada in 1870.

Rain and snow

Rain and snow are our most important sources of water. Without them, all the world's rivers, lakes and soils would be dry. Very few living things can survive in places where there is no rain or snow. They provide water for humans and other animals. Without rainfall, plants cannot grow properly. However, too much rain and snow can cause flooding that may destroy homes and damage crops.

▼ Much of India receives very heavy rains between the months of July and September. This period is known as the monsoon season. The rains are carried by warm, wet winds that sweep in from the Indian Ocean.

• If a lot of snow falls on a steep slope, it may start to slide downhill and produce dangerous avalanches.

Rain forms when water from the oceans evaporates (changes into a gas) and rises as water vapour. The rising water vapour condenses (cools) to form droplets of water. These droplets collect together to make clouds. You can see condensation for yourself if you watch your warm breath produce a thin layer of water on a cold window.

As clouds rise, they cool down and cannot carry as much water as when they were warm. This cooling causes the small drops of water to grow bigger as more vapour condenses on them. They may grow so heavy that they fall out of the sky as rain.

Drought and floods

Rain falls in most parts of the world, but the amount of rain that falls in a year differs from place to place. Desert regions may have no rain for many years, whereas some tropical areas, for example parts of India, can receive many metres of rain in a single year.

Sometimes a place may have less rainfall than expected, or even no rain at all. When this happens, the water level in nearby rivers and lakes drops. The ground may begin to crack, and the soil becomes dusty and dry. A long dry period

of weather like this is called a drought. During a drought, crops and other plants do not grow properly, and animals and often people may not have enough food to eat.

If too much rain falls over a very short period, rivers may not be able to carry the water back to the oceans and seas quickly enough. When this happens, water levels rise dramatically and floods occur.

Snow and hail

Snow is made up of tiny crystals of ice that stick together. This happens when the temperature is so cold that the water vapour in the air freezes. It forms small, fluffy, hexagonal-shaped ice crystals that fall out of the sky as snow. Snow may not melt for many weeks, and can collect in layers on the ground to become many metres thick. Snow that falls in high mountains or in the very cold polar regions might not melt at all, even during the warmer summer months.

Hail consists of pea-sized balls of ice that fall like rain. They can cause damage to houses, cars and crops. Hail is produced in tall thunderstorm clouds in which the air rises rapidly. The up-draughts of air can be so strong that they carry raindrops to the top of the cloud where the air is cold. The raindrops freeze into hailstones and drop out of the cloud faster than they can melt.

Frost

On very cold mornings you may find a white, sugar-like coating on the grass, on windows and on cars. This is called frost. It forms when the temperature of the air falls below the freezing point of water (0 °C). This causes moisture in the air to freeze onto cold surfaces.

▼ A snow scene in Japan. There are thousands of different shapes of snow crystal, but all have six points.

find out more
Climate
Clouds
Deserts
Ice
Water
Weather
Wind

Recording

Recording is a way of keeping sounds or video pictures so that you can hear or see them later. People record music and sound on cassette tapes or compact discs (CDs), and moving pictures on video. Professional recordings are made in specially designed studios. But you can make recordings at home with a tape recorder or a camcorder.

• Most music recordings are made in *stereo*. This means that there are two versions of the music on the recording, each containing different parts of the original music. When the tape or CD is played, the sounds of the tracks come out of different loudspeakers.

We hear sounds when vibrations in the air enter our ears. We see pictures when light enters our eyes. We cannot save sound vibrations or light rays directly, so they need to be saved in some other way. When we record something, the sounds and pictures are turned into electrical signals. These signals are then used to make the recording. On a tape, sounds and pictures are recorded as patterns in a magnetic coating. On a CD they are recorded as microscopic pits in the surface of the disc. A tape player, CD player, video player or computer turns the recording back into sounds or pictures.

Tape and CD recordings

A microphone can turn sounds into electrical signals; a video camera can do the same with pictures. To record on a tape, the electrical signals are sent to a recording head. A cassette tape is coated with millions of tiny magnetic particles. The recording head magnetizes these particles weakly or strongly, depending on the strength of the signal. In this way, the signal is recorded as a magnetic pattern.

A CD recording is a pattern made by millions of microscopic pits arranged in rings on the surface of the disc. When the disc is played, a laser beam in the CD player reads the pattern in a similar way to a bar code reader at a supermarket. Most CDs are 'read only': the recording on them cannot be deleted or recorded over. However, it is possible to record on to some kinds of CD, as with cassette tapes.

Analogue and digital

Any recording can be made either in analogue form or in digital form. An analogue recording is a direct copy or image of the electrical signal produced by the microphone or camera, recorded as a magnetic pattern. Until quite recently all recordings were analogue. Analogue recordings suffer from the problem that they can become distorted as they are copied or played back.

To make a digital recording, the signal is coded by turning it into a long list of numbers. This process is called *digitization*. It is carried out by an analogue-to-digital (A-to-D) converter. The converter measures the strength of the analogue signal thousands of times every second, and records each answer as a binary number (a number made up of only 0s and 1s). The long list of numbers is called a *digital signal*. Once a recording has been digitized, it is much less likely to be distorted or altered, and it can be copied exactly time after time.

Tape recordings can be either analogue or digital. On an analogue recording the magnetic pattern varies in just the same way as the original electrical signal. On a digital recording

▶ Analogue recording and playback.

microphone: sound waves make a crystal vibrate. This generates electric signals.

loudspeaker: electric signals make a coil vibrate. The coil's vibrations move the cone, which gives out sound waves.

recording

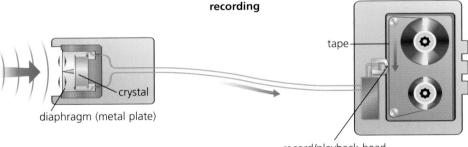

diaphragm (metal plate)

crystal

tape

cassette recorder: electric signals through the recording head put a magnetic pattern on the tape.

record/playback head

playback

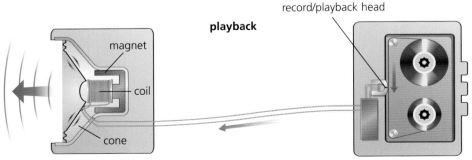

magnet

coil

cone

cassette player: the magnetic pattern on the tape generates electric signals in the playback head. The signals are boosted by an amplifier.

the binary numbers 0 and 1 are stored as on-and-off magnetic patterns on the tape. CD recordings are always digital. The microscopic pits in the surface of the disc represent the 1s of binary numbers, while the areas with no pits represent 0s.

Recording studios

Simple sound recordings can be made with a single microphone and tape recorder, but most music recordings are made in a recording studio. In the studio, different voices and instruments are picked up by different microphones and recorded separately. Each recording is called a *track*. The different tracks are mixed together to make the final recording.

In an analogue recording studio, tracks are recorded on wide magnetic tapes. In a digital studio, the signals are digitized and recorded on a computer. The sound engineer then mixes the tracks on a computer screen.

▶ FLASHBACK ◀

The first successful sound-recording machine was built in 1878 by the American inventor Thomas Edison. The machine, called a phonograph, recorded sound by making a groove on a cylinder covered in tin-foil or wax. The recording was made mechanically, because there were no electronics at the time. Flat discs (records) were first used for recording in 1888, and vinyl records in 1948. Magnetic tape was developed in the 1930s, and compact discs in the early 1980s.

◀ The sound-mixing desk in a large recording studio. Each of the sets of sliders controls the sound from one track of the recording. This is a 64-track studio – 64 tracks of sound can be recorded separately. It is also an analogue studio; in a digital studio the tracks are displayed on a computer screen and controlled through a keyboard.

Recycling

When we take waste products and turn them into useful materials, we are recycling them. Recycling materials saves energy and raw materials. As raw materials become scarcer and therefore more expensive, it will become more and more important to recycle. Recycling can also help to reduce damage to the environment.

Rubbish from homes and factories contains useful materials that can be recycled. More than half of the contents of the average family dustbin could be sorted from the rubbish and used again.

Glass is unique in that it can be used over and over again without any loss of quality. Broken or waste glass is mixed with sand, limestone and soda ash, and used to make new glass.

More than half of household waste is paper, and although recycled paper is not as good as the original, it still has many uses. Recycled paper and cardboard are used in the building industry, to make insulation materials and plasterboard.

Even before recycling became so economically important, there was a scrap-metal industry. People collected waste metal products, particularly iron, for sale to metal-producing firms. Some metals are easily separated from rubbish, and then melted down and reused. They include the tin coating on most steel food cans, as well as the valuable aluminium used to make soft-drink cans, metal foil and milk-bottle tops.

◀ Shredded waste plastic at a recycling plant. Plastic bottles, bags and containers can be recycled. It is important to recycle plastic because it does not rot, and can give off harmful gases when burned.

• Even the rubbish dumped in landfill sites can be recycled to provide an energy source. When the rubbish is compressed, it produces a gas called methane. This can be used as a fuel.

• If we recycled 75% of the world's paper, over 35 million trees would be saved each year.

Reformation

In 1500 all Christians in western Europe belonged to the Catholic Church, with the Pope in Rome at its head. Fifty years later, European Christians were bitterly divided into separate Churches. We call this change the Reformation.

Some people had been critical of the Catholic Church long before the Reformation. Popes often behaved more like powerful kings than religious leaders. Bishops and abbots of great monasteries were often wealthy landowners and also royal advisers at court. But ordinary priests were often so poor and ignorant that they could hardly do their job properly. For many ordinary people, visiting church must have been rather strange and mysterious. Churches were full of detailed pictures and statues, the altars were elaborately decorated with a cross and candles, and services were read in Latin, a language few understood.

Protest in the Church

The Church was further undermined by the row over indulgences (pardons for sins) which people could buy. In 1517 a German monk, Martin Luther, wrote a long list of reasons why he disagreed with indulgences, and pinned it on the church door in his home town of Wittenberg in Saxony. Perhaps this would have been just a local row if printing had not been invented. But Luther's list, and other churchmen's arguments against it, were printed throughout Germany. Luther's ideas spread.

The ruler of Saxony, and other German princes who wanted to be free of any interference by the Pope, backed Luther. They drew up a 'Protest' in 1529. Soon the 'Protestants' set up a separate Church. The nickname stuck.

Protestants

Luther taught that people must work out their own faith in God from the Bible, so they did not need the Pope or priests. People could only read the Bible for themselves when it was translated from Latin into ordinary languages, and when plenty of copies were printed. Protestant churches were plain and simple, and services were held in local languages by ministers in simple black gowns. Long sermons were preached to teach the Bible. In John Calvin's church in Switzerland church members chose their own ministers and lived simple, strict lives.

In time the Reformed and Non-conformist Churches developed from these movements. They include the Lutherans, especially in Germany, Calvinists in Switzerland and Scotland, and Anglicans (Church of England) and the Anglican Communion Overseas, which includes the Episcopal Church in the USA.

Counter-Reformation

The Catholic Church began to reform itself (the Counter-Reformation) and tried hard to win back Protestants. Both sides believed that they were right, and that those who disagreed with them would go to hell. Rulers did not want different Christian Churches in their kingdoms because of possible conflicts. So, in the 16th and 17th centuries, there were terrible religious wars and persecutions in Europe. It was a long time before Protestants and Catholics began to respect and tolerate each other.

▲ Martin Luther, the monk who started the Protestant Reformation in Germany. In Luther's Church bishops and priests were less powerful than in the Catholic Church. There were no monks, nuns, friars or pope.

• There were Christians who criticized the Catholic Church long before the Reformation. In England in the 14th century, John Wycliffe gained a following for his attacks on the wealth and power of the Catholic Church. He organized the first translation of the Bible from Latin into English so people could read it for themselves.

find out more
Bible
Christians
Tudor England

▼ The trunk and branches of this 'tree' represent the divisions in the Christian Church.

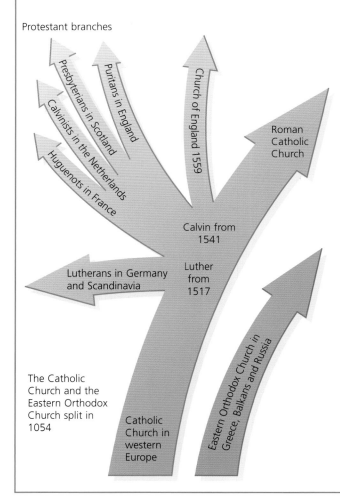

Protestant branches

Presbyterians in Scotland

Puritans in England

Calvinists in the Netherlands

Huguenots in France

Church of England 1559

Roman Catholic Church

Calvin from 1541

Lutherans in Germany and Scandinavia

Luther from 1517

Eastern Orthodox Church in Greece, Balkans and Russia

The Catholic Church and the Eastern Orthodox Church split in 1054

Catholic Church in western Europe

Refrigerators

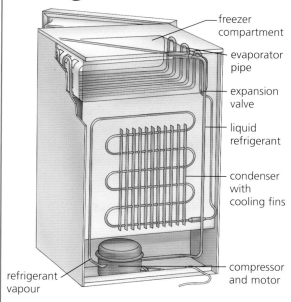

▲ In a compression refrigerator, a compressor pumps the refrigerant vapour through the condenser pipes, where it gives out heat and turns to liquid. As the liquid refrigerant passes through the evaporator pipe, it evaporates, taking in heat and producing a cooling effect. The vapour returns to the compressor and the cycle is repeated.

Labels on diagram:
freezer compartment
evaporator pipe
expansion valve
liquid refrigerant
condenser with cooling fins
compressor and motor
refrigerant vapour

Refrigerators ('fridges' for short) are machines for keeping things cold. Small fridges are used in people's homes to store fresh food, and sometimes small amounts of frozen food as well. Very large fridges may be fitted inside container lorries and in ships. They are used to transport perishable foods over long distances.

Refrigerators keep food at a temperature of about 5 °C (5 degrees above freezing). They work by evaporation. When a liquid changes to a vapour, it takes heat from its surroundings. Refrigerators move heat, taking it away from the inside, which becomes colder, and giving it to the outside, which gets warmer. This cooling process is done by evaporating a special substance called a *refrigerant*. The refrigerant circulates around a sealed system of pipes.

Some fridges use a device called a *compressor* to pump the refrigerant around the circuit of pipes. Others use the heat from a gas flame to circulate the refrigerant. Refrigerators like this have no moving parts and make no noise, but they are much less efficient than compression refrigerators and cost more to operate.

• Freezers work in the same way as refrigerators, but are more powerful and give a greater cooling effect. In a freezer, food stays frozen at about –18 °C.

• Early refrigerators used ammonia as a refrigerant, but this was poisonous, and corrosive if it leaked. Safer, synthetic refrigerants were not developed until the 1920s.

find out more
Gases, liquids and solids
Heat
Household equipment

Refugees

Refugees are people who flee from their homes in search of a better life. Many leave because their lives are in danger from war or famine, or because of persecution for their religion or politics.

There are more than 14 million refugees registered officially with the United Nations High Commission for Refugees. But millions of others who have fled their homes are not registered as refugees. Many are people who have moved to a distant part of their own country because of war, famine or persecution. Many others are not accepted as being refugees because they cannot prove that their lives are in danger.

Most refugees and displaced people arrive at refugee camps with nothing. They may have walked hundreds of kilometres. They need food, clothes, shelter and medical care. They may not be welcome in an area that is already poor. In time, the refugees may be able to go home because a famine is over or a war has ended. But some will have to stay where they are or resettle because they cannot return to their own country.

◄ Hundreds of Hutu refugees stream out of the Mugunga refugee camp in Zaire (now the Democratic Republic of Congo) in November 1996, heading for the Rwandan border. They had fled to Zaire in 1995 to escape fighting between the Tutsi and Hutu tribes in Rwanda. They returned to Rwanda when fighting spread to Zaire in late 1996.

• Millions of people became refugees during and after World War I and the Russian Revolution. Numbers increased again during World War II. There were more than 12 million refugees in 1945, mostly in Europe.

find out more
United Nations

Religions

Religions are made up of groups of people who share the same beliefs or way of life. Religions try to answer the questions in life which otherwise seem unanswerable, such as 'What happens to us after death?' or 'Why do people suffer?'

• Jews, Christians and Muslims believe that angels are spirits or beings created by God to be his servants and messengers. They believe that one of God's brightest angels, called Lucifer, wanted more power and rebelled against God. He was cast out of heaven and became the Devil.

Religions teach that the meaning of life is not only in our friends and families, our interests and work, but in something that will not die or change and is beyond, as well as related to, our world. This might be called God, the Transcendent One, or an eternal state of peacefulness called Nirvana.

God

Members of a religion share important ideas, such as belief in God. Religious people use the word 'God' to refer to the greatest good, the cause and final meaning of the Universe. God is called different things by different religions. Jews refer to *Ha Shem*, 'The Name'. Christians believe that God can be understood in a threefold manner, as the Father, his Son Jesus Christ, and the Holy Spirit. Muslims use the word *Allah* for God. To Sikhs, God is *Sat Guru*, the true teacher. Hindus use many different names and forms of God to help different people relate to God. Buddhists believe that their founder, Gautama Buddha, taught a path from suffering to peacefulness.

▼ Billy Graham is a famous American Protestant evangelist, seen here in Sheffield, England, in 1985. An eloquent speaker, he has preached to millions of people all over the world, persuading many to be 'born again' into a new commitment to God and the teachings of the Bible.

Beliefs

Many religious people believe that God has chosen certain men and women (prophets) to proclaim a message. Sometimes these prophets started a new religion. Some of the most famous prophets are those whose stories are told in the Jewish scriptures which are part of the Hebrew

▲ Zoroastrians (Parsis) belong to one of the oldest religions in the world. They follow the teachings of the prophet Zoroaster (Zarathusa), who may have lived as long ago as 1500 BC, in Persia (modern Iran). By taking the sacred cord in this initiation ceremony, this boy in Mumbai (Bombay), India, is confirming that he wishes to become a full Zoroastrian.

Bible. Christians believe that all the Jewish prophets, as well as John the Baptist, prepared the way for Jesus. Muslims accept all the Jewish prophets and Jesus: their names are mentioned in the Qu'ran (Koran). Muslims believe that Muhammad is the greatest and last of all God's prophets.

Members of different religions may also share a belief in reincarnation (being reborn in the next life as another human being or as an animal), in the teachings of prophets, and in heaven and hell. Many religious people believe that after death wicked people are punished and good people are rewarded. Heaven is the place of reward, a state of happiness and closeness to God. Hell is the opposite of heaven, a place of torture ruled over by the Devil, which also brings a separation from God.

Stories about reality

Teachers of all religions tell stories to help people understand the world and its meaning. These are sometimes called myths. Myths may be used to explain why the world exists, how it might end, and what are the best ways of living. The Hindu

story of Rama and Sita in the *Ramayana* is a myth. So is the Jewish story of creation in Genesis, the first book of the Bible. Some Christians think that the story of the birth of Jesus is a myth created to help them understand who Jesus was. Other Christians believe that the story of Christ's nativity is literally true.

A way of life

Whether or not people believe that these stories or myths are true, they can still affect the way people treat each other. All religions try to guide people, to show them the difference between good and bad, right and wrong. The story of Jesus' care for other people and his self-sacrifice on the cross inspire Christians to love and serve others. Muslims are encouraged to live honestly and bravely as Muhammad did. Hindus, Buddhists and Jains teach that no form of life should be harmed.

Worship

Most religions have a place where their members can meet for worship and social activities. This becomes an important part of people's lives, whether it is a Hindu temple, Christian church, Sikh gurdwara, Muslim mosque or Jewish synagogue.

Religious services are called rituals, rites or ceremonies. Usually they take place on a

particular day of the week: Fridays for Muslims, Saturdays for Jews, and Sundays for Christians. There may also be religious music, singing or chanting at the services.

In some religions, such as Christianity and Hinduism, specially trained men and women carry out certain rites during worship. In others, such as Sikhism and the Jewish faith, worship can be led by anybody.

Religion today

Religious differences have been the cause of many wars and much bad feeling. This is partly because religions often reflect racial and social differences. Members of different religious faiths today are making efforts to talk to each other and understand each other better. They are sharing in projects to help people all over the world. There are peace pilgrimages, environmental projects, and organizations such as the World Congress of Faiths which are bringing members of different religions together.

◄ A Baha'i temple in Haifa, Israel. Baha'is follow the teachings of Baha'u'allah (1817—1892), whose name means 'glory of God' in Arabic. They believe that God has helped the human race throughout history by sending prophets, such as Buddha, Baha'u'allah and Jesus, to teach us that there is only one God, that all religions are essentially equal, and that all people are equal.

◄ The Rastafarian hairstyle known as dreadlocks represents a lion's mane. 'Lion of Judah' was one of the titles of the Ethiopian emperor Haile Selassie (1892—1975), who Rastafarians believe was a living god. Rastafarians are both a religious group and a general movement for promoting the dignity of black people.

▼ A Mexican Devil mask. Most religious people today believe that the Devil is a symbol for wickedness, not a real being.

find out more
Buddhists
Christians
Hindus
Jains
Jews
Muslims
Shintoists
Sikhs
Taoists

Renaissance

Renaissance means 'rebirth'. It is the name used for the great discoveries in art, architecture and science that reached their peak in 15th- and 16th-century Italy. The influence of the Renaissance quickly spread throughout Europe.

For centuries in western Europe the Catholic Church had been the centre of learning and art. By the early 1400s, educated people were also beginning to find out more about the ancient civilizations of Greece and Rome. In Italy people could see the impressive remains of Roman buildings. Scholars learnt how to read long-forgotten documents in Greek, which opened up the great discoveries of the Greeks.

Greek learning seemed to be the key to finding out even more about the world. Learning and art became fashionable, as rulers and important churchmen in rich and powerful cities like Rome, Milan, Venice and Florence employed scholars and artists at their courts. Wealthy merchants also became patrons of the arts.

▼ Renaissance architects began to design buildings in the classical style, inspired by the Greeks and Romans. The Italian Renaissance architect Filippo Brunelleschi studied several classical domes, including the Pantheon in Rome built 1300 years earlier, as inspiration for the great dome for the cathedral in Florence. By 1436 he had built this octagonal brick dome which still soars above the city of Florence today.

▲ *The Grand Duke's Madonna* (1504) by the Italian painter Raphael, one of the greatest artists of the Renaissance. Renaissance artists discovered how to create space and distance in their pictures, as they worked out the rules of perspective. They also learnt how to use light and shade to make figures and objects look solid and realistic.

find out more
Architecture
Copernicus, Nicolas
Europe
Galilei, Galileo
Italy
Leonardo da Vinci
Michelangelo
Painting
Sculpture

▼ People in the time of the Renaissance felt there were no limits to knowledge. The artist Leonardo da Vinci was also a poet, scientist, architect and engineer. He even invented weapons, and acted as military adviser to the Duke of Milan. This is his design for a giant catapult.

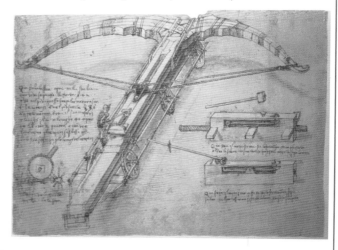

Reproduction *see* Sex and reproduction

Reptiles

Crocodiles, tortoises, snakes and lizards are all reptiles. They are cold-blooded, and usually have a tough, dry, scaly skin.

Reptiles are backboned animals (vertebrates) and breathe through lungs. Their body temperature, like that of all cold-blooded animals, goes up and down depending on the temperature of their surroundings. Most reptiles live in the warmer parts of the world. Although they have strong limbs, most reptiles are slow-moving animals.

In the breeding season, males use dances or bright colours to attract females. After mating, females lay their eggs in a sheltered, dry place. Most reptile eggs have a papery or leathery shell, but are otherwise very much like birds' eggs. Most reptiles leave their eggs to hatch in the warmth of the Sun, but some stay near the nest, and others, such as crocodiles and some snakes, look after their eggs and young. A few reptiles keep their eggs inside their bodies until they are ready to hatch. Baby reptiles look just like their parents.

In the past, many kinds of reptile flourished. The dinosaurs were reptiles and included the largest known land-living creatures. Today there are only four groups of reptiles.

- There are about 6000 different kinds of reptile.

- The largest reptile is the salt-water crocodile, which may grow up to 7 m.

- Big crocodiles and turtles may live to be 200 years old.

find out more
Crocodiles and
  alligators
Dinosaurs
Lizards
Snakes
Turtles and tortoises

◄ *Turtles and tortoises* are all armoured with a bony shell. Many swim well and live in water, but come onto land to lay their eggs.

▲ The *tuatara* lives on a few islands off the coast of New Zealand. It is the only survivor of a big group of reptiles which flourished at the time of the dinosaurs.

▲ *Lizards and snakes* are the best-known and the most abundant reptiles.

◄ *Crocodiles and alligators* are the biggest reptiles alive today. All live in or near water, although they have to come ashore to lay their eggs.

Rhinoceroses

Rhinoceroses, or rhinos, are large horned mammals that live in the tropical grasslands and forests of Africa and Asia. All five surviving kinds of rhinoceros are in danger of becoming extinct.

Rhinoceroses are different from other horned mammals in that their horns are not on the top of their heads but towards the end of their noses. And these horns are not bony, like the horns of cattle or the antlers of deer, but are made of compressed thick hairs. Rhinos are related to horses, and not to elephants and cattle.

Rhinos feed entirely on plants. Most rhinos are browsers – they eat leaves and twigs from bushes and trees which they pick using a grasping upper lip. But white rhinos are grazers – they feed on grass, which they crop with their distinctive broad lower lip.

All rhinos have good senses of hearing and smell, but they are short-sighted. They usually live alone and are suspicious of strangers, and may attack intruders without real cause.

Baby rhinos may be hunted by the big cats, but humans are the only enemies of the adults. In the past, dozens of kinds of rhinoceros lived in many parts of the world. Today, only five different kinds survive, and all of these have been hunted and poached to the point of extinction.

find out more
Africa
Grasslands
Mammals

◄ A white rhino and calf. White rhinos are in fact grey-brown in colour — the 'white' in their name comes from an Afrikaans word meaning 'wide', and refers to their broad lips.

Rivers and streams

A river travels from its source in the mountains or other highland area to the estuary where it flows into the sea. In the early stages of a river's journey, many small streams join up to form the main river, with other streams feeding in later on. Rivers and streams provide many different habitats for plants and animals. People have always settled along rivers too, taking advantage of the important travel routes they provide as well as using their water for drinking and washing, to water farmland and to make electricity.

People build roads and railways along river valleys, and dams are constructed to supply electricity. Large rivers can be used to transport food, fuel and goods. Dams, waterfalls and water wheels supply electricity for industry and domestic use.

How a river forms

A river is formed when water flows naturally between clearly defined banks. When rain falls or snow melts, some of the water runs off the land, forming trickles of water in folds of the land. These trickles eventually merge together to form streams, in mountain, lowland and woodland areas. The streams which join up to form the main river are called *tributaries*. As it flows towards the sea, a river becomes deeper and broader as more and more tributaries join it.

Rivers cut into the land and create valleys and gorges. Near its source, the river is well above sea-level and is flowing on steep slopes, so it has its greatest cutting power. Rocks, sand and soil (sediment) are swept along by the water, scouring the river-bed and banks. In the USA, the Colorado River has cut a gorge 1.5 kilometres deep called the Grand Canyon. The faster a river flows, the larger the rocks and the greater the load of sediment it can carry. When the river enters a lake or the sea, or when the valley floor becomes less steep, the river's flow is slowed down and it drops some of the sediment it is carrying.

When a river flows over bands of hard then softer rock, there will probably be one or more waterfalls or rapids where the different types of rock meet. The river will plunge off the resistant rock, and wear away the softer rock underneath even faster. The river will undercut the hard rock on top of the falls. Mountain rivers often have lots of waterfalls. The water rushes down steep hillsides, tumbling over boulders and rocky ledges in a series of small falls. Waterfalls are not so common at the coast, though they do happen when a river falls over a cliff into the sea. Spectacular waterfalls occur when a large river plunges into a gorge or falls from a high plateau.

- The Amazon River owes its name to the Amazon warrior women of Greek mythology. When the first European explorers landed in South America, they faced female and male warriors. Some people thought these must be descendants of the ancient Amazons, so the great river was named after them.

- In India the Ganges is considered a sacred river, and thousands of Hindu pilgrims travel each year to holy cities along its banks.

▼ The course of a river from its source in the mountains to its estuary at the sea.

Upper course The river is still small, and quite shallow. Its bed is full of boulders. It has great cutting power.

Middle course The river is fuller and flows more smoothly, often through a wide valley. It winds among the hills, cutting away the banks on the outside of bends.

Lower course The river becomes wide and sluggish, making huge curves called *meanders*. It may take a short cut across a meander, leaving the old bend as a lake (sometimes called an oxbow lake). The river spreads out and deposits sediment. As it enters the sea, it builds out a fan-shaped delta.

▲ West Indian manatees (sea cows) like this one live in the rivers of Florida, USA. Other large mammals, such as river dolphins and hippopotamuses, live in some tropical rivers.

River life

Some animals live on the river-bed, others in the open water, among the plants near or on the river bank, or on the bank itself. Herons, kingfishers and otters hunt for fish in the river, and swallows and bats swoop over the water to catch mayflies. The Amazon River alone contains over 2000 different kinds of fish, including piranhas, catfish, electric eels and the giant arapaima. Some river animals such as the Nile crocodile grow very big.

Dead plant and animal material washes into rivers from the land, and leaves and seeds blow into the water. This rotting material provides food for microscopic plants, worms, water snails, shrimps and mussels. These creatures in turn are food for fish, crayfish and turtles, and these animals may be eaten by otters, crocodiles and alligators. In very muddy water, it can be difficult to search for food. Electric catfish and electric eels use tiny pulses of electricity to detect their prey in the water.

River animals must avoid being washed away. Freshwater limpets cling fast to the rocks. Water beetles and mayfly nymphs have flattened bodies for hiding in crevices, and lampreys use sucker-like mouths to cling to rocks.

Floods

Prolonged heavy rains or the sudden melting of snow can cause rivers to overflow, creating a flood. In cold parts of the world, huge areas flood every spring when the winter snows melt. A landslide may dam a river, causing a flood when the dam collapses. Torrential rain is common in many parts of the world, especially in areas that have one short wet season each year. This rain swells the rivers and may flood land far away from the storms. After a flood, the river may settle on a new course.

The Huang He River in China has caused the world's worst floods. In 1931, over 3.5 million people were killed. The Huang He is the world's muddiest river. Its name means 'Yellow River'. A lot of the mud is dumped on the river-bed and at its mouth, which becomes clogged up. Melting snows each spring and heavy rains in summer threaten floods. For thousands of years, dikes have been built to hold back the water, and today the Huang He is controlled by huge sluice-gates.

The area that can be covered in water if a river floods is called its *flood plain*. The silt deposited over flood plains by large rivers provides some of the most fertile soil in the world, and many flood plains are important farmland today. For thousands of years, the Egyptians welcomed the River Nile floods which spread fresh fertile mud over the dried-up land.

▼ Flooded fields beside the River Severn in Gloucestershire, England. The river has burst its banks, covering the surrounding flood plain with water.

find out more
Hydroelectric power
Lakes
Water
Wells and springs

Longest rivers by continent

Africa
Nile, 6673 km
Longest river in the world, draining one-tenth of Africa.
Asia
Chang Jiang (Yangtze), 6276 km
Important waterway in China.
Europe
Volga, 3530 km
Frozen in parts during the winter.
North America
Mississippi–Missouri, 6019 km
Main inland waterway of the USA.
Oceania
Murray-Darling, 3718 km
Dries up in winter over much of its course.
South America
Amazon, 6570 km
More water than any other river in the world. Carries about a quarter of all the water that runs off the Earth's surface.

Roads

Modern motorways and ring roads help us to travel quickly from one place to another, avoiding busy city centres and residential areas. Yet many people feel that the building of new roads brings more traffic to an area, causing an increase in pollution. Local people often campaign very strongly against plans to build a new road in their area.

Motorways are fast roads with several lanes in each direction which are separated by a central reservation. They have no sharp bends, steep hills, crossroads or roundabouts. Traffic can travel a long way at high speeds without stopping. Many countries have motorway systems that link up the major cities. Dual carriageways are main roads with a carriageway

▲ These road workers in Nepal are spreading tar by hand onto the surface of a newly built road.

▼ This aerial photograph shows a busy intersection on the M62 motorway in northern England. At complex intersections like this one, the various roads are usually built on more than one level.

in each direction. Unlike motorways, they may have roundabouts and crossroads. Urban ring roads provide bypass routes around city centres to avoid traffic jams and residential areas. In country areas narrow, winding roads often follow the routes of ancient tracks.

Road construction

Before a new road can be built, the best route has to be chosen. This may not always be the most direct way between two places. Damage to the countryside, loss of wildlife habitats, inconvenience to local people, and the cost all have to be considered. Sometimes natural obstacles like rivers or hills have to be avoided.

When the route has been chosen, surveyors mark out the area ready for the huge earth-moving vehicles. A machine called a scraper loosens the top layer of soil, which is pushed aside by large bulldozers. The road has to be as level as possible, so cuttings are made through hills and the soil used to fill in small valleys and form embankments. Bridges and tunnels may also be needed.

The engineers then spread foundations of crushed rock to ensure the road can carry the weight of the predicted traffic. Sometimes cement or bitumen is added to the soil to form a solid base. Then a layer of concrete, called the base course, is put on the foundations. A machine called a spreader adds the top layer of asphalt or concrete slabs joined by bitumen. The concrete is often strengthened with steel mesh. Road markings, lights and direction signs are added to help control the traffic.

▶ FLASHBACK ◀

The first paved roads were built in Mesopotamia (now Iraq) in about 2200 BC. Two thousand years later the Romans began to build hard, straight roads paved with stones. These roads connected together the various parts of the empire, allowing soldiers to travel quickly across Europe and North Africa. In the 15th and 16th centuries, the Incas of South America created a network of highways and minor roads.

In the early 1800s John McAdam invented a new method of road building. The ground beneath the new road was drained and covered with small stones. Later, a coating of tar or bitumen was added to seal the surface, making it suitable for the rubber tyres of the motor car.

Robots

Most robots are machines that work in factories, doing jobs that would be boring, dangerous or very tiring for people. Androids are walking, talking robots that look like humans, but they are still a thing of the future. A robot would have to be very clever to do all the things you might do in a day!

Robots working in factories are called industrial robots. They work completely automatically, spraying cars with paint, cutting out car parts, stacking up heavy boxes, or welding pieces of metal together. Robot vehicles, including submarines and bomb-disposal robots, work in places which are too dangerous for people or too

difficult to reach, and are remote-controlled by an operator. In some car factories, automatic robot vehicles collect and deliver parts by following lines drawn on the factory floor. They have bump sensors which stop them if they run into anything.

How robots work

Robots are moved by electric motors, or they may be hydraulic or pneumatic (powered by water or compressed air). Their movements are controlled by computer. The computer sends instructions to each of the robot's joints, telling it which way to move, and how far. The computer checks that the robot's arm is in the correct position. Even the largest robots can be positioned accurately enough to thread a needle.

Before a robot can do a job, such as spraying a car with paint, it must be taught the correct movements. An engineer does this by holding the spray gun and carrying out the movements. The robot's sensors detect the movements, and the computer remembers them so that it can repeat them exactly over and over again.

• The word 'robot' comes from the Czech word *robota*, which means 'compulsory service'. It was made up by Czech writer Karel Čapek in 1920.

• Robotics researchers are trying to make a robot that can find its way about and identify objects with video eyes. With artificial intelligence, the robot's computer brain gradually learns from its mistakes.

◀ This robot arm has been programmed to perform welding tasks on a car production line. The vast majority of motor cars made in the developed world are now produced by robots.

find out more
Computers

Rockets

The first rockets were made about 1000 years ago in China. They were like the firework rockets of today. The huge rockets that launch spacecraft and satellites into space work in exactly the same way as these firework rockets.

Rockets are full of fuel which burns to make a lot of hot gas. The gas expands rapidly, and when directed downwards through a nozzle, the force of this expansion pushes the rocket upwards.

Space rockets

The first long-distance rocket, the V-2 war rocket, was designed by a German engineer, Wernher von Braun, in 1942. Almost all space rockets are

built along the same lines as the V-2. They have to be very powerful to escape from the pull of the Earth's gravity.

Space rockets usually have two or more sections called stages. Each stage has an engine and fuel supply. The first stage, at the bottom, lifts the rocket off the ground until the fuel runs out. It then falls away, and the second-stage engines take over, and so on.

Some space rockets burn a solid rubbery fuel. These are often boosters (extra rockets fixed to the side of the main rocket). But most space rockets use powerful liquid fuel. This will not burn without oxygen, so a second tank carries an oxygen supply. Most rockets can be used only once, but the booster rockets from the Space Shuttle are recovered and then reused.

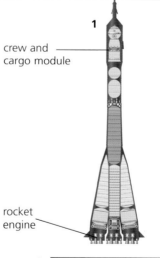

1

crew and cargo module

rocket engine

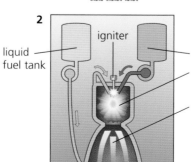

2

igniter

liquid fuel tank

liquid oxygen tank

combustion chamber

hot gases

◀ (1) A cutaway view of a liquid-fuel space rocket. It is carrying both the fuel and the oxygen (for burning) which it needs to work in space. (2) A diagram of a single rocket engine. The liquid fuel and liquid oxygen mix in the combustion chamber, then the igniter explodes the mixture.

• A speed of at least 40,000 km per hour, about 20 times as fast as Concorde, is needed to escape completely from the Earth's gravity.

find out more
Engines
Space exploration

Rocks and minerals

Rocks are the hard, solid parts that make up the Earth. You can find them all around you: in hillsides and mountains, in cliffs along the seashore, in the walls of large buildings, in the broken pieces of stone in the surface of the road. Rocks also lie beneath the oceans and seas, and under the ice in polar regions. Minerals are solid crystal shapes that are the building materials of rocks. Every kind of rock is made up of one or more minerals.

There are three main types of rock. *Igneous* rocks are formed at high temperatures from molten rocky material, either deep within the Earth or at the surface. *Sedimentary* rocks are formed from sand or mud (*sediment*) that has been laid down on land or in ancient rivers, lakes or seas. *Metamorphic* rocks are formed from sedimentary or igneous rocks that have been buried and heated up or put under great pressure.

Igneous rocks

Igneous rocks form from a hot molten mass of rocky material, called *magma*. Magma forces its way up through the Earth's crust from deep below the surface. Sometimes it reaches the surface as the lava (molten rock) which flows from an erupting volcano. When the magma cools, it hardens and forms rock. The kind of igneous rock that forms depends on what the magma is made of, where it cools, and how long it takes to cool. On cooling, the minerals in the magma form crystals. These crystals, like grains of sugar, have particular shapes depending on their chemical composition. The longer it takes the crystals to cool, the larger they become.

Igneous rocks formed deep in the Earth's crust are called *plutonic* rocks. A common type is granite, which consists of the minerals quartz, mica, feldspar and hornblende. Igneous rocks formed nearer the surface have finer grains and contain minerals such as olivine and magnetite but much less quartz. *Volcanic* rocks, which are formed at the surface, include basalt and pumice.

Sedimentary rocks

Soft and moving sands and muds at the bottom of rivers, lakes and seas form sedimentary rocks such as sandstone, mudstone and limestone. These rocks form part of the great cycle of erosion and deposition that takes place all the time. Rocks on land are broken down by the

Mohs' scale of hardness

The hardness of a mineral can be tested by seeing which other minerals it will scratch. Any mineral will scratch one that is softer than itself, but not one that is harder. The Mohs' scale was devised in 1812 by the German Friedrich Mohs (1773–1839).

Softest
 1 talc
 2 gypsum
 3 calcite
 4 fluorite
 5 apatite
 6 feldspar
 7 quartz
 8 topaz
 9 corundum
10 diamond
Hardest

• The igneous rock pumice began as volcanic lava filled with gases. When the gases escaped, they left behind tiny holes that filled with air, making pumice so light that it floats on water.

• Asbestos is a material made up of soft, silky fibres obtained by crushing asbestos rock. It helps to insulate things from intense heat or fire, and is woven into protective clothing for fire-fighters. Asbestos can be very harmful to health, so strict safety rules must be followed wherever it is used.

▶ How different kinds of rock are formed, and, above, an example of each of the three main types.

Granite is an **igneous** rock. It is rich in the mineral quartz. Granite is the most common type of rock in the Earth's crust.

Shale is a soft **sedimentary** rock formed from fine clay. The fossil of an animal has been preserved in the stone.

Schist is a **metamorphic** rock formed from mudstone and limestone. It consists of fine bands of different-coloured minerals.

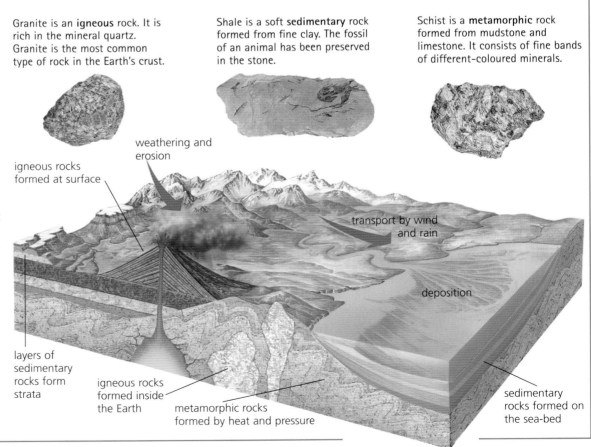

weathering and erosion

igneous rocks formed at surface

transport by wind and rain

deposition

layers of sedimentary rocks form strata

igneous rocks formed inside the Earth

metamorphic rocks formed by heat and pressure

sedimentary rocks formed on the sea-bed

◀ The rocks that form these cliffs at Eleonore Bay, Greenland, have been built up in layers. These rocky layers are known as *strata*.

action of wind, water, ice and plant roots. Small fragments of sand, silt or clay are then blown away or washed down into rivers or lakes. Over the years, millions of grains may be deposited (laid down) in a single place, building up into thick layers on land or underwater. The largest areas of sediment deposition are in the sea, where sediment is also eroded from the coastline by the action of the sea itself.

Sedimentary rocks also form when material from plants and animals that lived long ago is deposited, usually on the ocean floor. This kind of material is known as 'organic sediment'. On land, the plant material hardened to form beds of peat and coal. In the sea, the skeletons and shells of tiny animals hardened to form rocks such as chalky limestone. A famous example of this rock is the white cliffs of Dover, in southern England.

Two main changes have to take place in order for these sediments to form rock. First, the deeper layers of sediment are pressed down by the weight of sand or mud above, and the water is squeezed out of them. During the second stage, a kind of cement forms. The water that remains around the sediments contains dissolved minerals. As more water is lost, these minerals form crystals that fill the spaces between the rocky grains.

Metamorphic rocks

The word 'metamorphic' means 'later (or changed) form'. Metamorphic rocks have been altered by heat, or by heat and pressure. When magma forces its way up inside the Earth's crust, it heats the surrounding rock. If it passes through sandstone, this may be baked into hard quartzite. Limestone may be baked into marble. This process, which is called *metamorphism*, only affects small amounts of rock that are close to the rising magma.

Large-scale metamorphism can take place when mountains are forming. For example, when major plates of the Earth's crust collide, great pressures are created. Both pressure and heat may alter ocean-floor sediments like mudstone and sandstone to form metamorphic rocks such as slate and schist.

Minerals

When you look in detail at a piece of rock such as granite, you can make out smaller pieces of individual minerals, often in a variety of colours and shapes. Minerals include such everyday substances as rock salt, asbestos, the graphite used as pencil lead, the talc used to make talcum powder, and the china clay used to make crockery. They also include gold and silver, and the ores of metals such as copper, tin and iron. Minerals that are prized for their beauty and rarity, like diamonds, are known as gems.

Some rocks are made up of only one mineral, while others contain many. Scientists have identified more than 2500 different minerals, but some of these are quite rare. You can identify a mineral by the shape of its crystals as well as by its colour or lustre (the way it reflects light). You can also do a 'streak' test. When minerals are scratched against a rough white surface, many of them leave a distinctive streak of colour. Haematite, the commonest form of iron ore, always produces a red streak.

• During metamorphism, the tremendous heat can melt the rock into a liquid. When the liquid cools, impurities come together to form new minerals. A very unusual example of this is the formation of diamonds in coal layers that have been heated by igneous rocks.

find out more
Continents
Crystals
Diamonds
Earth
Erosion
Gems and jewellery
Geology
Metals
Mining
Mountains
Salt
Volcanoes

▼ Erosion by the wind has created these unusual sandstone rock shapes in the Arches National Park, Utah, USA.

Roman Britain

• Many museums have Roman exhibits. Some even have bits of buildings such as mosaic floors. Roman villas have been excavated in southern England. Some towns (York, London, Colchester) still have parts of their Roman walls, and Roman forts survive at Hardknott in Cumbria and along Hadrian's Wall. Many of today's main roads are Roman in origin.

In AD 43 the emperor Claudius invaded Britain and set about adding this new province to the Roman empire. A Roman way of life was established over the whole of England, but Wales and Scotland proved more difficult to conquer.

The emperor Claudius soon returned to Rome. Under his commander-in-chief, Aulus Plautius, the army gradually brought more of what is now England under Roman control. In AD 58 a new governor of Britain, Suetonius Paulinus, led an invasion of Wales.

Boudicca's revolt

While this invasion was going ahead successfully, the people in East Anglia revolted against their Roman masters in AD 60. Led by Boudicca, the queen of the tribe called the Iceni, they attacked Roman towns, villages and farms, burning and killing as they went. Eventually, after many setbacks, the Roman army took control and peace was re-established.

The area of Roman Britain changed over the years. By the middle of the 2nd century AD the Roman army had moved up the east coast of Scotland. But by the 3rd century it was back at the walled frontier established by the emperor Hadrian. In the 4th century the army had to build special forts along the southern and eastern coasts against invasions.

find out more
Anglo-Saxons
Caesar, Julius
Romans
Scotland
Wales

▼ All Roman towns had at least one bath house. The baths in Bath are the finest Roman remains in Britain. They were built soon after the Roman invasion. Bath's Roman name was *Aquae Sulis*.

▲ Roman Britain at its furthest extent, 2nd century AD.

Town and country

The governor of a province was in charge of the management of the province, the army and the law courts. It was the governor's job to see that towns were built in the Roman style. There had to be buildings for the local senate, and a forum (public square).

Towns had proper drains and streets, and several towns had theatres (like Colchester) or even amphitheatres (like Cirencester). In the countryside there were new villas. Britain exported some of its farm produce, such as wheat, but was also famous for its hunting dogs, woollen cloaks and metals. Many houses had fine painted walls and mosaic floors.

The end of Roman rule

By the beginning of the 5th century, there were attacks by barbarians in many parts of the Roman empire. The Roman army was spread all over the empire and had difficulty dealing with these attacks. Britain, too, was invaded by outsiders. The British army, without the Romans, expelled the invaders and ended Roman rule.

Romans

The Latini, a Latin-speaking people, took over the town called Rome from its Etruscan kings in 509 BC. As Romans they spread their way of life, their laws and their language throughout Italy and then over the Mediterranean area and much of Europe.

- The Latin language developed into many European languages spoken today, including Italian, Spanish and French. Roman law is the basis of the laws of many European countries. The English names for the months are Roman. The English alphabet is Roman and Roman numerals are often used.

- Romans liked their food with lots of spices, and the main meal of the day (eaten at about four o'clock in the afternoon) usually had three courses. Many people, especially those who lived in the flats, went out to fetch 'take-away' meals from the hot-food shops.

▼ In AD 79 the Roman town of Pompeii in Italy was buried under ash when the nearby volcano Mount Vesuvius erupted. This picture shows the forum (meeting place) with Vesuvius in the background. Many of the remains are remarkably well preserved and have told us a huge amount about Roman life.

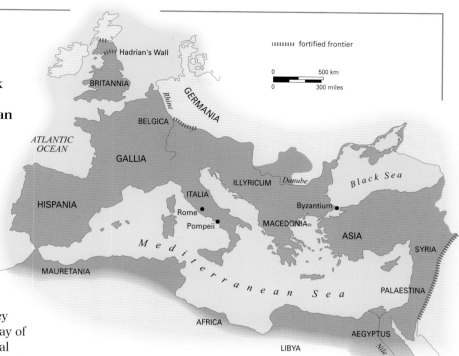

▲ This map shows the extent of the Roman empire in the 2nd century AD. The names of many modern countries come from the Latin names of the Roman provinces.

Wherever the Romans went as conquerors, they established their own way of life. Although many local customs survived, it is possible to talk about 'Roman everyday life' throughout the empire. Archaeologists often find the same sorts of evidence, either buildings or things that people used, all over the Roman world.

Town and country

Roman towns were usually well planned with straight streets dividing the town into regular blocks. A block of houses was called an *insula*, the Latin for 'island'. In the big towns and cities many people lived in blocks of flats or in apartments above shops or small factories. Those who were rich enough lived in private houses with rooms for slaves and a secluded garden. They may also have had mosaic floors and hypocausts (underfloor heating).

Roman towns usually had regular supplies of water and an efficient system of sewage disposal. Water pipes, of lead, wood or pottery, brought supplies from aqueducts to private houses, to businesses, and to fountains and public baths or basins in the streets.

The central government in Rome wanted farmers to work as much land as possible. New farmhouses and estates appeared. These villas had the same comforts as city houses.

The Roman army

Soldiers were organized into units called legions. Each legion was made up of about 5000 men and had a name and a number. The men trained and fought in groups of 80 with a centurion (the name for a commander of about 100 men) in charge of each. The legionary soldiers were well armed and fought on foot. Other army units, called the cavalry, fought on horseback. Some were trained to use artillery weapons such as catapults. Some were engineers.

The provinces

The army helped create the Roman world by conquering peoples, building forts and roads and keeping Roman-run countryside secure from attacks. Boundaries to the Roman world were established, sometimes using rivers, mountains or seas as a barrier, and in many places the Romans had to build a barrier. Inside the boundaries the Romans created provinces.

In the provinces the Romans encouraged the newly conquered peoples to live just like Romans. They introduced their religion into the provinces and built temples to gods and goddesses such as Jupiter, Minerva and Juno. Quite often,

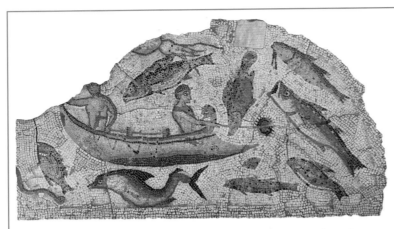

This Roman mosaic shows two fishermen surrounded by the fish they are catching. It comes from Utica, a Roman settlement in North Africa, and dates from the 4th century AD.

though, people in the provinces worshipped their own gods too. Celtic gods and goddesses were still worshipped in Roman Britain and in Gaul.

From republic to empire

At first Rome was a republic. Some people (men who owned property) were allowed to vote for the politicians who formed the government. At the head were two men, called consuls.

▼ Augustus put a great deal of time and money into making Rome a great city. He is said to have claimed that he found Rome a city of brick and left it a city of marble. This is the Forum Romanum (Roman forum) at the time of Augustus.

Each year one was elected to lead the government and one the army. They were the chief judges as well. A sort of parliament, called the senate, discussed the way the state was governed and made new laws.

In the 2nd century BC politicians began to fight each other for power and in the next century civil war broke out. Julius Caesar beat a rival politician, Pompey, and made himself dictator of Rome. The next dictator was Octavian, who in 27 BC made himself an emperor and called himself Augustus. This was the beginning of the period in Roman history called the empire.

Although men could still vote for their leaders it was not a proper democracy. The emperor decided who should rule and handed out jobs to people he could trust. Under the rule of the emperors, Rome gradually conquered an even greater area.

The end of an empire

Eventually this vast Roman empire was divided in two with one capital city in Rome and the other in Byzantium. Byzantium was established by the emperor Constantine as his capital in AD 330, and renamed Constantinople.

By the 5th century AD the western part of the empire had been overrun by Goths, Huns and Vandals. The eastern empire became the Byzantine empire and survived until AD 1453, when it fell to the Ottoman Turks.

• A Roman town might have a theatre, a stadium (for chariot racing) and even an amphitheatre. One of the spectacles at the amphitheatre was a cruel sport in which trained men, called gladiators, fought to the death in single combat. Sometimes animals were chased and killed in the arena, or even human beings. At various times, persecuted people, such as Christians, were 'thrown' to wild animals.

find out more
Augustus
Byzantine empire
Caesar, Julius
Greeks, ancient
Roman Britain
Slaves

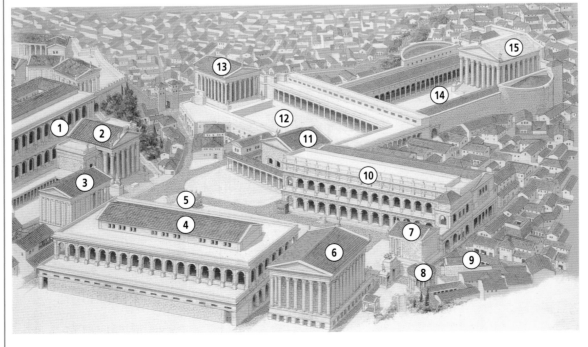

1 Tabularium (records office)
2 Temple of Concord
3 Temple of Saturn
4 Basilica Julia
5 *rostra* (the speaker's platform)
6 Temple of Castor and Pollux
7 Temple of the Deified Julius Caesar
8 Temple of Vesta
9 Regia (office of high priest)
10 Basilica Aemilia
11 Curia Julia (senate house)
12 Forum of Julius Caesar
13 Temple of Venus Genetrix
14 Forum of Augustus
15 Temple of Mars Ultor

Roosevelt, Franklin Delano

Franklin Delano Roosevelt was president of the USA from 1933 to 1945. He was the only president to be elected four times.

Roosevelt was already a well-respected politician when, at the age of 40, he developed polio. He never gained full use of his legs again. However, he worked hard to get himself fit, and he returned to politics. In 1928 he was elected governor of New York State, and in 1933 he became president of the USA.

This was the time of the Great Depression. One worker in four was out of work and many families faced poverty. Roosevelt promised a 'New Deal'. This was an economic programme to put the country back on its feet. He also began radio broadcasts to the nation, known as his 'fireside chats'. The success of these and later measures ensured his re-election as president in 1936.

In 1940 Roosevelt was elected for a third term. In December 1941 the USA entered World War II after the Japanese bombed the US naval base at Pearl Harbor in Hawaii. Roosevelt worked closely with the leaders of Britain and the Soviet Union, Winston Churchill and Joseph Stalin, to try and end the war. He won a fourth election in 1944, but six months later, with victory in the war in sight, he collapsed and died.

| Born 1882 in Hyde Park, New York State, USA |
| Died 1945 aged 63 |

◄ Franklin Delano and Eleanor Roosevelt in 1932. Eleanor Roosevelt was famous for her humanitarian work. She was a US delegate to the United Nations, and in 1946 she became the chairwoman of the United Nations Human Rights Commission.

find out more
Twentieth-century history
United States of America
World War II

Rubber

Rubber is a material used to make products as different as car tyres and surgeon's gloves. Its most important property is that it is elastic: it can be stretched or squeezed out of shape, but returns to its original form.

Natural rubber is made from a liquid called latex, obtained from the trunk of the rubber tree. The rubber tree originally grew in Central and South America. Today it is grown on plantations in hot parts of the world, particularly in South-east Asia. Since World War II synthetic rubber, made from chemicals obtained from oil, has become important. Over two-thirds of all rubber produced is now synthetic.

From tree to factory

Rubber is obtained from trees by a process called 'tapping'. The rubber tapper makes a shallow, diagonal cut in the bark of the tree. The milky latex slowly runs down from the cut into a cup fastened to the tree trunk. The latex is thickened and solidified into doughy sheets, then dried to make raw rubber.

Raw rubber is hard when cold and sticky when hot. It has to be processed before it is useful. The most important process is *vulcanization*. This involves mixing the rubber with sulphur. The resulting material is stronger and more elastic than raw rubber. Woven fabric or wires are often added to the material to strengthen it.

Over half of all rubber is used for vehicle tyres. Other uses include rubber gloves, hoses, tubing, elastic, tennis balls, and rubber seals to prevent leakage of water or oil in engines and pipelines.

◄ A rubber tapper in Indonesia. Once started, the latex will flow for a few hours, giving about 150 grams of rubber. A tapper can visit about 400 trees each day. Trees can be tapped only every two days, so each tapper looks after about 800 trees.

• Rubber balls were made by the Maya people in South America over 900 years ago.

• The vulcanization process was invented in 1839 by Charles Goodyear, when he accidentally spilled some rubber and sulphur on a hot stove.

find out more
Plastics
Springs

Russia

Russia is the world's largest country. It is almost the size of the USA and Canada combined. From east to west it is about 8000 kilometres and crosses 11 time zones.

The Ural Mountains separate European and Asian parts of Russia. The largest mountains are on Russia's southern borders and in the Far East along the Kamchatka peninsula, where there are active volcanoes. Three of the world's longest rivers flow through Russia. The River Amur forms the border with China as it flows towards the Sea of Japan.

Mineral wealth

Russia is rich in most of the minerals used by modern society. There are vast deposits of oil, natural gas, coal, copper, iron ore, gold, silver, platinum, lead and nickel. These minerals have helped make the Volga River region one of the world's major centres of industry. Factories get power from hydroelectric power stations on the Don and Volga rivers.

People

Russians make up the majority of the population, but there are more than a hundred other nationalities and languages. Most Russians live in the European part of the country. Moscow and St Petersburg are two of Europe's biggest cities. In the far north people have a more traditional way of life. People such as the Nenets, Yakuts and Komi keep reindeer herds or live by fishing. Many farmers live in the west, where the best farmland is. Wheat is a major crop.

- After the USA, Russia has the longest rail network in the world. It has almost 90,000 km of track. Its railways carry the most freight in the world: 2000 million tonnes a year.

▲ In parts of Russia the climate is very severe. Reindeer are kept in the snowy regions of Siberia in northern Russia. In the capital, Moscow, snow lies on the ground for five months of the year.

Key

- —— country boundary
- ◆ capital city
- ■ ● major cities and towns
- —— main roads
- —■— main railways
- ⊕ main airports
- ᴧᴧ ice cap
- ▲ highest peak (height in metres)

land height in metres

- 2000–5000
- 1000–2000
- 500–1000
- 200–500
- sea level — less than 200
- land below sea level

Russia's history

Over 1400 years ago there were tribes of Slav people living in parts of central and eastern Europe. In the 6th century AD some began to migrate further eastwards, where they found a great plain. Although the area was open to attacks from Huns, Scythians and Goths, some Slavs settled down as farmers. Others became pioneers, opening up new territory.

▲ Ivan IV (known as Ivan the Terrible) crowned himself first tsar of Russia in 1547. Although he did much to bring Russia in line with Europe, he is remembered most for his brutality. In his last years he had thousands of people executed. After killing his own son in a fit of rage, he became insane.

From the 6th to the 9th century, Vikings from the north came to trade in Kiev, Novgorod and other cities. Kiev also traded with Greeks in the south, and it was from the Greeks that the Russians took their Christian religion. In 988 Grand Prince Vladimir of Kiev was converted to Christianity.

In 1240 the Golden Horde of Mongol-Tartars from the Gobi Desert, in what is now Mongolia, overran Russia. They occupied the country for about 250 years. The princes of Moscow gradually beat them off, and in the 16th century Ivan the Terrible finally defeated the Tartars at Kazan. He became tsar (emperor) in 1547. After that the country turned more towards Europe than to Asia.

Rise of the Russian empire

After Ivan died, there were quarrels over the throne until Mikhail Romanov was made tsar. The Romanovs ruled Russia from 1613 until they were overthrown in 1917. Mikhail Romanov's grandson, Peter the Great, made Russia a world power, and introduced many political and social reforms. Before he died, in 1725, he brought Estonia and part of Latvia and Finland under Russian control.

In 1762 a young German princess took the throne. Catherine the Great ruled for 34 years. She expanded Russia southwards to the Crimea and Black Sea, eastwards into central Asia, and westwards to occupy Lithuania and much of Poland. At first she was a tolerant ruler, but she was scared by peasant revolts and the French Revolution of 1789. During the last years of her rule her government used secret police to arrest people who disagreed with its policy and exiled some to Siberia.

Russia in crisis

By the middle of the 19th century, Russia was in crisis. A costly war fought against Britain and France in the Crimea only revealed how backward its military was, and the country's serfs (poor peasants) had rebelled against the landowners. Many Russians wanted to modernize the country. In 1861 the tsar, Alexander II, freed the serfs and gave them land. However, most Russians were still very poor and there was a lot of discontent.

In 1905, factory workers marched on the Winter Palace in St Petersburg to present their demands for political reform to Tsar Nicholas II. They were met by troops, who shot and killed 130 of them. As news of this massacre travelled, a revolutionary movement swept the country. In order to keep the peace the tsar agreed to a few of

▼ The Winter Palace, St Petersburg, was taken by the Bolsheviks in 1917. The Russian Revolution brought to an end the Romanov family dynasty.

◄ Inside a gilded metro (underground) station in St Petersburg, which was built in the 1950s. The city was named after is founder, Peter the Great, but its name was changed to Leningrad after the Russian Revolution. It became St Petersburg again in 1991.

Commonwealth of Independent States
When the Soviet government voted itself out of existence, the republics became independent. Some of the republics thought it was important to keep in touch with each other. The Commonwealth of Independent States (CIS) was formed in 1991 to include 12 of the 15 republics of the former USSR both in Asia and Europe. Members meet to make agreements in areas such as trade, foreign policy, law enforcement, defence and transport.

the political demands. However, the unrest continued.

Russia's entry into World War I increased the nation's hardship and anger. Riots by starving people in February 1917 quickly spread. The tsar was forced to give up his throne, and Russia became a republic. For eight months a temporary government ruled, but it was overthrown by the Bolshevik Party led by Lenin. The new government had the tsar and his family shot in 1918. The Bolsheviks became the Communist Party. Under their rule all farms and factories were owned by the state.

The Soviet Union
The hopes of peace were short-lived. Civil war broke out and the new republic was invaded by foreign troops, including British and Americans. Millions of people died. At the end of the civil war the communist government divided the territories of the old empire into republics; the Republic of Russia was by far the largest of these. In 1922 the new country was named the Union of Soviet Socialist Republics (USSR), or the Soviet Union.

Under the harsh rule of Stalin, from 1924 to 1953, millions of people starved because the state-owned farms on which they were forced to work did not provide enough food. Anyone who opposed Stalin was either imprisoned or killed.

During World War II Germany invaded the Soviet Union, and 27 million Soviet people were killed. In 1945 Soviet armies liberated much of eastern Europe from German occupation.

Independence
Under the leaderships of Khrushchev from 1953 and Brezhnev from 1964 communist rule remained strong. In 1985 Mikhail Gorbachev became leader and tried to reform the Soviet Union. But he failed and in 1991 the Soviet Union collapsed. Boris Yeltsin then became the first president of the new Russian Federation, consisting of 21 self-governing republics, various territories, provinces, and a self-governing Jewish region. Yeltsin also organized the Commonwealth of Independent States.

Yeltsin's period as president was a troubled one. Not all of the nationalities of the Russian Federation wanted to stay part of it. The Chechens, who live in the Caucasus region, have been fighting the Russian army since the early 1990s to gain greater self-government. There has also been a steep drop in the standard of living of most Russians. In 2000 Vladimir Putin succeeded Yeltsin as president.

▶ President Boris Yeltsin negotiating with coalminers in 1991. Yeltsin tried to transform the country's economy and to give more choice and freedom to the Russian people.

Sailing

Sailing boats use the force of the wind to push them along. The wind blows across the surface of large sheets called sails. Sailing yachts are boats or small ships used for racing or leisure. Most have a crew of one or two, but the biggest ocean-racing yachts may have a crew of more than 20 people.

Sails used to be made of canvas, but strong lightweight synthetic materials such as nylon and Terylene are now normally used. A sail acts rather like the wing of an aircraft. As the air flows across it, pressure builds up on one side. By angling the sail, the sailor can use the sideways pressure to push the boat forwards. To move in a particular direction, the line of the sails is changed so that the wind blows across them. Sailors can use this effect to make their boats move in almost any direction.

The keel or centreboard stops the boat from being blown sideways when sailing across the wind. The boat can sail with the wind behind it, to the side of it, or even slightly ahead of it. It cannot sail directly into the wind. However, by tacking (zigzagging), it can move forwards against the direction of the wind.

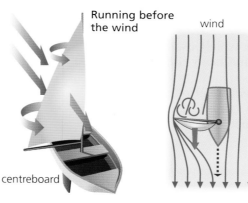
Running before the wind

centreboard

Sailing close to the wind

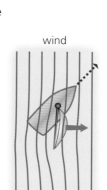
wind

wind

• The person who steers a yacht is called the helmsman. The people who help to adjust the sails are the crew.

······▶ boat moves this way
force on sail
wind

◀ A sail is pushed sideways when the wind blows across it. Sailors can use this effect to make their boats go in almost any direction.

find out more
Ships and boats
Submarines
Water sports

Saints

Saints are holy men or women who are singled out because of their wisdom and dedication to their faith. Throughout history and in many different religions, people who have led particularly good lives have been recognized as saints.

Followers of the ancient Chinese philosopher Confucius recognize certain 'holy rulers' from ancient times as saints. Buddhists believe that monks or others who attain *nirvana* (a state of peacefulness) are saints. Some Buddhists think that all people are capable of becoming saints. In the Hindu religion, holy people are often called *sadhu* ('good one'). Other people, including some saints who belong to other religions, are believed to be *avatar* – gods who descend to Earth in human form.

Christian saints provide particularly good examples of how God wants everyone to live. In the New Testament of the Bible the word refers to all Christians, but now it is used just for special people after they are dead. Christian saints normally model their lives on Jesus. They are unselfish and give up a lot to help other people. Many have died for their beliefs. They are then called *martyrs*. Many famous Christians have been officially canonized (declared to be saints) by the Church. Many people with the word 'Saint' (sometimes written as 'St') in front of their names belong to this group.

▼ St Francis of Assisi was a travelling preacher who spent his time with the poor, and with lepers and animals. In 1210 he set up a new order of friars (brothers) called the Franciscans, who were committed to a life of poverty, obedience and prayer. This painting, *St Francis Preaching to the Birds*, is by Giotto, a famous medieval artist.

Some famous saints
Bernard Patron saint of travellers
George Patron saint of England
Mary Magdalene Follower of Jesus
Paul Missionary traveller and writer of many letters (epistles)
Peter One of the 12 disciples of Jesus
Teresa of Avila A holy woman who saw visions and reformed the order of Carmelite nuns

find out more
Buddhists
Christians
Confucians
Hindus
Joan of Arc
Monks and nuns

Salt

Common salt is the most widely used mineral in the world. It has been estimated that there are 16,000 uses for it, including cooking and the manufacture of other chemicals. But common salt is just one of a large number of chemical substances called salts.

Salts are formed when the hydrogen in an acid is replaced by a metal. All these salts are made up of crystals. The chemical name for common salt is sodium chloride. It is used to preserve meat, fish and vegetables, and to make foods such as margarine and butter. Salt is used in the manufacture of dyes, paper, pottery, leather and many medicines. It is also spread on roads and pavements in winter to melt ice and snow and to prevent refreezing. This is because pure water freezes at 0 °C, but brine (salty water) freezes at a much lower temperature.

There is plenty of salt in the world, but it is not always easy to get at. 'Rock salt' comes from thick layers deep underground. These were formed long ago when prehistoric seas dried up. There

are famous salt mines in Canada, Poland, Siberia in Russia, and Cheshire in England. Sometimes rock salt is mined by digging for it underground. Usually, however, water or steam is pumped down the mine, forming brine. This is pumped to the surface, where the water is evaporated, leaving the salt.

• Roman soldiers were paid a *salarium* (allowance of salt). From this Latin name comes the modern word 'salary', which means a regular payment for work done.

◀ Salt is still mined today under old city ruins in Yemen in the Middle East.

• In some countries with hot sunshine, salt is obtained by trapping sea water in shallow pans or lagoons. When the sea water evaporates, 'sea salt' is left behind.

find out more
Acids and alkalis
Crystals
Oceans and seas
Rocks and minerals

Satellites

A satellite is an object that travels around a larger object. The natural satellites of planets are often called moons. Many artificial satellites are launched into space by rockets or the Space Shuttle. Some send out radio, television and telephone signals, others take photographs of the Earth's surface or look into the depths of space.

A satellite travels in space along a path called an orbit. The orbit can be a circle or an oval shape. A satellite keeps going round and does not fly off into space because the planet's gravity holds onto it.

A satellite 300 kilometres from the Earth goes round in about 90 minutes, while one that orbits at a height of 36,000 kilometres goes round in 24 hours. A satellite in *geostationary orbit* is one which is in orbit above the Equator and moves round the Earth in the same time that the Earth takes to spin around its axis once. It always stays directly above the same point on the Earth's surface. The International Telecommunications Satellite Organization (Intelsat) has a network of

communication satellites in geostationary orbit above the Earth. Other satellites travel round the Earth in a north–south direction. This is called a *polar orbit*. Each time the satellites come round, they pass over a different part of the Earth's surface.

Most artificial satellites get their power from panels of solar cells that turn sunlight into electricity. Some satellites are space stations where the crew can do experiments.

▼ The European Remote-Sensing Satellite (ERS-1) above the coast of the Netherlands. The satellite monitors shorelines and ocean currents. It can also be used to study crop growth and to detect oil spills.

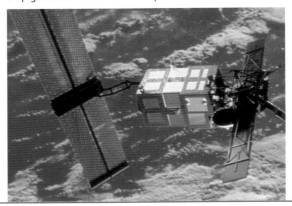

Types of satellite
♦ *Communications* satellites send telephone, television and radio signals between the continents.
♦ *Navigation* satellites send out radio signals that help aircraft and ships to find their way.
♦ *'Spy'* satellites take photographs of the land for military use.
♦ *Weather* satellites photograph cloud patterns and movements to help forecast the weather.
♦ *Scientific* satellites carry special measuring instruments.

find out more
Gravity
Moon
Navigation
Rockets
Solar System
Space exploration

Scandinavia

Scandinavia is a region of northern Europe that includes Norway, Sweden, Denmark, Iceland, the Faeroe Islands and Finland.

capital city

0   400 km
0   200 miles

The northern part of Scandinavia is in the Arctic Circle, but the cold climate is softened by a warm ocean current called the North Atlantic Drift. The western side consists of rugged mountains, some of which hold glaciers.

Landscapes

Along much of the Norwegian coast, the mountains are indented by long, deep inlets called fjords. Inland, the ancient rock mass is divided by the Baltic Sea and covered in thousands of lakes. Sweden alone has over 95,000 lakes.

While Iceland and the Faeroes are almost treeless, large areas of Norway, Sweden and Finland are covered in forests. Over half of Sweden's land surface is covered with dense forest, mostly pines.

Acid rain is threatening the forests of Scandinavia, while the Baltic Sea suffers from a build-up of industrial and agricultural chemicals.

Iceland was formed by volcanic activity over the last 16 million years. About 30 volcanoes have been active since records began, and the country has thousands of hot springs. Permanent ice covers about one-tenth of the land, much of which is rocky and barren.

Lands of the Midnight Sun

In parts of Scandinavia near and inside the Arctic Circle, people experience the 'Midnight Sun'. These are areas where the Sun never sets during June and July. In December and January, these places get the opposite effect and it is dark for almost 24 hours a day.

Scanners

Scanners are machines used in hospitals to take pictures of the inside of a person's body. Scanners produce pictures with more detail than an ordinary X-ray photograph. They 'scan' the body, one thin strip at a time.

• The beam from a CAT scanner is made as weak as possible because X-rays are harmful.

• Ultrasound scanners are used to look at an unborn baby inside its mother's womb. They provide a safer method than using X-rays, which might harm the growing baby.

CAT scanners (short for computerized axial tomography) X-ray a thin 'slice' of the body from many different angles. A computer processes the information to produce a picture of the slice. Doctors use CAT scanners to help them diagnose infections and broken bones as well as to detect certain diseases.

MRI scanners (short for magnetic resonance imaging) also take pictures of slices of the body, but without using X-rays.

The scanner sends out powerful radio signals that make certain atoms within the patient's body wobble. The atoms then give out their own radio signals, which are detected by the scanner. It converts the body's signals into an image on a monitor. MRI scanners are mostly used to take pictures of the head and spine.

Ultrasound scanners give less detailed pictures, but are much cheaper, and more convenient

for some jobs. They work by beaming sound waves into the body. A probe picks up the waves reflected from different layers inside the body, and the computer builds up its picture.

▼ Another method of taking scans is called positron emission tomography (PET). These scanners work by picking up the radiation from a radioactive material that is put into the patient's body. Here, the scanner's screen shows colour-coded images of 'slices' through the patient's brain.

Schools and universities

Every country in the world needs an educational system to train its young people. Young people go to university if they want to continue their education after they have completed the first stages of their schooling at primary and secondary level.

▼ Pupils coming to this village school in Sarangkok, Nepal, may have to walk for several kilometres every day for their lessons.

• Some of the poorer countries in Africa and Asia can afford to offer only 5 years of free schooling. Parents may have to pay for secondary education, and they usually pay for books and materials.

• After 3–4 years of study, university students take exams to obtain a degree, such as a Bachelor of Arts (BA), or a Bachelor of Science (BSc). Some go on to study for higher degrees. The highest degree is a doctorate, known as a PhD. Doctoral students must produce a piece of original research.

find out more
Children

What is taught in schools is called the *curriculum*. In some countries the curriculum is set down by the government. It means that children in all schools learn the same things. In other countries what is taught is decided at local level or by the schools themselves.

Primary education

Most countries give schooling to children at least up to the age of 11 or 12. These first schools provide primary education. In Britain children start primary school at 5, in the USA at 6, and in Russia at 7. In primary schools children learn to read and write in their national or regional language. For many Indians, Africans, Chinese and minority groups this may not be the language they speak at home. The kind of schooling given to children in primary schools differs from country to country.

Secondary education

Schooling for children in poorer countries usually ends at 11 or 12. Children then go out to work. For children in other countries there is secondary education until the age of 16, 17 or 18. The secondary curriculum includes sciences, computer studies, maths, history, geography and foreign languages. Pupils usually have the chance to take part in sports.

At the end of secondary school, pupils may take examinations set by public examination boards. In many countries, including Germany and the USA, teachers do the testing inside school. Pupils leave secondary school with qualifications that can help them to get a job or study at college or university.

Tertiary education

Universities and colleges make up a third level of education, known as tertiary education. The purpose of a college is to provide teaching and training. Many of the courses colleges offer are vocational, which means they teach skills for a particular job.

A university has three main purposes: first, to give its students qualifications that will help them to get a good job; second, to give them a better understanding of different ideas in the arts and sciences; and third, to provide a place where research can take place.

Britain's Open University, founded in 1969, was one of the first universities to allow students to study at home. Students follow lessons on television and radio and post work in to be marked. Other universities have copied this method. This means that people with full-time jobs or looking after families can also study for university degrees.

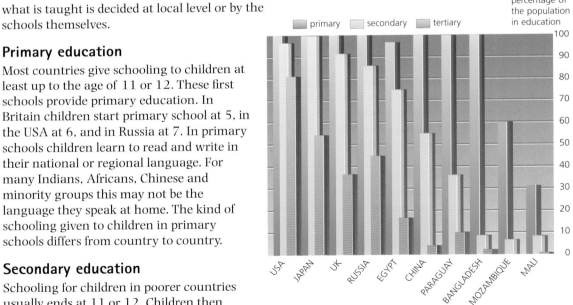

▲ This graph shows the percentage of people in primary, secondary and tertiary education in 10 different countries. In the USA most people go to school or college into their 20s, while in Mali fewer than a third even go to primary school. The height of each column shows the numbers going to school or college as a proportion of the total population in the particular age group.

Science fiction *see* Novels and novelists

Scientists

Scientists ask questions about the world around us and how it works. To find answers to their questions, they make observations and try out experiments. They investigate everything from the tiniest sub-atomic particles to volcanoes, stars and the human brain.

find out more
Astronomy
Biology
Biotechnology
Curie, Marie
Darwin, Charles
Ecology
Faraday, Michael
Genetics
Geometry
Mathematics
Medicine
Physics
Statistics

There are several different branches of science. *Chemists* investigate all the different substances in the Universe and also make new ones. *Physicists* are interested in the particles that make up the Universe, and in different forms of energy such as heat, light and electricity. *Biologists* study living things. They look at their structure, how they behave, how they evolve, and how they interact with each other and their environment. *Geologists* examine what our planet Earth is made of and how it has developed since it formed. *Astronomers* are interested in stars, planets and galaxies, and how the Universe itself began.

All scientific investigations begin with a question. What is water made of? How far away are the stars? The next step is to think up an experiment that might help to answer the question, and make measurements to try to find answers. From the results of their experiments scientists develop a theory about what is happening. Often the theory uses mathematics to describe how things behave. They then make predictions from the theory to test whether it is useful or not. They set up new experiments to check whether or not the predictions are correct.

▶ Not all scientific experiments are done in laboratories. This scientist with the British Antarctic Survey is taking snow samples in the Rutford Ice Stream, using his sledge as a makeshift ladder.

Scotland

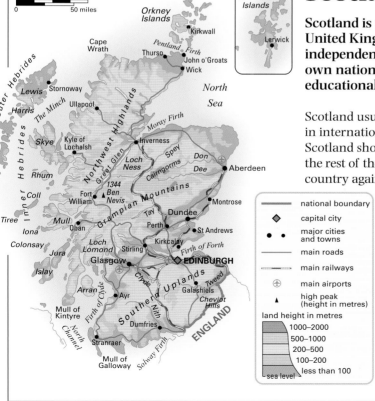

Scotland is the northern region of the United Kingdom. It was once a separate, independent kingdom, and it still has its own national Church, legal system and educational system.

Scotland usually competes as a separate country in international sport. Some Scots today feel that Scotland should have more independence from the rest of the UK, or even become a separate country again.

Highlands

The Highlands in the north are mostly mountainous, with many islands to the west (the Hebrides). Further north are the Orkney and Shetland islands. In the past, many Highland people spoke Gaelic, but it is now heard only in the north-west and in the islands.

The traditional Highland occupations are fishing and farming. Cattle and sheep graze on

Map legend:
- national boundary
- ◆ capital city
- •─• major cities and towns
- main roads
- main railways
- ⊕ main airports
- ▲ high peak (height in metres)

land height in metres
- 1000–2000
- 500–1000
- 200–500
- 100–200
- less than 100
- sea level

find out more
Britain since 1900
Celts
Europe
Industrial Revolution
Roman Britain
Stevenson, Robert Louis
Stuart Britain
United Kingdom
Watt, James

◀ Glencoe is a beautiful area of rugged peaks in the Highlands. In 1692 it was the site of a massacre of the MacDonald clan by the Campbells. The MacDonalds had delayed signing an oath of allegiance to the British crown, and the Campbells were acting on behalf of the British government.

the hills; and crops are grown in the valleys. Today many small farmers have a second job, often in tourism or another service. Fishing is important round much of Scotland. Fish are often deep-frozen and exported worldwide. Fish farming grew in the 1980s. North Sea oil has provided many jobs.

Lowlands and Southern Uplands

Most of Scotland's people and industry are in the Lowlands. Many of the coal mines here have closed, and other traditional industries such as steel-making are in danger. But there are newer industries, including chemicals, electronics and light engineering.

The Southern Uplands are more fertile than the Highlands. Crops grow in the Tweed valley and livestock farms are scattered throughout the region. In towns such as Galashiels people use local wool to make knitwear and tweed cloth.

Scottish history

The Highlands of northern Britain were the only part of the British mainland not to fall to the Romans. About AD 500 the area was settled by Scots from Ireland. Over the next 700 years the Scots, Britons, Angles, Vikings and Picts living north of the Roman barricade Hadrian's Wall were gradually brought together into a single Christian kingdom – Scotland.

An independent nation

Scotland's early kings struggled to keep out the English. When Alexander III died in 1286, Edward I of England began a series of wars to take Scotland. Led by heroic soldiers such as William Wallace and King Robert Bruce, the Scots eventually defeated the English in 1314.

Despite weak leadership and political unrest, the country prospered. By the reign of James IV (1488–1513), Scottish poets, educators, architects and engineers had a fine reputation

throughout Europe. Then, during Queen Mary's reign, conflict raged between Catholics and Protestants. Led by the religious reformer John Knox, the Protestants triumphed. Mary was removed and her son, James VI, restored order and authority.

One crown, two nations

In 1603 James VI became king of England and Wales as well as Scotland. In the 1650s Oliver Cromwell conquered Scotland and joined its government with England's. By 1707 Scotland's parliament had again been abolished and the country united with England and Wales.

At first Scots were uneasy about the union and the Jacobites (supporters of the Stuarts) rebelled in 1715 and 1745–1746. But wealth was increasing, new industries sprang up and Edinburgh became a centre of culture. Amid all this hope came the tragedy of the Highland Clearances. Poor farmers were driven off their land to make way for sheep farming. The Highlands became a fashionable tourist resort.

In the 20th century traditional heavy industries were replaced by North Sea oil, whisky manufacture and new high-technology industries. In 1997 the Scots voted in a referendum to have their own parliament again, which began to sit in 1999.

• Jacobites were people who continued to support Catholic King James II of England and his Royal House of Stuart after a Protestant revolution in 1688 had forced him into exile. Jacobite comes from *Jacobus*, Latin for James.

▼ Edinburgh is the capital of Scotland and an important financial city. Each summer there is an arts festival, and a splendid military tattoo in the famous castle. Glasgow is Scotland's other chief city. It is an industrial and commercial city, and it is much bigger than Edinburgh.

Sculpture

Sculptors create works of art that are three-dimensional – they are solid and substantial, instead of being flat like a painting. A piece of sculpture may be free-standing, so that you can walk around it and look at it from different angles. Sometimes you can touch it and feel its texture and shape.

Sculpture has been made from all sorts of materials, including plastics, fibreglass, bricks and even ice. Modern sculptors have sometimes used scrap material, including crushed car bodies. However, the traditional materials are wood, clay, stone and metal.

▼ This elegant ivory acrobat was made by an ancient Minoan sculptor of Crete in the 16th century BC. It may have been part of a bigger sculpture showing the acrobat leaping over a charging bull. Sport, especially bull-fighting, was very popular in Minoan culture, and the Minoans were skilled craftsmen and artists.

▼ This bronze sculpture of the head of a young man was made in Benin in West Africa in about 1550. It was produced from a wax mould.

Raw materials

Much sculpture has been made from wood. Hardwoods such as oak, walnut, yew, mahogany, ebony and cherry are all good for carving and have a wide range of colours and markings. But even the hardest wood may rot in the end, so most of the ancient sculpture that has survived is made of other materials.

Clays too have different textures and a variety of colours, including grey, reddish-brown, and blue-black. Stone also has a great range of colour, weight, strength and texture. Granite is the hardest and most weatherproof, so it has often been used for large outdoor monuments. It is difficult to carve, but can be polished to a mirror-like smoothness. Marble is a favourite stone for many sculptors because it produces such a beautiful surface.

Bronze is the most popular metal for sculpture because it can be worked easily. It has been used in virtually every civilization. Some of the most striking bronze sculptures have been produced in Africa and China. Several Greek bronze sculptures are in remarkably good condition after lying under the sea for more than 2000 years. Gold, silver, iron, steel and aluminium are other metals that sculptors use.

Subtracting or adding

Throughout most of the history of sculpture there have been two basic ways of shaping the materials: subtracting and adding. The first approach is to take a block of stone or wood and carve into it, subtracting the material you do not want and so creating a shape. It is almost as if the final sculpture were hidden inside, ready to be revealed by the skill of the sculptor.

The second way is to start with a lump of soft clay or wax and mould it into the shape you want. You can add on bits of material and join them together, so building up the model. When the model is finished, it can be fired in a kiln, like pottery, to make it hard and durable, or a mould can be made of it. This is then used to make a cast (an exact copy) of the model in metal.

Modern sculptors have added a third approach. They sometimes put together a sculpture from different materials by joining, welding, glueing, or simply grouping items together.

Traditionally sculpture has been solid and weighty, but modern artists have often used much lighter materials. Some of the 'mobiles' of the American sculptor Alexander Calder are made of thin sheets of metal hanging from strings so that they move even in quite gentle breezes.

Sculpture

► This marble statue of the goddess of love, Aphrodite — known as the 'Venus de Milo' (Venus is the goddess's Roman name) — dates from about 150 BC, and is a late example of the Greek classical style of sculpting. Greek sculptors of the 5th and 4th centuries BC sculpted the human figure in a calm and idealized way. Their female figures were more graceful, feminine and sensuous than those that had gone before. These sculptors were also skilled at moulding cloth to fall naturally, revealing the shape of the body beneath.

Forms and functions

Sculpture is a very ancient art. The earliest known examples include small stone figures of women, made about 25,000 years ago. Archaeologists think that they had a religious or magical purpose.

Since then sculpture has had many purposes. It has probably most often been used to create memorials to the dead. Most towns and cities have statues of important citizens. Many also have war memorials. Stone and bronze are very appropriate materials for such sculptures, as they can last for centuries.

Another important function of sculpture is the decoration of buildings. In almost all the great civilizations the most important buildings, especially churches and temples, have been richly decorated with carvings. The most breathtaking examples include some of the great Hindu temples in India. At Ellora, for example, there is a wonderful series of temples that have been sculpted out of rock cliffs rather than built in the normal sense.

find out more
Michelangelo
Picasso, Pablo
Pottery

Some great Western sculptors

Phidias was a Greek sculptor of the classical period. He lived in the 5th century BC and designed much of the sculpture that decorated the Parthenon in Athens.

Donatello (about 1386–1466) was an Italian Renaissance sculptor who produced marble and bronze figures of great power and character.

The Italian artist **Michelangelo** (1475–1564) is often regarded as the greatest of all sculptors. One of his best-known works is his statue of *David*.

The Italian Gian Lorenzo **Bernini** (1598–1680) is the most famous sculptor of the Baroque period. He designed many of the statues that adorn the cathedral of St Peter's in Rome.

The French sculptor Auguste **Rodin** (1840–1917) is famous for his bold and realistic figures, such as *The Thinker*.

The Romanian sculptor Constantin **Brancusi** (1876–1957) was one of the first sculptors to work with abstract forms.

The British sculptor Henry **Moore** (1898–1986) is famous for his massive figures that simplify the human form into smooth shapes.

Many artists have used sculpture, like painting, to express themselves and to experiment with materials, shapes and ideas. In the early 20th century, some sculptors have drawn particular attention to the natural beauty of their materials. Others have turned to waste material to show us how even junk can be transformed by a lively imagination.

▼ *Surrounded Islands*, Biscayne Bay, Greater Miami, Florida, USA, 1980–1983, by Christo and Jeanne-Claude, is an art 'installation'. An installation is not really a sculpture – it is a work of art constructed at a particular site, and it is designed to be temporary. The pink fabric used in the *Surrounded Islands* was chosen to complement the tropical environment. The project employed 450 people and, when completed, remained in place for two weeks.

Copyright Christo.

Sea birds

Almost three-quarters of the Earth's surface is covered by sea. The oceans are as rich in food as the land, so it is not surprising that birds take advantage of this food supply.

However, the open sea can be a harsh place for a bird and birds must come to land to breed. Only 300 or so of the 8700 different kinds of bird have come to depend on the sea.

Gulls are a particularly successful group of sea birds and many have benefited from humans. They eat our rubbish and some nest on our buildings. Gulls may be seen many kilometres from the coast and some kinds live entirely inland.

Albatrosses and shearwaters are great ocean travellers. The curious shape of their bill gives this group its name, the 'tubenoses'. The tube is an enlargement of the bird's nostrils and it may be used to gauge the strength of the air flow or to help the bird smell land or food. Albatrosses are spectacular gliders and only come ashore to breed.

gull

albatross

• A manx shearwater ringed in Wales was found in Brazil 16 days later. Its minimum flying speed must have been 740 km per day.

◄ Skuas are bird pirates. They are related to gulls and normally feed by following other sea birds and then chasing and harrying them until they drop a fish.

Another group of sea birds includes the cormorants, gannets, boobies and frigate birds. Their methods of finding food vary from the dramatic plunge of the gannet head-first into the water from a height of 15 metres or more, to the 'piracy' of frigate birds, which chase and rob other sea birds. ▶

cormorant

◄ Terns, sometimes called 'sea swallows', are close relatives of the gulls. Some of them are great travellers, like the Arctic tern which migrates from the Arctic to the Antarctic and back each year. Terns feed mainly on fish.

Penguins

emperor penguin

Penguins are flightless sea birds that live south of the Equator, especially in the Antarctic waters. Penguins have a layer of blubber (fat) below their skin as a protection from the cold. Their streamlined bodies and flipper-like wings help them to shoot along in the water like small torpedoes. Penguins are heavy and this helps them to dive. Emperor penguins can stay under water for up to 10 minutes. Most penguins hunt fish, although some kinds eat squid and krill. Penguins are social animals and live in large colonies.

find out more
Antarctica
Birds
Cliffs
Migration
Oceans and seas

▶ Atlantic puffins close to their burrows. Puffins nest in colonies. They breed from late May. The female usually lays a single egg in an abandoned burrow, or in a hole she digs herself with her feet.

little auk

Auks

Members of the auk family are all found north of the Equator. They look rather like penguins, but auks are able to fly. The puffin is a member of this family. Like penguins, auks swim and dive, and feed on fish. Many auks nest in huge colonies on sea-cliffs. Before they are fully grown, the young will flutter from their cliffs and disappear out to sea for the winter. The flightless great auk used to be a common member of this family, but was hunted for its flesh and became extinct in 1844, when the last surviving birds were killed.

Seals

Seals and their relatives the sea lions and walruses are sea mammals. Although they spend most of their lives in the water, they breathe air. Most of these animals live in the cold waters of the northern and southern oceans.

• There are 34 different kinds of seal, sea lion and walrus. The largest is the elephant seal, which sometimes grows up to 6 m long, and weighs up to 5000 kg.

find out more
Mammals
Oceans and seas

▼ Walruses use their huge tusks (up to 1 m long in males) to dislodge clams and other shellfish on the sea-bed. They then gather them with their mobile, whiskery lips.

Seals are slow and clumsy on land, but once in the water they are swift and graceful. Their bodies are streamlined, and they propel themselves through the water using their powerful flippers.

Seals can stay in the water for long periods. Beneath their skin they have a thick coat of special fat called blubber, which helps to keep them warm. When they dive, their heart rate slows to 4–15 beats per minute. This reduces the amount of oxygen that they use.

Most seals hunt fish, often those not valued by humans. A few kinds feed on krill, and walruses eat shellfish and sea urchins. Leopard seals feed on penguins and other seals.

Seals come to land to produce their young. They haul themselves ashore on islands or isolated beaches, which are traditional breeding places. Females produce only one baby, which grows quickly and is sometimes independent before it is three weeks old.

▼ Grey seals use their long whiskers to detect changes in water pressure as something swims past, so they can catch prey even in murky water.

484

Seashore

The seashore is where the oceans and seas meet the land. It is the part of the coast from the low-tide mark to just above the reach of the sea. In some parts of the world the tide does not go out very far and the seashore is only a few metres wide. In other places the tides go out up to 3 kilometres, and the seashore is very wide.

▼ Animals and plants on a rocky shore. The lower shore is wet and animals such as sea anemones, starfishes and sea urchins (1) live among the wet seaweeds in the rock pools. These seaweeds include sea kelp (2), serrated wrack (3) and thong weed (4). The rock pools are also home to small fishes such as blennies. Further up the shore seaweeds such as bladder wrack (5), knotted wrack (6) and spiral wrack (7) cling to the rocks. Mussels (8) fix themselves to the rock with tough threads. Crabs, sea slaters and shrimps survive by hiding in crevices. Limpets, periwinkles and barnacles (9) on the upper and middle shore have strong shells to protect them from the waves and the drying effect of the wind, and strong muscles to grip the rock. Channelled wrack (10) and lichens (11) flourish on the drier rocks.

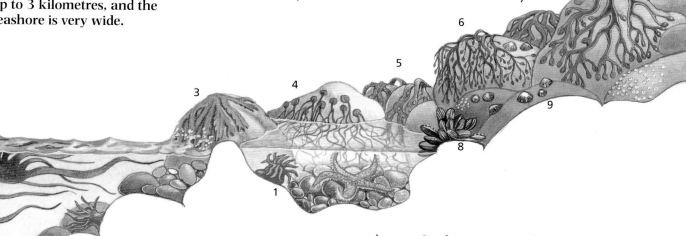

The lower shore is covered by sea water for much of the day, while the upper shore is covered for only a short time. The upper shore mostly dries out between tides. The animals and plants living there must be able to adapt to both wet and dry conditions, and to put up with rapid changes in temperature.

Rocky shores

Rocky shores have many pools, each with its own community of animals. The rocks are often covered with seaweeds. Seaweeds also fringe the rock pools, providing shade from the sun, and a place where small animals can hide from predators such as seagulls.

Most of the animals on rocky shores breathe oxygen from the water using gills, so they come out to feed when the tide is in. Crabs scavenge for seaweed and animal remains. Barnacles and shrimps filter food from the sea water using bristles on their legs. Mussels sieve the water with their gills, and limpets and periwinkles graze on the seaweeds.

Sandy and muddy shores

A sandy shore often appears to have very little life, but below the surface live a variety of burrowing animals. On muddier shores, there may be as many as 100,000 animals per square metre in the mud, out of sight of predators and protected from the sun and wind. The lugworm (sandworm) lives in a U-shaped burrow. It takes in water and food at one end, and pushes out waste at the other. Burrowing cockles and razor-shells sieve their food from sea water. Tube worms make themselves tubes of sand and mud, and put out sticky tentacles to trap food from the water. Small shrimps and crabs venture out to feed at high tide, but burrow in the mud before the tide goes out, so they are not swept away.

Where rivers meet the sea, there are huge expanses of mud. These shores can support an incredible amount of life. In just a square metre of mud, up to 1000 ragworms, 42,000 spire-shell snails, or 63,000 mud-burrowing sand-hoppers have been recorded (although not all together). Muddy shores and estuaries also attract large numbers of seagulls and wading birds (shore birds), which come to feed on the seashore animals.

find out more
Cliffs
Coasts
Crabs and crustaceans
Fishes
Jellyfishes and corals
Sea birds
Seaweeds

Seasons

As each season arrives, the length of daylight and the daily weather alter. Summer days are longer and warmer, while winter ones are shorter and cooler. Throughout the year, the different seasons bring changes to the world around us.

• In the night sky, the constellations you can see change day by day. The stars you see in the summer are quite different from the ones you can see in winter.

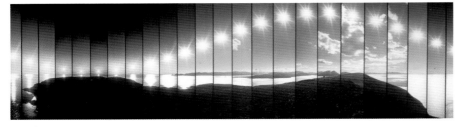

▲ This time-lapse photograph of the Midnight Sun was taken over northern Norway in midsummer. It shows the position of the Sun in the sky at one-hour intervals. Although the Sun is low in the sky at midnight, it never drops below the horizon.

Midnight Sun
Close to the North and South Poles, there are places where the Sun never sets for days or weeks in midsummer. These places experience the Midnight Sun. In midwinter, the opposite happens and the Sun never rises. This effect happens because the Earth's axis is tilted. The places that get the Midnight Sun lie inside the Arctic and Antarctic circles. The Antarctic has no permanent inhabitants, but people living near and inside the Arctic Circle have to adapt to long periods of continuous daylight or night-time.

find out more
Constellations
Earth
Time

In spring, after the short days of winter, the amount of daily sunshine increases as the Sun climbs higher in the sky. Summer is the warmest time of the year. The higher the Sun is, the stronger the warming effect of its rays. In autumn, the days shorten again, many trees drop their leaves, and the weather gets cooler as winter approaches.

Near the Equator, the number of hours of daylight does not change much through the year and it stays hot all year round. But the amount of rain that falls varies, so some tropical places have just two seasons: a wet one and a dry one. The seasonal changes are more extreme the further you are from the Equator. Near the Poles, there are enormous differences between the length of winter and summer days, but it never gets really warm because the Sun is not very high in the sky, even in midsummer.

The changing seasons
The Earth takes one year to travel around the Sun. We have seasons because the Earth's axis (an imaginary line going through the North and South Poles) is tilted to its path round the Sun at an angle of $23\frac{1}{2}°$. From about 21 March to 21 September, the North Pole is tilted towards the Sun and places in the northern hemisphere have spring followed by summer. At the same time, the South Pole faces away from the Sun. From September to March, the North Pole is tilted away from the Sun. Places in the northern hemisphere have autumn and winter while the southern hemisphere has spring and summer.

Each year, on or near 21 March and 23 September, the hours of daylight and darkness everywhere in the world are equal. These days are known as the spring and autumn *equinoxes* (equinox means 'equal night'). At midday on the equinoxes, the Sun is directly overhead at places on the Equator. The days when the number of hours of daylight is greatest and smallest also have a special name. They are called the *solstices* and fall on or about 21 June and 21 December.

▼ Places on Earth receive different amounts of sunlight during the year as the Earth travels around the Sun.

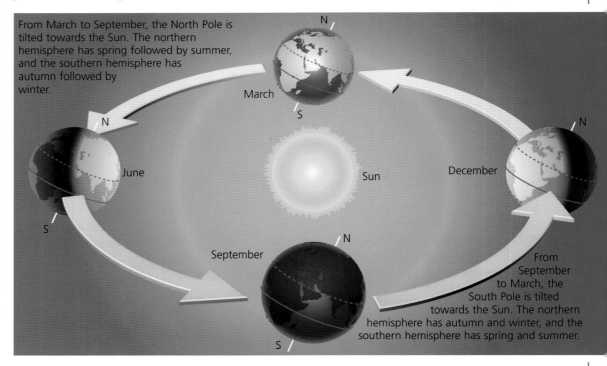

From March to September, the North Pole is tilted towards the Sun. The northern hemisphere has spring followed by summer, and the southern hemisphere has autumn followed by winter.

N

March

S

June

N

S

Sun

September

N

S

December

N

From September to March, the South Pole is tilted towards the Sun. The northern hemisphere has autumn and winter, and the southern hemisphere has spring and summer.

Seaweeds

Seaweeds are the plants you see growing on seashore rocks or washed up onto beaches after storms. They are not truly plants: they belong to a group of living things called algae.

The tiny cells that make up a seaweed are very simple. They do not have cell walls to strengthen them, so seaweeds can only stand upright when supported by water. Like plants, seaweeds make their food from water and carbon dioxide gas from the air, using the energy of sunlight. The process is called photosynthesis. So seaweeds can only grow near the water surface, where there is enough sunlight for photosynthesis.

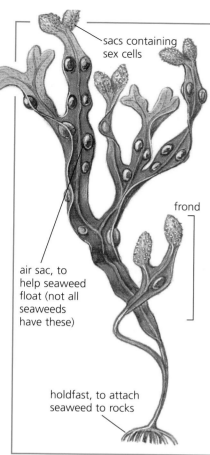

sacs containing sex cells

frond

air sac, to help seaweed float (not all seaweeds have these)

holdfast, to attach seaweed to rocks

◀ The structure of a typical seaweed.

Reproduction

Some seaweeds spread by breaking off fragments which grow into new plants. However, seaweeds can also reproduce sexually. The male and female sex cells are found in bladder-like sacs near the tip of a frond. The fertile sex cells are squeezed out through pores and mix together to form a fertilized egg cell. This grows into a new plant.

Zonation

Seaweeds living on shores between the tides have to cope with periods out of the water. Large kelp seaweeds growing at the bottom of the shore can survive out of the water for only a short time. Seaweeds at the top of the shore can survive drying for long periods. Between these two extremes, different seaweeds grow in bands or zones down the shore.

Useful seaweeds
Seaweeds gathered from the shore are used as fertilizers by farmers in many coastal areas. Glue-like substances called alginates, made from seaweed, are used in the food industry to help substances like ice-cream to 'set'. The Chinese and Japanese cook with seaweed. It is considered a very healthy food.

• Most seaweeds are brown or reddish in colour, although a few are green.

find out more
Algae
Plants
Seashore

Senses

Your senses tell you what is going on in the world around you. Human beings, like all animals, need this information to survive – to move and communicate, to find food and escape from danger. Your senses also enable you to take pleasure in your surroundings.

• Different animals have developed senses that equip them to survive well in their surroundings. Bats have such good hearing that they can fly in the dark and catch insects by sensing the echoes of bursts of extremely high-pitched sounds.

People have five main senses: sight, hearing, touch, smell and taste. Each of these senses is located in a part of the body, a sense organ. These sense organs pass information along nerves to the brain. The brain collects all the messages together to produce its 'picture' of the outside world.

You see with your eyes. Sight tells you what things look like and where they are. It also allows you to sense the colour and brightness of things. You hear with your ears. Hearing helps you to communicate and tells you where things are. Your inner ear is also important in helping you to balance. Your main organ of touch is your skin. Touch tells you what things feel like. You smell and taste with your nose and tongue. Smell and taste help you choose the right things to eat.

If one of the senses is damaged, other senses may become stronger to make up for it. For example, someone who has lost their sight may develop very good senses of hearing and touch.

find out more
Bats
Brains
Ears
Eyes
Noses
Skin

▶ This evening primrose flower has been photographed in ultraviolet light to reveal the 'honey guides', the dark lines and patches that guide bees to the nectar inside. Bees are able to see these lines, which are usually invisible to the human eye.

Seeds *see* Plants • **Senegal** *see page 638* • **Serbia and Montenegro** *see page 638*

Settlements

▲ A village street in Tibet, a region of south-west China. Tibet is very mountainous and isolated, and it is difficult to grow crops there. But the people who live in villages like this one cannot rely on nearby cities to provide them with goods and services. They must produce almost everything they need themselves.

• In India, three out of every four people live in villages. Many are farmers who have a small piece of land. Some rent land from a landlord in return for cash or part of their harvest. Others have no land of their own and work on a landlord's fields.

• Beijing was the first city to reach a population of 1 million, in 1800. Now the world has over 280 cities of this size. The largest urban regions – which can include several cities close together – are Tokyo, New York and Mexico City, all of which contain over 18 million people.

Settlements are the places where people live. They vary in size from small villages that can have populations of fewer than 100 people, to vast urban regions with over 20 million inhabitants.

Villages are usually found in rural areas, where about half the world's population lives. The other half lives in towns and cities.

Villages, towns and cities

Villages are traditionally places where farmers live so that they are close to the land they work on. They sometimes keep farm animals such as cows, oxen, pigs, chickens and ducks in the village. In some countries grain and other foods are kept in or near people's homes. Not everyone who lives in a village is a farmer. There may also be shopkeepers or teachers to serve the other inhabitants.

In developed countries, where few people are farmers, villages have changed. The people who live in them often travel to work every day in nearby cities. These *commuters* think that the time spent travelling is worthwhile because country villages are not as noisy or dirty as cities.

Towns are smaller than cities. A city is an important town where lots of people live and work. They are mostly employed in shops, factories and offices. A city may also have some things that small towns do not have. Cathedrals and universities, for example, are usually only found in cities.

Cities and towns that merge together are called *conurbations*. If such a conurbation covers a large region, it is known as a *megalopolis*. The area between Boston and Washington DC in the USA is a megalopolis over 600 kilometres long.

Every country has a *capital city*, where the country's government is usually found. The capital city is often the most important in the country, with the largest population and more businesses, shops and factories than anywhere else. Some countries have built their capitals specially, such as Canberra in Australia and Brasília in Brazil. Such capitals are often smaller than other, more established cities elsewhere in the country.

▶ A shanty town built on a swamp in San Juan, capital city of the Caribbean island of Puerto Rico. In stark contrast, the skyscraper buildings of the city's wealthy financial district rise up in the distance.

Settlement patterns

Settlements are found in different kinds of location. In Europe, for example, some villages are stretched out along a road or a river. Others consist of houses grouped together on a hilltop, originally for defence. In hilly areas villages were often built on the slopes, leaving the level land free for farming.

Cities start as small settlements and grow bigger because they have a particularly favourable site. Some cities, such as Paris, arise at a place where a large river is easy to cross. Others, including Sydney in Australia, have good natural harbours. Many big industrial cities grew up close to places where iron, coal or other natural resources were found. These resources were too bulky to move and had to be used on the spot.

A country's settlements can be arranged in a pyramid. There are more villages than towns, more towns than cities, and more small cities than big ones. This arrangement is called a settlement *hierarchy*.

◀ The city lights of the USA at night, as photographed by a satellite orbiting the Earth. The lights provide a clear picture of the country's varying population density.

A very small number of people do not live in any kind of permanent settlement. This group includes people such as nomads and hunter-gatherers.

Migration

Cities have grown big because people have migrated (moved) to them from villages and towns. When machines and more efficient methods of farming were invented, fewer people were needed to work the land. At the same time, factories in cities needed workers. This change happened in Europe and North America in the 19th century, and is happening in the developing world now.

Although there are not enough jobs for everyone in a city, people still move there. They have a better chance of finding work in cities than in rural areas. Cities also have better services, such as running water and hospitals, and entertainments, such as big sporting events.

City problems

As cities grow bigger, their disadvantages become greater. If cities expand too quickly, there may not be enough places for everyone to live. In much of the developing world, poor people have to make their own shelters, out of whatever

materials they can find. These settlements, crowded with dwellings made of wood or corrugated iron, are called *shanty towns*. When the poor have to build on land that does not belong to them, they create *squatter settlements*. If they can earn some money, they can gradually improve their shanties. Sometimes their governments help by providing materials, electricity and water.

As cities become bigger and more developed, there are more factories and cars, so the pollution and traffic congestion increase. The quality of the air and waterways often worsens, and so does the health of the inhabitants. Since polluted air carries chemicals such as

sulphur, which attacks stone, it also damages buildings. This is a major problem in Athens and Rome, where ancient buildings lie close to the city centre. To cope with this problem, cities such as Florence in Italy ban cars from the centre.

▶ FLASHBACK ◀

The first cities grew up in places where it was possible to produce a lot of food. These were usually near rivers which supplied good soils and plentiful water. They developed in different parts of the world: the Middle East, eastern China, the Indus Valley in what is now called Pakistan and India, Central America, and Peru.

Archaeologists are not sure which is the world's oldest city. It might be Çatal Hüyük in Turkey, which is now in ruins. Jericho, on the west bank of the River Jordan, is another candidate, and it is probably the city which has been lived in the longest – since 9000 BC. Byblos, in Lebanon, may have been inhabited for as long as Jericho.

• In some cities most of the residents live in squatter settlements. In Addis Ababa, in Ethiopia, 85% of the population are squatters, and in Bogotá, Colombia, 60% are squatters.

find out more
Countries
Government
Hunter-gatherers
Migration
Pollution
Population
Refugees

▼ Ponds of untreated waste surround the cardboard shacks of Haiti's Cité Soleil. This is the poorest part of the capital Port-au-Prince, the poorest city in the western hemisphere.

Seven Wonders of the World

find out more
Ancient world

Various ancient Greek writers compiled lists of the most impressive man-made structures known to them. The authors differed on what marvels (and how many) to include, but the seven here eventually became accepted as the standard list.

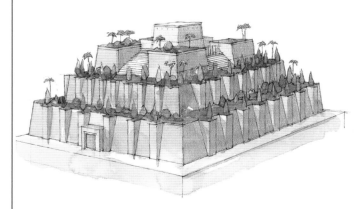

The Mausoleum of Halicarnassus, built in about 353 BC. Made of white marble, the tomb had a pyramid-shaped roof topped by a sculpture of a chariot drawn by horses.

The Hanging Gardens of Babylon. These spectacular gardens rose in a series of terraces. They were probably built by Nebuchadnezzar II, king of Babylon from 605 to 562 BC. Nothing remains of them.

The Pharos of Alexandria (280 BC). This Egyptian lighthouse was 135 metres tall and its light could be seen 65 kilometres away. It was destroyed by an earthquake in the 12th century AD.

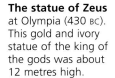

The statue of Zeus at Olympia (430 BC). This gold and ivory statue of the king of the gods was about 12 metres high.

The Colossus of Rhodes (304 BC). This huge bronze statue, about 30 metres high, represented the Sun god Helios and stood at the entrance to the island's harbour.

The greatest of the ancient **pyramids of Egypt** were these three, built at Giza in about 2600 BC. The oldest of the Seven Wonders, they are the only ones that survive virtually intact.

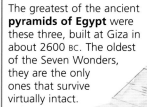

Building began on the **temple of Artemis** (Roman Diana) at Ephesus in 356 BC. It was enormous and beautifully decorated. Extensive remains of this site have been excavated.

Sewing and knitting

Sewing is used to join pieces of fabric or leather using a needle and thread. Knitting is a way of making a fabric by looping a yarn around needles.

Sewing is usually done with cotton, silk or synthetic fibres. Woollen yarn is most often used in knitting, although cotton, silk and synthetic yarns can also be used.

Sewing

Sewing is used to make and mend many everyday things, such as clothing, curtains, shoes and bags, and also for more specialized items such as sails for sailing boats and saddles and bridles.

The type of needle that you choose depends on what you want to sew. A thick needle, for example, might leave holes in a fine fabric. A *sharps* needle has a round eye and a sharp point. It is quite fine and is used for most sewing. Special curved needles are made for repairing chairs, tents, sails and lampshades.

Embroidery is a form of sewing, but the stitches used are just for decoration rather than for joining pieces of fabrics together. Embroidery stitches include running stitch, back stitch, chain stitch, cross stitch, stem stitch, French knots and satin stitch.

tacking stitch   back stitch

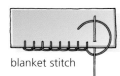
blanket stitch

herringbone stitch

Knitting

Knitting is a very ancient craft. Knitted sandal socks made in the 4th or 5th century AD have been found in Egypt. But knitting may have developed in Arabia before that.

Most knitting is done with two needles. They are usually made of aluminium, plastic or wood and vary in length from about 15–35 centimetres. There are many different kinds of knitting stitch, and beautiful patterns can be produced when different ones are used in special combinations.

Sewing and knitting machines

Although sewing and knitting can be very enjoyable, they are also very time-consuming. It is not economic to make most things by hand because not enough could be made to cope with demand and they would be too expensive for most people to buy. Fortunately, there is now a wide range of sewing and knitting machines, some for use in the home and others in factories. These can produce textiles and finished items quickly and cheaply.

▲ There are many different kinds of sewing stitch. *Tacking stitch* is used for temporarily holding seams or pieces of fabric together. *Back stitch* is used to replace machine stitching or to fasten off other stitches. *Blanket stitch* is used for neatening edges and to stop them from fraying. *Herringbone stitch* is used to secure a hem on thick fabric.

▲ A woman working in a jeans factory in Poland. She is using an industrial sewing machine that can cope quite easily with stitching thousands of heavy-duty garments.

The first sewing machine was invented in England in 1790. Nearly 50 years later a much better design was produced in France. This had a threaded needle that stitched the fabric on the top while a shuttle carried another thread below the fabric. The two threads became linked each time the needle pierced the fabric, thus producing a locked stitch which was very strong. Most modern machines are still based on this principle.

Knitting machines were first invented in 1589 in England, but it was not until the 19th century that more practical designs were developed. Today's knitting machines have a huge number of needles and can knit thousands of stitches a minute.

• Some modern sewing and knitting machines are computerized, which makes them very easy to operate. They can be programmed to produce all kinds of stitches and designs, or to create words or patterns with different coloured yarns.

find out more
Clothes
Cotton
Textiles
Wool

► French knots, chain stitch and cross stitch are embroidery stitches used for decoration.

French knots

chain stitch

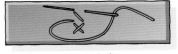
cross stitch

Sex and reproduction

The populations of many living things are divided into two sexes, male and female, and they reproduce (create new life) sexually. In animals, a sperm cell from the male joins with an egg cell from the female. In plants, the ovule (unfertilized seed) in the female part of one flower is fertilized by pollen from the male part of another flower, to produce seeds that grow into new plants.

Some living things do not have male or female parts, and reproduce non-sexually. This is called *asexual reproduction*. Amoebas, for example, simply split in two. Some sea anemones and their relatives can reproduce by *budding*. A small bud develops on the side of an adult and grows into a new animal joined to the parent by a stalk. Then the stalk breaks and there are two animals. Geraniums and many other plants can grow from a cutting. A stem cut from a big plant grows roots and becomes a new young plant.

Some plants, invertebrates (animals without backbones) and fishes are *hermaphrodite*. This means they have both male and female parts within them. Most hermaphrodites reproduce sexually with others of their kind rather than fertilize themselves. Slugs and earthworms, for example, simply exchange sperm when they mate, and both animals then lay fertilized eggs.

▶ Some male birds excel at courtship display. Some male birds of paradise hang upside-down, showing off their bright plumage to the female bird.

Genes

The cells of living things contain genetic material, which is made up of 46 chromosomes (coiled strands). These contain all the genes that determine how our bodies are built. Genes carry the information that makes a new living thing similar to its parents. One of the chromosomes also helps to decide the sex of the young. In human beings there are two sex chromosomes, called X and Y. All the female's eggs (ova) have an X chromosome but half the male's sperm have an X and half have a Y chromosome. If a sperm with an X chromosome fertilizes an egg the baby will be female. A male baby will develop if a sperm with a Y chromosome fertilizes the egg.

▲ Like most land animals, the male bear fertilizes the female bear internally, releasing sperm inside her body.

Courtship and mating

The physical action between male and female animals that brings about reproduction is called mating. Most animals only mate at certain times of year and they behave in different ways when they are ready to mate. Many male birds perform amazing displays to attract a female, and some arrange attractive collections of brightly coloured objects. This behaviour is called 'courtship'. Other animals make certain noises or calls to let the opposite sex know that they are ready to mate.

An animal's method of mating depends on whether the egg or eggs are fertilized outside the female's body (*external fertilization*) or inside the female's body (*internal fertilization*). Animals that fertilize externally, such as frogs and fishes, usually get close together or hold onto one another before eggs and sperm are released. This form of fertilization is common in water-living animals, but because eggs and sperm do not survive long in dry conditions, most land animals fertilize internally. With internal fertilization the male sperm are squirted into an opening in the female's body so they can reach the eggs inside her body. Insects, reptiles, birds and mammals use internal fertilization.

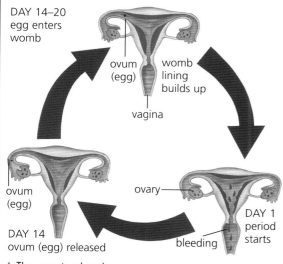

DAY 14–20 egg enters womb

ovum (egg)

womb lining builds up

vagina

ovum (egg)

ovary

DAY 14 ovum (egg) released

bleeding

DAY 1 period starts

▲ The menstrual cycle.

Human sexual reproduction

As with most other animals, male and female human beings have different sexual organs (*genitals*). A man has a penis. Below and behind the *penis* is a bag called a scrotum, containing two testes. In an adult, these produce several million sperm a day. The opening in a woman's body leading to her reproductive organs is called the *vulva*. It is surrounded by two thick folds of skin that protect the clitoris, a small bit of sensitive tissue. A channel called the *vagina* goes from the vulva to the *womb* (uterus). Two tubes link the womb to the egg-producing *ovaries*.

Mating between human beings has several names including 'making love', 'sexual intercourse' and 'having sex'. When people make love, many changes take place in their bodies. The man's penis grows bigger and harder. This is called an *erection*. The woman's vagina produces a fluid that makes it easier for the man to push his penis into it. Sliding the penis in and out gives both people feelings of pleasure; this usually leads to a peak called an *orgasm*, which involves strong muscular contractions in the sex organs. Orgasm in the man is necessary for fertilization to occur because it leads to *ejaculation*. This is when semen (the fluid containing sperm) squirts out from the penis into the vagina. The sperm swim into the woman's womb and up towards

her ovaries. If a sperm fertilizes an egg, the woman becomes pregnant.

Menstruation

Although humans may have sexual intercourse at any time, fertilization is only possible for several days each month. This is because a woman's reproductive systems works on a 28-day cycle. During a woman's reproductive years – usually between her early teens and middle age (45–50 years) – the ovaries release an egg about every 28 days. In the week after it is released, the lining of the womb grows thick with blood vessels to feed the egg. If the egg is not fertilized within a few days it will die. After about 14 days the womb lining will break away and flow out of the vagina with the egg and a little blood. This is called menstruating or having a 'period'. The period lasts about 5 or 6 days and the liquid is absorbed by sanitary towels or tampons.

Sexual responsibility

It is very important that care is taken to avoid the spread of dangerous diseases (such as AIDS) through sexual intercourse. The man can wear a *condom*. This is a thin rubber covering that fits tightly around the penis and is worn during sexual intercourse. It collects the semen and helps to protect against disease. Being careful in this way is called having 'safe sex'. A condom is also used to prevent the woman from becoming pregnant. There are various other ways of preventing pregnancy. These are known as forms of birth control or *contraception*. For example, a woman can take 'the pill'. These are special pills that stop her ovaries releasing eggs.

Sexuality

Sexuality is the word used to describe sexual feelings and behaviour. When people are emotionally and physically attracted to members of the opposite sex, they are heterosexual. Some people are not heterosexual but homosexual – they are attracted to people of their own sex. Homosexual men are often called gay, and homosexual women are called lesbians. There are also people who consider themselves bisexual – they feel attracted both to people of their own sex and to people of the opposite sex.

Because most societies have traditionally been based on heterosexual behaviour, homosexuals have often been unfairly treated, and in some countries homosexual relationships are illegal. However, homosexuality is now generally regarded as a normal kind of human sexuality.

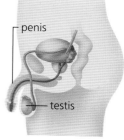

penis

testis

male

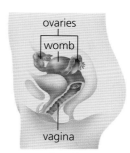

ovaries

womb

vagina

female

▲ The male and female sexual organs.

find out more
AIDS
Animals
Cells
Genetics
Growth and development
Human body
Plants
Pregnancy and birth

Shakespeare, William

William Shakespeare is the most famous playwright of all time. Between 1589 and a few years before his death in 1616, he wrote over 35 plays. All of them are still performed today.

Nobody knows how William Shakespeare earned his living in his early 20s, but it is certain that by 1592 he was earning money as an actor and playwright in London. He soon became a leading member of a theatrical company

called the Lord Chamberlain's Men, which later became known as the King's Men, and often performed at court. He remained with them for the rest of his working life.

Shakespeare is most famous for his tragedies, such as *Romeo and*

Juliet, Hamlet, Macbeth and *King Lear*, and his many popular comedies, such as *A Midsummer Night's Dream* and *Twelfth Night*. He also wrote historical plays, such as *Henry V*, part of a long cycle of eight plays dealing with English history from the reign of Richard II to the reign of Henry VIII. Other favourites often performed in the theatre are *The Merchant of Venice*, *Julius Caesar* and *The Tempest*.

Shakespeare's plays are mostly written in verse, although there are some scenes in prose, or a mixture of verse and prose.

◀ Between 1599 and 1613 the theatre company Shakespeare worked with was based at the Globe Theatre on the south bank of the River Thames. A reconstruction of the theatre, on the same site as the original, was completed in 1997.

Born 1564 in Stratford-upon-Avon, England
Died 1616 aged 52

● Shakespeare is famous for his poetry as well as his plays. He wrote 154 sonnets, which were published all together in 1609.

find out more
Drama
Theatres

Sharks and rays

Sharks, together with rays and skates, are different from other fishes. The most important difference is that their skeletons are made not of bone but of cartilage – the same material that is found in your nose and ears!

There are many different types of shark. Some, such as the bullhead sharks, are sluggish and feed on shellfish on the sea-bed. Others, such as the massive whale shark, filter the sea water for plankton. The best-known sharks are fast-swimming predators such as the great white. They feed mainly on fish, and the larger ones also eat seals and dolphins.

Sharks' eyesight and hearing are not very good, but they have a keen sense of smell, which they use to find their prey. They can sense vibrations produced by an injured or struggling fish. They can also detect electric currents in the water, which means they can trace prey by the electricity made in its body.

A flesh-eating shark may have up to 3000 teeth, but most of them are behind the front teeth. When one of these is damaged, it drops out and the next tooth moves forward to replace it.

Rays and skates are flat-bodied creatures that live close to the sea-bed. They move along by flapping their large 'wings'. They have a long thin tail, and eyes on the top of their head. Their wide mouths are on the underside of their heads. Stingrays have poisonous spines on their tails, which they use for defence. Other rays, called electric rays, produce an electric shock which they use to stun their prey.

stingray

blue shark

● Most sharks lay only a few eggs, and they are usually protected by horny egg cases. The 'mermaid's purse' which can be found on the seashore is the empty egg case of a small shark or a ray.

find out more
Fishes
Oceans and seas

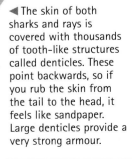

◀ The skin of both sharks and rays is covered with thousands of tooth-like structures called denticles. These point backwards, so if you rub the skin from the tail to the head, it feels like sandpaper. Large denticles provide a very strong armour.

Sheep and goats

Sheep and goats are naturally agile, sturdily built animals, related to cattle. They are now rare in the wild, but many domestic varieties have been bred from the wild species.

Most wild sheep and goats live in mountainous areas. Sheep are good climbers but less agile than goats, so they are generally found at lower and less rocky levels. Sheep and goats both have horns, which are larger in the males. They are used particularly in fighting for mates.

In the wintertime wild sheep grow a thick undercoat (fleece) of fine wool to keep them warm and dry. It is moulted (shed) completely in the summer. People started keeping sheep so that this fleece could be shorn off each year and used to make wool. There are now more than 800 breeds and over 800 million domestic sheep.

Wild goats live in herds. They have coats made of thick, often coarse hair. The coats of angora and Kashmir (cashmere) goats are used to produce wool for clothes. Many varieties of goats have been domesticated and kept for their milk, meat and skins.

▶ The alpine ibex is a goat that lives in high altitudes in mountainous regions of Europe. It is a very good climber and can easily leap from rock to rock.

▼ The mouflon from southern Europe and south-west Asia is the smallest of the wild sheep. It was domesticated about 9000 years ago and is the ancestor of domestic sheep.

find out more
Digestive systems
Mammals

• Sheep and goats are ruminants, like cattle and antelopes. This means they eat plants and then regurgitate the food to chew it again.

Shintoists

Shintoists follow Shinto, the folk religion of Japan. Shinto is one of the oldest religions in the world. It is so old that there is neither a founder figure nor any known date for its beginning.

Shinto is often translated as 'the *kami* (spirit) way'. According to Shintoism everything, including mountains, rocks and plants, as well as people, have spirits. The most important kami is Amaterasu, the Sun goddess. Japan is often called the 'land of the rising Sun', and Shinto has been Japan's state religion at certain times in history.

As well as worshipping spirits found in nature, Shintoists also worship the spirits of their dead relatives. Some families keep small Shinto shrines with pictures of deceased parents or grandparents in their homes. Some may have both Buddhist and Shinto shrines, as Shinto beliefs do not conflict with those of other faiths, and most Japanese follow both Shintoism and Buddhism.

There are also public Shinto shrines (places of worship) presided over by priests. All Shinto shrines have a *torii*, a special gateway marking the entrance to the sacred area. People pray there when they have personal problems, when they want to offer their thanks, or to meditate on the harmony there should be between the kami, nature and people.

▼ Before entering a Shinto shrine like this one in Kyoto, Japan, Shintoists cleanse themselves of evil thoughts and spirits. They do this by washing their hands and mouth in water. Once cleansed, they approach the shrine by clapping their hands twice and then bowing.

find out more
Japan
Religions

• Worshippers wishing for luck for a particular event, such as student exams or a future marriage, may leave their wish on a placard at a Shinto shrine.

Ships and boats

Ships are large, sea-going vessels, usually with engines that drive an underwater propeller. Ships used to carry sails and to rely on the wind, but there are very few large sailing ships in use today. Boats are much smaller craft and can be propelled by people using oars or paddles, by small sails or by an engine. Boats are used worldwide on rivers and along coasts.

Boats, which in the past were built of wood or reeds, are generally now made of materials such as aluminium, plastic, rubber and fibreglass. Modern ships are built of steel and other metals. Most have one propeller (also called a screw), but some ships have two or even three. Usually, the propeller is driven by a diesel engine, but a gas turbine or a steam turbine may be used instead. For a steam turbine, the steam comes from a boiler using the heat from burning oil or from a nuclear reactor.

Boats

Boats are small craft, often with little or no deck. They are not generally large enough to be used safely in the open sea. Coracles and canoes are small boats, with no keel, which are moved through water by a paddle or a sail. *Coracles* are made from a frame of woven wooden strips covered with canvas or flannel. A covering of tar or pitch makes the boat waterproof. *Dugout canoes* are hollowed out from tree trunks. Craft such as these are found in many parts of Africa and Asia. In West Africa, for example, they are used for fishing near the shore. The Inuit people of North America build *kayaks*, which are wooden-framed canoes covered with sealskin.

▲ A Tirio Indian uses an outboard motor to help his dugout canoe through some rapids on the Tapanahoni River in Suriname, South America.

Sailing ships

The earliest sailing ships had just one mast and sail. As ships grew larger, more and taller masts were added, and several sails were carried on each mast. Most large sailing ships were *square-rigged*, which means the sails were set at right-angles to the length of the ship. The square-rigged clippers were the fastest sailing ships of all. Small sailing ships are still used for trading in many parts of the world. For example, *dhows* are used in the Middle East and *junks* in the Far East.

Cargo and passenger ships

Most modern cargo ships are specially designed to carry one type of goods only. The cargo might be several hundred cars, containers packed with washing machines, or grain pumped aboard through a pipe. Passenger ships are either ferries or luxury liners taking people on holiday cruises. In the past, before air travel became popular, huge passenger liners provided regular services between all the major ports of the world.

▼ Different types of ship and boat. (These drawings are not to scale.)

coracle

rowing boat

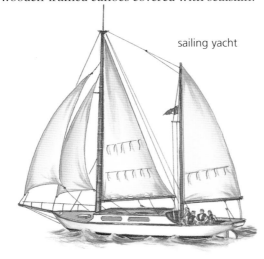

sailing yacht

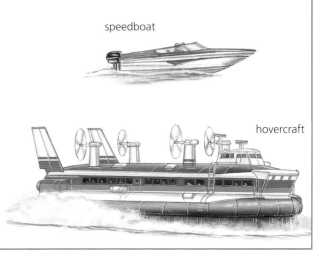

speedboat

hovercraft

Lifeboats

A lifeboat is a boat specially built for saving people who are in difficulty at sea. Lifeboats are self-righting, so that if they capsize, they will turn the right way again by themselves. A lifeboat needs to have powerful engines and must be strong enough to withstand the force of the waves. Many big lifeboats have now been replaced by small inflatable rubber boats. These are better suited to rescue work close to the shore, helping people in trouble on yachts and small fishing boats.

Hovercraft

Hovercraft carry people and goods over land and sea. Some are used as passenger and car ferries. They are sometimes called 'air-cushion vehicles' because they float on a cushion of air, which is made by pumping air downwards underneath the hovercraft. The vehicle is pushed forwards by propellers on top, usually driven by ordinary aircraft engines. Hovercraft are able to travel over any fairly flat surface and move easily from water to land without stopping. In Canada, for example, they work across land, water and ice.

► FLASHBACK ◄

The ancient Egyptians built long reed boats as far back as 4000 BC. The Greeks and Romans used long narrow galleys powered by lines of rowers. Between about 700 and 1000 AD, the Vikings

▲ A crowded ferry crosses the Mekong River in Cambodia, South-east Asia.

invaded much of northern Europe in their famous long ships. In the 16th century sailing ships called galleons were used to carry cargoes and as fighting ships.

Ships driven by steam engines started to replace sailing ships in the early 1800s. The first steamships were propelled by large paddle wheels. The engineer Isambard Kingdom Brunel had a major influence on modern ship design. His ship the *Great Britain* was a revolution in design. Launched in 1843, it had a screw-propeller and was built of iron. Steamships needed huge supplies of coal as fuel, so they became much bigger.

find out more
Engines
Gases, liquids and solids
Navies and warships
Oceans and seas
Ports and docks
Submarines

container ship

cruise liner

Shoes

Shoes are worn mainly to cushion the feet from impact with the ground when we walk. Yet there are a huge variety of shoes to suit many different purposes and tastes.

▶ Training shoes are made to support and protect the feet. Outer soles should be strong and hard-wearing. The tread moulded into the bottom grips the ground. Inner wedges and insoles provide support and flexibility, and they cushion the feet from impact against the ground. The upper provides support and, ideally, should both allow the foot to breathe and be water-resistant.

find out more
Dress and costume

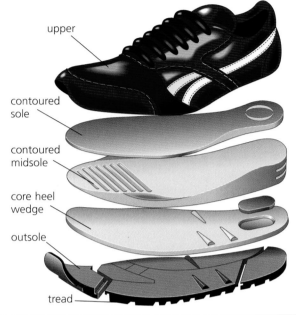

upper
contoured sole
contoured midsole
core heel wedge
outsole
tread

Many shoes made today have leather uppers and synthetic soles. More expensive shoes are lined with leather, and cheaper shoes have plastic uppers. Some shoes, such as sports shoes, have fabric uppers and rubber soles.

In a shoe factory, once an upper has been cut out it is 'closed' (stitched) and set on a 'last' (mould). The upper is attached to the sole with adhesive or, on more expensive shoes, the sole and upper are stitched together. The sole and heel are usually premoulded in one piece.

▶ FLASHBACK ◀

Shoemaking used to be a highly skilled craft. Cobblers would make strong shoes to last for years, as well as fashionable shoes in exaggerated shapes. Pointed toes and high heels have often been fashionable. In the 1470s pointed toes were longer than they have ever been since. Laws were even passed to restrict their length. The points were stuffed to keep them firm. Shoes with silk uppers were popular among fashionable ladies in the Stuart and Georgian periods. They wore shoes with a raised sole which were called pattens or clogs. Very poor people could only afford wooden clogs.

Shops

Shops are where we go to buy the goods and services we need. The business of selling to customers is known as *retailing*, and people who run shops are called retailers.

• Co-operative societies are special kinds of companies. Owners of co-operatives share the cost of starting a business, such as a shop. Then they share the profits (after deductions for expenses) among their members in proportion to the amount each spent.

▶ Sainsbury's is now one of the biggest chains of supermarkets, but when this store was opened in Guildford, England, in 1906 customers could sit on chairs while staff took their food orders.

find out more
Industry

Small corner shops may be run by just one person or by a family. They may sell everyday items, such as sweets, tobacco, newspapers, magazines and popular grocery items. Some of these independent retailers suffer because larger shops can offer the same goods at lower prices. So smaller shops often join a 'voluntary chain' or

'symbol group', where they can pool their resources to buy in goods more cheaply and to advertise themselves more effectively.

Some smaller shops in shopping centres specialize in one type of goods, such as books, shoes or toys. Most of these shops now belong to a chain, run by a large company. Some large chains have shops in many different countries. *Department stores* are shops which sell a wide variety of items in different sections or departments. Large, self-service food shops are called *supermarkets*. Larger, out-of-town supermarkets, which also sell non-food products, are called *hypermarkets*.

Sikhs

The Sikh religion began in the Punjab in northern India where most Sikhs still live. The most important thing for a Sikh is learning about God, and in the Punjabi language the word *sikh* means 'learner'.

The Punjabi word *guru* means 'teacher'. God is the 'True Teacher' and is described by Sikhs as the 'Eternal Being' beyond male or female. The title 'Guru' is also given to 10 important human beings in the history of Sikhism.

The Sikh Gurus

The first of the 10 Gurus was Nanak, who lived in the Punjab from 1469 to 1539. His background was Hindu, and Sikhs share the Hindu belief in a final liberation from repeated reincarnations. They also share some of the same festivals, such as Divali. Nanak taught that to reach unity with God, people should meditate, pray, sing hymns and follow the advice of a guru.

In 1604, the fifth Guru, Arjan, collected teachings from earlier Gurus into a book which became the sacred Scripture of the Sikhs. It is called the *Guru Granth Sahib* and passages from it are read aloud at all Sikh ceremonies.

Sikh beliefs

All the Gurus teach Sikhs three main things. First, they should remember God frequently by saying or singing his name. Secondly, Sikhs should work hard to earn an honest living. They usually marry and have families, feeling that this is the way God wants them to live. All Sikh men and women are equal and can perform any of the religious ceremonies. There are no monks or priests in Sikhism.

Thirdly, Sikhs should share their earnings and serve others, whatever their nationality, religion or social status. In the *gurdwara* (Sikh temple) everyone helps to prepare and serve food and drink from the *langar*, the guru's kitchen. Guests are welcome to stay and eat at any time, but especially after a service.

The five Ks

In 1699 the tenth Sikh Guru, Guru Gobind Singh, introduced five symbols for Sikhs to wear. The *kara* is a steel bangle worn on the right wrist to remind Sikhs that they are bound to God. *Kesh* is uncut hair, which is placed in a topknot by boys and men. Men usually wear a turban over the hair and women a long scarf. The hair must be kept tidy with a *kangha*, or comb. The *kachera* are shorts, usually worn under clothes. At the time of Guru Gobind Singh, shorts gave more freedom of movement for self-defence than other Indian clothes. The *kirpan* was originally a sword, but may now be small enough to be worn on the comb under the turban. It shows a willingness to help the weak and defend the truth.

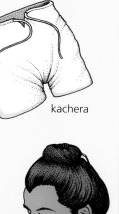

kirpan

kachera

kesh

kara

kangha

▼ The gurdwara is a Sikh place of worship and a community centre. Inside, everyone faces the *Guru Granth Sahib*, the Sikh holy book. The reader holds a *chauri* (a kind of fan) as a symbol of respect for the book.

• As Guru Gobind Singh lay dying in 1708, he declared that the Sikh holy book, rather than another human being, should guide the community after his death. Thus he became the last of the Sikh Gurus.

• The centre of Sikhism is the city of Amritsar in the Punjab, India. The Golden Temple of Amritsar is sacred to Sikhs, who make pilgrimages to see it.

find out more
Festivals and holidays
Hindus
Religions

Silk

Silk is a luxurious and expensive material. It is very strong and long-lasting. It is even used in the nose cone of the supersonic aircraft Concorde. The manufacture of silk is a slow process that involves a lot of hard work.

▲ To form the cocoon, the silkworm produces threads from its head which stick together with the help of a gummy material. The finished cocoon is about 3 cm long.

Silk is made from fine threads unwound from the cocoon (protective case) of the silkworm, which is the caterpillar of the moth *Bombyx mori*. A very large number of these threads are required for every centimetre of woven fabric. The silkworms feed exclusively on mulberry leaves. When the caterpillars reach their maximum size (about 8 centimetres), they start to spin cocoons. Inside the cocoon, the silkworm changes first into a pupa, and then into a moth, which (in its natural state) would break out of the cocoon.

To obtain the silk threads, the pupa in the cocoon has to be killed by hot air or steam. It would damage the cocoon if it tried to emerge as a moth. The ends of the two threads which form the cocoon are joined to the threads of another cocoon to form one complete silk thread. This thread is reeled off and wound into skeins, ready to be woven into silk fabric. The thread can be twisted in various ways to make different kinds of silk fabric.

▶ **FLASHBACK** ◀

Silk was first produced in the Far East over 4000 years ago. The Chinese empress Xi Ling is said to have discovered that the cocoons on her mulberry bush could be unwound to produce a fine fibre. Silk was brought to the West by early traders along the 'Silk Road' from the East to Venice and other busy trading ports. Only the nobles and very rich people could afford silk for their clothes.

▼ This textile worker is winding silk thread in a factory in Vietnam. Far Eastern countries still supply much of the silk used in the world today.

find out more
Butterfies and moths
Textiles

Silver

Silver is a brilliant-white shining metal. Along with gold and platinum, it is one of the so-called precious metals. Silver is widely used to make jewellery, tableware and ornaments. It is also used to coat other cheaper metals in a process called silver-plating.

• In many countries, objects made of silver, gold or platinum must be tested and hallmarked before sale. The hallmark guarantees that the object contains a high enough proportion of the precious metal. It may also give information on the manufacture and on the year and place in which the object was tested.

Some silver is found in the ground in its pure state, but it is mostly found combined with other substances. Silver can easily be beaten into shape or be given a highly polished surface. It is used to coat mirrors because it reflects light well. Silver is also a very good conductor of electricity. It is used in the electrical switches inside computers and other electronic equipment.

Silver has a special use in photography. When silver is combined with certain other substances, such as chlorine and iodine, it forms salts which are very sensitive to light. If a light shines on them, they turn black. For this reason, large quantities of silver are used to make photographic films and special, light-sensitive papers.

Many nations have at various times used silver coins. Nowadays, though, alloys (mixtures) of other metals are often used instead, except for coins to celebrate special events.

▶ A silver vesta box for keeping matches in. The four marks that make up the hallmark can be seen along the rim.

find out more
Metals
Money

Singing and songs

Singing is making music with the human voice. A song is a poem set to music which expresses different emotions and different experiences – like love or despair, going to war, having a night out, playing a game or lulling a child to sleep.

▲ Masai *moran* (warriors), women and children singing at their home in the Masai Mara, Kenya. African languages often have a musical quality, and speech and song frequently overlap.

Most songs are accompanied by instruments such as the guitar or piano, but some of the most effective songs stand alone, without accompaniment.

Styles of singing

Most singers, whether they are opera singers or pop stars, have to be trained to sing properly and to get the most from their voice. However, singing is very much to do with expressing emotions, and all singers bring their own personality to a performance.

Singers in different parts of the world develop singing styles which are most suited to their music. Arabic singers have a high nasal quality. Many folk musicians, especially country and western singers, often use a nasal twang to gain a different effect.

How we sing

When we sing, we breathe a column of air up from the lungs. The air passes across the vocal cords so that they vibrate to produce sound waves in the same way that a wind instrument does. These vibrations are then amplified in the throat, the mouth and the bone cavities in the face (sinuses). Finally the tongue and the lips alter the shape of the sound to form words.

Type and range of voice

Most children have high voices. As they grow older, boys' voices change. Between the ages of 13 to 16 they 'break' and get lower in pitch. Girls' voices also change very slightly. Men have lower voices because they generally have longer and thicker vocal cords than women.

Overall, voices are grouped into the following categories (from highest to lowest): soprano, mezzo-soprano, contralto ('alto') or counter-tenor (highest male voice),

tenor, baritone and bass. Some counter-tenors are also able to sing in an upper register using a falsetto voice.

Some kinds of song

Hymns are religious songs. They are used in many religions, but are especially popular in Christian churches and chapels. Gospel music is a form of Christian hymn-singing.

Carols are songs of praise and joy, and are usually used to celebrate Christian festivals. The best-known carols are songs celebrating the birth of Christ and telling the story of Christmas.

Anthems are pieces of music written around a passage of the Bible, to be sung by a church choir. Anthems were first developed in the 16th century, when English replaced Latin as the language used in church services. When the Bible was translated into English, many composers used verses from the Book of Psalms in their anthems.

A *national anthem* is a song or hymn that is special to a particular country. It is a symbol of the people's national pride, like the national flag, and it is played at public ceremonies, such as the medal presentation at the Olympic Games.

find out more
Choirs
Classical music
Jazz
Music
Operas and musicals
Pop and rock music

▼ Gospel singers in a church in Syracuse, New York, USA. Gospel-singing developed in the 1920s in black Baptist churches of the American South. Its musical roots are in spirituals and blues-singing.

Skeletons

Your skeleton is the frame of bones that supports your body. It gives you your shape and enables you to make distinct movements. Muscles are attached to the skeleton, and the skeleton and muscles together support the soft parts of the body such as the large organs.

Without skeletons most animals would be floppy objects with no distinct shape, and actions such as swimming, running, picking things up and chewing would be impossible. Skeletons provide animals with a wide range of body shapes, with distinct parts to carry out different functions.

Fishes, amphibians, reptiles, birds and mammals (the vertebrates) have internal skeletons made of bone and a softer, gristly substance called *cartilage*. All these animals have a backbone made up of a chain of vertebrae, and a skull. Most also have four limbs – legs, arms, wings or fins.

The skull and backbone support and protect the central parts of the nervous system, the brain and the spinal cord. Attached to the backbone are the ribs; these curve round to form the rib-cage, which protects the heart, guts and lungs. The shoulder and hip are bony connections between the backbone and the limbs. In different land animals the basic five-toed end of the limb has been adapted in many ways. In the horse, for instance, each leg has only a single functional toe, with a hoof (the toe-nail) at its tip.

Other skeletons

Animals without backbones (invertebrates) do not have bony skeletons. Worms and snails, for instance, have taut, fluid-filled bags inside their bodies which hold them upright.

Other invertebrates such as crabs, lobsters, spiders and insects have a skeleton on the outside of their body. Their soft bodies are supported by a stiff, jointed skin (*cuticle*), which gives them their shape.

Joints

Joints are the bending and sliding places where bones meet. The bones at joints are covered in smooth cartilage, lubricated by joint fluid, which allows them to move over each other easily. Different types of joint allow different types of movement. *Hinge joints*, such as the elbow and the knee, allow movements in two directions only. Where greater flexibility is needed, as in the shoulder and hip, *ball-and-socket joints* are found.

▲ This crab has just shed its cuticle. Cuticles are hard and do not allow an animal to grow. Underneath is a new, soft cuticle. Crabs have to shed their cuticles a number of times before they are fully grown.

skull
jawbone
collarbone
rib
breastbone
humerus
backbone
pelvis
radius
ulna
carpals
metacarpals
phalanges
femur
kneecap
tibia
fibula
tarsals
metatarsals
phalanges

◄ The human skeleton.

Rheumatism
Rheumatism is a term used to describe any illness which affects the muscles and joints. There is no one illness called rheumatism. It includes arthritis, gout and rheumatic fever. Arthritis occurs if the cartilage at the joints gets worn away and there is a build-up of joint fluid. The joints become swollen, stiff and painful.

find out more
Animals
Bones
Muscles
Teeth

Skin

Your skin is the protective outer surface which covers the whole of your body. Skin stops the body losing water, protects it against infection and is an important organ of touch. The bodies of most animals are covered by a layer of skin.

The outer layer of the skin, called the *epidermis*, is made up of dead skin cells. Its cells are constantly being worn away and replaced from below. The layer below is called the *dermis*. It contains blood vessels, nerves, hair roots, and sweat and oil glands.

Your skin helps to control your body temperature. It produces sweat to cool the body down and makes hair to keep you warm. There are also many nerve endings in the skin which send information about touch to the brain.

Some skin cells contain a dark pigment called *melanin*. People with dark skin have more of these than people with light skin. These dark cells protect the skin from cancer, as they block the dangerous ultraviolet rays in sunlight. Moles and freckles are clusters of cells containing melanin.

- A bruise is caused by bleeding under the skin. It is purple because the oxygen in the red cells that give the blood its normal colour has been used up.

- Leather is a material made from the skins (hides) of animals. Most leather is made from domestic animals such as cattle, sheep, goats, pigs, horses and camels. Leather is used to make many things, such as shoes, clothes and furniture.

find out more
Hair
Human body

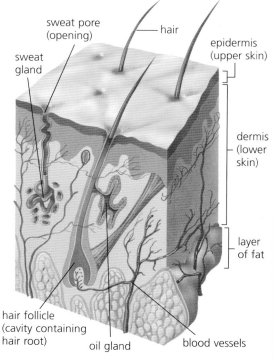

▲ A small piece of skin shown many times its actual size. The upper dead layer of skin wears away every time you touch something. But a layer of living cells replaces it as fast as it is removed.

Slaves

Slaves are people who are treated as if they were somebody else's property. They are bought and sold just like any object. There have been slaves in many different parts of the world, and at many different times in history.

- Spartacus was a gladiator who led a rebellion of gladiators and slaves in the 1st century BC. When he was defeated, over 6000 of the slaves who had joined him were crucified along the Appian Way, the main road into Rome.

The trade in slaves began long ago. The ancient Egyptians used people they had conquered as slaves, as did Greeks and Romans. Slavery continued in Egypt until the 19th century.

Ancient Greece and Rome

In ancient Greece, slaves often worked in rich people's houses. Women slaves cooked and cleaned, and served the lady of the house. They entertained guests at feasts as flute girls and dancers. Male slaves in Athens sometimes kept order in the streets like policemen.

The Romans too used slaves to run their homes, and to do hard and often dangerous jobs. Slaves also trained as gladiators who fought each other or wild animals, to entertain huge crowds in Roman theatres. Some well-educated slaves ran shops and became important government servants.

The Middle Ages

When the Roman empire broke up, slaves gradually disappeared in northern Europe. Powerful barons gave the people who worked for them a little land to live on. In return, these *serfs* had to work for their lord for fixed times, and could not leave their land. They were not owned, but otherwise they were like slaves.

However, slavery did not disappear in the Mediterranean. Slaves there were often black Africans or Slavs from the Balkans and further east. The word 'slave' comes from 'Slav'. ◆

◀ Romans could be very cruel to their slaves, whipping and branding them for disobedience. In this picture a slave has been killed just for an experiment. He is being weighed to find out whether the departing of the soul leads to weight loss (it doesn't!).

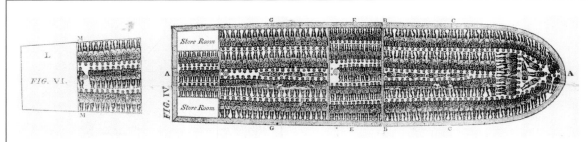

African slaves

There have been slaves in Africa for centuries. In East Africa, Arab traders sent slaves to Arabia and Asia, probably from the 12th century. In North Africa, from the 15th century, Muslims used white European Christians as slaves. Prisoners taken in wars between different tribes were used as slaves.

In the 15th century, European explorers reached West Africa. They discovered they could buy African slaves easily, and sell them across the Atlantic in the Caribbean, Brazil and North America. The Europeans soon found they could make a lot of money growing sugar in the West Indies and Brazil. But the fighting and the diseases they brought with them had killed off most of the native peoples, so they brought slaves from Africa to do the work. From the late 17th century, slaves began to work in tobacco and cotton plantations in North America. They also worked in the houses, cooking and cleaning.

Since slaves were so useful, owners sometimes treated them quite well. But they were harsh and cruel when they feared trouble, especially since there were soon many more slaves than there were Europeans.

▲ This is part of a plan of a slave ship which Christian MP William Wilberforce showed to the British parliament during his long struggle with the slave trade. An observer in 1788 wrote: 'The slaves lie in two rows close to each other like books in a shelf . . . the poor creatures are in irons . . . which makes it difficult for them to turn, or move . . . without hurting themselves or each other.'

An end to slavery?

Sometimes slaves rebelled against their owners. In Haiti, an army made up mainly of former slaves defeated the French and British soldiers and set up an independent country there in 1804. In the early 19th century, many white Americans and Europeans began to realize how wrong the slave trade was. The British parliament passed a law abolishing slavery throughout the empire in 1833. It came into effect in 1834, but some slaves in British colonies were not completely free until 1838.

In the USA there were few slaves in the northern states by this time, but Americans in the southern states fought for the right to own slaves. In 1863, during the American Civil War, Abraham Lincoln issued a proclamation for the freeing of all slaves. In 1865, after the end of the war, the Congress of the USA abolished slavery throughout the country.

• Harriet Tubman (1820–1913) escaped slavery at 29 and made her way north to Canada (where slavery was illegal) on the 'Underground Railroad.' This was not a real railway but a code name for a famous escape system. The organizers were called 'conductors' and Tubman became the most famous conductor of them all. She worked for 10 years, helping more than 300 slaves to escape, and was never caught.

• Many citizens of the United States are descended from West Africans who were taken to North and South America during the 17th, 18th and early 19th centuries to work as slaves. They used to be called negroes, but now prefer to be known as Afro-Americans, African Americans, or blacks.

◄ African slaves on plantations endured long hours cutting tough sugar canes under the blazing sun. Slaves also worked in the plantation owners' houses, cooking, cleaning and caring for their children. They looked after their carriages and horses and tended the gardens as well as working on the land.

find out more
Africa
Caribbean
Lincoln, Abraham
United States of America

Sleep

We do not really understand why we sleep. It may be that the body needs sleep to recover and repair damage, and the mind needs sleep to absorb the day's events and impressions.

During sleep, heart and breathing rates slow down and muscles relax. Our senses also fade: sight goes first, then hearing, and last touch. Our hearing is selective when we are sleeping. For example, someone might wake up if their name is whispered, but might stay asleep if there was a loud noise.

Scientists study sleep by measuring the pattern of electrical currents in the brain. They have found that there are different levels of sleep that alternate through the night.

Periods of *orthodox* (deep) sleep alternate with *paradoxical* (light) sleep, during which we make rapid eye movements (REM sleep). It is usually during REM sleep that people have dreams.

Dreams are images or thoughts that pass through your mind during sleep. Strange and vivid things can happen in dreams, and so they have always fascinated people. There are several theories about why we dream, but there are no clear conclusions.

Nightmares are very frightening dreams. Almost all children have nightmares at some time, but adult nightmares are not very common.

Hypnosis is when people are put into a deep sleep, but no one really understands how hypnosis works. It can be used to help people remember things they seem to have forgotten; to get people over unreasonable fears (phobias); and to cure them of addictions such as smoking.

▼ Dreams have fascinated many artists and film-makers, and they have tried to explore them in their work. This is a still from a dream sequence from Alfred Hitchcock's film *Spellbound* (1945). The sets were designed by the artist Salvador Dalí.

find out more
Hibernation
Human body
Psychologists

• Humans tend to sleep during the night and stay awake during the day. Some animals, however, are nocturnal – they sleep during the day and are active at night.

Slugs and snails

Slugs and snails form a highly successful group of animals that are found in large numbers both on land and in water. As a group, they are known as gastropods, which means 'stomach-footed' animals. This is because they all have a large muscular 'foot' which they use to walk or swim.

The main difference between snails and slugs is that in times of danger a snail can pull its soft body into a shell, which is usually coiled. Slugs may have a small shell, or an internal shell, but they cannot pull themselves into it for protection.

In most other ways, snails and slugs are very similar. Land slugs and snails ease their way on their foot with slime, which can be seen after the animal has passed. Both snails and slugs have simple eyes, which are sometimes on tentacles.

Both slugs and snails have a mouth on the underside of the head. This contains very many tiny teeth. Garden snails and slugs eat mostly decaying plants. You rarely notice the damage they do in the countryside, or in an untidy garden, where there is plenty of waste. It is only when there is no dead and dying material that they eat tender seedlings and young leaves.

Snails and slugs live in the sea as well as on land. Sea slugs are usually very brightly coloured, to warn other animals that their flesh is unpleasant-tasting and that they are best left alone. Unlike their land cousins, sea slugs do not feed on plants but on other animals.

• There are more than 35,000 kinds of slugs and snails.

▼ A garden snail may have up to 14,000 teeth in its mouth. They are arranged in rows on a ribbon-like tongue, which is called a radula. This works like a file, rasping away at food.

snail

▼ Sea slugs are almost all brightly coloured. Many of them feed on jellyfishes and use the powerful stinging cells of their prey to protect themselves.

▼ Whelks are snails that live in the sea. They feed on small fishes and other sea creatures, which they suck up through their long proboscis.

whelk

sea slug

find out more
Animals
Jellyfishes and corals

Smoking

People smoke tobacco either as cigarettes or cigars or in a pipe. There is now clear proof from studies that smoking causes ill health and early death.

Tobacco is a leafy plant originally from South America. Today it is grown in any area which has a high humidity, high temperature and plenty of rainfall. The leaves of the plant are placed in curing barns where they are heated and dried. Cured tobacco is rolled into cigars, or shredded and blended to make different brands of cigarettes and pipe tobacco.

Tobacco smoke contains tar with chemicals that cause cancers of the lungs, mouth, gullet and bladder. It also contains nicotine which raises blood pressure and makes blood vessels contract. This can cause heart disease. Nicotine is an addictive drug, which makes it hard for people to give up smoking.

Tobacco smoke can also harm non-smokers. When people do not smoke themselves but live or work with people who do, we say they are passive smokers. They may suffer higher rates of lung cancer and heart disease than non-smokers who live and work with other non-smokers.

▶ FLASHBACK ◀

The Spaniards introduced tobacco to Europe in the 16th century. At the time many people believed smoking was good for them. Towards the end of the 18th century, cigarette-smoking spread from Spain across the rest of Europe. Cigarettes became popular in the USA from the end of the 19th century.

▼ Despite the dangers, millions of people around the world continue to smoke. Here a stall in China is selling a wide variety of different makes of cigarette.

- About 850 million people around the world smoke tobacco, usually in cigarettes.

- 90% of lung cancers are caused by smoking, and 95% of people with bronchitis are smokers.

- Smokers are at least twice as likely to die of heart disease as non-smokers.

- Many countries are now imposing a ban on smoking in public places such as restaurants and bars.

find out more
Cancer
Diseases
Drugs

Snakes

Snakes are reptiles that have no legs. A number of snakes are burrowers, but most live on the surface of the ground. A few climb into trees, or even live in the sea.

Most snakes move by throwing their bodies into curves that push against any unevenness in the ground. Such snakes are helpless on smooth surfaces. Snakes are not slimy creatures. Their skin is dry and scaly. Every now and then, they moult (shed) their outer skin.

All snakes are flesh-eaters. They track their prey using their long, forked tongues, which flicker over the ground. The tongue picks up tiny traces of scent left by animals such as mice. Some snakes, like grass snakes, catch their food by grabbing and swallowing it. Others, like pythons, which are called constrictors, loop their powerful bodies round their prey and suffocate it. About a third of all kinds of snakes use poison to paralyse their prey.

Snakes swallow their food whole, and have a distinct bulge in their bodies after eating a meal. To take such a mouthful they have to unhinge their lower jaws at the centre and the sides. They can move each part of the jaw independently and so 'walk' their prey into their throats.

- In cool parts of the world snakes hibernate (go into a deep sleep) during the winter. In spring they look for mates. Males often compete with each other or put on displays for females. After mating, most female snakes lay eggs, although some give birth to live young.

find out more
Reptiles

▶ Vipers are examples of front-fanged snakes. They use the fangs to inject poison as they strike their prey. Each fang is on a movable bone, which allows it to be folded away: otherwise the snake could not close its mouth.

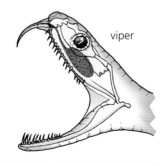
viper

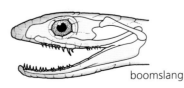
boomslang

▲ Boomslangs are examples of back-fanged snakes: they have small fangs towards the back of their mouth. This means that any prey they catch is partially swallowed before being injected with poison by the fangs.

▼ There are over 50 kinds of sea snake. Some are very poisonous, but they will only bite if they feel threatened or trapped.

sea snake

Soap

Soap is a natural detergent – a chemical that we add to water when we want to clean things. Soap helps the water to get right into the fabric of the things being washed, and to remove any dirt or grease. Synthetic detergents work in a similar way, by helping water to spread out and clean things.

• Soap was made from animal fats and wood ashes until the end of the 18th century. Then caustic soda was used in place of wood ashes, and plant oils such as olive oil and palm oil began to replace animal fats.

• The first synthetic detergents were developed during World War I (1914–1918). Household detergents became common in Europe and North America in the 1950s.

find out more
Acids and alkalis
Pollution

Washing soap is made by adding plant oil or animal fat to a strong alkali. Soap and a substance known as glycerol or glycerine are produced. The glycerine is washed out, and perfumes, preservatives and colourings are added. Finally, the soap is cooled and cut or shaped.

Soaps do not work well in hard water, which contains lots of calcium and magnesium salts. The soap reacts with these salts to form a 'scum'. This scum leaves rings on baths and a whitish film on glassware. Because they do not form a scum, synthetic detergents are now used instead of soaps for many cleaning purposes. They are made from chemicals obtained from oil. Other substances are added to detergents to make them clean better and to make the water look soapy.

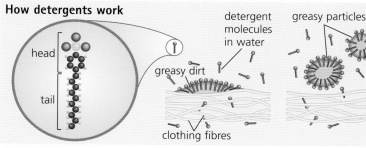

How detergents work

This is a magnified view of the structure of a detergent molecule. The head of the molecule is attracted to water, and the tail is attracted to grease.

When dirty clothes are washed in detergent, the tails of the detergent molecules bury themselves in any greasy dirt, leaving the molecule heads in contact with the water.

As the clothes move about, the greasy dirt breaks free from the fabric. Detergent molecules surround the greasy particles, which are rinsed away in the water.

Soil

Soil is a combination of rock particles of various sizes and decayed plant and animal matter. Different kinds of rock and different climates produce different types of soils. One square metre of fertile soil can contain over 1000 million living things, yet many are too tiny to see with the naked eye.

Soil is formed when rocks are slowly broken down by the actions of wind, rain and other weather changes. Plants take root among the rock particles. The roots help to bind the particles together, and protect them from rain and wind. When plants and animals living in the soil die, fungi and bacteria break down their remains to produce a dark sticky substance called *humus*. The humus sticks the rock particles together and absorbs water. You can find out about different types of soil by looking at a *soil profile* (a sample taken from the surface down through the soil). Each profile is divided into a series of layers called *horizons*.

The rock particles in soil have air spaces between them. The larger the particles, the bigger the air spaces between them and the faster water drains out of the soil. The air in the soil is important for plants because their roots need oxygen to breathe. The decaying plant and animal remains release minerals which are then absorbed by plant roots.

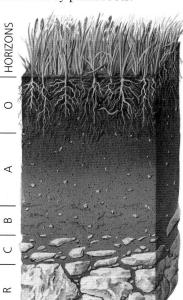

◄ A soil profile.

• In some parts of the world wind-blown dust accumulates to form a soil called *loess*. In parts of China the loess is as much as 300 m thick.

find out more
Erosion
Grasslands
Rocks and minerals

The *O horizon*, the surface layer, contains many animals and plant roots. It is rich in dark-coloured humus. It is thicker in rich soils than in poor soils.
The *A horizon* still has a lot of humus, but is a paler, greyish colour because many of the minerals have been washed out by rainwater. This process is called leaching.
The *B horizon* contains much less humus, but has some of the minerals washed out of the A horizon. Any iron left here may oxidize, producing a yellow or reddish-brown colour.
The *C horizon* is where weathering takes place, and the parent rock is breaking down.
The *R horizon* is the parent (original) rock.

Solar System

The Sun and all the things in orbit around it make up the Solar System. It includes a family of nine planets, most of which have one or more moons. Lots of other smaller objects, such as asteroids (minor planets) and comets, are also travelling around the Sun.

The Sun, which is a star, is by far the largest body in the Solar System. The nine planets are: Mercury, Venus, Earth, Mars, Jupiter, Saturn, Uranus, Neptune and Pluto. Planets are different from stars because they do not give out any light of their own. They shine because they reflect light from the Sun.

The nine planets

Mercury, Venus, Earth and Mars are small rocky planets that together make up the inner Solar System. Jupiter and Saturn are giant balls of gas. Uranus and Neptune are giant planets made of gas and ice. Pluto, the smallest planet, is composed of rock and ice. The diameter of Jupiter, the largest planet, is about one-tenth of the Sun's diameter. The Sun could contain a thousand bodies the size of Jupiter.

Some of the planets are surrounded by a system of rings. Saturn is circled by beautiful coloured rings made up of pieces of ice and rock and particles of dust. Uranus has a set of 10 very narrow rings, which were only discovered in 1977 when the planet crossed in front of a star and the rings cut out the starlight for a few moments.

All of the planets, except Pluto, have been visited or passed by spacecraft carrying cameras and scientific equipment.

The paths of the planets

The orbits of the planets round the Sun are not circles but have a squashed oval shape called an ellipse. A planet's distance from the Sun changes as it moves along its elliptical orbit. Most of the planets vary only slightly in their distance from the Sun, but Pluto varies from about 30 to about 50 times the Earth's distance. Although Pluto is further away than Neptune most of the time, a small part of its orbit crosses just inside Neptune's.

Apart from Pluto's, none of the planetary orbits is tilted by much, so the Solar System is like a flat disc. Pluto's orbit is tilted by 17°, so when it crosses Neptune's orbit it passes above Neptune and there is no danger of a collision. The way gravity acts means that the further a planet is from the Sun, the longer the period of time it takes to complete an orbit. The Earth takes one year, Mercury 88 days and Pluto nearly 248 years. The spaces between the planets are huge compared to their sizes. If the Sun were the size of a football, the Earth would be the size of this spot • and would be 30 metres away!

- The word 'solar' means 'to do with the Sun'. It comes from *sol*, the Latin word for Sun.

▼ The major planets in the Solar System, in order from the Sun, and a plan of their orbits around the Sun. The planets are drawn to scale, so their sizes can be compared with the Sun. (The distances between the planets are not drawn to scale.)

1 Sun
2 Mercury
3 Venus
4 Earth
5 Mars
6 Jupiter
7 Saturn
8 Uranus
9 Neptune
10 Pluto

Average distance of each planet from Sun, and time taken to orbit Sun

planet	million km	days
Mercury	58	88
Venus	108	224.7
Earth	150	365.3
Mars	228	687.0

planet	million km	years
Jupiter	778	11.86
Saturn	1427	29.46
Uranus	2870	84.01
Neptune	4497	164.8
Pluto	5900	247.7

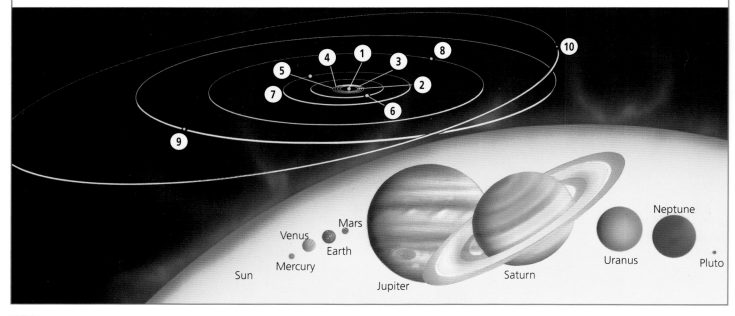

◀ This picture of Mars clearly shows the polar ice-cap that covers the planet's northern tip. The dark area around the polar region is a huge plain measuring about 10,000 km across. The plains in the northern hemisphere of Mars are lightly cratered, while those in the southern hemisphere have many more craters.

▼ In July 1997 the spacecraft *Pathfinder* landed on the surface of Mars. On board was this robot vehicle called *Sojourner*. It was powered by a solar panel, allowing it to move for a few hours each day. The 63-cm-long *Sojourner* carried equipment to study the planet's rocks.

• A year on Mars is nearly twice as long as an Earth year.

• Venus comes nearer to Earth than any other planet in the sky. You can easily find it by looking for a really brilliant object in the western sky in the evening or in the eastern sky in the morning.

• Jupiter, the giant of the Solar System, is wrapped in bands of swirling clouds. It has no solid surface but consists mostly of liquid hydrogen. Its largest cloud feature, called the Great Red Spot, has existed for at least 140 years.

Moons

Seven of the planets have moons that orbit around them. These moons are natural satellites, and altogether more than 100 of them are known in the Solar System. The biggest moons are the four major moons of Jupiter, Titan (one of Saturn's moons), and the Earth's Moon. Jupiter's moons were discovered by the astronomer Galileo and are called Io, Europa, Ganymede and Callisto. Another big moon is Triton, which orbits Neptune. Mars has two tiny moons called Phobos and Deimos.

Asteroids and comets

In the gap between the orbits of Mars and Jupiter, thousands of pieces of rock circle the Sun. These are the minor planets, or asteroids. The largest asteroid is Ceres, which measures about 940 kilometres across. However, most asteroids are much smaller than this, and

there are only about 200 asteroids with a diameter of more than 100 kilometres. Ceres is a round globe, but asteroids usually have an uneven shape. Most of them are likely to look like Gaspra and Ida, two potato-shaped asteroids covered with craters that were imaged by the Galileo spacecraft in 1991 and 1993.

Astronomers have recently discovered a number of icy asteroids beyond the orbits of Neptune and Pluto. These objects are probably part of a huge ring of icy bodies called the Kuiper Belt.

A comet is a lump of ice, dust and rock that travels through the Solar System. Comets usually travel in a very

• The smallest known asteroid, called '1991 BA', measures just 9 m across.

• When a new asteroid is discovered, it is given a label which indicates when it was found. For example, '2010 AA' will be allocated to the first asteroid found in the first half of January in the year 2010. When its orbit has been worked out, an asteroid is given a number and name, such as asteroid number 3200 called Phaethon.

◀ The surface of the asteroid Ida, imaged here by Galileo, is broken up by many craters, some of them very big. This suggests that Ida is quite old, because it has been hit many times by meteorites. Ida is 52 km long.

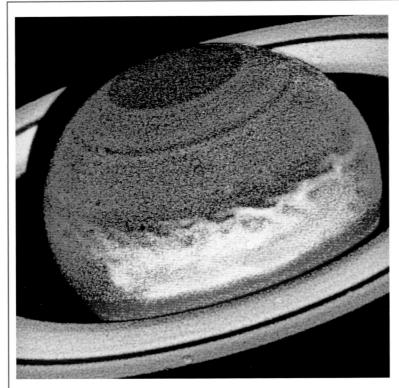

◀ This picture of Saturn was taken by the Hubble Space Telescope. The large, reddish-white area which stretches around the middle of the planet is a storm system called the 'white spot'. Scientists think that the clouds that form the white spot are made of ice crystals of ammonia.

stretched-out orbit around the Sun. Some of the comets come from the Kuiper Belt.

Astronomers think that others come from a huge cloud of icy bodies, called the Oort Cloud, which surrounds the Solar System and stretches out to a distance of about one light-year (about 10 million million kilometres).

Birth of the Solar System

Most astronomers believe that the Solar System was formed when a huge cloud of gas and dust fell together, pulled by its own gravity, just under 5 billion years ago. The cloud was spinning very slowly at first, but as it fell inwards, it began to spin faster and faster until it formed a central ball surrounded by a flattened sheet of gas and dust. As it continued to fall together, the central ball became hotter. Eventually it became hot enough to shine like a star and became our Sun.

In the surrounding sheet of gas and dust, tiny particles of

dust collided and stuck together to form small rocky or icy bodies. These then collided with each other to form complete planets like the Earth, and the cores (central parts) of the four giant planets (Jupiter, Saturn, Uranus and Neptune). Huge amounts of gas fell in to surround the core of each of the giant planets. Many of the remaining lumps of material collided with the newly formed planets and moons and blasted out craters on their surfaces. The lumps that were left over are the asteroids and comets that we see today.

▶ FLASHBACK ◀

The observations of the Danish astronomer Tycho Brahe in the 16th century led to a total rethink of the shape of the Solar System. From his observatory he made lots of measurements of the position of stars and planets, using only the naked eye. (A practical telescope was not available in his lifetime.) After Brahe's death

in 1601, his German assistant Johannes Kepler used Brahe's observations to produce a true description of the paths along which the planets move.

The Englishman William Herschel, one of the greatest astronomical observers ever, found the planet Uranus by accident in 1781. It was the first planet to be discovered with the help of a telescope. Herschel also discovered moons around Uranus and Saturn, assisted by his sister Caroline, who went on to discover comets on her own. In 1801 the first asteroid was found by the Italian astronomer Giuseppe Piazzi. It was named Ceres, after the Roman goddess of fertility.

● Galileo was the first person to see Saturn's rings when he looked through his telescope in 1610.

find out more
Astronomy
Comets
Copernicus, Nicolas
Earth
Galilei, Galileo
Gravity
Meteors and meteorites
Moon
Space exploration
Sun

▼ False colour has been added to this photograph of Io, one of Jupiter's moons. The dark areas are volcanic hot spots and may be flows of hot lava. Most of the moon's surface is covered with sulphur, which is represented in the photo by the red, orange and yellow areas.

Songbirds

Songbirds make up the largest group of birds. Of the 8700 different kinds of bird, about half are songbirds. There is great variety within the group, from tiny wrens to large crows, and from colourful birds of paradise to the dull grey dippers of North America.

• Not only do different kinds of songbird have different songs, but different individuals of the same kind also have slightly different songs. This helps scientists to identify an individual bird and may allow one bird to recognize another.

Most songbirds have a well developed voice-producing organ, called a syrinx. However, although they were named for their ability to produce vocal sounds, or 'songs', not all songbirds sing, and of those that do, some, such as the common crow, make a very unpleasant noise. At the other extreme are birds such as nightingales and larks, whose songs are famed for their beauty.

All songbirds have four toes on each foot, three pointing forwards and one backwards, and are nearly all land birds. A few are found around fresh water, but most only cross the sea during migrations.

A songbird's bill is adapted to suit its diet. The bill of a hawfinch, for example, is strong enough to crack open cherry stones. Crossbills have crossed tips to the bill to help them extract seeds from tough pine cones, and tree-creepers have fine bills for probing crevices in tree bark.

Courtship and mating

In most songbirds, only the male sings a true song, although the female can produce a variety of call notes and other sounds. Along with singing, the male may strike poses and dance or move objects around, in order to attract a mate. Birds of paradise are well known for their elaborate courtship behaviour. They hang upside-down to display their beautiful feathers and sing unusual songs, which may be soft or loud. Some can sound 'mechanical' and others explosive, rather like gun-fire.

Nests of songbirds are usually quite elaborate. Most build open, cup-shaped nests. Some kinds, such as the ovenbird of South America, construct ball-shaped, closed nests, with a small entrance.

When they hatch, the young of all songbirds are naked, blind and helpless. They are usually reared by both parents. A few songbirds, such as the cuckoo finch of Africa, are parasites, laying their eggs in the nests of other birds.

▶ Songbirds are found all over the world and include the majority of land birds.

black-headed weaver and nest (Africa)

waxwing eating berries (Europe and North America)

ovenbird and nest (South America)

scarlet tanager (North America)

Gouldian finch (Australia)

song thrush breaking snail shell open (Europe)

Sound

Sounds are caused by vibrations. They travel to our ears in the form of waves. Sounds can be high or low, loud or quiet. If they are too high, we cannot hear them. If they are too loud, they can damage our hearing.

If you pluck a guitar string, it vibrates, and the air next to it is squashed and stretched over and over again. As a result, lots of 'squashes' and 'stretches' travel through the air, rather as ripples spread across water. These are *sound waves*. You cannot see them, but when they enter your ears, they make your eardrums vibrate and you hear a sound. Sound waves can travel through solids, liquids and gases. But they cannot travel through a vacuum (empty space).

Speed of sound

Sound waves travel through air at a speed of about 330 metres per second, although this varies with temperature. Sound travels nearly a million times more slowly than light, which is why you see a distant flash of lightning before you hear it.

Supersonic aircraft travel faster than sound. When they do so, they create shock waves, rather like the bow wave at the front of a fast boat. You hear a 'sonic boom' as each shock wave passes you.

Echoes

Sound is reflected from hard surfaces. If you stand well back from a cliff and shout, you hear a reflected sound a few moments later. This is called an echo. Ships use underwater echoes to measure their distance from the sea-bed (or other objects). The system is called *sonar*. It involves sending out sound pulses and measuring the time taken for them to be reflected back. The longer the time taken, the greater the distance.

Frequency and pitch

When something vibrates, for example a guitar string, the number of vibrations per second is called the *frequency*. It is measured in hertz (Hz). A string that vibrates 1000 times per second has a frequency of 1000 Hz. The higher the frequency, the higher the *pitch* of the note – the higher it sounds to your ear.

The human ear can hear sounds between about 20 Hz and 20,000 Hz, although the upper limit becomes lower as you grow older. Sounds above the range of human hearing are called *ultrasonic* sounds. Some of these can be heard by dogs, cats and bats.

Loudness and noise

Big vibrations produce louder sounds than small ones. They make the air vibrate more. If a sound is too loud or unpleasant, we call it noise. Noise levels need to be checked because very loud sounds can permanently damage the ears.

▶ Scientists measure noise levels using the decibel (dB) scale. Here are some typical values on the scale.

• The speed of sound is called Mach 1. The aircraft Concorde cruises at Mach 2.2, which is more than twice the speed of sound.

▼ In factories, noise levels are checked to make sure that they do not go above the legal limit. Continuous loud noise damages hearing and may lead to deafness later in life.

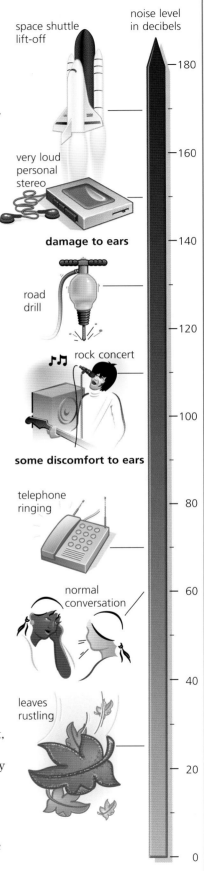

noise level in decibels

space shuttle lift-off — 180

— 160

very loud personal stereo

damage to ears — 140

road drill — 120

rock concert

— 100

some discomfort to ears

telephone ringing — 80

normal conversation — 60

— 40

leaves rustling — 20

0

South Africa

The Republic of South Africa is a country at the southern tip of Africa. It has many natural resources and is the richest country in the continent.

• The descendants of Dutch colonists in South Africa are called Afrikaners.

▼ Wild flowers in the Namaqaland Hills, Cape Province. This small region has probably the greatest diversity of flower species in the world. Many garden flower varieties originally came from the area.

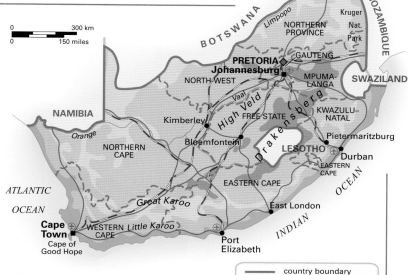

For many years South Africa was ruled by Europeans. Democratic elections were not held until 1994.

A rich landscape

At the heart of South Africa is a huge, grassy plateau called the high veld. To the north-east of it lies the Kruger National Park, one of several reserves where elephants, lions, zebras and other animals roam free. To the west, the high veld merges into the Kalahari and Namib deserts. In the east the high veld is bounded by the Drakensberg mountains, while to the south there are lower mountain ranges and the plains of the Great and Little Karoo.

South Africa has a pleasant climate, although nights can be cold on the high veld, and occasionally there is drought. The area in the south-west, around Cape Town, has a Mediterranean climate: hot, dry summers and mild, wet winters.

South Africa has huge reserves of gold, diamonds, chromium, platinum and other minerals of value to industrial nations. It also exports maize (corn), fruit, wine and other foods. It has busy, modern cities such as Cape Town and Johannesburg, with banks, stock exchanges, factories and skyscrapers.

South Africa's history

The first southern African people were hunters and gatherers. Their descendants are Bushmen (San) and Hottentots (Khoikhoi), together known as the Khoisan. The majority of today's black population speak Bantu (Nguni) languages. Their ancestors were living in southern Africa at least 1600 years ago. Two of the largest tribal groups are the Xhosa, who live mostly in the Transkei, and the Zulus, who are based in Natal.

Around 1652 the Dutch established the first European settlement in southern Africa, at the Cape of Good Hope. It provided food and sick care for sailors travelling to and from the Dutch East Indies. The Dutch brought in slaves, and they also forced the Khoisan to work for them.

During the Napoleonic wars of 1792 to 1815, Britain captured the Cape. English-speaking colonists settled there from the 1820s, fighting the Xhosa peoples for farmland. In the 1830s many Boers (Dutch farmers) wanted to control their own territory and to have more land. They moved north and founded the republics of the Orange Free State and the Transvaal. In Natal, Zulu chief Shaka (1787–1828), who controlled all the surrounding African tribes, strongly resisted the invading Boers.

Map legend

- country boundary
- province boundary
- ◆ capital city
- ■ ● major cities and towns
- main roads
- main railways
- ⊕ main airports

land height in metres
- 2000–5000
- 1000–2000
- 500–1000
- 200–500
- less than 200
- sea level

In 1877 Britain tried to take over the Transvaal, but was defeated in 1881. After bloody fighting, Britain defeated the Zulus of Natal. The discovery of diamonds (1871) and gold (1886) led to conflict between the British, led by Cecil Rhodes, and the Boers, led by Paul Kruger. This resulted in the Anglo-Boer war of 1899–1902, when the British defeated the Boers and took over their territory. South Africa became a self-governing British Dominion in 1910.

◀ Archbishop Desmond Tutu opposed the apartheid system for many years. When the ANC came to power, he was chosen as head of the Truth and Reconciliation Commission. The Commission encourages people who have been accused of crimes under the apartheid regime to admit to what they did.

Segregation of the races

Only white people could become members of the South African parliament, and only white people could vote. Black South Africans, (about 75 per cent of the population) were not allowed to vote: nor were Asians and people of mixed race (coloureds).

There were many rules for keeping whites and non-whites apart, and these became much stricter in 1948, when the National Party won the elections. Apartheid ('apartness') laws were passed, which meant that black Africans could not go about freely, and had to carry passes at all times. More than 3 million black people were moved to separate 'homelands'. Those blacks who did not live in homelands had to live in overcrowded townships on the edges of cities, and travel long distances to work.

Democratic government

The apartheid laws were condemned around the world. Within South Africa, the fight against apartheid was led by the African National Congress (ANC). For many years they campaigned peacefully. The ANC president in the 1950s, Albert Luthuli, won the Nobel Peace Prize for these campaigns. However, from the late 1950s the ANC organized acts of sabotage. In 1962 the new ANC leader, Nelson Mandela, was imprisoned.

As more and more countries refused to trade with South Africa, the government was forced to make some changes to the apartheid laws. They gave seats in parliament to coloureds and Asians, but blacks were still unable to vote.

In 1989 F. W. de Klerk was elected president, and things began to change. He released Nelson Mandela from prison and abolished the unfair apartheid laws. In 1994 South Africa held its first democratic elections, which were won by the ANC. Mandela was elected president for five years, with de Klerk as vice-president. Other countries began to trade with South Africa once more, and the homelands were abolished. Mandela retired as president in 1999.

Steve Biko

Steve Biko was the leader of the Black People's Convention, an organization that fought the oppression of apartheid. His activities brought him into conflict with the government and he was often arrested. In 1977, while under arrest, he was so badly beaten in the police cells that he died. He became a symbol of the anti-apartheid movement.

◀ Koffiefontein diamond mine, near Kimberley, South Africa. The area around Kimberley is one of the world's most important sources of gem diamonds.

find out more

South America

South America is the fourth largest continent in the world. It extends south from Colombia and covers 13 per cent of the world's total land surface.

• South America is sometimes called Latin America, because the Spanish and Portuguese languages still spoken there grew out of Latin. The phrase Latin America also includes Central America, which is part of the continent of North America.

▼ The village of Maras, in Peru, with the mountains of the Andes in the background. The Andes are a series of mountain ranges which start near the Caribbean Sea in the north, and go through Venezuela, Colombia, Ecuador, Peru and Bolivia. They then run along the border between Chile and Argentina down to Tierra del Fuego in the far south.

Amazonia and the other regions around the Equator are hot all year and very wet. Further south, on the wooded grasslands of the Gran Chaco, there are distinct wet and dry seasons. In the Brazilian Highlands the climate is much less extreme. In north-east Brazil frequent drought has created a landscape of low trees, thorny bushes and cacti, known as *caatinga*. South America stretches much further south than any other continent, so the far south is cool for most of the year. Really cold climates occur only in the extreme south of Argentina and Chile, and high up in the Andes.

Landscape

The Andes are the world's longest mountain range and, after the Himalayas, the second highest. They extend for over 7100 kilometres along the continent's western edge.

Snow-capped volcanoes such as the still-active Cotopaxi rise among the mountain peaks. Earthquakes are common.

Between the Andes and the Pacific coast there is an area of desert which stretches for 1600 kilometres from southern Ecuador to northern Chile. The

Atacama Desert is the driest place on Earth. Rain has never been recorded in some places.

There are three plateau areas in South America. The Guiana Highlands in the north are deep, forested valleys. They are largely uninhabited. The Brazil Plateau in the east is where most Brazilians live. Its western part forms the savannah grasslands of the Mato Grosso. In the south lies the dry plateau of Patagonia.

The lowlands of the Amazon basin are covered with dense rainforest, with a great variety of species of trees, insects, monkeys and parrots. Away from the Amazon the forest changes to wooded grassland (the Gran Chaco) and more

• French Guiana is an administrative district of France. This means that its people are French citizens.

• America was named after Amerigo Vespucci, an Italian navigator who explored the South American coast. The German mapmaker, Waldseemüller, first used the name because he believed Vespucci discovered America before Columbus. This is unlikely, but Vespucci was certainly one of the first to realize that the land might be a separate continent, not part of Asia as Columbus believed.

▼ Aymará Indians in Bolivia. More than half of all Bolivians are Native Americans. Bolivia was once part of the Inca empire and one of the languages still spoken in Bolivia, Quechua, was spoken by the Inca people.

fertile grasslands (the pampas) in the Paraná–Paraguay basin further south, and to the savannah lands (llanos) of the Orinoco basin in the north.

Countries

Brazil is by far the largest country in South America and contains half the population. Bolivia is the roof of South America. One-third of Bolivia is over 1.5 kilometres high. Argentina and Uruguay share the estuary of Río de la Plata, a great trading route to and from the continent's interior. South America exports many agricultural and mineral products. Chile is the world's leading producer of copper. Brazil produces the most coffee and is a leading exporter of sugar, cocoa, tin and fruit. Peru exports copper, lead and zinc.

People

Modern-day South Americans are descended from Europeans, Africans and Native Americans. Brazilians speak Portuguese. Most other South Americans speak Spanish. Many Native American languages are spoken, especially in the northern Andes and Amazonia. They include Aymará, Guaraní and Quechua.

Today, many Native Americans are moving to the

cities, but there they often earn low wages and live in shanty towns. The Native Americans of the tropical forests grow cassava root and vegetables in small clearings. Their villages are scattered to give each family a large area in which to hunt and gather plants. However, the forests are being cleared and people are losing their homes.

In the last 100 years other Europeans have settled in the continent, for example, Italians in Argentina and Japanese on the west coast. Most South Americans live near the coast in cities such as Rio de Janeiro, São Paulo, Buenos Aires and Lima. Roman Catholicism is the most important religion in South America.

South American history

In South America, before the arrival of European explorers, Native Americans developed large empires. Great civilizations came and went, including the Nazcas and Chimus. Agriculture supported the city populations of these great empires.

Native South Americans had their own forms of government and boundaries between nations. Their religions often taught a respect for nature.

▲ Huge deposits of metals and minerals, including gold, are found in the Amazon region. In order to exploit these resources, and also to provide farmland and housing, a lot of forest is being destroyed. Scientists are also concerned that the region's vast diversity of plants and animals will be lost.

Most people were peasant farmers who grew food for their own families, sold a small surplus at village markets, and gave the rest to government officials.

Conquering South America

The discovery of new lands in the west by Columbus in 1492 led to a race to claim and exploit them. Spain and Portugal were the main rivals for the new lands across the Atlantic Ocean. So in 1493 Pope Alexander VI drew an imaginary line on the map of the world called the Line of Demarcation. Spain was to have all the lands to the west of it, Portugal all the lands to the east. By the Treaty of Tordesillas, a year later, the line was moved westward, which gave Portugal the right to the area that is now Brazil.

In 1498 the explorer Christopher Columbus landed in South America on his third voyage, paid for by the Spanish. A Portuguese expedition reached the Brazilian coast

north of Rio de Janeiro in 1500. Spanish and Portuguese became the main languages of South America, and for the next 300 years Europe was to control South America.

Conquistadores

The conquistadores (conquerors) were inspired by a greed for gold, of which there was plenty in the Americas, and by a desire to bring the benefits of Christianity to the Native American peoples.

When the conquistador Francisco Pizarro arrived in Peru in 1532, he invaded and conquered the Inca empire, and within a few years the Spanish had begun to spread their rule over much of the continent.

The Spanish empire

At its height in the 16th and 17th centuries Spain's empire included half of South America, all of Central America and the Caribbean, and other parts of North America.

▼ Simón Bolívar (left) was a brilliant general who led the struggle against the Spanish rulers of South America. In 1825 he helped to defeat the Spanish armies in upper Peru, and the people decided to form a separate republic. They named it Bolivia, in honour of their liberator.

Many of the conquistadores married local Native American women. A class structure grew up. Those with all Spanish ancestors owned most of the wealth and had all the power. Those of mixed race often had small farms or were traders. The poorest of all were the Native Americans and African slaves, who were forced to work in the silver mines and sugar plantations, and to produce crops such as cotton and tobacco, which were exported to Europe. Many died of overwork in poor conditions, or from the diseases Europeans brought with them.

Wars of independence

The unequal wealth of the people in South American colonies led the citizens to rebel. The Wars of Independence began in 1809. At first they failed, but from 1816 onward were successful everywhere.

Two men were outstanding among the South American leaders. José de San Martín liberated Argentina, Chile and Peru. In the north Simón Bolívar won freedom for four countries: Bolivia, Colombia, Ecuador and Venezuela, helped San Martín defeat the Spanish in Peru.

There was no fighting in Portugal's South American colony, Brazil. In 1825 Portugal recognized Brazil as an independent empire. In 1889 the emperor left Brazil to seek refuge in Europe, and the Brazilians formed a republic.

The legacy of colonization

Many European immigrants flocked to South America, lured by the prospect of new land and a new life. Most inhabitants of South America today are descendants of European settlers who married Native Americans.

The only English-speaking nation in South America is Guyana, which was a British colony until 1966. Most people there are descended from African slaves or Indian labourers, brought to work on plantations. In Suriname many inhabitants are descendants of people from the Dutch East Indies (now Indonesia), brought to work there when Suriname was a Dutch colony. Suriname became independent in 1975.

▲ By treachery the Spanish conquistador Francisco Pizarro took the Inca emperor Atahualpa prisoner. Atahualpa filled his cell with gold to buy his freedom, but Pizarro had him killed anyway.

find out more
Argentina
Brazil
Caribbean
Columbus, Christopher
Grasslands
Incas
Magellan, Ferdinand
Slaves
See also individual
   South American
   countries in the
   Countries fact file,
   pages 613–645

Space exploration

• The USA is currently building a replacement for the Space Shuttle, the X-33 *VentureStar*. It will be fully reusable, with no expensive throw-away fuel tanks.

Since the beginning of the Space Age in October 1957, human beings have continuously looked for new ways of exploring space. Astronauts have walked on the Moon's surface, and can now live and work for months in space stations. Robot spacecraft have already explored nearly all of the planets in our Solar System, and have investigated the Sun, comets and asteroids. Despite these achievements, it would take any spacecraft thousands of years to reach the nearest star after the Sun.

The Space Age began in October 1957, when the Soviet Union launched the artificial satellite *Sputnik 1* into orbit around the Earth. One month later, *Sputnik 2* carried the dog Laika into space. By the 1960s rockets from both the Soviet Union and the USA were carrying men and women into orbit around the Earth.

Astronauts

▼ These astronauts are servicing the Hubble Space Telescope, which is docked onto the Shuttle *Endeavour*. Outside the spacecraft astronauts must wear a protective spacesuit. Its outer layers protect against radiation, and visors provide protection from the Sun. The backpack contains the air and power supplies.

Astronauts, or cosmonauts as they are called in Russia, are people who leave the Earth and travel into space. Before they go into space, astronauts train for a long time. They may spend many months in space on board a spacecraft or space station. Once they are in orbit, away from the pull of the Earth's gravity, astronauts become weightless and float around inside the spacecraft. Weightlessness affects their bodies so they have to exercise hard to keep fit.

In space, astronauts study the Earth below, the distant stars and galaxies, and the space around them. They launch and repair satellites. They measure the effects of weightlessness on themselves and other creatures, and they make things, such as certain kinds of medicine, that would be difficult to make on Earth.

Exploring the Moon

The exploration of the Moon began even before the first person had flown in space, when the unmanned Soviet spacecraft *Luna 1* flew past the Moon in January 1959. Over the next few years the Soviet Union and the USA launched many unmanned probes towards the Moon, which sent back tens of thousands of pictures and other information. In 1966 the probe *Luna 9* made the first soft landing on its surface.

▲ Astronaut Bonnie J. Dunbar floats weightlessly in the Space Shuttle's *Spacelab* science module. To stay in one place, astronauts must fix themselves to something, and they sleep strapped into sleeping bags.

In July 1969 three US astronauts flew to the Moon in the *Apollo 11* spacecraft. The main spacecraft, piloted by astronaut Michael Collins, orbited the Moon, while Neil Armstrong and Edwin Aldrin landed in the tiny Lunar Module. During five more Moon missions, the last in 1972, astronauts explored the Moon's surface, collecting rock samples and setting up scientific equipment. More recently, in 1994, the probe *Clementine* spent two months orbiting the Moon and mapping its surface.

The Space Shuttle

In April 1981 the first US Space Shuttle was launched. Unlike earlier spacecraft, the Shuttle can fly into space many times. Only the huge main fuel tank is new for each flight. The Shuttle takes off upwards like a rocket, but lands back on Earth like a glider on a runway. On board, astronauts conduct scientific experiments and launch satellites from the cargo bay. In 1990 the

Shuttle *Discovery* launched the space probe *Ulysses*, which flew over the north and south poles of the Sun. In the same year the Shuttle placed the Hubble Space Telescope into orbit.

Space stations

A space station is a home in space where astronauts can live and work. It contains everything that they need, including water, food and air, which must all be brought up from Earth. The first space station was *Salyut 1*, launched by the Soviet Union in 1971. The longest-lived space station was the Russian *Mir*, which was in orbit from 1986 to 2001. It was extended over the years by adding on extra sections (modules) sent up from Earth. Some astronauts spent more than a year on board *Mir*. In late 1998 the USA, Russia, Canada, Europe and Japan began to construct the International Space Station in orbit. Its completion has been delayed by the crash of the space shuttle *Columbia* in 2003.

Missions to the planets

Since the Moon missions, most space exploration has been carried out by unmanned spacecraft travelling to other planets. They take photographs and use radar and other instruments to collect information, which they send back to Earth by radio. Some spacecraft fly past planets, but others orbit or land on the surface.

The first successful planetary spacecraft was *Mariner 2*, which flew past Venus in 1962. The *Viking 1* and *2* spacecraft (1976) landed on Mars and dug up samples of soil. The two *Voyager* spacecraft sent back detailed pictures of Jupiter (1979), Saturn (1980–1981), Uranus (1986) and Neptune (1989) before passing out of the Solar System altogether. In 1997 the *Pathfinder* spacecraft landed on Mars. It released a tiny robot vehicle called *Sojourner*, which sent back high-quality photographs of the planet's rocky surface.

More space missions are planned for the future. *Cassini* is on a long mission to Saturn and its moons, and other spacecraft are intended to meet up with asteroids and comets.

◄ The probe *Galileo* was launched in 1989. It flew past Venus, using the planet's gravity to accelerate. *Galileo* then flicked past the Earth twice for further gravity boosts before flying to Jupiter. After launching a probe into Jupiter's atmosphere, it began a tour of Jupiter and its moons.

1 1989: launch
2 1990: flies past Venus
3 1990 and 1992: flies past Earth
4 1995: probe launched into Jupiter's atmosphere

Key
— planetary orbits
— *Galileo* flight path
— Earth's orbit

Space records
First person in space
On 12 April 1961 Yuri Gagarin of the USSR orbited the Earth once in *Vostok 1*, in a trip lasting 108 minutes.
First woman in space
In June 1963 Valentina Tereshkova of the USSR piloted the *Vostok 6* spacecraft. It made 48 orbits of the Earth.
First people on the Moon
In July 1969 Americans Neil Armstrong and Edwin 'Buzz' Aldrin landed the *Apollo 11* Lunar Module on the Moon.
Longest stay in space
Russian cosmonaut Dr Valery Polyakov returned to Earth on 22 March 1995 after spending 438 days on board *Mir*.

find out more
Moon
Rockets
Satellites
Solar System

519

Spain

Spain is the fourth largest country in Europe. It has a varied landscape and is home to a diverse population, a quarter of whom speak a language other than Spanish. It is also a country with an exciting and turbulent history.

Spain is one of the most mountainous countries in Europe. Madrid, at 646 metres above sea level, is Europe's highest capital city. It is near the centre of a high plateau called the Meseta. Rivers such as the Tagus and Duoro have cut deep valleys into this plateau. The Meseta is surrounded by high mountains which keep out the winds from the sea. This is 'dry Spain', with little rain, very cold winters and very hot summers. Northern Spain is 'wet Spain': a green, lush countryside facing the Atlantic Ocean. The southern province of Almería is very hot and dry, and contains Europe's only desert.

People and industry

Industry is mainly based in northern Spain, and Bilbao is Spain's most important industrial town. The main users of the steel industry are car manufacturers, and cars are Spain's greatest export. Lots of international companies are based in Spain and have factories there, making electrical goods, for example, or printing books.

Much of rural Spain is quite poor. Farming is still important, especially for crops such as oranges and olives which only grow in warmer climates. Wheat and barley grow in the Meseta.

There is a thriving tourist industry on the warm south and east coasts, and in the Balearic Islands in the Mediterranean and the Canary Islands in the Atlantic Ocean, which are also

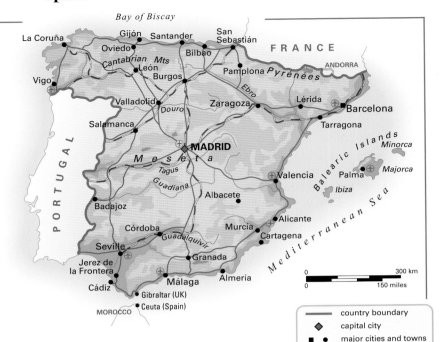

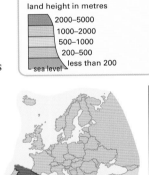

parts of Spain. Tourists buying local products, such as lace, leather goods and pottery, have helped these craft industries to survive.

Spain's history

By the 5th century BC, Phoenicians, Greeks and Celts had established small settlements in what is now Spain, but the country was divided among many small warlike tribes. It was the highly efficient Roman army that finally made the peninsula part of the Roman empire in 300 BC.

Roman rule lasted for almost 600 years. Then a Germanic tribe, the Visigoths, took over. They set up a kingdom whose nobles warred among themselves. In AD 711 one such noble, Count Julian, called in Berber warriors from Morocco to help him fight his king, even though they were Muslims, not Christians.

In just seven years the Berbers, helped by other Muslims – Arabs, Moors and Syrians – had conquered all but the north of the country. For nearly 500 years most of Spain was an Islamic country, although the Muslims were generally tolerant of Christians and Jews. The southern parts of Spain ruled by the Moors became famous for their universities, medicine, art and architecture.

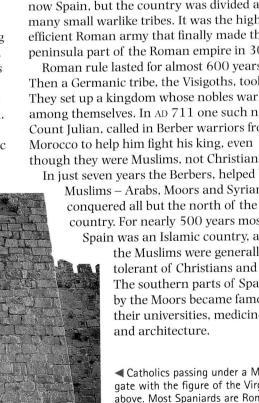

◄ Catholics passing under a Moorish gate with the figure of the Virgin Mary above. Most Spaniards are Roman Catholics, and festivals and processions take place on holy days and saints' days.

• Gibraltar is a tiny country linked to Spain by a narrow strip of lowland 3 km long. Gibraltar has been a British dependency since 1704.

• The Basques are a people who live in the border regions of France and Spain. In 1959 some Spanish Basques formed a group called ETA ('Basque-land and Freedom') to fight for independence. Spain created a Basque parliament in 1980, but terrorist attacks by ETA have continued.

The years of power

The Christian kingdoms of the north gradually reconquered Spain until only Granada in the south remained a Muslim state. Then, in 1492, three very important events occurred: the Muslims were driven out of Granada; the Canary Islands became part of Spain; and Christopher Columbus landed in the Caribbean. Queen Isabella of Spain had paid for Columbus's expedition, and so Spain reaped the benefits.

In the following 100 years Spanish adventurers, called conquistadores, conquered a vast empire in Central and South America, and an enormous amount of gold and silver was looted and brought back to Europe. In the late 16th century, under King Philip II, Spain enjoyed great wealth and power.

However, a series of disastrous wars and feeble kings weakened the country. It declined rapidly in the 18th century. In the 19th century its American colonies rebelled and became independent.

From dictatorship to democracy

In 1931 the king, Alfonso XIII, was driven into exile and a republic was set up. Five years later a military revolt against the elected left-wing government plunged the country into civil war. Spaniards suffered terribly during the three years of fighting between the Republicans and their allies on one side and the fascist 'Falange' on the other. In 1939 the fascists were victorious, and Spain fell under the rule of the dictator General Francisco Franco. However, before Franco died in 1975, he brought back the monarchy. Now Alfonso's grandson, King Juan Carlos, is head of a democratic monarchy.

◀ Troops supporting General Franco fire on rebels from a makeshift barricade in Toledo. Over 750,000 people were killed in the Spanish civil war.

find out more
Columbus, Christopher
Dictators
Europe
Magellan, Ferdinand
Muslims
Picasso, Pablo
South America
See also Countries fact file, page 639

Spices

Spices are used in cooking to add flavour and colour to our food. They come from a variety of different parts of different plants.

Spices are usually dried to preserve them and should be kept in airtight containers away from light. They may be used whole or ground. The way in which they are used affects their flavour.

The spice trade

Spices were known and used by the ancient Chinese, Egyptians, Greeks and Romans. Everywhere spices were very valuable. They grew in a small number of places such as the Spice Islands (now the Moluccas, part of Indonesia) and everyone wanted them.

They were used to preserve food, to cover up the taste of food which was going bad, and as medicines.

An important spice trade grew up between East and West. For a long time this was controlled by Venetians and merchants in the Middle East. Then, in the 16th century, Portuguese sailors discovered the Moluccas and took over the islands and the spice trade. A hundred years later the Dutch East India Company moved in. It controlled the trade until the islanders rebelled and the company went bankrupt. Indonesia is still the world's largest producer of cloves and nutmeg.

Some favourite spices

Peppercorns are the berries of the pepper vine. Black pepper is dried unripe fruit, and white pepper comes from fruit picked when almost ripe, with the dark outer skin removed.

Cloves are dried flower buds of a tropical evergreen tree. They are used to flavour some meats, such as ham, and sweet dishes.

Nutmeg and *mace* come from the fruit of an evergreen tree. Fresh nutmeg is enclosed in a hard brown shell which is itself enclosed in a crimson mesh called mace. Both are used in savoury stews and sweet food.

Chilli is the general name given to a variety of hot South American peppers. They may be green or red and are usually long and tapering and full of seeds. Chillis have a very fiery flavour.

Ginger is the dried, swollen underground shoots of a low-growing tropical plant. It is often used to flavour sauces and curries.

mace

nutmeg

ginger

chilli

pepper

cloves

find out more
Cooking
Food

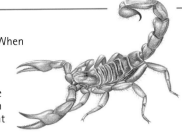

Spiders and scorpions

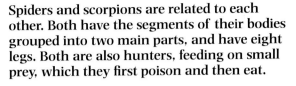

Spiders and scorpions are related to each other. Both have the segments of their bodies grouped into two main parts, and have eight legs. Both are also hunters, feeding on small prey, which they first poison and then eat.

• Over 30,000 kinds of spider are known; more are discovered every year. Scientists have discovered fewer than 1000 kinds of scorpion.

▶ A brown scorpion. When scorpions mate, they perform a special 'dance'. In the dance the male positions the female over the sperm he has dropped so that she can collect it.

Many people are frightened of spiders and scorpions, but although there are a few aggressive kinds, most are harmless to humans.

Spiders are found in most parts of the world. All spiders can make several kinds of silk, which they use in a variety of ways, including making traps, binding their prey, and protecting their eggs. Spiders have many ways of catching a meal. Apart from the familiar webs that many spiders use to catch their prey, some spiders hunt on the ground, some leap after their prey, and some spit silk to entangle it. Others drop a net-like

garden spider

web onto their meal, while bolas spiders swing a sticky 'fishing' line in order to trap it. Mating can be dangerous for a male spider, which is almost always smaller than his mate. The female often eats the male, but nevertheless she takes good care of their eggs and young.

Scorpions are found in warm parts of the world. They hide during the daytime, but at night they come out to hunt. They feed mainly on large insects, which they kill quickly using the poisonous sting at the tip of their tail. Eating the meal usually takes them several hours. Female scorpions do not lay eggs, but produce living young, which they carry about on their back for about two weeks.

▶ Tarantulas live in the south-west of the USA, in Mexico and in South America. They hunt mainly at night, catching insects and sometimes small frogs, toads and mice. They are not dangerous to humans.

find out more
Animal behaviour
Animals

Spielberg, Steven

Born 1947 in Cincinnati, Ohio, USA

Steven Spielberg is a film director and producer. He has worked on some of cinema's biggest box-office hits.

Spielberg started making amateur films when he was at school and college. When he was 21, he started directing television programmes, but his first big impact on the cinema came in 1975 with the tense thriller *Jaws*. This quickly made more money than any other film ever had before.

find out more
Animation
Films
Holocaust

After making the science-fiction film *Close Encounters of the Third Kind* (1977), Spielberg broke box-office records again with the success of *Raiders of the Lost Ark* (1981) and then with *ET* (1982), which made more than 700 million dollars. In *The Color Purple* (1985) he tackled a more sensitive story about racial conflict, and he won further praise with *Empire of the Sun* (1987).

Jurassic Park (1992), Spielberg's film about the return of the dinosaurs, was a huge financial success and won three Oscars in 1993. In 1997 the sequel, *The Lost World*, was released to equally great acclaim.

Schindler's List, an epic film about the Holocaust, established Spielberg as a director of serious cinema. It won seven Oscars in 1994, including ones for Best Picture and Best Director.

In 1996 Spielberg started up a new film company called DreamWorks SKG. His first feature film with the company, *Amistad* (1997), was a drama about a rebellion on board a slave ship in the 1830s.

◀ Spielberg directing the actress Julia Roberts as Tinkerbell in the film *Hook* (1992). The film was based on the story of Peter Pan. It starred Robin Williams as a grown-up Peter Pan.

Springs

Springs are usually made of metal and come in many different shapes – thin flat strips, wires or rods. Springs store energy that can be allowed to escape quickly or slowly. As energy escapes, the spring can move something or drive a piece of machinery around. Coiled-up springs are used in the 'clockwork' motors inside some toys.

A spring is usually made of a special type of steel so that it will return to its original shape, however much it has been squeezed, bent or stretched. The steel in the spring must also not crack or break after it has been bent a large number of times.

Springs are made of stretchy or springy materials that we call elastic. A rubber band is elastic. Wood, steel and plastic are much less stretchy than rubber bands but they are still elastic. For example, a plank of wood sags when you walk on it but straightens when you step off. Rubber and rubber-like plastics called *elastomers* can act as springs too. They are often used to cut down vibration. Engine mountings are usually made of rubber or elastomer, and some bicycles have suspension systems with elastomer springs. In some springs air is used as the elastic material. If you put your finger over the hole in a bicycle pump and push in the handle, you find that trapped air is springy. This idea is used in gas springs and in some vehicles.

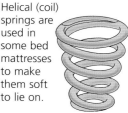

▼ Some different kinds of spring.

Helical (coil) springs are used in some bed mattresses to make them soft to lie on.

In a clockwork motor, a coiled-up strip of steel unwinds slowly to turn the wheels.

The spring in a door bell is a strip of bendy metal.

Some lorries have leaf springs made of bendy strips of steel that are clamped together.

- A material has passed its elastic limit when it stays out of shape, or breaks, when dented. Brittle materials such as china and chalk are hardly elastic at all. They break very easily because they cannot bend or stretch.

- Even your body has elastic fibres in it. For example, try pinching the skin on the back of your hand. As soon as you let go, the skin returns to its original shape.

find out more
Clocks and watches
Materials
Motor cars

Squids and octopuses

Squids and octopuses, along with their relatives cuttlefishes, belong to a group of molluscs called cephalopods. Unlike many other molluscs, such as snails and mussels, cephalopods do not have an outer shell to protect their soft bodies.

All cephalopods can escape their enemies quickly using jet-propulsion: they squeeze water out rapidly through the end of their bag-like bodies, and the force of this moves them forward.

Squids live in the open seas whereas octopuses are found mostly in shallow waters, hiding in rocky dens. Cuttlefishes also live in shallow waters, and hide by burying themselves in sand.

Cephalopods are hunters. Octopuses catch their prey with their eight arms, which are covered in suckers. Squids and cuttlefishes also have eight short arms, but they use two long tentacles to catch their prey. All cephalopods bite their prey, injecting it with a poison that makes it unable to move.

With their large, complex brains and big, sensitive eyes, cephalopods are able to spot danger quickly. They can also camouflage themselves. In their skin are bags of pigment that can swell and shrink in less than a second. This rapidly changes their body colour, warning off enemies or disguising the cephalopod in the flickering light of the ocean. If an enemy does come close, they can instantly release ink, creating a 'smoke screen' of black ink.

squid

- There are about 350 different kinds of squid, about 150 different kinds of octopus, and about 14 kinds of cuttlefish. The largest cephalopod is the giant squid, which can grow to an overall length of about 20 m.

find out more
Animals
Oceans and seas
Prehistoric life

octopus

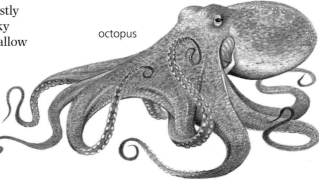

Squash *see* Tennis, etc. • **Squirrels** *see* Mice, squirrels, etc. • **Sri Lanka** *see page* 640

Stalin, Joseph

Joseph Stalin was leader of the Soviet Union from 1924 to 1953. He became a ruthless and much-feared dictator.

Joseph Vissarionovich Dzhugashvili was expelled from college at the age of 20. Two years later he joined the Russian Social-Democratic Workers' Party and became a revolutionary. His escapades led to him being imprisoned or exiled for a number of years. In 1912 he joined the Bolshevik (Communist) Party, and took the name 'Stalin' (man of steel).

In 1917 the Bolsheviks seized power and Lenin became ruler of the Russian republics (renamed the Soviet Union, or USSR, in 1922). Stalin became Secretary of the Communist Party in 1922 and took over as leader of the USSR after Lenin died in 1924.

In the years that followed, Stalin built a strong nation through a series of Five Year Plans, which were intended to industrialize and modernize the Soviet Union. His greatest achievement was to lead his country to victory over the Nazis in World War II.

However, all Stalin's reforms were done at great human cost. He had all of his rivals killed until he became dictator. Soviet people lived in fear of arrest, torture and execution by the secret police (later called the KGB). During the 1920s and 1930s, millions of people died of starvation, and millions more were sent to labour camps for opposing Stalin's wishes.

Born 1879 in Georgia, then part of the Russian empire
Died 1953 aged 73

find out more
Communists
Dictators
Lenin
Russia
Twentieth-century
  history
World War II

▼ The leaders of the Communist Party in Russia denounced Stalin in 1956, and in that same year his statue was pulled down in Budapest, capital of Hungary.

Starfishes and sea urchins

Starfishes are not really fish, but members of a big group of animals called echinoderms, which means 'spiny skins'.

starfish

▶ Sea urchins clearly belong to the echinoderm ('spiny skin') group of animals. They are sometimes protected by poison as well as spines. Swimmers must take care not to brush against them, nor to tread on them, because it can be very painful to have a spine in your foot.

Starfishes and their relatives are not obviously alike, but they have one feature in common: radial symmetry. This means their body is based around a circular plan, and if you divide it in half from above, the two halves are more or less identical.

Most starfishes have five arms. A few have a 'leading arm', but most move in any direction. If a starfish loses an arm, it can grow a new one. On the underside of starfishes and over the bodies of their relatives there are hundreds of little, soft bumps called tube feet. Each one is like a balloon, filled with sea water. Most have a sucker on the end, so the creature can hold food or grip onto the sea bed to walk.

Sea urchins are more rounded than starfishes, but you can imagine them as starfish with their arms tucked underneath. The structure of the arms can be seen on the shell as five double rows of tiny holes. Their tube feet emerge from the holes.

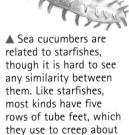

▲ Sea cucumbers are related to starfishes, though it is hard to see any similarity between them. Like starfishes, most kinds have five rows of tube feet, which they use to creep about on the sea bed.

• There are about 1600 different kinds of starfish in the world.

find out more
Animals
Prehistoric life

Stars

On a clear, dark night you can see hundreds of twinkling stars in the sky. These stars are huge glowing balls of gas like our Sun, but they are fainter because they are so much further away. Light from even the nearest stars takes years to reach us. We look up at the stars through air that is constantly blowing about, so their light is unsteady and they seem to twinkle.

Our Sun is one ordinary star among millions of other stars. In the centre of all stars, particles of hydrogen gas crash into each other and give off large amounts of nuclear energy. This process, called nuclear fusion, is what makes stars shine. The stars are all speeding through space but they look still to us because they are so far away. The patterns they make in the sky stay the same. Groups of stars that make patterns in certain parts of the sky are called *constellations*.

Some bright stars look quite red, while others are brilliant white or bluish; the Sun is a yellow star. The stars shine with different colours because some are hotter than others. The Sun's surface is about 6000 °C. The red stars are cooler and the blue-white ones hotter, at about 10,000 °C or more.

The birth of a star

Stars are being created all the time. They begin as clumps of gas and dust in space. Once this material begins to collect, the force of gravity makes it pull together even more strongly. In the middle it gets warmer and denser until the gas is so hot and squashed up that nuclear fusion can start. When this happens, a new star is born. Often, lots of stars form near to each other in a giant cloud to make a family of stars, which we call a *cluster*.

Giants and dwarfs

Astronomers have worked out that stars cover a huge range of sizes. They often call the large ones 'giants' and the small ones 'dwarfs'. The Sun is a smallish star, though some are even smaller. The kind of star called a *white dwarf* has a diameter

- About 5780 stars can be seen by the naked eye without a telescope. On a clear dark night around 2500 are visible from one place on Earth at any one time.

- In 1997 scientists discovered a new star in our galaxy, which is bigger than any other star yet discovered. It is over 100 thousand times as big as our Sun. If it were at the centre of our Solar System, it would engulf all the planets as far out as Mars. It is invisible from Earth because it is obscured by gas and dust.

▶ The birth and death of two stars. The top star, a massive star (red supergiant), will explode as a supernova and end up as either a neutron star or a black hole. The bottom star (red giant), which is more like our Sun, will end up as a white dwarf. The blue arrows show how the material blown off the stars is recycled into nebulas which become future stars.

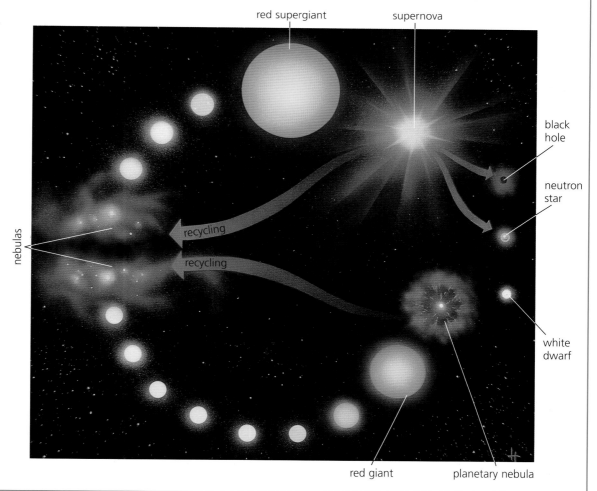

red supergiant

supernova

black hole

neutron star

white dwarf

planetary nebula

red giant

nebulas

recycling

recycling

less than one-hundredth that of our Sun. In contrast, there are some truly immense stars, called *red giants*, which are several hundred times the Sun's size. The bright red star called Betelgeuse, in the constellation Orion, is about 500 times bigger than the Sun.

Double stars

The Sun is a single star on its own, but most stars are in pairs. The force of gravity keeps them together and they orbit round each other like the planets going round the Sun. Sometimes the two stars in a pair pass in front of one another. This blocks out some of the starlight and makes the pair look fainter for a short time. The brightest star in the sky, Sirius, is a double.

The death of a star

Stars do not live for ever. Eventually the hydrogen gas fuel in their core is used up. When this happens, the star changes and eventually it dies. Old stars swell up into red giants. They can blow off some of their gas into space, like a big smoke ring. Astronomers can see stars like this at the centres of shells of glowing gas.

The Sun is already about 5000 million years old and is reckoned to be about half-way through its life. In the far future, the Sun will become a red giant and swallow up the planets near to it. After that, it will shrink until all its material is squashed into a ball about the size of the Earth. It will then be a white dwarf and fade away.

Stars rather more massive than the Sun finish up with a tremendous explosion, called a *supernova*. When a supernova goes off, it shines as brightly as millions of Suns put together for a few days. Only three supernovas have definitely been recorded in our own Galaxy during the past 1000 years.

Pulsars

When a supernova goes off, the inside of the exploded star that is left becomes a bleeping radio star, called a *pulsar*. Pulsars send out radio signals as a series of quick, short bleeps. They were discovered in 1967 by radio astronomers at the University of Cambridge, England. The most famous pulsar is in the middle of the Crab Nebula in the constellation Taurus. The Crab pulsar sends out 30 bleeps every second.

Star names

Many of the bright stars have their own names. Most of them have been handed down to us from Arab astronomers of centuries ago. Arabic names often start with the two letters Al, such as Altair, Aldebaran and Algol. Others come from Greek or Latin, such as Castor and Pollux, the 'heavenly twins' in the constellation Gemini. Stars are also called after the constellation they are in, with a Greek letter in front. Alpha Centauri, the nearest bright star after the Sun, is one example. Fainter stars do not have names and are known just as numbers in catalogues.

• In 1987 a supernova exploded in a galaxy very near to our own called the Large Magellanic Cloud, which can be seen from countries in the southern hemisphere.

find out more
Astronomy
Atoms and molecules
Black holes
Constellations
Galaxies
Gravity
Sun

◀ The Pleiades, or Seven Sisters, is one of the easiest star clusters to see in the night sky. It has six bright stars, and many more are visible through a telescope. The blue area of the picture is a cloud of cold gas and dust between the stars.

Starvation *see* Diets

Statistics

Statistics are sets of numbers, often called data, that record information in an organized way. Every day, people collect more and more data about the world and record it as statistics.

Statisticians organize and interpret statistics, using tables, charts and graphs. They use these to draw conclusions and make predictions. The *frequency table* below records the scores, in set bands, of children taking the same examination in two different schools. These numbers can also be plotted as a bar graph or *histogram*. The histogram (right) of the scores shows that, on average, the children at school A did better than those at school B. However, there is a much wider range of marks at school B. Statisticians call the range of numbers in the data its *distribution*.

• One kind of statistic that is often used is an average. An average is a single number, taken from a range of numbers and used to represent them. For instance, the average (mean) age of a group of children is found by adding all their ages together and dividing this number by the number of children.

find out more
Computers
Graphs
Numbers
Probability

	Band		Number of children	
			School A	School B
Examination score	0–9	1	0	0
	10–19	2	0	2
	20–29	3	1	5
	30–39	4	3	16
	40–49	5	6	32
	50–59	6	19	22
	60–69	7	40	16
	70–79	8	14	7
	80–89	9	3	3
	90–100	10	0	0

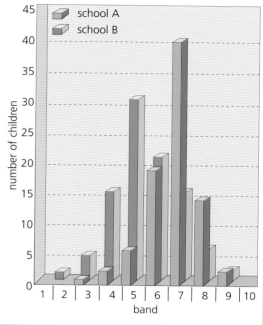

Stevenson, Robert Louis

Born 1850 in Edinburgh, Scotland
Died 1894 aged 44

Robert Louis Stevenson was a very popular author. He wrote fantasy adventure stories, horror stories, essays and verse.

Stevenson was brought up in Edinburgh. As a child he was frequently ill, and after he left university he spent most of his life abroad to try to escape the Scottish climate. Stevenson's first books described his tours in Belgium and France, and his journey to California to marry his wife.

He found fame as a novelist with his story *Treasure Island*. It first appeared in a boy's magazine before being published in book form in 1883. This thrilling adventure about pirates and the search for buried treasure has been popular ever since.

Three years later his fame soared when *The Strange Case of Dr Jekyll and Mr Hyde*, a fascinating horror story, was published. It tells the tale of a Dr Jekyll who takes a drug that changes him into the evil Mr Hyde. In that same year, his novel *Kidnapped* – an adventure story set in Scotland – was also published.

In 1888 Stevenson and his family travelled through the islands of the Pacific, before eventually settling on the Polynesian island of Samoa. He continued to write, and the islanders called him *Tusitala*, which means the 'storyteller'. He died suddenly of a stroke after living there for 4 years, and was buried on the island.

find out more
Stories and story-tellers

▼ A map showing Robert Louis Stevenson's *Treasure Island*.

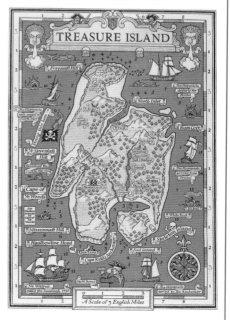

Stories and story-tellers

All over the world people tell stories. They tell them to make sense of the things that happen to them, and to entertain each other. People were telling stories long before books, or even writing, existed.

▶ The Asante people of West Africa tell stories about the trickster-god Anansi, who could take any shape he liked. Here Anansi is talking to the Banana Bird, whom he tricks into letting him have all the bananas in a big plantation. When Africans were taken to the Caribbean as slaves, they took the Anansi stories with them.

There are many different kinds of stories, including folk tales, fables, myths and legends, and fairy tales. Today people may read stories in books or magazines, watch them on television, listen to them on the radio, or even go to hear live story-tellers. Many of the stories still told today have a long history.

Folk tales

Some of the oldest stories are folk tales. The characters in folk tales are usually ordinary people who have extraordinary adventures. They frequently involve magic. Some tell of poor people who become rich through their cleverness or bravery. Others are about wicked people who are punished for their wrong-doings, or ordinary people who are made fun of for their foolishness.

Some of the same folk tales are told all over the world, although the names and other details change. One such story is about a person who is kind to a stranger or an animal, and is given three wishes as a reward. Instead of putting the wishes to good use, the person wastes them by wishing for silly things, often by accident. Another popular kind of story tells of a person who meets the Devil or a trickster in disguise. The ordinary character usually ends up tricking the trickster.

Fables and allegories

A fable is a type of folk tale that is short and amusing to listen to, and teaches us a lesson.

Fables often have one stupid and one clever animal in them, who speak to one another like humans. Over 100 fables are believed to have been written down by Aesop, a Greek slave who lived in the 6th century BC. These include the story of the 'Tortoise and the Hare', in which the Tortoise beats the Hare in a race by keeping going at a slow but steady pace while the overconfident hare falls asleep.

Allegories are similar to fables – they tell a story that is interesting in itself but which contains a deeper meaning. But they tend to be longer and more complicated than fables, and they are usually stories written by a single author, not folk tales. John Bunyan's *The Pilgrim's Progress*, published in 1678, tells of the journey of a man called Christian, but it also has a deeper message about how Christian people should live their lives.

Fairy tales

Fairy tales are seldom about fairies. They are stories in which magical things happen. They are often about people who do not fit in or who have been rejected, such as orphans, or girls who are ill-treated by a wicked stepmother. In fairy tales people who are kind or brave are usually successful and 'live happily ever after'.

Many fairy tales were originally folk tales, told in different versions in different countries. They became fairy tales when someone wrote them down and published them, often specially rewritten for children. The story we now know as 'Cinderella' was written down by the French writer Charles Perrault in the 17th century. The original English version was 'Cap o' Rushes'.

▶ This is an illustration from 'Aladdin and his Lamp', one of the tales of the *Arabian Nights*. A boy called Aladdin had an old lamp, which he thought was worthless. One day, when he happened to rub it, a huge genie (right) appeared, who became his servant and gave him everything he wished for.

find out more
Carroll, Lewis
Chaucer, Geoffrey
Myths and legends
Novels and novelists
Poetry
Stevenson, Robert Louis

The earliest known collection of fairy tales is the *Fables of Bidpai*, which were written down in India in the 3rd century AD. *The Arabian Nights' Entertainment*, or *A Thousand and One Nights*, is a very famous series of stories which were first enjoyed in the Middle East 1000 years ago. They include 'Sinbad the Sailor' and 'Ali Baba and the Forty Thieves'. Many of the European fairy tales popular today, including 'Snow White' and 'Rumpelstiltskin', were collected and published between 1812 and 1815 by two German brothers, Jakob and Wilhelm Grimm. In the 19th century the Danish story-teller Hans Christian Andersen published fairy tales that he invented himself. These include 'The Ugly Duckling' and 'The Little Mermaid'.

Story-tellers

There are many great story-tellers whose stories have remained popular for centuries. Homer, who probably lived in Greece in the 7th or 8th century BC, is thought to be the author of the epic poems *The Iliad* and *The Odyssey*. These tell many stories of the heroes of the Trojan War, including Achilles and Odysseus. The Roman poet Ovid, who lived in the 1st century BC and the 1st century AD is the author of *Metamorphoses*, a collection of stories about Roman gods, goddesses and heroes who undergo extraordinary changes. The 14th-century Italian poet Giovanni Boccaccio wrote a long poem called the *Decameron*, which includes 100 tales of adventure, deception and love.

More recently many story-tellers have written specially for children. The English writer Rudyard Kipling tells tales set in India, where he grew up. These include *The Just-So Stories* and *The Jungle Book*, which tells the story of Mowgli, the boy who is brought up by wolves. A story-teller who is very popular with children today is Roald Dahl, who has drawn some lively children as leading characters. They enjoy incredible adventures in stories such as *Charlie and the Chocolate Factory* and *Matilda*.

▼ This illustration by Quentin Blake for Roald Dahl's *Matilda* shows Matilda with her friend Miss Honey.

Stravinsky, Igor

Igor Stravinsky was a hugely influential composer. He ranks as one of the most remarkable and important composers of the 20th century.

Although Stravinsky showed an early talent for music, it was some time before he found his feet as a composer. His first great success came with the ballets he wrote for Sergei Diaghilev's Ballet Russes company between 1910 and 1913. *The Firebird*, *Petrushka* and *The Rite of Spring* made him the most talked-about composer in Europe. However, many people were outraged by *The Rite of Spring* and thought it was simply a horrible noise.

Because of World War I and the Russian Revolution, Stravinsky decided to leave Russia. He lived first in Switzerland and then in the USA. His music also took a new turn. It was still unmistakably Stravinsky's work, with interesting harmonies and exciting rhythms, but it was gentler than much of his earlier work. Some pieces, such as the concerto 'Dumbarton Oaks', sounded as though an 18th-century composer had suddenly stepped into the 20th century.

Even at the end of his life, Stravinsky was still experimenting with new ways of writing music. Many believe he was the most adventurous musical explorer of all time.

Born 1882 in Oranienbaum, Russia
Died 1971 aged 88

◀ The British Royal Ballet performing *The Firebird*. In this scene we see the hero, Prince Ivan, and the evil ogre, whom the prince eventually kills.

find out more
Ballet
Classical music
Music

Stuart Britain

The Stuart royal family inherited the English throne from the Tudors in 1603. They ruled until 1714, when the last of the Stuart monarchs, Queen Anne, died.

While the Tudors had provided strong government, there were so many difficulties between the Stuart kings and Parliament that they led to civil war. Neighbours, friends and even members of the same family sometimes found themselves on opposite sides.

Troubled times

Both King James I and his son Charles I were extravagant with money and often asked Parliament to raise extra taxes. But Members of Parliament (MPs) in the House of Commons were angered when the kings refused to listen to their complaints about royal spending and often voted against them. There were also religious disagreements. Many MPs were Puritans who wanted the Church of England to have plainer services and churches. The Puritans hated and feared Catholics. Charles I had a Catholic wife and Parliament was afraid he was going to make England Catholic.

Because of all these disagreements Charles I decided, in 1629, to rule without Parliament. However, in 1640 a Scottish rebellion forced Charles to call a Parliament to raise extra taxes. MPs immediately began to work to limit the king's power.

Civil war

These problems finally led to civil war. From 1642 to 1646, Cavaliers (for the king) fought Roundheads (for Parliament). Parliament's New Model Army won the war, and peace was restored. But when Charles I joined forces with the Scots in 1648 and fighting started again, Parliament decided they no longer wanted to be ruled by a king. In 1649 Charles was put on trial and executed.

For the next 11 years, England did not have a king. It was called a 'Commonwealth'. From 1653 Oliver Cromwell, who had led the army

▼ The execution of Charles I, 30 January 1649. This is the only time an English king has been put on trial and executed. Even many Roundheads were horrified at his death.

against the king, ruled as Lord Protector. He kept England peaceful and made it strong abroad. However, he too found it difficult to get on with Parliament, and had to raise taxes to pay for an army to help him rule.

Restoration of the monarchy

Cromwell died in 1658. In 1660 Charles I's son Charles II was invited back from exile and crowned as king. This was called the Restoration. The next king, James II, was a Catholic and ignored laws made by Parliament. His reign lasted only three years. In 1688 he was forced to escape into exile in France. Parliament asked his Protestant son-in-law and daughter, William and Mary, to become joint king and queen. They agreed to share power with Parliament. This change (which was peaceful in England, but not in Scotland and Ireland) is often called the Glorious Revolution. By the time of the last Stuart, Queen Anne, rulers of England had become 'constitutional monarchs' who had to obey Parliament's rules.

◀ In the civil war each side gave the other a nickname. 'Roundheads' were those who fought for Parliament. 'Cavaliers' were Royalists, who fought for the king.

1603 **James I** (James VI of Scotland)
1605 Gunpowder Plot
1625 **Charles I**
1642 1st civil war
1648 2nd civil war
1649 Charles I executed
1650 **Commonwealth**
1653 Cromwell Lord Protector
1655 Jamaica captured from the Spaniards
1660 **Charles II** Restoration of the monarchy
1665 Great Plague
1666 Fire of London
1685 **James II**
1688 **Mary II and William III**
1690 Battle of the Boyne. William III defeated James II in Ireland
1695 Mary II died
1702 **Anne**
1707 Union of England and Scotland
1714 Death of Queen Anne
The next king was George I. There is an article on Georgian Britain.

Stuart Britain

Stuart life

As the wealthy landowners and merchants in Parliament got even more say in running the country, they became even more powerful and prosperous. Change was much slower for ordinary people. They still could not vote or sit in Parliament. Times were often hard, especially when there was a bad harvest. But by the end of the 17th century, the country was generally more prosperous. Slightly fewer people died young, so the population increased.

London was the biggest city in Britain, with a population of about half a million by the 1660s. Slums full of filthy tumbledown houses grew up to the north of the city; the rich built grander houses to the west. There were fashionable new coffee houses, bull-baiting rings, bear-baiting pits, and theatres. The smoke from coal fires polluted the air. Disease spread easily. The Great Plague of 1665 was the last of several outbreaks of bubonic plague.

Trade

Trade grew enormously. At the beginning of the Stuart reign, England had only one important industry, the woollen cloth trade. Corn often had to be imported to feed everyone. By 1700 enough corn was grown to export some, and new goods, including tobacco, tea, coffee and chocolate, were imported. Much more sugar was coming into the country, and some of it was refined in London. Cotton, silks, fine china, dyes and jewels came from the East. Huge profits were made from the trade in slaves. Trade led to wars with Dutch and French rivals and to the establishment of colonies in North America and the Caribbean. The East India Company, which brought many of the luxury goods from the East, established settlements in India too. In the next century these colonies grew into an empire.

• Ireland was governed by English rulers. Most Irish were Catholics, except in Ulster where Protestant English and Scots settled. There was a Catholic rebellion in 1641. In 1649–1650 Cromwell led a harsh campaign to bring Ireland under English control again. By 1714 Irish Catholics owned only 7% of the land of Ireland. English landowners had taken the rest.

• Scotland had the same Stuart kings as England, but remained a separate kingdom. In 1650–1651 Cromwell defeated the Scots. Scotland was occupied. In 1707 the Act of Union united England and Scotland as part of a united kingdom. After the Glorious Revolution many Highlanders became Jacobites, who supported the exiled James II and his descendants.

• Wales was ruled in the same way as England, with similar law courts and counties.

◄ With wooden houses cramped together in narrow streets, fire was a common danger in Stuart London. This painting shows the most famous and devastating one, which raged across the city in 1666.

Submarines

Submarines are sea-going vessels that can travel underwater as well as on the surface. Most submarines are naval ones that patrol the oceans and can fire torpedoes or missiles. Special submarines called submersibles are used for engineering and exploration.

Submarines have long hollow ballast tanks, which can be filled with air or water. To dive and stay underwater, the tanks are filled with water so that the submarine can sink to a particular depth and then remain there. To return to the surface and float there, the water is blown out of the ballast tanks by compressed air. This makes the submarine lighter and so it rises again.

A submarine is driven forward by propellers, and fins called hydroplanes tilt to force it downwards or upwards. Submarines cannot use diesel or petrol engines when submerged, because these kinds of engine cannot work without oxygen. Instead, small submarines use electric motors and batteries. Larger ones are nuclear-powered. Their nuclear reactor boils water, producing steam that turns turbines to drive the propellers. Nuclear submarines can stay submerged for many weeks.

Submersibles

Submersibles can reach much greater depths in the ocean than a diver. They are used to collect scientific information as well as to carry out maintenance work on oil rigs and undersea pipelines. Most submersibles carry a small crew of people, although some carry only equipment, such as television cameras. The crew on board a manned submersible use movable arms to hold tools or to pick up objects and samples from the sea-bed.

▶ FLASHBACK ◀

The first vessel to travel underwater was built by the Dutch inventor Cornelius Drebbel. It was propelled by oars from Westminster to Greenwich on the River Thames in 1620. The first proper submarine was the *Turtle*, a wooden vessel built by the American engineer David Bushnell in 1776. In 1875 the Irish engineer John Holland built the first of a series of submarines in the USA. The modern naval submarine is descended from them. In 1958 the world's first nuclear submarine, the USS *Nautilus*, travelled under the Arctic ice and surfaced at the North Pole.

▲ This research submersible, the Johnson Sea-Link, is being launched for use in underwater exploration.

● When a submarine cruises just below the surface of the sea, the crew use a special telescope called a *periscope* to see where the submarine is going and to identify other vessels on the surface. The periscope is raised up like a hollow mast, and it has a sloping mirror at each end and lenses inside.

◀ How a submarine dives underwater and surfaces.

● The world's biggest submarines are the Russian Typhoon Class. They weigh over 26,000 tonnes.

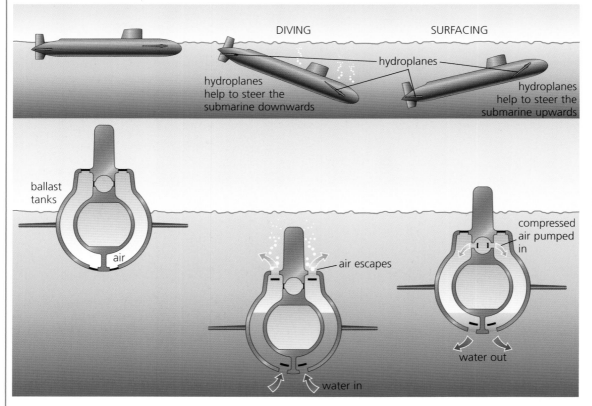

DIVING SURFACING

hydroplanes

hydroplanes help to steer the submarine downwards

hydroplanes help to steer the submarine upwards

ballast tanks

air

air escapes

compressed air pumped in

water out

water in

find out more
Navies and warships
World War II

Sudan

Sudan is the largest country in Africa. It stretches south from the Sahara Desert almost to the Equator. Northern Sudan is almost complete desert. But travelling south, the countryside gradually changes as the rainfall increases. In the far south, near the border with Uganda, there is tropical rainforest.

The River Nile runs south to north through Sudan. Without it, northern Sudan would be barren. But there is a narrow strip of land on either side of the river where farmers can grow crops. Further south the land changes through semi-desert to grassland, while in the far south the White Nile breaks up into a vast region of swampland called the Sudd.

People

The people of northern Sudan are mostly Muslims, who speak Arabic. In the south many people follow traditional African religions, and they speak a variety of African languages.

The Sudanese capital, Khartoum, is in the north, and most people in government are northerners. The southern Sudanese do not like being ruled by the Muslim north, and have been struggling for independence since 1963. Fierce fighting, together with droughts, has brought much suffering, and many refugees have fled to camps organized by aid agencies.

▶ A ferry across the Nile in Atbara, northern Sudan. The Nile is the only source of water in this desert region.

find out more
Africa
Aid agencies
Refugees
See also Countries fact file, page 640

Sugar

Sugars are sweet-tasting substances produced naturally by plants and animals. They belong to a chemical group called carbohydrates, made up of the elements carbon, hydrogen and oxygen. We use sugars and starch from our food to produce the energy we need.

Sugars are the simplest of the carbohydrates in our diet. The most common sugar is sucrose, usually known simply as 'sugar'. Sugar is made from both sugar cane and sugar beet. Sugar cane grows in tropical countries such as the islands of the Caribbean, Brazil and India. Sugar beet grows in temperate areas such as northern Europe.

The process used to extract sugar is similar for both cane and beet, and the refined white sugar made from each is exactly the same. This sugar is ground to give finer products such as caster and icing sugar. It is also compressed into sugar cubes. Some refined white sugar is coloured with molasses to make soft brown sugar. Brown sugars such as muscovado, Barbados and demerara are made from unrefined raw cane sugar. They have more flavour than ordinary soft brown sugar. Molasses and black treacle are by-products of the cane-sugar refining process.

sugar cane

cane cut and crushed

sugar beet

roots sliced up and soaked

sugary liquid

molasses from sugar cane

sugary liquid boiled and condensed

sugar crystals separated from liquid

sugar

Naturally occurring sugars
Fructose found in honey and some fruit
Glucose found in ripe fruits (e.g. grapes)
Lactose found in milk
Maltose found in barley malt
Sucrose found in sugar cane and beet and in maple syrup

◀ Sugar cane is cut and crushed. Sugar beet is sliced up. The strips are soaked and a sugary liquid is extracted. This liquid is boiled and condensed by evaporation. Sugar crystals separate from the liquid in centrifugal machines.

find out more
Caribbean
Chocolate
Diets
Food
Slaves

Sun

The Sun is a giant ball of hot gas, 150 million kilometres from the Earth. Although it is an ordinary star, like the thousands of others you see in the night sky, without it there would be no life on Earth. Human beings and all other livings things on the Earth need the heat and light energy from the Sun to stay alive. People have always recognized how important the Sun is and have often worshipped it as a god.

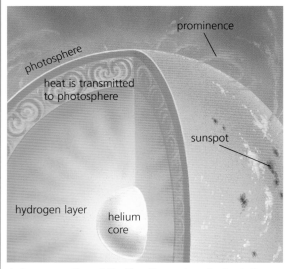

▲ A cross-section of the Sun. Energy travels slowly from the core through the thick hydrogen layer and heats the photosphere (surface).

The temperature near the outside of the Sun is about 6000 °C, but in the centre it is more like 16 million °C. Inside the core, enormous amounts of energy in the form of heat and light are produced by a process called nuclear fusion. This energy makes the Sun shine.

The Sun also gives out harmful X-rays and ultraviolet rays. Most are soaked up in our atmosphere and do not affect us. Sunlight is very strong and no one should ever stare at the Sun or look at it through any kind of magnifier, binoculars or telescope. Even with dark sunglasses it is still dangerous to look at the Sun. Astronomers study the Sun safely by looking at it with special instruments.

Activity on the Sun

Close-up pictures of the Sun show that it looks like a bubbling cauldron as hot gases gush out and then fall back. Some of the gas is streaming away from the Sun all the time into the space between the planets.

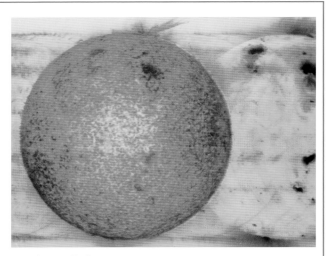

▶ Giant tongues of hot gas called *prominences* leap out violently from the Sun to heights of 1 million km or more. The prominence in this ultraviolet photograph of the Sun consists of glowing gases moving violently outwards from the Sun's surface.

Sometimes dark blotches called *sunspots* appear on the Sun's yellow disc. The average number of spots on the Sun goes up and down over a cycle of about 11 years. Near to sunspots, flares like enormous lightning flashes can burst out. When particles that shoot out from the Sun reach the Earth, they cause the lights in the night sky that we call an aurora.

▼ Solar panels on the roofs of buildings can trap the Sun's heat to provide hot water. When we use energy from the Sun as heat, or turn it into electricity, we call it *solar power*.

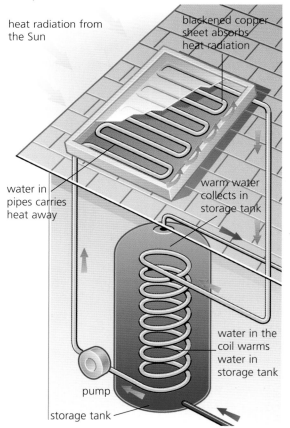

heat radiation from the Sun

blackened copper sheet absorbs heat radiation

water in pipes carries heat away

warm water collects in storage tank

water in the coil warms water in storage tank

pump

storage tank

find out more
Atmosphere
Atoms and molecules
Eclipses
Electricity
Energy
Heat
Light
Power stations
Seasons
Solar System
Stars

● Light from the Sun, travelling at 300,000 km per second, takes 8.3 minutes to reach the Earth.

● Solar cells can turn sunlight directly into electricity. Satellites in space have huge panels of solar cells to supply their electricity. In remote areas of some hot countries, solar cells provide electricity to pump water and to power appliances.

Swimming and diving

Swimming and diving are ways in which an animal pushes itself through water. A wide variety of animals can swim, including hedgehogs, cows and even moles. Many animals dive to find food or safety.

In order to swim, an animal must push the water back (to move forward) and down (to stay afloat). To thrust against the water effectively, it needs to maintain a good streamlined shape (more or less torpedo-shaped) so the water flows smoothly round its body.

Human techniques

Humans have developed several different methods of successful swimming. Four of these 'strokes' are used in competitive sport.

In *breast-stroke* the feet provide most of the thrust. They are brought together in a scissors motion. In the *front crawl*, the body lies flat on the surface of the water, and both arms and feet provide thrust. It is the fastest and most efficient stroke. In *backstroke*, swimmers lie on their back. The arms reach alternately above their head, and enter the water level with the shoulders. The *butterfly stroke* is used only for competitions. The arms are brought forward above the water, and the legs kick up and down.

Swimming is a good form of exercise, especially for the elderly and disabled, because the body is partly supported by the water. It puts little strain on the limbs while exercising the muscles and joints. It also strengthens the heart and lungs.

• The fastest human swimmers average more than 8 km an hour over a straight 50-m swim.

• Sperm whales are the deepest-diving mammals. They often dive to 360 m and have been known to reach depths of over 1000 m. They normally remain underwater for between 20 and 60 minutes.

▶ About 80 kinds of bird normally dive for their food. The common kingfisher, shown here, plunges through the water's surface at great speed to catch fish and water-living insects.

Animal techniques

Often an animal's feet, or sometimes the whole of its legs or arms, are shaped like paddles to provide a greater surface area to push against the water. Turtles and seals have flippers; dolphins and whales use their large tail flukes. Fishes have fins, and ducks, seagulls and otters have webbed feet. Many small shrimps and water insects have fringes of stiff bristles on their legs which produce a similar 'paddle' effect.

A few swimmers, such as jellyfishes and squids, use water-jet propulsion. This method of swimming involves taking water into their bag-like body and then forcing it out again, which propels them forward.

Many water-living animals and some kinds of bird dive below the surface waters to find food. Animals with gills have no problem when they change level because they get their oxygen from water. But mammals, which get their oxygen from air, have to protect themselves against a dangerous build-up of nitrogen gas in the blood. To do this they breathe heavily before they dive. This transfers oxygen to their muscles, where it will be needed, and reduces air in the lungs. With less air in their lungs they also lose some of their buoyancy (ability to float), so diving becomes easier. All deep-diving mammals are able to hold their breath for a long time. They regain the lost oxygen by panting as soon as they reach the surface and can breathe again.

◀ Without the help of scuba (self-contained underwater breathing apparatus), humans can only stay underwater for as long as they can hold their breath – about 3 minutes. Scuba is a portable oxygen supply. It was developed by the French underwater explorer Jacques Cousteau in the early 1940s.

Symbols

A symbol is something that represents something else. Anything – from an animal, to a colour, to an action – may be symbolic.

Many symbols are based on our experience of the world around us. One of the most important is the Sun, which is the source of light, warmth and energy – the source of life itself. It is traditionally associated with God's blessing. There are at least 14 countries in the world that have the Sun on their national flag.

In many cultures animals are symbolic. A cat, for example, can be a symbol for magic, because Europeans once believed that witches turned into cats. On the continent of Europe and in the USA, a black cat is considered unlucky, whereas in Britain it often stands for good luck.

Colours have great symbolic significance. White often symbolizes purity, and is traditionally worn by brides in Christian countries. In the same countries black is often associated with bad luck and death, but in India white is the colour of mourning.

Actions can also be symbolic. At the Last Supper, before Christ was crucified, he washed the feet of his apostles. By this symbolic act he showed that he loved and served them, and that they in turn should love and serve others.

▲ To Jews, Christians and Muslims a rainbow is a reminder that God created one after the great flood, as a symbol of the everlasting bond between himself and all life on Earth.

Some important symbols

A *lion* stands for courage and strength.

Oil, used to anoint a king or queen at a coronation, symbolizes the giving of wisdom through the grace of God.

A *swastika* is a prehistoric symbol of creative force; in Sanskrit it means 'so be it'. It was also used as a symbol by the Nazis in Germany.

A *wheel*, in Buddhism, represents the unending cycle of birth, life and death.

find out more
Buddhists
Designers

Taoists

Tao (dao) is a Chinese word which means 'the way'. It is used to describe both a way of life and to express religious belief in the Truth (God). The number of Taoists in the world is estimated to be around 50 million, mostly in China and other parts of Asia.

Taoists base their ideas and practices on the teaching of Lao Zi, who lived in the 5th century BC. Although the Tao, or Way, has never been put down in words, Lao Zi's ideas were written down in a book called the *Dao De Jing* or 'Book of Reasons and Virtue'. At only 5000 words long, it is the shortest of all sacred texts. In it Lao Zi states that 'the Tao that can be named is not the eternal Tao'. This means that, for believers, the true Tao is for them to discover within, not from books.

Taoism, like Confucianism, has influenced most Chinese people, whether or not they call themselves Taoists. It teaches harmony and balance between all opposites; these are called the yin and yang forces. Yin (dark side) is thought to be the breath that formed the Earth. Yang (light side) is the breath that formed the heavens. They symbolize pairs of opposites, such as female and watery (yin) and male and solid (yang). Taoists believe that by observing and learning from nature, people can find a way of always going gently, without using force.

• Taoism is usually pronounced 'Daoism' (although it can be pronounced with a 't' as well). It is sometimes also spelt with a 'd' (Daoism).

▲ The symbol of yin and yang. The two forces are opposites, but each has in it a small part of the other.

find out more
China
Confucians

◄ A Taoist shrine in China.

Taxes

Taxes are payments individual people and businesses have to pay to their country's government. Taxes are used to pay for things which benefit the whole country, such as defence (the army, navy and air force), health services, education and roads.

• Excise is any tax but especially one that is charged on goods before they are sold to the public. It may be charged when goods are brought into a country. Customs and excise officers are the people who collect the tax.

One of the main kinds of tax is income tax. People have to pay a certain percentage of their income (their earnings) to the government. Those who earn more money may pay a higher percentage of their income in taxes. Companies may have to pay tax on a proportion of their profits. These are examples of direct taxes on individuals and businesses. Inherited wealth may also be directly taxed.

Other taxes are added on to the price of goods and services. In Europe the main tax of this sort is called Value Added Tax (VAT) and in the United States it is called a sales tax. These taxes are charged on what people spend, rather than on what they earn. They are called indirect taxes. Indirect taxes can be used to change people's behaviour. If a government wants drivers to use unleaded petrol in order to reduce pollution, it may put higher taxes on leaded petrol. If it wants to discourage people from smoking, it might put a high tax on cigarettes.

find out more
Economics
Government

▼ Customs duties are taxes that have to be paid when moving goods from one country to another. Smugglers are criminals who avoid paying these taxes. Here customs officers in Essex, England, uncover a lorry load of beer that has been smuggled into the United Kingdom from mainland Europe.

Technology

The simple stone tools made over a million years ago by prehistoric people were the first examples of technology. Cars, concrete and computers are all examples of modern technology. Technology is about making things that can do useful jobs.

Technology firsts
1290 Mechanical clock
1712 Steam engine
1804 Railway locomotive
1826 Photograph
1839 Pedal bicycle
1876 Telephone
1879 Electric light bulb
1885 Petrol-driven car
1903 Heavier-than-air aircraft
1926 Television
1946 Electronic computer
1957 Space satellite
1959 Hovercraft
1971 Pocket calculator
1985 Genetic fingerprinting
1997 Cloned mammal (sheep)

find out more
Biotechnology
Industrial Revolution
Industry
Information technology

Sometimes scientific discoveries lead to new technology. For example, when X-rays were discovered, people soon realized that they could be used to take see-through photographs of bones. At other times, scientists do research so that new technology can be developed. Before the Space Shuttle could be built, scientists had to find materials able to cope with the heat generated by travelling through the Earth's atmosphere.

There are many different branches of technology. For example, materials technology develops new plastics, fabrics, metals and building materials. Food technology finds new ways to prepare, store and pack food. Engineers are technologists – they help to create vehicles, roads, bridges, chemical factories and machinery. Alternative technology is concerned with saving energy. It includes using wind and water to make electricity, or building with local stone instead of transporting bricks over great distances.

▼ A magnified photograph of an integrated circuit chip. Chips like these contain thousands of electronic parts, but they are often no bigger than the size of a pinhead. Integrated circuits control signals inside electronic equipment such as computers, televisions and pocket calculators. They are faster, cheaper and last longer than ordinary circuits.

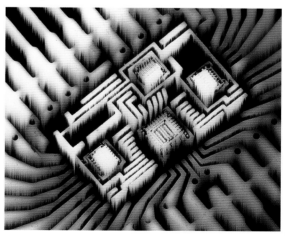

Teachers *see* Schools and universities

Teeth

Your teeth are the hardest part of your body. You use them every day for holding, cutting and chewing food, so they have to be very strong. If teeth are not well cared for, they will decay.

Most vertebrates (animals with backbones) have teeth. Different animals' teeth are adapted to different jobs.

▼ The part of a tooth that you can see is called the *crown*. Below the crown, hidden in the gums, is the tooth's root. This fixes the tooth firmly into the jawbone. Most of the tooth is made of hard material called *dentine*. The crown is coated with an even harder material called *enamel*. Inside the tooth is a cavity filled with pulp. The pulp consists of blood vessels and nerve fibres.

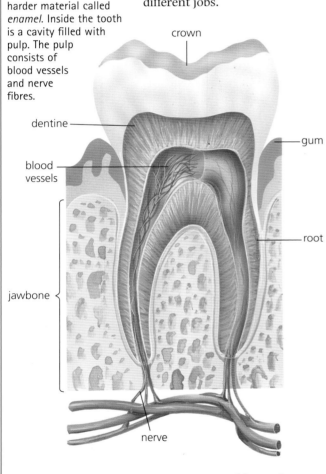

crown

dentine

blood vessels

gum

root

jawbone

nerve

Our upper and lower front teeth have straight chisel-shaped ends. They are called *incisors* and are used for slicing mouth-sized pieces from food. On each side of the incisors is a single pointed tooth. This is a *canine* tooth. The canines are more developed in meat-eating animals and are used for puncturing the skin of prey.

Our back teeth, behind the canines, are broad and bumpy. These are called *molars*. When you chew, you rub the upper and lower molars together, grinding food into small pieces for swallowing. In plant-eating animals the molars are large and have many ridges to enable them to grind tough grass and leaf material. Flesh-eating animals have special molars for chewing meat with the sides of their jaws. The edges of these teeth slide past each other like the blades of shears.

Caring for your teeth

It is very important to take proper care of your teeth. If you eat too much sugar and do not clean them regularly, your teeth will decay. Tooth decay occurs when small pieces of food, trapped around the teeth, are broken down by bacteria that live in the mouth. This produces acid which slowly damages the hard enamel coating the crown. Then it attacks the softer material (dentine), creating a hole or cavity. This causes toothache.

The best way to prevent tooth decay is to avoid eating too much sugar and to eat plenty of raw fruit and vegetables, such as apples and carrots. You should also brush your teeth at least twice a day and visit a dentist regularly.

A dentist's job is to care for your teeth and to treat them if they are diseased. If your teeth are decayed a dentist will remove the damaged parts and replace them with fillings. Sometimes they take out a whole tooth and replace it with a false one. The patron saint of dentistry is St Apollonia. Because of her Christian beliefs, she was tortured in AD 249 in Alexandria by having her teeth pulled out one at a time.

incisor   canine   premolar

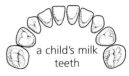

a child's milk teeth

molar

an adult's teeth

▲ The teeth develop inside the jawbones before birth and first appear at about 5 months. At about 6 years children have 24 teeth. Twenty of these are milk teeth, which will fall out between 7 and 11 years. They are replaced by larger permanent teeth.

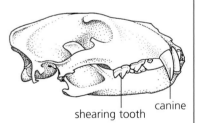

shearing tooth   canine

▲ **Lion (carnivore)**
Carnivores have long canines to kill prey and hold onto them. Massive shearing teeth crack bones and cut flesh.

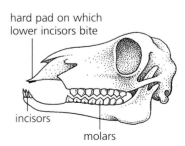

hard pad on which lower incisors bite

incisors

molars

▲ **Sheep (herbivore)**
Herbivores cut grass by moving their chisel-edged lower incisors sideways across a thick pad on the upper jaw.

find out more
Diets
Skeletons

Telephones

A telephone lets you talk to other people almost anywhere on Earth, simply by pressing a few buttons. There are hundreds of millions of telephones in the world. They are all linked by a complicated telecommunications network which carries telephone calls, fax messages, television and radio signals, and computer data.

When you speak into a telephone receiver, sound waves of your voice go into the mouthpiece. A microphone there changes the sounds into patterns on a tiny electric current, which are called signals. These signals travel from the receiver into the telephone network. When people telephone you, signals come from the network to the earpiece of your receiver. A thin metal diaphragm inside the earpiece vibrates to produce sound waves that enter your ear.

When you press the number buttons on your telephone, the receiver sends signals to your local telephone exchange. The exchange uses the numbers to route your call through the telephone network – to another local telephone, to another telephone exchange, or to the telephone network of another country.

Electrical and digital signals

Signals go from your telephone to the local exchange along copper cables. Most exchanges are linked by optical-fibre cables through which the signals travel as pulses of laser light. Microwave beams, sent between dishes on tall towers, link some signals. International calls go along undersea optical-fibre cables or via satellites high above the Earth.

Before they go through the telephone network, most signals are changed into digital signals (the changing electric current is changed into patterns of the digits 0 and 1). It is easy to send these as pulses of electricity or light microwaves. The digital signals turn back to normal signals before reaching your telephone. Signals from mobile telephones go by radio to a radio mast and then into the telephone network. Mobile phones only work when close to a radio mast.

▶ FLASHBACK ◀

The first device to send messages by electricity was the telegraph. The messages were sent by tapping out a special code, known as the Morse code. Invented by Samuel Morse in 1838, the code uses different combinations of short and

long bursts of electric current to represent different letters of the alphabet. The Scottish-American inventor Alexander Graham Bell was experimenting with a telegraph machine in 1875 when he realized it was transmitting sounds. In this way he invented the telephone almost by accident. The first telephone exchange, which connected 21 people, was opened in 1878. Although the first automatic exchange was built in the 1890s, operators still worked most exchanges until the 1920s. A transatlantic telephone cable was laid in 1956, and the first communications satellite, Telstar, was launched in 1962. Development of optical fibres carrying digital signals took place in the 1960s.

◀ Light beams emerge from the end of a cable of optical fibres. The fibres are made from flexible glass. Telephone conversations travel along optical-fibre cables as pulses of laser light. A thin optical-fibre cable can carry 40,000 digitized telephone calls at the same time.

find out more
Communication
Fax machines
Information technology
Radio
Satellites
Waves

▼ This illustration from a 1904 edition of *Le Petit Journal* shows the telephone exchange for the Paris Opera in France. Patrons used to call the Opera and listen to the evening's performance over the telephone.

Telescopes

When you look through a telescope, distant things seem nearer and bigger. A telescope collects light and funnels it into your eye, allowing you to see things that are too faint to be seen by the eye alone. A telescope also lets you see more detail than you would otherwise see. Telescopes range in size from simple tube-shaped ones that you hold in your hands to the huge telescopes used by astronomers to study the stars.

Telescopes that collect light are known as optical telescopes. The simplest kind, called a *refracting telescope*, has a tube with a lens at each end. The front lens collects light and brings light rays together to form an image of a distant object. The image is then magnified by the *eyepiece*, the lens that you look through. A *reflecting telescope*, or reflector, uses a concave (dish-shaped) mirror to collect light. The main mirror concentrates the light onto a smaller mirror which then reflects it into an eyepiece.

The bigger the main mirror or lens, the more light it collects, and the fainter the things it can see. Larger telescopes also show more details than small ones. The blurring effects of the atmosphere often prevent telescopes from showing as much as they should, so they are often built on high mountains or put into space.

Radio telescopes collect radio waves from distant stars and galaxies. These telescopes consist of big dishes to collect the radio signals. Radio telescopes can be used in daylight as well as at night.

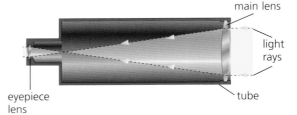

◄ A refracting telescope. The main lens focuses light from a distant object to form an image in front of the eyepiece. The eyepiece lens magnifies this image.

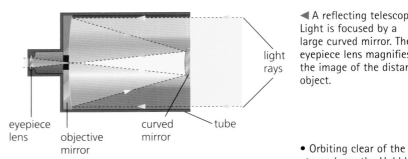

◄ A reflecting telescope. Light is focused by a large curved mirror. The eyepiece lens magnifies the image of the distant object.

• Orbiting clear of the atmosphere, the Hubble Space Telescope (HST) can see far more clearly than telescopes on the ground. Shuttle astronauts had to correct the main mirror in December 1993, and carried out further repairs to the telescope in 1997.

► FLASHBACK ◄

Hans Lippershey, a Dutch spectacle-maker, is usually said to have invented the first telescope in 1608. The next year, the Italian astronomer Galileo Galilei built a telescope and turned it on the sky. In 1671 Isaac Newton announced that he had made the first reflecting telescope.

Observatories

Observatories are buildings from which astronomers look at the sky. The two most important types of ground-based observatory are optical observatories and radio observatories. In space, unmanned observatories orbit the Earth on satellites.

Optical observatories have ordinary telescopes housed in big domes. At night, the dome opens and can turn to point the telescope at different parts of the sky. Many telescopes are now operated by computers. Optical observatories need to be built away from city lights and in cloud-free places. The best sites are on mountain-tops in warm places. The telescopes in radio observatories do not need to be inside buildings. Also, radio waves from space can pass through clouds, so it is not important where the observatory is built.

Thousands of years ago, astronomers watched the movements of the Sun, Moon and stars from observatories, long before the invention of telescopes. Over 4500 years ago Stonehenge was constructed in Britain, possibly for use as an observatory. At this time Babylonians watched the night sky from stepped towers called ziggurats.

Telescope records

Largest radio telescope
Puerto Rico, Caribbean: 300 m across

Most powerful radio telescope
Very Long Baseline Array (VLBA), USA: consists of 10 dishes spread along a line 8000 km long

Largest optical telescope
Keck telescope, Hawaii: 10 m across and weighs 270 tonnes

find out more
Astronomy
Galilei, Galileo
Lenses
Mirrors
Newton, Isaac
Satellites

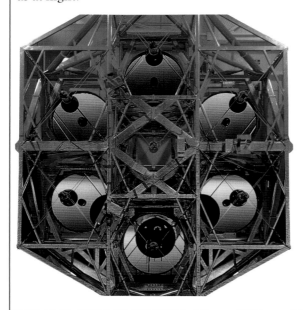

◄ A close-up view of the Multiple Mirror Telescope (MMT) on Mount Hopkins in Arizona, USA. One of the world's largest reflecting telescopes, it has six separate mirrors (each measuring 1.8 m across), which work together to form a single large mirror.

Television

Television is a way of sending moving pictures from one place to another. It lets us watch events from around the world as they happen, whether they are sporting competitions, wars or natural disasters. Television has a huge effect on the lives of many people. For most of us, it is our main way of getting news and entertainment. In developed countries, almost every home has a television set.

A television (TV) camera turns moving pictures into electrical signals. The signals are sent to your television set by radio waves, via satellites, or through cables under the ground. The television set uses the signals it receives to make a moving picture on its screen and to make sound through its speaker.

In Western countries most people watch a few hours of television each day. If they have the right receiving equipment, they can choose from dozens of channels broadcasting a wide range of programmes, from soap operas to wildlife films and current affairs discussions. Advertisers pay huge sums of money to have their products shown during the commercial breaks in television programmes, especially the programmes they know millions of people will be watching.

What is a TV picture?

Moving pictures are made by showing still pictures one after another very quickly. Each still picture, called a frame, is slightly different from the one before. Our eyes cannot react quickly enough to see one picture change to the next, and our brains are fooled into seeing a moving picture. Each frame is made up of hundreds of thin horizontal lines, and each line is made up of hundreds of coloured strips. You do not see the lines or strips because they all merge together to make up the complete picture.

In most of Europe, television pictures are made up of 625 lines, and 25 frames are shown every second. In the USA and Japan, pictures have 525 lines and 30 frames are shown every second. In a new kind of system, called high-definition television (HDTV), pictures are made up of thousands of lines instead of hundreds. This makes the pictures far more detailed.

From camera to TV set

The lens of a television camera collects light from a moving scene, just like an ordinary camera. ▶

• All TV pictures were in black and white until 1953, when the first successful colour pictures were broadcast in the USA.

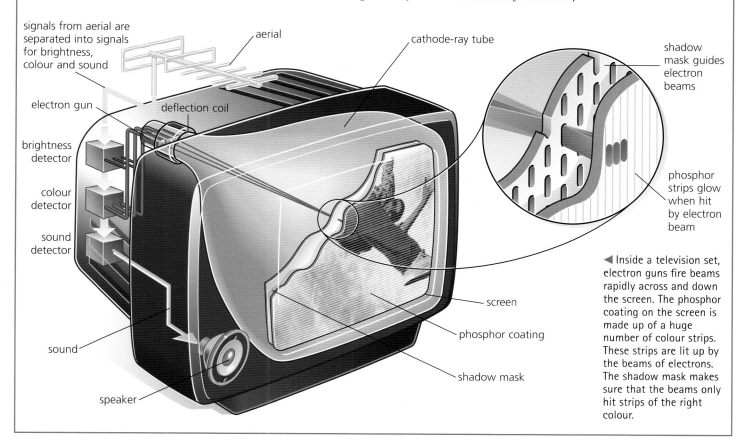

signals from aerial are separated into signals for brightness, colour and sound

aerial

cathode-ray tube

shadow mask guides electron beams

electron gun

deflection coil

brightness detector

colour detector

sound detector

phosphor strips glow when hit by electron beam

sound

screen

phosphor coating

shadow mask

speaker

◀ Inside a television set, electron guns fire beams rapidly across and down the screen. The phosphor coating on the screen is made up of a huge number of colour strips. These strips are lit up by the beams of electrons. The shadow mask makes sure that the beams only hit strips of the right colour.

- The largest TV screen in the world was built by Sony for an international exhibition in Tokyo. It measured 45 m by 24 m.

- The smallest TV screen is on a Seiko TV-wrist watch. It is black and white, and measures just 30 mm across.

TV pioneers

In 1926 a Scottish engineer John Logie Baird (1888–1946) gave the first public demonstration of television in England. He used a cumbersome mechanical camera, and the pictures produced were shaky and blurred.

Earlier, in 1923, a Russian inventor and engineer, Vladimir Zworykin (1889–1982), invented an electronic image-scanning device. In the 1930s it was developed into the cathode-ray tube. This all-electric system quickly replaced Baird's relatively crude device, and is still at the heart of every television set produced today.

▲ John Logie Baird was one of the pioneers of television. In 1929 his equipment was used to make the first television broadcast (without sound). He was also responsible for the first outside TV broadcast (of the Derby horse race in 1931).

satellite sends them down again, scattered over a wide area. To collect them, you need a small satellite dish. In *cable* television, the signals travel through electrical cables under the ground, straight to your television.

In *digital* television, television signals are made up of a list of numbers. This gives clearer pictures. In the future, all television will be digital. It will also be in widescreen format, just like movie pictures.

How a TV set works

Signals from many different television stations arrive at your television set. The first thing it does is pick out the signal from the station you want. This is called *tuning*. Next, it takes the signal apart to make signals for red, green and blue, and for sound. It uses these signals to re-create the picture on its screen and to make sound.

Behind a television screen there are three 'guns' which shoot streams of tiny particles called electrons at the back of the screen. The red, green and blue signals control the output of one electron gun each. The beams of electrons are not themselves coloured, but they make red, green and blue light when they hit the screen. The sound signal is sent to an amplifier and a speaker.

Inside the camera is a light-sensitive device which scans the pattern of light, line by line, strip by strip. It works out how much green, red and blue light there is in each strip, and codes this information in an electrical signal. When it has scanned one frame, it starts on the next. In this way, the moving scene is turned into an electrical signal. Sound is added to the signal later.

There are several ways of getting the signals from a television camera to your television set. In *terrestrial* (Earth-based) television, the signals are sent from a transmitter as radio waves and are picked up by a normal television aerial. In *satellite* television, the signals are sent by microwaves to a satellite orbiting the Earth. The

▶ In September 1997, thousands of people watched the funeral of Diana, Princess of Wales on giant TV screens in London's Hyde Park. Millions of people around the world saw pictures of the funeral on their television sets.

Tennis and other racket sports

In a number of sports, players use rackets to hit a ball (or shuttle) over a net. By far the most popular of these is tennis, which is a major professional sport and played for pleasure by millions around the world.

Another kind of racket sport involves hitting a ball against a wall, usually within an enclosed court. Today, squash is the most widely played sport of this kind.

► Because of the four-walled court, squash has never been a major spectator sport, but special transparent courts are used for important tournaments. Shown here in the foreground is Jahangir Khan of Pakistan, who won six world titles in the 1980s.

Tennis

Tennis is a game for two or four players, played indoors or outdoors on a grass, clay, wood or synthetic surface. The ball is put into play by *serving*. Standing behind the base line, the server has up to two attempts to hit the ball over the net so that it lands within the opposite service court. Play then continues until one player fails to return the ball into the opponent's court.

In order to win a *game*, a player must score four points and lead by at least two points. Six games are needed to win a set, provided that there is at least a two-game lead. If not, a *tie-break* game may be played when the game score is 6–6. Service changes to the other player after each game. The first player to win two sets, or three in some tournaments, wins the match.

'Real (royal) tennis' was first played inside French monasteries in the Middle Ages. In Britain in the 1860s some people took tennis outdoors and invented 'lawn tennis'. Today, all the top players are professional, and tournaments are played all over the world, with big prizes for the winners. The highlights of the tennis year are the US, French and Australian Opens and the Wimbledon Championships, which together make up the 'grand slam'.

Badminton and squash

Like tennis, badminton can be played as singles or doubles. The aim is to hit the shuttlecock ('shuttle') over the net so that it cannot be returned by the other player. The shuttle is very light and does not bounce, so (unlike tennis) it is always hit on the volley. Badminton is a very subtle and varied game, where big hits and gentle lobs all play their part.

Squash is usually played between two players in a four-walled court with a small soft ball. Players must hit the ball before it bounces twice, and must return it so that it hits the front wall. When the ball is in play, it can bounce from all four walls. It is a very energetic game, requiring quick bursts of speed to get to the falling ball or to intercept a hard shot.

◄ Martina Navratilova of the USA winning the last of her record nine Wimbledon singles titles in 1990. The record for singles titles in all grand slam events is 24, held by the Australian Margaret Court, who won the last of them in 1973.

▼ The tennis court. The areas between the singles and doubles side lines are used only in doubles matches.

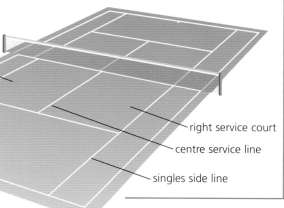

left service court
doubles side line
service line
right service court
centre service line
base line
singles side line

Teresa, Mother

Born 1910 in Skopje, Macedonia
Died 1997 aged 87

find out more
Christians
India
Monks and nuns

► Mother Teresa comforts a mother and child who have been poisoned by gas which escaped from a chemicals factory in Bhopal, central India, in 1984, killing 2500 people. Because of her dedication to some of the poorest people in the world, Mother Teresa was often known as the 'saint of the gutter'.

Mother Teresa was a nun who dedicated her life to caring for the poor and the dying. She was best known for her work with the street children in Calcutta, India.

Agnes Gonxha Bojaxhiu became a nun when she was 12 and took the name Teresa. In 1928 she was sent to India to teach at a convent in Calcutta. After several years, however, she felt that God wanted her to help the poorest people of the city. In 1948 she asked permission from the Roman Catholic authorities to leave the convent, and after two years it was granted.

By this time she had studied nursing, and with just a few rupees in her pocket she moved into the slums of Calcutta. There she gathered together five destitute children and sheltered them in a friend's flat. Gradually the number of children grew, and girls and teachers from her old convent came to help her. In 1950 the Church allowed her to found the Congregation of the Missionaries of Charity. She opened a Home for the Dying in Calcutta, as well as a leper colony called Shanti Nagar ('Town of Peace').

Mother Teresa opened over 60 schools, orphanages and homes for the dying all over the world. All the homes and settlements depend on gifts of money and other help.

In 1963 the Indian government awarded her the Padmashri ('Lord of the Lotus') for her services to the Indian people. In 1979 she received the Nobel Peace Prize, which she accepted on behalf of poor people everywhere. She was still actively serving the sick and dying at the time of her own death in 1997.

Terrorists

Terrorists are people who use violence or threaten to kill others to achieve some political aim. They try to create terror either to gain publicity for their cause or to force governments to do something.

Terrorist methods include bombing, shooting, taking hostages and hijacking (taking over by violence) vehicles, ships or aeroplanes. Hostage-taking and hijacking are often done in order to pressurize governments to release captured terrorists or to gain ransom money.

Some governments sometimes use methods that are similar to those of terrorists in order to intimidate groups that oppose them, either in their own or another country; but these actions are not usually called terrorist. Other governments have been accused of supporting terrorists, giving them arms, money and a safe place to live while they plan violence against other countries.

• Airports have been terrorist targets in many countries. Security is one way of combating this, particularly by searching people's luggage for weapons and explosives. Ways of searching include X-ray machines, metal-detection equipment, and dogs which can sniff out explosives.

find out more
Airports
Explosives

► In 1995 terrorists blew up this US government building in Oklahoma City, killing 168 people.

Textiles

Textiles are all around you. They form the clothes you wear during the day, and the bedding that you sleep in at night. Towels, carpets, curtains and furniture covers are made of textiles. Cars contain textiles on the seats and inside tyres. And textiles are used for many other useful things, such as belts, parachutes, tents, sails, and bandages.

A textile is a cloth or fabric made from fibres. These might be natural fibres that come from plants or animals, such as cotton, silk, flax and wool. Or they could be synthetic fibres made in factories, such as nylon, polyester and acrylics. Many textiles contain a mixture of natural and synthetic fibres.

Other kinds of textile

Denim: a strong woven cotton cloth used for jeans and other tough garments.
Linen: a fabric made from the flax plant.
Satin: a fabric woven with a smooth surface, so that it appears shiny.
Tweed: a heavy woollen cloth with a rough surface.
Lycra®: shiny fabric made with stretchy synthetic fibres, used to make sportswear.
Gore-Tex®: a 'breathable' waterproof fabric used for outdoor clothing and tents.

Making textiles

The first step in producing most textiles is to twist the fibres together to form a yarn or thread, like the cotton on a reel or the wool in a ball of wool. Yarn is made by *spinning* the fibres to twist them together, either by hand or using a machine. Most synthetic fibres are made from chemicals extracted from oil. The fibres are produced by forcing the chemicals through tiny holes in a nozzle called a *spinneret*. As the fibres emerge, they are spun to make yarn.

The yarn may then be dyed before being made into cloth or fabric. This is mainly done by *weaving*, in which lengths of yarn are criss-crossed on a loom, or by *knitting*, in which the yarn is linked in loops. A pattern can be formed by weaving or knitting different-coloured yarns together. *Felting* is a third way of making textiles, in which the fibres are matted together.

Once made, a textile may next need some kind of treatment – washing or cleaning to remove dirt and impurities, bleaching to whiten it, or waterproofing or fireproofing. Many textiles have patterns printed on their surface. This is done using large rollers which carry a pattern of coloured dyes.

Textile properties

The properties of a finished textile depend partly on the fibres from which it is made. Textiles made from natural fibres are generally softer, absorb moisture better and are more heat-resistant than synthetic fabrics. Synthetic textiles are stronger, harder-

▼ A Guatemalan woman using a simple loom. It is called a backstrap loom, because the warp threads are kept tight by a strap that runs around the weaver's back. With her left hand, the woman is lifting up one set of warp yarns to create a gap (the *shed*). With her right, she is pushing the weft tight, using a tool called a *reed*.

▶ Weaving involves passing a yarn, called the *weft*, over and under many parallel yarns, called *warp* threads.

1 Each warp thread is attached to a wire loop called a *heddle*.

2 Using the heddles, one set of warp threads is raised and another lowered. The weft is passed through the gap (the *shed*), using a *shuttle*.

3 The warp threads are reversed, so that the lower one is above, and the higher one is below. The weft passes through the shed again.

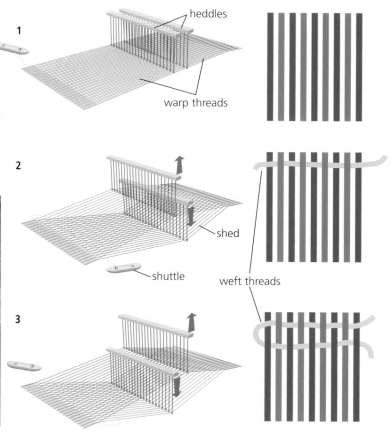

heddles
warp threads
shed
shuttle
weft threads

wearing and more crease-resistant than natural fabrics. Modern textiles may be made from a mixture of natural and synthetic fibres to give the best combination of properties for a particular product. Cotton–polyester shirts, for example, are soft and comfortable, but they are also hard-wearing and easy to iron.

▶ FLASHBACK ◀

Weaving was one of the first crafts. Remains of cotton seeds and clothes have been found that date back to 3000 BC. Cotton was grown in places as far apart as Mexico, northern India and China, and silk fabrics were woven 4000 years ago in China. In medieval Europe most textiles were made from wool, although the richest people wore silks. The Arabs introduced cotton fabric to Europe, but at first it was not very popular. Indian cotton became fashionable in Europe during the 17th century, and in the early 18th century cheaper cotton fabrics began to be made in England, using cotton grown in the USA.

During the Industrial Revolution, two important machines for making textiles were invented in the UK. These were the spinning jenny, which spun yarn, and the power loom, which wove cloth. These machines could spin and weave much faster than people. American cotton was shipped to Britain, where it was made into cloth using the new inventions.

The first synthetic fabric, rayon, was invented at the end of the 19th century. It was made from cellulose, a plant fibre that is extracted from wood pulp. Nylon was introduced in the 1930s, and in the 1940s many other synthetic fabrics were produced.

find out more
Clothes
Cotton
Dress and costume
Silk
Wool

▼ The quality of these synthetic yarns is being tested, using a machine that measures how strong a pull is needed to break the yarn.

Thailand

Thailand is a tropical country in South-east Asia. Much of the land is rice plains, mountains and rainforest. In recent years, large areas of the rainforest have been felled for timber.

find out more
Asia
Buddhists
See also Countries fact file, page 641

Central Thailand is a flat, damp plain, ideal for growing rice. Thailand is the world's leading rice exporter. The climate is hot and sticky for most of the year. Even in the 'cool' season, from November to February, average temperatures are about 26 °C. Between May and October more than 1500 millimetres of rain may fall.

Bangkok, the capital of Thailand, is a busy city of nearly 6 million people. Bangkok's streets are full of cars and modern buildings, but the city also contains the ancient Grand Palace of the king and queen of Thailand, and many Buddhist temples. Most Thai people are Buddhists. A majority of the men spend some part of their lives as monks, in one of the country's 27,000 *wat* (temples).

◀ A 'floating market' on the Chao Phraya river in Bangkok. The women sell fruit and vegetables directly from their boats.

Since the early 1980s Thailand's economy has grown fast, through new industries such as electronics. Thailand also exports textiles, rubber, tin and gems (rubies and sapphires).

▶ FLASHBACK ◀

Civilization is very old in Thailand. Bronze items dating back 6000 years have been found, and remains of the more ancient cities date back to at least AD 500. Thailand has been invaded by the Burmese and others, but it is the only country in South-east Asia which has never been a European colony.

Thailand was occupied by Japan in World War II. Since then, army generals have ruled for much of the time. Until 1939 the country was called Siam. The name Thailand means 'land of the free'.

Theatres

Theatres are places in which plays, ballets and operas are performed. Some theatres are permanent buildings, while others are much more simple and are put up for just a few days or weeks.

The word 'theatre' comes from the Greek word *theatron*, which means 'a place for seeing'. The first theatres in Europe were built in Greece about 2500 years ago. They were open to the sky, and often built against a hillside, with rows of stone seats rising up around a circular space for acting. Later theatres were built with surrounding walls, although many were still open-air. One of the most famous examples was the Globe Theatre in London. This was the theatre in which William Shakespeare's plays were first performed. A replica of the Globe has recently been rebuilt near its original site.

Modern theatres

Three basic types of stage are used in modern theatres. The most common type is the *proscenium stage*. The audience sits directly in front of the actors, who perform behind a 'picture frame' (called the proscenium arch). The *theatre-in-the-round stage* has the stage in the middle with the audience sitting all around, like at a circus. The *platform stage* has seats arranged on three sides of a stage that extends into the audience area. Both of these types of theatre allow the audience to get much closer to the performers.

Lighting

Lights are often used in theatres. At first people used candles, but they did not give much light, and sometimes theatres caught fire. Gas lighting was used in theatres during the 19th century, but these were still a fire risk. Electric lights were first fitted in 1887 and today they are a crucial element to most plays.

• Whatever a theatre looks like, it always has to fulfil the same requirement: this is to provide a setting in which people have an opportunity to watch and hear actors performing live drama. Some people who work in and visit the theatre prefer a simple, direct way of staging things, while others like to see beautiful and expensive costumes and scenery.

find out more
Ballet
Drama
Dress and costume
Greeks, ancient
Operas and musicals
Shakespeare, William

▼ A cutaway of a modern theatre with a proscenium stage.

1 The **proscenium arch** provides a picture frame through which the audience can watch the actors' performance.
2 **Lights** are used to help create different atmospheres on stage, or to highlight particular actors.
3 The **curtain** is opened to reveal the scene at the beginning of the performance.
4 The **safety curtain** is a fireproof screen that can be lowered if a fire breaks out.
5 **Trapdoors** are useful if actors need to make a surprise entrance or exit.
6 **Scenery and props** help to make a performance more realistic.
7 The performers put their make-up on and get dressed in **dressing rooms** before going on stage.
8 The costumes are made and stored in the **wardrobe room** until they are needed.
9 The **wings** are where the performers wait just before they make their entrance onto the stage.
10 The lighting director operates the lights from the **lighting control room**.
11 Scenery and props to be used for different plays are stored.

Tides

Tides are the rise and fall of the sea at regular intervals. At high tide, the sea rises high up the beach. At low tide, it falls low down the beach. Tides happen because the Moon's gravity pulls on the Earth and its seas.

▶ The Sun, Moon and Earth line up twice each month. Because the pull of the Sun adds to the pull of the Moon, this makes the sea rise and fall more than at any other time. These very high tides are called spring tides (but they do not only happen in spring). In between, there are neap tides when the change in sea level is smallest.

• High tides send a tidal wave, called a bore, up some rivers. One of the world's highest bores occurs on the Qiantang in China.

find out more
Gravity
Moon
Power stations
Water

Most places have two high tides a day, which take place 50 minutes later each day. The shape of the coastline can affect the tides. In enclosed seas like the Mediterranean the tides are very slight. The highest tidal range in the world is at the Bay of Fundy in Canada. The sea level can rise more than 15 m between low and high tides.

How tides are caused

The seas nearest the Moon are pulled most strongly by its gravity, so they bulge slightly towards the Moon. The seas furthest from the Moon are pulled less than elsewhere, leaving another bulge. There are high tides at the two bulges and low tides in between. As the Earth spins, places move in and out of the bulges and their sea level rises and falls.

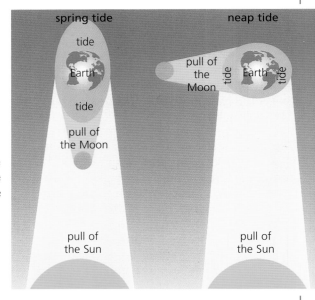

Tidal power

The use of tides as a source of energy to generate electricity is called tidal power. In a tidal-power scheme, a dam is built across the mouth of a river. As the tide comes in and goes out, water rushes in and out of tunnels in the dam. This flow of water turns huge turbines which drive generators.

Time

We see time passing in the natural world around us: the seasons and the weather change, plants grow, the stars shine at night and the Sun shines during the day. All over the world people need to keep to the same standard time and to measure it in the same way. International time is kept by atomic clocks in laboratories around the world.

• If we use a 12-hour clock, we have to add a.m. or p.m. to show whether a time is before or after the middle of the day. By using the 24-hour clock we can avoid confusion, so 1.00 p.m. is called 13.00 hours, 2.00 p.m. is 14.00, and so on.

• You will find a map of the international time zones on page 652.

find out more
Calendars
Clocks and watches
Einstein, Albert
Seasons

◀ In this view of the Earth taken from space, you can see the outline of California, on the west coast of the USA. The USA, which includes Alaska, spans a total of six time zones. When the time is 12 noon in New York on the east coast, for example, it is only 9 a.m. in Los Angeles, California.

The day is our most important period of time. Day begins when the Sun rises in the east, and night comes when the Sun sets in the west. Noon (midday) at a particular place occurs when the Sun reaches its highest point in the sky. As the Earth spins round, places across the world, from east to west, have noon one after the other. Places further east are already having their afternoon or evening while places further west still have not reached midday.

Measuring time

People used to measure time from when it was noon, but this meant that at every longitude in the world the time was different. In 1880, the whole of Britain adopted the average local time at Greenwich in London as its standard time. It was called Greenwich Mean Time (GMT). At an international conference in 1884, the world was divided up into 'time zones', each about 15 degrees of longitude wide. The standard time in each zone differs from the zones on either side by one hour. If you travel to another country, you usually have to alter your watch. The further you go, east or west, the bigger the time change.

Tools

We use tools around the home to prepare food, to work in the garden or to mend the car. A tool is any device which helps you do a job. In factories, much larger machine tools are used for cutting and shaping metals, plastics and other materials.

Hand tools use the force of your muscles. Power tools are driven by another energy source, such as electricity or compressed air. Specialized electric power tools include screwdrivers, hammer drills, chainsaws and hedge-trimmers. They are powered either from the mains or by rechargeable batteries. Extra parts can be attached to hand-held electric drills to convert them into jigsaws, circular saws, or sanders.

Machine tools are generally faster, more powerful and more accurate than hand-held tools. Many machine tools are now controlled by computers. Machine tools can make lots of identical parts one after another. Specific machine tools include lathes, grinders, shapers, planers, and drilling and milling machines.

For gripping
A high gripping force can be produced by lever action or by turning a screw thread.

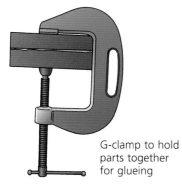

G-clamp to hold parts together for glueing

▲ A selection of commonly used hand tools and power tools.

For making holes
Hand drills have gearwheels to make the bit turn faster. Electric motors turn very fast anyway, so electric drills have gearwheels to slow the bit down.

electric drill for boring holes

bit

For shaping and smoothing
Some shaping and smoothing tools cut into the material with a sharp edge. Others have hundreds of tiny points to rub the material away.

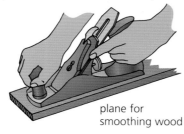

plane for smoothing wood

For hammering
A heavy metal head gives most force when hammering, but a wooden or plastic head is less likely to damage the material being struck.

claw hammer for driving in nails and pulling them out

For measuring and checking
Before materials are cut, drilled or fixed, it is important to check that all sizes and positions are correct.

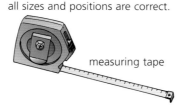

measuring tape

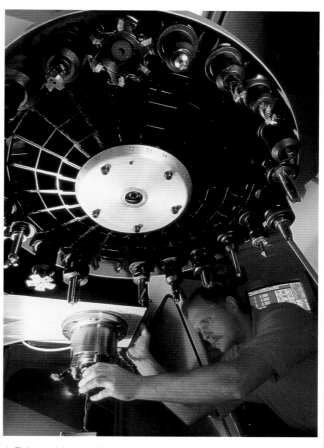

▲ This machine tool is controlled by computer. In the 1980s the computerized control of machine tools brought about a 'second revolution' in mass production.

For cutting
Some cutting tools have a sharp, smooth blade. Others have a jagged blade with small teeth along the edge.

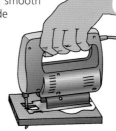

axe for chopping wood

electric jigsaw for cutting curves

For screwing and bolting
Nuts, bolts and screws have special tools to turn them. Tools like this must fit properly to give a firm grip, so they are made in a range of sizes.

straight-headed screwdriver for slotted screws

open-ended spanner

find out more
Machines
Prehistoric people
Robots
Wood

Tourism

Tourists are people who travel within a country or to another country for recreation. Tourists create many jobs in the places they visit, and tourism is now one of the most important industries in many countries.

find out more
Festivals and holidays
Industry
Pollution

About three-quarters of all tourists still come from the richest 20 countries, and most of them visit Europe and North America. However, a growing number of people are visiting other parts of the world, for example going on photographic safaris in Africa's game parks or back-packing through remote mountain ranges such as the Himalayas.

Although tourists help create employment, they can also bring problems to the places they visit. Many poorer countries have to spend a lot of money building roads, airports and other facilities for tourist resorts. This may mean that less money is available to spend on more essential services for the country's own inhabitants. Tourists can also cause damage and pollution to the areas they visit. The ancient monuments of Egypt and Greece attract many millions of visitors, but they are suffering damage from the traffic fumes the tourists bring with them.

◀ The beautiful Annapurna Valley is the most popular trekking destination in Nepal. But the booming tourist trade has brought problems as well as profit. In this picture rubbish left by campers pollutes the environment. Forests are being cleared for tourist lodges, and the deforestation leads to landslides and soil erosion. Local life is disrupted by the constant stream of foreign visitors.

Towers

Towers are buildings that are much higher than they are wide. They can stand alone or form part of a building.

• One of the most famous towers in the world is the Leaning Tower of Pisa, in Italy. It leans because its foundations, laid in 1174, are not secure and are 'settling' unevenly. Despite recent attempts to strengthen the foundations, the structure is still in danger of collapse.

Greater understanding of how structures work has been the key to constructing taller and taller towers. Some medieval builders built church towers that collapsed. The tallest medieval church tower still standing belongs to Lincoln Cathedral in England. It is 160 metres tall.

Buildings of over 10 storeys were made possible by the invention of lifts in the late 19th century.

Now, skyscrapers can be built that have over 100 storeys.

Some of the world's highest towers are radio and TV masts. The tallest free-standing tower is the CN Tower in Toronto, Canada, at 553 metres. The tallest building in the world is the Petronas Twin Towers, in Kuala Lumpur, Malaysia. It stands 452 metres high.

find out more
Architecture
Building
Seven Wonders of the World

Pharos of Alexandria, Egypt about 280 BC

Eiffel Tower, France 1889

Petronas Twin Towers, Malaysia 1996

height in metres

500

400

300

200

100

0

Great Pyramid of Khufu, Egypt about 2580 BC

Lincoln Cathedral, England 1307

Empire State Building, New York 1931

CN Tower, Canada 1976

Toys

Toys are playthings that have been used throughout the centuries by children for learning as well as for fun and entertainment.

Toys come in all shapes and sizes, and do not have to cost a lot of money or come ready made from a shop. Even something as simple as a stick or a round stone can be used by children as a toy. Many toys, games and sports have developed from such everyday items.

▲ Even very young children can enjoy working with today's computerized toys. This 3-year-old girl is concentrating hard on a game on her small computer.

From dolls to microchips

Some of the best-loved toys are dolls and teddy bears, which are really just miniature versions of humans and animals. Such toys encourage imaginative play and allow children to act out aspects of their own daily lives. Teddy bears have only been around since the beginning of the 20th century, but dolls have been played with since ancient times.

Dolls' heads used to be made of wood or clay, although in the middle of the 18th century porcelain and ceramic were used. The bodies were made of wood, or else of cloth or leather filled with sawdust. Today's dolls are usually made from moulded plastic and vinyl. They often have moving limbs, and modern technology has produced dolls which can move on their own and say simple sentences. Some of the best-selling dolls, such as Sindy, Barbie and Action Man, have many clothes and accessories for children to collect. Very often a successful film or television programme will lead to dolls being made of the main characters.

Some toys help children to learn skills that they will use in later life. Puzzles and board games sharpen children's minds and teach them to think quickly. Construction kits, such as Lego and Meccano, give children the chance to use their hands to build models of vehicles and buildings.

Many of today's toys and games use the same sort of microelectronic technology that has been developed by the computer industry. Computer games, with their increasingly brilliant colours and graphics, are particularly popular.

► FLASHBACK ◄

Archaeological evidence suggests that children in all cultures throughout history have played with toys, particularly miniature versions of real beings and objects, such as dolls and dolls' houses.

In the early days of toy-making, most toys were simply carved from wood. However, toy-making has always kept up with advances in technology and scientific knowledge. As clock- and watchmakers developed their craft, so clockwork technology was introduced into toys. Mechanical toys were developed as early as the 18th century, although it was many years before they were mass-produced so that many children could buy them. Then, in the 20th century, batteries and electricity made a huge impact on the range of toys that were produced.

▲ This beautifully dressed doll has a head made of china. Even though she was made about 100 years ago, she has many clever features, including movable legs and a voice box.

● Barbie dolls are the biggest-selling toy in the world today.

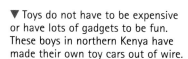

▼ Toys do not have to be expensive or have lots of gadgets to be fun. These boys in northern Kenya have made their own toy cars out of wire.

find out more
Children
Indoor games and sports

Trade

Have you ever swapped something of yours for something else your friend had? If so, you were trading. Trade takes place when people or countries exchange things. When things are swapped directly for other things, we call it barter. Today, most trade involves money.

▲ The New York Stock Exchange on Wall Street is one of the largest and oldest in the world. Stock markets are world markets where shares in companies or commodities (such as oil) can be bought and sold.

The last time you bought a bar of chocolate, yours was just the last in a whole series of trades. Before it was sold to you, the chocolate was probably bought from a bulk supplier (*wholesaler*) by the shopkeeper (*retailer*). In turn, the wholesaler bought it from the manufacturer, who also paid for the people and machines to make the chocolate. Before that, the ingredients had to be bought by the manufacturer and transported to the chocolate factory, probably from another part of the world.

International trade

Goods and services that are sold to foreign customers are known as *exports*, while goods and services bought from another country are *imports*. The trade in exports and imports is called international trade, and it is very important to all countries in the world.

Without international trade, consumers would only be able to buy a limited variety of goods. For example, people in Scandinavia would not be able to enjoy tropical fruits or rice because the climate in Scandinavia is unsuitable for growing such foodstuffs. There are also countries, such as Japan, which have very few energy sources of their own. It is vital for these countries to sell exports so that they can earn the money to buy the coal and oil they need. That is one of the reasons why so many Japanese goods are available in other countries.

Free trade and protection

When all countries specialize in producing the goods and services they are most efficient at producing, they are able to increase the output of goods and services throughout the world. And if there are more goods and services being produced, then the users of these things (*consumers*) will enjoy a higher standard of living. This is the main argument in favour of 'free trade', a situation where no country tries to prevent imports from another country.

Countries sometimes fear that imports of cheaper goods will mean that people making similar goods in the home country will lose their jobs. In the past, this has often led to countries trying to keep imports out. They have used *tariffs*, which are special taxes on imported goods. Tariffs make the imports more expensive, which stops consumers buying them. *Quotas* are also sometimes used. A quota is a limit on the quantity of imports of a particular item that a country will allow. The use of tariffs and quotas is known as *protectionism*, because the import controls are designed to protect the home industries from foreign competition.

find out more
Advertising
Economics
European Union
Money
Shops

• In 1948 trading countries set up the General Agreement on Tariffs and Trade (GATT). At GATT meetings trading nations agreed to make trade as free as possible by reducing tariffs and quotas. GATT has been replaced, since the beginning of 1995, by a new, permanent organization called the World Trade Organization, which has headquarters in Geneva, Switzerland.

▼ This woman in Sousse, Tunisia, is buying food supplies at a market stall. The produce she is buying was produced and sold, and will probably be consumed, locally. Millions of such small-scale transactions take place every day all over the world.

Trees and shrubs

Trees and shrubs are woody-stemmed plants. Trees usually have a single strong, woody trunk, supporting a mass of branches. By contrast shrubs often have a number of stems, giving them a bushy appearance.

Trees are the largest land plants. By growing tall, they can reach above other plants to the sunlight they need for growth. Their height also helps protect their leaves from ground-living browsers (animals that eat leaves and grass).

Shrubs or trees?

There is no real difference between shrubs and trees. The term 'shrub' is generally used for plants under 7.5 metres tall; anything taller is called a tree. Some species, such as hawthorn and hazel, can stay at shrub size if they are cut regularly or browsed by animals, but if they are left to grow they will eventually reach tree height. High in the mountains or on exposed coasts, even pine or oak trees will grow in a low, shrubby form.

Conifers and broadleaves

Trees and shrubs belong to two main groups of plants. Conifer trees, which have cones and needle-like leaves, belong to a division of the plant kingdom called the cone-bearing plants or gymnosperms. There are about 500 species, including the world's tallest trees (coastal redwoods) and the most massive ones (giant sequoias). Conifers are only distantly related to trees belonging to the flowering plants or angiosperms. These generally have wide, flat leaf-blades, and so are called broadleaves. Common broadleaf species include temperate trees such as the oak, ash, sycamore and holly, and tropical trees such as the many species of palm.

Trees that shed all their leaves for part of the year (generally the winter, but it can be the dry season in hot countries) are said to be *deciduous*. Shedding leaves helps protect the tree from frost damage or from drought. Other trees are *evergreen*, keeping some leaves on their branches throughout the year. Most deciduous trees are broadleaves, but a few conifers, such as larches, shed their leaves in winter.

Structure

Trees and shrubs have essentially the same structure, the main difference being the size of

the stem or trunk. The wood that makes up the stem, branches and parts of the roots is made from a mass of tube-shaped cells that transport water and food up and down the stem. Some of these tubes become thickened with a material called *lignin*. It is lignin that gives wood strength.

Roots

Usually there is as much mass of tree beneath the soil as above ground. Roots spread through the soil like underground branches. They have two basic functions. One is to form an anchor to stop the tree being blown over. The other is to absorb water and minerals from the soil. Most trees have a fungus partner that lives in their roots and helps them take the goodness from the soil.

Stem

Most of the stem of a tree or shrub is made of dead wood, which supports the plant even in strong winds. However, immediately beneath the bark is a zone of living cells, called the *sapwood*. A band of tubular cells in this zone transports water and mineral salts up and down the height of the tree.

The tubes are of two types. *Xylem* tubes carry water and minerals up the tree from its roots. The old, dead xylem tubes form the *heartwood* supporting the tree. Sap, carrying sugars made in the leaves, is transported down the tree in another set of tubes called the *phloem*. The sugars provide energy where the tree needs it, or can be stored as starch in the trunk or roots. Each spring, the tree produces new sapwood to carry sap to the opening buds. ◗

▲ Broadleaved trees like oak, beech and ash are quite slow-growing. They may take 150 years to reach their maximum height.

▼ Most conifers keep their leaves all year. A conifer's Christmas-tree shape helps it to shed snow, and its tough leaves can survive cold and ice.

Bark is the rough, grooved layer of dead, corky wood which covers the surface of trees and shrubs, protecting the living wood beneath. New bark is produced by a ring of living cells called the *bark cambium*. Older bark dies as it is pushed outwards by the expanding trunk.

Leaves

Leaves are tiny chemical factories, which make food for the tree in a process called *photosynthesis*. They take in carbon dioxide from the air and water from the soil, then combine them to make sugar. Light energy from the Sun powers this process, so the leaves are arranged to receive as much light as possible.

Leaves continuously leak water into the air by a process called *transpiration*. This sets up a suction, which draws water up from the roots through the xylem tubes, like sucking water up through a straw. Because no energy is involved, xylem can go on carrying water after the cells have died.

Fruits and flowers

Trees and shrubs reproduce (multiply and spread) by seeds. Conifers contain their seeds in a cone. When ripe, the seeds are shaken out and spread by the wind.

Like other flowering plants, broadleaves produce flowers. These may be colourful blossoms, or wind-pollinated flowers such as catkins. Some trees and shrubs, for example oak and hazel, produce separate male and female flowers. After flowering, the trees produce fruits, which contain the seeds. The fruits can be berries, nuts or dry, papery fruits which are spread by the wind.

Some shrubs or trees also spread using creeping underground stems which give off new trunks at regular intervals. All the elm trees in a hedgerow, for example, may have spread from a single tree.

The value of shrubs and trees

Trees and shrubs are valued by humans for their wood, and their fruits and leaves provide food for people and for many animals. When growing as forests, trees form an entire ecosystem, providing food high above the ground and creating a damp, shady woodland floor where other plants and animals can live.

People grow shrubs and trees in a tight mass to produce hedges. These act as a living green fence to control farm animals. Hawthorn is the commonest hedging shrub in Europe, sometimes with blackthorn or holly. Because they are expensive to look after and because farmers want larger fields, hedges are rapidly disappearing. More than a tenth of all English hedges was lost in the 1980s.

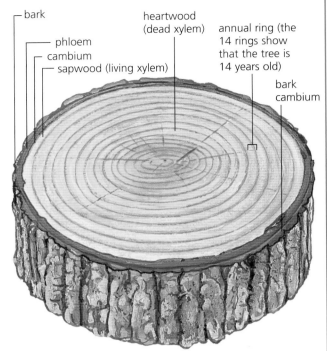

bark
phloem
cambium
sapwood (living xylem)
heartwood (dead xylem)
annual ring (the 14 rings show that the tree is 14 years old)
bark cambium

▲ Cross-section through a tree trunk. A ring of living cells outside the sapwood called the *vascular cambium* produces new xylem towards the inside of the trunk and new phloem on the outside. The xylem and phloem tubes grow to different sizes at different times of the year. This shows up as a series of rings through the wood. By counting these 'annual rings', it is possible to tell the age of a tree.

Cork

The light, waterproof layer of tree bark is made of cork. The cork we use to make bottle stoppers and tiles comes from the cork oak tree, which grows in the Mediterranean region. It has a thick, soft bark, made mostly of cork.

find out more
Flowering plants
Forests
Fruit
Plants
Wood

▼ A hedgerow in Clwyd, North Wales. Hedgerows are very important for wildlife. A good hedgerow is an excellent habitat for wild flowers, insects, birds and small mammals. The older a hedge, the more different types of shrub or tree it will contain.

Tudor England

The Tudors were a royal family who ruled England from 1485 to 1603. The first Tudor monarch was Henry VII, and the Tudor family dynasty which began with him ended with the death of Elizabeth I.

The first Tudor king, Henry VII, won his crown by defeating the unpopular Richard III at the battle of Bosworth in 1485. His victory ended the 'Wars of the Roses', a struggle for the throne between the families of York (one of whose badges was a white rose) and Lancaster (often represented by a red rose). In the unsettled 30 years of war before 1485 there had been five different kings.

Tudor rule

Henry VII was descended from the Lancastrians. Henry faced plots and rebellions, and his first son and heir died young. Fortunately, by the time Henry

▶ The Spanish Armada and the English fleet doing battle in 1588. Catholic King Philip II of Spain sent his ships to crush the Protestant English. The Armada failed and there was no Spanish invasion. But Philip rebuilt his fleet, and the war dragged on until 1604.

died in 1509, a second son, Henry, was old enough to inherit the throne.

Henry VIII became intent on producing a son and heir to the Tudor line. He went through three marriages and a major quarrel with the Pope before his son Edward was born, 27 years after he became king. Edward VI was only 9 when his father died in 1546, and was too young to rule by himself.

When Edward died in 1553, his only heirs were his two sisters, Mary and Elizabeth. Mary I married Philip of Spain, but she died, childless, five years later. When Elizabeth I became queen in 1558, she proved that a woman could be a successful ruler. She never married and so was the last Tudor monarch.

Ambitions beyond England

The Tudors ruled England reasonably successfully. They also tried to control more of the British Isles. Their family came from

◀ The Protestant Thomas Cranmer was Archbishop of Canterbury during Henry VIII's reign. When the Catholic Mary I became queen, she arrested him for heresy (not accepting the official Catholic teaching) and he was burnt at the stake for his beliefs.

Wales, and under their rule Welsh landowners had a better chance of doing well in England. In 1536 the Act of Union gave Wales the same local government as England, and made English the official language there, which made life difficult for ordinary Welsh-speaking people.

Henry VIII made himself King of Ireland in 1541 (until then English kings had been only 'Lords of Ireland'). Mary I and Elizabeth I tried to strengthen English control by giving Irish land to English settlers. This resulted in six serious rebellions in Ireland during Elizabeth's reign.

Scotland was an independent kingdom ruled by Stuart kings. The Scots had long defended themselves against English attempts to conquer them. Henry VII tried to make peace by marrying his daughter Margaret to the Scots king, James IV, in 1503. But this failed to bring peace, and Henry VIII tried unsuccessfully to conquer Scotland. However, when Elizabeth I died, Margaret Tudor's great-grandson James VI became James I, the first Stuart king of England. ▶

Richard III was the last English king of the Middle Ages.
1485 **Henry VII**
1509 **Henry VIII**
1534 Henry VIII Supreme Head of the Church of England
1536–1550 Monasteries destroyed
1538 English Bible printed
1542–1550 Wars with Scotland
1547 **Edward VI**
1553 **Mary I** Catholic Church restored
1558 **Elizabeth I** Church of England established
1568 Mary, Queen of Scots, imprisoned
1577–1580 Drake's voyage round the world
1587 Mary, Queen of Scots, executed
1588 Armada defeated
1596–1603 Rebellion in Ireland
1601 Poor Law
1603 Death of Elizabeth I
The next king was James I (Stuart). There is an article on Stuart Britain.

▲ Moor Field (now Finsbury Circus), London, 1553–1559. People can be seen drying washing, practising archery and setting up 'tenter' frames for stretching cloth.

Tudor life

In Tudor times most people still lived in villages and the local landowners were the most powerful people. The rich could afford to buy luxuries such as silks, spices, cotton, furs and carpets, which were brought to England from abroad. But for ordinary people life was much the same as it had been for centuries. Diseases were often killers; about one baby in five died before its first birthday. Poverty was a great problem. There were harsh punishments for beggars, and thieves were executed. Only at the end of the Tudor period, in 1601, did the new Poor Laws bring some relief to the poor.

Although some villages had schools, most poor children worked with their families in the fields. Wealthy boys often went to grammar schools in towns, but most girls just learned to read and prepared for marriage by helping their mothers at home.

A time of change

In Tudor times food prices increased because there were more people to feed. There was more unemployment because there were not enough jobs for everyone.

Printed books were becoming cheaper and more widely available, so information began to spread more quickly and there were probably more people who could read. The English Bible became a best-seller. Printed pictures began to appear too.

The Church changed as the Reformation spread to Europe. The Reformation was a movement to reform the Roman Catholic Church which led to the establishment of Protestant churches. After a dispute with the Pope, Henry VIII made himself Supreme Head of the Church in England and destroyed all the monasteries and sold all their lands. Mary I brought back the old Catholic faith and persecuted Protestants. Elizabeth's Church of England aimed to be a 'middle way'. However, Mary, Queen of Scots' ambitions to retake the English throne and Catholic King Philip II of Spain's attempt to invade England resulted in harsh laws against Catholics, who became very unpopular once more.

In Tudor times sailors and explorers travelled new sea routes to discover foreign lands. They brought back new goods such as tobacco and potatoes to England. Some explorers went to make a new life in North America and this was the beginning of England's colonies abroad.

▼ Mary, Queen of Scots, who, after 19 years of imprisonment, was found guilty of being involved in a Catholic plot to kill her Protestant cousin, Queen Elizabeth I, and take her throne. On Elizabeth's orders Mary was beheaded in 1587.

Tundra

find out more
Arctic

Tundra is the name given to Arctic areas that are free from snow and ice for only a few months of the year. The word tundra means 'treeless', which describes the area rather well.

◄ The tundra in summer, Alaska, USA. Although the summer is short, the Sun shines for 24 hours a day. The lush green vegetation provides plentiful food for the caribou (reindeer) that travel north each summer to breed.

Tundra forms a broad belt running through the far north of Europe, Asia and America, just south of the Arctic ice sheet. Tundra also occurs on the edge of Antarctica, and in high mountains beneath the height at which snow lies all year round.

Animals and plants

Lichens, mosses, grasses and sedges are the main plants of the tundra. But there are also a few flowering plants and small shrubs that can withstand the winter cold and flower in the short summer. Animals that live in the tundra all year include voles, shrews and lemmings. In winter they tunnel beneath the snow and dig up plant roots for food. Arctic foxes also stay all year, but polar bears wander more widely, hunting seals and walruses on the ice sheets. Musk oxen are pony-sized animals found in Canada and Greenland. They have long woolly coats and massive horns. They protect themselves from wolves by bunching themselves together in a circle, horns outwards.

When summer arrives, animals from further south come to the tundra to benefit from the rich feeding that is briefly available. Huge herds of reindeer (caribou) wander north, followed by packs of hungry wolves. And birds such as willow grouse, geese, swans, plovers and other shorebirds fly north to breed.

Tunnels

● The longest tunnel in the world is in the USA. It carries water 169 km from a reservoir to New York City, and was completed in 1944.

find out more
Canals
Explosives
Mining
Railways
Roads

► The Channel Tunnel consists of two main train tunnels, with a third service tunnel between them. Cross-tunnels link the main tunnels to each other and to the service tunnel.

Tunnels are underground passages that are built for different purposes. Tunnels in cities carry road and rail traffic beneath the streets and buildings. In the countryside, road and rail vehicles use tunnels to pass under rivers or through hills and mountains. Deep below the waters of the English Channel, the Channel Tunnel links Britain with the rest of Europe.

In cities, people use subways (short tunnels) to cross under busy roads. Tunnels also bring water supplies to the city and take away waste water or sewage. Narrow tunnels may contain telephone and other cables. Underground mines consist of tunnels dug into deposits of coal or minerals. Mines are by far the deepest tunnels of all.

Building a tunnel

Tunnels that are to lie just below the surface may be built by the cut-and-cover method. A large long ditch is dug, and then covered over to form a tunnel.

Most tunnels have to go deeper and are dug down into the ground. Cutting machines are used to gouge out soft rock or soil, or the rock is blown out with explosives. Supports or a lining made of steel or concrete prevent the tunnel collapsing. A tunnelling machine is often used to build a tunnel. Powerful motors push the machine forwards, and its cutting teeth or tools excavate the rock or soil.

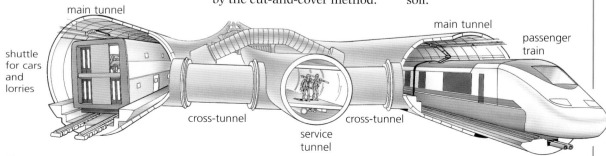

main tunnel

shuttle for cars and lorries

cross-tunnel

service tunnel

cross-tunnel

main tunnel

passenger train

Turkey

Turkey is a country at the eastern end of the Mediterranean, straddling two continents. A small part, Thrace, is in Europe. A much larger part, Anatolia, is in Asia. Dividing the two parts is a narrow strait: the Bosporus.

► Istanbul is a lively city with a busy port. On Istanbul's skyline you can see many towers and minarets of mosques such as the Hagia Sofia and the Blue Mosque.

find out more
Byzantine empire
Greeks, ancient
Kurds
Muslims
Ottoman empire
Romans
See also Countries fact file, page 642

Anatolia has a central plateau (a fairly level area of high ground) surrounded by mountains. The central area is largely agricultural, growing cereals and crops such as tobacco and cotton. Around the coast, the climate is milder in winter, and fruits and nuts can be grown. There is also extensive sheep farming. Tourism is an important industry for the country.

Turkey does not have a Muslim government, but most of its people are Muslims. Nearly 90 per cent of them are Turkish, but Arabs and Kurds live in Turkey as well.

Turkey's biggest city is Istanbul. It bridges the Bosporus, and is the only city in the world to be built in two continents. The city was called Byzantium by the Greeks, who founded the city in the

8th century BC. Later its name was changed to Constantinople. It was the capital of the late Roman empire and of the Byzantine empire.

► FLASHBACK ◄

From the 15th century, Turkey was ruled by the Ottomans, a Turkish tribe. By the 16th century the Ottoman empire included a large part of Europe and the Middle East and most of North Africa. The capital was Istanbul. The Ottoman empire slowly declined over the next 400 years and finally came to an end after World War I. Then, in 1923, General Mustafa Kemal (later called Atatürk) founded the modern republic, becoming its first president. He changed the alphabet to a Latin script and made Turkey a more westernized country.

Turtles and tortoises

Turtles and their relatives the tortoises and terrapins are among the most ancient of reptiles. They have survived since the days of the dinosaurs and have changed very little since then.

• Turtles live in the sea, tortoises live on land, and terrapins live in fresh water. There are about 240 different kinds altogether.

• Large land tortoises live for a very long time – some may live for over 200 years.

▼ The red-eared terrapin has red stripes on its shell and legs, and behind its eyes.

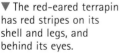

find out more
Reptiles

Turtles, tortoises and terrapins are easily recognized because of their armour-like shell. The shell encases and protects their body, and only their head, tail and legs show on the outside. Land tortoises can pull all of themselves into their shell. The shell is made of bone protected on the outside with horn. It is in two main pieces, one part covering the back, the other protecting the underside.

Tortoises, turtles and terrapins do not have any teeth. Instead they have sharp-edged, horny jaws with which they cut and tear their food. Tortoises are mainly plant-eaters, while terrapins feed chiefly on the flesh of various small creatures. Sea turtles eat sea grasses, seaweed and some animals.

After mating, females dig a hole in sand or soil with their hind legs, and then lay their eggs. Some kinds lay very few eggs while others lay up to 200 in a single clutch. Once the eggs are laid, the female covers the nest and leaves it. The young

◄ Hawksbill turtles are quite rare today because their shells have been used for making and decorating things. Use of 'tortoise-shell' is now illegal in many countries.

usually take several months to hatch out of their shells. They then have to fend for themselves.

▼ Hermann's tortoises are protected today because so many have been taken as part of the pet trade.

Turkmenistan *see page 642*

Twentieth-century history

The world changed at breathtaking speed in the 20th century. We invented flying machines, conquered many diseases, travelled into space, and sent words and pictures around the Earth in seconds.

In 1900 most people lived in villages. Important cities were much smaller than they are today. Over the century people moved into the rapidly expanding towns and cities. While for some town life was convenient and pleasant, for the poor living in city slums it could be grim and violent. By the 1990s some 30 million children lived on the streets.

Technology and religion

At the beginning of the century few houses had toilets, running water or electricity. Although millions still live like this, in the richer countries – Europe, North and South America, and East Asia – life was transformed by central heating, air-conditioning and a host of household gadgets, from washing machines to personal computers.

In some societies, particularly in Europe and communist China, the number of people regularly going to a place of worship greatly declined. However, in the Americas and the Muslim world religion was as important as ever. The last quarter of the century saw an alarming increase in conflicts between different religious groups.

Women's and children's rights

In 1900 most of the world's population could not read or write. Even in the West, most children had only a few years' early education. By the end of the century, the great majority of children went to school and many went on to college. As life became more complicated, people needed education to get jobs.

In 1900 women were largely seen as second-class citizens, without education or paid work. By the end of the century most governments agreed that men and women should be treated equally and given the same opportunities.

Communications

The arrival of cheap, mass-produced cars changed the way people lived and altered the shape of cities and the countryside. Air travel, telephones,

▲ A city street in Tokyo, Japan, in 1905 and in 1996. Modern forms of transport have speeded things up since 1905, but car exhaust fumes have filled the air with poisonous pollution.

radio, television and satellite communications also brought people closer together. Athletes met for international sporting events, such as the Olympic Games. In 1945 the United Nations was set up to help settle disagreements peacefully and tackle such problems as poverty and racism. Multinational companies began operating in dozens of different countries.

Conflict

Sadly, better communications did not bring less conflict. In two terrible world wars (1914–1918 and 1939–1945) cities were destroyed and millions were killed. World War II left the world dominated by the two 'superpowers' – the

• The 20th century was powered by the fossil fuels coal and oil. This made countries with large oil reserves, such as Saudi Arabia, rich and powerful.

• During the 20th century the world's population grew from around 1.5 billion to about 6 billion. The population explosion meant that more food had to be grown and distributed where it was most needed. It also led to serious environmental problems, such as forest clearance and pollution.

capitalist USA and the communist USSR. Their rivalry led to a period of dangerous tension known as the Cold War.

The Cold War cast a shadow over the second half of the century. Billions of pounds were spent on arms. Concrete and barbed-wire barriers divided eastern and western Europe. The struggle between capitalists and communists spread around the globe.

Nuclear weapons made another world war almost unthinkable. But there were many smaller conflicts, such as the Korean War (1950–1953), the Vietnam War (1963–1975) and the Afghan War (1979–1989). The Middle East saw a series of wars between Israel and its Arab neighbours (1948–1973) and a long, bitter war between Iran and Iraq (1980–1988).

The Cold War ended when the USSR collapsed in 1989. By this time relations between democratic nations and communist China had improved. Although a major war now seemed unlikely, bloody civil wars were fought in Yugoslavia, Somalia, Rwanda and the Russian province of Chechnya.

find out more
Aircraft
Britain since 1900
Communists
Dictators
Farming
Industry
Information technology
Motor cars
Peace movement
Pollution
Population
Refugees
Religions
Settlements
United Nations
Women's movement
World War I
World War II

Empires and nations

At the beginning of the century Britain and other European countries had empires stretching across the world. Europeans ruled most of Africa, the Caribbean, Oceania and huge areas of Asia. Before 1914 much of the Middle East was part of the Ottoman empire. Gradually these empires fell apart as the power of the European states grew less, and dozens of new nations won back their independence. Over the years many more independent states were created, sometimes after periods of conflict.

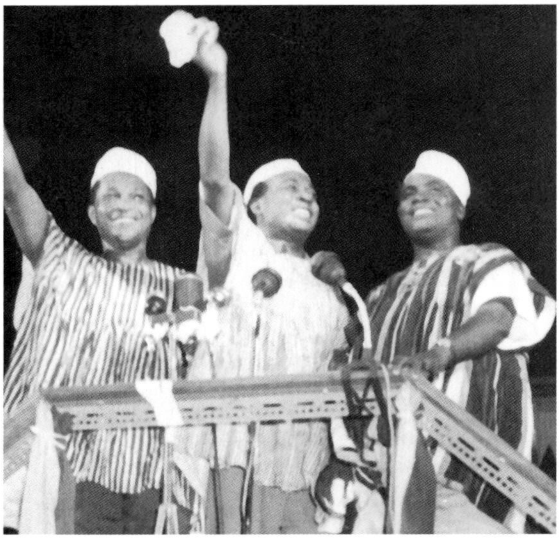

▶ In 1957 Ghana was the first black African state to gain independence, under its first president Kwame Nkrumah (centre).

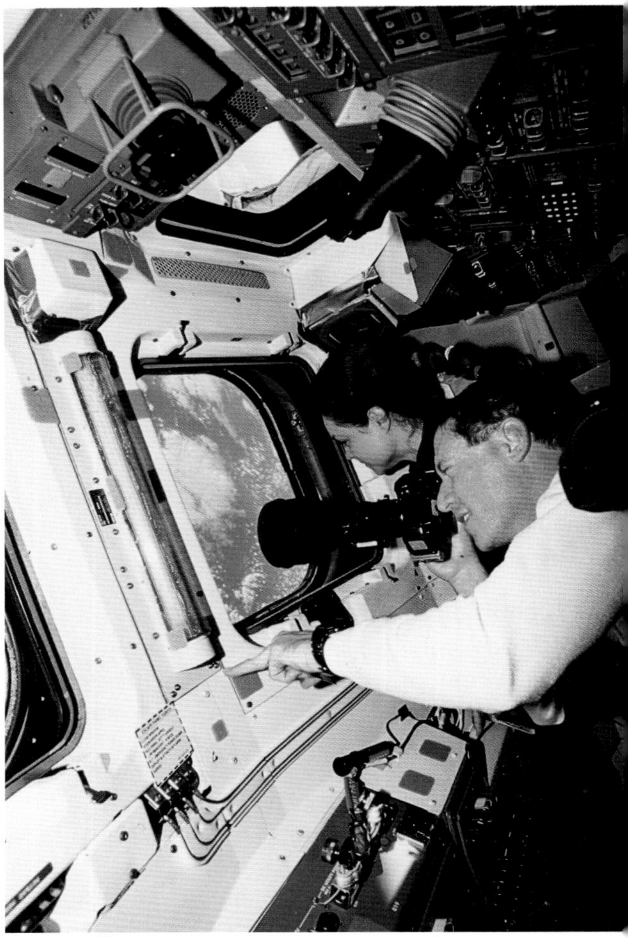

▲ At the beginning of the 20th century space exploration would have seemed fantastic and impossible. Today, orbiting astronauts can study the Earth below because of the huge technological advances science has made since then.

Mass killings of one group of people by another (genocide) haunted the 20th century. The Nazi destruction of some 6 million Jews was the worst example. But the massacres in Cambodia (1975–1979) and Rwanda (1994) were equally horrifying. By the end of the century most governments had laws to stop racism. The greatest anti-racist triumph was the fall of the all-white regime in South Africa in 1993–1994.

Unsolved problems

The 20th century was marked by the tragedies and triumphs of science. Huge technological advances were made, but many other difficulties remained. The gap between rich and poor was as wide as ever. Pollution threatened to poison the planet. People still turned to war to settle their differences. Learning to work together to solve these problems is the challenge of the future.

Type *see* Printing • **Typewriter** *see* Word processors

UFOs

A UFO is an Unidentified Flying Object. Since World War II, there have been thousands of sightings of strange lights and shapes in the sky. People often believe that these are spacecraft from outer space. However, many UFO sightings have been shown to have other explainable causes.

People have reported seeing strange objects in the sky for hundreds of years. But since the end of World War II, the number of sightings has been much greater.

In the 1950s and 1960s there were many thousands of UFO sightings, particularly in the USA. The US Air Force recorded over 12,000 UFO reports between 1948 and 1969. Since 1969 no official records have been kept, but UFO sightings continue in countries around the world.

There have been several scientific studies of UFO reports. One of the most important was published in 1969 by the US Air Force. The scientists were able to find natural explanations for many of the UFO sightings. Unusual cloud formations can look very like 'flying saucers'.

Other sightings were found to be meteors, rockets, artificial satellites, or reflections from cloud layers high in the sky.

Not all sightings could be explained in this way, but most scientists became convinced that UFOs are not from outer space. However, large numbers of people still believe in UFOs, and many books, films and TV programmes have been made about the subject.

• In 1947, a pilot over Washington DC in the USA reported seeing circular objects, like saucers, flying through the sky. As a result, 'flying saucer' became another name for a UFO.

◀ The white, cigar-shaped object in this photograph is a UFO.

find out more
Drama
Satellites
Space exploration

Ukraine

Ukraine is the second largest country in Europe. It is a country of vast treeless plains to the north of the Black Sea, and is dominated by the lowlands of the Dnieper and Donets rivers.

To the south-west are the foothills of the Carpathian Mountains and in the south are low plains. The Crimea, on the Black Sea, has a hot, dry climate which makes it very popular with tourists from eastern Europe and Russia. Many Ukrainians work on farms, which cover the fertile soils of the countryside. Wheat, barley, rye, maize, sugar beet and sunflower seeds are all major crops. The eastern part of the country has some large industrial cities, including Donetsk, Kharkov and Krivoy Rog. Beneath the basin of the River Donets is an important coalfield.

▶ FLASHBACK ◀

Kiev, the capital of Ukraine, is one of the oldest cities in eastern Europe. It was a trading centre as early as the 6th century AD, and it was part of a state called Kiev Rus in the 10th century. The Tartars conquered Kiev in the 13th century. Ukraine was later conquered by Poland, and then by the Russian empire. Under Soviet rule in the 1930s, more than 6 million Ukrainians suffered a terrible famine caused by the Soviet dictator Joseph Stalin.

During World War II Ukraine suffered heavily from the invading Germans. In 1991 it declared independence from the Soviet Union; this was confirmed the same year by a referendum of the people.

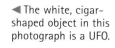

find out more
Europe
Power stations
Russia
See also Countries fact file, page 643

▶ Kiev, the capital of Ukraine, is built on the banks of the River Dnieper.

United Kingdom

The United Kingdom is a country in north-west Europe. It is often called simply the UK, but its full name is the United Kingdom of Great Britain and Northern Ireland.

The UK is made up of England, Scotland, Wales and Northern Ireland. The Channel Islands and the Isle of Man are also part of the UK, but they have their own laws and taxes.

Government

The king or queen is the formal head of state but entrusts the running of the country to the government and its ministers. The government is formed by the political party that has the

▼ The Channel Islands. Four main islands make up the Channel Islands, which are in the English Channel: Jersey (below), Guernsey, Alderney and Sark. Many Channel Islanders speak both English and French. A Norman-French dialect is also spoken, and many of the place names are French. The islands have a mild climate and are very popular with tourists.

most supporters in the House of Commons in London (Parliament). Members of Parliament, called MPs for short, are elected from areas, or 'constituencies', all over the UK. They make the UK's laws, but each law also has to be approved by another body, the House of Lords. The House of Lords is also in London, and its members are not elected.

In 1997 the people of both Scotland and Wales voted in favour of 'devolution'. This means that the central government in London now shares some of its powers with a new Scottish parliament in Edinburgh and a new Welsh assembly in Cardiff.

The UK joined the European Community, now known as the European Union, in 1973. It sends 87 elected representatives to sit in the European Parliament and recognizes certain types of laws passed there.

► FLASHBACK ◄

The British Isles were invaded by Celts, Romans, Saxons, Vikings and Normans. Each group of settlers brought their own language and culture.

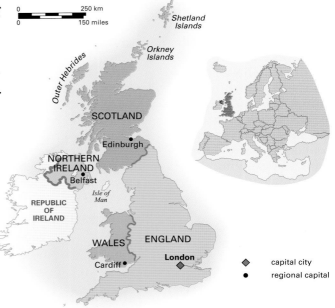

Wales resisted Norman rule but was eventually conquered and united with England in 1282. In 1603 James VI of Scotland became James I of England. England and Scotland have had a common parliament since 1707. In 1801 Ireland was united with the rest of the British Isles to form the United Kingdom of Great Britain and Ireland. After World War I, southern Ireland broke away to form a separate country, the Republic of Ireland.

• The British Isles became separated from the European mainland about 12,000 years ago, when the sea level rose after the last ice age. Many mainland plants and animals were prevented by the rising sea from reaching the British Isles.

▲ The national flag of the United Kingdom is the Union Flag ('Union Jack'). It was formed by combining the crosses of the patron saints of England (St George), Scotland (St Andrew) and Ireland (St Patrick). The flag was devised in 1801, when no separate recognition was given to the dragon of Wales.

find out more
England
Europe
Northern Ireland
Scotland
Wales
See also Countries fact file, page 643

United Nations

The United Nations (UN) is an international organization whose purpose is to maintain peace and security all over the world.

• An organization similar to the UN, called the League of Nations, was founded in 1919 after World War I. It was unable to keep the peace, partly because the USA decided not to join. Also, no action was taken against Japan, Italy and Germany when they invaded other countries in the 1930s, which led to World War II.

Some UN specialized agencies

FAO Food and Agriculture Organization
IMF International Monetary Fund
ITU International Telecommunication Union
UNESCO UN Educational, Scientific and Cultural Organization
UNHCR UN High Commission for Refugees
UNICEF UN International Children's Emergency Fund
World Bank
WHO World Health Organization

find out more
Balkans
Children
Korea
Refugees
Twentieth-century history

The United Nations tries to help countries settle disagreements by getting them to talk to each other. It also provides a place where the representatives of countries can discuss all sorts of problems. Nearly all the countries of the world are now members of the UN. There are now 191 member countries. The only major country that is not a member of the UN is Taiwan.

The General Assembly

Every member country of the UN has a seat in the *General Assembly*. Representatives discuss problems such as disarmament, environmental pollution and world poverty, and occasionally pass resolutions. At the heart of the UN is the *Security Council*. This is a body of selected member countries which takes decisions on behalf of all the members when there is a crisis. The *Secretary-General* of the UN

carries out decisions of the Security Council and works on the plans of the General Assembly. He also takes part in UN peace-keeping work.

Keeping the peace

Since 1945 the UN Security Council has tried to deal with many conflicts. Sometimes it sends a military force, made up of troops from different countries, to keep the peace between warring groups. UN forces have served in Korea, Cyprus, Lebanon, Cambodia and the countries of the former Yugoslavia. While the troops keep the warring groups apart, the Secretary-General and UN staff try to get the groups' representatives round a table

▲ The United Nations was founded in 1945 at the end of World War II. The idea arose among the allied nations who fought against Nazi Germany and Japan. At a conference in San Francisco, USA, they drew up a document called the Charter of the United Nations. The UN Charter has become its rule book.

to discuss solutions to their problems. Unfortunately, these peace-keeping efforts do not always succeed and the UN is often blamed when talks break down and wars continue.

Specialized agencies

Much of the work of the UN is carried out by specialized agencies. These deal with matters such as food aid, agriculture, health, education and finance. Member countries pay for the work of these agencies according to how rich they are. Some governments also give voluntary contributions to UNICEF and UNHCR for their work with children and refugees.

◄ Bosnian Serbs welcome a Russian United Nations battalion in Pale on 20 February 1994. UN peace-keeping troops were sent to the former Yugoslavia in the early 1990s, when wars broke out between different ethnic groups and the country divided into smaller states.

United States of America

The USA is the richest and most powerful country in the world. It consists of 50 states, each of which has its own elected government. These can set taxes and pass laws over many of the things that affect people's daily lives. A federal government organizes the whole country and conducts its relations with other countries.

Forty-eight of its states, from California in the west to Maine in the east, make up the main landmass. Alaska, the largest and most northerly state, is separated from the others by Canada. The volcanic islands that make up Hawaii are 3700 kilometres west of California in the Pacific Ocean. Because the USA is so huge, there is a time difference of 6 hours between Hawaii and Maine. While Alaska reaches into the Arctic Circle, with freezing winter temperatures, Florida shares the tropical climate of the Caribbean.

Mountains and deserts

Alaska and the western third of the USA are mostly mountainous. The Rocky Mountain range, which runs from Alaska to Mexico, is really a series of mountain ranges separated by plateaux and basins. But while the south-western states like Arizona are hot desert, the north-western states, such as Oregon, are the wettest in the country. Large rivers, such as the Colorado and Snake, have cut deep gorges and canyons through these ranges. In places the rivers have been dammed to provide water for irrigated fields and hydroelectric power for cities.

• Alaska and Hawaii are also in the USA.

CONN.	Connecticut
DEL.	Delaware
MARY.	Maryland
MASS.	Massachusetts
MISS.	Mississippi
N.H.	New Hampshire
N.J.	New Jersey
PENN.	Pennsylvania
R.I.	Rhode Island
VER.	Vermont
W. VA.	West Virginia

Plains and rivers

Much of the central and eastern regions of the USA are drained by the Missouri and Ohio rivers, which (along with many others) join the Mississippi River before it enters the sea in the Gulf of Mexico. Together, these rivers drain an area of over 3 million square kilometres. Although these rivers provide valuable routes for transporting goods, they often flood and cause great damage to settlements and farms.

Between the Mississippi and the western mountains lie the prairies, vast areas of grassland. Here are found some of the world's most important areas of wheat farming and, where there is less rainfall, cattle ranching.

The east coast is separated from the Mississippi basin by the Appalachian Mountains. These mountains contain deposits of coal which helped US industry develop.

People and cities

The USA has the third largest population of any country. Most Americans are descended from settlers and immigrants who came within the past 400 years, including Africans who were brought as slaves to work the sugar and tobacco plantations of the South. The majority of Americans live in cities, and this is where the country's great diversity of peoples can be seen most clearly. Larger cities such as New York, Chicago and Los Angeles have areas where people have decided to live together because they originally came from the same country. New York has a Chinatown, and in Miami there is a large Spanish-speaking population from Cuba.

The country is so big that there are still areas with very few people. Wyoming is about the same

▲ Central Park becomes a winter playground in the shadow of Manhattan Island skyscrapers in New York.

size as the United Kingdom but only has 100,000 residents. Other areas have been kept free of people to preserve landscapes, forests and wildlife. Much of the western USA is under some form of preservation.

Farms, mines and factories

Almost every kind of agricultural and industrial good is produced in the USA. It is a major world producer of maize (corn), soya beans, tomatoes, oranges, peaches, cheese, beef and chickens. The country has deposits of most of the natural resources useful to modern society. It mines more coal, copper, gypsum, salt, phosphates and sulphur than any other country. Alaska and the states around the Gulf of Mexico supply most of the country's oil and natural gas.

The world's three largest companies are American: General Motors and Ford (cars) and Exxon (oil). The country makes many goods associated with older, established industries such as chemicals and textiles. But it is also a leader in new industries such as electronics, software and biotechnology. Many important inventions associated with these products came about because of the USA's advanced space exploration and defence industries.

The USA and the world

The USA is the most important trading country in the world. It has signed a pact with its neighbours, Canada and Mexico, called the North American Free Trade Agreement (NAFTA) to make it easier for goods to cross their borders.

The country's influence is felt in other ways. American films and

• Two of the great plates which make up the Earth's crust, the Pacific and North American plates, meet along the west coast. This means that the region suffers from frequent earthquakes and, less often, volcanoes. The worst earthquakes happen along the San Andreas fault, which runs close to two big cities, San Francisco and Los Angeles.

• Los Angeles is one of the USA's most diverse cities in terms of nationality and language. Out of a population of 8.8 million, one in three was born in another country. Over a quarter speak Spanish and 210,000 speak Chinese. Los Angeles is home to the largest communities of Mexicans, Koreans and Iranians outside their countries of origin.

▼ The Colorado River has cut a spectacular gorge known as the Grand Canyon. It is 446 km long, and at its deepest point the river is 1870 m below the surrounding landscape. In some places the gorge is 29 km wide. The many layers of rock that form the canyon's sides record 2 billion years of geological history.

▲ Sprinkler systems create vast circular areas of irrigated farmland in Colorado, USA.

• In the USA people vote separately for their president and for their parliament, which is called Congress. The Congress has two houses: the Senate contains two people elected from each of the 50 states; the House of Representatives has 435 members, divided among the states according to their population size. Each state also has a congress and a governor.

television programmes are watched almost everywhere. American culture, from Hollywood movies to jeans and chewing gum, has become the international culture.

The military forces of the USA are the most powerful in the world. They are often sent to other countries to protect the USA's own interests or those of its allies.

History of the USA

The history of the United States began on 4 July 1776, when the 13 British colonies in North America declared themselves independent of Britain and its king, George III. After defeating the British in the War of Independence (1775–1783), the colonies wrote a constitution for their new country. This divided power between the states and a central (or 'federal') government, which was run by an elected president. The successful general George Washington became the first president of the United States of America and the new capital city, Washington, was named after him.

Across the continent

The USA expanded fast. Four new states had joined by 1803. In the same year President Jefferson doubled its size by buying a huge area of central America from France (the Louisiana Purchase). The USA now stretched from the east coast to the Rocky Mountains. It expanded south in 1819 when it bought Florida from Spain.

The USA continued to grow throughout the 19th century. It absorbed Texas in 1845. Three years later, following a war with Mexico, it took over territory that became the states of California, Arizona and New Mexico. Further states were added when Britain gave up its claim

to lands in the north-west, and in 1867 Russia sold Alaska to the USA for 7.2 million dollars.

Opportunity and repression

New territory brought new opportunities. Pioneer settlers moved west as farmers and cattle ranchers. In 1849 miners from all over the world flocked to California in search of gold. The population grew rapidly, boosted by thousands of European immigrants hoping for better lives in the New World. Towns and cities expanded and multiplied. The development of telegraphs and railroads speeded up communications across the vast country. The first railroad to cross the continent opened in 1869.

The new opportunities were not open to all. For the Native Americans, driven westwards and robbed of their ancestral lands by European settlers, it was a time of great hardship and misery. Until the Civil War (1861–1865), most African Americans were held in slavery and were often mistreated. Although slavery was abolished in 1865, African Americans were discriminated against for many years to come.

Industry and war

The USA changed dramatically in the years after the Civil War. Immigrants continued to flood into the country, including many from eastern Europe. As the population soared, so industry and business boomed. The world was flooded with new American inventions, from the sewing machine and typewriter to electric lighting and the combine harvester. The output of coal, iron and steel, machinery and, later, oil rose at a

▼ Sitting Bull, a Sioux Indian chief, is most famous for his defeat of General Custer at the battle of Little Bighorn in 1876, fought over Indian land rights.

spectacular rate. Grain from the Midwest was exported around the world. The development of canning and refrigeration greatly helped the meat industry.

By 1914 the USA had become the richest country in the world. But the industrial revolution brought problems too. Officials and politicians struggled to control child labour, slum dwellings, urban crime, pollution and corruption. Abroad, before the USA entered World War I in 1917, it used its new-found power to gain control over Puerto Rico, Hawaii, the Philippines and Cuba.

▲ The battle of Winchester (1864), fought between the pro-slavery southern states (Confederates) and the anti-slavery northern states (Unionists) during the Civil War of 1861–1865. The Unionists finally won, but only after terrible slaughter. One in 50 Americans (about half a million) died in the war.

Boom and bust

After World War I the USA went its own way. It refused the join the League of Nations, the peace-keeping body set up after the war, and it cut immigration and imports from other countries. The US economy flourished for a decade. The greatest advances were made in the oil and automobile industries. New factories, which attracted many African American workers from the south, turned out a vast range of consumer goods. The most famous, Henry Ford's Model T car, had sold 15 million by 1928.

The boom suddenly ended in 1929, throwing the USA into the worst depression in its history. Thousands went bankrupt, unemployment rocketed, factories ground to a halt, and farmland lay uncultivated. President F. D. Roosevelt's New Deal programme went some way to helping, but the USA did not really get back on its feet again until the outbreak of World War II in 1939.

Superpower and world leader

By 1950 the world was dangerously divided between communist nations, led by the Soviet Union and China, and democratic nations, led by the USA. Guided by its mistakes in the past, the USA accepted its new role. It supported the United Nations, and in order to deter communist aggression, it built up a huge arsenal of weapons.

The USA used force in Korea and Vietnam to try to halt the advance of communism. In 1962 President Kennedy brought the world to the brink of nuclear war when Soviet missiles were discovered on Cuba. The hostility between the USA and the USSR (known as the 'Cold War') lasted until the collapse of Soviet power in the late 1980s.

Modern America

The USA continued to prosper during the last half of the 20th century. Its scientists put a man on the Moon in 1969, and it dominated the new computer and software markets.

However, city centres deteriorated and sometimes flared into riot. Crime and drug-taking rose. Women and racial minorities, particularly African Americans and Hispanics, campaigned vigorously for equal rights. The Islamic terrorist attacks of 11 September 2001 on New York and Washington, in which over 3000 people died, were a major shock to all Americans. President George W. Bush declared a 'war against terrorism', attacking Afghanistan in 2001–2 and Iraq in 2003.

► The Statue of Liberty, which stands at the entrance to New York Harbour, was given by France to the American people in 1886. Her torch represents freedom and her book the law.

• Of the 43 presidents to 2003, all of whom were men, Franklin Delano Roosevelt served longest (1933–1945). Two of the most famous, Abraham Lincoln (1861–1865) and John F. Kennedy (1961–1963) were assassinated. Several had made their names as soldiers. Ronald Reagan (1981–1989) had been a film star and Jimmy Carter (1977–1981) a peanut farmer. Theodore Roosevelt (1901–1909) had the teddy bear named after him.

find out more

Edison, Thomas
Kennedy, J. F.
King, Martin Luther
Lincoln, Abraham
North America
Roosevelt, Franklin D.
Slaves
South America
Twentieth-century history
Vietnam War
World War I
World War II
See also Countries fact file, page 643

Universe

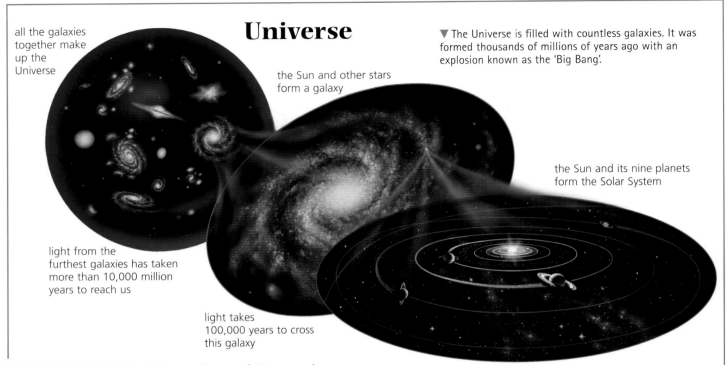

all the galaxies together make up the Universe

the Sun and other stars form a galaxy

▼ The Universe is filled with countless galaxies. It was formed thousands of millions of years ago with an explosion known as the 'Big Bang'.

the Sun and its nine planets form the Solar System

light from the furthest galaxies has taken more than 10,000 million years to reach us

light takes 100,000 years to cross this galaxy

light takes about one day to cross the Solar System

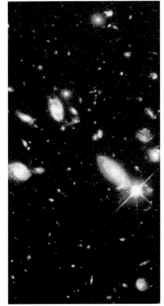

▲ This image is made up from over 200 separate pictures taken by the Hubble Space Telescope. It shows masses of very faint and distant galaxies.

find out more
Astronomy
Atoms and molecules
Galaxies
Solar System
Space exploration
Stars

We use the word 'Universe' to mean everything that exists, from the Earth to the most distant parts of space. The Universe contains countless galaxies of stars. The furthest ones we can see are so distant that their light takes billions of years to reach us.

People used to think that the Earth was the centre of the Universe. Although the Earth is important to us, we know now that it is a little planet going round the Sun, which is just one of millions of ordinary stars in our Galaxy. Because the light from the stars takes so long to reach us, we are seeing them now as they actually were long ago. When we look deep into space, we are looking a long way back in time as well.

The Big Bang
Scientists believe that the Universe started about 15 billion years ago with an event that they call the 'Big Bang'. This was an explosion in which all the matter and energy in the Universe were created. It was the beginning of time and space.

At first the Universe was incredibly dense and hot, but as it expanded, it began to cool down. Initially, it contained vast numbers of fast-moving particles called quarks and electrons. These joined together to form new particles called protons and neutrons, some of which combined into bunches. At this stage, matter in the Universe consisted almost entirely of the nuclei (central parts) of hydrogen and helium atoms.

Three hundred thousand years later, when the Universe was much cooler, the electrons had slowed down and the nuclei captured them to form atoms, the building blocks of everyday matter. Matter, light and other kinds of radiation spread out ever more thinly as space continued to expand. Huge clouds of gas began to collapse on themselves about a billion years later. Each of these clouds became a galaxy.

The Universe is still expanding, and the galaxies are moving further and further away from each other. If there is enough matter in the Universe, the pull of gravity will eventually halt the expansion and cause the galaxies to fall together until everything collides in a 'big crunch'. If the Universe does expand forever, thousands of millions of years in the future the stars will run out of fuel and will stop shining.

► FLASHBACK ◄
In 1929 the American astronomer Edwin Hubble showed that the galaxies are moving away from each other and the Universe is expanding. This discovery, known as 'Hubble's Law', forms the basis of the 'Big Bang' theory. A British physicist, Stephen Hawking, published his ideas on the Universe in 1988, in his best-selling book, *A Brief History of Time*. Hawking argues that our Universe, and an infinite number of universes like it, are all part of one great 'super-universe'.

Valleys

find out more
Erosion
Glaciers
Mountains
Rivers and streams

▼ Settlements scattered
along the Lauterbrünnen
Valley in the Alps,
Switzerland. Alpine
farmers move their cattle
up to high pastures in
spring as the snow
melts, bringing them
back down to the valley
floor in winter.

Valleys are formed when rivers or glaciers wear away the rocks of the high ground. As water or ice flows down the mountains, it carves out valleys, leaving ridges of rock on either side and giving the surrounding mountains their shape.

In mountain regions the valleys are the main areas where people live, because the climate is sheltered and the soils are more fertile. Valleys provide routes for roads and railways, and larger rivers can be used for transport.

How valleys are formed

Rivers flowing down steep gradients (slopes) cut deep into the rocks. Where the gradient of the river bed is less, the river flows more slowly and cuts a wider, shallower valley. Glaciers can carve out valleys much more powerfully than rivers. The ice may be hundreds of feet thick, so a great weight presses down on the valley floor. Rocks and boulders on the bottom of the glacier are pushed along by the ice.

Where the river follows a line of weakness in the rocks, such as a fault, it may cut a *gorge*. Some of the most spectacular gorges are the steep-sided canyons of the United States. In desert areas another kind of steep-sided valley forms when occasional heavy rainfall causes 'flash floods'. Because the hard, sun-baked soil cannot soak up the rainfall, powerful floods cut wide, deep channels called *wadis* or *arroyos*.

Valleys may also be drowned, for example where coastlines are sinking or sea levels are rising. When this happens long inlets of the sea called *rias* are formed. Where deep glaciated valleys are drowned, they form *fjords* with very steep sides and extremely deep water.

Life in valleys

The climate in a valley is usually much milder than in the hills around it. The valley sides provide shelter from wind, and often much of the rain or snow falls on the mountains, leaving the valley drier. In some valleys special mountain winds bring warm or cold air at certain times of year. The cold air sinks into the valleys, bringing more frost and fog than in the mountains.

In valleys near a river mouth, the soil is thick and contains sediments brought down by the river. Good crops can be grown in these fertile sediments. In mountain valleys the soils are usually thinner and not very fertile. Sheep farms are more common than crops. On very steep valley slopes, farmers may build terraces to prevent the water and soil rushing away.

Different kinds of valley

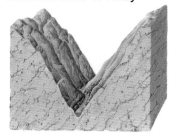

River valleys high up in the mountains have steep sides. They look V-shaped in cross-section. Further down the river course, they become wider and shallower.

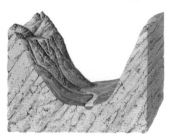

Glaciated valleys are gouged out by ice, rocks and boulders. They are U-shaped in cross-section, with very steep sides and a flat bottom.

Gorges are very deep valleys with almost vertical sides. One of the best-known examples is the Grand Canyon in the USA.

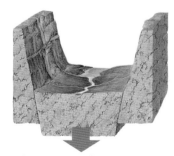

Rift valleys are formed in two different ways. Either huge blocks of rock rise up to form mountains, leaving a wide valley between them, or the block between drops down to form a valley floor. Two examples are the Rift Valley in Africa and the Rhine rift valley in Germany.

Vegetables

find out more
Beans
Diets
Food
Fruit

• Many vegetables have a very high water content. Lettuces, for example, are 96% water. Potatoes are about 80% water. But vegetables are also a good source of important vitamins and minerals.

Vegetables include many hundreds of plants or parts of plants which we can eat. Some vegetables, such as potatoes and aubergines, are always cooked. Some, like lettuce, are eaten raw. Others, like carrots and celery, can be eaten either way.

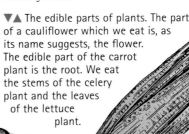

lettuce

The edible part of a plant may be those parts that grow underground, like roots, tubers and bulbs. Or they may be the stems, leaves, flowers and fruit which grow above the ground.

The idea of fruit as a vegetable may seem a little confusing. Courgettes, tomatoes, peas and aubergines are called vegetables by a cook, but,

strictly speaking, they are fruits. Rhubarb, on the other hand, is a stem vegetable which we use as a fruit and serve as a dessert.

All fresh vegetables contain vitamin C. Dark-green leaves, tomatoes and peppers have the largest amounts. Since vitamin C is gradually lost during storage, preparation and cooking, the sooner a vegetable is eaten after it is picked the better. Green and orange vegetables contain vitamin A. All vegetables are low in energy but high in dietary fibre.

cauliflower

carrot

▼▲ The edible parts of plants. The part of a cauliflower which we eat is, as its name suggests, the flower. The edible part of the carrot plant is the root. We eat the stems of the celery plant and the leaves of the lettuce plant.

celery

Victoria

Born 1819 in London, England
Died 1901 aged 81

Victoria was the queen of the United Kingdom from 1837 to 1901, and her long reign became known as the Victorian Age. During this time, Britain was one of the most powerful nations in the world.

• Despite her general popularity, Victoria survived six attempts on her life during the course of her reign.

• Victoria's reign was the longest in British history.

Victoria became queen when she was only 18, after her uncles George IV and William IV both died without heirs. Three years later she married her German cousin, Prince Albert. After her marriage she gradually became more serious and more conscious of her responsibilities as queen. She was devoted to her 'dearest Albert', and came to depend on him completely. They had nine children, many of whom married into European royal families. When Albert died suddenly of typhoid in 1861, Victoria was desperately unhappy. She refused to appear in public for some years, and wore black for the rest of her life. The prime minister, Benjamin Disraeli, finally managed to coax her into public life again.

During Victoria's 63-year reign, the British empire grew to a vast size, making Britain the richest country in the world. Victoria took great

interest in all the peoples of her empire, and her subjects around the world held her in great respect. She was delighted when she was given the title Empress of India in 1876. Her Golden and Diamond Jubilees, marking 50 and 60 years on the throne, were great events and causes for huge celebrations. Her death in 1901, marking the end of a glorious era, was an occasion of great public grieving.

▼ This photograph of Queen Victoria was taken in 1899 when she was 80 years old.

find out more
British empire
Victorian Britain

Victorian Britain

The Victorian period runs from 1837 to 1901, the years during which England was ruled by Queen Victoria.

▲ On 1 May 1851 Queen Victoria, with Prince Albert by her side, opened the first Great Exhibition in the Crystal Palace in London. On show were samples of industry from countries all over the world. Over half the exhibitors were British, because in 1851 Britain had a vast empire and was the leading industrial nation of the world.

• In Victorian times rich boys usually went to 'public' schools, which were not public but fee-paying. The North London Collegiate School founded in 1850 was one of the first to provide a good education for middle-class girls. The Church provided some primary schools, but not until 1870 were there 'elementary' schools for all children between the ages of 5 and 10. By 1901 these schools were free for everyone up to 12.

▶ Life for the poor in Victorian times was grim. Towns grew too fast for proper town planning. This meant overcrowding, poor water supplies and a lack of sewage and rubbish disposal. Disease thrived and cholera epidemics swept the country.

During Victoria's reign Britain's empire grew stronger than ever. The empire brought vast wealth for some and Britain ruled over millions of people. Many Victorians worked in India as soldiers, traders and government officials. Victorian explorers were beginning to go deep into Africa. Under Benjamin Disraeli, prime minister in 1868 and again from 1874 to 1880, Britain took control of the Suez Canal, the shortest route to India, and Parliament gave Victoria the title of 'Empress of India'.

Country life

Landowners continued to be the richest and most powerful people in Britain. The squire who lived in the big house in a village usually owned the villagers' homes, and most of them worked on his land. Owners of small farms were often well-off and quite independent. The poor, ordinary villagers lived in damp, cold houses with no indoor water supply.

Things began to change in about 1880. Cheap wheat and frozen meat began to be imported. Margarine was invented, and was cheaper than butter. All this competition hit British farming badly. Landowners did less well, wages fell and jobs were lost. More people left their villages to find jobs in the growing towns.

City and town life

Victorian Britain became the leading industrial nation in the world. More industry meant more cotton mills, bigger coalmines and more factories all over the country. Existing and new cities grew quickly. By 1880 the industrial town of Middlesbrough with 50,000 people had grown up on the River Tees. In 1830 there had been one farmhouse on the site.

This huge change in people's lives brought problems. Factories and mines were dangerous and unhealthy places to work. There were no rules about hours of work or wages. Workers' houses were built as cheaply as possible, huddled together with no taps or toilets indoors. Filthy drains were often close to

the pumps that provided drinking water.

For the better-off rail travel made it easier to get to work, and so suburbs grew up on the edge of towns, with bigger houses, trees and gardens. By 1901 big cities like Birmingham and Manchester had fine new town halls, libraries, art galleries and parks.

Struggles towards change

The 1830s were bad years for working people, with low wages and much unemployment. In 1836 a group of skilled workers in London, led by Francis Place and William Lovett, decided to draw up a Charter. This demanded several reforms by Parliament, in particular the vote for all adult males and payment for MPs so that working people could be elected to Parliament. Workers all over the country campaigned to get it accepted but the Chartists did not immediately get the reforms they wanted.

Gradually workers realized that if they joined a trade union, they could help each other, and perhaps force their employers to improve wages and working conditions. In the late 1880s, strikes by women making matchboxes (match girls) and dockers were both successful. But strikes were very

risky as employers often 'locked out' strikers, so they lost their jobs and their families starved.

Reforms

Many Victorians worked hard for reform, and most of the changes the Chartists wanted came about in the end. By 1884 most men over 21 could vote. By 1901 there were even a few working-class MPs, though MPs were not paid until 1911.

Many people began to realize that rules were needed to make

▼ The Chartists collected petitions, written requests signed by supporters of their cause, and took them to Parliament. This is the procession taking the 1842 petition. All three petitions were rejected.

▲ Victorian women had few rights. Working-class women lived hard lives and many worked as domestic servants. Most rich women found themselves dependent on their husbands. Better schools gave girls the chance to do more, and in about 1875 the first women studied at Oxford and Cambridge Universities. These women students are taking tea in their rooms at Holloway College, London, in about 1900.

towns healthy and workplaces safe. William Gladstone, prime minister four times in Victoria's reign, brought many reforms. In 1870, when he was in office, schools were provided for all children under 10 and in 1884 working men got the vote.

There were other reforms during Victoria's reign. By 1875 Parliament had passed laws enforcing clean water supplies, proper drains and dustbin collections. Cholera gradually disappeared.

The 7th Earl of Shaftesbury spent his life campaigning for laws to help people in the cities. These laws stopped children working in mines and factories and limited a factory worker's day to 10 hours. There were also rules about safety at work. Things improved, but poverty and disease did not disappear.

1837 Victoria becomes Queen
1840 Victoria and Albert marry
1851 Great Exhibition
1865 First woman doctor
1867 Workers in towns get the vote
1870 Education Act; Trade unions legal
1875 Public Health Act
1884 Workers in country get vote; Irish demand home rule
1892 Keir Hardie elected first Labour MP
1899 Britain fights Boer War with South Africa
1901 Death of Victoria

• Robert Peel was Britain's prime minister twice, but today he is best remembered for starting the police force in London. The arrival of 'Peelers', as they were called, in 1829 helped to stop a lot of petty crime.

find out more
British empire
Carroll, Lewis
Dickens, Charles
Grace, W. G.
Industrial Revolution
Nightingale, Florence
Victoria
Women's movement

Video

We use video recorders at home for recording and watching programmes and feature films. Camcorders record family events and holidays. Video is also used for television news reporting, for pop videos and for making adverts.

A video recorder plays video tapes on a television, and records television programmes so that you can watch them later. Video recorders record pictures on video tape as a magnetic pattern. The signals which are recorded are the signals that a television needs to create pictures on its screen. The signals are recorded on the tape in diagonal stripes.

A video camera records moving pictures that can be shown on television later. It uses a light-sensitive microchip to change the picture into electrical signals. The signals can be recorded on video tape to be played later. A camcorder records pictures on a mini video tape. Some camcorders are small enough to fit on the palm of your hand.

Video pictures can also be recorded digitally. Digital recordings code signals as numbers (digits). These signals can then be moved to a different medium, for example a computer, where they are converted back into signals for pictures or sounds, and called up onto the screen.

▶ When you load a cassette into a video recorder, levers wrap the magnetic tape around a metal drum. This has recording and playback heads. As the tape moves slowly past, the drum spins, making the heads move across the tape in diagonal lines.

find out more
Electronics
Recording
Television

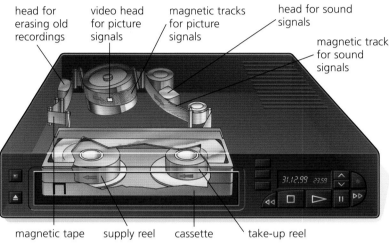

head for erasing old recordings
video head for picture signals
magnetic tracks for picture signals
head for sound signals
magnetic track for sound signals
magnetic tape
supply reel
cassette
take-up reel

31.12.99 23.59

Vietnam

Vietnam is a narrow, S-shaped country in South-east Asia. It is generally warm, with sandy beaches along the east coast and mountains to the west. During the 1950s and 1960s the country was divided by war, but since 1976 it has been a single nation.

Vietnam's climate is humid. The north has four seasons, with cool winters and hot summers, while the south is warm to very hot all year. Almost every year typhoons (hurricanes) from the east cause much damage. Less than a third of the country can be used for agriculture, but nearly three-quarters of the population work on the land. Rice, maize and sweet potatoes are the most important crops, but fishing and forestry are also important. Many trees are being planted to replace the 70,000 square kilometres of forest destroyed by war.

For many centuries the Chinese controlled Vietnam. Later an independent Vietnamese kingdom, called Annam, arose. In the mid-19th century Vietnam was part of French Indo-China. However in 1954, after a fierce struggle, two independent countries were formed: communist North Vietnam and pro-western South Vietnam. Throughout the 1960s the two countries were at war, the South being helped by troops from the USA. In 1973 the US troops withdrew, and three years later North and South Vietnam joined as one nation under a communist government.

▶ On the Mekong delta boats wait for customers. The Mekong in the south and the Song-Koi (Red River) in the north are Vietnam's most important rivers.

find out more
Asia
France
United States of
  America
Vietnam War
*See also Countries fact
  file, page 644*

Vietnam War

The Vietnam War was fought between the two halves of a divided country. From 1954 until 1975 communist North Vietnam fought against the US-backed South Vietnamese to unite the whole country.

During the 19th and early 20th centuries, Vietnam was part of France's empire in Indo-China. In 1946 communist leader Ho Chi Minh and his Vietminh forces declared war on the French. In 1954 Vietnam was divided into North Vietnam with Ho Chi Minh as president, and non-communist South Vietnam supported by the USA. Ho Chi Minh was determined to reunite the two. The North Vietnamese backed the South Vietnamese communists, the Vietcong, who were fighting their government and the Americans.

At war with America

The Americans believed in the 'domino theory' which said that if one country fell to the communists, the one next door would fall, then the one next to that, and so on. To stop this happening, the Americans decided to resist communists everywhere. In 1965 the US began to bomb North Vietnam. By the summer of 1967 there were 2 million US soldiers involved in the war.

The Americans were not trained to fight in the jungles and swamps of Vietnam, where their tanks and heavy artillery were useless. They tried massive air raids on North Vietnam and on neighbouring countries. Civilian targets were also

► This Vietnamese woman and her child were hit by a US grenade thrown into a bunker.

attacked. Huge areas of the jungle were destroyed with fire bombs and chemical weapons. But nothing stopped the Vietcong advance.

By 1968 the Americans realized they could not win, and in the following year peace talks began. By 1973, when a cease-fire was agreed, all American forces had been withdrawn. The cease-fire broke down in 1974 and a year later South Vietnam fell to the communists and the country was reunited.

find out more
Twentieth-century history
United States of America
Vietnam

Vikings

In the Middle Ages the word Viking meant a robber who came by sea. Today we use Viking as the name of Norse peoples who lived in the Scandinavian countries of Norway, Denmark and Sweden.

In their own countries the Vikings were farmers. In the 8th century AD they began to look for more land. They made raids across the seas and settled in other countries. They were great traders, too, reaching as far east as Byzantium (Istanbul) and westwards across the Atlantic to Newfoundland.

Everyday life

Most Vikings were farmers and they built the same sort of farmhouse wherever they settled. The most important part was the great hall. In earlier times this was where the family lived, ate and slept. Later the hall was divided into eating and sleeping rooms. Houses were often smoky inside because cooking was done over an open fire in the middle of the room.

Viking farmers grew all sorts of crops to eat, such as wheat, oats, barley and vegetables like cabbages, beans and carrots. They kept cattle, sheep, pigs and chickens, but they also hunted animals, birds and fish. Some of this food would be smoked in the roof of the hall, or dried or salted to eat during the winter.

Viking men and women liked bright clothes and decoration and jewellery. Women often wore headscarves, an ankle-length dress of wool or linen, with an overdress held on by great brooches. They might also wear necklaces, bracelets and rings. Men wore woollen trousers with a tunic on top.

Traders and raiders

The Vikings were famous for the goods they made themselves and for their trade with far-off countries. They traded as far north as Iceland and with the Lapps (for ivory and furs), as far south as Baghdad (for silk and spices) and into Russia (for slaves and furs).

▼ Archaeologists have found the remains of Viking houses at York (called Jorvik by the Vikings). This is a leather boot on a skate made of animal bone from Jorvik. The Jorvik Museum also contains reconstructions of Jorvik life using evidence found there.

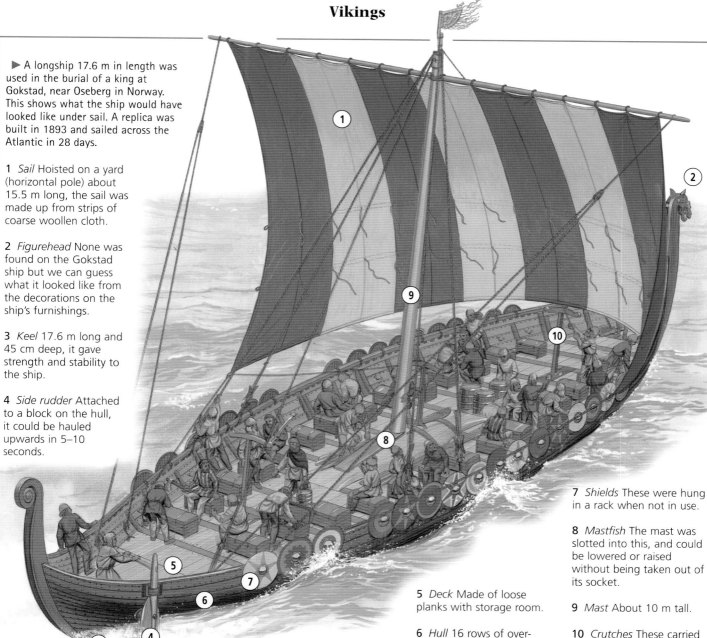

► A longship 17.6 m in length was used in the burial of a king at Gokstad, near Oseberg in Norway. This shows what the ship would have looked like under sail. A replica was built in 1893 and sailed across the Atlantic in 28 days.

1 *Sail* Hoisted on a yard (horizontal pole) about 15.5 m long, the sail was made up from strips of coarse woollen cloth.

2 *Figurehead* None was found on the Gokstad ship but we can guess what it looked like from the decorations on the ship's furnishings.

3 *Keel* 17.6 m long and 45 cm deep, it gave strength and stability to the ship.

4 *Side rudder* Attached to a block on the hull, it could be hauled upwards in 5–10 seconds.

5 *Deck* Made of loose planks with storage room.

6 *Hull* 16 rows of overlapping planks reinforced with ribs and cross-beams.

7 *Shields* These were hung in a rack when not in use.

8 *Mastfish* The mast was slotted into this, and could be lowered or raised without being taken out of its socket.

9 *Mast* About 10 m tall.

10 *Crutches* These carried the yard and mast when the ship was being rowed.

In towns, craftspeople made a variety of products; for example, pots and pans for the kitchen, clothes and jewellery, tools and weapons of bronze and iron. They exchanged goods but they also minted their own coins.

However, the Vikings are probably best known as fierce raiders of other peoples' lands. They first invaded Britain in AD 793. Raiders were looking for rich plunder, but also for slaves. Slaves, called *thralls*, worked on the farms for freemen, who were called *karls*. More important than freemen were the rich landowners, who were also chieftains. They were called *jarls*. Warriors on raiding parties were heavily armed with swords, shields, spears and axes. They wore helmets and chain mail.

Viking ships

The key to the success of the Vikings in trading and raiding was the ship. The Vikings built fast, strong ships that could withstand even an Atlantic crossing. In about AD 1000 the Viking explorer Leif Ericsson went all the way to Newfoundland in North America.

The Vikings built not only 'longships' for raiding (one of which held 200 fighting men), but also wider, deeper ships called *knarrs* for trade, and little rowing boats called *faerings*. Ships had both oars and sails.

● Norse myths are stories about the gods and heroes of the Norse people. The Vikings worshipped many gods including: Bragi, the god of poetry; Frigg/Freya, one of the twin gods of love; Loki, god of fire; Odin, king of the gods; Thor, the storm-god.

find out more
Anglo-Saxons
Archaeology

Virtual reality

Virtual reality (VR) is a way of simulating (re-creating) a world using pictures and sounds generated by a computer. You can enter this 'virtual world' by wearing a special headset that shows three-dimensional pictures in tiny television screens, and creates sounds through headphones.

Virtual reality makes you feel as if you are really part of the environment that the computer creates. In training and education, VR can simulate almost any situation in the real world. For example, a virtual aircraft can be used for pilot training and a virtual car for driver training. Virtual training is cheaper and safer than the real thing.

Objects in a virtual world do not have to be the same size as in the real world. Scientists have designed chemicals by joining huge virtual atoms which seem to float in mid-air. Manufacturers can construct virtual objects, such as cars, to test them before they make them for real. Amazing virtual worlds can be invented for computer games and for the rides found in some theme parks.

Creating a virtual world

Every VR system has a powerful computer. It needs to be quick at drawing the three-dimensional pictures. Plugged into the computer are a headset, containing television screens and headphones, and a hand-held controller. Data held in the memory of the computer describe the shape, size, colour and position of every object in the virtual world. The computer looks at this database so that it can draw the world. Finally, a computer program decides exactly what happens in that world.

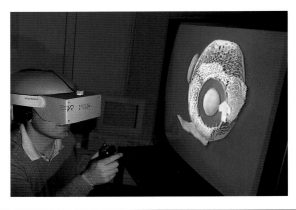

► A medical student uses a VR headset to practise techniques of eye surgery, without needing to operate on a live patient.

find out more
Computers
Information technology

Viruses

Viruses cause many diseases in animals and plants. They are very tiny and can only be seen through a microscope.

Viruses are made up of a coating of protein around the material needed for reproduction (genetic material). They can only reproduce by entering the nucleus of a living cell and inserting their genetic material into the genetic material of the cell. The cell then produces copies of the virus until the cell bursts, releasing them. These viruses then go on to infect other cells.

Unlike bacteria, viruses cannot be killed by antibiotics. But it is possible to be vaccinated against many diseases caused by viruses. A vaccine, made from a weak form of the germs that cause the disease, is put into your body. Your body then makes chemicals called antibodies that fight the disease.

One of the ways in which you are most likely to be attacked by viruses is when you catch a cold. Although you feel uncomfortable, a cold is not usually a serious infection. Colds are spread mostly by touch, rather than by coughing and sneezing. There is no cure for a cold because it is caused by one or more of over 200 viruses.

▼ A group of viruses, magnified many thousands of times. This image has been coloured to make the viruses easy to see. Their blue centres are the genetic material. The viruses shown here are adenoviruses, which can cause cold-like symptoms such as a runny nose.

Some human diseases caused by viruses
AIDS
Cancer (some forms)
Chicken pox
Glandular fever
Influenza (flu)
Measles
Mumps
Polio
Rabies
Shingles

find out more
AIDS
Cells
Diseases
Drugs
Immunity

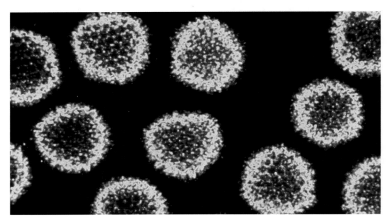

Volcanoes

A volcano is a mountain or hill made of lava which comes from deep beneath the Earth's surface. When a volcano erupts, lava and ash build up to make a cone. Some volcanoes give off clouds of ash and gas when they erupt. Others have streams of red-hot lava pouring down their sides.

The molten rock deep beneath the Earth's crust is called magma. It forces its way up through cracks and weak spots in the Earth's crust and spills out as lava. When a volcano erupts, pieces of broken rock and ash are often thrown out with the lava. Large lumps are called 'volcanic bombs'. As the rock and ash cool, they make layers of solid rock. As magma rises, gases separate out from the molten rock. These gases may collect near the surface and cause a great explosion.

Volcanoes can form on land or on the ocean floor. Some undersea volcanoes grow high enough to reach above sea level and become islands. Mountains can be formed when lava pours out of the ground, then cools and hardens to form hard, solid rock. Mount Fuji in Japan and Mount Vesuvius in Italy are examples of volcanic mountains.

Volcanoes eventually die. A volcano that has not erupted for a long time is said to be *dormant*, although there is always the danger that

it may suddenly erupt. When people think a volcano has finally died, then it is called *extinct*. Gradually, the volcano will be eroded. The softer rocks are worn away first, and in some places the only part left is the hard plug which filled the vent of the volcano.

The birth of a volcano

In Mexico, in 1943, some villagers were worried by earthquakes. Then a crack appeared across a local cornfield and smoke gushed out. The crack widened, and ash and rocks were hurled high into the air. Soon, red-hot lava poured out. After a week, a volcano 150 metres high stood where the cornfield had been, and the villagers had to leave. Mount Parícutin grew to 275 metres in a year, and to 410 metres after nine years.

▲ A thick cloud of smoke, ash and gases rises from Mount Ruapehu, on the North Island of New Zealand. The volcano erupted in September 1995.

● When Mount Vesuvius in southern Italy erupted in the year AD 79, the town of Pompeii was completely buried under volcanic ash. Today, the remains of the town have been dug out.

find out more
Continents
Earth
Islands
Mountains

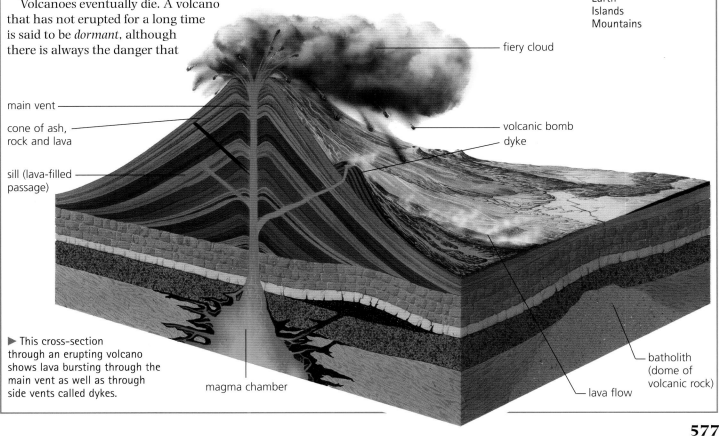

fiery cloud

main vent

cone of ash, rock and lava

volcanic bomb

dyke

sill (lava-filled passage)

▶ This cross-section through an erupting volcano shows lava bursting through the main vent as well as through side vents called dykes.

magma chamber

batholith (dome of volcanic rock)

lava flow

Volleyball

In the 100 years since it was invented, volleyball has rapidly established itself as a major international sport. It is relatively easy to play and requires little specialist equipment.

On beaches throughout the world, volleyball is played informally between teams of any number of players. As a competitive sport, the game is played on an indoor court between two teams of six players. The rectangular court is divided into two equal halves by a high net. The ball used is similar to a soccer ball but lighter.

The object of the game is to hit or knock the ball over the net with the hand or arm (or any part of the body above the waist) in such a way that the opposing team is unable to return it or prevent it from hitting the ground. Each team can hit the ball a maximum of three times before sending it back across the net. Players cannot catch or hold the ball, however, and the same player is not allowed to hit the ball twice in succession. The usual tactic is for the player making the second touch to put up a high ball close to the net, and for the third player to smash ('spike') it down into the opponents' side of the court.

If the serving side wins the rally, they gain a point. If they lose, service passes to the other side. The first side to reach 15 points by a margin of 2 points wins the set. The match is decided by the best of 3 or 5 sets.

Volleyball was invented in 1895 in the USA by a games instructor called William Morgan. He wanted to devise a game for businesspeople that was less strenuous than basketball. Its popularity soon spread throughout the USA and then to other countries.

● A version of the game known as beach volleyball is played two-a-side, on a sand court the same size as that used for the six-a-side game. It became an Olympic sport in 1996.

◀ Korea (in red) play Yugoslavia in the 1996 Olympics. A Korean player makes the spike, which the opposition attempt to block. Volleyball has been an Olympic sport for both men and women since 1964.

Wading birds

Wading birds are found along coasts worldwide, and on shallow inland waters, estuaries, marshes and mud-flats. Where food is plentiful, their numbers may build up to thousands. Long legs enable them to wade into water, and long bills help them to pick up small creatures, even those that are hiding in the mud.

Most of Britain's 'waders' are sandpipers and their relatives. In North America these are called 'shorebirds', while the word 'waders' is used for herons and egrets.

The size and feeding methods of wading birds vary. Snipe have extremely long, straight bills and probe deep into the mud for worms. Oystercatchers have long, strong bills for prising open mussels, clams and other shellfish. Plovers have short, stubby bills. They run, stop, bend and seize their prey from the surface.

Herons are large with long necks, legs and toes for climbing in trees and among waterside plants. They eat animals, often fish, which they grasp in their dagger-like bills.

Many wading birds live in the far north where food is plentiful in summer. The summer is short, but there is very little darkness and the young grow fast. Before the Arctic winter returns, the birds fly south.

◀ Wading birds find food in many different ways. Curlews probe deep into the mud (1). Pratincoles feed in the air (2). Turnstones search under stones (3). Phalaropes feed from the surface water (4), and avocets filter food from water (5).

find out more
Birds
Coasts
Migration
Seashore

Wales

Wales is a part of the United Kingdom, in north-west Europe. In the Welsh language Wales is Cymru. It comes from a Celtic word meaning 'fellow countryman'.

Much of Wales is mountainous and the highest peak (1085 metres) is Yr Wyddfa (Snowdon). Beneath the peaks of Snowdonia National Park are great caverns and slate quarries. There are also many lakes and rivers in Wales. Fast-flowing mountain rivers are used for hydroelectricity.

Industries

North Wales has a small population which lives mainly from farming and tourism. Sheep-farming is common. South Wales is industrial, and it is where most people live. Inland there are narrow valleys, in which houses and chapels cluster around the coalmines. There are few working coalmines now. New factories, built on the sites of 19th-century copper furnaces and on the coast, make cars, refrigerators and televisions.

People and languages

North and South Wales have different cultures. Traditions such as rugby football and choral singing are more common in the south. The northern and central areas are where most of the people who can speak Cymraeg (Welsh) live. About half a million people speak Cymraeg and English. A political party called Plaid Cymru works to protect Welsh culture and press for Welsh independence. Road signs and official documents are now in both languages. There is a Cymraeg-language television station and schools can teach in Cymraeg.

find out more
Celts
Europe
Henry VIII
Roman Britain
United Kingdom

• Welsh, one of the oldest languages in Europe, might have disappeared if people had not grown to love the language of the Welsh Bible, first translated in 1588.

▼ A granite quarry, near Porthmadog, North Wales. Mining landscapes like this one are common in Wales, where coal and slate mining were once major industries.

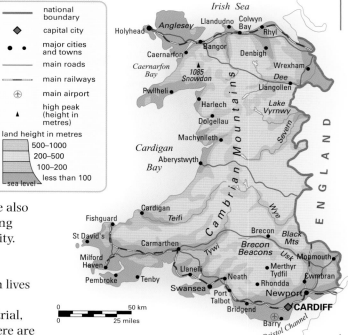

Welsh history

Wales first appeared in recorded history when the Romans attacked it in the 1st century AD. The people living there were Celts, with their own language and customs. The Romans conquered all but the mountainous heart of the country and introduced the Christian religion. The next wave of invaders, the Angles and Saxons, also failed to master Wales. So did the Normans.

The country was finally conquered after the death of Llywelyn ap Gruffudd in 1282. The new ruler, England's Edward I, built massive castles to keep the Welsh under control. Sometimes they rebelled and were penalized by harsh laws and heavy taxes.

Chapel and coal

In 1536 Wales was divided into counties and its government united with England's. The Welsh language was banned for all official business, but it did not die out.

The Welsh people eagerly accepted the Protestant religion. They did not take kindly to the Church of England, and in the 18th and 19th centuries thousands of non-conformist chapels (which refused to conform to certain Church practices) sprang up. Meanwhile, in the south a huge coalmining industry developed.

In the early 20th century demand for coal, steel and slate dropped and times were hard. But new businesses from Japan and other foreign countries are now moving into Wales, and in 1999 the Welsh elected a new assembly to discuss the country's own affairs.

Washing machines *see* Household equipment

Washington, George

George Washington was the first president of the USA, a post he held from 1789 to 1797. Before becoming president, he led the Americans against the British in the American Revolution.

At the time of George Washington's birth, America was divided into colonies. Some were ruled by Britain and some by France, but both countries wanted to be in control. Washington was born in Virginia, which was a British colony, and when he was 21 he joined the British army to fight against the French. His success as a leader made him well known in Virginia, and by the time he left the army he had become a colonel.

Washington settled down to be a farmer on his Virginia estate. However, like many others, he believed that people in the American colonies should be able to govern themselves rather than being ruled by the British. The only way for this to happen was to fight for their freedom. In 1775 he was made commander-in-chief of the American colonists' army. His job was to recruit men and train them to be soldiers. The American Revolution (War of Independence) began soon after. Washington's grit and perseverance kept his forces going. The British were finally defeated in 1783 and the United States of America was formed.

After the war, Washington went back to Virginia. Although he was a national hero, he did not want public office. Nevertheless, in 1789 he was unanimously elected as the first president of the USA and he dutifully accepted the job. He was re-elected in 1792 but refused to serve for a third term.

Born 1732 in Virginia, USA
Died 1799 aged 67

• The USA's capital city was named in George Washington's honour.

◄ After he died, it was said of Washington that he was 'first in war, first in peace, and first in the hearts of his countrymen'.

find out more
Georgian Britain
United States of America

Waste disposal

Every home produces large quantities of tin cans, waste paper, glass and other rubbish. Homes and factories also produce sewage (waste material from toilets). If this waste is not disposed of with care, it can become a hazard, causing disease and pollution.

Rotting rubbish not only looks and smells unpleasant, it also acts as a breeding ground for flies, rats and other carriers of disease. The easiest and cheapest method of disposing of rubbish is *tipping* it into a hole in the ground, such as one left by quarrying or open-cast mining. This kind of tip is called a *landfill* site. It is important that the rainwater running off it does not enter rivers, since it may contain poisonous substances. Tipping can be used to reclaim waste land or marsh land. The reclaimed land cannot be used for building for a long time because it may sink as the buried rubbish rots.

Waste can also be disposed of by *incineration* (burning). This greatly reduces the volume of the waste material, and the ash is clean and germ-free. The heat produced by burning waste can be used to generate electricity. However, the incinerators are expensive and produce some polluting gases. Ground-up waste can be turned into either solid fuel pellets or compost for farmland and gardens.

find out more
Pollution
Recycling
Water

▼ Waste water is carried by drains to the sewage works, where it is treated until it is clean enough to be pumped into a river or the sea.

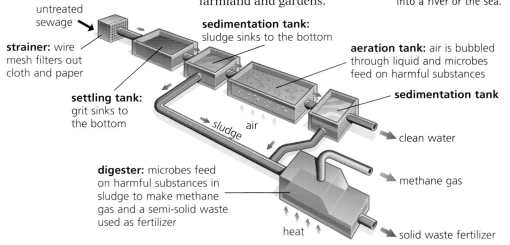

untreated sewage

strainer: wire mesh filters out cloth and paper

settling tank: grit sinks to the bottom

sedimentation tank: sludge sinks to the bottom

sludge   air

aeration tank: air is bubbled through liquid and microbes feed on harmful substances

sedimentation tank

clean water

digester: microbes feed on harmful substances in sludge to make methane gas and a semi-solid waste used as fertilizer

heat

methane gas

solid waste fertilizer

Water

Water covers almost three-quarters of the Earth's surface. The oceans, with an average depth of over 3 kilometres, hold about 97 per cent of the world's water. Frozen water forms the ice-caps at the North and South Poles. In the sky, clouds of water vapour bring rain, and where the rain falls and the rivers flow, plants and animals thrive. We use water in our homes for drinking, cooking, washing, cleaning, and flushing the lavatory. Factories need huge amounts of water for manufacturing things. Without water there would be no life on Earth.

Like many other substances, water is made up of molecules. These are so small that even the smallest raindrop contains billions. Every molecule of water consists of two atoms of hydrogen joined to a single atom of oxygen. Scientists say that the chemical formula for water is H_2O.

• In Europe, an average family of four people uses about 500 litres of water every day. You use 10 litres of water every time you flush a lavatory, and more than seven times that amount to have a bath.

▼ The water cycle. Only about 1% of the world's water is moving round the cycle at any one time.

Water and living things

Two-thirds of your body is water. Most of your blood is water. Your brain, heart, muscles and liver all contain water. Every day your body loses lots of water. About a litre goes down the toilet, and half a litre is lost as sweat and when you breathe out. You need about a litre and a half of water each day to stay alive.

Plants need water to grow. They usually take it in through their roots. They use water and other chemicals to make the substances needed for growth. They also use water to carry substances between their roots and leaves. The pressure of water in their cells helps plants to stay firm.

The water cycle

Water goes round and round in a process called the water cycle. In some parts of the cycle the water is a liquid (rain); in other parts it is a gas (water vapour) or a solid (ice). The warmth of the Sun evaporates water from seas, rivers and lakes, and also from the soil and plants on the land. The water turns into an invisible gas called

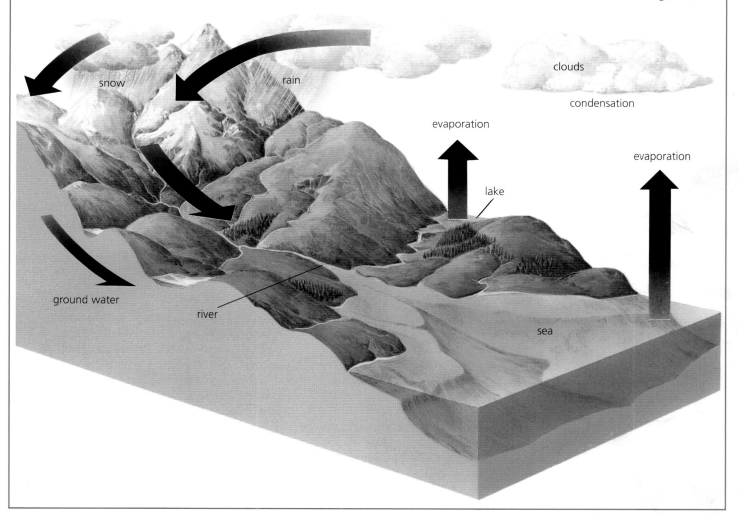

snow

rain

clouds

condensation

evaporation

evaporation

lake

ground water

river

sea

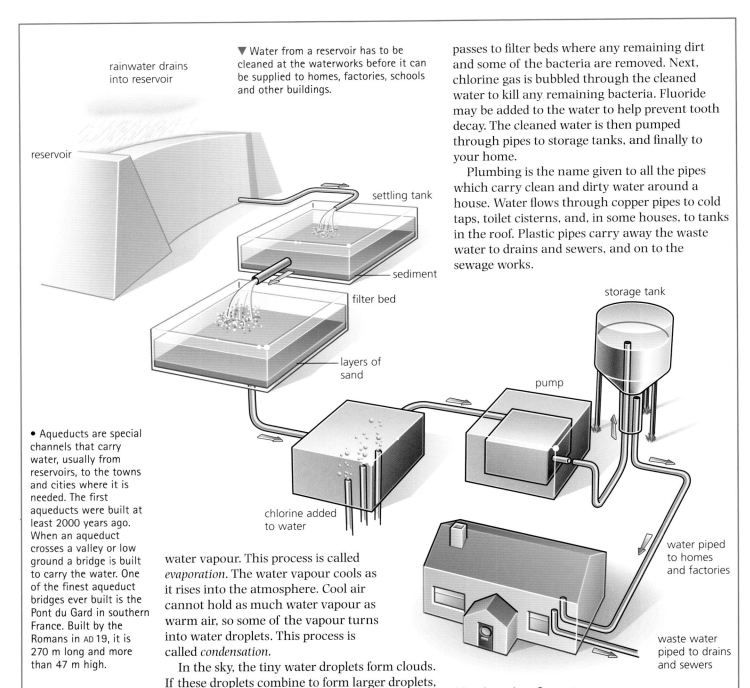

▼ Water from a reservoir has to be cleaned at the waterworks before it can be supplied to homes, factories, schools and other buildings.

rainwater drains into reservoir

reservoir

settling tank

sediment

filter bed

layers of sand

chlorine added to water

storage tank

pump

water piped to homes and factories

waste water piped to drains and sewers

passes to filter beds where any remaining dirt and some of the bacteria are removed. Next, chlorine gas is bubbled through the cleaned water to kill any remaining bacteria. Fluoride may be added to the water to help prevent tooth decay. The cleaned water is then pumped through pipes to storage tanks, and finally to your home.

Plumbing is the name given to all the pipes which carry clean and dirty water around a house. Water flows through copper pipes to cold taps, toilet cisterns, and, in some houses, to tanks in the roof. Plastic pipes carry away the waste water to drains and sewers, and on to the sewage works.

• Aqueducts are special channels that carry water, usually from reservoirs, to the towns and cities where it is needed. The first aqueducts were built at least 2000 years ago. When an aqueduct crosses a valley or low ground a bridge is built to carry the water. One of the finest aqueduct bridges ever built is the Pont du Gard in southern France. Built by the Romans in AD 19, it is 270 m long and more than 47 m high.

water vapour. This process is called *evaporation*. The water vapour cools as it rises into the atmosphere. Cool air cannot hold as much water vapour as warm air, so some of the vapour turns into water droplets. This process is called *condensation*.

In the sky, the tiny water droplets form clouds. If these droplets combine to form larger droplets, they will fall to Earth as rain, hail or snow. Much of the water that falls on the land flows to the sea in streams and rivers. Some soaks into the ground and some stays as ice. The water eventually finds its way into rivers and seas, where the water cycle begins again.

Water supplies

The water we use in our homes is rainwater from reservoirs, wells or rivers. Before this water can be pumped to your home, it must be cleaned at the waterworks. First, particles of sand, mud and grit sink and settle in a tank, and then the water

Hard and soft water

On its long journey to your home, rainwater washes over rocks and flows along rivers, dissolving gases from the air and many different substances from the rocks. Where there are chalk and limestone rocks, these dissolve in the rain and join with the dissolved gas, carbon dioxide, to form a substance called calcium bicarbonate. This and other similar chemicals produce 'hard' water. It is difficult to make a good lather with soap in hard water. Water that does not have these particular substances is called 'soft', but it still contains lots of different chemicals.

find out more
Atoms and molecules
Clouds
Dams
Hydroelectric power
Pollution
Rain and snow
Rivers and streams
Waste disposal
Wells and springs

Water sports

Water provides all sorts of opportunities for sport and recreation. Some water sports take place in a swimming pool, others on rivers and lakes or at sea.

Water sports such as swimming and rowing rely on muscle power. In others, like sailing and surfing, people harness the power of the wind or waves.

Pool sports

Swimming events were included in the first modern Olympic Games, in 1896, and today they form an important part of the Olympic programme. Competitive swimming calls for intensive training, and top swimmers may spend several hours a day in the pool.

There are swimming races for four different strokes: freestyle (front crawl is always used), breast-stroke, backstroke and butterfly. In major championships, freestyle events range from 50 to 1500 metres, and the other strokes each have 100-metre and 200-metre events. There are also relay races, and medley races, in which swimmers use a different stroke for each of the four legs (stages) of the race.

Another major pool sport is *diving*, which is also an Olympic sport. Springboard diving is done from a flexible board 3 metres above the water, while highboard diving is done from a fixed platform 10 metres above the pool. Divers perform dives of varying difficulty from a programme of more than 80 standard dives, and are marked by a panel of judges.

Other pool sports include *synchronized swimming*, in which women competitors perform ballet routines in the water in time to music; and *water polo*, in which two teams of seven players try to score by throwing a ball into their opponents' goal.

Surfing and windsurfing

Surfing is the sport of riding a surfboard towards the shore on the face of a wave. Surfboards are made of hard, light plastic foam, covered with resin and fibreglass. Professional surfers tour the world, competing for prize money in a dozen or more competitions.

The basic surfing position is with one foot in the centre of the board, the other pressing down at the back. By changing the position of the feet and body the surfer can change speed and direction. Surfers aim to catch

an unbroken wave and then slide down its face. The most exciting type of wave is the 'tube', which happens when a wave curls over itself. The surfer tries to ride into and through the tube.

Boardsailors (or windsurfers) combine the skills of surfing and sailing to steer their sailboards at high speed across the water. The boardsailor steers without a rudder by moving the sail, which is controlled by a 'wishbone' boom encircling it. In addition to racing, there are freestyle events, in which the boardsailors perform various routines and tricks.

Canoeing

Canoeing is an Olympic sport, with events for the two main racing craft. In the *Canadian canoe* the canoeist uses a single-bladed paddle first on one side, then on the other; in the *kayak* a two-bladed paddle is used.

In the Olympics races are held on still water over 500 and 1000 metres (the longer distance is for men only). Men

• It is vital to learn to swim before you take up any water sport. In sports that take place on the sea or on fast-moving rivers, life-jackets should be worn, even by good swimmers.

• British sailors saw Hawaiian Islanders surfing in the Pacific Ocean more than 200 years ago. Apart from Hawaii, some of the best surfing conditions are found along the coasts of Australia and California.

▲ Windsurfing (properly called boardsailing) was pioneered in the USA in the 1960s. Its popularity spread so quickly that it was accepted as an Olympic event in 1984.

▶ Against the spectacular backdrop of Barcelona at the 1992 Olympics, a woman diver moves into the 'pike' position while making a forward dive from the highboard.

and women race separately in singles, pairs and fours. Up to nine canoes take part in races, and each event has elimination heats before the final.

White-water racing takes place on a rough, rocky course. There are two main types. In *slalom* (an Olympic event) canoeists start at intervals and have to paddle through a number of 'gates' (pairs of coloured poles) hanging above the water. Competitors have to paddle through some gates downstream (with the current) and some upstream. In *wild-water racing* the object is to complete a helter-skelter course of rapids, rocks and other obstacles – at least 3 kilometres from start to finish – in the fastest possible time.

▲ The Whitbread Round the World Race, for large ocean-going yachts, is held every four years. The race always starts and finishes in the UK, but the course itself varies from race to race. The total distance covered is about 60,000 km.

▲ Kayaking on the Colorado River in the USA.

Rowing

Rowing is a sport for men and women in which long paddles called oars are used. The boats are light and streamlined. The oarsmen sit on sliding seats, and the oars are fixed in rowlocks on outriggers (projecting brackets). Each oarsman usually has a single oar, but in the form of the sport called *sculling* the scullers have one smaller oar in each hand.

Rowing boats have crews of two, four or eight oarsmen. Eights have an extra person called a cox who steers the boat, while pairs and fours are 'coxed' or 'coxless'. Events are held on lakes, rivers and coastal waters. For competition at the top level, such as the Olympics and the world championships, a purpose-built dead-straight course on flat water is required.

Sailing

Yacht racing goes back to 17th-century England, when it first became a royal pastime. Racing yachts range from simple one-person dinghies, which most people can afford, to ocean-going vessels that cost millions of pounds to design and build, and require a crew of 20 or more. Racing takes place both inshore and offshore. In major regattas and competitions, such as the Olympic Games, boats of a single type compete in a number of races over a triangular course marked by buoys.

Motor-powered water sport

Most water sports rely entirely on muscle power or the power of wind or wave. Some, however, involve the use of motorboats.

Powerboats range in size from small vessels just big enough to hold a single person to large craft that weigh several tonnes. The most powerful boats can reach speeds in excess of 240 km per hour. Different types (classes) of boats compete separately, and there are hundreds of races and regattas each year.

Motorboats are also used in *water-skiing*, to tow the skier by means of a long rope. Water-skiers compete in a form of slalom in which they ski in and out of a line of buoys. They also jump for distance, launching themselves from a ramp, and perform tricks, which involves doing various stunts and routines while being towed.

find out more
Sailing
Ships and boats
Swimming and diving

Watt, James

Born 1736 in
Greenock, Scotland
Died 1819 aged 83

find out more
Engines
Industrial Revolution
Railways

James Watt was a designer and engineer who helped develop the steam engine. Although he did not invent it, it was his improvements that made the steam engine the main driving force behind the Industrial Revolution.

◀ This painting shows the young James Watt being fascinated with the steam coming out of a kettle. It is supposedly based on a real-life event that marked the beginning of Watt's interest in steam.

James Watt's father had a workshop and it was there that Watt practised his early design and engineering skills. His love of machines led him into a career making mathematical instruments such as compasses, based at Glasgow University.

It was there in 1764 that he was given a model of Thomas Newcomen's steam engine to repair. Watt saw that it was a clever idea to use steam pressure to drive an engine, but it was clear that Newcomen's design did not work well: it was very inefficient and wasted a lot of fuel. Watt began to make improvements, and over the next 10 years he produced a

really good engine. In 1775 he went into partnership with a businessman to manufacture and sell his steam engines.

Watt's engines started to transform British industry. Iron manufacturers used them to drive the great hammers which crushed the iron. In the textile industry his engines were used to power new machinery. And in coal-mining, the coal was lifted to the surface by winding-gear powered by the Watt engine. This replaced the men and women who had previously had to carry sacks of coal up ladders from the coal-face.

Watt's improvements made the steam engine a much more effective and useful tool. Soon other new steam engines would be driving even heavier machinery, such as the one designed by George Stephenson for locomotives.

Waves

• A radio wave (a kind of electromagnetic wave) might have a frequency of 1 million vibrations a second: 1 million hertz (Hz), or 1 megahertz (MHz).

find out more
Light
Radiation
Radio
Sound
X-rays

▶ We can measure the speed, the frequency and the wavelength of a wave. Its *frequency* is the number of wave crests that pass a particular point every second. Its *wavelength* is the distance between any two crests.

The word 'waves' probably makes you think of waves on the sea. Yet there are many other kinds of waves. Sounds reach our ears in waves, and radio and TV programmes travel to our homes in waves, although you cannot see them.

Some waves are started by something that is wobbling in a regular way, for example a tuning fork or a guitar string. This wobbling or shaking is called *vibration*. When something that is wobbling makes the air near it vibrate, we may hear a sound. As the tuning fork vibrates, the air is alternately squashed and expanded, and the squashes travel out as waves.

An electric current is surrounded by invisible electric and magnetic fields. If the electric current wobbles, these fields vibrate too, and the wobbles travel as waves. These are called *electromagnetic waves*.

Waves in the sea
The wind makes waves at sea by pushing against ripples and making them bigger. The water in a wave does not move from place to place. It travels in a circle, upwards and forwards on the wave crest, then down and back as the wave passes.

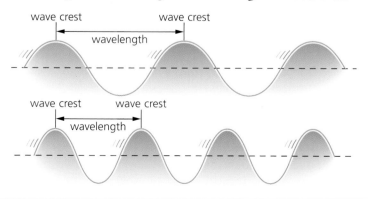

Longer waves
Longer wavelength: longer distance between crests
Lower frequency: fewer wave crests passing each second

Shorter waves
Shorter wavelength: shorter distance between crests
Higher frequency: more wave crests passing each second

Weapons

Since the earliest times, people have used weapons to defend themselves and their homes from attack by their enemies. Prehistoric people used simple weapons, such as sticks, stones and axes. Following the discovery of gunpowder, more powerful cannons and smaller firearms were developed. Modern weapons are very powerful and complicated, and some can kill many people at a time. The largest rockets can carry nuclear bombs to hit targets thousands of kilometres away.

▲ A catapult used by Roman soldiers to throw huge rocks at enemy castles.

Prehistoric people learned to use sticks and stones as weapons, then pointed sticks as spears and sharpened stones as knives and axes. When metal-working developed, bronze daggers replaced flint ones. Swords were made of bronze and, later, iron.

Bows were used as much as 20,000 years ago to fire arrows further and more accurately than a man could throw a spear. By the 10th century the Turks were making bows made from wood and animal bones. The crossbow was used across much of Europe during the 1100s. Later, the longbow was developed and was an important weapon in battles fought between the English and the French during the Hundred Years' War.

▲ The longbow had a range of 180 metres.

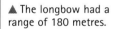

The first firearms

Before the discovery of gunpowder, weapons could only cut or hit. Now weapons could be developed which used the explosive power of gunpowder to fire a bullet or a shell. Firearms such as guns and cannons, and later bombs, started to appear.

Guns were developed in Europe in the 14th century, but the early ones were inaccurate, took several minutes to load, and could sometimes blow up in your face. In the 16th century they greatly improved with the development of the musket, which fired bullets that could penetrate a soldier's armour. In the 19th century a new development, the rifled barrel, made bullets spin in flight, so they could travel further, and in a straighter line. These new rifles could hit targets over 1000 metres away.

Cannons work in much the same way as guns but they fire bigger missiles over much longer distances. They were first used for attacking castles and fortified towns in the early 14th

▲ Musketeers fired their muskets from a rest stuck in the ground.

century. By the late 15th century no defences could withstand a cannon assault. During the course of 200 years they changed the face of warfare, and after their appearance most wars were decided on the battlefield. Field guns, which came after the heavy unwieldy cannons, were lighter and easier to transport. By the 18th century no army was complete without a battery of two-wheeled field guns. The basic design of the cannon remained unchanged until the 19th century, when breech-loading guns appeared. These were loaded at the rear, and fired shells that exploded on impact.

Weapons in the 20th century

Modern weapons have changed a lot from the early ones, although the guns carried by soldiers today are similar to those used in World War I. By the end of World War II the invention of the long-range rocket and the nuclear bomb changed the face of warfare. Today's firearms range in size from small hand pistols to large land guns with a barrel over 6 metres long. The explosive powder and the bullet are packaged together inside a *shell* or *cartridge*. Machine guns fire hundreds of bullets a minute, and modern rifles and pistols can fire bullets one after the other.

Bombs consist of a container, usually a metal case, filled with explosive material and a device called a fuse or detonator to set it on fire or make it explode. Aerial bombs, which were widely used in World War II and the Korean and Vietnam wars, are dropped from piloted aeroplanes and are filled with high explosives such as TNT. Newer types of bomb include anti-personnel cluster bombs, fuel-air explosive bombs, and laser-guided 'smart' bombs, which can hit small targets with accuracy. Nuclear bombs release the enormous energy produced during the processes of fission (the atom or A-bomb) or fusion (the hydrogen or H-bomb).

A *missile* is a weapon that is steered through the air to its target. With the help of radar and a computer, guided missiles can follow and hit a moving target, including other missiles. They can even can hit aircraft travelling at over 1800 kilometres per hour. They change direction using small wings, like aircraft, or by tilting their rocket nozzle. Long-range missiles, which carry nuclear bombs, are fired from land or from submarines. Some can travel over 8000 kilometres.

Land mines are explosive devices that are placed in the ground and cannot easily be seen. When a person steps on a mine, or when a vehicle drives over one, it explodes. In many recent civil wars, for example in countries such as Angola and the former Yugoslavia, millions of land mines have been left in the ground. Although originally intended to kill or injure enemy soldiers, land mines are often set off by passing civilian people, including children.

Weapon systems

Many different weapons are carried by ships and aircraft. A modern warship has large and small guns, guided missiles, torpedoes and depth charges to defend it. This use of many weapons together is called a weapons system. Tanks, ships

and aircraft are all *weapons delivery systems*. A modern tank can travel at over 60 kilometres per hour across muddy uneven ground, firing as it goes. Tanks can cross ditches and rivers, and some can even travel short distances under water.

There are two types of tank: large, heavy battle tanks and smaller, faster reconnaissance tanks used for scouting. A tank has one main gun, which is mounted on a rotating turret so that it can fire in any direction. The turret houses all the tank's crew apart from the driver, who sits at the front. The powerful diesel engine is at the rear.

Weapons for sport

In sports such as shooting and archery, people fire at targets with weapons. Weapons such as pistols and rifles are used in shooting. Archers use a bow and arrow to shoot at targets marked with coloured rings. The closer the arrow is to the centre of the target, the more points they score. Most bows are made of carbon or wood. The arrows used in target archery are usually made from a lightweight material like carbon or aluminium. This helps the arrow to fly through the air as quickly as possible.

▲ The US Apache helicopter carries massive firepower as a 'weapons delivery system'.

● Lighter firearms which can be used by a single person, such as pistols and rifles, are usually called *small arms*. Heavier military firearms, which are too big to be managed by one person, are known as *artillery*.

● The first aerial bombs were dropped on the Italian city of Venice from unmanned balloons by the Austrians in 1849.

● By the 15th century a large gun could fire a 300-kg cannon-ball several kilometres. One huge Turkish siege cannon was so heavy that it needed 100 oxen and 2000 men to pull it.

▼ The first tanks were used in 1916 in World War I. They were developed in Britain and France from the idea of the new tracked farm tractors.

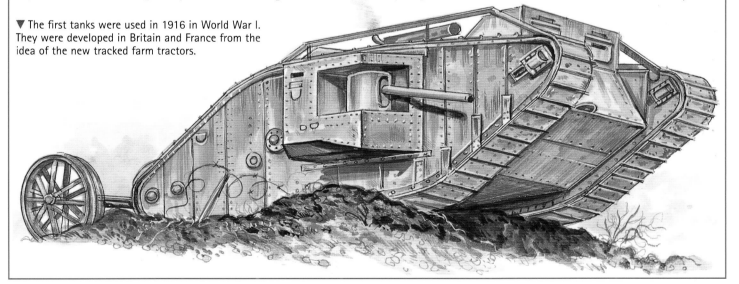

Weasels and their relatives

Although at first glance they look very different from each other, weasels, badgers, otters and skunks all belong to the weasel family.

• The weasel family contains 64 members, including 9 types of badger, 13 otters and 9 skunks. The rest of the family is made up of a variety of animals, such as weasels, stoats and polecats.

▶ Weasels are very fierce hunters. Some of them are so small that they are able to chase mice and voles down their tunnels.

Many of these animals, including some weasels, are small, active creatures with long bodies and short legs. But others, such as badgers and skunks, are larger and stockier. Members of the weasel family are found in most parts of the world and in many different habitats, both on land and in water.

Weasels

Weasels are fierce hunters, feeding mainly on small rodents. Their prey is killed with a bite to the base of the skull. They are often active during the daytime, for though they hunt mainly by scent, they have good senses of hearing and sight as well.

Young weasels may remain with their mother after they are weaned, and can sometimes be seen hunting together.

Skunks

Skunks live in the Americas. Most kinds are active at night, when they hunt for small rodents, insects, eggs, birds and plants. Their fur is black with white stripes or spots; this colouring acts as a warning to enemies. If a skunk is attacked, it defends itself by banging its front feet loudly on the ground and then doing a handstand and squirting a foul-smelling fluid from stink glands just beneath its tail. Most animals leave skunks well alone.

find out more
Mammals
Mice, squirrels and
  other rodents

▶ The striped skunk is the most common kind of skunk in the USA. Its stripes act as a warning to enemies.

Otters

Otters are more at home in the water than on land. Kept warm and dry by their dense waterproof coats, otters can close their nostrils and remain

▶ When it is swimming, an otter's long whiskers can feel movements in the water. This enables it to hunt in murky streams or in the dark.

underwater for up to 6 minutes. An otter's streamlined shape enables it to swim at speeds of up to 12 kilometres per hour.

River otters hunt small fishes, frogs and other water animals, which they catch in their mouth. Clawless otters, which live in tropical Asia and in Africa, use their sensitive fingers to feel in mud or under stones for crabs and similar animals.

Sea otters also use their forefeet to capture prey such as sea urchins, molluscs and other shelled creatures. The otter breaks open the shells by banging them on a stone which it rests on its chest.

Badgers

Badgers are shy creatures and are active at night. They are good diggers, using the long claws on their forelimbs to dig out food or make burrows called sets. European badgers usually live in groups of up to 12 animals. A set may be occupied for many generations and contain over 100 metres of tunnels, as well as a large number of entrance holes and living and sleeping chambers.

In spite of their powerful teeth, badgers feed mostly on small prey and plants. Their eyesight is poor, but they have excellent senses of hearing and smell. Badgers have special glands under their tails with which they mark or 'musk' familiar objects. Some kinds of badger have an unpleasant-smelling musk which they use to defend themselves.

▲ Despite having powerful teeth and claws, badgers are generally peaceable animals.

Weather

Rain, clouds, sunshine, wind: the conditions in the atmosphere and their day-to-day changes make up the weather. The weather affects our daily lives, and so we need to know in advance what it will be like. Weather forecasts aim to provide us with accurate details about weather conditions in the next 24 hours and for longer periods.

- The word 'meteorology' comes from two Greek words meaning 'study of what is high in the air'. (The word 'meteor' originally meant anything unusual that appeared in the sky.)

- It is likely that the weather affects people's moods. The warm, dusty sirocco wind of the Mediterranean and the mistral wind which blows down the Rhône Valley in France are famous for making people irritable.

Will it be safe to climb the mountain tomorrow? Do we need to grit the roads tonight? Will it be dry enough to harvest the crop this week? Everyone needs to know what the weather will be like in order to plan ahead. Information about future weather conditions saves money and can also save lives. Scientists who study the Earth's atmosphere and the weather are called *meteorologists*.

Weather recording

Reliable weather forecasting depends on a good supply of information about weather conditions all over the Earth. Thousands of separate pieces of weather information are collected several times a day from weather stations on land, from ships, from aeroplanes, from weather balloons up in the atmosphere and from satellites orbiting the Earth.

Weather observations are made at ground level by recording instruments located in weather stations. These stations need to be on open sites, away from buildings and trees which could influence the accuracy of readings. Observations must be precise and presented in a standard way so they can be compared with those taken at other sites and times. Some recordings are made by instruments carried up into the atmosphere by special weather balloons. The instruments can measure temperature, air pressure and wind speed, and transmit their readings back to Earth by radio.

▲ A satellite view of Hurricane Fran approaching the US mainland from the Caribbean in September 1996. The hurricane brought winds up to 190 km per hour. The day after this picture was taken the hurricane came ashore, killing 34 people.

Up in space, weather satellites photograph cloud patterns and movements, and the Earth's surface. Some carry instruments that can measure the heat given off by clouds and the Earth. Weather satellites of NOAA (National Oceanographic and Atmospheric Administration) in the USA provide most of the cloud pictures that we see on TV weather forecasts.

Weather forecasting

Forecasters have to know what is happening over the whole planet, because today's weather in America could affect the weather in Europe a week later. The data collected from all the different forms of weather recording are fed into a giant communications network called the Global Telecommunications System. The information is sent round the world at great speed by satellite, radio and cable. Weather forecasters in

▼ Some weather-recording instruments.

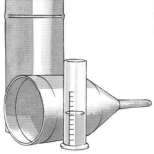

Rainfall is measured in a **rain gauge**. The amount of rain that falls in a day is measured in a cylinder marked in millimetres.

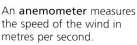

An **anemometer** measures the speed of the wind in metres per second.

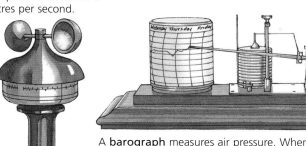

A **barograph** measures air pressure. When the air pressure changes, the top of the metal box (centre) bends and the movement is recorded on a rotating drum.

every country take from the system the data they need to make their own local forecast.

The information is first mapped on a 'synoptic chart', which shows the overall weather situation. Forecasters then make their predictions using their knowledge of how the atmosphere behaves, and with the help of computers which show what happened the last time when there were similar conditions. The forecasts must then be turned into maps and descriptions of what the weather will be like for the next 24 hours, for newspapers, television and radio.

Forecasts are becoming more accurate as time goes by, especially for short periods ahead. However, long-range forecasting is still difficult.

Cyclones and anticyclones

Cyclones and anticyclones affect the weather. A cyclone is an area of low air pressure, which means the air is rising. Cyclones often bring strong winds, stormy weather and even snow. They form over the sea, but as they move over large land areas cyclones gradually lose energy and fade out. Cyclones usually move faster than anticyclones. If you look at the weather maps for three or four days in a row, you can often follow the path of a cyclone.

Cyclones have different names in different parts of the world. In Britain they are usually called *depressions*. In tropical and subtropical areas a cyclone with very strong winds is called a *hurricane* or a *typhoon*. A tropical cyclone seen from a satellite is a great swirling mass of clouds. Its violent winds can do great damage as they roar across the oceans and islands.

In an anticyclone the air pressure is high because the air is sinking. Anticyclones bring more settled weather. In an anticyclone, high air pressure remains stable over a wide area. For example, a very large anticyclone stays over the vast area of Siberia in Russia every winter. It hardly changes its position from October to March, during which time the weather in Siberia is bitterly cold. Other parts of the world also have anticyclones in certain seasons. The weather map over the Sahara Desert often shows an anticyclone in the winter months.

• Many sayings about the weather are based on what the sky looks like. 'Red sky at night, shepherds' delight' is not always true, but 'Red sky in the morning, shepherds' warning' is usually reliable.

find out more
Air
Atmosphere
Climate
Clouds
Heat
Rain and snow
Satellites
Seasons
Wind

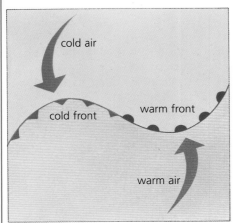

Before a depression: warm air meets cold air to form a warm front and a cold front.

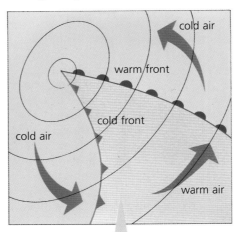

After a depression: the cold front catches up with the warm front. The different air masses mix, forming an occluded front.

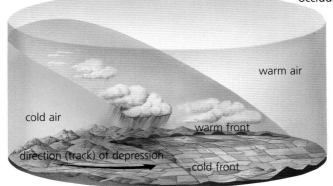

During a depression: the cold front pushes the warm air upwards. Large clouds form and heavy rain falls.

◄ A depression has two *fronts* (the lines where two different masses of air meet). The warm front is the forward edge of warm air pushing against cold air. The cold front is the following edge of cold air pushing against warm air.

Weeds

Any plant growing where it is not wanted is a weed. Even a rose bush might be considered a weed if it was growing in a vegetable patch. Most weeds are fast-growing plants that can spread to new areas quickly.

Weeds often produce large numbers of seeds that are easily spread. In dandelions, for example, each fruit has a tiny parachute to carry it away on the slightest breeze. The common garden weed groundsel goes on setting seed even after it has been pulled up. Other weeds, such as creeping buttercup, produce shoots, called runners, which root wherever they touch the ground, and help the plant to spread quickly.

Pioneer plants

When a piece of land is cleared, weeds are usually the first plants to grow. Their colourful flowers attract insects, and flocks of birds come to feed on the seeds. If the land is left long enough, other plants will eventually grow. But in places such as the verges of roads and railways, regular cutting stops other plants from getting established, and weeds take over.

Controlling weeds

Gardeners often control weeds by digging them up. But farmers usually use chemicals that kill the weeds but not the crop plants. There is now concern about the harmful effects of these chemical weedkillers.

find out more
Flowering plants

▶ Weeds growing on waste ground. The bush upper left is buddleia, the large pink flowers on the right are rosebay willowherbs.

Wells and springs

A water well is a deep hole dug or drilled in the ground to obtain water. Many people still get their water supply from wells, particularly in rural areas. A spring is the name given to any natural flow of water out of the ground. Long ago, villages frequently grew up around large springs.

Some of the rain that falls on the land sinks into the ground. The water soaks easily through rocks such as sandstone or chalk. These rocks are said to be permeable. But some materials, such as clay, stop the water sinking any further, and are said to be impermeable. The water that goes into the ground sinks until it reaches either a layer of impermeable material, or a rock that cannot soak up any more water. The level in the ground below which water collects is called the *water table*. If a hole is dug deep enough to reach below the water table, water will seep from the surrounding rocks into the well. The water is then drawn or pumped up to the surface.

Springs are often found where permeable rocks lie above impermeable ones, particularly at the foot of steep slopes. Many of the largest rivers begin their lives as springs.

Sometimes a layer of water-holding rock is sandwiched between two layers of impermeable rock.

London is built over rocks like these. At one time, if a well was dug down to the water table under London, the pressure underground was so high that the water came out of the well like a fountain. A well like this is called an *artesian well*.

• Long ago, people believed that many wells were holy or lucky. The Celts of western Europe frequently built altars and made sacrifices at wells, while the Romans dedicated their wells to goddesses.

◀ Water from this village well in India is drawn up in buckets attached to a moving chain. The chain is driven round by a wheel moved by the oxen.

find out more
Oil
Rocks and minerals
Water

Wetlands

Wetlands are damp, boggy areas where water lies on the surface, forming lakes or pools, or where plants have grown out into open water to form marshes or swamps. Wetlands support huge numbers of plants and animals, and their value to humans is enormous. For example, two-thirds of the fish caught around the world began their life in wetlands.

Wetlands are always changing. Once wetland plants begin to grow, they gradually build up and stabilize the ground, until eventually plants that grow on dry land can move in. In the same way, salt-marshes along coasts gradually extend out to sea. Wetlands disappear naturally as they become silted up, but at the same time new wetlands form in other places.

Types of wetland

There are many different kinds of wetland. Some are formed naturally, while others result from human activities.

Where rivers meander slowly over large flat flood plains, the slow-moving water drops the fine particles of soil and rock (sediment) into the water, and mudbanks gradually build up. River bends may get separated off, and form marshy

pools or lakes. Mud also builds up on the shores of estuaries, where rivers meet the sea. At the mouth of the largest rivers, this mud forms vast fan-shaped deltas. Plants which can cope with occasional flooding by salty sea water grow here, forming *salt-marshes*, which are home to many wading birds and other animals.

The coasts of some tropical seas are fringed with *mangrove swamps*. Mangroves are trees adapted to live in wet, salty places. Their roots stick up into the air from the mud. The plants take in oxygen from the air through these roots, because there is very little oxygen in the wet mud. Mangrove swamps are home to many different animals. Fiddler crabs scuttle about the mud, scavenging for the dead remains of plants and animals. Millions of tiny creatures live in the mud, which is enriched by dead mangrove leaves. The warm, shallow waters are a nursery for the young of many ocean fishes, which are hunted by crocodiles, alligators and birds such as storks, ibises and herons.

Large areas of the cooler parts of the world are covered in *peatlands*. These are formed by remarkable plants called bog mosses, which are able to grow in waterlogged areas. As they grow, bog mosses trap water amongst their leaves, like a natural sponge. In the waterlogged soil of the peatlands, plant material does not rot away. Bog mosses pile up and form a spongy material

• People are slowly learning the usefulness of wetlands. In some places, beds of reeds are being planted to act as a natural filter for sewage, instead of building expensive treatment works.

find out more
Conservation
Ecology
Moors and heaths
Rivers and streams

▼ Lesser flamingos on Lake Nakuru, a salty lake in Kenya, East Africa. Millions of birds come to the lake because the shallow water is full of the tiny insects, worms and crustaceans that they feed on.

known as peat. Peatlands are important areas for many breeding birds and insects.

Some wetlands are made by human activity. Disused gravel pits fill with water, and marshes develop around the edges of reservoirs. Many of these make valuable nature reserves. In warm countries, flooded paddy fields, made for growing rice, are home to fishes, egrets and herons.

The importance of wetlands

Wetlands are enormously rich food sources. Many small animals live in the soft ground, and provide food for shrews, frogs, toads and long-legged shore birds such as sandpipers and curlews. Insects thrive in wetlands, attracting insect-eating warblers and flycatchers. Seed-eating birds come to wetlands for the seed heads of the reeds and rushes, and large mammals come for water. Because of the water and rich feeding available, wetlands are important stopover places for millions of migrating birds.

Wetlands are valuable for humans as well as animals and plants. They soak up water during storms and let it drain away gradually. This reduces the effect of floods downstream. Peatlands 'lock up' carbon dioxide released by burning coal and oil, and so help reduce global warming. Mangrove swamps help to protect tropical coastlines, by forming a natural barrier against severe storms and hurricanes. They are also important to the fishing industry, as many commercially caught fish breed in them.

In some places, wetlands ensure that the water supply for local cities is good enough to drink. The mud acts like a water filter, removing impurities from the water that passes through.

Saving wetlands

In recent years, humans have been destroying wetlands at an alarming rate. It is estimated that half the wetlands that once existed have been lost, and many more are under threat. Many wetlands have been drained so that the land they occupy can be built on or farmed. Other areas have been filled in as rubbish dumps. Many wetlands have become polluted, as the rivers that feed them have picked up pesticides and other chemicals. Some peatlands are being destroyed by large peat-fired power stations, which use up the peat much faster than it can be replaced. Peat is also used by gardeners, which adds to the destruction of wild peatlands.

Conservationists and scientists are persuading governments to set aside wetlands for wildlife, because of their valuable role in protecting the environment. But simply leaving wetlands alone is not enough. Many would gradually silt up and disappear. Their water supply must be carefully controlled to prevent this, and to stop the water draining away to surrounding areas.

► Mudskippers are small fishes that live in mangrove swamps, scuttling over the mud on their front fins. They can stay out of water for long periods, breathing a mixture of air and water stored in their gill chambers.

Whales and dolphins

Whales may look like fishes, with smooth, streamlined bodies perfectly adapted for life in water, but in fact they are mammals – just like us. They are very intelligent animals, and they produce a single live young, which they feed on milk.

Smaller whales are generally known as dolphins and porpoises, but in most respects they are similar to their giant relatives.

Whales

There are two main types of whale. The *toothed whales* include the smaller dolphins and porpoises, as well as giants such as the sperm whale. These animals use their pointed teeth to catch and hold fish or squid. The *baleen whales* are all large and include the right whale and the enormous blue whale. These whales feed on shrimp-like creatures called krill, which they sift out of the water with huge fringed plates in their mouths. The plates are made of baleen, a material similar to our fingernails.

Whales live all their lives in water. They breathe through a blow-hole on top of their head and can only breathe when they come to the surface.

Whales can hear very well (even though they have no visible ears). Some use sounds we call whale songs to communicate with each other. They may also use ultrasound (sound waves that humans cannot hear) to locate obstacles and food.

Whales have always been an important source of food and oil to Arctic peoples, but commercial whaling has brought many kinds close to extinction. Most whales are now protected, although a few countries continue to hunt them.

Dolphins and porpoises

Dolphins are small, slender whales, some of which are capable of swimming at speeds of about 50 kilometres per hour. Most of them have a large, curved fin in the middle of the back that helps to stabilize them. They usually live in the open sea, though some come into inshore waters.

Most kinds of dolphin have a long snout crammed with up to 200 small pointed teeth, ideal for catching fish. The largest of the dolphins, the killer whale, sometimes hunts in packs to catch much bigger animals.

Porpoises differ from dolphins in a number of ways. They are generally smaller, and have rounded faces. They are all quite playful and can often be seen in small groups, called schools, cartwheeling in the water.

▼ A sperm whale (**1**), a right whale (**2**), a dolphin (**3**) and a porpoise (**4**), drawn to scale.

- Dolphins are thought to be among the most intelligent of animals. They are sometimes kept and trained to do tricks and to help underwater engineers.

- Whales are warm-blooded, like all other mammals. They are kept warm by a layer of blubber beneath the skin.

- There are 84 different kinds of whale, including 40 dolphins and 6 porpoises. The largest of these (and the largest animal in the world) is the blue whale, which grows to about 30 m in length and weighs over 100 tonnes.

find out more
Mammals
Oceans and seas

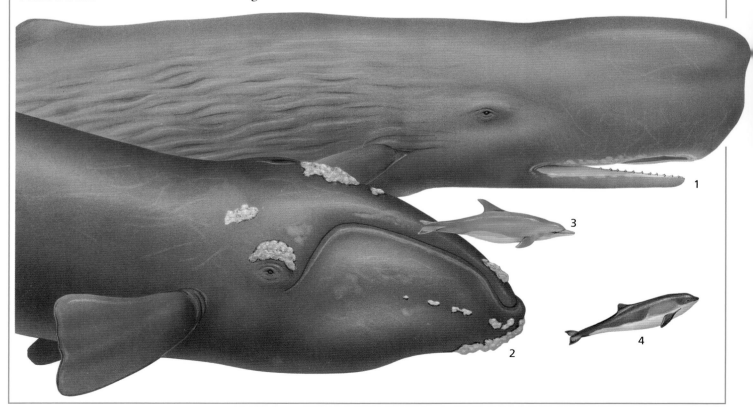

Wildlife

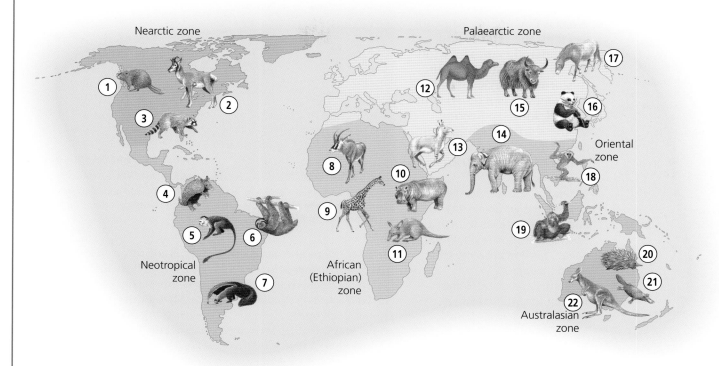

Nearctic zone

Palaearctic zone

Oriental zone

Neotropical zone

African (Ethiopian) zone

Australasian zone

The word 'wildlife' means all the plants and animals in the world that are not tame or domesticated.

If you were to travel about the world, you would notice a change in the kinds of plants and animals between one area and another. This is partly because of environment and climate, and partly because the big landmasses of the continents are separated from each other by water. The plants and animals in each one have evolved (changed) over millions of years and adapted to their separate environments.

Zones of life

The world can be divided into six *biogeographical zones* ('biogeography' means the geography of living things). Each zone tends to have many plants and animals not shared by the others, although they often have related species. Even when the same kind of habitat exists in different zones, there are usually different animals of a similar kind living in it. For example, the prairies of North America and the steppes of eastern Europe and Asia are both grasslands with hot summers and cold winters. In the steppes, susliks and marmots live in basically the same way as the related prairie dogs of North America.

▲ A map of the world's six biogeographical zones. The animals illustrated are found only in their particular zone, and nowhere else in the world.

In a few cases the same animals may be present in different zones. This happens in northern North America, northern Asia and Europe. If you were to take a trip round these cold regions, you would find reindeer (caribou), wolverines and brown bears in the whole area, although many of the small animals are different. The reason for this is that until about 10,000 years ago there was a land bridge between north-east Asia and Alaska. Animals were able to move from one great landmass to the other. Now the sea has broken through that bridge, and the American and Asiatic animals have been separated. But they have not been apart from each other for long enough to have changed very much.

It is easiest to see the biggest differences in wildlife among the mammals. Birds, which can fly, often move between two or more zones during migration, and some kinds, such as the swallow and the peregrine falcon, are found in almost all regions. Even plants can travel between zones, as their seeds can be carried by wind, water or birds (stuck to their feet or beaks, or in their droppings).

1 mountain beaver
2 pronghorn
3 racoon
4 armadillo
5 capuchin monkey
6 tree sloth
7 giant anteater
8 roan antelope
9 giraffe
10 hippopotamus
11 aardvark
12 Bactrian camel
13 onager
14 Asian elephant
15 yak
16 giant panda
17 wild horse
18 gibbon
19 orang-utan
20 echidna (spiny anteater)
21 duck-billed platypus
22 kangaroo

find out more
Conservation
Continents
Ecology
Food chains and webs
Islands
Marsupials
Migration

Wind

Wind is flowing air. You can feel it on the ground and high up in the air. The wind can be very destructive, in the form of hurricanes and tornadoes. It can also be put to work for us, powering sailing ships, windmills and modern aerogenerators which produce electricity.

▲ A tornado looks like a violent, twisting funnel of cloud which stretches down from a storm cloud to the Earth. The wind twists up within the tunnel at speeds of up to 650 km/h.

• In southern France, a cold northerly wind called the mistral often blows for several days at a time during March and April.

• In North America a warm dry wind called the chinook blows down the eastern slopes of the Rocky Mountains. It causes the temperature to rise quickly, often making snow thaw rapidly. The word Chinook means 'snow eater' in a local Native American language.

find out more
Climate
Rain and snow
Weather

When the Sun warms the ground, the air above it rises up and cooler air flows in to take the place of the air which has risen. This flowing air is what we call wind.

Many winds have names. Among the most constant winds are the 'trade winds'. These winds blow towards the Equator and blow most of the year round. They got their name in the times when much world trade was done by sailing ships. Ships always tried to avoid other areas in tropical oceans where winds hardly ever blow. These are called the 'doldrums'.

Hurricanes and tornadoes

Hurricanes are violent storms with winds that can blow at 250 to 350 km/h and bring torrential rain. They pick up moisture over an area of warm sea and hurtle towards the land. Such storms are called hurricanes in the Atlantic, but in the Pacific and Indian Oceans they are often called *cyclones* or *typhoons*. The swirling mass of winds spirals upwards around the 'eye' at the centre of the storm. The eye of the hurricane is a fairly calm area, but the strongest winds occur immediately around it.

Hurricane winds can uproot trees, destroy buildings, and even lift up boats and cars and throw them around. Along with the heavy rains and destructive winds, hurricanes bring very high tides. Today, hurricanes can be tracked on satellite photos. Each one is given a name, and warnings are issued in good time so that people can leave the area if necessary.

A tornado is quite different from a hurricane. It is a smaller, faster and more violent wind. A tornado (sometimes called a *whirlwind* or *twister*) is a terrifying wind which destroys everything in its path. It rushes across the land, sucking up dust, sand, and even people and animals like a giant vacuum cleaner into its twisting centre.

Wind power

For centuries, windmills have used the power of the wind for grinding corn and pumping water. In the Netherlands and the fens of eastern England, windmills were used to drain water from low-lying land. They are still used in many parts of the world for pumping water from wells and drainage ditches. Today, *aerogenerators* are using the wind's energy to generate electricity. Unlike oil and gas, the wind is an energy source which will never run out and does not cause any pollution.

Most aerogenerators have a tall, slim tower with huge propeller-like blades mounted on top. The blades can be over 20 metres long. As they spin in the wind, they turn a generator which produces electricity. Aerogenerators are placed on exposed sites on high ground to catch the maximum force of the wind. Large groups of them form 'wind farms' like this one at Altamont Pass in California, USA.

Wine *see* Alcohol

Winter sports

Winter sports take place on ice or snow. The most popular of these sports are skating, skiing and ice hockey.

The main competition for winter sports is the Winter Olympic Games, which are held every four years. As well as various skating and skiing events, the Games include the biathlon, which combines skiing and shooting, and two forms of sled racing (the bobsleigh and the luge).

Ice skating

Winter sports that involve skating on ice include figure skating, ice dancing, speed skating and ice hockey. All of these are major sports in the Winter Olympics.

Figure skating used to involve cutting 'figures' or patterns on the ice, but this is no longer a part of major competition. The three figure-skating events are men's and women's singles and mixed pairs. In each of these, competitors perform compulsory and free programmes to music.

The figure skate has a grooved blade with two edges, and skaters perform their movements – spinning, taking off and landing – on one or other of these. In pairs, the partners combine for jumps, lifts and spins, and also perform matching movements such as spins and jumps while apart. The skaters are awarded marks for style (artistic impression) as well as skill (technical merit).

▶ Short-track speed skaters at the 1994 Winter Olympics. Short-track races take place on a 111-m track, over distances from 500 to 3000 m.

Ice dancing is similar to pairs, with a man and a woman performing to music. However, the judges are looking for grace and artistry rather than athleticism.

In *speed skating*, men and women race separately over distances ranging from 500 to 10,000 metres. In long-track speed skating, on a 400-metre outdoor track, there are two lanes, and competitors race in pairs, switching lanes in a change-over zone on every lap. In short-track speed skating, four to six competitors race each other in knock-out heats leading to a final.

Skiing

Skiing is both a popular sport and a leisure activity in specialized ski resorts. Ski equipment includes skis, which are flat, narrow runners that curve up at the front, and ski poles, which are used for balance and for leverage.

▲ A competitor in the women's giant slalom at the 1996 world championships. In slalom racing, skiers weave between sets of poles, or 'gates'. Both feet must pass through the gate, but the skier is allowed to hit the gate poles themselves.

There are two main branches of ski racing. In *Alpine ski racing*, competitors ski down mountain slopes. They start at intervals, and the winner is determined on time. In downhill, they ski straight down the course. In the slalom events, they have to ski through a series of 'gates'.

Nordic skiing includes cross-country racing (langlauf) and ski-jumping. Nordic racers use lightweight skis and long ski poles. They start at intervals. Ski jumpers ski down a steep ramp before jumping. They are awarded points for style as well as distance.

- You can read about ice hockey in the article on Hockey.

- The sport of *tobogganing* is divided into two types, called lugeing and skeleton tobogganing. Both involve sliding down ice-covered tracks on small sleds. Speeds can exceed 120 km per hour.

- Bobsleighs are streamlined machines with mechanical brakes and steering. They are guided down specially prepared tracks of ice with banked bends, travelling at speeds in excess of 135 km per hour.

- Ice yachting involves travelling across ice in a craft that has runners and sails. The techniques are like those of ordinary sailing.

Witches

Witches in stories have pointed hats and black cats, and ride broomsticks through the sky. They chant magic spells. They are wicked, frightening women, until the hero or heroine tricks them and escapes.

If you had lived 400 years ago, you would not have laughed at stories of witches. Almost everyone believed that some women were the servants of the Devil.

If a child or an animal became ill, people sometimes thought that it had been cursed. They looked around for the guilty person – a witch. It was usually poor, old women who were accused of being witches.

One way of testing a witch was to tie her up and throw her into water. People thought that water rejected evil and that only the guilty would float. So the innocent drowned, and those who floated were killed. In most of Europe witches were burnt; in England they were hanged.

During the 17th century, witch-hunting became a mania. In parts of Germany there were a hundred burnings a year. In England over 200 women were hanged in just two years.

As scientific knowledge grew, belief in witchcraft faded, and there were few trials after 1700. In Salem, in Massachusetts in the USA, 30 people were executed for witchcraft in 1692. Only five years later, the judge and jury publicly admitted their mistake.

• A female witch is called a witch or a sorceress. A male witch is called a wizard, sorcerer or warlock.

• A witch who does good, like healing sick people, is often called a white witch.

◄ This German woodcut of 1555 shows three women accused of practising as witches being burned at the stake. They are condemned to suffer burning in death and in the afterlife (shown to the right). A demon is clutching one of them as she burns.

find out more
Myths and legends
Stories and story-tellers

Women's movement

For many centuries there have been people who want women to have the same rights as men. While different women's groups may campaign for different things, the movement as a whole is often called the women's movement.

From about 1850 there were campaigns in both the USA and Britain for married women to be able to own their own property, instead of everything belonging to the husband when they married. Women also campaigned for 'suffrage' or the right to vote. In Britain, many women became suffragettes to force a change in the law. By the end of the 1920s, the right to vote had been won by women in many countries.

After this, women's organizations campaigned for such things as childcare to enable them to work. In the 1960s, the women's liberation movement started in the USA. Feminists began to work for equal pay, equal education and equal opportunities.

In the 1990s women's groups are an accepted part of society. In business, sport, music, trade unions and many other areas, there are women's organizations which meet regularly and give positive advice and support to each other.

◄ Emmeline Pankhurst, suffragette leader, being arrested for an attack on Buckingham Palace, May 1914. The suffragettes, led by Emmeline and her daughter Christabel, became known for their dramatic publicity stunts. They burned empty buildings, smashed windows and chained themselves to railings.

Writing for women's equality

A Vindication of the Rights of Women, Mary Wollstonecraft (1792)
The Second Sex, Simone de Beauvoir (1949)
The Feminine Mystique, Betty Friedan (1963)
Sexual Politics Kate Millet (1969)
The Female Eunuch Germaine Greer (1970)
Women and Sex Nawal El Saadawi (1972)
The Beauty Myth Naomi Wolf (1992)

find out more
Peace movement

Wood

◀ Some buildings are constructed almost entirely of wood. This house being built in Montana, USA, has a wooden frame, and the walls are made of wood planking.

Wood is the material that makes up the trunks of trees and shrubs. People use wood for making all kinds of things, and for building. It is strong and hard-wearing, but can be cut and carved easily. Perhaps the greatest advantage of wood over other materials is that trees are a renewable resource – with care, we can go on using wood for ever, without supplies running out.

Each year, as a tree grows, it produces more wood in its trunk, and this yearly growth forms 'annual rings'. (You can tell how old a tree is by counting these rings.) The rings add an attractive pattern to the cut wood. This pattern is called the 'grain', and it also affects the wood's properties; for instance, it is easier to split along its grain.

Preparing wood

Foresters use power saws to fell (cut down) trees, and large machines to trim the branches off the tree trunk in seconds. At the sawmill, large saws slice the logs into planks. Before the timber can be used, it must be seasoned (dried), otherwise it will twist or shrink. Sometimes the planks are seasoned in the air. More often this is done in a special building called a kiln, where warm air is blown over the planks in order to dry them quickly.

Not all logs are cut into planks. Some are turned against a sharp blade so that thin sheets, called veneers, are peeled off. These veneers may then be used to make plywood, which is stronger and cheaper to produce than solid woods of the same thickness. Any waste wood left over at the sawmill can be made into chipboard. This is often covered with veneers or plastics and used for kitchen fittings and furniture. Another use of wood is for making paper. Vast quantities of softwoods are made into pulp for paper-making. Even trees with poor trunks can be used in this way, so in some countries forests are planted

▼ Carpenters who specialize in making furniture are often called cabinet-makers. Skilled cabinet-makers are still in demand for high-quality, decorative work.

where trees will never grow well, just for the paper industry.

Some wood products are made by breaking down the wood using chemical processes. They include charcoal for fuel; lignin for plastics and road-building materials; and wood pulp for rayon, paper and photographic film.

Types of wood

When we use wood for crafts or building, we call it *timber*. Timber is often divided into two main types: hardwood and softwood.

Softwood comes from coniferous trees such as spruce, pine and cedar. Foresters plant conifers because they grow quickly. Softwoods are easy to saw, drill, chisel and plane. They are useful for building, for packaging (for example, crates), for making chipboard and for papermaking.

Hardwood comes from slower-growing, broad-leaved trees such as oak, beech, ash and tropical trees such as teak and mahogany. They are hard to cut and shape, but very tough and resistant to rot. They often have beautiful grains. Hardwoods are used to make good furniture, and for special

items such as boats, musical instruments and cricket bats. Hardwood timber can also be sliced into thin veneers to cover softwood chipboard for cheap furniture. Tropical hardwoods are becoming very rare, because so many of the trees have been felled from the wild forests.

Carpentry

Carpentry is working with wood to make things. For instance, carpenters may produce furniture or help to build houses. The majority of wooden items, such as doors, window frames and most furniture, are made in factories using specially designed wood-cutting machines. However, there are still many types of wood-working that require a skilled carpenter.

Skilled carpenters are often called joiners. This is because one of the most important skills that carpenters have to learn is how to join pieces of wood together. By carefully cutting the pieces of wood so that they fit together precisely, a carpenter can make a strong joint. Added strength can then be given by gluing or screwing the pieces of wood together.

find out more
Building
Forests
Materials
Paper
Tools
Trees and shrubs

▼ Different ways in which wood is used.
1 The best wood (hardwood and softwood) is sawn into planks and other types of timber.
2 Poorer wood is sliced into veneers. Three or more veneers may then be used to make *plywood* and *blockboard*.
3 Waste wood is cut into chips, mixed with sawdust, glued and pressed into sheets to make *chipboard*. Smaller pieces are made into *hardboard*.
4 Softwoods are also pulped to make paper.

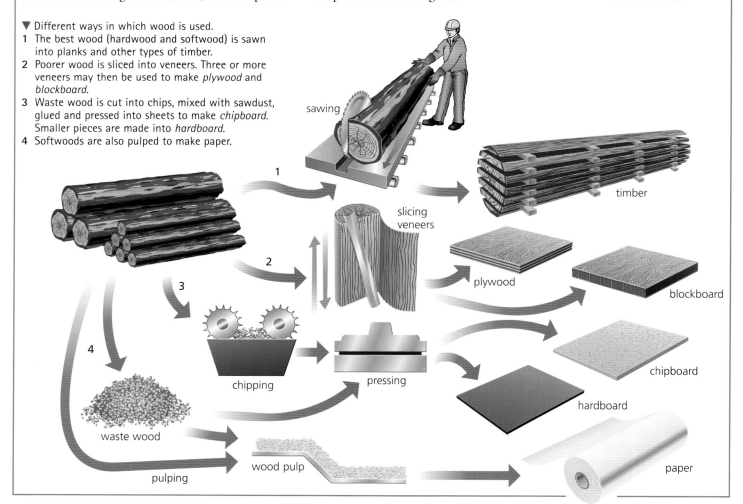

sawing

1

slicing
veneers

timber

2

3

plywood

blockboard

chipping

pressing

chipboard

4

hardboard

waste wood

pulping

wood pulp

paper

Wool

Wool comes from sheep, goats, llamas and some other animals. It is soft and resists dirt, static and tearing. Wool protects against both the cold and the heat. We use it to make strong, lasting fabrics for rugs, blankets and items of warm clothing such as coats, sweaters and gloves.

Wool has some unusual qualities which make it a very useful fibre. Wool is said to breathe because it stays in balance with the surrounding moisture even when no longer alive and growing. It absorbs and evaporates moisture.

Two kinds of yarn are made from wool for weaving and knitting. *Woollens* are spun from fibres which vary in length and are jumbled up together.

Worsteds are spun from wool that is combed to make a smoother, more even yarn.

Many countries have sheep and produce wool, but four countries dominate the world trade in wool: Australia, New Zealand, South Africa and Argentina. They export more than half their wool to countries in the northern hemisphere.

▶ FLASHBACK ◀

Prehistoric people wore sheepskins, but also made yarn and fabric from the fleece. From ancient to medieval times women spent time spinning, but weaving was considered more difficult and was left to men.

During the Industrial Revolution, cloth manufacture was revolutionized by the introduction of machines which could do work that had previously been done by hand.

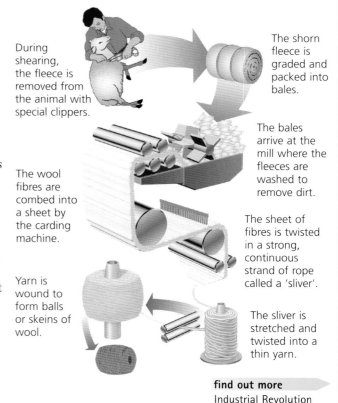

During shearing, the fleece is removed from the animal with special clippers.

The shorn fleece is graded and packed into bales.

The wool fibres are combed into a sheet by the carding machine.

The bales arrive at the mill where the fleeces are washed to remove dirt.

Yarn is wound to form balls or skeins of wool.

The sheet of fibres is twisted in a strong, continuous strand of rope called a 'sliver'.

The sliver is stretched and twisted into a thin yarn.

find out more
Industrial Revolution
Textiles

Word processors

A word processor is a computer which can be used as a typewriter. You type at the keyboard and the words and numbers (the text) appear on a screen. Some word processors can handle pictures (graphics) too. In offices across the world, reports, letters, magazines and newspapers are prepared using word processors. The articles in this encyclopedia were prepared in this way.

Word processors have now mostly replaced typewriters. Like a typewriter, most word processors have a 'qwerty' keyboard. It gets this name from the first six keys on the top row of letters on the keyboard. By using special keys, you can change the text and move it about. You can store or save the text on computer disk until you need it again. Some word processors have special spelling and grammar checkers. An electronic printer prints out the text on paper.

Most word processors plug into the mains electricity. Some run on batteries and are small enough to be used on trains and planes. These are usually small portable computers called *laptops*. Many word processors are just ordinary desktop computers with a special program in them for word processing. Some even 'learn' words you use a lot and complete them as soon as you have begun to type them.

Journalists use word processors to design and prepare whole pages for magazines and newspapers. This is sometimes called *desktop publishing*. At the printer's, signals from a word processor can be sent straight to the machine which makes the printing plates.

find out more
Computers
Information technology
Printing

● Many organizations use word processors to send out 'personal' letters. Everyone receives the same basic letter, but the word processor changes the name and address each time.

◀ This scientist is using a word processor to update scientific information on screen. The information appears on the World Wide Web, a computer network that connects tens of thousands of computers across the world.

World music

People all around the world make music. Some kinds of music are popular in many countries. Others are found only in a small area, or among a few people. Wherever it occurs, music helps people to say something about who they are, to remember their culture and beliefs, and to express their emotions.

Music is not a language, but it works like a language in some ways: sounds of different pitches and rhythms are put into phrases, and phrases go together to make longer pieces. Music is sometimes called a universal language because it has a similar effect on all people, regardless of where they are from.

Europe

There is a great variety of folk music in Europe. Some of the most famous kinds are Irish music and flamenco from Spain.

▶ Johnny Cash was a famous American country-and-western singer. Country-and-western music originated in the USA but was strongly influenced by the folk music of the English, Irish and Scottish people that settled in the USA in the 19th and early 20th centuries.

▲ In many parts of the world instruments and music have been influenced by foreigners living in the area. These Quechua Indians in Peru are playing violins and harps – instruments brought to the country by Spanish colonists during the late 18th and early 19th centuries.

In Irish music several performers meet to play through their favourite songs and dances, often in a pub. Traditional instruments include the guitar, violin, tin whistle, accordian and bodhran (an Irish drum).

In flamenco, performers express their deepest feelings through song and dance. They are accompanied by rhythmic guitar music, hand-clapping, and by cries of encouragement from the listeners.

The Americas and Oceania

In North America we can hear the music of the Native Americans, the music of people from many other parts of the world, and music created in the USA itself, including jazz, rap, barbershop, rock and country-and-western.

North America is made up of a great variety of people from many parts of the world. One reason why American popular music is so successful is that its composers and performers take ideas from the many different kinds of music they hear around them in American life.

Music in the Caribbean, Central America and South America is just as varied as that in North America. There are European, African and Asian musical traditions. There are also the musical styles of the native South American peoples, for example panpipe music from the Andes mountains, and newly invented forms like Caribbean steel-drum music.

All across the Pacific Ocean there are islands where people live and make music. In Australia, Aboriginal people sing to preserve and develop their religion and culture. The 'songman' is an important person who receives messages from the spirits of nature.

The people of the Solomon Islands have a long tradition of playing bamboo panpipes. The instrument is played either on its own or in a large group of many others, in a sort of panpipe orchestra. In the 19th century this music was banned by Christian missionaries from the West, but some musicians have kept it alive.

Asia and the Middle East

In South-east Asia, traditional percussion music is still very popular. The Indonesian *gamelan* orchestra has gongs, xylophones, drums and other instruments. It accompanies dance and song performances, and the theatre, where shadow-puppets act out exciting myths and legends.

Further north, in East Asia, we also find many theatrical traditions. The Beijing opera in China mixes speech, song, acting and acrobatics to make a very dramatic performance. In Korean *pansori*, on the other hand, one singer has to take all the parts in a story, and narrates the story as well.

Not all East Asian music is theatrical, however. Over the past three centuries Japanese composers have written many solos for the bamboo flute (the *shakuhachi*). The written music does not look like Western music, with its five-line stave. Instead, a vertical column of special symbols tells the performer exactly what to do. Much East Asian music is not written down at all. In Mongolian overtone singing, for example, one performer whistles a melody and sings a low note at the same time.

The music of the Middle East has been deeply influenced by Islamic culture. For instance, professional performers often belong to hereditary castes, and men and women may make music separately.

Improvisation is a key musical feature across this area. This means that although people compose new pieces, good musicians make old pieces sound new each time they play them. The musicians learn how to make up new tunes and rhythms while they play. In India, for example, a musician

▲ These musicians are from Rajasthan, a state in northeast India. In Indian music, players often take a raga (set series of notes) and tala (set rhythm) and improvise on it. Each raga and tala is associated with a particular time of day and type of emotion.

might take a *raga* (a scale of notes) and work with it to produce a very long and complicated performance.

Africa

There is an incredible variety of styles of music in Africa. Often, music is intimately connected with spoken language and with dance. Very little is written down, so the songs and ways of playing instruments have been passed down through families and the community.

One feature of African music is call-and-response: one

musician sings or plays a phrase and the others then reply. Many African pieces begin gradually as voices or instruments enter one by one. They may consist of short units repeated over and over in varied form. Particularly widespread instruments include the drum, the xylophone and the *mbira*, on which keys (strips of metal) are pushed down by the thumbs and fingers.

► This Swahili drummer from the Kenyan coast is surrounded by several types of drum. Drums are central to much African music, and their shape, size and sound vary enormously. In many societies only men may play them, though in a few societies certain drums are associated only with women.

Some top world-music artists

Europe
Bulgarka (Bulgaria)
Muzsikas (Hungary)
Tenores Di Bitti (Italy)
Shooglenifty (Scotland)
Gypsy Kings (Spain)

The Americas
Rumillajta (Bolivia)
Carlinhos Brown (Brazil)
Toto la momposina (Colombia)
Sierra Maestra (Cuba)
Milton Cardona (Puerto Rico)

Asia and Middle East
Jiang Jian Hua (China)
Ali Hassan Kuban (Egypt)
K. Sridhar K. Shivakumar (India)
Nusrut Fateh Ali Khan (Pakistan)
Ashkhabad (Turkmenistan)

Africa
Khaled (Algeria)
Alpha Blondie (Côte d'Ivoire)
Salif Keita (Mali)
Fela Kuti (Nigeria)
Youssou N'Dour (Senegal)
Miriam Makeba (South Africa)
Thomas Mapfumo & The Blacks Unlimited (Zimbabwe)

find out more
Music
Musical instruments
Orchestras and bands
Pop and rock music
Singing and songs

World War I

World War I was known at the time as the Great War. It started in August 1914 and ended in November 1918. For four years it was the biggest and most terrible conflict between nations that the world had ever seen.

▲ British troops going 'over the top' during the Battle of the Somme (1916) on the Western Front. Trenches provided some protection from enemy gunfire and were difficult to capture, but they were terrible places to live. They were often cramped, waterlogged and rat-infested. In battle soldiers ran across open ground ('no man's land') towards men firing rifles and machine-guns.

- Sea battles did not play an important part in World War I, as neither side wanted to risk serious damage to its fleet. The only major (but indecisive) sea battle was at Jutland in the North Sea in May 1916. The most effective sea warfare was the German submarine, or 'U-boat', campaign against ships used by Britain to import food and goods.

find out more
Britain since 1900
France
Germany
Ottoman empire
Russia
Twentieth-century
  history
United States of
  America
Weapons

▶ Britain and France's allies included Russia, USA, Romania, Belgium, Italy, Serbia, Japan and Portugal. On the other side were Germany, Austria-Hungary, Bulgaria and Turkey (the Ottoman empire).

The countries of Europe had been arguing for some time, jealous of each other's power. Conflict was almost inevitable. Then, on 28 June 1914, Archduke Ferdinand of Austria was killed by a Serb in the Bosnian capital, Sarajevo. Austria threatened Serbia, and by August Europe was at war.

The Western and Eastern Fronts

The Germans marched through Belgium, hoping to take France by surprise. The plan was to knock France out quickly and then turn to deal with Russia. The British and French stopped them. Where the two sides met, a 'front' developed which stretched from the English Channel to the Swiss border. Long trench battles were fought, and millions were killed and injured.

The same thing happened in the east, where the Austrian and German armies faced the Russians. The hardships caused by the war added to Russian discontent. This anger led to the Russian Revolution in 1917, after which the Russians left the war.

A world at war

In 1916 in the southern Alps the Germans and Austrians faced the Italian army, while at the Gallipoli peninsula in north-west Turkey British troops, with others from Australia and New Zealand (Anzacs), fought the Turks (the Ottoman empire was allied with Germany and Austria). Other troops came from countries of the British and French empires to fight in France on the Western Front. In Africa, British, French and African troops occupied the German colonies.

In the Far East, Japan declared war on Germany and occupied the Qingdao peninsula, which Germany held, and German island colonies in the Pacific.

In the Middle East, Britain encouraged the Arabs to revolt against their Turkish rulers. In 1917 an Anglo-Indian army entered Baghdad, the capital of Iraq. At the same time troops from Egypt, with Arab supporters (led by T. E. Lawrence – 'Lawrence of Arabia'), advanced into Palestine and occupied Jerusalem.

The end

In April 1917 the USA declared war on Germany. American weapons and reinforcements for the Western Front arrived from the USA. This was crucial in the final victory. In 1918 an armistice (end to the fighting) was called for at 11 a.m. on 11 November. Over 7 million people had died in the war.

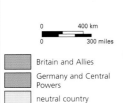

0   400 km
0   300 miles

Britain and Allies
Germany and Central Powers
neutral country

World War II

When the Nazi leader Adolf Hitler came to power, he gained popularity by saying that Germany should reclaim the land it had lost in World War I, and take over nearby lands where there were German-speaking people. It was this German expansion into neighbouring countries that eventually led to war.

Allies and neutral countries

German conquests and allies

Japanese conquests and allies

limit of Japanese conquests

▲ The countries allied to Germany were Bulgaria, Finland, Hungary, Italy, Japan, Romania and Thailand. The Allies were Australia, Belgium, countries in the British empire, Canada, China, Czechoslovakia, Denmark, France, Greece, the Netherlands, New Zealand, Norway, Poland, South Africa, USA, USSR and also countries in South America and the Middle East.

▶ The USA entered the war in December 1941, after the Japanese attack on Pearl Harbor. They gradually took island after island back from the Japanese in the Pacific. Here they are invading the island of Okinawa, about 500 km from Japan, in 1945.

Germany began its expansion in 1936 by reoccupying the Rhineland. Then in 1938 German soldiers marched into Austria, which was made part of Germany. In 1939 Czechoslovakia fell. Britain and France allowed these things to happen without much protest because they hoped that when Germany regained its 1918 position, it would stop threatening other countries.

War breaks out

In August 1939, the German Nazi government made an agreement with the Soviet Union so that if war came, the Germans would not have to fight Russia on their eastern front. In September 1939, German troops marched into Poland, as did others from the Soviet Union. The Germans used a tactic called 'Blitzkrieg', or 'lightning war': troops and tanks moved quickly, backed up by very effective dive-bombing. This time, Britain and France declared war.

▲ The Soviet Union suffered terribly in World War II. There were millions of civilian casualties, and Russians were badly treated by German troops. These grief-stricken Russians are searching for loved ones at Kursk after a Nazi massacre in 1943.

In spring 1940 the German army invaded Norway, Denmark, France, Belgium and the Netherlands, and the British army had to retreat in ships and small boats from the French port of Dunkirk. Germany was soon in control of most of Europe, and Britain stood alone, in danger of invasion.

USSR: the great patriotic war

In April 1941 German forces occupied Yugoslavia and Greece. Then, in June 1941, with western Europe under Nazi rule, the Germans invaded the Soviet Union, breaking the agreement made in 1939. German troops drove deep into Russia and besieged Leningrad (St Petersburg) and Stalingrad (Volgograd). The Russian losses were enormous.

The Germans had expected a quick victory, but the Russians resisted with determination. They were helped by the Russian winter, which killed

◄ Allied troops landing on 6 June 1944 (D-Day) on a beach in Normandy, northern France. British and Canadian troops landed on the eastern beaches and Americans landed to the west.

many German soldiers. In January 1943 the Germans were defeated at Stalingrad and over 90,000 German soldiers were taken prisoner. This was the beginning of the end for the Nazis, although two years of war were still to come.

Global war

World War II was a truly global war. Japan allied itself with Germany and overran several British and French colonies in the Far East. In December 1941 a Japanese air raid destroyed US ships at Pearl Harbor Naval Base in Hawaii, in the Pacific Ocean. After this attack, the USA entered the war on the side of Britain and the USSR.

Fighting went on across the Far East, the Pacific, the Atlantic Ocean, the Middle East and North Africa. American, Soviet, British and Commonwealth forces, together with 'Free' forces from France and other countries in German hands, fought against Germany, Italy and Japan in the conflict.

Land, sea and air

The main land weapon was the tank. Commanders tried to get their armies into positions where the tanks could be given freedom to travel across the countryside against the enemy. Great tank battles were fought, especially in Russia and the

deserts of North Africa. There were also heavy guns, and infantrymen marching on foot with rifles and bayonets.

By 1939 the big battleship was already becoming old-fashioned, because it was too easily attacked from the air. Aircraft-carriers and submarines became the most important fighting ships. Submarines ranged far from home, attacking cargo ships and warships. The Germans had a large and very effective fleet of submarines or 'U-boats'.

Commanders tried to get air supremacy – a situation in which their aircraft could roam the skies attacking targets at will. The 'Battle of Britain' was a battle for the skies over southern Britain in 1940. Had the British Royal Air Force lost, a German invasion would have been possible.

Victory

Once the Soviet Union and the USA were in the war, the defeat of Germany, Italy and Japan was only a matter of time. From early 1943, the Soviet Red Army rolled the Germans back towards their border and then pressed on to Berlin. In 1942 American forces began to recapture the Pacific islands taken by the Japanese. In November 1942 the British defeated the Germans and Italians at El Alamein in North Africa, and in 1943 Allied troops crossed the Mediterranean to invade Italy itself. Then in June 1944 came the long-awaited 'Second Front': the invasion of northern France by British and American troops on 'D-Day'.

Now Germany was under pressure from east, west and south. Gradually its troops were pushed back as far as Berlin, and Germany surrendered in May 1945. The Japanese surrendered in August after American planes dropped atomic bombs on the cities of Hiroshima and Nagasaki.

• As the great armies battled to and fro, millions of people were forced from their homes and took to the roads with their possessions. Many never succeeded in returning home, and many children lost contact with their families.

find out more
Britain since 1900
Churchill, Winston
Germany
Hitler, Adolf
Holocaust
Japan
Roosevelt, Franklin D.
Russia
Stalin, Joseph
United States of America

◄ Devastation in the city of Hiroshima in August 1945. Within one minute 80,000 people died. Around 70,000 more people were injured, of whom about 60,000 died within a year. The city was rebuilt, but there is a Peace Memorial Park on the site where the bomb exploded to remind the world of the true horror of war.

Worms

Worms have long bodies, often segmented into rings, and no limbs. There are many kinds of worms, which have little in common except their basic wormlike shape.

As their name suggests, earthworms burrow in the soil. They eat soil to extract tiny scraps of food. In doing so, they turn over the soil and let air spread through it, which is very important in keeping it fertile.

▲ Earthworms are long, thin animals whose bodies are very clearly made up of a series of similar segments, or rings. The head contains a brain and a mouth, which has tiny, horny jaws.

Flatworms, which are sometimes called flukes, usually live in water. Many of them are brightly coloured and are generally less than 1 centimetre long. Some kinds of fluke are parasites on other animals, and may cause serious diseases.

Tapeworms are related to flatworms. As adults they are parasites, living and feeding in the guts of another animal. Tapeworms are so called because they are long and flat, like a tape-measure.

Roundworms are usually less than 2 millimetres long. Huge numbers of them live in soil, in the sea and in fresh water. Some roundworms, called threadworms, can be parasites of animals, including humans, and often cause diseases.

Leeches usually live in ponds and streams. They hang onto plants or rocks using a sucker at the back end of the body. Many have a second sucker around the mouth. Most leeches feed by sucking blood from other animals, including humans. Leeches normally feed once every few months, but can go for a year without feeding.

▼ Leeches were once frequently used by doctors in Europe to suck blood from sick patients. Leech saliva contains a chemical which prevents blood from clotting. Diseases commonly 'treated' with leeches were mental diseases, headaches and tumours.

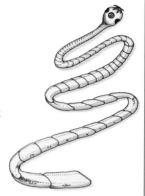

▲ Adult tapeworms cannot see, smell or hear. They are parasites and live protected inside the guts of pigs and other vertebrates (animals with backbones). Here they are surrounded by digested food, which they take in through their body wall.

find out more
Animals
Pests and parasites
Soil

Wren, Christopher

Christopher Wren was the greatest English architect of his time. One of his most famous buildings is St Paul's Cathedral in London.

Christopher Wren was originally a scientist who specialized in mathematics, physics and astronomy. In 1657 he was made professor of astronomy at Gresham College, London, and four years later he was appointed to the same post at Oxford University.

Wren's interest in architecture began when he was in his early 30s. At the time there was no architectural profession, and it was quite common for 'talented amateurs' to design buildings. Wren's skills as an architect soon became known, and for over 50 years he was the most productive and influential architect in Britain. The Sheldonian Theatre in Oxford and the chapel at Pembroke College, Cambridge, both dating from the early 1660s, were his earliest buildings.

Then, in 1666, the Great Fire destroyed most of London. Using his imagination and skill, Wren drew up a plan for rebuilding the entire city. His plan was never adopted, but he was chosen to rebuild St Paul's Cathedral. The construction of his magnificent design was begun in 1675 and completed in 1710. As well as St Paul's Cathedral, Wren also rebuilt or repaired 52 other churches that had been destroyed or damaged in the Great Fire. His background as a scientist and mathematician enabled him to come up with some ingenious solutions for many of the awkward and cramped sites.

Born 1632 in Wiltshire, England
Died 1723 aged 90

• As a young man, Wren would often get together with his friends to discuss scientific matters. Their discussions led to the foundation of the Royal Society in 1660. Many brilliant men were members, and the society still exists today.

◀ A portrait of Sir Christopher Wren in front of his most famous building, St Paul's Cathedral. Wren was knighted in 1672 for his great contribution to architecture.

find out more
Architecture

Writing systems

We write down words or ideas when we want to keep them and use them again later, or when we want someone else to read them.

Before writing was developed, many early people kept 'oral' records of their history or beliefs. Some people would learn the record by heart (perhaps in a long poem) and recite it to others in their society.

Early forms of writing

One of the earliest forms of writing was the *pictogram*, in which pictures of objects, such as a circle for the Sun, represented the object themselves. Another early form is the *ideogram*, in which the whole idea of the word is explained in a shape rather like a picture. The Chinese and Japanese writing systems use ideograms instead of an alphabet.

The earliest true writing was developed by the Sumerians in the land of Mesopotamia (now Iraq). The oldest examples date from about 3250 BC. The language was discovered on more than 250,000 clay tablets. The Sumerians used wedge-shaped signs on the tablets to develop a type of writing known as *cuneiform*. Cuneiform was used for about 3000 years.

Hieroglyphics

Hieroglyphics are a form of writing which uses pictures and symbols instead of words. The ancient Egyptians developed hieroglyphics around 3100 BC and used them for 3500 years, but other peoples have used them as well.

Egyptian hieroglyphics

The Egyptian written language started in a very simple way with pictures for objects such as the Sun or a flower. But it was difficult to explain complicated ideas with these, and so the Egyptians began to use the pictures to represent groups of things or ideas. For example, a soldier with a bow and arrow came to mean a whole army. It was a complicated way of writing. At least 700 different signs were used.

Egyptian hieroglyphs are found carved in stone on temples, painted on the wooden cases of buried mummies, and drawn on papyrus, a sort of paper made from crushed reeds.

In the 3rd and 4th centuries AD Greek replaced hieroglyphics as the written language used in Egypt. Soon people forgot what the hieroglyphic signs meant. Their meaning was rediscovered after 1799, when a stone slab was found in Egypt bearing a lengthy inscription. This became known as the Rosetta Stone. Because the stone was inscribed in both Egyptian and Greek (which people could understand), the hieroglyphs could be translated.

Mayan hieroglyphics

The Mayan people of Central America also used hieroglyphs for writing. They are preserved on a type of document, called a codex, made of folded strips of deerskin or tree-bark. These records tell us what the Mayans knew about the stars, about their religious ceremonies and about their calendar. The Spanish destroyed most of the codices when they conquered this ancient people in the 16th century.

horse

tortoise

to stand upright

▲ Chinese ideograms. The earliest forms were simple but recognizable drawings. Over the centuries they changed into stylized shapes that are easy to write.

▼ The hieroglyphs shown below represent particular sounds. To make a word the Egyptians used these signs and some of the other 700 pictures. The names of pharoahs were written in oval frames called cartouches. This is how Queen Cleopatra's name was written (bottom right).

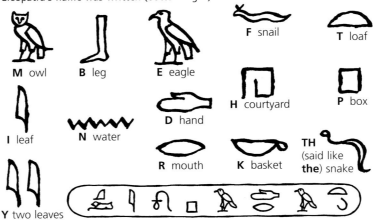

M owl **B** leg **E** eagle **F** snail **T** loaf

I leaf **N** water **D** hand **H** courtyard **P** box

R mouth **K** basket **TH** (said like **the**) snake

Y two leaves

Alphabets

Most languages today are written using an alphabet. The first true alphabet was probably developed in the 15th century BC by the Canaanite people of Syria. It had 32 letters.

The Phoenicians reduced the Canaanite alphabet to 22 letters and spread it through the Mediterranean. It is from this alphabet that the Greek, Roman, Arabic and Hebrew alphabets developed.

English is written in the same alphabet as Latin, the Roman language. The ancient Roman alphabet had 23 letters. After the collapse of the Roman empire the Latin language survived in changed forms in many countries in Europe. In most European countries people still use the Roman alphabet to read and write their language. It is the most widely used alphabet in the world today.

• The word 'alphabet' is made up from the first two letters of the ancient Greek alphabet, alpha (= a) and beta (= b).

The Cyrillic alphabet has 32 letters and is used in Russia, and some countries of the former Soviet Union.

АБВГДЕЁЖЗИЙКЛМНОПРСТУФХЦЧШЩЪЫЬЭЮЯ
абвгдеёжзийклмнопрстуфхцчшщъыьэюя

◄ The Cyrillic, Devanagari and Arabic alphabets are three of approximately 50 different alphabets used today. The letters in each alphabet are shaped differently. Most alphabets have between 20 and 30 letters. The Arabic alphabet is written from right to left.

The Devangari alphabet has 46 letters. It is the main alphabet of northern India.

ऋ ऋा इ ई उ ऊ ऋृ ए ऐ ओ औ अं अः क ख ग घ ङ च छ ज झ ञ
ट ठ ड ढ ण त थ द ध न प फ ब भ म य र ल व श ष स ह

The Arabic alphabet has 28 letters and is used by people all over the Arab world.

ا ب ت ث ج ح خ د ذ ر ز س ش ص
ض ط ظ ع غ ف ق ك ل م ن و هـ ي

find out more
Ancient world
Communication
Egyptians, ancient
Languages

X-rays

• Astronomers study the X-rays that come from the stars. These rays can show where black holes might be.

• X-rays have to be used carefully by people who work with them regularly. A screen, often made of lead, protects the X-ray machine operator while an X-ray picture is taken. You wear a lead shield to protect your body when your teeth are X-rayed.

find out more
Black holes
Radiation
Scanners
Waves

X-rays are a kind of energy which can be both useful and dangerous. The Sun and other stars produce some X-rays, but our atmosphere protects us from these. We use X-rays in hospitals, factories and laboratories.

X-rays are waves like radio waves and light, but they have much more energy. They travel at the same speed as light, but can go right through some solid things which light cannot penetrate.

Doctors and dentists use X-rays to take pictures of broken bones and growing teeth. X-rays make shadow pictures because they go through soft parts of your body, like skin, but are stopped by the hard bones or teeth. Computers can build up very detailed X-ray pictures of the inside of a patient's body. Doctors sometimes use carefully measured amounts of much stronger X-rays to kill cancer cells in the body.

X-rays can check inside machines for cracks or faults. Airport staff use them to check luggage for weapons and bombs. Scientists use X-rays to study how atoms are arranged in solid materials such as crystals.

► FLASHBACK ◄

Wilhelm Röntgen, a German physicist, discovered X-rays in 1895. He was experimenting with electric current flow inside a glass tube when he realized that rays were escaping from the tube. He found that these mysterious rays, which he called X-rays, passed through some solid materials.

▼ A radiologist (a doctor who specializes in using X-rays) takes accurate measurements of a human knee joint from a life-size X-ray picture. The measurements will be used to make an artificial knee joint to replace the patient's diseased one.

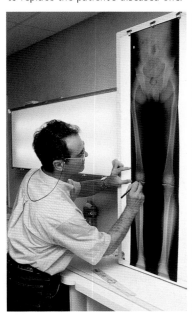

Yachts *see* Sailing *and* Ships and boats • **Yemen** *see page* 645

Youth organizations

Youth organizations exist to help young people channel their energy and enthusiasm. Many concentrate on sports or outdoor activities, and developing useful skills. Some are linked to political, military or religious organizations.

Before modern times education was only for the ruling classes. Children started work very young, helping at home or on the land, and women often had their first child before the age of 16. 'Youth' – the time between childhood and adulthood – was short and not very important.

In the 19th century, this began to change. More students were educated, staying at school or college into their teens and beyond. Many countries passed laws banning children from working, and couples married later. Millions of young people now spent years when they were neither children nor adults.

Gradually organizations were established that provided activities specially for young people. Sports clubs ran youth teams, and religious organizations formed groups like the Young Men's Christian Association (YMCA, 1844). The Youth Hostel Association provided young travellers with cheap accommodation around the world. Other organizations, such as the Young Farmers, were linked to work. The British Voluntary Service Overseas (VSO, 1958) and the American Peace Corps (1961) organized young people from privileged backgrounds to work in developing countries.

◀ These girl guides in Kenya are helping to renovate a centre for young disabled people.

Scouts and guides

The Scouts and Guides are perhaps the most successful youth organization. Robert Baden-Powell formed the Boy Scouts in 1908 and helped set up the Girl Guides two years later. The Cub Scouts and Brownies are for younger members. Today, the movement has millions of members in 150 countries. In recent years the Guide and Scout movements have lost many of their differences, and in some countries both boys and girls can become Scouts.

Political youth

Governments and political groups also sought the support of young people. Most democratic parties set up special youth sections. The armed services in many countries run junior sections in schools and colleges to train their future officers.

The German Nazis banned most ordinary youth organizations and replaced them with the Hitler Youth for boys and the League of German Girls for girls. Both organizations, which were made compulsory in 1939, arranged parades and meetings to spread Nazi ideas.

◀ In 1966 the Chinese leader Mao Zedong encouraged young people to join his Red Guards to defend the communist revolution. For a time gangs of Red Guards terrorized the streets, beating up members of the middle class and shouting slogans. They were so unpopular that a year later Mao used the army to bring them under control.

find out more
Children
China
Germany
Mao Zedong

Zoos

The word 'zoo' is short for zoological gardens. Zoos are places where people can go to see wild animals from many parts of the world. The first zoos were collections of animals made by ancient kings and noblemen. Today there are many types of zoo, some specializing in particular sorts of animals.

One of the most popular kinds of zoo is the oceanarium, which keeps dolphins and other sea creatures. However, some people believe that it is wrong to keep these large sea animals captive. Another type of zoo is the safari park, in which it is the visitors who are caged in their cars, and the animals have large areas in which to roam freely.

What zoos do

Apart from keeping animals for visitors to see, modern zoos have three main functions: to study the animals and find out as much as possible about their habits; to educate visitors; and to breed from the captives for return to the wild.

Breeding is an important part of the work of zoos. Many kinds of animal have such small numbers remaining in the wild that producing young in zoos can be the only way to save them

▼ In this oceanarium, a transparent tunnel allows visitors to walk right through a large tank containing sharks, rays and other ocean creatures.

▲ An Arabian or white oryx with its calf. Arabian oryx once lived in the deserts of the Arabian peninsula, but by the early 1970s the only animals left were in zoos. They were successfully bred in captivity, and in 1982 a herd of animals was reintroduced into Oman.

from extinction. If enough animals can be bred, groups can be returned to the wild in the areas where they have become extinct. This has been done with the Hawaiian goose (nene), Père David's deer and the Arabian oryx.

► FLASHBACK ◄

The first zoos were collections of animals made by kings and noblemen in the Middle East and China. In the past, zoo animals generally had a short life, for the right food and conditions were seldom available. When an elephant was first brought to Britain in 1254, it was housed in a special building 6 by 12 metres, which was certainly not big enough by modern standards. For centuries most zoos were miserable prisons for many animals, which were kept on their own. Such solitary confinement is the height of cruelty for social animals such as monkeys and apes.

In recent years many zoos have realized the importance of putting the interests of the animals first. The animals are fed adequate amounts of the correct food, and their enclosures are designed to imitate as far as possible the animal's wild home. In good zoos most animals live far longer than they would in the wild. There are still some bad zoos but fewer than there used to be.

• Zoos are extremely costly places to run. The animals have to be securely housed and kept warm. Their food may also be expensive.

• The Roman emperor Nero is said to have had a tame tigress called Phoebe, while the favourite of Charlemagne, who kept many animals, was an elephant called Abul Aba.

find out more
Animals
Conservation

DATA FILE

Contents

Countries fact file

The Countries fact file contains information about the sovereign countries of the world. (A sovereign country is a territory with its own government.) It lists all sovereign countries that are members of the United Nations.

Smaller countries in the fact file have a short list of statistics, plus a brief article about the country. These statistics include a grid reference relating to the world map on pages 646–647 (see map caption), and the GNP per person (see explanation below).

Countries that have an entry in the A–Z section have some extra statistics. 'Labour force' lists the percentages of people working in agriculture, in industry, or in services (office workers, shopkeepers, and so on). 'Population density' is an average figure, giving number of people per square kilometre of land. 'Urban population' is the percentage of people in the country that live in cities. 'Life expectancy' is another average – the average age to which people in the country live.

The following list includes some of the more specialized terms used in the Countries fact file.

colony: a settlement founded by a people from one country in another part of the world. These people are called colonists or colonials. Where this happens, a country is said to be colonized.

democracy: a form of government in which the people are able to elect their rulers freely.

ethnic group: an ethnic group is a large community of people, usually smaller than a nation, who believe themselves to share a common identity based on religion, place of origin or other factors.

federation: a form of government in which power is shared between a central (federal) government and the states or provinces that make up the country.

GNP (Gross National Product): the value of all a country's output of goods and services in a year. It is a measure of wealth for a country.

natural resources: physical things such as coal, timber and metals which humans can use to make goods or burn as fuel.

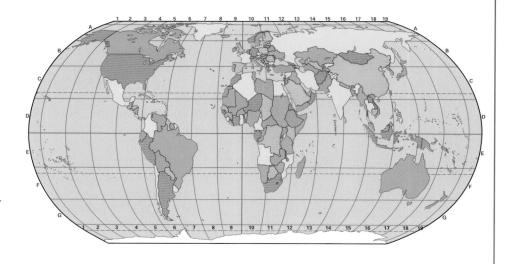

► The illustration shows the world map that can be found at full size on pages 646–647. Each country entry has a grid reference consisting of a letter and a number. The letter refers to the letters down the sides of the world map, the numbers to the numbers top and bottom of the map.

AFGHANISTAN

Grid reference C13
Capital Kabul
Population 20,500,000
Area 647,497 sq km
Language Pushtu, Dari
Religion Muslim
Currency 1 afghani = 100 puls
GNP per person $200

Afghanistan lies between Central Asia, South Asia and the Middle East. It is a land of high mountains and deserts. In the valleys farmers grow wheat, cotton and other crops. In the highlands herders keep sheep and goats. Although the population is mainly Muslim, they belong to many different ethnic groups, including Afghans, Pathans and Turkmen. From 1979 to 1989 the country was occupied by the former USSR. Civil war then followed, until the fundamentalist Islamic Taliban took control. They sheltered the terrorist group who attacked America on 11 September 2001. In 2002 US and other forces overthrew the Taliban.

ALBANIA

Grid reference B10
Capital Tiranë
Population 3,420,000
Area 28,748 sq km
Language Albanian, Greek
Religion Muslim, Roman Catholic, Greek Orthodox
Currency 1 lek = 100 qintars
GNP per person $340

Albania is a small country bordering the Adriatic Sea. Much of it is mountainous and forested, but in the valleys and along the coast farmers grow wheat, grapes, fruit and vegetables. Oil, copper and iron ore are the main natural resources. Many countries have fought over Albania throughout history. Between 1946 and 1991 it had a communist government. During this period, Albania became cut off from the rest of the world. In the 1990s democracy was introduced, but there was much fighting between different political groups.

ALGERIA

Grid reference C10
Capital Algiers
Population 28,580,000
Area 2,460,500 sq km
Language Arabic, Berber, French
Religion Muslim
Currency 1 dinar = 100 centimes
GNP per person $1600

Algeria is a large country in North Africa. Most of the people' live along the Mediterranean coast, where the most fertile lands are found. The Atlas Mountains separate this region from the Sahara Desert, which covers 85 per cent of Algeria. In the desert there are vast deposits of oil and natural gas, the country's main exports. But most Algerians are farmers or herders. Algeria was a French colony until 1962, when the people won their independence. In the 1990s fighting broke out between the government and their political opponents, and many innocent civilians were killed.

ANDORRA

Grid reference B10
Capital Andorra la Vella
Population 62,500
Area 453 sq km
Language Catalan, French, Spanish
Religion Roman Catholic
Currency 1 euro = 100 cents
GNP per person $14,000

Andorra is one of Europe's oldest and smallest states, situated high up in the eastern Pyrenees mountains between France and Spain. Andorra has an unusual government. The president of France and the Bishop of Urgel in Spain are joint protectors of the country. In reality, however, it is self-governing. Tourism, especially skiing, is an important source of income, along with some agriculture and mining. Andorra has low taxes and many businesses are based there and trade with the rest of Europe. Most of the people live in small settlements in just six valleys.

ANGOLA

Grid reference E10
Capital Luanda
Population 11,500,000
Area 1,245,790 sq km
Language Portuguese and African languages
Religion Roman Catholic, Protestant and traditional African religions
Currency 1 new kwanza = 100 iweis
GNP per person $410

Angola is a large country in south-west Africa, bordering the Atlantic. The coastal plain is fertile but dry. The inland plateaux are covered with tropical rainforest in the north, savannah grassland in the centre and dry plains in the south. Angola's natural resources include oil and diamonds. Most Angolans are farmers, producing coffee, sisal, sugar cane and palm oil. Since Angola gained its independence from Portugal in 1975 there has been civil war. A truce was arranged in 1996, but fighting has continued into the 21st century.

ANTIGUA AND BARBUDA

Grid reference D6
Capital St John's, Antigua
Population 63,900
Area 442 sq km
Language English
Religion Protestant, Roman Catholic
Currency 1 East Caribbean dollar = 100 cents
GNP per person $4870

Antigua and Barbuda are two small islands in the eastern Caribbean. Antigua is larger. It is hilly and surrounded by wide bays and coral reefs. Barbuda is a coral island surrounding an old volcano. A third island, Redonda, has no people on it and is a nature reserve. Columbus landed in Antigua in 1493. The islands later became a British colony. The British brought slaves from Africa, and most of the people on the islands today are descended from these slaves. The economy depends on sugar cane, cotton and tourism.

ARGENTINA

Grid reference F6–G6
Capital Buenos Aires
Population 34,770,000
Area 2,780,092 sq km
Language Spanish
Religion Roman Catholic
Currency 1 peso = 100 centavos
GNP per person $8030
Government Republic
Labour force Agriculture 21%, industry 31%, services 57%
Main industries Food, cars, textiles, chemicals, metals, steel, printing
Main farm and mine products Beef, wheat, maize (corn), sorghum, soybeans
Population density 12 people per sq km
Population under 15 years old 28%
Urban population 87%
Life expectancy 72 years

For main entry see page 37

ARMENIA

Grid reference B12–C12
Capital Yerevan
Population 3,700,000
Area 29,800 sq km
Language Armenian
Religion Armenian Church (Christian), Russian Orthodox
Currency 1 dram = 100 lumas
GNP per person $730

Armenia is a mostly mountainous country bordered by Turkey, Georgia, Iran and Azerbaijan. It is a small and ancient nation which has often been invaded. In 1915 over 1 million Armenians were massacred by Turkey, and between 1920 and 1990 it was part of the former USSR. Armenians are one of the oldest Christian peoples in the world and their culture is quite different from neighbouring countries, which are mostly Muslim. Armenia's main natural resources are copper, gold and silver. It also makes chemicals, electrical equipment and textiles, and produces wheat, grapes and cotton.

AUSTRALIA

Grid reference F16–17
Capital Canberra
Population 18,300,000
Area 7,692,300 sq km
Language English
Religions Roman Catholic, Protestant
Currency 1 Australian dollar = 100 cents
GNP per person $18,720
Government Federal state within the Commonwealth
Labour force Agriculture 5%, industry 26%, services 78%
Main industries Food, chemicals, steel, ships, cars and trucks, clothing, metals
Main farm and mine products Wool, beef, wheat, coal, gold, iron ore, uranium, zinc, copper, diamonds
Population density 2 people per sq km
Population under 15 years old 21%
Urban population 85%
Life expectancy 79 years

For main entry see pages 49–50

AUSTRIA

Grid reference B10
Capital Vienna
Population 8,050,000
Area 83,854 sq km
Language German
Religion Roman Catholic
Currency 1 euro = 100 cents
GNP per person $26,890

Austria is one of the most mountainous and forested countries in Europe. It is situated between the eastern Alps and the Danube river valley. The valley farmlands support wheat, dairy cattle and pigs. Austria also has natural resources such as coal and iron ore, and dams produce hydroelectric power. The Alps attract skiers and climbers. Tourists also visit historic towns such as Salzburg, where Mozart was born. Until 1918 Austria was the centre of the Austro-Hungarian empire. After 1945 it developed as a peaceful and prosperous country. In 1995 Austria joined the European Union.

AZERBAIJAN

Grid reference B12–C12
Capital Baku
Population 7,500,000
Area 86,600 sq km
Language Azeri, Russian
Religion Muslim
Currency 1 manat = 100 gopik
GNP per person $480

Azerbaijan is a former republic of the USSR located between the Caspian Sea and the Caucasus mountains. Part of the country, Nakhicevan, is separated from the rest by Armenia, which also claims control over the Nagorno-Karabakh region inside Azerbaijan itself. Although most of the people are Azeris, there are Russian, Armenian and other minorities. Cotton is raised in the lowlands, but the country also manufactures many products based on minerals such as copper, lead and zinc. Oil is the main natural resource, and recent new discoveries have made the country important to the outside world.

BAHAMAS

Grid reference C6
Capital Nassau
Population 275,700
Area 13,934 sq km
Language English
Religion Protestant, Roman Catholic
Currency 1 Bahamian dollar = 100 cents
GNP per person $11,940

The Bahamas is a long string of 700 islands and over 2000 coral reefs and sandbanks stretching south-east from Florida almost to Cuba. The islands are very flat and there is not enough fresh water on them for farming. People live on only 30 of the largest islands. Tourism, fishing, cement-making and oil-refining provide many of the jobs. Taxes are very low, so thousands of businesses, especially in banking and finance, have their headquarters there. Often these are no more than tiny offices – the real work is done abroad. Because the Bahamas are so low-lying, hurricanes can cause a lot of damage.

BAHRAIN

Grid reference C12
Capital Manama
Population 586,109
Area 678 sq km
Language Arabic, Farsi, Urdu
Religion Muslim
Currency 1 Bahrain dinar = 1000 fils
GNP per person $7840

Bahrain consists of one large island and over 30 smaller ones in the Persian Gulf. Bahrain is very sandy and rocky, there is little water, and trees are rare. Most of the people live in the north, where the main farmlands and industries are found. Oil was the main natural resource, but after 50 years little now remains. Trading and banking provide alternative sources of income. About a third of the people are migrants from Asia and other Arab countries who came to work in the petroleum (oil) industry. Bahrain has a single ruler (an emir), but the 1990s brought growing demands for greater democracy.

BANGLADESH

Grid reference C14
Capital Dhaka
Population 129,147,000
Area 143,998 sq km
Language Bengali, English
Religion Muslim, Hindu
Currency 1 taka = 100 paisa
GNP per person $240
Government Republic
Labour force Agriculture 65%, industry 14%, services 21%
Main industries Textiles, food, steel, fertilizers, glass
Main farm and mine products Jute, rice, wheat, tea
Population density 824 people per sq km
Population under 15 years old 39%
Urban population 21%
Life expectancy 56 years

For main entry see page 55

BARBADOS

Grid reference D7
Capital Bridgetown
Population 264,300
Area 430 sq km
Language English
Religion Protestant
Currency 1 Barbados dollar = 100 cents
GNP per person $6560

Barbados is a small island in the Atlantic Ocean. It is the furthest east of any of the Caribbean islands. In the 1600s it was settled by the British, who introduced African slaves to work on sugar plantations. The people today are mainly descended from these Africans. For such a small island, Barbados has a big population. Many are farmers, who grow sugar, bananas and cotton on the rich volcanic soils. Tourism now accounts for most of the island's economy. Many islanders migrate to Britain and the USA, often returning to Barbados when they retire. Barbados became independent in 1966.

BELARUS

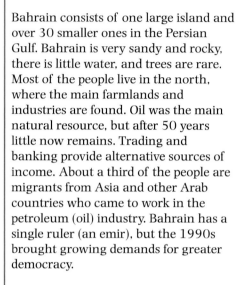

Grid reference B11
Capital Minsk
Population 10,400,000
Area 207,600 sq km
Language Belarusian, Russian
Religion Roman Catholic, Russian Orthodox
Currency 1 Belarusian ruble = 100 kopec
GNP per person $2070

Belarus, or Belorussia, was part of the former Soviet Union located between Russia, Poland, Ukraine and the Baltic states. It is low-lying, with many lakes and rivers. A third is covered by forest, and large marshes lie in the south. Summers are cool and the winters often very cold. Where the land has been drained, farmers grow flax, sugar beet and potatoes. The cities are the centre of manufacturing, including machinery, textiles and chemicals. Belarus has often been occupied by neighbouring states such as Poland and Russia. Since independence in 1991, it has kept close links with Russia.

BELGIUM

Grid reference B10
Capital Brussels
Population 10,140,000
Area 30,540 sq km
Language Flemish, French, German
Religion Roman Catholic
Currency 1 euro = 100 cents
GNP per person $24,710

Belgium is a small country in north-west Europe. Apart from dunes along the coast and the Ardennes mountains in the south, Belgium is mostly low-lying farmland. Agriculture, together with textiles, coal-mining and international trade, have made the country prosperous. Belgium has developed an advanced industrial economy as well as being an important business centre. The European Union Commission and many international organizations are based in Brussels. The country is divided into a Flemish-speaking north and a French-speaking south.

BELIZE

Grid reference D5
Capital Belmopan
Population 209,500
Area 22,963 sq km
Language English, Spanish, Garifuna, Maya
Religion Roman Catholic, Protestant
Currency 1 Belize dollar = 100 cents
GNP per person $2630

Belize is a small Central American country bordering the Caribbean Sea. The coast is protected by a long barrier reef and in the south there are good natural harbours. Belize's interior is heavily forested. The climate is warm and wet, and hurricanes are a hazard to low-lying areas – one reason why the capital was moved inland from Belize City to Belmopan. The region was once part of the Mayan empire before being colonized by Spain and then Britain. Belize's people are now a mix of Indians, Africans and Europeans. The economy depends on timber, sugar cane, bananas and citrus fruits. Oil has been found offshore.

BOLIVIA

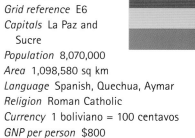

Grid reference E6
Capitals La Paz and
  Sucre
Population 8,070,000
Area 1,098,580 sq km
Language Spanish, Quechua, Aymar
Religion Roman Catholic
Currency 1 boliviano = 100 centavos
GNP per person $800

Bolivia is a large country in South America. The Andes mountains are in the west, while to the east and north lie tropical rainforest. Many rivers which flow into the Amazon begin here. Most Bolivians live on the Altiplano, a cold, high plateau between the Andes and the rainforest. Lake Titicaca, the largest lake in the continent, is divided between Bolivia and Peru. Bolivia was once part of the Inca empire, and 40 per cent of its people are South American Indians. The Spanish overthrew the Incas and exploited the country's mineral wealth, especially tin, which is still a major export. There is also oil.

BENIN

Grid reference D10
Capitals Porto Novo and
  Cotonou
Population 5,460,000
Area 112,622 sq km
Language French, Fon, other African languages
Religion Traditional African religions,
  Christian, Muslim
Currency 1 CFA franc = 100 centimes
GNP per person $370

Benin is a long, narrow country in West Africa, stretching inland from a small sandy coastline to wooded lowlands and savannah grasslands. Parts of Benin suffer from drought and are turning into desert. It was a French colony until 1960. The four main ethnic groups, the Fon, Adja, Yoruba and Bariba, live in different parts of the country. Benin's economy is mainly based on agriculture. Farmers produce palm oil, cocoa and cotton for export, and maize (corn), cassava, yams and beans for food. Benin has few natural resources, and it is a fairly poor country.

BOSNIA AND HERZEGOVINA

Grid reference B10
Capital Sarajevo
Population 4,370,000
Area 51,129 sq km
Language Serbian, Croatian, Bosnian
Religion Muslim, Serbian Orthodox,
  Roman Catholic
Currency 1 dinar = 100 paras
GNP per person $3200

Bosnia and Herzegovina is one of the new countries created by the break-up of Yugoslavia in the 1990s. Before 1918 the region had been part of the Turkish and then Austrian empires, leaving it with a mix of people, including Serbs, Croats and Bosnian Muslims. These communities lived in peace until the 1990s. An international peacekeeping force now prevents fighting. Most of the country lies in the Dinaric Alps. The people grow grains, vegetables and grapes. There are many natural resources, such as coal, copper and manganese.

BHUTAN

Grid reference C14
Capital Thimpu
Population 600,000
Area 46,600 sq km
Language Dzongkha, Nepalese
Religion Buddhist, Hindu
Currency 1 ngultrum = 100 chetrum
GNP per person $420

Bhutan is a small kingdom on the slopes of the Himalayas between India and China. The north is cold and mountainous, and there are peaks over 7000 m high. People herd cattle and yaks. The south is more tropical, and farmers grow rice, wheat and maize (corn) for food. Most of Bhutan is forested, and there are large timber plantations. Few people live in towns and cities. For centuries Bhutan had very little contact with the rest of the world, and even now the numbers of foreigners allowed to visit is limited. Traditional customs, such as wearing national dress, are widely followed.

BOTSWANA

Grid reference F11
Capital Gabarone
Population 1,400,000
Area 581,730 sq km
Language English, Tswana
Religion Traditional African religions, Christian
Currency 1 pula = 100 thebes
GNP per person $3020

Botswana is a large country in southern Africa, parts of which lie in the Kalahari Desert. The Okavango swamp in the north is one of the world's most important wildlife habitats. Most people live in the east, where there are hilly grasslands and the soils are better for farming. In drier areas people raise cattle. In the centre of Botswana there is a major game reserve which attracts tourists. The country has also recently discovered mineral reserves, notably diamonds (it is the world's third largest producer), nickel and cobalt. Botswana was a British colony until 1966.

BRAZIL

Grid reference E7–F7
Capital Brasília
Population 174,469,000
Area 8,511,965 sq km
Language Portuguese
Religion Roman Catholic
Currency 1 real = 100 centavos
GNP per person $3640
Government Republic
Labour force Agriculture 23%, industry 23%, services 54%
Main industries Textiles, clothing, shoes, chemicals, steel, cars, aircraft, machinery
Main farm and mine products Coffee, cocoa, soybeans, beef, timber, iron ore, coal, minerals
Population density 17 people per sq km
Population under 15 years old 31%
Urban population 76%
Life expectancy 62 years

For main entry see page 71

BRUNEI DARUSSALAM

Grid reference D15
Capital Bandar Seri Begawan
Population 276,300
Area 5765 sq km
Language Malay, English
Religion Muslim, Buddhist, Christian
Currency 1 Brunei dollar = 100 sen
GNP per person $13,890

Brunei is a small country on the northern coast of the island of Borneo in South-east Asia. Its only land neighbour is the Malaysian state of Sarawak. It is hot and humid all year round, and rainfall increases the further inland you go. The people mainly live on a narrow coastal strip. Most of Brunei is tropical rainforest, which has been altered little by logging or development. Brunei was once the centre of a powerful empire in the region. It is ruled by a sultan, one of the world's richest people. Brunei has huge oil and gas fields along its coast, which are the source of its great wealth.

BULGARIA

Grid reference B11
Capital Sofia
Population 8,430,000
Area 110,912 sq km
Language Bulgarian, Turkish
Religion Bulgarian Orthodox, Muslim
Currency 1 lev = 100 stotinki
GNP per person $1330

Bulgaria is in south-east Europe. It has a coastline on the Black Sea and its northern border follows the Danube river. Bulgaria is crossed from west to east by the Balkan and the Rhodope mountains, which are separated by the fertile Maritsa valley. The high ground is wooded, but in the plains there are fields of wheat, tobacco, grapes and flowers. Bulgaria has an industrial economy, based on natural resources such as oil, coal, iron ore and zinc. The region was once part of the Turkish empire. Between 1946 and 1990 Bulgaria was a communist country allied with the former Soviet Union.

BURKINA

Grid reference D9
Capital Ougadougou
Population 10,000,000
Area 274,200 sq km
Language French, African languages
Religion Traditional African religions, Muslim, Christian
Currency 1 CFA franc = 100 centimes
GNP per person $230

Burkina, known as Upper Volta until 1984, is in West Africa. The north lies in a semi-desert region. The southern highlands are drained by the headwaters of the Volta river. Frequent droughts and the presence of tsetse flies, which prey on cattle, make farming and cattle-raising difficult. Wood is also scarce. There are many different peoples: some are nomadic herders; others are farmers, who grow cotton and peanuts for export, and millet, maize (corn) and rice for food. The region became independent from France in 1962.

BURUNDI

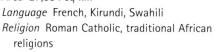

Grid reference E11
Capital Bujumbura
Population 5,360,000
Area 27,834 sq km
Language French, Kirundi, Swahili
Religion Roman Catholic, traditional African religions
Currency 1 Burundi franc = 100 centimes
GNP per person $160

Burundi is a small, crowded country in central Africa, to the north-east of Lake Tanganyika. The land is mostly hilly grasslands. The Ruvubu river, which runs through the country, is the source of the Nile. Most people are small farmers, growing maize (corn), cassava, sorghum and beans. Coffee is the major export. Over the past 500 years the region has often been torn apart by conflicts between the Hutu majority and the Tutsi minority. Bloody warfare returned in the 1990s. Thousands of people were killed and many refugees fled to neighbouring countries.

CAMBODIA

Grid reference D15
Capital Phnom Penh
Population 9,860,000
Area 181,035 sq km
Language Khmer, French
Religion Buddhist, Muslim
Currency 1 riel = 100 sen
G*NP per person* $270

Cambodia, called Kampuchea between 1975 and 1989, is in South-east Asia. The centre of the country is a vast plain covered in rice fields, which are watered by the annual monsoon rains. This plain is drained by the Mekong river. Western Cambodia is more mountainous and forested. The area was ruled by the Khmer empire from the 6th to the 15th century. Between the 1970s and 1990s Cambodia suffered from civil war and the ruthless actions of the Khmer Rouge government (1975–1979). Three million people died under this regime.

CAMEROON

Grid reference D10
Capital Yaoundé
Population 12,200,000
Area 475,442 sq km
Language French, English and African
    languages
Religion Christian, traditional African
    religions, Muslim
Currency 1 CFA franc = 100 centimes
GNP per person $650

Cameroon is a country in equatorial Africa. The northern parts are dry plains, where cattle are raised and cotton is grown. The central plateau is mainly grassland. Most people live in the south, where the best farmlands are. They grow crops such as coffee, bananas, palm oil, and especially cocoa, which is the country's main export. The many different peoples include nomadic herders and pygmies. Cameroon used to be made up of two colonies – one French, the other British. It became independent in 1960.

CANADA

Grid reference B3–7
Capital Ottawa
Population 29,960,000
Area 9,971,500 sq km
Language English, French
Religion Roman Catholic, Protestant
Currency 1 Canadian dollar = 100 cents
GNP per person $19,380
Government Confederation within the
    Commonwealth
Labour force Agriculture 3%, industry 25%,
    services 72%
Main industries Food, wood and paper, cars,
    chemicals, petroleum, metals,
    telecommunications
Main farm and mine products Wheat, barley,
    fish, asbestos, zinc, nickel, oil and natural
    gas, aluminium
Population density 3 people per sq km
Population under 15 years old 21%
Urban population 77%
Life expectancy 79 years

For main entry see pages 86–87

CAPE VERDE

Grid reference D8
Capital Praia
Population 420,000
Area 4,033 sq km
Language Portuguese, Crioulo
Religion Roman Catholic
Currency 1 escudo = 100 centavos
GNP per person $960

Cape Verde is a group of islands 620 km off the coast of West Africa. They are volcanic, but only Mount Fogo (2830 m) is still active. The main economic activities are fishing for tuna and lobster, and farming. Farmers raise maize (corn), beans and manioc for food, and bananas and coconuts for export. But the soils are poor and some of the smaller islands have no natural water supplies. Severe drought in the 1970s forced over half a million islanders to leave and work abroad in Portugal and Italy. The money they send back helps the islands' economy. Cape Verde was a Portuguese colony until 1975.

CENTRAL AFRICAN REPUBLIC

Grid reference D10–11
Capital Bangui
Population 3,070,000
Area 622,984 sq km
Language French, Sangho
Religion Christian, traditional African religions,
    Muslim
Currency 1 CFA franc = 100 centimes
GNP per person $340

The Central African Republic is in the middle of Africa. A high plateau divides rivers flowing south into the Congo from ones flowing north to Lake Chad. There is thick tropical forest in the south-west and semi-desert in the north-east. Most people are farmers. They grow maize (corn), manioc and sorghum for food, and cotton, coffee and tobacco for export. The country also produces diamonds and timber. The region was a French colony until 1960. The many different peoples speak a variety of languages. Sangho is used between the groups, but French is the official language.

CHAD

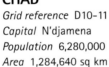

Grid reference D10–11
Capital N'djamena
Population 6,280,000
Area 1,284,640 sq km
Language Arabic, French, African languages
Religion Muslim, Christian, traditional African
    religions
Currency 1 CFA franc = 100 centimes
GNP per person $180

Chad is a large country in north central Africa. The northern half lies within the Sahara Desert. Nomadic herders such as Tuaregs and Berbers live there. Lake Chad, on the western border, changes greatly in size between the wet and dry seasons. Most people are farmers who live in the south, where there are rivers and more rainfall. Cotton is the main crop grown for export, but there are also natural resources such as tungsten, uranium and oil. Chad was a French colony until 1960. Since the 1970s it has often fought with Libya over control of parts of the Sahara.

CHILE

Grid reference F6–G6
Capital Santiago
Population 14,660,000
Area 756,626 sq km
Language Spanish
Religion Roman Catholic
Currency 1 Chilean peso = 100 centavos
GNP per person $4160

Chile is an unusually long and narrow country, lying between the Andes mountains and the Pacific Ocean, and stretching from the tropics to the southern tip of South America. In the north lies the cold Atacama desert, which includes the driest places on Earth. There are glaciers and volcanoes in the mountains. The middle of the country, around Santiago, has a milder climate, and this is where most people live. Chilean farmers grow crops such as wheat, maize (corn) and grapes, and there is also a big fishing industry. The main exports are minerals: Chile is the world's largest producer of copper.

CHINA

Grid reference C13–15
Capital Beijing
Population 1,273,000,000
Area 9,597,000 sq km
Language Mandarin and other Chinese dialects
Religion Atheist, Confucian, Taoist, Buddhist
Currency 1 yuan = 100 jiao
GNP per person $620
Government Communist People's Republic
Labour force Agriculture 74%, industry 15%, services 11%
Main industries Iron and steel, weapons, textiles, toys, shoes, fertilizers, electronics
Main farm and mine products Rice, potatoes, sorghum, fruit, tea, poultry, coal, iron ore
Population density 117 people per sq km
Population under 15 years old 26%
Urban population 34%
Life expectancy 70 years

For main entry see pages 105–107

COLOMBIA

Grid reference D6
Capital Bogotá
Population 34,500,000
Area 1,140,105 sq km
Language Spanish
Religion Roman Catholic
Currency 1 Colombian peso = 100 centavos
GNP per person $1910

Colombia occupies the north-west corner of South America. It has coasts on both the Pacific Ocean and the Caribbean Sea. Three great ranges of the Andes mountains run from north to south through the country. These ranges are separated by high valleys, where many of the people live. There is a narrow coastal plain in the west and a large area of tropical forest to the east. The climate is hot and Colombia is one of the wettest places in the world. The country has good agricultural lands. Farmers grow coffee, one of the country's main exports. Oil, gold and silver are important natural resources.

COMOROS

Grid reference E12
Capital Moroni
Population 490,000
Area 1862 sq km
Language Arabic, French, Kiswali
Religion Sunni Muslim, Roman Catholic
Currency 1 Comorian franc = 100 centimes
GNP per person $470

Comoros consists of three volcanic islands, called Njazidja, Nzwani and Mwali, all located between mainland Africa and Madagascar. Most people are farmers, growing tropical fruits, potatoes, yams, manioc, rice and spices. For centuries people migrated there from Africa, Madagascar, Malaysia, Arabia and Europe. But poverty and overpopulation are now forcing many to leave for Africa and France. Since independence from France in 1975, there has also been much political unrest and many military coups. In 1997 Nzwani tried to break away from the other islands.

CONGO, DEMOCRATIC REPUBLIC OF

Grid reference E10–11
Capital Kinshasa
Population 45,260,000
Area 2,234,585 sq km
Language French, Swahili and other African languages
Religion Roman Catholic, Protestant, Muslim, traditional African religions
Currency 1 zaire = 100 makuta
GNP per person $220
Government Republic
Labour force Agriculture 65%, industry 16%, services 19%
Main industries Textiles, shoes, food, cement, wood
Main farm and mine products Coffee, sugar, palm oil, casssava, quinine, rubber, diamonds, copper, gold
Population density 20 people per sq km
Population under 15 years old 48%
Urban population 29%
Life expectancy 47 years

For main entry see page 130

CONGO, REPUBLIC OF

Grid reference D10–E10
Capital Brazzaville
Population 2,940,000
Area 341,945 sq km
Language French, Kongo, Téké
Religion Christian, traditional African religions
Currency 1 CFA franc = 100 centimes
GNP per person $680

Congo lies on the northern banks of the Congo river in central Africa. The centre is covered with dense tropical forest and has few inhabitants. Most people live along the Congo River in the south, where the main railroad and highway are located. Congo is rich in minerals, including diamonds, oil, gold, lead and zinc. Farmers produce coffee, sugar cane, cocoa, palm oil and tobacco. It was a French colony before becoming an independent state in 1960. Since democracy was established in 1991, there has been fighting between different political groups.

COSTA RICA

Grid reference D5
Capital San José
Population 3,370,000
Area 51,022 sq km
Language Spanish
Religion Roman Catholic, Protestant
Currency 1 Costa Rican colón = 100 céntimos
GNP per person $2610

Costa Rica is a small, mountainous country in Central America, between the Pacific Ocean and the Caribbean Sea. The Caribbean lowlands are covered in dense rainforest. The Pacific coast is drier, and there are many cattle ranches. Most people live on the central plateau. Small numbers of Native Americans follow traditional ways of life in the jungles. Costa Rica is mainly an agricultural country, exporting coffee, bananas, sugar and fruits. It was a Spanish colony until independence in 1821. Compared with other Central American countries, it has been peaceful and politically stable.

CÔTE D'IVOIRE

Grid reference D9
Capital Yamoussoukro
Population 13,720,000
Area 322,462 sq km
Language French, Akan, Kru
Religion Traditional African religions, Muslim, Christian
Currency 1 CFA franc = 100 centimes
GNP per person $660

Côte d'Ivoire (Ivory Coast) is in West Africa. Its name was given by the Europeans who, from the 15th century, traded in ivory and slaves along the coast. The south has a wet, tropical climate and is forested, although much of the forest has been cleared for farmland. There are large plantations of coffee, cocoa and bananas, which are grown for export. It is one of the world's largest producers of cocoa. The north is a drier, grassland region, where people grow sorghum, maize (corn) and peanuts. From 1889 to 1960 Côte d'Ivoire was a French colony.

CROATIA

Grid reference B10
Capital Zagreb
Population 4,840,000
Area 56,540 sq km
Language Croatian
Religion Roman Catholic, Eastern Orthodox
Currency 1 kuna = 100 lipa
GNP per person $3250

Croatia was part of the communist state of Yugoslavia until it broke away and declared its independence in 1991. Fighting between the Croats and the Serbs followed independence, causing many civilian deaths and forcing thousands of refugees to flee. Peace was made in 1995. Croatia has a long coastline on the Adriatic, which was a popular tourist area before the fighting. The coast is separated from the inland plains by the hills of the Dinaric Alps. A third of the land is forested. Croatia has a big manufacturing economy, partly based on natural resources such as oil, coal, bauxite and copper.

CUBA

Grid reference C5–6
Capital Havana
Population 10,980,000
Area 110,860 sq km
Language Spanish
Religion Roman Catholic
Currency 1 Cuban peso = 100 centavos
GNP per person $1370

Cuba is the largest island in the Caribbean and is the region's most populated country. South-east Cuba is mountainous, but most of the country consists of plains. The climate is warm all year and the soils are very fertile. Farmers grow sugar cane (Cuba is the world's second biggest exporter of sugar), coffee, tobacco and rice. There is also nickel. In 1959 Fidel Castro led a revolution, and introduced a communist government. Since then, Cuba and the USA have been hostile to each other. Thousands of Cubans opposed to the government have fled to Florida, USA.

CYPRUS

Grid reference C11
Capital Nicosia
    (Lefkosia)
Population 729,800
Area 9251 sq km
Language Greek, Turkish
Religion Greek Orthodox, Muslim
Currency 1 Cyprus pound = 100 cents
GNP per person $9820

Cyprus is an island in the eastern Mediterranean. Over the past 6000 years it has been settled by many different peoples, and there are many important archaeological sites. Two mountain ranges enclose a fertile plain in the centre. The coasts, especially in the south, have become tourist areas. Cyprus was a British colony until 1960. After independence, relations between the Greek and Turkish Cypriot groups grew worse. In 1974 Turkey invaded the north of the island. Cyprus remains divided and UN troops guard the boundary between north and south.

CZECH REPUBLIC

Grid reference B10
Capital Prague
Population 10,330,000
Area 78,864 sq km
Language Czech
Religion Roman Catholic
Currency 1 koruna = 100 halér
GNP per person $3870

The Czech Republic is in central Europe. The western region, known as Bohemia, is mountainous. Moravia and Silesia, the other two regions, are largely plains and farmlands. Farmers raise cattle and pigs, and grow rye and potatoes. Bohemia and Silesia also have coal. The country has a strong manufacturing economy, based on steel, machinery, chemicals and cars. Between 1918 and 1993 it was joined with Slovakia to form a single country, Czechoslovakia, and was an ally of the former USSR. After the USSR collapsed, the people of Czechoslovakia voted to separate into two new countries.

DENMARK

Grid reference B10
Capital Copenhagen
Population 5,300,000
Area 43,076 sq km
Language Danish
Religion Lutheran
Currency 1 Danish krone = 100 øre
GNP per person $29,890

Denmark is a small, low-lying country in northern Europe. It consists of a peninsula called Jutland, and a number of islands in the entrance to the Baltic Sea. Copenhagen, the largest city, is on the island of Zealand. The soils are very fertile and farming is important. Milk and dairy products are Danish specialities. It also has a huge fishing industry. Denmark provides very good health-care, pensions and other services for its citizens. It was once part of the Viking world, and it has close cultural ties with Sweden and Norway. Greenland and the Faeroe Islands are self-governing parts of Denmark.

DJIBOUTI

Grid reference D12
Capital Djibouti
Population 586,000
Area 23,200 sq km
Language Arabic
Religion Muslim
Currency 1 Djibouti franc = 100 centimes
GNP per person $690

Djibouti is a small, desert country in north-east Africa. It is one of the hottest places in the world. Agriculture is found only in isolated areas along the coast and around inland oases. In between these places nomads herd cattle. Along the coast there are fishing communities. There is not much industry. The port of Djibouti city lies where two sea routes, the Red Sea and the Gulf of Aden, meet. It has been important in trade between surrounding countries for centuries. There are two main ethnic groups, the Issas and Afars. Djibouti was a French colony between 1896 and 1977.

DOMINICA

Grid reference D6
Capital Roseau
Population 74,200
Area 751 sq km
Language English, French
Religion Roman Catholic, Protestant
Currency 1 East Caribbean dollar = 100 cents
GNP per person $2990

Dominica is an island in the Caribbean between Martinique and Guadeloupe. There are high volcanic peaks covered in lush forests in the centre. The highest point is Monte Diaboltin (1447 m). The rich volcanic soils and the tropical climate make the land suitable for growing bananas, citrus fruits and cocoa in large plantations. But hurricanes have caused a lot of damage to crops and buildings. The original inhabitants were called Caribs, but they died out after Spain, France and Britain occupied the island. Today's Dominicans are mainly descended from Africans brought there as slaves.

DOMINICAN REPUBLIC

Grid reference D6
Capital Santo Domingo
Population 7,770,000
Area 48,442 sq km
Language Spanish
Religion Roman Catholic
Currency 1 Dominican peso = 100 centavos
GNP per person $1460

The Dominican Republic occupies the eastern half of the Caribbean island of Hispaniola. Haiti forms the western half. The country is very mountainous: Pico Duarte (3175 m) is the highest point in the Caribbean. Columbus landed on Hispaniola in 1492. He and his crew were the first people to report back to Europe about the existence of the Americas. Modern-day Dominicans are mainly descended from Spaniards, and slaves brought from Africa. Sugar is the most important crop. Tourism, nickel mining and manufacturing are also significant. Many Dominicans have migrated to the USA.

ECUADOR

Grid reference E6
Capital Quito
Population 11,700,000
Area 270,699 sq km
Language Spanish, Quechua
Religion Roman Catholic
Currency 1 sucre = 100 centavos
GNP per person $1390

Ecuador is in north-west South America. The Andes run through the middle of the country. They separate a coastal plain on the Pacific from a region of tropical rainforest. There are many active volcanoes in Ecuador, and earthquakes are common. Oil is the major natural resource. Along the coast farmers grow tropical crops such as coffee and bananas. Half the population are Quechua Indians, who were once part of the Inca empire. The Galapagos Islands, 970 km off the coast, belong to Ecuador. They were where Darwin made important findings that contributed to his theory of evolution.

EGYPT

Grid reference C11
Capital Cairo
Population 69,537,000
Area 1,001,449 sq km
Language Arabic
Religion Muslim, Christian
Currency 1 Egyptian pound = 100 piastres
GNP per person $790
Government Republic
Labour force Agriculture 43%, industry 23%, services 34%
Main industries Textiles, food, tourism, chemicals
Main farm and mine products Cotton, rice, maize (corn), oil
Population density 60 people per sq km
Population under 15 years old 37%
Urban population 46%
Life expectancy 61 years

For main entry see page 178

EL SALVADOR

Grid reference D5
Capital San Salvador
Population 5,050,000
Area 21,476,000
Language Spanish
Religion Roman Catholic
Currency 1 colôn = 100 centavos
GNP per person $1610

El Salvador is the smallest country in Central America. It lies on the shores of the Pacific Ocean. El Salvador is mountainous, with many volcanoes and frequent earthquakes. A severe earthquake in 1986 destroyed large areas of San Salvador. Agriculture is the main economic activity. Coffee is grown on large plantations in the highland valleys, while along the coast farmers produce sugar and maize (corn). El Salvador is also a major producer of balsam. The region was once part of the Aztec empire, before coming under Spanish rule in 1524. El Salvador became independent in 1841.

EQUATORIAL GUINEA

Grid reference D10
Capital Malabo
Population 420,000
Area 26,016 sq km
Language Spanish, African languages
Religion Roman Catholic
Currency 1 CFA franc = 100 centimes
GNP per person $380

Equatorial Guinea is a tiny country in West Africa. It includes a mainland area, called Rio Muni, and some islands in the Gulf of Guinea. The capital is on the island of Bioko (once called Fernando Po), but most people live on the mainland. The coast is swampy and lined with mangrove forests. Inland it is mountainous and heavily forested. The climate is very hot and humid, and over 2000 mm of rain fall each year. Cocoa, grown on Bioko, is the main export crop. Farmers also grow coffee, bananas, cassava and palms. The country was colonized by Portugal, Britain and then Spain, before independence in 1968.

ETHIOPIA

Grid reference D11–12
Capital Addis Ababa
Population 55,000,000
Area 1,251,282 sq km
Language Amharic
Religion Muslim, Ethiopian Orthodox, traditional African religions
Currency 1 Ethiopian birr = 100 cents
GNP per person $100

Ethiopia is a large country in north-east Africa. Apart from desert regions in the north and east, it is very mountainous. Two large, dry plateaux are separated by the northern part of the Great Rift Valley. They are drained by many rivers, including the Blue Nile. Drought and famine have been common throughout history, notably in the 1980s. Ethiopia was Africa's first Christian country, and one of its oldest independent states. Between the 1970s and 1990s there was civil war between the country's regions, leading to Eritrea breaking away in 1993.

ERITREA

Grid reference D11
Capital Asmara
Population 3,530,000
Area 93,700
Language Tigrinya, Tigray, Amharic
Religion Muslim, Coptic Christian
Currency 1 Ethiopian birr = 100 cents
GNP per person $105

Eritrea is one of the world's newest countries. After two decades of fighting, it won independence from Ethiopia in 1993. The war devastated the country, causing widespread destruction to the environment and forcing many people to flee to Sudan. Most Eritreans live in farming villages, but some are also nomadic, herding goats and cattle. Frequent and severe droughts make farming difficult. The coastal strip is very hot and dry, and few people live there. Eritrea's economy relies on foreign aid, but it also produces textiles, leather goods and salt.

FIJI

Grid reference E18
Capital Suva
Population 803,500
Area 18,333 sq km
Language English
Religion Christian, Hindu, Muslim
Currency 1 Fijian dollar = 100 cents
GNP per person $2440

Fiji (or Viti) is made up of over 300 islands, 100 of which are inhabited, in the Pacific Ocean. Some islands are volcanic, others are coral reefs. The largest island, on which most Fijians live, is Viti Levu. The climate is hot, humid and rainy. The islands produce a lot of sugar cane, and also bananas, ginger and copra. Many tourists visit Fiji. Native Fijians belong to the Melanesian and Polynesian peoples. They are now outnumbered by Indians, descended from labourers brought to Fiji in the 1900s. Relations between the communities got worse after native Fijians staged a military coup in 1987.

ESTONIA

Grid reference B11
Capital Tallinn
Population 1,600,000
Area 45,100 sq km
Language Estonian, Russian
Religion Lutheran
Currency 1 kroon = 100 senti
GNP per person $2860

Estonia is a small country in northern Europe, on the Gulf of Finland and the Baltic Sea. There are many small islands off the coast, and over 1000 lakes on the mainland. The largest of these is Lake Peipsi (Peipus). Large areas are wooded, and forestry, along with dairy farming, is an important economic activity. A type of coal called bituminous shales supplies some of the country's energy. Factories make farm machinery and electric motors. Estonia was ruled by Russia, and after a brief period of independence (1918–1940), became a republic of the former USSR. It became independent again in 1991.

FINLAND

Grid reference A11
Capital Helsinki
Population 5,120,000
Area 338,145 sq km
Language Finnish, Swedish, Saame
Religion Lutheran
Currency 1 euro = 100 cents
GNP per person $20,580

Finland is in northern Europe, in Scandinavia. Parts of Finland lie within the Arctic, and the whole country has been altered by glaciation. It is very flat and covered in thousands of small lakes and streams. Two-thirds of the country is forested. Heavy snows fall in winter. Most Finns live in the southern coastal region, although there is a Lapp (Saami) minority in the north. They herd reindeer. Wood (for making paper and for building) is the main natural resource, along with iron and copper. Finland was ruled by Russia between 1809 and 1917, and joined the European Union in 1995.

FRANCE

Grid reference B10
Capital Paris
Population 58,000,000
Area 551,000 sq km
Language French
Religion Roman Catholic
Currency 1 euro = 100 cents
GNP per person $24,990
Government Republic
Labour force Agriculture 5%, industry 30%, services 65%
Main industries Steel, machinery, chemicals, cars, aircraft, electronics, tourism, food
Main farm and mine products Wheat, sugar beet, wine, beef, potatoes, dairy products
Population density 104 people per sq km
Population under 15 years old 19%
Urban population 73%
Life expectancy 78 years

For main entry see pages 228–230

GABON

Grid reference D10–E10
Capital Libreville
Population 1,010,000
Area 267,667 sq km
Language French, Fang and other African languages
Religion Christian
Currency 1 CFA franc = 100 centimes
GNP per person $3490

Gabon is on the coast of West Africa. It lies on either side of the Equator. The climate is hot and humid, with heavy rainfall all year round. Thick forests cover most of the land, which is made up of mountains and plateaux. The Ogooué river drains most of Gabon. There are over 40 different ethnic groups in Gabon, but most of them speak one of the Bantu languages. The majority are farmers, growing coffee, cocoa, rubber and palms. The country also has oil, natural gas, manganese and iron ore. It gained independence from France in 1960, and is one of West Africa's most developed countries.

GAMBIA

Grid reference D9
Capital Banjul
Population 1,090,000
Area 11,295 sq km
Language English, Mandinka, Wolof, Fula
Religion Muslim, Christian
Currency 1 dalasi = 100 butut
GNP per person $320

Gambia, in West Africa, is a long, narrow country located on either side of the Gambia river. Except for a small coastline, it is entirely surrounded by Senegal. During part of the 1980s the two countries were joined together as Senegambia. The land is mostly flat, covered in savannah grassland, forest and farmlands. It is rainy, but hot throughout the year. The people are mostly farmers, growing cotton, groundnuts, rice, millet and fruit. The Mandinka are the largest of the many ethnic groups. Gambia was a British colony until 1965. It is a popular destination for European tourists.

GEORGIA

Grid reference B12
Capital Tbilisi
Population 5,430,000
Area 69,700 sq km
Language Georgian, Russian
Religion Georgian Church
Currency Lari
GNP per person $440

Georgia lies in the Caucasus mountains, bordering the Black Sea. Until 1991 it was a republic of the former Soviet Union. The land is mountainous, and 40 per cent of the country is forested. Georgia's climate is warm in the summer and mild in the winter. It is famous for its orchards and vineyards, as well as its holiday resorts along the Black Sea coast. Georgia also has a strong industrial sector, making chemicals and iron and steel. Since independence from the Soviet Union, the regions of South Ossetia and Abkhazia have fought to break away. Many civilians have fled the fighting.

GERMANY

Grid reference B10
Capital Berlin
Population 81,540,000
Area 357,868 sq km
Language German
Religion Lutheran, Roman Catholic
Currency 1 euro = 100 cents
GNP per person $27,510
Government Federal republic
Labour force Agriculture 6%, industry 41%, services 53%
Main industries Iron and steel, cars, chemicals, machinery, electronics
Main farm and mine products Wheat, potatoes, barley, rye, wine, beef, pork, coal
Population density 228 people per sq km
Population under 15 years old 16%
Urban population 88%
Life expectancy 76 years

For main entry see pages 245–247

GHANA

Grid reference D9–10
Capital Accra
Population 16,470,000
Area 238,537 sq km
Language English, Akan, Ewe, Ga
Religion Christian, traditional African religions, Muslim
Currency 1 cedi = 100 pesawas
GNP per person $390

Ghana is in West Africa. Southern Ghana is mainly forest, partly cleared to grow cocoa, coffee, groundnuts and food crops. It is one of the world's leading exporters of cocoa. Northern Ghana is a savannah grassland region. Lake Volta, created by a dam in the Volta river, is one of the largest reservoirs in the world. It supplies electricity to Ghana's industries. A number of powerful states have ruled the region. The last was the Ashanti kingdom, overthrown by the British in 1874. In 1960 Ghana became the first British African colony to gain independence.

GREECE

Grid reference C11
Capital Athens
Population 10,400,000
Area 131,957 sq km
Language Greek
Religion Greek Orthodox
Currency 1 euro = 100 cents
GNP per person $8120

Greece is a Mediterranean country, made up of the southern end of the Balkans and several islands. Crete is the largest of the islands. Greece is a mountainous country, with farming confined to small areas. Farmers grow olives, wheat, fruit and many food crops. Sheep and goats are often kept in highland areas. The Greek economy mainly depends on services, tourism, trade and shipping. It has one of the world's largest shipping fleets. The region has been the centre of many cultures and civilizations since prehistoric times. Its ancient artists, philosophers and politicians have had a major influence on the world's ideas.

GRENADA

Grid reference D6
Capital St George's
Population 96,000
Area 344 sq km
Language English, French patois
Religion Roman Catholic, Protestant
Currency 1 East Caribbean dollar = 100 cents
GNP per person $2980

Grenada lies at the southern end of the Windward islands in the Caribbean. The island is volcanic, and has two lakes which occupy the craters of extinct volcanoes. The country also includes two islands of the nearby Grenadines, which lie to the north. Grenada was colonized by the French and British, who introduced African slaves and crops such as cocoa, bananas and especially nutmeg. There is high rainfall and a warm climate, which is good for farming. Most people are of African origin. In 1983 the USA invaded, overthrowing the communists and establishing political stability.

GUATEMALA

Grid reference D5
Capital Guatemala City
Population 10,620,00
Area 108,889 sq km
Language Spanish, Quiche, Cakchiquel, Kekchi
Religion Roman Catholic, Protestant
Currency 1 quetzal = 100 centavos
GNP per person $1340

Guatemala is in Central America and was once part of the Mayan empire. The ruins of magnificent Mayan cities can be seen among the tropical forests in the north. About 40 per cent of the people are Indians, speaking many different languages. Most Guatemalans live on the high central plateau. The Pacific coast is forested and few people live there. The country experiences volcanic eruptions, earthquakes and hurricanes. Farming is the main activity, producing coffee, bananas, cotton, sugar and rice. There are also big cattle ranches. Since the 1950s there have been several military takeovers.

GUINEA

Grid reference D9
Capital Conarky
Population 6,500,000
Area 246,048 sq km
Language French, Fulani, Malinké
Religion Muslim, traditional African religions
Currency 1 Guinean franc = 100 cauris
GNP per person $550

Guinea is in tropical West Africa. Along the Atlantic coast is an area of heavy rainfall, where most people live and where rice, bananas and coconuts are grown. Inland there is a drier plateau region, where cattle are raised. The north-east is drier still. Tropical forests extend to the south. Although most Guineans are farmers, the country is also rich in bauxite, gold and diamonds. The region was once part of the Mali and then Songhai empires, and later a French colony. It became independent in 1958. The largest ethnic groups are the Fulani and Malinké peoples.

GUINEA-BISSAU

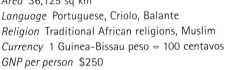

Grid reference D9
Capital Bissau
Population 1,060,000
Area 36,125 sq km
Language Portuguese, Criolo, Balante
Religion Traditional African religions, Muslim
Currency 1 Guinea-Bissau peso = 100 centavos
GNP per person $250

Guinea-Bissau is a small country in West Africa, located where the Corubal and Geba rivers enter the Atlantic. There are many small and forested islands off the coast. Much of the country is low-lying and marshy. Many people live by fishing. Rice is grown in the watered areas, and cattle, nuts and palms are cultivated in the drier regions. Guinea-Bissau's climate is tropical. From November to May it is very dry and winds from the Sahara Desert blow across the land. Guinea-Bissau was a Portuguese colony, and was politically united with the Cape Verde islands until 1980.

GUYANA

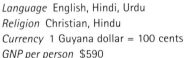

Grid reference D7
Capital Georgetown
Population 730,000
Area 214,969 sq km
Language English, Hindi, Urdu
Religion Christian, Hindu
Currency 1 Guyana dollar = 100 cents
GNP per person $590

Guyana is a former British colony on the Atlantic coast of South America. Almost all the population live on a narrow coastal plain, which is where the main farmlands are. People have built dams and ditches to irrigate fields of sugar and rice. The south is mountainous and heavily forested, and is home to some Indian tribes. Guyana has two rainy seasons: April to July and November to January. Most people are descended from African slaves and workers brought from India in the 1900s. The two communities keep fairly separate. Since independence in 1966 they have often been political rivals.

HAITI

Grid reference D6
Capital Port-au-Prince
Population 6,760,000
Area 27,750 sq km
Language French, Creole
Religion Roman Catholic, Voodoo
Currency 1 gourde = 100 centimes
GNP per person $250

Haiti forms the western half of the Caribbean island of Hispaniola. The Dominican Republic makes up the eastern half. In the mid-17th century it became a French colony, but in 1804 the African slaves rebelled and declared the Caribbean's first republic. In the 20th century, Haitians suffered under dictatorships and endured social and political unrest. This has prevented development. The clearance of forests for farmlands has also caused severe soil erosion. Farms produce bananas and coffee for export. The widespread poverty has led many Haitians to migrate abroad or to flee to the USA as refugees.

HONDURAS

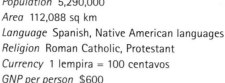

Grid reference D5
Capital Tegucigalpa
Population 5,290,000
Area 112,088 sq km
Language Spanish, Native American languages
Religion Roman Catholic, Protestant
Currency 1 lempira = 100 centavos
GNP per person $600

Honduras is a Central American country. Eighty per cent is rainforest and high mountains, rising to 2865 m at Patuca. The ruined Mayan city of Copàn is in the west, and there is still a small Indian population. But most Hondurans are descended from Spanish colonial settlers. Honduras is a major producer of bananas, and it also grows coffee, tobacco and maize (corn). The country mines silver, lead and zinc, and is developing offshore oil. Between the 1960s and 1980s the country had military rulers and the army fought with left-wing rebels. In the 1990s there was greater stability.

HUNGARY

Grid reference B10–11
Capital Budapest
Population 10,210,000
Area 93,033 sq km
Language Hungarian
Religion Roman Catholic, Protestant
Currency 1 forint = 100 fillér
GNP per person $4120

Hungary is in central Europe. The Danube river flows along its northern border, and then runs south, dividing a range of hills running east to west. The largest region is a great plain, called the Alföd, an area of rich farmlands. Hungary's farms produce grain, potatoes, sugar beet and wine. It also makes chemicals, machines and textiles. The medieval kingdom of Hungary was founded by the Magyar peoples, but for much of its history it was part of the Ottoman and then Habsburg empires. Between 1949 and 1989 Hungary was a communist state, and Russian troops put down an uprising in 1956.

ICELAND

Grid reference A9
Capital Reykjavik
Population 267,800
Area 103,000 sq km
Language Icelandic
Religion Lutheran
Currency 1 króna = 100 aurar
GNP per person $24,950

Iceland lies between the Atlantic and Arctic oceans. Beneath the island the Earth's crust is very active, so Iceland has many volcanoes, hot springs and geysers. The land itself is very flat and treeless, and an ice-cap covers much of the south-east. Blizzards often occur. All along the coast there are steep inlets called fjords. Norse people settled Iceland in the 9th century. Today, almost half the islanders live in the main city, Reykjavik. The country has few good farmlands and few natural resources. Fishing, especially for cod and herring, is the main export activity.

INDIA

Grid reference C13–D13
Capital New Delhi
Population 1,030,000,000
Area 3,166,829 sq km
Language Hindi, English, Urdu, Punjabi and others
Religion Hindu, Muslim
Currency 1 Indian rupee = 100 paisa
GNP per person $340
Government Federal republic
Labour force Agriculture 65%, industry 16%, services 19%
Main industries Textiles, chemicals, food, steel, cars, cement, machinery, tourism
Main farm and mine products Tea, rice, wheat, sorghum, millet, cotton, cattle, poultry, pulses, coal, iron ore
Population density 288 people per sq km
Population under 15 years old 34%
Urban population 26%
Life expectancy 60 years

For main entry see pages 282–284

INDONESIA

Grid reference E15–17

Capital Jakarta

Population 191,360,000

Area 1,906,200 sq km

Language Bahasa Indonesian, Javanese, Dutch

Religion Muslim

Currency 1 Indonesian rupee = 100 sen

GNP per person $980

Government Republic

Labour force Agriculture 55%, industry 14%, services 31%

Main industries Petroleum, textiles, shoes, rubber, plywood, cement

Main farm and mine products Rice, cassava, peanuts, rubber, cocoa, palm oil, oil and natural gas

Population density 100 people per sq km

Population under 15 years old 32%

Urban population 40%

Life expectancy 62 years

For main entry see page 285

IRAN

Grid reference C12

Capital Tehran

Population 63,200,000

Area 1,648,000 sq km

Language Farsi, Kurdish, Turkic and others

Religion Muslim

Currency 1 Iranian rial = 100 toman

GNP per person $2190

Government Islamic republic

Labour force Agriculture 33%, industry 21%, services 47%

Main industries Petroleum, chemicals, textiles, metals, weapons

Main farm and mine products Wheat, rice, sugar beet, fruit, cotton, caviar, oil and natural gas

Population density 37 people per sq km

Population under 15 years old 45%

Urban population 58%

Life expectancy 68 years

For main entry see page 295

IRAQ

Grid reference C12

Capital Baghdad

Population 19,410,000

Area 434,925 sq km

Language Arabic, Kurdish

Religion Muslim

Currency 1 Iraqi dinar = 1000 fils

GNP per person $2140

Government Republic

Labour force Agriculture 30%, industry 22%, services 48%

Main industries Petroleum, chemicals, textiles, construction, food

Main farm and mine products Wheat, barley, rice, vegetables, dates, cotton, cattle, sheep, oil and natural gas

Population density 45 people per sq km

Population under 15 years old 48%

Urban population 77%

Life expectancy 67 years

For main entry see page 295

IRELAND, REPUBLIC OF

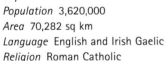

Grid reference B9

Capital Dublin

Population 3,620,000

Area 70,282 sq km

Language English and Irish Gaelic

Religion Roman Catholic

Currency 1 euro = 100 cents

GNP per person $14,710

Government Republic

Labour force Agriculture 14%, industry 28%, services 57%

Main industries Food, drink, textiles, clothing, chemicals, computers, glass, tourism

Main farm and mine products Root crops, barley, potatoes, meat, dairy products, peat, natural gas

Population density 52 people per sq km

Population under 15 years old 23%

Urban population 59%

Life expectancy 76 years

For main entry see pages 296–297

ISRAEL

Grid reference C11

Capital Jerusalem

Population 5,710,000

Area 20,770 sq km

Language Hebrew, Arabic

Religion Jewish, Muslim

Currency 1 shekel = 100 agorot

GNP per person $15,920

Government Republic

Labour force Agriculture 4%, industry 32%, services 64%

Main industries Food, textiles, clothing, chemicals, weapons, diamond cutting, tourism

Main farm and mine products Fruit, cotton, sugar beet, beef, potash

Population density 271 people per sq km

Population under 15 years old 29%

Urban population 90%

Life expectancy 78 years

For main entry see page 300

ITALY

Grid reference B10–C10

Capital Rome

Population 57,270,000

Area 301,255 sq km

Language Italian

Religion Roman Catholic

Currency 1 euro = 100 cents

GNP per person $19,020

Government Republic

Labour force Agriculture 10%, industry 32%, services 58%

Main industries Iron and steel, chemicals, cars, clothing, ceramics, food, tourism

Main farm and mine products Fruit, vegetables, olives, grapes, potatoes, sugar beet, wheat, maize (corn)

Population density 190 people per sq km

Population under 15 years old 15%

Urban population 67%

Life expectancy 78 years

For main entry see pages 300–301

JAMAICA

Grid reference D6
Capital Kingston
Population 2,500,000
Area 10,957 sq km
Language English, Creole
Religion Protestant
Currency 1 Jamaican dollar = 100 cents
GNP per person $1510

Jamaica is one of the larger and more populated Caribbean islands. Much of the land is mountainous, notably the Blue Mountains in the east. The west is formed by a plateau. Jamaica has important natural resources – bauxite and limestone – from which aluminium and cement are made. Farming is also important, especially sugar, bananas and tropical fruits. The northern coast has beautiful beaches and is a popular place for tourists. Most Jamaicans are descended from Africans brought by the British to work sugar plantations. Many have migrated to the UK and USA.

JAPAN

Grid reference C16–17
Capital Tokyo
Population 125,570,000
Area 377,728 sq km
Language Japanese
Religion Shinto, Buddhism
Currency 1 yen = 100 sen
GNP per person $39,640
Government Constitutional monarchy
Labour force Agriculture 7%, industry 33%, services 60%
Main industries Steel, metals, cars, ships, electronics, textiles, telecommunications
Main farm and mine products Rice, sugar beet, vegetables, fruit, pork, fish
Population density 332 people per sq km
Population under 15 years old 16%
Urban population 78%
Life expectancy 80 years

For main entry see pages 302–303

JORDAN

Grid reference C11
Capital Amman
Population 4,100,000
Area 96,188 sq km
Language Arabic
Religion Sunni Muslim
Currency 1 Jordanian dinar = 1000 fils
GNP per person $1510

Jordan is a small kingdom in the Middle East, surrounded by larger and more powerful countries. Ninety per cent of the country is desert, with hot summers and annual rainfall under 200 mm. The area to the west of the Jordan river and the Dead Sea, known as the West Bank, has been under Israel's control since 1967. Jordan is short of water, and cereals and citrus fruit are only grown in a few places. Much of the land is used to raise sheep and goats. But Jordan also exports potash and phosphates. The ancient city of Petra, whose buildings are carved out of rock, is in southern Jordan.

KAZAKHSTAN

Grid reference B12–13
Capital Astana
Population 16,500,000
Area 2,717,300 sq km
Language Kazakh, Russian, German
Religion Muslim, Russian Orthodox
Currency tenge
GNP per person $1330

Kazakhstan, in Central Asia, lies between China and the Caspian Sea. There are vast grassland plains and desert plateaux across most of the country, rising to mountains in the south-east. The Aral Sea lies partly within Kazakhstan. There are fields of cotton, wheat and tobacco, and on the plains Kazakhs raise cattle. The region also has many minerals, such as coal, iron and copper. Kazakhstan was a republic of the former Soviet Union, but is now developing relations with China and the USA. These countries are keen to develop Kazakhstan's newly discovered giant oilfields.

KENYA

Grid reference D11–E11
Capital Nairobi
Population 26,440,000
Area 580,367 sq km
Language English, Swahili and other African languages
Religion Protestant, Roman Catholic, traditional African religions
Currency 1 Kenyan shilling = 100 cents
GNP per person $280

Kenya, in East Africa, lies across the Equator. The coast is hot and rainy, but inland it is much drier. Part of the Great Rift Valley runs through western Kenya. Where there are mountains, the climate is cooler and the land is suited to growing crops such as tea and coffee. Parts of Kenya are also covered in grasslands, home to many wild animals. Game reserves attract many tourists for safari holidays. Kenyans are members of several different ethnic groups. Some are farmers, while others herd cattle. Kenya became independent in 1963.

KIRGYZSTAN

Grid reference B13
Capital Bishkek
Population 4,460,000
Area 198,500 sq km
Language Kirgyz, Russian
Religion Muslim
Currency som
GNP per person $700

Kirgyzstan is in Central Asia. It was one of the republics of the former USSR until 1991. The Tien Shan, Altai and Pamir mountain ranges cover most of the country. They include some of the most remote places in the world – areas which are very dry and often desert-like. Most of the people live in valleys between the mountains, where the main roads are located. Fields of wheat, cotton and tobacco are found here. The country also possesses natural resources such as gold, lead, zinc and coal. Kirgyzstan was ruled by Russia from the 1860s, and there are many Russians still living there.

KIRIBATI

Grid reference D18–E18
Capital Bairiki
Population 80,000
Area 717 sq km
Language English, Gilbertese
Religion Roman Catholic, Protestant
Currency 1 Australian dollar = 100 cents
GNP per person $920

Kiribati is made up of 33 islands and coral atolls scattered over 3 million square kilometres in the central Pacific Ocean. The main island, on which most people live, is Tarawa. The islands were once part of a British colony called the Gilbert and Ellice Islands. The people are mainly farmers, growing coconuts, bananas, fruits and food crops. People also fish, especially for tuna. The main natural resource, phosphate, is almost all gone because of over-mining. But the surrounding sea-bed may contain valuable mineral resources.

KUWAIT

Grid reference C12
Capital Kuwait City
Population 2,020,000
Area 17,818 sq km
Language Arabic
Religion Muslim
Currency 1 Kuwaiti dinar = 1000 fils
GNP per person $17,390

Kuwait is a small state at the northern end of the Persian Gulf. Almost all of Kuwait is low-lying desert. It was once a British colony. Since independence in 1961 it has been ruled by the al-Sabah family. Oil was discovered there in the 1940s, and Kuwait has become very wealthy and developed. Over 40 per cent of the population have come from other countries, especially South Asia, to work in the oil industry. Between 1990 and 1991 Kuwait was occupied by Iraqi forces, which were driven out by a UN-led alliance. The war caused great damage to the environment, with oil spills on land and sea.

LAOS

Grid reference D15
Capital Vientiane
Population 4,580,000
Area 236,800 sq km
Language Lao, French, tribal languages
Religion Buddhist, Lao-Theung
Currency 1 kip = 100 at
GNP per person $350

Laos is a mountainous country in South-east Asia. The Mekong river flows north to south, forming the border with Thailand. Most of Laos away from the Mekong valley is heavily forested. Between 1953 and 1975 Laos was torn apart by civil war, with the USA and Vietnam supporting rival sides. A communist government was set up in 1975. Laos is a poor country due to war, drought and floods. Most people are farmers, who grow rice, tobacco, cotton and coffee. Laos plans to build dams to produce hydroelectricity for Thailand and make more use of its timber resources.

LATVIA

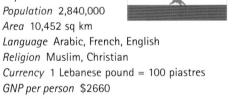

Grid reference B11
Capital Riga
Population 2,490,000
Area 64,600 sq km
Language Latvian
Religion Lutheran
Currency 1 lat = 100 santims
GNP per person $2270

Latvia lies between Estonia and Lithuania, on the shores of the Baltic Sea in northern Europe. The inland areas are mainly low-lying and wooded, and are dotted with many lakes and marshes. The Zemgale plain in the south has the best farmlands. They produce cereals, meat and dairy products. Latvia's industries make machines, motorcycles, electronics and chemicals, although industrial pollution is a serious problem. It was ruled by Russia between 1721 and 1918, and was a republic of the former USSR from 1940 to 1991. There is still a large Russian minority in Latvia.

LEBANON

Grid reference C11
Capital Beirut
Population 2,840,000
Area 10,452 sq km
Language Arabic, French, English
Religion Muslim, Christian
Currency 1 Lebanese pound = 100 piastres
GNP per person $2660

Since ancient times, the region now known as Lebanon has been an important centre for trade in the Mediterranean. Over the centuries many different peoples have settled there, including Muslims and Arabs. Relations between the communities broke down in the late 1950s and a long period of civil war followed. Syria, Israel and the USA all became involved. Parts of southern Lebanon are still controlled by Israel. There has been peace since 1993, allowing the economy to flourish again. Lebanese farms produce many fruits, olives and wheat, and its factories make chemicals and textiles.

LESOTHO

Grid reference F11
Capital Maseru
Population 2,110,000
Area 30,355 sq km
Language Lesotho, English, Zulu
Religion Roman Catholic, Protestant
Currency 1 loti = 100 lisente
GNP per person $770

Lesotho is a small southern African kingdom. It is entirely surrounded by South Africa. Lesotho is mostly mountainous, and soil erosion is a big problem. Farmers grow wheat, sorghum and maize (corn) in the western lowlands. Cattle are raised in the highlands. There are few natural resources, apart from diamonds. Many people migrate to South Africa to work. Almost all the residents of the country belong to the Basotho people. They fought for independence against both Zulus and Boers (Africans of Dutch descent) in the 19th century. Once a British colony, Lesotho became independent in 1960.

LIBERIA

Grid reference D9
Capital Monrovia
Population 2,830,000
Area 111,370 sq km
Language English, African languages
Religion Traditional African religions, Muslim, Christian
Currency 1 Liberian dollar = 100 cents
GNP per person $390

Liberia is a small country in West Africa, founded in the 1820s as a homeland for freed African slaves from the USA. It became an independent country in 1847. Only a small number of Africans from the USA settled there. The coast is low-lying, and is fringed by lagoons and mangrove marshes. Inland there are mountains covered in thick forest. There are large rubber plantations in Liberia. Iron ore, gold and diamonds are the main natural resources. Most Liberians are farmers, growing cassava, coffee, cocoa and other crops. In the 1990s the country was torn apart by civil war.

LIBYA

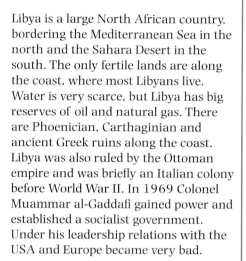

Grid reference C10–11
Capital Tripoli
Population 5,590,000
Area 1,758,610 sq km
Language Arabic
Religion Sunni Muslim
Currency 1 Libyan dinar = 1000 dirhams
GNP per person $5350

Libya is a large North African country, bordering the Mediterranean Sea in the north and the Sahara Desert in the south. The only fertile lands are along the coast, where most Libyans live. Water is very scarce, but Libya has big reserves of oil and natural gas. There are Phoenician, Carthaginian and ancient Greek ruins along the coast. Libya was also ruled by the Ottoman empire and was briefly an Italian colony before World War II. In 1969 Colonel Muammar al-Gaddafi gained power and established a socialist government. Under his leadership relations with the USA and Europe became very bad.

LIECHTENSTEIN

Location see Europe map (page 195)
Capital Vaduz
Population 30,923
Area 160 sq km
Language German
Religion Roman Catholic
Currency 1 Swiss franc = 100 centimes
GNP per person $33,510

Liechtenstein is a tiny country in the European Alps, lying between Austria and Switzerland. The River Rhine forms its western border. Most of the country is hilly and the more mountainous areas are forested. The state of Liechtenstein has existed since 1342, and for many years it was part of the Holy Roman Empire. It became fully independent in 1866. Liechtenstein is a monarchy. It produces high-technology goods, medical products and metal goods for export. Many international banks and companies have their headquarters there.

LITHUANIA

Grid reference B11
Capital Vilnius
Population 3,710,000
Area 65,200 sq km
Language Lithuanian
Religion Roman Catholic
Currency 1 litas = 100 centai
GNP per person $1900

Lithuania is a country in northern Europe, bordering the Baltic Sea. In medieval times it was a much larger kingdom. Between 1385 and 1795 it was united with Poland. From 1940 to 1991 Lithuania was a republic of the former USSR. The country is mainly low-lying or hilly, with many forests, marshes, lakes and streams. The Nemunas river drains much of the land. Its farms specialize in cattle, pigs and poultry, although they also produce grains and vegetables. Its factories make many types of machines, plastics and fertilizers, and there are also shipyards and port industries.

LUXEMBOURG

Grid reference B10
Capital Luxembourg
Population 412,800
Area 2586 sq km
Language French, German, Letzeburgish
Religion Roman Catholic
Currency 1 euro = 100 cents
GNP per person $41,210

Luxembourg is a very small country in Europe, bordered by France, Belgium and Germany. The head of state is called the Grand Duke. Various countries, including France and the Netherlands, have ruled over Luxembourg, but it became fully independent in 1867. Since then it has become a rich and peaceful country. Its wealth came from trade, and later from iron and steel, based on big reserves of iron ore. In the 20th century Luxembourg became a major centre of international banking and business. Many people from neighbouring countries travel to work there.

MACEDONIA (FYROM)

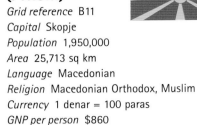

Grid reference B11
Capital Skopje
Population 1,950,000
Area 25,713 sq km
Language Macedonian
Religion Macedonian Orthodox, Muslim
Currency 1 denar = 100 paras
GNP per person $860

The modern country of FYROM (Former Yugoslav Republic of Macedonia) dates back to only 1991, when it separated from the former Yugoslavia. But in ancient times Macedonia was the centre of a powerful empire. One of its rulers was Alexander the Great. It is a mountainous country and the Vardar river runs through it. In its valley farmers grow wheat, barley, maize (corn) and rice. In the highlands herders keep sheep and goats. Most inhabitants are Macedonians, but there are Albanian, Serb and Turkish minorities. The break-up of Yugoslavia has strained relations between these communities.

MADAGASCAR

Grid reference E12–F12
Capital Antananarivo
Population 13,500,000
Area 587,041 sq km
Language Malagasy, French
Religion Traditional African religions, Roman Catholic, Protestant
Currency 1 Malagasy franc = 100 centimes
GNP per person $230

Madagascar is a large island off the south-east coast of Africa. Mountains run down the centre of the island. They are covered in dense tropical forest on the wetter coast and grasslands to the east. It has many unique plants and animals, such as lemurs. It was first settled by people from South-east Asia, and later by Africans, Arabs and Europeans. It was a French colony until independence in 1960. Farmers grow rice, coffee, bananas and sugar. There is severe soil erosion because much of the forest, which naturally protects soils, has been cut down.

MALAWI

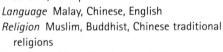

Grid reference E11
Capital Lilongwe
Population 11,000,000
Area 118,484 sq km
Language English, Chichewa
Religion Christian, traditional African religions, Muslim
Currency 1 kwacha = 100 tambala
GNP per person $170

Malawi is one of the smaller countries of southern Africa, to the west and south of Lake Malawi, Africa's third largest lake. The land is very varied, including forested, tropical mountains, high plateaux and grasslands. The highest mountains, over 2500 m, are in the far south. The region was once part of the Zimbabwe empire, and later occupied by Portugal and then Britain. It changed its name from Nyasaland before it became independent in 1964. Ninety per cent of the people are farmers. They grow food crops, sugar, tea and cotton.

MALAYSIA

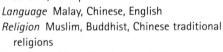

Grid reference D15
Capital Kuala Lumpur
Population 21,300,000
Area 329,749 sq km
Language Malay, Chinese, English
Religion Muslim, Buddhist, Chinese traditional religions
Currency 1 Malaysian dollar = 100 cents
GNP per person $3890

Malaysia is a federation of 13 states, including nine states on the mainland peninsula of South-east Asia, and two (Sabah and Sarawak) on the island of Borneo. The peninsula is divided along its length by granite and limestone mountains, which are heavily forested. The Borneo states are also very mountainous and covered in tropical forests. Since the 1970s the country has developed very rapidly. Its economy has moved from depending on natural resources such as rubber and tin, to advanced industries such as electronics, cars, oil and banking.

MALDIVES

Grid reference D13
Capital Malé
Population 253,300
Area 300 sq km
Language Dhivehi, Arabic, Hindi, English
Religion Sunni Muslim
Currency 1 rufiyaa = 100 laaris
GNP per person $990

The Maldives are an island chain in the Indian Ocean, lying between India and the Equator. Only 200 or so of over 1100 islands are inhabited. Many of them are small and very low-lying. Nowhere is more than 2 metres above sea level, so the Maldives government is campaigning to stop global warming and prevent any rise in sea level. The people are descended from migrants from India and Arabia, and the country was a British colony until 1965. There is little vegetation apart from coconut palms, and no important natural resources. Fishing, farming and tourism are the main economic activities.

MALI

Grid reference C9–D9
Capital Bamako
Population 9,200,000
Area 1,240,192 sq km
Language French, Bambara and other African languages
Religion Muslim
Currency 1 CFA franc = 100 centimes
GNP per person $250

Mali is in West Africa. Its northern region lies within the Sahara Desert. Tuaregs and other nomadic herding people keep sheep, goats and cattle on the dry desert lands. In the south, the Niger and Senegal river lowlands support farming of sorghum, maize (corn) and millet for food. There is little industry in Mali, but fishing is important along the rivers. The Mali empire reached its peak in the 14th century, when it was a major centre of trade in goods such as gold, salt and ivory. Later, Mali was a French colony, and it gained independence in 1960.

MALTA

Grid reference C10
Capital Valletta
Population 376,330
Area 316 sq km
Language Maltese, English
Religion Roman Catholic
Currency 1 Maltese pound = 100 cents
GNP per person $7240

Malta lies in the central Mediterranean Sea. The two main inhabited islands, Malta and the smaller Gozo, both have rocky coastlines with plenty of natural harbours. Neither has any permanent rivers. Because of its location, Malta has been important to many of the region's trading peoples over the centuries. These included Phoenicians, Romans and Arabs. Between the 16th and 18th centuries it was governed by a Christian religious order, the Knights of St John. Malta was famous for resisting the German air force in World War II. The main industries include tourism, ship repair and agriculture.

MAURITANIA

Grid reference C9–D9
Capital Nouakchott
Population 2,330,000
Area 1,029,920 sq km
Language Arabic, French, African languages
Religion Muslim
Currency 1 ouguija = 5 khoums
GNP per person $460

Mauritania is in West Africa. Two-thirds of the country lies within the Sahara Desert, and is covered in sand dunes and rocky plateaux. Between the desert and the wetter region along the Atlantic coast there are savannah grasslands, where Berber and Arab nomads herd cattle, camels, sheep and goats. Most people live in the south, along the Senegal river. Here they grow sorghum, millet and rice. Mauritania was once part of the Ghana and Mali empires, and between 1903 and 1960 was a French colony. Its most serious problem is drought and the spread of deserts into the dry grasslands.

MAURITIUS

Grid reference F12
Capital Port Louis
Population 1,130,000
Area 1865 sq km
Language English, French, Hindi, Urdu
Religion Hindu, Roman Catholic, Muslim
Currency 1 Mauritian rupee = 100 cents
GNP per person $3380

Mauritius is made up of one large island, 800 km east of Madagascar, and 25 smaller ones, all lying in the Indian Ocean. The islands are old volcanoes. They rise steeply from the coast, which is fringed with coral reefs, lagoons and mangrove swamps. They were uninhabited until the 16th century, after which the Portuguese, Dutch, French and British fought over them. They set up sugar plantations and brought workers from India and Pakistan. Sugar is still a major industry, but the islands also export tea, cut diamonds, textiles and watches. Mauritius is very popular with tourists.

MEXICO

Grid reference C4–5
Capital Mexico City
Population 91,120,000
Area 1,978,800 sq km
Language Spanish, Native American languages
Religion Roman Catholic
Currency 1 Mexican peso = 100 centavos
GNP per person $3320
Government Federal republic
Labour force Agriculture 28%, industry 27%, services 45%
Main industries Food, drink, iron and steel, petroleum, cars, chemicals, tourism
Main farm and mine products Maize (corn), wheat, tobacco, soybeans, fruit, tomatoes, cotton, oil and natural gas, silver
Population density 41 people per sq km
Population under 15 years old 36%
Urban population 77%
Life expectancy 74 years

For main entry see page 342

MOLDOVA

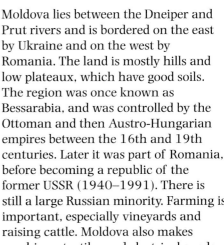

Grid reference B11
Capital Chisinau
Population 4,400,000
Area 33,700 sq km
Language Moldovan, Ukrainian
Religion Russian Orthodox
Currency leu
GNP per person $920

Moldova lies between the Dneiper and Prut rivers and is bordered on the east by Ukraine and on the west by Romania. The land is mostly hills and low plateaux, which have good soils. The region was once known as Bessarabia, and was controlled by the Ottoman and then Austro-Hungarian empires between the 16th and 19th centuries. Later it was part of Romania, before becoming a republic of the former USSR (1940–1991). There is still a large Russian minority. Farming is important, especially vineyards and raising cattle. Moldova also makes machines, textiles and electrical goods.

MONACO

Grid reference B10
Capital Monaco
Population 29,970
Area 1.95 sq km
Language French, English, Italian, Monegasque
Religion Roman Catholic
Currency 1 euro = 100 cents
GNP per person $16,000

Monaco is a tiny state on the shores of the Mediterranean Sea, bordered on all sides by France, which protects the country. Ever since 1297 it has been ruled by the Grimaldi family. Almost all of the narrow strip of land has been built on, so there is no farming. Banking, tourism and some manufacturing make up the economy. Monaco has a world-famous casino, as well as a motor-racing grand prix held on its narrow streets. Luxury yachts are moored in its harbour. Natives of Monaco are called Monegasques, but resident foreigners, mainly from France and Italy, outnumber them four to one.

MONGOLIA

Grid reference B14–15
Capital Ulaanbaatar
Population 2,300,000
Area 1,566,500 sq km
Language Khalka, Russian, Chinese
Religion None officially
Currency 1 turgik = 100 möngö
GNP per person $310

Mongolia is a large country in Central Asia, centred on the Gobi Desert. There are steppe grasslands to the north and south of the desert. In the west lie the Altai Mountains, which are rich in minerals such as copper, tin and coal. Mongolia has long, cold winters and short, hot summers. Sheep, goats, horses, yaks and cattle are herded on the grasslands. In the 13th century the nomadic Mongols were united by Genghis Khan and established a vast, but short-lived, empire stretching from Europe to China. Between 1924 and 1990 Mongolia was a communist state, allied with the former USSR.

MOROCCO

Grid reference C9
Capital Rabat
Population 26,100,000
Area 409,200 sq km
Language Arabic, Berber, French, Spanish
Religion Muslim
Currency 1 Moroccan dirham = 100 centimes
GNP per person $1110

Morocco is a country in North Africa with coasts on the Mediterranean Sea and the Atlantic Ocean. The dry Atlas Mountains lie in the south, inhabited by nomads called Berbers. The coastal plain is more fertile, and supports the farming of citrus fruits, wheat, grapes and other crops. Morocco is the world's leading exporter of phosphates, which are used to make fertilizers. It also has desposits of zinc and lead. In the Middle Ages it was the centre of a powerful Muslim Arab empire, which included parts of Spain. France and Spain later colonized the country, but it became independent in 1956.

MOZAMBIQUE

Grid reference E11–F11
Capital Maputo
Population 16,000,000
Area 799,380 sq km
Language Portuguese, Swahili, Bantu dialects
Religion Traditional African religions, Roman Catholic, Muslim
Currency 1 metical = 100 centavos
GNP per person $80

Mozambique lies in south-east Africa. It has a tropical climate, with a rainy season from December to March and is warm all year. The people mainly live on a wide coastal plain. From there the land rises to plateaux and mountains inland. The Zambezi River flows through Mozambique, and it has been dammed to form Lake Cabora Bassa. Farming is the main activity. Farmers grow tea, cotton, sugar, nuts and other crops. Mozambique was a Portuguese colony, but after independence in 1975 a civil war set back its economic development.

MYANMAR (BURMA)

Grid reference C14–D14
Capital Yangon (Rangoon)
Population 44,740,000
Area 678,576 sq km
Language Burmese
Religion Buddhist
Currency 1 kyat = 100 pyas
GNP per person $200
Government Military regime
Labour force Agriculture 65%, industry 14%, services 21%
Main industries Textiles, shoes, wood, petroleum
Main farm and mine products Rice, maize (corn), sugar cane, oil seed, pulses, copper, tin, tungsten
Population density 66 people per sq km
Population under 15 years old 37%
Urban population 28%
Life expectancy 56 years

For main entry see page 373

NAMIBIA

Grid reference F10
Capital Windhoek
Population 1,510,000
Area 824,292 sq km
Language English, Afrikaans, African languages
Religion Lutheran, Roman Catholic, Dutch Reformed Church, traditional African religions
Currency 1 Namibian dollar = 100 cents
GNP per person $2000

Namibia is a large country in south-west Africa with few inhabitants. The Namib Desert runs along its coast. Much of inland Namibia lies within the Kalahari Desert, where there are herders and hunters. Most people live in the central plateau and the north, where there is more rainfall and rivers. The country has valuable deposits of diamonds as well as uranium, copper and other minerals. These are mainly mined by foreign companies. From the 1960s to 1990, Namibia was illegally run by South Africa and there was a long guerilla war to gain independence.

NAURU

Grid reference E18
Capital Yaren district
Population 8100
Area 21.3 sq km
Language Nauruan, English
Religion Protestant, Roman Catholic
Currency 1 Australian dollar = 100 cents
GNP per person $10,000

Nauru is a small coral island in the Pacific Ocean, east of New Guinea and just south of the Equator. It is fringed by sandy beaches and a narrow strip of land, suitable for farming. Islanders grow tropical fruits, coconuts and vegetables. The centre of Nauru consists of a deposit of guano, a substance produced by sea birds' droppings, which are rich in phosphates and potassium. These chemicals supply almost all the island's income, which is used to provide health, housing and education. But the guano is nearly exhausted, and the only alternative source of income is fishing.

NEPAL

Grid reference C14
Capital Kathmandu
Population 19,280,000
Area 145,391 sq km
Language Nepali, Maithir, Bhojpuri
Religion Hindu
Currency 1 Nepalese rupee = 100 paise
GNP per person $200

Nepal is a kingdom in the Himalayas lying between India and China. It rises from the Ganges river basin to over 8000 m. Mount Everest lies partly within it. There is a fertile central valley, the Vale of Kathmandu. The country's lower slopes are covered in rainforest. Many different crops are grown, including rice, jute, cereals and potatoes. Farmers also raise sheep and buffalo. Tourism is a growing industry, but the country is still poor. Nepal consisted of many small states until the 19th century. It then came under British control, which lasted until 1947.

NETHERLANDS

Grid reference B10
Capital Amsterdam
Population 15,420,000
Area 33,929 sq km
Language Dutch
Religion Roman Catholic, Dutch Reformed
  Church
Currency 1 euro = 100 cents
GNP per person $24,000

The Netherlands lie at the mouth of the Rhine and other rivers where they enter the North Sea. Over a quarter of the land lies below sea level. For centuries the Dutch have built dykes and canals to reclaim land from the sea. On such fertile soils the Dutch maintain very productive farms, specializing in vegetables, flowers and dairy products. In the 16th and 17th centuries the Netherlands was one of the world's most powerful countries. Today, the country remains a major centre of international business. Rotterdam, for example, is the world's largest port.

NEW ZEALAND

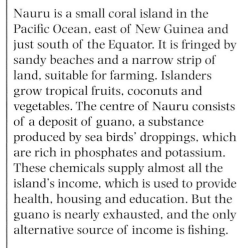

Grid reference F18–G18
Population 3,660,000
Area 268,812 sq km
Capital Wellington
Language English, Maori
Religion Protestant, Roman Catholic
Currency 1 New Zealand dollar = 100 cents
GNP per person $14,340
Government Independent state within
  Commonwealth
Labour force Agriculture 10%, industry 25%,
  services 65%
Main industries Food, wood and paper,
  textiles, machinery, banking, tourism
Main farm and mine products Wool, dairy
  products, wheat, barley, potatoes, fruit, fish
Population density 14 people per sq km
Population under 15 years old 23%
Urban population 87%
Life expectancy 77 years

For main entry see page 382

NICARAGUA

Grid reference D5
Capital Managua
Population 4,400,000
Area 148,000 sq km
Language Spanish, Indian languages, Creole
  English
Religion Roman Catholic
Currency 1 córdobaoro = 100 centavos
GNP per person $380

Nicaragua is in Central America and has coasts on both the Pacific Ocean (the Mosquito coast) and on the Caribbean Sea. A volcanic mountain range runs along the Pacific coast. Although it is drier, most people live here. Two large lakes separate this region from the central highlands, where there are few people. There are few Native Americans: most Nicaraguans are _mestizos_, descended from both Europeans and Native Americans. Farming for cotton, coffee, rice and sugar is the main economic activity. There are small deposits of oil, gold and silver too.

NIGER

Grid reference D10
Capital Niamey
Population 9,460,000
Area 1,267,000 sq km
Language French, Hausa, Songhai and other
  African languages
Religion Muslim, traditional African religions
Currency 1 CFA franc = 100 centimes
GNP per person $220

Niger lies on the southern edge of the Sahara Desert, in Africa. Its southern regions are grasslands. The only major river is the Niger. Berber and Tuareg nomads raise cattle, sheep and goats in the dry areas. Most people are farmers, growing crops such as millet, sorghum and cassava. There are natural resources such as uranium, tin, phosphates, coal and salt. Dust storms, drought and the cutting-down of too many trees to provide fuel are major environmental problems. There are several ethnic groups. The largest of these are the Hausa, Djerma, Songhai and Fulani.

NIGERIA

Grid reference D10
Capital Abuja
Population 97,220,000
Area 923,768 sq km
Language English, Hausa, Yoruba, Ibo, Fulani
Religion Muslim, Christian, traditional African religions
Currency 1 naira = 100 kobos
GNP per person $260
Government Military regime
Labour force Agriculture 43%, industry 7%, services 50%
Main industries Petroleum, textiles, cement, shoes, chemicals
Main farm and mine products Palm oil, peanuts, cotton, sorghum, cassava, sugar cane, oil and natural gas, columbite, tin
Population density 96 people per sq km
Population under 15 years old 45%
Urban population 36%
Life expectancy 54 years

For main entry see page 383

NORTH KOREA

Grid reference B16-C16
Capital Pyonyang
Population 23,260,000
Area 122,098 sq km
Language Korean
Religion Officially atheist
Currency 1 won = 100 chon
GNP per person $923
Government Communist People's Republic
Labour force Agriculture 36%
Main industries Machines, weapons, chemicals, textiles
Main farm and mine products Rice, maize (corn), potatoes, soybeans, coal, iron ore
Population density 188 people per sq km
Population under 15 years old 30%
Urban population 64%
Life expectancy 70 years

For main entry see page 312

NORWAY

Grid reference A10
Capital Oslo
Population 4,400,000
Area 323,895 sq km
Language Norwegian, Lapp
Religion Lutheran
Currency 1 Norwegian krone = 100 øre
GNP per person $31,250

Norway is a very wealthy country in northern Europe. Its long coastline on the northern Atlantic is deeply cut by fjords and dotted with islands. Northern Norway lies inside the Arctic, but an ocean current called the North Atlantic Drift keeps the coast fairly warm and wet. Because the land is mainly mountainous and forested, there are few farmlands. Norway's wealth comes from oil and natural gas, extracted from beneath the North Sea, and a large fishing industry. Vikings lived in Norway, but after them the country was ruled by Denmark and Sweden until its independence in 1905.

OMAN

Grid reference C12–D12
Capital Muscat
Population 2,140,000
Area 300,000 sq km
Language Arabic, English, Baluchi, Urdu
Religion Muslim, Hindu
Currency 1 Omani rial = 1000 baizas
GNP per person $4820

Oman occupies the south-eastern corner of the Arabian peninsula, with coasts on the Arabian Sea and the Gulf of Oman. This position has made it an important centre of trade around the Indian Ocean and Arabia over the centuries. The Rub Al Khali desert covers much of Oman, and the Jebel Akhdar mountains lie on the northern coast. Where there is rain, farmers grow dates, sugar cane, wheat and other crops. Oman's main source of income is oil and natural gas. Workers from Pakistan make up a fifth of the population. Oman is ruled by a sultan, and there are no legal political parties.

PAKISTAN

Grid reference C13
Capital Islamabad
Population 130,200,000
Area 803,943 sq km
Language Urdu, Punjabi, Sindhi and others
Religion Muslim
Currency 1 Pakistan rupee = 100 paisa
GNP per person $460
Government Republic
Labour force Agriculture 56%, industry 18%, services 26%
Main industries Textiles, food, drink, clothing, paper
Main farm and mine products Cotton, wheat, rice, sugar cane, salt
Population density 150 people per sq km
Population under 15 years old 42%
Urban population 32%
Life expectancy 58 years

For main entry see page 408

PALAU

Grid reference D16
Capital Koror
Population 18,000
Area 494 sq km
Language English, Palauan
Religion Roman Catholic, Modekngei
Currency 1 US dollar = 100 cents
GNP per person $2260

Palau, or Belau as it is also called, consists of about 350 coral islands in the Pacific Ocean, north of New Guinea and east of the Philippines. There are many reefs and lagoons around the islands, and the seas are rich in marine life. During World War II Japan and the USA fought over the islands and many thousands of people fled abroad. After the war it came under US protection, and then became a Free Associated State with the USA. This means that it runs its own affairs, but it allows the USA to have military bases there. Farming, fishing for tuna and tourism are the main sources of income.

PANAMA

Grid reference D5–6
Capital Panama City
Population 2,330,000
Area 77,082 sq km
Language Spanish, English, Cuna, Chibchan, Choco
Religion Roman Catholic
Currency 1 balboa = 100 cents
GNP per person $2750

Panama, in Central America, was one of the centres of the ancient Chibcha civilization. Later it became a Spanish colony, then part of Colombia, until it broke away in 1903. This allowed the USA to build a canal across Panama, linking the Caribbean Sea and the Pacific Ocean. Since the canal's opening in 1914, Panama has benefited from it and the extra trade it brings. Panama itself has one of the world's biggest shipping fleets. Elsewhere, the country is mountainous and forested. Native American peoples live in the forest and on the islands along the northern coast.

PAPUA NEW GUINEA

Grid reference E17
Capital Port Moresby
Population 3,850,000
Area 462,840 sq km
Language Pidgin English, Motu, Tok Pisin and about 750 local languages
Religion Protestant, Roman Catholic, traditional religions
Currency 1 kina = 100 toea
GNP per person $1160

Papua New Guinea includes the eastern part of the island of New Guinea and a number of smaller islands in the western Pacific Ocean. The mainland is mountainous and heavily forested. There are mangrove swamps around the coast. In the remote highlands there are many tribes who had very little contact with the rest of the world until the 1950s. There are big gold, silver and copper mines at Ok Tedi and on Bougainville. Most people live by fishing or farming. Coffee, cocoa and rubber are grown for export.

PARAGUAY

Grid reference F7
Capital Asunción
Population 4,900,000
Area 406,750 sq km
Language Spanish, Guaraní
Religion Roman Catholic
Currency 1 guaraní = 100 céntimos
GNP per person $1690

Paraguay is in the centre of South America, entirely surrounded by Brazil, Argentina and Bolivia. The Paraguay river flows south through the middle of the country. There are dry grasslands (called the Gran Chaco) in the west, and wetter forest and savannah grassland in the east. Farming is the main activity. Cattle are raised in the west, and soybeans, wheat, tobacco and maize (corn) are grown in the east. There are few natural resources. The Guaraní Indians form only a small minority of the population, but most people can trace their ancestors back to both Spanish colonists and Guaranís.

PERU

Grid reference E6
Capital Lima
Population 23,850,000
Area 1,284,640 sq km
Language Spanish, Quechua, Aymarà
Religion Roman Catholic
Currency 1 new sol = 100 céntimos
GNP per person $2310

Peru lies in tropical South America. From a narrow and mainly dry coastal strip the land rises steeply to the Andes mountains, which run north to south. About half the population lives on the plateau between these ranges. They grow maize (corn) and potatoes or herd alpacas and llamas. Many Peruvians are Quechua and Aymarà Indians. Eastern Peru lies within the Amazon rainforests. Peru was the centre of the great Inca empire until its overthrow by the Spanish in 1524. It is rich in minerals, including zinc, copper, lead, silver, gold, iron ore and oil. The Pacific waters off Peru are good for fishing.

PHILIPPINES

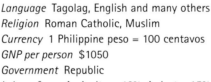

Grid reference D16
Capital Manila
Population 69,800,000
Area 299,679 sq km
Language Tagolag, English and many others
Religion Roman Catholic, Muslim
Currency 1 Philippine peso = 100 centavos
GNP per person $1050
Government Republic
Labour force Agriculture 46%, industry 15%, services 39%
Main industries Textiles, medical products, chemicals, wood, electronics, tourism
Main farm and mine products Rice, coconuts, bananas, pineapples, maize (corn), sugar cane, fish, copper, gold
Population density 233 people per sq km
Population under 15 years old 38%
Urban population 59%
Life expectancy 66 years

For main entry see page 413

POLAND

Grid reference B10–11
Capital Warsaw
Population 38,610,000
Area 312,683 sq km
Language Polish
Religion Roman Catholic
Currency 1 zloty = 100 groszy
GNP per person $2790
Government Republic
Labour force Agriculture 28%, industry 32%, services 40%
Main industries Machines, ships, iron and steel, chemicals, glass, drinks, textiles
Main farm and mine products Potatoes, wheat, meat, dairy products, coal, zinc, lead, sulphur
Population density 125 people per sq km
Population under 15 years old 22%
Urban population 62%
Life expectancy 72 years

For main entry see page 424

PORTUGAL

Grid reference C9
Capital Lisbon
Population 9,900,000
Area 91,630 sq km
Language Portuguese
Religion Roman Catholic
Currency 1 euro = 100 cents
GNP per person $9740

Portugal lies on the Atlantic coast of the Iberian peninsula. It also includes two island groups in the Atlantic, the Azores and Madeira. The north is wet and mountainous, an area of intensive farming, especially vineyards, olives and wheat. In the south the land is drier and lower, where there is more sheep-farming and cork-making. In the 15th century Portuguese explorers sailed the world, finding many new routes and places unknown to Europeans. In the 20th century Portugal suffered periods of dictatorship and military rule. Since joining the European Union in 1986 its economy has developed rapidly.

QATAR

Grid reference C12
Capital Doha
Population 539,000
Area 11,437 sq km
Language Arabic
Religion Muslim
Currency 1 Qatar riyal = 100 dirhams
GNP per person $11,600

Qatar is a small country in the Persian Gulf, consisting of a low-lying peninsula and some nearby islands. The climate is hot and humid. Much of the water comes from desalination plants, which turn sea water into fresh water. The land has too much sand and gravel to grow many crops or to herd animals. Discoveries of oil in the 1940s, and later gas, have made Qatar rich and have paid for free health care, education and social services for the people. Only one quarter of the population are native Qataris. The rest are mostly from South Asia and Egypt, working in the oil, chemicals and construction industries.

ROMANIA

Grid reference B11
Capital Bucharest
Population 22,730,000
Area 237,500 sq km
Language Romanian, Hungarian, German
Religion Eastern Orthodox, Roman Catholic
Currency 1 leu = 100 bani
GNP per person $1480

Romania is a large country in south-eastern Europe with a coast on the Black Sea. The Carpathian Mountains occupy much of the land. These are heavily forested. The rest of Romania is covered in plains. The River Danube flows along the southern border. Romania has good farmlands, as well as oil, natural gas, iron ore and coal. Its many factories make metals, chemicals, textiles and electronics. After World War II Romania was run by communist governments, allied to the Soviet Union. In 1989 the people rebelled, overthrew the dictator Nikolai Ceausescu and held democratic elections.

RUSSIA

Grid reference B11–A19
Capital Moscow
Population 147,500,000
Area 17,075,400 sq km
Language Russian, 100 others
Religion Russian Orthodox, Roman Catholic
Currency 1 rouble = 100 kopecks
GNP per person $2240
Government Republic
Labour force Agriculture 14%, industry 42%, services 34%
Main industries Petroleum, chemicals, machines, steel, aircraft, weapons, trains, textiles
Main farm and mine products Wheat, fruit, vegetables, sugar beet, meat, coal, oil and natural gas, iron ore, timber
Population density 9 people per sq km
Population under 15 years old 21%
Urban population 78%
Life expectancy 63 years

For main entry see pages 472–474

RWANDA

Grid reference E11
Capital Kigali
Population 7,460,000
Area 26,338 sq km
Language French, English, Kinyarwanda, Kiswahili
Religion Christian, traditional African religions, Muslim
Currency 1 Rwanda franc = 100 centimes
GNP per person $180

Rwanda is a small, crowded country in the middle of Africa. The land is mountainous, and many rivers flow through steep, forested valleys. Most people grow cassava, beans and rice for themselves and their families, but also some coffee and tea for export. Rwanda was torn apart by a civil war which broke out in the early 1990s between the two major ethnic groups, the Tutsis and Hutus. Millions fled to countries nearby. Peace came in 1994. Since then the UN has been trying to help Rwandans return to their villages.

ST KITTS–NEVIS

Grid reference D6
Capital Basseterre
Population 43,350
Area 269 sq km
Language English, Creole English
Religion Protestant, Roman Catholic
Currency 1 East Caribbean dollar = 100 cents
GNP per person $5170

St Kitts (sometimes called St Christoper) and Nevis are two small volcanic islands in the Caribbean. They were governed as a single colony by Britain from 1882 to 1983. The centres of both islands are mountainous, rising to around 1000 m. They have a warm, tropical climate, with high rainfall and average temperatures of 26 °C. On the volcanic soils farmers grow sugar cane and cotton, as well as food crops. Factories makes shoes, clothes and electrical goods. The inhabitants of the islands are descended from Europeans, and from Africans brought there as slaves to work the sugar plantations.

ST LUCIA

Grid reference D6
Capital Castries
Population 140,900
Area 616 sq km
Language English, French patois
Religion Roman Catholic, Protestant
Currency 1 East Caribbean dollar = 100 cents
GNP per person $3370

St Lucia is a volcanic Caribbean island that lies between Martinique and St Vincent. None of the volcanoes is now active, and they are covered in lush tropical forest. The island has two cone-shaped peaks formed by the lava plugs. These were left after the rest of the volcano had eroded away. The peaks are called Gros Piton (798 m) and Petit Piton (750 m). Farming and tourism are the main economic activities. Bananas, coconuts, cocoa and mangoes are important crops. The farmlands were devastated by hurricane Debbie in 1994 and have recovered only slowly. Independence from Britain came in 1979.

SAN MARINO

Location see Europe
map (page 195)
Capital San Marino
Population 24,003
Area 61 sq km
Language Italian
Religion Roman Catholic
Currency 1 euro = 100 cents
GNP per person $17,000

San Marino is a tiny country surrounded by Italy, 20 km from the Adriatic Sea. Mount Titano rises in the centre. It was founded when Saint Marino settled on the mountain in AD 300. The inhabitants live by farming, industry and tourism. The main industries include making bricks, tiles and a kind of pottery called majolica. Over 3 million tourists visit every year. The largest town and centre of industry is Serravalle. The capital, San Marino, sits high up on the western side of Mount Titano and has to be reached by cable railway.

ST VINCENT AND THE GRENADINES

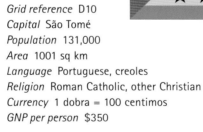

Grid reference D6
Capital Kingstown
Population 109,000
Area 390 sq km
Language English, French patois
Religion Protestant, Roman Catholic
Currency 1 East Caribbean dollar = 100 cents
GNP per person $2280

St Vincent is an island in the Caribbean. The country also includes six islands of the nearby Grenadines, which lie to the south. St Vincent is a volcanic island and the highest peak, Soufrière, is still active. It erupted in 1979 and people had to be evacuated. The country produces crops such as sugar and bananas on large plantations. It is also a leading producer of arrowroot, used to thicken sauces in cooking and in making paper. Between 1763 and 1979 it was a British colony. The people are mainly descended from Africans who were brought there as slaves in the 18th and 19th centuries.

SÃO TOMÉ AND PRINCIPE

Grid reference D10
Capital São Tomé
Population 131,000
Area 1001 sq km
Language Portuguese, creoles
Religion Roman Catholic, other Christian
Currency 1 dobra = 100 centimos
GNP per person $350

São Tomé and Principe are volcanic islands that lie off the west coast of Africa. The country also includes a number of smaller islands. The main islands are mountainous and heavily forested. They are hot all year round and have plenty of rainfall. Most people work on farms, which produce coffee, cocoa and coconuts. An oil called copra is made from coconuts and is sold abroad. The islands were uninhabited until the 16th century, when they were colonized by the Portuguese, who brought slaves from Africa to work on the plantations.

SAMOA

Grid reference E1
Capital al-Aioun
Population 163,000
Area 2842 sq km
Language Samoan, English
Religion Protestant, Roman Catholic
Currency 1 tala = 100 sene
GNP per person $1120

Samoa is made up of two large islands, Savai'i and Upolu, and several smaller ones in the Pacific Ocean. They are volcanic in origin, and surrounded by coral reefs. The climate is tropical, with cool, dry winters and hot, wet summers. On the fertile soils farmers grow food crops such as taro, yams, breadfruit and bananas. They also export copra (dried coconut), wood and textiles. Many tourists visit Samoa. From 1899 the islands were administered by Germany and then New Zealand, before becoming independent in 1962. Samoa changed its name from Western Samoa in 1997.

SAUDI ARABIA

Grid reference C12–D12
Capital Riyadh
Population 16,900,000
Area 2,331,000 sq km
Language Arabic
Religion Muslim
Currency 1 Saudi Arabian riyal = 100 halalah
GNP per person $7040

Saudi Arabia is a large country that occupies most of the Arabian peninsula between the Red Sea and the Gulf of Persia. Deserts in the north and south are separated by highlands and a fertile plain. Water is scarce and there are only tiny pockets of irrigated, cultivated land where wheat, dates and other crops grow. The country's wealth comes from oil. Saudi Arabia has about a quarter of the world's known supply. The Muslim prophet Muhammad was born here and Makkah (Mecca) is the holiest city in Islam. Each year tens of thousands of Muslims from all over the world go there on a pilgrimage.

Scotland *see* United Kingdom

SENEGAL

Grid reference D9
Capital Dakar
Population 7,970,000
Area 196,790 sq km
Language French, African languages
Religion Muslim
Currency 1 CFA franc = 100 centimes
GNP per person $600

Senegal lies between the Senegal river and the Atlantic Ocean in tropical West Africa. The country of Gambia lies within its borders. The land is mainly savannah grassland or semi-desert, but there are forests along the southern border. Three-quarters of the population work in agriculture. They grow sorghum, maize (corn) and millet to eat, as well as groundnuts and cotton to sell abroad. The country has a big fishing fleet, and there is oil and natural gas in the coastal waters. Senegal was part of the Mali empire in the 14th and 15th centuries, and was a French colony between 1895 and 1960.

SIERRA LEONE

Grid reference D9
Capital Freetown
Population 4,460,000
Area 71,740 sq km
Language English, Krio
Religion Muslim, traditional African religions
Currency 1 leone = 100 cents
GNP per person $180

Sierra Leone lies in West Africa, bordering the Atlantic Ocean. The coast is often swampy, but there are wide sandy beaches in some places. Inland, the tropical forests have been largely cleared for farming. Farmers grow rice, coffee, cocoa and citrus fruits. In the more mountainous eastern part there are minerals, including titanium, gold and diamonds. Since independence from Britain in 1961, the country has had little political stability. Fighting for control of the diamond mines broke out in the 1990s. However, peace and democracy were restored with the help of British troops.

SERBIA AND MONTENEGRO

Grid reference B10–11
Capital Belgrade
Population 10,540,000
Area 102,173 sq km
Language Serbian, Albanian, Hungarian
Religion Serbian Orthodox, Roman Catholic
Currency 1 dinar = 100 paras
GNP per person $3000

'Serbia and Montenegro' is the name adopted in 2003 by what remained of the old country of Yugoslavia. Serbia and Montenegro, two of the six states which until 1991 formed a single nation, retained the former name until 2003. Old Yugoslavia broke up in the 1990s following tensions between the different peoples. Serbia then fought wars against the breakaway states of Slovenia, Croatia and Bosnia. In 1995 the UN and NATO forced the Serbs to stop their aggression in Bosnia. Then Serbia turned against Albanians living in the province of Kosovo. NATO stopped this in 1999 by bombing Serbia.

SINGAPORE

Grid reference D15
Capital Singapore City
Population 2,990,000
Area 618 sq km
Language English, Malay, Chinese, Tamil
Religion Buddhist, Muslim, Christian, Hindu, Taoist
Currency 1 Singapore dollar = 100 cents
GNP per person $26,730

Singapore is an island state on the Malay peninsula in South-east Asia. It is joined to Malaysia by a thin strip of land. In 1819 the island was bought by a British politician, and became Britain's key trading centre in the region. Merchants and workers came there from China, and the Chinese outnumber the native Malays today. Since independence in 1965, Singapore has become one of the world's major ports. Industries include oil-refining, food processing, banking and chemicals. It is now very wealthy.

SEYCHELLES

Grid reference E12
Capital Victoria, on Mahé island
Population 73,850
Area 455 sq km
Language Creole, French, English
Religion Roman Catholic
Currency 1 Seychelles rupee = 100 cents
GNP per person $6620

The Seychelles is made up of 115 tropical islands and islets spread out over 600,000 sq km of the Indian Ocean close to the Equator. The groups of islands are separated by deep ocean trenches. The largest is the Mahé group, where most people live. Farmers produce tropical crops such as cinammon, copra (coconut oil) and cassava. Tourism is very important. Because the islands are small and have only limited water, the number of tourists allowed in is limited. There are many rare birds, animals and plants found nowhere else in the world.

SLOVAKIA

Grid reference B10–11
Capital Bratislava
Population 5,370,000
Area 49,035 sq km
Language Slovak, Czech, Hungarian
Religion Roman Catholic
Currency 1 Slovak koruna = 100 halura
GNP per person $2950

Slovakia once formed the eastern half of the central European country of Czechoslovakia. After World War II Czechoslovakia was run by communist governments. Following the overthrow of communism in 1989, the two parts of the country voted to separate, which they did in 1993. The Carpathian and Tatras mountains cover much of the north, while the south is drained by the Vah and Danube rivers. On the plains cereals, wine and fruit are produced. The country also has a large industrial sector, centred on Kosice. Its factories make iron and steel, as well as weapons and machinery.

SLOVENIA

Grid reference B10
Capital Ljubljana
Population 1,980,000
Area 20,251 sq km
Language Slovene, Croatian
Religion Roman Catholic, Protestant, Eastern
   Orthodox
Currency 1 Slovene tolar = 100 paras
GNP per person $8200

Slovenia was created after the break-up of Yugoslavia in 1991. Slovenes are a Slavic people who have lived in the region since the 6th century. Throughout history they have mostly been governed by outsiders, including the Austro-Hungarian empire. It is a mountainous country, covered with forests. Cattle-raising and agriculture are important. Its many natural resources, including iron, coal and lead, have enabled it to develop many industries. Compared with other parts of the former Yugoslavia, it is wealthy as well as peaceful.

SOLOMON ISLANDS

Grid reference E18
Capital Honiara, on
   Guadalcanal
Population 349,500
Area 27,566 sq km
Language English, pidgin English and other
   local languages
Religion Protestant, Roman Catholic
Currency 1 Solomon Islands dollar = 100 cents
GNP per person $910

The Solomon Islands lie to the east of Papua New Guinea in the Pacific Ocean. There are several hundred coral and volcanic islands, the largest of which is Guadalcanal. They are mainly mountainous and forested, and contain some active volcanoes. The people live by farming and fishing. Widespread clearance of the forests has caused severe damage to the environment. The government has now banned log exports. The Solomon Islands were a British colony, but they gained independence in 1978.

SOMALIA

Grid reference D12
Capital Mogadishu
Population 9,200,000
Area 637,357 sq km
Language Somali, Arabic
Religion Muslim
Currency 1 Somali shilling = 100 cents
GNP per person $150

Somalia occupies the coastal regions of the Horn of Africa, which juts out into the Arabian Sea. Most of the land is semi-desert, although there are good farmlands along the northern coast and in the southern river valleys. There are frequent droughts. The main traditional way of life is nomadic herding of camels, sheep, goats and cattle. Modern Somalia was formed when Italian and British colonies were united in 1960. But there has been fighting ever since, first with Ethiopia over land, and then among different clans within the country. Northern Somaliland declared independence in 1992.

SOUTH AFRICA

Grid reference F11
Capitals Cape Town,
   Pretoria, Bloemfontein
Population 41,540,000
Area 1,233,404 sq km
Language English, Afrikaans, Xhosa, Zulu and
   others
Religion Christian, traditional African religions
Currency 1 rand = 100 cents
GNP per person $3160
Government Republic
Labour force Agriculture 30%, industry 29%,
   services 35%
Main industries Cars, metals, machines,
   textiles, chemicals
Main farm and mine products Maize (corn),
   wheat, fruit, vegetables, cotton, gold,
   platinum, chromium
Population density 34 people per sq km
Population under 15 years old 36%
Urban population 49%
Life expectancy 59 years

For main entry see pages 513–514

SOUTH KOREA

Grid reference C16
Capital Seoul
Population 44,610,000
Area 98,913 sq km
Language Korean
Religion Christian, Buddhist
Currency 1 won = 100 chon
GNP per person $9700
Government Republic
Labour force Agriculture 21%, industry 27%,
   services 52%
Main industries Electronics, cars, ships,
   chemicals, steel, textiles, shoes, clothing
Main farm and mine products Rice, root crops,
   barley, fruit, fish
Population density 443 people per sq km
Population under 15 years old 23%
Urban population 84%
Life expectancy 73 years

For main entry see page 312

SPAIN

Grid reference B9–C9
Capital Madrid
Population 40,460,000
Area 504,750 sq km
Language Spanish, Catalan, Galician, Basque
Religion Roman Catholic
Currency 1 euro = 100 cents
GNP per person $13,580
Government Constitutional monarchy
Labour force Agriculture 11%, industry 30%,
   services 59%
Main industries Cars, clothing, shoes, food,
   drink, metals, chemicals, ships, tourism
Main farm and mine products Wheat,
   vegetables, olives, wine, fruit, beef, fish
Population density 80 people per sq km
Population under 15 years old 16%
Urban population 77%
Life expectancy 78 years

For main entry see pages 520–521

SRI LANKA

Grid reference D14
Capital Colombo
Population 17,900,000
Area 65,610 sq km
Language Sinhala, Tamil
Religion Buddhist, Hindu, Christian, Muslim
Currency 1 Sri Lankan rupee = 100 cents
GNP per person $700

Sri Lanka is a large island off the southern tip of India. Before 1972 it was called Ceylon. The island has two main regions separated by central highlands. The south-west is wetter because of monsoon rainfall. Large plantations of tea, rice, rubber and coconuts are found here. The north-west is drier and flatter. Farming, fishing and mining for gems are important economic activities. Although most of the population are Buddhist Sinhalese, one-fifth are Hindu Tamils. Since independence from Britain in 1948, the Tamil minority has waged a bloody war for independence in the north of the island.

SUDAN

Grid reference D11
Capital Khartoum
Population 28,900,000
Area 2,505,870 sq km
Language Arabic, African languages
Religion Muslim, traditional African religions
Currency 1 Sudanese dinar = 100 piastres
GNP per person $400
Government Republic
Labour force Agriculture 80%, industry 10%, services 10%
Main industries Textiles, cement, shoes, soap
Main farm and mine products Cotton, sugar, oil seed, sorghum, millet, wheat, sheep, gum arabic, copper, lead
Population density 12 people per sq km
Population under 15 years old 46%
Urban population 27%
Life expectancy 55 years

For main entry see page 533

SURINAME

Grid reference D7
Capital Paramaribo
Population 407,000
Area 163,265 sq km
Language Dutch, Hindi, Javanese
Religion Hindu, Christian, Muslim
Currency 1 Surinamese guilder = 100 cents
GNP per person $880

Suriname is one of the smaller countries in South America, lying on the north-eastern Atlantic coast between Guyana and French Guiana. The coastal strip is swampy and often flooded, but it contains rice fields. Inland there is savannah grassland, which merges with a more mountainous and forested region to the south. Here there are deposits of bauxite, which is processed into aluminium and exported. The people include descendants of native Caribs, African slaves, Asian Indians and Javanese. It was a Dutch colony, and after independence in 1975 many people emigrated to the Netherlands.

SWAZILAND

Grid reference F11
Capital Mbabane
Population 850,630
Area 17,363 sq km
Language Siswati, English
Religion Christian, traditional African religions
Currency 1 lilangeni = 100 cents
GNP per person $1170

Swaziland is in southern Africa, lying between Mozambique and South Africa. In the west it is mountainous. The lower areas in the east are covered in hills and bush vegetation. Large rivers run towards the Atlantic. They provide both hydroelectric power and irrigation. Most people grow crops such as sorghum, maize (corn), tobacco, cotton and groundnuts. Many Swazis work in South Africa and send money home. The Swazi kingdom was formed in the 19th century after fighting with Zulus and Boers (Africans of Dutch origin). It was a British colony before gaining independence in 1968.

SWEDEN

Grid reference A10–B10
Capital Stockholm
Population 8,840,000
Area 411,479 sq km
Language Swedish, Finnish, Lapp
Religion Lutheran
Currency 1 Swedish krona = 100 øre
GNP per person $23,750

Sweden is a large country in northern Europe, and is part of Scandinavia. The northern tip lies within the Arctic. There are thick forests south of the Arctic region. The centre is the most industrial area. Sweden produces modern goods such as cars, trucks, aircraft, chemicals and electronics. Factories use hydroelectric power. The south is more agricultural. Sweden was once a powerful kingdom in the region, but in the 19th century many Swedes migrated to the USA. In the 20th century it recovered its wealth. Swedes now enjoy excellent welfare services such as health, education and housing.

SWITZERLAND

Grid reference B10
Capital Bern
Population 7,020,000
Area 41,228 sq km
Language German, French, Italian, Romansch
Religion Roman Catholic, Protestant
Currency 1 Swiss franc = 100 centimes
GNP per person $40,630

Switzerland is a mountainous country. The Alps lie in the south and the Jura Mountains in the north. In between there is fertile lowland. There are many large lakes in Switzerland, and the Rhine and Rhone rivers rise there. It has a unique form of government. It is a federation of 20 cantons. Each has a large degree of independence, which has allowed the many different religious and linguistic groups to exist together peacefully for centuries. As well as farming and industries such as watch-making and engineering, the strong economy includes important banks and international organizations.

SYRIA

Grid reference C11
Capital Damascus
Population 14,620,000
Area 185,180 sq km
Language Arabic, Kurdish
Religion Sunni Muslim, other Muslim sects, Christian
Currency 1 Syrian pound = 100 piastres
GNP per person $1120

Syria is a Middle Eastern country. Most of it receives very little rainfall and is covered in semi-desert and plateaux. But there are good farmlands along the coast and in the south. Syria grows cotton, cereals, grain and fruit, and some fields are irrigated by waters from the Euphrates river. The main export is oil. The region was once part of the Phoenician and Ottoman empires, and there are many ancient sites, including Crusader castles. Since independence from France in 1946, it has been involved in many of the region's wars, including fighting with Israel and occupying Lebanon.

TAIWAN

Grid reference C16
Capital Taipei
Population 21,500,000
Area 36,000 sq km
Language Mandarin Chinese, Taiwanese
Religion Taoist, Buddhist, Christian
Currency 1 New Taiwan dollar = 100 cents
GNP per person $10,180

Taiwan is an island off the east coast of China. A mountain chain runs from north to south. Most people live on the coastal plains. Following the war between nationalists and communists in China, the defeated nationalist government fled to Taiwan in 1945. They joined a large Chinese community which already outnumbered the native peoples. Since then relations between the mainland and Taiwan have been very tense. Despite this, the economy became rapidly industrialized, and it is now a major centre of manufacturing. It produces textiles, electronics, oil products and plastics.

TAJIKISTAN

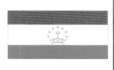

Grid reference C13
Capital Dushanbe
Population 5,700,000
Area 143,100 sq km
Language Tajik, Russian
Religion Sunni Muslim
Currency Tajik rouble
GNP per person $340

Tajikistan lies in Central Asia. The Tien Shan, Pamir and Gissar-Alai mountain ranges cover almost all the country. The highest point is Communism Peak (7495 m). Although much of Tajikistan is dry, the river valleys are warmer and wetter, and there are wide areas of irrigated farmland. They grow cotton for export. There are also many natural resources, including uranium, oil, coal, lead and zinc. Tajikistan came under Russian control in the mid-19th century, and between 1924 and 1991 it was a republic of the former USSR. Since independence, war has led thousands to flee abroad.

TANZANIA

Grid reference E11
Capital Dodoma
Population 29,700,000
Area 945,087 sq km
Language Swahili, English, African languages
Religion Christian, Muslim, traditional African religions
Currency 1 Tanzanian shilling = 100 cents
GNP per person $120

Tanzania was formed in 1964 by the union of Tanganyika, a large mainland area, and Zanzibar, a smaller island in the Indian Ocean. It is hot and receives a lot of rainfall. Inland there is a large, dry plateau covered in grasslands. There are mountains in the north and, around the shores of Lake Victoria, good farmlands. The famous Serengeti and Ngorongoro Crater wildlife reserves are found here. There are over 100 different ethnic groups in Tanzania. Most are poor farmers, growing crops such as rice, sorghum, coffee and sugar.

THAILAND

Grid reference D14–15
Capital Bangkok
Population 58,340,000
Area 513,115 sq km
Language Thai, Malay
Religion Buddhist
Currency 1 baht = 100 satang
GNP per person $2740
Government Constitutional monarchy
Labour force Agriculture 57%, industry 17%, services 26%
Main industries Textiles, electronics, tourism, furniture, plastics, jewelry
Main farm and mine products Rice, cassava, pineapples, bananas, rubber, tobacco, tungsten, tin
Population density 113 people per sq km
Population under 15 years old 25%
Urban population 22%
Life expectancy 69 years

For main entry see page 546

TOGO

Grid reference D10
Capital Lomé
Population 3,500,000
Area 56,790 sq km
Language French, Ewe, other African languages
Religion Traditional African religions, Christian, Muslim
Currency 1 CFA franc = 100 centimes
GNP per person $310

Togo is a long, narrow country in West Africa, with a short coast along the Gulf of Guinea. The land rises from coastal lowlands to the Atakora mountains in the north. Most people live in the lowlands, growing manioc, maize (corn), palms and bananas. In the north there are coffee and cocoa plantations. The rainy season is between May and October. Togo also has natural resources such as bauxite, and iron ore. The Ewe, the traditional inhabitants of the region, suffered greatly during the slave trade. Togo was a German and then a French colony. It became independent in 1960.

TONGA

Grid reference E19–F19
Capital Nuku'alofa
Population 103,000
Area 646 sq km
Language Tongan, English
Religion Methodist, other Christian
    denominations
Currency 1 pa'anga = 100 seniti
GNP per person $1630

Tonga is made up of 169 islands, 36 of which are inhabited, lying in the Pacific Ocean east of Fiji. They were named the Friendly Islands by Captain James Cook when he landed there in 1773. The islands were united into a single country by Chief Taufa'ahua in the 1820s. He founded the royal family which still rules today. Tonga was under British protection until 1970. About half the population lives on the largest island, Tongatapu. They grow cassava and yams for food, and coconuts, sugar cane and vanilla to sell abroad. Tourism and craft industries are the other main economic activities.

TURKEY

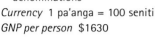

Grid reference C11-12
Capital Ankara
Population 62,530,000
Area 779,452 sq km
Language Turkish, Kurdish, Arabic
Religion Muslim
Currency 1 Turkish lira = 100 kurus
GNP per person $2780
Government Republic
Labour force Agriculture 46%, industry 23%,
    services 31%
Main industries Textiles, food, steel, wood and
    paper, glass, cement
Main farm and mine products Cotton, wheat,
    olives, fruit, vegetables, coal, chromite,
    copper, boron
Population density 81 people per sq km
Population under 15 years old 32%
Urban population 59%
Life expectancy 72 years

For main entry see page 558

TRINIDAD AND TOBAGO

Grid reference D6
Capital Port of Spain
Population 1,270,000
Area 5128 sq km
Language English, Hindi
Religion Roman Catholic, Protestant, Hindu
Currency 1 Trinidad & Tobago dollar = 100 cents
GNP per person $3770

Trinidad and Tobago are at the southern end of the Lesser Antilles island chain in the Caribbean Sea. They lie close to the coast of Venezuela. Trinidad is the larger island and is crossed from west to east by three mountain ranges separated by rivers. There are large sugar and cocoa plantations. Tobago is a small, volcanic island with dense forests. The population is divided into two main communities of roughly equal size, one descended from African slaves and the other from Indian migrant workers. Oil and oil products are the main source of income. Tourism is also important.

TURKMENISTAN

Grid reference C12–13
Capital Ashkhabad
Population 4,500,000
Area 488,100 sq km
Language Turkmen, Russian
Religion Muslim
Currency 1 manat = 100 gapik
GNP per person $920

Turkmenistan is found to the east of the Caspian Sea in Central Asia. Over 80 per cent of the land lies in the Kara Kum ('black sands') desert. It is an area of sand dunes and oases, where nomads follow their herds of sheep, horses and camels. The Kara Kum canal diverts water from the Amu Darya river to irrigate the cotton fields in the south. Turkmenistan also has natural resources such as oil and natural gas, sulphur, potassium and salt. The region was part of the Persian, Mongol and Russian empires, and became a republic of the former USSR in 1924. It became independent in 1991.

TUNISIA

Grid reference C10
Capital Tunis
Population 8,800,000
Area 164,150 sq km
Language Arabic, French, Berber
Religion Muslim
Currency 1 Tunisian dinar = 1000 millèmes
GNP per person $1820

Tunisia lies on the Mediterranean coast of North Africa. It was settled by Phoenicians in the 12th century BC, and since then has been part of many empires, including the Carthaginian, Roman and Ottoman empires. There are many good harbours along the coast, and fertile farmlands in the north. Farmers grow olives, grapes, wheat and fruits. In the central mountains there are communities of nomadic shepherds. Southern Tunisia lies in the Sahara Desert. It has deposits of phosphates, salt and iron ore. Tunisia became independent from France in 1956. Its monarchy was abolished in 1957.

TUVALU

Grid reference E18
Capital Funafuti
Population 10,900
Area 26 sq km
Language Tuvaluan, English
Religion Protestant, Roman Catholic, Baha'i
Currency 1 Australian dollar = 100 cents
GNP per person $970

Tuvalu is made up of nine low-lying coral islands spread out over the Pacific Ocean, east of Papua New Guinea. They were known as the Ellice Islands and were governed by Britain, along with the Gilbert Islands, until 1975. Tuvalu became independent in 1978, although it still uses Australian currency. The people live by farming and fishing, which provides enough food to eat and some coconuts and copra (dried coconut) for export. Tuvalu raises money from marketing postage stamps, collected by enthusiasts all over the world. It also sells fishing rights to foreign trawler fleets looking for tuna.

UGANDA

Grid reference D11–E11
Capital Kampala
Population 16,670,000
Area 241,038 sq km
Language English, Swahili, Luganda, Ateso, Luo
Religion Roman Catholic, Protestant, traditional African religions
Currency 1 Ugandan shilling = 100 cents
GNP per person $240

Uganda is in East Africa on the northern shores of Lake Victoria. The centre is a fertile plateau, surrounded by lakes, swamps, mountains and volcanoes. The River Nile flows north from Lake Victoria. The country is hot all year round, with plenty of rainfall. Wide areas of farmlands produce rice, maize (corn) and cassava for food, and coffee, tea, cotton and tobacco for export. Lake Victoria is rich in fish. There are also copper mines. The population is made up of many different ethnic groups. Uganda was a British colony until 1962.

UKRAINE

Grid reference B11
Capital Kiev
Population 52,140,000
Area 603,700 sq km
Language Ukrainian, Russian
Religion Ukrainian Orthodox, Catholic
Currency 1 hryvna = 100 kopiykas
GNP per person $1630
Government Republic
Labour force Agriculture 21%, industry 33%, services 46%
Main industries Electrical goods, metals, machinery, chemicals
Main farm and mine products Wheat, potatoes, rye, flax, vegetables, sugar beet, coal, salt
Population density 86 people per sq km
Population under 15 years old 20%
Urban population 68%
Life expectancy 67 years

For main entry see page 561

UNITED ARAB EMIRATES

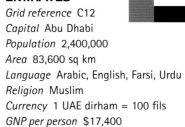

Grid reference C12
Capital Abu Dhabi
Population 2,400,000
Area 83,600 sq km
Language Arabic, English, Farsi, Urdu
Religion Muslim
Currency 1 UAE dirham = 100 fils
GNP per person $17,400

The United Arab Emirates (UAE) is made up of seven small states on the Arabian peninsula, with a coastline on the Persian Gulf. They were known as the Trucial States until they became united as an independent federation in 1971. Abu Dhabi is the largest state. Each one is ruled by an emir. Most of the land is barren and rocky desert, with a few oases and rivers which are often dry. Where there is water, farmers grow dates, fruits and vegetables. The coast is lined with coral reefs and sand dunes. The country's wealth is based on huge oil and natural gas fields found in this coastal region.

UNITED KINGDOM

Grid reference B9
Capital London
Population 58,780,000
Area 244,755 sq km
Language English
Religion Protestant, Roman Catholic
Currency 1 pound sterling = 100 pence
GNP per person $18,700
Government Constitutional monarchy
Labour force Agriculture 2%, industry 28%, services 71%
Main industries Machinery, electronics, cars, aircraft, chemicals, textiles, tourism, banking
Main farm and mine products Wheat, barley, potatoes, beef, poultry, fish, oil and natural gas, coal
Population density 240 people per sq km
Population under 15 years old 20%
Urban population 90%
Life expectancy 76 years

For main entry see page 562

UNITED STATES OF AMERICA

Grid reference B4–C4
Capital Washington, DC
Population 278,059,000
Area 9,160,454 sq km
Language English, Spanish
Religion Protestant, Roman Catholic
Currency 1 US dollar = 100 cents
GNP per person $26,980
Government Federal republic
Labour force Agriculture 3%, industry 25%, services 72%
Main industries Petroleum, steel, cars, aircraft, telecommunications, computers, chemicals
Main farm and mine products Wheat, maize (corn), fruit, vegetables, cotton, beef, poultry, coal, iron ore, oil and natural gas, copper
Population density 29 people per sq km
Population under 15 years old 22%
Urban population 75%
Life expectancy 76 years

For main entry see pages 564–567

URUGUAY

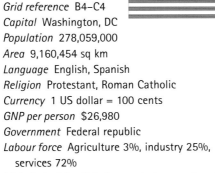

Grid reference F7
Capital Montevideo
Population 3,200,000
Area 176,215 sq km
Language Spanish
Religion Roman Catholic
Currency 1 New Uruguayan peso = 100 céntisimos
GNP per person $5170

Uruguay lies on the Atlantic coast of South America, on the northern shore of the Río de la Plata estuary. Grassy plains and low hills cover most of the country. The damming of the Río Negro has formed a large artifical lake in the centre. The climate is warm in summer and cool in winter, with plenty of rainfall. There are cattle and sheep ranches in many areas, and meat, hides and wool are important exports. The original inhabitants were Charrúa, Chaná and Guaraní Indians, but most people are descended from Spanish and Italian settlers. A third of the population live in Montevideo.

UZBEKISTAN

Grid reference B13–C13
Capital Tashkent
Population 22,200,000
Area 447,400 sq km
Language Uzbek
Religion Muslim
Currency sum
GNP per person $970

Uzbekistan is in Central Asia, to the south of Kazakhstan. Dry plains cover the north and west of the country, while the south is mountainous and wetter. Half of the Aral Sea lies within northern Uzbekistan. So much water has been taken from this inland sea that it is shrinking and leaving huge areas of salt-covered land. Dry winds blow the salts across the country, harming people's health. Uzbekistan has natural resources such as coal, oil, natural gas, gold and other minerals. It was part of the Russian empire from the late 19th century, and a republic of the former USSR between 1925 and 1991.

VENEZUELA

Grid reference D6
Capital Caracas
Population 20,410,000
Area 912,050 sq km
Language Spanish, Italian, native languages
Religion Roman Catholic
Currency 1 bolivar = 100 céntimos
GNP per person $3020

Venezuela is a large country in South America. Most Venezuelans live in the hilly and mountainous north, where there are huge reserves of oil around Lake Maracaibo. Around the Orinoco valley in the centre there are grasslands called llanos, an area of livestock farming. In the far south lie the Guinea Highlands, a sparsely populated region of tropical rainforest. Angel Falls, the world's highest waterfall, is found here. There are rich deposits of bauxite, iron ore, gold and diamonds. There is a small Native American population, but most of the inhabitants are descended from Spanish and Italian immigrants.

VANUATU

Grid reference E18
Capital Port Vila, on Efate island
Population 160,000
Area 14,763 sq km
Language Bislama, English, French
Religion Protestant, Roman Catholic, local religions
Currency 1 vatu = 100 centimes
GNP per person $1200

Vanuatu is a long chain of 12 islands and many smaller coral atolls in the Pacific Ocean west of Fiji. There are active volcanoes throughout. Most people live on just four of the islands. They are mostly farmers, growing crops such as yams, breadfruit and taro to eat, and cocoa and coffee to export. The seas around Vanuatu are full of fish, and factories on the islands process them for animal food. Captain James Cook visited the islands in 1774 and claimed them for Britain. Under British rule, which ended in 1980, Vanuatu was called the New Hebrides.

VIETNAM

Grid reference C15–D15
Capital Hanoi
Population 74,000,000
Area 329,566 sq km
Language Vietnamese, French, Chinese
Religion Buddhist, Taoist, Confucian
Currency 1 dông = 100 xu
GNP per person $240
Government Socialist republic
Labour force Agriculture 72%, industry 14%, services 14%
Main industries Textiles, toys, machines, glass, tyres, fertilizers
Main farm and mine products Rice, maize (corn), potatoes, rubber, soybeans, poultry, coffee, fish, oil
Population density 195 people per sq km
Population under 15 years old 36%
Urban population 20%
Life expectancy 67 years

For main entry see page 573

VATICAN CITY

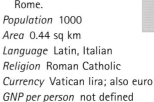

Location see Europe map (page 195) for location of Rome.
Population 1000
Area 0.44 sq km
Language Latin, Italian
Religion Roman Catholic
Currency Vatican lira; also euro
GNP per person not defined

Vatican City is the world's smallest state. It is located on a hill within the Italian capital, Rome. It is the centre of the Roman Catholic Church, which is headed by the Pope. Within its boundaries are the Papal Palace, the basilica of St Peter's, the Sistine Chapel and the offices of the Church. The Pope used to rule a large area of Italy, called the Papal States, but over the years these have become part of Italy itself. The Pope's sovereignty over the Vatican was established in the Lateran Treaty of 1929. Vatican City has its own police force, the Swiss Guard, and issues its own stamps and coins.

YEMEN

Grid reference D12
Capital Sana
Population 15,800,000
Area 531,570 sq km
Language Arabic
Religion Muslim
Currency 1 Yemeni rial = 100 fils
GNP per person $260

Yemen occupies the southern end of the Arabian peninsula. It has shores on the Red Sea and the Gulf of Aden. The modern country was formed in 1990 from the unification of two states, North and South Yemen, following many years of hostility between them. Beyond the coastal region, the land is mainly dry and mountainous, with large areas of desert. The economy is mainly based on agriculture, with cotton and coffee being the major crops. The capital, Sana, is a historic centre of trading and Islamic religion. It contains many beautiful buildings.

ZAMBIA

Grid reference E11
Capital Lusaka
Population 8,940,000
Area 752,613 sq km
Language English, Tonga, Kaonde, Lunda and other African languages
Religion Christian, traditional African religions
Currency 1 kwacha = 100 ngwee
GNP per person $400

Zambia is a large country in south central Africa. Most of the land is high plateau over 1000 m, drained by the Zambezi river. The Kariba dam, on the river, supplies hydroelectric power. The Victoria Falls lie on the border with Zimbabwe. Zambia's main economic activity is mining, especially for copper. But most of the people are farmers, growing maize (corn), tobacco, groundnuts, cotton and other crops. There are over 70 ethnic groups. Most speak a Bantu language. Zambia was a British colony (Northern Rhodesia) until its independence in 1964.

ZIMBABWE

Grid reference E11–F11
Capital Harare
Population 11,500,000
Area 390,759 sq km
Language English, Ndebele, Shona
Religion Christian, traditional African religions
Currency 1 Zimbabwe dollar = 100 cents
GNP per person $540

Zimbabwe is a country in south central Africa. Most of the country is a high plateau of rolling hills. The population is concentrated in the highveld region, where the soils are more fertile. The northern border with Zambia is formed by the Zambezi river. Victoria Falls lie on the border. Zimbabwe was a mighty kingdom between the 12th and 16th centuries. Between 1923 and 1980 it was a British colony, known as Southern Rhodesia, and later Rhodesia. Robert Mugabe has been president since 1980. Many people have criticized him for behaving more and more like a dictator.

Map of the world

This map shows all the countries listed in the Countries fact file on pages 613–645. For each country in the fact file there is a grid reference consisting of a number and a letter, which can be used to find the country on the map. Malaysia, for example, is D15. The letter refers to the letters down the sides of the map, the number to the numbers along the top and bottom of the map. To find Malaysia look across the page from the letter D at the side of the map and down the page from the number 15 at the top of the map. The square where these two bands meet is D15.

Where there is not enough space to print the name in full, countries are shown by the first few letters of their name, or by their initials. The abbreviations used are shown below.

A	Albania
AR	Armenia
AU	Austria
AZ	Azerbaijan
B	Belgium
BD	Brunei Darussalam
BE	Benin
BH	Bosnia and Herzegovina
BU	Burkina
C	Croatia
CAR	Central African Republic
CON	Congo
CZ	Czech Republic
G	Gambia
G-B	Guinea-Bissau
H	Hungary
I	Israel
L	Lebanon
LI	Lithuania
LU	Luxembourg
M	Macedonia (now FYROM, Former Yugoslav Republic of Macedonia)
N	Netherlands
Q	Qatar
R	Romania
S	Slovakia
SL	Slovenia
SM	Serbia and Montenegro
SW	Switzerland
T	Tajikistan
TU	Turkmenistan
U	Uganda
UAE	United Arab Emirates
ZIM	Zimbabwe

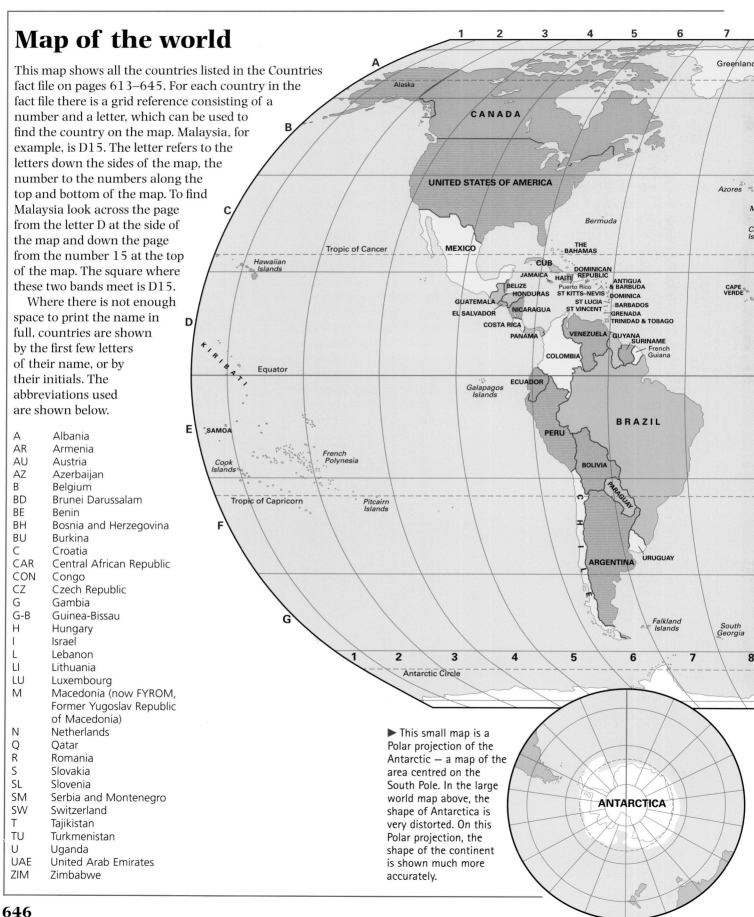

▶ This small map is a Polar projection of the Antarctic — a map of the area centred on the South Pole. In the large world map above, the shape of Antarctica is very distorted. On this Polar projection, the shape of the continent is shown much more accurately.

646

Map of the world

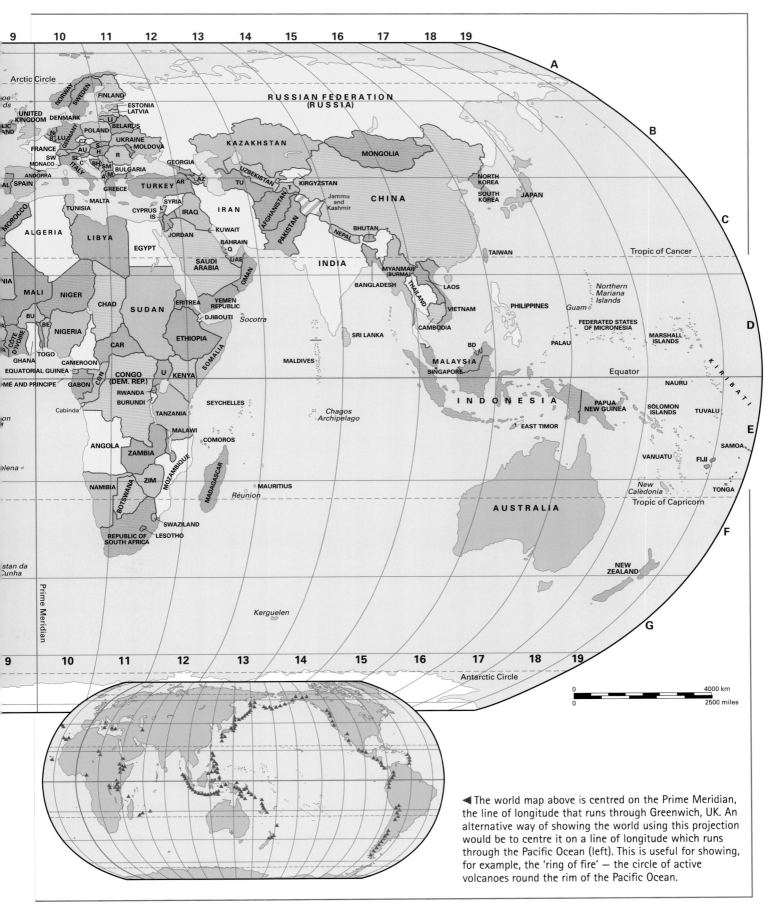

The world map above is centred on the Prime Meridian, the line of longitude that runs through Greenwich, UK. An alternative way of showing the world using this projection would be to centre it on a line of longitude which runs through the Pacific Ocean (left). This is useful for showing, for example, the 'ring of fire' — the circle of active volcanoes round the rim of the Pacific Ocean.

World history

	Before 10,000 BC	10,000 BC	5000 BC	3000 BC	2000 BC
Asia	· Hunter-gatherers · A variety of stone tools used – knives, axes, needles, harpoons	· Rice and millet farming begins and spreads · Pottery made in Japan and China	· Horses domesticated on steppes (grasslands) · Cities in China · Decorated pottery made in Japan · Jade worked in China	· Silk weaving in China · Cities of Harappa and Mohenjo-daro in Indus valley · Cotton grown in Indus valley	· Aryans invade northern India · Beginnings of Hindu religion ▲ The Hindu god Shiva
Americas and Oceania	· Hunter-gatherers · Cave drawings in Australia from about 40,000 BC	· Hunter-gatherers · Canoes and sledges used	· Maize (corn) cultivated in Mexico · Pottery first made in South America · Llamas domesticated in Andes · Root crops cultivated in New Guinea	◄ A sailing canoe · Temples and monuments built in Peru, and cotton cultivated · Colonization of Pacific islands by canoe begins	· Metalworking and cotton weaving in Peru · Colonists reach Samoa in the central Pacific
Africa and Middle East	· First humans · From about 100,000 BC people spread through all continents · Cave drawings in south-west Africa from about 27,000 BC · Female figurines made · Bow invented	· Cereals farmed from about 9000 BC · Grain ground with hand mills · Wheel invented · Dogs, cattle, sheep and goats domesticated · Woven textiles · Copper used about 6000 BC	· Plough invented · Horses and camels domesticated · Sails used on River Nile · Bronze made · Writing invented · Wheeled vehicles made · Pottery made in East Africa	► The Great Pyramid at Giza, built 2600 BC · Pyramids built in Egypt · Sumerian civilization · Stone cities in Middle East · Troy founded	· New kingdom in Egypt · Hittites establish empire · Beginnings of Jewish religion
Europe	· Hunter-gatherers · Cave paintings from 30,000 BC · Female figurines made · Bow invented	· Farming in Balkans and Greece from 7000 BC · Canoes and sledges used · Animals domesticated and herded	· Standing stones and circles built · Flint mines worked · Farming spreads · Ploughs drawn by animals	· Bronze objects made · Sailing boats in Aegean · Megalithic ('large stone') tombs built	◄ Golden burial mask from Mycenae ('Mask of Agamemnon') · Minoan civilization in Crete · Mycenaean civilization in Greece

World history

1000 BC	750 BC	500 BC	250 BC	AD 1 AD 249
· Zhou dynasty in China · Taoism founded in China · The epic poem, the *Mahabharata*, composed in India	· Iron working in China · Confucius (Kongzi) and Buddha lived ◄ Statue of Buddha	· Mauryan empire in India · Alexander the Great invades India	► Terracotta horse from the tomb of the Chinese 'First Emperor' · Great Wall of China built · Qin dynasty unites China · Great Silk Road across Asia opens	· Han dynasty in China · Buddhism reaches China and South-east Asia · Paper invented in China · Emperors in Japan
· Settlements in Polynesia · Chavin culture in Peru · Pottery made in North American Arctic	· Olmec civilization in Mexico	· Olmec civilization ends	· City of Teotihuacán founded in Mexico ◄ A Mayan hieroglyph · Early Maya culture in Central America · Hieroglyphic writing develops in Mexico	· Large states in Central America · Large temples built in Peru
· Kingdom of Kush in East Africa · Assyrian empire · Kingdom of Israel	· First coins in Lydia, Turkey · Persian empire established · Zoroastrian religion develops in Persia · Assyrians conquer Israel	· Nok culture in Nigeria · Persian empire conquered by Alexander the Great · Alexandrian Library founded	· Romans destroy Carthage, and conquer Syria, Palestine and Egypt · Birth of Jesus	· Jews expelled from Jerusalem · Beginnings of Christianity · Kingdom of Axum, Ethiopia ◄ Colosseum, Rome, completed AD 80
· Celts move into Germany and France · Etruscans settle in northern Italy	· Greek alphabet develops · Greek city states · Roman republic founded · Hillforts in western Europe	· Great age of Athens · Alexander the Great conquers Greece · Romans conquer Etruscans, rule all Italy, and conquer Spain	· Growth of Roman empire · Julius Caesar conquers Gaul · Augustus first Roman emperor	· Roman empire reaches greatest extent · Christianity spreads

World history

	AD 250	500	750	1000	1250
Asia	• Gupta empire in India • Horse-collar harness first used	• Large Chinese empire under Tang dynasty	• Beginning of Fujiwara period in Japan • Tang dynasty in China • Chinese invent gunpowder • Printing invented in China	• Genghis Khan creates Mongol empire • Mongol Golden Horde conquers Russia • Muslim conquests in northern India • Khmer kingdom in South-east Asia	• Yuan (Mongol) and Ming dynasties in China • Conquests of Tamerlane • Russia defeats Mongols • Growth of Vietnam state • Portuguese reach India via southern Africa
Americas and Oceania	• Maya civilization in Central America growing • Nazca civilization in southern Peru	• Maya civilization at its height	• Toltec civilization in Mexico	• Vikings sail to North America • Polynesians settle Hawaii, New Zealand and Easter Island • Growth of Inca empire, Peru	◀ A Khmer temple, Angkor, Cambodia • Aztec and Inca empires at their height • Columbus reaches America
Africa and Middle East	▶ Madonna and child from a Byzantine icon • Byzantine empire succeeds Roman empire in east	▶ Islamic mosque, Persia • Muhammad founds Islam • Sassanid (Persian) empire at its height • Arab conquests in northern Africa	• Abbasid caliphate rules from Baghdad • Empire of Ghana, West Africa • Cairo founded by Fatimids • Great Zimbabwe founded, East Africa	• Christian crusaders invade Middle East • Saladin defeats crusaders • Turks conquer Palestine	• Mongols destroy Abbasid caliphate, Baghdad • Empires of Benin and Mali powerful in West Africa • Black Death ▶ Bronze cast from Benin
Europe	• Collapse of Roman empire in west • Spread of Christianity continues • Frankish kingdom founded	• Gregory the Great establishes the power of the pope • Muslims conquer Spain	▶ A Viking longboat • Viking raids and settlement • Empire of Charlemagne • England united • Beginning of Holy Roman Empire	• Break between Roman and Greek (Byzantine) Churches • Normans conquer England and Sicily	• 100 Years War between England and France • Ottoman Turks capture Constantinople • Black Death • Fall of last Muslim state in Spain • Printed books made • Beginning of Renaissance

World history

1500	1600	1700	1800	1900 2000

- Babur founds Mughal empire
- Beginning of Sikh religion in Punjab, India

- Qing (Manzhou) dynasty in China
- Tokugawa shoguns (governors) in Japan
- Taj Mahal built in India
- European trading forts established
- Russian expansion reaches the Pacific

- Qing dynasty continues
- Decline of Mughal empire
- British defeat French and control much of India

- Europeans dominate trade in Asia
- Opium Wars in China
- Taiping rebellion in China
- Indians rebel against British
- Japan begins to modernize

- China becomes a republic, then a communist state
- Rise and fall of Japanese empire
- India and other countries gain independence
- Vietnam War

- Spanish conquer Aztec and Inca empires, and establish colonies in Caribbean
- Fleet led by Ferdinand Magellan finds a route round the Americas and sails round the world

- Europeans found colonies in North America
- Slavery grows

- British defeat French in Canada

▲ The first US flag, 1776

- USA gains independence
- First European settlers in Australia

- Spanish and Portuguese colonies gain independence
- USA expands through Louisiana Purchase and Mexican War
- American Civil War
- European settlement of Australia and New Zealand

- USA becomes leading world power
- Civil rights movement grows
- *Apollo 11* puts first astronauts on Moon
- Technological revolution in industry, transport and communications

---

- Ottoman (Turkish) empire at its height under Suleiman the Magnificent
- Atlantic slave trade begins

- Slave trade expands
- Dutch settlers in South Africa

◄ The Globe Theatre, London, where Shakespeare's plays were performed

- Atlantic slave trade continues to grow
- Ottoman power declining
- Ashante kingdom in West Africa

- Africa divided into European colonies
- Atlantic slave trade ended
- Suez Canal opened

▼ Stephenson's 'Rocket', an early steam locomotive

▲ A communications satellite

- Turkey becomes a republic
- African and Arab states gain independence
- State of Israel founded
- South Africa adopts and later abandons apartheid

- Reformation (split between Catholics and Protestants)
- Ottomans invade central Europe
- Wars of Religion
- Shakespeare's first plays

- Netherlands gain independence
- Thirty Years War
- France replaces Spain as greatest power
- Civil wars in Britain
- Isaac Newton explains law of gravity

- England and Scotland united
- Russia dominant in northern Europe
- Rise of Prussia
- French Revolution
- Big advances in farming
- Start of Industrial Revolution

- Napoleonic wars
- Industrial Revolution continues
- Italy united
- Germany united
- Growth of railways
- Rise of socialism

- Einstein's theory of relativity
- World Wars I and II
- Russian Revolution
- Ireland gains independence
- Eastern Europe under Soviet communist control
- European Union founded

651

Time zones

▶ Because the Earth spins, places across the world have day and night at different times. But if everyone used different local times it would be very confusing. Because of this the world is divided up into 24 'time zones', each of about 15° longitude.

Key
Numbers indicate how many hours ahead or behind Greenwich Mean Time (GMT) a place is.

- even no. of hours different from GMT
- odd no. of hours different from GMT
- $\frac{1}{2}$-hour difference from adjacent zone
- less than $\frac{1}{2}$-hour difference from adjacent zone

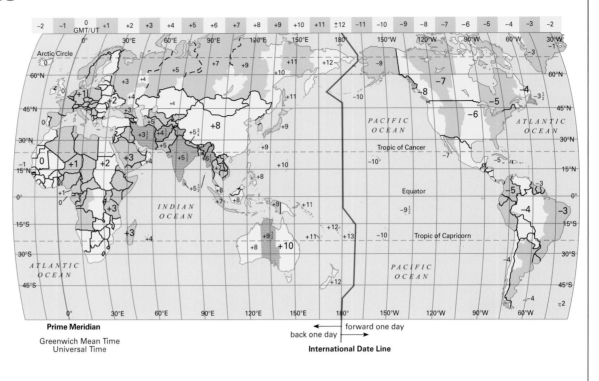

Prime Meridian
Greenwich Mean Time
Universal Time

back one day ← | → forward one day
International Date Line

Units of measurement

Metric to Imperial units

Length
1 kilometre (km) = 0.6214 mile
1 metre (m) = 1.094 yards
1 metre = 3.647 feet
1 centimetre (cm) = 0.394 inch
1 millimetre (mm) = 0.039 inch

Area
1 hectare (ha) = 2.471 acres (1 ha = 10,000 m^2)
1 square metre (m^2) = 1.196 square yards

Volume (liquid)
1 litre (l) = 0.22 gallons*
1 litre = 1.76 pints*
1 millilitre (ml) = 0.002 pint

Mass
1 tonne = 0.984 tons (1 tonne = 1000 kg)
1 kilogram (kg) = 0.1575 stone
1 kilogram = 2.205 pounds
1 gram (g) = 0.0353 ounces

* The Imperial pint and gallon are not the same as the pint and gallon measures used in the USA. An American *liquid* pint is 0.473 litre, and a gallon is 3.784 litres; an American *dry* pint is 0.550 litre.

Imperial to metric units

Length
1 mile (1760 yards) = 1.609 kilometres
1 yard (3 feet) = 0.9144 metres
1 foot (12 inches) = 0.3048 metres
1 inch = 2.54 centimetres
1 inch = 25.4 millimetres

Area
1 acre (4840 square yards) = 0.405 hectare
1 square yard = 0.836 square metre

Volume
1 gallon* (8 pints) = 4.546 litres
1 pint* = 0.568 litre
1 pint = 568 millilitres

Mass
1 ton (160 stones) = 1.016 tonnes
1 stone (14 pounds) = 6.35 kilograms
1 pound (16 ounces) = 0.4536 kilogram
1 ounce = 28.35 grams

Metric prefixes
In the metric system, the basic unit of length is the metre. Mass, time and other quantities also have a basic unit. Units smaller or larger than the basic unit have a prefix, which indicates a multiple or fraction of the unit:

1 *micro*metre (μm) = 1 millionth of a metre

1 *milli*metre (mm) = 1 thousandth of a metre

1 *centi*metre = 1 hundredth of a metre

1 *kilo*metre = 1000 metres

1 *mega*metre = 1 million metres

British royal family

▼ Elizabeth II became queen after her father's death in 1952. She is one of the longest-serving monarchs of the United Kingdom. As queen, she is the head of state and undertakes more than 400 public engagements a year, many of them abroad. In her free time she loves country life and being around dogs and horses.

▼ Charles, Prince of Wales (centre), is the heir to the throne. He works for many charities and travels widely as a representative of the crown. He is particularly interested in architecture and in the environment. In 1981 he married Lady Diana Spencer, who became Princess of Wales. The couple had two sons: William (left) and Harry (right).

▼ Diana, Princess of Wales, was born in 1961. She was the daughter of Earl Spencer. Diana worked actively for many charities, especially those connected with children, and was immensely popular. Diana and Charles separated in 1992 and later divorced. On 31 August 1997 Diana was killed in a car crash in Paris, France. She was only 36.

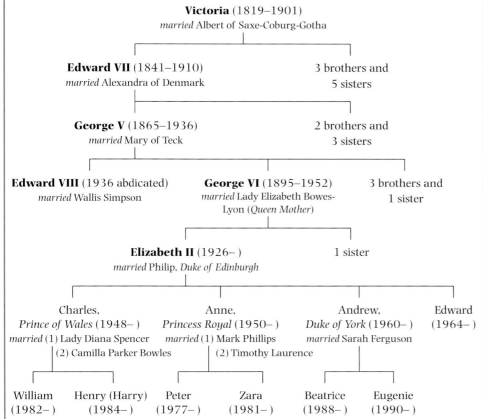

Victoria (1819–1901)
married Albert of Saxe-Coburg-Gotha

Edward VII (1841–1910)
married Alexandra of Denmark

3 brothers and 5 sisters

George V (1865–1936)
married Mary of Teck

2 brothers and 3 sisters

Edward VIII (1936 abdicated)
married Wallis Simpson

George VI (1895–1952)
married Lady Elizabeth Bowes-Lyon (*Queen Mother*)

3 brothers and 1 sister

Elizabeth II (1926–)
married Philip, *Duke of Edinburgh*

1 sister

Charles, *Prince of Wales* (1948–)
married (1) Lady Diana Spencer
(2) Camilla Parker Bowles

Anne, *Princess Royal* (1950–)
married (1) Mark Phillips
(2) Timothy Laurence

Andrew, *Duke of York* (1960–)
married Sarah Ferguson

Edward (1964–)

William (1982–)

Henry (Harry) (1984–)

Peter (1977–)

Zara (1981–)

Beatrice (1988–)

Eugenie (1990–)

Rulers of England and of the United Kingdom

Saxon kings	
Alfred	871–899
Edward the Elder	899–925
Athelstan	925–939
Edmund	939–946
Eadred	946–955
Eadwig	955–959
Edgar	959–975
Edward the Martyr	975–978
Ethelred the Unready	978–1016
Edmund Ironside	1016
Danish (Viking) kings	
Canute (Cnut)	1016–1035
Harold I	1035–1040
Hardicanute (Harthacnut)	1040–1042
Saxon kings	
Edward the Confessor	1042–1066
Harold II (Godwinson)	1066
House of Normandy	
William I (the Conqueror)	1066–1087
William II	1087–1100
Henry I	1100–1135
Stephen and Matilda	1135–1154
House of Plantagenet	
Henry II	1154–1189
Richard I	1189–1199
John	1199–1216
Henry III	1216–1272
Edward I	1272–1307
Edward II	1307–1327
Edward III	1327–1377
Richard II	1377–1399
House of Lancaster	
Henry IV	1399–1413
Henry V	1413–1422
Henry VI	1422–1461
House of York	
Edward IV	1461–1483
Edward V	1483
Richard III	1483–1485
House of Tudor	
Henry VII	1485–1509
Henry VIII	1509–1547
Edward VI	1547–1553
Mary I	1553–1558
Elizabeth I	1558–1603
House of Stuart	
James I of England and VI of Scotland	1603–1625
Charles I	1625–1649
Commonwealth (declared 1649)	
Oliver Cromwell, Lord Protector	1653–1658
Richard Cromwell	1658–1659
House of Stuart	
Charles II	1660–1685
James II	1685–1688
William III and Mary II (Mary died 1694)	1689–1702
Anne	1702–1714
House of Hanover	
George I	1714–1727
George II	1727–1760
George III	1760–1820
George IV	1820–1830
William IV	1830–1837
Victoria	1837–1901
House of Saxe-Coburg-Gotha	
Edward VII	1901–1910
House of Windsor	
George V	1910–1936
Edward VIII	1936
George VI	1936–1952
Elizabeth II	1952–

Prime ministers and presidents

Prime ministers of Great Britain and of the United Kingdom

(1721)–1742	Sir Robert Walpole	*Whig*
1742–1743	Earl of Wilmington	*Whig*
1743–1754	Henry Pelham	*Whig*
1754–1756	Duke of Newcastle	*Whig*
1756–1757	Duke of Devonshire	*Whig*
1757–1762	Duke of Newcastle	*Whig*
1762–1763	Earl of Bute	*Tory*
1763–1765	George Grenville	*Whig*
1765–1766	Marquis of Rockingham	*Whig*
1766–1768	William Pitt (the Elder)	*Whig*
1768–1770	Duke of Grafton	*Whig*
1770–1782	Lord North	*Tory*
1782	Marquis of Rockingham	*Whig*
1782–1783	Earl of Shelburne	*Whig*
1783	Duke of Portland	*coalition*
1783–1801	William Pitt (the Younger)	*Tory*
1801–1804	Henry Addington	*Tory*
1804–1806	William Pitt (the Younger)	*Tory*
1806–1807	Lord William Grenville	*Whig*
1807–1809	Duke of Portland	*Tory*
1809–1812	Spencer Perceval	*Tory*
1812–1827	Earl of Liverpool	*Tory*
1827	George Canning	*Tory*
1827–1828	Viscount Goderich	*Tory*
1828–1830	Duke of Wellington	*Tory*
1830–1834	Earl Grey	*Whig*
1834	Viscount Melbourne	*Whig*
1834	Duke of Wellington	*Tory*
1834–1835	Sir Robert Peel	*Conservative*
1835–1841	Viscount Melbourne	*Whig*
1841–1846	Sir Robert Peel	*Conservative*
1846–1852	Lord John Russell	*Whig*
1852	Earl of Derby	*Conservative*
1852–1855	Earl of Aberdeen	*coalition*
1855–1858	Viscount Palmerston	*Liberal*
1858–1859	Earl of Derby	*Conservative*
1859–1865	Viscount Palmerston	*Liberal*
1865–1866	Earl Russell	*Liberal*
1866–1868	Earl of Derby	*Conservative*
1868	Benjamin Disraeli	*Conservative*
1868–1874	William Gladstone	*Liberal*
1874–1880	Benjamin Disraeli	*Conservative*
1880–1885	William Gladstone	*Liberal*
1885–1886	Marquis of Salisbury	*Conservative*
1886	William Gladstone	*Liberal*
1886–1892	Marquis of Salisbury	*Conservative*
1892–1894	William Gladstone	*Liberal*
1894–1895	Earl of Rosebery	*Liberal*
1895–1902	Marquis of Salisbury	*Conservative*
1902–1905	Arthur Balfour	*Conservative*
1905–1908	Sir Henry Campbell-Bannerman	*Liberal*
1908–1916	Herbert Asquith	*Liberal*
1916–1922	David Lloyd George	*coalition*
1922–1923	Andrew Bonar Law	*Conservative*
1923–1924	Stanley Baldwin	*Conservative*
1924	Ramsay MacDonald	*Labour*
1924–1929	Stanley Baldwin	*Conservative*
1929–1931	Ramsay MacDonald	*Labour*
1931–1935	Ramsay MacDonald	*coalition*
1935–1937	Stanley Baldwin	*coalition*
1937–1940	Neville Chamberlain	*coalition*
1940–1945	Winston Churchill	*coalition*
1945–1951	Clement Attlee	*Labour*
1951–1955	Sir Winston Churchill	*Conservative*
1955–1957	Sir Anthony Eden	*Conservative*
1957–1963	Harold Macmillan	*Conservative*
1963–1964	Sir Alexander Douglas-Home	*Conservative*
1964–1970	Harold Wilson	*Labour*
1970–1974	Edward Heath	*Conservative*
1974–1976	Harold Wilson	*Labour*
1976–1979	James Callaghan	*Labour*
1979–1990	Margaret Thatcher	*Conservative*
1990–1997	John Major	*Conservative*
1997–	Tony Blair	*Labour*

Presidents of the United States of America

1789–1797	George Washington	*Federalist*
1797–1801	John Adams	*Federalist*
1801–1809	Thomas Jefferson	*Democratic-Republican*
1809–1817	James Madison	*Democratic-Republican*
1817–1825	James Monroe	*Democratic-Republican*
1825–1829	John Quincy Adams	*Independent*
1829–1837	Andrew Jackson	*Democrat*
1837–1841	Martin Van Buren	*Democrat*
1841	William H. Harrison	*Whig*
1841–1845	John Tyler	*Whig*, then *Democrat*
1845–1849	James K. Polk	*Democrat*
1849–1850	Zachary Taylor	*Whig*
1850–1853	Millard Fillmore	*Whig*
1853–1857	Franklin Pierce	*Democrat*
1857–1861	James Buchanan	*Democrat*
1861–1865	Abraham Lincoln	*Republican*
1865–1869	Andrew Johnson	*Democrat*
1869–1877	Ulysses S. Grant	*Republican*
1877–1881	Rutherford B. Hayes	*Republican*
1881	James A. Garfield	*Republican*
1881–1885	Chester A. Arthur	*Republican*
1885–1889	Grover Cleveland	*Democrat*
1889–1893	Benjamin Harrison	*Republican*
1893–1897	Grover Cleveland	*Democrat*
1897–1901	William McKinley	*Republican*
1901–1909	Theodore Roosevelt	*Republican*
1909–1913	William H. Taft	*Republican*
1913–1921	Woodrow Wilson	*Democrat*
1921–1923	Warren G. Harding	*Republican*
1923–1929	Calvin Coolidge	*Republican*
1929–1933	Herbert C. Hoover	*Republican*
1933–1945	Franklin Delano Roosevelt	*Democrat*
1945–1953	Harry S. Truman	*Democrat*
1953–1961	Dwight D. Eisenhower	*Republican*
1961–1963	John F. Kennedy	*Democrat*
1963–1969	Lyndon B. Johnson	*Democrat*
1969–1974	Richard M. Nixon	*Republican*
1974–1977	Gerald Ford	*Republican*
1977–1981	James E. Carter	*Democrat*
1981–1989	Ronald W. Reagan	*Republican*
1989–1993	George H. W. Bush	*Republican*
1993–2001	William J. Clinton	*Democrat*
2001–	George W. Bush	*Republican*

Prime ministers of Australia

1901–1903	Edmund Barton
1903–1904	Alfred Deakin
1904	John C. Watson
1904–1905	George Houstoun Reid
1905–1908	Alfred Deakin
1908–1909	Andrew Fisher
1909–1910	Alfred Deakin
1910–1913	Andrew Fisher
1913–1914	Joseph Cook
1914–1915	Andrew Fisher
1915–1923	William M. Hughes
1923–1929	Stanley M. Bruce
1929–1932	James H. Scullin
1932–1939	Joseph A. Lyons
1939	Earle Christmas Grafton Page
1939–1941	Robert Gordon Menzies
1941	Arthur William Fadden
1941–1945	John Curtin
1945	Francis Michael Forde
1945–1949	Joseph Benedict Chifley
1949–1966	Robert Gordon Menzies
1966–1967	Harold Edward Holt
1967–1968	John McEwen
1968–1971	John Grey Gorton
1971–1972	William McMahon
1972–1975	Edward Gough Whitlam
1975–1983	J. Malcolm Fraser
1983–1991	Robert J. L. Hawke
1991–1996	Paul J. Keating
1996–	John W. Howard

Prime ministers of Canada

1867–1873	John A. Macdonald
1873–1878	Alexander Mackenzie
1878–1891	John A. Macdonald
1891–1892	John J. C. Abbott
1892–1894	John S. D. Thompson
1894–1896	Mackenzie Bowell
1896	Charles Tupper
1896–1911	Wilfred Laurier
1911–1920	Robert L. Borden
1920–1921	Arthur Meighen
1921–1926	W. L. Mackenzie King
1926	Arthur Meighen
1926–1930	W. L. Mackenzie King
1930–1935	Richard B. Bennett
1935–1948	W. L. Mackenzie King
1948–1957	Louis Stephen St Laurent
1957–1963	John George Diefenbaker
1963–1968	Lester B. Pearson
1968–1979	Pierre Elliott Trudeau
1979–1980	Joseph Clark
1980–1984	Pierre Elliott Trudeau
1984	John Turner
1984–1993	Brian Mulroney
1993	Kim Campbell
1993–2003	Jean Chrétien
2003–	Paul Martin

Prime ministers of New Zealand

1856	Henry Sewell
1856	William Fox
1856–1861	Edward William Stafford
1861–1862	William Fox
1862–1863	Alfred Domett
1863–1864	Frederick Whitaker
1864–1865	Frederick Aloysius Weld
1865–1869	Edward William Stafford
1869–1872	William Fox
1872	Edward William Stafford
1872–1873	George Marsden Waterhouse
1873	William Fox
1873–1875	Julius Vogel
1875–1876	Daniel Pollen
1876	Julius Vogel
1876–1877	Harry Albert Atkinson
1877–1879	George Grey
1879–1882	John Hall
1882–1883	Frederick Whitaker
1883–1884	Harry Albert Atkinson
1884	Robert Stout
1884	Harry Albert Atkinson
1884–1887	Robert Stout
1887–1891	Harry Albert Atkinson
1891–1893	John Ballance
1893–1906	Richard John Seddon
1906	William Hall-Jones
1906–1912	Joseph George Ward
1912	Thomas Mackenzie
1912–1925	William Ferguson Massey
1925	Francis Henry Dillon Bell
1925–1928	Joseph Gordon Coates
1928–1930	Joseph George Ward
1930–1935	George William Forbes
1935–1940	Michael J. Savage
1940–1949	Peter Fraser
1949–1957	Sidney G. Holland
1957	Keith J. Holyoake
1957–1960	Water Nash
1960–1972	Keith J. Holyoake
1972	John R. Marshall
1972–1974	Norman Kirk
1974–1975	Wallace Rowling
1975–1984	Robert D. Muldoon
1984–1989	David Russell Lange
1989–1990	Geoffrey W. R. Palmer
1990–1997	James B. Bolger
1997–1999	Jenny Shipley
1999–	Helen Clark

Subject index

General index

If an index entry is printed in **bold**, it means that there is an article under that name in the A–Z section of the encyclopedia or in the Countries fact file. When an entry has more than one page reference, the most important one may be printed in **bold**. References in *italic* indicate that there is a map, photo or other illustration relating to the entry on that page.

Where people are listed in the index, their birth and death dates are given in brackets; 'b.' stands for 'born' and 'd.' stands for 'died'.

C

U

V

W

X Y Z

Acknowledgements

Key

t top; b bottom; c centre; r right; l left; back background; fore foreground

Artwork

All flags courtesy of The Flag Institute.

Allen, Graham: 426b
Allington, Sophie: 511
Ambrus, Victor: 259br; 375t
Arlott, Norman: 64c; 65b; 578b
Baker, Julian: 4; 118cl; 142t; 184t; 185b; 249b; 254b; 289; 314tr; 320b; 328; 333; 397b; 409; 429t; 445b; 448b; 454; 465b; 475t; 478b; 486b; 507t; 532b; 536t; 540t; 545br; 600; 601t
Barber, John: 226b; 344b
Beckett, Brian: 59t
Beckett, Brian/Gecko Ltd: 292
Beckett, Brian/James Sneddon: 99b; 138
Berridge, Richard/James Sneddon: 439cl
Black, Brad: 161b; 527tr
Bull, Peter: 377; 587; 496–497b
Cameron, Jo: 314b
Connolly, Peter: 148bl; 258bl; 470b; 575
Cottam, Martin: 168–169b; 194–196fore
Courtney, Michael: 199tr; 435
Doherty, Paul: 508
Frank Kennard: 155bl; 277t; 309tc; 324b; 379b; 502b
Gaffney, Michael: 483–484
Hiscock, Karen: 57b; 232b; 607tl
Gecko Ltd: 52t; 53b; 78; 82b; 84t; 97; 144; 145b; 206t; 265bl; 266b; 279t; 313b; 359; 361b; 416t; 430tr; 433; 444t; 498t
Gecko Ltd/James Sneddon: 414b; 421
Hardy, David: 133b; 357b; 378; 519; 525; 534tl; 568t
Hawken, Nick: 10b; 260t
Hinks, Gary: 96b; 121b; 122b; 172b; 248b; 299b; 363c; 395b; 462; 466; 507b; 569tr; 577b; 581; 590
Hook, Richard: 440b; 586
Jonatronix: 7b; 30b
Jones Sewell Associates: 42t
Jones Sewell Associates/James Sneddon: 491; 368–370
Linden Artists: 217c
Loates, Mick: 212t; 213
Luff, Vanessa: 521b
Madison, Kevin: 227cr
Milne, Sean: 33br; 38b; 96t; 150b; 175tr; 217tl; 221b; 225; 232t; 233b; 255tc; 261b; 266t; 417t; 484b; 485; 487t; 495t; 595; 436–437b
Milne, Sean/James Sneddon: 176t
Moore, David: 554tr
Murray, David: 108t
Murray, David/James Sneddon: 533b
Ovenden, Denys: 156
Oxford Illustrators: 17b; 45; 46br; 61br; 84b; 122t; 123b; 174b; 182b; 190b; 191b; 216c; 274bl; 298b; 315t; 457t; 523tr; 549; 557b; 654–656
Oxford Illustrators/James Sneddon: 325
Oxford University Press: 311br; 608tr
Oxprint Design : 366t; 24–25; 436–437back
Parsley, Helen: 104b; 147b; 180cl; 261t
Polley, Robbie: 3; 93; 172; 180t; 275; 386b; 490 ; 547 ; 550b; 648–651
Raw, Stephen: 393b; 608b
Hutchins, Ray: 163b
Raynor Design:
548t
Richardson, Paul: 29b; 33tl; 83b; 148t; 155tr; 171t; 291cl; 355; 494b; 594; 595; 94–95
Robbins, Jim: 44b; 56tr; 262; 285cr; 286
Roberts, Steve: 3; 28fore; 29c; 32b; 60t; 63cl; 178cr; 215t; 323t; 343tr; 344tr; 373t; 381b; 505b; 506br; 522t; 523b; 524b; 558b; 588; 595
Robinson, Andrew/James Sneddon: 131b; 437tr
Rothero, Chris: 39t
Sanders, Martin : 263br; 589
Saunders, Michael: 63tr; 171b; 365b; 390b; 493tr; 503t; 506bl; 538cl
Seymore, Steve: 240tl
Sneddon, James: 11t; 15b; 16t; 28back; 43b; 47t; 55br; 57tr; 73cr; 89b; 123tr; 126b; 128b; 129t; 140t; 153b; 154b; 177t; 183t; 188; 214; 219b; 220t; 222t; 223tl; 224tr; 237b; 239b; 240tr; 241; 242; 252b; 257t; 265cr; 270br; 293b; 318b; 322; 326b; 351; 394t; 400b; 420back; 449b; 450b; 456b; 512cr; 534br; 541; 543br; 573t; 580b; 582; 585b; 194–196
Spenceley, Annabel: 120b; 224b; 431t
Visscher, Peter: 28, 193b; 322; 396; 420fore
Ward, Catherine : 209; 211t
Weston, Steve: 67b; 70bl; 72; 249tr; 263bc; 264b; 281t; 493tl
Wheatcroft, Andrew: 39b
Wiley, Terry: 157; 197b; 438tl
Woods, Michael: 23b; 100b; 135b; 186br; 272bl; 343tl; 538tr
Woods, Michael/Gecko: 461t; 499t; 607tr
Woods, Michael/James Sneddon: 98b; 418b; 570t
Woods, Rosemary: 528t

Photographs

The Publishers would like to thank the following for permission to use photographs:

Aardman Animations Ltd 1993: 30t
Action Plus Photographic: 43t (Glyn Kirk); 44t (Glyn Kirk); 56tl (Al Messershmidt); 69bl (Mike Hewitt); 69tr (Glyn Kirk); 251bl (Mike Hewitt); 313tr (Richard Francis); 362t (Richard Francis); 543bl (Chris Barry); 543t; 578tr (Glyn Kirk); 583b (Peter Tarry); 583t (Mike Hewitt); 597b (Glyn Kirk); 597t (Glyn Kirk)
AKG London: 91b; 107b
B. & C. Alexander: 294tr
Allsport: 584t (Stephen Munday)
Ancient Art and Architecture: 127tl; 179bl; 234tr (Ronald Sheridan); 441tr (Ronald Sheridan); 481tr (Michelle Jones); 482tl (Ronald Sheridan)
Heather Angel: 218br; 553br; 553tr
Apple Computer, Inc.: 151tc
Apple Corporation Ltd: 58br
Arcaid: 234bl (Richard Bryant)
Architectenbureau Alberts & Van Hunt: 35tl
Associated Press: 101b
Associated Press/Topham: 181b (A. Bradlow)
Jan Baldwin: 68tr
Bibliotheque Nationale, Paris : 136tl; 146t
William Sturgis Bigelow Collection, Courtesy Museum of Fine Arts, Boston: 374
Bridgeman Art Library: 20bl (Museo e Gallerie Nazionali Di Capodimonte Naples); 48cr (Museo Archeologico Nazionali, Naples); 59br (Private Collection); 60br (Bibliotheque Nationale, Paris); 81bl; 102br (Private Collection); 142br; 147tr (Downe House, Kent); 159br (Lauros-Giraudon); 167b (Graphische Sammiung Albertine, Vienna); 167t (by permission Henry Moore Foundation/Bonhams); 187cr (Woburn Abbey, Bedfordshire); 200t (The Maas Gallery, London); 243bl (Crown Estate/Institute of Directors); 267tr (Walker Art Gallery, Liverpool); 287t (Walker Art Gallery, Liverpool); 305cl (Private Collection); 308tr (Jean Auguste Dominique Ingres); 310b (The British Library, London); 319t (Louvre, Paris, France); 337b (Glasgow University Library); 338tr (Lambeth Palace Library, London); 339tl (Private Collection); 347br (The British Library, London); 354tl (Private Collection); 366 (Museo di San Marco dell'Angelico, Florence); 375b (Arthur Rackham Estate/Chris Beetles Ltd); 376b (Christie's Images); 379tl (National Maritime Museum, London); 392t (Novosti); 404b (Vatican Museum and Galleries,Vatican City, Italy); 404tl (National Gallery, London); 405t (Victoria & Albert Musem, London); 406bc (ADAGP Paris and DACS London, 1998); 406tl (Christie's Images); 414t (Vatican Museum and Galleries,Vatican City, Italy); 416b (DACS, 1998); 422b (Doumo, Florence); 422t (Palazzo Ducale, Mantua); 423 (Fitzwilliam Museum, University of Cambridge); 426cr (Bibliotheque Nationale, Paris); 456tr (City of Bristol Museum and Art Gallery); 460br (Biblioteca Ambrosiana, Milan); 460tr (Palazzo Pitti, Florence); 475br (Giraudon); 504bl (The British Library, London); 528b; 531bl (Museum of Fine Arts, Budapest); 531tr (Private Collection); 555tr (National Maritime Museum, London); 556br (Victoria & Albert Musem, London); 571b (Royal Holloway and Bedford New College, Surrey); 571t (Stapleton Collection); 585tl (Waterhouse and Dodd); 607br (Private Collection); 338b (The British Library, London); 402tr (The British Library, London)
Copyright The Brontë Society: 391tc; 391tr
Christie's Images: 303b; 405bl; 431bc; 432br; 551tr
Christo 1983: 482br (Wolfgang Volz)
CNRI/Science Photo Library: 70tr
Bruce Coleman: 269bl (Jules Cowan); 269tl (Harold Lange)
Colorific: 19br (Michael Yamashita); 353tr (Enrico Ferorelli); 495br (Nik Wheeler/Black Star); 501br (Rob Crandall); 520bl (Raghubir Singh)
Corbis: 108b (Gunter Marx); 238tr; 253b (Steve Raymer); 317cl (Adam Woolfitt); 332tr (Earl Kowall); 459bl (Richard Nowitz)
Corbis Bettmann/UPI: 222b; 270bl
Corbis/Getty Images: 270t
DeBeers: 151b
Dickens House Museum: 152tc; 152tl
The Walt Disney Company Limited: 161tr
Dominic Photography: 53br (Zoe Dominic); 53t (Catherine Ashmore); 146cr (Catherine Ashmore)
Mike Dudley: 500br (Mike Dudley)
E. T. Archive: 109cr
Mary Evans: 11br; 48bl; 51br; 92tr; 102t; 111tc; 111tr; 130t; 135tr; 144tr; 159tl; 198tr; 243tr; 244br; 244tl; 248tr; 311cl; 321t; 335tr; 347t; 357t; 365t; 383b; 384bl; 389bl; 389tr; 392b; 398br; 417br; 473c; 494tl; 503br; 517bl; 527bl; 527br; 580tr; 598tc
Mary Evans/Explorer: 124tl (Plisson)
Mary Evans/ Sigmund Freud Copyrights: 446tl (Max Halberstadt)
Fortean Picture Library: 561t
Diane Fress, FRS: 437cr
Geo Science Features/Dr B. Booth: 466c; 467br; 467tl
Getty Images: 17tr; 18bl; 18cr (Chuck Keeler); 34br; 54cr; 55bl; 66br (Billy Hustace); 74b; 85b (Frank Herholdt); 103t (Michael Rosenfeld); 110b (Oliver Benn); 110tl (Alan Seith); 113tr; 152br; 165b; 166t (Glen Allison); 203tl (Kevin Horan); 204b (Mitch Kezar); 205tl (Gary Braasch); 219tr (Ian Murphy); 230tr; 245b (Hans Peter Merten); 246b; 247t; 250cl (Tony Hutchings); 250tr; 254tr; 271b; 271tr; 294bl; 297br; 316t (David Young-Wolff); 321b; 323br; 326tl; 336t (Seth Resnick); 348b (Nabeel Turner); 349t; 350bc (Graeme Norways); 352bl (Michael Rosenfeld); 380tr; 397tr (James Wells); 402bc; 415t; 446br (David Hanson); 450tr (Paul Chesley); 452b; 453b (Christopher Arneseh); 471t; 472t (Natalie Fobes); 486tl (Arnulf Husmo); 491cl (Steven Weinberg); 530br; 531tl; 551cl (Bob Thomas); 552b (Lorne Hesnick); 552tl (Jon Riley); 555bl; 559cr (Peter Seaward); 559t; 561b (Jerry Alexander); 570br; 572t; 598bc; 599b (John Garret); 606tl
Giraudon: 324tr
Robert Goble & Son Ltd.: 370tl
Governor and Company of the Bank of England, 1989: 381tl
Sally and Richard Greenhill: 239tl; 506tr (Sam Greenhill)
Greenpeace: 260br (Sims)
Guardian: 290b (Don McPhee)
Hanny/Gamma/FSP: 441br
Robert Harding: 13t (G. Renner); 14bl (Sassoon); 14t (Robert Cundy); 20cl (Nedra Westwater); 36b (Gavin Hellier); 41bl (Nevada Wier); 41br (Duncan Maxwell); 41tr (Thomas Laird); 54bl (Michael J. Howell); 55tr (Nigel Gomm); 61bl (J. H. C. Wilson); 71cr (David Lomax); 76bl (Advertasia); 76tr (G. Hellier); 77b (Jerry Alexander); 77tl (Alain Evrard); 79tl (M. Leslie Evans); 79tr (Nigel Frances); 81tr (Robert Frerck); 90t (John Miller); 91t (Fred Friberg); 105br (Gavin Hellier); 105tr (Nigel Gomm); 106tr (T. Megarry); 109tl (Adam Woolfitt); 111tl (G. R. Richardson); 113bl (T. Gervis); 116bc (Gavin Hellier); 116tr (Philip Craven); 120t (Gina Corrigan); 121tr (Nigel Temple); 127bl (D. Beatty); 130b (Yoram Lehmann); 149c (Robert Francis); 178br (Philip Craven); 192tr (Paul Hadley); 193tr (Jennifer Fry); 207b (G. & P. Corrigan); 220b (Luca Invernizzi Tettoni); 229b (Nigel Frances); 229tr (David Martyn Hughes); 233cr (Rainbird); 238br (David Beatty); 246t (Gavin Hellier); 259tl (Tony Gervis); 263tl (C. Rennie); 264tr (Adam Woolfitt); 285tr (Nigel Gomm); 292tr (N. A. Callow); 295tl (Paolo Koch); 296b (Roy Rainford); 300tl (E. Simanor); 302tl (J. H. C. Wilson); 306br (Photri); 306tr (A. S. A. P.); 307br (Richard Nowitz); 307tl (E. Simanor); 329tr (D. Holdsworth); 335br (Christopher Rennie); 341tl (Michael Short); 346b (Peter Scholey); 352tl (Kodak); 356t (Explorer); 371b (Mohamed Amin); 373br (James Strachan); 382b (Julian Pottage); 383t (D. Maryk); 385tr (Adam Woolfitt); 390t (David Lomax); 394b (Liba Taylor); 407b; 408bl; 410br (C. Bowman); 430b (Robert Francis); 441t (Adam Woolfitt); 451br (John Miller); 453t (J. H. C. Wilson); 460bl (Philip Craven); 464tr (Gavin Hellier); 468b (D. Beatty); 478t (C. Rennie); 480b (Rolf Richardson); 480t (C. Bowman); 488tl (Thomas Laird); 513b (T. Waltham); 535b; 546b (Advertasia); 546t (Bildagentur Schuster); 558t (Adam Woolfitt); 567br (Simon Harris); 569bl (Lorraine Wilson); 573b (Steve Benbow); 579b (Duncan Maxwell); 591br (Financial Times); 603t (Tony Gervis); 610b (Paolo Koch)
Michael Holford: 25b; 25tl; 26tr; 35b; 36tl; 51tr; 98tr; 179tr; 180cr; 258tr; 287bl; 316b; 340 ; 368t; 386t; 469bl; 470tl; 481bl
Hutchinson Library: 208br; 332bl (Juliet Highet); 353br (Leslie Woodhead)
Image Bank: 18t (Erik Simonsen); 19tl (Chris A Wilton); 49b (Peter Hendrie); 49t (Michael Coyne); 50tr (Jeff Hunter); 61tr (John P. Kelly); 73tl (Alan Choijnet); 79br (Walter Bibikow); 85t (Margaret Mead); 86tr (Andre Gallant); 123br (T. Chinami); 133tr; 136b (Jurgen Vogt); 164tr (Jeff Hunter); 168cl (Carlos Navajas); 168tr (Alvis Upitis); 198bl (Roland Dusik); 208tc; 211tl (G. K. & Vikki Hart); 214cr (Chris Hackett); 250bc (Marc Romanelli); 288tr (HMS Images); 301tr (Marc Romanelli); 323bl (J. Du Bisberran); 356b (Wendy Chan); 388br (Stuart Dee); 388tl (Eric Meola); 393tr (Anthony Edwards); 403tl (Steve Allen); 410tr; 421tr (Marc Romanelli); 425br (Yiu Chun Ma); 430cl (John Banagan); 432t (Wendy Chan); 445t (Grant Faint); 459br (C. Brown); 459tr (P.-E. Berglund); 464bl (Steve Allen); 471b (P. & G. Bogwater); 472t (Harald Sund); 500tr; 512bl (Jaime Villaseca); 514b (Guido A. Rossi); 549tr (Ted Kawalerski); 565bl; 565tr (John P. Kelly); 584b (John P. Kelly); 596br (Steve Proehl)
Images: 163tr; 268tl
Images of Africa: 62t; 118t; 150t; 203br; 205tr; 276t (Johann Van Tonder); 501tl; 551br; 603b
Images of India: 104tr (Roderick Johnson); 186tr; 268bl (Roderick Johnson); 282br; 283br; 283cl (Roderick Johnson); 284tl; 288b (Michael Ravinder)
Irish Embassy: 137t
Japanese Information Cultural Centre: 115b; 166cr
Jersey Tourism: 562b
Bragi Por Josefsson: 411t
Katz/Mansell Collection: 317br; 494tr
David King Collection: 318tl; 329br; 524tr; 605tr
Kobal: 101t (United Artists); 210tl (MGM); 210tr (Selznick/MGM); 442tr (Paramount); 505cr (Selznick/United Artists); 522bl (Columbia)
Peter Lawson: 537tr
Link Picture Library: 283tr (Eric Meacher); 284b
Charlotte Lippmann: 345tr
Lucasfilm/20th Century Fox: 210b
Matsumoto/Sygma: 606b
Latha Menon: 201b
Milepost 92_: 452t
National Geographic Image Collection: 10tr (Sam Abell); 13br (George F. Mobley); 34tr (Kenneth Garrett); 37br (O. Louis Mazzatenta); 71bl (Brooks Walker); 88br (George F. Mobley); 88tl (Dean Conger); 107t (James L. Stanfield); 145tl (Volkmar Kurt Wentzel); 200br (George F. Mobley); 251tc (James L. Stanfield); 280b (Medford Taylor); 281b (Stephen L. Alvarez); 295br (Lynn Abercrombie); 303tl (David A. Harvey); 312b (Otis Imboden); 342br; 342tl (Walter Meayers Edwards); 442br (Stanley Breeden); 476tr (Thomas J. Abercrombie); 488br (Stephanie Maze); 489br (James P. Blair); 496tr (Wilbur E. Garrett); 497tr (David A. Harvey); 532tr (Jonathan Blair); 533t (Jonathan Blair); 596tr
National Maritime Museum Picture Library: 164br
National Motor Museum: 360b
The National Museum, Copenhagen: 99t
National Postal Museum, London: 319b
Natural History Photographic Agency: 21t (M. I. Walker); 23tr (Daniel Heuclin); 27bl (G. I. Bernard); 27tr (Steve Robinson); 31b (Jonathan Chester); 32cl (Steve Robinson); 56bc (Stephen Dalton); 58c (John Shaw); 64bl (Orion Press); 64tr (Alan Williams); 65t (L. Hugh Newman); 80bc (John Shaw); 80tr (Anthony Bannister); 87tr (John Shaw); 94tr (Stephen Krasemann); 95tr (Gerard Lacz); 100tr (Douglas Dickins); 131tr (Kevin Schafer); 132br (David Woodfall); 138tr (Jeff Goodman); 139bl (B. Jones & M. Shimlock); 149t (Anthony Bannister); 156bl (Daniel Heuclin); 162bl (Michael Leach); 175tl (Kevin Schafer); 176b (Norbet Wu); 178t (E. A. Janes); 186bl (Anthony Bannister); 199bl (Daniel Heuclin); 199br (Stephen Dalton); 212bl (Norbet Wu); 216b (Stephen Dalton); 218cl (John Shaw); 218tr (Stephen Dalton); 221tr (Daniel Heuclin); 226tl (Rod Plank); 231cr (Stephen Dalton); 255br (Stephen Dalton); 255tl (Laurie Campbell); 256bl (Christophe Ratier); 256tr (John Shaw); 267br (Hellio & Van Ingen); 272tr (Christophe Ratier); 277b (Christophe Ratier); 278bl (Laurie Campbell); 278tr (Manfred Danegger); 291br (Anthony Bannister); 305br (B. Jones & M. Shimlock); 327tr (E. A. Janes); 333cl (A. N. T.); 350tr (B. Jones & M. Shimlock); 354bc (Daniel Heuclin); 358br (Michael Leach); 358tc (David Woodfall); 396bl (Norbet Wu); 412bl (Anthony Bannister); 413b (Douglas Dickins); 413t (Dr Ivan Polunin); 415b (Stephen Dalton); 418t (Karl Switak); 419b (David Middleton); 419t (John Shaw); 420tr (G. I. Bernard); 447bl (Silvestris Fotoservice); 447tr (Daniel Heuclin); 448c (T. Kitchin & V. Hurst); 461bc (Kevin Schafer); 484cr (Melvin Grey); 492bl (Bruce Beehler); 492cr (David E Myers); 500tr (Anthony Bannister); 535t (Silvestris Fotoservice); 550t (David Woodfall); 554bl (David Woodfall); 557tl (Rich Kirchner); 591tr (E. A. Janes); 592b (John Shaw); 593 r (Dr Ivan Polunin); 593tr (Stephen Krasemann); 599t (Stephen Krasemann); 611tr (Daniel Heuclin)
Peter Newark's Pictures: 87br; 566br; 567cr
NMB Bank: 35tr
Novosti: 473b
Oxfam: 15t (Nic Dunlop)
Oxford Scientific Films: 125t; 139t (Harold Taylor); 162tr (David C. Fritts); 172t (Hjalmar R. Bardarson); 437tl (Douglas Faulkner)
Palazzo Publico Siena / E. T. Archive: 301bl
Ann & Bury Peerless: 458tr; 536b
Performing Arts Library: 400t (Kate Mount)
Planet Earth Pictures: 173t; 327b (Geoff du Feu); 463tl (James D. Watts); 502tr (David Maitland)
Popperfoto: 126tr; 158br; 223tr (Sam Mircovich); 252t (Gary Cameron); 276b; 317t; 349b; 362b (Sutton); 412tr; 514t (Juda Ngwenya, Reuters); 521t; 604tr
Popperfoto/AFP: 22tc (Adalberto Roque)
Press Association: 653 (John Stillwell)
Q. A. Photos Ltd: 75tr
Queen Productions Ltd.: 428bl
Redferns: 114 (Mick Huston); 145tr (Pankan Shar); 146bl (Mick Huston); 304br (Chuck Stewart); 304tl (David Redfern); 370br (Mick Huston); 398tl (David Redfern); 401b (Graham Diss); 401t; 427bl (Fin Costello); 427br (Richie Aaron); 427tr (David Redfern); 428br (Marc Marnie); 455t (Suzi Gibbons); 602b (David Redfern)
Rex Features: 141bl (Robert Kock); 153tr (David Manning); 169br; 169cl; 170br (C. Brown); 187bc; 230b; 247br; 253t (Marianella/Prisma); 310tr; 411br; 458bl (Bob Steerwood); 474b; 542br; 544br (Charles Sykes); 544t (SINH); 577tr (Arthur Pengelly); 653 ; 653
RSPCA : 204t
Sainsbury's Archives: 498b
St Edmundsbury Borough Council/West Stow Anglo-Saxon Village Trust: 26bl
Peter Sanders: 371tr; 372bl; 372tr; 499b
Science and Society Picture Library: 190t
Science Photo Library: cover (Sally Bensusen); back cover (D. Roberts), (Eye of Science); 1b (Vaughan Fleming); 5b; 16br (Dr George Gornacz); 22bc (Eddy Gray); 42br (Space Telescope Science Institute/NASA); 46t (Patrice Loiez); 47b (Los Alamos National Laboratory); 62b; 66tl; 67tl (Ken Eward); 83tr (Jean-Loup Charmet); 89tl (Geoff Tompkinson); 103b (Maximilian Stock Ltd); 119bl (Peter Ryan); 119tr (Alexander Tsiaras); 124b (Tony and Daphne Hallas); 125b (NASA); 128t (David Parker); 129b (Los Alamos National Laboratory); 132tr (NASA); 143 (Jeremy Burgess); 143 (Eye of Science); 158tl (Hattie Young); 160cr (EM Unit, VLA); 160tl (Mark Clarke); 170tl (Larry Mulvehill); 173b (NASA); 177br; 181t (Jean-Loup Charmet); 182tr (Adam Hart Davis); 184b (Nelson Morris); 185tc (Vaughan Fleming); 189br (Peter Menzell); 189t (Department of Energy); 191t; 202br; 227bl (Sinclaire Stammers); 235bl (US Naval Observatory); 235br (Dr Steve Gull); 236t; 237tr (Richard Folwell); 240b (Philippe Plailly/Eurelios); 257bl (NASA); 265t; 273bl (Malcolm Fielding); 273tr (Peter Menzell); 279b (Martin Bond); 280tr (Pekka Parviaien); 290t (James King-Holmes); 298tl; 299t (Douglas Faulkner); 315br (Will & Deni McIntyre); 320t (Richard Nowitz); 326br (Alex Bartel); 331b (M-SAT Ltd); 334b (NASA); 336b (Jean-Loup Charmet); 337t (Ed Young); 341b (John Mead); 345b (Dr Jeremy Burgess); 357br (NASA); 360t (Martin Bond); 364 (W. Bacon); 378bl (David Parker); 384cr (Geoff Tompkinson); 399bl (Geoff Tompkinson); 399tr (Hank Morgan); 403tr (James King-Holmes); 407t (Rosenfeld Images Ltd); 416t (David Parker and Julian Baum); 424b (Philippe Plailly); 425tr (NOAA); 434br (Sandia National Laboratries); 434tl (Martin Bond); 435br (Ron Sutherland); 436tr (John Reader); 443t (Pascal Nieto); 449t; 455b (James King-Holmes); 463br; 465cr (David Parker); 476br (European Space Agency); 477br (Will & Deni McIntyre); 479t (David Vaughan); 487br; 489tl (National Snow and Ice Data Centre); 509b (NASA); 509tc (NASA); 509tl (US Geological Survey); 510br (NASA); 510tl (NASA); 518bl (NASA); 518tr (NASA); 526br (Tony and Daphne Hallas); 526t; 534tr (NASA); 537br (Alfred Pasieka); 539br (Jean-Loup Charmet); 539tr; 540b (David Parker); 542tl; 548bl (NASA); 560tr (NASA); 566tl (Jim Gipe); 568cl (Space Telescope Science Institute/NASA); 576b (Omikron); 576t (Hank Morgan); 589tr (NASA); 601br (David Parker); 609br (Abeles Bsip)
Shell Oil: 151tr
Joey Shelley: 610t
South American Pictures: 515b; 516bl; 516tr; 517tr; 545bl; 602t
Museum of London: 293t; 556tl
Spectrum Colour Library: 207tr
Spice Girls Ltd: 428tr
Peter Spilsbury: 269br (Peter Spilsbury)
Suzuki: 361tr
Telegraph Colour Library: 111br (S. Djukanovic); 297tl (V. C. L.); 380br (Japack Photo Library)
The Coca-Cola Company: 151tl
Topham: 39cr; 69bl; 74tr; 82tr; 141tr; 174tr (Y. Shimbun); 202tr (G. Marinovich); 231tr; 236br; 308br; 309br (Ray Hutchinson); 328br; 424t; 425br (Kurt Adams); 457b (Associated Press); 529cr; 560b; 563b; 574tr (Associated Press); 605b;
Trek Bikes: 334tr
Twentieth Century Fox: 165t
United Feature Syndicate Inc., 1993: 92b
United Nations: 563tr
Vardon Attractions: 611br
A. P. Watt Ltd/Quentin Blake: 529t
Weidenfeld Archives: 572b
Wilberforce House, Hull City Museums: 504t
Reg Wilson: 115t; 529bl
York Archaeological Trust: 574br
ZEFA: 109bl